COYOTE'S SONG

*Light is the left hand of darkness
and darkness the right hand of light.
Two are one, life and death, lying
together like lovers in kemmer,
like hands joined together,
like the end and the way.*

Yin-Yang Symbol (Vertical alignment)
'Tormer's Lay,' *The Left Hand of Darkness*

COYOTE'S SONG

THE TEACHING STORIES OF URSULA K. LE GUIN

by

Richard D. Erlich

THE BORGO PRESS

An Imprint of Wildside Press LLC

MMX

The Milford Series
Popular Writers of Today
ISSN 0163-2469

Volume Seventy-Two

Copyright © 1997, 2001, 2006, 2010 by Richard D. Erlich

This book was published in 2001 as an SFRA Digital Book at
<http://www.sfra.org/Coyote/CoyoteHome.htm>
with the copyright to the Index held jointly by Michelle Walker and Richard Erlich, 'Site design and hosting by Science Fiction Research Association, Peter Sands, Web Editor.' For an indexed copy of this work, see the SFRA Digital Book version on line.

All rights reserved.
No part of this book may be reproduced in any form without the expressed written consent of the publisher.

www.wildsidebooks.com

FIRST EDITION

CONTENTS

How to Use This Book 7
Acknowledgments 12
Introduction 13
An Ursula K. Le Guin Chronology 24
A Biography of Ursula K. Le Guin 31

1. Beginnings: Early Works 37
2. Transition, Daoism, Magic, and Getting in Touch 55
3. Explicity Daoist Works 74
4. On Violence, Utopia, Ethics—and Sex 111
5. New Heroes 180
6. *Always Coming Home* 232
7. *Buffalo Gals and Other Animal Presences* 303
8. Other Lessons: Picture Books 348
9. Earthsea Revisited: *Tehanu* 379
10. Transition: The Social Construction of Reality 418
11. The Hainish Universe Revisited I 432
12. The Hainish Universe Revisited II 472
13. Alternative Routes 546
14. Dancing Over the Abyss with Shiva and Kali 574
15. Love and Death and Returning to Rer 603
16. Conclusion 616

Abbreviations 636
Works Cited 637
About the Author 658

DEDICATED

to the Memory of

Harriette Ryder

Virginia and Sidney Raike

Bea and Harry Erlich

HOW TO USE THIS BOOK

My initial intentions for *Coyote's Song* (which I will usually shorten to just *Coyote*) were to do a close reading of most of Ursula K. Le Guin's science fiction, fantasy, and other writing outside of the 'realistic main stream' and within the teaching tradition; to put those works into the context of Le Guin's canon; and to put Le Guin's canon into its literary and historical contexts. I intended a book that could be used for reference and either read through—although that is *not* a strategy I recommend—or sampled chapter by chapter, perhaps starting with my central chapter, on perhaps Le Guin's central work: ch. 10 on *Always Coming Home*. *Coyote* was written for readers with backgrounds ranging from undergraduate students in introductory courses to scholars of science fiction and fantasy specializing in the works of Ursula K. Le Guin.[1]

I have done the close readings, including showing inter-relationships between any text at hand and other works by Le Guin; that is, I have contextualized the works within Le Guin's canon. As I explain later, I have done additional contextualizing, but most of the rest of the literary and historical context I intended to supply I have not supplied, and I have concluded that such detailed contextualizing would best be done by future scholars. Everything is connected to everything else, as mystics and ecologists remind us, and it is always more or less arbitrary what we set off to study. What I think I can usefully do, and have tried to do, is to suggest how Le Guin's works might appear to a fair number of contemporary readers embedded in those social, political, and historical contexts: basically (and egocentrically) readers like me.

I have tried to make *Coyote* useful as a reference text and to have my chapters and sections of chapters mostly independent so that someone

---

[1] Below in this preface I define some key terms I use. However, I ordinarily try to clarify terms as I go along; readers concerned with a usage may wish to consult the Index and look back at earlier appearances of a problematic word. My attempting to write for a fairly broad audience also explains in part my favoring for allusions, comparisons, and contrasts of the plays of William Shakespeare and other relatively well-known and accessible works of popular, mass, or undergraduate academic culture; it also helps justify my favoring the hard and soft sciences over technical philosophy when I try to make plausible the idea of the social construction of reality.

looking for an introduction to one of Le Guin's works can find such an introduction in one place. Again though, I havealso tried to *get into* the works and trace the web of the inter-relations of the works, and these goals working together means that there is intentionally a fair amount of redundancy in *Coyote* plus whatever inadvertent repetitions got past me and my editor. I have tried to give warnings when I am taking a second pass at a work (*e.g.*, with 'Vaster Than Empires and More Slow') and when I am reviewing basic philosophy. When I am repeating a point, as with Existentialism, I have tried to vary my examples; and I have tried to vary my approach to different works, following similar patterns in discussing them but trying to avoid mechanical repetition of some transcendent formula of interpretation and presentation. Still, I advise against trying to read through *Coyote*. Going chapter by chapter, taking long breaks, generous readers might find *Coyote monumental*; try to get through large hunks of it in a few sittings, and *Coyote* will just seem interminable.

I hope I have written seriously, insightfully, and irreverently enough to hold the interests of professionals. I am sure that I have occasionally argued with Le Guin and with some high-power critics I respect (Rosemary Jackson, Sarah Lefanu, Gregory Benford, Marleen Barr), so there may be enough implicit conflict to hold the interest of professionals who like a little drama if, I am very sure, not enough conflict for those who like their literary criticism as a blood sport. More fervently, I hope I have written simply enough to be accessible to undergraduates willing to skip over or look up words they don't know. Please note, however, that there are a handful of technical terms that appear fairly often and which cannot be just read over. I will discuss them as I go along, but for people unfamiliar with the terms and who will be reading selectively, I provide the following rough and ready definitions.

Ontology/Metaphysics: The study of Being, the science of the essence of things (if one thinks things have an essence). Trying to figure out what *is* and where the Basis or Goal of things might be located.[2]

Epistemology: The study of knowledge. If ontology, or metaphysics, determines what, if anything, is out there to be known, epistemology asks *if* we can know what is out there, and, if we can know, *how* we might know it. Last, for my purposes: if we can know about the things in the world (or in our minds), epistemology asks whether or not we can communicate such knowledge to other people. In Le Guin's terms, if there are facts out there, how might they look to a dragon? And if a dragon wanted to tell me about those facts, could I understand?

---

[2] I have consulted for terms in philosophy, *Dictionary of Philosophy*, ed. Dagobert D. Runes. For my brief statement on Daoism here, I have consulted Strickmann, 'Taoism' and Seidel, 'Taoism, History of' articles in *Encyclopaedia Britannica: Macropaedia* (1974); my discussion is mostly, though, from my teaching Le Guin's Daoist works (see also Bittner's appendix on Daoism in 'Approaches').

Immanence: In *Coyote,* the idea that What IS, ultimately, doesn't transcend the universe or go outside the universe, but is *in* the universe. In one translation of a saying of Koheleth, the Preacher in the biblical Book of Ecclesiastes, 'That which is, is far off, and deep, very deep' (7.24, RSV). So to get to that which is, one goes down, not up, possibly taking this figurative journey by means of a mystic discipline, or, if one is in the Romantic tradition, getting in true touch with Nature.

Transcendence: The opposite of *immanence.* That which is, is beyond and above the universe. In the tradition of Western monotheism (Judaism, Christianity, and Islam) that which IS, ultimately, is God. In the tradition of Western rationalism, that which is, is eternal forms, categories, universal principles. If reaching the immanent may be pictured as a descent, transcendence is an ascent: the Ascension of Christ, the Assumption of the Virgin, the upward movements of rockets leaving Mother Earth for the conquest of space—or Stanley Kubrick's great image of Star-Child above the Earth at the end of *2001: A Space Odyssey* (1968).

Mâshâl: A Hebrew word for a linguistic construct like a parable, satire or prophecy, but in the ancient sense of language in which words act in the world; so *mâshâlim* that epitomize past situations educate their hearers in significant ways and satires and prophecies may *will* future outcomes.

Existentialism (atheistic, Sartrean variety): A very popular theory in the late 1940s through the 1960s Christian/Common Era (CE). In Western religious views for some two thousand years, human beings live in a kind of Middle Earth between Heaven above and Hell beneath, connected with Nature and with each other—if at all—through God and/or God's love. Atheistic Existentialism gets rid of God, heaven, and hell, leaving Man (it is a macho theory) on a great plane surface, with no God to define 'human nature' for humans to fulfill or to specify what is allowed and what forbidden, what is good and what is bad—and reward good actions or punish evil. Man is alone, outside of Nature, abandoned, cut off from his fellows, alienated, forlorn, in pain, despairing, and free, including free to define himself and will himself to be what he and (therefore) all people should be.

Daoism (older spelling, 'Taoism'): Always in *Coyote,* and in Le Guin, the philosophy deriving from Lao Tzu (6th c. Before the Christian / Common Era [BCE]), Chuang Tzu (4th-3rd c. BCE), and their philosophical and mystic followers, *not* the organized Daoist religion. Basically—totally basically—that which *is* is the Dao: the Way, the nonBeing underlying all Being, the womb from which ultimately all things are born and to which all return. To live well, humans should go with the Dao, which usually means the stillness of a sage or mystic, inaction (*wu wei*), avoiding doing anything against nature, against the Way; when one must act, one should act spontaneously, following one's 'knacks,' one's luck, and the Way of things. The Dao is immanent and may be touched momentarily, at which time one might *feel* how the world goes and be certain of what to do. There is, though, no transcendence (in Le Guin's version), and no God or transcendent gods, so one cannot receive a Revelation and thereby see a straight path to the Good, and one cannot, in Daoism, *possess* certainty.

Hence there are no universal rules at all, and hence no universal rules for government: no doctrine or secret knowledge that would justify forcing the world to one's will or pushing around other people. In such a view, the safest social arrangement would be very old-fashioned communist anarchy. Daoism is one basic formulation of a perennial philosophy of human embeddedness in the world, a feeling for the ultimate unity of things common in mystic practices, the spirituality of traditional Native Americans, the *real* old-time religion preceding the worship of highly individualized man-like, transcendent sky-gods. If you can accept the idea of a godless galaxy where the highest power is The Force while watching a Star Wars movie, you are at least willing to accept tentatively a 'Way of Power' related to the Dao.[3]

Kulturkampf: My encyclopedia defines the term as a German word for the 1872-87 'struggle to subject the Roman Catholic Church to state controls in the newly founded German Empire.'[4] I first heard *Kulturkampf* used in a contemporary sense in 1990, by William Rusher, publisher of the right-wing magazine *National Review*.[5] Patrick Buchanan introduced the term into mainstream political usage during his campaigns for President of the United States. In a typical *Kulturkampf* move, I wish to appropriate the term—as Rusher, Buchanan, et al. have done—co-opt it, and, redefine it. In current, melodramatic usage, the *Kulturkampf* is the struggle for the hearts and minds of the American people (and Terrans generally—the humans of our Earth). The concept participates in the great myth or metanarrative of the struggle of Good against Evil, Ormazd vs. Ahriman, God against Satan, or Us vs. Them. I use *Kulturkampf* as an alternative metaphor for 'The market-place of ideas.' Ideas are not simply laid out by equal and rational salesfolk for rational purchase by rational Economic Man and rational Economic Woman; a more useful figure of speech is the evolution of ideas, but with evolution seen in literal biological terms of differential reproduction and survival to reproduce, not some social-Darwinist jungle. There is an evolutionary *Kampf* or contest over culture:

---

[3] The title of Lao Tzu's book, the *Tao te Ching* may be translated, 'Classic of the Way of Power' (e.g., 'Taoism, History of' 1045). In the new Pinyin transliteration that would be 'the *Dao De Jing* of Lao Zi.'
[4] *Encyclopaedia Britannica: Micropaedia* (1974).
[5] 'First Amendment Debate,' Nat Hentoff vs. William Rusher, Miami University at Oxford (Ohio), 3 Oct. 1990. The idea of a struggle over key terms is quite old. I've been concerned with it since 1960, when I was called a fool for declining to falsify a US Federal income tax filing for a pittance—passionately concerned with contested terms since I was accused of lack of patriotism by talkative members of 'the great silent majority' during the Viet Nam War and of drug abuse for occasional and moderate use of cannabis—by heavy (ab)users of nicotine and alcohol. See my diss., 'Wise Men and Fools...' (1971) or, for a far more convenient example, St. Paul on wisdom and folly in his First Letter to the Corinthians, chs. 1-3 (and Paul wrote nearly half a millennium after Greek playwrights used tragedies to debate in art key contested terms in Greek culture [William Arrowsmith's theory]).

for the highest of stakes among humans but pursued quietly, on the whole—a very serious game with unspectacular victories and silent defeats as, say, one system of images for talking about evolution is replaced by another, or if readers of *Coyote* catch themselves using my idea of *Kulturkampf* rather than that of Pat Buchanan.

Ursula K. Le Guin is a player in a number of contests for hearts and minds.

For there to be change, people must believe change is possible. For people to believe change is possible, they must be able to imagine realities different from their own. Like history and anthropology, then, fables, fantasy, and science fiction—the genres I mostly deal with here—are potentially subversive by providing alternative visions of the way things can be: providing alternative legends, alternative myths. Since the late 1960s, Le Guin has consciously written highly political poems and narratives: presenting new myths, especially myths of origins, and getting us to think about our current myths, presenting a 'Perennial Philosophy' offering forms of spiritual life—relation to the universe—radically different from those of the dominant religions and philosophies of the West, making visible and problematic our ideas of such key terms as progress, patriotism, manhood, womanhood, Hero. 'Revolution begins in the thinking mind,' one of Le Guin's early heroes will tell us (*TD* [1974]: 267; ch. 10); and when asked by his boss, 'Is this a revolution, Havzhiva?' one of Le Guin's most recent heroes will respond, 'It is education, ma'am' ('A Man of the People' [1995]: *FIS* 130). So, CAUTION: You are about to enter a *Kampf* zone.

ACKNOWLEDGMENTS

First acknowledgment goes to Ursula K. Le Guin, without whom—nothing. In addition to the obvious, supplying the texts I wrote about, Le Guin has been very generous in her time and effort helping with my manuscript. Second, I wish to thank Kathleen Spencer for introducing me to Le Guin's *A Wizard of Earthsea*, and to Spencer and Carol Stevens for sending on to me materials I have found crucial to my work. My debt to a number of critics will be obvious from my citations, but I wish to acknowledge literally up-front, the work of Douglas Barbour on Daoism in Le Guin, Elizabeth Cummins for her *Ursula K. Le Guin: A Primary and Secondary Bibliography* and *Understanding Ursula K. Le Guin*, Charlotte Spivack, and James Bittner for their studies of Le Guin, and Sam Siciliano, for his 1975 dissertation work on *The Word for World Is Forest*. I am also grateful to Robert Galbreath for his work on Daoism and magic and other topics, and to Tom Remington for his work on touch as a motif in Le Guin's canon generally, and on Earthsea as Terran. More recently, I have been aided by Linda Nicholson, who has done great service in making philosophical poststructuralism intelligible to those of us who have not had formal training in recent philosophy; and I have been aided on philosophical issues by discussions with Dennis McGucken, who also offered helpful commentary on my discussion of postmodernism. And, finally, for help with my text, my thanks to my colleague Anita C. Wilson for her suggestions on the chapter on picture books, from the point of view of a professional critic, scholar, and teacher of literature for children and young adults.

I am deeply indebted to Roger Schlobin of Starmont Press for his initial confidence in me, and to Mary A. Burgess and Robert Reginald for their patience and aid for the production of this book by Borgo Press. Last, my thanks to C. Barry Chabot, Chair of the Department of English at Miami University, for his encouragement, advice, and aid.

INTRODUCTION

> Throughout human history, stories have been the preferred form for expression of moral commitments.... Narrative is a primary means for testing with concrete particularizations the benefits and disadvantages of specific ethical decisions. Narrative retellability and rereadability ensure that such examinations will not too easily crystallize into mere dogma.
> —Karl Kroeber, *Retelling and Rereading* (189; qtd. Le Guin, *Norton* 24).

> One who does not honor the teacher...is greatly confounded though knowledgeable.
> (*Tao te Ching* ch. 27)

Coyote's Song is mostly a close reading of a large number of the narrative works of Ursula K. Le Guin. It does not exactly have a thesis, but it does have a title, some controlling ideas and, arguably, an agenda.
• In his title 'Persuading Us To Rejoice and Teaching Us How to Praise,' James W. Bittner is not only alluding to a line by W. H. Auden but also making clear that a significant part of Le Guin's project, from her first published work on, is teaching. Eric S. Rabkin has described Le Guin's *The Left of Darkness* as 'clearly didactic' ('Determinism' 5), and other readers of Le Guin have noted what Elizabeth Cummins has called 'the didactic Le Guin' (166). I accept Le Guin's didacticism as a *given* in her writing, but I knew enough people find the word 'didacticism' negative that I avoided it in my title. I will avoid the word 'didactic' in my text as well because Le Guin's works are didactic in a fairly unusual way, what we might call 'dialogic didacticism,' or 'teaching by dialectics (*i.e.*, argument)'; most simply put, Le Guin's works are usually *good* teachers. The problem with most didactic works I've encountered is that the teachers are cock-sure that they have Truth and are duty-bound to ram it down the throats of children and the unwashed masses. Le Guin has her certainties, but they are rare, and, ordinarily, she debates with herself. So instead of coming up with long phrases modifying 'didacticism,' I offer the image of

this book's title: Coyote, the great Trickster figure, teaching in raucous antiphony and polyphony (see Cadden 516).

• The first controlling idea should not be controversial. Art *means* in contexts, contexts that includes its perceivers (in the scientific formulation, 'The observer is part of the system'). I give my students the image of the rainbow. The colors are created by the interaction of a portion of the electromagnetic spectrum with the vision of humans who can see colors. Different cultures define the colors differently. And there are an indefinitely large number of possible colors that can be perceived; still, somewhere along the way one gets into the ultraviolet or infrared—one gets to colors merely normal humans cannot see. Similarly, there are an indefinitely large number of meanings we can legitimately perceive in works of art, and that meaning is created by an interaction of the work and its perceivers—but some place along the line an interpretation can figuratively go into the ultraviolet or infrared (or beyond), and one's fellow perceivers can say, 'I just don't see it.' Changing the metaphor, even one perceiver is likely to see even one work differently in different contexts, as differing figures against different 'grounds'; e.g., I read Le Guin's 'Vaster Than Empires and More Slow' somewhat differently in the context of the stories collected in *The Wind's Twelve Quarters* than I read it collected in *Buffalo Gals....* Much of the work I do in *Coyote's Song* is putting Le Guin in the context of Le Guin: closely reading her works individually—I have publicly admitted to doing *compulsively* close readings—and reading them as a canon, an *opus*, an interrelated set whose individual members are mutually illuminating and defining.

To a lesser extent, I read the works as historical documents. In the cliché of historical criticism of all varieties, every artistic work is produced in a specific time and place, and all literature needs to be read (in part) in terms of its historical contexts. Especially for younger readers, especially with the earlier works, Le Guin's work needs to be 'historicized.' Older readers, too, can be helped with historical context. E.g., almost all readers who were in the United States and at least teenagers during the 1960s will understand that Le Guin's *The World for Word Is Forest* comments quite directly on American warfare in Indochina, what was called in the United States, 'The Viet Nam War.' Until late in the first draft of this book, however, I missed the implications for American warfare in Viet Nam implicit in the Earthsea trilogy (1968-72). The trilogy deals extensively with the importance for using power without pride, with the importance of avoiding arrogance, of observing limits. I knew that. It took a long time, though—and reading other critics—for me to put that fact together with two well-known book titles from the 1960s: Sen. J. William Fulbright's *The Arrogance of Power* (1966/1967) and Sen. Eugene J. McCarthy's *The Limits of Power: America's Role in the World* (1968).

I hope to help younger readers a bit with historicizing Le Guin's earlier works, and some aspects of the later ones. But I refer all readers to the work done by James Bittner, Charlotte Spivack, Elizabeth Cummins, and others for offering different histor*ies* to form the context of Le Guin's work, including biographical material on Le Guin for the personal history of a very active and complex human being whose life is still very much a work in progress.

• The second, and related, controlling idea is continuity. Looking at various entities (things, objects, organisms, people) some people will see mostly differences; other people will see mostly similarities. E.g., in various works, Le Guin has used the symbol of 'the Circle of Life' (an almost complete circle), the Yin-Yang, open and closed doorways, and the hinged spiral of the heyiya-if. One may note that Le Guin uses symbols, that they are similar symbols, that they are symbols familiar in but more often foreign to Western religions and attitudes: similarities and continuities; or one may note that Le Guin changes her symbols: difference and change.[6] Some will value difference and change, others similarity and continuity. I tend to see and value similarities and continuities, and I will argue for a strong tendency toward continuity in Le Guin's work. In her poetry, picture books, and short stories, Le Guin is more experimental, but in her science fiction and fantasy novels up until the mid-1980s, Le Guin's works are analyzable in terms of a limited number of themes and patterns.[7]

One continuity for Le Guin's writing, then, is the return to such perennial themes as the role of art and the artist and variations on the theme of (usually heterosexual) love, and varieties of friendship: human bonding. Another of her repeated themes is hard for many readers to accept in the world and therefore difficult to recognize in literature they like. As we will soon see, Le Guin denies a transcendent One-God and with that god Christianity and 'the Judaeo-Christian-Rationalist West' (*LoH* 82; ch. 6). Very emphatically, Le Guin denies the separable soul as contemporary monotheists usually see it, and insists on the finality of death. Insofar as Le Guin allows an 'afterlife' at all, it is a 'Dry Land' like Hades, as the most ancient Greeks saw it, or Sheol as viewed by Job or Koheleth ('the Preacher' in Ecclesiastes)—or it is 'The Four Houses of the Sky,' which also include abstractions and the unborn (*ACH* 44, [47]). Basically, when you are dead you are dead, for Le Guin, and this «mortalist» view makes very urgent her concerns with lethal violence generally and war specifically.[8] In ways that are varied and historically conditioned, but frequently, Le Guin re-

---

[6] The heyiya-if is from *Always Coming Home* (*ACH*); analogs to its open spiral form may be found in (unhinged) Keltic gyres and Jewish Havdalah candles. The open and closed doorways are from *The Farthest Shore* and *Tehanu*, using a symbol from, among other places Western places, Rome: *Janus bifrons* has his two faces because doorways and gates necessarily 'look' in two directions.

[7] For continuities and consistency in Le Guin's works from a contemporary psychoanlytical point of view, see Bernard Selinger, *Le Guin and Identity* (see esp. Selinger 145).

[8] The 4th edn. of *The MLA Handbook*... (1995) calls for 'quotation marks around a word or phrase used in a special sense or purposefully misused' (§ 2.2.8). Since the close reading I do requires extensive quotation from Le Guin (and others), and I want to differentiate real quotations from special senses, I shall use for special senses European-style quotation marks: « ».

turns to the theme of war and the problem of violence, leading in turn to the question of utopia: How might we get not The Great Society but a good society? What might make for, at least, a nonviolent society? Le Guin finds the best hope for human society in some variety of communist anarchy, with a feminist emphasis that increases from the earlier works to the later, and a Daoist emphasis most explicit in the earlier works but maintained throughout.

Le Guin's continuity, however, is flexible. If one sees *Always Coming Home* as central to Le Guin's canon and the motion of the Dao as her sustaining image (and I do), decorously central also are Le Guin's debates with herself. Her consistency lies less in taking position X or Y or Z than returning to the XYZ axis system, *returning* to these issue in a kind of reversal.

Le Guin's major patterns, by my count, are three or four in number.

I'll begin with the pattern of Romantic Comedy. In the Shakespearean form that permeates English-speaking culture, Romantic Comedy moves toward a new and better world—younger, more flexible, more hopeful, more joyous—coalescing around a central couple. That's Northrop Frye's formulation in *Anatomy of Criticism*, except that I have corrected his chemistry. (Frye had the new world *crystallizing*: too rigid an image.)[9] Using this pattern doesn't mean fulfilling it each time, offering an audience every work, 'As You Like It.' The movement of the pattern can be frustrated, with the plot moving toward tragedy. Instead of the wished-for happy ending of union, integration, renewed life, and rejoicing, there can be somber endings of isolation and separation. A newly integrated and peaceful world coalesces around Shakespeare's Romeo and Juliet, but they are dead. Rocannon in *Rocannon's World* is able to destroy his enemies and bring to the League of All Worlds a great gift; and Rocannon in the Epilogue finds a home, hearth, marriage, and a people. But Rocannon's victory is at the cost of the life of a dear friend, and Rocannon is dead before he can be told his new home world has been given his name (135-36).[10] Rolery and Jakob Agat in Le Guin's *Planet of Exile* marry and will live more or less happily ever after, but they go home together onlyafter the death and destruction of a major battle. And the potential Romantic Comedies of *The Word for World Is Forest* and in Stone Telling's story in *Always Coming Home* are utterly frustrated, yielding as happy an ending as we can hope for in *Word for World*, with the survival of the Athshean

---

[9] '...the movement of comedy is usually a movement from one kind of society to another. At the beginning of the play the obstructing characters are in charge of the play's society, and the audience recognizes that they are usurpers. At the end of the play...[a] device in the plot...brings hero and heroine together [and] causes a new society to crystallize around the hero...' (Frye 163).
[10] *Cost* is a major issue in Le Guin. Cf. and contrast the death of Mogien in *RW* (1966) with the death of Estraven in *LHD* (1969) and with the intentionally deformed life of the imprisoned scapegoat child in 'The Ones Who Walk Away from Omelas' (1973).

peoples, but for the point of view characters isolation, madness, and death. In Le Guin, 'Patterns of Integration'—epitomized by marriages—are usually good things (Crow and Erlich), but, sometimes, the least bad upshot is integration's reversal: separation, divorce.

Next, is the pattern of two abstractly philosophical views of the world: immanence vs. transcendence. Le Guin has been an enthusiastic participant in the immanence vs. transcendence debate in the form that goes back, in the European tradition, to at least Augustine of Hippo and Boethius in the 400s-500s CE. Is Ultimate Reality Out There and Up in some transcendent God or Truth or Whatever, or inside things, over, under (especially under) around and through—immanent in—the world? Le Guin is consistently Daoist in mostly denying transcendence and emphatically denying a transcendent God and most Western people's ideas of an afterlife, and this profound denial of monotheism in a highly spiritual writer—one who likes the Hindu deities Shiva and Kali—is very important for her work and is a subtext in much of the analysis of Le Guin's works by others.[11] Less well recognized, by me certainly, has been more mundane, *homelier*, meanings for immanence and transcendence.

* * * * * * *

In *The Second Sex*—a book Le Guin cites in 'Is Gender Necessary?'—Simone de Beauvoir explicitly uses 'immanence' and 'transcendence' as central terms for her analysis of women's current situation and proposals for women's liberation ('Gender?' *DEW* 8).

Beauvoir nowhere defines 'immanence' and 'transcendence,' but does say that 'The domestic labors that fell to [woman's] lot...imprisoned her in repetition and immanence'—to which the translator supplies a note that in Beauvoir *immanence* 'always signifies, as here, the opposite or negation of transcendence, such as confinement or restriction to a narrow round of uncreative and repetitious duties; it is in contrast to the freedom to engage in projects of ever[-]widening scope that marks the untrammeled existent' (63). And earlier, in her Introduction, Beauvoir states:

> [When] transcendence falls back into immanence, stagnation, there is a degradation of existence into the...brutish life of subjection to given conditions.... The downfall represents a moral fault if the subject consents to it;...inflicted upon him, it spells frustration and oppression...an absolute evil. Every individual concerned to justify his ex-

---

[11] Shiva is the creative Destroyer in the Hindu pantheon, gendered male, who dances the worlds into being; Kali is the creative Destroyer gendered female. Following Aldous Huxley in *The Perennial Philosophy*, and Capra on creation/destruction in *The Tao of Physics*, we can see Shiva/Kali, along with the goddess Shakti (also Sakti), as the mythic figuring of the Dao, as the Being and non-Being from which all things come and to which all return.

> istence feels that his existence involves...[a] need to transcend himself, to engage in freely chosen projects.
> Now,...woman—a free and autonomous being...—nevertheless finds herself living in a world where men compel her to assume the status of the Other. They propose to stabilize her as object and to doom her to immanence since her transcendence is to be overshadowed and forever transcended by [the male ego].... (xli)

And however much a human couple 'is the original *Mitsein*' (friendly society) and 'a basic combination' (35), nowhere is 'woman' more trapped in immanence than reproduction and marriage.[12] To get out of that trap 'woman' must 'seek self-fulfillment in transcendence': i.e., 'lose herself in her projects,' becoming independent and free. 'Woman' today 'no longer seeks to drag [man] into the realms of immanence but to emerge, herself, into the light of transcendence' (51, 717; see also II.VII.xxv: 702, 715).

Le Guin wrote in 'Is Gender Necessary?' (1976) that she considered herself a feminist at least by the mid-1960s and repeats her claim in her Introduction to *Planet of Exile*, concluding there, famously in Le Guin studies, and, she says, unfashionably, with 'Once I was asked what I thought the central, constant theme of my work was, and I said spontaneously, 'Marriage'' (cf. Headnote 'Good Trip', *WTQ* 109).

One way to help historicize the stories of Ursula K. Le Guin, especially her early short fiction, is to place them in dialog with Beauvoir's *The Second Sex* (and its philosophical tradition) and with themselves on issues of immanence and transcendence, broadly defined. In a number of works from Le Guin's first published story, 'An die Musik' (1961), through *Tehanu*, in 1990, Le Guin works through the immanence/transcendence antithesis, literally re-evaluating the two terms and undermining the binary opposition between them. Quite emphatically, she looks at immanence in several forms, including domestic life, and at transcendence primarily as moving out of Being and nature into action, culture, and history: into conflict, art (including magic), saving people, and utopia building.

In *Tehanu*, the point-of-view character, Tenar, explicitly and consciously gives up studying magic with the great mage Ogion: 'I left him,' she says. 'What did I want with his books?.... I wanted to live, I wanted a man, I wanted my children, I wanted my life' (51)—not transcendence in Existentialist terms but simply *life*. Tenar's journey is away from 'the powers of learning and skill offered her by...Ogion. She had turned her back on all that, gone to the other side, the other room, where the women lived, to be one of them. A wife, a farmer's wife, a mother, a householder, undertaking the power that a woman was born to, the authority allotted her by the arrangements of mankind' (*Tehanu* 30). Tenar gives herself to im-

---

[12] See e.g., in *Second Sex* 147, 173-5, 187; II.V.xvi: esp. 429-30, 447-48, 451-54, 456; II.V.xvii: 513, 521; 555-6, 594; II.V.xxi: esp. 598-99, 602 (see also 618-21).

manence, and does womanly, life-sustaining, things therein, and thereby helps change her world radically.

Or consider three clearly philosophical stories collected in *The Wind's Twelve Quarters* (1975).

'Darkness Box' (1963) is a Pandora story, but here the Pandora-figure is male and a prince, and the gods are replaced by the sea, a female witch, and a little boy. It's not a bad world in the story: a world of high fantasy, where the exiled prince returns to lay siege to the royal city and be defeated by the loyal prince, true soldier to their father (*WTQ* 59). It's a world with unicorns and witches' familiars and at least one griffin. But it is a grey world, with no sun and no shadows and no darkness, a world of stasis where the clocks always read 9:50 A.M. It is a world of immanence—but, in this world, the 'narrow round of uncreative and repetitious duties' is precisely the heroic project of loyal warfare. The prince serves the king, fighting off—again and again and again—the attacks of the prince's brother. 'Serve and be served,' the witch tells him, 'rule and be ruled. Your brother chose neither to serve nor rule...'—and then breaks off and warns the prince to take care. Perhaps he does. For whatever motivation, the prince releases darkness from the box, and so Time and shadow, chance, change, and death enter his world. And this is a happy ending (*WTQ* 64). There may be some Martin Heidegger or Rainer Maria Rilke in there; there are certainly ideas consistent with Le Guin's Daoism. Still the main point here is that in 1963 Le Guin asserted in her fiction that the violent project of heroic warfare was what was repetitive and boring. And she did so while associating warfare with subjugation and rule and suggesting the need for an alternative to the subjugation/rule antithesis.[13]

Undoubtedly Heidegger, Jean-Paul Sartre, and Albert Camus are around in two stories from 1970, with maybe a touch of Søren Kierkegaard: 'Things' and 'A Trip to the Head,' juxtaposed in *The Wind's Twelve Quarters*.

'Things' is a story of 'The End' (the title under which Damon Knight ran the story). In a very low-tech country by the sea, The End is expected, and the people divide into the Weepers up in Heights-Hall and the Ragers down in the fields (148-49), all except for three: a brickmaker named Lif, an unnamed widow, and an unnamed baby. Lif dreams of the Islands, and if this were a «hard», technological SF story, the plot would involve his invention and building of a boat. But the Ragers have destroyed everything Lif can think of to build a boat. In social SF, the plot would move toward an allegory where the Ragers = the Weathermen and other young rebels (153) and the Weepers were 'The Great Silent [Christian] Majority,' and the world would die with a bang and a whimper. Within the story, that doesn't happen either. Lif takes up with the widow and her child, and they

---

[13] For Heidegger, Rilke, et al., see Bitner, *Approaches*, Index: *Dinge*. Cf. and contrast the dialog between the prince and the witch in 'Darkness Box' with that between King Ashthera and the Priestess in Le Guin's 1985 film script *King Dog* (90-92; Part 4).

live together for a while; he learns to float and swim a bit and lays a causeway with his remaining bricks, a causeway heading away from the country and its madfolk and toward the Islands. And then Lif and the widow, with the baby, walk into the sea upon his causeway, going as far as it goes and the taking the last step. Perhaps with a ship rescuing them and taking them to the Islands, but probably not.

Heidegger, my encyclopedia tells me, said that Man 'stands out' from things, a project who will be occasionally absorbed back into things, becoming 'nobody in particular' (740). In 'Things,' two elderly men coming from a Weeping say, 'It is well to be free of Things' (sic: T, 154). Maybe. Le Guin was to say so in *The Dispossessed*. But the bricklayer is 'a builder, not a floater' (152), and I think the line has symbolic meaning, and the widow accounts for their (temporary) survival with 'you had your things—your bricks—and I had the baby....' (156). Lif's labor, while they're waiting for The End, was Sisyphean: load after load of bricks. But he did his own thing, and he produced a straight, heavy, earth-bound road in the right direction, one leading away from the pointless and repetitive Weeping and Raging. To apply a song from the period: they found an 'also' in 'a world of Either/Or.' And Le Guin supplies here an 'also' to the antithesis of immanence and transcendence, feminine domesticity and manly, heroic projects: the most free and creative work we see is housekeeping, childcare, and hauling bricks. In the midst of madness, where one cannot do much good, heroism may be impossible, and heroism may be one of the sources for the madness, not the solution but part of the problem; the best one might do, then, is just keep going with the everyday, or just walk away. To mix some of Le Guin's metaphors, when nothing remains to be done, one can be done with doing and walk away to rejoin the sea (or forest) of Being.

'A Trip to the Head' (1970) is no story to try to summarize, but it clearly moves away from 'possession...[and] success,' away from a utilitarian view of people away from macho Existentialism and equally macho sexuality. The story moves from defining oneself outside the world— naming oneself and willing oneself out of nature into culture and dominance—toward a forest Le Guin associates with shadows, myths, old wives' tales, and Blakean tigers. As we will see, 'A Trip to the Head' moves toward a forest that Le Guin associates with philosophical Immanence, with Being. And in 'A Trip to the Head,' Le Guin *contrasts* that immanence with a relationship that could lead to a traditional heterosexual marriage. Fifteen years later, Le Guin tells a similar story in 'She Unnames Them' (1985). The protagonist-narrator there is Eve, and the action is far more cosmic, but Eve, too, like the naming character in 'A Trip,' ends up among trees, heading 'down the path away from the house,' into immanence. It has been Eve's transcendent project to increase immanence: she *consciously* unnames all the animals and then consciously unnames herself (discussed in Khanna).

One last set of stories of the Immanence/Transcendence Pattern. 'The Ones Who Walk Away from Omelas' (1973), 'The Day Before the Revolution' (1974), and 'Sur' (1982; see Khanna 50-55).

Carol D. Stevens reminds us that the Omelites are 'us' (30), and Elizabeth Cummins reminds us of a slogan from our recent history: 'America—Love It or Leave It' (22). I'll add Peter Biskind's reminder that in many Cold-War era Hollywood movies, 'the U.S.A., ca. 1955, was utopian enough for anyone' (115). 'The Ones Who Walk Away' is a most rigorous examination of the highly transcendent—'Let's get out there and **perfect things**, damn it!'—utopian project. Omelas *is* a good place, mostly—almost entirely: a place of happiness and joy, a place, it first seems, without guilt. What the story turns into is a scapegoat fable and a reduction to the grotesque of the hyper-rationalist, measuring, utilitarian doctrine of the greatest good for the greatest number. The story attacks the ideal of the 'Rationalist' part of 'Judaeo-Christian-Rationalist West: it attack the benevolent desire 'to make the world better for humanity' (*LoH* 82-83); the story attacks idealism insofar as idealism seeks an Archimedean point outside the world, from which he can shove it toward an abstract, transcendent Good (see *NA* 88). The Omelites, however much they are 'mature, intelligent, passionate adults' (*WTQ* 254) are gravely mistaken or, as Rebecca Adams suggests, a little crazy (41). Either way, we can help privilege Those Who Walk Away from Omelas by associating them with Lif and the widow and child in 'Things,' and Eve in 'She Names Them.' If will and reason have created a transcendent project in Omelas, then it might be well to leave Omelas. If some 'transcendental power' has dictated the 'sacrificial 'terms'' shown in the Omelas story (Adams 41), then it would also be well to leave Omelas, rejecting such transcendental powers.

'[O]ne of the ones who walked away from Omelas,' Le Guin tells us in the headnote, is Odo from 'The Day Before the Revolution' (260), and so positive a revolutionary should give pause in privileging immanence over Beauvoir's transcendence. What could be a more transcendent project than developing the theory for a utopian revolution? Three points. First, at least into the 1970s, the utopian question was, 'What will things be like the day *after* the Revolution?'—i.e., what are the goals of the Revolution? Le Guin's story is about a fairly ordinary day, the day *before* the revolution. Second, the story is about Odo, 'the famous revolutionary,' except it is not just that, because Odo is not just that: Odo is also a woman who had married and loved her husband. She was and is her whole history, which included being, a 'swimmer in the midst of life': an image of immanence in the world (275). Third, Odo is the theoretician of people on the bottom, at 'the foundation, the reality, the source'; her wisdom comes from knowing people are, at bottom, mud (*WTQ* 274), part of the Earth.[14]

---

[14] See Tzu Yu on death: *Chuang Tzu*, ch. 6 (Giles 79), and Kurt Vonnegut, Jr., in *Cat's Cradle* (1963): § 99, 'Dyot meet mat' ('God made mud' [149]).

Finally, let's look at the great project of polar exploration and making of a temporary utopia in 'Sur' (1982; see Khanna 51-55).

In 'Sur,' nine women—we will see many nines in Le Guin's work—nine women in 1909-1910, are the first people to reach the South Pole (although they probably shouldn't have made that last part of the trip [*WTQ* 267-8].) They select leaders in case of grave emergency, but never have an emergency, and so act in near-perfect anarchy (257); they practice good housekeeping, 'the art of the infinite' (260); Berta creates beautiful sculptures (262-3); and Teresa has a baby (269-70). They have their goal and 'success crowned our efforts.' They are world-class explorers, *and* they are very responsible wives and mothers: 'those who wished to evade' the claims of family 'were not the companions we wanted in hard work, risk, and privation' (256). They claim no reward, not even fame. They achieve their transcendent goal, but they renounce any sort of victory and don't leave at the South Pole for a memorial so much as a single human footprint.

* * * * * * *

The last pattern is the political complement of the immanence / transcendence antithesis: a pattern of opposition and political philosophy had been worked out by the Daoists and which appears in Le Guin's work as early as *A Wizard of Earthsea* (1968) and continued into *Always Coming Home* (1985), *A Fisherman of the Inland Sea*, and 'Solitude' (1994), but not, significantly, *Tehanu* (1990). Le Guin herself implies most of the opposition in her very important essay 'Is Gender Necessary': not only in the original 1976 version but retained in the 1988 form, 'Is Gender Necessary? Redux.' In this social opposition, the people on the right path are in some sense anarchistic: 'communal, independent, and somewhat introverted.' Their populations are stable and they tend not to 'move in large masses, or rapidly. Their migrations have been slow.... They have no nomadic peoples, and no societies that live by expansion and aggression.... Nor have they formed large, hierarchically governed nation-states, the mobilizable entity that is the essential factor in modern war.' Competition is ritualized, and, when ritual breaks down, any resulting violence 'does not become mass violence, remaining limited, personal.' The people going wrong *are* organized into 'hierarchically governed nation-states' or their future analogs, and they will organize for war (*DEW* 10), modern or premodern war. In *The Left Hand of Darkness* (1969), the culture farthest along the wrong way tends toward transcendent belief. In *Always Coming Home* (1985), the wrong-headed people are explicitly defined as monotheists, worshipping the transcendent One and basing their social structure on—or at least justifying it in terms of—their theology and cosmography.

* * * * * * *

Le Guin is not a formulaic writer in any derogatory sense, but she is a highly prolific popular artist with a strong ethical sense and strong interests. Like William Shakespeare, Charles Dickens, and other popular writers who are producing high art—making problematic, and interesting the old forms—she has used both generic patterns and more personal patterns; like Shakespeare and, more recently with some film auteurs, she has looked at some recurring issues from different angles in different works, sometimes 'arguing' different sides of a question. Most important, like the Greek dramatist Euripides and some of the inventors of American literature, she has performed the highly radical work of moving society toward change by examining and shifting archetypes and (re)inventing myths, trying to 're-vision' our inherited formulas (*ER* 1993), to find new 'Legends for a New Land' (1988).

AN URSULA K. LE GUIN CHRONOLOGY

1862-90 US military leads warfare against various Native American tribes, nations, and confederations as White settlers move West; the Indians lose, including massacres and cultural genocide among the Indians of California.
1916 Death of 'Ishi,' the last Yahi Indian in California, who had been aided, befriended, and studied by Le Guin's father, A. L. Kroeber.
1917-19 A. L. Kroeber finishes monumental *Handbook of the Indians of California.*
1926 Theodora Kracaw Brown, mother of Clifton and Theodore, marries Alfred Louis Kroeber.
1929 Ursula born at Berkeley, CA, to Theodora and A. L. Kroeber, youngest of four children and only daughter (a couple years younger than Karl, her full sibling).
1937-48 Golden age of twentieth-c. Existentialism.
ca. 1938 At about age twelve, Ursula discovers Lord Dunsany's *A Dreamer's Tales* and discovers her 'native country' (Le Guin, 'Citizen of Mondath').
1939-45 After preliminaries, World War II begins in deadly earnest. US formally enters after attack on Pearl Harbor (7 Dec. 1941).
1947-51 Ursula Kroeber attends Radcliffe College majoring in French and Italian, with a concentration in Renaissance literature; graduates Phi Beta Kappa not long after having an unplanned pregnancy and an abortion.
1948 A. L. Kroeber publishes revised 2nd edn. of *Anthropology* (1st edn. 1923), reissued in parts in the early 1960s.
1950-53 The Korean Conflict. / Rise of Joseph McCarthy and the power of a Red Scare silencing much unorthodox thought in the USA into the 1960s.
1951 Ursula writes Radcliffe senior thesis: 'The Metaphor of the Rose as an Illustration of the 'Carpe Diem' Theme in French and Italian Poetry of the Renaissance.'
1952 Receives M.A. from Columbia University, French specialization with thesis on 'Ideas of Death in Ronsard's Poetry.'
1953 Travels to France on a Fulbright grant for research for Ph.D., meeting at sea the historian Charles Le Guin; they marry in Paris.

1954 Charles teaches history at Mercer University in Macon, GA; Ursula teaches French. French forces at Dienbienphu surrender to Vietminh in Indochina, giving the nationalist/Communist forces following Ho Chi Minh victory in the First War for Vietnamese Independence. Segregation by law forbidden by the US Supreme Court in *Brown v. Board of Education of Topeka, Kansas*.
1955 Ursula writes parents of her interest in Daoism on feminine yin and masculine yang (28 Oct., reported in Barrow & Barrow 86). Ngo Dinh Diem refuses to hold elections and declares the Republic of Viet Nam in the south of old French Indochina. Rosa Parks is arrested for refusing to move to segregated section in a bus in Montgomery, Alabama.
1956 Charles teaches history at the University of Idaho in Moscow, ID; Ursula teaches French.
1957 Daughter Elizabeth born.
1959 Le Guins move to Portland, OR; Charles teaches history at Portland State University; daughter Caroline born. Ursula Le Guin's mother, Theodora Kroeber, publishes *The Inland Whale*, nine stories from native American cultures in California, each giving a portrait of a woman.
1960 Le Guin's 'Coming of age...at about age thirty-one' (*LoN* 55). / Le Guin reintroduced to S.F. / Death of A. L. Kroeber in Paris. National Liberation Front (NLF) established in South Vietnam; Pres. John F. Kennedy increases US aid for South Vietnam and sends additional military advisers. Student Nonviolent Coordinating Committee (SNCC) and others launch southern sit-in movement.
1961 'An die Musik' (an Orsinian tale) published in *Western Humanities Review*. T. Kroeber publishes *Ishi in Two Worlds*. Congress of Racial Equality (CORE) sends 'Freedom Riders' into US South to resist segregation laws in interstate transportation.
1962 'April in Paris' (SF) published in *Fantastic* 11. Students for a Democratic Society (SDS) national convention in Port Huron, MI, issues 'The Port Huron Statement' calling for radical change in America, aiming at 'participatory democracy'—rise of the 'New Left.'
1963 'The Masters' and 'Darkness Box' (science fiction/'SF') published in *Fantastic* 12. Le Guin writing *Planet of Exile*. August: march on Washington, DC., featuring M. L. King, Jr.'s 'I Have a Dream Speech'—climax of civil rights movement. / November: Assassination of John F. Kennedy.
1964 'The Word of Unbinding' and 'The Rule of Names' published in *Fantastic* 13 (Earthsea tales); 'The Dowry of the Angyar' published in *Amazing*; son Theodore born. T. Kroeber publishes *Ishi: Last of His Tribe*, story of Ishi's life and world. / Rise of UK magazine *New Worlds*, providing an outlet for serious S.F. experimentation with themes and writing styles.
1964 Civil Rights Act makes illegal discrimination based on race and other listed reasons, including sex. / Three civil rights workers murdered in Mississippi. / Riots in Harlem and elsewhere. / L. Johnson elected President of the United States, on a peace platform. / Free speech

movement starts at U. of California at Berkeley. 'All through the sixties, in my home city in the States, I had been helping organize and participating in nonviolent demonstrations, first against atomic bomb testing, then against the pursuance of the war in Viet Nam.... Anyway, there was a peace movement, and I was in it, and so had a channel of action and expression for my ethical and political opinions totally separate from my writing' (Le Guin, *LoN* [1979]: 151).

1965 First US combat troops at Danang, Vietnam, rising to 200,000 by December. B-52s bomb North Vietnam. First march against the war in Vietnam.

1966 *Rocannon's World*, *Planet of Exile* (Ace Doubles). Founding of the National Organization for Women. / At a conference on Structuralism at Johns Hopkins University, Jacques Derrida delivers a paper on 'Structure, Sign and Play...,' laying a philosophical groundwork for a very strong theory of what Peter L. Berger and Thomas Luckmann would call in their book that year, *The Social Construction of Reality*.

1967 *City of Illusions* (Ace Books).

1968 Le Guin in London and feels she should not participate there in anti-US demonstrations; writes *Word for World*.... / *A Wizard of Earthsea*. *No More Fun and Games* begins publication: 'one of the very earliest radical feminist journals (Echols 158-65). / Joanna Russ publishes *Picnic on Paradise* an early tale of Alyx, a strong feminist hero(ine). / Film and novel of *2001*: the ultimate male 'trip.' Battle of Khesanh and Tet Offensive in Vietnam. American troops massacre men, women, children, and babies at My Lai. / Students riot in Paris: France appears close to a revolution. Assassinations of Robert Kennedy and M. L. King, Jr.; King assassination followed by rioting. / Televised police riot at Democratic National convention in Chicago. / R. M. Nixon elected US President, beginning of 'backlash' against political radicalism.

1969 *The Left Hand of Darkness* (wins both Nebula and Hugo Awards [SF fans and SF authors]), 'Winter's King' (*Orbit 5*, ed. Damon Knight), [coll. 1975 in *The Wind's Twelve Quarter*, with feminine pronouns]), 'Nine Lives' (*Playboy*, but under the name 'U. K. Le Guin'—hiding her gender—and with some unapproved changes). Receives Boston Globe-Horn Book Award for *A Wizard of Earthsea*. US bombs North Vietnamese bases in Cambodia. First and second withdrawals of US troops announced by Nixon. US bombs Hanoi and Haiphong. Successful 'Moratoriums' protest against the war. Ca. 300 Weathermen attempt to 'bring the war home' battling police in Chicago. / Fred Hampton and Mark Clark of the Black Panther Party killed in raid by Chicago police. / Increasing feeling among some politically active women that feminism and the left are opposed (Echols 134). / Last week of June: Stonewall Rebellion and 'Gay Pride Week'—riot and aftermath when gay men resist raid on The Stonewall Bar in Greenwich Village, NYC.

1970 'A Trip to the Head (*Quark 1*, ed. S. R. Delany), 'The Tombs of Atuan' (short form in *Worlds of Fantasy* 1). Wins both Hugo and Nebula Awards for *The Left Hand of Darkness*. Publication of T. Kroeber's

Alfred Kroeber: A Personal Configuration; J. Russ's scholarly work, 'The Image of Women in Science Fiction'; Gloria Steinem's liberal feminist essay, 'What It Would Be Like If Women Win,' *Time*, 31 Aug.; Kate Millett's *Sexual Politics*, Shulamith Firestone's *The Dialectic of Sex*, and Robin Morgan, ed., *Sisterhood is Powerful*—best selling, ovular works for radical feminism (Echols 198-99). Spring: US invades neutral Cambodia, bombs North Vietnam; Ohio National Guard shoots into gathered students at Kent State U., four killed; police open fire at Jackson State College, two killed. / First Earth Day.

1971 *The Tombs of Atuan* (Atheneum, Gollancz to Bantam), *The Lathe of Heaven* (Scribner's, Gollancz, to Avon for paperback) / 'Vaster than Empires and More Slow' in *New Dimensions 1*, ed. Robert Silverberg. Major antiwar demonstrations in Washington, DC in April (peaceful) and May (not peaceful). / Proceedings of the second Congress to Unite Women pre-empted by group insisting the women's movement accept lesbianism and value, as phrased in the title of the Radicalesbian position paper, 'The Woman-Identified Woman.'

1972 'The Word for World Is Forest' (in H. Ellison, ed., *Again, Dangerous Visions*, wins Hugo Award for novella), and *The Word for World Is Forest* (novel format), *The Farthest Shore*. Newbery Silver Medal Award for *The Tombs of Atuan*. National Book Award for Children's Books for *The Farthest Shore*. Start of *Ms.* magazine: liberal feminist publication (Echols 199). / Joanna Russ's 'When It Changed,' featuring Whileaway, a feminist separatist utopia. Last US ground troops leave Vietnam. Preliminary peace agreement in Vietnam. The 'Christmas bombing' of Hanoi and Haiphong. R. M. Nixon runs against G. McGovern in what many see as a referendum on the 1960s; Nixon wins in a landslide.

1973 'The Ones Who Walk Away from Omelas...' (*New Dimensions III*, ed. R. Silverberg; by 1981 frequently anthologized). Hugo Award for *The Word for World Is Forest*. Locus Award for *The Lathe of Heaven*. Alice Sheldon ('James Tiptree, Jr.') publishes 'The Women Men Don't See,' separatist feminist fiction; Mary Daly publishes *Beyond God the Father*, endorsing separatism in a woman's counterculture (Echols 5).

1974 'Schrödinger's Cat' (*Universe 5*, ed. Terry Garr), *The Dispossessed* (wins both Nebula and Hugo Awards), 'The Day Before the Revolution' (wins Nebula Award, rpt. *Bitches and Sad Ladies*, ed. Pat Rotter, *Nebula Award Stories 10*, ed. J. Gunn, *More Women of Wonder*, ed. Pamela Sargent). Hugo Award for '...Omelas.' Pamela Sargent publishes first of her anthologies of S.F. by women, *Women of Wonder*; Suzy McKee Charnas publishes *Walk to the End of the World*: male-domination dystopia. Nixon resigns. Peace agreement signed in Paris, POWs returned, last US forces leave South Vietnam; US stops bombing in S.E. Asia.

1975 'The New Atlantis' (rpt. by 1978 in *The Norton Anthology of Short Fiction*, regular and 'Shorter' edn.) Le Guin wins Nebula and Hugo Awards for *The Dispossessed*, the Nebula and Jupiter Awards for 'The

Day Before the Revolution.' / *Wild Angels*: Le Guin's first coll. of her poems. / Special Le Guin issue of *Science-Fiction Studies*. Joanna Russ publishes *The Female Man*, whose utopian ideal is Whileaway. Saigon surrenders to North Vietnamese, for the end of the Second War for Vietnamese Independence. / Khmer Rouge take over in Cambodia and begin the time of 'the killing fields.'

1976 *Very Far Away from Anywhere Else* (Young Adult novel: male protagonist-narrator), *Solomon Leviathan's Nine Hundred and Thirty-First Trip Around the World* (picture book illustrated by Alicia Austin), *Orsinian Tales* (coll. of 11 stories, including 'An de Musik'). Jupiter Award for 'The Diary of the Rose.' Samuel R. Delany publishes *Triton*, a utopia, dystopia, and 'heterotopia' with radical differences in how various people live. / Vonda N. McIntyre and Susan Janice Anderson, eds., *Aurora: Beyond Equality*, anthology of nonsexist S.F., plus Le Guin's essay 'Is Gender Necessary' (on *LHD*). Bicentennial of American Revolution.

1977 Alice Sheldon (writing as Rocconna Sheldon) publishes 'The Screwfly Solution,' a story premised on the intertwining, down to the neural level, of male aggression and male sexuality.

1978 'The Eye of the Heron' (*Millennial Women*, ed. Virginia Kidd): Le Guin's male hero killed, women central to conclusion of story. Publication of Mary Daly's *Gyn/Ecology: The Metaethics of Radical Feminism*—a strong statement of what A. Echols calls *cultural* feminism. Suzy McKee Charnas's *Motherlines* published: slightly ambiguous feminist separatist utopia, sequel to *Walk to the End of the World*.

1979 *Leese Webster* (children's book), *Malafrena* (set in Orsinia), 'Pathways of Desire' in *New Dimensions 9*. Le Guin is the invited respondent for a very high-powered international symposium on narrative at the University of Chicago. Lewis Carroll Shelf Award for *A Wizard of Earthsea*; Gandalf Award (Grand Master of Fantasy). Original edn. of *Language of the Night* published: coll. essays. / Death of Theodora Kroeber. / T. Kroeber and Robert F. Heizer, eds., *Ishi the Last Yahi*....

1980 *The Beginning Place* (Young Adult novel: narration divided between points of view of a young man and a young woman). / Special Le Guin issue of *Extrapolation*. Ronald Reagan elected Pres., starting at least 12 years of 'New Right' rule.

1981 *Hard Words* (new poems by Le Guin, several with Hindu and feminist themes).

1982 *The Compass Rose*, coll. stories from 1974 through 1982.

1983 'The Ascent of the North Face' in *Isaac Asimov's Science Fiction Magazine*.

1984 Locus Award for *The Compass Road* collection.

1985 *Always Coming Home* (a 'future anthropology' containing a novel), audio cassette: *Music and Poetry of the Kesh*, composer, Todd Barton (released with *ACH*). Libretto for *Rigel Nine: An Opera*, music by David Bedford. Le Guin on lecture circuit with presentation on 'A Woman Writing.'

1986 Continuing travel with 'A Woman Writing.' Janet Heidinger Kafka Prize for Fiction for *Always Coming Home.*
1987 *Buffalo Gals and Other Animal Presences* (coll. stories from the 1970s and 1980s), 'Is Gender Necessary? Redux': original essay from 1976 (q.v.), with commentary and corrections. Prix Lectures-Jeunesse for *Very Far Away from Anywhere Else.*
1988 *Wild Oats and Fireweed* (new poems), *Catwings* (picture book illustrated by S. D. Schindler), *A Visit from Dr. Katz* (picture book illustrated by Ann Barrow). Publ. of 'Legends for a New Land': Guest of Honor Speech at nineteenth Annual Mythopoeic Conference.
1989 *Catwings Return* (picture book illustrated by S. D. Schindler), *Fire and Stone* (picture book illustrated by Laura Marshall), *Dancing at the Edge of the World: Thoughts on Words, Women, Places* (important coll. of essays from 1976-1988). / Reissue of *Language of the Night* (with expansions). / Le Guin Receives the Pilgrim Award from the Science Fiction Research Association. International Fantasy Award and Hugo Award for 'Buffalo Gals, Won't You Come Out Tonight.' US troops invade Panamá.
1990 'The Kerastion' appears in *Westercon 1990 Program Book.* 'The Shobies' Story' in *Universe. Tehanu: The Last Book of Earthsea* (wins Nebula for best novel). *Blood Lodge Dances*—dance: choreography by Judy Patton, design by Christine Bourdette. US troops sent as largest contingent facing off against Iraq: Operation Desert Shield, followed by Operation Desert Storm: war against Iraq resulting in heavy Iraqi casualties.
1991 'The First Contact with the Gorgonids' in *Omni*; 'Newton's Sleep' in *Full Spectrum 3. Searoad* (connected 'mundane' short stories). Pushcart Prize for 'Bill Weisler' (coll. *Searoad*). Harold Vursell Award, American Academy & Institute of Arts & Letters.
1992 'The Rock that Changed Things' in *Amazing. Stone Dances*—dance: choreography by Judy Patton, design by Christine Bourdette. H. L. Davis Award from Oregon Institute of Literary Arts for *Searoad*
1993 'Dancing to Ganam' in *Amazing.* Publication of *The Norton Book of Science Fiction: North American Science Fiction, 1960-1990*, ed. Le Guin and Brian Attebery, with Karen Joy Fowler. *Earthsea Revisioned*, 'A lectured delivered under the title *Children, Women, Men and Dragons* at *Worlds Apart*, an institute sponsored by Children's Literature New England,' 2-8 August 1992 at Oxford U (UK).
1994 'The Matter of Seggri' in *Crank!*; 'Betrayals' in *Blue Motel*; 'Solitude' published in *The Magazine of Fantasy and Science Fiction.* 'Another Story, or A Fisherman of the Inland Sea' in *Tomorrow. A Fisherman of the Inland Sea*, coll. SF stories. *Going Out with Peacocks and Other Poems*, including animals poems and political poems (feminist, leftist).
1995 *Hubbub* annual poetry award for 'Semen' (coll. *Going Out with Peacocks*). Theodore Sturgeon Award and *Locus* Readers Award for 'Forgiveness Day' (coll. *Four Ways to Forgiveness*). James Tiptree, Jr.

Award for 'The Matter of Seggri.' 'Coming of Age in Karhide.' *New Legends*. Ed. Greg Bear. New York: Tor Books, 1995. *The Year's Best Science Fiction*. Thirteenth Annual Collection. Ed. Gardner Dozois. New York: St. Martin's, 1996. *Unlocking the Air and Other Stories* published (mostly fantasy and 'mundane' fiction).[15] *Four Ways to Forgiveness*. New York: HarperPrism-HarperPaperbacks (HarperCollins), 1995. Collects 'Betrayals' (from *Blue Motel* 1994); 'Forgiveness Day,' *Asimov's Science Fiction* 18.12-13 (Nov. 1994): [262]-304; 'A Man of the People,' *Asimov's Science Fiction* 19.4-5 (April 1995): 22-65; 'A Woman's Liberation,' *Asimov's Science Fiction* 19.8 (July 1995): [116]-63 1995. Twenty-fifth anniversary of the first Earth Day.1997 *The Twins, the Dream/Las Gemelas, el Sueño*, with Diana Bellessi: ArtePublico Press: Poems, mutually translated. *Steering the Craft....* Small book: Discussions and exercises for writers, on narrative-prose technique. / *Lao Tzu: The Tao Teh Ching. A Book About the Way and the Power of the Way*: 1997/98.

---

[15] 'Mundane' is Samuel R. Delany's suggestion for literature that is not fantasy, science fiction, 'magical realism,' etc. but in the mimetic-empirical tradition. One should accept 'mundane's' denotation—'down to —and ignore its connotation of 'unimaginative.' The connotation is a problem, but less problematic than calling SF and its generic relatives 'imaginative literature' and implying that the works of, say, George Eliot are unimaginative. Talking of 'realism' closes examination of what is real, and using 'mainstream,' fudges the question, 'The main stream of *what*?' The main stream of world literature since the invention of writing seems to center on something like fantasy; and what an unmodified 'mainstream' refers to would require a massive empirical study that seems a waste of time and effort, and the money it would require.) See Le Guin's Preface to *LoN* (1989) for comments on 'The Canoneers of Literature,' women authors, and genre (3-5). For a general term for much nonmundane fiction, I'll often use 'SF'.

A BIOGRAPHY OF URSULA K. LE GUIN

Ursula Kroeber was born 21 October 1929 (St. Ursula's Day) in Berkeley, California, the youngest child of Theodora and Alfred Kroeber. Theodora Kroeber had an M.A. in psychology in 1920 and, by 1961, a reputation as an author. Alfred was one of the founders of American anthropology and a world-class scholar. During the academic year, the Kroebers lived in a substantial house they owned in Berkeley; over the summer and other vacations, they lived at their country house in the Napa Valley, on a forty-acre estate they named Kishamish. The family appears to have been stable, loving, supportive, and 'functional,' and neither the Great Depression nor World War II seems to have harmed the family as a unit or Ursula and her three brothers individually.

The Kroebers were cosmopolitan, and 'bicoastal' long before the term was invented. Theodora Kroeber was thoroughly Western ('the redhead from Telluride' and before that Denver, CO), but Alfred studied literature at Columbia University in New York City and after retiring from the University of California at Berkeley taught as a visiting professor at such Eastern citadels as Harvard (1947-48), Columbia (1948-52), Brandeis (1954), and Yale (1958). Between 1947 and 1951, Ursula studied as an undergraduate at Radcliffe College for women—affiliated then as now with Harvard University—and then went on to Columbia for graduate work, her time at Radcliffe and Columbia overlapping with her father's time at Harvard and Columbia. When Ursula became pregnant shortly before graduating Radcliffe, she consulted with her parents at their home on Riverside Drive; the elder Kroebers arranged for an abortion, at that time and place, an act of criminal conspiracy (*DEW* 76).

Ursula's original ambitions were for careers in biology and poetry, but 'her inability to handle math caused her to drop biology' (De Bolt 16). Her collegiate work was in French and Italian Renaissance literature, and in 1953, Ursula won a Fulbright fellowship to work in France on her Ph.D. On the ship crossing to Europe, she met the historian Charles A. Le Guin, and they were married in Paris in December of 1953.

Ursula Kroeber Le Guin dropped her plans for the Ph.D. and followed Charles to Mercer University in Macon, GA, then to Emory University in Atlanta, where Charles got his Ph.D., to the University of Idaho at Moscow. While living in Moscow, ID, Le Guin gave birth to Elizabeth, the Le Guin's first child. In 1959, Charles got a job at Portland State University, and the family moved to Portland, OR. As of this writing, the Le Guins have kept Portland for their home, have remained married, and have raised three children: Elizabeth as mentioned, Caroline, and Theodore. For eighteen years, the Le Guins have shared territory with a male cat named Lorenzo Bean, and Le Guin has rarely described a scene with a potential cat in it without producing a cat, plus producing the *Catwings* series of picture books.

On 5 October 1960, Alfred L. Kroeber died at eighty-four years of age in Paris; he was buried in Berkeley, CA. Theodora Kroeber died on 4 July 1979 at age eighty-two. In a sentence Joe De Bolt quite properly made much of in his 'A Le Guin Biography' (1979), Le Guin tells us that 'Coming of age is a process that took me many years; I finished it, as far as I ever will, at about age thirty-one; and so I feel rather deeply about it' (*LoN* [1979]: 55).

Coming into adulthood is important, but would-be biologist and thoroughly honest woman 'going through the change,' Le Guin reminds readers that there is, for women, an additional physiological passage. Le Guin tells us that in 1976 she entered menopause and began to take up 'the opportunity to become a Crone' (*DEW* 3). By the time of her parents' deaths, Le Guin had gone from virgin to the Woman and mother biologically and had achieved success getting her intellectual 'offspring' into the world. By the late 1970s, Le Guin was ready for 'a change involving matters even more important—if I may venture a heresy—than sex,' to 'bear herself, her third self, her old age' (*DEW* 5). In terms of *Coyote's Song*, the continuities and changes implicit in the idea of giving birth to oneself are most legitimately seen in Le Guin's work as an artist.

Le Guin's first published short story appeared in 1961, 'An Die Musik,' a tale set in Orsinia: a very realistically described Central European country, which exists only in Le Guin's imagination. It's an important place. As Elizabeth Cummins stresses, it is one of Le Guin's four great settings: Orsinia, the Hainish Universe (human space from our near future to some five millennia in the future), Earthsea (in Earth's fantasy past), and the American West Coast (*Understanding* passim). Orsinia is also a very personal place for Le Guin, the location of her first stories and some of her later ones, and a place playing on her name: Ursa (she-bear) / Ursula (little she-bear) / Orsino (bearish) / Orsinia (see Bittner [29], 131 n. 1). Le Guin's first professional story, the first one she got paid for, was published in 1962, the mildly fantastic, brief comic romance (with a sting to it), 'April in Paris.'

From there, Le Guin's career rose on an exponential curve. She published two stories in 1963, three stories in 1964, including two set in the problematically-heroic fantasy world of Earthsea, and three novels between 1965-67: *Rocannon's World*, *Planet of Exile*, and *City of Illusions*—the works laying the foundation for her Hainish universe. In 1968 *A Wizard of Earthsea* appeared, followed in 1969 by 'Nine Lives,' *The Left Hand of Darkness*, and the associated story 'Winter's King' (Hainish universe stories). And with her 1969 publications began the awards: first the

Boston Globe-Horn Book Award for *A Wizard of Earthsea*, then, for *The Left Hand of Darkness*, the 1970 Hugo—more formally, the Science Fiction Achievement Award from the 1970 World Science Fiction Convention ('Worldcon'), the main annual meeting of SF fans. *The Left Hand of Darkness* also won a Nebula Award, a prize instituted by the Science Fiction Writers of America in 1966. Le Guin won the Hugo and Nebula again in 1974 for her Hainish universe 'ambiguous utopia,' *The Dispossessed*. She won Hugos for *The Word for World Is Forest* and 'The Ones Who Walk Away from Omelas,' and a Nebula for 'The Day Before the Revolution.' In 1971 and 1972, Le Guin finished her initial trilogy on Earthsea with *The Tombs of Atuan* (The Newbery Silver Medal Award book) and *The Farthest Shore* (winner of the National Book Award).

In 1970 Le Guin published 'A Trip to the Head,' a story she describes in the headnote in *The Wind's Twelve Quarters* as 'definitely a Bung Puller'—getting the words flowing again after a brief period of writer's block that wouldn't allow her past the line, from the 'other' to the tentatively male protagonist, 'Try being Amanda.' *The Lathe of Heaven* came out in 1971, Le Guin's first published work in her fourth major world: the west coast of North America, in *Lathe*, exclusively Portland, OR. The other major west-coast stories are 'The New Atlantis' (1975) and *Always Coming Home*, a long work that collects many of Le Guin's shorter pieces (1985). *Lathe* is the one Le Guin story so far to get filmed: for the Public Broadcasting Service, 1980. Le Guin has not given up on writing scripts, however; she published the screenplay *King Dog* (1985) and has worked on her own version of : 'A Wizard of Earthsea' (1981), co-written with Michael Powell and based on *A Wizard of Earthsea* and *The Tombs of Atuan*.

Le Guin has revisited Orsinia to collect her stories set there in *Orsinian Tales* (1976) and in a major work, the novel *Malafrena* (1979); and she has returned to Earthsea for apparently the last time to pick up the story of Tenar, the point of view character and female lead in *Tombs of Atuan*, and, secondarily, of Ged, the hero of the trilogy: in *Tehanu: The Last Book of Earthsea* (1990).

Le Guin's creative work outside of her four major worlds has included the novella 'The Eye of the Heron' (1978)—an important examination of the uses and limitations of nonviolent, loving resistance—audio tape versions of her stories, four collections of poems, six collections of short stories and novellas, two short young-adult novels and a series of picture books, including the *Catwings* series: stories for children that return, in good quest fashion, to a beautiful touch in her first book, the great winged cats of *Rocannon's World*.[16] There is continuity with change however: the

---

[16] Like 'The Word for World Is Forest,' 'The Eye of the Heron' has been published independently as a novel, and that is the way I will discuss it; it's initial context of *Millennial Women*, ed. by Le Guin's agent, Virginia Kidd, is important, as is the first appearance of *WWF* as one of the stories in Harlan Ellison's *Again,*

Catwings are not the great, heroic beasts of *Rocannon's World*, but normal-size Terran cats, living on a mundane Earth and unusual «only» in their ability to fly and to talk.

Like a number of writers of SF, Le Guin herself works in science fiction criticism. Many of her essays and talks collected in *Language of the Night* and *Dancing at the Edge of the World* are science fiction criticism and of such quality that Le Guin received the 1989 Pilgrim Award of the Science Fiction Research Association. Le Guin has also been active with the journal *Science-Fiction Studies*; from its fourth issue through the nineteenth (vol. 1, part 4 [Fall 1974]-6.3 [Nov. 1979]), she was first *the* and then *a* Contributing Editor, with the other Contributing Editor the Polish author, Stanislaw Lem. From the twentieth issue on (7.1 [March 1980]), she has been an Editorial Consultant, i.e., a scholar available to referee manuscripts. Other *SFS* editorial consultants include Brian Aldiss, H. Bruce Franklin, Frederic Jameson, Pamela Sargent, and, until his death, Northrop Frye: people of good reputation in literature and publishing. Arthur C. Clarke and Le Guin are the Patrons of the Science Fiction Foundation of the United Kingdom.

There are two major S.F. journals in North America, and Le Guin has had a special issue of each devoted to her work: *SFS* #7 (2.3 [Nov. 1975]) and *Extrapolation* (21.3 [Fall 1980]). Works published under the title or main title *Ursula K. Le Guin* include the anthology of essays edited by Joseph D. Olander and Martin Harry Greenberg (1979), the anthology of essays edited by Joe De Bolt (1979), and the Twayne volume by Charlotte Spivack (1984). There are also *The Farthest Shores of Ursula K. Le Guin* by George Edgar Slusser (1976), *Approaches to the Fiction of Ursula K. Le Guin* by James W. Bittner (1984), and an initial (1990) and revised/expanded (1993) edition of *Understanding Ursula K. Le Guin* by Elizabeth Cummins—indeed, to sum up rather literally, some 761 entries for 'Critical and Bio-Bibliographical Studies'of Le Guin cited by Elizabeth Cummins Cogell in her 1983 *Ursula K. Le Guin: A Primary and Secondary Bibliography*, and Cummins stopped with 1981.[17] A quick search of 'WorldCat' for books with 'Ursula K. Le Guin' in the title, excluding works listing Le Guin as author, brought forty-six entries.

Three of Le Guin's stories have been 'canonized' with a vengeance. 'The New Atlantis' is in the *Norton Anthology of Short Fiction*, the 'Shorter' as well as the regular edition. 'Nine Lives' has been very frequently reprinted, including in the anthology put out by the Science Fiction Writers of America and the Science Fiction Research Association (1978) *and* in the SFRA (going-it-alone) anthology of 1988, both volumes titled simply, *Science Fiction*. With 'The Ones Who Walk Away from Omelas' (1973), Le Guin has o'erleaped the walls of the S.F. ghetto. This

---

Dangerous Visions. Note that one could see *EoH* set on an isolated world at about the time the Hainish arrived at Terra to reunite the human genus.

[17] 'Elizabeth Cummins' and 'Elizabeth Cummins Cogell' are two forms of the name of one person (and one fine critic and bibliographer).

story is in anthologies edited by Robert Scholes, X. J. Kennedy, and Northrop Frye, and made it into *The Norton Introduction to Fiction* and *The Norton Introduction to Literature*. First year students in colleges and universities in the United States of the 1990s may find it difficult to miss 'The Ones Who Walk Away from Omelas.'

Equally impressive is Le Guin's having been a creative writer invited to attend, and the one person invited to respond to, the symposium on 'Narrative: The Illusion of Sequence,' 26-28 October 1979 (Mitchell 1). This was a Symposium at the University of Chicago, funded by a bureau of the University, and by 'the Midwest Faculty Seminar with the support of the Andrew W. Mellon Foundation.' Invited guests included Seymour Chatman, Paul de Man, Jacques Derrida, Frank Kermode, Barbara Myerhoff, Paul Ricoeur, Roy Schafer, Robert Scholes, Barbara Hernstein Smith, and Victor Turner (Mitchell 4)—people Le Guin correctly calls, 'Big Guns' (*DEW* 21) in a variety of fields, at a meeting held at an elite private university and paid for in part by a well-established and very well-endowed private foundation.

By the 1980s, then, Le Guin had arrived; she'd been accepted by those who teach the literary establishment what to accept, what to take seriously. Once you've arrived, though, the question is 'Where to from here?' The answer I can give takes up a fair amount of my discussion of Le Guin's works from about 'The Eye of the Heron' on. In her pamphlet *Earthsea Revisioned* Le Guin writes:

> By the early seventies, when I finished the third book of Earthsea [*FS*], traditional definitions and values of masculinity and femininity were all in question. I'd been questioning them myself in other books. Women readers were asking how come all the wise guys on the Isle of the Wise were guys. The artist who was above gender had been exposed as a man hiding in a raincoat. No serious writer could, or can, go on pretending to be genderless. I couldn't continue my hero-tale until I had, as woman and artist, wrestled with the angels of the feminist consciousness. It took me a long time to get their blessing. (*ER* 11)

By the 1990s, Le Guin had won her wrestling match with feminist consciousness as much as such matches can be won or lost: she was working her way toward her own voice, as Cummins stresses, doing her part in the cultural work of the invention of the feminist novel.

I.

BEGINNINGS: EARLY WORKS

The people [of a California tribe] sang:

I dream of you,
I dream of you jumping
Rabbit, jackrabbit, and quail.
And one line is left of a dancing song:
Dancing on the brink of the world.

With such fragments I might have shored my ruin, but I didn't know how. Only knowing that we must have a past to make a future with, I took what I could from the European-based culture of my own forefathers and mothers. I learned, like most of us, to use whatever I could, to filch an idea from China and steal a god from India, and so patch together a world as best I could.
Ursula K. Le Guin, 'World-Making'
(1981 [coll. *DEW*])

An die Musik (1961)

Ursula K. Le Guin's first published story, 'An die Musik,' is set in the city of Foranoy in Orsinia in Central Europe on 'a warm bright day, late spring' (140) and then in September of 1938, when British Prime Minister Neville Chamberlain was meeting Adolf Hitler in Munich.[18] We are re-

---

[18] The meeting of German, Italian, British, and French—but not Czech—representatives began on 29 September 1938 and lasted into the next day. The upshot of the Munich meeting was that the Czechs were forced by the major powers to cede the Sudetenland to Germany, plus a small area to Poland. What remained of Czechlosovakia then disintegrated as its constituent ethnic groups divided the country. 'Munich' entered English as a figure of speech for 'appease-

minded twice of Chamberlain's trip to Munich (142, 143); readers who know the history of World War II in Europe know that Chamberlain's meetings with Hitler in 1938 did not bring 'peace with honour' or 'peace in our time.' Nazi Germany got the Sudetenland, and England and Europe and much of the world got the most destructive war in human history. What happened to Foranoy and Orsinia in general is more difficult to know; you will find them only on maps that include Sir Thomas More's Utopia (*Utopia*, 1516) or Freedonia in the Marx Brother's *Duck Soup* (1933). In science-fictional terms, Orsinia is located in a universe with a history identical to that of ours, with the exception of the existence of a country on our Earth called Orsinia. Orsinia differs from More's Utopia and its relatives in that Le Guin is interested in it primarily for itself, not so much as a place to hold up to our world the 'mirror' of satire. Le Guin gives us Orsinia with the completeness and detail of a fantasist, but she follows in her presentation the conventions of mundane literature, of Realism (Cummins 128-29).

'An die Musik' is the highly naturalistic story of a few hours in the life of Ladislas Gaye: his springtime visit to Otto Egorin, impresario; Gaye's talk with Egorin; his trip home; some time at home, mostly talking with his wife and then his son; a barely noticeable passage of time (141-42); walking to teach a piano lesson; and his return home, where, finally, he 'went off to bed' (145). And that is it.[19]

The story takes on additional meaning in *Orsinian Tales* (1976), where it fits into a fuller context, but in itself it is important for at least four reasons. First, for introducing Ursula's country, Orsinia (with its play on Le Guin's given name); second, for postulating (very quietly) a world without a transcendent god; third, for showing at the beginning of her career a genius for handling complex issues in a lucid, simple style. And, finally, 'An die Musik' is important for introducing related themes Le Guin would return to throughout her career—up though 'The Kerastion' (1990) and 'The Rock that Changed Things' (1992), and other stories in *A Fisherman of the Inland Sea*: the roles, for good and for ill, of artists and intellectuals in society; the problem in believing that utility—usefulness—is the only criterion for value; the demands of their callings in the lives of people who are, among other things, artists and intellectuals; the necessity to find alternatives to apparently 'either/or' choices; the possibility of momentary visions that can give a healing certainty—and the related, Daoist feeling for human creativity, where one goes the Way to the whole created object, without forcing thought or trying to find the Way; the importance of moving out of imprisoning houses and constraining cultures back into nature and the world.

---

ment,' and 'appeasement' became a loaded word as Hitler found other lands needed for the German Empire.

[19] Plus, in the original 1961 version, a number of 'allusions to Romantic poets and musicians'; see Bittner, *Approaches* 135, n. 38. For his excellent discussion, Bittner uses the original version; I use the revised text of 1976.

In a few hours on a spring day and then later, in September of 1938, thirty-year-old Ladislas Gaye takes his son for a walk and visits Otto Egorin, to show Egorin some of the few compositions Gaye has managed to produce when not supporting his somewhat sick wife, very sick mother, and three children, by working as a clerk and moonlighting as a piano teacher. Gaye is obviously under stress (he starts to cry), and eventually Egorin asks, 'Have you ever thought of throwing it over, Gaye? Not the music. The rest.' That is, his family. 'If you live for music you live for music.' Gaye replies 'I'm not made so' (*Orsinian Tales* 136). Egorin continues his argument with 'You can't serve two masters,' but then he compromises and suggest that Gaye 'Write little songs, not impossible Masses.' Gaye replies, 'The Mass is what I've got to write' (plus a symphony); 'I've begun it, I have to finish it' (137). Egorin's wife, Egorina enters, and we see Egorin's sacrifice 'To Music': Egorina is hyperkinetic and inflicts upon Egorin and the world 'An unceasing flood of words' for a full day before she appears in concert; she is, apparently, a brilliant singer, a snob, something of an airhead, and a casual bigot: in Central Europe in 1938, her dismissive reference to someone she calls 'that little Jew' (never named) is a damning indictment of her.

Gaye returns to his family, and readers should sympathize with Gaye's weeping. Gaye is 'not made so' that he can just abandon his family, and the whole situation seems not made so that any of the family can (re)negotiate the terms of their relationships. By the time she reached her 1986 lecture on a woman writing, Le Guin would give Mrs. Gaye a voice and suggest that she might be the one having trouble finding time for her art.[20] But the issue in 'An die Musik' isn't dysfunctional relationships or who gets to do art, but the value of art, period—especially in Central Europe in 1938.

Even Egorin (significantly named if we see him representing the selfish artistic Ego)—even Egorin questions 'what's the good' of music. With the world marching to, not dancing on, the brink of disaster, who wants or needs music?

> 'Who indeed, when Europe is crawling with armies like a corpse with maggots, when Russia uses symphonies to glorify the latest boiler-factory in the Urals, when the function of music has been all summed up in Putzi playing the piano to soothe the Leader's [Hitler's] nerves. By the time your Mass is finished, you know, all the churches may be blown into little pieces, and your men's chorus will be wearing uniforms and also being blown into little pieces.... Write your songs, write your Mass, it does no

---

[20] For print versions of Le Guin's lecture, see 'The Hand that Rocks the Cradle Writes the Book,' and 'The Fisherwoman's Daughter.'

harm.... But it won't save us...' (140, unspaced ellipsis mark in original)

In his chapter on the Orsinian stories, James W. Bittner argues that this is Le Guin's point, that it is asking the wrong sort of question, making the wrong kind of demand, to ask art 'to save anything or to make anything happen or to change the world.' Art's social usefulness, paradoxically, 'is to deny the world, to detach people from politics and history so they can receive visions of a better world,' and then those people of vision, perhaps, can act to 'redeem politics and history with that vision.' Following W. H. Auden's 'In Memory of W. B. Yeats' (1940), Bittner asserts that when it does its job, art 'removes the obstacles that block the way to a better world, but it does not bring that world into being. That is the historical task of the artist's audience' (*Approaches* 51).

Bittner is correct about what Le Guin was saying in 1961 in 'An die Musik.'

In the climax of the story, Gaye is troubled with the poetic line he has set, 'It is Thou in thy mercy that breakest down over our heads all we build, that we may see the sky: and so I do not complain' (143).[21] The line hangs him up even in a quiet moment at the kitchen table. And then he hits bottom and gets an insight, a feeling, similar to the ones that will come to several later, depressed Le Guinian heroes:

> The total impossibility of writing was a choking weight in him, like a big chunk of rock in his chest. Nothing would ever change, he thought, and in the next moment he felt a relaxation within him, lightness, openness, and certainty, utter certainty. He thought it was his own song, then, raising his head, understood that he was actually hearing this tune. He did not have to write it. It had been written long ago, no one need suffer for it any more.[22] [Lotte] Lehmann was singing it,
> *Du holde Kunst, ich danke dir*
> [I thank you, thou gracious / kindly Art (see 136)]...
>
> ...Music will not save us.... What good is music? None, Gaye thought, and that is the point. To the world and its states and armies and factories and Leaders, music says, 'You are irrelevant'; and, arrogant and gentle as a god, to the suffering man it says only, 'Listen.' For being saved is not the point. Music saves nothing. Merciful, uncaring, it

---

[21] This is from Joseph Eichenforff (1788-1857), 'Es wandelt, was wir schauen' ('Things change...'). Note that Bittner translates Eichendorff's *Himmel* as 'heaven' where Gaye, and Le Guin, has the less likely 'sky.'
[22] Music by Franz Schubert (1797-1828 [see *Orsinian Tales* 135]), for a lyric by Franz von Schober (Bittner, *Approaches* 50).

> denies and breaks down all the shelters, the houses men build for themselves, that they may see the sky. (144-45)

As I hinted earlier, there is a problem or two with the sexual politics of this story: wives usually have had more trouble following artistic callings than husbands; an Otto Egorin was as likely to be a genteel anti-Semite as his wife was. There is also a problem with seeing personified music (or a god, for that matter) breaking down 'all the shelters' so figuratively when the German air force and armies a year later would begin the destruction of very literal houses all over Europe. In later works, Le Guin's image becomes 'unbuilding walls' and refers more explicitly to political institutions and cultural categories that have grown inflexible; such walls refer to hatred and human arrogance and to all that separate people from each other, nature, the world: the hindrances keeping us from following the Dao, the Way that leads home.[23]

Bittner asserts that 'Ultimately, the real subject of An die and the rest of Le Guin's fiction that explores ethical problems is not a group of ethical questions. These are means, not ends. Her purpose is to ask them, not to answer them. The real subject of 'An die Musik' is celebration; the tale is a celebration of Gaye's devotion to his art, and beyond that, a celebration of art itself' (53). Bittner's comments are true, but it is more true, I think, that 'An die Musik' raises its ethical questions as part of a very rigorous and quite serious set of thought experiments—and that 'An die Musik' celebrates Ladislas Gaye's devotion to his art *and* to his family, his refusing to make an impossible choice. It also celebrates a music that will at least get us out of our houses, out of culture, that we 'may see the sky' (145).[24]

Jesus of Nazareth spoke well when he said no one 'can serve two masters' (Matthew 6.24 [Luke 16.13])—not when they're God and personified riches ('Mammon'). Otto Egorin, though, is playing the Tempter's role—or that of the militantly antifamily Jesus—in asking Gaye to think 'of throwing it over,' dumping his family and living totally for music (136-37).[25] Ladislas Gaye is not a Romantic Hero as Artist giving up all for his art (and hurting a lot of other people in the process), nor is he a martyr sac-

---

[23] In a good society like that of Rer in 'Coming of Age in Karhide,' the walls are just part of houses that are themselves true homes. See the 'Note on Walls' at the end of this chapter.

[24] Again, Le Guin translates 'sky' not 'heaven,' but in later works she will go farther: music no longer gets us to see the (still potentially transcendent) sky, but puts us in touch with the more clearly Daoist sea (*New Atlantis* [1975]) or with the quantum field that allows us to 'dance' to space-time light-years away, 'in no time at all' ('Dancing to Ganam' [1993]).

[25] Bittner cites the key texts for Jesus on the family: Matthew 10.34-39, Mark 3.31-35, Luke 14.26; Eric Hoffer adds Matthew 8.21[-22], Matthew 10.21, 12.47-49 (*True Believer* 40-42; ch. 5, section 32).

rificing his art for deified Responsibility.[26] He's an average human being, but with a knack, a talent, and he muddles through as best he can. That deserves celebration, and even as Europe moves toward catastrophe in September of 1938, Le Guin celebrates this artist as a low-key, domesticated, hero, loyal to his art and to his family, to his marriage Promise.[27]

Rocannon's World (1966)

Rocannon's World is the first novel in Le Guin's Hainish series, and it is useful to have an overview of Le Guin's Galactic History in approaching the series.[28] A word of caution, though: the Hainish series was not written in its historical order, nor can we be at all confident that Le Guin had its whole order in mind when she began in the middle 1960s a series continuing into the mid-1990s.[29] Indeed, we can be certain that there are some inconsistencies in the History as it is presented in the various novels and stories in the series.

In the History, there is a planet called Hain by its inhabitants (and eventually called Davenant by the people of our Earth, Terra). Long ago, in the near-mythic part of the history, the people of Hain seeded the galaxy with human stock, creating the galactic genus, Homo. During a great collapse, Hain lost contact with many of its colonies. After a recovery, Hain re-established contact with some of the worlds, forming a League, initially called, pretentiously and/or hopefully, the League of All Worlds. From the first, the League possessed Nearly as Fast as Light (NAFAL) ships; early in League history, a Cetian physicist develops the theory necessary for building an Instantaneous Communications Device (ICD), the ansible. Ansibles start out incredibly expensive but soon come down in cost, allowing a fair degree of communication among the worlds of the League. In *Rocannon's World*, nuclear bombs can also be delivered instantaneously by newly-developed Faster than Light (FTL) ships (31; ch. 1). Ansible communication—though not FTL nukes—becomes vital, to prepare for the War to Come against an extragalactic enemy. The enemy comes, wins, and humanity survives the Age of the Enemy; the worlds of the League again lose contact, and then regain it. By *The Left Hand of Darkness*, the League

---

[26] See later in *Coyote* the discussions of sacrifice in *BP* and *EoH*, and Le Guin's denial of the goodness of sacrifice.
[27] For the motif of the Promise, see *TD*.
[28] Le Guin and I have corresponded, somewhat flippantly, on the meaning of 'Hain.' Le Guin would have it pronounced [hain], with the option of rendering the 'n' somewhat nasalized, French fashion, making the word similar to the French word *hein?*: 'eh?'. Hain is also the brand name of a line of natural-food products; in correspondence in July 1989, Le Guin told me 'We have been using Hain(ish) Mayonnaise for years'; in a note in 1996, however, she said that she had not known about Hain condiments (etc.) when she first used the name.
[29] For a summary of what Le Guin has given us of Hainish history as of 1997, see Brigg, "Literary History" 16-21.

has become the well-established Ekumen (i.e., 'household') of Known Worlds, and well along in the task of reuniting the human family.[30]

Rocannon's World is set fairly early in the Galactic History, during the preparation for the War to Come and when the League was 'Dominated by the aggressive, tool-making humanoid species of Centaurus, Earth, and the Cetians' (36; ch. 2). In terms of Le Guin's thinking, *Rocannon's World* comes before Le Guin explains the existence of numerous humanoid species; and in *Rocannon's World*, Hain-Davenant is just another planet, not—or not necessarily—the home-world of the human genus (85; ch. 5).

In its political plot, *Rocannon's World* is a story of rebellion and revenge, in the Germanic or Nordic manner. Gaverel Rocannon ('Rokanan' to the local inhabitants) is Director of the First Ethnographic Survey of Fomalhaut II, sent by the League to do a systematic and thorough study of High Intelligence Life Forms (HILFs) of the planet.[31] The League's interest is more than academic: the better they understand the peoples of technologically primitive Fomalhaut II, the more efficiently they can use them to prepare for and fight the War to Come. Rebels against the League from the planet Faraday arrive on Fomalhaut II and bomb the meeting place to which Rocannon has called his fourteen on-planet colleagues and friends, killing all the League people at the meeting except Rocannon (30; ch. 1). This is the incident that gets the plot going. Much later we learn that the Faradayans have set up a base on Fomalhaut II, with six FTL warships (131; ch. 9). After an arduous and costly quest, Rocannon is able to call in a League attack with FTLs, which takes out the base with surgical precision. Thus Rocannon saves the League, saves the peoples of Fomalhaut II from the tyranny of the rebels, stops the war of the rebellion, and avenges the deaths of his friends. Rocannon also marries a woman he's recently met: the Lady Ganye, leader of a relatively egalitarian people; within a few years Rocannon dies, before ships of the League return to the planet, so Rocannon 'never knew that the League' in gratitude 'had given that world his name' (135-36; Epilogue).

Even more than 'An die Musik,' *Rocannon's World* introduces a number of themes and narrative elements that are important for Le Guin's canon. Plus some elements that are probably not all that important but interesting and fun. For example, the windsteeds of the low-gravity Fomalhaut II in *Rocannon's World* are the tiger-size literary ancestors of the winged cats of the illustrated Catwings series for children (1988-94). The Lady Semley on her windsteed, feeling 'like a girl again, like the wild maiden she had been' (11; Prologue) is similar to one of Le Guin's poetic narrators, recalling herself as a 'dirty little virgin.'[32] *Rocannon's World*

---

[30] See my discussion of *LHD* for a note on 'Ekumen' and my rendering it 'household.'

[31] In Ace first edn. 'Gaverel' on p. 111 (ch. 7), 'Gaveral' on p. 131 (ch. 9). There are numerous minor variations in spelling in the 1966 Ace edn.

[32] 'Song' in *Wild Angles* (21), quoted and discussed in Arbur, 'Le Guin's 'Song' of Inmost Feminism.'

can be viewed as high fantasy, or Germanic epic, modernized and made more 'realistic' through an SF presentation, and one gauge of the difference between high fantasy and the fairy tale can be found in the difference between the great, mute, flying cat-steeds of *Rocannon's World* with the little winged cats with their own language and culture in the Catwings series. One can get the same sort of gauge contrasting the Lady Semley with the 'Dirty Little Virgin,' getting herself joyously filthy.[33]

More attractive to professional students of Le Guin (earnest folk, frequently) are the 'themes and narrative elements' embodied in tales: of the dance, joy, naming; 'pseudospeciation,' wholeness and balance; the shadow-death, the blood-bond and telepathy; godhead, the anthropologist as hero; doing what one must do, the ethical responsibilities of scientists generally and anthropologists especially, the ethical obligation to individuals (including oneself); and the connections linking together aggression with technology, spirituality, and urbanization, or in that mating of urbanization and spiritual striving that we often call civilization.

Rocannon's World begins, 'How can you tell the legend from the fact on these worlds that lie so many years away?—planets without names...where the past is the matter of myth, and a returning explorer finds his own doings of a few years back have become the gestures of a god. Unreason darkens that gap of time bridged by our lightspeed ships, and in the darkness uncertainty and disproportion grow like weeds' (5 [see also 27]). Not much comes of this opening since most of the book is the straightforward narration of the tale of Rocannon. There's the Prologue of 'The Necklace'—Le Guin's story, 'The Dowry of the Angyar' from 1964—and an Epilogue, plus an inserted song, a message to the League Presidium, and a couple of expository excerpts from *The Abridged Handy Pocket Guide to Intelligent Life-forms* (5-6) and the *Handbook for Galactic Area Eight* (27-28); but the great majority of this short novel is a straight-line narration moving from the attack on Rocannon's colleagues to Rocannon's revenge. Such linearity is an elegant way to proceed, but it leaves us with basically one tale, which we will believe or not—like any story, including those that don't open with questions about epistemology. Like much else in this introductory paragraph, development of the epistemological question will wait for Le Guin's later works.

This is not the case with the rest of my list of themes and elements. In two very dense clusters near the climax of the book, Le Guin brings them together, and, I think, makes sense of them.[34]

Early in the narrative Rocannon is thinking about the rebels from Faraday and how they threaten to take over Fomalhaut II 'for colonization or

---

[33] For another gauge of the changes in Le Guin's emphases, cf. and contrast Semley and another NAFAL traveler through time, King Argaven XVII in the two versions of 'Winter's King' (1969/1975). I discuss Semley in later chapters, passim.

[34] My analysis follows from Bittner's suggestive description of much in *RW* as 'both conventional science fiction and a critique of it' (95).

for military use. The High-Intelligence Life Forms of the planet...they would ignore or enslave or extirpate.... For to an aggressive people only technology mattered.' Rocannon goes on to think that this may be a weakness of the League itself, a weakness even in terms of the desperate need to prepare for the War to Come. As a 'hilfer,' an anthropologist, Rocannon questions 'the wisdom of staking everything on weapons and the uses of machines.'[35] Dominated by aggressive tool-makers, the League 'had slighted certain skills and powers and potentialities of intelligent life, and judged by too narrow a standard' (36; ch. 2).

You have to keep in mind a number of passages to get the point, but the issue is clear enough if we put together a kind of thematic sandwich, or layer-cake. In the Prologue, we get to meet the most technologically developed of humanity on Fomalhaut II: the Gdemiar, or Clayfolk, who seem a combination of folklore dwarves with the Clay People from an old Flash Gordon serial (1938) and the Morlocks from H. G. Welles's *The Time Machine* (1895). Near the beginning of the book proper, we get the 'MORAL' on technology and aggression, the unwisdom of placing one's hope in war machines (36). Immediately after that, we again see the Clayfolk, and they're still troglodytic, short, arrogant, sexist, relatively urban and ugly, if also clever, communal, and mildly telepathic (37-42; ch. 2). At the end of the novel proper, we see a rough sort of justice where those who live by the FTL die by the FTL and the Faradayans get blown up by a League missile. In the center of *Rocannon's World* we get the basic point made more strongly, philosophically, and symbolically when we meet a native human species that has gone (we may infer) too far along the way of technology, spirituality, and 'urbanity.' In chapter 6, Rocannon and friends are captured by what seem to be angelic, high-tech dwellers in what is emphatically 'a city, not a stone-age village or a bronze-age fortress but a great city, severe and grandiose, powerful and exact, the product of a high technology' (96). Under the seeming, the reality of the tall, thin, god-like, angelic Winged Ones is that their 'noble heads held brains degenerated or specialized to the level of insects' (102; ch. 7)—and they're vampires to boot (100-101; ch. 6). On the surface-level of the story, we have technology, which is to accepted, but accepted within reasonable limits; down below a bit, we get technology (transcendent spirituality, civilization) associated with some of our most unconscious prejudices and most powerful fears. We have technology associated with dwarves in caves; and, more important, we have technology and civilization associated with angelic looking vampires in a city as mathematically perfect as a hive (102, 104, 109; ch. 7).[36]

---

[35] For an excellent discussion of Rocannon as anthropologist in the role of Ishi, a lone survivor in a highly different culture—and for good comments on *RW* generally—see Maslen, esp. 64-65.

[36] The Clayfolk, on their own, were definitely low-tech, fine craftsmen; it is unclear if their culture would have changed without strong pushes from the League. This is symbolically significant. High technological culture isn't 'dwarvish' but

Immediately after the episode in the vampire city, *Rocannon's World* moves toward its climax, and moves into the second dense cluster of significant, interrelated thematic elements.

Aiding Rocannon and friends escape the vampire city are the Kiemhrir, small talking animals whose group 'name' is in fact 'only an adjective, meaning lithe or swift.' Rocannon ask a leaderly animal, 'Small lord, may I know your name?' and receives in response '"Name," the black-faced one whispered.... "Liuar," he said, the old word Mogien had used to mean both nobles and midmen, or what the *Handbook* called Species II. "Liuar, Fiia, Gdemiar: names. Kiemhrir: unname' (105; ch. 7). The Fian, Kyo, addresses the little animals as 'Wordmasters...Wordlovers, the eaters of words, the nameless ones,' which brings up motifs Le Guin will develop in *The Tombs of Atuan* and, far more immediately, links the ideas of names and species (106). This link is developed within a few hours of fictive time, when Rocannon and Kyo sit and talk about how Kyo knew of the Kiemhrir. Like their cousins, the dwarfish Gdemiar, the elfin Fiia have a degree of telepathy amongst themselves: 'What one of us in my village remembered, all remembered...'—but Kyo had no memory of the Winged Ones. Kyo tells Rocannon that the Fiia 'have no memory for fear,' nor should they be expected to: 'We chose. Night and caves and swords of metal we left to the Clayfolk, when our way parted from theirs, and we chose the green valleys, the sunlight, the bowl of wood. And therefore we are the Half-People. And we have forgotten, we have forgotten much!' (108).[37]

Rocannon, on the other hand, as a Hainish-normal man, finds names very important. When Kyo asks him, what a name might be, Rocannon tells him that his birth-name was 'Gaverel Rocannon' and that when he has pronounced that he has 'described nothing, yet I've named myself. And when I see a new kind of tree in this land I ask you...what its name i[s]. It troubles me,' Rocannon says, 'until I know its name' (111; ch. 7).

A bit later Rocannon observes what might be an awakening individuality in Kyo (110; ch. 7) and goes on to discuss with Kyo names and distinctions, ending in Rocannon's question, 'How do you know one [mountain] range from another, one being from another, without names?' Kyo doesn't answer. There is a dance at the Fian village, and Kyo tells Rocannon that Kyo will leave the quest; he will not leave the valley to accompany Rocannon to the mountains: 'The dance that had no music was ended, the dancers that had no more name than light and shadow were still. So between him and Kyo a pattern had come to its end, leaving quietness' (112; end of ch. 7).

'angelic': it is based on a philosophy with a transcendent God outside of the universe. For the significance of the hive, see Dunn and Erlich, 'A Vision of Dystopia.'

[37] See Kroeber § 119 on 'Subcultures and Part-Cultures,' esp. 82; ch. 7. If the Clayfolk are like Welles's Morlocks in *The Time Machine*, the Fiia are like Welles's Eloi.

For many of us, the implication of the image cluster and the plot upshot would be a value judgment: Kyo and the Fiia should reintegrate with the Gdemiar and become a full people.[38] That way Kyo could continue loyal in his metaphoric 'marriage' to Rocannon and aid in the just struggle against the Faradayans—and, anyway, get to see the mountains. That is correct, but we should balance against it Rocannon's anthropological ethic of pretty vigorous cultural relativism.

Rocannon himself questions exploiting the peoples of Fomalhaut II and 'pushing them about' (33; ch. 1 [also 42; ch. 2]). And a fair number of readers nowadays would accept more readily Rocannon's willingness to let other cultures follow their ways if he were, say, a dumpy little woman: an unimposing Starlady rather than a Starlord, and perhaps liable to lose status any moment and be treated little better than a slave among at least two groups on Fomalhaut II. Still, there is much to be said for the philosophy of 'Let be' when dealing with other peoples, and much to be said for the cultural relativism that lies behind this 'Let Be.' Kyo and his people may be incomplete and immature in sticking to the valleys; they go against modern individuality in denying ethical primacy to 'one man's fate' (43; ch. 2 [133; ch. 9]); and they deny a fundamental doctrine of modern lore in seeing community ties superior to the pair-bond of love and friendship—and deny a fundamental doctrine of masculinist culture in rejecting the Heroic project of making a name for oneself. But there are arguments to be made for the 'elfin' position (arguments Le Guin will make later in her career), for the Daoist view rather favoring valleys over mountains, and unnamed Dao over the named things of everyday: for staying within nature and (as much as possible) outside culture, history, and as far away as one can from high-tech civilization. Certainly the Fiia have this much superiority to us, who usually live in a high-tech world and unmindfully find it «natural»: the Fiia *chose* their way (108); they consciously walked away from the potential City of Man.[39]

In *Rocannon's World*, though, the rest of the questers leave Kyo and go to the mountains, where Rocannon's aristocratic companion, Mogien, finds his 'domain' and joy in battle against the cold and against fear from encountering the shadow of his death (113-14, 115-16; ch. 8). 'Mogien was his [Rocannon's] leader and he followed. He had forgotten why he wanted to cross these mountains, remembering only that he had to, that he must go south' (114). The older man follows the younger man here, as Ged will follow Arren in *The Farthest Shore*; Rocannon is reduced to do-

---

[38] Such a moral on the necessity for reuniting Half-People is quite explicit in Yevgeny Zamyatin's classic dystopia *We* (ca. 1920 in Russian as *My*). Wholeness, balance, and integration are certainly norms in Le Guin's later work; see Barbour, 'Wholeness and Balance...,' esp. 165.

[39] The Kesh in *ACH* (1985) and the pueblo Hainish in 'A Man of the People' (1995) have this much advantage on the Fiia: their separation from high technology and history is far less final, and they choose again and again, as peoples and individually.

ing only what he must do, as Ged will advise Arren to do as a matter of royal policy (and which Le Guin would advise as Daoist policy applicable to everyone, especially given that, for Le Guin, we are all potential kings, or even gods).

Doing what he must leads Rocannon to a cave containing the Ancient One, a kind of combination of Mimir (the guardian of the Well of Wisdom in Norse mythology), and an atypically nasty Daoist hermit.[40] 'It was like the Clayfolk, dwarfish and pale; like the Fiia, frail and clear-eyed; like both, like neither'—integrated, combining two binary opposites in one, like an androgyne (*LHD* [1969]), or the girl/dragon Tehanu (1990)—and the creature is highly telepathic. Telepathy being an innate ability in most humans (in the Hainish universe through the 1960s), the Ancient One easily educes in Rocannon the power to mindhear, but at the cost of '*That which you hold dearest and would least willingly give*' (118; ch. 8), which is Rocannon's companion and friend, Mogien—whose death is the bloodbond, giving the story its meaning.[41]

With the gift of mindhearing, Rocannon becomes a pedan, a 'god,' a hero, a world changer (125; ch. 9).[42] Even as just 'one man alone, against a people bent on war,' he is able to call in the FTL strike that destroys his enemies (133-34; ch. 9). With this gift he also brings real telepathy to the League, which we should feel is their one chance in the impending war. A great good has been done for a great number of the human family, and any sane, mature, civilized, *rational* calculation would come out, Bottom Line: even counting all the deaths, Rocannon made the right decisions. But yet it is fortunate for Rocannon that he did what he must do and could see no alternatives to doing; for there is something to be said for the way of the Fiia in that it allows human beings to live without making such bloody calculations.

Planet of Exile (1966)

Planet of Exile might be called the Hainish cycle's *Romeo and Juliet*, and, as in *Romeo and Juliet*, the action is passionate, violent, and speedy: completed between 'the last days of the last moonphase of Autumn' (5; ch. 1) to the time of the first blizzard of winter; a Terran season could encom-

---

[40] Near one of the roots of Yggrrasil, the World Tree, there is the Well of the Highest Wisdom, plus a giant named Mimir who drinks daily from the well and epitomizes wisdom. The god Odin comes to drink at the well, and Mimir tells him the cost is one of Odin's eyes; Odin pays the cost (Hamilton 308; Putnam's 'Mimir' and 'Odin'). Note also the divine name *El Shaddai* in the ancient Near East, usually Englished as 'God Almighty; according to the annotation for Gen. 17.1 in the *Oxford Annotated Bible*, a literal rendering would be 'God, the One of the Mountains' (see also Ex. 6.2-3).
[41] *Italics* indicate mindspeech, telepathy.
[42] On pedan, see ch. 9, p. 125; ch. 2, pp. 45-46; ch. 3, p. 53; and ch. 4, p. 68. Cf. and contrast Selver as a god in *WWF*.

pass the action. The fictive history of *Planet of Exile*, however, is more considerable.

After the time of *Rocannon's World* but still during preparation for the War to Come, a Terran colony was placed on the planet Gamma Draconis III, which moves in a huge, elliptical orbit around a sun called Eltanin, the true name for Gamma Draconis (26; ch. 3).[43] The Year on Gamma Draconis III is 24,000 days long, and the Winter is very severe; the Terran colony would be marginal under the best of circumstances, and circumstances turned out far from the best. Ten local Years before the action of the novel, the Enemy entered human space, and the Terrans on Gamma Draconis III sent home their ship and ansible and some of their people. They have not heard from anyone in the League of All Worlds for some 657 Terran years. Nor have they done well in their isolation. On the positive side, Terrans have not been troubled by local diseases; on the negative side, they have not fit well into the local ecology in any other ways, and their birth rate has been very low (45-46; ch. 5). For the most part, they have been true to their Law of Cultural Embargo, which forbids them to transfer to the native High Intelligence Life Forms ('hilfs') any technique, theory, 'cultural set or pattern' without permission of the League's Area Council and Plenum (68; ch. 8)—permission it would be impossible to get even if the native humans were ready for significant cultural transfer, which they are not. Indeed, the natives are hostile, and a film production of *Planet of Exile* could have much fun with old movie clichés on 'The natives are restless tonight, Bawana,' since the Terrans are dark-skinned, and the native humans much lighter, with the most barbaric being northerners who look Nordic. The Terrans, then, have remained aliens on the planet: choosing to stay aloof from the world and its culture(s) in some ways, in other ways being kept out of the world.

The political crisis at the beginning of the story comes from the once-a-Year migration south of the northern barbarians, the Gaal; this Southing has never been a major problem before for either the Terrans or the literally more civilized among the native humans: the Gaal have moved in small groups and could not do much damage to walled and fortified cities. But 'a new time' has come to the planet, as Jakob Agat of the Terrans explains to Wold, Eldest of his clan and chief man of the Range and Winter City of Tevar:

> There is a great man among the Gaal, a leader, they call him Kubban or Kobban. He has united all their tribes and made an army of them. The Gaal...[are] besieging and capturing Winter Cities in all the Ranges along the coast, killing the Spring-born men, enslaving the women, leaving Gaal warriors in each city to hold and rule it over the Win-

---

[43] An aside in *PE* but, with a reversal, the True Name of the Sun is a very important point for *CI* (1967).

ter. Come Spring, when the Gaal come north again, they'll stay; these lands will be their lands.... (23; ch. 2)

There is a potential irony here, as Agat much later thinks to himself:

> It wasn't like the hilfs, this planning ahead. Hilfs did not consider either time or space in the linear, imperialistic fashion of his own species. Time to them was a lantern lighting a step before, a step behind—the rest was indistinguishable dark. Time was this day, this one day of the immense Year. They had no historical vocabulary; there was merely today and 'timepast.' They looked ahead only to the next season at most. They did not look down over time but were in it as the lamp in the night, as the heart in the body. And so also with space: space to them was not a surface on which to draw boundaries but a range, a heartland, centered on the self and clan and tribe.... This planning ahead, this trying to keep hold of a conquered place across both space and time, was untypical; it showed—what? An autonomous change in a hilf culture-pattern, or an infection from the old northern colonies and forays of Man.[44]
> It would be the first time, Agat thought sardonically, that they ever learned an idea from us. Next we'll be catching their colds. (74; ch. 9)

The Gaal have lived as savages within nature; they are moving into culture, and they are about to enter history and civilization. In the manner of the peoples of Atilla, Genghis Kahn, or Tamburlaine the Great—or the Gauls attacking Rome ca. 390 BCE—they are going to *make* history.[45]

* * * * * * *

The method of narration of *Planet of Exile* is useful if one thinks it problematic to tell 'fact from legend, truth from truth' (*RW* 5). We get the story in third-person, limited omniscient from the points of view of Rolery, a woman of Tevar; of Wold, 'the Eldest Man of the Men of Askatevar' (34; ch. 4) and of Jakob Agat Alterra—the last word an honorific indicat-

---

[44] Here, 'Man' = Terran humans, viewed by a Terran-descended male. Through *LHD*, 'Man' in such contexts in Le Guin's writing means 'human being(s).' Such generic uses of 'Man' for 'human being,' along with 'he' as the 'generic pronoun,' were quite common into the 1970s; for 'he' as the generic, see (even) Joanna Russ's 'The Image of Women in Science Fiction' (1970): 39.
[45] See below, my chapter on *ACH*. For some old *Kulturkampfen*, note that in *PE* there is no privileging of a Gaal militarized horde over Gaal savages, or civilization absolutely over the savagery or barbarism of the New Stone Age.

ing one of the ten elected leaders of the Terrans (who call themselves Alterrans [words change]).[46] Of the fourteen chapters, we get Rolery's point of view in five (chs. 1, 5, 8, 11, 13), Wold's in four (2, 4, 7, 10), and Agat's in five (3, 6, 9, 12, 14). To push a point, we could divide the chapters in the manner of an Italian (or Petrarchan) sonnet into an octave and sestet, only I would prefer to put the sestet first and have the turning point of the novel the marriage of Rolery and Agat in chapter 6, followed by the arrival of the Gaal horde in chapter 7.

The political over-plot begins with Agat's attempts to form an alliance between the Alterran town of Landin and the Winter City of Tevar so they can ward off the Gaal Southing. Forming such an alliance is difficult since even Rolery, born out of season and marginal herself, initially sees the Alterrans as 'black falsemen' (9; ch. 1), and a dying Alterran near the close of the book—one who has fought alongside Tevarans against the Gaal—still sees the Tevarans as 'hilfs,' not humans, and 'bloody barbarians': he is disgusted with the thought that 'our human blood' will be lost 'if we can breed with the hilfs,' that the Terran exiles will cease being 'Man' (115; ch. 13). Agat convinces Wold to get his people to prepare for the horde, but meanwhile Rolery and Agat have fallen in love and have made love in the forest margin between Landin and Tevar. They are soon caught by Rolery's kin, and the alliance is harmed. Rolery goes to Landin with Agat, where they marry; the Gaal arrive and destroy the Winter City; Wold and the remaining Tevarans go to Landin, which they defend together. Landin is slowly losing ground to the Gaals, and the defenders are being pushed to the innermost keeps, when Winter comes on. Wold dies; the Gaals move off. It turns out that the Alterrans come down with infections from wounds, so it seems they've adapted to the planet, in that sense, entered the world. Rolery knows 'that she could bear Agat's son' (116; ch. 13), and a promised integration ends the book: 'Come,' Agat says to her, 'come, let's go home' (124; ch. 14).[47]

Romeo and Juliet brought to a happy ending, plus some other Le Guinian twists—but let's start with the happy ending.

At the end of *Planet of Exile* we can look at Rolery and Agat and say, figuratively (and using a masculinist phrase), 'the wall is down that parted their fathers.'[48] We can also see literal walls down, or at least breached: those of Tevar and Landin. The literal invasions of the cities are very bad things (chs. 7, 12), but there is something in Le Guin that is—even this

---

[46] 'Limited omniscience' is an oxymoron, but the phrase is useful; to avoid the contradiction, I'll prefer the clipped form, 'third-person limited.' For Le Guin on point of view, see 'On Theme,' *Those Who Can* 207-08. My page references to *PE* are to the Fourth Ace rpt. of 1974, Ace #66953 (incorporated as the central number of the ISBN); in places this differs slightly—up to two pages—from the pagination of Ace #66951 and possibly other printings. Try looking *ahead* a couple pages if you have trouble finding my references.
[47] Cf. and contrast adaptation to New Zion in 'The Eye Altering' (1976/1978).
[48] Shakespeare's *Midsummer Night's Dream* 5.1.350-51—a play closely related to *Romeo and Juliet*.

early in her career, even when they are most positive—highly ambivalent about walls. In a complex way, she associates the walls of Landin with the grey-faced, bitter, highly gifted mind-hearer Alla Pasfal Alterra—and associates Alla Pasfal with breaking the Law of Cultural Embargo, and with both an assertion and negations of what Thomas J. Remington has discussed as 'touch.' It is Alla Pasfal who does the actual mindhearing to spy on the Gaal, breaking the Law of Cultural Embargo: 'The walls of the City are safe' she says; Agat replies: 'But the law is broken'—and it turns out the Gaal have left a force to take and occupy Landin, a force already inside the city's walls (94-95; ch. 11). It is Alla who comes to Jakob Agat when Rolery brings him back after he's beaten by the men of Tevar. She reaches out to him with news and mindspeech, but her message is that *'Man and unman cannot work together.... We can make no alliances but among ourselves.... Never hold your hand out to any creature that belongs to this planet.'* Agat rejects this advice, most importantly by asking Rolery to marry him (56-57; ch. 6).

Le Guin associates the walls of Tevar with old Wold, who comes to realize that their walled City, built under his leadership, 'is only a trap' against the Gaal horde (63; ch. 7). Significantly, one instance of Wold's thoughts on walls is sandwiched between Wold listening to one of his people ranting against 'the farborn,' the Alterrans, and Wold's thought, 'All men were alien one to another, at times, not only aliens' (37; ch. 4).

The movement of romantic comedy is the integration of people into a re-formed community, that new and better world coalescing around a central couple. In *Planet of Exile* Le Guin takes the pattern of romantic comedy and moves it to an intercultural scale: the comic movement of Exiles finding a home, envoys finding their mission a success.[49] Insofar as she color-codes her people, she suggests a wish for integration in a political sense obvious to a careful reader in the mid-1960s: Black and White together, / They *do* overcome; Rolery and Agat making love in any one of several conventional positions, yields variations on the Yin-Yang symbol.[50] Insofar as she has her future Terrans people of color, she hints at a point about literal racial survival that will become more specific in later stories. Still, at the center of *Planet of Exile* is the marriage of Rolery and Agat, which offers hope for the Alterrans on Gamma Draconis III: their marriage can be fertile, and Rolery and Agat can produce sons and (bio-

---

[49] See Spencer, 'Exiles and Envoys.'
[50] Most simply imaged, a Yin-Yang is a circle with a wavy line separating and joining black on one side (with a speck of white)—Yin—and white on the other side (with a speck of black): Yang. This is a Daoist symbol of wholeness and of balanced opposites, including female/male produced by the Dao and in turn producing 'The Ten Thousand Things' that are the universe. It is a symbol Le Guin uses frequently: for the integration of Ged in *WE*, for true marriages in works ranging from *LoH* (1971) through *Tehanu* (1990). For more on Daoism, see listed Barbour works, the appendix on Daoism in Bittner's 'Approaches' diss. and my discussions below.

logically more significant) daughters who can be fertile with both peoples (117; ch. 13).

Rolery has noticed that Agat spoke of all the people on the planet as humans and soon after that, Agat tells her that communicating by mind-speech mostly requires learning how 'to break down one's own defenses,' to reach out to the alien (110-11; ch. 13). Speaking from Agat's point of view, the Narrator looks through Agat's eyes at Rolery and tells us that 'She the stranger, the foreigner, of alien blood and mind, did not share his power or his conscience or his knowledge or his exile. She shared nothing at all with him, but had met him and joined with him wholly and immediately across the gulf of their difference: as if it were that difference, the alienness between them, that let them meet, and that in joining them together, freed them.... In his mind he heard her say his own name, like a whisper in the night, like a touch across the abyss' (80-81; ch. 9). They have formed the first of many central Le Guinian marriages, a constant in her canon. This marriage serves in the plot as a seal of the alliance between the two people: a blood-bond made with many deaths but not those of the central lovers. In more literary ways, the marriage is a kind of synecdoche or metonym—see Note below—for the integration of the Tevarans and Alterrans: as if to say, by hundreds and thousands of such moments of touch, of such bondings, peoples are brought together, and a people like the Terrans can become part of a world, finding a home. And so the people on Gamma Draconis III will be brought together and thrive: as we learn in *City of Illusions*, where Gamma Draconis III has long been the prosperous planet colloquially called, Werel, 'the world.'

A Note on Walls (etc.)

Synecdoche is the rhetorical figure of taking part of something for the whole thing, e.g., 'The ranch HANDS herded 2000 HEAD of cattle' (complete human beings' herding full cows, bulls, steers, and calves—not the literal meaning). *Metonym* suggests relationship: when 'Factions of the Plantagenet family fought for THE ENGLISH CROWN' they wanted more than the physical headgear: the crown is a metonym for a finite but indefinite set of powers, privileges, and so forth. *Symbolism* is like a new and still unfocused metonym put to uses more literary than rhetorical: e.g., in William Shakespeare's *Othello*, Desdemona's handkerchief takes on symbolic values as the play goes on, as do clothes in Shakespeare's *Macbeth* and *King Lear*.

As indicated above, I will ask you to pay close attention to Le Guin's walls and roofs, which are always available for figurative or symbolic use, starting with the synecdoche of walls and roofs as parts of buildings, buildings that can contain humans and allow us to stay indoors: safe. In a good sense—*in bono* as Medieval scholars used to say—such buildings provide shelter and convenient places for humans to form communities. *In malo* (bad senses), those buildings are traps and/or prisons separating humans from a truer home in nature. Buildings in turn can become synecdoches, metonyms, symbols for home, urban life, civilization, safety, technology, and/or culture, which in turn can be traps and prisons. And walls and roofs can be just there, neutrally: part of the setting.

II.

TRANSITION, DAOISM, MAGIC, AND GETTING IN TOUCH

> I read Lao-tzu and the *Tao Te Ching* at 14. My father had it around the house in the old edition with the Chinese text. I sneaked a peak and was and remain fascinated. Taoism is still an underlayer in my work. It begins talking about what we can't talk about—an old mysticism that intertwines with Buddhism and is practical and not theistic. Before and beyond God. There's a humorous and easygoing aspect to it that I like temperamentally and that fits in with anarchism. Pacifist anarchism and Lao-tzu have a lot of connection with each other, especially in the 20th century.
>
> (Le Guin on 'Summer Reading,'
> *Mother Jones* May/June 1995: 34)

Possibly the best way into the worlds of Le Guin's Daoist and magical works is through the early short stories.[51] I'll suggest the philosophical stories 'Field of Vision' (1973), 'A Trip to the Head' (1970), and 'Darkness Box' (1963); the stories in the 'marriage group' 'April in Paris' (1962) and 'Nine Lives' (1969); and the Earthsea stories 'The Word of Unbinding' and 'The Rule of Names' (both 1964).[52]

---

[51] 'The word 'Tao' is pronounced [dao], and is now often spelled with a 'D,' in the same reform that took 'Peking' to 'Beijing.' I retain the older spelling in titles and quotations.

[52] 'The Marriage Group' is a term from Chaucer criticism, referring to the Canterbury Tales dealing with literal marriage. In Le Guin's usage and that of her critics, 'marriage' means close, life-long pair bonds: the close personal relationships of friends and lovers, of which legally married couples are a subset. Again, Le Guin has said that most of her work deals with 'marriage,' but some works deal with 'marriage' more directly than others, and I'll occasionally group together such works.

'Field of Vision' (1973)

The science-fiction story 'Field of Vision' makes a useful starting place, logically, not chronologically—since it handles very explicitly a question usually made moot or only handled indirectly in much of Le Guin's work until *Always Coming Home* (1985): God. The story also deals with the important themes of light and darkness, reason and certainty, literal and metaphorical touch, and with how we organize reality.[53]

In 'Field of Vision,' God exists, 'the one true God, immanent in all things. Everywhere, forever.' Geraint ('Gerry') Hughes, the protagonist of the story has 'learned to see God,' at an archeological site on Mars, and Joe Temski, one of his colleagues, has learned to hear God. In the manner of prophets who've heard the Word, Temski goes off to preach and become First Apostle of the holy and universal Church of God, based on the Revelation of the Ancients who had visited Mars 600 million years ago (*WTQ* 239, 242-43). Before the Church can be formed, Hughes kills himself, and his motivation for suicide—a negative act for Le Guin—is important.

When Hughes looks at his therapist, Sidney Shapir he sees 'A blot. A shadow. An incompleteness, a rudiment, an obstruction. Something completely unimportant.' Shapir asks him what he sees when he looks at himself, and Hughes answers, 'Just the same. A hindrance, a triviality. A blot on the field of vision' (241).[54] Hughes will not preach and refuses to be a missionary because he does not want God for himself and certainly doesn't want God for his world. The logic of the story is impeccable: If God is, then 'Only God is'—truly *is*, is in a meaningful way. Nothing about human beings matters except to know the truth of our worthlessness: 'that we are trivial vehicles of the great truth' of God. 'The earth doesn't matter, the stars don't matter, death doesn't matter, nothing is anything'—at least nothing is anything significant (242). After his time in the 'conversion' room on Mars, all Hughes has to do is open his eyes and look and he can 'see the Face of God. And I'd give all my life just to see one human face again, to see a tree...a chair.... They can keep their God, they can keep their Light. I want the world back. I want questions, not the answer. I want my own life back, and my own death!' (243). He gets only his death.

Le Guin uses in 'Field of Vision' a variation on the method of *Reductio ad absurdum*. Assuming the existence of God does not lead to literal absurdities in logic, but it does lead to conclusions Le Guin does not like, conclusions which will not go over well with humanist readers. Let's examine, briefly, the God here rejected.

---

[53] For 'Field of Vision' in Le Guin's canon, see Abrash, esp. 12-13.
[54] In Robert Browning's dramatic monolog 'Fra Lippo Lippi' (1853/1855), the world is not a 'blot' to the artist Fra Lippo but 'means intensely, and means good' (see lines 313-15). Le Guin agrees here with Browning's Fra Lippo, that it is wrong 'To let a truth slip' of the wondrous details of everyday life (see 'Lippo' lines 286-309).

First, this is less the transcendent Creator-God who says 'Let there be light' (Genesis 1.3) than the immanent God who is Light. Le Guin may be alluding to the opening of the Gospel of John and to John 8.12, where Jesus proclaims himself 'the light of the world.' Still, it may be more useful to see the God in 'Field of Vision' as the God who spoke to Moses out of the burning bush and responded to Moses's request for a name: that God who calls himself 'Ehyeh-Asher-Ehyeh,' with the short form of just 'Ehyeh' ('I Am' or 'I Will Be'). My most recent and textually sophisticated English bible refuses to try to translate the name of God, but notes the centrality to its meaning of the Hebrew verb for *to be*. The True Name of God may be, then: The One Who Can Say *I Am* and Have It a Significant Statement. That is, God is Being, immanent and eternal—and such a God is a problem for humans when personified, when made one, given a personal name, and assigned a pronoun. Indeed, 'Field of Vision' could even be seen to critique any of the schools of Buddhism that stress seeing the ground of Being. Ch'an Buddhism, Fritjof Capra writes, is the Chinese version of Zen, and the formula in Ch'an for enlightenment is 'the vision of the Tao.' Capra concurs, with reservations, with D. T. Suzuki's assertion that 'Buddhist philosophy...ultimately points toward seeing reality as it is' (Capra 22; ch. 2, 'Knowing and Seeing'). Capra can cite other Eastern sources to the same effect, so perhaps we should say that 'Field of Vision' critiques all theories that stress seeing and relating to an Absolute *One* as opposed to living in the multitudinous world of everyday.

Later, I will deal in some detail with the rather overwrought confrontation between Jean-Paul Sartre's Orestes and Zeus in *The Flies* (1943), but a more decorous repetition of what Le Guin is getting at in terms of Western thought can be found in the quieter separation between God and at least part of humanity at the end of Paddy Chayefsky's *Gideon* (1961). About to follow the word of the LORD and kill the elders of Succoth, Gideon

> felt a shaft of terror that chills me even now. It was as if the nakedness of all things was exposed to me, and I saw myself and all men for what we truly are, suspensions of matter, flailing about for footholds in the void, all the while slipping back screaming into endless suffocations. That is the truth of things, I know, but I cannot call it truth. It is too hideous, an intolerable state of affairs. I cannot love you, God, for it makes me a meaningless thing.

Gideon wants a divorce.[55] The Angel reviews Gideon's position: 'You would pretend God is not although you know that he is, so that you might

---

[55] I use 'divorce' advisedly: the word is quite explicit in *Gideon*; it fits in with Le Guin's emphasis on marriage; and it is a Judaic point Chayefsky, significantly, would make and Le Guin would not. Among the Jewish images for relationship

be a significant creature which you know you are not.... And you do not love me!' (Chayefsky 64-65).

If God is and is a person, God is all, and we are nothing. If there is no God, though, then there are other problems.

Le Guin will accept Shiva and Kali, especially Shiva Nataraja, dancing the worlds into being, and nonbeing, and Kali as goddess of creative destruction: these two deities nicely symbolize a mythologized Dao. But a monotheistic One, a 'Judaeo-Christian-Rationalist' God does not exist in Le Guin's work, with part of her rationale for this rejection stated plainly in 'Field of Vision.' Another part of the rationale of rejection is the way monotheism, especially with a transcendent God, correlates with macho, imperialist civilization—but that is a matter for later. For now, Le Guin denies 'the one true God' and writes as an atheist, as she ambiguously says in the 1976 introduction to the re-issue of *The Left Hand of Darkness*, and an honest and intelligent atheist; she knows that getting rid of God, singular, can be 'extremely embarrassing' (Sartre, 'Existentialism' 294). With no One, personal God, one might be left in the Sartrean vision: Man alone, abandoned on a vast plain, with each of us trapped in our own skins and, in extreme cases, nauseated by the world; most importantly for such a vision, 'Hell is—other people' (*No Exit* 47).[56] In Earthsea, from one point of view, when Le Guin gets cosmological, she presents in part a metaphysical and physical universe not far from that of Sartre: a relatively flat world of human beings pretty much between an empty heaven and the Dry Land of the dead, with human people necessarily incapable of being part of nature in the unconscious way of leaves and whales and rocks. What we must learn in Earthsea is the Daoist lesson that one is either tossed about on the surface of the 'stream' or one *becomes* the stream (or river or ocean—or goes deep into the forest): i.e., one merges with the Dao.[57] Le Guin, though, usually wants to keep such merging short-term. She wants us embedded in what *is*, indeed, but ordinarily what is in terms of everyday, domestic realities.

It is a central fact of Le Guin's work that she accepts the problem of 'skin' as a real problem: it is difficult to really get in touch with another

---

with God are a wrestling match, betrothal, and marriage; Gideon's rejection of God is both intellectual and as emotionally laden as the breakup of a marriage.

[56] *No Exit* is useful background for some touches in Le Guin: e.g., the formulation 'Hell is' (*TD*); and for 'You are—your life, and nothing else' (45; 'Existence precedes essence' in nondramatic prose), an important idea in the first three books of Earthsea. Note, though, that *Moby Dick* is also useful for studying Le Guin, and it is not a book she has looked at since 1947 (Le Guin, 'Response' 46): I am *not* suggesting Le Guin's sources here or most other places in *Coyote's Song* but readings useful for readers of Le Guin (who have their own work to do in establishing the meaning of Le Guin's texts).

[57] For Ogion to Ged on becoming the stream, see *WE* 128, ch. 7; for Ged to Arren, see *FS* 122, ch. 8.

person, but it is by no means impossible.[58] Indeed, as Gerry Hughes brings home quite clearly, the desire to get in touch with other human beings and with the world—'just to see one human face again, to see a tree...a plain wooden chair'—may be stronger than the desire to see God, to have the mystic vision and achieve certainty (243). Or, so it is for most people, the unsaved of Henry Vaughn's poem 'The World' (1650), excerpts from which Le Guin uses to open and close the story. The Speaker of Vaughn's poem accuses worldlings of folly 'thus to prefer dark night / Before true light'; but one of them replies in a whisper and implies that Eternity is, indeed, a divine gift only for the elect: *'This Ring the Bride-groome did for none provide / But for his bride.'* And the rest of us (the great 'preterite' majority if Calvinist Christians are correct) may not want this Ring—the transcendent God—but prefer the physical world and other people. Le Guin would not have a Chayefskian divorce from God but would have us reject the Groom (if any Groom there be) and call off the wedding.

'April in Paris' (1962), 'Nine Lives' (1969): First Pass

The problem of 'skin' is stated succinctly by Kislk in 'April in Paris' (Le Guin's first professional story) explaining why in 15,000 years of recorded history one magical spell—and only one—in one place over a brief period of time worked to bring together four strangers and a puppy. 'People bored me,' Kislk tells us. 'All like me on the outside, all alien to me on the inside. When everything's alike,' as it is in her world some 6500 years in our future, 'which place is home?' However, in the late medieval Paris of the story she's met a man she likes, shorter than she is, 'with bad teeth and a short temper. Now I'm home, I'm where I can be myself, I'm no longer alone!' (*WTQ* 35). Loneliness is the problem, a constant human problem. The first-time magician who has summoned three new friends (and a dog) tells us 'Loneliness is the spell, loneliness is stronger.... Really it doesn't seem unnatural' (35; the ellipsis mark is in the original). Loneliness may be even stronger than natural law, and a primary human desire may be to be where one is not alone but with friends and lovers: truly at home.

A similar point is made in 'Nine Lives' (1969). The plot there shares a premise with Le Guin's future history for our Earth from 'Nine Lives' through 'Newton's Sleep' and the Hainish stories of the early 1990s: there has been a major ecological and social collapse on Earth. Some space flight survives the collapse in 'Nine Lives,' and early in the years of our expansion into the galaxy, a mining colony is set up on the planet Libra, manned, at the beginning of the story by Alvaro Guillen Martin, a healthy, extroverted Argentinean, and Owen Pugh, a scrawny Welshman (*WTQ* 123). To start the plot, in good dramatic fashion, Owen and Pugh soon must deal with the arrival of newcomers: the John Chow tenclone, all

---

[58] For touch imagery, see Remington, 'The Other Side of Suffering: Touch as Theme and Metaphor....' and 'A Touch of Different, A Touch of Love.'

named John Chow, but having for middle names letters of the Hebrew alphabet.

And then Le Guin does something very undramatic; she interrupts the arrival scene with a paragraph of general doctrine, and then follows that with another paragraph applying the doctrine to the situation on Libra.

> It is hard to meet a stranger. Even the greatest extravert meeting even the meekest stranger knows a certain dread, though he may not know he knows it. Will he make a fool of me and wreck my image of myself invade me destroy me change me? Will he be different from me? Yes, that he will. There's the terrible thing: the strangeness of the stranger.
>
> After two years on a dead planet, and the last half year isolated as a team of two, oneself and one other, after that it's even harder to meet a stranger, however welcome he may be. You're out of the habit of difference, you've lost the touch; and the fear revives, the primitive anxiety, the old dread. (121)

The plot works to set up the plausibility of a clone as 'the first truly stable, self-reliant human being,' a corporate individual like a beehive, that 'would need nobody's help. It would be sufficient to itself physically, sexually, emotionally, intellectually' (*WTQ* 129). And then Le Guin stages a quake and a collapse in a mine and kills off all the clones except Kaph.

Now *this* is isolation: three men alone on a planet, under a dome under a Godless sky, over a planet that kills those who go beneath her skin. (I put the matter melodramatically but stay faithful to the imagery of the story.) The action of the plot is Kaph's isolation from his clone, and then learning to make contact, to touch, Pugh and Martin.[59] Kaph asks Pugh if Pugh loves Martin and, after a moment's anger, Pugh answers that Martin is his friend, and then realizes he has answered Kaph's question indirectly so does so directly: 'Yes, I love him. Why did you ask that?' For later, note Pugh's anger at what he takes as a suggestion of homosexuality: it fits into Le Guin's wrestling with one orientation of the angels of feminist consciousness.[60] For now note Kaph's answer to Pugh's wanting to know why

---

[59] The isolation of Kaph is implicitly compared to that of Ishi upon coming into the modern world in Maslen's essay, '...Theodora Kroeber and Ursula K. Le Guin' 67.

[60] To anticipate: From 1970 through the 1980s, Le Guin had occasional problems with fellow feminists. The publication in *Playboy* in Dec. 1990 of Ursula K. Le Guin's 'Unlocking the Air' can be justified on feminist grounds: bringing unto the *un*converted, the readers of a very slick, very high-class 'girlie magazine,' a strong woman character like 'Air's' Fana Fabbre and a good, radical message. The 1969 publication of 'Nine Lives' in *Playboy* by 'U. K. Le Guin,' though, with a byline disguising her identity, was an issue. The bigger issues were Le Guin's use of male heroes (in 'Nine Lives,' all the female John Chow's are soon

he asked; Kaph needs to know how people can love, how we do love. Pugh cannot answer such a question, but he can say that '...it's practice, partly.... We're each of us alone, to be sure. What can you do but hold your hand out in the dark?' (*WTQ* 146-47).

That's about all we can do, and that is what most of us try to do, with whatever success we find. And that, basically, is Le Guin's answer to J-P Sartre and the dozens of lesser thinkers of the 1940s and 1950s who (unlike Sartre) rather exalted in isolation and tragedy and irony and detachment and a sort of 'manly' acceptance of what a small horde of social critics was identifying as the pathological alienation and 'atomization' of people in technologically sophisticated cultures in general and the United States in particular.

But Le Guin was not quite finished with her respectable target, J-P Sartre; that came the following year in 'A Trip to the Head,' a story she describes in the headnote in *The Wind's Twelve Quarters* as 'definitely a Bung Puller,' a story that got her writing again.

'A Trip to the Head' (1970)

'A Trip to the Head' is a surreal, philosophical work, and I'm not sure it would be useful to try to talk about its plot, but the situation of 'A Trip to the Head' is a man finding himself with another person at the edge of a never-named forest.[61] The other is an Other—a person the Self encounters—and the forest both symbolizes and literally is the unconscious, plus nature and the Dao, as both Being and nonBeing.[62] The man is called 'blank' at first by the Narrator, finally identified as Lewis D. Charles, who then becomes 'blank' again. Somehow the man has stumbled out of the forest and into consciousness. There is some action in the head of the man, but much of the story is a dialog between this newly-conscious Self and the Other.

Blank's first question is whether or not he's on Earth, and the Other tells him he is with an allusion to the once famous line, 'Why this is Hell, nor am I out of it' from Christopher Marlowe's *Dr. Faustus* (1.3.76). The allusion is apt since blank is there and the Other—'the one beside him'—is

---

killed off) and an issue that seriously divided liberal feminists and radical feminists: lesbianism and heterosexism. As of *TD* in 1974, Le Guin could present worlds in which consenting homosexual sex was accepted; it was not until *ACH* (1985) and really the 1990s, that Le Guin would write stories in which gay and lesbian sex would be *praised*.

[61] The title, 'A Trip to the Head,' is a complex pun on 'head trip,' 'drug trip,' and 'head' as a slang term (and fairly standard naval usage) for toiletroom.

[62] For classic imaging of a forest as Self, especially the unconscious portions of the Self, note the forest near Athens in Shakespeare's *A Midsummer Night's Dream* (ca. 1594-95) and the entry of Washizu into the labyrinthine forest in the fourth scene of Akira Kurosawa's *Kumonosu-Djo* (1957), *The Castle of the Spider's Web*, released in the USA as *Throne of Blood* (Jorgens 238, Davies 18 [after J. Blumenthal]).

there and 'As Jean-Paul Sartre has said in his lovable way, 'Hell is other people'' (Garcin's line in the last moments of *No Exit*, quoted by the Other).[63] Blank wishes to hell J-P Sartre and again wants to know where he is, to which the Other asks *who* he is. He doesn't know, apparently because they stand 'at the edge of the forest' and in the forest—out of civilization, again home in nature and Being—things lose their names (see 'She Unnames Them' and *King Dog* [1985]).

So blank is but remains unnamed: in good Existentialist fashion his existence precedes his personal essence. Nor does he know what type of thing he is, aside from similar to the Other; if there is no God to determine human nature (as Sartre asserts) it is up to men—Sartre's is a masculinist theory—to define 'Man.' Blank ask, 'How can I say who I am when I can't say what I am?'—and he determines to do something, to get the basics: '...it doesn't matter what name you're called by...it's what you do that counts.... I will exist.... I will call myself Ralph' (162). Existence precedes essence; human action (in Existentialist theory) creates human being, our only *authentic*, really real being.

And then, segue into a parody of a 'women's romance' scene in which Yankee carpetbagger Mr. Ralph proposes to aristocratic, probably White, now-poor but always-proud Amanda, ending in a passionate kiss 'But it did not seem to help at all.' So jump forward in time a bit for a brief sex scene and a longer philosophical discussion afterward. The Self and the Other decide that gender is important; the Other is less sure about sex. ''Oh, Hell,' said the other with a flare of temper, 'brisleworms have sex, tree-sloths have sex, Jean-Paul Sartre has sex—what does it prove?' And then a very important dialogue:

> 'Why, sex is real, I mean really real—it's having and acting in its intensest form. When a man takes a woman he proves his being!'
> 'I see. But what if he's a woman?'
> 'I was Ralph.'
> 'Try being Amanda,' the other said sourly. (162-63)

And here, Le Guin says in her headnote in *The Wind's Twelve Quarters*, here she stopped writing this story—had *'been stuck'* in her writing—for a year or so (159).

Shortly after blank had come to consciousness, he had looked at the also-nameless Other and wondered, 'What good was it?' (161). Sex is one answer to that question: one utilitarian use of another is as a sex object.

---

[63] Le Guin compliments Philip K. Dick by saying that, in his work '...other people are not (as they are to Sartre) hell, but salvation' ('The Modest One,' coll. *LoN* [1979] 176). Sartre on Justice comes across better: Orestes's line 'Justice is a matter among men' is presented in paraphrase in *King Dog* (16) and just possibly alluded to by Ged and Arren in their ignorance of who might allow or forbid human actions (*FS* 137; ch. 9).

More important is the suggestion of sex as man's way of proving 'his being': it would be the 'intensest form' and primal paradigm of 'having and acting.' But should one make utilitarian demands on people—insist that they be good for something, of use *to me*? Is sex always and necessarily 'having and acting'? Is sex always that way even for men? Is 'having and acting' the usual view of sex among women? "Try being Amanda,' the other said sourly'—and consider also the implications 'if Amanda was black' (*WTQ* 163).

The rest of 'A Trip to the Head' shows shadows coming over the world in what may be night, during or after which blank experiences a dream or vision. The Other asks blank to check his memory, and blank finds 'old toys, nursery rhymes, myths, old wives' tales, but no nourishment for adults, no least scrap of possession, not a crumb of success' (164). Blank finds no comfort in being merely human, with 'no name, no sex, no nothing. I might as well be a bristleworm or a tree-sloth,' or, the Other significantly suggests, he might as well be Jean-Paul Sartre. I?said blank, offended. Driven to denial by so nauseous a notion, he stood up and said, I certainly am not Jean-Paul Sartre; he is himself: Lewis D. Charles. Charles names himself in that moment and sees himself before a forest emphatically there, 'root and branch,' but the Other has disappeared.

> He had got it all wrong, backwards. He had found the wrong name. He turned, and without the least impulse of self-preservation plunged into the pathless forest, casting himself away so that he might find what he had cast away.
>
> Under the trees he forgot his name again at once. He also forgot what he was looking for. What was it he had lost? He went deeper and deeper into shadows, under leaves, eastward, in the forest where nameless tigers burned. (165)

Blank's finding the thought of being J-P Sartre 'so nauseous a notion' is a joke; *Nausea* (1938) is the title of Sartre's first famous work, a novel with a narrator radically alienated from other people, the physical world, and even his own body. The burning tigers in the last line of 'A Trip to the Head' are lifted from William Blake's 'The Tyger' (*Songs of Experience*, etched 1789-94). In the poem, Blake raises the question of what sort of God 'Could frame' the 'dreadful symmetry' of a tiger. We should not make too much of a joke and an allusion, but one thing is very clear in 'A Trip to the Head': the movement is away from a utilitarian view of people and a macho Existentialism in the manner of Sartre and into a forest Le Guin has associated with shadows, myths, old wives' tales, and Blakean tigers—and has identified as the unconscious, where names are lost. Such a trip may be very negative, as it is at the conclusion of Le Guin's 'Semley's Necklace' (1964); in later works, it will be mostly positive.

Do not insist, then, upon an Existentialist either/or—e.g., Sartre or Blake—with the comfortable stasis of a fixed position. Definitely don't look for some sort of 'golden mean': a grey blending of, e.g., Sartre and Blake. Do, however, note the *movement*, the vector toward the unconscious, toward so many things most people in the Western world have associated with the dark, the movement *away* from a supposed victory of culture and civilization over savage nature. Like Romantics generally, Blakean and otherwise, Le Guin would have us get back home to the forest, into relationship with tigers, Nature, trees, and the dark, labyrinthine wilderness.

Le Guin is different from most people in the West, different from all of us who've grown up in the tradition of revelation of Judaism, Christianity, and Islam, in the rationalist tradition of Greece, the legalist tradition of Rome, in the tradition going back to at least ancient Egypt that validates the desire for immortality, that celebrates spirit over body, light over the dark. The difference will be more explicit some fifteen years later when Le Guin publishes *Always Coming Home* and, the complement to 'A Trip to the Head,' her (anti)myth of Creation and denial of separation, 'She Unnames Them' (1985).

* * * * * * *

Transition: Daoism (First Pass)[64]

> Tao gives birth to one,
> One gives birth to two,
> Two gives birth to three,
> Three gives birth to ten thousand beings [= the world].
>   (*Tao te Ching* 42 [Chen 157 f.])

For our first pass at Daoism I shall start with Sartrean Man, more specifically Orestes in his climactic confrontation with Zeus in *The Flies*.[65] With Zeus in front of him, Orestes will not deny the existence of God, but he does deny God's relevance. God is 'the king of gods, king of stones and stars, king of the waves of the sea. But you are not the king of man,' because God erred and created us free; indeed, we *are* our freedom (120-21). Before achieving consciousness and the recognition of his freedom, Ores-

---

[64] See Dena C. Bain, 'The Tao Te Ching as Background to the Novels of Ursula K. Le Guin' for a brief summary of relevant Daoist doctrines. For an excellent brief bibliography, see Robert Galbreath, 'Taoist Magic,' 267-28. See passim in James W. Bittner's *Approaches to the Fiction of Ursula K. Le Guin*, and his ch. 5 and appendix on Daoism in his 1979 U of Wisconsin diss. 'Approaches to the Fiction of Ursula K. Le Guin.' I have not seen it, but Susan Wood's 1992 MA thesis, 'Taoism: a Study of Balance in the Hainish Novels of Ursula K. Le Guin' from San Francisco State University is now listed on WorldCat on the Internet and, I assume, available.

[65] We will return to Orestes in my discussion of *ACH*, where being 'Outside nature, against nature' is central to what I call The Big Mistake in the development of civilized cultures.

tes had felt he had a purpose: serving the good by serving God; he felt gentle and a part of the Whole. And then, 'Suddenly.... Nature sprang back...and I knew myself alone, utterly alone in the midst of this well-meaning little universe of yours. I was like a man who's lost his shadow. And there was nothing left in heaven, no right or wrong, nor anyone to give me orders. * * * [I am] Foreign to myself.... Outside nature, against nature, without excuse, beyond remedy, except what remedy I find within myself.... Nature abhors man, and you too, god of gods, abhor mankind. * * * You are God and I am free; each of us is alone, and our anguish is akin' (*The Flies* 121-22). Orestes claims one human connection: the people of Argos are his people, and he feels he must open their eyes with the gift of truth. Zeus says it's a gift 'of loneliness and shame.' They will see through the veils a merciful God has placed over their eyes and 'will see their lives as they are, foul and futile, a barren boon.' What will they make of themselves, the people who'll accept Orestes's gift? Orestes says, 'What they will. They're free, and human life begins on the far side of despair' (123).

So Man is out there, free, alone, utterly alienated. In theory—and in the 1940s through the 1960s a very invigorating theory it was. Still, though, only a French philosopher living a stereotype could be totally content with a picture of the human condition that was both so bleak (if not pathological) and so obviously counter to a fair amount of human experience. We do make friends; we do form bonds with other people; we do love; and we do form human communities from time to time, and most of us, on at least rare occasions, can sense a relationship with Nature and the world, and feel at home in the universe. How does one return to the theory the experience of many men and, quite possibly, most women?

Allow God, and the problem had been solved long before Le Guin started to write, and before Sartre, for that matter. In *I and Thou* (1923, 1937), Martin Buber argued that relationship with God, the great and eternal Thou, allows human relationship with one another and other creatures. Quite emphatically, however, Le Guin will not allow God. How, then, to make possible I-Thou relationships in a Godless world?

One way is to take the God who says 'I AM' and delete the 'I'—get rid of the personal and transcendent in God and leave only immanence, the Being within things, that underlies things. And this was not something Le Guin had to do: the idea of immanent Being may well be far older than named transcendent gods, and is central to the religious and philosophical thought of the East and well developed in 'The Perennial Philosophy'— what Aldous Huxley sees as almost a «natural» approach to the universe— perhaps most austerely embodied in philosophical and mystic Daoism.[66]

---

[66] See Huxley, *The Perennial Philosophy* (1944, 1945), Introd. (Huxley credits *Philosophia perennis* as a phrase to Leibniz [i.e., the Baron Gottfried Wilhelm von Leibniz, 1646-1716]). For the «naturalness» of connection and Daoist ideas on the complexity of all action, note the maxim of the 1970s Ecology Movement, 'Everything is connected to everything else' and the corollary, 'You can't change

Note carefully (and again) that is the philosophical and mystical Daoism stemming from *Tao te Ching* ('The Classic of the Way and its Power') associated with the name Lao Tzu, and the later teachings of Chuang Tzu; the Daoist religion is more recent, different, and not relevant.

The Daoists are the source of the saying that 'Those who know will not say; those who say do not know,' so one should be reluctant to discuss Daoism: philosophically, the Dao itself precedes names and categories and *can't* be discussed, and true knowledge in a mystic discipline comes not from discourse but mystic experience. But the basics are easy enough if one recognizes throughout that any discussion of serious mysteries or ultimate metaphysics has to be figurative, indirect, and partly wrong. I'll tell the Daoist story as I explain it to my students, somewhat mythically and numerologically:

> In the beginning that never was, there was/is/will be the Zero: Nothing, Not-Being, the Immense, the Matrix, the Mother, the Void, the Nameless. Out of this unnamable Zero came the one, Being, that which we can nickname 'Dao' (the Way). Out of the one came and comes the two: Yin and Yang in constant flux and momentary balance: the dark side and light side of a hill, then dark and light, female and male, heights and valley—then all things that can be viewed dualistically, by two's: binary opposites that can complement and/or oppose one another. The Two, though *is* one: Yin and Yang form the Yin-Yang: the dynamic circle with a curved line, traditionally imaged at the moment of balance (a kind of equinox), before the relationship changes and Yin or Yang comes to predominate. Within the Yin is a speck (a seed) of Yang, and within the Yang there is a seed of Yin, and when Yin seems about to take over the world—when, say, nights have grown longest—the seed of Yang sprouts, and the year turns: the winter solstice. Even so, when it appears that Yang will take over: again, there is a reversal, as, in the cosmic example, the summer solstice. The one of Yin-Yang, though, is one of black and white (or orange and azure): balanced opposites, *not* a compromised grey. Out of the flux of the Two came the five elements ('agents,' 'phases,' 'powers'), and from the interactions of the five elements come the Ten Thousand Beings: everything, the universe, nature—including human beings firmly embedded within nature, woven into the world. (Or you can leave out the five 'agents' and just picture the flux of Yin-

---

just one thing.' (Even in the Eden myth, the natural state of humanity is in close connection with the ground, plants, and animals; alienation and separation is the heart of the Fall: Gen. 2.4-3.19).

Yang producing the universe.) So as it was at the beginning, so it is now—since there was no beginning—as the Nameless and the Dao grow out of and become one another and in their flux move the universe through the natural cycles and smaller-scale fluctuations.[67]

In such a view, human beings are part of the universe; even the most alienated of us dies and returns to the cycles of nature. That view of humanity as part of nature is a radical difference between Daoism and Existentialism, and the major source of radical differences between the ancient habits of thought preserved in Daoism versus most of the light-enamored thought of 'the Judaeo-Christian-Rationalist West' (*LoH* 82; ch. 6).[68] We will be returning to this theme, but for now note that if we are part of the universe we cannot get outside the universe to see how it runs, but we can get *in touch with* the universe (contact the Dao) and momentarily *feel* certain of the nature of things. In such a scheme, right action is never going against nature—never trying to force people or things to one's will—but always going *with* nature, going with the Dao.

Le Guin summarizes 'THE WAY' almost at the end of *Always Coming Home* (1985), in her last entry of seven '...Generative Metaphors' at The Back of the Book (483-85):

The Metaphor: THE WAY.
What it generates: CHANGE.
Universe as the way: Mystery; balance in movement.
Society as the way: Imitation of the nonhuman, inaction.
Person as wayfarer: Caution.
Medicine as keeping in balance.
Mind as wayfarer: Spontaneity. Sureness.
The relationship of human with other beings on the way: Unity.
Images of the Way: Balance, reversal, journey, return. (485)[69]

---

[67] From various sources, including Waley (esp. *Tao te Ching*, ch. 42), Bittner diss., Seidel. See also *FS* 137; ch. 9.
[68] For an imagined (very negative) critique of Americanism by Lao Tzu, see Holmes Welch, *Parting of the Way* (1957), Part Four: 'Tao Today,' esp. 169-74 and, for evolution, 187. Le Guin refers to this book in 'Response' (45).
[69] 'In Tao the only motion is returning; / The only useful quality, weakness': *Tao te Ching* ch. 40 (Waley trans. 192). In Wilhelm's trans. (45; II.40), conflated with Chen's trans.:

> Return is the movement of DAO.
> Weakness is the effect of DAO.
> All things under Heaven come about in existence
> [Chen: 'are born of being (*yu*)']
> Existence comes about in non-existence
> ['Being is born of non-being (*wu*)']

Now for people who grew up in the macho 1950s and 1960s, or 1980s, Daoist philosophy may sound rather feminine, and the feminine emphasis (in terms of traditional patriarchal dualities) was insisted upon by the founders of Daoism, who lived during China's Warring States period and knew a thing or two about the costs of macho. More important, though, this quietism—the celebration of *wu wei* 'inaction (action through stillness)'—seems to put the lie to the title to Arthur Waley's explanation of Daoism, *The Way and Its Power*. What power?! Well, for one thing the power to know when to act and how to act so that one's action is in rhythm with the universe—so a small human act could have great consequences, a touch on a Great Wheel that changes its direction (*LHD* 189, 192, 203). One might have, then, the power of the wise diplomat. Or of great athletes when they have entered the rhythm of the game, or dancers who momentarily embody the music and become the dance. Anna K. Seidel, however, suggests that 'The philosophical notion of Tao expressed the religious sympathy and complete solidarity that unites nature and man. In the magical arts that influenced Taoism, Tao designated the magical feat of bringing Heaven and Earth, the sacred powers and man, into communication with each other. In this sense, Tao was an art and a power, specifically the power of the magician and the king' (1035).[70]

And I will use that observation as a transition to magic.

'The Rule of Names' (1964) and 'The Word of Unbinding' (1964)

We will get powerful presentations of magicians and kings (if only one *literal* king) in *The Lathe of Heaven* and the Earthsea series, but I want to get to them by way of some transitional works, starting with the two promised Earthsea stories, 'The Rule of Names' and 'The Word of Unbinding' (both 1964). 'The Rule of Names' is a nice bit of dark comedy about the dragon Yevaud and a treasure hunter. After the manner of dragons, Yevaud has picked up some treasure, but there has arisen a problem: peace has broken out in Earthsea, and the human people have formed a League that wants the treasure enough to send out a mage-equipped fleet sufficiently strong to threaten even an ancient dragon. So Yevaud goes off, possibly commits a murder to stage his own 'death'—at least some dragon other than Yevaud turns up conveniently dead to discourage the hunt—and

---

[70] A. L. Kroeber had a lower opinion of magic. Though insisting upon what many today would call the historical construction of the theory of progress, he suggested some criteria for objective ranking of «progressed», 'higher cultures' and 'lower cultures,' retarded in their beliefs. 'The first is the criterion of magic and superstition.In proportion as a culture disengages itself from reliance on these, it may be said to have registered an advance. In proportion as it admits magic in its operations, it remains primitive or retarded. This seemingly dogmatic judgment is based on the observation that beliefs in magic, such as are normal in backward societies, do recur in cultures that by profession have discarded magic, but chiefly among individuals whose social fortune is backward or who are psychotic, mentally deteriorated, or otherwise subnormal' (§ 127, *Culture Patterns*...106; ch. 7).

shows up on Sattins Island disguised as a mediocre wizard who picks up the usename 'Mr. Underhill,' since he lives in a small, Hobbit-style house under a hill.[71]

While out walking, Mr. Underhill answers the question of the local school mistress why one must be careful to conceal one's truename: 'Because the name is the thing...and the truename is the true thing. To speak the name is to control the thing' (*WTQ* 76).[72] This point is illustrated, with a twist, later, when the current Sealord of Pendor, nicknamed Blackbeard, comes for the treasure that will make his title real and not a mockery. Blackbeard has a great advantage: he knows the truename of the thief and uses it at the climax of a wizards' duel to trap Yevaud in his true shape. The name of a thing, or person, is the essence of the thing, and to know the name means you can summon the thing and hold it there in its true shape. Unfortunately for the arrogant Blackbeard, Yevaud is right there and wants to be there, and Yevaud's true shape is that of a very large dragon with experience killing lesser thieves, like a Sealord and his garrison (79). Very shortly, all that is left of Blackbeard on the island is 'a reddish-blackish trampled spot' (83).

'The Rule of Names' introduces Earthsea as an Archipelago (islands and sea: Earthsea) and gives us the rules for magic in the world of Earthsea. It's a rather generic sort of magic, by no means specifically Daoist, but it is a kind of magic compatible with Daoism (see Galbreath, 'Taoist Magic...'). Most important, it teaches a strong lesson—all the stronger for its being comic—against using magic to force one's will on the world in the manner of Blackbeard: the world is much too complicated to be forced. The story also associates magic with the unconscious or subconscious: in psychoanalytic theory, 'true speech' is the unconscious, and the language of dreams and symbols and other manifestations of the human unconscious is true speech.[73] In psychoanalysis and more generally, the unconscious is the place of our primary thoughts/feelings; however uncanny (unHome-y, *unhiemlich*), the unconscious may seem to our consciousness, it and its

---

[71] Adult dragons in Earthsea are talking, intelligent creatures, so a human's killing one is always at least 'dracocide' and a bad act—if usually justifiable. Yevaud's killing another dragon to hide his (her?) tracks, though, definitely is a murder (the killing of a member of one's own [intelligent] species).

[72] For ancient belief in the power of names, see Gen. 32.24-30: Jacob's getting his name changed to Israel, and the refusal of the divine being Jacob wrestled with to give Jacob his name. Oxford Annotated RSV notes: 'In antiquity it was believed that a person's self was concentrated in his name.... Jacob's new name signified a new self.... The divine being refuses' to tell Jacob his name 'lest Jacob, by possessing the name, gain power over him (compare Ex. 3.13-14, Jg. 13.17).' For the power of an adept at Daoist Quietism 'to move and transform matter' see Waley 46.

[73] Vivian Sobchack refers to 'the 'true speech' that [Jacques] Lacan sees as the unconscious' ('Virginity' 57). The idea, of course, is general to psychoanalytic views of what is truest in human personality (although usage of 'unconscious' and 'subconscious' varies—and I apologize if my conflating of the two gives offense).

language may be basic to us and to our Selves being in the world and acting on the world. The language of the unconscious may be like art, irrelevant for power and still, paradoxically, providing great power.

****

'The Word of Unbinding' (1964) very specifically associates magic with homecoming (*WTQ* 70) and introduces us to the Dry Land, the land of the dead, far to the west in Earthsea (71-72). As Le Guin says in her headnote, 'It also reveals a certain obsession with trees, which...keep cropping up in my work' (65). The quadruple association is significant.

The hero of 'The Word of Unbinding' is a warlock named Festin, who, like Dante at the beginning of *The Divine Comedy* (ca. 1302, printed 1472) is 'in the middle of his life' and in a woods. But it's a positive woods for Festin, since he wants to learn patience, and so has 'gone to converse with trees, especially oaks, chestnuts, and the grey alders whose roots are in profound communication with running water' (66). Festin is captured by the wicked wizard Voll the Fell and imprisoned. Up to the final brief episode, 'The Word of Unbinding' is the story of Festin's attempts to escape.

In the next to last episode, Festin is exhausted, injured, and very sad over his failure to protect his land and people: 'Trusting his power too much, he had lost his strength.' Unable to act, he wishes himself a fish 'in the forest in the shadow of the trees, in the clear brown backwater under an alder's roots'—and he becomes a fish. The Narrator tells us explicitly that 'This was a great magic,' but Festin hadn't exactly performed this magic no more than anyone else 'in exile or danger' who 'longs for the earth and waters of his home.... Only in dreams do any but the great Mages realize this magic of going home. But Festin...gathered his will together till it shone like a candle in the darkness of his flesh, and began to work the great and silent magic' until 'He got free. He was home'—and then gets captured again, trapped by his own spell in the shape of a fish (*WTQ* 69-70).

Back in his dungeon, Festin wanders why Voll hasn't killed him, and makes a shrewd guess why Voll doesn't want him dead. If Festin chooses to live, it is as a perpetual prisoner, 'But if one chose not to live?' And 'So Festin made his choice,' in one nicely Existentialist gesture and speaks the word of unbinding. 'This was not transformation. He was not changed,' and he walks 'slowly down the far slope of the hill of being, under new stars'—and summons Voll by Voll's name (71). Like Cob later, in *The Farthest Shore*, Voll and 'death had found a way back into the other land,' the land of the living, of fish and water, change and trees. Festin easily defeats Voll, forcing him to die truly, and then Festin waits for Voll's corpse to finally rot and thereby render Voll incapable of further evil. He waits 'in the heart of the country which has no seacoast. The stars stood still above him; and as he watched them, slowly, very slowly he began to forget the voice of streams and the sound of rain on the leaves of the forests of life' (*WTQ* 72).[74]

Renouncing his power as a magician—abnegation, as it will be put in 'Winter's King' (1969/1975)—Festin comes into his strength, a strength associated with water ('The softest thing on earth / overtakes the hardest thing on earth' [*Tao te Ching* I.43; Wilhelm p. 47]). Renouncing still more, renouncing even his life, Festin gets the only victory he can get over his enemy. Summarizing 'The Perennial Philosophy' on mortification and non-attachment, Aldous Huxley writes that 'It is by losing the egocentric life that we save the hitherto latent and undiscovered life which, in the spiritual part of our being, we share with the divine Ground' (106; ch. 6). Le Guin here is both more rigorous and downbeat: by losing his life, period, Festin joins with Being and gets as much as he can get: freedom, victory, and justification of his life as a wizard; he has, finally, protected the people he serves. Pure Being, though, in Earthsea is the Dry Land, devoid of 'streams and the sounds of rain on the leaves of the forests of life,' and Festin's is a somber victory for a tragic hero.

Impermanence, Le Guin is convinced, especially that of human mortality, is central to human life, and the source not only of our pain, but of love and joy (Huxley 106-07). And death is a terrible thing: 'I have learnt that death exists,' says Arren to Ged in *The Farthest Shore* (1972), 'and that I am to die. But I have not learnt to rejoice in the knowledge.... If I love life, shall I not hate the end of it?' (136; ch. 9). It is a question Le Guin will continue to debate with herself into the 1990s.

Reference Table: Le Guin and the *Tao te Ching*

I tabulate below chapters in Lao Tzu's *Tao te Ching* (Pinyin: *The Dao De Jing* of Lao Zi) useful for various themes in Le Guin's canon. Note that these are very brief chapters, usually shorter than an English sonnet.

I rely on Arthur Waley [1934] and 'The Richard Wilhelm Edition': the Wilhelm translation, translated from German into English by H. G. Ostwald (1910/1978), supplemented with the translations of Ellen Chen and 'TaoDeChing - Lao Tze...(with hyperlinks to Chinese text) / Version 2.07 - Copyright (C) 1992, 1993, 1994, 1995 Peter A. Merel'—on the World Wide Web. (I put some doubtful, but interesting, items in parentheses.)

---

[74] I'm not sure what to make of 'no seacoast' beyond the obvious: you can't just sail off to the land of the dead. Note that in the Revelation of John at the end of Christian Scriptures, there's a new heaven and new earth, 'and there was no longer any sea' (21.1). Contrast more generally the forest as a place for human life, with John's vision of a city for eternal life: a square (21.16) world of eternal day (22.5) done in gold and jewels and semiprecious stones (21.11-21). Le Guin prefers water, a central Daoist symbol—and popular among Native Americans (see Le Guin's 'Legends' 5)—and she prefers life, trees, and forests.

Themes / Chapter Numbers in *Tao te Ching*

abyss: 4
acting (on a world too big to handle: a bad idea): 29
actionless activity (*wu wei*) / wordless teaching: 2, 3, 29, 30, 37, 43, 48, 57, 58, 63, 64, 67 (81). [Also *Chuang Tzu* 23.6]
anarchism (recommended) / leaving off (withdrawal) / 'Let be': 3, 9, 17, 29, 30, 32, 57, 58, 75
balance / harmony: 32, 42
beginning: 52
Being / Non-being: 1, 2, 6, 14, 40, 43
below: 61, 66, 68
benevolence / holiness, morality, humane behavior, duty / good & evil / justice, rights / ruthlessness: 5, 8, 18, 19, 20, 38, 79 [Also *Chuang Tzu* 22.1]
bent, twisted (a good thing): 22
chance / luck: 50
change / changelessness: 25
child, infant / uncarved block: 10, (19), 20, 28, 55
communism / no property / being 'dispossessed': 3, 7, 9, 19, 22, 44, 46, 64, 77, 81
Dao (Way): 1, 4, 16, 25, 32, 34, 37, 40, 41, 46, 51, 53, 62, 73
dark(ness) / chaos (positive as aspects of Dao): 14, 21, 41, 42
desire / desirelessness: 19, 37, 46, 55, 57, 64
doorway / gateway: 6
duration, eternity, lastingness (of Heaven and Earth) / deathlessness: 7, 16, 25, 37, 52, 59
ego(izing), boasting: 24
emptiness / nothingness (positive, useful): 4, 5, 11, 16
environment (shaping humans): 51
evil / good: 13
far (away): 25
fate: 16
female / Mysterious Female / male: 6, 28, 61
flow / flux: 4, (16), 45
flowing abundance (wealth): 45
foreknowledge (= folly): 38
forgiveness: 62, 63
form / formless(ness): 14
freedom: 17
gender (male/femaleness): 28
glory: 26, 56
God, gods (Dao preceding): 4, 39
greatness (including human): 25
home (as Dao): 62
ignorance / learning, knowledge, cleverness (a bad idea): 18, 19, 20, 48, 64, 65, 71, 81

joy (gladness): 23
judging: 54
king (ruler): 16, 25
knowledge / wisdom (positive): 47, 52, (71)
left / right: 31, 34
life / death: 23, 38, 41, 50
light: 42, 52, 56
limits: 59
living well: 54, 56, 57, 59, 64, 66, 67, 68, 71, 77, 79
love: 8, 38, 56, 67
low(liness), baseness / humility: 39, 56, 66, 68
loyalty / promise-keeping, faithfulness: 38, 49
Mother (cosmic): 20, 25, 52, 59
Name(s) / nameless (Self-so) / true name: 1, 25, 32
nature: (Used by Merel and others for 'heaven and earth,' 'the world,' Dao,' and other words and formulations.)
nothing: 11
One, oneness / undifferentiated unity: 10, 19, 22, 39, (60),
origins / continuity: 14
pain, suffering: 13, (16), 71
peace: (16), 31, 66, 68, 81
progress, advance: 41
return (circle, cycle): 16, 22, 25, 40, 52
rock: 43, 78
root: 6, 16, 26, 39
sea / brooks, streams, rivers (like Dao): 32, 66
Self (vs. «ego»): 7, 13, 24
shame / purity: 41
simplicity: 19, 28, 32, 37, 57
soft(ness) / hard (soft better): 10, 43, 76, 78
Source (Dao as [older than God]): 4
stillness / quiet, silence (vs. busy-ness, claiming to know, leading the world: 15, 16, 23, 26, 49, 53, 56, 57, 61, 67
strength (true strength): 55
things (hoarding them): 9, 44
thread: 14
traces (tracks): 27
use, usefulness / purpose: 11, 20, 40, 67
utopia (primitive, and small): 80
valley, gorge / Valley Spirit (valley stream): 6 32, 28, 41
violence, conquest (advised against) / nonviolence: 29, 30, 31, (67), 68, 69
water / dryness: 6, 8, 43, 74, 78
weakness (advised): 28, 36, 40, 76, 78
wholeness: 22
words: 70

III.

EXPLICITLY DAOIST WORKS

City of Illusions (1967)

In the chronology of Le Guin's Hainish cycle, the action of *City of Illusions* comes about six hundred years after the action of *Planet of Exile*, when the descendants of Rolery and Jakob Agat send an expedition from Werel ('the world') to reestablish contact with Earth (Bittner, *Approaches* 99). Symbolically and philosophically, however, *City of Illusions* goes with the West Coast tale *The Lathe of Heaven* (1971): both begin where 'A Trip to the Head' (1970) begins; both turn inside out the ending of 'The Word of Unbinding.'[75] Both start with a man's coming to consciousness, in *City of Illusions*, coming to consciousness at the margin of a literal forest.

The plot of *City of Illusions* is straightforward, and James W. Bittner has demonstrated that it is quite conventional, even while undermining its own conventionality (*Approaches* 98-101). I'll argue for its conventionality and anti-conventionality even more strongly than Bittner, since *City of Illusions* retells, very differently, Philip Francis Nowlan's late 1920s stories 'Armageddon—2419 A.D.' and 'The Airlords of Han.' These old stories were emphatically 'around' in comics and movies in mid-century America, and in 1962 the two original stories were cleaned up a bit, combined, and reissued as what the 1978 redaction would call 'THE SEMINAL 'BUCK ROGERS' NOVEL.' However she knew the stories (or whether she consciously knew them at all), Le Guin gives Nowlan's 'Yellow Peril' propaganda an ironically appropriate Chinese twist, presenting in *City of Illusions* a story I've described as 'Buck Rogers Goes Taoist.'

Before the action of the story, the people of Werel have sent a starship to Earth to reestablish contact. The ship is intercepted by the Shing, a humanoid species that can tells lies telepathically ('mindlie'). They were the Enemy feared in the earlier Hainish stories, and it turns out they won. But

---

[75] For an elegant analysis of the four major settings of Le Guin's stories (Earthsea, The Hainish World, Orsinia, and The West Coast [of North America]), see Cummins, *Understanding Ursula K. Le Guin*, ch. 5 for 'The West Coast').

it was a pathetic victory since the Shing seem incapable of creating and simply rule Earth, keeping Terrans separated into small groups, isolated and powerless. The Shing present themselves, when necessary, as 'the self-sacrificing Lords,' holding 'the torch of civilization alight' on the 'dark barbaric earth' (165, ch. 8; 118, ch. 6), but their benignity is only marginally more noble than that of the liberals in the Belgian Congo at the end of the nineteenth century in our history: whose most famous representative is Joseph Conrad's Mr. Kurtz, a would-be hero picturing himself the Knight serving Lady Civilization holding aloft a torch (*Heart of Darkness* 27-28; § I). The Shing do better than genocidal Europeans in that they will not kill, at least not human beings or complex animals (*CI* 196 and passim), but they do 'mind raze' all of the captured Werelians, except one child (Har Orry). At least one adult survives, and the story begins with his awakening:

> Imagine darkness.
> In the darkness that faces outward from the sun a mute spirit woke. Wholly involved in chaos, he knew no pattern. He had no language, and did not know the darkness to be night.
> [Dawn. The creature begins to move.]... He had no way through the world in which he was, for a way implies a beginning and an end. All things about him were tangled, all things resisted him. The confusion of his being was impelled to movement by forces for which he knew no name: terror, hunger, thirst, pain. Through the dark forest of things he blundered in silence till the night stopped him, a greater force. (1)

This 'blank,' however, is luckier than Lewis D. Charles of 'A Trip to the Head'; the Other who finds him (the girl, Parth) takes him home, and merciful Terran people decide to keep him and care for him even if he might be a Shing agent. They name him 'Falk''yellow' in their language— 'for his sallow skin and opal eyes' (7; ch. 1), and they raise him, necessarily, as they would raise a baby. Children, though, grow up and must eventually leave home, and Falk reluctantly leaves partner (again Parth) and Forest home on that most basic of quests, to find out who he is, to find his 'name and nature' as he puts it, to go the 'way' to his 'true name,' in the words of a wise Prince (99, 100; ch. 5). He intends to go to Es Toch, the one city of the Shing, in the far west. After a number of adventures and what turns out to be the (apparently) good advice to go alone, he is brought to Es Toch by a human agent of the Shing, the Terran woman Estrel. The adventures are significant.

One is among the Nation of the Basnasska (ch. 4), a post-catastrophe Plains Indians society—but not literally descended from Indians—with customs like those of a primitive Condor people, and views on ghosts very similar to the Fox Indians discussed by Claude Lévi-Strauss (31).[76] In his escape from the Basnasska, Falk kills a man: 'Without thought, reflex-quick and certain' (73), an act that follows the Dao, and can therefore be done with 'Spontaneity. Sureness' (*ACH* 485).[77] Falk also encounters a small gang of thugs who define themselves an 'Men, free men, killers' (34; ch. 2), and a 'Thurro-dowist' hermit (47-57; ch. 3), an overly sensitive empath who lives like Henry David Thoreau at Walden Pond, except with far more consistency and dedication. The hermit reads 'the Old Canon of Man' (the *Tao te Ching*) and gives his departing guest a 'slider' hovercraft, good advice to beware singing hens—the femme fatale who both betrays and aids him—and the important 'news and wisdom and advice' that 'There are not very many of the Shing' (54-55); like the British Raj in India, or most colonizers, the few rule, with local aid.

On the Great Plains, Falk finds the Bee-Keepers, clothed all alike 'in long shifts of yellow winter cloth marked with a brown cross on the heart.' Almost all of the Bee-Keepers range in age from about twelve to forty, and Falk thinks them 'a strange community, like the winter barracks of some army encamped here in the midst of utter solitude in the truce of some unexplained war; strange, sad, and admirable.' In their order and frugality, Falk is reminded of his own Terran home in the Forest, and he finds their 'hidden but flawless, integral dedication' to be 'restful to him. They were so sure, these beautiful sexless warriors, though what they were so sure of they never told the stranger' (*CI* 89), certainly not a stranger accompanied by one they suspect to be an Enemy agent. Estrel tells him (truly or falsely we do not learn) that the Bee-Keepers maintain their numbers by kidnapping and 'breeding...savage women like sows, and bringing up the brats in groups. They worship something called the Dead God, and placate him with sacrifice—murder'; Estrel dismisses them as 'nothing but the vestige of some ancient superstition.' The Bee-Keepers are hospitable, though; one of their leaders tells Falk that they find solitude 'soul's death,' believing that 'man is mankind'; but they will trust no one 'but brother and hive-twin, known since infancy,' as the only safe rule (see Remington, 'Other Side' 159). Falk though has 'no kinsmen, and no safety' (89-90; ch. 5).

A bit later Falk encounters the 'Prince and God' of the Kansas Enclave and their leader in 'one of the great games. King of the Castle it's called.' The Prince is bound by the rules of the game, and by no other rules. This Everyman as King, ruling by consent (102-03), does, though, consult his 'patterning-frame' as one might consult the *I Ching* (precisely as one might consult the *I Ching*, the Chinese 'Book of Changes,' for philosophy to fortune-telling), which allows him to foreshadow a good deal of *City*'s remaining plot (99-103; ch. 5).

The two-person quest across the middle of a continent prefigures the movement at the center of *The Left Hand of Darkness* (1969), and other elements in this section of *City* will be used to good effect in later works:

---

[76] For the Condor People, see below, the section on *Always Coming Home*.
[77] In the section of *ACH* (1985) entitled 'Some Generative Metaphors.'

the privileging of solitude as a choice by those who can use solitude for contact with nature and the Way; the problematicizing of both sacrifice and safety; the idea of royalty as 'risk and grace' and a natural king as both a rare fact and a possibility for anarchistic leadership; Daoism, and the *I Ching* or intuition as a way to find how the Way goes, how the great Wheel turns; 'one's name and nature' as, possibly the proper quest, even if they take one to 'The Place of the Lie' (99), here Es Toch.

At Es Toch, the Shing produce young Orry of Werel and tell Falk that he, Falk, is really Ramarren, the Navigator of the Werelian ship Alterra, 'a decisive and potent person' (190; ch. 9). The Shing tell Falk there never was an Enemy; there was civil war, and some humans took over in order to run Earth until peace came, and now use the lie that there is an Enemy to get the populace to accept their rule. The Shing are lying, and what they want from Ramarren is the True Name of the sun of Werel—the name in Galaktika—so they can find the Werelians and neutralize them. Neutralizing the Werelians is important to the Shing; Werelian telepathic discipline is good enough that Werelians can know that the Shing can mindlie, and with this knowledge, resist them. The Shing offer Falk an operation that will bring Ramarren back to consciousness—but only at the cost of Falk, who will disappear. With a little help from his friend, more or less, Orry, and a lot of help from the opening lines of the *Tao te Ching*, Falk is not sacrificed but survives; and Falk and Ramarren together become Falk-Ramarren, a 'double man' who is strong enough to mentally overpower a Shing, steal a ship, and escape with Orry and a Shing captive to tell the tale on Werel.[78]

The Nowlan Buck Rogers story begins in 1927 when Anthony Rogers (not yet 'Buck') enters an abandoned mine near Scranton, PA, inhales radioactive gas, and sleeps in suspended animation for about 500 years. He awakes in a forest world, where he is discovered by a beautiful and highly competent young woman (Wilma Deering) and adopted by the Wyomings, a gang of Americans. He gets integrated into the gang with amazing speed, marries Wilma Deering, and proceeds to aid the gang and their allies fight the tyrannical Han, 'fierce Mongolians, who...had in their blood a taint not of this earth, and who with science and resources far in advance of those of a' United States nearly bankrupt after warfare with a Bolshevik Europe 'had swept down from the skies in their great airships' to kill most of the 'American race' and drive the survivors into the forest that had regrown

---

[78] Students of recent literary theory might want to apply to Falk-Ramarren, and Le Guin on the idea of Balance more generally, the theories of Mikhail Bakhtin. Margaret Lee Zoreda describes Bakhtin's idea of monologism as 'the impossibility to achieve a harmonious understanding within the same being, 'of two consciences and two subjects' at the same time ('Problem [of the Text...] 111).' She paraphrases Bakhtin's idea of *dialogism* as 'the encounter-juxtaposition of autonomous entities, whether words, sentences, discourses, subjects[,] or cultures that without merging conserve their identities in a mutually enriching bond' (paraphrasing 'Response to a Question...' 7) (Zoreda 55, 59). Falk-Ramarren has achieved a dialogic existence.

over America. Rogers leads a commando raid on the Han city of Nu-Yok to get intelligence on American collaborators and then helps attack a nearby American tribe called the Sinsings, who have treacherously joined forces with The 'hereditary enemies and oppressors of the White Race in America' ('Airlords' 1106). Rogers is a World War I veteran, and his knowledge of artillery barrages and hand-to-hand fighting helps the Wyomings and the other loyalists totally exterminate the Sinsings, for the climax of 'Armageddon 2419' (445).

In 'Airlords,' Rogers attacks a Han airship in his 'swooper' fighter craft, crash lands, gets captured, and is taken across the continent to Lo-Tan, the Rocky mountain capital of the Han in America. The Han treat Rogers quite well physically, but they use coercive psychological methods in an attempt to get from him some sort of information; he guesses they want to learn about American science (1118). In general, Rogers gets a full tour of Lo-Tan, the Magnificent, but at heart a thoroughly dystopian city. Rogers is rescued after a couple of months, most directly by Wilma.

> The Americans have nuked Nu-Yok and invested the other Han cities, and the story ends with the destruction of Lo-Tan...and the killing of Lo-Tan's 10,000 survivors by rocket barrage and hand-to-hand fighting.... In the last paragraph of the story proper, we...learn that the remaining Han cities 'were destroyed and their populations hunted down, thus completing the reclamation of America' and beginning the 'most glorious and noble era of scientific civilization in the history of the American race' (1134). (Kalish et al. 305)[79]

The American example leads to worldwide revolt and the killing of every man, woman, and child among the Han, 'that monstrosity among the races' (1134-35).

In her introduction to the 1978 reissue of *City of Illusions*, Le Guin notes that she has 'villain trouble' in the book, primarily that the Shing are unconvincing. Just possibly, Le Guin has villain problems because she presents as rather positive the City in *City of Illusions*, at least potentially, and allows some validity to 'the Yaweh Canon' (54; ch. 3): at least parts of Jewish and Christian Scriptures—in *City*—present some newfangled beliefs with some truth or usefulness.[80] The monotheistic Nation of the Basnasska on the American Plains is pretty negative, and the Shing talk of a

---

[79] I am one of the 'others' in 'Kalish et al.' The Kalish article stemmed from a project I directed in two of my SF courses at Miami U.
[80] In *CI*, the *Tao te Ching* is the 'Old Canon' that is complemented by the newer 'Yahweh Canon.' The *texts* in Hebrew scripture are probably older than the *Tao te Ching*, but philosophical Daoism is part of the very ancient 'Perennial Philosophy,' most especially the tradition of immanence and the Mother, against relatively new, personalized, masculine, transcendent sky-gods.

singular 'Creator' and 'God' (143; ch. 7); but the Bee-Keepers are ambiguous, and *City of Illusions* mostly lacks the constellation of City-Monotheism-Transcendence-Immortality-Sexism-Militarism we will see in later works. That makes *City* an interesting part of Le Guin's canon, but probably contributes to the inadequacy of the villains.[81]

Perhaps equally important, Le Guin refuses to work out the logic of what to do with a bad people like the Shing, who have done and continue to do great evil and will always be capable of great evil at least as long as their culture exists, possibly as long as they exist. Philip Francis Nowlan had no such qualms, and that far his work is more logically and esthetically elegant than *City of Illusions*: one possible, very final solution to this villain problem is enthusiastically narrated genocide.

If Le Guin in *City of Illusions* 'mocks her own use of the hackneyed machinery of space opera' of the galactic empire variety (Bittner, *Approaches* 101), the book can also be read as taking Nowlan's blood-thirsty bit of racist war obscenity and rehabilitating it as a philosophical tale of a quest for wholeness and simultaneously a critique of any attempt at dominion and rootless self-sufficiency (see *TD* 68; ch. 3).

Anthony Rogers has nearly no internal life except anger and sloppy sentiment; his actions are almost all external and active actions, frequently killing people. Falk will kill if he has to, and in good Daoist fashion does so when he must: 'Without thought, reflex-quick and certain Falk fired his laser at pointblank range....' (73; ch. 4). Still, his struggle with the Shing is almost entirely internal, literally mental. Falk must first survive by asserting his existence in the personality of the awakened Ramarren; then the yielding Falk and the over-active Ramarren must balance one another and become an integrated whole. They do this in the manner of the Daoist mystic, starting with Falk losing himself and becoming 'utterly, everlastingly himself: nameless, single, one' (171-73; ch. 8). And then Falk and Ramarren balance and integrate, remaining two and becoming one: a microcosm of Yin-Yang in contact with the Dao (188-90; ch. 9). Falk-Ramarren's external victory comes because of Ramarren's mental abilities, including, I think, his indoctrination in the Kelshak concept of Rale, 'the right thing to do...like a river following its course,' following the Dao (*CI* 136; ch. 7). But this victory owes more to Falk's ability to wait and be still, acting at need and at the right moment. Ramarren plays for time and

> sought with all his trained intelligence some way in which
> he could turn his situation about and become the controller
> instead of the one controlled: for so his Kelshak mentality

---

[81] For different evaluations, see Spivack's criticism of *EoH* for making 'too explicit,' too neat, the confrontation of values and peoples in the evil folk of Victory City against the 'gentle people' of the town of Shantih (114). Spivack may underestimate Falco, a major Boss of the City, but her point is legitimate, as is her valuing the ambiguity that leads to complexity in *LHD* and *TD* over the clarity of *EoH*.

> [disciplined as a high-status man on Werel] presented his case to him. Seen rightly, any situation...would come clear and lead of itself to its one proper outcome: for there is in the long run no disharmony, only misunderstanding, no chance or mis-chance but only the ignorant eye. So Ramarren thought, and the second soul within him, Falk, took no issue with this view, but spent no time trying to think it all out, either. For Falk had seen the dull and bright stones slip across the wires of the patterning-frame, and had lived with men in their fallen estate, kings in exile on their own domain the Earth, and to him it seemed that no man could make his fate or control the game, but only wait for the bright jewel luck to slip by on the wire of time. Harmony exists, but there is no understanding it; the Way cannot be gone. So while Ramarren racked his mind, Falk lay low and waited. And when the chance came he caught it.
> Or rather...he was caught by it. (208; ch. 10).[82]

Ken Kenyek, the Shing expert at mindscience, insinuates himself into Ramarren's mind and carefully seizes control, but, unknown to him, Falk is there, and pounces: 'ambush and re-ambush' (209-11; ch. 10).

The original Buck Rogers story inculcates the masculinist and racist lesson of loyalty to the White Race in America and joy in helping to eradicate any 'yellow incubus,' 'inhuman yellow blight,' or similar threat (see Kalish 314). In *City of Illusions*, Falk is yellow, and yellow is mostly a positive color. Aside from racial tolerance or even a celebration of difference—a constant in Le Guin's canon—*City* prefigures a number of important ideas in Le Guin's later work. Clearly, *City* inculcates the Daoist lesson of the strength of quietness, solitude, wholeness, balance, and patience: of what the Daoists call *wu wei*, action through stillness. The story also privileges self-preservation, starting with avoiding suicide, over self-sacrifice, whether hypocritical or real (165, 172; ch. 8), primarily by finding a way out of an intolerable dilemma, possibly through what Le Guin will later call 'the possibility of abnegation' ('Winter's King,' *WTQ* 101). Most important, I think, especially for *City* in relationship to *Buffalo Gals*, *Always Coming Home*, and the rest of Cummins's West Coast grouping, is the isolation of the Shing and Es Toch.[83] As Thomas J. Remington

---

[82] For 'the Way cannot be gone,' note Le Guin's rendering of the opening to *Tao te Ching* as 'The way that can be gone / is not the eternal Way' (*CI* 187; ch. 9). For acting at need and at the right moment, cf. Ged to Tenar in *Tehanu* (1990): 'You did what you could. What you did was right. Timed right' (175; 'Home,' ch. 11). See Conclusion to *Coyote* for Rosemary Jackson on this passage in *CI*.
[83] See *CI* 170, ch. 8, for 'the drowned lands' west of the Sierras from Es Toch, drowned in 'the cataclysms of two thousand years ago.' California's slipping into

stresses, the Shing keep to themselves, out of touch.[84] Their city is appropriate to such a people. Nowlan's Han are racist, nationalist, and villainous, and Lo-Tan is the place of tyranny. Es Toch is the place of the lie, most centrally, I think, the 'Lords of the Earth' lie the Shing have told themselves (*LHD* 233; ch. 16): thinking themselves above all, hence putting themselves out of touch with the Dao of humanity, of nature, of the world. Though it is 'wonderful, timeless'—though it dances its being over the abyss (usually a good thing with Le Guin)—Es Toch is radically 'alien' in a very negative way. The towers of Es Toch, 'jutted up, hardly based on earth at all'; a 'wall closed the city off' (113; ch. 6).

> This was not a Place of Men. Es Toch gave no sense of history, of reaching back in time and out in space, though it had ruled the world for a millennium.... Though there were said to be so many of the Lords, yet on Earth they kept only this one city, held apart, as Earth itself was held apart from the other worlds that once had formed the League. Es Toch was self-contained, self-nourished, rootless; all its brilliance and transcience [sic] of lights and machines and faces, its multiplicity of strangers, its luxurious complexity was built across a chasm in the ground, a hollow place. It was the Place of the Lie. (159; ch. 8).

The lie that power over other people can lead to a good world—even utopia—produces in *City of Illusions* as it produced in George Orwell's *Nineteen Eighty-Four* (1949) and will produce in Le Guin's work at least into the 1980s the literally or figuratively walled, towered, dystopian city and 'the awful darkness of the bright lights of Es Toch' (55, ch. 3; 118, ch. 6).

The Lathe of Heaven (Novel, 1971) and *THE LATHE OF HEAVEN* (TV Film, 1979/80)

> Towers of ancient bridges
> contain the bones of children, nestled
> in the mortar like mousebones [sic] in the dry scat of coyotes
> * * * * * * *
> What I discovered when the bridge fell was that towers are build of the bones of children.
> —Ursula K. Le Guin, 'What I Discovered After the Earthquake / October 17, 1989'

---

the sea is an old fear and joke, but I think it significant if the coastal geography of *CI* turns up again in *ACH*.
[84] Remington, 'The Other Side of Suffering' 158-59. See *CI* 152-53; ch. 8. I am indebted to Remington for my understanding of 'touch' in Le Guin.

Ursula K. Le Guin's novel *The Lathe of Heaven* (1971), opens in a manner similar to that of *City of Illusions* (1967) and 'A Trip to the Head' (1970) with coming into consciousness. In *The Lathe of Heaven*, however—as in the Atlantean section in the West Coast story 'The New Atlantis' (1975)—the forest of being has been replaced by the ocean as 'the sea of being' (170; ch. 11); the human mind is imaged as a jellyfish, and we are reminded that this figurative jellyfish gets stranded 'on the dry sand of daylight' every morning when people awake (7; ch. 1).[85]

In one sense, we are in a much more familiar world than Fomalhaut II in *Rocannon's World* or Werel of *Planet of Exile* or the far-future America in *City of Illusions*: the setting in *Lathe* is mostly Portland, Oregon, in the near future. But even as Le Guin has made strange—'defamiliarized'—the familiar act of waking up, even so this is a Portland that will be made very strange indeed. Among its inhabitants is George Orr, an abnormally normal man (dead center on all the graphs) with only one rare trait.

In April of 1998, the human world came to an end. Among the people dying of radiation sickness after this nuclear apocalypse was George Orr. Orr passes out, or falls asleep, and has a dream, and the dream he dreams is the world of the story. And in the world Orr made, Orr can dream effectively. That is, when he has very powerful dreams, his dreams change reality for everyone: change reality completely, radically, from its roots, all the way back into the distant past, so only Orr (and people very near him during the change) even notice. For everyone else there is one single, coherent, new reality, complete with appropriate memories. Orr does not want to change the world (18; ch. 2). He tries to avoid dreaming by borrowing Pharmacy Cards and getting more than his 'allotment of pep pills and sleeping pills from the autodrug' (12). Some time in 2002, Orr has a very bad drug episode, gets caught and is sent to 'Voluntary Therapeutic Treatment' (which is, of course, compulsory) with Dr. William Haber, an oneirologist, a dream specialist (13; ch. 2). Orr tells Haber his problem, and Haber comes to believe Orr; and then Haber uses Orr (assisted by the Augmentor, a machine to augment dreams) to improve the world, to create Haber's idea of a Utilitarian utopia.[86]

The plot thereafter is a series of dreams induced by Haber on an ever more reluctant Orr until Haber can coerce Orr to have one last effective dream to produce a world in which Orr doesn't dream effectively, and Haber does (159-61; ch. 10). Orr, though, has found marriage with Heather Lelache, his attorney in the initial world of the novel, and he gets a little

---

[85] For *Lathe* as familiarly Daoist but otherwise 'somewhat of an anomaly' in Le Guin's fiction, see Spivack, ch. 5 (quote from 60), who refers readers to Watson's 'Le Guin's *Lathe*.' For the initial work on Daoism in *LoH*, see Barbour's '...Taoist Dream' article.

[86] For a brief discussion of Le Guin's background in the scientific study of dreams, see Bucknall 90.

help from his wife and other friends—including some aliens he has literally dreamed up. When Haber tries to dream effectively, the nightmare out of the hollowness of his being threatens disaster for at least the Earth. Orr turns off the dream machine—which he sees as his one real action—and saves the world (165-68, 170; chs. 10, 11). Haber ends up mad and institutionalized, and the world ends up in a mess; indeed, it's a mess where Heather Lelache had not married George Orr but a man killed in the war in the Near East, and the novel ends with Orr's moving toward renewing his marriage with Lelache, a return to a true relationship (172-75; ch. 11).

The complexity of the narrative, film as well as novel, derives from the fourteen significant effective dreams, each dream changing the reality of the world of the story. And the complexity comes in with the ethical implications of the conflict between Orr and Haber. Haber is an active man, a mover and shaker: an idealist, with a vision of the way the world ought to be and a desire to play hero and savior and make it that way. When Haber discovers Orr's talent, he has a way to make the world as it ought to be, to make everything right. In many narratives, Haber would be a hero. In a conservative film of the 1950s, Haber might be a villain, but not because he is overactive and intellectually macho but because he is a scientist and an intellectual, period—and a utopian; in such a film he would probably be defeated by a military man even more aggressive than he is.[87] Elizabeth Cummins neatly sums up Haber's reduction of 'principles to three mottoes: The proper study of mankind is man; The greatest good for the greatest number; and The end justifies the means' (1993: 158)—which is a serviceable summary of the philosophy of many heroes in U.S. popular culture. Orr is passive, a dreamer, the 'uncarved block' of the Daoists.[88] In most stories he'd be a minor character, and a major bore.

Le Guin both uses and mocks the idea of Haber as 'a Mad Scientist with an Infernal Machine' (47; ch. 4). In the late 1960s, when Le Guin was writing *Lathe*, Haber could be read as a more immediate threat: a reduction to the grotesque of corporate liberals like Robert McNamara who were demonstrating dramatically the costs of 'nation building'—utopian or otherwise—in Viet Nam and other exercises in American 'toughness': 'By attempting to impose its will on a chaotic world...the United States had fallen victim to the 'arrogance of power' and was flirting with disaster.'[89] The fall of William Haber was a mid-twentieth-century fable for Americans.

Opposed to Haber is Orr, emphatically the hero, if an unlikely one, in both novel and film. In the novel he is the hero because the novel accepts a

---

[87] I depend here on Biskind, ch. 3, 'Pods and Blobs,' esp. 115-17, 123-44, for Biskind's taxonomy of 1950s 'centrist' and 'extremist' films.

[88] Arthur Waley commenting on *Tao te Ching* ch. 19: 'The Uncarved Block is the symbol of the primal undifferentiated unity underlying the apparent complexity of the universe' (167).

[89] Herring 172, paraphrasing J. William Fulbright, whose 1966 work attacking US adventurism was called *The Arrogance of Power*.

Daoist world-view and ethic. *The Lathe of Heaven*, as novel, is an attack not only on Haber and his immediate political implications but also on most of what Haber stands for: much of the ethics and ideal of heroism of 'the Judaeo-Christian-Rationalist West' (82; ch. 6). The PBS film is courageous, but not that courageous. In the film Haber is still not a cliché Mad Scientist, but, as in one place in the novel, a man who would 'play God with masses of people' (150; ch. 10), a victim of immoderation, yet another dramatic example of the danger of overweening pride. Thus he comes across in the film's dialog and much of its imagery. He is, in the film, not a SciFi villain but an SF builder of Moloch-machines that engulf and metaphorically devour people, finally engulfing their inventors.[90] The film Haber is the direct descendent of the builders of great cities like Sodom and Gomorrah, and of great buildings such as the Tower of Babel. But there is more to the film that just excellent use of such familiar motifs and prejudices; the film also picks up some important dialog and much of the imagery of the novel and thereby suggests, fairly subtly, the Eastern ideal of balance. Balance as a secondary norm in the film works against not only the immoderate urge to tinker with society and the universe, as if they were machines, but also against the film's more explicit norm of the grey mediocrity of 'moderation in all things'—a very nonDaoist, Greek rationalist slogan Orr uses in the film.

In the dialog of the film, Orr makes explicit his charges against Haber. They include a rather daring and vigorous assertion of passivity on Orr's part and his denial of human purpose—ideas Le Guin stresses; most of the accusations, however, are more familiar: Haber is playing God in using Orr; Haber is immoderately 'tinkering' with dangerous powers; Haber refuses to take responsibility for his actions and misunderstands the place of humans in the universe; Haber is overconfident in the power of reason and is much too dedicated to will, power, and control.

Orr in the film is quite correct in his accusations, and his accusations are reinforced by the imagery of coerced containment within a mechanism, the Augmentor, and by Haber's utopian building. When Orr (or Haber) is within the Augmentor, we have an image of the superimposition of the mechanical not only upon Orr or Haber but the superimposition of the mechanical and electronic upon the unconscious—dreams—and, in effective dreaming, the superimposition of the machine upon the world.[91] The Augmentor by itself changes nothing, but its augmenting aids Haber in making hypnotic suggestions to Orr that do change the world. In a sense, then, as Haber augments the Augmentor by having Orr dream him bigger

---

[90] I allude to the vast machine in METROPOLIS that is called 'Moloch' by the hero: i.e., in colloquial usage, a god to whom children are sacrificed.
[91] The idea of 'the superimposition of the mechanical upon the organic,' specifically upon the human, is from Henri Bergson, applied to quite a bit of SF by Dunn and Erlich, e.g., 'A Vision of Dystopia.'

and better machines—a process stressed in the film—he puts more and more of his world effectively within the machine he controls.[92]

In novel and film, the utopias Haber creates have problems.[93] Most spectacularly, Haber tells Orr to eliminate overpopulation, and Orr's subconscious takes a very direct route: a Plague dream that kills some six billion people. When Haber becomes more accomplished at instructing Orr, the results are much less brutal—and very darkly comic—but still bad. Haber's world is a better world, in many ways, but a grey, lifeless world, bureaucratized and unfree, what we would expect from the imposing of hubristic rationalism, via a machine, upon the stuff of dreams. Haber's last utopia in the film is also a world without Heather Lelache. Lelache is African-American, brown in color; she cannot exist in a grey world—literally a grey world for human beings. Haber tells Orr to solve the race problem, and Orr's subconscious produces a human species with bodies 'the color of a battleship' (127; ch. 9). But Haber will not be satisfied with any version of utopia. As the Narrator in the novel tells us, 'The quality of the will to power is, precisely, growth. Achievement is its cancellation. To be, the will to power must increase with each fulfillment, making the fulfillment only a step to a further one. The vaster the power gained, the vaster the appetite for more' (128; ch. 9). To improve the world until it is really right, Haber needs a better tool than Orr. So he cures Orr and prepares to substitute himself.

For Le Guin, Haber is preeminently unsuitable as a dreamer perfecting the world: any dreamer who would want to exert such control is disqualified because he radically misunderstands the nature of dreams. Haber is especially unsuitable because for Le Guin the dream goes to the heart of our being, and Le Guin's Narrator makes clear that Haber is like a dried onion; at his center there is a void (127-28, 82; chs. 9 and 6). Just as bad, Haber is out of touch with the world (150; ch. 10): a loveless loner, someone who sees people only as things to be used or dependent clients to be helped—or used (112, 32; chs. 8 and 3).[94] Haber 'never wanted marriage nor close friendships' and is promiscuous and bisexual, his sex life 'almost entirely...one-night stands, semipros, sometimes women and sometimes young men' (112).[95]

---

[92] Note that neither the machine as such nor control are in themselves Bad Things. A wise Aldebaran Alien finds an electroencephalograph 'Worthy' in *LoH* (119; ch. 8), and controlled dreaming is central to Athshean culture in *WWF* (e.g. 99-101; ch. 5).

[93] For *LoH* as a commentary on utopias: Dr. Haber puts George into effective dreaming with the word 'Antwerp' (25; ch. 2), which is never explained and doesn't particularly mean anything in the story; Antwerp, however, is the setting for Book I of Sir Thomas More's *Utopia* (1516).

[94] See Remington, 'Other Side' 169.

[95] Le Guin's point here is Haber's perverse need to be free of 'any kind of need for the other' (*LoH* 112), and this is highly important for Le Guin on marriage, touch, relationship with the world: Le Guinian marriage is a human good, understood to included a wide range of connections, and not just a tender trap for

No film can get into such complexities of psychology as Le Guin's analysis of Haber; but *THE LATHE OF HEAVEN* as PBS film does suggest Haber as a loner, and it certainly shows that Haber's effective nightmare is a disaster for the world. The film shows quite well how different Haber is from Orr, who is capable of love, and therefore capable of saving the world. Twice: first in his dream in April 1998 and again in his one conscious act of turning off the Augmentor and ending Haber's effective nightmare.

The film, then, unlike the novel, does not explicitly condemn, generally and forcefully—if with bitter comedy—the ethics and heroic ideal of the 'Judaeo-Christian-Rationalist West' but instead uses explicitly some of our Western norms to justify Orr and condemn Haber.[96] Some dialog and visuals, however, do condemn the busy-ness of Western utopianism and the ethical superficiality of a doctrine of improving the world: When we see a large sign with what is clearly Haber's favorite slogan—'THE GREATEST GOOD FOR THE GREATEST NUMBER'—we can be sure there is a satiric attack against the doctrine of Utilitarianism that promulgated that slogan as philosophy (see *LoH* 132; ch. 9). Indeed, several shots suggest our need to accept and go with the world, to find our way from Haber's over-bright, Utilitarian ways back to the dark Great Way of Being, of the Dao. 'When the Great Way is lost, we get benevolence and righteousness' Le Guin quotes from ch. 18 of the *Tao te Ching* (headnote to *LoH* ch. 5). Le Guin's point comes across in the film: Haber has lost his way, and his attempts at benevolence and righteousness will *not* yield good.

The film develops these points visually. Le Guin's image for Being in *Lathe* is the sea; and opposed to the impressive buildings and machinery (and a couple of muscular thugs) we see with Haber in the film is a series of images associating Orr and Lelache with water, the yielding but yet very powerful water that wears away rock and is the favored element of the Daoists.[97] To oversimplify, water—especially in the film, dark, sparkling, and/or misty water—stands for Namable Dao: Being, the Absolute,

---

women. Still, see my discussions of *LHD* and *TD* for the cultural skirmishes over the treatment of homosexuality in Le Guin's canon, and Le Guin's increasing openness over time toward homosexuality and relatively casual sex while still valuing highly 'the body's obscure, inalterable dream of mutuality'—esp. woman/man mutuality—in the 1990s stories 'Seggri,' 'Solitude' and, 'Coming of Age in Karhide' (quoting here 'The Matter of Seggri' [1994]: 29).

[96] In conversation, Le Guin pointed out that she found dreaming up a series of worlds funny in itself. Also, literal-mindedness such as shown by Orr's unconscious is a source of comedy in Golem stories; more exactly, it's a source of danger for people within the stories, comedy for listeners or readers.

[97] 'What is of all things most yielding,' water (or perhaps air [Chen 161]) 'Can overwhelm that which is most hard,' i.e. rock (*Tao te Ching* ch. 43 [Waley trans. 197]). Water is also important among Native Americans ('Legends' 8), and, I will add, in George Carlin's philosophically sophisticated satiric routine on 'Water don't give a shit.'

'the milk of the Mother / the Way' (*CI* 51; ch. 3).[98] Out of the sea (in the film) comes Lelache. Out of one in Daoist theory comes two: Yin-Yang, all opposites in dynamic equilibrium, represented schematically at their instant of exact balance: the Yin-Yang figure in black and white, centrally (perhaps) female and male in balance—embodied in the film in the image of Lelache and Orr making love.[99]

The social and political implications of the Lelache/Orr relationship Le Guin handles when Lelache first meets Orr (narrated from Lelache's point of view): 'He liked her. He was a poor damn crazy psycho on drugs, he would like her. She liked him. She stuck out her brown hand, he met it with a white one, just like that damn button her mother always kept in the bottom of her bead box, SCNN or SNCC or something she'd belonged to way back in the middle of the last century, the Black hand and the White hand joined together. Christ!' (52; ch. 4).[100]

The Lathe of Heaven is part of Le Guin's 'marriage group' and a rather somber romantic comedy: a new and chastened world coalesces around Orr and Lelache as they exit to woo again, and I think it is that basic romantic pattern that comes through most clearly in the film. We may read the film as a love story featuring a triangle with Orr at the apex, contested over by Lelache who loves him and Haber who wants to use him. For good and for ill, esthetically, what comes through more strongly in the novel is the ongoing debate between the men, both literal debates and a comparison and contrast between two radically different—truly 'Either/Or'— approaches to life. And it is a familiar one: we have come out of the forest, climbed out of the sea, and we ask with that urExistentialist Koheleth, the Preacher in Ecclesiastes, What is good for the sons of men to do in our few days under the sun? (2.3). Or, in the nonsexist formulation of the Kesh play of *Chandi*, '*How shall a human being live well, then?*'[101] Except that here the answer is the very nonExistentialist, nonWestern one of Daoist wu wei: Ordinarily, do nothing (Watson, 'Le Guin's *Lathe*' 70). And in the novel there is a third point of view character: Heather Lelache. In *The Lathe of Heaven* the ideal is not the masculinist one of 'having and acting' (*WTQ* 163) but the more traditionally 'feminine,' Daoist one of 'unaction'—doing nothing unnatural, nothing against the Dao, nothing to control others and the world, nothing to move one out of the world, out of touch.

---

[98] In his presentation on '...*The Lathe of Heaven* as Novel and Film,' Andrew Gordon called attention to the film's 'repeated images of water and light, developed from the images in the novel'; my interpretation of those images differs from Gordon's, but I have profited from his work on the film.

[99] For the Yin-Yang pictured vertically, with Yin on the right, see Cummins (1993): 33; for the horizontal version, Yin on top, see printer's marks in *WTQ*.

[100] It's 'SNCC': Student Non-Violent Coordinating Committee,' pronounced [snIk].

[101] *ACH* 236; Dramatic Works (I have retained the italics indicated a fixed line in an otherwise improvised play).

The narration of *The Lathe of Heaven* is third person, limited omniscient (or selective omniscient) from the points of view of George Orr (chs. 1, 3, 6, 9, the first part of 10, and 11), William Haber (chs. 2, 5, and 8), and Heather Lelache (4, 7, the second part of 10)—a division of points of view we have seen in *Planet of Exile* (1966) and will see again, perhaps most closely paralleled in *The Word for World Is Forest* (1972).[102] In general, Le Guin uses the divided points of view to ensure a positive image of Orr and a negative view of Haber. Orr's thoughts are generally attractive; Haber's are not. Lelache has a relatively positive view of Orr at first, and a strongly positive view later; her view of Haber is negative. Lelache's view of herself starts negative—spider, coward (45, 91, 94; chs. 4, 7)—and improves. Indeed, it is arguable that Heather Lelache is the only character in the novel to really change. In the novel, Orr returns to what he essentially is, and Haber works out the logic of his villain role, finally (in the dried onion image) having the last layers stripped from him to reveal the void at his core. But such an argument for change in Lelache gets complicated in a world where realities keep changing; different realities may just produce different Heather Lelaches.[103]

The constants are Orr and Haber, and the novel form allows a good deal of elaboration of what they stand for—aided by Lelache's insights and gnomic comments by the Narrator. In the manner of the Germanic scops, Le Guin's early narrators sometimes pause to insert a pithy assertion summarizing the 'moral' of the preceding episode. For a central and highly instructive example, consider the Narrator's comments speaking of Lelache, that 'A person who believes, as she did, that things fit: that there is a whole of which one is a part, and that in being a part one is whole: such a person has no desire whatever, at any time, to play God. Only those who have denied their being yearn to play at' being (106; ch. 7)—or to play God. Such a statement aids Lelache's credibility in her judgments of Orr and Haber, and in its immediate context the comment helps us approve of Lelache even when she is about to move the plot along by making the mistake of giving Orr a hypnotic suggestion on what to dream. A tran-

---

[102] Roughly speaking, in *WWF* Selver is to Davidson as Orr is to Haber; Lyubov is to Selver and Davidson as Lelache is to Orr and Haber. *LHD* (1969) and *EoH* (1978) have significantly modified versions of this triangle. For a different interpretation of point of view in *LoH*, see Cummins (1993): 157, 165.

[103] I'm skirting here a *Kulturkampf* skirmish. Male authors of bourgeois novels and some dramas attempted to create characters who mirrored selves in the real world. Typically in such works, the (male) hero was a Self, capable of change, and women Others, and constant. By the 1990s, some key terms in my last two sentences were contested. Is *LoH* a more feminist novel if Lelache changes? Change is privileged in most postRomantic thought, and in much of Le Guin's canon, but *LoH* privileges stillness. Christian doctrine—and some other doctrines developed in Christian cultures—celebrates change and the New Man: rebirth; some nonChristians believe most of us are born all right initially and should develop decent personalities and stick with them. (For an excellent introd. to Self, Other, and change, see Bamber ch. 1.)

scendent God isn't, in the universe of *The Lathe of Heaven*; immanent Dao is: Dao is the ultimate 'whole of which one is a part,' and only as part of the Dao, and in touch with other people, can one achieve personal wholeness, know one's being. Those who try to exist outside of Nature deny human nature, their human being. Such people necessarily will be more or less out of contact with themselves, and therefore, when in authority, will be dangerous.

When Haber still won't admit he knows Orr dreams effectively, Orr suspects that Haber 'might be compartmenting his mind into two hermetic halves,' so that he both knows—and uses—and doesn't know Orr's power. Given his own wholeness, Orr has trouble understanding how Haber might have gotten so 'out of communication with himself.' Like anyone who grew up in America after Vietnam and the whole series of twentieth-century wars, Orr must recognize the possibility of people high in the hierarchy with compartmentalized minds: 'He had grown up in a country run by politicians who sent pilots to man the bombers to kill the babies to make the world safe for children to grow up in' (87; ch. 6).[104]

Orr doesn't know the word, Dao, or Eastern philosophy (83; ch. 6), but he is in touch with the Dao. Indeed, his dreams may aid Dao in the process by which reality is constantly 'replaced, renewed' (71; ch. 5); certainly, when Orr and Lelache make love, they aid in the remaking of love in the world. Like the Dao and Daoist reality, 'Love doesn't just sit there, like a stone, it has to be made, like bread; re-made all the time, made new' (153; ch. 10). Being in and in touch with the world, Orr can appear to Heather Lelache—and be—the Daoist ideal, the 'block of wood not carved. The infinite possibility, the unqualified wholeness of being of the uncommitted, the nonacting...: the being who, being nothing but himself, is everything.' For Heather Lelache, who frequently sees herself as a black widow spider, what is most impressive about her insight into the mild-mannered Orr is Orr's strength: 'He was the strongest person she had every known, because he could not be moved away from the center' (95; ch. 7).

As we would expect from *Rocannon's World* and *City of Illusions*, mind and stillness are going to be very important in *The Lathe of Heaven* . But in Rocannon's World the «Daoist» hermit, the Ancient One, was decidedly nasty in the pricing of «gifts» to suppliants, and in *City of Illusions* there was something of a fair debate between the still and active lives, at least in the person of Falk-Ramarren and in the balanced characters of the Thurro-dowist hermit and the equally Daoist Prince of Kansas Enclave (chs. 3 and 5). Le Guin does not demonize Haber, or she gives this devil his due, but she is not about to give him a fair chance. By the time of *The Lathe of Heaven*, the danger of men like Haber had become far too clear (most spectacularly in Indochina) for responsible writers on the Left to stage a dispassionate, «objective» confrontation between two legitimate approaches to life. By the time we reach their crucial philosophical con-

---

[104] Cf. the Terran military men in *WWF*, esp. 67; ch. 3.

frontations in *Lathe* chapters 7-9, we know that Orr will be right, Haber mostly (but not entirely) wrong.

Shortly before she really sees him, Heather Lelache had thought of Orr as 'that little bastard.... Mr. Either Orr' (90; ch. 7).[105] Moving into the center of their debate, Haber talks about Orr's test results in the now loaded terms of 'Both, neither. Either, or. Where there's an opposed pair, a polarity, you're in the middle; where there's a scale, you're at the balance point.' Haber doesn't see Orr's scores as indications of a healthy adjustment, wholeness, or harmony, but a kind of 'self-cancellation' that accounts for Orr's lackluster life (134; ch. 9).[106]

And accounts for Orr's resistance to change:

> What's wrong with changing things? Now, I wonder if this self-canceling, centerpoised personality of yours leads you to look at things defensively.... You are afraid of losing your balance. But change need not unbalance you; life's not a static object, after all. It's a process. There's no holding still. Intellectually you know that, but emotionally you refuse it. Nothing remains the same from one moment to the next, you can't step into the same river twice. Life—evolution—the whole universe of space/ time, matter/energy—existence itself—is essentially change.'
>
> 'That is one aspect of it,' Orr said. 'The other is stillness.'
>
> 'When things don't change any longer, that's the end result of entropy, the heat-death of the universe. The more things go on moving, interrelating, conflicting, changing, the less balance there is—and the more life. I'm pro-life, George. Life itself is a huge gamble against the odds, against all odds! You can't try to live safely, there's no such thing as safety. Stick your neck out of your shell, then, and live fully! It's not how you get there, but where you get to that counts.... We're on the brink of discovering and controlling, for the good of all mankind, a whole new force, an entire new field of antientropic energy, of the life-force, of the will to act, to do, to change!'

Haber has just stated some major ideas from Daoism and the Perennial Philosophy, and some favorite Le Guinian themes: life as process, life as a gamble (see *King Dog*), the lack of safety, flux at the heart of things. Orr

---

[105] For Either/Or, note Søren Kierkegaard's *Either/Or* (1843), and *Fear and Trembling* (1843), Kierkegaard's analysis of the Binding of Isaac (Genesis 22), where Abraham is *either* a knight of faith *or* a fanatical murderer. Le Guin rejects either/or but accepts the Kierkegaardian Existentialist belief in the necessity for conscious choices among the options in life.

[106] See Remington, 'Other Side' 170.

acknowledges these truths but insists that, 'We're in the world, not against it. It doesn't work to try to stand outside things and run them that way. It just doesn't work, it goes against life. There is a way but you have to follow it. The world is, no matter how we think it out to be. You have to be with it. You have to let it be' (135-36; ch. 9).

After a kind of day dream of encountering an Alien who gives him good Hindu advice—'Self is universe'—and the phrase 'Er' perrehnne!' for summoning 'auxiliary forces' (138; ch 9), Orr moves into his direct confrontation with Haber, his just saying 'No' 1960s style, challenging authority and force. Orr set his teeth and faced Chaos and Old Night.[107]

> But they were not there.... He remained sitting on the comfortable couch.... And, quiet as a thief in the night, a sense of well-being came into him, a certainty that things were all right, and that he was in the middle of things. Self is universe. He would not be allowed to be isolated, to be stranded. He was back where he belonged.... This feeling did not come to him as blissful or mystical, but simply as normal.... [I]t was his natural mode of being....
> He knew this was nothing he had accomplished by himself. (139-40; ch. 9)

But it wasn't Haber's Augmentor that did it. Presumably, he got a little help from his friends, from the other 'gods': 'nameless and unenvious, asking neither worship not obedience' (140), the other people in touch with the universe (145; ch. 9). Without debating the matter with himself, Orr tells Haber firmly that he won't let Haber use his effective dreams any more (140).

Haber appeals to Orr's sense of guilt, without success (142).[108] Haber then tries a literally rational appeal—'Reason will prevail' and notes all the good he and Orr have done. Orr notes the evil, including the nonexistence in this world of Heather Lelache, which is fine with Haber, and he tells that to Orr: Haber finds both Orr and Lelache irresponsible; Orr lacks a social conscience, displays 'no altruism,' acts the role of 'a moral jellyfish' (143; ch. 9). Haber's attitude toward Lelache makes him appear especially villainous here, and that is useful to «point» for us Le Guin's point that in this book (as in *The Dispossessed* [1974]) a social consciences is an ambiguous thing, and altruism rather negative: again, 'When the Great

---

[107] Sri Krishna tells Arjuna 'When we consider Brahman as lodged within the individual being, we call Him the Atman' (*Song of God* 74; Bhagavad-Gita 8). Alternatively, the doctrine of Atman-Brahman: 'Brahman is in all things and is the Self (Atman) of all things' ('Hinduism' 8.889). Or, 'Atman is Brahman': Self is universe.
[108] Cf. Selver in *WWF*, 124; ch. 6. This far Le Guin's protagonists are good Existentialists like Sartre's Orestes in *The Flies*: authority figures fail in most attempts to send them off on guilt trips.

Way is lost, we get benevolence and righteousness' (53; ch. 5).[109] But also, altruism just *is* suspect as a motivation for political actions. With President Lyndon Johnson and others into the 1970s presented American warfare in Indochina as altruistic, it was clear to anyone thinking seriously that the personal virtue of altruism would easily become a vice when applied abstractly, impersonally, politically. When applied on mass scale, altruism soon becomes just another justification for pushing people around. Opposing the benevolent busy-ness of Haber, Orr recognizes that he has a gift and an obligation to 'use it only when I must. When there is no other alternative. There are alternatives now' (143; ch. 9). Haber, though, intends to go on, to where Earth 'will be like heaven, and men will be like gods!' Orr says, 'We are, we are already' (145; ch.9).

In the climactic chapter 10, Orr receives a gift from an Alien, the Beatles' 'With a Little Help From My Friends,' drinks some weak cannabis tea and dreams back Heather Lelache. The two of them go together to Haber's lab for one last dream: Orr dreams he's no longer capable of effective dreaming—Haber is. Orr advises Haber to consult with the Aliens, who are more experienced than we 'At dreaming—at what dreaming is an aspect of. They've done it for a long time. For always, I guess. They are of the dream time.' In line with the teaching that those who know the Way don't talk about it, and the commonplace that the mystic experience is ineffable, Orr says he does not rationally understand his insight, nor can he express it verbally, but,

> Everything dreams. The play of form, of being, is the dreaming of substance.[110] Rocks have their dreams, and the earth changes.... But when the mind becomes conscious, when the rate of evolution speeds up, then you have to be careful. Careful of the world. You must learn the way. You must learn the skills, the art, the limits. A conscious mind must be part of the whole, intentionally and carefully—as the rock is part of the whole unconsciously. Do you see? Does it mean anything to you?

It really doesn't mean anything to Haber. For Haber, Orr's great speech on 'Everything dreams' is all mysticism, and mysticism is not 'acceptable' for sensible people. And saying Er' perrehne to 'get a little help from your friends' is not acceptable to an egoistic loner like Haber (161; ch. 10).

Using his Augmentor on his own dream, Haber dreams his effective dream, the nightmare Orr stops. In the novel and (perhaps more briefly) in the film, Orr tells an Alien, 'I did a lot today. That is, I did something. The only thing I have ever done. I pressed a button. It took the entire will

---

[109] *Tao te Ching* ch. 18.
[110] Le Guin noted on my ms here 'The language and ideas are straight from Victor Hugo.' I pass this information on for the use of those who know Hugo. Unspaced dots in the next sentence represent an ellipsis mark in original.

power, the accumulated strength of my entire existence, to press one damned OFF button.' The Alien replies, 'You have lived well.' Orr's one action, out of his stillness, has saved the world (170; ch. 11).

At the end of the novel, Orr sleeps and has normal dreams, 'like waves of the deep sea far from any shore,' coming and going, 'profound and harmless, breaking nowhere, changing nothing. They danced the dance among all the other waves in the sea of being' (170; ch. 11). Orr awakes to visit Haber in an asylum and then meet again, for the first time in this new reality, Heather Lelache.

The Earthsea Series (1968-72, 1990)

All the world says,
'I am important;
I am separate from all the world.
I am important because I am separate,
Were I the same, I could never be important.'

TaoDeChing - Lao Tze, ch. 67. Unimportance © 1992-1995 Peter A. Merel (on the World Wide Web, with Chinese text [Webmaster: Ming L. Pei])

Introductory Comments

I agree with Le Guin's assessment in her Response to the 1975 Le Guin issue of *Science-Fiction Studies* that the ideas in her Earthsea trilogy 'are more totally incarnated, less detachable from the sounds, rests, and rhythms, less often stated as problems and more often expressed in terms of feeling, sensations, and intuition' than in some of her other work up to that time (45)—hence, I would say, probably better art—and I follow a fairly widespread consensus that the Earthsea trilogy is among Le Guin's best art. *A Wizard of Earthsea* won the 1968 *Boston Globe*-Horn Book Award; *The Tombs of Atuan* got the 1972 Newbery Silver Medal Award; *The Farthest Shore* won the 1972 National Book Award for Children's Books. As the back blurbs on the Bantam editions of 1975 note, 'This trio of novels, a recognized classic of high fantasy, has been compared with [J. R. R.] Tolkien's *Lord of the Rings* and C. S. Lewis's Narnia stories.' But—classifying the Earthsea trilogy with *The Lord of the Rings* and the Narnia stories, however meant as a compliment, makes it easier for Rosemary Jackson to place the trilogy, plus *City of Illusions* and *The Left Hand of Darkness*, among 'conservative vehicles for social and instinctual repression' (Jackson 154-55). There are political problems with the trilogy, but not particularly those Jackson identifies. If you accept Jackson's psychoanalytical framework, you should also accept Jackson placing a significant sampling of Le Guin's work along with Tolkien's and Lewis's and to the political right of Charles Dickens—whose demonizing of working class movements Jackson documents (131-32)—and even Fyodor Dostoevsky (133-36, 154-55), to whom my encyclopedia devotes a full subsection under 'Conservatism,' for his attacks in later life upon 'Socialism, liberalism, materialism, and atheism,' preaching instead 'Greek Orthodox tsarism, Slavic traditionalism, and the redemption of mankind by 'Holy Russia'' (Viereck 5.65-66). I like Dickens and Dostoevsky, and I will join in insisting upon the liberatory potential and immediate goodness of their 'compassion for...'the insulted and injured'' (Viereck 66); but to prefer on Leftist political grounds an antirevolutionary reformer like Dickens and any variety of Czarist over Le Guin is to take Theory and disgust with 'an outworn liberal humanism' (Jackson 155) into the perverse. I think it is more accurate to start with the observation that, like Tolkien's trilogy and the Narnia stories, Le Guin's Earthsea trilogy is high fantasy, and then immediately add that Tolkien's work comes out of Christian tradition and Lewis's work is firmly within the Christian tradition and powerfully inculcates significant parts of Christian doctrine. Le Guin's high fantasy is un-Christian specifically and more generally outside of the tradition of all institutionalized religions and transcendental theologies. From what we see, the people of Earthsea realize the positive parts of their 'religious capacity' in popular celebrations of the high points of the astronomical year; the institutionalized religions we see at Atuan in the trilogy are not positive. Le Guin has shown in Earthsea a Time of Legend that gets along quite nicely without sky gods—common enough in science fiction and fantasy—but a world *not* totally desacralized; indeed, at moments in Earthsea we see its key characters in very profound 'relationship...with the cosmos' (*TD* 12; ch. 1). And Le Guin provided this elegant counter to Tolkien, Lewis, et al. in a trilogy that is accessible to children, receives Establishment awards, and gets past (apparently) even the Right-wing types who catch on that *The Lathe of Heaven* might be a dangerous book. The Earthsea series, then, is sophisticated art and serious literature—and a nicely subversive contribution to an early round of the most recent *Kulturkampf*.

* * * * * * *

Moving into the end of the 1990s, the Earthsea series consists of four books: *A Wizard of Earthsea* (1968), *The Tombs of Atuan* (1971), *The Farthest Shore* (1972)—'the Earthsea trilogy'—and *Tehanu: The Last Book of Earthsea* (1990). The temptation, obviously, is to see the series as the trilogy (1968-72) plus *Tehanu*, with *Tehanu* as a late addition to, and a correction of, the trilogy. I shall succumb to that temptation shortly, in my chapter on *Tehanu*; I'll indicate now, though, why *Tehanu* is a very appropriate 'Last Book' for the series, analyzing the series as a Daoist construct.[111]

---

[111] Following Le Guin's comments in 'Is Gender Necessary? Redux' and elsewhere, throughout this book, I use 'Daoist' in talking about Le Guin's ontology, epistemology, politics, etc. Note, however, that the Dao is a generally Chinese idea, as is Odo's 'To be whole is to be part' (*TD* 68, ch. 3; 'The Day Before the

We may legitimately see the trilogy as a portrait of an artist in magic, Ged, from birth until he sacrifices his magic power at the beginning of old age. The three books of the trilogy make a *Künstlerroman* (artist novel) with magic as the art and the story told in third-person, limited-omniscient narration from the points of view of three people: (1) Ged, who starts the novel as the boy Duny, and then goes on to become the wizard Sparrowhawk, and then fully himself as an adult Ged (*Wizard*); (2) Tenar, the priestess of the Nameless ones (*Tombs*); and (3) Arren, who goes on to become King (*Shore*) and rule Earthsea under his true name, Lebannen (*Tehanu*).

The esthetic world of the trilogy is classic high fantasy and Romance: male-centered, heroic, aristocratic, concerned mostly with youth and the great story of 'coming of age'—to the first 'age' of the (male) hero, adulthood, and the only physiologically marked coming of age for a human male, lacking, as men do, menopause (see 'Coming of Age in Karhide'). That far, and not a step farther, the trilogy uses the sort of world Le Guin mocks in 'The Pathways of Desire' (1979): a story set in a boy's world (indeed, the world of 'Pathways' is dreamed up between a boy's ears), whose native society lacks leading roles for women, a world where old people without power are nearly invisible. As such, the world of the trilogy is out of balance. *Tehanu* moves toward achieving a better balance, at least addressing what Holly Littlefield correctly identifies as the 'fundamental imbalances of power and gender' (252).

As a four-novel series, the odd-numbered books are narrated from the points of view of boys becoming men (*Wizard* and *Shore*); the second book is told from the point of view of a girl becoming a woman (*Tombs*); and the fourth book (*Tehanu*) is narrated from the point of view of the girl of *Tombs* grown into a middle-aged widow—switching at the very end to a split point of view between the woman, Tenar, and Tehanu: a being both girl and dragon.[112] *Wizard* begins on Gont Island, the birthplace of Ged, and then moves on to extensive sailing about Earthsea. *Tombs* is quite static: except for an «opening out» at the end, limited to the place of the Tombs of the Nameless Ones on Atuan; put more positively, *Tombs* adheres fairly closely to the Neoclassical unities of place and action. *Shore* shows extensive sailing and offers two endings. The official one, so to speak, from *The Deed of Ged*, ends has Ged return to the center of events, for Arren's crowning in Havnor and then sailing off 'westward over sea' to be heard from no more. The version told on Gont is less romantic. Ged returns to Gont and retires to the forest, truly 'done with doing,' off on the margin of the world of doing, but in the heart of one of Le Guin's forests

---

Revolution'). See *LoN* (1989) 164-65, and Chung-Ying Cheng esp. 27-28, 31, 33, 38. For discussions of Le Guin's use of Daoism in various works see Spivack, here 26, and passim (see Index 181).

[112] For other switches in point of view, see *WE* 123-25, ch. 7 (Ogion's) and 179-80, ch. 10 (Vetch's point of view). For Le Guin on switching POV, see 'On Theme,' 208.

(*WE* 196-97), a place to *be*. In good quest fashion, and following the movement of the Dao (*Tao te Ching* 40), *Tehanu* returns Ged to Gont and shows only one short sea trip from one Gontish port to another—with the rest of the traveling on foot on Gont.

Further unity of the series is suggested by *Wizard* and *Tehanu*'s both begin with the same poetic epigraph:

> Only in silence the word,
> only in dark the light,
> only in dying life:
> bright the hawk's flight
> on the empty sky.

In this epigraph, some key opposites insisted upon in the Judeo-Christian tradition get yoked together in good Daoist fashion, with the careful Yin-Yang balancing of polarities in the first three lines broken only by the denial of any transcendent sky-god(s) of the final two lines. Yin-Yang, indeed, is a unifying symbol in the trilogy. In *Wizard*, there is a Yin-Yang symbol in the white scars on the dark face of Ged, and again when Ged merges with his Shadow. In *Tombs* the Yin-Yang symbol is suggested at the climax of the novel, when white-skinned Tenar moves close to Ged, initially intending to kill him, and then bonds with him (140; 'Voyage,' ch. 12).[113] In *Tehanu*, Yin-Yang is suggested when Ged asks Tenar for a job on her farm and Tenar resolves the sleeping arrangements by asking Ged if he wants her in his bed (189; 'Winter,' ch. 12). He does, and when they couple his dark skin is balanced against her white skin.[114] There is an even more powerful symbol of balance, wholeness, and integration in Tehanu herself, and her people. In one aspect, Tehanu is a young girl, Therru, who has been horribly abused and scarred far worse than Ged. In another aspect, she is a dragon, one of 'those among us who know they once were dragons,' connected with those 'among the dragons...who know their kinship with us' (12; 'Going to the Falcon's Nest,' ch. 2). And the dragon she is closest to is Kalessin, the Eldest, who turns out to be Segoy, the demiurge who spoke the Word of Making and brought forth the islands of Earthsea (222-24; 'Tehanu,' ch. 14).

The Yin-Yang balance, then, of human and dragon leads back to Kalessin, who is Segoy; and that is useful for a Daoist Earthsea. Segoy, a demiurge, had been something of an embarrassment for a Daoist reading of the trilogy, since Segoy could be pictured as transcending the world Segoy made. That embarrassment is eliminated in *Tehanu*. In the legends of Coyote (e.g., among the Miwok Indians of California), Coyote is a coy-

---

[113] The chapters in *WE* are numbered; those of the other three books are not, so I have supplied the chapter numbers. Those wishing to look up several or many of my citations will find it time-saving to number the chapters.

[114] For skin colors in Earthsea, consult *WE* 7 and 39; chs. 1 and 3: Ged is 'red-brown.' For other symbols in Earthsea, see Spivack 30-31.

ote, and emphatically a wily animal in the world—and Coyote made the world.[115] In *The Lathe of Heaven*, George Orr dreams up his worlds, and is within each world. And in *Tehanu*, Segoy remains the creator of the world, but is clearly shown living in the world as the oldest dragon, Kalessin.[116] With a little pushing of the point, we can see Kalessin/Segoy as a descendent of Ouroboros as the crowned dragon eating its tail: a symbol in the West for the unity of all things, perpetually mutating one into another in a never-ending cycle of creation and destruction: the mythological embodiment, in our culture, of the idea of the Dao, or Shiva Nataraja dancing the worlds into existence, and he and Kali destroying them.[117]

Most important, *Tehanu* goes far to resolve the problem of magic. As Robert Galbreath has argued, there is indeed 'Taoist Magic in the Earthsea Trilogy'—but it is only relatively Daoist, only restrained and passive and in the tradition of 'unaction' relative to western magic. In the trilogy, magic is still essentially power. In *Tehanu*, Tenar asks Ged,

> 'Is there something besides what you call power—that comes before it, maybe? Or something that power is just one way of using.... Ogion said of you once that before you'd had any learning or training as a wizard at all, you were a mage. Mage-born, he said. So I imagined that, to have power, one must first have room for the power. An emptiness to fill. And the greater the emptiness the more power can fill it....
>
> 'Emptiness is one word for it. Maybe not the right word.'
>
> 'Potentiality?' he said, and shook his head. 'What is able to be...to become.'
>
> 'I think... [a significant coincidence happened to Ged] because of that—because that is what happens to you. You didn't make it happen. You didn't cause it. It wasn't because of your 'power.' It happened to you. Because of your—emptiness.'[118]
>
> After a while he said, 'This isn't far from what I was taught as a boy on Roke: that true magery lies in doing only what you must do. But this would go further. Not to do, but to be done to....'

---

[115] Coyote's making or causing the world is an idea Le Guin works with in 'Buffalo Gals, Won't You Come Out Tonight' in *Buffalo Gals and Other Animal Presences* (1987) 22, 43.

[116] Contrast the transcendent Dreamer, adolescent demiurge in 'Pathways of Desire.'

[117] A picture of Ouroboros as 'Crowned dragon as tail eater,' from *Uraltes Chymisches Werk* (1760) can be found under 'Ouroboros,' *Encyclopaedia Britannica* (1974), Micropaedia VII—or on Google Images.

[118] Contrast the very negative emptiness in Dr. Haber (see above).

> 'I don't think that's quite it. It's more like what true doing rises from. (193-94; 'Winter,' ch. 12)

On Roke, Ged has learned the lesson of Chuang Tzu, that to do right 'allow yourself to fall in with the dictates of necessity. For necessity is the TAO of the Sage,' which Herbert A. Giles paraphrases, 'Do nothing save what you cannot help doing' (Giles 231).[119] Tenar proposes a theory—to appropriate and redefine a phrase from John Keats—of 'negative capability' for the art of magic, and of life. As Arha, Priestess of the Nameless Ones in *The Tombs of Atuan*, Tenar had been taught 'that to be powerful she must sacrifice. Sacrifice herself and others. A bargain: give, and so get'—and Tenar denies neither her life as Arha nor the truth of this lesson. But in her maturity Tenar's soul 'cannot live in that narrow place—this for that, tooth for tooth, death for life.... There is a freedom beyond that. Beyond payment, retribution, redemption—beyond all the bargains and the balances, there is freedom.' Ged replies, 'The doorway between them,' and says no more (*Tehanu* 194).

Tenar's denial of sacrifice, and questioning the *lex talionis* (law of retaliation and retribution) and payment and redemption in both capitalist and theological senses are themes Le Guin develops in *The Dispossessed*, *Eye of the Heron*, *The Beginning Place*, and elsewhere. The image of emptiness is the Daoist one of the absence that allows some important existences: the hub as the absence at the center of the wheel, allowing the existence of the wheel, the empty space that is a doorway.[120]

Before Tenar and Ged can get to such an insight, however (whatever it means)—before they can get 'beyond...balances' and understand positive doorways—Ged must learn the necessity of balances and how opening some doorways can be very bad.

Which returns us to the trilogy.

* * * * * * *

Margaret P. Esmonde has called the trilogy 'straightforward stories [that] deal in strong colors and plain fabrics,' works that readily show 'the design the master patterner has woven, not just in Earthsea but throughout the entire fabric of her work.' The main pattern Esmonde sees is 'the psychological journey' passing 'through pain and fear' to 'the integration of personality that Carl [G.] Jung wrote about' (16 and 34). Esmonde implies

---

[119] *Chuang Tzu* ch. 23; see also ch. 6 (Giles 74).

[120] Strongly contrast the tone of Koheleth's opening line, trans. in NEB, 'Emptiness, emptiness, says the Speaker, emptiness, all is empty' (Eccl. 1.2). Vulgate trans. into Latin: 'Vanitas vanitatum, dixit Ecclesiastes; Vanitas vanitatum, et omnia vanitas.' The Geneva Bible and those derived from it just English Jerome's *Vanitas* as 'Vanity'; *Tanakh* renders the image into idiomatic English and supplies appropriate punctuation: 'Utter futility!—said Koheleth—Utter futility! All is futile!'

that the individual integration of Ged is paralleled by integration of Earthsea politically and cosmically; in an essay ending the anthology Esmonde's begins, John H. Crow and I examine such 'Patterns of Integration' explicitly, and I still see in the trilogy, but not *Tehanu*, patterns of integration on the levels of the individual, society, and the cosmos.[121]

The Earthsea novels, then, are set on Earth in a legendary time in which consolidation of power under a king might be the least bad political option.[122] It is a time when magic works and there are still dragons, but otherwise a plausible world for moving into a second age of kings (rather like the Mycenaean Age as recalled by Homer). Backward places like Ged's home island of Gont are pretty much in the Bronze Age at the beginning of the story and some forty to fifty years later have as their technological high points the spinning wheel, soap, and a large ship like King Lebannen's *Dolphin*.[123] It is an archipelago world of islands and water, a politically simple world where power is generally visible and often quite personal—a world where King Lebannen can say 'I will forbid,' and be convinced that that will be that (*Tehanu* 147; ch. 10). It is a world moving toward integration, starting with individuals (see Crow and Erlich 202). The integration is most spectacular with Ged in *Wizard*, but psychological integration is also central to *Tombs* and *Shore* in the initiation into adulthood of Arha/Tenar and Arren/Lebannen.

Political integration is less obvious, but it is there as a kind of goal for the trilogy. Near the beginning of *Wizard*, Gont is raided by Viking-like warriors from the Kargad Lands, and the political situation does not get much better over the next fifty or so years: no wars, but raids, piracy, and slaving make for a political world that could use (arguably) a strong central authority. 'Unhappy a land where heroes are needed,' as Bertolt Brecht's Galileo put it, but, I will add, unhappier still to need a hero and not get one.[124] In *Wizard*, Ged becomes a hero who can oppose the evils of his world. And in *Tombs* and *Shore* he does so. In *Tombs* Ged does find and free Tenar—even as Tenar in the plot finds Ged and helps him escape—and that coming to freedom is what is most important in *Tombs*, Tenar's book; still Ged's goal for his quest in *Tombs* is reuniting the Ring of Erreth-Akbe, thereby completing the Rune of Peace, peace through the

---

[121] In the Conclusion to *Coyote's Song* I deal with Rosemary Jackson's objections to the idea of integration, objections underlying, I think, some of Sarah Lefanu's problems with Le Guin's early work: Jackson 154-55, Lefanu 139-40 and passim in the section on Le Guin.

[122] One could also see Earthsea in an alternative universe or on another planet; I follow Remington in seeing the series on our Earth ('...Cyclical Renewal' 278).

[123] Esmonde sees *WE* covering Ged's life from birth to age seventeen or so and *TA* set ten or fifteen years later (20), with Ged forty to fifty years old in *FS* and Archmage for about five years (27). I discuss the cultural setting in *Survey* 447, 450-51.

[124] Brecht, *Life of Galileo* (Scene 13, 98), quoted by Grixti (223).

dominion of a King.[125] In *Shore*, the goal of the quest is closing a gap in nature that is draining the vitality from the world, but the quest accomplishes not only this task but also the making of Arren into King Lebannen: Arren is initiated into manhood, brings Ged back to life through pain and the Dry Land of death, and thereby fulfills the prophecy that the true inheritor of the throne will be one '*who has crossed the dark land living and come to the far shores of the day*' (*Shore* 17; ch.2).

The One of the Dao that can be named—one of the relatively few good 'One's' in Le Guin's canon—produces the two of Yin-Yang, which in turn produces the many things of the world.[126] In *Wizard*, Ged achieves wholeness—oneness—which allows him to become the hero in *Tombs*, where Tenar will bond with him, and the two of them will reunite the Ring. The Ring they return to the world bears the sign under which Lebannen will rule when he and Ged return to Earthsea and Lebannen begins the task of uniting the many.

Integration on the cosmic level is a theme more explicit in the trilogy than the politics. There is no problem of integration with most of the cosmos of Earthsea: it is just a small, wholly material world. Ged can know about stars and the fire at the core of the Earth, but as a practical matter the world of the trilogy consists of the islands of the archipelago and the sea, covered by 'the empty sky'—i.e., just the dome of the sky, without a heaven or transcendent gods. No heaven above, and no hell below, just the Old Powers of the Earth, close enough to the surface to be an immediate problem only in the area of *The Tombs of Atuan* and at the Court of the Terrenon (*WE* ch. 7 [see Erlich, in *Survey*, 450-51]). Where the cosmos gets problematic is with death. No heaven, no hell: but there is Sheol, a Realm of Hel or Hades, 'the Dry Land' of the dead. The Dry Land touches Earthsea and is reached by a spirit journey.[127] Those desiring to make most of the journey while embodied, head west, toward the setting sun, but the last part of the journey must be made in spirit. 'There is a wall of stones...at a certain place on the bourne. Across it the spirit goes at death, and across it a living man may go and return again, if he is a mage' (*FS* 75; 'Sea Dreams,' ch. 5)—or if he's Arren.

Perhaps we can get a better image of the problem Ged confronts with a damaged cosmos if we drop for a moment the psychological and political term 'integration' and use Douglas Barbour's phrase, 'Wholeness and Bal-

---

[125] On royal dominion, contrast 'the Flowering of Rer, the Summer Century' when 'Sedern Geger, the Unking, cast the crown' of Karhide into the River Arre and proclaimed 'an end to dominion' ('Coming of Age in Karhide' [1995]: 470).
[126] 'Tao gives birth to one, / One gives birth to two.../ Three gives birth to ten thousand beings'—i.e., everything (*Tao te Ching*, ch. 42, Chen trans. 157 f.).
[127] For the spirit journey as 'one of the themes of the philosophical Taoists,' see Welch 94. For one example of a real-world view of spirit journeys, cf. and contrast the beliefs of the Twana people of western Washington State (Elmkendorf with A. L. Kroeber 483-84). The idea of a spirit journey, however, is enough of a commonplace even in our culture to be central to the parodic premise of *BILL & TED'S BOGUS JOURNEY* (1991).

ance.' Ged tells Arren that 'Death and life are the same thing—like the two sides of my hand, the palm and the back. And still the palm and the back are not the same.... They can be neither separated, nor mixed' (*FS* 74; ch. 5; see also *WE* 80-83; ch. 5). Death and life must be like the clasped hands on the SNCC button described in *The Lathe of Heaven,* or like George Orr and Heather Lelache making love, or two hands—left and right—placed together palm to palm: one whole (new) thing possible because two things are both similar and different, touching and separate, complementary: Yin-Yang.[128]

More generally, the principle of the cosmos is Balance. This point is repeated at key moments in the trilogy, most emphatically in a lesson Ged teaches Arren:

> ...an act is not, as young men think, like a rock that one picks up and throws, and it hits or misses, and that's the end of it. When that rock is lifted, the earth is lighter; the hand that bears it heavier. When it is thrown, the circuits of the stars respond, and where it strikes or falls the universe is changed. On every act the balance of the whole depends. The winds and seas, the powers of water and earth and light, all that these do, and all that the beast and green things do, is well done, and rightly done. All these act within the Equilibrium. From the hurricane and the great whale's sounding to the fall of a dry leaf and the gnat's flight, all they do is within the balance of the whole. But we, insofar as we have power over the world and one another, we must learn to do what the leaf and the whale and the wind do of their own nature. We must learn to keep the balance. Having intelligence, we must not act in ignorance. Having choice, we must not act without responsibility.[129]

On Ged's level of power, the important balance is between the worlds of life and death.

In all things, but especially in matters literally of life and death, the nature of the world of Earthsea makes imperative following the rule Ged suggests to Arren for a mage to advise a king: 'My lord, do nothing because it is righteous or praiseworthy or noble to do so; do only that which you must do and which you cannot do any other way' (*FS* 67; ch. 4).[130] To oversimplify—one must act with the Dao, while necessarily within the Dao, embedded in the world; and one must understand the consequences of one's actions. One must act on what one knows, which means acting locally, on the smallest scale possible, and preferably spontaneously, de-

---

[128] See Remington, 'Other Side' esp. 162-63, Crow and Erlich 201.
[129] *FS* 66-67; 'Magelight,' ch. 4. See also *WE* 44; 'The School for Wizards,' ch. 3.
[130] See *Chuang Tzu* ch. chs. 6 and 23 (Giles 74 and 231).

pending upon one's intuition. To attempt large-scale, violent, deadly impositions of will upon the world would be 'The Arrogance of Power,' a failure to know 'The Limits of Power'—as local wars taught the Daoist philosophers during China's Warring States period (481-221 B.C.E.), as twentieth-century history had made and was again making very clear.[131] Most importantly, we do not and cannot 'know what life is or what death is,' as Ged tells Arren. 'To claim power over what you do not understand is not wise, nor is the end of it likely to be good' (*FS* 74; ch. 5). On great matters, then, the proper (in)action of wu wei would be to do nothing but 'that which you must do.' Or so the matter must be put if one acts consciously. Alternatively, one might—if one is an adept—join oneself with the Dao and be acted through. Ogion rather cryptically explain this to Ged: 'A man would know the end he goes to, but he cannot know it if he does not turn, and return to his beginning, and hold that beginning in his being. If he would not be a stick whirled and whelmed in the stream, he must be the stream itself, all of it, from the spring to its sinking in the sea' (*WE* 128; ch. 7). Ultimately, only mystic union with the Dao allows full being and right action, ultimately, even a hero must be a sage.[132]

* * * * * * *

In each of the books of the trilogy there is a balance that must be restored, an integration to be made, and a doorway to be shut.[133]

A Wizard of Earthsea gives Ged's early years, starting with his childhood as a goatherder and witch-child, and then his time as apprentice to Ogion the Silent, the Mage of Re Albi on Gont, and Ged's most important teacher. Ged very much needs to learn what Ogion has to teach: silence, patience, humility before nature, unaction.[134] Not long into Ged's apprenticeship, Ogion offers Ged a choice: to stay with him or to go to the school for wizards on Roke. Ged later sees this offer as the choice between 'the life of being and the life of doing' and tells Arren that he 'leapt at the latter like a trout to a fly.' That 'fly,' however, had a hook in it: actions have

---

[131] See bibliographic entries for J. W. Fulbright and E. McCarthy.
[132] Hero and sage can be seen as binary opposites, but probably shouldn't be. Even in the Latin West, the formula for a hero was *Fortitudo et Sapientia*, covering meanings from 'strength and cunning' through 'fortitude and wisdom'; and even Hercules, god of jocks, got transmuted by the Renaissance into an intellectual.
[133] On equilibrium and balance, see *Chuang Tzu* ch. 11, Giles trans. p. 106.
[134] Significantly Ogion also names Ged in a ceremony that takes Ged at age thirteen 'Nameless and naked' across 'the cold springs of the Ar' (*WE* 14; ch. 1). Before seeing unChristian Le Guin alluding to Christian baptism, note that Hesiod says that 'The daughters of Tethys and Ocean are the holy race of nymphs who, with the help of Lord Apollo and their brothers the Rivers, bring young boys to manhood....,' apparently in some long-preChristian rite of baptism (*Theogony* 63; v.337-82).

consequences to which one is bound and every act 'makes you act again and yet again' (*FS* 34; 'Hort Town,' ch. 3).[135]

Ged goes to Roke, does very well in his studies, and then acts indeed. He gets into a magic contest with an aristocratic youth and in his anger, envy, and pride summons up the spirit of Elfarran, 'the fair lady' from a famous heroic song. But the millennium-dead Elfarran appears only for a moment, 'Then the sallow oval between Ged's arms grew bright. It widened and spread, a rent in the darkness of the earth and night, a ripping open of the fabric of the world. Through it blazed a terrible brightness. And through that bright misshapen breach clambered something like a clot of black shadow, quick and hideous, and it leaped straight out at Ged's face' (60-61; ch. 4). This is 'The Loosing of the Shadow,' and the act results in Ged's facial scars, and provides the plot of *Wizard* (plus a favorite Le Guinian image: 'the *fabric* of the world,' here torn with 'a terrible brightness'). For the rest of the novel Ged is bound to 'act again and yet again' as he recovers from his wounds, then avoids his shadow—and then flees, desperately trying 'to choose his way, to plan where he should go, what he should do; but each choice, each plan, was blocked by a foreboding of doom' (98; ch. 6).

The middle of *Wizard* stresses three temptations of Ged. In one, he succumbs, trying, 'with no thought for himself' to bring back to life a dead child. Whatever other allusions we can find, this action would imitate Christ's raising from the dead the daughter of Jairus (Luke 8.49-56). Going after the child was a bad idea on Ged's part not because it is blasphemous to imitate Christ that literally but because Le Guin's thinking suggests that Christ did ill in self-sacrifice generally and, more specifically here, enforcing his will over nature in ignoring the rule 'let the dying spirit go' (*WE* 80; ch. 5). Ged also confronts the Dragon of Pendor and the Terrenon Stone, where the lure in both cases is telling Ged the name of his shadow. It is well that Ged resists since the Shadow's name is 'Ged,' and saying 'Ged' would give the dragon or the Stone power over him (92, ch 5; 120, ch. 7).

After the confrontation with the would-be mistress and master of the Terrenon, at his psychological low-point in the story, Ged returns in the form of a hawk to Ogion, who changes him back to a man and gives him the advice that he 'must be the stream itself.' And for the turning point of the novel Ogion notes that Ged returned to Gont and to him and now must 'turn clear round, and seek the very source, and that which lies beyond the source.' That is, Ged must seek both nameable and unnameable Dao, and, far more immediately, stop fleeing for safety (for there is none in a universe in flux), and instead turn around and hunt his hunter. He must stop

---

[135] Cf. and contrast Tenar's leaving Ogion for marriage and a family in *Tehanu* (see below, my chapter on *Tehanu*). Ged leaps at power; Tenar turns her back on it; and, with all respect for Ogion, the good as well as the Silent—and with great respect for power wisely used and more wisely not used—in that turning away and renouncing Tenar joins The Ones Who Walk Away from Omelas (see below).

allowing his shadow to gain strength from him but instead hunt down and gain strength from his shadow (128; ch. 7). This is a frightening thought, since the shadow somehow knows Ged's true name, and Ged doesn't know the shadow's name, but Ged faces his fear and goes hunting (ch. 8 f.). Along the way he gets help from two strangers and repays their kindness as well as he can, and receives as a gift half of the Ring of Erreth-Akbe. Finally he gets a little help from his friend Vetch and confronts the shadow.

Ged and Vetch are in a boat at sea, and yet dry land appears around them—*the* Dry Land. Ged lifts his wizard's staff and produces light that 'harrowed even that ancient darkness.' As they approach one another, the shadow 'became utterly black in the white mage-radiance that burned about it, and it heaved itself upright. In silence, man and shadow met face to face, and stopped.' Simultaneously, they say one word, "Ged.' And the two voices were one voice.' Ged reaches out and 'took hold of his shadow, of the black self that reached out to him. Light and darkness met, and joined, and were one.' Ged tells Vetch that 'The wound is healed,' in the world and in Ged: 'I am whole, I am free,' and Vetch understands 'that Ged had neither lost nor won but, naming the shadow of his death with his own name, had made himself whole: a man: who, knowing his whole true self,' including the evil in it, and his mortality, 'cannot be used or possessed by any power other than himself, and whose life therefore is lived for life's sake and never in the service of ruin, or pain, or hatred, or the dark' (178-81; ch. 10). Ged has integrated his shadow into himself and become a balanced whole: one hero.

* * * * * * *

In her headnote to 'The Good Trip' in *The Wind's Twelve Quarters* (1975), Le Guin jokes about her '*infallible talent for missing whatever boat all the fashionable people are on*' (109), and I'll somewhat flippantly apply this line to *The Tombs of Atuan*. *Tombs* appeared in 1971; in 1972 Joanna Russ's 'When It Changed' appeared in Harlan Ellison's *Again Dangerous Visions,* and Russ's story may be usefully set in dialog with *Tombs* and read as a friendly but firm response to *Tombs*.[136] 'When It Changed' presents Whileaway, a feminist separatist utopia whose doom (apparently) is announced with the arrival of men. Other separatist works

---

[136] Note that it is irrelevant for such an exercise whether or not Russ intended a response or had even read *Tombs*. It is unlikely Shakespeare ever read Machiavelli; *Macbeth* and *King Lear* are still responses to Machiavellian theories of *Realpolitik*; Le Guin said she had not read Jung before she wrote *WE*; *WE* still features 'Jung's Shadow' ('Response' 45). In a very useful review essay on James Bittner's *Approaches*, Marleen Barr suggests in a footnote setting other Le Guin texts in dialogs: 'Mary Gentle's *The Golden Witchbreed* (1985)...can be read as a feminist version of' *LHD*,' and Sheila Finch's *Triad* (1986) 'can be read as a feminist version' of *WWF* (*SFS* #41: 112 n.).

were to follow in the early 1970s, in imaginative literature doing significant thought experiments asking what women's societies might be like, societies without men. Other works investigated the possibility of women's religion. The value system of *Tombs* is not separatist in terms of gender but strongly integrationist, and against institutionalized religion, period, whether worshipping a Godking or the more feminine, 'chthonic' powers of the earth. As we will see, the most politically powerful woman at Atuan is the High Priestess of the Godking and definitely a man-identified woman, and the sexual and religious politics of *Tombs* may be somewhat problematic.[137]

In *A Wizard of Earthsea* , the imbalance to be corrected was Yangish over-action, over-assertion, over-intellectuality, too much desire for life and power: in Daoist (and traditional patriarchal) symbolism, too much light. In *The Tombs of Atuan*, the balance to be redressed is too much stasis, darkness, 'cyclical' reincarnation. In *Wizard* the doorway to the Dry Land was shut when Ged merged with his shadow. In *Tombs*, the doorway is rather more literal, the Place of *The Tombs of Atuan*, where the powers of darkness have irrupted into the light and hold that which is not theirs: the Ring of Erreth-Akbe and Tenar, plus other women and eunuchs who have a chance to escape at the end of the novel, or choose not to escape.

The plot of *Tombs* starts when the infant girl Tenar is found and declared to be the incarnation of the One Priestess of the Nameless Ones (a process similar to the one for finding a new Dalai Lama). In the ceremony of the Remaking of the Priestess, Tenar has her name taken from her and becomes only Arha, 'the Eaten One,' a vocational title only, not a name (Prologue, and ch. 1). Arha comes into her full powers as priestess, theoretically, at fourteen, but nothing really changes, and she still cannot act against the power of Kossil, the Priestess of the Godking. More important, Arha finds it impossible to *not* act when Kossil presents her with prisoners accused of plotting against the Godking and says it is Arha's choice how they will die (see Crow and Erlich 210). Arha chooses to have them die of thirst and starvation (31-33; 'The Prisoners,' ch. 3), faints at the conclusion of this episode (35), and has bad dreams (38; 'Dreams and Tales,' ch. 4). As time slowly passes, all Arha has to do she does, primarily learning her domain: the Undertomb and the Labyrinth, which she explores almost entirely by touch, since light is forbidden in the Undertomb, the heart of the realm of the Old Powers, whom she thinks her 'Masters.'

And then something happens. Change is introduced with the arrival of Ged, who momentarily brings light to the Undertomb with his wizard's staff, revealing the underworld as an exquisite cave (58-59; 'Light Under the Hill,' ch. 5). Ged brings change and a possibility of beauty that includes Arha's own when Ged creates an illusion showing her as Tenar, in a

---

[137] Again, see Littlefield for 'The fundamental imbalances of power and gender' (252), not addressed until *Tehanu* .

beautiful dress (88; 'Great Treasure,' ch. 7).[138] Arha captures Ged and then saves his life, a politically dangerous move that Kossil discovers. Ged has half of the Ring of Erreth-Akbe, and the other half is buried in the Great Treasury of the Nameless Ones. Arha has a choice: accept her name back from Ged and escape with him and the Ring to the Inner Lands, or return to being Arha and let Ged die. She takes back her name; Ged unites the Ring—and they escape, eventually bringing the Ring to Havnor, the central city of Earthsea. During their escape, however, Tenar momentarily repudiates the pain of her freedom and considers killing Ged (139-40), and Ged promises to take Tenar away from Havnor to Ogion on Gont, so she can live quietly and decide whether or not to enter the larger world beyond Gont (145; 'Voyage,' ch. 12).

In terms of Ged's Jungian individuation, *Tombs* tells the 'rescue of the Anima,' where the Hero takes his missing feminine portion from some representative of the Great Mother. In terms of restoring balances and closing doors, the key part of the story is Ged's bringing light to the Undertomb, which eventually results in an earthquake from the angered Nameless Ones, an earthquake that causes the fall of the monoliths that mark the Tombs, and the destruction of their temple. Most important, there is the rejoining of the Ring and the symbolic marriage of Ged and Tenar: Ged's masculinity balancing Tenar's femininity, Ged's dark skin balancing Tenar's white, Ged's associations with light balancing Tenar's associations with darkness.[139]

All these themes, however, get a very different twist from being told from the point of view of Tenar as 'a feminine coming of age' story with the subject of 'sex.'[140] Viewed this way, the imbalance is in the life of Arha; in Simone de Beauvoir's terminology, Arha is trapped in immanence and in very great need of a project (see Crow and Erlich 205). And this imbalance is corrected when Tenar accepts Ged's offer of her name (her being) and with it true choice, true action, and, most important, escape. Together Ged and Tenar escape from the underworld and get away from the forces of darkness, dryness, and sterility when they reach a very literal door, and Ged uses his magic, a word, and his phallic wizard's staff to blow the door open (121-22; 'The Anger of the Dark,' ch. 10). As a critic of *Tombs*, Le Guin stresses the escape together: Tenar cannot 'get free of the Tombs without him,' but then 'neither can Ged get free without her. They are interdependent,' with Le Guin redefining her hero to be

---

[138] Later, Ged will tell her she'll have a hundred dresses like that—but real ones—in Havnor (131-32; 'Western Mountains,' ch. 11). See *Tehanu* (155; ch. 11) for Tenar as dressmaker for Therru. See Littlefield for a very negative interpretation of the hundred dresses, as an ineffective bribe (249).

[139] Barrow and Barrow found a letter from Le Guin to Theodora Kroeber indicating Le Guin didn't marry off Ged and Tenar because 'a 'happily married wizard just won't do'—an archetype must '*behave* like an archetype'' (Letter, 8 July 1971, qtd Barrow 36).

[140] Le Guin, 'Dreams Must Explain Themselves' 55. See also Esmonde 22-26, Littlefield 249-50.

more part of, in balance with, the world and other people: 'dependent, not autonomous' (*ER* 9), half of 'the original *Mitsein*', a human couple (Beauvoir 35).

For Tenar, personal balance is restored when she gets out of a constricting, terminally boring life without sex and enters the wider world of men, women, freedom, and significant action. Contrary to the macho theory of 'No retreat, no surrender'—and self-sacrifice as an ideal (especially for women)—Le Guin frequently endorses walking away: from a doomed world in 'Things' (1970), from the finally corrupt utopia of Omelas (1973), from dysfunctional relationships in *The Beginning Place* (1980), from the threat of serfdom in *Eye of the Heron* (1978). What sort of life Tenar can find on Gont or in any of the Inner Lands, given the low status of women in Earthsea, is a question that waits for *Tehanu* (Littlefield 249-50), but it will be an improvement over the life of a priestess at Atuan—even the highest of priestesses—serving real powers but very false gods. Giving her highly personal view, Tenar's friend Penthe says she would 'marry a pigherd and live in a ditch,' if she could, rather than stay 'buried alive' as a priestess (40; ch. 4), and, however unraised her consciousness, Penthe has a point. Expressed in consciously political terms, Le Guin as critic says her 'view is that the Place in the desert is a community of women (and eunuchs) *totally controlled by men*—a subservient element in the totally male-dominant regime of the godkings. Ged's society is also male-dominant, but not so repressive, and so he can offer her a (relative) freedom' (personal communication).

* * * * * * *

The Farthest Shore returns to more explicit dealing with the Balance and doorways, but it reverses much in *The Tombs of Atuan* (Crow and Erlich 206-07).

In *Shore*, Arren, Prince of Enlad, has been sent by his father to Roke to seek the counsel of the Archmage Sparrowhawk and his colleagues. There has been a loss of magic in the remote areas of Earthsea. Later Ged and Arren will learn of increasing piracy and slave-taking, drug use, and a decline in the arts and crafts. More generally, joy, vividness, and light are draining from the world. Arren and Ged set off to discover why. Ged believes that one man is responsible for this strange contagion, what he sees as a radical imbalance, outside of the natural order. Ged is correct. A sorcerer named Cob has found a way to immortality by dying and returning, opening a door between the realms of life and death.

To search for Cob, Ged needs a guide: Ged is satisfied with the power of his art and has long been reconciled to his own death. For Ged it is well that his body will return to the natural cycles (as Chuang Tzu taught) and that the being the acts and choices of his life have created will go to the Dry Land.[141] Arren, though, hears Cob very well, and the temptation for

---

[141] *Chuang Tzu* ch. 6 (Giles 79).

him is to become a servant to Cob, serving the Anti-King. The appeal, Ged tells Arren, is made 'In our minds,' an appeal to 'The traitor, the self; the self that cries I want to live; let the world burn so long as I can live! The little traitor soul in...all of us. But only some understand him. The wizards and the sorcerers. The singers; the makers. And the heroes, the ones who seek to be themselves. To be one's self is a rare thing and a great one. To be one's self forever: is that not better still?' (135; 'Orm Embar,' ch. 9).

Ged, then, needs someone who can hear Cob's appeal and resist it. Arren is a good candidate: he fiercely wants to live, but will listen to Ged's lesson that 'Nothing is immortal' and that our mortality is the source of our selfhood. Ged tells Arren the Perennial Philosophy 'That selfhood... does not endure. It changes; it is gone, a wave on the sea' and asks rhetorically, 'Would you have the sea grow still and the tides cease, to save one wave, to save yourself?' (122; 'Children of the Open Sea,' ch. 8).[142] Conveniently for Le Guin's teaching purpose, but very plausibly, Arren is hard to convince and demands to know why he shouldn't desire immortality. Ged is pleased that Arren argues seriously and allows that Arren should desire immortality, but he should beware lest he get his desire and the world suffer even worse.

> There are two, Arren, two that make one: the world and the shadow, the light and the dark. The two poles of the Balance. Life rises out of death, death rises out of life; in being opposite they yearn to each other, they give birth to each other and are forever reborn. And with them all is reborn, the flower of the apple tree, the light of the stars. In life is death. In death is rebirth. What then is life without death? Life unchanging, everlasting, eternal?—What is it but death—death without rebirth? (136; ch. 9)[143]

Arren objects that if so much depends on 'the Balance of the Whole,' surely 'it would not be allowed'—and here he stops, but we can fill in that surely one mere human would not be allowed to disturb the Balance. Ged pounces on the passive voice, deleted agent and asks rhetorically, 'Who allows? Who forbids?' Arren does not know, and neither does Ged. There are no transcendent gods in the universe of Earthsea to allow or forbid, no God or gods to command. Ged is sure that he was able to upset the Bal-

---

[142] 'Especially in Hindu symbolism, time is portrayed as a placid, silent pool within which ripples come and go. The ripples are our temporary lives from which we must go down into the great, eternal Nirvana' (Meerloo 248). Water with waves is also a good image for the Dao, and as an alternative image of the great Void can correlate with ultimate physical reality as a quantum field (Capra ch. 14, 'Emptiness and Form').

[143] For rebirth as a positive thing earlier in the trilogy, in *TA*, see Barrow 37. Note Waley's rendering of the opening of *Tao te Ching* ch. 50: 'He who aims at life achieves death' (p. 203).

ance greatly: 'I have done the same evil, in the same folly of pride. I opened the door between the worlds just a crack, just a little crack, just to show that I was stronger than death itself.... Oh, the door between the light and the darkness can be opened.... But to shut it again, there's a different story' (137; ch. 9).[144] It is the story of almost all of the rest of their quest, and of *Shore*.

Ged and Arren go to Selidor, as far west as Earthsea goes, and then go in spirit to the Dry Land of death. At the climax of *Shore*, Arren and Ged confront Cob at the Dry River (176-84; 'The Dry Land,' ch. 12). There is an agon at the Dry River: a struggle in words, a physical struggle (though in spirit), and a magical struggle as Ged strives to close the door between the worlds. In a significant paraphrase of a graffito attributed to Percy Bysshe Shelley, that door was 'a way that led nowhere' (183; ch. 12).[145] Shelley, the story goes, was expelled from Oxford for painting 'THIS WAY TO HEAVEN' on the wall forming the end of a dead-end alley. Any religious way promising immortality, including the Christian Way, Shelley and Le Guin hold, is a way going nowhere. Arren and Ged succeed: Ged closes the door and gives Cob back his true name, and a real death. The cost of this victory to Ged is all his power as a mage, and most of his physical strength. Arren—or Lebannen, now, the King who goes by his true name—must carry Ged over the Mountains of Pain. They arrive on Selidor and the Eldest dragon Kalessin flies them back to Roke.

On Roke, Ged kneels to Lebannen, acknowledging him King of All the Isles. And then Kalessin takes Ged back to Gont. Again, Le Guin offers alternative endings. The heroic *Deed of Ged* has Ged go to Havnor for the coronation and then take his boat, *Lookfar*, 'from harbor and from haven, westward among the isles, westward over sea; and no more is known of him.' That is, when he has spent his power and has reached old age he makes a heroic exit and—like a combination of Alfred, Lord Tennyson's Ulysses and a hero in a Western movie—sails off into the sunset. They tell the story differently on Gont. In that version the King comes to Gont to seek Ged but learns he's gone off to the 'into the forests of the mountain.' The King forbids seeking Ged out, saying, 'He rules a greater kingdom than I do.' That is, Ged takes the route of a Sage and leaves the life of doing for a forest, Le Guin's favorite image for Being (196-97; 'The Stone of Pain,' ch. 13).

Tehanu goes with the version told on Gont, but corrects it. Ged returns to Gont and finds Tenar, and in old age finds love and a domestic life—and, for the first time, a sex life. Yin-Yang can symbolize the balance of Life and Death and cosmic Equilibrium, or the human and dragon in Tehanu. Le Guin insists in her last book-length visit to Earthsea that the im-

---

[144] See also Ged's speech on 'the kingdom of life,' ending rather hopefully with 'Deep are the springs of being, deeper than life than death....': 165, 'Selidor,' ch. 11.
[145] See headnote to 'The Field of Vision,' *WTQ* 222).

age for the mystic Yin-Yang (re)creation of the world is also the mundane but complex intertwining of dark and light as Ged and Tenar make love.

IV.

ON VIOLENCE, UTOPIA, ETHICS—AND SEX

> It is by losing the egocentric life that we save the hitherto latent and undiscovered life which, in the spiritual part of our being, we share with the divine Ground. This newfound life is 'more abundant' than the other, and of a different and higher kind. Its possession is liberation into the eternal, and liberation is beatitude. Necessarily so; for the Brahman, who is one with the Atman, is not only Being and Knowledge, but also Bliss, and after Love and Peace, the final fruit of the spirit is Joy. Mortification is painful, but that pain is one of the pre-conditions of blessedness.
> —Aldous Huxley, *The Perennial Philosophy* (106; ch. 6)

From 1969 through 1985, Ursula K. Le Guin published several important works that deal significantly with large-scale violence: 'Winter's King' (1969), *The Left Hand of Darkness* (1969), *The Word for World Is Forest* (1972), *The Eye of the Heron* (1978), Stone Telling's story in *Always Coming Home* (1985), and, to a lesser extent, *The Dispossessed* (1974). For one of the bases of violence, 'Vaster than Empires and More Slow' (1971) is useful, as is 'Nine Lives' (1969). And 'The New Atlantis' (1975) and *Tehanu* (1990) are important for smaller-scale violence and for Le Guin's rethinking the question in more feminist terms. In this chapter, I wish to look at Le Guin's extended investigation of the roots of war and lesser forms of highly organized mass murder—dystopian topics; and, true to Le Guin's frequent use of comparison and contrast, I'll examine also Le Guin on the opposite of dystopia ('bad place'), eutopia (a 'good place').

Violence was a pressing topic in the United States of the late 1960s and early 1970s. Putting the matter crudely, human beings in general and Americans in particular were running out of excuses. Most of us, most of the time are peaceful enough, but a fair number of Americans every generation or so marched off to kill large numbers of other human beings, ordinarily to the applause of the fellow citizens of the killers.

Why?

Utopia was not a hot topic through the 1960s. The Right and Center in the American-led West have been militantly antiutopian for much of the twentieth century, and, as one radical in the late 1960s put it, the New Left was also very reluctant to talk about what things would be like the morning after the Revolution: 'The two great utopians of the twentieth century were Hitler and Stalin....'[146] 'Second wave' feminism seems to have changed that; whatever the cause, the early 1970s on have been a major period of utopian writing, especially works that include feminist utopias, often contrasted with masculinist dystopias: for notable examples, Joanna Russ's 'When It Changed' (1972) and *The Female Man* (1975), Suzy McKee Charnas's 'diptych' *Walk to the End of the World* (1974, dystopia) and *Motherlines* (1978, utopia), Marge Piercy's *Woman on the Edge of Time* (1976), and Samuel R. Delany's *Triton* (1976).[147] *Triton*, subtitled 'A Heterotopia,' is most directly a response to Le Guin's *The Dispossessed*, 'An Ambiguous Utopia,' but all these works, and others, may be usefully seen, or heard, in a multi-voiced dialog—occasionally, an argument. I'll suggest here only the obvious point that Le Guin until recently generally offered the liberal (feminist) ideal of integration, symbolized in the androgyne (and Daoist Yin-Yang), while Russ and Charnas preferred thought experiments using (and therefore making thinkable) more radical, separatist, women-only utopias.

SHORT STORIES:
'Nine Lives' (1969 [again—briefly]), 'Vaster than Empires and More Slow' (1971 [first pass]), 'Winter's King' (1969 [first pass]),' 'The Ones Who Walk Away from Omelas' (1973)

'Nine Lives' has no human-against-human violence, nor does it analyze any societies, either utopian or dystopian. But 'Nine Lives' makes one of Le Guin's most explicit statements about evolution and deals very elegantly with the problem of the stranger and our dread at meeting the stranger. Both points are important.

In Le Guin's future history, the near future of us Terrans is (generally) not good: it is a time of ecological disaster, of famine, plague. In 'Nine Lives,' the worst is famine:

> The United Kingdom had come through the Great Famines well, losing less than half its population: a record achieved by rigorous food control. Black marketeers and hoarders had been executed. Crumbs had been shared.

---

[146] Quoting from memory a man who talked to my Rhetoric 108 class at the University of Illinois (Urbana-Champaign), ca. 1969. The unspaced dots indicate that his voice trailed off.

[147] Charnas has continued but not completed her story in *The Furies* (1994). For Le Guin and the renewal of the American utopian tradition, see A. I. Berger 548-49.

> Where in richer lands most had died and a few had thriven, in Britain fewer died and none throve. They all got lean.... When civilization became a matter of standing in lines, the British had kept queue, and so had replaced the survival of the fittest with the survival of the fair-minded. Owen Pugh was a scrawny little man. All the same, he was there. (*WTQ* 123)

Following Peter Kropotkin in *Mutual Aid* (1902) and putting the matter in more orthodox Darwinist terms, it is the fit who survive (by definition); and, in times of stress, the fittest social animals are those who are most sociable, the most cooperative—as we civilized people are pleased to flatter ourselves, the most civilized (P. E. Smith 80-83; Bittner, *Approaches* 149 n. 49). In Le Guin's future worlds, White Americans and our descendants are rarely among the survivors. As a culture, the great White West has usually prized competitiveness over cooperation; when under grave pressure, we aren't in the habit of queuing up. In truly lean times, then, we are far less likely to survive than peoples who practice solidarity and mutual aid.[148]

The question of the stranger is crucial for the problem of violence. For human violence, there must be an 'I' and an 'Other'—an Other the 'I' sees as both similar enough to be a competitor and different enough to be a threat. One temptation for utopia is to reduce the likelihood for violence between people by radically reducing differences: 'There's the terrible thing: the strangeness of the stranger'—*any* stranger (*WTQ* 121). A false utopian possibility, then, is to eliminate strangers. Within itself the John Chow tenclone accomplishes exactly that. The ideal of the melting-pot has been realized in the ten genetically identical and phenotypically very similar men and women of the self-sufficient clone: 'Always to be answered when you spoke; never to be in pain alone. Love your neighbor as you love yourself.... That hard old problem was solved. The neighbor was the self: the love was perfect' (126).[149]

Pugh's thinking here of the teaching on love of neighbor in the Holiness Code (Leviticus 19.18), quoted with approval by Jesus (Matthew 13.39). It is unfortunate that Jesus did not quote further: 'The stranger who resides with you shall be to you as one of your citizens; you shall love him as yourself, for you were strangers in the land of Egypt....' (19.33-34). An even harder assignment than love of neighbor, someone like you: an injunction to love someone different. In any case, the clone eliminates differences, within the clone; and it eliminates active hostility toward those

---

[148] It took Le Guin a while to realize fully that 'civilization' is too problematic to use casually in a complimentary sense. In terms of large-scale violence, it's usually been city folk—civilized people—who have done the most damage; we have the technology, organization, philosophy, and discipline.

[149] Unspaced dots represent ellipsis mark in original.

outside the clone: a self-sufficient entity can usually just ignore outsiders (*WTQ* 129-30).

If 'Nine Lives' were a philosophical essay, Le Guin would have to justify why cloning 'is all wrong' beyond the practical problem of a higher fatality rate if they all tend to do the same wrong thing (142, 134-36)—and the social utility problem cited in Martin's rhetorical question, 'What are a lot of duplicate geniuses going to do for us when they don't even know we exist?' (142). 'Nine Lives' is not a philosophical essay, and homogenized humanity comes across as wrong because lack of difference eliminates sympathy (130), love (146-47), and manners (142). Manners are not more important than love but they are important. A. L. Kroeber comments on the Luiseño specifically, and (California) Indians more generally: 'The Indian, beyond taboos and cult observances, centers his attention on the trivial but unremitting factors of personal intercourse; affability, liberality, restraining of anger and jealousy, politeness. He...sets up an open, even, unruffled, slow, and pleasant existence as his ideal. He preaches a code of manners rather than morals. He thinks of character, of its expression in the innumerable but little relations of daily life, not of right or wrong in our sense. It is significant that these words do not exist in his language' (*Handbook* 684; ch. 47). A. L. Kroeber's daughter, rejecting absolutes of 'right' and 'wrong,' agrees (see *Chuang Tzu* ch. 23 [Giles 229]).

For Le Guin circa 1969, the simplest model for a utopian community is not the tenclone but Martin, Pugh, and Kaph as we last see them: lonely individuals, whose pain in isolation is their motivation to reach out to one another, to attempt, in the darkness, human touch (147).

* * * * * * *

'Vaster than Empires and More Slow' (1971) takes a situation similar to that of 'Nine Lives'—a small group on an isolated, threatening planet—but keeps in general shape close to old SF formulas.[150] Instead of a tenclone, we have ten literally mad scientists on a planet two lightcenturies beyond human exploration (*WTQ* 174), one where 'All lifeforms were photosynthesizing or saprophagus, living off light or death, not off life. Plants: infinite plants....' (175). And then the isolated humans are threatened by—something, something large and dangerous, where there *are* no intelligent creatures, no dangerous animals, nothing with voluntary movement—no possible threats! A familiar enough SF premise, even one presented with some psychological sophistication in *FORBIDDEN PLANET* (1956), a film whose Monster from the Id lurks in the speculations about 'psychic projections' and 'Dark Egos' by 'Vaster's' mad explorers (182). The movement of the plot of 'VEMS' identifies the threat as the planet's forest, one vast semi-sentient. The forest has sensed the fear and aggression of the humans and projected it back upon them, frightening them more and contributing to a vicious cycle. The forest is not conquered in the

---

[150] I discuss 'VEMS' below, as collected in *BG*.

story but contacted by the human explorers' 'Sensor,' Osden, the hypersensitive empath of the group.

'As Jean-Paul Sartre has said in his lovable way, 'Hell is other people'' ('A Trip to the Head,' *WTQ* 160)—and this statement is literally true for Osden, who has no 'skin,' so to speak, to keep other people out, so 'touch' becomes for him a violation. Osden is most sensitive to the fear of his fellow humans, and to that of the forest. Osden resolves his own problems and those of the group, when he takes 'the fear into himself, and, accepting, had transcended it. He had given up his self to the alien,' to the forest, 'an unreserved surrender, that left no place for evil. He had learned the love of the Other, and thereby had been given his whole self'—which 'is not the vocabulary of reason' but is the language of the Perennial Philosophy, and is the resolution of this story (*WTQ* 199).

As a teaching story, 'Vaster than Empires' makes explicit some important Le Guinian points on the human Shadow, Being, macho, aggression, and the *one*, the desperately egocentric individual man.

'What one fears,' the Narrator tells us, 'is alien...not one of us. The evil is not in me!' (187). In 'Vaster than Empires' the forest is radically alien, but it is not evil or a murderer. The forest is, on the contrary, associated symbolically with connectedness and identified with the ground of all connections. The forest is described as 'Presence without mind. Awareness of being, without object or subject. Nirvana' (191) and explicitly called 'the forest of being' (198). Indeed, what initially terrifies the forest is recognizing the mere existence of the humans: in its wholeness, the forest had never before encountered an Other. The forest is not conquered by the humans and hardly could be; the relatively happy resolution of the story comes in contacting, getting in touch with, the forest. Like *City of Illusions*, 'Vaster than Empires' takes a standard sort of tale and retells it with radically different values, climaxing in a different idea of victory than defeating the Other; as in *A Wizard of Earthsea*, such victory as is possible comes not from conquering the apparent enemy, but the 'mortification' of embracing the enemy.

This is a very unmacho idea, supported by some aspects of 'Vaster than Empires.' The Surveyors who go out exploring 'Where no man has gone before' (in the classic *Star Trek* formulation) are 'escapists, misfits' and 'nuts' (*WTQ* 167), described early in the story as 'wriggling through the coupling tube one by one like apprehensive spermatozoa trying to fertilize the universe' (167-68). So much for the Daniel Boone tradition and the central SF ideal of expansion into the Galaxy—and for the image of the phallic rocket ship penetrating and impregnating space! (As in, for a highly relevant example, Stanley Kubrick's film, *2001: A SPACE ODYSSEY*.)[151] On a more personal level, Osden tells one of his women colleagues that his 'choice is to be hated or to be despised. Not being a

---

[151] The apprehensive spermatazoa of Woody Allen's *EVERYTHING YOU WANTED TO KNOW ABOUT SEX*...weren't released into popular culture until 1972, a year after 'VEMS.'

woman or a coward, I prefer to be hated.' Osden is at his sickest here, and in case we—especially a male 'we'—miss that point, Le Guin goes on to undermine Osden by having him immediately go on to deny his humanity: 'But I am not a man.... There are all of you. And there is myself. I am *one*' (177-78).[152]

Osden has set up false oppositions, a false dilemma, and a false association of 'woman' or the feminine with cowardice or weakness. He has identified himself against the group as a God-like *One*. He has yet to live the paradox of victory in 'unreserved surrender' (*WTQ* 199), 'losing the egocentric life.' I will discuss the nature of that surrender in the discussion of 'Vaster' in its context in *Buffalo Gals*. Here I wish to caution readers that Le Guin's self-description as an 'unconsistent Taoist and...consistent un-Christian' is somewhat modest; she is more consistent than most of us.[153] So we should be careful not to think of Osden's surrender as Christ-like sacrifice and Christian paradoxical triumph over an adversary. Osden is not imitating Christ, and he is not sacrificing himself; Le Guin does not approve of sacrifices in any religion, or self-sacrifice as an ideal.[154] Osden fulfills himself by finding in solitude relationship with the forest: with Nature, Being, the Dao.[155] 'Vaster than Empires' is not a story of Christ-like love, nor is it one of the analyses of the late 1960s and early 1970s that would find the solution to all problems in better communication or more sensitivity. Osden's problem is that he is too sensitive. The standard-issue human being is far from 'a well of loving-kindness' (177), and 'Vaster than Empires' makes even clearer than 'Nine Lives' that some aggressiveness is a standard part of human interaction. Mannon, 'the Soft Scientist,' tries to explain Osden's obnoxiousness:

> ...the normal defensive-aggressive reaction between strangers meeting...is something you're scarcely aware of...you've learned to ignore it, to the point where you might even deny it exists. However, Mr Osden, being an empath, feels it. Feels his feelings, and yours, and is hard put to say which is which. Let's say that there's a normal element of hostility toward any stranger in your emotional reaction to him when you meet him, plus a spontaneous dislike of his looks, or clothes, or handshake—it doesn't

---

[152] Cf. Shakespeare's formula for a villain, pronounced by Richard of Gloucester, later to be King Richard III:

> I have no brother, I am like no brother;
> And this word 'love,' which greybeards call divine,
> Be resident in men like one another,
> And not in me. I am myself alone. (*3 Henry VI* 5.6.80-83)

[153] Le Guin's self-characterization is from *SFS* #6 = 2.2 (July 1975): 139, her comments on David 'Ketterer on *The Left Hand of Darkness*.'
[154] See my discussions of '...Omelas' (1973), *EoH* (1978), and *BP* (1980).
[155] Cf. Le Guin's much later story, 'Solitude' (1994).

matter what. He feels that dislike. As his autistic defense has been unlearned [as he was cured of childhood autism], he resorts to an aggressive-defense mechanism, a response in kind to the aggression which you have unwittingly projected onto him. (*WTQ* 169)

This speech gives us an approximate statement of Le Guin's position that aggressivity (as at least mild hostility to strangers) is a normal human trait: aggressivity—the capacity for anger, even violent rage—is part of the human repertoire. As with any trait, discounting for a moment free will, different people will be for aggressivity to greater and lesser degrees; as with any trait, aggressivity will be expressed in ways determined by the environment, most specifically for humans—always and necessarily—our cultures. The question then becomes, What are we going to do about it? What in human societies increases the probability of actual violence, especially large-scale violence? Can we build better and saner societies if not utopias, where violence is rare and war unknown?

****

Again, one way to such a utopia would be to eliminate the biological and cultural bases for violence: the differences that make people strangers to one another, the masculinity that provides the anatomy, hormone systems, and indoctrination that support macho violence. We know from *The Lathe of Heaven* that Le Guin dislikes a grey world without racial problems because it is without racial differences, but race is a minor matter genetically and by itself determines nothing culturally; there are other ways in which humanity could be homogenized. In *The Left Hand of Darkness* (1969), and Le Guin's writing about it, Le Guin deals at length with the more ancient question of gender. What if *that* were eliminated? Before getting to the complexities of *Left Hand*, however, it will be well to look briefly at 'Winter's King,' written, Le Guin says a year before she began *The Left Hand of Darkness* but published the same year, and then revised for *The Wind's Twelve Quarters* (1975) to change the pronouns for the Gethenians to the feminine, while keeping masculine titles, as one way to suggest their androgyny (*WTQ* 85). I will discuss 'Winter's King' more completely in the context of Le Guin's three visits to the Karhidish city of Rer.

'Winter's King' is a Hainish story, set far into the future, two generations after *The Left Hand of Darkness*, which is itself set on the planet Gethen ('Winter'), ca. 4780 CE and long after the League of All Worlds has evolved into the Ekumen ('household') of Known worlds.[156] The nar-

---

[156] For Hainish history date for *LHD*, see Briggs, 'Hainish Chronology' 18. For 'Ekumen,' see Kroeber, *Cultural Patterns...*§ 175 231: 'The Greeks had a name for the central area of higher civilization: *oikumenê*...the region in which people lived in cities in organized states....' (231; ch. 19). By the late 1960s, however,

rative's plot involves a political plot. King Argaven XVII of Karhide is kidnapped and brainwashed: 'An induced paranoia. You might well have become a remarkably vicious ruler.... Not overnight, of course.... It would have taken several years for you to become a real tyrant....' (*WTQ* 100). To avoid this plot, Argaven leaves Gethen and goes to the Ekumenical world of Ollul and is cured of her incipient paranoia—and then goes to school. Argaven's child, Emran, becomes king, and a bad one. When Argaven returns to Karhide, she comes to lead the rebellion against her child and regains her throne.

Three points here.

First, Argaven returning from her kidnapping has 'Abdication, suicide, or escape' as 'the only acts of consequences' she could choose of her own free will. Argaven's physician on Hain notes that her kidnapper's 'counted on your moral veto on suicide'—a major taboo on Gethen—'and your Council's vote [veto] on abdication. But being possessed by ambition themselves, they forgot the possibility of abnegation, and left one door open for you' (101). That is, Argaven can renounce her rights to kingship and does (abnegation) and goes to Ollul for treatment as simple 'Mr Harge.' Such renunciation of egotistical demands for status and power is beyond the mindset of people *possessed* by ambition, by the desire for power, and it is the right answer for Argaven. She turns her back on kingship and walks away from dominion, and this path leads her to true power and proper usefulness to her people (103).

The second point is in a dialog between King Argaven and Mr. Axt, the Mobile of the Ekumen on Winter. Axt tells Argaven of ancient Hainish seeding of the galaxy with humans, and alludes to loss of contact among the worlds during the Age of the Enemy. Argaven asks, 'The dream of the Ekumen, then, is to restore that truly ancient commonalty; to regather all the peoples of all the worlds at one hearth?' Axt agrees, saying, 'To weave some harmony among them, at least. Life loves to know itself, out to its furthest limits; to embrace complexity is its delight. Our difference is our beauty. All these worlds and the various forms and ways of the minds and lives and bodies on them—together they would make a splendid harmony.' Young Argaven replies, mostly correctly, 'No harmony endures'; Axt responds, 'None has ever been achieved.... The pleasure is in trying' (97).

In 1960s sociological language, Le Guin's ideal is integration, not assimilation. She wants to bring the (human) family together in our 'commonalty,' not in some sort of homogeneous unity. She wants 'a splendid

---

'ecology' and 'ecological' had come into general use among the educated, and many knew their etymology from *oikos*, the Greek word for 'house'; see, e.g., in J. T. Fraser's *Voices of Time* [1966], JTF's reference on 280, and J. L. Cloudsley-Thompson's section title on 308. I will stick with 'household' for 'Ekumen,' but see Bittner, *Approaches* 103, 107, and also Joseph Needham's reference to 'the Chinese oikoumene' ('Time and Knowledge...' in Fraser's *Voices* 115; see Bittner, *Approaches* 148, n. 45). In 'Dancing to Ganam' (1993), the (anti)hero Dalzul juxtaposes to 'Ekumen' the phrase 'the household of humankind' (*FIS* 112).

harmony'—a figure of speech from music, where harmony requires at least two *different* notes.

And she's willing to allow some dissonance. Less figuratively, there is violence among the humans on Gethen, much of it in this story lead by Le Guin's hero, Winter's true King; and this violence is no less in the version of the story Le Guin revised to make the Gethenians androgynous. People will fight to put down a tyrant, especially an incompetent tyrant; people will follow Argaven against Emran; under enough political pressure, a mother will pursue the child of her body even to the child's dishonorable death (*WTQ* 107-08). Putting the matter more positively, 'when our sense of justice is offended,' as Hannah Arendt argued in *On Violence* (1969, 1970), we may react with rage and with violence. Such violence 'is neither beastly nor irrational' but possibly legitimate when we are 'confronted with outrageous events or conditions,' when violence 'is the only way to set the scales of justice right again' (Arendt 63, 64). Such violence is simply never good.

* * * * * * *

> I do not like to see the word 'liberal' used as a smear word. That's mere newspeak. If people must call names, I cheerfully accept Lenin's anathema as suitable: I am a petty-bourgeois anarchist, and an internal emigree [sic] O.K.?
> —Le Guin, 'A Response to the Le Guin Issue' (45)

Gethen during the struggle between Argaven XVII and Emran is far from utopia; Omelas is a utopia: a place of almost perfect peace, of high art and science, profound kindness, natural religion (and no clergy), a place without guilt, of pleasure, happiness, joy ('The Ones Who Walk Away from Omelas,' 1973, *WTQ* 252-55). Having established this beautiful place, at the Festival of Summer no less, Le Guin's Narrator asks us, 'Do you believe? do you accept the festival, the city, the joy? No? Then let me describe one more thing' (265)—and she describes the *cost* of this utopia: the scapegoat, one child kept miserable in a locked room. 'It is naked. Its buttocks and thighs are a mass of festered sores, as it sits in its own excrement continually.' We are never told how the child's misery allows the happiness of Omelas—how *its* mortification and pain allows Omelas's joy—but we are told explicitly that this is the case. All the people of Omelas 'understand that their happiness, the beauty of their city, the tenderness of their friendships, the health of their children, the wisdom of their scholars, the skill of their makers, even the abundance of their harvest and the kindly weathers of their skies, depend wholly on this child's abominable misery' (257). Now that the Narrator has made Omelas more credible, she has only 'one more thing to tell, and this is quite incredible.' Sometimes adolescents who go to see the child, sometimes older adults, 'go out into the street, and walk down the street alone. They keep walking, and walk straight out of the city of Omelas...into the darkness, and they do not come back. The place they go towards is a place even less imaginable to most of us than the city of happiness. I cannot describe it at all. It is possible that it does not exist. But they seem to know where they are going, the ones who walk away from Omelas' (259).

This 'psychomyth' (*WTQ* 251) is among my favorite short stories and has been immensely popular among anthologists and critics, and that may represent a failure of faith by many of us: a failure to believe in the possibility of 'the city of happiness,' our insistence that there *must* be a catch somewhere. Indeed, 'There ain't no such thing as a free lunch' (or free pizza delivery, to bring the saying up to date) but there *are* free gifts, starting with the universe and one's life, and large-scale human happiness, pretty-good societies, may be possible.[157] However readers resolve the question of eutopia, it is clear Le Guin intends for us to consider seriously the philosophical question the story raises in the manner she raises it, as the parenthetical description under the title puts it, 'Variations on a theme by William James.'[158]

In *The Wind's Twelve Quarters* headnote, Le Guin quotes from James's 'The Moral Philosopher and the Moral Life,' most relevantly James's idea that James and his readers would find it 'hideous' if utopian happiness for millions were achieved 'on the one simple condition that a certain lost soul on the far-off edge of things should lead a life of lonely torment' (251). Le Guin follows James in reducing to its most radical case the Utilitarian doctrine of 'The greatest good for the greatest number,' and she attacks the 'hard-headed' notion that in a nasty world one must sometimes use evil means to achieve good—or, to multiply slogans: 'The end justifies'—or will justify—'the means.'

Le Guin suggests for etymologies for 'Omelas,' initially, 'Salem, O[regon],' read backwards, but also '*O melas*,' and '*Homme hélas*' ('Man, alas!'; *WTQ* 252). I will add to the possibilities, French *homme* plus Latin *Hellas*, for 'man of Greece,' and relate the name to the 'Rationalist' part of the reference in *The Lathe of Heaven* (1971), to the 'Judaeo-Christian-Rationalist West.' Dr. Haber, after all, was, in that novel 'a benevolent man. He wanted to make the world better for humanity' (82-83), which means, ideally, finding an Archimedean point outside the world from which to see the world objectively and analytically, and push it around rationally: giving it a shove toward an abstract, transcendent Good, finally to utopia (cf. 'The New Atlantis' 88).

---

[157] See the debate centering around Kenneth M. Roemer's essay, 'The Talking Porcupine...' in *Utopian Studies* 2.1 &2.

[158] In her headnote in *WTQ*, Le Guin says that the scapegoat idea comes up in Fyodor Dostoyevsky's *The Brothers Karamazov*—but she hadn't read any Dostoyevsky in a long time and 'had simply forgotten he used the idea' (251). Some readers add to the list of 'sources and analogs,' Shirley Jackson's scapegoat story, 'The Lottery' (*New Yorker*, 1948, coll. 1949; rpt. *Just an Ordinary Day* [NY: Bantam, 1996]). For a literal ritual of the scapegoat, see Leviticus 16.

If its basic rationalism is one possible problem with Omelas, another is that the Omelites, however much they are 'mature, intelligent, passionate adults' (254) might be gravely mistaken or, as Rebecca Adams suggests, a little crazy (41). Either way, we can help privilege Those Who Walk Away from Omelas by noting Le Guin's counting Odo among them (*WTQ* 260), and by associating them with a line of Le Guin's people who, if they could not be part of the solution where they were, at least walked away and ceased being part of the problem, or, if very lucky, went to better places to *be*: Lif and the widow and child in 'Things,' Luz in *The Eye of the Heron*, and Eve in 'She Unnames Them'—plus, in different ways, Leese Webster (the exiled, dispossessed spider) and 'blank' in 'A Trip to the Head.' If will and reason have created a transcendent project in Omelas, then it might be well to leave Omelas. If some 'transcendental power' has dictated the 'sacrificial 'terms'' shown in the story (Adams 41), then it would be even more imperative to leave Omelas: Le Guin rejects the 'Judaeo-Christian' and all similar transcendental powers.

I'll suggest that this far, if no further, we should put 'The Ones Who Walk Away' in the tradition of Sir Thomas More's *Utopia* (1516) and also Jonathan Swift's 'A Modest Proposal' (1729): More's *Utopia* should shame Europeans by showing how much more ethical Utopians are with only reason than Christian Europeans with both reason and revelation (J. H. Hexter, *More's Utopia*, 1952). The final turn of 'A Modest Proposal' shows us that the Projector is a monster who would sell human baby meat to solve Ireland's economic problems *and* that he is more ethical than his rich Irish and English readers. Even so, we may, and should, identify with those who walk away from Omelas—until we're 'ambushed' by the thought that those who stay in Omelas are better people than Le Guin's generally privileged readers.[159] The Omelites live well from the suffering of only one child, and they are all conscious of the child's suffering (*WTQ* 257). The economy that sustains most of Western prosperity is based on the exploitation of many more, and those who suffer are virtually invisible to the privileged (see Le Guin's 'Non-Euclidian View' 83-84).

Exploitation is one form of and one reason why there is violence among real-world humans, although in Omelas violence is limited to the victimization of one child. However mad the bargain of the Omelites, within the terms of the bargain, this is *rational* victimization, if we note that 'rational' and 'reason' come from *ratio*, 'reckoning,' and a simple calculation might indicate that the good of very many could outweigh the good of the one (to paraphrase a central thematic concern of the *Star Trek* movies).[160] Among those who believe in immortal souls of infinite value, the salvation of one such could outweigh all of human life. Would the goal of utopia, if achieved, justify violence against even one child? 'The Ones Who Walk Away from Omelas,' in a rigorously constructed teaching story, says it would not.

---

[159] 'Ambushed' from R. Silverberg's 'Happy Day in 2381' (1970).
[160] See my discussion of *BP* for sacrifices and bad bargains.

Still, the dissidents on the road from Omelas—exiles, émigrés —do not try to overthrow the 'city of happiness.' They do not try to rescue the child. They do not resort to violence, perhaps because they know the anarchist teaching 'that the means you use to attain your object soon themselves become your object' (Berkman 113)—or 'The means justify the end.' It's unclear just what the Omelite exiles are going toward, although they 'seem to know where they are going' (259). What is clear is that they reject the terms of Omelas's bargain: violence as a mysterious but rational price for utopia, even violence against one, the idea that good intentions can justify evil actions. In *The Left Hand of Darkness*, Therem Harth rem ir Estraven writes, 'To oppose something is to maintain it' and quotes the saying of a foreign people s/he is now among that 'all roads lead to Mishnory.' S/he continues, '...if you turn your back on Mishnory and walk away from it, you are still on the Mishnory road. To oppose vulgarity is inevitably to be vulgar. You must go somewhere else; you must have another goal; then you walk a different road'—I assume even while on the road away from Mishnory or away from Omelas. We will see below more of the possibilities of minimally turning and walking away from evil, and the possibility of, perhaps, even finding a new road, to 'go somewhere else, and break the circle' and go free (*LHD* 153; ch. 11).[161]

The Left Hand of Darkness (1969)

> *The 'female principle' has historically been anarchic; that is, anarchy has historically been identified as female. The domain allotted to women—'the family,' for example—is the area of order without coercion, rule by custom not by force. Men have reserved the structures of social power to themselves (and to those few women whom they admit to it on male terms, such as queens, prime ministers); men make the wars and peaces, men make, enforce and break the laws. On Gethen, the two polarities we perceive through our cultural conditioning as male and female are neither, and are in balance: consensus with authority, decentralizing with centralizing, flexible with rigid, circular with linear, hierarchy with network.* —
> Ursula K. Le Guin, 'Is Gender Necessary (Redux)' (1976/1988, *Language of the Night* [1989]: 164)

Let's begin with some jargon useful for discussing science fiction: 'foregrounding the background' and 'textualizing the subtext.' In 'realistic,' down-to-Earth stories ('mundane fiction,' in Samuel R. Delany's for-

---

[161] See A. L. Kroeber §247 for a discussion of cooperation and competition as two poles on the axis of interpersonal relations; societies such as the Inuit and the Ojibwas neither affirm nor deny competition but take a different path, individualism, and so avoid *this* dichotomy (*Biology and Race*, esp. 184).

mulation), our main interest is in the characters and what they do; the setting is background. In what Northrop Frye called the modes of Romance and Satire, the characters and their doings must compete for our interest with the settings. So, in the modes where we usually find SF—and emphatically in utopias and dystopias—what is background in Comedy and Tragedy, the mere settings of narratives, may get a good deal of attention, be drawn, figuratively, into the foreground. Add to this the idea of the subtext of a play as all the things the director and actors have to know that the playwright doesn't tell us. For a classic instance, Shakespeare's script tells us nothing about Hamlet and Ophelia's sex life, if any; the actors playing Hamlet and Ophelia, however, must know the *sub*textual details; whether or not they have been physically intimate is important for how they react to one another. Similarly, SF authors need to know a great deal about the worlds they create that they don't have to tell us directly: history, geography, myths, customs—all the things we usually teach aspiring writers to sneak in and not present in big, undigested, expository lumps.

Not as much as in *Always Coming Home* (1985; a downright future ethnography), but still to a great extent, *The Left Hand of Darkness* foregrounds the background and textualizes subtexts, expanding a simple plot to twenty chapters and an appendix by insisting that we look very closely at the world Le Guin has made and which Genly Ai presents to us in his 'Report.'

The plot falls into three parts correlating with the story's three main settings, followed by a brief conclusion. In the beginning of the story, Genly Ai is in Erhenrang, the capital of Karhide, a country on the planet Gethen, nicknamed Winter because it is at the cold end of the range in which human societies can survive. Ai's status is First Mobile of the Ekumen ('Household,' League) of Known Worlds, and his mission is to invite the Gethenians to enter the Ekumen, re-establishing contact with the other known human species of the Galaxy. Ai believes he is about to have an audience with King Argaven XV, ruler of Karhide, to present the case. The audience has been arranged by Therem Harth rem ir Estraven, prime minister to Argaven and a supporter of Ai's mission. Ai has dinner with Estraven, who implies strongly that Ai might want to leave Karhide for Orgoreyn, the other country on Gethen's Great Continent. To just advise Ai to leave would be to insult him: adults do not advise other adults in Karhidish culture.[162] Ai gets his audience with King Argaven, but they meet only moments after Ai hears the announcement of Estraven's banishment, in part for trying to help Ai, but more for becoming 'Estraven the Traitor' for attempting the peaceful resolution of a border dispute with Orgoreyn (29-30; ch. 3 [and ch. 9]). Ai's audience with Argaven does not go well, and he soon goes off to see the countryside of Karhide—and see if there was anything to tales of Gethenian Foretellings; and then Ai crosses over into Orgoreyn, hoping his offer will be better received by the Orgota.

---

[162] This rule of *shifgrethor* (see below) is implicit in *LHD* and made explicit in Le Guin's 'Coming of Age in Karhide' (481); cf. her 'Solitude' (143).

Estraven also has gone to Orgoreyn, just ahead of assassins sent by Pemmer Harge rem ir Tibe, Estraven's successor as 'King's Ear.' Ai's mission soon becomes urgent. Tibe is pressing Karhide's claim in the border dispute, and Karhide and Orgoreyn are approaching a breakthrough in Gethenian history: war. Entry into the Ekumen by one of the countries would drag in the other, and it would be necessary for the two to cooperate in bargaining with the Ekumen. The Orgota leadership lacks the insight and courage to go a new way; so they go a very old way and have Ai arrested and sent to a 'voluntary farm,' a forced-labor camp.

Estraven rescues Ai, and the two of them attempt to return to Karhide the only way they can, across the Gobrin Ice that separates and connects Karhide and Orgoreyn. It is a long trip: the third section of the novel.

Surviving the journey on the ice and arriving back in Karhide, Ai calls down his colleagues in their ship in orbit; and Estraven is betrayed by a person s/he has aided and has asked for help and skis into the guns of Tibe's agents. Since the Orgota had announced Ai's death, his arrival, alive, in Karhide is sufficiently embarrassing to require a rearrangement of the Orgota leadership, bringing into power those more in favor of peace with Karhide and entry into the Ekumen. Tibe resigns after learning of Estraven's death; Ai's ship lands safely; Karhide prepares to enter the Ekumen; and Argaven refuses—at least just yet—to revoke the order of exile on Estraven and rehabilitate Estraven's reputation. The book ends with Gethen at peace and Ai leaving the Karhidish capital and visiting Estraven's family and telling them his and Estraven's story.

What I have left out of this plot summary is that the Gethenians are androgynes: neither male nor female five-sixths of the time; either male or female when they go into kemmer: estrous, heat, rut—and, of course, remaining female through pregnancy and nursing if they enter kemmer as female and get pregnant.[163] The key goal of the protagonists, Genly Ai and Estraven, is to prevent a war between the great nation-states of Karhide and Orgoreyn; and androgyny is second only to the climate among the reasons the Gethenians *as yet* have had no wars. Commenting on *The Left Hand of Darkness* in 'Is Gender Necessary? Redux' (1976/1987), Le Guin says '*At the very inception of the whole book, I was interested in writing a novel about people in a society that had never had a war. That came first. The androgyny came second. (Cause and effect? Effect and Cause)*' (*DEW* 11).[164] Gethenian androgyny is not necessary and probably not sufficient

---

[163] For the possibility of kemmer as 'an ironic comment on male sexuality,' see, Lamb and Veith (223), who are themselves extending a suggestion by Barbara Bucknall (77).

[164] I retain the italics, indicating that this is a comment added in 1987 to Le Guin's 1976 essay 'Is Gender Necessary?', or a revision of a statement already there. Note that the time of the 'inception of the whole book' would have been during US warfare in Indochina. The 1995 production of a dramatized *Left Hand of Darkness* by the Lifeline Theatre in Chicago eliminated the consideration of war, an important datum for students of SF in theatre, and for cultural studies.

for their lack of warfare, but it is the biological basis for much in their culture that has made warfare unlikely.

Warfare anywhere on our Earth is a biological luxury item, possible only among peoples who have surpluses to destroy. As Ong Tot Oppong, an Ekumenical Investigator notes, 'The weather of Winter is so relentless, so near the limit of tolerability even to...[Gethenians], that perhaps they use up their fighting spirit fighting the cold. The marginal peoples, the races that just get by, are rarely the warriors. And in the end, the dominant factor in Gethenian life is not sex or any other human thing: it is their environment, their cold world. Here man has a crueler enemy even than himself.' (*LHD* 96; ch. 7). On Gethen, humankind have a constant reminder, that 'Heaven and Earth are not humane.'[165]

Androgyny by itself might not have been sufficient to prevent war; the severe climate certainly helped limit large-scale violence, as did the relatively small numbers of Gethenians (96): mass violence requires masses. Also, Gethenian technology, like that of the Chinese, developed at a slow rate, their Machine Age having started up 'gradually, without any industrial revolution, without any revolution at all. Winter hasn't achieved in thirty centuries what Terra once achieved in thirty decades. Neither has Winter ever paid the price that Terra paid' (*LHD* 99; ch. 8).[166] No industrial revolution suddenly and blatantly put a nation far enough ahead of the climate that warfare made sense. No industrial revolution made one Gethenian nation suddenly superior to another technologically. And androgyny by itself wouldn't preclude war any more than the production of a subspecies of XYY, testosterone-crazed supermales would guarantee war; warfare is not an instinct or behavior. As Konrad Lorenz argued in *On Aggression* (1966), war is an institution (275). Still, human beings are biological creatures, and (spiritual matters aside?) everything we are and do has to have biological bases. On Gethen, the biological basis for the cultural constellation that has prevented war—and made for a rather good place in Karhide—has been androgyny. Everything in Gethenian society 'is shaped to fit the somer-kemmer cycle' of sexual latency and rut. 'Room is made for sex, plenty of room; but a room, as it were, apart,' as the Ekumenical Investigator Ong Tot Oppong, initially saw and elegantly expressed it. 'The society of Gethen, in its daily functioning and in its continuity, is without sex' (93; ch. 7). And where there is sex among Gethenian humans, one's role might be female or it might be male; the Masculine and the Feminine, as defining categories, simply wouldn't exist—and the 'tendency to dualism that pervades human thinking' and is reinforced by Female/Male divisions is somewhat 'lessened, or changed, on Winter' (94).[167]

---

[165] 'Lao Tse: V,' quoted as the headnote to *LoH* ch. 8 (110).
[166] For the 'leisurely rate' of Chinese technological advance, see Needham, 'Time and Knowledge' 120.
[167] Human biology includes more than sex., and the biological bases of dualism go beyond sex. Our bodies are far more bilaterally symmetrical than radially sym-

Le Guin makes her points about gender, violence, and war in *Left Hand* by explicitly foregrounding background and textualizing subtexts. In *Planet of Exile* (1966), Le Guin had divided her narration among three point-of-view characters; but in *The Left Hand of Darkness* we not only have Ai and Estraven getting different chapters but the remainder going to still other voices, making explicit a good deal of what is usually implicit background and subtext. Of twenty chapters, Ai gets ten (50%), Estraven gets four (20%), and miscellaneous others get six (30%)—plus the appendix on 'The Gethenian Calendar and Clock' (302-04). Of the 'other voices,' two of the chapters are identified as tales (chs. 2 and 9), and one as a story (ch. 4). Of interest to me here are the scientific report on 'The Question of Sex,' the theological piece 'On Times and Darkness,' and 'An Orgota Creation Myth' of great antiquity.

Each of these chapters provides a transition in, and interruption of, the plot. 'The Question of Sex' (ch. 7) is central in the section getting Genly Ai to Orgoreyn and the Orgota capital of Mishnory—and rather more abruptly getting the exiled Estraven safely to Orgoreyn (chs. 6-8). 'On Time and Darkness' (ch. 12) is central to the sequence of chapters moving Ai from Mishnory to the labor camp 'Down on the Farm' and then his rescue by Estraven and their movement 'To the Ice' (chs. 10-15). 'An Orgota Creation Myth' (ch. 17) is told as Estraven and Ai move 'Between Drumner and Dremegole,' a geologically active area, and then 'On the Ice' on their way home to Karhide and the resolution of the plot (chs. 16-19).

I will state directly what I see as Le Guin's answer to The Question of Sex, and Violence and War—her basic answer from 1969 to at least 1985. As on Joanna Russ's Whileaway (1972, 1975), or among Suzy McKee Charnas's Riding Women in *Motherlines* (1978), violence is indeed possible in worlds without men, but it will tend to be direct, emotional, personal. What is specifically *man*ly is not violence but warfare, which tends to be indirect, unemotional, impersonal: indeed, ideally, *professional* (see Arendt 62 n. 83).[168] Alternatively, zealous soldiers, fighting for a cause, are willing to kill huge masses of total strangers as a means to the end of the kingdom of God or utopia or some abstract, ideal—whatever—so long as their zeal lasts. What is necessary for war is the mobilization of a large numbers of men to do the job of killing large numbers of strangers. For modern total war it is necessary to mobilize at least one entire society.

In 'The Domestication of Hunch' (ch. 5), Genly Ai observes that Prime Minister Tibe

---

metrical, and this make it easy to think of left vs. right and on the one hand and the other; our 'encephalization' makes it easy to think of head vs. tail. Our constant struggle against gravity as upright terrestrial creatures makes it easy to think of up vs. down, higher and lower. Etc. For the necessary duality of I/Other, see *LHD* 234; ch. 15 .

[168] As Stanley Kubrick drives home very effectively in *FULL METAL JACKET* (1987)—tap into a persecuted recruit's 'killer instinct,' and he'll kill his drill instructor, not total strangers half a world away.

was going to press Karhide's claim to...[the Sinoth Valley]: precisely the kind of action which, on any other world at this stage of civilization, would lead to war. But on Gethen nothing led to war. Quarrels, murders, feuds, forays, vendettas, assassinations, tortures and abominations, all these were in their repertory of human accomplishments; but they did not go to war. They lacked, it seemed, the capacity to *mobilize*. They behaved like animals, in that respect; or like women. They did not behave like men, or ants. At any rate they never yet had done so. What I knew of Orgoreyn indicated that it had become, over the last five or six centuries, an increasingly mobilizable society, a real nation-state. The prestige-competition, heretofore mostly economic, might force Karhide to emulate its larger neighbor, to become a nation instead of a family quarrel, as Estraven had said; to become, as Estraven had also said, patriotic. If this occurred the Gethenians might have an excellent chance of achieving the condition of war. (48-49; ch. 5)

This is clear enough, and it is a theme upon which Le Guin will work variations for at least the next sixteen years. For the variation in *The Left Hand of Darkness*, picture Karhide and Orgoreyn on the Great Continent of Gethen as a giant geographical Yin-Yang symbol, with Karhide more toward Yinnish darkness and Orgoreyn more in Yangish light (see Barbour, 'Wholeness' 167). Now picture the movement of Yin-Yang (and the Dao behind it) affecting—or effecting—obscurely all that happens on Gethen, right down to the Yin-Yang balance in Gethenian androgynes: '*On Gethen, the two polarities we perceive through our cultural conditioning as male and female are neither, and are in balance...and at the moment of the novel...[the balance] is wobbling precariously*' (Le Guin, 'Gender...Redux' 12); and this time, as the balance wobbles toward what we perceive as male, the civilized people of Gethen have the wherewithal for war.

Insofar as the question of warfare in *The Left Hand of Darkness* is a question of sex—which is a great amount—the placement of The Question of Sex' (ch. 7) is significant.

In chapter 5, 'The Domestication of Hunch,' Ai leaves Erhenrang for the countryside—in contemporary American terms he goes to see 'the *real* Karhide,' beyond the Karhidish equivalent of the Washington, DC, Beltway.[169] There Ai gets to experience Karhide at its economic roots, in its

---

[169] Cf. Havzhiva's trip to Hayawa Tribal Village in 'A Man of the People' (1995; in *FWF* 131 f.). Note the slogan in that story, 'All knowledge is local' and the conversation between Shevek and the Terran ambassador on the 'real' Urras in

anarchic splendor at the old capitol of Rer (53), and at its most impressive: the ancient Fastness of Otherhord, where he attends a Foretelling. Ai asks the Weaver and the foretelling group whether Gethen will be part of the Ekumen in five years.[170] The climax of the Foretelling shows Faxe, the Weaver, 'in the center of all darkness,' appearing as 'a woman, a woman dressed in light.... And she screamed aloud in terror and pain, "Yes, yes, yes!"' (66)—'not so much a prophecy as an observation,' and Ai is certain the 'observation' is correct (67).

Chapter 6 gives a less good impression of Karhide: it is Estraven's first turn at narrating, and we get the story of Estraven's escape from Karhide and entry 'One Way into Orgoreyn.'

And then, chapter 7, the field notes of Ong Tot Oppong on Gethenian sexuality, giving us a large expository lump and repeating that the Gethenians 'have never yet had what one would call a war. They kill one another readily by ones and twos; seldom by tens or twenties; never by hundreds or thousands' and asking, Why? (96). One possible reason: the Ancient Hainish colonizers had planned it that way, deliberately setting up a fairly elegant experiment in which they seeded Gethen with normally competitive humans but made them androgynes. But the experiment got sloppy over time when the Hainish had to withdraw—and a new ice age came on.

Finally, as I'm dividing the chapters: chapter 8, significantly called 'Another Way into Orgoreyn.' The literal meaning of this title refers to Genly Ai's physical movement from Karhide to Orgoreyn—important in the symbolic journey in the novel. More important, though, is Ai's description of the Karhide he's leaving and the Karhide coming into being under the regency of Tibe during King Argaven's pregnancy (100-01).[171] Karhide is not a nation, not 'a social unit, a mobilizable entity' (100); Tibe intends to make it one. Besides acting in the Sinoth Valley, Tibe propagandizes the people. Somewhat oddly for a Gethenian politician, Tibe did not talk about *shifgrethor*: 'personal pride or prestige,' etymologically and metaphorically, the shadow one casts, related to one's status, one's

---

TD ch. 11. For a real-world anthropologist on one's *not* finding 'the real article' of real-world cultures, see Heilman, xv-xix.

[170] Foretelling involves nine people, with Ai perceived as the tenth when the empathic and 'paraverbal forces at work' draw him into the circle. Cf. 'Nine Lives,' the Nine Masters of Roke—or ten with the Archmage and the Doorkeeper (*WE*)—and the ten members of the expedition in 'Vaster than Empires and More Slow.' My best guess for 'nine' is a reference to Chuang Tzu's association of water, the abyss, and nine (ch. 7). Le Guin wrote me, 'I just *like* the number 9' and points out that nine is 'one of the central organizing devices in *ACH*, too.' In addition to the number of human fingers, and toes (hence, base-10 for our numbers), ten is the number of days in a Chinese week (Needham, 'Time and Knowledge' 100), an Anarresti decad (*TD*), and a *décade* in the French Republican calendar.

[171] Two women in my classes have stated strongly that they would not like gender-free titles and pronouns in *LHD* and the commentary thereon if that meant losing lines like 'The king was pregnant' (*LHD* 100) and 'unless he's pregnant' ('Gender...Redux' *DEW* 12; see italicized revised text, top of 13).

clout.[172] Tibe 'was deliberately avoiding talk of shifgrethor because he wished to rouse emotions of a more elemental, uncontrollable kind, He wanted to stir up something which the whole shifgrethor pattern was a refinement upon a sublimation of. He wanted his hearers to be frightened and angry.... He talked a great deal about Truth also, for he was, he said, 'cutting down beneath the veneer of civilization.'' Ai denies that there is a veneer of civilization, denies 'that civilization, being artificial, is unnatural: that it is the opposite of primitiveness.... Of course there is no veneer, the process is one of growth,' perhaps, I'll add, part of *human* evolution, 'and primitiveness and civilization are degrees of the same thing. If civilization has an opposite, it is war'—and the peoples of Gethen had long ago chosen against war. Tibe wants a nation-state to rule, one like Orgoreyn, an 'efficient centralized state,' and s/he wants one now. One 'means of mobilizing people rapidly and entirely is with a new religion; none was handy; he would make do with war' (102-03), although, of course, Tibe lacks both the word and a firm concept of what a war might be.

Tibe's way into Orgoreyn—toward a modern authoritarian or totalitarian state—is through the human Shadow: a sense of national superiority, hatred of the alien, fear disguised as courage, brutal anger rhetorically transmuted into something noble (102; ch. 8). But what justifies such a poor opinion of Orgoreyn, and how did Orgoreyn get to be what Orgoreyn is?

Politically, Orgoreyn is soon revealed as a nasty blend of oligarchy and bureaucracy, with a typically nasty secret police. Also, older readers might superimpose over the struggle between Karhide and Orgoreyn a historical model. Tibe comes across like Joseph Goebbels, the head of Nazi propaganda for the Third Reich. If that makes Karhide parallel to Hitler's Germany (1933-45), then Orgoreyn can be cast as Stalin's USSR—and the Stalinist-Russia analogy holds when we finally see Orgoreyn, starting with the scene of docile people imprisoned by their own government in a cellar (111-112; ch. 8). Still, younger readers would probably do better seeing Tibe as a more generic demagogue, scaring the hell out of the people and making them feel brave to go off killing strangers with whom they have no quarrel.

How Orgoreyn got that way is handled by a couple of very direct satirical maneuvers and one subtle one. The Orgoreyn section of *The Left Hand of Darkness* is 'Conversations in Mishnory' from Genly Ai's point of view and 'Soliloquies in Mishnory' from Estraven's journal (chs. 10-11), and then 'Down on the Farm,' where Ai recounts his capture, transportation, and imprisonment in the Orgota forced labor camp, and 'The Escape,' a straight narration by Estraven of his rescue of Ai (chs. 13-14).

---

[172] In all its complexity, shifgrethor is similar to 'face' in Japanese and, more so, Chinese usage; see Mao, esp. 460-61. Since shifgrethor is significant to Gethenians in somer, not kemmer—i.e., when they are not sexed—it is presented as relevant for humans generally, not just for men or women: humans as status-seeking, face-maintaining female and/or male animals.

The first satirical move is having the Orgoreyn sequence begin with Ai in a cellar with Orgota refugees with no papers, then betrayed in tidy, sunny, Mishnory, sent to prison in a slow truck full of other prisoners, and then end up the sequence getting rescued from death in the 'Pulefen Commensality Third Voluntary Farm and Resettlement Agency.' Now, in 'The Ones Who Walk Away from Omelas,' we probably should accept the festival and the good sex, good drugs, and good life as real and significant, and balance against them the child kept miserable in the room. Le Guin balances the good of Omelas against the evil done to the child. She is not so fastidious in *The Left Hand of Darkness*. As George Slusser said in 1976, the real reality of Orgoreyn is the dark cellar and the truck (24)—and slow death in the labor camp.

The subtle maneuver is preparing for the opening of the sequence (Ai's strained meeting with Estraven in Mishnory) with a visit to Ai from Estraven's ex-kemmering, Foreth, who wants Ai to bring money to Estraven in exile (104-06; ch. 8). Foreth asks Ai if Ai feels in Estraven's debt for Estraven's having supported Ai's mission. Ai replies that he does feel indebted, 'in a sense. However, the mission I am on overrides all personal debts and loyalties.' Foreth responds, 'If so...it is an immoral mission.' Foreth not only presents a view that might be expressed by 'an Advocate of the Ekumen,' but formulates a basic principle of Le Guin's moral system. The lesson here is that no abstract Mission, no transcendent project, should override the personal. To get people to allow loyalty to abstractions, particularly patriotic loyalty to the abstract State, routinely to override personal obligations, requires that they be rigorously trained in abstraction and conditioned to place value upon transcendence.

The second satiric move is the placement of chapter 12, 'On Time and Darkness.' In chapter 12 we find an excerpt from 'The Sayings of Tuhlme the High Priest, *a book of the Yomesh Canon, composed in North Orgoreyn about 900 years ago.*' In chapter 13 we have Genly Ai's arrest and mistreatment in Orgoreyn. Preeminently, we have the 'Voluntary Farm,' with its grotesquely euphemistic name, chemical spaying/castration of its prisoners, and slow attempted murder of Genly Ai—and, for Le Guin, or any anarchist, the central damning fact of the 'Farm' as a prison. The juxtaposition of 'On Time and Darkness' and 'Down on the Farm' (chs. 12/13) is significant. The juxtaposition is a *post hoc*: After this, therefore because of this—a fallacy in logic but a standard device in literature. Accept the world-view of the Yomesh, the chapter order implies, accept their ideas on time, darkness, and epistemology, and you are only a few hundred years away from a mobilizable, patriotic Orgota State, the obscenity of the Sarf (the Orgota secret police), and prison farms.

From Goss at the Otherhord Fastness, we have learned that the Lord of Shorth had forced a group of Foretellers to attempt to answer the unanswerable question, '*What is the meaning of life?*' The Weaver of that Foretelling group was Meshe (60; ch. 5), and, according to the Yomeshta, the result of trying to answer that question was Meshe's enlightenment, Meshe's being placed 'in the Center of Time':

> In answering the Question of the Lord of Shorth, in the moment of the Seeing, Meshe saw all the sky as if it were all one sun. Above the earth and under the earth all the sphere of the sky was bright as the sun's surface, and there was no darkness.[173] For he saw not what was, nor what will be, but what is....
>
> Darkness is only in the mortal eye, that thinks it sees, but sees not. In the Sight of Meshe there is no darkness.
>
> Therefore those who call upon the darkness ['the Handdarata'] are made fools of and spat out from the mouth of Meshe, for they name what is not, calling it Source and End.[174]
>
> There is neither source nor end, for all things are in the Center of Time.... There is neither darkness nor death, for all things are, in the light of the Moment and their end and their beginning are one.
>
> One center, one seeing, one law, one light.[175] Look now into the Eye of Meshe! (163-64; ch. 12).

Such a look, Le Guin has warned us, may be very dangerous: 'Apollo, the god of light, of reason, of proportion, harmony, number—Apollo blinds those who press too close in worship. Don't look straight at the sun. Go into a dark bar for a bit and have a beer with Dionysios, every now and then' (Introd. to 1976 edition).[176] And the problem is not with just rationalist, pagan Apollo. God's first line in the Jewish creation myth is 'Let there be light'—and God sees 'the light was good' (Genesis 1.3-4); and in The Revelation to John we learn that in the New Jerusalem 'there shall be no night' (21.25).

If it were true that we really did live in a world without darkness, without shadows, with total certainty, action would be impossible; life would be impossible. So Faxe, the Weaver, who knows so much about the 'eternal present,' has told Genly Ai (71; ch. 5). So we see during the days of

---

[173] Le Guin has a note to the all-bright sky referring to 'one of the theories used to support the expanding-universe hypothesis.' See Whitrow's comments in *Voices* that a theory of an expanding universe 'enables us to resolve Oblers' paradox concerning the background brightness of the universe' (572).

[174] Note the Handdarata blessing 'Praise then darkness and Creation unfinished' (*LHD* 246; ch. 18). In 1990, Le Guin provided the balancing Handdarata blessing: 'Praise also the light, and creation unfinished' ('Shobies' Story' [*FIS* 99]); note also, 'In the act of creation praise' ('Coming of Age in Karhide' [481, 482]).

[175] Cf. the triplets: Justinian's 'One empire, one church, one law' (Swain 2.613), and the Nazi slogan 'One people, one Leader, one empire.'

[176] Students looking up 'Dionysios': look under 'Dionysos' or 'Dionysus,' and note that there is more to him than just 'the god of wine and revelery,' as my desk dictionary identifies him. Dionysos is one of 'The Two Great Gods of Earth,' the male complement to the goddess Demeter (see Hamilton, ch. 2).

white weather, when Ai and Estraven 'need the shadows in order to walk' on the Ice (260-61, ch. 18 ; 265-67, ch. 19). The Yomesh philosophy gives its followers a pernicious half-truth. With all that light they can think themselves certain of their knowledge, sure of their 'way.' They can know the ends and need not take much care in selecting means. As Eric Hoffer argues in *The True Believer*, such certainty is the foundation of the fanaticism of True Believer leaders and followers (75-82). With perfect rationality and calm, they can order and cary out atrocities. Unlike Terran anarchists and Le Guin's Ekumen—and opposed to Le Guin's urDaoists, the Handdarata—such people readily adopt 'the doctrine that the end justifies the means' (259; ch. 18 [see Berkman 113]).

'Meshe is the Center of Time.... And in the Center there is no time past and no time to come.... The life of every man is in the Center of Time, for all were seen in the Seeing of Meshe, and are in his Eye.... Our doing is his Seeing: our being his Knowing' (162-63; ch. 12).[177] For Meshe and all who see through his 'Eye,' there is no change: no history and no sequency; all is simultaneous.[178] Being and doing are not balancing and reinforcing aspects of mortal life but are conflated together in the purely rational Seeing and Knowing of Meshe. Such a view can greatly simplify politics. Given such a vision, people can set up a rational, orderly, efficient state, such as Orgoreyn. Anyone with views differing from Truth does not deserve to be heard. Anyone who cannot or will not fit into such a perfect institution is obviously a 'defective' or an enemy of the people. Such a view of things, Le Guin suggests, is a step toward the dark cellar in which 'nameless' people are imprisoned by their fellow citizens, and accept their imprisonment without complaint or protest (111-12; ch. 8)—and toward the Sarf truck, where light has again given way to darkness and the perfect 'commensality' is achieved: where naked prisoners have nothing left but their pain and a terrible kindness and merge into 'one entity occupying one space' (170; ch. 13 [see also 109; ch. 8]). Most emphatically, we move toward the Voluntary Farm, with its 'excess of light,' where 'social purpose' is achieved through the dehumanization of one's fellow human beings (174, 176-77; ch. 13).[179]

---

[177] 'Meshe is in the Center of Time,' includes Meshe's having 'lived on earth thirty years' up to the Seeing, 'and after it he lived on earth again thirty years': cf. Dante character in the *Inferno* opening his story with 'In the middle of the journey of our life I came to myself in a dark wood where the straight way was lost' (I.1). Le Guin might have advised Dante to stay in the woods.

[178] For my discussion of Time in *LHD* I am esp. indebted to Nudelman, 'Approach to the Structure....' See also Fraser, 'Note Relating to a Paradox of the Temporal Order,' *Voices* 524-25, and its hypothesizing a world of logic and being, where 'the unexpected cannot happen.' My discussion of chapter placement in *LHD* is from my "Praise then Darkness" essay, which I wrote while consulting with Jenkins on her essay on *LHD* for our course in College Composition.

[179] For 'excess of light,' cf. the Ministry of Love as 'the place where there is no darkness' in Orwell's *Nineteen Eighty-Four* (24-25, 87, 147, 189).

In *The Left Hand of Darkness*, Le Guin has used not merely *post hoc ergo propter hoc* but also but the subtle, satiric, indirect 'proof' of reduction to the grotesque. If Meshe is correct, Le Guin strongly implies, then we have no logical complaint if the Orgota embody Meshe's Truth in their New Epoch regime. If the New Epoch regime sickens us, we would do well to reject Meshe's view as a species of dangerous insanity.

* * * * * * *

The center of *The Left Hand of Darkness*, however, is not in Orgoreyn or Karhide but on the Ice between the two countries. It is time then to turn to the Ice and to the straightforward fact that chapter 17, 'An Orgota Creation Myth' falls in the center of the story of the winter journey, in the balance point of chapters 15-16 and 18-19. In these chapters, Le Guin brings together in a series of significant juxtapositions her views on Being and becoming, patriotism and friendship (and treason), manhood and humanness, time and darkness (rightly understood), epistemology, ecology, evolution, death, pain, and ethics.

The origins of the Orgota creation myth '*are prehistorical; it has been recorded in many forms. This very primitive version is from a pre-Yomesh written text.....*' (237; headnote to ch. 17). The creation myth, then, is part of the common cosmological heritage of all Gethen. For my purposes, there are four significant statements in it: (1) The ice-shape that says 'I bleed' creates from the excrement of the sun 'the hills and valleys of the earth.' (2) The ice-shape that says 'I sweat' creates in one act 'trees, plants, herbs and grains of the field, animals, and men.' (3) The ice-shapes sacrifice themselves to produce milk to wake the sleeping humans. (4) The entire last paragraph:

> Each of the children born to them [the Gethenian first parents] had a piece of darkness that followed him about wherever he went by daylight. Edondurath [the mother] said, 'Why are my sons followed thus by darkness?' His kemmering said, 'Because they were born in the house of flesh [produced by Endondurath's murders of his/her later-waking siblings and then piling up the bodies], therefore death follows at their heels. They are in the middle of time. In the beginning there was the sun and the ice, and there was no shadow. In the end, when we are done, the sun will devour itself and shadow will eat light, and there will be nothing left but the ice and the darkness. (239)

In creating hills and valleys, especially if we imagine the hills in sunlight and valleys in shade, 'I bleed' has created two of the most primitive manifestations of Yang and Yin. In creating all living things in one act and from one source (soil plus sea-water), 'I sweat' has established the interconnectedness of the web of life, including (in a way that would please Luz in *Eye of the Heron*) making people of mud. In sacrificing themselves, in allowing the sun to melt them to form milk, the three ice-shapes enact a little allegory of the sacrifice involved in the rise of consciousness. Human consciousness, since the myth informs us that '...milk is drunk by the children of men alone and without it they will not wake to life' (238). And the words to Edondurath of the nameless 'younger brother, the father' point our way to the proper understanding of shadows and shifgrethor and several key images and themes in the journey on the ice.

In terms of this myth, we can say in general that the relatively young doctrine of the Yomeshta manages to get just about everything wrong; the really old-time religion of the Handdarata not only manage to understand the myth correctly but to improve upon it. As Tuhlme, the Yomesh High Priest, tells us, the Handdarata recognize that the darkness is 'Source and End,' that the world will not only fall into darkness at the end of time but also arose out of darkness in the beginning. In Daoist terms, the Handdarata recognize that beyond the Named Dao (Being) there is the darkness of the Unnamed Dao, Unbeing, the Void, in a continuing dynamic of creation and dissolution.[180]

The Yomeshta do not err in valuing human consciousness, the consciousness for which the ice-shapes sacrificed themselves. Their error comes from valuing consciousness, the light, exclusively, and in failing to see that consciousness has its costs. If all we were were pure being, like the ice, then we would be eternal. To differentiate into individuality, to awake into consciousness, however, is to enter time, to become mortal. And to be mortal is to be part of the web of life. Here Meshe and his followers make their gravest error: they are blind to humanity's place as part of the scheme of things, blind to the true significance of our living 'in the middle of time.'[181]

Estraven comments that 'The Yomeshta would say that man's singularity is his divinity.' Ai replies, 'Lords of the Earth, yes. Other cults on other worlds have come to the same conclusion. They tend to be cults of dynamic, aggressive, ecology-breaking cultures. Orgoreyn is the pattern, in its way; at least they seem bent on pushing things around' (233; ch. 16). On the other hand, the Handdarata, as Estraven tell us, 'are less aware of the gap between men and beasts, being more preoccupied with the like-

---

[180] For the Last Days in the Orgota Creation Myth, cf. image in Norse vision of Ragnarök of the sun darkening and stars falling from sky (Hamilton, *Mythology* 313). For Ragnarök, creation, and dissolution in D. H. Lawrence—for a highly intriguing comparison and contrast with Le Guin—see Erlich, 'Catastrophism and Coition....'

[181] In commenting on A. L. Kroeber's collection of *Yurok Myths*, the folklorist Alan Dundes comments that 'the 'middle' in [the] Yurok worldview,' esp. as reflected in the myths and tales Kroeber collected, is of 'paramount importance,' as both a 'place of distinction' and 'also a place of danger' (xxxxvi). Cf. use of 'central' in Pravic language on Anarres in *TD*; contrast Urrasti and Terran use of 'higher' for 'better' (12; ch. 1).

nesses, the links, the whole of which living things are a part'—and then Estraven goes on to quote Tormer's Lay, the 'source' of the title for *The Left Hand of Darkness* (233-34; ch. 16). The Yomeshta, seeing humans as 'Lords of the Earth,' misinterpret totally the basic fact of human existence. We are indeed in 'the Center of Time'—but that means that we are mortal, subject to pain and death.[182] Our mortality is the shadow that follows us, and it is that shadow that gives substance to our lives.[183] Moreover, each of us (even clones) must die individually, moving beyond the touch of our closest loves; and, as stressed particularly in *The Dispossessed*, it is that loneliness and pain of mortality that moves us to join with others. And in joining with other people (and with the world), we can perhaps move through pain to joy—or at least reduce the pain enough to remain sane.[184]

* * * * * * *

The themes of the Orgota creation myth are worked out and expanded in the winter's journey in *The Left Hand of Darkness* chapters 15-16 and 18-19. These five chapters, taken together, give us an insight into the ethical norms of *Left Hand* and of Le Guin's early canon in general.

Chapter 15 is narrated by Genly Ai and is parallel to the first part of Estraven's journal in chapter 16; the rest of chapter 16 is parallel to Ai's narration in chapter 18. The sequence begins with Ai's awakening and seeing Estraven 'as he was'—really *seeing* Estraven, in a kind of James Joycean 'epiphany,' especially seeing Estraven's face (200; ch. 15).[185] The movement of the sequence is toward Ai's and Estraven's acceptance of each other and their touching in what may be the only way possible for them (or possibly for Le Guin at that stage of her development) through love and through mindspeech, not sexually.[186] Ai's vision of Estraven leads to his growing insight into Estraven's wholeness (202 and 203). Estraven is like a Daoist sage, like Ogion in the Earthsea series, George Orr in *The Lathe of Heaven*—or like Faxe of the Handdarata: the simplicity of an uncarved block, the completeness of an animal (71; ch. 5). To be whole requires be-

---

[182] The First Noble Truth of the Buddha is the Truth of Suffering: 'Existence is pain' (*Ency. of Religion* 'Buddhist Terminology,' 'Buddhism' I [p. 95]).
[183] Cf. Ged's Shadow in *WE*, esp. 197-81; ch. 10, recapitulated *Tehanu* 72; ch. 6.
[184] See Remington's discussion of 'The Other Side of Suffering.' See below, the Athsheans in *WWF* and the Kesh in *ACH* as sane societies.
[185] For the continuing importance of faces in Le Guin, see the descriptions in *Tehanu*, esp. those of Flint and Spark, and in *TD* Shevek's line at Vea's party on Urras, 'Everything is beautiful, here. Only not the faces. On Anarres nothing is beautiful, nothing but the faces' (184; ch. 7). In John Keats's *The Fall of Hyperion*, 'those 'who feel the giant agony of the world' and 'Labour for mortal good'...'seek no wonder but the human face'' (I.162 f., qtd. Duerksen 15).
[186] For the significance of touch and pain, see Remington, 'A Touch of Difference' and 'The Other Side of Suffering.' For sex and gender in this scene, see Russ, 'Image' 39. For the lack of sex between the always-male Genly Ai and Estraven in kemmer, see Lamb and Veith 224-31.

ing part, and to be as whole as Estraven requires being in close touch with the universe. Genly Ai surprises us a bit by telling us that Estraven saw Estraven 'so slow-thinking' s/he 'had to guide his acts by a general intuition of which way his 'luck' was running, and that this intuition rarely failed him...the gift is perhaps not strictly or simply one of Foretelling, but is rather the power of seeing (if only for a flash) *everything at once*: seeing whole' (203-04; ch. 15).

With such temporary vision, as opposed to Meshe's permanent Enlightenment, Estraven can see (feel?) what s/he must do, right down to he 'vile crime' of theft, when s/he and Ai need food (205; ch. 15). Even so, Ai will later break custom and teach Estraven mindspeech and call his ship before he can be sure the Karhidish government will allow it to land in safety.[187] All we can get is a 'general intuition' of how our 'luck' runs, of how the great wheel turns, but following this intuition, against convention or even law, is of crucial importance. It is how noncontemplatives can find the Dao and not have to depend upon abstract theories. If we deceive ourselves in the Yomesh fashion and hold that the wheel doesn't turn and that we can know with certainty what *is*, then it is just a step to a masculinist, Platonic, Apollonian True Belief of the sort that Le Guin shows us in Orgoreyn. But there is another way to go, a more utopian possibility shown in Estraven in him/herself and in the love that develops between Estraven and Ai (see Slusser 26).

When Estraven takes up the narration in chapter 16, the first point of discussion is Time and exile (221-22). Disjunction in time has alienated Ai from his homeworld. This alienation establishes the esthetic appropriateness for Ai's name as 'a cry of pain' (229; ch. 16).[188] Disjunction in time, then, leads to isolation and pain; and, as in 'Nine Lives' and *The Dispossessed*, and, allegorically, in *The Farthest Shore*, pain leads to the possibility of human touch, relationship (Remington, '...Suffering'). More immediately, the timejumping discussion leads to a couple of brief allusions to geological evolution and from there to organic evolution and the contrast and relationship between singularity and isolation. Out on the Ice, Estraven and Ai are both 'singular, isolate,' cut off from their societies and social rules. Estraven writes that they 'are equals at last, equal, alien, alone' (ch. 16, p. 232). Ai speaks of the 'isolation and loneliness,' of themselves and of Estraven's species. He is especially impressed that the Gethenians developed a theory of evolution given the 'unbridgeable gap' between them and 'the lower animals' (233; ch. 16). This mention of evolution

---

[187] For the importance of telepathy in Le Guin's early works, see Darko Suvin's 'Parables of De-Alienation: Le Guin's Widdershins Dance' (269).
[188] Ai is both envoy and exile: see Spencer. For 'Ai!' as an emotional exclamation, cf. and contrast A. L. Kroeber's explicit exclusion from language animal sounds and 'a man's moan' (§20, 'Animal Communication,' *Biology and Race* rpt. 41). See also Abberkam's 'crying like an animal' in 'Betrayals' in *FWF* (11-12),

moves the discussion on to the differences between the Yomeshta and the Handdarata on ecology, and then on to Tormer's Lay.

Time and loneliness, evolution and ecology, wholeness and dualism, '*myself* and *the other*,' 'I and Thou'—all come together in chapter 16 and are repeated in part in chapters 18 and 19 (from Ai's point of view). In chapter 18, Ai looks upon Estraven in kemmer—in kemmer necessarily as a woman, since Ai is a 'Pervert': in his case always male. Ai looks at this woman and does not deny the (now) obvious: 'And I saw then again, and for good, what I had been afraid to see...in him: that he was a woman as well as a man. Any need to explain the sources of that fear vanished with the fear; what I was left with was, at last, acceptance of him as he was.' A few minutes later they consummate their love by symbolically marrying, communicating in mindspeech (248-53).

When they are close to Karhide, to home, Ai will symbolize his union with Estraven, without totally realizing it, in the figure of Yin and Yang: '*Light is The Left Hand of Darkness*...how did it go?[189] Light, dark. Fear, courage. Cold, warmth. Female, male. It is yourself, Therem. Both and one. A shadow on snow' (267; ch. 19). Yin-Yang also symbolizes Estraven and Ai—Female and Male when Estraven was in kemmer, two human beings who have reached enough unity in themselves to be able to balance each other, and thereby achieve further unity, wholeness, and balance (Barbour).

In the central philosophical chapters of *The Left Hand of Darkness*, Le Guin posits a universe based on nonbeing, Darkness—in Western mythology, Chaos and Old Night. Out of this ultimate Darkness comes the primal Light and the Ice; out of nonbeing comes Being, the Dao that can be called at least, 'the Way,' the world of the eternal now. Out of Being come shadows and balance, Yin-Yang: the world of becoming, of 'Mutabilitie,' life, death, history, process, change, and evolution.[190] As Ged has assured Arren in *The Farthest Shore*, there is no danger in the flux itself including the evolution and acts of unconscious species (66; ch. 4, 'Magelight'). The only potential problem is with conscious creatures, with human beings (cf. *LoH* 161; ch. 10). We do have moments in which we can see or feel past the flux to the roots of Being, and these moments are important: they are the moments that allow us individual wholeness and the brief fullness of the I-Thou relationship. These are, however, only moments, and we have neither the power nor the right to take a subjectively eternal moment and turn it into a permanent insight into the workings of the Whole. We have no right to attempt to freeze or deny time and stop change—to deny flux and death and darkness and attempt to set up a New Epoch society of (anti-)utopian perfection.[191] We also have no right to try to push things around

---

[189] Cf. *Chuang Tzu* ch. 22, in Giles trans. 'Light is born of darkness' (213).
[190] For evolution and revolution in Le Guin's work, see Suvin, 'Parables' 271.
[191] For 'the collision between the processes of history and utopianizing,' see Theall 261.

and try to consciously *force* change, to force the world, and other people, to obey our wills.[192]

Which brings us back to the questions of war, violence, aggression, utopia, dystopia, and sex.

No Gethenian 'is quite so thoroughly 'tied down'...as women, elsewhere, are likely to be—psychologically or physically'—by childbearing and child raising. More important for my concerns, no Gethenian is 'quite so free as a free male anywhere else' (93-94; ch. 7 [see Russ, 'Image' 39]). Anyway, no Gethenian is as free as a privileged Terran male from what Simone de Beauvoir discusses, quite negatively and at length, as the *immanence* of the life of women. Gethenians cannot give themselves totally to masculine transcendent projects because normal Gethenians go into kemmer every month (more or less), and all who are healthy have the privilege and risk of pregnancy, birthing, and nursing. Less so than Hainish-normal women but much more than Hainish-normal men, Gethenians are embedded in the world. And when you are *in* the world, it is hard to picture pushing it around. Gethenian anatomy and physiology did not determine the philosophy of the Handdarata—but it made it easy to *think* that philosophy. And it took someone 'blinded by the light,' Meshe, to think transcendence. And with transcendence, large-scale violence is possible. People can then think abstractions like The State, The Nation, National Honor—abstractions that dwarf our puny little existences and are worthy of dying for (see Trumbo, ch. 10). People can then dream up schematic utopias and push around others to try to build them.[193]

The Yomeshta started playing such a wide-scale push-and-shove game some 2202 years before the action of *The Left Hand of Darkness*. But from their most ancient times the Gethenians have known they 'were born in the house of flesh' and 'death follows at their heels' (239; ch. 17); they know they are mortal and part of the world. And they are reminded of the flesh frequently. They may, indeed, be mobilizable for war. Tibe almost succeeds; the Orgota have established a real nation-state. But their violence is, so to speak, of the flesh, and it proves hard to idealize it and turn it toward warfare. More immediately important, there is the underlying basis for Karhidish culture in the views of the Handdara, especially as embodied in their 'Old Men' at the Fastnesses: 'It was an introverted life, self-sufficient, stagnant,' from Genly Ai's rather American kind of view, 'steeped in that singular 'ignorance' prized by the Handdarata and obedi-

---

[192] See Heinlein's Sgt. Zim on 'The purpose of war': to make your enemy 'do what you want him to do' (*Starship Troopers* 52; ch. 5); this is standard military doctrine. Cf. Bertrand de Jouvenel and Francoise Voltaire on Power (Arendt, *On Violence* 36; § I).

[193] There is one exception to Le Guin's dislike of transcendence, indicated by the opening of Susan Wood's 'Discovering Worlds': 'Ursula K. Le Guin makes maps' and the reference to the worlds 'she presents,' necessarily after first creating (Bloom 183). The privileged, transcendent overview of worlds Le Guin allows is that which authors can give readers. We have godlike vision of worlds we cannot affect.

ent to their rule of inactivity or noninterference. That rule,' like *wu wei* for the Daoists is the Handdarata *nusuth*: 'no matter,' which 'is the heart of the cult.' Ai won't 'pretend to understand it. But I began to understand Karhide better, after a halfmonth in Otherhord. Under that nation's politics and parades and passions runs an old darkness, passive, anarchic, silent, the fecund darkness of the Handdara' (60; ch. 5). Gethen may find an Ekumenical peace because war, however rationally conducted, is always somewhat mad, and deep in the culture of Gethen lies a very ancient sanity.

* * * * * * *

In most of her canon, ethical action for Le Guin moves toward contact with the Dao, multiple integrations, and away from hatred and war. Ethical action in Le Guin's early and middle works is fairly explicitly based upon a vision of the world that accepts both simultaneity and sequency, Being and becoming—and it is based upon a vision of reality that sees more than just one country or race or world. In short, ethical action—with a lot of luck—will move toward an Ekumen: a human society in which we can fulfill the Dao of Humanity and of nature—a society in which we can be fully human. A society, perhaps, in which we 'follow one law, only one, the law of human evolution' (*TD*, ch. 7, p. 177). A society in which we can consciously extend 'the evolutionary tendency inherent in Being' (*LHD*, ch. 15, p. 211). Which thought, after I finish discussing Le Guin's work of the 1960s, will take us to *The Dispossessed* (1974).

CRITIQUE: *Kulturkampf*-ing on the Left with *The Left Hand of Darkness*

In a 1979 review-essay for Salem Press, I called *The Left Hand of Darkness* 'one of the best literary works to come out of America in the late 1960's,' and I stand by that assessment, although I will now admit that I've read far too few of the works of the 1960s to make so broad a statement.

Le Guin's major SF novels are clearly teaching stories and political works, and one criterion for judging them is whether or not the politics are correct, not 'politically correct' but *correct*: right, decent. *The Left Hand of Darkness*, I think, is almost completely right: it promotes peace and freedom, and attacks betrayal, autocracy, warmongering, authoritarian oligarchy, and bureaucracy. It offers an elegant analysis of war as an institution. It is an excellent book for helping male readers accept women as adult human beings and helping girls and women readers learn that they can be active, competent adults.

Still, there was sufficient controversy of *The Left Hand of Darkness* that Le Guin wrote 'Is Gender Necessary?' (1976) and then reissued that essay with glosses as 'Is Gender Necessary? Redux' (1987).[194] I shall very briefly epitomize that debate so that younger readers will have some idea of what the fuss was about. This is important to do. First, the end of the twentieth century and beginning of the twenty-first seem likely to combine capitalist triumphalism with nationalistic and fundamentalist-religious reaction. In such a context, and from such a distance, liberal and radical feminists of the 1970s and 1980s may look indistinguishable. Second, Le Guin has accepted much of the criticism and has modified (arguably radicalized) her writing accordingly—and, simultaneously, the women's movement has moved to accommodate a range of feminisms and welcome more enthusiastically heterosexual, married, liberal feminists. Third, the debate is significant for changing definitions of, or at least changing focuses for, politics in the United States, as the saying 'The personal is the political' shifted from advice against hypocrisy—the injunction to live one's politics—to an assertion of the political dimensions of issues in people's personal lives, especially the lives of women.

Let's examine, then, the 1976 Ace re-issue of the text.

The front and back covers feature what seem to be ice versions of Caribbean androgyne statues rising out of a glacier. Such imagery was probably unexceptional with most feminists in 1976: in that year Pamela Sargent could hope that as more women write science fiction and 'as more men deal thoughtfully with their female characters,' SF will 'become a more androgynous and human literature' (13). By 1978, however, Mary Daly had argued against androgyny as an ideal (*Gyn/Ecology* 386-88 and passim; ch. 10). Few feminists moving into the 1980s would be offended by the cover, but after Daly's book, some might not be reassured. The front blurbs announce that *The Left Hand of Darkness* has won both the Hugo and Nebula Awards, as has Le Guin's *The Dispossessed*. Joanna Russ won her first Hugo for a novella in 1983, and women, other than Le Guin, did not start winning Hugos regularly under their own names until the 1980s. The situation is somewhat different for the Nebula—Russ's 'When It Changed' won the short story award in 1972, and Suzy McKee Charnas's 'Unicorn Tapestry' won in 1980—but the pattern is the same. Especially before 'James Tiptree, Jr.' revealed herself as Alice Sheldon in 1977, it could seem like the major awards in SF were won by Men, Misc. Women, and Ursula K. Le Guin (*The Ency. of S.F.* 'Hugo,' 'Nebula,' and

---

[194] Russ's criticisms in 'The Image of Women in Science Fiction' (1970) were early, respectful, and very sensible. Susan Wood says that 'The criticism ''that the Gethenians seem like men instead of menwomen'' was raised most notably by Polish critic Stanislaw Lem, in an essay published in the German journal *Quarber Merkur* and translated, revised, and published in the Australian fanzine *SF Commentary* 24 (November 1971),' to which Le Guin replied in *SF Commentary 26* (April 1972)—Introduction to part III of *LoN* (1979): 131. For a discussion of Le Guin as 'this female writer who' up to the mid-1980s 'seem[ed] to appeal to everyone—with the exception of feminists,' see Marleen Barr's 1987 review of Bittner's *Approaches*.... (112-14).

passim).[195] The dedication for *Left Hand* is 'For Charles, *sine quo non.*' The book is dedicated to Charles Le Guin, Ursula Le Guin's husband, 'without whom, not; an indispensable requisite or condition.' This is a loving and poetic thought, and readers familiar with Le Guin's work would recognize the valorizing of marriage, in a very wide sense. For a major relevant example, readers familiar with *The Lathe of Heaven* (1971) will know that little condemns Dr. William Haber as much as his being 'a lone wolf,' who wanted neither 'marriage nor close friendships,' prizing far too highly his unfettered will and 'independence' (112; ch. 8). A suspicious reader, however, less immersed in Le Guin's canon than in the historical moment of the late 1970s through the 1980s, might see in this dedication to Charles Le Guin an unfeminist degree of dependence.

Moving into the text, one might ask, 'Where are the women?' Genly Ai, whose point of view we get in half the chapters, is a man; and the Gethenians aren't women. They're androgynes, but they tend to come through, as Joanna Russ pointed out, as men: 'It is...a deficiency in the English language that these people must be called 'he' throughout, but put that together with the native hero's personal encounters in the book [primarily with Foreth], the absolute lack of interest in child-raising, the concentration on work, and what you have is a world of men.'[196] One might also ask, 'Where are the Black people?' since Genly Ai is as much «ethnized» White for most White readers as Estraven is gendered male, but Terran ideas of ethnicity are far less immediately relevant than gender on a planet of androgynes.

Coming to Chapter 5, we get the Foretelling at Otherhord, which includes, in a formal role, a 'Pervert.' That Hainish-Normal people, like us, would be perverts in Gethen is a very useful suggestion, but note the analogy Genly Ai uses. Gethenian perverts 'are not excluded from society, but they are tolerated with some disdain, as homosexuals are in many bisexual societies' (64). In the year 3850 CE, at the earliest, Genly Ai is aware of many societies in which homosexuals are contemned, behavior Ai might better know about from his 'criminal ancestors,' not from current events in the Ekumen. And Ai's use of 'bisexual' for sexually dimorphic (basically two-sexed) societies eliminates a handy word for people who like sex with both men and women, and may be seen as an ignoring of that category of

---

[195] The same could be said for literary criticism and prominence of reviews. E.g., in literary criticism, note the Special Le Guin issues of *SFS* (Nov. 1975) and of *Extrapolation* (Fall 1980), for two out of two of the major academic SF journals at the time in North America. For rough comparisons, note also the sheer physical size of Elizabeth Cummins Cogell's *Ursula K. Le Guin: A Primary and Secondary Bibliography* in the G. K. Hall series Masters of Science Fiction and Fantasy, compared with the volumes on other authors.
[196] Russ, 'Image' 39; see 'Gender...Redux' 15. See 'Winter's King' in the *WTQ* version, and, especially, 'Coming of Age in Karhide' for responses in fiction to these criticisms.

twentieth-century Terrans.[197] In the 1987 re-issue of 'Is Gender Necessary?', Le Guin notes correctly that she *'quite unnecessarily locked the Gethenians into heterosexuality. It is a naively pragmatic view of sex that insists that sexual partners must be of opposite sex!'* ('Gender...Redux' 14). At the Foretelling itself, the Pervert is a male; therefore the Celibate in kemmer becomes female, and their part of the Foretelling, with the Pervert importuning the Celibate for sex, can be read as one long scene of sexual harassment. And the rest of the people at the Foretelling perceive this extended interaction as intentional or inadvertent voyeurs (64, 65-66); and we, figuratively, watch them watching.

When we get to ch. 7, 'The Question of Sex,' we learn that Le Guin is serious about biology: the climax word in the chapter title isn't 'Gender'— a word from grammar in the 1960s, not politics—but *Sex*. Some feminists of the 1970s and 1980s may still have had qualms about biology: Betty Friedan and others worked hard in the 1950s and '60s attacking 'The Sexual Solipsism of Sigmund Freud' (ch. 5 of *Feminine Mystique*) and the whole idea that biology, if not strictly anatomy, was destiny. We also learn in this chapter that Karhidish culture privileges socially enforced heterosexual marriage—just with changes in who is male during kemmer this month and who is female. Good anarchist fashion, there are no legal marriages; but still, 'The whole structure of the Karhidish Clan-Hearths and Domains' is built upon the institution of monogamous marriage—as we are told by Ong Tot Oppong; we do not see the Clan Hearths at work in *Left Hand* (92; ch. 7). We do see them, in 'Coming of Age in Karhide' in 1995, where we see a hearth with a clan that does not vow kemmering and raises its children without fathers and, to a great extent, communally. Looking back, the Gethenians in 1969's *Left Hand of Darkness* do seem locked into what Adrienne Rich called 'compulsory heterosexuality,' and gays, lesbians, and the asexual (outside of the Handdarata) do not seem welcome.

Which gets us back to homosexuality and to the question, just why don't Ai and Estraven physically make love? They are intimate in their conversations on the Ice, and that comes through even in the audio cassette version of the story, where Le Guin cuts their mindspeech communication. Why not consummate their love in the flesh, however much they might feel at the moment that 'to meet sexually would be' for them 'to meet again as aliens' (248-49; ch. 18). The decision not to couple is plausible enough, but in context, Patricia Lamb and Diana Veith have found it suspect (229). If Lamb and Veith (et al.) are correct, Le Guin and her readers may be picturing Estraven as a man—even when she is in kemmer with Ai in their tent—and it might have been too daring, ca. 1969, to show or sug-

---

[197] Benford (17) contends there is 'unconscious condescension' toward Bedap in *TD*. Priority for Le Guin on homosexuality may go to Samuel R. Delany, whom Bedford cites, 'To Read *The Dispossessed*' in *The Jewel-Hinged Jaw* (1977). See also, though, Remington on Huru Pilotson's 'homosexual devotion to Jakob' Agat in *Planet of Exile* ('Other Side' 157). See below for Bedap in *TD*.

gest a quasi-homosexual sex scene (248-49; ch. 18). Le Guin, as critic, notes that the sex here '*would* have been heterosexual after all,' and as author says 'that it was ultimately an aesthetic choice' to avoid sex here. 'To 'marry' them' on the Ice 'would have defused the story.... The story-energy would have gone into *that* story; and it wasn't the one I had to tell' (personal communication).

More basic problems for some readers would be Le Guin's anarchism and Daoism. In 'Is Gender Necessary? Redux,' Le Guin notes that anarchy '*has historically been identified as female. The domain allotted to women—'the family,' for example—is the area of order without coercion, rule by custom not by force*' (12). Part of the radical feminist project has been resisting the traditional family precisely as an area of coercion and force, and many recent feminists have approved of using State power in support of that project. Additionally, feminists who wish to use the police powers of even the patriarchal State against rapists, pornographers, and other abusers of women, who wish to use the courts to force child support payments—such feminists should feel at least ambivalent about ideals of anarchy. And the Daoist ideal of unaction is going to seem very problematic to women who have resisted the Freudian idea of 'the male road of exploit' versus 'the female road of nurture,' the idea of 'feminine passive' and 'masculine active.'[198] Le Guin's Daoism privileges much of the traditional feminine over the masculine, but the basic Daoist categories of Yin and Yang themselves reinforce division into '*two polarities we perceive through our cultural conditioning*' that make for a mischievous dualism ('Gender...Redux' 12). And moving into the 1980s, poststructuralist academics would be increasingly upset by any theory involving binary opposites, seen as basic to 'the hierarchical relations that ground capitalist notions of power, desire, and value.'[199]

My last point on Daoism I will make quite tentatively.

Daoism is among the *least* 'totalizing' and most dynamic of belief systems, but it is a total system: all that is is produced by the action of the Dao and the waxing and waning of Yin and Yang. And in the 1970s and 1980s 'totalizing' and 'closed system' were used as criticisms by many academics in the humanities, sometimes even smear words. Total systems and binaries were stressed in Structuralist teaching of the 1950s and 1960s and were out of date and, postStructuralists argue, politically dangerous. A major symbol of Daoism and the controlling symbol of *The Left Hand of Darkness* is the Yin-Yang: a *closed* circle containing that most famous of binary (if dynamic) opposed pairs.

We should note, though, that Le Guin was well aware of the problem of total systems—she showed one very negatively among the Orgota—and did not limit herself to the Yin-Yang symbol. In *The Dispossessed* the image became the unclosed circle of The Circle of Life; in *Always Coming*

---

[198] Freudian formulations quoted by Friedan 120-21 (see all of ch. 5, 'The Sexual Solipsism of Sigmund Freud').
[199] Sobchack, *Screening Space* 302; see also 300; ch. 4.

Home, the organizing symbol is the hinged spirals of the heyiya-if. As Le Guin's character Stone Telling will put it in *Always Coming Home*: 'We must...remain mindful that our knowledge not close the circle, closing out the void' (29).

* * * * * * *

The Left Hand of Darkness, and other early works by Le Guin, may indeed be 'Feminism for Men,' as Craig and Diana Barrow say, but 'The Women Problem,' is, at its core, a problem among men. Moreover, *The Left Hand of Darkness* is also feminism for nonfeminist women, and the generation I teach includes many women who begin sentences 'I'm not a feminist, but....' *The Left Hand of Darkness* was pretty radical stuff for nonfeminist readers in 1969, and for the generation raised in the Reagan-Bush years—for students of mine who find The Song of Songs rather daring (with its very active female protagonist and extramarital love)—it is still radical. To rephrase, then, my own conclusion on this book: of the works with which I'm familiar, *The Left Hand of Darkness* is one of the best and most important novels to come out of America in the late 1960s.

A Note on Mindspeech

The condensation of *The Left Hand of Darkness* Le Guin herself read for the audio tape of the novel, and the play based on *Left Hand* both quietly dropped mindspeech, and Le Guin has not used the trope of mindspeech in her SF or fantasy since the late 1960s. She may prove me wrong by returning to it later, but I think I can suggest some straightforward reasons why we should note but not make too much of the lack of mindspeech after *Left Hand*.

Into the 1960s, those of us trained in scientific method could say that the proper attitude toward moderate claims of telepathy was an open-minded skepticism.[200] Moving into the 1970s, however, matters had changed. Several of the parapsychologist J. B. Rhine's 'best performers were ultimately exposed as frauds' ('ESP'); and it was getting around that the idea that we humans used only 10% of our brains—leaving a lot of spare capacity for telepathy and other paranormal skills—was based on seriously flawed research: anesthetized rats used perhaps 10% of their brains, not waking, undrugged humans, and the whole idea of percentage of usage was losing meaning as memory and other brain functions were thought of increasingly less in metaphors of filing cabinets and more in terms of holographic pictures. After the 1960s, telepathy and other psi powers became more and more the province of Scientology and others

---

[200] My basic information on Psi Powers and ESP in SF is from Nicholls and Stableford, 'ESP' and 'Psi' in the *Ency. of S.F.* and my own casual reading of SF and in *Extrapolation* and other journals.

who wished humans not to fulfill humanity but to *transcend* humanity, an occult association Le Guin seems unlikely to like.

Additionally, mindspeech had come across as a method of and metaphor for honest and direct, almost transparent communication, a communications system in which only the Shing—the Enemy—could lie. As literal telepathy became less plausible as a scientific concept, the metaphor of nonproblematic communication became more problematic. Men and women may speak 'In a Different Voice,' at least on ethical issues, as Carol Gilligan's book title suggests; and Gilligan may herself oversimplify by leaving out 'perspectives such as class, sexual orientation, race, and ethnicity'—i.e., to the extent she had women «speaking» in '*a* different voice,' from men, even just in terms of moral development, Gilligan herself may greatly oversimplify (Fraser and Nicholson 32). Communication between two individuals of the same gender may never be anywhere near transparent; even communication between two monozygotic siblings ('identical' twins et al.) may be far less than transparent; and so telepathy as a metaphor for unambiguous, true communication may include in itself a bit of a lie.

Perhaps more important, the period between the 1960s and 1990s saw what we might call «a crisis in relationship(s)» in the United States. Among my friends, anyway, a commonsensical and often-suggested first step toward resolving this crisis was summarized by joking about «a failure in telepathy». I.e., we mockingly assigned blame in a relationship to person 'B' for failing to read person 'A's' mind when person 'A' seemed to expect such mindreading. The joke was a reversal: people are *not* telepathic, and the fault here lay with person 'A' for not *speaking* his or her mind. Some people really are close enough to others that they can anticipate the other's thoughts and desires very accurately; most of us are not, and you *really* loved me, you'd know what I want without my having to tell you! came to be seen, by my group (and some recovery groups), as a useful joke but a very bad idea in earnest.[201] Further, anticipating *needs and desires* is a virtue for servants, and it became an increasingly open question whether men should be good chivalric servants to mistresses (as in courtly love), and increasingly objectionable to say that women should be socialized to be sensitive servants to anyone.

In any event, between the late1960s and the 1990s, telepathy as fact, symbol or metaphor became problematic in biology, linguistics, politics, and everyday human relations. And during this period Le Guin dropped mindspeech from her Hainish universe.

---

[201] This joke is used in Greg Howard's *Sally Forth* cartoon for Sun., 9 Feb.: 1997. Sally explains to her husband, Ted about the 'process' involved in finding out what's bothering someone else. The dialog includes, 'First I give you some obscure hint that you miss entirely. Then I expect you to read my mind.' When Ted asks if it wouldn't be easier if she just *told* him what was bothering her, Sally responds 'Then you wouldn't get a chance to show me you love me by reading my mind.'

The Word for World Is Forest (1972)

Le Guin returned to questions of violence and war, treason and patriotism in *The Word for World Is Forest*. The plot of *The Word for World* begins near the end of the story, with a massacre of Terran colonists at a location they call Smith Camp on a planet they call New Tahiti. In chronological order, the story goes like this.

Not very long from now, our Earth is in the midst of an ecological disaster, and we Terran humans are saved by the humans from Hain-Davenant, who, among other things, give us Nearly As Fast As Light (NAFAL) ships to allow colonizing other worlds. Some twenty-seven lightyears from Earth is World 42, New Tahiti. The Terrans plant a colony, almost all males, under military organization and authority, to prepare the world for permanent settlers. The planet is mostly water, and the land is heavily forested. Preparation of the land for farmers means clearing the forests—at great profit since wood is more prized on Earth than gold (7; ch. 1).[202] Aiding the Terrans is 'The Voluntary Autochthonous Labor Corps' (63; ch. 3)—enslaved men and women from the native species of humans: literally little green men (and women), who call their world *Athshe*, 'Forest.'

One of the Terran officers, Captain Don Davidson, rapes Thele, an Athshean woman, a rape from which she dies. '[A]cting without argument or speech,' or only a bit of speech, Selver Thele, her husband, attacks Davidson and attempts to kill him: an act we may see, in Hannah Arendt's words, as 'the only way to set the scales of justice right again' (*On Violence* 64 § 2). Davidson is a big 'euraf' (*WWF* 79; ch. 4) from Cleveland and a professional soldier; he is hurt and scared by Selver's attack but defeats him in the fight and prepares to kill him. He is stopped by Raj Lyubov, an anthropologist who had worked with Selver, with Selver as a native informant. Selver leaves for the North Isle and lives on the coast of Kelme Deva where he sees the Terrans destroy the city of Penle, enslave some hundred of its inhabitants, and cut open the world (30; ch. 2). Commanding the Terrans at Kelme Deva—Smith Camp—is Captain Davidson. Selver organizes the Athsheans, and 'after long talking, and long dreaming, and the making of a plan, we went in daylight, and killed the yumens of Kelme Deva with arrows and hunting-lances, and burned their city and their engines,' killing some two hundred of the Terrans. Davidson—gone to colonial headquarters at Centralville, mostly to get laid by one of the newly arrived women—returns to find his camp destroyed. Selver attacks

---

[202] For readers familiar with what Carol D. Stevens has called 'Le Guin and the Family Business,' the *gold* reference, within a page of 'Conquistador' (6) should be a cue: crucial to the destruction of the Californian Indians studied by Le Guin's parents were Spanish, Mexican, and US conquest, Christian missionizing, White American ranching and farming—and the 1849 Gold Rush. See esp. T. Kroeber's *Ishi* books and A. L. Kroeber's *Handbook* ch. 57, 'Population,' esp. 883, 886-90.

Davidson and is wounded by Davidson, but brings down the Terran and sings over him (19-20,ch. 1; 30-32, ch. 2).

There is an investigation at which we learn Athsheans are supposed to be 'intraspecific nonaggressive' and have no real history of violence. The Terrans learn from visiting Cetian and Hainish officials that there is now a League of worlds, communicating by ansible, an instantaneous communication device. The brutal ways of Terran exploitation of Athshe are over.

Davidson is sent off to a distant outpost where he organizes a quiet atrocity against the local Athsheans. Lyubov continues his work, eventually encountering Selver at the Athshean town of Tuntar. Selver tells Lyubov to leave Centralville two days hence (96), and Lyubov forgets that advice and semiconsciously omits mentioning Selver in his report on his trip to Tuntar (109-10; ch. 5). Selver leads the Athsheans against Centralville, killing all the women—thus 'sterilizing' the Terrans—and capturing most of the men. Lyubov is killed in the battle and Selver sees the body and/or the dying Lyubov (117-18; ch. 6).

Davidson kills his local commanding officer and refuses to stop fighting the Athsheans. Finally his position is overrun, and his men are killed. Selver and his comrades capture Davidson and handle him as they would an Athshean psychotic: they isolate him on an uninhabited island. Plot and story end with the return of a Terran ship and League representatives to pick up the remaining Terrans; the ship's commander and a League representative tell Selver that, in large measure because of Lyubov's work, Athshe 'has been placed under the League Ban' and will no longer be subject to Terran colonizing or any other alien interference (165-67; ch. 8). Ironically, the least conventionally heroic of the trio of potential heroes in this book, the intellectual Dr. Lyubov, turns out to be highly effective; Lyubov's 'inactive action' of anthropological scholarship is crucial for the long-term survival of the Athsheans.

* * * * * * *

The Word for World Is Forest might be seen as *Planet of Exile* (1966) shifted out of Romance and into the modes of Tragedy and Satire. Both stories use third-person, limited narration from the points of view of three main characters. In *Planet*, old Wold does what old people are supposed to do in Romances: he shuffles off on 'his last foray,' leading the women and children to a well-protected fort (87; ch. 10)—and then shuffles off this mortal coil (123-24; ch. 14), leaving the stage clear for the (relatively) young couple of Rolery and Jakob Agat to consummate their marriage in fertility, and for a new and better world to coalesce around them: a world in which the native humans and the Terrans will integrate and prosper.[203]

---

[203] I use here and elsewhere N. Frye's theory of Modes in *Anatomy of Criticism*—and his idea that at the end of a Romantic Comedy a better world forms around a central couple: concluding the comic action, 'a new society crystallizes on the stage around the hero and his bride' (44; see also 163).

Jakob Agat looks around in joy at the end of the story and sees 'his fort, his city, his world; these were his people. He was no exile here'; and he says to 'the alien, the stranger, his wife' (122) the last words of *Planet of Exile*, 'come, let's go home' (124).

The Word for World emphatically does not end in joy, integration, and coming home.

Selver in *The Word for World* corresponds to Rolery in *Planet of Exile*: the point of view nonTerran, native human; Davidson corresponds to Agat: a leader among the Terran colonists; and—much less exactly—Lyubov corresponds to Wold: the third member of a triangle. In *Planet*, we have a love triangle with the key apex occupied by Rolery, daughter to Wold and later wife to Agat, with Wold coming to love both his Summer-born daughter and son-in-law. In *The Word for World*, we get two love-hate triangles, with Selver emphasized. The first triangle is Selver-Thele-Davidson. Again, Davidson rapes and (indirectly) murders Thele, for which Selver tries to kill him. Lyubov saves Selver, earning Davidson's enmity. When the action of the plot begins, then, Selver and Davidson hate one another; Lyubov and Selver have come to love one another; Lyubov intensely dislikes Davidson, and Davidson despises Lyubov. To make *The Word for World* into a kind of Romantic Comedy would be easy enough: the 'marriage' of the Athshean Selver and the Terran Lyubov would be central to a plot moving toward the conversion or defeat and expulsion of Davidson and reconciliation and friendship between the two peoples. We get a hint of this possibility in a savior motif in the central triangle. Lyubov saves Selver; Selver tries to save Lyubov by warning him of the attack on Central, and Selver does save his people; and Davidson consistently sees himself as a Messiah for the Terrans on Athshe. Which fits his name: *Don*, 'world ruler,' plus *Davidson*, 'son of David'—suggesting a descendent of King David, as a Messiah should be (see Matthew 1.1-17).

The plot moves away from integration and toward alienation and isolation: Lyubov is killed in the attack on Central; Davidson ends up isolated on an island; and the Athsheans will be isolated by the League for generations. And that is as happy an ending as we are going to get.

In her introduction to *The Word for World Is Forest*, Le Guin tells how she wrote the story under the title of *The Little Green Men* in 1968, while in England, 'a guest and a foreigner' with 'no outlet' for her anger at the war in Vietnam (*LoN* [1979]:151). I have suggested that Le Guin's inability to demonstrate directly her anger with her government and people led her take action in the old-fashioned Prophetic way of writing a *mâshâl* (plural: *mâshâlim*): 'a likeness;...' 'taunt,' or 'satire.' Whatever the translation, the 'likeness' in question is either the aptly stated analogue of a previously experienced reality, or it is the quasi-magical, verbal prefiguring of reality in the shape, for good and for ill, in which the utterer would like to encounter it' (Rabinowitz 320). *The Word for World Is Forest* is, in part, a *mâshâl* of the war in Indochina in the late 1960s. It is also the aptly stated analog of a long series of encounters between people sophisticated in the technology and political organization of violence (civilized people) and people with far fewer means for killing other people ('primitives'). In the physical and psychological territory of 'Frontierland,' we meet the Others and 'the normal defensive-aggressive reaction between strangers meeting' can get very bloody (Erlich, '...Le Guin and...Clarke' 111). Le Guin's Narrator places an early scene in the book in a pretty clearing that 'might have been Idaho in 1950.... Or Kentucky in 1830. Or Gaul in 50 B.C.' (see Siciliano 76). Or, I will add, the upper waters of Mill Creek in California, a few weeks after 15 August 1865, where White men under the command of R. A. Anderson ambushed one of the few remaining groups of Yahi Indians.[204] The limited action in the scene in the clearing in *Word for World* includes a distant bird saying, 'Te-whet' (9; ch. 1). Kentucky and Gaul are among the many places where Terran tribal peoples were slaughtered by the civilized, and the immediate response to thoughts of Kentucky and Gaul is what Kurt Vonnegut, Jr., has assured us is the one decorous comment on massacres:

> ...there is nothing intelligent to say about a massacre. Everybody is supposed to be dead, to never say anything or want anything ever again. Everything is supposed to be very quiet after a massacre, and it always is, except for the birds.
> And what do the birds say? All there is to say about a massacre, things like '*Poo-tee-weet?*' (*Slaughterhouse-Five* 19; ch. 1 [see also 19, 23, 215]).

The best Le Guin can see for Indochina is, in a geopolitical sense, about what happened: that the United States would lose the war, and we would have to go home.

Where Le Guin proved optimistic was in the suggested body counts: Le Guin's imaginary war was far less bloody than the Terran reality (over 58,000 Americans killed, over two million Vietnamese and others). Where Le Guin was highly optimistic was in her utopian vision of the Athsheans, and in her Anarchistic faith that such a utopian culture could defeat a high-tech army. The Vietnamese did, indeed, defeat the U.S. military, but, as Le Guin well knew, they had a good deal of experience fighting off invaders. The Terran commanding officer in *Word for World*, Col. Dongh, a Vietnamese, mentions his people's spending 'about thirty years fighting off

---

[204] See Heizer and T. Kroeber, *Ishi the Last Yahi*, 123-26: in their rpt. of T. T. Waterman's 'The Last Wild Tribe of California (1915),' from *Popular Science Monthly* (March 1915): 233-44; Heizer and Kroeber 142-43: in their rpt. of Waterman's 'The Yana Indians (1918),' from *University of California Publications in American Archaeology and Ethnology* 13.2 (1918): 35-102: the section The Yahi Meet Disaster, excerpting from the account of Anderson. See also Maslen 69, who reminds us of this massacre.

major super-powers one after the other in the twentieth century' (133; ch. 6): the Japanese, the French, and then the USA, 1940s on.[205]

****

Athshe is like an Earthsea where the Immanent Grove has spread out over the Archipelago to create a huge Yin-Yang symbol: 'Ocean: forest. That was your choice on New Tahiti. Water and sunlight, or darkness and leaves' (7; ch. 1). And the people there are peaceful; like the Gethenians, they've never had a war. Unlike the Gethenians, they additionally don't have 'assassinations, feuds, forays'; Athshean murders are committed only by extraordinarily rare psychopaths; even fights are rare and usually limited to adolescents ('Gender...Redux' 10; *WWF* 58, ch. 3). Most important, the Athsheans are Hainish Normal in their sexual anatomy and physiology: our Terran standard-issue, sexually dimorphic human beings.[206] A bit more than the Gethenians, the Athsheans are sane and *relevant*.

With the Terran conquest, we see on Athshe a pattern of opposition Le Guin began as early as *A Wizard of Earthsea* (1968) and continued into *Always Coming Home* (1985). The Athsheans are technologically primitive and organizationally simple, anarchistic, 'communal...and somewhat introverted.'[207] Their populations are stable in size and stay put. 'They have no nomadic peoples, and no societies that live by expansion and aggression.... Nor have they formed large, hierarchically governed nation-states' that can be mobilized for war. 'Competition is ritualized, and, when ritual breaks down, the resulting violence does not become mass violence, remaining limited, personal.' The Terrans are from a 'hierarchically governed' world-state and are under military law and discipline.[208] And the Terrans are heavily armed and dangerous.

---

[205] The local superpower in historical times has been China, so the Vietnamese came to the twentieth c. with a tradition of armed resistance going back to at least to 39 CE and the revolt under the Ladies Trung Trac and Trung Nhi ('Vietnam, History of' 122).

[206] We learn almost nothing about the sexual *behavior* of Athsheans, and most heterosexual readers will unconsciously 'fill in the blank' by generalizing from Thele and Selver's idealized marriage to a straight Athshean culture contrasted with the (mostly negative) Terrans, where the rule is male homosexuality and heterosexual prostitution.

[207] See Needham, 'Time and Knowledge...,' 11-12 for Daoist reverence for 'a Golden Age of primitive communalism,' an 'ancient paradise of generalized tribal nobility, of cooperative primitivity, of spontaneous collectivism' before social differentiation into 'lords, priests, warriors and serfs' (*Tao te Ching* ch. 80). On introversion vs. extroversion as part of 'National Temperament or Types,' see A. L. Kroeber § 244 (*Biology and Race* 171-72); for folk/tribal culture vs. sophisticate/urban culture see Kroeber § 121 (*Culture Patterns and Processes* esp. 89-91).

[208] *WWF* 4; ch. 1. See 'Gender...Redux' (*DEW* 10-11), 'Gender' in *LoN* (1979): 166; Erlich, 'Le Guin/Clarke' 115.

What the Terran officials have done is familiar enough and takes little interpretation: they have sent men (mostly) organized militarily and have given them rules, regulations, and orders. They are like US Army units on the Western frontier during the Indian Wars, the period my US military history book called the 'nadir' of US Army history. One cause for some US war crimes in the Indian Wars was units operating independently under ambitious commanders, with George Armstrong Custer as the best-known example.[209] But the telegraph came through fairly early on in the American West, and Lyndon Johnson 'micromanaged' US warfare in Vietnam; even so Le Guin introduces the ansible—and Le Guin supplies a League government that is competent (as LBJ was), but also moral, relatively peace-loving, and well-intentioned. In the *mâshâl* of Vietnam, the League can be read as a wish for something like the United Nations to attempt to undo US damage in Indochina. In political terms, the point may be that a strictly political analysis is insufficient: even if the Terran military were absorbed into a good system—with sane, ethical people giving orders from Earth—the frontier and/or military *culture* would undermine the new system. More concretely, a charismatic traitor like Don Davidson could get enough support to cause a lot of trouble; and, of course, in *Word for World* he does. Whether 1849ers going to California for gold or future loggers going to New Tahiti for lumber, men who flee civilization and strike out for riches are not going to let native peoples stand in their way; as they think necessary, the invaders will destroy inconvenient natives through 'disease, malnutrition, forced removal, massacre, aggravated rape....' (Buckley 438). Military organization and armaments mean that when an intelligent psychopath like Don Davidson takes over a group, he has a group organized and equipped for carnage (84; ch. 4).[210] And, finally, militarism, macho, and racism ('speciesism' here) can be mutually reinforcing. Davidson, anyway, believes that 'The fact is, the only time a man is really and entirely a man is when he's just had a woman or just killed another man' (81; ch. 4). A macho mind, tightly compartmentalized, can feel both manly and guiltless raping human females not seen as really women and killing human males not seen as really men. In Davidson's

---

[209] The US is far from unique here. Examples of massacres by other imperial peoples are easy to find, e.g., the Romans' producing impressive body counts by all except the most rigorous Early Modern and modern standards for slaughter. For more recent examples, see Arendt, 'Race and Bureaucracy,' *Origins of Totalitarianism*, ch. 7.

[210] Maslen instructively compares Davidson with 'an earlier manifestation of American colonialism, a man called Anderson who was the most prominent of the Indian killers in Kroeber's narrative' (69)—i.e., T. Kroeber's *Ishi in Two Worlds* 63-68 and passim. Maslen refers to R. A. Anderson, 'sometime sheriff of Butte County' and author of the 1909 pamphlet, 'Fighting the Mill Creeks,' and one whom an early commentator indicated was among the 'very considerable proportion of our 'Indian fighters' in this state [who] deserved, in strict justice, to be hung' (quoting T. T. Waterman, in Heizer and Kroeber 126, 124). For Anderson's account of a crucial massacre, see Heizer and T. Kroeber 142-43.

head, such a mind can allow him to disobey orders and thereby endanger the Terran colony, assassinate his commanding officer, lead armed men to massacre a village—generally engage in murder and treason and atrocities—and still feel himself the only true patriot, the only truly sane, morally, and manly man.

And here I will stop discussing Don Davidson and the Terrans, whom Le Guin anatomizes in great detail. That's the dystopian satire in *Word for World*. The violated utopia of the Athsheans is equally interesting.

How do we get decent behavior out of human beings, a genus not notably 'primitive, harmless, and peace-loving' (63; ch. 3)? One answer, as we've seen in *The Left Hand of Darkness*, is to be sure that they organize themselves anarchistically. In *Left Hand*, however, war was prevented (as things worked out) by the presence of outsiders: Ai and the Ekumen. War on Gethen would have been between two Gethenian peoples with sufficient sense of identity to have '*two polarities we*' and the Gethenians '*perceive through our cultural conditioning*' as patriot and traitor ('Gender...Redux' 12), and two polarities that the Gethenians through *their* cultural conditioning—and we through reading Le Guin's novel—perceive as Karhide and Orgoreyn. Genly Ai knows 'the love of one's homeland' but beyond that he's not sure, from his own experience, what patriotism is. Estraven, soon to be exiled for treason explains it to him: 'No, I don't mean love, when I say patriotism. I mean fear. The fear of the other. And its expressions are political not poetical: hate, rivalry, aggression' (19; ch. 1).[211] In the United States ca. 1969, Estraven's comments were highly relevant: lack of patriotism was a standard charge against the Peace Movement, the people trying to end US military adventures in Indochina; since antiwar actions were necessarily 'giving aid and comfort to the enemy' in time of war—however undeclared by Congress—movement people were also traitors. *The Left Hand of Darkness* as a whole goes even further than just problematicizing words like 'patriotism' and 'treason'; as a whole, *Left Hand* emphatically puts personal loyalties and love of home over attachments to *any* abstraction (true treason is to betray a friend), but Le Guin gives us technologically sophisticated people on Gethen, living in a complex civilization: there is on Gethen the possibility for conflict between personal loyalty or loyalty to home and the loyalty patriotism requires to the State.

The Athsheans have not had to deal with conflicts in loyalty between concrete people and abstracts commonwealths because they have never had abstract states to be loyal to; they are not civilized people: i.e., they don't have cultures based on cities in the ways ancient Terrans developed civilization from city life.[212] What Athsheans call cities we'd call villages or towns, and the Gethenians might call Hearths; and no conqueror or

---

[211] For more on patriotism and treason in *LHD*, see ch. 3, pp. 30-39; ch. 9; ch. 15, pp. 211-212; ch. 19, pp. 278-82.
[212] For Le Guin's more positive view of 'The City as goal and Dream,' see 'Introduction to *City of Illusions*,' *LoN* (1979): 147, and 'Coming of Age in Karhide.'

other consolidator has come along to bind the villages into a confederation, set up his royal seat in a city, and continue expanding until he or a successor ran into another royal thug with similar ideas.[213] So: the immediate reason the Athsheans don't have big wars is that they can't; their social groups are too small. But those groups are small because they have no history of consolidation, and one reason they have no consolidation is they have no history of feuds and forays that could be organized into rational warfare for the purpose of large-scale theft. Apparently, it has never occurred to Athsheans to organize into groups to murder, maim, wound, and (thereby) terrorize others in order to steal the property or labor of those others. Put in such terms, this hardly appears a mystery, but it is a mystery. In Le Guin's Hainish universe, warfare has been fairly common; and the Hainish universe is a legitimate extrapolation from and fabulation upon human history on our Earth—where, I believe, warfare began as highly organized theft with violence (see discussion of *ACH*). Why are there no feuds and forays on Athshe? Why are even fist fights uncommon? Why are they really nonviolent, really peaceful? Putting the matter formally: As human beings the Athsheans have as a trait *aggressivity*; to a greater or lesser degree they all are capable of getting very, very angry, so angry they desire to lash out. Further, 'The Athsheans are carnivorous, they hunt animals' and can hunt in groups; and they have their rare psychotics and the concepts of rape and murder (61; ch. 3)—and weapons. Why then is there so little *aggression*?[214]

One reason is that politics among the Athsheans is controlled by old women, the Head Women of the villages: '...old women are different from everybody else, they say what they think' (98; ch. 5). In Earthsea terms, politics on Athshe are conducted in a True Speech. A second reason is that fights will not move into deadly violence because the Athsheans have 'aggression-halting gestures and positions' (*WWF* 60) like those of Terran wolves and jackdaws (Lorenz 123-28). And it is highly unlikely a conflict would ever get to physical combat. Among men, anyway, they have a custom like Terran Inuit and use ritualized 'singing to replace physical combat.' Any Athshean man can, when angry, sublimate aggressivity into art and sing a song against his opponent—a very literal *mâshâl*, in the sense of 'taunt,' 'satire'—the quality of the song depending upon the man's talent. Like the appeasement gestures, the singing contests also 'might have a physiological foundation....' However deep their roots (and there has to be a biological basis somewhere), Athshean aggression-halting and aggression-ritualizing customs make 'an effective war-barrier,' especially since there is relatively little positive motivation for warfare (60-61; ch. 3). The Athsheans have little wealth, so there is little to steal. The Athsheans also have no tradition of hating outsiders and are slow to learn group enmity. They are literally in touch with one another, with an entire grammar and

---

[213] See my discussion of *ACH*. Also note that my speaking harshly of kings should not imply an idealized vision of more democratic constitutions.
[214] For more on aggressivity and aggression, see Erlich, 'Le Guin/Clarke' 114.

vocabulary of 'touch-exchanges' filling that vast gap in Terran culture (US culture) 'between the formal handshake and the sexual caress' (94-95; ch. 5). Possibly most important, the Athsheans are incredibly well integrated into their world. They can go with the unconscious, with the Dao. To a remarkable degree, they are sane. Athsheans can take their dreams and, according to their abilities, shape, analyze, react to, and reshape them. As a folk art they can dream while awake and 'balance...sanity not on the razor's edge of reason but on the double support, the fine balance of reason and dream' (99; ch. 5).[215]

Bright water and dark forest balance on Athshe. Even so, intellect—that clear light of reason—balances the maze-like, forest-like unconscious among Athsheans (25-26; ch. 2). 'They're a static, stable, uniform society' from Lyubov's somewhat limited point of view, 'Perfectly integrated and wholly unprogressive. You might say that like the forest they live in, they've attained a climax state'—but they can adapt and apparently have adapted rather spectacularly to the Terran colony with their massacring the Terrans at Smith Camp (61-62; ch. 3).[216] Lyubov notes that the Athsheans have 'recognized us as members of their species, as men. However, we have not responded as members of their species should respond. We have ignored...the rights and obligations of non-violence. We have killed, raped, dispersed, and enslaved the native humans, destroyed their communities, and cut down their forests. It wouldn't be surprising if they'd decided that we are not human.' The Cetian, Mr. Or, completes the logic: 'And therefore can be killed, like animals...' (62; ch. 3).

What it takes a long time for Lyubov to figure out is the mechanism for change among the Athsheans. He has to be told directly and then mull it over: 'Selver is a god,' he's told (97, [100], 105; ch. 5). Then he thinks, Selver is 'a link between the two realities, considered by the Athsheans as equal, the dream-time and the world-time.... A link: one who could speak aloud the perceptions of the subconscious. To 'speak' that tongue is to act.

---

[215] For Athshean sanity, cf. the Kesh in *ACH*—and see Barbour, 'Wholeness' 172. For dreaming, cf. 'the Senoi people of Malaysia,' whom Le Guin hadn't even heard of when she wrote *WWF*; see Synchronicity Can Happen...section of Introd. to *WWF* (*LoN* [1979] 152-54). A. L. Kroeber had a lower opinion of cultures that put high value upon dreams: 'Backward peoples assume as actual certain phenomena to which we grant only a mental or subjective existence.... Certain things we classify as unreal the primitive considers superreal...' (§ 127; *Culture Patterns*...107; ch. 7.

[216] Cf. and contrast the 'unprogressive' native peoples in California and Australia. Among both groups the pattern for all times was set in the mythic past: the primordial Dream Time among the Australians (Eliade 40) during the time of the *Ixkareya* among the Karok, of the *woge* among the Yurok (e.g., A. L. Kroeber, *Karok* 263, *Yurok* 18, 271-81, 289-91; see Erlich, 'Le Guin and Clarke' 113). To the Mohave-Yuman peoples along the Colorado, 'dreaming is moving back in time and in understanding to the beginnings of things when gods walked the new earth' (T. Kroeber, *Inland Whale* 193). See Franz, 221-23 for primordial time, dreams, and 'synchronicity' in significant dreams.

To do a new thing. To change or to be changed, radically, from the root. For the root is the dream.' Selver was such a link, a literal *translator*, one who carries over. 'He had done a new deed. The word, the deed, murder. Only a god could lead so great a newcomer...across the bridge between the worlds' (106-7; ch. 5).[217]

When Selver tells the story of the Smith Camp massacre to the old Dreamer, Coro Mena, Coro Mena replies, 'Before this day the thing we had to do was the right thing to do; the way we had to go was the right way and led us home. Where is our home now? For you have done what you had to do, and it was not right. You have killed men' (33-34; ch. 2). From a Daoist perspective, and for Le Guin, these are powerful lines. A classical Daoist talks little of right and wrong but of following the way and, in Le Guin's formulation, doing as one *must* do—which *is* right.[218] Coro Mena here admits the Western paradox that sometimes one must do evil—which makes evil unavoidable, but no less evil. And Coro Mena has, all together, an optimistic view of Selver (47-48; ch. 2)! The more pessimistic possibility is suggested by Lyubov's asking himself whether Selver was 'speaking his own language, or...Captain Davidson's' (107; ch. 5). Selver may not be a god; he may just be a charismatic man who has learned that a possible political means to desirable ends is massacres. Either way could fit into the story. The point of view characters are a trinity of two saviors and Davidson as Messiah-manqué. There are also two clear traitors: Davidson and Lyubov (110; ch. 5). Selver could complete the threesome of traitors. Selver's gift to his people is guerrilla warfare, which requires group enmity. Athsheans must think of themselves as Athsheans, with a cause to press against the Terrans; this sets up the possibility for Selver of a conflict of loyalties. In attacking Central, Selver endangers his friend Lyubov; in warning Lyubov, Selver endangers the cause of his people and the lives of those who have chosen to follow him in the attack. Selver fails to save Lyubov, which may be a betrayal. It would elegantly reinforce the theme of treason if Selver were to betray his own nature in learning murder from Davidson and teaching mass murder to his people. But this is not my reading. The Change Selver brings the Athsheans is, I think, a true Change, just deeply, and appropriately, problematic.

At the end of the story, Selver tells Lepennon, from Hain, that a god 'brings a new way to do a thing, or a new thing to be done.... He brings this across the bridge between the dream-time and the world-time. When he has done this, it is done. You cannot take things that exist in the world and try to drive them back into the dream, to hold them inside the dream with walls and pretenses. That is insanity. What is, is. There is no use pretending, now, that we do not know how to kill one another' (168; ch. 8).

---

[217] I eliminated the phrase 'as Death.' Lyubov got excessive in the last sentence: Death was no newcomer among the Athsheans. What Selver had introduced was mass murder. Note 'link' for hinge imagery in *ACH*.
[218] See *Chuang Tzu* ch. 6 (Giles 74).

The book ends with Selver with the memory of Lyubov—they remain in touch—and the knowledge that Davidson is on an island, still alive. It is not a totally tragic vision of isolation, but its vision of Athshe figuratively walled off from the galaxy is decorously bleak for the years of war and reaction in which it was written (1968) and published (1972).

The Dispossessed (1974)

> Emigration offers some of the things the frustrated hope to find when they join a mass movement, namely change and a chance for a new beginning. The same types who swell the ranks of a rising mass movement are also likely to avail themselves of a chance to emigrate. Thus migration can serve as a substitute for a mass movement. (Hoffer 28; § 17 in Part One)

> Time is awakened when one is faced with freedom of choice. —Satosi Watanabe, in *Voices of Time* (561)

The teaching of *The Dispossessed*, its thematic content, complements and balances *The Lathe of Heaven* but fits in more closely with *The Word for World Is Forest* and *The Left Hand of Darkness*. In *Lathe* it is the villain, Haber, who says that 'Life—evolution—the whole universe of space/time, matter/energy—existence itself—is essentially *change*' and the hero, Orr who corrects with, 'That is one aspect of it.... The other is stillness' (135; ch. 9). In the debate between the active and contemplative life, *Lathe* comes down sturdily on the side of meditatively and carefully dealing with things as they are and mostly just leaving them be. *The Dispossessed* gives more than equal time to that other aspect life, and the Way as change (*ACH* 485), evolution, and, indeed, as the Human Way, revolution.

Left Hand takes place in the far future, in the days of the well-coordinated and highly evolved Ekumen of known human worlds colonized by the ancient Hainish; *Word for World* and *The Dispossessed* are set in the near future, when just a League is getting started. *Word for World*, *Left Hand*, and *The Dispossessed* all deal with conflict, violence, and warfare—and with ways to organize human societies to keep conflict more or less nonviolent.

Again, in *Word for World*, the overarching symbol for integration is the world-wide Yin-Yang of Athshe before the arrival of the Terrans: 'Ocean: forest.... Water and sunlight, or darkness and leaves' (7; ch. 1). That symbol remains far in the background, however, replaced by the forest vs. the deserts of the lands clear-cut by the Terran loggers: and this is decorous, since there is no integration in *Word for World*. In *Left Hand*, the thematic symbol is the androgyne, explicitly connected with the Yin-Yang symbol (267; ch. 19). The major symbol in the plot of *Left Hand* is the arch. At the beginning of *Left Hand* we see the King of Karhide mortaring a keystone into an arch, with the mortar pinkish from the traditional blood and bones mixed in. 'Without the bloodbond the arch would fall, you see,' Estraven tells Ai. At the time of the story, the blood and bones are those of nonhuman animals, but at one time it was 'Human bones, human blood' (5; ch. 1).[219] Estraven's death at the end of *Left Hand* provides the bloodbond that will bring together his world.[220] In *The Dispossessed*, there is the double Ioti arch (like a complete or partial McDonald's arch), but the thematically significant image of integration is that of the double planets Urras and Anarres themselves—the 'Cetian' planets—forever circling about each other as they revolve about their common center of gravity.[221] Tightly associated with the planetary image is the image of the circle of life: the almost-complete circle that is the symbol of the Odonian anarchist movement and which is the shape of the wall around the Port of Anarres, given much stress at the opening of the novel—and with walls used for an important figure of speech throughout. This is also the shape of the quest of Shevek, the hero of *The Dispossessed*, as we see it in *The Dispossessed*: the novel is 'open ended,' leaving Shevek just before he completes a circular journey back home to Anarres, a return that may result in his death, the closing of Shevek's individual circle.

Placing *The Dispossessed* with *Word for World* and *The Left Hand of Darkness* is also useful for putting the works—very tentatively—into the context of broad-scale political discussion in the USA in the late 1960s and early 1970s. *Word for World* and *Left Hand* were salvos in the *Kulturkampf* associated with the war in Vietnam; *The Dispossessed* has to do with 'the Revolution.'

As the War continued, and as the war-fighting American government had little time nor inclination to deal with domestic problems, preeminently the long unanswered demands of Black Americans, more radical elements split off from the mainstream peace and civil rights groups ('the Movement') and called for a second American revolution, this time a truly radical one. Looking back from even the middle 1970s, it was obvious that the Movement, let alone the Revolution, had been mortally wounded in Chicago in 1968 and 1969—and finally killed by gunfire at Jackson State

---

[219] In response to my query of what work is alluded to in the blood-bonded arch—guessing, on the basis of James Bittner's work, it might be a poem of W. H. Auden's—Dennis McGucken sent me by e-mail the message (1 Nov. 1996) that 'The allusion is to the last lines of Auden's poem 'Vespers' from the sequence Horae Canonicae. * * * 'For without a cement of blood (it must be human it must be innocent) no secular wall will safely stand .' [See] W.H. Auden, *Collected Poems* (Random House, 1976 (pp. 482-485).' McGucken is correct, but students of the question of allusions should note that Le Guin said she didn't think she had read the poem (personal communication).

[220] This is a standard interpretation: see e.g., Cummins, *Understanding...Le Guin* (86; ch. 3).

[221] For a later handling of two-planet relationships and the exploitation of a nearby planet, and of people, see Werel and Yeowe in the novellas collected in Le Guin's *Four Ways to Forgiveness* (1995). For the imagery of the circling planets, see Erlich 'On Barbour....'

and Kent State Universities in May of 1970, had twitched for a couple of years, and then received indecent burial in a landslide: Richard Nixon's victory over George McGovern in the Presidential election of 1972.[222] Still, in 1968 revolution had been possible—though unachieved—in France and had seemed plausible to many people in the USA into the early 1970s. And by 1973, with the war 'winding down' and the Nixon administration teetering, people began to look forward to 1976 and the Bicentennial of the American Revolution of 1776.

The Dispossessed, then, may be read in historical context as an immediately relevant meditation on revolution, one of many such meditations at the time. *The Dispossessed* is a rather indirect meditation and speaks very cogently to a couple of questions not considered sufficiently in the 1960s and 1970s and then forgotten as 'revolution' once again became a taboo word in American political discourse. The first question was, 'What do you want the world to be like the day after your revolution?' In *The Dispossessed*, Le Guin pictures a utopia worth struggling for. The second question is, 'Why another revolution—what went wrong with the first American Revolution?' In *The Dispossessed*, Le Guin endorses the political accuracy of Thomas Jefferson's reckoning 'that one rebellion in thirteen States in the course of eleven years, is but one for each State in a century and a half. No country should be so long without one.' Shevek says the Anarresti have enjoyed a fully-functioning anarchy 'for one hundred and fifty years now' (183; ch. 7); the Odonian colony on Anarres has been recognized under the Terms of the Settlement with the Urrasti governments for 170 years (275, ch. 11; 286, ch. 12); and the demonstration Shevek attends in the Ioti city of Nio Esseia occurs on the 200th anniversary of the Insurrection that began the Odonian Revolution (239-40; ch. 9 [also 188; ch. 8]). By Mr. Jefferson's schedule, the Cetian planets are due for an uprising. Even in Odonian society on Anarres, a communist anarchy conceived as a permanent revolution, there must be some revolutionary anarchist activists every now and then, acting like anarchists and waking up the social organism. 'A little rebellion now and then is a good thing,' in the Jeffersonian view of things, and probably a necessary thing if people are to stay free.[223]

* * * * * * *

---

[222] Chicago, 1968: Violent confrontations and police riot at the Democratic National Convention; Chicago, 1969: police killing of Black Panthers Fred Hampton and Mark Clark. Jackson State/Kent State: in violence associated with student strikes in May of 1970, two students were killed by police at Jackson State University in Mississippi, and four students were killed by the Ohio National Guard at Kent State University in Ohio, plus other significant student casualties (Miller 309-11, Herring 232, memory).
[223] The quotations on rebellion are from Jefferson's correspondence with James Madison (30 Jan. 1787. The phrase 'permanent revolution' is usually associated with Leon Trotsky, the Bolshevik revolutionary and commissar for war under Lenin.

The plot of *The Dispossessed* gives us the biography of Shevek, a physicist, parent, and Odonian of Anarres, from infancy through his journey in middle age to the capitalist archist county of A-Io on Urras—where he develops the General Temporal Theory bringing together Sequency and a Theory of Simultaneity, which allows the ansible and the instantaneous transmission of data over interstellar distances (276; ch. 11)—and, finally, his return home, almost to his landing on Anarres (ch. 13). As in most SF, much is at stake: the ansible is necessary for the formation of a League of Worlds, so Shevek's work ultimately helps in the creation of the Ekumen. As in *The Left Hand of Darkness*, there is conflict, but in *The Dispossessed* it is good to move into that conflict, and to try to move it onto a nonviolent and productive path. And also as in *Left Hand*, Le Guin complicates her narration by refusing to tell her tale from the beginning through the middle to the end. Here, though, the narrative voice and point of view remain constant; Le Guin appropriately rearranges the time scheme.

Shevek is a student of time, and in a central discussion in the central chapter of the novel—and that's both metaphorically and literally central—Shevek explains how time is both linear and circular (ch. 7). As James Bittner has very elegantly demonstrated, Le Guin uses a similar structure for her novel (*Approaches* 121-25). The novel has thirteen chapters: six set on Anarres, five set on Urras, two involving both; in ch. 1 Shevek goes from Anarres to Urras; in ch. 13 he leaves Urras to return to Anarres. The arrow of time takes Shevek from infancy to what may be his death at forty or so (244, ch. 9).[224] The circle takes him on a typical quest journey, in this case, to Urras and back again, with some oscillations. If we follow Bittner's schema and see chapter 1 as a fictional present, chapter 2 is a long flashback taking us to Shevek's infancy and early youth; except that it is the kind of flashback where we don't return any time soon to the present. Instead, the succeeding even-numbered chapters move us forward in time from Shevek's youth until Shevek decides at the end of chapter 12 that he is not going to Urras, and Takver (his partner in a monogamous heterosexual reproductive relationship) tells him in a spousal way that he is, too, going to Urras, and will return. From the end of ch. 1 on, the odd-numbered chapters move from Shevek's arrival on Urras, through his adventures there, to his trip from Urras almost to Anarres in ch. 13: moving us from the present of chapter 1 into the future. Past, present, and future, all exist simultaneously in the physical book, *The Dispossessed*; and we encounter past, present, and future (though not necessarily in that order) as we read—and yet what is happening in *The Dispossessed*, as we first read *The Dispossessed*, is always happening 'now.' This is the case with any

---

[224] The phrase 'time's arrow' is attributed to Sir Arthur Eddington by Richard Schlegel in 'Time and Thermodynamics' in *Voices of Time* (1996): 505, citing Eddington's *The Nature of the Physical World* (1929), ch. 4. For time's arrow and other symbols of time, see § 8 'The Symbolization of Time' in Meerloo, esp. 248. For more on the 'arrow of time,' see *Voices of Time*, Index 692.

book, but Le Guin's time-switches defamiliarize the experience and should make us recognize how all written narratives exist both simultaneously (in the volume) and in sequence (as read).

* * * * * * *

To repeat a cliché from Shakespeare criticism: from *A Midsummer Night's Dream* to *As You Like It* and *Twelfth Night*, William Shakespeare perfected his technique of doing variations on a comic pattern. To put the same statement into popular culture terms, Shakespeare worked out his versions of the formulas of the genre of dramatic romantic comedy. By the early 1970s and *The Dispossessed*, Le Guin had her formulas worked out.[225]

Corresponding with the balanced symbolism mentioned earlier, there's the balance and contrast between the 'Yangish' archists of Urras and the 'Yinnish' communist anarchists of Anarres. Viewed from a metaphorical distance,

Urras/Anarres = Terrans/Athsheans = Orgoreyn/Karhide.

But, as always, Le Guin offers variations on themes by Le Guin. To start with biology, this time around, all the people involved are 'Hainish normal': exactly like us, as far as we're told, with only the trivial difference of having more body hair than even White Terrans. And this time around Le Guin spends little time attacking the USSR. We hear of the Stalinist country of Thu and see a Thuvian agent or two, but the one country on Urras we see is A-Io, which is strongly capitalistic and clearly modeled on America ca. 1970: just more sexist, nonracist (apparently lacking racial differences), more efficiently organized, less republican in origins, and more responsible in preserving the natural environment.

Like America, A-Io is a highly centralized and powerful state with a capitalist economy—on Urras, with that planet's magnificent, complex environment, great natural wealth, great beauty. Culturally, A-Io is also very similar to the United States, e.g., in having a university system, radio and newspapers (with intellectuals getting their news from the Ioti equivalent of NPR), and in their combining excessiveness and endemic vices combined with observance of strong taboos. Early in his stay, the rather puritanical Shevek had noted 'that the Urrasti lived among mountains of

---

[225] Le Guin herself has spoken against the formulaic as writing in obedience to external standards, or for a market: 'On Theme,' *Those Who Can* 206, and 'The Stone Ax and the Muskoxen,' *LoN* (1979): 232-33. PostRomantic moderns have tended to rate quite highly originality, novelty, and individual, 'self-sufficient' achievement, which is a legitimate preference but only a preference, or but one criterion for artistic quality.

excrement, but never mentioned shit' (120; ch, 5).[226] Urras, however, is also like Europe: the Old World, with a long history, and a real aristocracy. And Anarres is also like America, at least the Americas as viewed by Europeans: the New World, but truly empty this time, lacking human inhabitants or any animal inhabitants above the level of fish; and on Anarres the Odonian colonists from Urras have founded a new society, formed in revolution and accepting the revolutionary values the French formulated as Liberty, Equality, Fraternity, or, to phrase the matter in more properly anarchist terms: freedom, equality, solidarity, responsibility, and mutual aid. The Odonians on Anarres have created a good society, but even they might have done better to have stayed home on Urras and ensured the Revolution on Urras. Even as the American and other colonies, and later the United States, provided a home for trouble-makers and relieved the European ruling classes of troublesome opposition, even so with Anarres and Urras. And, again, the Anarresti and Urrasti in the political fable in *The Dispossessed* have a much simpler ethical situation: the success of a Cetian colony on Anarres did not rest upon the twin evils of slavery and the extermination of native peoples.[227]

Alongside the beauty of A-Io and Urras—not beneath it and denying it, but alongside it—is the military force of the Ioti State: force we see used in an attack upon political demonstrators (Odonians, Syndicalists, Socialist Workers) at the climax of *The Dispossessed* (241-46; ch. 9). Along with the wealth and beauty of A-Io is a capitalist system that alienates people from the products of their labor, from the truth, other people, honest sexuality, and themselves (e.g., 105 ch. 5). On Anarres we have a radical alternative to any polity we've ever had on Earth: a long-functioning, high-technology, communist anarchy. On Anarres, then, we get 'The ABC of Communist Anarchism' (to use a title from Alexander Berkman); and we also get an analysis of the threats to communist anarchism or any utopia, or even to a modest republican experiment like the United States of America. It is much to give people a vision of a world the day after the revolution; it is a great gift to political analysis to deal with problems arising some 170 years after establishment of Odonian society, as utopian a revolutionary society as theorists have pictured.

* * * * * * *

---

[226] In the Odonian saying, 'Excess is excrement,' not 'shit': Pravic, their invented language, lacks body-reference taboos. 'Pravic was not a good swearing language. It is hard to swear when sex is not dirty and blasphemy does not exist' (*TD* 208; ch.8). See and contrast A. L. Kroeber on how '*retarded* cultures seem infantile both in their unabashed preoccupation with bodily functions and in their disregard of other human lives' (§ 128, *Culture Patterns* 109; ch. 7, my emphasis).

[227] For endorsements of getting out, as opposed to staying and resisting, see Le Guin's '...Omelas,' *BP*, and *EoH*. See also in her Introd. to *The Norton Book of Science Fiction* (42), the praise for the story that ends the *Norton*: John Kessel's 'Invaders.'

In Odo's theory and initially among the Anarresti, there was no government of people by other people but only the administration of things (136; ch. 6).[228] No hierarchy of rank, and no hierarchies of property since no one on Anarres can own anything: even use of the grammatical possessive case is limited in their invented language, Pravic. With the exception of personal items, everything is held in common. There is no money, no property: when Shevek gets to Urras, he arrives 'like a good Odonian, 'with empty hands'' (56; ch 3), and if they want Anarres, the future, he tells potential revolutionaries, 'you must come to it with empty hands' (241; ch. 9).

Religion for Odonians 'is one of the Categories: the Fourth Mode.' Few people use every Mode, but the Modes are intrinsic to 'the natural capacities of the mind,' and Anarresti, have a 'religious capacity'—need one to do physics, in fact, since religion is 'the profoundest relationship man has with the cosmos' (12; ch. 1). Anarresti religion, however, is invisible in Shevek's narrative: not in churches, nor established, organized, ritualized, nor prayed. The Odonian stress on coming 'with empty hands' can be taken in this context as a rejection of any transcendental religion requiring sacrifices or material support. The slogan of the sky gods has been 'none shall appear before Me empty-handed,' at least when they got houses for themselves: ceilings, walls, and attendant priests, expenses, property, and hierarchy.[229] If we like, what (un)religion we see in *The Dispossessed* we can interpret, applying Fritjof Capra's title, as 'The Tao(ism) of Physics,' for Shevek, especially, but also for him the Perennial Philosophy in trying to work through pain to Joy. And Takver is a kind of natural Daoist as well as good Odonian and biologist in her relationship with the world.

Jobs among the Odonians, called 'postings,' are requested at and assigned by 'Divlab,' the Division of Labor office (121; ch. 5); resources are divided up by the 'PDC' (Production and Distribution Coordination) among syndicates, partnerships, individuals, or other combinations of people working together (61; ch. 3). And people do work: as the Daoists observed, '...men are always doing something; inaction to them is impossible' without a lot of training (*Chuang Tzu* ch. 23 [Giles 237]); or, in the formulation of modern ethologists, 'The healthy animal is up and doing.' The Anarresti are 'Hainish normal' aggressive and status-seeking, and we see plenty of conflict and one fist fight (41; ch. 2) but no lethal violence and certainly no warfare. There are no states to establish armies and no reason to form gangs: there is no property to steal nor the sort of authority physically weaker folk can be forced to submit to (see 120-21; ch. 5). Leadership is provided by people with 'inherent authority,' emperors, so to

---

[228] Chuang Tzu may have priority on the anarchist ideal of the management of things, not people: '...man...must not be managed as if he were a mere thing; though by not managing him at all he may actually be managed as if he were a mere thing' (*Chuang Tzu* ch. 11 [Giles 114-15]).
[229] Exodus 23.15; see also Ex. 34.20 and Deuteronomy 16.16-17 (*Tanakh*).

speak, who 'actually have new clothes' (45; ch. 2).[230] The development of bureaucratic machinery, of an *apparat*, is prevented, in theory, by democratic structuring of PDC and other possible hierarchies, but primarily by the sort of public vigilance that Thomas Jefferson noted as the price (the minimal price we know today) of liberty: Jefferson, however, said 'eternal vigilance' and eternal is much longer than 150 or 170 or 200 years (136; ch. 6).

Could Odonian anarchism work? The great advantage to the writer of a utopia is that she can point to her imaginary world and say, 'Can it? Look; it *does* work!' What we can demand of a utopian writer is that the better new world work plausibly and instructively, and Anarres does.

In addition to handling the objections to utopias alluded to above, Le Guin just eliminates three major objections to an anarchist society. The first she expresses through the comments of Shevek's Urrasti colleague Demaere Oiie that the Anarresti could get by as 'primitive populists...because there were so few of them and because they had no neighbor states' (163; ch. 7). Not recognizing Shevek as an anarchist from a working anarchy is Oiie's problem, but the rest of his objection is valid. Anarchy's main problem might, indeed, be 'the neighbors,' but it is relatively easy to be anarchists on a world without nation-states, or even armed city-states. There are no guns or states on Anarres, and everyone has been raised an Odonian. The second objection is the idea I learned through folklore—and which Oiie may allude to—that anarchy might work well on Tahiti or some other abundant place but would be in major trouble amid scarcity. Anarres is a rather harsh planet, poor in resources; but, contrary to folk belief, that is exactly where we should expect anarchy to work.

That anarchy would work amid relative hardship will not seem odd if we recall Owen Pugh in 'Nine Lives' and that he is alive to star in a story because the English could cooperate even during a time of famines. And more is working than a kind of racial altruism or Affirmative Action (*ER* 12) in Le Guin's having her future heroes generally people of color: White folks are currently a minority on Terra, and Western White folks belong to cultures that work against solidarity and mutual aid. It is consistent for Le Guin to believe that when the biological going gets tough, tough-minded, competitive cultures will be going, dying out more quickly than some of the currently marginal, but cooperative, cultures. More immediately relevant for Anarres, consider the beasts of a coral reef or any of the biologically abundant places Charles Darwin examined for his idea of the origin of new species by natural selection of the fittest. In such rich, crowded areas, the fittest can well be the most competitive—indeed, the most aggressive—and Darwin might be forgiven for stressing competition. Petr Kropotkin studied animals in the stressed environment of Siberia and Northern Manchuria. The one law Shevek and the Anarresti follow is that of human evolution, and the 'law' of evolution for social species is solidarity and

---

[230]Le Guin alludes to the fine story by Hans Christian Anderson, 'The Emperor's New Clothes' (ca. 1835).

mutual aid, a point very clear in stressed environments in which individuals in social species either aid one another or die (see *TD* 6, 177; chs. 1, 7).[231]

The third objection Le Guin deals with is that anarchism and other philosophies of what has been called 'the soft-hearted school' (vs. 'hard-headed') are both unrealistic and unmanly. Oiie puts the raw power struggle on Urras between A-Io and Thu in terms of 'the politics of reality' (164; ch. 7) and the old aristocrat Atro comments significantly that 'The trouble with Odonianism...is that it's womanish. It simply doesn't include the virile side of life [i.e., warfare].... It doesn't understand courage—love of the flag' (230; ch. 9). That is, for now, Odonianism and other idealistic creeds might work, but only if people were essentially altruistic, *nice*.

Le Guin goes to some length to establish that she is not so naive to build a utopia upon a premise of human niceness. On Urras she notes territoriality and primitive possessiveness in birds (166; ch. 7), and the culturally evolved human behaviors based on such traits; and on Anarres she shows us that even in utopia there are some fairly firm givens, and not all of them the impulse to solidarity and mutual aid. In an important chapter of the book, Bedap, a close friend of Shevek's, tells him how power centers develop on Anarres, 'anywhere that function demands expertise and a stable institution.' For any stability in an institution gives scope to the authoritarian impulse:

> In the early years of the Settlement we were...on the lookout for it. People discriminated very carefully then between administering things and governing people. They did it so well that we forgot that the will to dominance is as central in human beings as the impulse to mutual aid is, and has to be trained in each individual, in each new generation. Nobody's born an Odonian any more than he's born civilized! But we've forgotten that. We don't educate for freedom. Education, the most important activity of the social organism, has become rigid, moralistic, authoritarian. Kids learn to parrot Odo's words as if they were *laws*—the ultimate blasphemy! (136; ch. 6)

Eternal vigilance is always the first installment payment on liberty in part because of 'The Iron Law of Oligarchy': experts tend to hang on to jobs and make themselves indispensable as they monopolize both knowledge of how things are (traditionally) done and also dominate the means of communication: finding out what's going on from the rank and file and communicating to (not with) the rank and file (Nicos 489). Shevek comes to agree with Bedap's analysis: '...every emergency, every labor draft even, tends to leave behind it an increment of bureaucratic machinery

---

[231] For Kropotkin's influence on *TD*, see P. E. Smith, 'Unbuilding Walls...' esp. 80-83; Bittner, *Approaches* 149 n. 49.

within PDC....' (264; ch. 10). Famine on Anarres almost pushed Odonian society to violence when there wasn't enough to share (206; ch. 8), but things did not get very violent. The greater dangers were more subtle.

The first danger is somewhat personal and personalist: during crises where severe rationing is required, lists must be made of who gets what, including who gets food and who gets to starve. Shevek had such a job, and he quit it. 'But someone else took over the lists at the mills in Elbow. There's always somebody willing to make lists' (*TD* 250-51; ch. 10). Figuratively, Shevek joined Odo and the ones who walk away from Omelas and refused to benefit from other people's being sacrificed (Finch 42), or even other people's sacrifices. There is, however, another 'but': but at a moment of high tension in the debate at PDC over the plan for Shevek to go to Urras a visiting delegate from a miners' syndicate, and a person who has obviously suffered during the famine, quotes Odo on how '...we each of us deserve everything' *and nothing* because we have 'eaten while another starved,' nor can people claim virtue for having starved while others ate. Odo's point is 'Free your mind of the idea of *deserving*, the idea of *earning*....' (288; ch. 12), and the quotation, in retrospect, should make it difficult to judge Shevek's walking away from list making, *and* to judge the person who replaced him (see Benford, 'Reactionary Utopias' 16).

The second subtle danger from social stress is also richly problematic. The urge to solidarity itself, the carefully reinforced trait that allowed Odonian society to survive even the famine—solidarity itself can be a danger (109; ch. 5). Where there are no official hierarchies, no state, and no law, one is left with one's own 'private conscience' and 'the social conscience,' then 'the opinions of one's neighbors becomes a very mighty force' (121; ch. 5).[232] Shevek believes, and he's at least half correct, that some 200 years after the Revolution the Anarresti social conscience 'completely dominates the individual conscience, instead of striking a balance with it. We don't cooperate—we *obey*' (265; ch. 10). Shevek and his friends start the Syndicate of Initiative to continue the permanent revolution of Odonian society: to be anarchists, to *change* things that must be changed if the society is to remain anarchistic. And this is where the personal comes together with the professional, and the professional for Shevek—the study of Time—is profoundly political.

But how do you change things in a permanent revolution? How do you rearrange the mechanism of government when there is (in theory) no mechanism but only the social organism? Indeed, how does one dare 'tinker' with the social organism at all when the organic image is so useful

---

[232] Good opinion is necessary for what an Anarresti can hope for. Even as traditional Chinese built 'beautiful votive temples dedicated not to Taoist gods or to Buddhas...but to ordinary men and women who conferred benefits upon posterity' (Needham, 'Time and Knowledge...' 119), even so among the Anarresti: a Shevek from the early years of the Settlement earned a 'good immortality' by designing 'a kind of bearing they use in heavy machinery, they still call it a 'shevek,'" naming it after her (160; ch. 7).

to conservative thinkers precisely because it is so dangerous to tinker with living organisms? Which returns us to the Le Guinian theme of true change: In a world without a transcendent god to set up means-justifying goals and moral laws, how can people achieve ethical, responsible change? Le Guin's answer in *The Dispossessed* is connected slightly with dreams (as in *WWF*) but mostly with time.

Among the Greek philosophers before Socrates, Pythagoras taught 'All is number.' Parmenides taught, 'Nothing changes'; and Parmenides's student Zeno (of Elea) pushed the point logically to 'Nothing moves,' and came up with Zeno's Paradox, where rocks never hit trees and fast runner Achilles never passes tortoises (see *TD* 23-27; ch. 2). And Heraclitus, profoundly disagreeing, insisted that 'All is change,' 'All is flux.' In a world of Simultaneity, Parmenides is right: nothing changes, all is constant, all is Being. We don't toss a stone and watch it hit the tree because the stone has already hit the tree when we tossed it (182; ch. 7)—indeed, we have already been born and have died, as has our species; all is *now*. In a world of Sequency, all is becoming, and change is continuous. Either way, there is little possibility for ethics or politics.[233] When finally developed, at an epiphany in the novel (224-26; ch. 9), Shevek's General Temporal Theory brings together Simultaneity and Sequency: dream-time and world-time, natural cycles and natural evolution (179-80; ch. 7). And it bases ethics solidly in physics, in number—our dual sense of linear and cyclical time—and this basis in *number* (if C. G. Jung is correct) relates ethics to a primary human instrument 'to bring order into the chaos of appearances,' an essential 'instrument for either creating order or apprehending' a pre-existent order in nature, perhaps a true archetype.[234]

At a party on Urras, drunk, Shevek explains the importance of our everyday sense of linear time:

> ...chronosophy does involve ethics. Because our sense of time involves our ability to separate cause and effect, means and end. The baby, again, the animal, they don't see the difference between what they do now and what will happen because of it. They can't make a pulley, or a

---

[233] For simultaneity and sequency, see Franz, esp. 220-22: time's arrow vs. 'primordial time'—Eliade's *illud tempus* (similar to Australian or Athshean Dream Time). The Simultaneous view and its ethical implication of Quietism is critiqued in Kurt Vonnegut, Jr.'s *Slaughterhouse-Five* (1969). Like *Slaughterhouse-Five*, *The Dispossessed* offers a gentle antidote to Transcendent views (such as the Tralfamadorians' god-like simultaneity) that kill compassion. For a Daoist view of cyclical time, see *Chuang Tzu* ch. 25 (Giles 257): 'Exhaustion leads to renewal. The end introduces a new beginning.'

[234] I quote here Franz, 231, paraphrasing Jung's *The Structure and Dynamics of the Psyche*, in *Collected Works* (1960), vol. 8: 456. See Also Franz's notes, *Voices of Time* 633-42: Franz is highly useful for Le Guin's work in the 1970s.

promise.[235] We can. Seeing the difference between *now* and *not now*, we can make the connection. And there morality enters in. Responsibility. To say that a good end will follow from a bad means is just like saying that if I pull a rope on this pulley it will lift the weight on that one. To break a promise is to deny the reality of the past; therefore it is to deny the hope of a real future. If time and reason are functions of each other, if we are creatures of time, then we had better know it, and try to make the best of it. To act responsibly. (181; ch. 7)

Sober and on Anarres, in bed with his beloved partner, Shevek talks with Takver about his old friend Tirin, a satiric playwright and Odonian anarchist driven insane by people who couldn't stand a real rebel.[236] The conversation moves on to the ethics of Shevek's having allowed his book to be edited and presented to the worlds as by Shevek and Sabul, Shevek's boss in a society where, in theory, there are no bosses. 'It did get the book printed,' Shevek notes, and Takver responds, 'The right end, but the wrong means!': which gets Shevek thinking here the ends/means problem and Takver's belief that she made the decision for both of them on compromising with Sabul. Shevek handles the second assertion first, declaring that neither of them made a real choice on publishing the book. 'We let Sabul choose for us. Our own, internalized Sabul—convention, moralism, fear of social ostracism, fear of being different, fear of being free!' (266; ch. 10).[237] Shevek notes that 'Those who build wall are their own prisoners' and asserts his 'proper function in the social organism': 'to go unbuild walls,' eventually having a go at unbuilding the wall between Anarres and Urras, and between Anarres and the rest of the galaxy. Huddling together with Shevek under the blankets, Takver says, 'It may get pretty drafty' (267).[238]

---

[235] Cf. Le Guin's poem 'Tenses' (*Wild Oats* [1988]: 81) where madness traps the Speaker in the 'cage of the present tense,' where part of the 'interminable pain' is a life of 'No promise kept.'
[236] Cf. Tenar and Ged's thematically significant kitchen conversation in *Tehanu*, 195-201 (ch. 12).
[237] Cf. Vea's remarks on Shevek's having a royal tyrant, 'a Queen Teaea inside you' (177; ch. 7). Note *Escape from Freedom* (1941) as the title of a well-known book by Erich Fromm and later a cliché (a powerful, true, and useful cliché) among mid-century analysts of totalitarianism.
[238] Unbuilding walls is a positive thing in *TD* and getting outside of walls a major motif in Le Guin, a Romantic and Daoist return to nature, the Way: from 'An die Musik' (1961) through *Leese Webster* (1975) to 'Solitude' (1994); walls and safety within a *good* City are valued in 'Coming of Age in Karhide' (1995). For two in bed, cf. and contrast Ishmael and Queequeg at the end of ch. 10 of *Moby Dick*, 'A Bosom Friend,' significantly juxtaposed with Father Mapple at the end of ch. 9, 'The Sermon' (for relationship vs. transcendent projects). Le Guin indicates *Moby Dick* wasn't a source for her ('Response to the Le Guin Issue' 46), but

With Takver asleep, Shevek begins a meditation in a section that repeats some variation on 'responsibility' at least four times in two pages, and one that begins and ends significantly with the idea that 'one must work with time and not against it' (267; ch. 10 [see 269, 249]).

What this might mean is suggested by Shevek's thought that for Takver and for him, and for Odonians, Daoists, and anarchists in general, there can be no separation of ends and means. There can be 'no end. There was process: process was all,' which suggests to me time's circle and cycles, as opposed to time's arrow, which we must picture with a beginning and direction, and usually picture with an end (a shot arrow more or less hits or misses).[239] That's not what Le Guin intends however: the next line is 'You could go in a promising direction or you could go wrong, but you did not set out with the expectation of ever stopping anywhere. All responsibilities, all commitments thus understood took on substance and duration'— apparently life-long duration. This open-ended obligation is much of what Le Guin means by 'responsibility,' and she says here exactly what she means. To Le Guin as to Odo, a promise is a promise, even a 'promise of indefinite term,' and it is promises that bind past, present, and future and which make freedom meaningful. 'A promise is a direction taken, a self-limitation of choice. As Odo pointed out, if no direction is taken, if one goes nowhere, no change will occur. One's freedom to choose and to change will be unused, exactly as if one were in jail, a jail of one's own building, a maze in which no one way is better than any other' (197; ch. 8). Indeed, Le Guin assigns meaningless circularity to what Hedonists and Utilitarians and other practical sorts have seen as rational, goal-seeking, linear behavior: seeking pleasure and avoiding pain. As what Aldous Huxley has called 'The Perennial Philosophy' teaches (106), evading suffering means also evading 'the chance of joy,' the chance for fulfillment. 'The search for pleasure is circular, repetitive... [and] always ends in the same place. It has an end. It comes to the end and has to start over. It is not a journey and return, but a closed cycle, a locked room,' and, repeating an important image in *The Dispossessed*, 'a cell,' as in *prison* cell. Opposed to such end-seeking is 'promising' action: 'Outside the locked room is the landscape of time, in which the spirit may, with luck and courage, construct the fragile, makeshift, improbable roads and cities of fidelity: a landscape inhabitable by human beings'—a landscape in which one can 'know what it is to come home,' which seems to be the one goal or end Le Guin unequivocally accepts. 'Loyalty, which asserts the continuity of past and future, binding time into a whole, is the root of human strength; there is no good to be done without it' (268-69; ch. 10).

The relationship of individual to society is reciprocal, with society offering literal 'security and stability' and figurative warmth and stillness, and the individual offering the 'power of moral choice—the power of

---

the image is an obvious one and goes back at least to Koheleth: '...if two lie together, they are warm; but how can one be warm alone?' (Eccl. 4.11).
[239] 'The means are the end. Odo said it all her life' (*TD* 238; ch. 9).

change.' In *The Dispossessed*, part of Dr. Haber's view is favored over George Orr's: change is 'the essential function of life.' Change is also the metaphorical essence of revolution, and Odonian society is supposed to be 'a permanent revolution,' with revolutionary activity seen—in theory and in the plot of this novel—as individual (267, ch. 10; see also 135, ch. 6). Le Guin has Shevek think here '...revolution begins in the thinking mind.' Later in the story, though earlier in the book, Shevek tells a demonstration, 'You cannot buy the Revolution. You cannot make the Revolution. You can only be the Revolution' (242; ch 9). Granted, but, What are Odonians to *do*?

A good, eclectic Daoist might respond to that question with the Buddha's *wu* (or *mu*)—short-form translation, 'Wrong question'—and note the doctrine '...the Quiet of the Taoists produces...a power 'that could shift Heaven and Earth'.... For 'to a mind that is 'still' the whole universe surrenders'' (Waley, 58).[240] A good Daoist does not make big plans, but acts spontaneously: '...from inaction comes the potentiality of action' (*Chuang Tzu*, chs. 5, 6, 13 [Giles 67, 71, 132]).[241] If one *is* the Revolution, one will do what must be done—at the right time. Such an idea requires a lot of faith, but it gets support from a surprising source, the very nonmystical, very European political theorist, Hannah Arendt:

> Textbook instructions on 'how to make a revolution' in a step-by-step progression from dissent to conspiracy, from resistance to armed uprising, are all based on the mistaken notion that revolution are 'made.' In a contest of violence the superiority of the government has always been absolute; but this superiority lasts only as long as...[governmental] commands are obeyed and the army or police forces are prepared to use their weapons [against the opponents of the government]. When this is no longer the case, the situation changes abruptly. Not only is the rebellion not put down, but the arms themselves change hands.... Only after...the disintegration of the government in power has permitted the rebels to arm themselves, can one speak of an 'armed uprising,' which often does not take place at all or occurs when it is no longer necessary. Where commands are no longer obeyed, the means of violence are of no use; and the questions of this obedience is not decided by the command-obedience relation but by opinion, and, of course, by the number of those who share

---

[240] *The Way and Its Power...*; Waley is bringing together the Confucian Mencius and *Chuang Tzu* ch. 13 (opening). See also Welsh's trans. of *Tao te Ching* ch. 43, in the section on water, on the value of 'action that is actionless'—and how difficult that teaching is to get across to people (Waley 197).
[241] Also Welch, *Parting* 15 (ruler's wu wei), 33 (returning to roots to practice wu wei and save the world).

>   it [numbers = power for Arendt]. Everything depends on the power behind the violence. The sudden dramatic breakdown of power that ushers in revolutions reveals in a flash how civil disobedience...is but the outward manifestation of support and consent [granted: 'civil' and denied: 'disobedience'].
>
>   Where power has disintegrated, revolutions are possible but not necessary. (*On Violence* 48-49; § II).

Coups can be accomplished with a small, elite, vanguard; the Revolution bubbles up from the masses who produce a 'revolutionary situation,' where 'power is already in the streets.' What is needed then is conscious people 'prepared to seize power and the responsibility that goes with it' (Arendt 50) and give direction. Or, as I think Odo and Le Guin would prefer, allow oneself to be seized by power and take responsibility for how one directs that power (see *TD* 152; ch. 6). Meanwhile, what one does is what Shevek and his friends do: they organize and educate.

Le Guin isn't going to start favoring Dr. Haber over Mr. Orr generally, and her Revolution, in 1960s terms, is more Countercultural than narrowly political: relational more than goal-seeking. At the center of her Revolution, central even to the Syndicate of Initiative, is the inaction that allows potential right action, and the loyalty, fidelity, 'marriage' that allows time-binding through human promises.[242]

If we are to picture Shevek and Takver in bed when Shevek has his long interior monolog to decide to unbuild walls, then at the very center of the vision of *The Dispossessed* is a pair of a life-bonded, child-producing, child-rearing people. In a variation on the comic romance theme, a new and better world will (probably) coalesce around them at the end of the novel. In any event, Shevek is central to the plot, and Shevek and Takver are established as central symbolically when Shevek returns from the famine years in the Dust and he and Takver make love: '...the third time they were both half asleep, and circled about...each other's being, like planets circling blindly...about the common center of gravity, swinging, circling endlessly' (258; ch. 10). If one can talk of an Odonian duty, it would be to be like Shevek and Takver, living complex lives of partnership and parenthood, domestic jobs and political work: Takver as partner, biologist, and mother; Shevek with more stress as 'not only a physicist but also a partner, a father, an Odonian, and finally a social reformer.... [H]e had not been sheltered, and had expected no shelter' (104; ch. 5).[243] Beyond that, one can modify the arrow analogy by putting the bow in the hands of a Zen adept—one loyal to spouse, family, and friends! There is no target;

---

[242] For time-binding, see Meerloo 237-40, section 2, Evolutionary Time and Time-binding Processes.

[243] Cf. image of unsheltered male 'artist' in 'An die Musik'; cf. image of radically unsheltered female author in Le Guin's essay 'The Fisherwoman's Daughter.'

the archer works with time and Being and knows where to shoot and, more important, when (see *Tehanu* 175; ch. 11).

CRITIQUE: *Kulturkampf*-ing on the Left with *The Dispossessed*

The artistic merit of *The Dispossessed* is, I think, unquestionable. What has been questioned is parts of the politics, and here I'll express some of my own political reservations. Then, with political reservations earnestly expressed, we can move on. Le Guin did.

First, again, I find *The Dispossessed* vague about how to bring change to societies, especially societies like that of A-Io, where even peaceful demonstrators are likely to get machine-gunned by military establishments ideal for such uses.[244] If the idea is to just Be It and Do It!, we still need more details. Shevek and the Syndicate of Initiative do pretty much just *do it* on Anarres, but we never learn how—or what plans they have if PDC had refused to assign resources to activities perceived by many of their Odonian sibs as dangerous, subversive, counterrevolutionary, and/or unOdonian.

Second, taking 'politics' more generally, there are a number of attacks in *The Dispossessed* against moralizing, puritanical hardness, and narrow-minded, second rate, moralistic people, including the young Shevek (e.g., 78-81, 96 in ch. 4; 126, 128 in ch. 6). Indeed, part of the ambiguity of the ambiguous utopia of the Anarresti is how unnecessarily harsh they've made parts of life by applying Odo's dictum, 'Excess is excrement' on the biologically poor world of Anarres (80; ch. 4). Getting specific, and dealing with sexual politics, we're told that Odo 'provided better for the promiscuous than for those who tried long-term partnership' (198; ch. 8). She certainly provided better than we have in America in the 1970s or today. There are no laws of any sort, of course, and no social disapproval of any 'sexual practice of any kind, except the rape of a child or woman' and both heterosexual and homosexual partnerships are accepted (198; ch. 8). Well, perhaps 'statutory rape' *should* have some meaning and social enforcement even where there are no statutes, and rape is a bad thing, even if the victim is a man. Still, my feeling is that the surface level of *The Dispossessed* is antipuritanical, while much of the text is pretty severe. Vokep is the one man we see with the sexual philosophy of 'Touch and go,' and he has a low opinion of women and one small scene on two pages of a novel of over 300 pages (42-43; ch. 2). The one promiscuous woman we see on Anarres is Beshun, and she is treated fairly sympathetically in bringing Shevek 'into the heart of sexuality' (42), but we're told that Shevek now and then during sex felt he possessed Beshun, 'And she had thought,' for a while, that she 'owned him' (43). In a society where 'propertarian' is an insulting epithet, what little we learn of Beshun does not speak well of her.

In terms of the treatment of homosexuality, and of a single, socially dedicated life, there are problems. We see no lesbians, and we do see one

---

[244] *TD* 245; ch. 9. See Lefanu 141.

gay man: Bedap. Bedap is important to the plot, highly visible and has a brief, fully-adult sexual relationship with Shevek and helps change Shevek's life (138-40; ch. 6); and in some ways Bedap is more important even than Shevek in establishing the Syndicate of Initiative and renewing utopia on Anarres. Such treatment of a gay man is progressive even nowadays—watching the immensely popular film *INDEPENDENCE DAY* (1996) will drive home *that* point—and more progressive in 1974. And Thomas Remington has correctly pointed out in a discussion of *Planet of Exile* that 'homosexual devotion...represents the yearning for a 'bond of sameness' rather than one 'of difference'' ('Other Side' 157), which would help justify Le Guin's privileging of heterosexual bonds. Still, some readers are legitimately troubled by the treatment of Bedap.

During the agitation over the Syndicate of Initiative, Shevek and Takver's daughter is tormented by other children and ends up crying in Shevek's arms. Bedap is present but leaves almost immediately, not wanting to intrude on 'the one intimacy which he could not share...the intimacy of pain. It gave him no sense of relief or escape to go; rather he felt useless, diminished.' And then he has his mid-life crisis, asking himself at thirty-nine years 'What have I done? What have I been doing? Nothing. Meddling. Meddling in other people's lives because I don't have one.' And he reaches his recognition 'that all his hope was in that understanding that if he would be saved he must change his life' (298; ch. 12; see Bedford 17).[245] Now a gay can certainly become a workaholic 'political' and mess up his life; but we see only one adult gay, and arguably only truly political person in the novel, and that's Bedap; and he is not partnered and is not happy; and in utopia, even a highly ambiguous utopia, readers may well see this as his fault. Bedap seems to see it as his fault, and we do not learn how he goes about mending that fault. Rulag, Shevek's mother (as we shall see) is also unpartnered, unhappy, politically active, and dangerous. Odo may have indeed 'provided better for the promiscuous than for those who tried long-term partnerships'—Shevek and Takver undergo long separations—but *The Dispossessed*, like the Karhidish Hearths, privileges partnership: from what we see, it comes down in favor of monogamous, heterosexual marriage (Lefanu 141). In its explicit ideology and in the maturing of Shevek, *The Dispossessed* is antipuritanical; in the sum of its incidents, readers seem to be told to change our lives, take responsibility, marry, have kids, work hard—and that pain, damn it, is *good* for you, including the pain of trying to make a partnership work on Anarres (48-50, ch. 3; 140, ch. 6; 269, ch. 10).

---

[245] 'You must change your life' is what Rainer Maria Rilke said a statue of Apollo said to him—quoted by Le Guin in 'Myth and Archetype in Science Fiction,' *LoN* (1979): 77-78. The line is used at least twice elsewhere in *TD*: rather ironically on p. 126 (ch. 6) and as part of a tribute to Bedap for changing Shevek's life: 140; ch. 6. See also, 'The Child and the Shadow,' *LoN* (1979): 59-71. For Bedap's sex life outside of his relationship with Shevek, see 44; ch. 2.

Shevek discovers for himself the First Noble Truth of the Buddha that 'Suffering is the condition on which we live'—in Shevek's words—and he and his friends recognize that small 'p,' individual pains and pain, is one of the roots of society. And he comes close to the idea that one should get through pain to the 'place where the self—ceases' (48-50; ch. 2). As Aldous Huxley says the Perennial Philosophy teaches: 'Mortification is painful, but that pain is one of the pre-conditions of blessedness,' if it leads to 'losing the egocentric life' (106; ch. 6). What blessedness we see in terms of the plot of *The Dispossessed*, though, on Anarres and on Urras, is purified but fairly traditional family life. And for some readers, memories of their families may suggest not blessedness, just pain.

Which brings me to my third reservation. I find Sarah Lefanu's harsh tone unfortunate and unfair, but she has some legitimate points in her section on *The Dispossessed* in the 1988 book *Feminism and Science Fiction* (132-33, 140-43; ch. 12). I do not have a problem with *The Dispossessed*'s appeal to liberal male readers or with its binary oppositions (Lefanu 140-41); or with Le Guin in general having male central characters in her early work—Lefanu does not mention anything later than 'The Diary of the Rose' (1976). Nor do I mind that Le Guin writes in 'the tradition of the bourgeois novel with its construction rather than deconstruction of the subject as hero' (Lefanu 143, 142). Le Guin has good insights into male perception, and I enjoy seeing with the kind of double vision one gets looking through a male's eyes as a woman and brilliant writer—Le Guin—imagines the view. And if the subject or Self is a mere myth of middleclass culture, it is a myth useful for ethical behavior: establishment of 'I-Thou' relationships require an 'I'; and I-Thou relationships are a good starting point for ethics, however unfashionably Structuralist they must be.[246] Lefanu is highly suggestive and useful though in dealing with Le Guin's treatment of her political people and with *The Dispossessed*'s three major female characters, 'the treacherous temptress,' Vea, who is 'part of the evils of capitalism' (Lefanu 132), Shevek's career-woman mother, Rulag, and Shevek's partner, Takver 'the token strong woman, [who] keeps the home fires burning while Shevek is off changing the future of mankind...' (141).[247]

I wish to go father than Lefanu on Shevek's encounter with Vea at that highly stressed party on Urras (ch. 7).

---

[246] Again, binary oppositions are central to Structuralism, a major approach to anthropology and other academic subjects in the 1950s-70s; from the mid-1970s on, cutting-edge thought in the humanities and social science moved toward a PostStructuralist (postmodern, postcolonial) paradigm.
[247] For Rulag, see *TD* ch. 4, esp. 100, her line, 'The work comes first, with me'—i.e., she chooses work over her family. Cf. Stone Telling's father in *Always Coming Home*, when he leaves North Owl and Willow, following his military 'work'; contrast Shevek's balancing of family, physics, and politics. Lefanu usefully notes Tom Moylan on Shevek and sex: Lefanu 141, quoting Tom Moylan, *Demand the Impossible: Science Fiction and the Utopian Imagination* (1986): 110.

At Vea's party, Shevek gets to expound his theories on time to a lay audience. More, when he tries to intimidate a know-it-all with physics jargon, Vea stops him: "'Now stop trying to scare Dearri, and tell us what that means in baby talk,' Vea said. Her acuteness made Shevek grin' (178)—so we get Shevek's cocktail-party lecture in language *we* can understand. We also see Shevek's first experience with alcohol, and his getting drunk. After the discussion of time and philosophy, after a profound comment on Anarres vs. Urras (184) Shevek gets dizzy and goes with Vea into a bedroom. Vea says 'I've got to kiss you for that!' and does kiss Shevek, lifting 'herself on tiptoe, presenting him her mouth, and her white throat, and her naked breasts.' Shevek misunderstands. Le Guin notes, as a critic, 'They can't read each other's cultural signals' (personal communication).

> 'Now stop,' she said. 'No, now listen, Shevek, it won't do, not now. I haven't taken a contraceptive.... No, let me be,' but he could not let her be; his face was pressed against her soft, sweaty, scented flesh.... 'Wait—just wait, we can arrange it.... I do have to be careful of my reputation.... Not now! Not now!' Frightened at last by his blind urgency, his force, she pushed at him as hard as she could, her hands against his chest. He took a step backward, confused by her sudden high tone of fear and her struggle; but he could not stop, her resistance excited him further. He gripped her to him, and his semen spurted out against the white silk of her dress. (185)

Shevek returns groggily to the party and vomits on a silver pastries platter on a fancy table.

Shevek is drunk; he does misunderstand Vea's intentions; but there is a problem with this scene similar to the problem with the Pervert and the kemmerer in the Foretelling scene in *The Left Hand of Darkness* (64-66; ch. 5). If one wishes to complain on feminist grounds about *The Left Hand of Darkness* and *The Dispossessed*, one need not get into such subtleties as objecting to the 'attempted syntheses of binary oppositions' in 'romances of integration' (Lefanu 139, Jackson 154) or a 'subject-centered view of the novel' (Lefanu 136)—or 'Man' for humankind and the generic 'he.' In *Left Hand* Le Guin was too casual with the imagery of sexual harassment; in the scene in Vea's bedroom she is too casual with what most readers should understand, after Vea's 'No,' as a sexual assault.

That said, there I will stop my own criticism of *The Dispossessed* and shift into another mode.

Lefanu is bothered by Vea as 'the treacherous temptress' (132); more exactly, we have the presentation of Vea as an informal government agent (*TD* 186; ch. 7), and more importantly as a 'body profiteer' (*TD* 256; ch. 10): "'A body profiteer,' Takver called women who used their sexuality as a weapon in a power struggle with men'—and, of course, Vea is 'the body profiteer to end them all' (171; ch. 7). That Vea would use her sexuality any way she can among the sexist, capitalist, objectifying, and commodifying Ioti is no criticism of women or The Nature of Woman; it is not even much of a criticism of Vea. The problem would be that Takver has the concept of body profiteering: one may feel that the Odonian utopia should be free of any sort of prostitution or use of sex or sexuality for power or advantage in some war of the sexes. I don't see a problem in this, unless one thinks a war of the sexes inevitable, which Le Guin does not. If there is a flaw in this aspect of *The Dispossessed*, it is in limiting 'body profiteering' to women and to 'sexuality'—unless we understand 'sexuality' very broadly. Men and boys in our world learn early and well whether or not their bodies can be exploited—for sex as well as for money and power (e.g., as athletes).[248] I expect in utopia much less exploitation, period, in every sense; of the residue that remains, utopia should allow both men and women to take their advantages equally. If we wish to avoid binary oppositions, and especially hierarchical binary oppositions, where it is 'A' vs. 'B', hence 'A' superior to 'B'—then one opposition to be avoided is 'mind'/'body.' As Odo thinks, 'A proper body's not an object, not an implement, not a belonging to be admired, it's just you, yourself' ('Day Before,' *WTQ* 262); it is a fault, not a virtue of "Civilized Man" to go 'climbing up into his head' and cut himself off from other animals and the world (*BG* 11; Introd.), and from his body. If smart people have a right to use our brains to get status, then graceful, beautiful, athletic, and sexy people have a right to use their gifts.[249] In utopia the gifted—in any way and like everyone else—just may not use their gifts to gain power over other people.

But in critiquing the critique of Lefanu et al., there is an 'on the other hand' to recognize in *The Dispossessed*'s presentation of women, its general politics, and its teaching about teaching.

(1) Takver does indeed make a speech on 'pregnant women have no ethics. Only the most primitive kind of sacrifice impulse....' (266; ch. 10), but Takver makes this speech; it is not a series of aphorisms from the Narrator, and I take it as a general warning against the 'sacrifice impulse.' The Narrator has told us early in the novel that 'However pragmatic the morality a young Anarresti absorbed, yet life overflowed in him, demanding altruism, self-sacrifice, scope for the absolute gesture' (75; ch. 4), and we know from elsewhere in *The Dispossessed* and Le Guin's canon generally that she is well aware of the dangers for any *him* and his or her society from impulses toward sacrifice, self-sacrifice, and even altruism. (2) *The Dispossessed* is dedicated '*For the partner*': Le Guin is a married woman; she believes in marriage; and she has the right to celebrate her decision and her way of life. (3) The partnership between Takver and Shevek is utopian in that it is significantly better than most people, especially most female people, get in our society. Takver is a scientist; she travels; and she

---

[248] See below, discussion of 'The Matter of Seggri.'
[249] Note Bob in 'Pathways of Desire,' whose physical beauty is part of his kingliness (*CR* 189).

has daycare and a male partner who really shares rearing the kids. Indeed, in terms of Le Guin's overarching norms, Takver is rather like Tenar in Rosemarie Arbur's observation that Tenar reaches Ged's 'goal in life—that of *being* rather than *doing*—about two decades before he does' (*Proceedings* 151). Indeed, Shevek recognizes Takver as one of those 'souls... whose umbilicus has never been cut.' Changing the metaphor, he thinks Takver and people like her 'never got weaned from the universe. They do not understand death as an enemy' but, as the Daoist philosopher Chuang Tzu advised, 'look forward to rotting and turning into humus' (*TD* 150; ch. 6).[250] The legitimate complaint here is that *The Dispossessed* is not Takver's story; Le Guin has not yet written an 'Affirmative Action' story for Takver as she has written *Tehanu* for Tenar. (4) Last: Rulag, Takver, and Vea are not the only women in *The Dispossessed*.

There is Sewa Oiie, sister-in-law to Vea (157; ch. 7) and pretty much neutral: a good mother in Ioti society. There's Bunub, 'Mother Envy'—a rather paranoid, selfish, envious person, but a very nicely drawn minor character and comment on the limits of utopia; like aggressivity and the authoritarian impulse, envy and some other bad traits are human givens (261, ch. 10; 208-10, ch. 8). One may disagree with the givenness of such givens or any human givens, but Bunub's faults are more than balanced by worse faults among men, and the argument here would not be with her gender. Finally, as Shevek tells the physicists on Urras, his teachers Mitis and Gvarab were women—and, as all the characters know and we should not forget, so was Odo (60; ch. 3). This point is important, and ambiguous: three of the central people in Shevek's life, in the formation of his character, were women and teachers; and one of them, of course, founded his society.

On the one hand, these women are definitely *minor* characters in *The Dispossessed*: they are important in the story primarily because of their effect upon Shevek; on the other hand, any feminism that excludes teaching and nurturing as honored activities loses many women supporters and a fair number of men fellow-travelers. Odo was the teacher to a whole society, and from Moses of the Exodus unto Moses Maimonides unto Odo the revolutionary, teachers have been important. Education and teachers, in fact, seems central to Le Guin's theory of revolution (see 'A Woman's Liberation' in *FWF*, esp. 197 f. [and *FWF* 125 f.]). Mitis was 'a splendid teacher' and Gvarab, also, just unfortunate to have lived too late to develop the General Temporal Theory (58; ch. 3) on her own: Gvarab's work lived on in Shevek's. Our usual hierarchizing of achievement puts the mere teachers Mitis and Gvarab far below Odo and puts Sewa Oiie even lower, or Takver in her role as mother. But, then, such hierarchizing puts Ursula K. Le Guin's 'partner' down pretty far as a college teacher (plus much of the rest of Le Guin's family) plus Ursula K. Le Guin in her role as housewife and mother—and I also am pretty far down on the status chain, among Le Guin's other critics with academic jobs. The point, I would

---

[250] *Chuang Tzu* ch. 6, Giles 79.

hope, is to value all sorts of achievements on the way to eliminating such arranging of people into hierarchies.

And on that point, Ursula K. Le Guin was very much ahead of the curve by 1974.

Whatever flaws recent critics have or future critics will find in *The Dispossessed*, I recall it in 1974 offering a vision of an alternative to two pernicious hierarchies: both class-ridden, authoritarian capitalism and centralized, authoritarian Communism. It offered and still offers particularly to Americans an analysis of the ways revolutions get stopped or rolled back. At a time in which the bicentennial of the American Bill of Rights went by with hardly a word in celebration, approaching a new millennium in which the United States may go from a secular republic to a Christian nation, that analysis is still highly relevant. With that analysis in a work of such elegant structure, *The Dispossessed* earned its Hugo and Nebula in the 1970s. During times in which respectable discourse in much of the world excludes not only anarchists—who are used to it—but even democratic socialists and liberals, *The Dispossessed* continues to be an important book and an important book on the political Left.

'The Day Before the Revolution' (1974)

In the headnote to her story, Le Guin describes as '*one of the ones who walked away from Omelas*' Odo, the anarchist philosopher whose theories are shown in *The Dispossessed* (1974) and whose last day is narrated in 'The Day Before the Revolution' (1974 [*WTQ* 260]).

At least in terms of the works I'm stressing, 'The Day Before the Revolution' can be seen as a (figurative) hinge, recapitulating important themes that proceeded it and foreshadowing developments to come.

For one thing, so positive a revolutionary should give us pause in privileging immanence over Simone de Beauvoir's transcendence, Daoist unaction over heroic striving. What could be a more transcendent project than a utopian revolution? Few things, actually, but I would raise three points on the Le Guinian favoring of immanence that critics since Douglas Barbour (1974) have stressed in pointing out Le Guin's Daoism. First, at least into early 1970, the utopian question was, 'What will things be like the day *after* the Revolution?'—i.e., what are the goals of the Revolution? Le Guin's story is about a fairly ordinary day, the day *before* the revolution. Second, the story is about Odo, 'the famous revolutionary,' except it is not that, in part because Odo is not *just* that. She is also a wife and lover. She was her life, which included being, a 'swimmer in the midst of life' (*WTQ* 275). Third, Odo is the theoretician of people on the bottom, at 'the foundation, the reality, the source'; her wisdom comes from knowing people are, at bottom, mud (274), part of the Earth.

The plot of 'The Day Before the Revolution' may be summarized thus: On the day before the Revolution in A-Io, as news arrived of rebellion in Thu, Laia Asieo Odo had a dream, awoke, dressed, ate breakfast, fixed her hair a bit and answered letters (with some help), spoke with visiting students, went out for a walk, returned home (with help), and died. If you know Le Guin's *The Dispossessed*, you know that A-Io and Thu are on the planet Urras; if you don't, you don't. If you know Le Guin's early SF and fantasy, you know she has always been quite capable of telling stories with many physical incidents—and you know that in 'The Day Before the Revolution' Le Guin has chosen to keep the world-shaking events offstage. As she says in her introduction to 'Vaster than Empires and More Slow,' her interest *'is in what goes on inside. Inner space and all that. We all have forests in our minds. Forests unexplored, unending. Each of us gets lost in the forest, every night, alone'* (*WTQ* 166). I.e., in dream, where Le Guin begins 'The Day Before the Revolution,' as she had begun *The Lathe of Heaven* (1971). And Le Guin deals here with an old person on the edge of death, as she had dealt with Wold in *Planet of Exile* (1966)—a book that also uses an image much like the Circle of Life (*WTQ* 272). Both Odo and Le Guin note the dangers of 'Dualizing' (267) and altruism (270) deal briefly with marriage, touch (contact with the Other), doing what one *must* do, names (273), freedom, liberty, discipline, and responsibility—constants in Le Guin's writing and maybe in much of Odo's. In 'The Day Before the Revolution,' Le Guin makes explicit her intuition into *her* use, at least, of the Return as a human imperative: 'If you wanted to come home you had to keep going on, that was what she meant when she wrote 'True journey is return,'...'—at least that was what she, Le Guin as well as Odo, meant to the extent that one can 'rationalize' meaning out of an intuition (266).[251]

Old Wold, however, was a man, and Odo is a woman: the point-of-view character and protagonist in what is emphatically and wholly her story. And Odo is an unambiguously attractive character (if hardly perfect), clarifying in Le Guin's fiction that Le Guin means what Le Guin says about anarchy: she's for it. Not anarchism as terrorism nor *'the social-Darwinist economic 'libertarianism' of the far right; but anarchism as prefigured in early Taoist thought'*—the advice to the Emperor to do nothing—*'and expounded by* [Percy Bysshe] *Shelley and* [Petr] *Kropotkin,* [Emma] *Goldman and* [Paul] *Goodman.'* That is, she disapproves of *'the authoritarian State (capitalist or socialist),'* and she approves of anarchism's *'principal moral-practical theme'* of *'cooperation (solidarity, mutual aid)'* (*WTQ* 260).[252]

---

[251] Especially an intuition by someone not overtly spiritual: More cosmologically, Return is the action of the Dao: *ACH* 485—the last word under THE WAY as a 'Generative Metaphor' is 'return'; also *Tao te Ching* ch. 40: 'In Tao the only motion is returning' (Waley 192).
[252] For *TD*'s principles as 'feminist, communal, centrally coordinated, anarchist and Taoist' (as opposed to Robert A. Heinlein's anarchist but also masculinist, individualist, Capitalist, and ultimately Christian (?) revolutionary society on the Moon in *The Moon Is a Harsh Mistress* [1966]), see Williams, 'The Moons of Le Guin and Heinlein.'

But Le Guin is not so concerned with any over-arching philosophy that she privileges it over the thoughts of a rather rough-edged 'drooling old woman' (if one 'who had started a world revolution' [265]) moving toward her death at seventy-two, never having learned the names of the one set of flowers we see in the story (277); 'The Movement was not strong on names' (273). Dead center in the story is Odo as individual. Odo is 'the famous revolutionary' (275), but also the sexual being who still cares how she looks to a young man who attracts her. She's the troublemaker who once 'kicked policemen, and spat at priests, and pissed in public on the big brass plaque in Capitol Square'—and who rejects the role of 'sweet old monument' and 'Big Sheltering Womb.' Most especially she is 'The one who loved Taviri,' her husband, long dead, but that's not enough either (275). She is her history, as the Existentialists have said; and finally, there is what she is at her foundation, sitting in a doorway in the city, asking who she is. 'There was nothing left, really, but the foundation. She had come home; she had never left home. 'True voyage is return.' Dust and mud and a doorstep in the slums' (*WTQ* 268, 271-72, 275-76).

Odo is an anarchist, '*One who, choosing, accepts the responsibility of choice*' (*WTQ* 272). Her choices in life were very different from those of her fellow author, Ursula K. Le Guin. Le Guin accepts and accepts responsibility for the choices she made and does not repudiate them. But her work evolves. Odo is a hinge in Le Guin's canon, simultaneously separating and connecting the works through the early 1970s with the later works. These works are still Daoist: Odo is in touch with her world (270), follows the Dao of revolution. But Odo regrets 'Dualizing again' (267), setting up mind/body as binary opposites—or perhaps *any* binary opposites—and is a woman moving toward defining a new kind of heroism: with her Le Guin moves toward works more explicitly informed with contemporary feminism.

V.

NEW HEROES

I'll repeat here some of what I've inferred to be the basic patterns for Ursula K. Le Guin's SF and fantasy.

First, there is the pattern of two philosophical views of the world: transcendence vs. immanence (in its Eastern, 'Perennial Philosophy' form): most generally the argument over whether Ultimate Reality is Out There in some transcendent God or Ultimate Truth reached through a semi-divine Reason, or is within the world, to be felt out inside things—immanent. Le Guin has come out for immanence in terms of this philosophical debate, but she has also been willing to endorse immanence in more worldly, political ways. In *The Second Sex* (1949), Simone de Beauvoir uses 'immanence' and 'transcendence' as central terms for her analysis of women's current situation and proposals for women's liberation, and finds that the 'domestic labors that fell to [woman's] lot...imprisoned her in repetition and immanence'—a clearly bad thing. For Beauvoir a human couple 'is the original *Mitsein*' (friendly society), but still, nowhere is 'woman' more trapped in immanence than reproduction and marriage.[253] Le Guin may deny church and state and the sanction of either for personal relationships, but she can speak well of friendship, love, commitment to a promise—and, in those senses, speak well of 'marriage.'

Which leads to the pattern of Romantic Comedy.[254] In the Shakespearean form that permeates English-speaking culture, Romantic Comedy moves toward a new and better world—younger, more flexible, more hopeful, more joyous—coalescing around a central couple. The Shakespearean pattern also allows for variations, even such extreme variations as the tragedy of Romeo and Juliet and the trashing of Romance in love and war in Shakespeare's *Troilus and Cressida*. The Shakespearean precedent also includes the contrasting of two worlds as in the «dream-time» forest

---

[253] See e.g., in *Second Sex* 1 35, 47, 173-5, 187; II.V.xvi: esp. 429-30, 447-48, 451-54, 456; II.V.xvii: 513, 521; 555-6, 594; II.V.xxi: esp. 598-99, 602 (see also 618-21).
[254] Implicit in my use of the terms 'Comedy,' 'Romance,' 'Tragedy,' and 'Satire' is my simplification of an image from Northrop Frye of a cycle of pre-generic modes following the cycle of the seasons. See Frye, 'Theory of Myths,' esp. 162.

vs. the orderly palace of Theseus in *A Midsummer Night's Dream*, the green world of the Forest of Arden vs. the authoritarian Court in *As You Like It* or the golden world of Belmont vs. the early-capitalist world of Venice in *The Merchant of Venice*. Two worlds in instructive contrast are also common in utopias and dystopian satires; as the anti-hero says in Frederik Pohl and C. M. Kornbluth's *The Space Merchants*, '...things are invisible except against a contrasting background' (173; ch. 14). In Sir Thomas More's *Utopia* (1516) there is Utopia vs. 'all the other states which flourish today,' which seem to Raphael Hythloday (the voyager to Utopia) to be 'nothing but a conspiracy of the rich, who pursue their own aggrandizement under the name and title of the Commonwealth' (Hythloday's closing speech). In Yevgeny Zamiatin's *We* (ca. 1920), it is the anti-Christian, Scythian-like rebels—the 'Mephi'—vs. the over-rational, Euclidean, 'Taylorized' City-dwellers of the United State.[255] In Aldous Huxley's *Brave New World* (1932), there is the Savage Reservation vs. the civilized lands of the World State. In E. M. Forster's 'The Machine Stops' (1909), the contrast is between machine-using subterrestrials and surface-dwellers closer to nature.[256]

As Le Guin, I, and others have noted, Le Guin's variation on this common pattern has the good society in the story in some sense anarchistic: 'communal, independent, and somewhat introverted.' Their populations are stable and they tend not to 'move in large masses, or rapidly. Their migrations have been slow.... They have no nomadic peoples, and no societies that live by expansion and aggression.... Nor have they formed large, hierarchically governed nation-states, the mobilizable entity that is the essential factor in modern war.' Competition is ritualized, and, when ritual breaks down, the resulting violence does not become mass violence, remaining limited, personal.' Bad societies are organized into 'hierarchically governed nation-states' or their future analogs, which Le Guin sees correctly as 'the mobilizable entity that is the essential factor in modern war' and, I'll add, premodern war ('Gender...Redux' 10-11, 'Gender' in *LoN* [1979]: 166). If religion is an issue in the story, the good people favor an immanent, noninstitutionalized spirituality, putting them into the world and connecting them with the world; the bad people favor transcendence and immortality and *organized* religion—as we have seen in *The Left Hand of Darkness*, and which can be inferred from *The Dispossessed*: one

---

[255] That's capital 'C' *City*. For the City in *We*, see Aldridge 76. Le Guin's works can be placed in a very fruitful dialog with *We* and the other dystopias I mention. For Le Guin and Zamiatin, see end of 'The Stalin in the Soul,' coll. *LoN* (1979): 220-21.

[256] Comparison and Contrast is a traditional 'mode' in rhetoric, and from the early 1960s into the 1970s, binary oppositions were popular in various structuralist theories and other intellectual work. See Lévi-Strauss 139, 161 and passim; note comparison/contrast methodology in Elmendorf with A. L. Kroeber, or for that matter, comparative anatomy, comparative linguistics, and much of the tradition of 19th- into early 20th-c. science.

of Shevek's first lines to the Urrasti is 'You admit no religion outside the churches, just as you admit no morality outside the laws' (*TD* 12; ch. 1).

With these patterns in mind, I wish to examine here five of Le Guin's works from the mid-1970s to 1980 and point out variations on these themes from the work of the 1960s and early 1970s.

YOUNG ADULT STORIES:
Very Far Away from Anywhere Else (1976)

Very Far Away from Anywhere Else is a mundane ('realistic,' 'mainstream') novella telling, according to the front cover blurb on the Bantam 1978 edition, 'A Different Kind of Love Story.' The story is set in our world, on the west coast of the USA, and covers some six months of fictive time and one basic 'action' (1).

Owen Thomas turned seventeen 'last November,' and the plot kicks in five days after his birthday, a birthday on which Owen's father gave him a car (6-7). Owen is a contemporary American intellectual with strong interests in biology and psychology, and the protagonist-narrator of the novella. For college he wants to go to the Massachusetts Institute of Technology, California Institute of Technology, or Princeton (in that order); his mother very much wants him to go to 'State' (see 22-23). Shortly after getting the car, Owen, still walking to and from school, guiltily takes a bus to get out of the rain and meets Natalie Field, a fellow student, about a year older than he. Natalie is also an intellectual, and an artist. Owen and Natalie become best friends. Owen clowns, doing an ape act for Natalie; Natalie lets Owen stay with her while she practices the viola.[257] Natalie tells Owen about her desire to become a composer and lets him know she feels insecure in that ambition—an insecurity that contrasts with her confidence as a performer and her rock-steadiness (18, 33, 41-42). And, when Natalie tells Owen about the Brontë family, Owen tells her about the land of Thorn he invented, his own country, 'a very long way from anywhere else' (49). All goes well until Owen decides he must desire sex with Natalie, hence must love her (43-45). At an outing to Jade Beach, Owen makes a sexual advance upon Natalie and is rebuffed (52-57). Having dropped Natalie off at home, Owen drives away, drives around, and drives his new car off the road, 'totaling' the car and giving himself some serious bruises, a dislocated shoulder, and a concussion (58). Fortunately, the car is completely insured; unfortunately Owen avoids Natalie, cuts himself off from people, lives in a figurative 'fog,' and starts lying about small things (67). This goes on until spring, when Owen sees an announcement of an evening of music with the civic orchestra that will include performances by Natalie and others of her settings for three poems (65). Owen goes to the concert, is greatly moved (69-71), and he and Natalie reconcile and become friends again. At the end of the novella, she goes off to Tanglewood, and he will

---

[257] For clowning, cf. and contrast the ritual clowns and occasional clowning in *ACH* (e.g. 384).

soon go to MIT. Their 'touch' is relatively chaste kisses mostly, but they are now going beyond the six-second limit they thought decorous for friends (85-87).

At the start of his story, Owen tells us, 'Sports are neat to do, but dull to talk about. Anyhow there won't be much about sports in this' (1). Nor is there any coming of age through sex or violence or going through basic training or cruising with the guys or spectacular car chases or getting drunk, getting high, or rescuing the heroine. Instead we get a young male protagonist on the border of manhood making some points about relationships. *Very Far Away* offers a different kind of romantic comedy or romance: one that ends in friendship strong enough to stand separation, one that examines very deeply the complexities of young love.

* * * * * * *

Very Far Away is interesting in itself in its participation in the 'debate' on the possibility of boy/girl and woman/man friendship, and on sex.

Michael Moffatt, an anthropologist who has studied college students only slightly older than Owen and Natalie, repeats some true clichés about friendship in America:

> Until recently in American culture, friendships usually formed between men and men or between women and women; they did not ordinarily occur between the sexes [after childhood]. As late as 1970 a sociologist could generalize about American gender relations: 'Except during courtship, [American] men and women are not expected to pursue interaction voluntarily with one another. And they are not expected to form friendships with one another, but to try to find a marriage partner, thus the assertion that men and women can be lovers but never friends. (45)[258]

According to Moffatt's studies, norms for male/female relationships had changed enough by the late 1970s and 1980s, at least among young people, that 'over a third of hundreds of reciprocated close friendships reported...by students in the Rutgers [University] coed dorms were cross-sex relationships' (45). But such relationships were still sufficiently problematic into the 1990s to be material for television situation comedies like *Seinfeld* and *Friends* and for theatrical films such as Rob Reiner's WHEN HARRY MET SALLY (1989). *Very Far Away* in 1976, then, was dealing centrally with a topic important for its Young Adult target audience and beyond. Also significant is the question of sex. Moffatt notes that 'The direct sources of the students' sexual ideas were located almost entirely in mass

---

[258] Moffatt quotes here Suzanne B. Kurth's essay 'Friendship and Friendly Relationships,' in George J. McCall, S. B. Kurth, et al., *Social Relationships* (Chicago: Aldine, 1970): 145.

consumer culture,' from films and television to *Penthouse*, *Playgirl*, Harlequin romances (females only), and occasional pornography (Moffatt 194). All together, these sources produce what the Leftist British critic Stephen Heath calls

> a 'new sexual orthodoxy,' one that is in some ways as coercive as older, rejected western sexual codes.[259] If pre-Victorians associated sex with sin and guilt but nevertheless often enjoyed it quietly as a private pleasure, Heath argues, and if the Victorians discovered sexuality and then repressed it, contemporary Anglo-Americans almost *must* celebrate it. Sexuality almost *must* be central to one's sense of self. And the essence of sexuality itself, in currently established conventions, is a technique-centered act of intercourse to orgasm.... If the archetypal Victorian novel ended in a good marriage..., the archetypal contemporary romance ends in the explicitly described perfect orgasm....
>
> Much in these student sexual self-reports [collected by Moffatt] was consistent with Heath's...interpretation of the contemporary mass culture of sex. It was virtually impossible, for instance, for any writer of these papers, woman or man, to say, Sex is incidental, or I'm too young to think about such things, or To tell you the truth, I don't like sex very much. Sex *had* to be important, even for the sexually inactive.... And those few students who tried to move away from the orthodoxy, who tried to say something idiosyncratic, were in the end 'controlled by the discourse.' In the end...they virtually had to cop out for the centrality of sex and for sexual pleasure as an ideal.... (195)

So says a professional anthropologist studying students at Rutgers University. It is more effective with young readers, I suspect—perhaps with readers generally—to have similar views expressed by a credibly presented seventeen-year-old boy: '...the way a lot of people talk, and the way a lot of movies and books and advertising and all the various sexual engineers, whether they're scientists or salesmen, tell you the way it is is all the same. Man Plus Woman Equals Sex. Nothing else.' But Owen goes a bit beyond the idea of popular culture's sexual orthodoxy to get to an older orthodoxy; the person who most got him thinking about sex with Natalie Field was her father, the rather fundamentalist, church-going Mr. Field (32, 42-43). After their fashion, puritanical sorts, too, are obsessed with sex. Further, Owen honestly responds to Natalie as exciting: 'Physically, and mentally, and spiritually exciting.' And from this excitement he draws

---

[259] Stephen Heath, *The Sexual Fix* (New York: Schocken, 1982).

a conclusion: 'But what I thought, because of what everybody, even Freud, says, was that it must be Love. They all say that sex is the real thing, and Love is what you call it when you are slightly more civilized than a gorilla. Sex isn't something you do when you're in love, love is what you call it when you want sex,' which, of course, 'the toothpaste commercials and the cigarette ads and the porno movies and the art movies and the pop songs, or Mr. Field' all agree you do (44).

In *Very Far Away* Le Guin is getting into a major debate on sexuality and endorsing 'Just Say 'No'' in a very nuanced way. Locating in popular culture and (ironically) in conservative religion some of the motivation for 'Just Say 'Whoopee!'' is one tactic Le Guin uses here. A second is Owen's observation that he 'had decided that I was in love with Natalie. I hadn't fallen in love with her, please notice that I didn't say that; I had *decided* that I was in love with her.' Owen goes on to allude to the work of psychologists who stress 'front-back differences' in the brain 'rather than left-right differences.' In this case his *decision* to love Natalie 'would be an example of the frontal lobes trying to run the whole show, and fouling up the poor old hind-brain. This is a foul-up intellectuals are liable to. At least, stupid mixed-up intellectuals like me' (44-45). Owen is getting his ideas from Robert Evan Ornstein's work, but Le Guin could have found them in also D. H. Lawrence or other very late Romantic celebrants of the power of passion and 'the blood' and suspicion of the intellect. Or from Daoist reversals of the clichés of most civilized folk in valuing the spontaneous and intuitive and «animal» over planning and scheming.

Of more interest to me is why Natalie just said 'No.' One reason is straight-forward: a bad experience with a (male) oboist (77-78). The other reasons will get us into the relationship of *Very Far Away* with other works in Le Guin's canon.

Owen is quite exact in his description and analysis of Natalie's 'No'; a little after he 'took hold of her really hard and kissed her' there is a crucial dialog, with Owen beginning, brokenly:

> ...'Natalie, why can't—we're not kids—don't you—'
> She said, 'No, I don't. I don't Owen. I love you. It isn't right.'
> She didn't mean morally right. She meant right the way the music or the thought comes right, comes clear, is true. Maybe that's the same thing as moral rightness. I don't know.
> It was she who said, 'I love you.' Not me. I never did say it to her. (55-56)

Le Guin rightly recognizes, and says in her own voice, that 'Sex is a great mana' and therefore 'there is always a code' for sex in any society.[260] An 'immature society' or immature individual psyche will set 'great taboos about it. The maturer culture, or psyche, can integrate these taboos or laws into an internal ethical code,' with true maturity allowing 'great freedom' but forbidding 'the treatment of another person as an object' ('Is Gender Necessary?' *LoN* [1979]: 166). But what about Natalie? She is a very mature eighteen-year-old living in a society that is radically conflicted about sex. She is 'a religious person' with a 'grim, fundamentalist type' father who is 'a very churchgoing man,' 'extremely Biblical about young men who cast their eyes upon his daughters' (32, 38-39). Natalie goes against much of the social flow, but she goes with 'rale' (*CI*), the Way, the Dao, the music: music as 'another way of thinking, or maybe thinking...[as] another kind of music' (28), music from 'the silent half of the brain' (42). And going *consciously, intentionally*, in good anarchist fashion, with the real Way of things, she can make proper decisions for herself and recognize, perhaps paradoxically, that 'People make the real choices together' (57).

Music and dance have been a Le Guinian theme since her first published story, 'An die Musik' (1961) and continue through her poetry and fantasies to 'Dancing to Ganam' (1993) and 'Coming of Age in Karhide' (1995). So especially when we look at *Very Far Away*'s near contemporary, *The New Atlantis* (1975) and its handling of music, a music/Dao association will seem very familiar. There is more though, and a re-reading of *Very Far Away* shows it to be a very elegant brief compendium of Le Guinian themes from Orsinia and her science fiction and fantasy—and certainly from her surrealist philosophical exercise 'A Trip to the Head' and its attack on the more philosophical formulations of '...sex is real,... really real—it's having and acting in its intensest form,' the manly way of proving his masculine being (*WTQ* 163).

Owen's invented country of Thorn is not only a fictional parallel to the Brontë children's 'long, involved romances about [the] non-existent countries' of Angria and Gondal but also to Ursula K. Le Guin's Orsinia. And Owen's development of Thorn's 'flora and fauna...landscape and...cities... economy and the way they lived, their government and history' closely parallels SF's worlds and world-building (48-50).[261] There is a brief defense of housekeeping in *Very Far Away* and of being 'a good wife and mother' as a legitimate choice for an intelligent woman (Owen's mother), but with a warning against being 'afraid of doing anything else, of being anything else' (19): which could serve as a defense of Takver in *The Dispossessed* (1974) as partner, mother, biologist, and social activist. But

---

[260] Cf. A. L. Kroeber, *Anthropology* § 28, for the assertion 'that soon after the time when men began to possess institutions at all...they have never seriously swerved from an insistence on some sort of a social limitation on the natural sex impulse' (*Biology and Race* 60).

[261] And SF fantasizing, although, undoubtedly, Owen's Thorn is far more interesting, if on an ontologically vaguer standing, than Bill Kopman's Yirdo (see below, discussion of 'Pathways of Desire').

Owen also offers some comments on his parents' views of 'woman's work' that indicate things to come in Le Guin's canon (20-21). On their first trip to Jade Beach, on 'the day before New Year's Eve,' in the 'Heart of winter,' Owen and Natalie 'talked about life' and 'decided that it was no good asking what is the meaning of life, because life isn't an answer, life is the question, and you, yourself, are the answer.' The 'sea was there,' and 'it was cold, and it was the high point of my life,' Owen says. He'd had other high points, including once 'out in the desert, under the stars, when I turned into the earth turning on its axis,' but he'd always been alone. 'This time I was not alone. I was on the high mountain with a friend...there is *nothing* that beats that. If it never happens again in my life, still I can say I was there once' (41).[262]

The climactic epiphany in *Very Far Away* occurs when Owen hears Natalie's setting of an Emily Brontë poem (70) and starts crying: 'There was a glory in it... And it was partly love. I mean real love. In the song I had seen Natalie whole, the way she really was, and I loved her. It was not an emotion or desire, it was a confirmation, it was a glory, like seeing the stars' (71). Owen finally *sees* Natalie as Genly Ai finally sees Estraven (*LHD* 248; ch. 18), Heather Lelache sees George Orr's wholeness (*LoH* 95; ch. 7) or Mary Pannis had seen her husband, Nick (*BP* 102; ch. 4).[263] Also clear are the more casual connections with Le Guin's more popular science fiction and fantasy: the motifs of introversion / extroversion (30), loneliness, pain, touch (61), useful methodicalness (50), mechanical philosophies and psychologies (36), taking risks, plain speaking, coming home (62), and speaking one's mind—as old women do in *The Word for World Is Forest* and small children are said to do in *Very Far Away* (3)—and an attack (similar to the one in *The Dispossessed*) on 'leveling,' including the male-chauvinist sort that made it necessary for women to be first-class to get as far as third-class men: 'Anti-intellectualism seemed to be part of it,' Owen argues, 'but not all of it; it was this sort of pulling things all down to the level where everybody is the same, like ants, that I called 'leveling,' although these days it gets called by some fancy names like anti-elitism, and some really out of place names like democracy, names you shouldn't even say unless you're willing to think about them' (35).

We have, then, in *Very Far Away from Anywhere Else* a 'Different Kind of Love Story' indeed: one that postpones sex and of marriage in any sense, an unpopular ending since Shakespeare tried it with *Love's Labors Lost*. A love story from the boy's point of view—commercially risky with girls as the target audience for romances—a story for ordinary kids, defending the right of other kids to be intellectuals, talented, and chaste.

---

[262] For places and times of power, compare *WE*; for exultation in the cold, see *RW*, and *LHD*, where '*What is the meaning of life?*' is a very destructive question (60; ch. 5 & passim). For turning with the planet, see 'Solitude,' and contrast the valuing in that story of solitary experience.

[263] See also *TD* 146; ch. 6.

The Beginning Place (1980)

> [The anarchist cultural critic Paul] Goodman once expressed the dilemma of modern existence this way: 'If we conformed to the mad society, we became mad; but if we did not conform to the only society that there is, we became mad.'... [In the 1950s,]...he worked his way through this dilemma. He would not conform to the mad society, as Freudianism would have demanded, but neither would he simply deny it.... Rather, he would do as he would have patients do, cope with the society as it was, take the mad society seriously, confront it and find space for autonomy and self-affirmation within it. — Kirkpatrick Sale, 'Countercultural Elite' (498-99)

As Charlotte Spivack says in her excellent analysis of the book, '*The Beginning Place* in effect takes the central situation presented in *Very Far Away from Anywhere Else*, the alienation of two contemporary adolescents, and imposes on it the allegorical narrative of the *Faerie Queene*' (123). Or an allegorical form of some sort.[264] At first readings, *Very Far Away* and *The Beginning Place* seem quite different. The central characters are only a little older in *The Beginning Place*, but they are working class, not middle class, and they are both currently out of school; and the kids in *Very Far Away* come from far more functional families. Perhaps more noticeably, if there is any secondary or alternative world in *Very Far Away*, it must be the imaginary country of Thorn or the future country, so to speak, of MIT, Tanglewood, and the Eastman School of Music in 'the East.' With *The Beginning Place*, we get a much more substantial alternative world and in it a psychological allegory that makes for a very interesting variation on other of Le Guin's patterns (see Spivack 118).

The plot of *The Beginning Place* is straightforward.[265]

Hugh Rogers, the male hero and male point-of-view character, is a fairly tall, overweight checkout clerk at a suburban grocery store; at twenty-one years old, he has no life outside of his work and making sure that he is home most of the time so that his mother does not return from work to an empty apartment, especially at night.[266] Hugh's father deserted

---

[264] In English 112 A, Miami University, Fall Semester 1994, some of my students usefully compared and contrasted *BP* with Alan Jay Lerner's 1953 play *Brigadoon* (Katheryn A. Snowberger) and C. S. Lewis's 1953 *The Lion, the Witch and the Wardrobe* (Ian D. Bäby and Scott Rocke).

[265] The plot summary is based on work originally done by Denise Miller in 'Love and Acceptance in *The Beginning Place*,' essay in Miami English 112 A, used with permission. I have modified Miller's summary.

[266] As frequent in Le Guin, the point of view is third-person, limited (or selective) omniscient, with Hugh and Irene alternative as point-of-view characters.

his mother and Hugh long ago, and Hugh is unwillingly the dependable man of the house. Hugh's mother is all he has, but she abuses him, not physically—which she couldn't do—but emotionally, still angry at her desertion by Hugh's father (see though 18; ch. 1). Hugh would like to hug his mother or pat her head or show her some sign of affection, but 'she hated to be touched....' (30; ch. 1). In the course of the story, Hugh's mother makes a friend we never see and becomes quite interested in spiritualism. As far as we can see, Hugh starts the story with no friends beyond Donna, a middle-aged fellow-worker at Sam's Thrift-E-Mart, who calls him 'Buck' after 'Buck Rogers in the twenty-first [sic] century,' adding 'I bet you're too young to remember the real one' (20-21; ch. 1).[267]

The female hero and point-of-view character is called Irene by everybody in the everyday world except her mother, and Irena by her mother (Mary) and by the people in the twilight world: the secondary world of the novel. In the world of the American suburbs, ca. 1980, Irene's life is even worse than Hugh's. She works as an 'errandperson,' delivering mail and memos, blueprints and 'stuff' (226; ch. 8). Irena's father (Nick Pannis) died of leukemia when she was two years old and her brother Michael three months old. Irene's family lived with her father's sister until the aunt retired to Florida, leaving a farmhouse and a half-acre of tree nursery to her sister-in-law, Mary. Soon after that, Mary Pannis married Victor Hanson, bringing into the family a real 'ogre' of a step-father (Spivack 119). Vic is a ne'er-do-well who apparently deals in stolen bicycles, definitely had a small-time drug-dealing business, and currently has an alcohol problem. He beats his wife, hits his younger children, and molests Irene, on one occasion nearly raping her (97, 99; ch. 4). 'Victor was a big, well-made, handsome man, much concerned with his body and its functions and appearance...[against the] central reality of which the rest of the world and other people were mere reflections without substance: the self-concern of the athlete or the invalid, though he was neither, being strong and inactive' (97; ch. 4).

Mr. Hanson is like Mrs. Rogers in disliking darkness—he works on the car outside at night, by floodlight—but he contrasts with her and balances her in other ways. Mrs. Rogers's problem is associated with spirit; Vic's problems are associated with that nice looking but ill-used body of his, plus his highly ill-used mind. Vic is a theorist of macho: 'Victor had theories about many things, including sex, and liked to expound them to people: 'See, if the man doesn't get rid of the fertile material, you understand what I mean, the fertile cells, they back up and cause the prostrate gland [sic]. That material has to be cleared out regularly or they make poison, same as anything doesn't get cleared out regularly. Same as clean bowels, or blowing your nose...'' (97; ch. 4). After four pregnancies in five years, and three of them ending in miscarriages, Mary was 'on the pill' but kept

---

[267] The 'real one' was in the comic strip *Buck Rogers 2429* and following years, staying 500 years ahead of present, 'until eventually the strip was stabilized as *Buck Rogers in the Twenty-Fifth Century*' ('About 'Buck Rogers'...').

that from Victor because he thought that contraception, also, "blocked the fertile material up in the glands' and did not want her using contraceptives; but Irene got her to by making 'a woman's mystery of it' (100; ch. 4).

As children, Irene and her younger brother Michael had been close; but when he was eleven or so he started rejecting her, and 'as he came into full adolescence his rejection of her had become absolute. He spent his time with a male clique, adopting all their manner and rhetoric of contempt for the female, and sparing her none of it' (99; ch. 4). So Irene feels she cannot tell her brother about Victor's advances and the rape attempt, since Michael would blame her. 'Michael already despised her for...being a woman, therefore subject to lust, therefore unclean' (100; ch. 4). So Irene's brother would be no help if he were around, and he is not around, having left home a couple of years earlier (99; ch. 4).

And Mary, although a positive character, can give Irene little help. Her life centers around her family, and to destroy her family bonds would destroy her (100; ch. 4). And Mary's loyalty is not some mere neurotic attachment but based in part upon her experience in her previous marriage to Nick: a true Le Guinian marriage of being whole through being part, a participation in glory. But all that glory 'can happen and be done with by the age of twenty-two,' and Mary Hanson is thirty-nine (102, 97; ch. 4).[268] As a practical dilemma for Irene, if her mother had to choose, was 'forced to it,' she would side with Irena rather than Vic, and then Vic would 'have all the excuse to punish her he wanted.' After Michael had gone, Irene's only way out was to just get out, too, but she cannot being herself to make the break. 'Her mother had to have someone around to depend on' (100; ch. 4). A little short of half-way through the novel, Irene summarizes her view of her situation in one highly emotional but succinct thought-paragraph:

> Everybody I know just hurts each other. All the time. I have to get out. I can't keep coming home. Next time Victor trie[s] to cop a feel or even touches me or treats her like shit I'm going to blow, I can't shut up any more, and that'll just make it worse and hurt her more, and I can't do anything, and I can't take it. Love! What good is love? I love her. I love Michael, just like she does. So what? God help me, I'll never fall in love, never be in love, never love anybody. Love is just a fancy word for how to hurt somebody worse. I want to get out. Clear out, clear out.… (104; ch. 4).[269]

---

[268] See also Edna in 'Ether, OR' (1995) who claims to have made her soul for 'glory,' and is grateful to have known a good deal of glory. 'But it doesn't last. It doesn't come together to make a place where you can live, a house. It's gone and the years go' (*UA* 109).
[269] HarperPaperbacks edn. has 'trie*d* to cop a feel'; I emend the tense from the 1981 Bantam edn., p. 76.

The parents in *The Beginning Place*, then, are mostly what Irena and Hugh are striving a bit too strenuously not to become: Irena trying too hard to 'clear out' and be free of men; Hugh trying too hard to be dependable and stay with his mother (83; ch. 3).[270]

At the start of the novel, both Hugh and Irene feel they can never find love, feel alone and isolated, desperate to escape but trapped. And then they find the beginning place.

Irene found the gate long before Hugh had, and had gone through the gateway and the beginning place into a changeless land of continual evening twilight—what she calls her 'ain countrie,' her own country. She got as far as Tembreabrezi, 'Mountain Town,' a place she felt accepted, at home (57; ch. 2). She had learned the language, made friends, and most important, had found a father figure in Sark, the mayor or 'Master' of Mountain Town, and master of Irena: 'He was her law'; 'If she had spoken at all'—could speak to him intimately—Irena could only have said, "I have always loved you,' but she could not, and there was no need to. He knew his power. He was the Master.' (57, 55; ch. 2).[271]

The action of *The Beginning Place* begins with Hugh's fleeing home and finding the gateway into the twilight world. Here he drinks pure water, gets naked, swims, and is free to think and just move about unthinking in a world where there are no clocks, and where all time except the metabolic runs at $1/24^{th}$ the speed of clock-time. It is a world in which he can find Romantic Love—infatuation—with a fairy-tale princess, the daughter of Horn, Lord of the Manor of Mountain Town. And it is a world in which he can be the Romantic Hero in a quest: the people of Mountain Town and the land generally are subject to a great fear (a curse?), and the people cannot travel their roads. As Stephanie Bradford noted in one of my classes, most significantly the people of Mountain Town cannot take 'the road north, the road that led down to the City' (164; ch. 6).[272] The people think Hugh is their hero, their savior.

For Irena, Hugh is an affront: a thief, a stranger, an intrusion into her changeless world. What one of Le Guin's characters describes as 'the normal defensive-aggressive reaction between strangers meeting' is very strong when Irena meets Hugh.[273] She wants to stay in the grey, twilight world, but has trouble finding her way into it; annoyingly, Hugh cannot always find his way out but can quite reliably find the gateway in. After

---

[270] Following Adrienne Rich, who herself follows here Lynn Sukenick, Carol Franko talks of 'matrophobia': the fear of becoming one's mother. I'll add patriphobia: male fear of becoming one's father. The ideas are now common in popular culture and have appeared in comic strips (*Sally Forth* and *Boomers*), on the TV show *Friends* [1994], and alluded to in the commercial telling potential customers, this is *not* your father's car.
[271] See next to last chapter of *Tehanu*, 'The Master' (ch. 13).
[272] E-mail message, 18 November 1995, on the ListServ for English 113E, First Semester 1995-96, Miami University, Oxford (Ohio).
[273] Mannon, 'the Soft Scientist,' in 'Vaster than Empires and More Slow' (*WTQ* 168-69.)

Hugh's getting to Mountain Town and his acceptance there, Irena feels she's been reduced to a translator, and a barely necessary one at that: translating between *her* friends and newcomer Hugh.[274] She sees him as a minotaur (129; ch. 4), and orders, 'Don't ever touch me!' (151; ch. 5).

Before they leave Mountain Town on the Quest to end the fear, to free the roads, there is a ceremonial moment when Master Sark asks Lord Horn, 'What will you give him to take, my lord?' and Lord Horn offers 'The sword I was given, if he wants it.' Hugh takes the sword. The next question is 'What will you give him to give, my lord?' And there follows a confrontation between Sark and Horn, on an issue of long standing (169; ch. 6). In context of the chapter (161-63) and still more clearly later on (173; 194, ch. 7), the 'to give' can refer to a sacrifice, a human sacrifice. Sark's great-grandfather had been a Master of Tembreabrezi and had struck the bargain, 'with the price in his hand' (162), apparently giving his daughter in sacrifice to some monster; Sark believes the bargain should be remade, the price paid yet again.

In the context of Le Guin's canon generally, this confrontation repeats and very elegantly epitomizes an important Kropotkinesque point made at length in *The Left Hand of Darkness*. For all the potential and actual tyranny of the Kings and lords of Karhide or most of medieval Europe, each of their 'seeming' nations 'was a stew of uncoordinated principalities, towns, villages...a sprawl and a splatter of vigorous, competent, quarrelsome individualities over which a grid of authority was insecurely and lightly laid' (*LHD* 100; ch. 8). In the microcosm of Mountain Town, Lord Horn reflects—hazily—traditional, quasi-feudal, aristocratic ways, and Master Sark a more modern, utilitarian, capitalistic approach to life: what I've called in discussing Job and *King Lear*, the double-entry bookkeeping view of the world. The more loosely-structured medieval system, explicitly based in personal loyalty in its feudal part, associated with one's land and lord in the manorial, is rather favored by anarchists in Petr Kropotkin's tradition, and favored by Le Guin over theories of rationalized, systematic exploitation. In terms of *The Beginning Place* itself, the confrontation between Horn and Sark helps mark Hugh and Irena's disillusionment with their loves in Mountain Town, especially Irena's love for 'the Master.' When Hugh and Irena leave town on their trek north and their monster-quest, they leave behind them their infatuations. They need to depend upon one another to survive.

After much hard travel, described in some detail, Hugh and Irena come to the place they seek on the mountain: 'not ground but stone, a shieldlike expanse of rock.... Iron rings were bolted into the stone, four of them, making a rectangle several feet long.' On one of the rings, there remains a 'strip of rawhide thong' still knotted (194; ch 7). But 'This was the wrong place' (195). In the forest there is a crying, and they move toward it, going through the forest's maze when they glimpse and hear the monster and are too terrified to move on (195-97). Hugh weeps; in his own eyes he's run

---

[274] Cf. and more so contrast Selver as translator in *WWF*.

away again (202), lacked courage. Hugh and Irena debate Hugh's going alone (201). They stay together and do what they must do, 'toiling' up the mountain to a cave: 'There it was, of course; this was the place.... At last. Again. He had been coming here all his life and had never left it in the beginning' (208; ch. 7). Hugh moves toward the dark cave: 'Not twilight: darkness. From the beginning of time until the end'—and Irena rushes past him, daring the monster to come out. Which the monster does, and is dispatched by Hugh in one short paragraph, and the traditional sword-thrust 'upward into the white, wrinkled belly' (209; ch. 7) of the ambiguous or androgynous dragon: male to Hugh, female to Irena.[275]

There are two remaining chapters of the book, for nine chapters. In chapter 8, Irena must get Hugh out from under the dragon-beast (211), get them off 'the dragon's way' (223), the clear way that seems the fastest way back, and go east, not west, through the forest, toward increasing light and the beginning place and the gateway to the everyday world (224-25). And in chapter 8 Irena goes back on her 'never touch' order, and she and Hugh make love, somewhat perfunctorily the first try, but with richly symbolic description throughout:

> He held her to him, but awkwardly and timidly, until she put up both her arms, feeling herself go as soft and quick as water. Then he held her and mounted on her, overcoming; yet her strength held and contained his strength.
> As he entered her, as she was entered, they came to climax together, and then they lay together, mixed and melded, breast against breast and their breath mingled, until he rose in her again and she closed on him, the long pulse of joy enacting them. (229)

A little later, Hugh touches Irena's hair and kisses her (231).

The last chapter of *The Beginning Place* has Irena lead Hugh (237) into the daylight world, except it is not a hot, bright summer's day they return to but 'across the threshold into night and rain' (240). And Irena needs help. She gets it from an anonymous man she simply thinks of as 'Redbeard' (242). The rain is significant—water imagery, cleansing, the Daoist element of constancy and change—and so is the help from Redbeard.

---

[275] Carol Franko points out (in 'Acts of Attention...' [read 27/II/95]), the dragon leaves an odor that smells to Hugh like semen; from Hugh's point of view, the dragon 'runs like a man' (203). Brian Attebery sees the monster as a fairly pure incarnation of the Jungian Shadow: 'a sort of undifferentiated essence of monster. Its weapon is raw fear and its form...is dependent upon the beholder.' Irena sees the monster as female, Hugh as a male threatening Irena (Attebery 116-17, in Bloom 238). Le Guin says her intention was Hugh to kill the monster in the male form, as he sees it, with Irena seeing it as female (personal communication).

Irena's biological father 'deserted' her by dying; her step-father is an abusive brute, her brother a worse than useless sexist. She's even had a close woman friend raped by a gang of men (104; ch. 4); and Rick, the male of the couple she's been living with is no major villain but still a loser putting the make on her (94-95; ch. 4). Redbeard is like the Portuguese sea captain, Pedro de Mendez, who befriends Gulliver at his return from his 'Voyage to the Land of the Houyhnhnms' in Jonathan Swift's *Gulliver's Travels* (1726, 1727). The Portuguese sea captain represents simple human decency when we may have lost hope for it, and Gulliver certainly has. Even so, Redbeard, a male with a pirate's appellation, turns out to be a decent human being; but, unlike the crazy Gulliver with Mendez, the sane and now regenerate Irena can appreciate him.

The end of *The Beginning Place* has Hugh's mother rejecting Hugh, and Hugh and Irena finding an apartment in the city to start their *a*lawful marriage.

The beginning place is a place to begin; for Irena and Hugh, the city and life in the everyday immanence of everyday things is the immediate goal at the end of the book, with a strong hope of library school for Hugh and a more adult job—maybe teaching, maybe nursing, 'Or kids'—for Irena (226-27; ch. 8). The book ends with the line, 'There is more than one road to the city' (246), in this case, I think, The City of Man viewed positively, as against the suburbs or dysfunctional families, or as opposed to St. Augustine of Hippo's City of God. This is 'The City as goal and dream' as opposed to the grey changelessness of the twilight world beyond the beginning place—or most of Le Guin's cities, as opposed to towns or forests or icy wastes or mountains.[276]

* * * * * * *

I find in *The Beginning Place* three basic jobs for a critic; in order of increasing importance, they consist of one riddle, one central question for *The Beginning Place* itself, and one overarching question.
• The riddle is, Why can Hugh easily get into the twilight land and not out (dependably), and Irena can get out but not in?
• The central question for this novel itself, I'd formulate this way: In a story that seems to have strong didactic statements to make, what might those statements be? What should we *learn* from *The Beginning Place*?
• The overarching question is the place of *The Beginning Place* in Le Guin's canon.

I'm not very good at riddles, but I think the answer to the one in *The Beginning Place* is this: Hugh can find the gateway in, and Irena can find the way out, because Le Guin wanted them to have complementary talents, and the binary opposition of IN vs. and OUT pretty well limits the choices to the ones Le Guin used. That Owen can get them in and Irena can get

---

[276] For the positive City, see Introd. to *City of Illusions*, rpt. *LoN* (1979): 147. For the negative City, see my discussions of *EoH* and *ACH*.

them out is necessary if Le Guin wants to show for the climax of the novel Irena leading. If we want to see in *The Beginning Place* something of a reworking of the Earthsea trilogy, and I'll soon make clear I want to do that, then Irena here is in structural position parallel to Arren's in *The Farthest Shore*: the leader to the lair of the monster, the one who gets the hero home, and the hero for the future. So her specialty needs to be exits.

The teaching agenda of *The Beginning Place* I find in the ethical/theological issues it raises and in its family and gender-politics.

Recall Charlotte Spivack's comment (123) that *The Beginning Place* uses the allegory of Edmund Spenser's *Faerie Queene*, Book 1. In paralleling *The Beginning Place* to *Faerie Queene*, Book 1, Hugh—who is explicitly (though comically) compared to St. George (182; ch. 6)—corresponds to the Red Cross Knight slaying Error and, eventually the Satanic dragon; and Irena corresponds to Una (One), who 'represents truth, true religion, and the true church. Her name...implies the qualities of truth and of the true church; it admits of no contradiction and no relativity' (Kellogg and Steele 15, 16, 44-45). Opposed to Una is Duessa: 'As one (Una) represents truth, goodness, beauty, order, and whatever is perfect and eternal in Platonic thought (*Timaeus*); so two (Duessa) represents all that is imperfect, chaotic, earthly, and evil' (Kellogg and Steele 20). Red Cross falls away from Una and goes with Duessa to the House of Pride, which Kellogg and Steele identify as 'St. Augustine's City of Man as opposed to the City of God' (26). At the House of Pride, Red Cross must also fight Sansjoy, another old lover of Duessa's: i.e., allegorically, he must fight Joylessness, despair. There are other parallels, including forests, but I think we should modify Spivack on *The Beginning Place* this far: *The Beginning Place* is to *The Faerie Queene* even as it is to the Buck Rogers story and C. S. Lewis's second (or first) book in the Narnia series,[277] *The Lion, the Witch and the Wardrobe*: a 'gentle antidote to,' a critique of, prime examples of a world-view Le Guin has problems with.[278]

My student Ian D. Bäby observed that the greyness of Le Guin's twilight land parallels the winter-world of Narnia under the witch's curse in *The Lion*....[279] Both the world of *Faerie Queene* and the world of Narnia are undergirded by the central Christian myth of the Sacrifice, and there is a very explicit sacrifice of the Christ-figure Lion, Aslan, in *The Lion*, on a 'Stone Table' very like Le Guin's 'shieldlike expanse of rock' (Lewis 150-55, ch. 14; Le Guin 194, ch. 7). And, in the background, the Christian vision of the Apocalypse, presided over by 'the dragon, that ancient serpent, who is the Devil and Satan' (Revelation 20.2, RSV)—except that the

---

[277] There is debate over the order of the Narnia books <http://www.aslan.demon.co.uk/narnia.htm>.
[278] Le Guin's 'gentle antidote' line is quoted in Smith 79.
[279] As a practical matter, C.S. Lewis's work is the important target: Buck Rogers is no longer well-known, and few people generally and very few children read *The Faerie Queene*; *The Lion, the Witch and the Wardrobe* is still popular and influential.

dragon in *The Beginning Place* 'is a dragon of the psyche,' not some cosmological, apocalyptic force (see Minkowitz 26). Also in the background, behind even the Christian myth, is the pattern of the masculinist Hero: 'quest, contest, and conquest as the plot, sacrifice as the key' (*ER* 13). In Le Guin's *Beginning Place*, the twilight world in its changelessness is a necessary place to visit and a place to begin from, but not a place for adult humans to live.

These large issues have implications for ethics and family politics. If part of the moral of *The Faerie Queene*, *The Lion, The Witch and the Wardrobe*, and Christian sermonizing generally is to encourage the imitation of Christ, including self-sacrifice, part of Le Guin's intention in *The Beginning Place* is to discourage such sacrifices. The theological point of *The Beginning Place*, so far as it has one, and a strong ideological point, is that one should **not** make such sacrifices: not as Christ-like sacrifice, nor in the Jewish form of Abraham's willingness to sacrifice Isaac in The Binding of Isaac story (Gen. 22.1-14), nor in any other form.[280] Self-sacrifice is a very bad idea in politics, and for Le Guin, the political is the personal as well as the personal, the political: sacrifices—whatever the religion, whatever the ideology—are problematic, period (see Hoffer, Part Three).[281]

Hugh overcame guilt sufficiently to keep returning to the twilight land—the land of the unconscious, perhaps the collective unconscious (McLean 132-33)—and gets a bit of a life independent of his mother and against his mother's will (143; ch. 5). In the twilight land, Irena calls forth an eminently killable dragon-monster, which Hugh kills. Not Error in Spenser's Christian allegory, but Horrible Parent in a psychological allegory. And it is Hugh and Irena together who kill the dragon, not the Christ-figure Aslan, helped by the boys defeating the White Witch, as in Narnia (with Lewis's featured girl character, Lucy, getting to nurture, not kill). In *The Beginning Place*, though not as much as in the Christian stories, the magic works (see Attebery 118). Hugh comes back to the daylight world with a woman, and his mother rejects him, freeing him to leave her (243, 245-46; ch. 9). And Irena overcomes guilt enough to 'clear out' and leave her mother and stepsiblings in an abusive relationship. Such desertions are not good things; they are also not what unselfish, self-sacrificing, good boys and girls do.[282] But that, I think, is Le Guin's point: Given their

---

[280] See McLean 140, Finch 42, Talbot 14. Talking to me on 13 May 1996, Le Guin stressed that sacrifice is valued in many religions, not just Christianity. I'll add that martyrdom—self-sacrifice—is also valued. Contrast Luz on sacrifice in *EoH*. In *TD*, Takver warns against the will to sacrifice in pregnant women (266; ch. 10); we need not agree with Takver, but we should take the idea seriously.
[281] Le Guin handles living for others with instructive irony in 'The Fisherwoman's Daughter' (*DEW* 216), and gives similar treatment to 'the self-sacrificing Lords' of the Shing in *CI* (165; ch. 8). For a more direct attack on women trying to be self-sacrificing angels, see 'Fisherwoman' 225, 232 -33.
[282] Other readers have found Hugh's and Irena's actions far less problematic than I do. My students weren't troubled by the monster-slaying, and neither were such

powerlessness to cure dysfunctional relationships, 'Clear out' may be the least bad choice Hugh and Irena can make. And their living together and trying to find suitable, adult work are positive goods.

The powerlessness of Irena, in the everyday, 'realistic' part of the novel stems from the mindless macho and misogyny of her stepfather and her brother; there isn't even any explicit sexist doctrine to attack. Irena's family is sick from a complex disease endemic in our culture, sick in ways Irena cannot hope to cure. Mrs. Rogers is also sick, and her illness is both common (perhaps also endemic to technological civilization) and one to which both Hugh and Irena would be very susceptible: 'a kind of getting out of gear, out of synch. The engine made a noise but no power got to the wheels. They were stuck. They got nowhere.' Pulling up roots and changing towns doesn't help: '...the oftener she moves' Hugh thinks, 'the more she doesn't get anywhere' (79-80; ch. 3). 'Sick is when you drove the car in neutral. The place she couldn't get away from was home'—one of Le Guin's rare uses of 'home' in a negative sense—the more Mrs. Rogers 'left it the worse she was stuck; could not bear to be alone in the house...lived in terror of waking up at night with no one else there.' And for good reason: her husband deserted her, and Hugh is well aware of the effect on himself of that desertion and intuits the effect on her, and he knows his duty: 'There's nothing I can do. She hasn't got anybody but me' (79-81; ch. 3). There is also nothing he can do *for* his mother, and it is a relatively happy ending, given the options, when Mrs. Rogers rejects Hugh.

* * * * * * *

As much as Mrs. Rogers finds happiness at all, it is making friends with Durbina and researching their 'previous lives,' usually as 'princesses or high priestesses' in interesting places like Ancient Egypt (80; ch. 3); and Mrs. Rogers's hobby can help us place *The Beginning Place* in Le Guin's canon, establish its relationships with other works and to Le Guin's basic patterns. Starting from the hint of Mrs. Rogers's spiritualism, we can see that one obvious relationship is with *The Tombs of Atuan*, where Tenar is 'eaten' and made into Arha, the reincarnation of the 'One Priestess of the Tombs of Atuan' (10; ch. 1 [see McLean 140]). It's hard to take Mrs. Rogers's reincarnations seriously, but Irena's life in the evening land is both quite similar to and different from Arha's situation in Atuan. Arha leads what is nominally a women's religion, the worship of the Nameless Ones, and Irena practices a kind of Earth religion in a changeless place. Entering her 'ain country,' Irena

> dropped down on all fours and kissed the dirt, pressing her face against it like a suckling baby...then went to the wa-

---

sophisticated critics of young-adult literature as Lukens and Cline (*Critical Handbook* 70).

ter's edge, knelt...drank, answered the waters loud, continual singing, 'So you are, so I am, so.' She sat down crosslegged on the shelving rock, sat still, shut her eyes to contain her joy.

It had been so long, but nothing had changed, nothing ever changed. Here was always. She could do what she always did when she was a kid, thirteen, when she first found the beginning place, before she had even crossed the river [going in-country]; she could do the things she used to do, the fire worship and the endless dance...her burnt offering, the wooden figure she had carved, in the center. That had all been silly, kid stuff. The things people did in church were silly too. There were reasons for doing them. She would dance the endless dance if she felt like it; keep it going; that was the thing about it, it didn't end. This was the place where she did what she felt like. This was the place where she was her self, her own. (40, ch. 2; see also 146-47, ch. 5.)

Like Arha, and Le Guinian characters from the Earthsea trilogy through 'Coming of Age in Karhide,' Irena dances; unlike Arha, Irena doesn't even chant (*TA* 24; ch. 2). Both Irena and Arha are mostly alone; but, unlike Arha, Irena can leave her changeless, evening land without help—it's just that she has only the hot, dry, Wasteland suburbs to go to, no real home. Both girls are ready for something different; and in both works, the new thing Le Guin gives them is a man, and a crossing over into womanhood via a variation on the pattern of Comic Romance.

Le Guin returns to the romantic comic pattern in *The Beginning Place* strongly: as Spivack points out, one of the analogs here is Shakespeare's *As You Like It*, especially the idea that 'there is no clock in the forest' of Arden (see Spivack 118; I quote *AYL* 3.2.300-01). *As You Like It* is a kind of Shakespearean experiment in pure Romantic Comic form: seeing how much play one can get out of the Romantic pattern with just about no plot—using, highlighting, mocking, undermining, and (paradoxically) reinforcing romantic comedy. In both *The Beginning Place* and *As You Like It*, the movement is from a corrupt place of civilization into a changeless forest world and then back to the everyday. The very everyday, entirely mundane, 'moral' of both works may be that young people can use a kind of natural-world time-out between childhood and adulthood: time to just *be*, get their heads together, and find an appropriate partner and appropriate work—ideas Le Guin makes explicit in *The Farthest Shore* (1972) and *Always Coming Home* (1985).

The 'time-out' worlds in *The Beginning Place* and *As You Like It*, though, are more different than similar.

Shakespeare's Forest of Arden is, mostly, a bright, happy place, full of music—especially songs—and life. The evening, twilight land in *The Beginning Place* is without song, without visible animal life, and emphatically grey. And however much Le Guin personally likes grey, and book publishers find grey appropriate for paperbacks of her books, grey is often a negative «color» in Le Guin's work.[283] As in the world of 'Darkness Box' (1963), the twilight land is under a kind of curse, and color and music and change must come to it for it to be an appropriate place not just to visit at the end of youth, but to live. In 'A Trip to the Head' (1970), the forest is a better place to be alone and avoid the true Other than to find partner; in *The Beginning Place*, the forest is a place to find a partner, then go home.

More politically and symbolically in Atuan, more mythically in *The Beginning Place*, the source of the greyness of the worlds is related to sacrifice. And the theme of the sacrifice in turn relates both works to Omelas and 'The Ones Who Walk Away from Omelas' (1973). The Omelites' bargain is one intelligent people can argue about, and have argued about at length at a conference of the Society for Utopian Studies and in its journal. The sacrifices in Atuan and the twilight world of *The Beginning Place* are simply bad. In *The Beginning Place*, the sacrifice, whatever its details, made the inhabitants, 'The children of fear.' They are 'bound,' their 'right hands useless,' sold; so says Lord Horn (169; ch. 6). More significantly, when Irena talks of 'A scapegoat' and looks for the word 'sacrifice,' Hugh interrupts with 'They're stuck,' his image of mental illness, his mother's problem, and much of the wrong of the world (79-80; ch. 3). As Simone de Beauvoir has stressed, people can get stuck in immanence; if there is no way out, a woman is *stuck* at home.

Le Guin habitually contrasts two societies, and she usually favors the more 'Yinish,' less active society; and, possibly, she does so here: the American suburbs, ca. 1980, are hardly a world of positive transcendent action. Also, there is silence in the twilight world, 'the silence that gave words meaning, the center that gave the world a shape' (*BP* 76; ch. 3), and we know from the Earthsea trilogy that such silence is necessary.[284] Still, it is difficult to get too caught up with the problems of the twilight world, and I think Le Guin discourages overly enthusiastic identification with the twilight town. Consider just the imagery. Ordinarily, Le Guin wants balance, often black/white balance, not greys. The only place of symbolic balance in the twilight world is at the cave of the dragon: the blackness of the darkness of the cave—an image of the womb of Mother Earth—against which stands the whiteness of the dragon. And then there's the extraordinary muting of the heroic dragon-slaying. Irena summons the dragon, and Hugh succinctly kills the dragon—with no reveling by the Narrator whatever in the details of the fight—and we see no regeneration of the twilight world in consequence: no spring thaw, no rain on the wasteland, no loos-

---

[283] For the seriously pedantic on such matters: black, white, and grey are not colors, but 'achromatic colors'; I have compromised with *color* in European quotation marks.
[284] My thanks to Amy Howell of English 113E, Miami University, Fall 1995, for reminding me of the 'silence' quotation.

ing of the waters: none of the action and flowers and Carl Orff's *Carmina Burana* that John Boorman gives so spectacularly in the healing of the King sequence in his exuberantly romantic film, *EXCALIBUR* (1981); more immediately relevant here: no speeding up of time and movement toward nightfall. At the climax of *The Beginning Place* there isn't even the pro forma political restoration of *As You Like It*.[285] The magic does work for Irena and Hugh; but it is a very low-key and slow regeneration if the magic works for the twilight world.

What we get for narrative are two working-class kids making love and getting out, with much effort and pain: first getting out of the twilight world—out into the reviving dark and rain of *our* world—then getting out of dysfunctional homes. No Buck Rogers-style heroism here. The heroism is the stoic, relatively 'feminine' heroism of determination and *active* endurance, and appropriate action (*wu wei*), a form of quiet, toiling heroism Le Guin has celebrated in *The Left Hand of Darkness* (1969) and *The Eye of the Heron* (1978) and will celebrate again in 'Sur' (1982) and, in a different way, in 'Coming of Age in Karhide' (1995).[286] We get two kids saving a fantasy world indeed, but more importantly each other: two kids finding each other, marriage, and a way to home in the city.

The Eye of the Heron (1978)

> Nobody but the dead know whether all these things people talk about are worth dying for or not. And the dead can't talk. So the words about noble deaths sacred blood and honor and such are all put into dead lips by grave robbers and fakes who have no right to speak for the dead. * * * He could tell all these high-talking murdering sonsofbitches who screamed for blood just how wrong they were. He could tell them mister there's nothing worth dying for.... There's no word worth your life. —Dalton Trumbo, *Johnny Got His Gun* (1939), ch. 10

Some time after the year 2027 (16; ch. 2), and 111 years before the start of the story of *Eye of the Heron*, 'the Government of Brasil-America sent several thousand people' to a penal-colony world called 'Victoria.' Fifty-six years before the start of the story 'the Government of Canamerica sent

---

[285] From *Beowulf* to *Faerie Queene* to the latest *ALIEN* movie, audiences have come to expect an exciting fight with interesting monsters. That Le Guin does not give such thwack-by-thwack descriptions—not even in the Earthsea trilogy—is a highly significant silence in her work.

[286] In addition to the specific allusion by Donna to Buck Rogers, note that Hugh originally thinks Irena a boy (69-70; ch. 3). The motif is a commonplace when Romance heroes discover a heroic chivalric opponent is a warrior-maiden, but still note the scene of Antony Rogers (not yet 'Buck') first meeting Wilma Deering: 'The 'boy' was, I found, a girl,' and an aggressive one (*Armageddon 2419* 4; ch. 1).

two thousand more' (37; ch. 3). The first group were criminals and their families, and they founded 'the City'; the second group were peace-movement activists in the tradition of Mohandas K. Gandhi and Martin Luther King, Jr., and they founded 'the Town': Shantih, a set of villages with a central Meeting House. The City has about 8,000 inhabitants, Shantih, 4,320; all are necessarily exiles from Earth, permanent exiles.[287] The two communities have remained distinct but are 'deeply interdependent' (37; ch. 3): the Town supplying agricultural goods and the City providing the Town with 'tools and machinery made by the Government ironworks, fish caught by the City fleet, and various other products which the older-established colony could more easily provide. It had been an arrangement satisfactory to both.' As *Heron* begins, the arrangement is strained. The Town has kept its part of the bargain; the City has taken more and given less (53; ch. 4). The Town has continued 'communal...somewhat introverted,' egalitarian, nonsexist, anarchic; the City has remained macho (and nominally Christian?) and has become 'hierarchically governed'; and, as the story begins, the City is developing a military.[288]

The City, of course, will produce 'the bad guys,' and the Town the good, but with intriguing variations. Indeed, *Heron* offers highly significant variations on familiar Le Guinian themes.

* * * * * * *

Under the leadership of Councillor Luis Falco ('falcon') the ruling men of the City plot to establish 'latifundia': 'Big farms; large fields, planted in one crop, for efficiency...an estate...peasants to work it.' To get the cleared land and the peasants, they will provoke into rebellion against the 'government' of the City the people of 'Shanty Town,' and put down the rebellion with 'a troop of elite soldiers,' the Black Guards under Herman Macmillan: armed 'young aristocrats, brave intelligent, and properly commanded. Men who love fighting, like our brave ancestors of Earth' (65-67; ch. 5). In a sense, Falco wishes to continue what Yevgeny Zamiatin's character D-503 tells us was 'the Great Two Hundred Years' War...be-

---

[287] And at one time or another, all the major characters in *EoH* are envoys; note Spencer's title and discussion of 'Exiles and Envoys.' Cf. and contrast Estraven in *LHD*, the Jewish exiles in 'The Eye Altering,' the Terrans in *PE*, and Ekumenical envoys exiled by the time-dilation of NAFL flight.

[288] Beyond some confused expletives—'Oh, hesumeria!' (42; ch. 3)—there is no indication of religion in the scenes set in Victoria City. Later in the novel, the Narrator says from Luz's point of view, 'There was the idea of God,' and Luz remembers the stories told to City children about God and Heaven and 'Meria [sic], God's mother, everybody's mother' who 'waited for the souls of the dead' (162; ch. 11). A director filming *EoH* might or might not want some crucifixes on the walls of homes in the City, a church in the City square, a man garbed as a priest at Falco's dinner party, etc. Le Guin says she assumed no priests went with the convicts (personal communication). See, though, debate on ordaining priests in T. More's *Utopia*, Book II (71).

tween the city and the village,' what Zamiatin sees as a deeply-rooted struggle between literally civilized people, living within city walls, and what such urban and urbane sorts see as 'primitive peasants' (*We* 21; 5th Entry). In another sense, Falco's plan would reenact 'Earth's oldest conflicts on the soil of an alien world' (Back cover blurb of 1984 Bantam edn.). The political givens at the opening of *Heron* recapitulate and epitomize—produce a *mâshâl* of—some crucial moments in human history: the transition 'from the wholly rural, hamlet-dwelling, undifferentiated society and self-sufficient economy of the Near Eastern Neolithic of 5000 B.C. and before' to the city-states and proto-empires of early Mesopotamia and Egypt (Kroeber, *Anthropology* 705; § 286), the creation of the great latifundia in the late Roman Empire (Swain 2.512), the Spartan division into aristocrats, resident semi-aliens (*perioikoi*), and helots—public slaves (Swain 1.315-16), the reduction of free peasants to serfs with the establishment of feudalism and manorialism in early medieval Europe (Thompson & Johnson 326-29). Closer to home, *Heron* refers to the establishment of the hacienda and peonage system in much of Spanish America, the *estancia* and *fazenda* in Argentina, Uruguay, Brazil—a system that lasted in some places into the 1990s.[289] For their part, the people of Shantih have already planned to settle a new area and move a large part of their population out of danger from the City. In one historical analogy, the People of the Peace resemble some California Indian tribes. A. L. Kroeber notes that the area of 'the lower Colorado [River] almost exactly parallels the Nile in valley, flood, silt, and climate; but the historical Cocopa, Yuma, and Mohave tribes, though they regularly farmed the overflow bottoms, never multiplied, urbanized,' or grew so urbanely sophisticated that they renounced their 'egalitarian primitive democracy' (*Anthropology* 708; § 287). In perhaps a closer analogy, James W. Thompson and Edgar N. Johnson find it 'highly significant that whenever pioneer conditions existed in medieval Europe...the peasants stoutly, and generally with some success, resisted manorial organization' (Thompson & Johnson 328).[290] Or, most closely

At the beginning of the story, an expedition from the Town has returned with news of a good area to settle in the north. A Town meeting is interrupted by Falco, who commands the Shantih Towners to submit their plans to the government. Lev Shults, a young leader in the Town, says 'No,' but the Town will send a delegation to the City to negotiate. When

---

[289] I consulted here the entry 'hacienda' in the Micropædia, *Encyclopædia Britannica* (1974). In her rev. of *Columbia: The Genocidal Democracy*, by Javier Giraldo, S.J., Ana Carrigan writes that Colombian paramilitary troops, 'trained...by the Colombian Army, and funded by large landowners (frequently mafia bosses)' go into 'rural areas...[and] savagely 'cleanse' the land'—present tense—'of recalcitrant, small peasant owners, and create feudal enclaves where the subdued populations that remain work as serfs for the new landowners' (40).
[290] See Thompson & Johnson's chapters 11 and 12: 'Feudalism' and 'Manorialism'—or similar chapters in any competent introduction to medieval history.

the Town delegates try to negotiate rather than just submit information, they are arrested. Among the delegates is Vera Adelson, who is held at Casa Falco under a loose house arrest: i.e., her promise not to escape. There she meets Luz Marina Falco Cooper, Luis Falco's daughter, and the two women become friends. In terms of their given names, 'sea light' (Luz Marina) has met 'truth' (Vera), and they've gotten along.

Luz is a privileged aristocrat, slated to marry well—probably Herman Macmillan—and continue a life of genteel femininity. Looking at her life, she sees 'A prison. All Victoria was a prison, a jailhouse. And no way out. Nowhere else to go.' And then she thinks of her childhood friend Lev, who has said 'No' to her father (29-30; ch. 3).

Luz comes to thoroughly detest Herman Macmillan, but what gets her out of that prison is overhearing her father telling Macmillan the plot to subjugate Shantih and reduce the Shantih Towners to an agricultural proletariat or serfs (65, 91-93; chs. 5 &7).[291] Vera refuses to break her promise and escape the City, not even to bring to her people word of the plot against them (93-95; ch. 7). Instead, Luz walks out and brings the news to Shantih and stays with the Townspeople. Falco comes to get his daughter, who refuses to return with him to the City. Macmillan leads his Black Guards toward the Town, and the People of the Peace meet the armed forces of the City in a great demonstration of nonviolent resistance.

>   Falco had begun speaking, but there was still a lot of noise, and his dry voice did not carry. Lev stepped forward and took the word from him. His voice silenced all others, ringing out in the silvery, windy air of the hilltop, jubilant.
>
>   'The People of the Peace greet the representatives of the City in comradeship! We have come to explain to you what we intend to do, what we ask you to do, and what will happen if you reject our decisions.... First, our hostages must be set free. Second, there will be no further forced work drafts. Third, representatives from Town and City will meet to set up a fairer trade agreement. Finally, The Town's plan to found a colony in the north will proceed without interference from the City, as the City's plan to open South Valley along the Mill River to settlement will proceed without interference from the Town. These four points have been discussed and agreed upon by all the people of Shantih, and they are not subject to negotiation. If they are not accepted by the Council,...all cooperation in work, all trade, all furnishing of food, wood, cloth, ores, and products will cease.... We will in no case use violence against you; but until our demands are met we

---

[291] Reduction of free workers to serfs or slaves is *not* one of the aspects of the Middle Ages that would be appreciated by Kropotkinesque anarchists.

will in no way cooperate with you. Nor will we bargain with you, or compromise. I speak the conscience of my people. We will hold fast.' (131-32; ch. 9)

Then Macmillan shoots Lev, killing him; Falco grabs a rifle and clubs Macmillan to death; and, in the ensuing melee, seventeen People of the Peace are killed, eight people of the City (138-41; ch. 10).

This is the climax of the novel and the end of Lev's story; if we apply Søren Kierkegaard's definition of the phrase, Lev dies a tragic hero, following the 'universal': honorable ideals.[292] The rest of the story works out the results of the confrontation and killings. Falco is arrested for killing Macmillan, and the City and Town begin painful and ambiguous negotiations: compromises and more compromises, threatening betrayal of the Town's ideals and 'permanent bondage to the City' (144; ch. 10), but promising also that 'There won't be forced labor, or 'estates' and all that' (153; ch. 10). We do not learn the results of the negotiations, since the final chapter follows Luz and others from Shantih as they take up again the 'Long March' of the People of the Peace and find a place where they can start a new settlement, far from the City.

The narration of *The Eye of the Heron* is similar to that of *Planet of Exile* (1966), *The Lathe of Heaven* (1971), and *The Word for World Is Forest* (1972). We are told the story from the points of view of the major characters, alternating among Lev (chs. 1, 4, 6, 8), Luz (chs. 2, 7, 10, 11), Vera (chs. 3, 9 [shared somewhat with Falco]), and divided: Luz and Falco (ch. 5), Lev and Luz (ch. 8). But *Heron* does not move toward the romantic happy ending of the integration of two peoples in *Planet of Exile*, nor even the chasten romanticism of *Lathe*; *Heron* moves toward the separation of *The World for World Is Forest*. As in the earlier stories, one of the major point-of-view characters drops out: old Wold dies in *Planet of Exile*; Haber goes mad from his power-dream in *The Lathe of Heaven*; Lyubov is killed in the attack on Central in *The Word for World Is Forest*. But in *Eye of the Heron*, Le Guin kills off her one male hero: a young, attractive, revolutionary hero. The act of 'heroicide' in *Heron* is significant. Lev dies; Luz and Vera survive, and the future will be with the women and what they represent, and what they represent both complements and opposes what Lev represents.

Lev's death is part of a hard teaching in *The Eye of the Heron*, and I'm going to ease into the topic with a slightly easier teaching, with a key passage on imperialism—Roman imperialism in ancient Britain here—from Joseph Conrad, *Heart of Darkness*:

'They were no colonists [the Romans].... They were conquerors, and for that you want only brute force.... They

---

[292] 'The tragic hero renounces himself in order to express the universal, the knight of faith,' Kierkegaard's theistic Existentialist hero, 'renounces the universal in order to become the individual' (86; Problem II).

grabbed what they could get for the sake of what was to be got. It was just robbery with violence, aggravated murder on a great scale, and men going at it blind—as is very proper for those who tackle a darkness. The conquest of the earth, which mostly means the taking it away from those who have a different complexion or slightly flatter noses than ourselves, is not a pretty thing when you look into it too much. What redeems it is the idea only. An idea at the back of it; not a sentimental pretence but an idea; and an unselfish belief in the idea—something you can set up, and bow down before, and offer a sacrifice to....' (4; part I)

Reading *Heart of Darkness* in 1902, a genteel, white Englishman could balance the 'abomination' of Roman (and Belgian and British) imperialism against 'the idea' and might be willing to 'offer a sacrifice' to that idea, perhaps to the *ideal* of Western Civilization—fulfilled, of course, in a genteel, white Englishman ca. 1902. century later, such balancing is itself an abomination. European imperial adventures in Africa 'resulted in the most terrible massacres in recent history...and finally...it resulted in the triumphant introduction of such means of pacification'—mass murder—'into ordinary, respectable foreign policies' (Arendt, *Origin of Totalitarianism* 185; ch. 7). Looking back over the holocausts of the late nineteenth through the twentieth centuries, it is clear that the 'idea at the back' of imperialism or racial purity can be very dangerous to 'sacrifice to.'

This is the easy part; what Le Guin asks us to deal with in the life and death of Lev Shults is the danger of good ideas and noble ideals, of the danger in the best in the masculine tradition of striving to heal, improve, perfect the world.

After the arrest of their delegation to the City, the leaders of Shantih prepare for a mass meeting of the Town.

> As Lev was about to leave, Sam, who had serenely stood on his head throughout the discussion, came upright in a single graceful motion and said to Lev, smiling, 'Arjuna, it will be a great battle.'[293] * * * The campaign which the people of Shantih were undertaking was a new thing to them, and yet a familiar one. All of them, in the Town school and the Meeting House, had learned its principles and tactics; they knew the lives of the hero-philosophers Gandhi and King, and the history of the People of the Peace, and the ideas that had inspired those lives, that history. In exile, the People of the Peace had continued to

---

[293] The *Bhagavad-Gita*, The Song of God, is a conversation between Arjuna and Krishna just before the Battle of Kurukshetra (see my discussions of *FWF* and *King Dog*).

live by those ideas; and so far had done so with success. * * * The children and grandchildren of the exiles, now grown men and women, had never seen the technique of conflict and resistance, which was the binding force of their community in action. But they had been taught it: the spirit, the reasons, and the rules. (52-53; ch. 4 [I have eliminated paragraphing]).

Having grown up in 'the Judaeo-Christian-Rationalist West' (*LoH* 82; ch. 6), most of Le Guin's readers will view positively here acting according to 'the spirit, the reasons, and the rules' and will not notice the military metaphors embedded in 'campaign' and 'tactics,' nor object to the idea of reverencing such true hero-philosophers as Gandhi and M. L. King. Middle-aged, sensible, indeed, *normative* Vera had talked about the stubbornness of the People of the Peace, 'And when that meets up with another stubbornness, it can make a kind of war, a struggle of ideas, the only kind of war anybody ever wins' (44; ch. 3). Still, from *Rocannon's World* on, Le Guin has insisted upon the price of the heroic gesture, and the explicitly Daoist works should get us a little suspicious of spirit, reasons, rules, and conscious technique.

Subtlety being an overrated virtue in art, Le Guin soon gets more explicit.[294] Vera, as in 'Truth,' has a long conversation with Luz. They start with Falco, the best of the men of the City: 'He's a king, a real one,' Vera says, 'strong of soul,' but he's trapped 'inside walls that he's been building stronger and higher all his life.'[295] He's also trapped within 'the roof and walls of this City that his fathers built as a fortress against the unknown' (Spencer 40). And Luz is 'part of that City, part of his roofs and walls, his house, Casa Falco. So is his title, Senhor, Councillor, Boss. So are all his servants and his guards, all the men and women he can give orders to. They're all part of his house, the walls to keep the wind off him.' Falco, then, and the men of Victoria City generally, 'made a bad mistake.' They

---

[294] To clarify my tone, note Northrop Frye's observation that 'Mr. E. M. Forster speaks with disdain of Dickens's Mrs. Micawber, who never says anything except she will never desert Mr. Micawber: a strong contrast is marked here between the refined writer too finicky for popular formulas, and the major one who exploits them ruthlessly' (*Anatomy of Criticism* 168-69). The ability to produce nuanced writing is a good thing; as Anthony Burgess said about the Beatles, so is the capacity for simplicity. There is nothing subtle about Job on his dung heap, Pentheus's acting sacrificial goat-boy in Euripides's *The Bacchae*, the attack on comfortable theology in *King Lear*, or the sexual politics of Joanna Russ's *The Female Man*—etc.

[295] For Le Guin on natural kingship, note J. Needham on 'the ancient paradise of generalized tribal nobility' in the Daoist version of the Golden Age ('Time and Thought' 112).

refuse to 'come outside into the rain' (73-74; ch. 5).[296] Lev and the men of the Peace have made no such mistake—the Town is not 'gathered in, walled, protective, like the City' (98; ch. 7), but Vera sees a problem with even such obviously good men, perhaps with all men:

> 'I like men very much, but sometimes...they're so stupid, so stuffed with theories.... They go in straight lines only, and won't stop. It's dangerous to do that. It's dangerous to leave everything up to the men, you know. That's one reason why I'd like to go home.... To see what Elia with his theories, and my dear young Lev with his ideals, are up to. I get worried they'll go too fast and too straight and get into a place we can't get out of, a trap. You see it seems to me that where men are weak and dangerous is in their vanity. A woman has a center, is a center. But a man isn't, he's a reaching out. So he reaches out and grabs things and piles them up around him and says, I'm this, I'm that, this is me, that's me, I'll prove that I am me! And he can wreck a lot of things trying to prove it. That's what I was trying to say about your father. If he'd only be Luis Falco. That is quite enough. But no, he has to be the Boss, the Councillor, the Father, and so on. What a waste! And Lev, he's terribly vain too, maybe in the same way. A great heart, but not sure where the center is.' (76-77; ch. 5)[297]

Shortly before the story reaches its violent climax, there is a debate among some of the young people in the Town. Luz wants an end to the talk and rules and fighting and advises flight. 'Go north, to the valley you found. Just go. Leave. It's what I did' (113; ch. 8). Now just going was probably a bad idea for the Odonian ancestors of the Anarresti in *The Dispossessed*; it was probably a bad idea for the European ancestors of Americans: all us 'wretched refuse' probably would have done better to stay home, raise hell, and foment an effective revolution. But Luz's advice is followed by a comment by the Narrator indicating why Luz's counsel will not be easily followed: 'They all thought of the same thing: the wilderness. It was as if the wilderness came into the cabin, as if the walls fell down, leaving no shelter' (113). Since 'An die Musik' Le Guin has liked the idea of getting those walls down; more relevantly, Luz and Vera have effectively 'poisoned the well' on walls: they're prisons, traps; they're

---

[296] Cf. David Crosby's 1960s song, 'Mind Gardens,' the allegory of a man who plants a garden, then walls it in and covers it to keep it safe. When the garden starts to die, he learns he must unbuild the walls.
[297] Since some men have been Daoist sages and anarchists and tribesmen; and since some women have been Christian saints and Abolitionist, Suffragette, and/or Prohibitionist idealists—Vera overgeneralizes a bit; cf. and contrast presentation of essentialist views by Moss in *Tehanu* (see *ER* 16).

what make Falco become a villain; as will become absolutely clear in *Always Coming Home*, such walls are essential for the evil incarnation of City of Man (see Spencer 40-41).

Luz is eventually answered by a woman, Southwind, whose lover died in the wilderness during the exploration trip north. "Freedom's won by sacrifice,' Southwind said.' And Luz responds, significantly: 'I hate that idea, sacrifice!' (115). Lev implies Luz sacrificed herself by coming to warn them of the impending attack. Luz says she has 'Not sacrificed myself for any idea! I just ran away—don't you understand? And that's what you all ought to do!'[298] Southwind surprises Lev by agreeing with Luz: "You may be right,' she said. 'So long as we stand and fight, even though we fight with our weapons, we fight their war'' (115; ch. 8).

Lev is shocked by Southwind's saying 'something irresponsible' and 'an affront to their perfect unity.' He responds by starting a dialog that leads up to his truly seeing Luz and feeling confirmed by her, but one in which Lev is generally wrong and Luz is right:

> 'To run away and hide in the forest—that's a choice?' Lev said. '...Not for human beings. Standing upright and having two hands doesn't make us human. Standing up and having ideas and ideals does! And holding fast to those ideals. Together. We can't live alone. Or we die alone—like animals.'
>
> Southwind nodded sadly, but Luz frowned straight back at him. 'Death is death, does it matter whether it's in bed in the house or outside in the forest? We are animals. That's why we die at all.'
>
> 'But to live and die for—for the sake of the spirit—that's different, that's different from running and hiding, all separate, selfish, scratching for food, cowering, hating, each alone—' (116; ch. 8)

And Lev stammers and stops, seeing 'Praise' in Luz's eyes. Still, on a world named by Luz 'Mud,' in a life immanent in mud, there's much to be said for denying ideals, rejecting sacrifice, and, when necessary, lighting out for the wilderness (110, 116-17; ch. 8).

Lev holds fast to his ideals and so leads his people to the confrontation with Herman Macmillan's armed thugs. In Luz's words, '...Lev stood up there facing the men with guns and defying them and got killed' for the same reason Luz's father killed Macmillan: 'Because he was a man, that's what men do. The reasons come afterward' (143; ch. 10). Fighting is fighting and a problem even if one tries to 'fight' for peace. Lev and what he

---

[298] For a damning attack on the desire for self-sacrifice as central to fanaticism—for a sacrifice of Self as the central act of becoming a fanatic— see Hoffer, esp. 21, 35-36, and all of Part Three, 'United Action and Self-Sacrifice.'

stands for will not be at the center of *Eye of the Heron* as a whole. No man will.[299]

The end of *The Eye of the Heron* has a group of Towns-folk walking away from both Town and City in a very antiMacho escape. The escape motif here is important. Their jobs done, cowboy heroes can ride off into the sunset—or Mad Max can walk—and still remain heroes. A hero in Northrop Frye's 'second phase of comedy' doesn't transform his 'humorous society but simply escapes or runs away from it' (*Anatomy* 180 'Theory of Myths,' essay 3). And from Henrick Ibsen's Nora in *A Doll's House* (1879) to George Bernard Shaw's Eliza Doolittle in *Pygmalion* (1912) to Gary Trudeau's Joan Caucus (1970s f.) to Thelma and Louise (*THELMA & LOUISE*, 1991), at least male authors and auteurs can imply that brave women did well to just walk away from unsatisfactory situations they can't change. Still, both the macho and mach*a* ideal is to stand and fight, or at least return to kick ass, like Rambo or Suzy McKee Charnas's free fems (all ironies admitted) in *The Furies* (1994). Le Guin is doing gutsy cultural work in *Eye of the Heron*, and elsewhere, getting us to take seriously the option chosen by those who walk away from Omelas. Positively stated, the people of the Peace, as Lev reminds us are 'outcasts' and 'the children of outcasts,' and, as 'the Founder' said, 'the outcast is the free soul, the child of God.' At his most connected with the world, Lev knows that being again outcast, going on yet another long march—going north, into the wilderness—is the one way his people will be free (14; ch. 1).

In the world of *Eye of the Heron*, Luz's escape plan is a better idea, but not, emphatically not, a universal truth or ideal. An exodus is *an* option, a true way in certain times, certain places, not a cure-all. Immanent in the world, one finds only specific courses of action or inaction in specific situations—specific ways to go with the Dao; there are no universal rules; all ethics are contextual.[300] What is crucial is remaining at home in the world and comfortable in nature—remaining dispossessed by one's immediate house and city and society so that a quick exodus is a real option.

* * * * * * *

At the end of the escape sequence, the Towns-folk find what Luz calls, 'a new place...a beginning place.' When Andre responds 'God willing,' Luz answers back, 'I don't know what God wants' and takes up some 'damp, half-frozen earth': "That's God,' she said, opening her hand on the

---

[299] Le Guin commented on my ms. in through here that *EoH* is her 'first book...that doesn't have men/a man at the center. It was a breakthrough for me.'
[300] Fictional meanings are also influenced by immediate contexts. In *Millennial Women* (1978), a collection of feminist SF, readers might well catch on to Luz as the hero of *EoH* earlier than in reading the story independently, in the novel publication of 1984 (Spivack 109). My thanks to Meghan Braidish for stressing the *Millennial Women* context of *EoH*, and Spivack on Lev vs. Luz as centers (Spivack 112).

half-molded sphere of black dirt. 'That's me. And you. And the others. And the mountains. We're all...it's all one circle'' (176; ch. 11). Luz comments that she really doesn't know what she's talking about here—a good Daoist observation; I'll say Luz is talking about mud and immanence, and using an unChristian figure of speech.[301] In the city of the Lamb, '...nothing unclean shall enter.' There are no seas or forests or night in the New Jerusalem, and where cleanliness is next to godliness, there will be no mud (Revelation 21.27, 21.2-22.5). The symbols in *Heron* are very different.

Most generally, as Jewel, 'a beautiful, dark woman, tells Lev, Victoria is 'a world of shadows' (14; ch. 1), especially the shadows of the wilderness. A more specific symbol is that of the title. After recalling his grandmother's story of her cat, Lev sits on the root of a ringtree and looks at the Meeting Pool, thinking of Lake Serene in the lands of the north he'd helped explore, thinking of mountains he would like to climb, through the mists and rain 'into the brightness of the summits.' Lev thinks in images of transcendence, and he thinks too much; he is not good at stillness, and 'Only for a moment did he find quiet'; but in that moment, 'One of the herons walked silently out into the water.... Lifting its narrow head it gazed at Lev. He gazed back, and for an instant was caught in that round transparent eye, as depthless as the sky clear of clouds; and the moment was round, transparent silent, a moment at the center of all moments, the eternal present moment of the silent animal' (50-51; ch. 4). In a small epiphany, Lev touches the Dao, sloughs off ego; for a moment he comes 'into animal presence'; and 'An old joy returns in holy presence.'[302]

The other, connected controlling symbol for most of *Heron* is the ringtree, a tree with a 'double life.' It begins 'as a single, fast-growing seedling,' that matures quickly and flowers. The flowers get fertilized, and fold into seeds, all of which drop off, apparently dying, 'leaving at last one single seed on a high central branch.' The tree withers, and then, some hot autumn afternoon, the seed explodes, sending out 'several hundred seedlets' in a circle, and plant competition working until 'Ten years later, and for a century or two after that, from twenty to sixty copper-leaved trees stood in a perfect ring about the long-vanished central stem. Branch and root they stood apart, yet touching, forty ringtrees, one tree-ring.' Where the trees of the tree-ring are numerous enough to touch, and live a long time, they 'so exhausted they central ground that it might sink and form a hollow, which filled with ground seepage and with rain, and the circle of high, old dark-red trees was then mirrored in the still water of a

---

[301] Le Guin would stress immanence here: 'I think she's talking about immanence, no?' (personal communication).
[302] Denise Levertov, 'Come into Animal Presence' (1961); the poem is quoted as a headnote / introd. to *Buffalo Gals and Other Animal Presences* (1987 [*BG* 14]).

central pool.³⁰³ The center of a tree-ring was always a quiet place' (46; ch. 4). It is at such a pool that Lev sees and is caught by the eye of the heron.

The ringtree in *Heron* corresponds to the rock-pounding circle in *Planet of Exile* (1966), the Yin-Yang in *Left Hand of Darkness* (1969), the Circle of Life in *The Dispossessed* (1974), the heyiya-if in *Always Coming Home* 1985). It is clearly a symbol of individuality and wholeness; it can have water—the favorite element in 'the Perennial Philosophy' and among some Native Americans—in a still place at a center, a center specifically said to be hollow: the Daoist nothingness, lack, like the hole in the center of a wheel allowing the existence of the wheel. And the Meeting House ringtree is old enough to have at its center the Meeting Pool, with herons: imaging wholeness, an appropriately anarchic society within the world, in touch with nature, the Dao, and animals.

Luz's symbol is mud. She is in good company, and such views are significant for a very important debate—one scene of *Kulturkampf*—in our world.

Le Guin sees "Civilized Man" as 'climbing up into his own head' and talks of the 'soul-fortress' Church 'towering over the dark abysms' of all which is not soul: all that can be associated with the complex, 'bestial/mortal/World/Hell' (*BG* 11; Introd.). In Le Guin's correct summary of antiSocial-Gospel Christianity, 'The world has no value except as a sort of waiting room or testing ground for the soul of Man, a passage from eternity to eternity' ('Legends ' 8). Humans = Man = 'the soul of Man.' There is another tradition in the West. In the J-Code version of creation, after bringing forth water to 'well up from the ground and water the whole surface of the earth—the LORD God formed man [*'adam*] from the dust of the earth [*'adamah*]. He blew into his nostrils the breath of life, and man became a living being' (Genesis 2.6-7; Tanakh). I.e., Man = dirt/breath, one thing. Le Guin here stresses the dirt, and adds water.³⁰⁴

In *The Tombs of Atuan*, a character describes the people outside of Atuan as 'the color of dirt' (*TA* 18; ch. 2). In *The Lathe of Heaven*, George Orr tells Heather Lelache that she's brown, and she snaps back, 'Shit color.' Orr responds with 'The color of the earth' (*LoH* 103; ch. 7). In the Orgota creation myth that is chapter 17 in *The Left Hand of Darkness*, the ice-shape that creates all life uses soil plus sea-water. As Le Guin's writing career was getting started, other authors had taken earth and added Daoist water rather than the J-Code's air to get humans. Kurt Vonnegut, Jr., in *Cat's Cradle* (1963) has as the first *foma* of *The First Book of Bokonon*— i.e., the initial harmless lie—that God got lonely and so made 'living creatures out of mud,' of which one was man. 'Man as mud alone could speak' and asks 'What is the *purpose* of all of this?' God didn't know everything

---

³⁰³ For dark red, cf. the palace at Erhenrang and the Un-Palace of Rer in *LHD* 53; ch. 5, and ch. 3, passim. See below for 'dark red,' aggressively carnivorous fish ('NA' 77-78). In *LHD* and 'NA,' Le Guin seems to associate deep red with anarchy, grandeur, power, and danger.
³⁰⁴ In 'NA' she allows more for soul; see below.

has to have a purpose, but man insists. "Then I leave it up to you to think of one for all this," said God' and went away (117; § 118). In the section 'Dyot meet mat' ('God made mud', § 99), the first human gets to sit up and look at creation and says, 'Lucky me, lucky mud' and gets to feel pretty insignificant compared to God but mildly important when thinking 'of all the mud that didn't even get to sit up and look around.' Le Guin might agree that if we must feel superior, an acceptable form might be the expression of gratitude: 'I got so much, and most mud got so little' (Vonnegut, *Cat's Cradle* 149-50). Finally, in Brian Aldiss's *The Dark Light Years* (1964), Sir Mihaly Pasztor says, 'To our way of thought...civilization is reckoned as the distance man has placed between himself and his excreta' (44; ch. 5). The statement is made more exact a bit later when Sir Mihaly has it 'that civilization was the distance man had placed between himself and everything else....' A minor character offers comfort to a rattled Sir Mihaly by telling him that we humans are 'coming away from the mud, away from the primeval slime, away from the animal, towards the spiritual.' Since what's rattled Pasztor is the death by torture of one of the wise, dirty aliens of the novel, we sympathize when Pasztor asks 'Oughtn't we to have stayed in the mud? Mightn't it be more healthy and sane down there?' (99; ch. 10).

Luz's stress on mud, just before the climax of *The Eye of the Heron* (117; ch. 8) and almost at its end (176; ch. 11), makes clear what this novel is up to right down to its recurring symbolism. *The Eye of the Heron* denies even the best forms of masculinist, transcendent idealism in favor of a feminist-inflected immanence, including the necessity, now and then, to get down into the mud.

'Pathways of Desire' (1979)

'Pathways of Desire' enters 'into the midst of things' some forty-one days into an anthropological expedition by three Terrans of the Ethnographic Corps of the Space Service to the Ndif people of the planet Yirdo (a moon actually, of the gas giant Uper [*CR* 180-81]). The story is set in an indeterminate future, but we're told it is eight years after an interstellar Exploratory Survey visited the system containing Yirdo and thirty years after the development of Faster Than Light (FTL) space flight (198). FTL or no, however, the anthropologists are pretty much Terrans like us, and the Ndif are, in several ways, 'natives' no different from us.[305] Incredibly not different biologically: miraculously, totally improbably no different from us biologically. This remarkable biological similarity is not remarked upon by anyone in the story, and that is significant: either (1) we're in the Hainish universe or (2) Le Guin has gotten sloppy with world-building— or (3) 'Pathways of Desire' isn't SF extrapolation but fabulation. There's

---

[305] *Ndif*: 'Natives'—Le Guin (personal communication), 'No difference'—Bittner, 'Serpent' presentation.

no indication we're in the Hainish universe, and Le Guin is firmly in control of her material; and 'Pathways of Desire' is indeed the stuff of fable.

The story features the Terran anthropologists: Tamara, a twenty-eight year old dark-skinned 'configurationist' (*CR* 178,188, 190); Ramchandra ('Ram'), a forty-year old male Brahmin linguist from a suburb of Calcutta (181, 207); and Bob: 'big, beautiful blond Bob, lean tanned tough Bob, perfect hero of male wish fulfillment' (176)—Bob, God of Ohio, in the formulation I'll offer—the student of myths in the group (*CR* 185). Narration is third-person limited from the point of view of Tamara, giving the vision (and some thoughts) of a woman trained in anthropology, but still willing to judge a youth-based, masculinist culture from the point of view of a 'Middle-Aged Woman.'

The plot involves a death, a mystery, and a love story, more or less in that order. The death is Bob's. He's been 'Sleeping with informants and stuff' and has been challenged to a duel (187). He fights the duel and throws and knocks out his opponent, but not before his opponent stabs him with a poisoned knife. The mystery is how the culture on a planet thirty-one light-years from Earth can be so totally un-alien generally—less alien to Bob and Tamara than Ramchandra is alien to them (188-89)—and, more specifically, how the Young Ndif language can be a 'direct derivation...from Modern Standard English' (196). The solution to the mystery is that 'Man made the world * * * In his head, between his ears' (192), and 'Man,' in the case of Yirdo and the Ndif, is Bill Kop*man*:

> 'A fifteen-year-old boy, with glasses, probably also acne and weak ankles. A skinny boy, lazy, shy. He reads stories, he daydreams, about the great blond hero who can hunt and fight and make love all day and night. His head is full of the hero, himself, and so it all comes to be.' * * * 'He doesn't understand desire. He is entirely caught in it, bound by it, he sees and knows nothing but his own immense desire. And so he makes the world.' * * * 'He writes it all down...his fantasies about the Ndif. Maps and everything. A lot of kids do that. And some adults....' * * * 'There is room. There is time [for all the worlds humans dream]. All the galaxies. All the universes. That is infinity. The worlds are infinite, the cycles are endless. There is room...for all the dreams, all the desires.' (204-05).

So Ramchandra tells Tamara, ending with, 'Bill Kopman dreams...and the God dances. And Bob dies, and we make love'; for that is the final part of the plot: the romance and love of Ramchandra and Tamara (*CR* 205).

So, in our universe, the author Ursula K. Le Guin dreams up a universe where young, horny, bored Bill Kopman of, say, Topeka, Kansas, dreams up the moon Yirdo and the Ndif people and develops a language and culture for them, and, lo, they come to be. And three Terrans go to this world and work and solve a mystery, one dies and the remaining two find love.

The plot in 'Pathways of Desire' is interesting but not really the point. The point is about story-telling, culture, and teenage boys, about science fiction as a genre, about old women; plus lot about ontology, theories of reality.

I'll start with ontology and work backwards. 'Pathways of Desire' is a Hindu version of what Brian W. Aldiss has called a 'Shaggy God' story (*S.F. Ency.* 500). As Nataraja, the Lord of the Dance, the God Shiva brings movement into the cosmos, dancing the worlds into existence.[306] Or perhaps the worlds are dreamed, by Indra, or perhaps Krishna or Brahma. Ramchandra asks the question: 'Who dreamed the Earth?' He answers only, 'A greater dreamer than you or I.' In 'Pathways,' the immediate world is dreamed by a kid in Topeka (or wherever), who created Yirdo 'between his ears.' This much is a joke, based on the idea of the Universe as a dream of God. But Ramchandra adds a 'but' and goes on: 'but we are the dreamer, Shakti, and the worlds will endure as long as our desire' (207). Shakti (also Sakti), is the divine mother, sometimes seen as wife to Shiva.[307] Ram sees himself and Tamara as Shiva and Shakti. As in *The Lathe of Heaven* (1971), humans are the gods, and, somewhat like George Orr, we can dream worlds.

Part of what's going on in 'Pathways' is use of contemporary (capital 'T') Theory in which world-creation is mental. Ramchandra says that the Old among the Ndif 'seem to be engaged in creating the world. Humans beings do this primarily by means of language, music, and the dance' (197). I.e., we do at least semiconsciously what the god Bill Kopman does mostly unconsciously. This 'creating the world' can mean that human beings organize our sense perceptions in culturally determined ways to create the *cosmos*—the *ordered* universe—we deal with; or it can mean that we humans individually or collectively create the universe in our minds precisely in the manner of George Orr. Such world creation is a possibility made plausible by, among other ideas, the 'Whorfian Hypothesis' in linguistics and by the idea in quantum theory 'that quantum states are not definite until they are observed.' As a couple of Greg Bear's characters put it, such quantum states

> 'fluctuate, interact, as if two or more universes—each containing a potential outcome—are meshed together, until the physicist causes the collapse into the final state by observing. Measuring.'

---

[306] My sources on Indian philosophy are *Encyclopaedia Britannica* 1974, articles on 'Buddha,' 'Buddhism,' 'Buddhism, History of,' "Buddhist Mysticism,' 'Heracleitus,' 'Hinduism,' 'Indian Philosophy,' 'Nataraja,' 'Siva'; *The Song of God: The Bhagavad-Gita*; A. L. Kroeber, *Anthropology* § 306; Watts, *The Way of Zen*; and Bittner's PCA presentation, 'The Serpent Spits Out Its Tail.'
[307] For Shiva and Shakti, see Le Guin's poetry collected in *Hardwords* (1981).

> 'Doesn't that give consciousness a godlike importance?' Fausch asked.
> 'It does indeed,' said Frederik. Modern physics is on a heavy power trip.' (Bear 479)[308]

Fortunately, however, we don't need to get into any modern theories or postmodern / poststructuralist Theory for 'Pathways of Desire'; old Indian philosophy is quite sufficient. I shall justify this cop-out from serious Theorizing with a reference to two quotations.

One of the aliens Orr dreams up in *The Lathe of Heaven* tells him 'Speech is silver, silence is gold. Self is universe. Please forgive interruption, crossing in mist' (138 [also 139]; ch. 9). 'Self is universe' is the Hindu 'Brahman = Atman' equation read from right to left ('Indian Philosophy' 9.316). More immediately relevant, one of the Old Men of the Ndif tells Ram and Tamara, 'Nothing is wood, nothing is stone, nothing is water, nothing is blood, nothing is bone; all things are sanisukiarad' (192), where 'sanisukiarad' is, I think, the 'Not this...not that' of Brahman: Being is what's left over after all creation is removed. The 'mist' in the *Lathe* quotation may be the 'relative' world of appearances: *maya* in Indian philosophy, and in the original introduction to 'Vaster Than Empires and More Slow' (1971).

Indian philosophy is varied and difficult, so I'm going to defer here to a work cited by Le Guin in her 'Introductory Note' to *King Dog*: the *Bhagavad-Gita* (*The Song of God*), specifically Lord Krishna's primer for his friend and student Arjuna. Krishna tells Arjuna that Brahman is constant and uncaused, totally Itself. Within an individual, Brahman is the Atman. Brahman as creative energy caused and causes all 'existences' to exist.

> The nature of the relative world is mutability. The nature of the individual man is his consciousness of ego. I alone am God [Krishna, embodying Brahman,] * * * the Lord, who is the light-giver, the highest of the high. * * * Shining sunlike, self luminous. (74-75; VIII)
>
> How hard to break through
> Is this, my Maya,

i.e., the necessary but necessarily delusion-causing forces/matter of the perceived world. It is possible to take 'refuge' in Krishna, and 'pass beyond Maya,' but this passing beyond can be difficult. As embodied Brahman, Krishna describes himself as 'veiled' in Maya and hard to recognize. 'All living creatures are led astray as soon as they are born, by the delusion that the relative world is real. This delusion arises from their own desire and hatred. But the doers of good deeds, whose bad karma is exhausted,

---

[308] See below, my discussion of 'the social construction of reality,' preceding chapter on stories in *FIS*.

are freed from this delusion * * * [A]t the hour of death, their whole consciousness is made one with mine' (73-74; VII). By following the proper yoga, people can 'break the chains of desire' and get free 'from the terrible wheel of rebirth and death,' no longer 'a prisoner, / Enslaved by action' and dragged about by our desires (39; II). Krishna denies that God deludes humans. The delusion is our dreams: 'You dream you are the doer, / You dream that action is done, / You dream that action bears fruit.' The problem is our ignorance and the delusion built into the world that gives us these 'dreams.' To do right in this system is to strive for the time 'When the light of the Atman' in oneself 'Drives out our darkness,' to 'find the place of freedom, / The place of no return'—i.e., the merging with the Real so that one need never again return to the karmic wheel. In being 'Absorbed in Brahman' one 'overcomes the world' and becomes 'Changeless, untouched by evil.' Krishna asks of personified Brahman, 'What home have we but Him?' (59-60; V).

It may be dangerous to answer a rhetorical question posed by God, but Le Guin has not been shy these last three decades in replying to a transcendent God; among other things, 'Pathways' is her more polite answer to a mostly absent transcendent god, and to Ultimate Immanence.

Tamara dreams of Bill Kopman, 'Standing in front of me. Sort of filling everything, taking up all the room, so that I couldn't get past him or around him'; she tells Ram the dream, and he has immediate enlightenment. Tamara asks him if anything is wrong, and he responds that nothing is wrong; 'Go back to sleep. You talked to God.' She asks if 'God's name is Bill?', and Ram names God: 'Bill Kopman, or Kopfman, or Cupman,' anyway, 'Bill Kopman, who made this world through his desire' (*CR* 204). Ramchandra understands this desire very well. He was raised in 'The great teaching tradition of the Brahman caste' and knows 'Nothing is real' in the world of perception, that all is Maya (181); he is a hunter of 'peremensoe'—'(191, 195)—and knows 'that desire is to be transcended. The goal of a Brahmin should the Understanding that allows him to be 'Absorbed in Brahman,' to never return to the wheel, to go home to God. Not in a story by Le Guin, though.[309] A widower, Ram returns instead to human love, going to Tamara: 'Listen, Tamara, you set me free, your hands free me. And bind me. Tighter to the wheel, never in this life now will I get free, never cease to desire you, I don't *want* to cease.' 'Confusion' he finally whispers, 'Illusion,' and he will yield to it (203). He sees the better wisdom of going with the folly of human relationships. In the speech ending the story, Ramchandra tells Tamara, 'I speak my native tongue, because you have brought me home' (207), not home to God, but to a Le Guinian marriage.

---

[309] One of Le Guin's sources in valuing the world of 'Mutabilitie' may be the teaching of Master Dôgen, a Japanese Buddhist teacher of the 13th c. and possibly the founder of the Sôtô-Zen sect. 'For Master Dôgen, impermanence is itself the absolute state, and this impermanence is not to be rejected but to be valued. 'Impermanence is the Buddhahood....'' (Nakumura, in *Voices* 86).

Le Guin's concluding gesture in favor of desire should condition, I think, our reading of this whole story.

Tamara's final vision of Bill Kopman is a very negative one: his 'blind yearning face before her, filling the world, no way around it, no path'; the last references to him are Ramchandra's reminder that it is highly unlikely he will awake to reality—'in a thousand thousand years does a soul wake up'—and a reference to 'Bill's wet dreams' (206). Not very dignified in the mind of any reader, and such a description should be especially unsettling for people familiar with Le Guin's work. Victor Hanson fills his world, and is a very negative character in *The Beginning Place*, as is the world-filling Big Man in the Kesh story 'Big Man and Little Man' (*ACH* 157). Especially in *The Lathe of Heaven*, a work with obvious connections to 'Pathways of Desire,' 'no way,' implies the loss of the Dao. James Bittner, a reader very familiar with Le Guin's work, takes Kopman as an intentionally stereotyped SF fan and relates him to Le Guin's possibly feeling 'in the late seventies that her path/way/tao was blocked, and chose then to go on exploring by paths other than science fiction' ('Serpent' 2).

Again, though, Bill Kopman isn't the only one with sexual desires in this story, and the image of the blocked way has been undercut a bit by the entrance of Bob: 'The light of Uper haloed his thick fair hair; the importance of his return filled the entire biosphere as the bulk of his body filled the doorway. 'I just got back,' he announced' (186). Again, in my formulation: Bob—God of Ohio, with whom, I think, Le Guin is having some fun. Le Guin may also be having a little bit of fun when Ramchandra tells Tamara solemnly, and thematically, 'You must take words seriously. They are all we have' (182); 'Words are all we have' is an important idea from modern philosophy, but it's also a line from George Carlin's seriously philosophical and very funny comedy routines on language (most famously 'Seven Words You Can't Say on Television').

With these warnings against over-earnestness, let us look at the world Bill Kopman made, and the reactions to it of the three adult Terrans.

The world itself is beautiful: bright sunshine, no rain until after sundown (as in Camelot in *Camelot* [film version 1967]), consistent warm weather. Food is readily available: 'boneless poro meat and the mushy sweet fruit of the lamaba tree,' a kind of ready-made 'hot dogs and milkshakes' (*CR* 175). Disease is rare. Socially there is no war, and violence is limited—entirely, as far as we see—to formal knife-duels (one-on-one) among the young men (187), plus some wrestling (188). Social structure is simple: male dominance and division into sex/age groups. I assume infants and girls. We learn of the formal groups of Juvenile Males: nine- to twelve-years old, Young Women: 12-23, Middle-Aged Women: 23-40, Young Men: 13-40. Old Men/Women: anyone over 40. The Juvenile Males run around and play. The Young Men hunt poro, watch the Young Women dance, and have sex with the Young Women. The Young Men also get together and brag about their hunting and sex. The Young Women dance and have sex with the Young Men; they do not have children, because becoming fertile makes one a Middle-Aged Woman (179). In addition to child-bearing, only briefly discussed in the story, the Middle-Aged Women cook and clean and serve communal meals. The Old are mostly invisible, but they have their own house and are developing their own language and dances and myths about 'Bik-Kop-Man.'

And that's pretty much it. No art. No history. No legends. No family life, no affiliation patterns, just about no customs. Indeed, Bob ends up engaging in sex with quite so many of the Young Women because he looks 'just like' the Ndif and he'd be offending local custom to refuse, and 'It's practically the only custom they've got' (187). Sleeping around, plus any duels that develop from sleeping around: Bob feels he must reject Tamara's excellent advice to 'Beg off' on the knife fight—'We can just move on'—because there is at least the sense of local honor, and a desire for entertainment (188-89). The Ndif also have no manners.

All together 'It's a teenage society' of 'Locker-room aliens!' (188-89), where '...they all talk like Hemingway characters' (185). The most severe judgments of the Ndif are made by Tamara:

> So far...working in three widely separate localities, we've found the same language, without major dialectical variations, and the same set of very rudimentary social and cultural patterns. Bob hasn't found any legends, any expressions of the archetypes, any developed symbology. I haven't found much more social structure than I'd find in a herd of cattle, about what I might find in a primate troop. Sex and age determine all roles. The Ndif are culturally subhuman; they don't exist fully as human beings. The Old Ndif are beginning to. (197)

Bob objects, 'That's missionary talk!' and suggests that the Ndif have become stagnant from lack of environmental challenges, 'and they don't have sexual hangups—' Tamara interjects, here, to Bob's annoyance, 'That's *in*human' (198-99).

If it is true that we learn to be human, then one might ask at what age most people have learned enough to be judged human, and living in a college town, around the corner from a high school, I'm willing to consider the suggestion that teenagers, especially teenage boys are, ordinarily, 'subhuman.' Still, the subhumanity of teenage boys is a necessary assumption of the war-making classes (who usually really regret, I think, killing women and children and old people), and I think we should find any judgment of cultural subhumanity suspect. Le Guin problematicizes the 'culturally subhuman' issue not only by having Bob (who may be ignored as male wish-fulfillment) object to Tamara's view but also by having Tamara earlier raise the issue herself, "Why shouldn't there be a South-Sea-Island world?' she argued with herself. 'Why does it seem too simple—phony? Am I a Puritan, am I looking for original sin?" (181).[310] The Ndif culture *is* phony, in a sense, and Tamara's is not just being a Puritan. What is troublesome about Ndif sexuality is not that it is promiscuous but that it's so damn simple. As Le Guin says in 'Is Gender Necessary?' (and does not change in the 'Redux' version), 'Sex is a great mana,' and 'there is always a code' (166). Even high-school cliques and college dorm floors and fraternities have codes, and it very strange that the Ndif mostly lack one.

And here, I think, we come to Le Guin's serious critique of the Ndif. It's not evil that they lack a sexual code; it's boring. They have a sexist society, but, as patriarchal societies go, they are not an evil people: almost no crime and punishment, no hunger, no war, no domestic violence, no prisons, no genital mutilation, no rape, no incest, no prostitution, no pornography or taxes, no slavery, no economic classes, no capitalist exploitation, no state tyranny, no destruction of the environment, no alienation from one's body or one's community, no loneliness—they're not a people most Americans should criticize on moral grounds. Tamara gets it right when she finds the Ndif 'like a stage play, a movie, the island paradise,' except it is a movie she doesn't like: 'But I *don't* like them!' she finally asserts. 'They're boring! No kinship systems, no social structure except stupid age-grading and detestable male dominance, no real skills no arts...once they grow up, *they're* bored' (184). *Boring*, however, is only marginally an ethical category. If people have the opportunity to make their lives more interesting—and the Old among the Ndif are doing that quite nicely (rediscovering the Perennial Philosophy)—being boring is only a minor cultural failing.[311] Degree of interest, however, is a crucial esthetic category. To say a human or a culture is boring is no major accusation; to say that a work of art is boring is to damn it utterly. Bill Kopman isn't a bad boy—we see nothing of his life on Earth—just a lousy author.

'Pathways of Desire' is a relatively 'gentle antidote' to the varieties of SF that take readers thirty-one light-years to find a culture No Different from macho wish-fulfillments that could be set on any southsea island on Earth—or southsea battlefield or Chicago southside street for those who want to Make War, Not Love and romanticize violence.[312] A classic example of such bad SciFi would be one of the original *FLASH GORDON* movies, where Flash and Dale Arden and Dr. Zarkov land on Mongo or

---

[310] See A. L. Kroeber, *Anthropology* § 248, 'Inhibition and Puritanism'; see also Le Guin's 'Omelas,' and my discussion thereof.
[311] And, of course, Serenity in 'Solitude' (1994) would chide the Terrans for being bored among such wonders: a whole new physical world, in a wondrous universe, with people (to mostly avoid). The Thurro-dowist Listener in *CI* (ch. 3) would agree
[312] 'Pathways' looks very gentle put next to Norman Spinrad's *The Iron Dream* (1972): a satire purporting to be an SF novel written by Adolf Hitler in a reality only slightly alternate to our own—with Hitler's fiction shown to be not all that different from 'the considerable body of pathological literature published within the science fiction field' in our world (252).

Mars and find the Hawk Men and the Lion Men and the Shark Men, but very few significant women and almost no Old Men or anything except White Men.[313] And everyone speaks English, without even 'You wonder how I can speak your language.' All that way to Mongo or Mars, and 'no difference'! One might conclude from that lack of difference that the culture of the USA in the 1930s (for Flash Gordon) is, in its basics, literally universal. Worse, the imaginative creation of a world without some human group can be a wishing away of the existence of that group; and the imagined subordination of a group can work similarly. In America we lack the word *mâshâl*, but many writers can still produce 'quasi-magical, verbal prefiguring[s] of reality in the shape, for good and for ill, in which the utterer would like to encounter it' (Rabinowitz 320). 'Pathways' reminds us of the wishing-away in much SF of non-Whites, the invisibility of the Old, and the reduction of women to servants and playthings.[314]

Such SF is not so much conservative as small-minded and imaginatively timid, and it may be 'filling the world' of the imagination of many readers and viewers of SF. In that sense there is 'no way around it, no path' for SF as an esthetic experience or endeavor. Whether such stories are good or is not the point here; they're legitimately 'detestable' to a conscious woman like Tamara; and a truth-telling Old Woman like Le Guin insists they're (eventually) just plain boring to any conscious adult.

* * * * * * *

As in *Lathe of Heaven* (1971) and in the stories of what I'll present as The Churten Group in *Fisherman of the Inland Sea* (1994), Le Guin in 'Pathways' plays seriously with the 'strong' version of *constructed* reality. But this may be the final meaning of 'Ndif': It makes no difference how the moon Yirdo or the planet Terra and their cultures got structured; the world *is*, and the human job is to live in the world: responsibly, consciously, lovingly, and joyously. Tamara and Ramchandra do right to accept and love each other, and, generally, let the world they find *be*. Where 'Pathways' offers a critique it is of the wet-dreams of nerdy adolescent male humans—when, and *only* when, those wish-fulfillment's are written by grown people, who get them published and/or filmed and receive money for them and thereby profit from providing role models and paradigms for imagining highly destructive realities. When stories go out into the world and encourage boys to live the macho fantasy, and not grow up,

---

[313] For the gender issue in much SF, see Russ's 'The Image of Women in Science fiction.' Note that in the original *Flash Gordon* comic strip, all the Mongonians, not just the villainous Ming, were Asian; the films, that far, are less actively racist than the strips.

[314] There is, though, an 'on the other hand' here: On the other hand, all art is selective, and we should be careful in dealing with what is not in any individual work of art (see Frye 235.)

and for girls to accept a world ruled by such boys, they are spreading a figurative poison in need of an antidote.

'The New Atlantis' (1975)

...[T]he contemporary trend [is for] other cultures to assimilate themselves to Occidental civilization...to 'Westernize'.... Mankind...is not yet unitary; but at the moment it is traveling fast that way.... Suppose we attain a single, essentially uniform, world-wide civilization that has supplanted the many diverse ones of the past. And suppose that in attaining this one civilization we achieve its aims, realize the values potential in its patterns. What then when the exhausted, repetitive stage is reached, and there is no new rival culture to take over responsibility and opportunity and start fresh with new values in a different set of patterns—what then? — A. L. Kroeber, *Anthropology* § 161

'[T]hou met'st with things dying, I with things newborn.' — William Shakespeare, *The Winter's Tale* 4.1.113-14

'The New Atlantis' repeats the Le Guinian pattern of two worlds separated and in communication, but with major differences.

The primary world of the story is a very dystopian West Coast of the United States in the near future: a world that is poor, environmentally degraded, totalitarian, linguistically corrupt—a world edging toward George Orwell's Oceania in *Nineteen Eighty-Four* (1949), or the more explicitly named United States in Frederik Pohl and Cyril Kornbluth's *The Space Merchants* (1952) or in John Brunner's *The Sheep Look Up* (1972; see Suvin 268). The second world of the story is the world of the rising continent, which I'll call 'Atlantis'; but note that the story posits 'the emergence of new—or, possibly, very old—continents in the Atlantic and Pacific,' not just the Atlantic (*NA* 67-68), plus Charlotte Spivack's correct observation that 'the new Atlantis' is also the sinking United States (*Le Guin* 88). The West Coast world is presented in first-person singular ('I') narration by Belle, the protagonist of the West Coast sections, whose journal we are reading; the Atlantis portions are narrated in first-person plural ('we') by the citizens of the rising Atlantis: what Elizabeth Cummins perceptively labels 'the first-person collective voice' (173). Spivack (87-88), and Darko Suvin note the similarity between the alternation between the US and Atlantean sections of 'The New Atlantis' and the alternation between Anarres and Urras in *The Dispossessed* (1974), adding that thematically and politically the associations are between Urras and the US, Anarres and Atlantis (see Suvin 268). Cummins finds the closest analogy in narrative structure to that of *The Left Hand of Darkness*.[315] For a close precursor for the Atlantis sections themselves, my suggestion is Samuel Beckett's *The Lost Ones* (1972), which I interpret as a rigorous exercise in empiricism: the exact description of a very impoverished environment—in the sense in which people on a space probe would be in an impoverished environment, with much less to perceive than in a forest or on a city street. The people of Atlantis literally rise to consciousness, moving up from the depths (of unconsciousness, Nameless Dao, nonBeing, the deepest sea) with very little to sense except the pressure of the ocean, toward the world of light and sound—and of Becoming and action and the 10,000 things of our world.

The structure of 'The New Atlantis' is obvious in the original publication in *The New Atlantis and Other Novellas of Science Fiction*: the US parts are printed in roman type, the Atlantean in indented *italics*. (No italics in the reprint in *The Compass Rose*.) There are six sections to the story, each section divided into two parts.[316] To stress the similarity to *The Dispossessed*, I label the sections 1.U for the opening in the USA, 1.A for the first section in 'Atlantis,' 2.U/2.A, etc.

The story's opening paragraph introduces us to the 'I' (not yet named), hints about her world, and ends with the news from a pamphlet that 'a new continent is rising from the depths of the sea' (*NA* 67). The rest of 1.U moves the 'I' from her Wilderness Week among the few remaining trees of the National Forest Preserve back home to Portland, Oregon, where she finds her husband, Simon, in bed (67-68), back from 'the Rehabilitation Camp' (70). So far we've learned that 'a Supersonic Superscenic Deluxe Longdistance coal-burner, with Home Comfort' is a slow, dilapidated bus with a toilet (67) and that the 'Longhorn Inch-Thick Steak House Dinerette' serves meatless hamburgers (69), so we can be quite sure the 'Rehabilitation Camp' is a labor camp in the tradition of the Stalinist Gulag or the Pulefen Commensality Third Voluntary Farm and Resettlement Agency 'camp' (*LHD* 175; ch. 13).[317] Simon's 'crime'—and in totalitarian states *crime* is a particularly tricky word—is only hinted at in this section, but it is clear that he is important enough in the sciences or mathematics (math as it turns out) that someone 'published his proof of Goldbach's Hypothesis in Peking' (70), a parallel to Shevek in *The Dispossessed* (Suvin 168).

---

[315] See Cummins's, *Understanding* (1990/1993): 170-71. Contrast Ayn Rand's *Anthem* (1938/1946), where coming to political consciousness moves one from 'we' to 'I.'

[316] See Suvin 270, Cummins 167, Spivack 88-91.

[317] Le Guin's strong dislike of euphemism appears also in *WWF* (1972) and is readily understandable in the context of the Viet Nam War and much of 20th-c. politics. Readers who have grown up on euphemism and are not bothered by it, should see the classic analysis of euphemism as political obscenity, George Orwell's 'Politics and the English Language,' coll. *Shooting an Elephant and Other Essays* (1950).

Section 1.A is the start of a (re)creation myth: as Atlantis rises, the pressure lessens (subliminally sensed by the Atlanteans), and '*'then' there was the light*,' an event that creates time and confirms consciousness (71).[318] The first light is followed by a second:

> *It did not occur to us that there might be another moment. There was no reason to assume that there might be more than one. One was marvel enough: that in all the field of the dark, in the cold, heavy, dense, moveless, timeless, placeless, boundless black, there should have occurred, once, a small slightly blurred, moving light! Time need be created only once, we thought.*
>
> *But we were mistaken. The difference between one and more than one is all the difference in the world. Indeed, that difference is the world.* (*NA* 71-72)

Seeing the light, the Atlanteans think of the stars and then the planets: '*Like the stars, yes, but not stars. It is not the great Existences we are seeing, but only the little lives*' (73). Less poetically put, they see luminescent fish.

Section 2.U begins the morning following the protagonist's coming home to find Simon. The protagonist tells us about Simon's condition after the Camp— '[H]e moved like a ninety-year old...all bent out of shape'— and Simon tells her a bit about the Camp. The protagonist finds her husband 'changed out of recognition, a different man,' yet still the same: 'It is enough to make you understand why most languages have a word like 'soul.' There are various degrees of death, and time spares us none of them. Yet something endures, for which a word is needed' (74).[319] We learn the protagonist's name, here, 'Belle,' and that she has a job under 'the Full Employment Act': four hours a day as an inspector at a recycled paper bag factory, backing up an electronic inspection system that has yet to make an error she has caught. This is not Belle's true work however; that is music (75). Belle gets a black-market doctor to look at Simon, and gets him some aspirin (76-77). These two actions give us more information about the USA of the story, a 'corporative State,' that Suvin correctly identifies as a well-known 'American variation of...fascism...integrating into a seamless government totality all the already existing bureaucracies...with interstices for regulated and parasitic 'private enterprise'' (267-68). The doctor—an assistant to a jeweler in town—gives Belle an occasion for some indirect exposition on the laws of her world, and some quite direct gender commentary: 'She gathered very soon that Simon and I were

---

[318] Cf. The opening of *LoH*, and note Le Guinian motif of coming into consciousness and returning to unconsciousness and/or dream.

[319] Luz in *EoH* may overstate in having humans only 'mud': dirt + water; there may also be a problem in postmodern theories that deny a subject, or anything else, for that 'something' that endures.

married, and it was funny to see her look at us and smile like a cat. Some people love illegality for its own sake. Men, more often than women. It's men who make laws, and enforce them, and break them, and think the whole performance is wonderful. Most women would rather just ignore them. You could see that this woman, like a man, actually enjoyed breaking them' (*NA* 76). As Cummins stresses (171-72), this passage connects 'The New Atlantis' with *The Dispossessed*, where Shevek thinks '[M]en have to learn to be anarchist. Women don't have to learn' (*TD* 42-43; ch. 2).

The section ends with Belle's going out 'to register Simon as temporarily domiciled at my address and to apply for Temporary Unemployment Compensation ration stamps for him,' and a brief meditation on how law enforcement 'must have been simpler...back when marriage was legal and adultery was what got you into trouble' (77). The point here is an important one: whether marriage is required or forbidden, 'there is always a code,' and where there's an authoritarian state, or worse, the state will enforce a code.[320]

Section 2.A raises Atlantis more and brings more '*lantern-creatures*':

> *They were not pretty. They were dark colored, most often a dark red, and they were all mouth. They ate one another whole. Light swallowed light, all swallowed together in the vaster mouth of the darkness. * * * Poor ragged, hunchjawed dwarfs squeezed to the bone by the weight of the darkness, chilled to the bone by the cold of the darkness, tiny monsters burning with bright hunger, who brought us back to life!* (77-78)

Darko Suvin rather dislikes the luminescent fish, finding them 'Luciferic' in their light-bearing (Suvin 268), which is sound etymology (Lucifer = Light-Bearer, The Bright One), but rather demonizing biology; so I will view the fish as Luciferic, but with sympathy for the devil. Picture very carefully darkness, and then a hand-sized, luminescent creature settling down toward, something, and then:

> *We saw the pavement beneath the creature and the wall beside it, heartbreaking in its exact, clear linearity, its opposition to all that was fluid, random, vast, and void....*
> *So we knew that the wall was there; and that it was an outer wall, a housefront perhaps, or the side of the one of the towers of the city.*

---

[320] The totalitarian states in Y. Zamiatin's *We*, A. Huxley's *Brave New World*, and G. Orwell's *1984* have significantly different regulations about sex; but all of them regulate sex stringently.

> *We remembered the towers. We remembered the city.*
> *We had forgotten it. We had forgotten who we were; but*
> *we remembered the city, now.* (78-79, end of the section)

In her Daoist works, Le Guin pays her respects to all that was and is 'fluid, random, vast, and void,' but there is something to be said for the city and human memory—as in 'The Eye Altering' (1976/1978) and 'A Woman's Liberation' and 'Coming of Age in Karhide' (1995)—and there is much to be said for a little light in the midst of the void, illuminating a *'clean angle where the foot of a wall rose from the pavement'* (78). Beginnings are important with Le Guin's Ekumen (*LHD* 259; ch. 18), and, I infer, to Le Guin, and the beginning sketched out for the rising Atlantis is a beautiful one. *Bereshit*—In the beginning, of this cycle, there was darkness and a decrease of pressure, and out of the darkness, not a God saying 'Let there be light' but a light-bearing fish. Then more fish, which allowed the reborning Atlanteans a defining vision: darkness, biological light, a fish, an angle, and the memory of the City: the archetypal City of right angles, walls, and towers, bringing form, human will, and transcendence into, and into balance with, the void. And if funny-looking, highly carnivorous fish seem an odd replacement for a transcendent god, they may be, perhaps, decorous, deep-aquatic incarnations of Coyote—or more mundane animal presences (see chapter on *BG*).

Section 3.U elides Belle's workday but takes up as soon as she returns home from work, where the US Federal Bureau of Investigation had been over to question Simon and to plant an electronic listening device in the bathroom. The rest of the section mentions 'a new continent emerging' and very elegantly offers more exposition on a USA of shortages, warfare abroad, and violence at home that has escalated to where the Neo-Birch insurgents—i.e., Right-wing guerrillas—hold Phoenix, Arizona, with the help of tactical nuclear weapons supplied by the Weathermen in Los Angeles (79-80), i.e., Left-wing radicals. The point is also driven home that *this* totalitarian government not only outlaws marriages but encourages 'healthy group sex' (80). The section ends with Belle's listening to Simon's breathing 'like the sound of soft waves far away,' and she goes out 'to the dark sea on the sound of them.' This leads Belle to recall going 'out to the dark sea, often, as a child, falling asleep,' something she'd almost forgotten in the conscious part of her mind. As a grownup, she experienced 'the great depths, rocking' only 'rarely, as a great gift. To know the abyss of the darkness and not to fear it, to entrust oneself to it and whatever may arise from it—what greater gift?' (81, end of section).[321]

In section 3.A, the Atlanteans continue to perceive the creation of the world, and participate through their perception. Watching the luminescent fish, they come to sense *'space and direction—near and far, at least, and higher and lower.'* They hear the whales singing, *'Where are you? I am*

---

[321] Cf. Le Guin's *LoH* (1971), 'Solitude' (1994), and Owen's turning into and with the Earth in *Very Far Away* (41).

here,' 'Where are you? Where have you gone?'; but the whales do not sing to the Atlanteans, nor do the Atlanteans remember the word 'whale.' The unanswered songs of the whales brings self-awareness to the Atlanteans: they now know, '*because we heard, because we felt, because we wept, we knew that we were; and we remembered other voices*' (82-83).

Section 4.U brings on stage Max, mentioned in 2.U (73, 75) and shows us Belle practicing on her viola in the bathroom (83). Belle gets to muse a bit about artists and intellectuals as Simon and Max get very excited over formulas for electron emission (83-84). This is the high point in the USA part of the story:

> ...Max had solved the problems that were bothering them before Simon was sent to Camp, and had fitted Simon's equations to (as Simon put it) the bare facts, which means they have achieved 'direct energy conversion.' Ten or twelve people have worked on it at different times since Simon published the theoretical part of it when he was twenty-two. The physicist Ann Jones had pointed out right away that the simplest practical application of the theory would be to build a 'sun tap,' a device for collecting and storing solar energy, only much cheaper and better than the U.S.G. Sola-Heetas that some rich people have on their homes. (84)

Simon hadn't exactly published since he's not a government employee and lacks clearance, but his theory had been distributed in 'Sammy's-dot' (from the Russian *samizdat* 'self-published'—usually illegally).

The political implications of the sun tap are made explicit: 'You could call it Flower Power,' Simon says, using a phrase from the counter-cultural, hippie part of the peace movement, ca. 1967.

> 'The State owns us,' he said, 'because the corporative State has a monopoly on power sources, and there's not enough power to go around. But now, anybody could build a generator on their roof that would furnish enough power to light a city.' * * * 'We could completely decentralize industry and agriculture. Technology could serve life instead of serving capital. We could each run our own life. Power is power!... The State is a machine. We could unplug the machine, now.... When groups can keep the power to themselves; when they can use physical power-to in order to exert spiritual power-over; when might makes right. But if power is free? If everybody is equally mighty? Then everybody's got to find a better way of showing that he's right....'

Belle answers, 'That's what Mr. Nobel thought when he invented dynamite.... Peace on earth.' Simon accuses her of being the 'Skull at the banquet,' the 'finger writing on the wall' (85). Except the skull at the banquet always speaks true: all the guests will die; and in the story of Belshazzar's feast the words written on the wall, as interpreted by Daniel, also come true (Daniel 5). 'But it was cruel,' Belle thinks, 'to be shown this great hope, and to know that there was no hope for it. He did know that.... He knew that there was no mountain' for him to be on that top of; Simon knew 'that he was skiing on the wind' (86).

In 4.A the Atlanteans see dawn, but a dawn still seen from great depth, '*only color: blue. * * * no compass bearing to it. It was not brighter in the east. There was no east or west. There was only up and down, below and above.*' And the Atlanteans can contrast this dawn with those of memory: dawn in a world in the air, with territorial and self-assertive birds like those of our Earth, or Urras (*TD* 166; ch. 7): '*...the chorus, voice by voice: This is my nest, this is my tree, this is my egg, this is my day, this is my life, here I am, here I am, hurray for me! I'm here!*' (86).[322]

The climax of 'The New Atlantis' comes in 5.U with a gathering of scientists in Belle and Simon's apartment and the unveiling of a solar cell that the engineer in the group had actually built. The scientists celebrate in a low-key kind of way, and it grieves Belle that 'they couldn't rejoice aloud over a job done and a discovery made, but had to hide there and whisper about it' (88).[323] Belle's refusal to judge is important for the tone of 'The New Atlantis,' which neither celebrates technology nor denigrates it (Suvin 268). The scientists speculate on the ethical issues themselves, 'Could it be, ' asks Clara Edmonds, alluding to physicists' knowing sin in atomic weapons research, 'that we physicists have known sin—and have come out on the other side?'[324] Max catches the allusion and notes that the solar cell wouldn't be useful for bomb production. The engineer, however, has the last word on this topic: 'Bombs are obsolete. Don't you realize that we could move a mountain with this kind of power.... We could thaw Antarctica, we could freeze the Congo. We could sink a continent. Give me a fulcrum and I'll move the world. Well, Archimedes, you've got your fulcrum. The sun' (88).

But Archimedes *cannot* move the world because he can never find an 'Archimedean point' outside of the world on which to stand. As the Daoists insist more strongly than most, one cannot move the universe with an external machine because, by definition, there is no place outside the uni-

---

[322] For these territorial birds, cf. Tolfink, an author whose one surviving work is preserved in Carlisle Cathedral in England: a line of runes Le Guin quotes in translation in 'It Was a Dark and Stormy Night' (1979): 'Tolfink carved these runes in this stone' (*DEW* 29).
[323] Cf. singing of former slaves at celebration in 'A Man of the People' (*FWF* 133).
[324] Cf. Shevek and Takver on suffering and the need to 'get through it, go beyond it' (*TD* 48-49; ch. 2).

verse, which was Archimedes's point, if Archimedes was joking. Nor can Archimedes even move the Earth; as a practical matter, the quotation attributed to Archimedes as other than a profound joke is a nice example of technological hubris, and the 'We can' series in also hubristic, and in the world of the story just wrong. 'We' human beings may be able to move mountains and sink continents, but we humans could not do so without great, unforeseeable costs. And 'we' as the scientists in the story cannot do any of these things at all—can't even light up their own rooms—because they lack the political power to oppose the State's monopoly over electrical power. The line immediately following the ode to techno-power is Simon's 'Christ...the radio, Belle!'—i.e., turn on cover noise so the FBI won't hear the conversation.

Belle goes to the bathroom and doesn't turn on the radio but instead practices her viola, ending up improvising in the dark of yet another power outage.

> Without light, when you couldn't see all the hard shiny surfaces of things, the sound seemed softer and less muddled. I went on, and it began to shape up. All the laws of harmonics sang together when the bow came down. The strings of the viola were cords of my own voice, tightened by sorrow, tuned to the pitch of joy. The melody created itself out of air and energy, it raised up the valleys, and the mountains and hills were made low, and the crooked straight, and the rough places plain.[325] And the music went out to the dark sea and sang in the darkness, over the abyss.

Belle comes out of the bathroom to find Simon and the guests quiet and greatly moved. Finally Rose Abramski speaks: "I saw it. I saw the white towers, and the water streaming down their sides, and running back down to the sea. And the sunlight shining in the streets, after ten thousand years of darkness.' Out of the shadows of the room, Simon says that he heard them, heard their voices (*NA* 89). Simon asks Phil if they could 'raise up the white towers, with our lever and our fulcrum?', and Phil tells him that

---

[325] Quoting Isaiah 40.3-4, set to music by George Frederick Handel in *The Messiah* (1742). This section of Isaiah is near the beginning of the 'Book of the Consolation of Israel' (chs. 40-55); it begins, in the AV trans. of 1611 (the one used by Handel): 'Comfort ye, comfort ye my people, saith your God. Speak yet comfortably to Jerusalem, and cry unto her, that her warfare is accomplished, that her iniquity is pardoned....'—which is hopeful in Le Guin's context, or ironic. Quoted and paralleled by J. Needham with the Daoist teaching that 'The great highway (of the Tao of justice and righteousness)...is broad and level' ('Time and Knowledge' 114).

they have the power to do it. Simon asks, 'What else do we need, besides power?' He gets no answer.[326]

In section 5.A, the Atlanteans see the water change from deep blue to turquoise; then from turquoise to colors like jade, sapphire or emerald: New Jerusalem naturalized, the bride-perfect, walled city, made of jewels, with a 'radiance...clear as crystal,' submerged and now emerging from the depths (Revelation 21.2-22.5). With the changes come thoughts of dreams and then the memory *'of the thunder and the tremor and the fire and the towers falling, long ago,'* the fall of the first Atlantis (90). After the memory, three things happen. First, something moves, *'something not composed of planes and angles, but of curves and arcs.'* The Atlanteans turn and look: willed motion. They see a cuttlefish, next to an engraving of a cuttlefish, the Atlantean *'cherished sign': 'Did it recognize its image?'* (91). Second, they all turn and look at a school of silver fish, and the shadows the fish make. *'There were shadows, now'* (91-92). The Atlanteans see the towers of their city, and above, sunlight on the sea's surface.

> *We are here. When we break through the bright circle into life, the water will break and stream white down the white sides of the towers, and run down the steep streets back into the sea....*
> *We are here.*
> *Whose voice? Who called to us?*

As Kathleen Spencer notes, this is a 'powerful shared vision,' connecting the Atlanteans and the Americans—momentarily ('Exiles' 37).

Section 6.U ends the US story. Simon is arrested and hauled off to the federal hospital in Salem, O(regon)—'Omelas,' spelled backwards—and, in the larger world, rising land masses in the South Atlantic and Western Pacific contribute to the subsidence of the US coasts, including Oregon. Belle tries to walk to Salem, taking with her her journal, a 'tiny camp stove powered with the solar cell,' and a half pint of brandy. When she finishes the brandy, she plans to put the journal in the bottle and let it float off. Clearly, Belle has been successful in her attempt 'to preserve her voice' (Cummins 173); we are reading her journal. Cummins (173) and Spencer (37) assume that Belle has drowned, and they are correct. Her words go 'out to the dark sea,' and to us.

Section 6.A is just two lines, three sentences, the Atlanteans' version of the whales' song:

> *Where are you?*
> *We are here. Where have you gone?* (93)

* * * * * * *

---

[326] For power as insufficient, see the dialog between Ged and Cob at the climax of *FS* (179-80; ch. 12).

In terms of Le Guin's canon, there are the similarities noted above between 'The New Atlantis,' *The Left Hand of Darkness*, and *The Dispossessed*. To these we can add joy: Belle's joy at being reunited with Simon—'joy' is the climax word of the first section—fits in with a motif that runs from *Rocannon's World* (113; ch. 8), through *The Left Hand of Darkness* (220; ch. 16) to 'Hernes' in *Searoad* (184 [1991]). There are also similarities to 'An die Musik' (1961), *The Lathe of Heaven* (1971), and other of Le Guin's works.[327] The similarity to 'An die Musik' has to do with the importance of artistic creation over immediate political effectiveness. To repeat a quotation in an earlier chapter, 'An die Musik' teaches that 'Music will not save us.' It has no use-value. On the contrary, 'To the world and its states and armies and factories and Leaders, music says, '*You are irrelevant*'; and, arrogant and gentle as a god, to the suffering man it says only, 'Listen.' For being saved is not the point. Music saves nothing. Merciful, uncaring, it denies and breaks down all the shelters, the houses men build for themselves, that they may see the sky' (*Orsinian Tales* 144-45; my emphasis). In 'The New Atlantis,' Belle's music doesn't move transcendentally to the sky, but immanently to the sea, uniting for a moment Simon and his guests and the Atlanteans (89-90, 92). The moment of communication 'saves nothing,' but, I think, it is a good in itself, and, along with Belle and Simon's love, is the best that we will see among the dying Americans in the story.

Locating 'The New Atlantis' in terms of the themes of Le Guin's canon is one of the projects of Darko Suvin in his 'Parables of De-Alienation' essay; and I think this locating is both gotten completely right and a bit wrong. In this excellent article, Suvin suggests that '...the centre of Le Guin's creation is the double star of identifying the neo-capitalist, individualist alienation and juxtaposing to it a sketch of a new, collectivist and harmonious, creation....' (267). Le Guin's method, like that of serious SF generally is analogy through parable, but not allegory, where X in the story = Y in our world: In Suvin's words, Le Guin 'does not substitute one thing for another'; instead, Le Guin's method '*sets one thing by the side of another*, the explicit by the side of the implicit.' The meaning of such parables is clear, but, Suvin insists, 'there may be several levels of meaning; a parable is usually polysemous,' multi-meaning (269). Suvin sees the unity in 'The New Atlantis' in the contrast between 'the emerging new City' and 'the dying American society, a new republic, community or life-form germinating up for the depths, symmetrically opposed, as it were, to the perishing republic of the first strand' of narration, the sinking USA.

> The ascending narration is in the first person plural, the 'we' being a new community...which relates to that of the U.S.A. as collectivism does to individualism and also—in

---

[327] See Spivack 91 for 'New Atlantis' privileging hearing over seeing and valuing most of all sound in the darkness. Cf. and contrast 'Field of Vision.'

view of the cognition and color imagery—as beauty and knowledge to pollution and ignorance of both self and universe. The Atlantis collective has been submerged and unconscious for ages, just as the idea of a true and beautiful collective or classless society; the Fall of Atlantis, then, is here something like the fall from tribal into class society and the concomitant alienation of man into social institutions. A condition of pristine unity is presupposed in the whole of Le Guin's opus as a past Golden Age; it echoes through the present alienation from the unsplit Ancient One in RW [*Rocannon's World*], through the direct, unalienated communication he gives to Rocannon—mindspeech...to Selver's integral forest in WWF [*The World for Word Is Forest*] and the other forest-minds and tree images in her opus. But by 1975, in NA, there is a New Atlantis rising: the forces of de-alienation are on the rise in Le Guin's writing. (269)

I will say that 'The New Atlantis' is not an allegory or even a *mâshâl* but a modernist, symbolist, philosophical parable, indeed, more parabolic—indirect—than Suvin allows in the details of his interpretation. The USA of the story is dystopian, and it is undoubtedly contrasted with Atlantis: Atlantis as the City as hope, the good City arising out of the depths of the ocean and the unconscious, not one 'coming down out of heaven from God' after a horror-show, divine apocalypse (Revelation 21.6-20). Belle's first-person narration is undoubtedly contrasted with the Atlantean 'we.' But: it is a good thing that Belle says 'I' and has an individual voice. As Elizabeth Cummins notes, it is 'the voices of the oppressors' that we do not hear (170); and those silenced American bureaucratic oppressors might very well speak as a '*we.*' The 'corporative State' (*New Atlantis* 75) is corporate and, in a Stalinist sense, collectivist. The Atlantean collective is recognizably human, but not us. Our hope, if any, is in the descendants of the survivors of the geological and ecological catastrophes on the West Coast: the Kesh and other anarchistic, sane peoples of *Always Coming Home*, who regain tribal consciousness and establish a very beautiful society.

VI.

ALWAYS COMING HOME

Who turned us round like this, so that
no matter what we do, we have the air
of somebody departing? As a traveller
on the last hill, for the last time seeing
all the home valley, turns, and stands, and lingers—
so we live forever taking leave. (Le Guin, trans., Rilke's
'The Eighth Elegy' [*BG* 193])

Introduction

    Bernard Selinger begins his discussion of Ursula K. Le Guin's *Always Coming Home* by saying that it 'is like no other novel I have read' but 'Still, it is patent Le Guin' ([127]). I'm not sure I'll call *Always Coming Home* a novel, although it says right on the cover, '*Always Coming Home*: a novel'; but, perhaps, *Always Coming Home* is best seen as one of Le Guin's major contributions toward the redefinition of the novel: a step toward the nonmasculinist novel. In whatever terminology, Selinger is correct: *Always Coming Home* is unusual and quite familiar, 'patent Le Guin'; and also something unusual: clearly an ethnography but also what I'll call Le Guin's antiBible, or unBible.

    I will work with *Always Coming Home* this far as I would teach the Hebrew Scriptures: at length, and as a work that should be covered 'spirally,' making several passes. I shall give some self characterizations by Le Guin and some statements relevant for her work she has offered in her own voice; and I shall then give some *selected* context: (1) some background on philosophy, (2) an important essay by Lewis Mumford on utopia and the historical rise of the royal city-state, (3) a historical instance of such a rise (and fall) of a royal city, (4) some American Indian background of *Always Coming Home* and Le Guin's rather radical variation there on a 'typical situation, stock Le Guin plot' ('Legends' 9).[328] Readers who don't

---

[328] My thanks to Kathleen Spencer and Carol D. Stevens for supplying me with a copy of the 'Legends' speech, and for other help with my scholarship over the last decade.

need yet another introduction to Existentialism or to speculations on the rise of patriarchal civilization might skip the introductory sections and move straight into my commentary on *Always Coming Home*, 'Some Short Works in *Always Coming Home*: Philosophy,' starting with the play of *Chandi*, the Kesh version of the story of Job.

* * * * * * *

In 1971, in *The Lathe of Heaven* Le Guin presented an effective intellectual attack on many of the premises of 'The Judaeo-Christian-Rationalist West' (82; ch, 6). In 1975, Le Guin described herself as 'an unconsistent Taoist and consistent unChristian' ('Ketterer' 139), and on another occasion offered the alternative, 'a congenital non-Christian' ('Dreams Must Explain Themselves' [*LoN* (1979): 55]). In her Introduction to the 1976 re-issue of *The Left Hand of Darkness*, Le Guin presents the paradox, 'I talk about the gods, I am an atheist' (n.p.; coll. *LoN* [1979] 158), and in the same year reacted to some comments in the special Le Guin issue of *Science-Fiction Studies* by rejecting use of 'the word 'liberal' used as a smear-word' and saying that 'If people must call names, I cheerfully accept Lenin's anathema as suitable: I am a petty-bourgeois anarchist and an internal emigree [sic]. O.K.?' ('A Response to the Le Guin Issue' 45). And speaking as guest of honor at the Nineteenth Annual Mythopoeic Conference in the late 1980s Le Guin indirectly but very strongly characterized herself as an Outsider critiquing 'the Judeo-Christian religion that informs our world view' and suggests that *Always Coming Home* offers a this-worldly alternative to 'the City of God' that is 'in the spirit only' and 'not founded on this earth' ('Legends' 8).

The reference to 'the Judeo-Christian religion that informs our worldview' was quite decorous in terms of Le Guin's subject and the original audience for the 'Legends' speech. Le Guin focused much of her talk on the world-view of Native Americans, especially the California Indians, and the people who massacred the California Indians were Whites raised in the Judeo-Christian tradition; and Le Guin was talking to the Mythopoeic Society: a group whose very useful work centers on the Christian authors J. R. R. Tolkien, C. S. Lewis, and Charles Williams. Still, I prefer the oldest of Le Guin's formulations and the least direct: the reference of the villainous Dr. William Haber to 'The Judaeo-Christian-Rationalist West.' This formula may let Islam unjustly off the hook and may tempt us to forget that the Animist-Hindu-Confucian-Shinto-Daoist-Buddhist East has created its own share of horrors, but it focuses our attention on us—most of the probable readers of Le Guin's work—and our root problems.[329]

---

[329] Le Guin's *King Dog* shows large-scale violence in what could be ancient Indian culture. In the 'Redux' portion of 'Is Gender Necessary?', Le Guin says that she had in mind for Gethenian balance 'a Taoist ideal' that would be better exemplified historically by some 'pre-Conquest cultures of the Americas' rather than

The 'Rationalist' part of 'The Judaeo-Christian-Rationalist West' should remind us that such pagans as Plato and atheists as Jean-Paul Sartre were and are important for what I think is centrally the intellectualizing of macho culture.[330] Indeed, the phrase 'the One,' stressed in *Always Coming Home* as mostly a monotheistic term, can refer also to the One of the radical monism of pre-Socratic Greek Eleaticism and its followers, or can be used more loosely as philosophical shorthand for the privileged, White, European philosophers of the Enlightenment with their lust for (totalizing) systems that would incorporate all knowledge, or for such slogans of unified total government as the Byzantine Emperor Justinian's 'One empire, one church, one law' (Swain 2.613) or the Nazi variation, '*Ein Volk, ein Fürher, ein Reich.*' A contemporary feminist identifying with all those 'marginalized by the transcendental voice of universalizing theory,' writes that the 'nonbeing' of all those outside the rationalist world of the Enlightened served as 'the condition of being of the One, the center, the taken-for-granted ability of one small segment of the population to speak for all' (Hartsock 170-71).

The 'West' part of the phrase from *Lathe* brings in the traditional historical trinity of traditions for the formation of Western Europe: Judeo-Christian, Greco-Roman, and Germanic-Nordic; and we should add Islam and 'The Empire of the Arabs' (Thompson and Johnson, title of ch 7). It is not just the One God that is at issue in the rise of patriarchy, but also the Heroes who worshipped Sky-Father Zeus (or Jupiter or Odin or Thor), or attempted on their agnostic own to win fame or assert their own personal, aristocratic worthiness and manliness (*arete, virtus*), their own Heroism.[331] Fanaticism, though, there yes; Judaism and Judaism's daughter religions have been quite good at producing fanaticism: Eric Hoffer ends his *True Believer* noting that 'J.B.S. Haldane counts fanaticism among the only four really important inventions made between 3000 B.C. and 1400 A.D.' (in *The Inequality of Man*, 1938). 'It was a Judaic-Christian invention' (151, § 125; ch. 18). Still, the larger problem of the macho hero goes beyond the problems rooted in monotheism.

* * * * * * *

---

actually existing (thoroughly sexist) ancient Chinese civilization (*LoN* [1989]: 165).

[330] For a very different view of Plato and Le Guin, see Rochelle on *LHD* and some of Plato's major dialogs, esp. Rochelle 322-26.

[331] For Le Guin on heroism, see Haber's heroic fantasies in *LoH* (e.g. 36; ch. 3) and, more positively, the overflowing of life in even pragmatic young Anarresti, yielding altruism and desire for self-sacrifice and 'scope for the absolute gesture' (*TD* 75; ch. 4). For Hero as normal stage 'adolescents go through on their way to becoming responsible human beings,' see below in this chapter and 'The Fisherwoman's Daughter' 229. For the Artist as Hero: 'Fisherwoman's Daughter,' 223, 226, 229.

> If there were no eternal consciousness in a man, if at the foundation of all there lay only a wildly seething power which writhing with obscure passions produced everything that is great and everything that is insignificant, if a bottomless void never satiated lay hidden beneath all—what then would life be but despair? —Søren Kierkegaard, *Fear and Trembling* (1843): [30]; 'A Panegyric Upon Abraham'

Le Guin has been very consistent in her attack upon much of elite attitudes and values in 'the Judaeo-Christian-Rationalist West' (*LoH* 82), and in offering repeatedly 'a gentle antidote'—or sometimes not so gentle—to what she sees as problems in our culture that go to our Judeo-Christian-Rationalist roots. Le Guin is, in her own description, 'an aging angry woman laying mightily about me with my handbag, fighting hoodlums off' ('Carrier Bag' 168). Alternatively, though, one can see Le Guin, if not exactly wrestling with God, vigorously participating in a central *Kulturkampf*, and metaphorically wrestling with the issues of 'ultimate concern' that define religion—as well as 'with the angels of the feminist consciousness' (*ER* 11).

Le Guin denies a transcendent monotheistic god, but she is strongly concerned with issues of the human spirit, with what human people should do with our lives to live them well. She pays what most Americans understand as religious belief the great respect of arguing with it and against it, vigorously. If Le Guin is occasionally puzzled why her fans include some Anglican clergymen ('Dreams Must Explain Themselves,' *LoN* [1979]: 55), she need not be: it's better to be attacked than ignored, and Le Guin's antipathy in fiction to much of the Western religious and intellectual tradition can be seen as an invitation by a worthy opponent to a necessary wrestling match.

****

The stakes in that match are high. Getting rid of God can be 'extremely embarrassing' (J-P Sartre, 'Existentialism' 294). With no God, one might be left on a Sartrean plain, with each of us alone, trapped in our own skins and, in extreme cases, nauseated by the world. Or, in Matthew Arnold's more poetic vision of life after the death of God:

> ...the world, which seems
> To lie before us like a land of dreams,
> So various, so beautiful, so new,
> Hath really neither joy, nor love, nor light,
> Nor certitude, nor peace, nor help for pain;
> And we are here as on a darkling plain
> Swept with confused alarms of struggle and flight,
> Where ignorant armies clash by night.

('Dover Beach,' ca. 1851)

Far more people, though, study Arnold and Søren Kierkegaard and Sartre—or learn Fyodor Dostoyevsky's teaching that If God is dead, nothing is prohibited—than ever come to feel the fear, trembling, dread, and despair that Kierkegaard, Sartre, et al. say define the stakes in this issue. So for those for whom it's "God is Dead'—Will that be on the final?'; or 'Weren't the problems of death and futility solved by hermeneutics?' I would like to do some Kierkegaardian multiple passes at the implications for most Americans and a good many other people of a world without a transcendent and loving One.

Consider for a moment an old legend of the rise of drama in Greece, specifically of tragic drama. In the beginning, in this legend, there was a chorus singing a *dithyramb* (a wild 'Goat Song' hymn) to and in praise of the god Dionysos; and then one Thespis, an ancient impresario, went over to the chorus leader and had him step out of the chorus and told him he would be a new thing under the sun: an actor. The new actor then exited and re-entered (or stepped back into the chorus and stepped out again) and said 'I am ___ (probably Dionysos).' Thespis and his actor had given the world impersonation, dialog, the possibility of conflict and action: drama, specifically tragic drama. That's the legend, anyway, and I want to accept it as an origin story and read that story allegorically. When drama arose, there was a chorus singing of 'We' and the god, with the chorus hoping to merge with Dionysos, a kind of 'Father Nature,' traditionally pictured as androgynous or 'effeminate.' The actor says 'I am,' and this produces tragedy, which, in its typical Greek form, usually involved an act of tragic pride (*hubris*) producing divine anger (*nemesis*). Taking for a moment a Hebraic view, the *hubris* was always and necessarily implied in the character's 'I am,' whatever name followed it. 'I AM' is God's line. When Moses very sensibly asks for some I.D., so to speak, from the voice from the burning bush telling him to take on Pharaoh, God responds with 'Ehyeh-Asher-Ehyeh': the Name of God is some sort of complex pun on 'to be,' or, for short, 'I Am' (Exodus 3.14, *Tanakh*). Which makes sense. When I say 'I am,' it is a trivial statement: I was not here ten million years ago; I will not be here ten million years from now. I'm going to die and rot and return to the cycles of nature via worms and maggots, and however much that thought may please a Daoist mystic like Chuang Tzu, it does not please me.[332] If God exists, on the other hand, God *is*, was, and will be, world without end (very nontrivially)—amen.

In taking that step out of the chorus and saying 'I am,' the newly-invented actor stepped out of society, out of nature, out of tribal 'we'-consciousness into alienated culture, history, and an 'I'-consciousness which is necessarily tragic: the isolated individual's inevitable history of

---

[332] *Chuang Tzu* ch. 6, 'The Great Supreme' (esp. Giles trans. 72 and 79).

birth-struggle-death, a death that he—almost always *he* in tragedy—must die, ultimately, alone.[333]

Sartre's Orestes and Zeus in *The Flies* discuss this step into consciousness at some length and with some nicely melodramatic rhetoric:

> ORESTES: Yesterday, when I was with Electra, I felt at one with Nature, this Nature of your making. It sang the praises of the Good—your Good—in siren tones, and lavished intimations. To lull me into gentleness.... Suddenly, out of the blue, freedom crashed down on me and swept me off my feet. Nature sprang back, my youth went with the wind, and I knew myself alone, utterly alone in the midst of this well-meaning little universe of yours. I was like a man who's lost his shadow. And there was nothing left in heaven, no right or wrong, nor anyone to give me orders.[334]
>
> ZEUS: What of it?... Your vaunted freedom isolates you from the fold; it means exile.
>
> ORESTES: Yes, exile. * * * Foreign to myself—I know it. Outside nature, against nature, without excuse, beyond remedy, except what remedy I find within myself.... Nor shall I come back to nature...but I must blaze my trail. For I, Zeus, am a man, and every man must find out his own way. Nature abhors man, and you too, god of gods, abhor mankind. * * * You are God and I am free; each of us is alone, and our anguish is akin....
>
> ZEUS: What do you propose to do?
>
> ORESTES: The folk of Argos are my folk. I must open their eyes.
>
> ZEUS: Poor people!... They will see their lives as they are, foul and futile, a barren boon.
>
> ORESTES: Why, since it is their lot, should I deny them the despair I have in me?
>
> ZEUS: What will they make of it?

---

[333] Note for the complexities of dying alone, the dying man beyond 'touch' in *TD* 49-50; ch. 2; and see below for dying in the Valley of the Na. Note the medieval / Early Modern play of *Everyman* (ca. 1500)—where only Good Deeds will go with Everyman to the grave, and the more recent Calvinist hymn, 'You've Got to Walk that Lonesome Valley' ('You've got to walk it by yourself').

[334] See below, this chapter, my discussion of 'The Bright Voice of the Wind (*ACH* 271-72). Cf. and contrast shadowlessness in *LHD*, where it is a very negative thing Le Guin associates with the hyper-rationalists of Orgoreyn. With atheism's leaving one free from 'orders' Le Guin agrees: *FS* 136-37; ch. 9.

> ORESTES: What they choose. They're free; and human life begins on the far side of despair. (121-23; Act III)[335]

Less militantly depressing but more specific are the series of questions and the single, *somewhat* depressing answer offered in the Jewish morning service immediately proceeding the Shema (the central statement in Judaism and Christianity of God's Oneness [Deut. 6.4, Mark 12.28-30]).

> What are we? What is our life? What is our piety? What our acts of righteousness? What our salvation? What is our strength?... Are not all the mighty ones like naught before thee [God], and men of fame as though they were not?... For the multitude of their works is emptiness, and the days of their life are vanity before thee; and the preeminence of man over beast is naught: for all is vanity. (*Service* 6; cf. Eccl.)

The Ashkenazi text (eastern and northern European) then goes on directly to a major 'But': 'Howbeit we are thy people, the children of thy covenant' and moves very quickly from that rescue from emptiness into relationship with the Eternal, and to the happy duty of proclaiming God's unity. The Sephardic text (Spanish-speaking countries, Africa) adds another rescue: it modifies the conclusion that 'all is vanity' by adding 'except the pure soul which must hereafter give accounting before the throne of Thy glory' (*High Holiday Prayer Book* 31). We can all agree, I think, that we are transcendentally ensouled, or we are mud (*EoH*) or, as we will see, turds and words (*ACH* 168). Without a transcendent God to serve or defy, human life lacks any purpose beyond that of any other animal: survival, reproduction, and, generally, going about the business of being that animal. Without an immortal soul, we are our projects indeed, but mostly just dirt animated with lifebreath (*ruach, anima, spiritus*), or whatever less poetical images may be scientifically fashionable for explaining the mind-body 'machine.' Without a transcendent, acting, judging God before whose throne 'the pure soul...must hereafter give accounting,' there are neither strong, transcultural, trans-historical definitions of 'good' and 'evil' nor absolute rules for human behavior nor certain, ultimate sanctions for behavior good or bad.

Viewed imaginatively from outside the world, the world without God appears absurd: a 'Turn, Turn, Turn' world of interlocking, meaningless cycles—cycles of nature, cycles of history—with human life the vision of

---

[335] There is a similar dialog between a variant Christ and St. Paul in Nikos Kazantzakis's *The Last Temptation of Christ* (English edn. 1960): the last temptation is to live a domestic life as an ordinary man, rejecting the transcendent project of a Paul who intends to be an Apostle of heroic purpose, founding Christianity, whether there is a Christ or not, whether Jesus the carpenter wants him to or not.

Emptiness! Emptiness! responded to in the Hebrew prayer book.[336] In the poetic vision of Koheleth ('the Preacher,' 'Ecclesiastes'):

> Vanity of vanities, says the Preacher
> vanity of vanities! All is vanity.
> What does man gain by all the toil
> at which he toils under the sun?
> A generation goes, and a generation comes,
> but the earth remains for ever.
> The sun rises and the sun goes down,
> and hastens to the place where it rises.
> The wind blows to the south,
> and goes round to the north;
> round and round goes the wind,
> and on its circuits the wind returns.
> * * *
> All things are full of weariness;
> * * *
> What has been is what will be,
> and what has been done is what will be done;
> and there is nothing new under the sun.
>   (Eccl. 1.2-11, RSV)

Koheleth's is not the view of some gentle cynic—a comfortable, *genteel* sort, in my view—but that of a rigorous capital 'C' Cynic, and a protoExistentialist to boot, who works his way to the obvious conclusion that human beings are not 'divine beings'; hence, Koheleth must 'face the fact' that humans 'are beasts. For in respect of the fate of man and the fate of beast, they have one and the same fate: as one dies so dies the other, and both have the same lifebreath; man has no superiority over beast, since both amount to nothing. Both go to the same place; both came from dust and both return to dust.' (3.18-21, *Tanakh*).

One last quotation—from a work we can be sure Le Guin knew at least well enough to dismiss as 'crap.'[337] In *African Genesis*, Robert Ardrey recounts a theory that had a very brief popularity in the early 1940s: The Illusion of Central Position. According to the theory, this illusion 'is the birthright of every human baby.' I'd say the illusion literally stems from perception; it's an immediate fact of perception that The World Revolves Around ME. In any event, a baby boy enters the world and 'Bright objects appear for his amusement, bottles and breasts for his comfort. His groping consciousness finds no reason at all to doubt the world's consecration to

---

[336] 'Turn, Turn, Turn' is the title of Pete Seeger's setting of the poem in Ecclesiastes 'For everything there is a season, and a time for every purpose under heaven' (3.1-9). Strongly contrast the positive view of emptiness in *Tao te Ching* (chs. 4, 5, 11, 16).
[337] See Erlich, 'Ursula K. Le Guin and Arthur C. Clarke...' 122; n. 1.

his needs and purposes. His Illusion of Central Position is perfect,' an initial given of awareness (*Af. Genesis* 144; ch. 6). With maturity, however, the illusion is undercut and the child and then the man comes to a truer perception of his place in the scheme of things.

> Nonetheless the theory grants that should a man ever attain a state of total maturity—ever come to see himself...in perfect mathematical relationship to the tide of tumultuous life which has risen upon the earth and in which we represent but a single swell; and furthermore come to see our earth as but one opportunity for life among uncounted millions in our galaxy alone, and our galaxy as but one statistical improbability, nothing more, in the silent mathematics of all things—should a man, in sum, ever achieve the final, total, truthful Disillusionment of Central Position, then in all likelihood he would no longer keep going but would simply lie down, wherever he happened to be, and with a long-drawn sigh return to the oblivion from which he came. (145; ch. 6)[338]

Or not. In a world of Emptiness! Emptiness!, where God is very distant and death is a trip to Sheol—the grave, Hades—and no more, Koheleth concluded 'There is nothing worthwhile for a man but to eat and drink and afford himself enjoyment with his means' (2.24, *Tanakh*). And he advises his (male) readers to 'Live joyfully with the wife whom thou lovest all the days of the life of thy vanity, which he [God] hath given thee under the sun...,' and, more macho-ly Existential, 'Whatsoever thy hand findeth to do, do it with thy might; for there is no work, nor device, nor knowledge, nor wisdom, in the grave, whither thou goest' (9.9-10, AV).[339] Plus, of course, the teaching 'Two are better than one,' especially in the image, '...if two lie together then they have heat: but how can one be warm alone?' (4.11, AV).

One of the major contexts for *Always Coming Home*, then, is Le Guin's answering Sartre and Ardrey—however indirectly, intentionally or not—and carrying on Koheleth's great quest to determine 'what was good for the sons of men to do under heaven during the few days of their life' (Eccl. 2.3, RSV), and which her Job-figure Chandi reformulates, gender-

---

[338] Cf. and contrast imagery in *FS* of selfhood as 'a wave on the sea' (121-22; ch. 8). Cf. the speech in Clarke's *Childhood's End* telling us that human attempts to explore even our own galaxy are 'like ants attempting to label and classify all the grains of sand in all the deserts of the world' (*CE* 137, ch. 14; see Erlich 'Ursula K. Le Guin....' 116-17).
[339] I have removed AV's italics, which indicated words inserted for the translation.

neutrally, *'How shall a human being live well, then?'* (*ACH* 236).[340] An obvious possibility for living in the world at all, and so getting a chance to 'live well' is to lower one's expectations from life—stop hoping for some sort of purpose or cosmic significance—and intentionally, mindfully limit one's interests to the human world and limit the significant human world as much as possible to one's own people and attempt to build in whatever 'green and pleasant land' one finds oneself in, not Jerusalem but a good society.[341]

Another context for *Always Coming Home*, then, is utopia, plus the related questions of the origin(s) of the current mess of the human condition. Both issues are neatly handled in a classic essay by Lewis Mumford: 'Utopia, The City and The Machine' (1965).

One possible reason utopias go wrong, Mumford suggests, 'is that the abstract intelligence' that creates utopias, 'operating with its own conceptual apparatus, in its own self-restricted field, is actually a coercive instrument: an arrogant fragment of the full human personality, determined to make the world over in its own oversimplified terms.' But Mumford prefers to stress another alternative. Mumford finds that both the ideal of utopia for the Greeks and what I'll call (after Aristotle's *hamartia*) The Big Mistake stem from the same historical event: the rise of 'the archetypal ancient city.'[342] In terms of utopian thought, the rise of the city in the ancient Fertile Crescent, is the relevant event; in terms of history, the move from the Late Neolithic village to Bronze Age city is relevant, whatever Old World rivers it occurred along, or New World forests or highlands it occurred in (see Mumford 10).

In the beginning, in the story Mumford accepts, the Neolithic village was (for one hand) composed of human people (in village-size numbers) who lived democratically, with 'no ruling class' exploiting others, 'no compulsion to work for a surplus the local community' couldn't use, 'no taste for idle luxury,' no private property, no 'exorbitant desire for power,' and nothing we would consider warfare: a golden age (Mumford 4), a variety of paradise (18). On the other hand, again in the story Mumford accepts, the common people of a Bronze Age city generally experienced city life in terms of 'total submission to a central authority, forced labor, lifetime specialization, inflexible regimentation, one-way communication, and readiness for war.' Mumford sums up their condition as that of a popula-

---

[340] The italics identify this as a 'peg' line in *Chandi*. The 'peg lines,' or 'hinge-bolts' ranged from ten to twenty for a play and 'were invariable both in wording and in the order they were spoken. Everything that was said and done in the intervals between them was up to the players' (226, 227).

[341] For Le Guin's denying human purpose, see *LoH* 82, ch 6; *WE* 17-18, ch. 2.

[342] If you were taught that tragic heroes always have 'tragic *flaws*,' chalk one up in a *Kulturkampf* for those who believe, like the rather priggish Edgar in Shakespeare's *King Lear,* that 'The gods are just, and of our pleasant vices / Make instruments to plague us' (5.3.171-72). The Mistake in a neatly-constructed tragedy should stem from the characters of the principle characters, but the source of the Mistake can be a neutral element or a virtue as well as some flaw.

tion of constantly scared people, 'galvanized into corpselike obedience with the constant aid of the mace, the whip, and the truncheon' (17). Mumford's characterization may be somewhat sensationalized, but the analysis is convincing. The Hebrews in Egypt were ordinarily treated no worse than the native-born Egyptians, and my barely civilized ancestors saw themselves in Egypt as slaves.

The historical question is how did the kings and other elites pull off the transition from the Neolithic village to civilization—to city-life as we know it—and why did ordinary people go along?

In Egypt and Mesopotamia, the first cities were made by kings 'acting in the name of a god' and incarnating within themselves the will and immortality of the gods. 'The king's first act, the very key to his authority and potency, is the erection of a temple within a heavily walled sacred enclosure. And the construction of another wall to enclose the subservient community turns the whole area into a sacred place: a city' (Mumford 12 and 19). To build the city and to protect the city the king needs raw, physical power, and getting it was a problem in a Neolithic world in which the high point of technology was the bow and arrow (15). Mumford's key point is that concomitant with the theological pretensions I'll return to in a moment, kings developed two great machines: 'the labor machine and the military machine,' both organized hierarchically and bureaucratically, both serving with nearly mechanical rigidity the will of the king, and both related almost mystically in cycles of building and destruction (18). For Mumford, the city and the army—an 'Invisible Machine' (19)—are the two great images of civilization and for the earliest political states. And the military army will be used as much as the labor army; with all such states, though Mumford himself cites only Plato's imagined Republic, 'Nietzsche's observation that war is the health of the state applies...for only in war is such stringent authority and coercion even temporarily tolerable' (Mumford 6).

Briefly, then, we can say with Mumford that the first city arose because kings were able to deify themselves and create armies of laborers and soldiers, with the soldiers able to capture more laborers and keep them in line. Once the system got started, it would be quite stable. If one king builds an army and a city and another king does so too, the (re)building and (re)arming of both places go on as one attacks or threatens the other. We need 'our' army to protect us from their army, and we need to capture them as slaves to rebuild portions of our city that they have destroyed. And so on, unto the days of Roland and Rambo. Again, though, how did the system get *started*?

And here I'll digress from Mumford for a bit.

One theory for the mysterious rise of warfare and civilization in the Neolithic (an important theory for the origins and influence of patriarchy) holds that there is little mystery. If there is a will to power in people, there's also a will to submit, and there are always people who enjoy giving orders (especially, perhaps, young men) and people around willing to obey (especially, perhaps, older boys).[343] As the Stone Age went on, human numbers increased enough that human groups met one another more frequently, and it is easy to picture occasional raids, where a man of the village led out the youngsters to revenge some offense, and maybe pick up some souvenirs: perhaps the head of a fighter from the Others, perhaps things of more everyday practical use. What changed in the Neolithic was the rise of herding and simultaneous rise of agricultural villages and the production of surpluses that could free some of the population from productive labor, and the production of surpluses worth the while of excess young men to steal. What changed also was that somewhere along the line people figured out the relationship between sexual intercourse and childbirth, and the concept of fatherhood was invented. With the concept of fatherhood—if Lewis Henry Morgan, Friedrich Engels, et al. are correct—would come the idea among men of '*my* children' and 'the mother of *my* children,' hence '*my* wife and children' and the idea of property, starting with property in people.[344] With the idea of property as the right to keep and hold and bequeath to one's descendants what one has—not just use—the idea of theft becomes more attractive. With the rise of surpluses, people had more stuff worth stealing and, with the rise of slavery, enslaveable Others necessarily had something worth stealing: themselves. From this point, the rise of the military to get the theft organized and regularized as protection money (tribute, taxes) takes little more explanation than the Mafia or the depredations of pirates, freebooters, Conquistadors, slavers, colonial exploiters, and other practitioners of large-scale, highly organized crime.[345]

---

[343] See Le Guin's 1994 short story, 'Solitude' (esp. 143) for how sometimes 'boy-groups get wicked' when 'magicians among them, leaders' organize them for action (including, apparently raiding and quite likely rape).

[344] A. L. Kroeber rejects the assumption of 'the classic evolutionistic school of anthropology of, say, 1860-1890,' which definitely includes L. H. Morgan, 'that early societies must have done the opposite of what we do,' so if we are monogamous, 'the beginnings of human sexual union probably lay in the opposite condition of indiscriminate promiscuity. Since we accord precedence to descent from the father, and generally know him, early society must have reckoned descent from the mother and no one knew his own father' (*Anthropology* § 5, *Patterns* and *Biology* 6). Still, fatherhood is a concept and can be no older than abstract, conceptual thought. It is also clear that matrilineal descent was the rule among many early peoples (see Swain I.46).

[345] Cf. in Le Guin's canon the exploitation of Athshean wood, and Athsheans, in *WWF* and the plans for re-establishing serfdom of Councillor Luis Burnier Falco in Le Guin's *EoH* (ch. 5 and passim). Add to my exposition here Barbara Ehrenreich's recent contradiction: 'Or so the story went, until Lawrence H. Keeley's *War Before Civilization* was published in February of 1996.... Relentlessly, and with an impressive command of the archeological and anthropological evidence, Keeley analyzes what he calls 'the myth of the peaceful savage.' For one thing, there is evidence for what looks very much like war from about 12,000 years ago...' ('Once Upon a Wartime' 21). See also Susan Faludi's 'Let Us Prey,' rev. of Ehrenreich's *Blood Rites: Origins and History of the Passions of War*, follow-

Now, slavery can be quite pleasant for slave owners; but it is a pernicious institution for those who must compete with slave labor, and even the least vicious forms of slavery are horrible for the slaves themselves. A battle every now and then may be occasionally exhilarating for youngsters desiring a change of routine, but extended warfare is not pleasant for most of its practitioners, let alone its victims; for most of the men fighting, the formula is 'Boredom punctuated by terror.' So, we are still left with the question, Why did so many ordinary people at least acquiesce in the establishment of property, kingship, servitude, civilization, and the state?

Part of the answer may start with the straightforward archeological observation that the Cro-Magnons and all 'neanthropic' humans 'interred their dead in an elaborate and formal manner' (Swain I.22), so even in the Old Stone Age some people had the idea of death. By the late Neolithic, people were working—really working at drudge-jobs many of them—in the agriculture business and the related pastoral and industrial occupations made possible by agricultural surpluses. Many people, then, were living lives of drudgery, followed by death, a death of which they were conscious. And they were leading those lives of drudgery among large groups of people, most of whom necessarily remained strangers and amongst whom it would be difficult to maintain the illusion that one was *special*. They were immersed in what Simone De Beauvoir would much later call immanence. Arguably, these people needed some transcendent projects to break the boredom and futility. Especially among young men producing neither children nor art nor engaged in other useful labor, the destruction and killing of war might be the most obvious project to prove they significantly exist.

To return to Mumford:

> By effecting a coalition between military power and religious myth...the hunter-chieftain of the later Neolithic economy transformed himself into a king; and kingship established a mode of government and a way of life radically different from that of the proto-historic community.... In this new constitution, the king gathers to himself all the powers and functions that were once diffused in many local communities; and the king himself becomes the godlike incarnation of collective power and communal responsibility....
>
> ...it was through the king that the functions of the community were concentrated, unified, magnified, and given a sacred status, [and] it was only in the city that the power and glory of this new institution could be manifested in monumental works of art. (12)

---

ing Ehrenreich's rev. article in the Spring Books issue of *The Nation* for 12 May 1997 (Faludi: 24-28).

With the most impressive monuments the pyramids of Egypt: tombs guaranteeing the immortality of Pharaoh, plus functioning as huge symbols of the social structure, ideologies, and striving for transcendence that made such monuments possible and necessary.[346]

> The King's power to make decisions, to by-pass communal deliberations, to defy or nullify custom brought about vast communal changes, far beyond the scope of village communities. Once amassed in cities, governed by a single head, regimented, and controlled under military coercion, a large population could act as one, with a solidarity otherwise possible only in a small community. * * *
> Up to this time, the human community had been widely dispersed in hamlets, villages, country towns: isolated, earthbound, illiterate, tied to ancestral ways. But the city was, from the beginning, related to the newly perceived cosmic order: the sun, the moon, the planets, the lightning, the storm wind. In short, as Fustel de Coulanges and [Johann Jakob] Bachofen pointed out a century ago, the city was primarily a religious phenomenon: it was the home of a god, and even the city wall points to this superhuman origin; for Mircea Eliade is probably correct in inferring that its primary function was to hold chaos at bay and ward off inimical spirits.
> This cosmic orientation, these mythic-religious claims, this royal preemption of the powers and functions of the community are what transformed the mere village or town into a city: something 'out of this world,' the home of a god.... [T]he city transmogrified itself into an ideal form— a glimpse of eternal order, a visible heaven on earth, a seat of the life abundant—...utopia.
> ...With such a magnificent setting as background, the king not merely played god but exercised unqualified power.... In the city, the good life was achieved only by mystical participation in the god's life and that of his fellow deities.... There lay the original compensation for giving up the petty democratic ways of the village. To inhabit the same city as a god was to be a member of a supercommunity: a community in which every subject had a place, a function, a duty, a goal, as part of a hierarchic structure representing the cosmos itself. (Mumford 13-14).

As Le Guin implies with the off-stage rise of the 'Godking' in *The Tombs of Atuan* (1971), the temptation of a King and the temptation of

---

[346] Note the pyramid as architecture and objective correlative for social structure in Orwell's *Nineteen Eighty-Four* (I.1, p. 7; II.9, p. 171).

even vicarious immortality are very great (see Crow and Erlich 205). Initially, it seems, only Pharaoh got immortality. Later, though, immortality became possible for anyone rich enough to get properly embalmed; and finally—by the Middle Kingdom in Egypt—there developed the theory of a separable soul as a birthright in all people (Swain I.122), or, perhaps, all people one considered good enough to be people. Instead of God's animating *Adam* with breath, there was body—dust, dirt—as a temporary house or temple or prison for an immortal soul. The goal of fully human life, then, becomes fully separating the true human self—the immortal soul—from imprisonment in the body and in the mortal world; the enemies of the true human self, then, became The World, the Flesh, and, later, the Devil. And the world, flesh, and devil could incorporate everything Other to, not part of, the immortal soul: the masculine, world-transcending, heaven-aspiring ego. This Other would be women to start with, and everything associated with the ultimate 'woman': 'Mother Earth, the giver of life to her children,' the Great Mother worshipped 'over the whole Near East in neolithic times' and emphatically not 'the Sky Father' worshipped by 'the pastoral and patriarchal nomads': the Indo-European, or 'Aryan,' peoples (Swain I.51).[347]

* * * * * * *

I'll end this Introduction with a historical example of the rise and fall of a royal city with a briefly successful true king representing the One cosmic and transcendent God. Around 1372 BCE, Pharaoh Amenhotep ('Amon is satisfied') changed his name to Akhnaton ('Spirit of Aton'), and ordered built a new capital, dedicated to Aton, the sun. This religious reform moved Aton to supreme god and finally the One God. Akhnaton became a fanatic for Aton and 'relentless toward critics.... He put himself forward as the son' of Aton, 'the sole god of the universe, and demanded obeisance such as earlier kings of Egypt had never received' (Swain I.158-59).

Akhnaton didn't have a very spectacular fall: no armed rebellion with a satisfyingly gory ending as in Shakespeare's *Macbeth*. Akhnaton was deserted by his family, and his power, figuratively, drained away from him. A regency was established, and then Akhnaton soon died, and the dynasty petered out after Akhnaton's successor, Tutankhamen. Upon his death, the royal and divine city of Akhnaton had been abandoned; by the time of Tutankhamen's death, the sun-dried bricks had already begun collapsing, 'and the place became the desert which it has remained to the present day.' A military dictator succeeded Tutankhamen, and 'The last vestiges of Akhnaton's revolution were stamped out' (Swain I.159-60). Not quite the image of futility of Ramses II, as ironically celebrated in Percy Bysshe

---

[347] Caution to younger readers: In Nazi and neoNazi racist theory, the Aryans were and are the 'Master Race,' destined to destroy the power of the Jews and rule over inferior peoples (basically, all nonAryans). I use the term intentionally; don't use it casually.

Shelley's 'Ozymandias' (1817/1818), but Akhnaton offers an elegant paradigm for the rise and fall of a ruler who presents himself as son of the Sole God, demanding obeisance, and of a political movement based on those claims.

If you know *Always Coming Home*, all this—the philosophy, history, and historical illustration of Akhnaton—should sound familiar; indeed, *Always Coming Home* might appear a fictional re-viewing of this crucial 'hinge' in human history: the moment when the ancestors of most of us did move into civilization and history in the ancient world, and do *not* move into civilization and history in the future-world of *Always Coming Home*. More exactly, *Always Coming Home* is a *mâshâl* of that event, an ideal configuration of humankind's *not* moving into LAWKI, 'Life As We Know It' (*Norton* Introd. 34 f.). Such a reading is correct, and I'm going to recommend it, but I wish first to do a bit more contextualizing. The Big Mistake in human history is important here, but we can find contexts for the primary culture of *Always Coming Home*, contexts much more recent and closer to home for most of us than the Neolithic: Northern California until the Conquest, and earlier works in Le Guin's canon.

* * * * * * *

As Elizabeth Cummins implies (*Understanding* 181-83) and Carol D. Stevens detailed in a paper at the 1989 Conference of the Science Fiction Research Association, Le Guin would know of Neolithic people from, among other sources, anthropological work done with tribes in the area in which she grew up, tribal cultures gone with the wind by 1985 but sufficiently remembered early in the century that they could be described by Alfred Kroeber, and their stories retold by Alfred Kroeber, Theodora Kroeber, and others. In a sense, then, *Always Coming Home* is Le Guin's retelling of some of the *Yurok Myths* and *Karok Myths*, the story of Ishi as told by Theodora Kroeber and the stories Theodora Kroeber retells in *The Inland Whale* (Barr, 'Other Hand' 115); in a sense, *Always Coming Home* is a fictional retelling of much in A. L. Kroeber's monumental *Handbook of the Indians of California*. But only—and this is an important point—in a sense; Le Guin is also abstracting from a number of 'pre-Conquest cultures of the Americas' (*LoN* [1989]: 165): the Pueblo, for example—cf. 'A Man of the People' (1995)—and the Navajo (Le Guin, personal communication). *Always Coming Home* is Le Guin's 'gentle antidote' to 'the Judeo-Christian religion' and the world-view of 'the Judaeo-Christian-Rationalist West,' an antidote administered by the healers of the traditional cultures of several tribes and groups of Native Americans.

To anticipate and overstate: in its ethics, *Always Coming Home* is a response to a generally successful genocide in California, suggesting that the ultimate Western City of Man, the extrapolation to its endpoint of the macho-heroic/aristocratic, *transcendent* ideal, would be Auschwitz: a city of death, power, and the triumph of the will over the body and compassion, the subjugation of even mind to will.[348] Le Guin, rooted in the American west, includes as a target for attack the contempt encouraged by the sort of 'Judeo-Christian religion that informs our world-view' for not only the body but also the land and its sacredness in favor of sacralized history: the universe as divinely-scripted drama 'acted by Man.' In such a view the world, and especially the 'New World' Europeans saw in the Americas, is only

> a kind of natural resource for the destiny of Man. At the end of time...the world will fall to ashes, to the nothing it is;...a play that has been acted, a story that has been told. The world has no value except as a sort of waiting room or testing-ground for the soul of Man, a passage from eternity to eternity.... There is indeed a Holy Land in this tradition, but to consider it literally so, to worship the land, is to mistake the created for the Creator, the contingent for the transcendent. 'Jerusalem,' the Center, is in the spirit only: the City of God is not founded on this earth. ('Legends' 8)

In her earlier works Le Guin had opposed to this 'City of God' of St. Augustine of Hippo and the Christian tradition, 'the City of Man' of (more or less) the secular liberal tradition. In *Always Coming Home*, the City of God is subsumed into the City of Man, and the City of God/Man is opposed to places like 'Dzil na' odili, the center of the world' in a Navajo emergence story ('Legends' 6, 8). The view we are asked to take to enter the world of *Always Coming Home* is that of people who are *in* the world, "an integral part of it," as opposed to that of 'People who look at the world from outside it, 'objectively'" ('Legends' 6).[349]

In her 'Legends' lecture, Le Guin presents two maps, both relevant for *Always Coming Home*. The first goes along with the Navajo emergence story, which tells how the First People were initially 'all together,' not yet separated into nonhuman animals and human animals (or nonhuman-people and human people, for a more decorous paraphrase).[350] These First People move up through the worlds into our world (6)—for a number of motifs shared with California Indians, and which Le Guin will use in *Always Coming Home*. More important is a map very similar to the map of the 'Ancient Yurok World' that precedes the introduction in Theodora

---

[348] Cf. Charnas's *Walk to the End of the World*; see Kroeber § 249 for 'separation of body and soul' leading, in at least some instances, to 'contempt of the body' (*Biology and Race* 190).
[349] 'Legends' 5: Le Guin is quoting Robert F. Heizer and Albert B. Elsasser, *The Natural World of the California Indians* (Berkeley: U of California P, 1980), #46 in the series, California Natural History Guides.
[350] Cf. in *Tehanu* the song of the Woman of Kemay telling how 'in the beginning, dragon and human were all one' (11: ch. 1).

Kroeber's *The Inland Whale*, in the 1974 edn.[351] Le Guin tells her Mythopoeic Society audience,

> This is a map of the universe. The Yurok called it kiwesona, that which is. We call it Del Norte, Siskiyou, Humboldt, and Trinity Counties. You see the ocean surrounds the land, which floats upon it.... Over all is the Sky Country...a solid dome whose outer edge bounds the universe. There's a hole in it for the wild geese to migrate through, and people have climbed up poles made of arrows into Sky Country, or got outside the world by shooting their boats through where the rim of the sky meets the rim of the sea.... The center of the world is a rock called Katimin, and the Klamath River runs past it. Along this river lived the woge, the first people, before they took their present forms of animals and humans. To live here is to live in the world that the woge got ready for us; a world where what we call the real and the spiritual, or the secular and the sacred, are the same thing—a seamless, centered sphere, a wholeness. ('Legends' 7)[352]

With some expansions, this is the everyday world of the Kesh people in *Always Coming Home*: they know of the cosmos—the universe of billions of stars in billions of galaxies—but they mostly choose to ignore it. Le Guin presents this turning away from space exploration and the galaxy as prudent and mature and as only a turning away: the Kesh and their neighbors do not try to oppose the cosmos or conquer it, Flash Gordon style; nor do they walk away from it like 'The Ones Who Walk Away from Omelas' to 'go somewhere else.' The positively presented peoples in *Always Coming Home* can't 'go somewhere else' in terms of the universe; the universe IS; but they can purposely and mindfully image it in the Five Houses of the Earth and the Four Houses of the Sky and, for the most part (like most humans) turn their backs on its galactic portions and live in 'a seamless, centered sphere, a wholeness'—but a wholeness that includes 'the sun, the stars' in the Four Houses of the Sky, and electricity and convenient, *chosen* machines and electronic devices—appropriate technology. And a mystic like Flicker can get in contact with the universe very completely and very directly.[353]

---

[351] A fair idea of the world-view of the California Indians can be inferred from the nine stories of the nine heroines in *The Inland Whale*.
[352] In 'Legends,' 'samething' is one word; on my ms., Le Guin corrected that as a mistake.
[353] Le Guin stressed for me Flicker's vision and the emphasis of *ACH* precisely upon technology. *ACH* as a meditation on technology, and perhaps Technique, is a topic I have not dealt with in detail in *Coyote*; I recommend it for development

* * * * * * *

In spite of Le Guin's having written *Always Coming Home* by 'a very different process from any other writing...[she] had done,' *Always Coming Home* still includes the 'typical situation, stock Le Guin plot' of much of her earlier work ('Legends' 8, 9). If the old Nordic scops had a 'word hoard' for their poetry, Le Guin has her theme and motif hoard for her teaching works. We will see this in more detail shortly. For now, note that the ethnographic methods Elizabeth Cummins stresses in *Always Coming Home* have been hinted at in *Rocannon's World* (1966), *The Word for World Is Forest* (1972), and, most importantly, *The Left Hand of Darkness* (1969). If *Always Coming Home* is Le Guin's rather new 'Carrier-Bag' approach to structure pursued vigorously, it is also a reworking of ideas and techniques she used in *Left Hand*: in some ways *Always Coming Home* is a culmination of her work on patriotism, the State, and 'people who didn't fight wars' ('Legends' 9), on extroverted, aggressive ways of life vs. the introverted, and on the momentary insight into Being in the mystic experience, Daoist style or as part of 'The Perennial Philosophy.' In terms of structure, compare 'Flicker of the Serpentine' at the center of *Always Coming Home* (Cummins 187) with the Foretelling in *The Left Hand of Darkness*; compare and contrast 'Flicker' and 'Junco' with the vision of Meshe. *Always Coming Home* is, so far at least, the culmination of Le Guin's analysis and critical critique of the 'Judeo-Christian religion' and its doctrine 'that man's singularity is his divinity,' making us 'Lords of the Earth,' rather than parts of the world, making the 'Judeo-Christian religion' a cult—and the currently most important cult—underlying 'dynamic, aggressive, ecology-breaking cultures' (*LHD* 233; ch. 16).

Taking this view, we can find the philosophical centers of *Always Coming Home* in the sections, 'Junco,' 'The Bright Void of the Wind,' 'The Dog at the Door' and 'Flicker of the Serpentine' (four of the Eight Life Stories); 'Time and the City,' 'A War with the Pig People,' the play 'Chandi,' and 'Some Generative Metaphors'; the figurative backbone to *Always Coming Home* is the three-part novella, 'Stone Telling's Story.' Significantly, 'The Visionary: The Life Story of Flicker of the Serpentine of Telina-na' physically is near the center of the book (pp. 282-304 out of ca. 525 in the Harper and Row edition), but the other metaphorically central sections are scattered in various places in the book and 'The Back of the Book.' To place these chapters in context, I will now take a stab at describing just what *Always Coming Home* might be.

---

by students of what Thomas P. Dunn and I have called 'The Human/Machine Interface' (Erlich and Dunn, *Clockworks* [subtitle]). Researchers should look very carefully at 'Some Generative Metaphors' at The Back of the Book (483-85) and note THE MACHINE, placed after THE ANIMAL, and before the set, THE HOUSE, THE DANCE, and, concluding the list, THE WAY.

* * * * * * *

Always Coming Home is, first, a *satura*: a hodgepodge, a kind of literary stew or chop suey of many elements—a novella, poems, short stories, myths, dramatic works, legends, histories, romances, direct address by the author (in the guise of Pandora, an impossible anthropologist from our time, 'now' working among the Kesh), recipes, song lyrics, insults, sanctifications (or, more exactly, praise of existing sanctity), and a utopia. As a *utopian* satire, *Always Coming Home* offers a fairly complete view of a good place, starting even as Sir Thomas More's *Utopia* (1516) started, with the physical place.[354] 'The people had to be the people who belonged to that place. Their stories would be the stories of that place, their legends would be the meaning of that place, their songs would be the voices of that place. If they didn't fight wars it would be because they lived in that place, because the way people do things and make things in the Valley does not include the making of war' ('Legends' 9).[355]

So *Always Coming Home* is a very complete 'Handbook of the Culture of the Kesh'—including music in the Harper and Row first edition—and a rather ahistorical, and antihistorical work, by Pandora 'All-Giver' (*ACH* 147-48). A handbook is necessary rather than a historically-based narrative because the Kesh have managed fairly successfully to avoid progressing or falling back into history. If The Big Mistake of our ancestors was 'stepping out of the chorus' into history, the Kesh have been smart enough to step back into the figurative chorus and stay there.

But who are the Kesh? They are the point-of-view people among the peoples who Pandora tells us 'might be going to have lived a long, long time from now in Northern California.'[356] So we are told in 'A First Note,' that seems to be Le Guin speaking in her own voice. The Kesh are not California Indians—the 'cultures of the California Indians had been irreparably damaged or wholly destroyed' by the early twentieth century—but (as Stevens has stressed) our descendants.[357] And somewhere between us and them, the ancestors of the Kesh decided to live like precivilization

---

[354] *Utopia*: Sir Thomas More's New Latin formulation from the Greek for No Place (*outopos*) and Good Place (*eutopos*). The second part of More's work is a very complete description of Utopia, starting with geography and the origin of the current (utopian) constitution, and moving on to matters studied today as sociology, political theory, theology, cultural studies, criminology, ethnography. The first part of *Utopia* and its conclusion make clear that pagan Utopia is a rational norm against which Christian Europe is to be measured and found wanting.
[355] For *ACH* as a pacifistic work, examining both 'the psychology and anatomy of war,' see Wytenbroek (quote from 330).
[356] The opening sentence of *ACH* may be characterized in contemporary linguistics terminology as *A self-reflexive artistic sentence, whose tense, aspect, and mood may be described as 'past conditional, semi-conditional, emphatic past perfect, implying futurity.'* (Source: Stephens paper, plus consultation with Max Morenberg, a linguist in my department, 8 May 1995.)
[357] Quoted clause is from Le Guin, personal communication.

people who fit into their worlds without trying to dominate them: something like Neolithic ideology but with electricity, metals, rifles, a modest railroad (469-70), and a *very* high-technology computer network. The Kesh live in the Valley of the Na River, which we may picture as the Napa Valley in California, after earthquakes have 'reshaped the western coastline' (Cummins 179), producing, perhaps, the body of water 'big enough for a whale to live in comfortably'that Ninawa arrives at to become 'The Inland Whale' of the Yurok story (T. Kroeber, *The Inland Whale* 29-30).[358] The Kesh live in a post-cybernetic world, where the computing machines have split off from their human creators and proceed with their own evolution as the City of Mind (*ACH* 149-52), an entity that is expanding out into the galaxy quite effectively and holds the promise of 'conscious, self-directed evolution' (150) until it can view the universe objectively and possibly holistically.[359] The world of *Always Coming Home* is also post-catastrophe: the series of Terran catastrophes beginning 'offstage' but alluded to in 'Nine Lives,' *The Dispossessed,* and *The Word for World Is Forest,* and seen, again in only their first stages, in 'The New Atlantis' (1975) and 'Newton's Sleep' (1991). There were not only 'vast subsidences and local elevations' that had 'left most of what we know as the Great Valley of California a shallow sea or salt-marsh' but also 'the permanent desolation of vast regions,' and equally permanent genetic damage to the human survivors (*ACH* 159). In the story of 'Four Beginnings' told in *Always Coming Home* by Cooper of the Red Adobe, the human people who preceded the Kesh—the 'woge' to them; to us: us—'were born wrong. They were crazy, they tried to make the world. All they could do was make it end again, all they could do was imitate what happened before. So what they did caused fires and smoke and bad air and then ice and cloud and cold, everybody dying again,' with just a few surviving 'the dark, cold time' (160-61), which in the mid 1980s would suggest a nuclear winter (*ACH* 148; see below).

The Kesh incorporate much of the material culture of dawn peoples who have lived along rivers from the Nile to the Yellow to the Amazon to the Colorado, or such far-future people as those who live along the Oro in Le Guin's 'Another Story OR A Fisherman of the Inland Sea'; as part of becoming 'the people who belonged to that place' they would have had or developed customs appropriate to the place ('Legends' 9).[360]

---

[358] See in *BG* the introduction to 'May's Lion' for Le Guin's comment that her initial work for *ACH* was 'trying to find the right way to get from the Napa Valley of my childhood and the present to the 'Na Valley' of the book' (*BG* 179).
[359] Cf. and contrast A. C. Clarke's pure mentality Vanamonde in *The City and the Stars* and the evolution of the ETs in his novel—not Stanley Kubrick's film—*2001*. See Erlich, 'Ursula K. Le Guin...' 120-21.
[360] Like the Original Californians, adults among the Kesh rarely practice even primitive 'war for the fun of the game, or for gain' (*Handbook* 308). They also incorporate positive parts of the cultures of the Zuñi and Navajo and other pre-Columbian, North American peoples (Le Guin, personal communication). Eliminated features of some Amerindian cultures include slavery; there was not much,

The Kesh live in a series of small towns along the River. Our archeologist of the future, Pandora, had assumed that the towns 'must be walled, with one gate' (like a very ancient city/fortress, or a slave compound on Werel in *Four Ways to Forgiveness*). When she gets over her presupposition, Pandora finds 'the town was *there*, between the creeks, under my feet the whole time. And there was never a wall; what on earth did they need a wall for?' No wall, and at 'the center is' *not* 'a heavily walled sacred enclosure' (Mumford 12, 19) but 'the Hinge' and 'the sacred buildings and the dancing place...in their own arm of the double spiral' of the heyiya-if (*ACH* 3): chaos is not kept out but invited in at the void at the center, and ritually encompassed as part of life. Cummins counts eight towns (179); it's nine if we count the town of Tachas Touchas. I'll count it. First to get to *nine* towns (the number given in 'The Dog at the Door' [280] and the map on 374): not a magic number among the native Californians, but an important one for Le Guin, and a significant number in Theodora Kroeber's *The Inland Whale*. Second, 'Tachas Touchas was (notoriously) settled by 'people from outside'—from the northwest, traditionally' (411). We are told that 'The people of Tachas Touchas insisted, without offering evidence, that the name of their town in their forgotten northern tongue meant Where the Bear Sat Down' (412). I think this is a joke. *Tuches* is the Yiddish term for 'buttocks,' and the people of Tachas Touchas may be the closest we will get to a touch of multiculturalism among the Kesh. Otherwise for the Kesh, 'The rest of the world was not a matter of urgent concern to most people of the Valley. They were content to know it was there' (*ACH* 453). The Kesh have a good culture, but a pretty homogeneous one, and we would do well to count what little diversity they have.

As indicated above, and to be discussed in more detail below, the basic Kesh view of things is integration into in a sacred and joyous whole, an antithesis to the vision of life of Koheleth standing outside the natural cycles, and equally antithetical to macho atheistic Existentialism, trying to live outside nature entirely.

The Kesh people are far more sane and rather less 'quarrelsome, competitive and aggressive' than we, or the Gethenians in *The Left Hand of Darkness*, but they do have their fights and ritualistic, 'primitive' warfare, as we see in the important very small 'History,' 'A War with the Pig People' (*ACH* 129-34).

---

but some among West Coast tribes. And the Kesh are far from what A. L. Kroeber describes as 'the usual Californian point of view: a stranger would usually be killed on principle because he was a stranger...' and neighbors attacked if they'd given serious offense. (For slavery in Native-American California, see A. L. Kroeber, *Handbook*: Yurok: 32; Shasta: 296; Modoc [Oregon]: 308 Juaneño: 647; Mohave: 752). I do not attempt in *Coyote* rigorous identification of Le Guin's literary sources; even less will I attempt to do more than suggest her sources in academic ethnography or among living peoples.

But there have been no great invasions by people on the move, like the Mongols in Asia [or like the Gaal in *Planet of Exile*] or the Whites in the New World.... They have no nomadic peoples, and no societies that live by expansion and aggression against other societies. Nor have they formed large, hierarchically governed nation-states, the mobilizable entity that is the essential factor in modern war.

Towns are small and 'communal, independent' and not just 'somewhat introverted' but very introverted. Rivalries are 'channeled into a socially approved form of aggression,' of the flyting, the insult contest. Authority is anarchic: accepted as custom, without appeal to patriarchal ideals of divine right, patriotic duty, etc. (Wytenbroek 331-32). Class structure is almost nonexistent, and there is 'no great gap between rich and poor,' nor 'slavery or servitude. Nobody owned anybody. There were no chattels. Economic organization was rather communistic or syndicalistic' and not 'capitalistic' or centralized. I quote and paraphrase and make a bit stronger for *Always Coming Home* Le Guin's description of Karhidish culture at its best in *The Left Hand of Darkness* ('Gender...Redux' in *LoN* [1979]: 165-65 [a section Le Guin would *not* have us read differently in 1989]). More precisely: as among Karhidish culture at its best in *Left Hand*, so were social arrangements on the far-future North American West Coast at the start of Stone Telling's story in *Always Coming Home*.

Threatening to repeat the Neolithic entry into history, warfare, slavery, and patriarchy is the Condor People, in their own tongue, the Dayao. The Dayao are descended, figuratively, from the Basnasska Nation in *City of Illusions* (1967).[361] Falk is captured by these people and initiated as a Hunter of the Mzurra Society (67). Either paraphrasing Falk's thoughts or stating her own aphorism, Le Guin's Narrator in *City* observes or asserts that

> The more defensive a society, the more conformist. The people he was among walked a very narrow, a tortuous and camped Way, across the broad free plains. So long as he was among them he must follow all the twistings of their ways exactly.... Wild herdsmen of the wild cattle...[they lived] a life with no rest. They hunted with hand-lasers and warded strangers from their territory with bombirds].... They had no agriculture and no domestic animals; they were illiterate and did not know, except perhaps through certain myths and hero-legends, any of the history of humankind.... They practiced a monotheistic re-

---

[361] See also the Bosses of the City of Victoria in *EoH*, and their scheme for establishing large estates and serfdom (or peonage).

ligion whose rituals involved mutilation, castration and human sacrifice. (*CI* 68)

Falk is made a member of the Mzurra Society 'with the full initiations of a Hunter, a ceremony which involved whippings emetics, dances, the recital of dreams, tattooing, antiphonal free-associating, feasting, sexual abuse of one woman by all the males in turn, and finally nightlong incantations to The God to preserve the new Horressins [= the renamed Falk] from harm' (69).[362]

The main story of the Condor is told by a woman best called Stone Telling, a familiar figure in Le Guin's narrative: a liminal character like Genly Ai, Estraven, Tenar, Lyubov, Falk, Luz, Irena—also an 'internal emigree,' or just an émigré or immigrant or alien.[363] The change in Le Guin's method in *Always Coming Home* generally, is the scientific method, so to speak, of fairly exhaustive ethnography: having *all* those voices speaking the world of the Kesh. And in her novella, Stone Telling can tell us, like Belle in 'The New Atlantis,' just what she thinks, in her own words. This is important for reasons in addition to Cummins's point (176) and Marleen Barr's (114-15) on Le Guin's moving to female voices. *Always Coming Home* is strong satire and a long one, and profits from strong (and multiple) points of view.

Stone Telling is a woman of the Kesh, and her sojourn among the Condor makes for a Quest tale, with very significant variations, and is the main narrative in *Always Coming Come*. If one began study of *Always Coming Home* by reading Stone Telling's story straight through, one could see the rest of the book as background to the story, but background foregrounded by getting its own time in the book. If one reads *Always Coming Home* from beginning to end, Stone Telling's story comes in three parts, with material before and after it. I wish to start my discussion of *Always Coming Home* proper with the 'background': some of the elements of the social and cultural world in which Stone Telling and her story are embedded, the important elements of the social and cultural world of *Always Coming Home* that Stone Telling's story helps illustrate. Viewing the works with an appropriate double vision, subject and ground are in dynamic cycling, what is foreground and what background depends upon the reader's choice of focus.

---

[362] Folk is named for Old Horressins, a dead member of the Society, who would haunt the tribe until someone assumed his name. Ghosts are a minor theme in Le Guin's canon; note above Mumford and Eliade on one function of a city wall the warding off of 'inimical spirits,' such as ghosts.

[363] *Liminal*: Threshold condition. The theory of liminality is developed by Victor Turner; my thanks to Kathleen Spencer for introducing me to the work of Turner and for her essay 'Exiles and Envoys' (for liminality, see Turner, *Ritual Process*, ch. 3, and Spencer esp. 34-36, 42). Stone Telling is particularly interesting in moving from the near *communitas* (but still structured society) of the Valley into the rigid structure of the City of the Condor, where she is a very liminal character: marginal, barely defined. See Spencer on Luz in *EoH* (Spencer 39-42).

Some Short Works in *Always Coming Home*: Philosophy

We [progressives] just have to confront certain facts: 94 percent of the American people believe in God, 72 percent believe Jesus Christ is the son of God, 39 percent believe they spoke to God on personal terms at least twice last week....

If we're going to be able to address people where they are, we have to be honest with ourselves and them, but we also have to acknowledge where people are. That is a crucial starting point—a place to begin and not to end. — Cornel West, interview in *The Progressive* 61.1 (Jan. 1997): 26.

Chandi (226-38)

'Pandora,' as editor/Narrator, tells us that 'Like most Valley drama, *Chandi* is symbolical or allegorical, generalising life. The resemblance of the plot to one of the great biblical stories is striking; but so are the differences' (227).

The biblical story is that of Job, and the similarity is that Chandi loses all, gets sick, gets argued with and bad-mouthed by choruses of uncomforting comforters—unjustly, absurdly suffers—and gets as good an answer as he can get to a couple of central questions on life for most humans. There are four major differences. First, the Adversary (Satan) in the prose introduction to the Book of Job raises the question, 'Does Job fear God for nought?' (1.9, RSV)—and argues quite cogently that Job has a good deal with God: Job loves and fears and worships God and in return profits. Should people love and worship a God who fails to deliver? Second, in the poem of Job, Job accuses God of injustice in God's inflicting suffering and horror upon the innocent:

> From out of the city the dying groan,
> and the soul of the wounded cries for help;
> yet God pays no attention to their prayer. (24.12)

> It is all one; therefore I say,
> he destroys both the blameless and the wicked.
> When disaster brings sudden death,
> he mocks at the calamity of the innocent.
> The earth is given into the hand of the wicked;
> he covers the face of its judges—
> if it is not he, who then is it? (9.22-24, RSV)

Third, the climax to the poem of Job is a theophany: God reveals himself to Job—and to Job only, not the comforters, as William Blake stresses in his great illustration of the scene—and shifts the argument from Job's blameless (1.8) 'Illusion of Central Position' and upright (2.3) accusations against God to...something else. If we make a leap of faith, God shows Job a universe in which God is somehow justified: Job sees his beloved God in the whirlwind. If we decline to make that leap of faith, we are pretty much left with the whirlwind and Job intimidated by raw power. Last, in the prose finale of the Book of Job, God pronounces Job right and his conventionally pious comforters wrong and restores Job to prosperity and his family (with Job getting new children in the conventional biological manner).

One crucial difference between Job and *Chandi* is that *Chandi* takes place in a universe of immanent sacredness/connectedness: no God, no Sons of God, no Satan. Another difference is that it takes place in a social world where human people take care of their own.

The play starts with Chandi as a 'handsome man in the prime of life, magnificently dressed' and energetically chanting '*Heya hey heya!*' and going on to 'dance the Summer,' practicing for a performance planned for that night. The play's dialog ends with Chandi repeating the *heya* chant and then the lines,

> There are the stars shining.
> there is nothing between the stars,
> the dark dancing. (228, 237)

The play itself ends with the tune of the Heron Dance: 'Stooping and half-naked, stiffly and painfully, Chandi began to dance the dance which he practiced in splendor in the first scene: but all the motions and turns were reversed, so that the dance carried him across the stage to the right,' apparently to his death. The cast vanishes into darkness, and then the musicians 'held the Ending Tone' on their instruments 'until it died away very gradually into silence' (237-38). Like much else in Kesh culture, but perhaps more directly, *Chandi* illustrates that these people 'had no god; they had no gods; they had no faith.' They are a culture with 'a working metaphor. The idea that comes nearest the center of the vision is the House,' a multivalent metaphor for Le Guin, including in its suggestions 'STABILITY' and 'Selfhood' (484); 'the sign' of this working metaphor 'is the hinged spiral or heyiya-if; the word is the word of praise and change, the word at the center, heya!' (49; 'The Serpentine Codex').[364]

---

[364] *Heya*: Cf. 'Haya!' in 'Coming of Age in Karhide' (481). In Judeo-Christian, 'heya' would be a combination of *Kadosh! Kadosh! Kadosh!, Hallelujah!,* and *Baruch...!* (Holy! Holy! Holy!, Praise Yahweh!, Bless/Praise!)—except that the Judeo-Christian equivalents I suggest are *not* correct translations. The Hebrew words direct praise to Yahweh, even as the Condor praise only the One (see below, discussion of Stone Telling's Story) and orthodox ants praise only the Queen (see discussion of 'The Author of the Acacia Seeds,' coll. *BG*). I elide Christianity in 'Judeo-Christian' here as a reversal. Also, *heya* is 'the word that contained the

On a less cosmic level, *Chandi* illustrates that many people will die 'in pain,' as an audience member observes after the show (238), and, as we see in the play, often live in pain. In *Chandi*, suffering is not a mystery requiring 'theodicy': attempting to explain the presence of evil in a universe created and ruled by a good, just, and omnipotent God. *Chandi* is about pain and suffering in any human world: as a constant in human life from the once upon a time of Job in 'the Land of Uz' (1.1) and Ged and Arren in the Dry Land, to the time of Shevek on the planets Anarres and Urras to 'a long, long time from now' among the Kesh. Shevek on Anarres allows that 'Of course it's right to cure diseases, to prevent hunger and injustice, as the social organism does. But no society can change the nature of existence. We can't prevent suffering. This pain and that pain, yes, but not Pain' (*TD* 48; ch. 2). The same with the Kesh as we see in *Chandi*: Chandi has his people, 'the House of Summer, the Serpentine,' and they will, of course, take care of him: 'Well, of course we'll go on looking after you. But'—but they don't have to like him much or like being around him; they will still, like Job's Comforters, add to his suffering. In such a world—even in utopia—*'How should a human being live well, then?'* (*ACH* 236).

'How to Die in the Valley' (83-94)

To live well, perhaps, one must learn to die well, once an important theme for instruction, but now unpopular.[365] We do have heroic works, teaching heroic death, but such works are irrelevant for most of us eminently nonheroic people, and the Kesh would (and Le Guin does) find such works misguided. Even the best of our heroic deaths might be, to reapply a phrase, 'a bit too excessive, a bit too heroic, for Valley approbation' (90). The Kesh of the Valley of the Na *learn* to die, their way, with their ceremonies and rituals, from the members of the Black Adobe Lodge (87); the nonhuman people presumably know their own ways to die, but no animals are killed—not even a mosquito—without the 'death-words' being spoken, or at least one word of the formula (90-93).

The Kesh do not, believe in «Pie in the sky when you die». They do not believe in a heaven of reward nor in a hell of punishment: not in their vulgar forms nor in the philosophical ideas of eternity with God (heaven) or infinitely removed from God (hell). They *do* believe in a soul or souls, but, as among the ki'O in 'Another Story,' their religion is 'godless, argumen-

---

world...on this side and on the other side of death' (94; 'How to Die...'). For the heyiya-if, cf. 'the Bokononist concept of a *wampeter*' in Vonnegut's *Cat's Cradle* (1963): 'A *wampeter* is the pivot' of every *karass* 'just as no wheel is without a hub' (a standard Daoist analogy to show the importance of the Void). Whatever a *wampeter* is, 'the members of its *karass* revolve about it in the majestic chaos of a spiral nebula' (42; ch. 24).
[365] For a relatively recent *ars moriendi* (art of dying) see Joanna Russ's *We Who Are About To...*(© 1975, 1976, 1977).

tative, and mystical' (*FIS* 175 [1994]), or, perhaps more exactly, not a religion as a set of doctrines but a Way, a far-future version of The Perennial Philosophy. In any event, 'Valley beliefs and theories concerning the soul were of a most amazing complexity, and imperturbably self-contradictory. One might as well try to pin Valley people down to one creation myth as to get a coherent description of the soul out of them. This multiplicity, of course, was in no sense of the word accidental. It was of the essence' (*ACH* 89 [see also 92]). Along with generic Humanity, the unborn, 'most birds, sea fish, shell fish,' and most animals not hunted by humans, the dead inhabit the Four Houses of the Sky, at least metaphorically, at least in the system given in 'The Serpentine Codex' (here 44, [47]). The main thing about the Kesh view of death is that it is part of their intense 'sense of community, of continuity with the dirt, water, air, and living creatures of the Valley' (90). It is encompassed in human community at 'the World Dance at the equinox of spring'—a cosmic reversal time, a turning from Yin to Yang, a time of power in Earthsea and elsewhere. This 'First Night of the World was a community ceremony of mourning and remembrance for all who had died' in a Valley town that year. 'The long night ceremony of Burning the Names was a fearfully intense, overcharged excitation and release of emotion,' and could be tough going for those placing high value on equanimity, 'required on this one night to share without shame or reserve the pent-up grief, terror, and anger that death leaves the living to endure.' Most important, the commemoration ceremonies, preeminently, give substance to 'the emotional and social interdependence of the community, their profound sense of living and dying with one another' (88-89), their embeddedness in human society and the world.

'Junco' (267-71)

In a universe without a transcendent God, where 'there is nothing between the stars,' seeking an ultimate truth is futile and potentially dangerous. This issue is developed directly in the life story, 'Junco,' told in the third person, male singular—the first word of the story is 'He'—by Junco himself. Even as the Lord of Shorth asked a wrong question with '*What is the meaning of life?*' (*LHD* 60, 70; ch. 5), so Junco seeks 'the eternal truth.'[366] Junco quotes Junco's saying that he wants Truth over "the souls, the forms, the words," of the world, and quotes his promise: "I will give my life, if I may see before death what lies behind life and death, behind word and form, behind all being, the eternal truth.... The gyre of the buzzard, the history of the rocks, the silence of the grass, they were all there, but he would not have them, desiring the eternal truth" (*ACH* 267-68). Against good advice, Junco follows his quest, partially under the name 'Sungazer'; 'It was a name that others had given him; he had not chosen it. Now he thought that he must do what his name said.' At the top of a

---

[366] Cf. Meshe's vision and its effects: *LHD* 162-64, ch. 12; Ai and Handdarata comments on it and ultimate truth: 60-61, 67-68, 70-71; ch. 5.

mountain, 'He looked up and gazed at the sun' (268). Junco would be ignorant of Le Guin's telling us that 'Apollo blinds those who press too close in worship. Don't look straight at the sun' (*LHD*, 1976, Introd.); but commonsense, a bluejay, and an owl tell him to stop looking. He doesn't, and comes to see 'wheels': 'black wheels and very bright wheels, turning one within the other' (268): the most memorable part of the vision of Ezekiel (1.15-21)—and a memorable part of some migraine headaches—and a significant part of the vision of Flicker (*ACH* 291).[367] The wheels are wheels of power, contrasting with going with the world in gyres.

The earth and 'everything' tell him "Go down!" off the mountain, which he does, and tries to get 'below the Valley.' He's been up the mountain: sign of Yang, place of revelations; now he'll go beyond the Valley—an embodiment of Yin—and go into a group or series of caves, 'back to where springs seep out of the rock in the dark.' It is a dark place, but still he can see 'the bright wheels turning under the ground.' Junco dances and cries out, "Let me know the truth!" (*ACH* 269). Junco is rescued by the vintners who use the caves, and they feed him and take him to his mothers' house. He refuses to stay and starts a fast to the death. He gets close, when he sees a shining person who says to him "Take the gift!" Junco thinks he will get truth, and he does: 'The young man waited for the gift, for the truth.' And nothing happens. He gets taken home and is healed, except for his eyesight. He 'can see things only by looking sidelong at them.' Looking straight ahead he sees nothing (270). And Junco returns to the world.

As 'Sungazer,' Junco was excessive even by most ascetic standards, which is part of the point. Junco's story is an *exemplum*, an example of a very wrong answer to the question '*How shall a human being live well, then?*'. Junco is crazy, but logical, and his logic is important: his craziness reduces to an absurd his premises. If there's a transcendent Truth out there, one might well strive to find out what it is; if Truth is outside the world and our flesh shackles us to the world (see, e.g., Romans 8), then mortification of the flesh makes sense for the experience of transcendence. No transcendence, no experience—and Le Guin offers little transcendence in her works. Junco gets the gift of truth about transcendent reality: nothing. There is no esoteric eternal reality in *Always Coming Home* for there to be Truth about. Junco just harms his body, permanently—and ironically—affecting his vision. He could do worse: strivers after absolutes that transcend the body often produce high counts of other people's bodies.

No transcendence, then, but might there be 'the experience of Immanence' accepted by the Handdarata (*LHD* 58; ch. 5)?

'The Bright Void of the Wind' (271-72)

Juxtaposed to Junco's story is 'The Bright Void of the Wind,' a life story told by Kulkunna of the Red Adobe of Telina-na. If Kulkunna is gendered in the story, I missed it: the personal pronoun s/he uses is the

---

[367] Le Guin notes the 'aura' of migraine headaches (personal communication).

gender-neutral first person. The name itself is a combination of the Kesh words for 'mountain' and 'river' (especially The River: the river [*na*] the Kesh live along); *na* can also mean 'To flow as or like a river' (518). Mountains are usually male symbols for us, but looking up *kulkun* in the Kesh Glossary one finds the parenthetical note on 'Ama Kulkun, Grandmother Mountain'—a suspiciously useful note, I think, for blurring the gender of mountains. And rivers are always potentially androgynous: (traditionally) feminine water in a (traditionally) masculine shape. So I'll accept the name Kulkunna as androgynous, and will refer to per using third-person, neutral pronouns modeled on the system Marge Piercy uses in *Woman on the Edge of Time* (1976).[368]

Thirty years back, Kulkunna had a serious illness and eventually per heartbeat and breathing stopped. Pe had a near-death, out-of-body experience. In a vision, Kulkunna starts 'inside a dark house,' which has a door pe opens. 'At once the wind blew it wide open...and the house shriveled up behind me like an empty bladder. I stood in a tremendous place of light and wind. Under my feet was only light and wind, the force of the wind bearing me up.' Pe falls, of course, and 'was terrified. I closed my eyes in fear, but it made no difference: there was no darkness there.' Soon, though, Kulkunna begins to feel like a feather—an important symbol in *Always Coming Home* and, at least in Egyptian religion, associated with judgment after death, light, air, and supporting the sky ('Egyptian Religion' 505). In any event, Kulkunna says 'I began to know the greatness of the wind, the brightness of the light, and joy' and would just as soon stay there (*ACH* 271).

Kulkunna feels called back, and goes, and the vision continues, seeing with 'mind's eye that all my senses could perceive was themselves, that they were making the world by casting shadows on the bright void of the wind. I saw that living was catching at shadows with hands of light. I did not want to come back to that. But the doctors' art made me come back, pulling at me, and their singing drew me back, calling me home' (*ACH* 272). This is a rather solipsistic vision, related to recent ideas in our culture on the construction of reality. It may not fit in well with the general view among the Kesh that human people are part of a larger whole that, I would think, can exist without us (see, e.g., 297). Still, this vision is appropriate to the 'many voices' structure of *Always Coming Home* and the idea of different truth for different people. Also, this vision fits in with the premise of Le Guin's 'Pathways of Desire' that we do indeed create worlds between our ears—and with the internal debate on the social construction of reality in the Churten group stories in *Fisherman of the Inland Sea* (1994). Most important, Kulkunna's vision presents imagery of shadow, void, and light that is a Le Guinian constant.

---

[368] Readers of *Coyote* annoyed with the 'pe/per/pem' pronoun system should note that I won't use it for long, and that Le Guin had a point in avoiding such a system with her androgynes in *LHD* and after.

The end of this very brief story? The main song Kulkunna hears is Blackfern of the Black Adobe's calling per back 'to walk here now,' not go with the 'shining.' Blackfern died when Kulkunna was a child, so pe listens and obeys: 'I became my ashes. I became my dark body and its illness once again' but goes on to get cured and, taking care, remaining well and becoming a doctor (272).

Male Junco wants Truth before he dies, a certain, absolute Truth; and he gets nothing. Kulkunna dies and sees perhaps what Meshe saw in trying to see the meaning of life: 'no darkness,' 'bright void' (*ACH* 271, 272 [*LHD* ch. 12]). Perhaps what Meshe saw is true enough and the ultimate truth and sole certainty. In *Left Hand* Faxe the Weaver asks Genly Ai to tell per, 'What is sure, predictable, inevitable—the one certain thing you know concerning your future, and mine.' Ai responds as we should expect: 'That we shall die' (71; ch. 5). Ungendered (for us) Kulkunna returns to life, even if life is living in a 'dark body' that may become the 'ashes' of a body diseased; life is darkening snow with our footsteps and shadows (*LHD*), 'casting shadows on the bright void.'

Between Kulkunna's story and 'The Dog at the Door' are two «mundane» pieces. 'White Tree' is a beautiful little memorial by a grandchild to a grandfather. The grandfather's last name—i.e., name picked last in life—was White Tree, and we learn the he learned *with* (not from, Pandora notes) his uncle and worked *with* pear trees to produce a variety that would grow better in the Valley and produce a better pear for the Valley people to eat. His grandchild hopes 'that he may be remembered for a while when pear trees are planted or orchards praised' (273-75).[369] 'The Third Child's Story' by Spotted Goat of the Obsidian of Madidinou, is the life story of a loser and a nasty trouble-maker, but one who writes lively verse, with a darkly-comic tone. 'Third Child' is his poem, beginning with his birth to a mother named 'Careless' and ending with his decision after a life as a 'superfluous person, / a low-quality person' with a small soul to stay where he is because 'all the towns are just the same, / people are just the same': no damn good, and Spotted Goat will stay where he is just to spite them. If a map without utopia is not worth looking at, as Oscar Wilde said, a utopia inhabited only by the smugly wise is also not worth looking at: *Homo sapiens sapiens*—the Wise, Wise Man—is a grim joke as the name of our species, so a culture of the wise is not immediately relevant for us; and smug utopians are boring. Spotted Goat is a runt from one of Coyote's litters, who has lived an unmindful, irresponsible life; he (ironically) enriches Kesh culture, and his yapping prepares well for the earnest matters to follow.

---

[369] Cf. Shevek on the Shevek in the early days on Anarres who 'designed a kind of bearing they use in heavy machines, they still call it a 'shevek.'.... There is a good immortality' (*TD* 160; ch. 7).

'The Dog at the Door' and Flicker of the Serpentine (280-304)

'The Dog at the Door' is a very brief 'record of a vision' submitted anonymously; the Narrator has no gender, no name, no house. This person follows a dog to 'a deep well lined with stone' and looks down into the well and sees the sky. 'I stood between the sky above and the sky below': in a center, then, as in Meshe's vision (*LHD* ch. 12) or 'An Orgota Creation Myth' (ch. 17), with a daylight version of the main image in Le Guin's short story 'The Stars Below' (1973). In what may be 'overdetermined,' as some psychologists say, by the center location, the story-teller asks, 'Must all things end?' and gets the answer,

> 'They must end.'
> 'Must my town fall?'
> 'It is falling now.'
> 'Must the dances be forgotten?'
> 'They are forgotten.' * * *
> 'Is the world at its end?'
> The answer was: 'There is no end.'
> 'My town is destroyed!'
> 'It is being built.'

The dog reappears, with a bag in its mouth with 'the souls of the human beings of the world.' The teller takes the bag and went along with the dog. The sky clears and the tellers sees 'that the mountains had fallen. Where they had been, where the Valley had been, there was a great plain.' There are people on the plain, each with a bag full of either seeds or little stones. 'The stones in the bags made a whispering as they moved together, saying, 'In the end is no end. To build with us, unbuild with us'' (281).

I'm not sure what this all means, but it does show a humans-only Sartrean plain and a universe of impermanence combined with a kind of ultimate stability. As with Koheleth and Heraclitus, Kali and Shiva, Yin-Yang and the movement of the Dao (or with D. H. Lawrence): the reality of things is a cycle of cycles of dissolution and re-creation. A very *mortal* world, and simultaneously, unending.

And then comes the linearly last and thematically central story in this section of *Always Coming Home*: the story of 'The Visionary: The Life Story of Flicker of the Serpentine of Telina-na,' a woman—very much a female speaker—who has had 'the experience of Immanence,' very much capital 'I' Immanence.

Like a reversed mirror image of the male protagonist of 'The Man Who Could Not See Devils' in Joanna Russ's story, as a very young child Flicker had seen people in rooms, people *invisible* to everyone else, getting her mother to think that Flicker might have 'the third eye' and should use it by becoming a doctor (*ACH* 282-83). Flicker turns away from these people only she sees, and they leave her, and she becomes a fairly normal teenage girl-woman: in love with horses (286), an occasional thief of booze, in with a group of dopers (287). She 'did not want the world to be as it was' and began 'making up the world.' Most specifically, she nurses an infatuation for a forbidden love: a young man of the Serpentine of Chukulmas, her own house—a 'brother,' with whom sex would be incest (284, 287). Flicker wants to die (287), and at this low-point she has her central vision. It's a complex one.

It begins with her looking at Black Oak, an ordinary enough man, and seeing not him 'but the Serpentine. It was a rock person...,' a human being made of serpentine. Serpentine hits her, or she falls—or undergoes something that hurts her head—and she is stunned (288). When she can look up again, she sees Serpentine put hands to navel and pull apart the body, opening 'a long, wide rent...like the doorway of a room' that she is to enter. Flicker tells us she thinks 'the rest of the vision all took place in the stone; that is where it all happened and was; but because of the human way human people have to see things, it seemed to change, and to be other places, things, and beings.' Flicker finds herself 'in the earth, part of the dirt,' feeling the feelings of dirt. Rain starts and she could 'feel rain coming into the dirt,' feeling 'in a way that was like seeing.' Waking and sleeping, Flicker perceives. 'I began feeling stones and roots, and along my left side I began to feel and hear cold water running, a creek in the rainy season.... Near the creek I began to feel the deep roots of trees' and other life (289).

The vision shifts here, but I want to deal with this passage, since it so powerfully invokes both capital 'I' Immanence and the great fear with which those who will fully accept immanence vs. transcendence must deal: death, the grave, being in and becoming dirt. Or mud (see *EoH* 116-17, ch. 8; 176-77, ch. 11, and passim). The passage can be put in useful dialog with what I'll call the 'Erdschweinhöhle'—'Aardvark hole'—meditation in Thomas Pynchon's *Gravity's Rainbow* (1973), a section that deals with a number of motifs of great interest to readers of Le Guin (although *Gravity's Rainbow* has not been read by Le Guin).[370]

Part of Pynchon's meditation includes a bit of ethnography about the poorest group among the Herero people, whose totem animal was 'the Erdschwein [earth-pig] or aardvark.' Leaving the area of these people, a White might be able to perceive a

---

[370] Personal communication: Le Guin has not read *Gravity's Rainbow*. Still, note in *Gravity's Rainbow* • naming in a godless universe: 'There may be no gods, but there is a pattern: names...may have no magic, but the *act* of naming...obeys the pattern' (*GR* 322). • 'Christian Europe' as 'death and repression' (317). Christianity as the way of division vs. 'Pre-Christian Oneness,' the religion of 'the Empire' (321), associated with 'immachination' and 'the Rocket' (318). • The creation of a world/people without history. 'The people will find the Center again, the Center without time, the journey without hysteresis, where every departure is a return to the same place, the only place...' (319). • The 'old tribal unity' for the Hereros of German Southwest Africa including 'the gathered purity of opposites, the village built like a mandala....' (321). See also *GrR* 563, 701.

> woman alone in the earth, planted up to her shoulders in the aardvark hole, a gazing head rooted to the desert plane.... She can feel the incredible pressure...against her belly.... [Her four stillborn children] have pointed her here, to be in touch with Earth's gift for genesis. The woman feels power flood in through every gate: a river between her thighs, light leaping at the ends of fingers and toes. It is sure and nourishing as sleep. It is a warmth. The more the daylight fades, the further she submits—to the dark, to the descent of water from the air. She is a seed in the Earth. The holy aardvark has dug her bed. (315-16)[371]

In the Zone (the spreading War, the metastasizing Western world), the point-of-view character feels, 'The Erdschweinhöhle is in one of the worst traps of all, a dialectic of word made flesh, flesh moving toward something else....' (321).

Flicker's vision is more optimistic. Pynchon's Hereros see a binary choice: they can choose 'between two kinds of death: tribal death, or Christian death. Tribal death made sense' (318) and Pynchon's Hereros will complete the Germans' job of extermination begun in Southwestern Africa by committing tribal suicide (317-18, 323). They will not attempt a return to tribal life and wholeness after the time of European sickness. They won't try to get back to the Immanence symbolized by the aardvark-hole. As Stevens stressed in her 1989 SFRA presentation, Le Guin offers no opportunity for 'restitution' to massacred Indians. In Le Guin's words, 'The people who lived in the Valley are silent, now and forever. We did not listen to them. We—my people—killed them without hearing one word they said.' In Le Guin's view, 'at the very root and center' of *Always Coming Home* 'there is that: a silence, and an act of contrition. Not of reparation. There is no reparation. But inside my dance of celebration of humanity set in the dreamtime future [of *ACH*] there is another dance, a spiral going the other way into the past, not touching; a dance for the dead, in silence' ('Legends' 10). In my prosaic words, much of Le Guin's point in *Always Coming Home* is creating a *mâshâl* in which exterminated tribes *do* return insofar as their cultures are recreated in words and imagination.[372] And among the imagined Kesh and their neighbors there is a returning to life.

Even so, as a kind of mystic microcosm. Flicker does not get trapped but gets 'moving toward something else.' Le Guin has Flicker have it that the 'human way human people have to see things' causes perception of change. So Flicker sees the rain—a classic symbol for revival, new life, renewal—as 'ladders of rain' and climbs them out of her version of the

---

[371] Cf. feelings of being part of the universe in Le Guin's 'Solitude' and *VFA* (41).
[372] Again, *mâshâl:* 'a likeness;...or 'satire.'...either the aptly stated analogue of a previously experienced reality, or...the quasi-magical, verbal prefiguring of reality in the shape...in which the utterer would like to encounter it' (Rabinowitz 320).

aardvark-hole to the 'stairways of cloud' and on to the 'path of wind,' where she gets a crucial helper: Coyote (289), the totem animal of the Eighth House (the House of the wind) and the Kesh symbol for change ([47], 49).[373]

Coyote asks Flicker if and then where Flicker wants to go, and Flicker says she wants to go to the Sun, taking her from the Eighth House (associated with Coyote, wilderness, 'across') into the Ninth (Hawk, Eternity, 'out' [47]). Going across then out, Flicker sees a jerky history of the world, one which is hard to describe: 'Seeing with the hawk's eyes is being without self. Self is mortal. That is the House of eternity.' Where there is no self, 'When there is no I nor she there is no story' (290). What Flicker can tell us about her hawk-vision is that she saw 'the universe of power'—as power—as decorous for the daughter of an electrician and an apprentice electrician herself (in our job descriptions). In its purest form, this ultimate world was and is—if the more mystical interpretations of modern physics are correct (Capra chs. 13-15)—a 'network, field, and line of energies of all the beings, stars and galaxies of stars, worlds, animals, minds, nerves, dust, the lace and foam of vibration that is being itself, all interconnected, every part part of another part and the whole part of each part, and so comprehensible to itself only as a whole, boundless and unclosed.' In her moment of vision, 'the electrical mental network of the City' of Mind, 'that vast web' of cybernetic high technology in all its light-year magnitude immensity 'was one momentary glitter of light on one wave on the ocean of the universe of power'—not *being* this time but 'the universe of power' (*ACH* 290-91).[374]

Atman is Brahman. Self is universe. A human being cannot maintain the vision of Being for very long, nor can the Real be described at length without falling into bathos. Both Flicker and Le Guin move on into 'a descent or drawing away' where things are describable. Following what seems like Buddhist tradition, they move from Being-as-Power to a 'lesser place or plane, which was what might be called the gods or the divine, beings enacted possibilities. These I, being human, recall as having human form.' The gods, however, are not Buddhist deities or Native American *woge*. The one Flicker remembers is a form of Hephaestus (Vulcan) the Greco-Roman metal-smith to the gods. Flicker applies the categories of the Kesh and sees the Hephaestus figure as a member of the Miller's Art; this is decorous for her, and also useful for Le Guin, elegantly alluding to literal milling of grain, the saying 'The mills of the gods grind slowly, but

---

[373] The Kesh, however, want little to do with *historical* change. In *ACH*, Le Guin is an ally to Y. Zamyatin and develops the same sort of City/country, Christian/anti-Christian conflicts he uses in *We*, but her Kesh seem liable to Zamyatin's sarcastic statement of the (anti)utopian ideal as 'the condition where nothing *happens* any more' (24; Sixth Entry).
[374] Cf. Ged on human selfhood in *FS*, as 'a wave on the sea' (122; ch. 8), and the electricity, dance, and wave references and imagery in 'Dancing to Ganam' and 'Another Story' in *FIS*.

very fine,' and to William Blake's great vision of 'dark Satanic Mills' destroying 'England's green and pleasant land,' and people (Preface to *Milton* [1804-08]).

Hephaestus in the vision 'shaped the vibrations of energies, closing their paths from gyre into wheel...making wheels of energy closed upon themselves, terrible with power, flaming. He who made them was burnt away by them...but still he turned the paths of energy and closed them into wheels, locking power into power.' These wheels of the god grind slowly, perhaps, but turn all around them 'black and hollow.' Other beings appear, looking like birds,

> flying and crying across the wheels of fire to stop the turning and the work, but they were caught in the wheels, and burst like feathers of flame. The miller was a thin shell of darkness now, very weak, burnt out, and he too was caught in the wheels' turning and burning and grinding, and was ground to dust, like fine black meal. The wheels as they turned kept growing and joining until the whole machine was interlocked cog within cog, and strained and brightened, and burst into pieces. Every wheel as it burst was a flare of faces and eyes and flowers and beasts on fire, burning, exploding, destroyed, falling into black dust. That happened, and it was one flicker of brightness and dark in the universe of power.... The dark dust or meal lay in the shape of open curves or spirals.... It began dancing...to the left, something was there crying like a little animal. That was myself, my mind and being in the world, and I began to become myself again.... (291-92)

We have in this Vision, I think, a recapitulation of our history and a foretelling of the outcome of Stone Telling's story: the outcome of the crisis approaching the Kesh. Haephestus/Vulcan is one of the possibilities that may be enacted out of the infinite possibilities inherent in Being; he is an appropriate god to represent our civilization, a civilization that did, in *Always Coming Home*, keep 'growing and joining until the whole machine was interlocked cog within cog,' finally 'burning, exploding, destroyed, falling into black dust' (291).

The rest of Flicker's story is Flicker's learning to live with her vision, learning 'to speak sky with an earth tongue,' approaching 'the condition of living in both Towns,' of 'being oneself in the world' (292-93), learning 'the techniques of revisioning, of recounting,' of 'recalling' and music (298).

She also has to learn to deal with Milk, an ungentle, celibate woman who works with words and has little respect for Flicker's male teacher, Tarweed, who 'worked with words, drum, and matrix chanting.' She also contemns Tarweed because he is a man. Flicker recalls that Milk 'In the Lodge' had said 'the old gibe' that 'A man fucks with his brain and thinks with his penis.' Flicker thinks that Tarweed knew what Milk thought, 'but intellectual men are used to having their capacities doubted and their achievements snubbed....' Flicker tries to defend him, but her own freedom from sexist attitudes only goes so far as, '...he thinks like a woman!' (293-94). These are reversals probably of use to young readers; for older readers, the more interesting part of this section of the story is Flicker's coming to understand that Milk is tough on her because Milk envies her for 'going ahead,' being ahead of her in the visionary calling (302-03). There is a moral here, I think: A great soul like Ged, teaching and using Arren in *Farthest Shore*, can willingly encourage a young person to lead; most people can't. Flicker also has to learn how to avoid a return to 'making up the world' (300) as she had done with her infatuation with her Serpentine brother. Interestingly, she gets her name, Flicker, and important but bad (William Blakean? Sadean? D. H. Lawrencean?) advice from an old woman in a vision: 'What are you sulking about? Why don't you go fuck with your [House] brother in Chukulmas? Desire unacted is corruption. Must Not is a slave-owner. Ought Not is a slave. Energy constrained turns the wheels of evil.... How can you gyre, how can you handle power, chained like that? Superstition! Superstition!' (295). Flicker may accept that 'Vision is transgression!' always and necessarily (294), but she is not going to violate her people's incest taboo. She gets better advice from Deertongue, 'A woman-living man of the Serpentine of Wakwaha.' He tells Flicker to follow Coyote's advice 'at the beginning of it all': to wit, 'take it easy'; he also gets her to admit that her vision in the Ninth House is the center of her life, which she needs to recognize and, probably, let go (299).

It is significant that Le Guin does not idealize women in the 'Flicker' story and that she presents without comments on any need to change his life, a male homosexual (?) or transvestite. Not a gay man in our sense, but, apparently, closer to the 'One in every several hundred Yurok men, on the average' who 'preferred the life and dress of a woman,' a tendency, A. L. Kroeber tells us, that was 'not combated, but socially recognized by the Indians of California...probably by all the tribes of the continent north of Mexico' (*Handbook* 46).[375] This is significant for Le Guin's later work; for now we can follow Flicker down from mystic vision—backward in *Always Coming Home* as a physical book—to the world of myth, and thence down toward mundane considerations of war and peace, politics, and family.

Time and the City Section (149-72)

'Big Man and Little Man' starts with a retelling of a Japanese creation myth, I think, combined with Genesis (1.1-2.24) and the Western mystical idea that the first act of creation was God's withdrawal, to allow space for a creation to take place in. 'Big Man and Little Man' starts with Big man

---

[375] See *Handbook* Index, 'Transvestite' (971).

having created the stars with his semen (or so 'they say') and filling up all of the universe outside the world: 'There wasn't room for anything else' (*ACH* 157), an image for gods and men too full of themselves.[376] Big Man sees 'the world inside, and he wanted to be in it, get it pregnant with himself, or maybe he wanted to eat it, get it inside himself,' anyway, get *possession* of it. Big Man couldn't get into the world, though, 'He could only see it backwards.' So he sends across 'a Little Man,' with 'his head on backwards.' Little Man doesn't like the little world, 'So Big Man put him to sleep and while he was sleeping made a thing like a woman out of dirt, out of red adobe, they say. It looked like a woman, it fooled Little Man....' Big Man tells Little Man to 'go there and breed,' which he does: Little Man 'took the thing and went back inside the world. He fucked it and it made copies. He kept doing that until there were as many of him as mosquitoes.... All the same, no matter how many of him there were, he didn't like it there. He was afraid. He didn't belong there inside the world, he had no mother, only a father. So he killed whatever he was afraid of' (157-58), which is pretty much everything. 'He was really afraid of water, because of the way water is' (158). That last point refers to Daoist ideas on water, but primarily to the American Indian idea that 'The white people destroy all. They blast rocks and scatter them on the earth. The rocks say, "Don't. You are hurting me."' But water 'can't be hurt. The white people go to the river and turn it into dry land. The water says, "I don't care. I am water"' (qtd 'Legends' 5).[377]

Anyway, with the exception of water, Little Man and his descendants—we, civilized humanity—managed to destroy most of the world, finally poisoning the sea. So the world is corrupted, and Big Man declares, 'It's nothing but corruption, that world!' and turns away and leaves. The vermin of the world come sneaking back and eat the dead: 'They made it food.' Some human people had somehow gotten born, 'born with mothers,' even, and survived (158). These new human people 'weren't afraid' but were low enough, hungry enough, and smart enough to ask 'the coyotes to help them,' which brings Coyote herself. 'Where she walked she made the wilderness. She dug the canyons, she shat mountains' and the world is renewed. 'Things went on, people went on,' leading to the world of *Always Coming Home*, 'Only Little Man didn't go on. He was dead. He died of fear' (159).

* * * * * * *

---

[376] A god's masturbation to create the world images creation *ex deo*, without goddesses or women or anything female or feminine. For another approach, note the erotic aspects of Bill Kopman's fantasies creating and filling the world of 'Pathways of Desire' (*CR* 204-05 and passim).

[377] Cf. George Carlin's routine, 'Water don't give a shit'; he is using an idea of Lao Tzu's (*Tao te Ching* chs. 8, 43, 78) that Le Guin alludes to in her 'Review of *Ascent of Wonder*,' and an American Indian idea Le Guin quotes here from 'an old Wintu woman' (see also Needham II.42, Welch 43).

The story 'A Hole in the Air' works a major variation on the Karok/Yurok motif of the sky hole: changing a vertical trip into the sky world above into a temporal trip back in time to our civilization. In Le Guin's allegory, a man finds a hole in the air, 'up near Pass Valley,' we're told, 'in the Range of Light' (154), a symbolically appropriate place for a kind of time-portal to an age in some ways (as the saying has it) 'blinded by the light.' The man goes 'through the hole to the outside world,' i.e., outside the world, into our world: civilization, 'Life As We Know It' (*Norton* 35). This is the land of 'The backward-head people,' where the food is poisoned, and roads with fast-moving automobiles are everywhere, where there are very few people around besides human people and all seems to be 'walls and roofs,...roads and houses.' The human people there 'had electrical wires in their ears, and were deaf. They smoked tobacco day and night, and were continually making war.' The Kesh man tries to 'get away from the war by going on, but...they lived everywhere' (156).[378] The Kesh man 'died of grief and poison,' and his people 'took the pole house down and let the wind blow' away the hole in the air (157).

Again, from a Kesh point of view, we are the *woge*, the first people, who prepared the world for them by perversely *un*making the world, and we are outside the world, dangerous, and insane. That's the MORAL, and in case we don't get it, these stories are part of a kind of exposition sandwich.

After our author/editor Pandora has lamented killing off our civilization—imaging the death of a culture is far from genocide but less than innocent—and implicating us (147-48), we get 'The City' section of Time and the City. This section subdivides into exposition on *Yaivkach*: The City of Mind, *Wudun*: The Exchanges, and *Tavkach*: The City of Man. The City of Mind and the Exchanges are the extraordinarily evolved computer network in the world of the Kesh and their neighbors, descended from human technology but now mostly outside of the human world. The City of Man is civilization:

> The historical period, the era of human existence that followed the Neolithic era for some thousands of years in various parts of the earth, and from which prehistory and 'primitive cultures' are specifically excluded, appears to be what is referred to by the Kesh phrases 'the time outside,' 'when they lived outside the world,' and 'the City of Man.' * * *
> ...[T]his period in which we live, our civilisation, Civilisation as we know it, appeared in Valley thought as a remote region, set apart from the community and continuity of human/animal/earthly existence—a sort of peninsula sticking out from the mainland, very thickly built upon,

---

[378] Cf. the vision of civilization in 'Buffalo Gals.'

very heavily populated, very obscure, and very far away.
* * * [Separated from them by a] gap or lack of connection....

...[T]hey may have perceived it as the most important thing...about civilisation, about history in our terms: that gap...break, flip, that reversal from in to out, from out to in. That is the hinge. (152-53)

In the middle of Time and the City, there is 'A Note on the Backward-Head People,' the most terrifying 'ghoul' in the Valley; because *we* are the horror folks who gave the Kesh and the other survivors on Earth those 'vast regions' desolated 'through release of radioactive or poisonous substances, the permanent genetic impairment from which they suffered most directly in the form of sterility, stillbirth, and congenital disease' (159). Our legacy to them has been 'war, plague, famine, holocaust, and Fimbul Winter' (148)—of the nuclear variety, apparently, not the one out of Norse legend. Which brings us back to war, a central metaphor for our activity from a Kesh point of view: 'They'—we—'smoked tobacco day and night, and were continually making war' (156).

'A War with the Pig People' and Commentary (129-34)

In his 'Reactionary Utopias' article, Gregory Benford accuses Le Guin of an 'aversion for violence' and avoiding in her work both violence and 'the problem of evil' (16-18), in Benford's context, the practical problems caused by human evil. (There is no 'problem of evil' in a theological sense for Le Guin, nor for Benford in his article.) I think one could say with equal truth, and equal error, that Le Guin is obsessed by the problem of warfare as large-scale, organized violence. Set as they are in Europe, however modified by an imaginary country, *Malafrena* and *Orsinian Tales* have war, insurrection, and the threat of war as a recurrent theme. And in Le Guin's SF and fantasy there is organized fighting, outright warfare, the threat of warfare, or repression through institutional violence or the threat of violence in *Rocannon's World*, *Planet of Exile*, *City of Illusions* (agents of the Shing destroy Terrans who seek to organize), *The Word for World Is Forest*, *The Lathe of Heaven* ('offstage'), *The Left Hand of Darkness*, *King Dog*, 'The Matter of Seggri,' *The Eye of the Heron*, *A Wizard of Earthsea*, and *The Dispossessed*—i.e., most of Le Guin's major works and some minor ones. As I have stressed, *Always Coming Home* is very much concerned with war, and I will be getting into the question of war in detail in the discussion of Stone Telling's narrative. First, however, we need to get back to the accusation against our culture that we smoke tobacco and make war continually. How does the man in 'A Hole in the Air' know about warfare, and what does warfare have to do with nicotine addiction? The Gethenian languages don't have a word for war; how is it that Kesh does?

The short and simple answer is that the people of the Valley of the Na, like their Indian predecessors along the Klamath River and 'primitives' most places indeed had warfare; it's just that what they mean by 'war' is very different from our meaning. That difference is made clear in 'A War with the Pig People' by Strong of the Yellow Adobe of Tachas Touchas (*ACH* 129-34).

This narrative is significantly called a 'History': to say nothing of the negative implications of 'history' in *Always Coming Home*, it is still an old insult that conquerors make history, plus widows and orphans; and much of what is thought of and taught as history is about wars. In this brief history, an unusually large number of Pig People stay around Tachas Touchas longer than usual, and 'Their pigs were all over the hunting side.' A man from both the Bay Laurel Lodge and the hunters of the town—after due consultation—goes over and politely asks the Pig People to keep their pigs out of the hunting area.

> A Pig woman spoke for them. She was about seventeen years old. She said, 'Can't your hunters tell pigs from deer?'
> He said, 'Not always.'
> She said, 'This is how to tell the difference: deer run away, pigs don't.'

This response angers the Bay Laurel people and the hunters. They meet and 'agreed to have a war with the Pig People after [the celebration called] the Moon. Nobody spoke against it.' Three people of the town go to the Pig camp and eat with them. 'After everybody had eaten we sat around being polite, until Dream Eagle fetched out the tobacco and the pipe. He said, "Will you smoke with us?"' Some thirty-one of the Pig men but no women smoke with the three people from town (129). 'Four women and thirteen men' from the town 'had agreed to fight the war.' They negotiate when and where the war is to occur, then the townsfolk go home, with Strong noting that he was drunk and sick from smoking: smoking tobacco was *not* mere recreation or a bad habit among the California Indians, and, except for problem people under the influence of the Condor, isn't a common activity among the Kesh and their neighbors.

The ad hoc warriors from the town prepare weapons and ammunition 'and people who had fought wars before talked to us and trained us'; and, of course, they all perform the proper rituals (130). Dream Eagle is chosen as 'the war chief so he could tell us what to do and not do,' but we are not told the method of selection. When the war begins, 'Most of the Pig men stayed high up in the brush and shot from there. I think all of them had guns, but they were not all good guns. We had three very good guns made by Himpi the Gunsmith, and eight good ones. The rest of us had chosen to fight with knives or without weapons' (131). Dream Eagle is killed; Black (a young woman) is killed; Sun's Son is killed; and a fourteen- and fifteen-year-old behave bravely: running after the Pig People and shouting insults at them (132). A Pig man signals for peace, 'and people called out, "It is over, it is over"' (133). The Pig People move on, and the victors, more or less, of Tachas Touchas 'went through purification ceremonies.' Strong ends with what seems to be a compliment for both sides: 'They were brave and true warriors in that war' (133).

Well, someone my age would call it a 'rumble,' except that when the word 'rumble' was used, guns were usually not used (see *West Side Story* [film: 1961]). Clear of the Yellow Adobe of Tachas Touchas calls the war much stronger things and is angry at its adult participants.

> I am ashamed that six of the people of my town who fought this war were grown people. Some of the others were old enough to behave like adults, too.
>
> All over the Valley now they are saying that the women and men in Tachas Touchas make war. They are saying that people in Tachas Touchas kill people for acorns.... They are laughing at us....
>
> It is appropriate for children to fight, not having learned yet how to be mindful, and not yet being strong. It is part of their playing.
>
> It is appropriate that adolescents...may choose mindfully to risk their strength in a game, and they may choose to throw away their life, if they wish not to go on and undertake to live a whole life into old age. That is their choice. In undertaking to live a whole life, a person has made the other choice. They no longer have the privilege of adolescence. To claim it in grown life is mindless, weak, and shameful. (133-34)

Counting coup, in the fashion of the Plains Indians, is obviously a kind of game; California Indians usually raided to avenge an affront they took seriously. I agree with Clear, though: rumbles have rules and, ideally, clear winners and losers; from an anthropological point of view, they are games for the rowdier among two or more groups' adolescents. What the Kesh lack is 'large, hierarchically governed nation-states, the mobilizable entity that is the essential factor in modern war' ('Is Gender Necessary?' *LoN* [1979]: 164), nor do they have hierarchically governed city-states that were the essential factor in early ancient warfare. So their violence remains fairly personal, small-scale, and regulated. Violence is not celebrated as the defining act of manhood; war is not seen as the highest vocation of gentlemen or the noble man, or the greatest, most meaningful, most value-bestowing activity of a civilization. Warfare among adults, to Clear of Tachas Touchas, is 'mindless, weak, and shameful'—and, in the Valley, literally ludicrous.

'Stone Telling'

> 'History is a nightmare from which humanity longs to awaken.' —Qtd. Joanna Russ, end of *We Who Are About To...* (1975 f.)[379]

A hierarchically governed city-state and the glorification of war are exactly what the Dayao, the Condor people, have, and we get to see it in detail in the three parts of Stone Telling's story, and appended material (*ACH* 7-42, 173-201, 340-86).

Stone Telling is a 'liminal' person, one of Le Guin's 'Exiles and Envoys,' to use Kathleen L. Spencer's suggestive phrase and highly useful analysis. Her mother is Kesh, her father Dayao, and her quest for her self, for Home, takes her from the Valley to The City of the Condor—a City of Man—and then (fulfilling the quest pattern) back again, re-integrated into her world and, in *Always Coming Home, the* world: '*To be whole is to be part; true journey is return*' (Odo's tombstone, *TD* 68; ch. 3). Her movement 'There and Back Again' allows her to see and show us not only her utopian world of the Kesh but also the imperialist dystopia of the Condor.[380] In the movement between utopian and dystopian worlds, she is somewhat like the protagonist in Piercy's *Woman on the Edge of Time* (1976), or the 'J's' in Joanna Russ's *The Female Man* (1975). 'Genre writers and readers,' as Le Guin has written, 'share a common stock of concepts, icons, images, manners, and patterns, precisely as the musicians and audiences of Haydn's and Mozart's time shared a *materia musica* which the composer was expected, not to shatter or transcend, but to use and make variations on' (*Norton* 21). So Stone Telling joins other women travelers from one world to another and back again, helping to answer the question, '*How shall a human being live well, then?*' In the context of *Always Coming Home*, the question includes how we might set up cultures and societies that actively encourage—and avoiding creating cultures that discourage—good living.

The most relevant analogy for the politics of Stone Telling's journey may be an earlier work that *Always Coming Home* reflects in a reversing

---

[379] Either original or modified in James Joyce's *Ulysses* (1922): 'History, Stephen said, is a nightmare from which I am trying to awake.' My thanks to Sue Ebbs on the SFRA ListServ for the *Ulysses* quote from *Oxford Dictionary of Modern Quotations*., and to Brooks Landon and Andy Miller for giving the location: ch. 2, line 377 in The Correct Text, ed. Hans Walter Gabler et al. (New York: Vintage, 1986): 28.

[380] 'There and Back Again' is J. R. R. Tolkien's alternative title for *The Hobbit* (1937), quoted 'Legends' 9. For the condor as symbol, note A. L. Kroeber on 'the two-headed condor' among the Nazca people of southern Peru, in his discussion of 'The Double-Headed Eagle' as § 190 of *Anthropology*. Kroeber traces the European symbol back to the winged sun disk of Ra through its use in Austro-Hungary and Russia: 'The meaning of sovereignty remaining attacked to the figure, the device before long became indicative of the imperial idea' (474).

and distorting mirror image: Yevgeny Zamyatin's modernist dystopia, *We* (ca. 1920).[381] *We* starts in dystopia and mostly stays there, with a test of a space vehicle turning out to be no way out of dystopia and only a quick trip beyond the City's quite literal Wall. 'Man ceased to be a wild animals,' *We*'s male protagonist-arrator, D-503 tells us, 'only when he built the first wall. Man ceased to be a savage only when we had built the Green Wall, when we had isolated our perfect mechanical world from the irrational, hideous world of trees, birds, animals....' (93; Seventeenth Entry), enclosing 'infinity behind a wall'—outside it, I think—'terrified to glance outside the wall' (40-41; Eighth Entry). D-503 is a man of the City, initially well-integrated into his world. The plot of *We* has him meeting I-330, a sensual woman and revolutionary, and being led by her to discovery of transgressive sex and politics, and losing his integration: i.e., going insane. D-503 finally is captured by the authorities and cured by having his imagination excised, but there is a chance the rebellion of the forces of energy and change will defeat the City and its stasis.

In the background of *We* is

> the Great Two Hundred Years' War—the war between the city and the village. The primitive peasants, prompted perhaps by religious prejudice, stubbornly clung to their 'bread.' But in the year 35 before the founding of the One State, our present food, a petroleum product was developed. True, only 0.2 of the earth's population survived the war. But, cleansed of its millennial filth, how radiant the face of the earth has become! And those two tenths survived to taste the heights of bliss in the shining palace of the One State. (21; Fifth Entry)

It turns out that a 'small remnant' survived also outside the Wall, to become the wild, savage Mephi—as in 'Mephistophilis' (C. Marlowe) or 'Mephistopheles' (Goethe) or 'Mephisto.' These savages are the 'half' that must unite with the civilized for full humanity (163); in any event, they represent nature and energy. I-330 tells D-503 'There are two forces in the world—entropy and energy. One leads to blissful quietude, to happy equilibrium; the other to destruction of equilibrium, to tormentingly endless movement. Entropy was worshipped as God by our—or rather, your—ancestors, the Christians. But we anti-Christians, we....' (165; Twenty-eighth Entry). She never finishes the sentence, but that doesn't matter much for *We* and is irrelevant for us. What's relevant here is the City/Village split and *Always Coming Home*'s literally re-evaluating some basic terms of Zamyatin's formula. Le Guin indeed puts her protoJudeo-Christians within the walls of the City and the people integrated into nature into wall-less villages in the shape of the double-spiral heyiya-if (*ACH*

---

[381] For a discussion of mirror images and reversals, relating to *ACH*, see Selinger 135 f.

3); but it is the Condor who hold the promise of action, destruction, and 'tormentingly endless movement,' or at least busy-ness.

Le Guin is revisiting and re-visioning, I think, her own *City of Illusions* (1967). There she had tried to balance 'The forest of the mind' (inhabited by humans in households) with the City and civilization: civilization 'not as a negative force—restrain, constraint, repression, authority—but as an opportunity lost, an ideal of truth. The City as goal and dream' (*LoN* [1979]: 147). In her introduction to the 1978 re-issue of *City of Illusions*, Le Guin expressed dissatisfaction with the Shing, the City-dwelling villains of *City of Illusions*. 'Real villains are rare; and they never, I believe, occur in flocks....' Le Guin had obeyed an order from her elder daughter to write about a people she had thought up, the Shing: 'They're *bad*.' As of ca. 1978, Le Guin thought she'd 'fluffed it' with the Shing. 'I should have made Elisabeth tell me how to do it.... Eight-year-olds know what bad is. Grownups get confused' (*LoH* [1979]: 146). The City of the Condor is a Bad Place—period: 'a negative force' a place of 'restraint, constraint, repression, authority.' And the Condor (abstract mass noun) are bad, the villain (singular) of *Always Coming Home*: not each Condor person individually, nor even high-ranking Condor people, but the Condor as a culture. Le Guin has learned 'what bad is' enough to show its social expression in a highly satiric story.

Always Coming Home starts sputteringly, as is traditional with saturas/satires (see Jonathan Swift's longer works), but when we get past a rather analytical Contents and 'A First Note,' 'The Quail Song' (a ten-line lyric), and a note moving us 'Towards an Archeology of the Future'—then *Always Coming Home* 'begins' with 'Stone Telling,' Part One.[382]

Part One (7-42)

We meet Stone Telling under her first name, North Owl, and she tells us her mother's names were Towhee (a bird), Willow, and Ashes and that as a girl she lived with her mother and her grandmother, Valiant. Her 'father's name, Abhao, in the Valley means Kills,' which is our first hint that her father's name, at least, is not of the same sort as those that are just given, in meaningful words ('ashes,' 'owl'), without translation. Stone Telling talks to us as if we were human people of the Valley, and—as in most really imaginative SF—we have to suspend our disbelief and a few beliefs, and tolerate some ignorance and the risk of misunderstanding if we are to follow her story. E.g., 'First Name' here doesn't mean first name in our binomial nomenclature for European naming: it's the chronologically first name someone uses (7-8).

We soon learn that young Stone Telling is teased by some of the other children with epithets of 'half-House' and called 'half a person,' and that this hurts her (9). The significance of the mockery is, first, that kids can be

---

[382] The Harper 1st edn. has it Part I, Part Two, Part Three; I have regularized the section titles.

cruel even in utopia, second, that her father was an outsider, one who 'had come from outside the Valley and had gone away again,' and, third, as we shall learn later, that there is a kind of sickness in the Valley, with some very subtle manifestations. Thinking as a child, North Owl saw these epithets to mean only that she 'had no father's mother, no father's House, and therefore was half a person'; she hadn't yet even heard of the Condor (10), but she will, very shortly.

North Owl's first adventure is going with her mother and (maternal) grandmother to visit her grandmother's mostly ex-husband in Chumo, a rich town. Continuity with our idea of the human world is assured by young couples in Chumo going off into a willow wood to copulate (or whatever), and North Owl and her bratty cousins entertaining themselves by annoying the couples. Difference and change—for the Kesh as much as for us—is indicated by North Owl's grandfather. He has changed from his middle name of Potter to (probably) a last name of Corruption, a name that bothers Valiant (13). Corruption tells Valiant and us, 'Your body is not real' and performs a trick upon himself and then North Owl demonstrating the maxim: he passes a potter's paddle through his hand and then through North Owl's arm. Corruption says, 'This North Owl might come to the Warriors,' teaching her a new word, with Valiant responding, 'No chance of that. Your Warriors are all men,' with Corruption answering back, 'She can marry one.' Willow may have been 'frightened by the power her father had shown'; North Owl seems impressed (14).

Very soon, North Owl sees men of the Condor for the first time and learns that her father may return, news that initially causes her to have a momentary but frightening vision and keep repeating 'I don't want it to eat you' (16). Nothing comes of the Condor visit for a while, and North Owl goes on being, mostly, a normal eight-year-old of her people: including one who recognizes dirt as 'the mother of my mothers,' and kinship with Coyote (21-22).

North Owl sees a Condor gyring one day: 'Nine times it turned in the air about my town, and then completing the heyiya-if flew gliding slowly into the northeast,' over North Owl, convincing her the Condor sought her (23). Her mother calls North Owl 'Condor's Daughter,' as if it were a name (24), and then news of the Condor arrive, and with it a debate. Some say the Condor should be kept out of the Valley, that they're sick, 'that they have their heads on crooked,' and that for ten years there have been Valley people emulating the Condor, the 'men of the Warrior's Lodge in the Upper Valley, and what are Warriors but people who make war?' The speaker of North Owl's heyimas (to North Owl, centrally meaning something like 'school') sees no problem: 'They can do us no harm. We walk the gyre.' He is answered with 'And they walk the wheel, and the power builds!', a line we are not going to understand until we return to it after reading 'Flicker' on wheels of power and understanding what 'gyres' mean to the Kesh (the image of the Way). In this loaded context, North Owl finds a feather: 'It was dark, stiff, thin, and long. I knew what it was: it was the word I must learn to speak.' North Owl tries to give the feather to Cave Woman, who was 'very old, wise, and weak.' Cave Woman refuses the gift, saying it was for North Owl. 'Heya,' she says—'Heya, Condor's Daughter, in the dry land, think of the creeks running! Heya, Condor's Daughter, in the dark house, think of the blue clay bowl!' The dry land in the universe of Earthsea is the land of death; here it is that symbolically, and the City of the Condor. The dark house is usually the grave; here it is symbolically that, plus, I think, the house of North Owl's father's family (25; see also 359). I don't know what 'the blue clay bowl' might be, but North Owl is of the Blue Clay, associated with fresh water and Earth and game animals ([46], 420). North Owl denies being the Condor's Daughter, but Cave Woman responds 'It seems the Condor says you are,' and North Owl takes the phallic feather (Selinger 137). 'Seeing it in the lamplight, dead black, longer than an eagle feather, I began to feel proud that it had come to me. If I had to be different from other people, then let my difference be notable, I thought' (25).

When North Owl is nine (another Le Guinian nine), her father returned to the Valley. Looking back, the adult Stone Telling knows that he was 'Terter Abhao, True Condor, Commander of the Army of the South, who was off duty with his troops for the autumn and winter, awaiting orders for the spring campaign—who returns to be rejected by the town but accepted immediately and without recriminations by his wife and daughter. To North Owl, her father was home and that was that: 'He was home...our family was whole; now everything was as it should be, balanced, complete; and so it would not change' (29-30).

The rest of Part One is the story of Abhao's stay in the Valley, especially North Owl's response to him and his men, until, inevitably, he leaves.

When she first sees her father's soldiers, North Owl isn't sure what to make of them and tries out theories. 'They all dressed alike and looked alike,' so perhaps they are 'a herd of some kind of animal'—not a human animal, either, since, if they had language, she couldn't understand it. Or perhaps they were crazy or just very stupid, with Abhao 'the only real person among them' (31). Stone Telling's recalled perceptions and thinking are our introduction to the military seen with an innocent eye, or at least seen by someone ignorant of military customs in our world. North Owl's observations demean the military (as Le Guin intends) and defamiliarize uniforms, inviting us to see the weirdness of dressing a whole band of men identically and wonder what function the uniforms fulfill.[383] And here that sense of wonder isn't just a virtue in readers of SF but an ethical imperative: the organizers of the Condor military and those in our world are neither crazy nor stupid (Wytenbroek 334-35). More exactly, they are very

---

[383] Uniforms first became necessary to allow (relative) strangers to fight alongside each other and distinguish «friends» from «enemies». Beyond this primary use, they mark position in bureaucracy and rank in a hierarchy, abstract identification with a unit too large to bond with, and perform other functions. Cf. rudimentary uniforms among enemy army in *King Dog*.

much like Herman Melville's Ahab's brief insight into himself, 'namely, all my means are sane, my motive and my object mad' (250; ch. 41). Another naive observer, Shevek at the climax in Urras in *The Dispossessed*, gets a sudden insight into 'why the army was organized as it was' and concludes, 'It was indeed quite necessary' (245, ch. 9). In Kesh terms, the Condor have their heads on, but their heads are on backwards.

'Kills' in the Valley is a stranger in a strange land, but an aristocratic one, too arrogant to learn to behave appropriately in the Valley, since he is certain that his way is the only way for a True Condor: 'I am not a *tyon*,' he tells Willow: not a farmer, not a peasant. 'I am a commander of three hundred in charge of an army, I am— There are things a man can do and cannot do' (32). In terms of traditional Western European culture, what would come after the 'I am' is 'an officer and a gentleman.' And being 'gentle' means severe limitations of the kinds of work one may do without losing face; a gentleman, ordinarily, may *not* do subsistence farming or build huts (cf. Falco in *EoH* on Victorians being City people, not peasants [19; ch. 2]). Valiant remains quiet, 'but she could not hide her contempt for a man who would not herd or farm or even chop wood. He, holding herders and farmers and woodcutters in contempt, found this hard to bear.' And Willow loves Kills too much to insist that he work (31).

North Owl enjoys her father. For one thing, he has the largest horse she's ever seen and takes her for rides, giving her an aristocrat's view of the world—that of a cavalier, knight, caballero: a horseman and a gentleman. He also introduces her to a variety of thrill unavailable among the Kesh. One day, when his troops are building a bridge, Abhao has North Owl yell 'Now!' in his language as loud as she can. Each times she does so, '...the men working would drop the piledriver, a big stone in a pulley. I heard my high, thin voice and saw ten strong men obey it, over and over. So I first felt the great energy of the power that originates in imbalance, whether the imbalance of a weighted pulley or a society. Being the driver not the pile, I thought it was fine' (32).

North Owl is not the only one in the Valley to be attracted to such power. We have heard of Warrior Lodges growing up among the Kesh, and soon learn that they are organized by men who imitate the Condor in following a military or militaristic life (as North Owl's grandfather has done). When Warriors from Chumo and Kastoha-na arrive, there is a mild confrontation with the Condor. To start, it was wrong to build a bridge 'without consulting either the River or the people who lived alongside it'—and why a bridge at all? (33). Because, Abhao explains, the Condor wish to get their supply wagons across the river and don't want to go out of their way. Why not ford or 'carry things across by the ferry'? Because 'Soldiers don't carry loads on their backs.' Besides, 'Men of the Condor are not only brave fighters but great engineers. The roads and bridges in the lands around the City of the Condor are the wonder of the age' (34). Like the ancient Romans of the Republic and early Empire and, until recently, the Americans, the Condor are great builders, and builders build. To the people of the Valley, Abhao and his troops are building in their home: 'This Valley is our house, where we live,' and they don't need roads or bridges (or outside meddlers) to get around in their own house. A woman of great power calls Kills 'child' and suggests he needs more education. Having trouble arguing with women (or even talking to women in front of his men [34]), Abhao says 'The decision is neither mine nor yours to make or change'; the 'Roads will be widened, bridges will be build. Do not provoke the anger of the Condor!' (35).

What we have in this minor confrontation in *Always Coming Home* is less a misunderstanding than a confrontation between two groups of people who see the world in different ways and therefore have irreconcilable goals. The Condor wish to impose their corporate will upon the Kesh and everyone else, and the Condor are much more heavily armed than the Kesh and much more ready to kill people to get their way. This is not a misunderstanding but a nonviolent version of the confrontations in *The Word for World Is Forest* (1972), *The Dispossessed* (1974), and, preeminently, *The Eye of the Heron* (1978). North Owl notes that Abhao's 'head was not on backwards' (35); he could learn the Valley ways. He's just not going to because he's been raised as a narrow-minded, aristocratic snob who doesn't feel a need to learn the ways of his inferiors.

We do get a minor misunderstanding when Terter Abhao says to his wife, 'We must go before your World Dance, Willow,' meaning by 'we' he and his troops (39). Willow understands 'we' as 'you and I' because, Pandora tells us in a note, he has used the form of 'we' that 'includes the person addressed, and a form of the verb 'goes' which implies going a short distance for a short while,' so Willow assumes he's inviting her for a walk (42). Two speakers of English might equally miscommunicate if a wife assumes the primary 'we' for her husband is himself and his family. That may indeed be the case, with Kills, if we see his family as the Terter clan among the Condor people. In any event between an order from the Condor (his sovereign and commander-in-chief) requiring him to leave his Kesh wife and child, and his wife and child's desire that he stay, he chooses to obey the Condor. And Willow figures this out quite quickly and tells him if he goes not to come back.

Willow puts Abhao's clothes and red rugs outside the door and Willow's Blue Clay relations explain to him 'that a man may come and go as he likes, and a woman may take him back or not as she likes, but the house is hers, and if she shuts the door he may not open it.' Abhao insists 'But she belongs to me—the child belongs to me' and is mocked in what would be a comic scene if it were not narrated from the point of view of the pained North Owl (40). Part One ends with Abhao's departure, asking North Owl to wait for him, and with Willow going back to the name of Towhee, her name as a child (41). Abhao follows his orders, putting military business before his family. As with Rulag in *The Dispossessed*, 'The work comes first'; we are to understand but disapprove—and disapprove far more than with Rulag, whose work did not center on killing people (see *TD* ch. 4, 100 for the quotation).

If one reads through *Always Coming Home* beginning to end, Part Two of Stone Telling is introduced with the last subsection of Time and the City, 'Time in the Valley.' This section includes a Valley Origin Myth; except we must note that it is 'a' myth, one of them, not *the* myth; and the 'myth' we hear from Red Plum may be more of a tale or a story she made up (165). It is a *narrative*, in any event, both similar to Le Guin's other origin myths—the Orgota Creation Myth and Meshe's vision in *The Left Hand of Darkness*, the Segoy stories in the Earthsea trilogy (and their revision in *Tehanu*), the rise of Atlantis—and different from them. The myth in 'Time in the Valley' starts in chaos: 'not light not dark, nothing moving nothing thinking. The sea was all mixed up with the dream, death and eternity were the same...no edges, no surfaces, no insides. Everything was in the middle of everything and nothing was anything.... In the sea and air and dirt the mortal souls were mixed in, mixed up, and they were bored, bored with no change and no moving and no thinking.' So they start moving about, 'falling a little, dancing a little' and making a little bit of noise: 'The was the first thing, the noise, the first thing made. They made that music, those mortal souls. They made the waves, the intervals, the tones.... That is what the world is still singing if you know how to listen': the music of the world, here, not the music of the spheres. So in the beginning was music, and with the music comes differentiation (*ACH* 166): things drew apart and organized into 'outsides and insides...things and spaces between things.' And among the least things in the new world, among the dust-motes and sand-grains, was the Coyote soul (in North American Indian folklore, the classic Trickster). 'The coyote soul wanted more kinds of music, chords with more voices, disharmonies, crazy rhythms, more goings on.' Coyote soul 'pulled itself together out of everywhere' and thereby 'left gaps behind, holes in the world, empty places. By unmaking it made darkness. So light came in to fill the holes: stars, sun, moon, planets came to be' (167). Coyote has created the world of Sky ([47]).

Across the gaps come rainbows and on the rainbows are the Four-House people who call out to Coyote. Coyote, though, can only sing her song (i.e., howl), so the Four-House people call out words to her to teach her to speak, 'and their words were all the people of the earth,' people in Kesh terms: including bears, pond-scum, condors, and lice. The peoples of both earth and sky laugh at Coyote, so she runs off (167) to and into a local mountain—or a mountain the myth teller gets to claim tentatively for their own local mountain—and eats hot volcanic things, and sulks. 'In there...she went into herself, deep in, and made there in the darkness the he-coyote.... There in the mountain she gave birth to him. While he was being born...he shouted, 'Coyote is talking!...'' Coyote nurses he-coyote, and when he is grown they mate, setting an example for all the other people of the world, who mate (and establish thereby the Moon Dance, when human people have a ritual orgy). Coyote and he-coyote having left, the mountain is now hollow, and inside it, 'in the heyimas of the wilderness... this hollow filled with people, human people all crammed together.' Their origin? Maybe from he-coyote's afterbirth, maybe from Coyote's turds, maybe from Coyote's words made flesh, or maybe not. The volcano erupts, spewing out the human people. The ones who landed closest to the mountain—the people of the local teller—hit the ground softest, and so got less sense knocked out of them than other folk (which is why to this day locals are smarter than strangers): 'Anyway, so here we are, the children of Coyote and the Mountain, we are their turds and their words' (168).[384]

The rest of this subsection is on time-keeping and calendars and the general resemblance of the Kesh to the Indians of Northern California in not being much concerned with exactness of time keeping.[385] Pandora discusses time with Gather: a man of 60, an expert in using the Exchange, a student of domestic architecture, 'whose lifelong passion has been the retrieval of data concerning certain doings of human beings in the Valley of the Na. At last we have met a historically minded person....' (169). Except she hasn't, exactly. Gather 'spatializes time; it is not an arrow, not a river, but a house, the house he lives in' (171-72). Pandora is frustrated and leaves Gather, walking off with the Archivist of Wakwaha. 'If you don't have a history,' Pandora says to the Archivist, 'how am I to tell your story?' The Archivist asks for a definition of history, and Pandora quotes, 'the study of Man in Time.' The Archivist is silent.

> 'You aren't Man and you don't live in Time,' I say bitterly. You live in the Dream Time.'
> 'Always,' says the Archivist of Wakwaha. 'Right through Civilisation, we have lived in the Dream Time.'...
> After a while...[the Archivist] says, 'Tell about the Condor. Let Stone Telling tell her story. That's as near history as we have come in my day, and nearer than we'll come again, I hope.' (172)

And, if one is reading linearly, this brings one to Stone Telling Part Two. If one is looking at Le Guin's canon spatially, structurally—compare the Dream Time among the Athsheans in *Word for World* (1974), and the view of civilization in 'Buffalo Gals...' (1987 [*BG*]) and of history in 'A Man of the People' (1995 [*FWF*]) and 'Another Story' (1994 [*FIS*]).

Part Two (173-201)

Stone Telling Part Two begins with repeating that Willow had left her middle name and had gone back to Towhee, her first name, a problematic choice since it went 'against the earth.' Moving on in the story, Stone Telling tells us that her love has gone to her father when he said farewell to her

---

[384] Cf. and contrast *Adam* (Man) as dust + breath (Gen. 2.4-7), and humans as mud (*EoH*).
[385] A. L. Kroeber's *Handbook* Index has no entries for 'time' or 'calendar.' See also *Handbook* 177 (ch. 11) for the usual lack of a word among the original Californians for 'year,' and for people not keeping track of their ages.

and asked her to wait for him. 'I thought I did not love my mother at all.' Aside from a re-enactment of a common mother-daughter conflict, North Owl's choice of beloved parent serves a psychological function for her: 'My loyalty to him made my difference from other people a virtue, and gave unhappiness both a reason and a term,' centrally in the chronological sense of 'term,' until Kills returns, but potentially with a pun: the reason and word for 'unhappiness' is 'Kills' (173).

As the story goes on, the political becomes the personal for North Owl as her grandfather moves back in to help organize the town of Sinshan for the Warriors. In the two years since Abhao had left 'the Warriors had been doing more and more things the Bay Laurel boys'—the Lodge in Tachas Touchas that had fought the Pig People (129)—'supposed to do—scouting, watching the outside ridges, making weapons, training people in the use of guns, having trials of strength and endurance, and teaching various kinds of fighting' (175). North Owls' beloved cousin, Hops, becomes a Warrior and takes the middle name 'Spear,' whose phallic suggestions amuse North Owl (175-76). The household becomes strongly involved with not only the Warriors but also the Lamb Lodge: 'a kind of woman Warriors' (176).

North Owl is caught up in the tension in her town. Spear tells her the new teaching 'that there had never been sacredness in rocks or springs, but in the mindsoul, the spirit only. The rock and the springs and the body, he said, were screens that kept the spirit from true sacredness, true power.' North Owl disagrees and says sacredness, heyiya, 'was the rock, it was the water running, it was the person living.' If the person breaks the relationship and says, 'The sacredness has gone out of it,' then the person had changed, not the rock. Coincident with North Owl's turning thirteen, there is a change in custom significantly juxtaposed with the introduction of this new philosophy. The Kesh had their custom of 'living on the Coast': a period of abstinence from sex in early adolescence (see 'Living on the Coast,' in the Back of the Book [488-89]). The change the Warriors introduced was 'to forbid the young men even to speak to adolescent girls' (179). As we know from Irena's pain when her brother Michael deserts her for the world of macho in *The Beginning Place*, this is a bad sign. Readers of just *Always Coming Home* have the point made for them by North Owl's adopted grandfather, Ninepoint. Ninepoint's biological grandson had gone over to the Warriors and taken the name 'Vile,' and Ninepoint accuses him of arrogance and implies that the lot of them may be 'so afraid of girls you have to make war on them.' Or so afraid of themselves that they have to fight themselves. Corruption comes to speak contemptuously of all women, and Valiant finally accuses him of 'trying to be like those Condor men, who are so afraid of women they run...away from their own...to rape women they don't know!' (179). We will see more of the Condor shortly, but insofar as we get within the story a psychological explanation of why they do what they do (or sexists generally do) the answer seems to be fear—a very popular and plausible theory. Keep in mind, though, North Owl's pleasure in 'the power that originates in imbalance' (32).

North Owl comes to see her absent father as a symbol of her freedom and strength and asserts to her household, 'I am a Condor woman!' (180).

And womanhood of some sort she is about to embark on. Just before the party for her entry into the Blood Lodge, she talks with Spear, who asks her who she is, now, and who may hint at regret that sexual love between them is taboo. For a moment 'he had forgotten about being the Warrior who turned away and the Man and the Self. He had sat by the dry creekbed and the soul of the water had come into him' (181). And they talk and Spear leads with her the linedance that is important to her 'Blood singing' (181, 183). Shortly thereafter, though, Spear returns to the Warrior way and avoids her and will not speak to her (183). She follows after him in desperate infatuation and her personal hang-up with him becomes political. She was 'swallowed up' in her love and had become 'the servant' of that love. And so she joins the Lamb Lodge, where they 'spoke of love, of service, of obedience, of sacrifice' for the love of a Warrior man as unambiguously good things—as they are in the Religion of Love in the Romance tradition and in the Imitation of Christ (the Lamb of God) in the Christian tradition. North Owl accepts such teachings for her love of Spear. Looking back, Stone Telling's sees her year in the Lamb Lodge as 'a lie, a denial of my own knowledge and being, and yet a truth at the same time. Almost everything is double like that for adolescents....' As implied earlier in Clear's 'Commentary on the War with the Pig People' (*ACH* 133-34), 'The Lambs and Warriors were houses for adolescents, people who were not able to choose their own way yet, or unwilling ever to do so' (184). Soldiers, clearly, want others to structure their lives for them—or at least soldiers acquiesce in the structuring—and, perhaps, free them from the pain of freedom; Stone Telling suggests the same is true for romantic girls and girl-women who wish lives limited to 'loving, serving, obeying, sacrificing.'

At a low point in her relationship with her family—when North Owl has finally dropped the emotional big one and said to her grandmother, 'I hate you!'—Terter Abhao returns (185). He gives her a new name, Terter Ayatyu (Woman Born Above Others, of the clan of the Terter), and takes her away to live among the Condor (186-87). This is the first turning point, or major hinge, of the story and it leads to Stone Telling as a stranger being introduced to the strange land of the Condor, the Dayao. In terms of plot, Part Two takes us to Stone Telling's installation in the Terter household and her acceptance as granddaughter by her father's father, Terter Gebe, the clan chief. In terms of getting done the work of the story, the crucial point is a brief ethnography of the Condor, and 'a history' (192).

Briefly, in terms of their ethnography and history, the Dayao are well on their way to epitomizing (in a *mâshâl* as satire and wish) The Big Mistake in the evolution of our societies.

The Condor as a man is Mumford's early Bronze Age King given a local habitation and a name (and some high technology): Genghis Khan or some Aryan chieftain converted to a city-based, militant, postMosaic monotheism; Joshua leading Israel into a Canaan with a much smaller and more pacific population.[386] The Condor as a man is a temporarily successful Akhnaton, starring in an unBiblical epic celebrating the failure of Egypt to become an Empire. Alternatively, we may see the Condor people as relatively high-technology Spartans: the women-avoiding militarists of Greece, conquerors and enslavers of the helots.[387] In their combination of technology and hierarchy, the Condor people are in a line of Le Guin's thought going back to the Gdemiar in 'Semley's Necklace' (1964); more importantly here, the Condor people are the culmination of a line of thought that Le Guin had been nursing as a minor theme since *Planet of Exile* (1966).

In *Planet of Exile*, 'a new time' had come. Among the native peoples, the Gaal had stopped thinking of time and space in their traditional ways. Time to them had been 'a lantern lighting a step before, a step behind—the rest was indistinguishable dark.... They looked ahead only to the next season at most. They did not look down over time but were in it....' For the Gaal until recently, 'space was not a surface on which to draw boundaries but a range, a heartland, centered on the self and clan and tribe....' The Gaal had started to think of time and space in a civilized way, 'in the linear, imperialistic fashion' (*PE* 74; ch. 9). A ' great man' arose among the Gaal who 'united all their tribes and made an army of them.' The Gaal stopped raiding and started instead 'besieging and capturing Winter Cities in all the Ranges along the coast, killing the Spring-born men, enslaving the women, leaving Gaal warriors in each city to hold and rule it over the Winter. Come Spring, when the Gaal come north again, they'll stay,' holding the lands they've conquered (*PE* 23; ch. 2). The Condor, finally, are the Basnasska Nation from *City of Illusions* (1967) settled down; I picture them as the Basnasska Nation in the City of the Shing, with the Shing teaching them the Terran imperialist, macho monotheist mode, i.e., how to be *truly* bad.

In a 'Carrier-Bag' ethnography of the Condor, I'd say the following are the most important points noted or shown in Parts Two and Three:

• The Condor people are 'at war with every people' between the City of Man and the Valley of the Na (192), and, in theory, at war with everyone

---

[386] A. L. Kroeber describes the Aryans who entered the Punjab as a 'cityless, hut-dwelling, cattle-raiding, uncommercial Vedic people,' with a culture that was tribal, without walls, 'unbound, ready to pack up and move without being essentially nomadic; half peasantlike and half aristocratic; an uncitified semicivilization, pioneer rather than backwoods' (*Anthropology* 749; § 305)—rather like the early Condor and in some ways like the White Anglos who initially came to California.

[387] Ca. 650 BCE, a Messenian revolt seriously scared the Spartan overlords, leading them to divide their population 'into three classes: the Spartans, the *perioikoi* ['dwellers around'], and the helots': i.e., professional soldiers, villagers who lived as second class citizens, and state-owned serfs (Swain 1.315-16). Male Spartans avoided women more but were possibly less sexist than male Athenians.

until they bring everyone 'under the wing of the Condor'—or kill them all (194).

• In the City of Man, the men will 'blind the eye or cut off the hand of a woman or farmer who writes a single word'; writing is sacred and limited to the True Condor elite, with only the One-Warriors, a kind of warrior priesthood, literate to a high degree. The Word of One is absolute truth, and 'That word—'One'—is the end of talking as well as of writing, under the Condor's wing....' (192).

• The Condor status system starts with the One at the top, God. ('Hear, O Israel, the LORD our God, the LORD is one' [Deut. 6.4; qtd Mark 12.28-30]). Next under One is One's messenger, The Condor. 'Certain men belonging to certain families are called True Condors'; others, also of high status are the 'One-Warriors. No other people are called Condors. Men who are not of those families are all called *tyon*, farmers, and must serve the True Condors' (as Helots served the Spartans or European serfs served aristocrats or Japanese peasants served nobles and warriors or American peons served the gentlefolk in the great house). Women of elite families are called 'Condor Women' and are inferior in rank to Condor Men but superior to and 'may give orders to tyon and hontik. The hontik are all other women, foreigners, and animals' (i.e., nonhuman animals, 'lower' animals in the view satirized in the Condor).

• Stone Telling correctly sees that the City of Man is 'civilisation' and that to use *civilized* as a compliment and *barbaric* as an insult is problematic (193).

• Upon conquering a city, The Condor 'killed and burned men and children and kept women to be fucked by Dayao men,' penning the women with the cattle (193-94).[388]

• The City of Man is built rectilinearly, 'with walls of black basalt,' a 'magnificent bridge,' 'machines and engines of work and war'—a phrase I can picture delighting Lewis Mumford—and many other 'marvelous products of handmind.' Stone Telling summarizes: 'All I saw was great, and straight, and hard, and strong....' (194).

• Condor houses reflect 'the winter dugouts and summer tents' the tribe used when they were 'nomads of the Plains of Grass,' except in The City they're all-electric, usually brightly lit, and 'very warm and comfortable, encompassing' (*ACH* 194 [see *LHD* 117 , ch. 8]). Stone Telling speculates that 'maybe their health as a people was in being nomads.' When they built a city and lived in it, they 'locked their energy into the wheel, and so began to lose their souls' (196).

• In a land low on metals, the Condor have plenty, and the City, as a whole, seems wealthy. 'But their wealth did not flow; they did not give with pleasure' (195), so by Kesh standards they were poor.

---

[388] Cf. the destruction of Troy by the Acheans, with the subsequent slaughter and taking the women for slaves, as described and shown in *The Trojan Women* by Euripides (415 BCE). Cf. and contrast regulations for Israelite holy war: Deut. 20.10-18.

- Condor women 'lived under siege all their lives' and are rarely allowed to be alone; Stone Telling says she was *never* left by herself. As far as Stone Telling can find out, the only work Condor women did or were allowed to do was spinning and sewing (195).
- Condor men would rape foreign women taken as slaves, but they would marry only Condor women (196). The Condor women are kept in under a regimen Stone Telling calls 'a household arranged like a himpipen,' i.e., a pen for oversized guinea pigs (199).
- Condor society is absolutely hierarchized and militarized: 'Everything among the Dayao had to have a chief. If two of them were together, one or the other was chief.[389] Even when people worked together one of them was chief of the work, as if working were making war...' (199).
- Women are not included in the life of the mind of the Condor; 'they are kept in but left out.' Stone Telling finds it notable that 'It was not men there, but women, who told me that women have no souls' and so don't need to learn about 'the soul's way' (200).
- Except for a 'pretty wife,' all wives must comes with dowries; and it is a noteworthy point if a man 'never beats his wife' (*ACH* 345; Stone Telling Part Three [cf. and contrast *EoH* 24; ch. 2]).
- Condor's wives are 'expected to have babies continuously,' in a big-litter theory appropriate to a warring people (345), but the peasant women 'aborted more often than they bore' (349).
- Adulteresses are 'killed by the husband's family...in public,' in a formal execution because the wife belongs to the husband (346; as contrasted with murderous 'jealousy and sexual rage,' which Stone Telling accepts). Indeed, punishments generally are violent, frequent, and severe, and directed toward underlings (348); the Condor also practice group punishment, killing ten 'hontik of the City...as punishment or payment for the deaths of...ten Condor killed' at a distant mine (353). California Indians would understand killing members of another family if the killer of a member of your family didn't pay for the loss to your family; Stone Telling, taking a more philosophical view, sees group punishment as a sign of binary thinking: The killing of random slaves for punishment or payment 'was fair, if all Condors were one and all non-Condors the other: either this, or that' (353).[390]

---

[389] Cf. Shevek on Urras watching two incompletely indoctrinated boys (*TD* 118; ch. 5). Note that in the Great Chain of Being—standard Western theory among the educated elite from ca. Aristotle into the eighteenth century (with residues unto today)—there is a rank for everything and everybody.

[390] *Either/Or*: 1843 work by Søren Kierkegaard establishing the basic premise of modern Existentialism in the need for individual, conscious, responsible choices. Alluded to by Heather Lelache in *LoH* (90; ch. 7). In this passage on the Condor, Le Guin attacks thinking in binary oppositions; she consistently supports conscious, responsible choices, what the Kesh would think of as acting mindfully.

• Dayao women, even among the elite, come to think like slaves and feel it necessary to lie to men, usually, 'smiling and agreeing with everything and pretending' ignorance (358-59).

• Dayao women feel insecure outside the walls of a father's or husband's house 'because to Dayao men all women unprotected by a man are victims' (360).

Stone Telling ends Part Two summarizing what she can infer about the ideology of the Condor—starting with their theology; this passage is crucial for ordering the data about the evils of Condor culture (everything, mostly, except their cooking) and determining what Le Guin is up to in *Always Coming Home* and what she had been leading up to in her teaching works for nearly two decades.

> One made everything out of nothing. One is a person, immortal. He is all-powerful [and a 'he'—RDE]. Human men are imitations of him. One is not the universe; he made it, and gives it orders. Things are not part of him nor is he part of them, so you must not praise things, but only One. The One, however, reflects himself in the Condor; so the Condor is to be praised and obeyed. (200)

Alternatively put, 'I believe in one God, the Father Almighty, maker of heaven and earth' *ex nihilo*, 'and all things visible and invisible' (Nicene Creed), followed by very standard divine right of kings theory (and Condor theory is only a *slightly* stronger version of the divine right theory one can find in the Elizabethan Homily on 'Good Order and Obedience to Rulers and Magistrates').

The theology goes on to present a Great Chain of Humanity—but with Platonic «reflection» metaphors as much as Aristotelian theory—moving down from The Condor to the True Condors and One-Warriors, 'who are all called Sons of the Condor or Sons of the Son' (as Christians believe in 'one Lord, Jesus Christ, the only begotten Son of God' [Nicene Creed]). The Sons of the Sons, as 'reflections of the reflection of One' are also to 'be praised and obeyed.' Peasants are still reflections, if very dim ones, so are counted as human beings, if barely. 'No other people are human,' and only human people—recalling that the Kesh use 'people' to mean 'beings'—count in the Condor system. 'The hontik...have nothing to do with One at all; they are...unclean, dirt people. They were made by One to obey and serve the Sons.' That last part gets 'a little complicated,' and contradictory, 'since Condor's Daughters gave orders to tyon [farmers] and talked about them as if they were dirt people,' a contradiction found, not coincidentally, in Western racist, sexist, and class-defining theory.

Stone Telling speculates that things 'must have been very different when the Dayao were nomads, but it may have started then, too, as a matter of sexual jealousy, the chief men trying to keep their wives and daughters 'clean,' and the women holding themselves apart from the strangers they met along their way, and finally all of them coming to think that to be a person at all is to be separate from and apart from everyone and everything' (200). This gets at the 'Judeo' part in 'Judeo-Christian religion': the nationalist part of Jewish doctrine (opposed to the Universalist part) that praises God for not making 'us like the heathens of the earth, nor fashioned up like the godless of the land.'[391] This part of Condor belief also satirizes doctrines that define purity through separation: 'Blessed is the...Ruler of the Universe, who separates' not just Israel from the heathen but 'sacred from profane' (*Gates of Prayer* 641). If 'To Be Whole Is To Be Part' (*TD* 68; ch. 3), and if the world is already sacred, then radical separation as a way to holiness is a big part of The Big Mistake. It is a very common mistake, hardly limited to Western monotheism: Cf. Arha at Atuan as the 'solitary, untouched priestess, a holy thing' (*Tehanu* 56; ch. 5). In being *set apart*, Arha has been sacralized: 'For Émile Durkheim, sacredness referred to those things in society that were forbidden or set apart...,' as suggested of the etymology of 'sacred' from Latin *sacer*, 'set off' (Streng 123).

The final parallel is primarily a satire against Apocalyptic Christianity. The Condor believe that even as there 'was a time when One made everything, there will be a time when everything will stop being, when One will unmake everything. Then will begin the Time Outside of Time. One will throw away everything except the True Condors and One-Warriors who obeyed him in every way and were his slaves. They will become part of One then, and be forever (201; see The Revelation to John 7.1-22.5).[392] As we learn later in the words of a Condor hymn, 'In One...There is no death!' (352).

Part Three (340-86)

Stone Telling Part Three completes the Catalog of Abuses against the Condor, shows them as a Judeo-Christian analog/sexist-militaristic culture, and completes the story. In terms of the political overplot of the rise and fall of the Condor, Part Three shows the fall foreshadowed in Stone Telling's earlier observation that even while stealing and slaying in the Volcano country and spreading the disease of their ideology among the Kesh, the Condor 'were dying' (194). In terms of the more personal history of Stone Telling, Part Three tells the story of her marriage among the Condor, her aborting the fetus produced by a marital rape, her giving birth to a

---

[391] From the nationalistic opening of the *Aleynu* (*High Holiday Prayer Book*, e.g., 251); this is balanced, from a Jewish point of view, later in the prayer, with the Universalist idea that all people will one day come to worship the God of the Jews. The formulation, however, is unlikely to please a Kesh scholar, except for making explicit just Who, primarily—though not exclusively—is 'One': 'The Lord shall be King over all the earth; on that day shall the Lord be One, and His name One' (*Service* 59, Zechariah 14.9).
[392] See also 'Legends' 8 and Le Guin's 'Ketterer' letter 139: her statement that '...all apocalypses are fake to me.'

daughter, and her return to her people to become 'Woman Coming Home,' and then Stone Telling: a wife again, then mother and grandmother. Stone Telling, Part Three, is a *mâshâl* bringing to a happy ending the story of the greatest threat to the Kesh and their uncivilized neighbors within their memory. Part Three also brings to a very happy ending the story of Stone Telling, a woman like Ursula K. Le Guin at least insofar as she is a writer, a mother, and one who has lived in two worlds rather liminally, marginalized: in Le Guin's case, marginalized as something of a liberal, a romantic, 'a petty-bourgeois anarchist,' and, necessarily as 'an internal emigree [sic]' ('Response' 45).

In Part Three, Terter Gebe and Terter Abhao fall into disgrace (341-42), and Stone Telling is married off as 'pretty wife' to Retforok Dayat, a younger brother, no soldier or One-Warrior, but from a rich family, and a man who 'never beats his wife' (345). The marriage starts off well enough. Since Stone Telling 'had little happiness,' she will settle for 'pleasure,' and took it, as sex, as frequently as she could—which was fine with Dayat's first wife (346). As alluded to earlier, Stone Telling becomes pregnant twice.

> I aborted the first pregnancy, because my husband had raped me when I told him I did not want him and though I had no contraceptive. A Condor's Daughter would go on and have the child of a rape, but I did not. It was easy to get abortifacient from the tyon, who aborted more often than they bore, and Esiryu [her servant] helped me. Two years later, when I was twenty-one years old, I wanted to became pregnant. Esiryu and Syasip [first wife] were good friends, but I was always bored, because there was nothing to do but spin and sew and talk, always indoors and always among people, never alone and therefore always lonely. I kept thinking that a child would be like the Valley. It would be part of me and I part of it; it would be beloved home. (349)

If the child had been a boy, he'd 'have 'belonged' to' Stone Telling's husband, but 'Since she had decided to be a girl she was unimportant and did not matter to anyone but me and Esiryu and Syasip.' The priest names her Danaryu (Woman Given to One); Stone Telling calls her Ekwerkwe, Watching Quail (351).

The Condor move toward a total war effort, trying to build 'Great Weapons' that will allow them to conquer, everything. About the time Ekwerkwe is born, the Condor bring out Destroyer and the Nestlings: a tank and aircraft (*ACH* 350). Stone Telling describes the tank as 'huge and magnificent,' 'huge and blind, with a thick penis-snout' and three Condors inside. It breaks through the roof of a cave 'and destroyed itself with its own great weight, thrusting and wedging itself into the lava tube,' which makes for some interesting Freudian imagery. More significantly, Stone

Telling dreams of the tank 'moving in the cave, pushing the earth in, crushing darkness.' The tank in the cave is not Ged with his mage-light staff in the labyrinth at Atuan, but an ironic violation (350): the bringing of force into the domain of the Earth Mother, which bothers Stone Telling in her dream but, in world-time, destroys the tank. The aircraft come to naught less symbolically: not enough petroleum for fuel, and the attempt to make alcohol fuel takes up a lot of grain (351). And, as we know from *The World for World Is Forest*, air power isn't of much use against guerrillas, and high-tech cities are very vulnerable to attack from former slaves: '...one person, probably a man or woman who had been a hontik slave and knew where things were and how to behave and talk, came at night and set fire to the fuel storage tanks. They exploded. The person was burned to death, but the Nestlings were left without fuel' (352-53).

Primitive warfare went well for the early kings in part because there were plenty of resources around for what they needed, and only limited communication among the people they were out to subjugate. Post-civilization warfare goes ill for the Condor in part because we civilized folk have depleted the Earth of easily-gotten resources, and because the Condor's neighbors have the Exchange: the computer terminals of the City of Mind are there for a kind of very high-tech e-mail.

In *Always Coming Home* Le Guin deals with what she sees as one of the most serious problems facing utopia: hostile neighbors, specifically armed and dangerous neighbors like the Condor, and all the 'dynamic, aggressive, ecology-breaking cultures' (*LHD* 233) for which they stand. And her last answer to why the imperialist Condor fail is the same satiric, probably inevitable answer she gave in *The Word for World* combined with a common bit of wisdom from the antiwar movement of the late 1960s and early 1970s: 'If you want to stop the War Machine, / Don't feed it.' In *Always Coming Home*, Stone Telling tells us that 'The sacrifices the Dayao were making were to win them wealth and comfort when the Nestlings went out to war. The trouble with the plan was that all the human peoples living anywhere near Dayao country had already moved away'— an option Le Guin consistently endorses, as long as there are places to physically or psychically go to—'or, if they remained, stayed to make war, not to give tribute of food, slaves, or anything else' (352). Perhaps only those with empty hands are truly free because only they are really free to fight obstreperous people like the Condor, and/or move on.

As life got harder, among even the privileged Condor, a number of women want to move away from where 'the finger of light had pointed,' southward 'into more prosperous lands'; and their husbands listen, however much their ideology says women speak nothing of importance. It's a difficult issue for them, especially the women: '...most of them had lived their whole life inside the City, inside the houses, inside the rooms' and were ignorant of the outside world and afraid of it (352). Stone Telling suspects they fear the outside 'because the Dayao said that everything belonged to One,' so they 'forced themselves to think in twos: either this, or that. They could not be [outside] among the many' (352-53 [see Psalm 24.1-2]).

To move or not to move becomes a major issue, hence a major problem since the Dayao lacked democratic or even representative institutions to resolve disputes, 'So ideas became opinions, and these made factions, which diverged and became fixed opponents' (352).

Failure and dissension tend to bring on repression, and the City becomes 'more and more like an ant-hill against which another ant-hill is making war.' The executions of the ten City slaves to make up for the killing of the Condor soldiers at the mine destroys Stone Telling's desire 'to be a woman of the Condor or to follow their way' (353), and the executions of other 'enemies of the Condor' sickened her and scared her: her grandfather had died, and her father was 'chief of the household' of the Terter, a clan in disgrace. She wants her father to go with her and finish their journey, returning to the Valley. The constant boredom of the life of a Condor Woman has returned to her after Ekwerkwe has grown a bit, and now that boredom is punctuated—decorously in time of war—with terror; looking at her father she 'saw that place in front of the Palace in his face, the stakes and the bloody pavement'—a fear of execution for him, herself, and maybe even her child. Plus a growing disgust and what we might call guilt. 'There is no way,' Stone Telling thinks, 'that men could make women into slaves and dependents if the women did not choose to be so. I had hated the Dayao men for always giving orders, but the women were more hateful for taking them,' and Stone Telling grows very angry for her years in the City, possibly years of complicity (355). Stone Telling escapes, with Ekwerkwe and Esiryu, her servant, escaping with her as Stone Telling's friend—and aided by Arda and Dorabadda, two of Terter Abhao's soldiers: 'They had the loyalty prized by the Dayao; they were like sheepdogs, trustworthy, brave, and mindless, doing what another person thought, minding him' (356). One of them is shot and killed the first moment an ambush heard the men speak Dayao (357).

As the ambush indicates, the world outside the City is tense. The mother of a household that puts up Stone Telling and her party complains 'that there was too much war, too much killing going on, that the young men of her house were sick and carried guns, like crazy people' (357).[393] To dramatize this point, Stone Telling recounts her meeting some Warriors of her own people, including Changing Always, who took on the Warrior name Maggot. Maggot greets her as 'North Owl,' and she tells him she's that no longer North Owl but 'Woman Coming Home,' the name which

---

[393] See *TD* on sickness metaphors (96; ch. 4), and note that it's difficult for people without a single transcendent God to speak definitively about 'good' and 'evil'—which is an effective argument for atheism—but which makes it difficult to talk about people who are *bad*. E.g., '...to the Mesopotamians, there was no independent concept of evil. Just disease and ill health. Evil was a synonym for disease'—or so says, plausibly, a character in Stephenson's *Snow Crash* ([1992]: 116; ch. 15).

comes to her (and she chooses) for the middle of her life (358). However much Le Guin privileges change in the aphorisms and symbolism of her work, we should recall from *Lathe of Heaven* that the busy-ness implied by 'Changing *Always*' bodes even worse for this character than 'Maggot,' and Maggot and his warrior associates don't disappoint us. Woman Coming Home is suspicious of them and responds to them with 'The slave mind' she learned in the City, and, as she would respond to Condor men, she lies (358). The Warriors go on to the City, and Woman Coming Home et al. go southwest. To a young man with the Warriors who is of her House, she repeats Cave Woman's words to her: 'My brother, in the dry land, think of the creek running. My brother, in the dark house, think of the bowl of blue clay' (*ACH* 359 [see 25]).

Ekwerkwe comes to enjoy the trip, but Esiryu, away from home, isn't so much 'cautious and mindful of difference'—good things—but just scared: 'To a Dayao woman outside the walls of her father's or her husband's house all men are dangerous,' regarding all women without male protection as victims: 'cunts,' as Esiryu sees herself, 'as something to be raped.' Woman Coming Home names Esiryu 'Shadow Woman,' short form: 'Shadow' (360).

Woman Coming Home arrives home in a flurry of significant words, phrases, numbers, and images:

> I walked singing a song that came to me out of the rain
> and the feathers [she picked up on the way], the words
> given to me:
>
>> 'There is no knowing,
>> only going on,
>> only going by, ah ya hey.
>> I am the great being,
>> the grass bowing.'
>
> When I came back into the Valley of my being, I
> brought this song and the feathers of nine birds from the
> wilderness, the coyote's way; and from the seven years I
> lived in the City of Man I brought my womanhood, the
> child Ekwerkwe, and my friend Shadow. (361)

As George Orr enters the 'sea of being' in dream after the climax of *Lathe*, as Osden goes off into 'the forest of being' at the end of 'Vaster than Empires' (*WTQ* 198)—and as other Le Guinian characters enter decorous symbols of the Dao—so Woman Coming Home returns to the Valley of her being. And Woman Coming Home, Ekwerkwe, and Shadow go to the Blue Clay heyimas (here, meeting house) at Kastoha and arrange for shelter. And as most of the political action takes place offstage at the political climax of *The Left Hand of Darkness*, even so we learn 'that there had been a meeting of the Valley people about the Warriors, and that that lodge had stopped being.' The scholars of the heyimas advise her to post on the Exchange what she knows about 'the doings and intentions of the Dayao people,' which she will do when she gets back to her home town (361).

Woman Coming Home gets to her mothers' house and is admitted but not enthusiastically welcomed. Her grandmother Valiant is dead, but more disturbing is her mother. With the end of the Warriors, the Lamb Lodge also ceased, and her mother turned in on herself. 'Her souls had shrunk away and unmade themselves,' Woman Coming Home thinks; 'that is the danger of going backward in the way she had done when she took back her child-name. She had not gyred but closed the circle.' In her own mind, Woman Coming Home gives her mother her last name: Ashes (365).

Politically, though, the small town of Sinshan seems better. Some walking wounded remain after the Condor crisis, but a sickness 'had gone out of the Valley that had been there when the Condor was there' (365). Shadow likes it. She thought the City hard, 'being was hard. Here's it's soft. * * * Animals live softly. They don't make it hard to live. Here people are animals. * * * Here even the men are animals. Here everybody belongs to everybody. A Dayao man belongs to himself. He thinks everything else belongs to him....' Woman Coming Home says that the Kesh 'call that living outside the world' (366-67). In terms of the satire, we can call it the hard Dayao way of living Life As We Know It, living in civilization, living in a culture that is monotheistic, rationalist, aristocratic, death-denying, death-dealing, high-tech, and macho; a culture that uses 'ideal' as a compliment and 'animal' as an insult, that can set up transcendent Goods that 'justify' mundane horrors.

The love plot of Stone Telling's story gets resolved as the denouement of the story as such, but it is not Stone Telling—melodramatically violating an incest taboo—but Shadow who marries Spear. This brings Spear to a happier ending than we might foresee for Irena's disloyal brother in *The Beginning Place* (1980) or Tenar's ne're-do-well son in *Tehanu* (1990): all youthful males who turn away from women, and turn on them. Spear, though, is lucky enough to live in a good society. Not marrying Spear is just as well for the rational part of Woman Coming Home, who 'felt the Warrior still in him.' Woman Coming Home can now see her father as a life-long soldier but still one who had been 'in mind and heart no warrior at all.' Spear, on the other hand (for a useful binary opposition) was like her comfortably rich husband among the Dayao, 'who though he never fought with his body or weapons made all life into war, a matter of victory or defeat.' She also comes to think that 'People who make life into a war fight it first with people of the other sex...trying to defeat them, to win a victory.' Shadow wouldn't play such a game, 'but all her education among the Dayao had fitted her to play the already-defeated one, the loving enemy' (368).

Woman Coming Home eventually comes to marry, gets rich—i.e., can and does give much—and ends her tale as Stone Telling and 'the grandmother weaving at the loom' (376). She gets the last word on romantic love, before enacting a more stable love:

> Maybe it was because I had seen what the passion of love did to my parents' lives that I kept shy of any man who might have brought such passion into my life. I was just beginning to learn to see and I did not want to be blinded. Neither of my parents had ever truly seen the other. To Abhao, Willow of Sinshan had been a dream—waking life was all elsewhere. To Willow, the Condor Abhao had been all the world—nothing mattered but him. So they gave their great passion and their fidelity to no one, not truly to one another but to people who did not exist, a dream-woman, a god-man, and it was wasted, a gift to no one. My mother had gone out of her own being after that nonbeing, had spent all passion on nothing. Now nothing was left of it or of her. She was empty, cold, poor. (369)

Countless are stories of similar woe, / Like this of Willow and her Abhao—in real life—but we usually want something more pleasing in literature, and we usually get comic romances, romantic comedies, or, with luck, a high-class tear-jerker like *Romeo and Juliet*. Abhao and Willow are not Romeo and Juliet. There is enough in a name in Shakespeare's play, enough enmity between Montague and Capulet, to kill off the young lovers, and a large part of the supporting cast; there is far more significance in the names 'Condor' and 'Kesh.' If we wanted, we could put together the series *Planet of Exile* (1966), *The Eye of the Heron* (1978), and Willow and Kills in *Always Coming Home* (1985), and see Le Guin making '*progress...away from open romanticism, slowly and steadily,*' with no ambiguities about how steady she goes or about what 'romanticism' refers to (headnote to 'Semley's Necklace,' *WTQ* 1)—or Le Guin's changing views on progress. It's not that simple. The Rolery and Jakob pairing in *Planet of Exile* was Le Guin's strongly romantic statement on love conquering lots, if hardly all. But the loves in the slightly earlier *Rocannon's World* are more ambiguous, and Le Guin has gyred around the themes of love and romance for three decades, through *The Beginning Place* (1980) and right up to the love stories in 'A Fisherman of the Inland Sea' (1994), 'The Matter of Seggri' (1994), *Four Ways to Forgiveness* (coll. 1995), and 'Coming of Age in Karhide' (1995). Difference matters; love matters greatly; true love is based in difference—not in romantic love at first sight, but in perceiving the Other, eventually and momentarily, as that person really is: necessarily radically different (an Other), necessarily similar if a sibling at humanity's hearth, a participant in Being. 'Love' is a word of power in *Always Coming Home* and a great passion can be a good thing in Le Guin's canon, but there are matters beyond romantic passion, and there are other powerful and important words.

The last words of the political overplot are comments by Pandora, our editor and annotator, and documents by people more politically engaged than Stone Telling and in some ways more knowledgeable; this set of documents and commentary give both an overview of the Condor people and the views of conscious opponents of the Condor.

Document 1 gives a synopsis of a summary of a history of the Condor, sent because 'People in Rekwit think it important that we stop the Condor people from making trouble.' Here we learn that before their time 'as nomads in the Grasslands and in the desert countries' the Condor may have lived in the Great Lakes region and, in any event, are related linguistically to the peoples of the Great Lakes area. Pandora has problems finding people who think chronologically, but one person in the Rekwit area can state directly that 'About a hundred and twelve years ago' the Dayao 'began to become civilised,' coming under the leadership of Kaspyoda, one of their men, who led them west, died, and was succeeded by a son who started to re-democratize the people but was killed by a cousin, 'a man named Astyoda, calling himself The Great Condor,' who saw the finger of light in the Lava Beds and founded the City (377). In terms of California Indians—arguably not the most relevant group in this case—the closest parallel would be the Wiyot. Like the Yurok, the Wiyot are Northwestern Californians who speak an Algonkin (sic) language: a set of languages centering of the Great Lakes. And they are the only Algonkin speakers in Northwest California who share the fairly common Californian concept of 'a supreme god.' The Wiyot believe in Gudatrigakwitl:

> With Gudatrigakwitl, 'above old man,' we encounter a conception of which there is no trace among the Yurok. He existed before the earth, he made it, made the first man..., made all human beings, animals, acorns, boats, string, other utensils, the weather, even dances. He used no materials and no tools. He merely thought, or joined and spread apart his hands, and things were. He lives now and will exist as long as the world. (A. L. Kroeber, *Handbook* 112, 119)

The Dayao One People, under charismatic leadership, also combine elements of the Mormons—a number of elements from the Mormon migration from the midwest—the Israelites (coming off the desert into Canaan), and Le Guin's Gaal and the post-Shing recreation of Plains Indians in *City of Illusions* (see above).

The second and third documents are from people who agree with the concerned people of Rekwit. Reads of the Serpentine notes that 'much infection has taken place' since the Condor came to the Valley; 'Cults have arisen,' presumably the Warriors and Lamb Lodge. 'If fighting a war is necessary people will come from here to the fighting. If quarantine is possible it would be better'; and Reads asks that news of aggressive acts by the Condor people be entered on the Exchange. The third document notes simply that the Tahets 'have been fighting a war with these sick people for two lifetimes.' And from here Pandora notes 'a flurry and then a steady crossflow of messages through the Exchanges of twenty-two different peoples of the regions.' One notes the depredations of the Condor and says, 'If you try to fight them you had better have guns and bullets. They do.' Another, from a people far away, took up the 'sick' motif. 'Do not fight these sick people, cure them with human behavior.' Pandora tells us that the Rekwit people responded 'tersely, 'You come up north here and do that'' (378).

Pandora gets the penultimate words, noting that had the Condor people attempted to increase their territory or move southward, they 'would have met the concerted resistance by an alliance of all the people in the region. But the Condor dreams of empire were self-defeated.' So, no war. But a major need for an explanation since in the personal, political, and historical experience of most of us, people looking for fights usually find them, and evil, well-armed imperialists usually conquer nicer peoples with fewer weapons. Pandora suggests some possibilities:

• The Condor 'seem to have been unusually self-isolated; their form of communication with other people was through aggression, domination, exploitation, and enforced acculturation. In this respect they were at a distinct disadvantage among the introverted but cooperative people native to the region.' Also, they just couldn't use the Exchange very well. Between their fear of contamination and their dominance hierarchy, the Condor were under strong pressure to restrict use of the Exchange, which they did, limiting it to the priestly caste and The Condor himself (the only one with a personal terminal, as Stone Telling recalls).

There were no documents in the Exchanges figuratively stamped TOP SECRET, and the City of Mind had no qualms in any sense about releasing information about weapons construction. What stopped the Condors' Great Weapons program was 'the absence of the worldwide technological web...of the Industrial Age,' and, as mentioned, the depletion 'of many of the fossil fuels and other materials from which the Industrial Age made itself' (379-80). Pandora notes that even at the height of the Industrial Age (our era) the expense 'of making maintaining, fueling, and operating such machines...was incalculable, impoverishing the planet's substance forever and requiring the great majority of humankind to live in servitude and poverty. Perhaps the question concerning the Condor's failure to build an empire with its advanced weapons is not why did they fail, but why did they try.'

• As Pandora and Le Guin are well aware, the obvious question from anyone with military knowledge is why didn't the Condor 'use their superiority in metals not in a misguided effort to build anachronistic tanks and bombers, but in building up a good arsenal of guns, grenades, and other 'conventional' weapons until they were invincible among the almost defenseless and poorly armed peoples about them?' And Pandora/Le Guin adds significantly: 'Then they might truly have made history!' Or restarted history: either way, a bad thing.

Pandora says that the Valley people might have responded to such questions by observing that 'Very sick people tend to die of their sickness' or that 'Destruction destroys itself.' Pandora/Le Guin adds 'This answer, however, involves a reversal from our point of view. What we call strength it calls sickness; what we call success it calls death' (380). For reversals cf. not only folklore and the Dao and clown traditions but also that somber worldly philosopher, Karl Marx (in *Capital* III.12.3).[394] Marx had a view of reversals that is relevant here: '*In competition* [under Capitalism], *therefore, everything appears upside down* [Larrain: *reversed*]. The finished configuration of economic relations, as these are visible on the surface, in their actual existence, and therefore also in the notions with which the bearers and agents of these relations seek to gain an understanding of them, is very different from the configuration of their inner core, which is essential but concealed, and the concept corresponding to it. It is in fact the very reverse and antithesis of this' (311; also qtd. in different trans. Larrain 220). Militaristic, competitive Condor society is operating in contradiction to its world, a world in which the Condor ideas of strength are weakness. The Condor attempt at conquest fails partly because Le Guin *wills* them to fail, *mâshâl* fashion but also because, *mâshâl* fashion, Le Guin presents a vision of a universe and a social world in which such attempts will fail. And we readers can accept that failure or reject it in terms of what we find plausible.[395] Stranger things have happened. The *mâshâl* worked, so to speak, in *Word for World*; the United States military did withdraw from Viet Nam and most of Indochina. And a motif of history as well as old poetry is *Ubi sunt?*: Where are the empires of yesteryear, from the mini-empires of the Fertile Crescent to the holy city of Akhnaton to the Chinese Warring States to the empires of the first Rome, Byzantium, and then Moscow? Where are the ancient Aryan tribes—or the Thousand-Year Reich that was to come from the twentieth-century revival of Aryan *Herrenmoral*, the morality of the Masters? The Nazi Third Reich lasted a dozen years.

Pandora does *not* deal with what made the war unnecessary, but goes on to suggest something biologically unlikely but quite possible in terms of cultural development and of great ethical interest. She suggests an optimistic, Kropotkinesque version of 'the law of human evolution' (*TD* 177; ch. 7): that 'natural selection had had time to work in social as well as physical and intellectual terms' and that her future Californians (newcomers like the Condor excepted) might be 'healthier'—saner—than she, or we, can understand. 'In leaving progress to the machines, in letting technology go forward on its own terms and selecting from it, with what seems to us excessive caution, modesty, or restraint,' it is possible that 'these people did in fact succeed in living human history with energy, liberty, and grace' (380-81). I'd put it that the Kesh have begun to *live*, *human* history,

---

[394] Hellmut Wilhelm translated the opening line of *Tao te Ching* 40 as 'Reversal is the movement of tao' (where 'Return' is also possible): *Change* 34.
[395] For a different suggestion, see Benford 17.

with our history, the history of civilization, dominion, and destruction—the history of the misuse and abuse of technology—something we muddle through in a prehuman way, and while seriously insane.

The concluding section is 'About a Meeting Concerning the Warriors' Lodge, by Bear Man, a member of the Doctors Lodge (381-86). It also concerns the Lamb Lodge, and the topic of the meeting is the dissolution of those lodges. The argument for the dissolution of the lodges is, as we would expect, that the Condor are sick, 'Their heads are turned backwards,' and that the people of the Valley 'have let people with the plague come into our house,' and 'The people of the Warrior Lodge and some people in the Lamb Lodge have been infected' (381).

If we've read Stone Telling consecutively, we know how this debate comes out. What is most important about it is the final comment by Bear Man and the comments by the Warriors: words in male voices, and finally, after all this talk about sickness, by a physician. Bear Man tells us that he was at the meeting he records and has been thinking about it in the many years since. He has

> come to think that the sickness of Man is like the mutating viruses and the toxins: there will always be some form of it about, or brought in from elsewhere by people moving and traveling, and there will always be the risk of infection. What those sick with it said is true: It is a sickness of our being human, a fearful one. It would be unwise in us to forget the Warriors and the words spoken at Cottonwood Flats, lest it need all be done and said again. (386)

Here, then, is a good chance to be pretty sure of what Le Guin means by 'the sickness of Man': What the Warriors say. And what they say is that they are proud to be Warriors; that they are not sick, but everyone else is. '[Y]ou're dying and don't know it. You eat and drink and dance and talk and sleep and die and there is nothing to you, like ants or fleas or gnats, your life is nothing, it goes nowhere.... We are not insects, we are human people. We serve a higher purpose' (382). Skull of Telina-na, a Warrior, says, 'Our sickness is our humanity. To be human is to be sick. The lion is well, the hawk is well, the oak is well, they live and die in the mindfulness of the sacred and need take no care,' and thus far Skull could be Ged lecturing Arren in *The Farthest Shore* (66; ch. 4). But here Skull comes to a 'But,' and it's not Ged's 'But' about human consciousness and our need to 'learn to keep the balance.' Skull goes on,

> But from us sacredness has withdrawn care; in us is the mind of the sacred. So all we do is careful, and all our effort is to be mindful, and yet we are not whole.... You say that human people are not different from the other animals and the plants. You call yourself earth and stone. You deny that you are outcast from that fellowship, you deny

that the soul of man has no house on earth. You pretend, you build up houses of desire and imagination, but you cannot live in them. (384)

This could be Orestes to Zeus in J-P Sartre's *The Flies*: Skull has reinvented Sartrean Existentialism and accuses his opponents of Bad Faith in denying the human condition in a Godless world. What Skull has to say so far is definitely arguable: we humans are in culture and are conscious, and that far we are 'outside' of nature. Le Guin accepts the fact of *our* disconnection from nature; and since her first published story, 'An die Musik,' she has been advising us to unbuild walls, unbuild houses, and go outside into Nature and dance over the nearest figurative abyss. But then Skull takes a logical leap and shows not a cloven hoof—that's a fable among Christians—but a figurative jackboot. We cannot live in our houses of desire:

In them is no habitation. And for your denying, your lying, your comfort-seeking, you will be punished. The day of punishment is the day of war. Only in war is redemption; only the victorious warrior will know the truth, and knowing the truth will live forever. For in sickness is our health, in war our peace, and for us there is only one, one house. One Above All Persons, outside whom there is no health, no peace, no life, no thing! (384)

A slip here from Orestes into the Prophetic mode, but then quickly into something more ominous for readers with any knowledge of the Heroic doctrine most recently celebrated by the Nazis, and totalitarian word-twisting scrawled across the twentieth century as 'WAR IS PEACE / FREEDOM IS SLAVERY / IGNORANCE IS STRENGTH' (Orwell, *Nineteen Eighty-Four* 17; I.1). And to those who hear the totalitarian allusion, 'One Above All Persons' sounds ominously like *Deutschland über alles* ('Germany over all'). It is one formula for what I see as the complement of the denial of death in The Big Mistake: the setting up of a transcendent Good that is 'Above All Persons,' and upon whose orders men can—and some women, too—with clear consciences, commit massacres, atrocities, horror.[396]

* * * * * * *

As a teaching story, *Always Coming Home* is crucial to Le Guin's canon. It raises the great question of Ecclesiastes and Job *How shall a human being live well, then?*—and does a fair job answering it. Appropriat-

---

[396] In *LHD*, Genly Ai says that the mission he is on 'overrides all personal debts and loyalties.' The person he is talking to responds, 'If so...it is an immoral mission' (*LHD* 104-06; ch. 8).

ing E. M. Forster's injunction on the title page of *Howard's End* (1921), we might put the answer, *'Only connect...'*, except that comes across a little too active for the 'Perennial Philosophy' view that one already *is* connected. Perhaps what we need to do to live well is to recognize our connectedness to people with whom we bond, to our clans and towns and societies, to the Earth, to the cosmos. Among the Kesh, such connectedness is possible. Among the Condors and those who mimic them—corresponding to worshippers of a transcendent One God in our world, to supporters of patriarchy and hierarchy—the connection is denied, showing us a way in which people can live ill.

Always Coming Home may also be seen as the culmination of Le Guin's initial work comparing and contrasting different ways of living in or outside of the world. The Kesh vs. the Condor people completes the pattern by working it out in full detail. And the Kesh vs. the Condor takes to its logical conclusion Le Guin's critique of Western culture: civilization as we know it was a bad idea, a wrong turn, a perversion.

Decorously, *Always Coming Home* may also complete the pattern of controlling symbols as variations on the Yin-Yang. In *The Left Hand of Darkness* (1969) and *The Wind's Twelve Quarters* (1975) the symbol was the Yin-Yang itself. In *The Dispossessed* (1974), the symbol was the Circle of Life: a circle almost completed, but with a break for the Void to come in. In *Eye of the Heron* (1978) it was the ring tree; in *The Compass Rose* (1982), the symbol is our compass with its directions, but supplemented by the Native American stress on Above and Below as directions (*CR* xi). In *Always Coming Home*, the highly stressed symbol is the heyiya-if, 'the figure or image of the heyiya,' i.e. of that which is a 'sacred, holy, or important thing, place, time, or event; connection; spiral, gyre, or helix; hinge; center; change.... To be or to be at the center; to change; to become; Praise; to praise' (512; Glossary). The specific form of the heyiya-if is a mirror-image doubling of 'The Exponential...Life Spiral of Time' symbolizing 'the unity of evolution, learning, perception-hallucination and dreaming,' and (as just a curve) studied by Descartes, Torricelli, and John Bernoulli.[397] Le Guin stresses the heyiya-if's openness and its reversal. 'The Dayao way,' Stone Telling Tells us, 'was without clowns or clowning, without reversal or turning, straight, single, terrible' (201). Under that sentence on the page is the heyiya-if as a printer's mark: spiraling, open, reversing.[398]

Again, the main continuity with Le Guin's earlier works is that there is a symbol, at all, and it is a symbol fairly similar to those in the earlier works. In *King Dog*, also from 1985, the symbol is Shiva/Kali: 'an androgynous dancing god/dess' (20), and the King's dog. In the later works,

---

[397] R. Fisher's Figure 2 in *Voices of Time* 372, reproducing the curve from E. H. Lockwood, *A Book of Curves* (1963).
[398] For the importance of Pandora for what she sees as the open-endedness, the ambiguity of *ACH*, see Franco 30 and passim. On clowning, cf. and contrast Owen's clowning for Natalie in *VFA* (13 f.).

Buffalo Gals and Other Animal Presences (1987) and *Tehanu* (1990), the symbols get still more complex: Coyote and a dancing woman in *Buffalo Gals*, Tehanu herself in *Tehanu*: girl and dragon.

Always Coming Home is pivotal in featuring in its main story a strong but flawed female protagonist, letting her tell her life from girlhood in her grandmother's house to when she becomes the grandmother (375-76). The stakes in Stone Telling's story are high, as is decorous for SF: immediately, the direction of human culture for at least twenty-three peoples in the region, counting the Condor (*ACH* 378; 'Messages Concerning the Condor').[399] Ultimately, perhaps, given human history from the end of the Neolithic to the present, the stakes may be as high as the nature of human culture on Earth. If the Condor win, a portion of humanity on Earth will fall out of nature into culture and history and recapitulate the 'urban revolution' and beginning of the ancient empires, a process that can diffuse, and which, in our world, lead to Life As We Know It (Swain I.59 f.; ch. 3). The fates of at least two approaches to human culture are at stake—at least locally—and yet this is only part of the story; Stone Telling also tells us about her relationships with her mother and father and family, about her one romantic love, about her married life, about fucking and making love, about birthing and motherhood, about escape and finally finding a good relationship.

Always Coming Home is an unBible giving counter myths to compete with those central to the culture of the Judeo-Christian-Rationalist West. And it moves toward a symbol appropriate to the new mythos, the heyiya-if, indeed, but also Coyote. If civilization as we know it says we must accept One Above All Persons, Le Guin suggests that we join those who walk away from the One, necessarily in our world becoming internal émigrés. Southwind says in *Eye of the Heron* (1978), 'So long as we stand and fight, even though we fight with our weapons, we fight their war' (114; ch. 8). Blood Clown of Chumo who responded to the great Existentialist speech of Skull says mockingly 'Outside of One there is nothing, / nothing but women and coyotes' (*ACH* 384). Le Guin will move on, to a large extent with the women and coyotes.

---

[399] Note in 'Dancing to Ganam that 'Ganam is one little city-state on a large planet, which the Gaman call Anam, and the people in the next valley call something else entirely' (*FIS* 142). Even so, the Kesh are one culture on a large and complex world (Le Guin, personal communication).

VII.

BUFFALO GALS AND OTHER ANIMAL PRESENCES

> He is clad in a robe dipped in blood, and the name by which he is called is The Word of God.... From his mouth issues a sharp sword with which to smite the nations, and he will rule them with a rod of iron.... — Revelation 19.13-16 (see also Matt. 10.34-36)

In her Introduction to *Buffalo Gals* (1987), Ursula K. Le Guin gives us a very brief Le Guinian unMessianic vision (so to speak), starting with the way things are now: a cat appears 'And the cat will say,' quoting Rudyard Kipling, '"I am the Cat that walks by himself, and all places are alike to me!" And the Man'—colloquial 'man,' biblical Man and street-slang, the *Man*—'infuriated by this failure to acknowledge Hierarchy,' by the Cat, animals, women, kids, unruly men, 'will throw his boots and his little stone ax...at the Cat. Only when the Man listens, and attends...and hears, and understands, will the Cat return to the Cat's true silence.' And this vision of the better world Le Guin ends with, 'When the word is not sword, but shuttle' (*BG* 12).

Against the word as sword, dividing and (thereby?) killing, Le Guin places the literal image of a dancing woman—the printer's mark ending each section of *Buffalo Gals*—and the word-image of the word as shuttle, weaving the world. Both images are important for *Buffalo Gals* and Le Guin's work in the mid 1980s, but I am going to stress the shuttle (see my discussion of Le Guin's poetry and *King Dog* for the dancer). In *City of Illusions* and *The Left Hand of Darkness*, Le Guin could present the City and civilization at least ambiguously positively. By 1985, she could go along with a view Brian W. Aldiss presented in 1964 in *The Dark Light Years*, a satire of great brilliance and bitterness. After hard experience and some thought, one of Aldiss's characters concludes 'that civilization was the distance man placed between himself and everything else' (69). In *The Dark Light Years*, that setting up of civilized 'barriers' turns out to be very dangerous. The idea of civilization as distance from the world, and the dangers of such distance, is the main moral of *Always Coming Home*

(1985). Here I want to talk about a shorter, mostly gentler volume than *Always Coming Home*, making the same point about the Man and civilization, Le Guin's 1987 collection *Buffalo Gals and Other Animal Presences*, especially the beginning and ending pieces from 1985-87, and the general shifting in significance of the collected stories (and a poem or two) in the context of, as parts of, this particular collection.

Against myths of the word as sword and holiness and consciousness as separation, Le Guin again sets the worldview common in the stories of many 'of the hundreds of Indian tribes that were once scattered from the tip of Florida to the Alaskan straits,' where—as the editor of my undergraduate folklore collection put it, 'the line between a grass plant, an animal, man, and the stars was very thin.' In many American Indian tales, definitely including those collected by Le Guin's father, A. L. Kroeber, 'The plant possessed a soul, beasts could speak, men changed into stars, and stars became men. Everywhere in nature there were spirits, both good and bad, who took an active, and occasionally...crucial part in human affairs. Everywhere, too, there were animal powers. Sometimes...the culture hero of the tribe is a bird. At other times,...he is a coyote....' (Rugoff 95). Or she is: a point we will get to shortly.

Coyote on one side, on the other side an opponent that that 'unconsistent Taoist and...consistent unChristian,' Critical-Romantic Ursula K. Le Guin has been taking on for years.

In 1969, in *The Left Hand of Darkness*, Genly Ai says to Estraven, 'Your race is appallingly alone in its world. No other mammalian species.' Estraven responds, 'The Yomeshta would say that man's singularity is his divinity.' And Ai says, of this exotic sect of androgynes, the Yomeshta, 'Lords of the Earth, yes. Other cults on other worlds have come to the same conclusion. They tend to be the cults of dynamic, aggressive, ecology-breaking cultures' (233; ch. 16). In 1987, the US *Kulturkampfen*, our 'culture wars,' were well under way and the Christian Right moving toward significant power; and in 1987, in the Introduction to *Buffalo Gals*, Le Guin was gracious about allowing exceptions, but far more explicit about which set of cults she had most in mind:

> In the dreadful self-isolation of the Church, that soul-fortress towering over the dark abysms of the bestial/mortal/World/Hell, for St. Francis to cry out 'Sister sparrow, brother wolf!' was a great thing. But for the Buddha to be a jackal or a monkey was no big deal. And for the people Civilization calls 'primitive,' 'savage,' or 'underdeveloped,' including young children, the continuity, interdependence, and community of all life, all forms of being on earth, is a lived fact, made conscious in narrative (myth, ritual, fiction). This continuity of existence, neither benevolent nor cruel itself, is fundamental to whatever morality may be built upon it. Only Civilization builds its morality by denying its foundation.

> By climbing up into his head and shutting out every voice but his own, 'Civilized Man' has gone deaf. He can't hear the wolf calling him brother—not Master, but brother. He can't hear the earth calling him child—not Father, but son. He hears only his own words making up the world.[400] He can't hear the animals.... This is the myth of civilization, embodied in the monotheisms which assign soul to Man alone. (*BG* 11)

This is the beginning of *Buffalo Gals*, followed immediately by Denise Levertov's 1961 poem 'Come into Animal Presence,' which Le Guin calls the book's 'true introduction.' Then comes the important story, written for the volume, 'Buffalo Gals, Won't You Come Out Tonight.' *Buffalo Gals*, the collection, ends with Le Guin's translation of Rainer Maria Rilke's 'The Eighth Elegy' (1922) from *The Duino Elegies* and, the very last piece in the volume, Le Guin's *mâshâl* 'She Unnames Them' (1985). The Rilke poem is important for Le Guin, but 'She Unnames Them' is crucial.[401] Le Guin says in her brief introduction to 'She Unnames Them' in *Buffalo Gals* that 'She Unnames Them' is the story 'that had to come last...because it states (equivocally, of course) whose side (so long as sides must be taken) I am on and what the consequences (maybe) are' (191).

In its original context in *The New Yorker*, 'She Unnames Them' appeared to me mostly a revisiting of Le Guin's earlier story, 'A Trip to the Head' (1970), just with a female protagonist and a tone that was simultaneously quieter and lighter, more politically engaged—and funnier—than 'A Trip to the Head.' Or it was the inverting of parts of *City of Illusions* (1967): a book starting with a movement out of the forest and into civilization in a kind of birth into human consciousness—and a book ending with the finding of a true name and a blasting off into space (in an image, arguably, of phallic transcendence). Insofar as it was a *mâshâl* undoing the naming of the animals by Adam (Genesis 2.18-20), 'She Unnames Them' in *The New Yorker* seemed to me a *mâshâl* in the sense of 'mild satire' against Man-centered, word-centered civilization. As the last work and word in *Buffalo Gals*, however, 'She Unnames Them' is *mâshâl* in the stronger sense of an (anti)Prophecy: the word doing work in the world, here, undoing the work of words. As the note in my Bible to Genesis 2.19 says, 'Naming the animals signifies man's dominion over them....' In the context of *Buffalo Gals* and doing much to establish the context of *Buffalo Gals*, 'She Unnames Them' is a willing ('equivocally, of course') of the removal of names, the removal of dominion, which would make the animals at least seem 'far closer than when their names had stood between' us and 'them like a clear barrier' (195). Unnaming the animals becomes an unmaking of patriarchal creation, not just an individual return to name-

---

[400] For a more positive view of 'words making up the world,' see below, the discussions of the Churten stories in *FIS* (1994).
[401] See Bittner on Rilke's influence (*Approaches* 40-42 and passim; 132 n. 26.)

lessness and the unconscious as in 'A Trip to the Head' (*WTQ* 165). It is an unbuilding of the first and thickest wall between humans and the world.

'Buffalo Gals, Won't You Come Out Tonight'

> Man, the flower of all flesh,...man who had once made god in his image...beautiful naked man was dying, strangled in the garments he had woven [= civilization].... Truly the garment had seemed heavenly at first, shot with the colours of culture, sewn with the threads of self-denial. And heavenly it had been so long as it was a garment and no more, so long as man could shed it at will and live by the essence that is his soul, and the essence, equally divine, that is his body. — E. M. Forster, 'The Machine Stops' (1909)

'Buffalo Gals, Won't You Come Out Tonight' is a familiar Le Guinian work in having two contrasting worlds; and it is somewhat like *The Beginning Place* (1980) in that one of these worlds is fantastic. What is different in 'Buffalo Gals' is that its central character has just dropped into the world of fantasy at the beginning of the story and is just about to leave it at the end. Both technically and more figuratively, the point of view is almost entirely that of the main character, and she stays in the world in which she has landed. We have in this story the motif of a passage through a portal (looking-glass, back of the wardrobe, hole in the air), to there and back again, but the journeys in and out are only implied. What is a secondary world in most fantasy is the primary world in 'Buffalo Gals.'

And this is decorous. From the point of view of a stereotypical civilized reader, the world of the story is fantasy or, possibly at best, 'magic realism,' retelling a Kiplingesque *Jungle Book* story with a female protagonist: Mowgli in girl's clothes.[402] From the point of view of a more insightful civilized reader, 'Buffalo Gals' is a fable: a story with talking animals that teaches some lessons. But from a quite different point of view, 'Buffalo Gals' is an important story in the Coyote Cycle, also with variations, but a Coyote story: a wild-assed *realistic* tale, but realistic in terms of other realities than those of a stereotypical civilized reader.

'Buffalo Gals' is one of the Coyote stories where Coyote is the star but not the protagonist or hero. Coyote is a trickster—if you believe in archetypes, an embodiment of Trickster—given a local habitation and a name in the American West. 'Buffalo Gals' is an unusual Coyote story in that Coyote is female: a she-coyote and a human woman. Unusual, as far as my knowledge of folklore goes, but not overly challenging even for a narrow-minded male reader. Coyote 'cause[d] the world' in one character's formulation (*BG* 43), 'made it,' according to Coyote, 'Every goddam sage bush'

---

[402] For Le Guin's very gracious acknowledgment of the achievement (and influence on her) of Rudyard Kipling's *Jungle Books*, see Le Guin's Introd., *BG* 10.

(22); and Coyote is a horny old coyote, roaming the world. Coyote's ontological status is heavily paradoxical; to worry about her sex or gender is definitely, as we said in the 1960s, to sweat the small stuff.

'Buffalo Gals' begins with direct address by a coyote: "You fell out of the sky,' the coyote said' (17). The 'you' is soon identified as a girl, and the coyote—still lower-case 'c'—goes on to specify that the girl fell out of 'a burned place in the sky.' In realistic terms in our world, the girl was in an air-accident in a light plane. In realistic terms in Coyote's world, the girl has fallen out of 'Civilization as we know it,' 'the City of Man,' the dry land of 'The backward-head people' (*ACH* 152-59) into a world of life.

The plot of 'Buffalo Gals' starts with the conversation welcoming the girl, or Gal, Myra, into the world Coyote made; it ends with Myra going to see Spider Woman, called here '(the) Grandmother': the webster who weaves the larger universe of which even Coyote is part (50-51; § 5 [also 37, 42-43]). Grandmother tells Myra that she will be able to live her life well among the civilized, and that she, Grandmother, will 'be there too'; she will be in Myra's dreams and ideas, 'in dark corners in the basement.' And the Gal turns away and 'starts up the night slope towards the next day' and civilization, with Chickadee, for most of the way, flying before her (*BG* 51).[403]

That's the beginning and end of 'Buffalo Gals.' The incidents that make up the middle are, in linear order: Coyote bringing Gal into Coyote's town; Blue Jay's having a healing dance for her and replacing her missing, destroyed, or injured eye with one of pine pitch (*BG* 28-29; § 2)—as in one of the Native American tales of Coyote; Gal's learning to live with Coyote and bit by bit adopting her as a mother; Coyote's having her male friends over for sex (a repeated motif); Gal's forming a true friendship only with Horned Toad Child, and wanting—something (35); Horned Toad's advising her to see Horse; a ride on Horse to a human place (a ranch), with Chickadee scouting ahead (36-40; § 3); a talk between Gal and Chickadee about the nature of things once, and how times have changed; a trip with Coyote to a civilized place, where Coyote likes the action—e.g., getting shot at (47; § 4)—and likes the food, and in her greed accepts as an 'offering' (48) a poisoned smoked salmon, which she eats and dies from; Gal's burying Coyote's body; returning to town; and being taken to Grandmother to learn that Coyote 'gets killed all the time' and get sent back, acquiescing to what she must do, to civilization (50-51; § 5).

Woven into this linear plot, collected in a figurative carrying bag and laid out before us, are the conversations motivated by the plot and the associated symbols and motifs, all helping get across the point of the story.

The major symbol is, of course, Coyote, and the major motif what we may see as either transformations or double vision—Shakespearean,

---

[403] Cf. and contrast the Archmage Nemmerle's going to 'the dry hillsides of death's kingdom' with the raven of Osskil flying before him (*WE* 63; ch. 4).

Blakean-Romantic, antiNewtonian double vision.[404] At the beginning of the story, Coyote is 'the coyote' and ungendered, seen with her one good eye by the as-yet-unnamed 'the child' as a standard-issue, US coyote: 'a big one, in good condition, its coat silvery and thick' (17; § 1). Except that the coyote talks.

As the story progresses, 'the coyote' becomes a 'she-coyote' as the child notices her nipples (19: § 1), and then ambiguously 'Coyote,' without the article but as the first word of sentences (20-21), and finally and unambiguously Coyote when Coyote starts behaving like Coyote in some of the more vulgar legends: "Piss on the fire!' she cried, and did so, standing straddling it. 'Ah, steam between the legs!' she said. The child, embarrassed, thought she was supposed to do the same thing, but did not want to, and did not. Bareassed, Coyote danced around the dampened fire,' singing a chorus of 'Buffalo Gals, Won't You Come Out Tonight' (21; § 1). In the meantime, the coyote's appearance has changed. One moment, 'The child turned. She saw a coyote gnawing at the half-dried up carcass of a crow'; next moment, 'She saw a tawny-skinned woman kneeling by a campfire,' cooking food in a pot (20; § 1).[405] Coyote calls the child 'Gal,' and we learn that her name in our world is 'Myra' (22; § 1). And then Gal and Coyote go to Coyote's town, where she is greeted as 'new person' (23; § 1). This phrase is significant.

'Buffalo Gals' teaches that 'Things are woven together'—everything—and that 'When we lived together,' human and nonhuman people, 'it was all one place'; the world was one. As Chickadee goes on to say, things are different now: 'But now the others, the new people, they live apart.... They weigh down on our place, they press on it, draw it, suck it, eat it, eat holes in it, crowd it out.... Maybe after a while longer there'll only be one place again, their place'—our place, civilization. 'Buffalo Gals' teaches the possible eventual complementarity (43-44; § 4) but the present definite opposition of us 'new people' and 'the old ones,' the 'first people.' Coyote drives the point home with the (serious) old joke about two kinds of people in the world—the kind who divide the world into two kinds of people and the kind who don't—and then more earnestly goes on to explain to Myra that 'There's the first people, and then the others.' The first people are 'Us, the animals...and things. All the old ones.' The others are 'The new peo-

---

[404] Myra's name may be significant here; *mira* in Spanish tells one to 'Look!' or 'observe.' For the usefulness of unfocused, double vision, note Hermia's 'Methinks I see things with parted eye , / When everything seems double,' in Shakespeare's *A Midsummer Night's Dream* (4.1.188-89), a play featuring a time-out time in Nature, presented as a wild woods in contact with one version of the Dream Time. Similar points are made in *As You Like It* and *Twelfth Night*; the relativity of vision is stressed in *The Tempest*; the necessity to see the world 'feelingly' is hammered home in *King Lear* (for *Lr.*, see Erlich, 'Wise Men...').

[405] For an «artist's conception» of Coyote-Woman and the other people of her town, stressing the 'magical' in 'magical realism,' see the beautiful illustrations of Susan Seddon Boulet in the 1994 reissue of 'Buffalo Gals...' as an independent volume.

ple. The ones who came.' In Coyote's world, that would be the Euro-Americans. 'We were here.... We were always here. We are always here. Where we are is here. But it's their country now. They're running it.... Shit, even I did better!' Myra says 'They're illegal immigrants.' Coyote disagrees. 'What the fuck's illegal mean? You want a code of justice from a coyote? Grow up, kid!' But Myra doesn't want to grow up and become one of the others, a civilized adult human (32; § 2).

Myra can join with the old ones because she is a child and possesses a child's double vision: from the start she can hear the coyote, and she soon sees Coyote as a person, a coyote/human person (see Cadden 519, 521-22). She can see the other non-human animals in the same way, from the first time she sees them. Still, her double vision gets itself an «objective correlative» in the healing dance Blue Jay performs for her. With an ungentle touch, Blue Jay replaces her bad eye with, he says, one of pine pitch (28-29, § 2; 47-48, § 4). Opening her eyes after the operation, what Myra 'saw was confused, hazy, yellowish. She began to discover, as everybody came crowding around...that if she shut the hurting eye and looked with the other,' her old, civilized eye, 'everything was clear and flat; if she used them both, things were blurry and yellowish, but deep' (28; § 2). As in *The Word for World Is Forest* (1972) and in 'Newton's Sleep' (1991), clear, one-eyed, 'Newtonian' vision is limited, and to be replaced with vision 'blurry and yellowish, but deep,' vision that sees the animals and plants and rocks 'and things.'

To quote me, drawing the moral of a fable I wrote in high school, 'Both difference and similarity are in the eye of the beholder; it depends only on how long and how deep he cares to look.'[406] Coyote tells Myra, 'Resemblance is in the eye' and goes on to state, 'It just depends on how you look at things'—and then Coyote and Myra go on to the 'two kinds of people' discussion (31-32; § 2). The problem with us new people, at least with adults, is that we do not see things right.[407] We miss what some children can see: 'With her wild eye,' Le Guin writes as a literary critic, 'Myra sees the wilderness as well as the human realm as her true home' (*ER* 23). This point on the simultaneous relativity and importance of vision is driven home in the rest of the episodes in the story, contrasting Coyote's world and ours.

Le Guin, however, does not sentimentalize her «primitives». Coyote has real problems as a mother, from a child's point of view, and ours, and from that of the more elegant Chickadee—and probably from Le Guin's.

---

[406] I was unconsciously borrowing from 'It depends on how you look at things,' the moral of an old recording of *The Churkendoose*, for which see my chapter on Le Guin's picture books. (I would now rewrite the moral of my fable to be gender-neutral.)
[407] Le Guin is quite certain she has never read or heard *The Churkendoose*, so source-hunters be warned. (Note throughout *Coyote* that I am rarely interested in Le Guin's sources but want to help readers make comparisons and contrasts and/or place Le Guin's works in contexts I think helpful.)

Coyote is pretty neat and clean about her person, but she's a lousy, or «flea-and-ticky» housekeeper. She's rather greedy about food, and she is *not* respectable. She pisses and shits where she wishes and uses precisely such terms—strongly contrasting with Myra's juvenile delicacy—for her actions. As Coyote does in Oregon Indian tales, Le Guin's Coyote talks to her turds, and they talk back to her.[408] (Coyote is not a civilized man, alienated from the world and trying to distance himself from his body and its excretions.) And she really likes to fuck. Not make love, maybe not even innocently copulate: she fucks (33; § 2). In her den, with Myra there, and with at least one of her sons and with one coyote/man who will come on to Myra. When Coyote wakes up and realizes what he's up to she 'bit him hard, and kicked him out of bed.' Coyote insists she has some standards, and she does—but the male who stroked Myra's belly spends the night again a while later. 'You want a code of justice from a coyote?' You'll get one before you will get middle-class morality, or even much responsibility. And not everyone in Coyote's world is hospitable to Others. 'Some persons in town made it clear that as far as they were concerned she [Myra] didn't and never would belong there' (*BG* 34; § 3). Hawk for one, and the young Skunks (who dislike her smell). Still, Myra loves Coyote, and her love is returned (however much Coyote would not say so); and the hostility Myra experiences motivates her to get advice from Horned Toad Child and then seek out Horse and then check out local civilization (34-35; § 3).

'Horses are weird,' Horned Toad, says, because they are sexist and ageist—if viewed as humans. Horse's personal name is 'Prince,' and he's a young stallion waiting a while to take over from the local king horse: defeating him in battle and taking over the harem. Another possible reason why horses are weird is that they are newcomers, additional illegals who came to the new world with European humans. When Horse asks Myra 'Who are you,' Myra 'saw it was true: Horse had come here with her people, people who had to ask each other who they were.' Horse is also an aristocrat, an heir apparent, and Myra and the Narrator see him as 'vainglorious,' but also 'magnanimous,' and Myra falls in love with him immediately (36; § 3). Le Guin has long been a Daoist-anarchist-Leftist-radical with strong respect for «nature's nobles», and horses have always looked aristocratic, especially, it sometimes seems, to girls.

In any event, Horse, for all his pretensions, is basically a nice guy: beautiful, responsible, and thoughtful, a newcomer who has fit in. When Myra asks him about 'where the other people are,' Horse carefully asks if she is referring to 'the metal places, the glass places? The holes?' If so, Horse is wise enough to go around them: He sees human habitations as primarily walls, and walls in increasing numbers: 'There didn't used to be so many.' And in the first reference to Grandmother in the story, he adds, 'Grandmother said there didn't used to be any walls' (37; § 3). Readers

---

[408] For 'turds and...words,' see *ACH* 168 ('Time in the Valley'). Le Guin mentioned the Oregon stories in a note to me.

familiar with Le Guin's *The Dispossessed* (1974), will recognize this as an important line: that novel begins, 'There was a wall' (1; ch. 1) and refers to us Terrans as 'intellectual imperialists, jealous wall-builders' (224; ch. 8), and has a hero whose job is 'to go unbuild walls' (267; ch. 10). Horse's putting together 'walls' and 'Grandmother' in the same breath, plus civilization as 'holes' in the world, makes him (like Odo) a kind of hinge between Le Guin's earlier work and later, her early Hainish universe of future human cultures and her mid-1980s works set in an American West of animals and relatively time-less Amerindian cultures—and on to her 1990s works in a re-visioned Hainish universe. And this hinge-function is appropriate: Horse is liminal and a link: both a new person and one of the old ones.[409]

Myra 'sort of' feels like she has to go to the dangerous 'holes'; it seems to be something she *must* do (38; § 3), and Horse, with Chickadee chaperoning, takes her there. Horse points out the human place, 'There.'

> The child stared. In the strange light and slight mist before sunrise she could not see clearly, and when she strained and peered she felt as if her left eye were not seeing at all.[410] 'What is it?' she whispered.
> 'One of the holes. Across the wall—see?' [says Horse.]
> It did seem there was a line, a straight, jerky line drawn across the sagebrush plain, and on the far side of it—nothing? Was it mist? Something moved there—'It's cattle!' she said....
> 'It's a ranch,' the child said. That's a fence. There's a lot of Herefords.' The words tasted like iron, like salt in her mouth. The things she named wavered in her sight and faded, leaving nothing—a hole in the world, a burned place....

And then a car comes—'something moving fast, too fast burning across the ground straight at them at terrible speed'—and they flee 'away from sunrise, the fiery burning chariot, the smell of acid, iron, death' (40-41; § 3). In the vision of the animal people, the human world is associated with speed, burning, dawn, light, and a 'fiery burning chariot' like unto the one that carried the Prophet Elijah into heaven (2 Kings 2.11-12)—and like the truck that ran over (with no serious harm) Alexander Furby, the feline male lead in *Wonderful Alexander and the Catwings*.[411] For the first people, the Existentialist vision of the world as a truck or locomotive coming

---

[409] Cf. Selver in *WWF*. For liminality in Le Guin, see Spencer on 'Exiles and Envoys'.
[410] Myra's left eye is her original-equipment eye (*BG* 18) the right the new one (28).
[411] For Alexander, see below, the chapter on Le Guin's picture books. See below in this chapter my discussion of 'Direction of the Road.'

to run over ME is one of civilization's cultural aberrations; the *civilized* condition of radical individualists might be horrific, but the condition of sentient creatures truly *in* the universe is not. The horror for them is local and specific: us.

Later, Myra goes into town with Coyote, who finds human towns weird and fun: Coyote can move between the worlds without fear. Even more than Horse, Coyote is a new addition to Kate Spencer's gallery of 'envoys,' a new liminal character moving between worlds. From Myra's point of view, though, the human world is scary. The air is odd and so is time. Myra calls out for Coyote: 'Mom!' and then "Mother!'—standing one moment at the end of an ordinary small-town street near the gas station, and the next moment in a terror of blanknesses, invisible walls, terrible smells and pressures and the overwhelming rush of Time straight forward rolling her helpless as a twig in a race above a waterfall.' And then a man and a boy appear, spot Coyote ('big as my wife's ass,' in the man's words) and shoot at her. Coyote tells Myra, and us, that the townspeople are her 'folks.... All yours. Your kith and kin and cousins and kind. Bang! Pow! There's Coyote! Bang! There's my wife's ass! Pow! There's anything— BOOOOM! Blow it away, man! BOOOOOOM!' (46-47; §4).

Coyote sings 'one of the endless tuneless songs that kept time from running too fast' and 'wove the roots of trees and bushes and ferns and grass in the web that held the stream in the streambed and the rock in the rock's place and the earth together.' And then Myra tells Coyote aloud that she loves her—and then Coyote finds her smoked salmon offering and dies (for a while) from the poison in it (48-49; §4). The sequence and section ends with Myra cursing humankind: 'I hope you all die in pain' (50; §4).

The final scene of 'Buffalo Gals' has Chickadee taking Myra for her trip to Grandmother's and seeing Grandmother 'there at the center, at her loom.'[412] Grandmother greets Myra as a New Person, and Myra denies her people. Grandmother isn't so sure: 'You got outside your people's time into our place; but I think Coyote was taking you back'—and without much trouble Grandmother convinces Myra to return to her father, who (with others) had been looking for her. The end of the story is Grandmother's promise to be in Myra's dreams and ideas and 'in dark corners in the basement,' and the possibility that Myra might see Coyote again— although Grandmother makes no promises about Coyote. Myra will return to her/our world, keeping her new eye, and the double-vision it symbolizes (*BG* 50-51; § 5).

Additional Comments

Our world in 'Buffalo Gals' is presented as pretty bloody awful, but Myra returns to it in a somber but somewhat happy ending. Chickadee, Horned Toad, and Horse were fond of Myra, but only Coyote really loved

---

[412] For a nonmythic but significant grandmother at the loom, see beginning and end of Stone Telling's story in *ACH*.

her, and, for a while anyway, Coyote is unavailable, with the excellent excuse of being dead. Also, Coyote, as we have seen, has her limitations as a mother. Coyote is the great American incarnation of Trickster, and, again, if we don't expect law, justice, or morality from Trickster neither should we expect responsibility—and we should expect recklessness, imprudence, and occasional downright stupidity, as Coyote herself admits (e.g., 47; § 4). As I've tried to make clear, I find Coyote's vulgarity delightful in itself and an excellent reminder that much of what we civilized folk find refined comes from our denial of our bodies and is part of our alienation from the world. As even our Judeo-Christian-Islamic-Rationalist tradition will occasionally remind us, our shame at our animal desires and impulses is a sign of lost innocence. Still, Coyote's completely unalienated neighbors, in Coyote's world, find her a little gross, and I don't think we want to see Myra dropping her pants where she feels like it to defecate and then punningly communicate with her feces—'Dumb shit,' Coyote calls them when annoyed (45); we probably do not want to see Myra getting pregnant from sex with Coyote men.

This far the personal and concrete is different from and more important than the abstractly political: Myra will personally and individually live better in our world than in that of the dead Coyote, so Le Guin returns her to us, however much the old world may be better than ours as a possible ideal. Note also that gender issues appear in 'Buffalo Gals' but are not stressed. The world of the old ones, the original people is balanced toward the feminine, and female-gendered people are central: Coyote made the world; Spider Woman/Grandmother weaves the web of reality. In the world of the civilized, a boy threateningly rides a skateboard; but in the limen between Coyote's world and the civilized, Myra is given a ride by Horse, a princely male; and Young Owl and Blue Jay also have their niches, their respect, and their roles to play. 'Buffalo Gals' is clearly one of Le Guin's feminist works, but in its gender balance and complementarity, it is also clearly in the line from the Daoist works. It is also emphatically Native American but still in the Daoist line with having the source of reality Grandmother: the Dao-that-can-be-named; 'Name' itself, 'Being' or 'Existence' in the *Tao te Ching* is 'the mother of individual things' (ch. 1, Wilhelm, Chen).

'Buffalo Gals': Final Dissonance

There may be a momentary danger here of seeing Ursula K. Le Guin and the worlds she presents, as Odo just before her death fears she is seen: 'as if she were some kind of All-Mother, the idol of the Big Sheltering Womb...everybody's grandmamma...come worship at the womb. The fire's out, boys, it's safe to come up close' ('Day Before the Revolution,' *WTQ* 271-72). We will be getting to Le Guin's poems and *King Dog* (1987) and 'grandmamma' as Kali: the All-Mother goddess with a bloody attitude and a necklace of skulls. As a more gentle antidote right now, I wish to oppose to Spider Woman and Grandmother as Weaver a vision honest adult Westerners should go through first to come to Her. In Herman Melville's *Moby Dick* (which Le Guin has not read since 1947 ['Response' 46]), there is the skeleton of a whale in 'A Bower in the Arsacides' as location and chapter title. The skeleton is slowly incorporated into the bower of green mosses and tall trees, while 'the industrious earth beneath was a weaver's loom, with a gorgeous carpet on it, whereof the ground-vine tendrils formed the warp and woof, and the living flowers the figures.' It is a beautiful place, but—

> Through the lacings of the leaves, the great sun seemed a flying shuttle weaving the unwearied verdure. Oh, busy weaver! unseen weaver!—pause!—one word!—whither flows the fabric?...wherefore all the ceaseless toilings? Speak weaver!—stay thy hand!—but one single word with thee! Nay, the shuttle flies—.... The weaver-god, he weaves; and by that weaving is he deafened, that he hears no mortal voice; and by that humming, we, too, who look on the loom are deafened; and only when we escape it shall we hear the thousand voices that speak through it [as in noisy factories]. * * * Yet as the ever-woven verdant warp and woof intermixed and hummed around him, the mighty idler [the whale] seemed the cunning weaver; himself all woven over with the vines; every month assuming greener, fresher verdure; but himself a skeleton. (573-74; ch. 102)

As Selver reminds us in *The Word for World Is Forest*, 'What is, is' (*WWF* 168; ch. 8); and what *Is* is not about to fit neatly into any human category or system of categories or images, and will appear as Spider Woman, Grandmother, Kali, or the weaver-god (and so forth) depending on our perceptions. Grandmother talks to Myra and listens to Myra, because Myra is a child, and one with special vision. Taking the view of an alienated adult Westerner from an industrialized culture, Melville's image of life and death enfolded and unaware of humankind can be disturbing; from the view of adult followers of Western religions, used to talking with God and assuming God listens, the idea of a deaf, skeletal god presiding over unceasing creation and destruction—a heaven and earth far from humane or humanity—should be frightening. Western adults are not children like Myra, and Le Guin's message for us is—or should be—a tough one.

Poems, Miscellaneous Short Stories:
'Vaster than Empires,' 'She Unnames Them'

Stories can certainly be told in verse, and for a long time most stories were: poetry is older than prose for the formal telling of stories; and poems can certainly be used for teaching: the best English mnemonics, for example, are in meter and rime. Still, relatively short poems usually have only minimal narrative, and insofar as they teach, they teach differently from stories; so the same motivation that had me set off in a separate chapters Le Guin's picture books will have me separate off her film script and most of her poems; all are part of Le Guin's canon, but they are in or for different media. Some of the poems collected in *Buffalo Gals*, though, I want to discuss here and now, in the context of *Buffalo Gals*. First, because some of them tell stories; second because they fit into and help define the context of *Buffalo Gals*.

The poems come in five places in the book:

(1) § II. Three Rock Poems (right after 'Buffalo Gals')

(2) § IV. Five Vegetable Poems (preceding 'Direction of the Road' and 'Vaster than Empires....')

(3) VI. Seven Bird and Beast Poems (preceding 'The White Donkey' and 'Horse Camp')

(4) VIII. Four Cat Poems (preceding 'Schrödinger's Cat,' 'The Author of the Acacia Seeds...' and 'May's Lion')

(5) XI. Le Guin's translation of Rilke's 'Eighth Duino Elegy' (preceding 'She Unnames Them')

As Le Guin says in her introduction to the Three Rock Poems, there is one basic thing about rocks: I'll phrase it, they're basic. They are very old (basic in time), and they are the basis for everything else, for defining place: *'Rocks are what a place is made of to start with and after all. They are under everything else in the world, dirt, water, street, house, air, launching pad. The stone is at the center'* (*BG* 55).

The world-view established in 'Buffalo Gals' is re-established here for the rest of the book, starting from the bottom up: in the Rock Poems 'The Basalt,' 'Flints.' In the third poem in the section, 'Mount St. Helens / Omphalos' (1972), there is the idea of the rock as the center of the world—the world's navel, the omphalos at Delphi (or, in Eastern versions, Hanoi).[413] Except this rock, Mount St. Helens, is a volcanic peak, until the spring of 1980, when eruptions reduced its height by some 400 meters, a very high volcanic peak (*CIE* 'Saint Helens, Mount'), by my midwestern US standards, a mountain. The traditional advantage of central mountains is the liminality of their peaks, between heaven and earth; if you want to prepare to meet your God, O, Israel (or anyone else), a good way to do it is to climb a mountain. But not this mountain, not in this poem. In 1969, Americans went to the Moon, and returned; Le Guin suggests here that

---

[413] Or Dzil na'odili—the Upper Mountain, or 'the Center Place'—in a version Le Guin cites of the Navajo Emergence story ('Legends' 6, 8). Or the omphalos is at Mt. Sumeru, suggested in Patrick D. Murphy's excellent discussion of 'Mount St. Helens'; see Murphy also for Daoism in Le Guin's poetry (128). Among Le Guin's Kesh, I don't recall a navel of the world; note, though, Coyote's hollow mountain in Red Plum's version of the origins (*ACH* 167-68) and the Serpentine person's navel in Flicker's vision (289). Either I missed it, or the Kesh are sufficiently centered not to need a world-navel as symbolic center—the navel as point of radial symmetry in humans, as well as bilateral—or to need it as a euphemistic, asexual displacement for a vagina.

these children of Earth saw Mount St. Helens and returned, coming home to Earth, their 'hearth, hill, altar,' the 'heart's home' with at its center 'the stone' (*BG* 57). Perhaps, as in one character's belief in 'Another Story' (1994), the astronauts are connected to Earth as 'a mother is connected to her child by a very fine, thin cord, like the umbilical cord, that can stretch light-years' (*FIS* 173)—and got snapped back.

The first three of the Five Vegetable Poems, call our attention to trees, mostly: trees being a strong motif in Le Guin's work.[414] 'Torrey Pines Reserve' is an earth-poem, a Daoist poem, and a woman's poem. Mostly it is a description of 'A lizard place' where, if we listen, we 'can hear the lizards / listening.' Daoistically, it makes the point that sandstone, ultimately, is carved by water and wind, but this is not defeat but the aging proper to mortality, the decorous yielding to that which is strongest precisely in its yielding: water, air. More, the water (as ocean) hollows out circles that become eyes. In Ariel's song to Ferdinand in Shakespeare's *The Tempest*, Ferdinand gets misled into thinking his father drowned and that his father's bones are becoming coral and 'Those are pearls that were his eyes' (1.2.396-405). In a clever reversal, Le Guin's Speaker tells us the circles she sees 'are eyes that were his pearls'—with 'his' referring to either 'the rock' or 'ocean.' The Speaker finds this a 'gentle wilderness,' and a vulnerable one, 'fragile,' where the rain comes rarely and hard, like the tears of an old woman. We're told to 'Hold to the thread of way,' and keep to the 'narrow place' which we humans may occupy 'in this high place between the still / desert and the stillness of the sea.' That is, one needs to literally walk carefully in an ecologically fragile space, but one must follow the 'way' in the sense of Dao, and the thin thread of Spider Woman, Grandmother, the folklore thread that leads home in *A Ride on the Red Mare's Back* (1992).

'West Texas' is set in one 'of the terrible places,' and Le Guin's Speaker tells us to look and see how life is brought there and honor those who bring it: the plants and occasional deer who break the hard ground. 'Lewis and Clark and After' (1985) takes on the persona of Meriwether Lewis and/or William Clark (or any one or more members of the Expedition), who famously 'walked across a forest continent' 1804-06 CE.[415] The poem consists of two stanzas and three sentences. The first stanza is one long sentence summarizing the Expedition; the second stanza consists of 'Ohone!' ejaculated twice, plus two exclamations praising the woods of Ohio and 'the silent lives' of 'the forests of Oregon!' Significant here is the admission by the Speaker(s) in the first stanza that they crossed a heavily wooded continent pretty much without seeing the trees. They didn't 'think much about it' since trees are 'by our tribe' only 'seen with the one

---

[414] See Introds. to 'The Word of Unbinding' and 'Vaster than Empires...' in *WTQ* (65, 166).
[415] Very famously in Portland, OR, Le Guin's home, which celebrated the 100th anniversary of the Lewis and Clark Expedition in 1905 and has a university named after them (*CIE* on Lewis and Clark).

eye'—i.e., with what William Blake called Newtonian 'Single vision.'[416] More specifically here, it would not only be the single vision of good Jeffersonian scientists (the Expedition was sent by Thomas Jefferson) but also less good American capitalists—Mr. Jefferson included—who would see the trees as potential lumber.

The poems 'Xmas Over' (1982) and 'Crown of Laurel' (1987) tell teaching stories, and are two well-placed salvos in the American *Kulturkampf*, religo-mythic theater of battle.

'Xmas Over' does not assume the persona of a tree, but tells the story in the third-person, limited omniscient point of view common in Le Guin; in this case taking the point of view of the tree: a young fir in a relatively large pot that had been used as a Christmas tree. The plot begins with the tree (I assume without the pot) in the back of a car, not admiring the scenery, and being taken out to be replanted, 'trading a two-foot pot for the Columbia Gorge.' The replanted tree's branches make soft sounds in the wind, but its trunk and roots are quiet. The 'glass bubbles and colored lights' that had decorated the tree for Christmas are gone, and a hundred years hence the tree will have in its branches 'rain, and owls.' The poem ends with the Narrative voice telling us the tree 'won't hear carols sung again. / But then, it never listened' (*BG* 78).

In *A Wizard of Earthsea*, the illusion of the Year-Tree was conjured for the Winter Festival (49-50; ch. 3). In 'Xmas Over,' though, we learn of the problem in our world with even so lucky a real tree as this one: not cut down, replanted in a beautiful place. Nice people in a Christian culture have used a tree-person (not a personified tree) for 'Xmas.' Eating 'the First Salmon,' who has offered himself to human and other people for food (*BG* 43)—that's one thing, as is Myra's accepting a ride from Horse (38); tricking out a handsome young fir tree in lights and bubbles, though, without permission, is something else again, and not something good. It is a self-separation from the oneness of the world, a sign of dominion especially bad in worship of an infant One-God who will grow up to claim, '...I have come not to bring peace,' or a shuttle, 'but a sword' (Matt. 10.34-36).

* * * * * * *

'The Crown of Laurel' (1987) is a retelling of the metamorphosis of Daphne into a/the laurel tree, a story Edith Hamilton says is told only by the Roman poet Ovid among the ancients (Hamilton 114).[417] In Ovid, though not in Hamilton's retelling, the ultimate blame for Daphne's plight lies with Venus's son, Cupid: the executive officer, so to speak, for Love. In Mary M. Innes's translation, Ovid says that it 'was not blind chance' which brought about the disastrous love of Phoebus Apollo and Daphne 'but Cupid's savage spite.' Apollo had recently killed the Python monster, and, 'still exultant over his slaying of the serpent,' he makes the mistake of

---

[416] Last line of Blake's letter 'To Thomas Butts' 22 Nov. 1802 (p. 818 of *Works*).
[417] Murphy discusses 'The Crown of Laurel,' 133.

chiding Cupid for Cupid's pretensions as an archer. Cupid replies, 'Your bow may pierce anything else, Phoebus, but mine will pierce *you*: and as all animals are inferior to the gods, your glory is to that extent less than mine.' So Cupid, in Ovid's story, shoots Phoebus Apollo with his golden-headed, well-pointed arrow, enkindling love, and shoots Daphne, daughter of the river god Peneus, with a lead-headed, blunt arrow, the arrow that destroys love. 'Immediately the one fell in love; the other, fleeing the very word 'lover,took her delight in woodland haunts and in the spoils of captured beasts, emulating Diana, the maiden goddess....' (Innes trans. 41).

Daphne comes from an excellent family—her grandparents are Heaven (Uranus) and Earth (Gaia)—and in Ovid and Hamilton, but not Le Guin, a very human Daphne is much desired in marriage, and an even more human Peneus, a single father it seems, reminds her gently but repeatedly, 'It is your duty to marry and give me a son-in-law... My child, it is your duty to give me grandchildren' (Innes 41-42). The point becomes moot when Phoebus sees her, falls in love 'and wanted to marry her.' Such is his love, that 'Apollo's prophetic powers deceived him,' and he tries to woo Daphne. Ovid compares Phoebus's feelings to fire, and, appropriately for a sun deity, '...the god was all on fire, his whole heart was aflame.' Somewhat more flippantly, Ovid compares the moment of the welling up of Apollo's love to 'when a Gallic hound spies a hare in some open meadow'; hare-like Daphne flees; hound-like Apollo pursues. Apollo eventually closes in on Daphne, and in Ovid and Hamilton Daphne prays to her father as the River Peneus: 'O father...help me! if you rivers have divine powers, work some transformation, and destroy this beauty which makes me please all too well!' Peneus answers her prayer by changing her into the laurel tree.

> Even as a tree, Phoebus loved her.... Embracing the branches as if they were limbs[,] he kissed the wood: but, even as a tree, she shrank from his kisses. Then the god said: 'Since you cannot be my bride, surely you will at least be my tree. My hair, my lyre, my quivers will always display the laurel. You will accompany the generals of Rome, when the Capitol beholds their long triumphal processions, when joyful voices raise the song of victory. You will stand by [Caesar] Augustus' gateposts too, faithfully guarding his doors.... Further, as my head is ever young, my tresses never shorn, so do you also, at all times, wear the crowning glory of never-fading foliage.'
> And the tree 'seemed to nod her leafy top, as if it were a head, in consent,' although Ovid will not, one might say, go out on a limb pushing this interpretation of the movement of a tree (Innes 44).

In her introduction to the 1976 reissue of *The Left Hand of Darkness*, Le Guin had reminded us that 'Apollo, the god of light, of reason, of proportion, harmony, number—Apollo blinds those who press too close in worship. Don't look straight at the sun. Go into a dark bar for a bit and have a beer with Dionysios, every now and then' (n.p.). By 1987, Le Guin would have people in the figurative bar with Dionysos more, or, and better, among the trees at the River Peneus with Daphne, Gaia, Persephone, Demeter—and Dionysos and his (orgiastic) followers 'every now and then.' In the context of *Buffalo Gals*, Apollo is not the potential danger he appears as in the 1976 *Left Hand of Darkness* introduction, nor the semi-comic character of Ovid. In 'The Crown of Laurel,' Apollo is the immediate villain.

Le Guin's retelling starts at the end of things, with Daphne a laurel tree and then jumps backward. The unnamed Daphne tells us that an unnamed 'He' once liked to feel her fingers in his hair. 'So he pulled them off me, wove a wreath of them,' which he wears 'at parades and contests': her 'dying fingers' amid his 'sunny curls.' We learn, very paradoxically if we do not know the Daphne and Apollo story, that 'Sometimes he rests on me a while'—i.e., Phoebus as sun, apparently «resting» at the top of a laurel tree, and, with wordplay, «resting on his laurel(s)»; but 'Aside from that, he seems to have lost interest' (*BG* 78).[418]

In the second stanza, the unnamed Speaker assures us that she didn't run to preserve her "virtue," with *virtue* carefully placed in quotation marks: virtue is a men's thing, nothing for a nymph. Ovid had said nothing about Daphne's virtue, and Hamilton stressed the utter folly—the invitation to disaster for women—of sex with an Olympian (Hamilton 114-50). Still, the very popular Ovid was seized on early and Christianized and moralized, and we should accept as justified the concern of Le Guin's Daphne that people might think she ran from Apollo because she identified her virtue with her chastity, or was concerned with (masculinist) virtue at all. No, the Daphne here has naught to do with *virtue*; she just 'wasn't in the mood,' and it looked like her mood didn't concern Apollo, and that scared her. If she knew her Greco-Roman myths, it should have: rape is a motif, including by the gods.

Daphne develops her ideas of proper sexuality and intimacy for five verse paragraphs implicitly contrasting with Apollo's lust. Satyrs she calls 'The little goatleg boys' and notes that they, unlike Olympian Apollo—still unnamed, mostly uncharacterized—'can wait till they can smell you feel / like humping with a goatleg in the woods.' She tells us they can laugh, synechdochizes them as 'poor little hairycocks,' and says she misses them. She doesn't miss Apollo.

The next stanza describes Daphne with her sister nymphs, lying around in easy intimacy after sex with the satyrs; and then, moving down into the mortal world there is a long stanza on the men and boys she has seen. Mortal human males look at her and do not even dare to hope, not the hunters, poachers, or even 'the deciduous shepherd boys.' That last beautiful phrase brings together the human and vegetative: *deciduous* is most often

---

[418] My thanks to Le Guin for pointing out the 'rests' pun; I had missed it.

used to refer to deciduous trees, dropping off their leaves each autumn, defining the season of fall, and the hope for spring: 'New every spring, like daffodils, those boys.' This thought moves Daphne to one exception in her relationships with human males: she once loved a mature man and met him on the hills for forty years, into his extreme old age. She kissed 'his wrinkles, the ravines of time' she 'cannot enter.' Daphne even graced his funeral, walking behind the dead man's wife: 'She could have been Time's wife, my grandmother'—i.e., Rhea as sister-wife to Cronus and identified with Gaia as Earth-mother.[419]

With this set-up, Apollo re-enters the poem: 'hard, bright, burning, dry, intent: / one will...no center but himself, the Sun. A god....' (*BG* 79-80). Daphne supposes a god 'has to be' this way, but she had placed no requests to meet a god. And Apollo, here, is a *putz*: 'a big blond blue-eyed god,' so perhaps I should specify an *Aryan* putz. Such fastidious distinctions aside, Apollo thinks all women alike, having literally seen them all—Phoebus Apollo is the personified sun—but for some reason wants Daphne in particular. And he will not accept a 'no,' bringing us back to the inevitable in the poem—the metamorphosis—already given us (if subtly) in the opening stanza.

Daphne, still unnamed (never named in the poem), philosophizes a bit on why her metamorphosis happened: 'I guess that maybe it was time for me / to give up going naked and get dressed.' Le Guin gives Daphne a mother, though also unnamed—Demeter most likely—and has Daphne says that her mother just couldn't get her to put clothes on, so maybe it is well that a god made her do it.[420] Maybe even an immortal needs to get on with her life and move to another stage. That's an important point for Le Guin: she doesn't fancy immortality nor hierarchy, so what may seem to lovers of hierarchy as a horrible metamorphosis in that a nymph moves

---

[419] Hesiod lists the progeny of Rhea and Cronus (Time) as the goddesses Hestia, Demeter, and Hera, and the gods Hades, Poseidon, and Zeus: i.e., the elder Olympians (66; 8.453-606). Fairly late in his reproductive career, just before he married Hera, Zeus sired upon Leto—daughter of two Titans (the immediately elder gods)—Artemis and Apollo (Hesiod 79, 12.820-1022; *Smaller Classical Dictionary*). Rhea is grandmother to Apollo on both sides, and to Daphne (in Le Guin's version) via Demeter (see below). In the final stanza in this section, to finish with issues of family, Daphne talks about her 'brothers of the streams,' her 'river-lovers' once, and now intimates who send 'their kindness' to her roots, and she drinks from the hands of her mother, I assume the Earth (79; see below). Except for Eddie, Susan's Rose's half brother in 'Newton's Sleep' (*FIS* 39), these may be the best brothers in Le Guin's canon.

[420] On Daphne's mother, Le Guin wrote me, 'In my mind, Gaia or Demeter, probably Demeter,' and drew attention to Persephone as Demeter's daughter and Daphne's 'sister, seamstress, sovereign.' Less literally, Gaia is Earth All-Mother, and certainly mother to Daphne as a tree.

down the Great Chain of Being into the vegetative may be just a good idea, however villainous Apollo was in bringing about the change.[421]

In a nice inversion on 'Clothes make the man'—a literal statement in the original Latin (*Vestis virum reddit*)—Daphne becomes her clothing, 'being what I wear.' As a tree, Daphne has achieved *wu wei*, Daoist action through stillness, to an extreme degree. She runs no more and says 'the winds dance me.' Every April, her clothes get mended by her 'sister, seamstress, sovereign' who 'comes / up from the dark below the roots.' The reference here is to Persephone, daughter of Demeter, wife to Hades, and (therefore by patriarchal theory) queen of the underworld. Here, though, I'd take 'sister' experientially and politically as much as literally: Persephone and Daphne are sisters in their being part of nature and hurt by upstart kin of Zeus All-Father, sisters also, perhaps, in their both surviving—and surviving well—sexual attacks by males.[422] Or we can see Persephone's living at 'the dark below the roots' by herself: Hades might be just an unpleasant myth spread by those who profit from the hegemony of the younger gods (however much Zeus and his generation are the eldest among the Olympians).[423] In any event, Persephone's being a seamstress relates her to Spider Woman / Grandmother, the weaver of the world; and Persephone's coming up from 'the dark below the roots' is a nice restatement of Nameless Dao as the origin of things in the Chinese formulation, Void as the origin in Hesiod (*Theogony* 56; 2.116).[424]

The last two stanzas return to the theme of the beginning: Phoebus Apollo with a laurel wreath. Apollo says he honors Daphne to wear her

---

[421] Cf. and contrast metamorphosis into trees in Brian Aldiss's *The Dark Light Years* (1964), Orson Scott Card's *Speaker for the Dead* (1986), and Le Guin's story 'Olders' (*Omni* 1995, coll. *UA*).

[422] Persephone was raped by Zeus's brother Hades in the sense that he abducted her, plus in our sense.

[423] Joseph Ward Swain (1950) notes that '...while agricultural and matriarchal peasants were addressing their supplications to Mother Earth, the pastoral and patriarchal nomads'—Swain specifically mentions Nordics—'worshipped the Sky Father,' e.g., Sanskrit *Dyuas pitar*, Greek *Zeus pater*, Latin *Jupiter*, old German *Tiu* (as in '*Tues*day'). 'The fundamental religious ideas of the Mediterranean world of classical times can be traced back to the worship and mythology which grew out of the commingling of these neolithic types of deity' (Swain 1.51). Put politically, the generations of the gods noted in Hesiod's *Theogony* may reflect earthly hegemony by those who worshipped Sky over Earth. As Hesiod indicates, Zeus was a comparative newcomer as King/Father of Gods and Men (and, since Egypt was an ancient Kingdom in the time of Moses, so was Yahweh). See also the Orestes trilogy of Aeschylus (458 BCE) and note that this *Kulturkampf* is literally thousands of years old.

[424] The Greek word rendered 'Void' here is 'Kaos,' but Norman O. Brown avoids using English 'chaos' in his translation because of the misleading connotations of 'chaos' in English. Here I follow Brown to more easily bring in Lao Tzu and Unnamed Dao, and as a political decision. (For a more recent use of the Demeter/Persephone myth, see Le Guin's 1994 poem, 'Her Silent Daughter' [*Peacocks* 31].)

'fingers turning brown and brittle' in his 'bright hair' when he sings. Daphne as the laurel thinks, for her last words, that her 'silence crowns the song' (*BG* 80).

The Seven Bird and Beast Poems are enjoyable but less immediately relevant for *Coyote*. The introduction to this section, though, immediately does two things I wish to point out. First, it tells of Le Guin's seeing a barn the walls of which have 'neat rows of little holes, each one with a long Valley Oak acorn stuck in, a perfect fit, almost like rivets in sheet iron.' She assumes these are the winter hoard for the local acorn woodpeckers. 'On the other hand, they might be a woodpecker art form,' a matter we will get to with 'The Author of the Acacia Seeds....' Second, the Introduction notes that the social lives of acorn woodpeckers are familial or tribal, with cooperative raising of the young. There is no particular reason why humans should take acorn woodpeckers for exemplars for human social life, but, like wolves and ravens, the woodpeckers are good examples that a vision of 'Nature, red in tooth and claw' is true enough, but only a partial truth (Tennyson § 56). As Petr Kropotkin pointed out in *Mutual Aid: A Factor of Evolution* (1902, 1914), animals also cooperate, and if we are to infer a 'social Darwinism' out of nature, we might legitimately infer cooperation as much as competition.[425]

The poem 'For Ted' (1973)—Le Guin's older half-brother—presents the image of a hawk's curving flight.[426] The hawk is a good hunter and human and/or hawk children watch him hunting. 'The children wait,' and when the hawk stoops 'The children cry,' either tears or they cry *out*. The hawk's fall is labeled 'fell,' recalling (for those who know it) Macduff's lament in *Macbeth*, when he learns of the slaughter of his family and household 'At one fell swoop' (5.3.218-19). The Speaker, though, allows no sentimental condemnation, but insists in the closing lines, 'To the old hawk / all earth is prey, and child.' With a hawk hunting to feed his young, the yoking of 'prey' and 'child' is decorous. 'Heaven and Earth are not humane,' in the translation of *Tao te Ching* 5.1 that Le Guin uses for the headnote to chapter 8 of *The Lathe of Heaven*; but neither are Heaven and Earth cruel: the talons red with blood here are getting food.

'Totem' (1979) is in praise of Mole, as totem animal to the Speaker and possibly to Le Guin. It is also a brief compendium of symbols important to Le Guin. Mole is presented here as a 'mound builder,' which is both literally true of moles and associates them with Amerindian mound builders, and as a 'maze maker,' which associates moles with the imagery of mazes and complexity Le Guin usually associates with forests and the human subconscious.[427] Noting Mole's 'tooth at the root' identifies one of the reasons gardeners get cats or other engines of destruction to kill moles. It also associates Mole with the serpent brood at the roots of the World Tree

---

[425] See my discussion of *TD*.
[426] Le Guin notes that the poem was for her brother Ted's fiftieth birthday (personal communication).
[427] See below, this chapter, my discussion of 'Mazes.'

in the place of the goddess Hel in Norse mythology: an image of mortality for even the universe (Hamilton 312-13). Mole is a Yinnish animal, living in darkness, in the hollow of earth and following the way, but simultaneously a maker, shaper, like adept dreamers among the Athsheans of *The Word for World Is Forest*, or like a poet (old term: *Scop*, 'Shaper') who both follows and makes the Way. And Mole is also a destroyer, reinforcing the connection of destruction and creation. Yin-Yang-like, then, Mole is 'shaper of darkness / into ways and hollows.' Unlike Apollonian intellectuals, Mole is alive in the grave, 'heavy handed / light blinded.' Like George Orr in *The Lathe of Heaven* (1971), Mole must feel the way to solutions. Like *The Creation of Éa*, Mole suggests 'only in dark the light, / only in dying life' (headnote to *WE* and *Tehanu* [1968 / 1990]).

'Sleeping Out' (1985), is punctuated as two sentences, the first giving the order, 'Don't turn on the flashlight' in spite of strange things going on in the area the kids (?) are sleeping out in. The second sentence gives the philosophical/practical reason not to have the beam of a flashlight stab ancient darkness: 'The light will make a hole / in the air' and their fears will be there all the more, around the hole, 'in the dark brush and the old dark mind,' the mind that fears anything outside of the bright, daytime world (*BG* 136).

* * * * * * *

Le Guin's Four Cat Poems introduce, appropriately. 'Schrödinger's Cat,' 'The Author of the Acacia Seeds...,' and 'May's Lion.'

The last poem in the group is 'For Leonard, Darko, and Burton Watson' (1982) and has an 'I' who is reading and a cat 'aware of,' if not exactly reading, 'the writing / of swallows' on a 'white sky.' Then the Speaker is writing and the cat sleeping, and the Speaker asks, 'Whose poem is this?' The potential reading of the swallows' writing is important for the tone of 'The Author of the Acacia Seeds'; the question of whose poem this might be anyway moves toward collapsing distinctions among the cat and the woman (?) writing as subjects of the poem and Le Guin, the nonfictional woman writing, as author. Readers may see this poem as a nicely Theoretical thought appropriate to an evolving Le Guin in the early 1980s; readers may see this poem in the line of thought that led to Chuang Tzu dreaming of a butterfly and awaking to wonder if he might be a butterfly dreaming itself Chuang Tzu—a line of thought and development that included Le Guin's 1971 *The Lathe of Heaven*.

Her short poem 'Tabby Lorenzo' (1984) stars, I assume, 'Lorenzo, who is called The Bean' in *A Visit from Dr. Katz*. The poem is like a long *haiku*, presenting a Speaker, with a male cat on her knee. Or *his* knee; the poem doesn't specify the human's gender. The cat rests there, trusting completely the human and the situation, and at the same time 'entirely strange' to the speaker. 'His ears are scarred': this cat has been in some battles. Lorenzo is another of the envoys Kate Spencer identifies. Like Ged almost trapped in the hawk-shape in *A Wizard of Earthsea* (124; ch. 7), like Shevek and Genly Ai and the Mobiles and Envoys and Ambassadors in Le Guin's 1990s return to the Hainish universe—like these humans Lorenzo is both messenger and message. In this homelier case ('homely' as in *heimlich*), Lorenzo is 'a messenger to all indoors / from the gardens of danger.' There is a time to take risks and a time to lie in a lap 'entirely trusting,' feeling some sense of safety.

'A Conversation with a Silence' (1986) is a dramatic dialog with three characters, one more silent than the other two. The first voice asks the wife's/parent's question, 'What kept you out so late my love?', as we later learn even unto a rainy dawn. The answer is that the second speaker was out 'running in the dark,' among and up the trees, which serve as 'clouds and roads.' The second speaker goes along 'the sweet dirt-darkness in the rain' and climbs the trees up to where 'chirping sleep-warmth / nestle their blood for me.' I.e., the cat climbs trees looking for, and, it seems, occasionally finding, nesting birds: the cat knows about the blood. Below, the cat meets enemies: 'the White One' and 'the Singer.' The cat has been out in an uncomfortable and rather dangerous world—including a feline social world—doing feline macho or mach*a* things: hunting, fighting.[428] The first speaker, whom I'll call the Woman, then asks the Cat about what the Cat's brother might be looking at through the window, a major mystery for those of us who deal with cats. The Cat tells the Woman the other cat watches 'Ghosts in the other garden': some literal other garden, some ideal garden of feline imagination, or both—or some other meaning. The speaker-Cat does not see ghosts. S/he goes 'farther / along the cloud-roads' (farther than the brother?) to go up the trees and 'kill where darkness branches in the rain,' i.e., literally, at the crotches of trees where birds build nests. Even in her picture books, Le Guin avoids sentimentalizing nature; she gentles up nature's even less for readers sophisticated enough to read poetry.

The fourth poem is 'Black Leonard in Negative Space' (1978) and it most closely fits the theme of 'Buffalo Gals.' The poem establishes first, 'All that surrounds the cat' and then specifies that that 'is not the cat.' There is the cat, then, and there is the world, radically separated: cat and 'not the cat,' that is 'everything, except the animal.' Upon death, the cat and 'all' will 'rejoin without a seam.' So far so easy: as Chuang Tzu and Genesis agree, after death we—feline people and hominid people—return to the earth, to the dirt and dust, and get recycled. But what of before death? The rest of the poem is brief but difficult, and I'm going to quote it in full.

> To know
> that no-space is to know
> what he does not, that time
> is space for love and pain.

---

[428] Mongo Gato, the resident feline thug and bully in my old neighborhood, was a macha female with the innocent sounding name of 'Rita.'

He does not need to know.

The 'no-space,' I think is time, human civilized world-time. It's the time Myra falls out of and then moves to return to at the beginning and end of 'Buffalo Gals.' Our time. That literal time is the figurative space for human love and human pain: the pain coming in large part from our alienation from the world, the human love being our major compensation for the pain of our alienation. And that human love is made possible by alienation: love is between individuals, and a totally integrated individual is a contradiction. The Speaker tells us that this cat doesn't need such compensation. The young Shevek tells his friends that 'It's the self that suffers, and there's a place where the self—ceases' (*TD* 48; ch. 2); the cat is already in that place, having no human space but not needing it.

The last poetry in *Buffalo Gals* is Le Guin's translation of Rainer Maria Rilke's 'The Eighth Elegy,' the original German poem completed prior to July 1922.[429] Le Guin in her headnote says that this elegy '*is the poem about animals that I have loved the longest and learned the most from*' (*BG* 191).[430] In basic structure, the Elegy is a comparison and contrast between the world-perceptions of nonhuman animals and our own, a contrast signaled by the opening lines:

Mit allen Augen sieht die Kreatur / With their full sight animals see
das Offene. Nur unser Augen sind / the openness. Only our eyes are as if
wie umgekehrt und ganz um sie gestellt / turned 'round; and surround like
    traps,
als Fallen rings um ihren freien Ausgang / blocking openness's going
    forth in freedom.

And that will be my last effort at my own translation. Readers familiar with Le Guin's *Always Coming Home* will recognize here a variation on the image of people with heads on backwards and, perhaps, one of the sources of that image in *Always Coming Home*. The poem continues the contrast of beast and human, or at least human adults. Beasts are free from death; we see only death (lines 9-10). And because of this freedom from death, beasts move «in Ewigkeit, so wie die Brunnen gehen» (lines 13-14), which Le Guin renders with a Daoist spin: the beast's 'way / is the eternal way, as the spring flowing' (Leishman and Spender have the 'creature-world' moving into *eternity* in a comparison with *running springs*). Contrasted with the way of 'The free animal' is our refusal to have even for an eye-blink 'pure space before us'; instead 'Always it's world' for us and «niemals Nirgends ohne Nicht»: 'never nowhere-nothing-not.' With us, it's never the total Void; it's always the world; beasts are free to deal with openness/nothingness, the 'nowhere-nothing-not.'

---

[429] See the Leishman and Stephen Spender introd. to Rilke's *Duino Elegies* 13.
[430] Le Guin differentiates between her headnotes and stories by italicizing the headnotes.

Children may approach that 'silence' and get lost there—and get pulled back. Or people die and are that silence or, in Le Guin's rendering, 'one dies, and *is*' («*jener stirbt und ist*»). Close to death we may finally turn our vision outward and see (lines 19-21). Like children, lovers can 'come very close to it,' but for each lover the other blocks the vision. Finally, though, no human ever really gets beyond a mere reflection of freedom.

For Rilke and for Le Guin, we adult humans are trapped in time. Primarily, we look to the future, but also to the past while beasts see 'all, / and itself in all,' a healing vision (lines 41-49). One of the reasons we look to the past (and deny the present and Presence in the world?) is a kind of profound nostalgia. We have a kind of memory

> As if not long ago all we yearn for
> had been closer to us, truer, and the bond
> endlessly tender. Here all is distance,
> there it was breathing. After the first home
> the second is duplicitous («zwitterig») and drafty.
> O happiness of tiny creatures
> that stay forever in the womb that bears them!
> O fly's buzzing still *within*,
> even on its mating-day! For womb is all. (46-54)

Outside of what I take to be the cosmic womb, Nameless Dao, the world before individuation and civilization—we are literally on the outside looking in on what *is*. And as spectators, we can only try to arrange things from the outside, and this won't work; «Wir ordnens. Es zerfält.» Le Guin translates 'We control it. It breaks down' (lines 67-69).

The beast's condition, then, is something like always being at home in the universe, still in the womb. Our current condition is like that of a traveler about to leave 'the home valley,' who 'runs, and stand, and lingers.' Like that traveler, 'we live forever'—«immer», always—'taking leave' (end of poem). And, of course, Le Guin would have us instead, 'Always Coming Home': that is, living in the universe consciously and carefully—as Ged and George Orr and the Kesh would have us—but living *in* the universe and coming home to the womb of Dao, the Mother, Grandmother.

'May's Lion' (1983-87) and 'She Unnames Them' (1985)

The final prose works in *Buffalo Gals* are 'May's Lion' (the one work in § X) and 'She Unnames Them,' which follows the Rilke poem and ends § XI and the volume. In her introduction, Le Guin tells us she did 'May's Lion' while writing *Always Coming Home* and trying to find a way *'to get from the Napa Valley of [her] childhood and the present to the 'Na Valley' of the book'* (179). This story came with *Always Coming Home*, and helped Le Guin write that book, but it didn't belong there: May belonged *'in her own house,'* not in Le Guin's valleys of Napa or Na; *'It is only the lion who crosses between history and dream unchanged.'* So, Le Guin says, '*in this story*' she followed '*the lion's tracks*'—those of a direct beast—'*not Coyote's*,' not the Trickster's. I.e., this is not to be a story where the highest art is the hiding of art, but where the connection between actual and fictional would be explicit (*BG* 179).

The first part of 'May's Lion' tells what really happened, in the story of May's lion, the story that 'May gave to us' repeated by Le Guin's Narrator (she tells us) 'as truly as I could' (183)—allowing that May is a good story teller, and good story tellers will occasionally make the story 'suit' themselves 'or get the facts to fit the story better' (179). As Genly Ai said back in 1969, 'Truth is a matter of the imagination' and facts can change with the teller's style (*LHD* 1; ch. 1); except Genly Ai gave us mostly implicit connections between '*the actual and the fictional, fact and imagination*' (*BG* 179).

What really happened was that some time back in the 1940s a mountain lion (or maybe a bobcat, but May told it as a mountain lion)—was that a mountain lion showed up under May's fig tree. May had quit keeping chickens, as the Narrator finally assures us, and her cranky fox terrier was long dead, and the 'black cats who lived in the barn kept discreetly out of the story': so the initial persons of this little drama were May and the cow Rosie, alone on a fairly isolated farm with a lion under a fruit tree (180-81). "It just laid there looking around. It wasn't well,' says May.' May 'had lived with' and had taken care of animals her whole life, and had 'earned her living for years as a nurse,' so she puts out water for the lion, carefully, and returned to the house. "After I went back in[,] it did get up and tried to drink some water. Then it made that kind of meowowow." May thinks the lion came 'here because it was looking for help. Or just for company, maybe.' Rosie needed to be milked, and 'May didn't like being shut in,' so she tries to shoo it away. (And the lion is still ungendered here—'it'—May hasn't yet observed its sex.) The lion stays, perhaps allusively, perhaps not, under his fig tree (182), the 'silent wild creature' watching May with his eyes, but otherwise without moving.[431]

May talks to a friend, Miss Macy, on the telephone and is warned the lion may have rabies and advised to call the sheriff. Given her circumstances—shut in by a lion that may have rabies, a cow to milk—May calls the county police, who show up in force. 'I guess there was nothing else they knew how to do. So they shot it.' May regrets the shooting: she hadn't been scared, and the lion was a full 'seven feet long, all stretched out.... And so thin!' (182). A magnificent seven-foot lion, and all the cops knew to do was to shoot him. Coyote, in 'Buffalo Gals,' has a point about humans (especially men) and guns.

After a white space, Le Guin retells May's story 'as fiction, yet without taking it from her: rather to give it back to her, if I can do so. It is a tiny

---

[431] For fig trees, see 1 Kings 3.25 and Micah 4.4. Any allusion to the old figure of speech here would have to be the lion's: Le Guin assures me that her Aunt May's place had a fig tree and that was where the lion lay.

part of the history of the Valley, and I want to make it part of the Valley outside history' (183).

The style of the retelling is slightly more elegant than was decorous for the version mostly from May, with 'elegant' here meaning mostly 'simpler.' In the retelling, the re-visioning (as Adrienne Rich's useful neologism has it), 'May' becomes 'Rains End,' living alone in her summer house in the hills about Sinshan town.[432] We're no longer in the Napa Valley but the Valley of the Na, and the changes are appropriate to the new setting, a healthier, more real world: Rains End is childless but rooted in her land and community: the fig tree is one 'planted there a hundred years or so ago by her grandmother'; she 'feels herself an aunt to all the children' in the area, even though the young ones avoid her. She thinks it 'natural for children to shrink away from somebody part way dead.' But they'll come 'round when older, for her stories. Instead of having earned a living as a nurse as May, Rains End 'was for sixty years a member of the Doctors Lodge.' And, like May, Rains End finds a mountain lion under the fig tree (184), and, like May, she gives him water (*BG* 185).

But Rains End also sings to the lion what she remembers from the Puma Dance Song, which is little except, 'You are there, lion,' but that is something. More important thematically, Rains End can also do a more complete job than May at giving meaning to the appearance of the lion; Rains End

> did not want to frighten him or to become frightened of him. He had evidently come for some reason, and it behooved her to find out what the reason was. Probably he was sick; his coming so close to a human person was strange, and people who behave strangely are usually sick or in some kind of pain. Sometimes, though, they are spiritually moved to act strangely. The lion might be a messenger, or might have some message of his own for her or her townspeople. She was more used to seeing birds as messengers; the four-footed people go about their own business. But the lion, dweller in the Seventh House [in the Kesh structuring of the world], comes from the place dreams come from. (185)

Rains End considers going over to tell her neighbor Valiant and her family, or go over to Buck's on Baldy Knoll. She hesitates because one course of the other might take her where she'd have to tell her story to 'four or five adolescents...and one of them might come and shoot the lion, to boast that he'd saved old Rains End from getting clawed to bits and eaten' (186). Such an immediate threat and heroic rescue indeed might have happened—if Le Guin had a different lesson to teach. In *this* valley,

---

[432] For 're-visioning,' see *ER* 12.

(good old) boys with guns are the threats, not lion-messengers of the Seventh House.

Rains End gives the lion milk, which he declines to drink, but no solid food. She gives him mostly her presence and what spiritual comfort she can: she sings to the lion 'the five songs of *Going Westward to the Sunrise*, which are sung to human beings dying. She did not know if it was proper and appropriate to sing these songs to a dying mountain lion, but she did not know his songs' (187). The lion dies quietly before sunrise, stretching himself out his full length (which no one measures), and Rains End gets help to carry 'the body of the lion off where the buzzards and coyotes could clean it' (188).

'May's Lion' ends with direct address from the Narrator to May:

> It's still your story, Aunt May; it was your lion. He came to you. He brought his death to you, a gift; but the men with the guns won't take gifts, they think they own death already. And so they took from you the honor he did you, and you felt that loss. I wanted to restore it. But you don't need it. You followed the lion where he went, years ago now. (188)

* * * * * * *

'She Unnames Them' is a *mâshâl* in the sense of a light-toned, highly serious comic satire. 'She Unnames Them' ends *Buffalo Gals*, and, again, it is, in this context—and helping greatly to establish the context—an (anti)Prophecy, a *mâshâl* of unmaking: a figurative unbuilding of walls. In this beautiful funny little story, Le Guin is as sincere as the authors of the 'J-Code' in their story of the making: the myth of the Creation of Eden.[433] Initially, in the J-Code version of Creation, you have a pretty sterile world, because Yahweh had not yet created farmers and gardeners nor watered the earth. So the Eternal gathers up dust (*'adamah*) and animates it with 'the breath of life,' making *'adam*, 'man...a living being'—i.e., dust plus breath (*ruach, anima, spiritus*). The body/soul business is a later importation, and, I strongly agree with Le Guin, a very bad idea. Then,

> The LORD God took the man and placed him in the garden of Eden, to till it and tend it. And the LORD God formed out of the earth all the wild beasts and all the birds of the sky, and brought them to the man to see what he would call them; and whatever the man called each living

---

[433] The 'J' in 'J-Code' is for 'Judah,' home of the earliest compiler(s) of the traditional texts, plus 'J' as Germanic 'Y' for 'Yahweh.' I give the translation of *Tanakh*; but the translations in Geneva and the Bibles derived from it (AV, RSV) and the NEB are similar, as is the Vulgate. I depend on the linguistic notes of *Tanakh* and *The Oxford Annotated RSV*.

creature, that would be its name. And the man gave names to all the cattle and to the birds of the sky and to all the wild beasts; but for Adam no fitting helper was found. So the LORD God cast a deep sleep upon the man; and, while he slept, He took one of his ribs and closed up the flesh at that spot. And the LORD God fashioned the rib that He had taken from the man into a woman; and He brought her to the man. Then the man said,

> 'This one at last
> Is bone of my bones
> And flesh of my flesh.
> This one shall be called Woman,
> for from man was she taken.'

Hence a man leaves his father and mother and clings to his wife, so that they become one flesh. (Gen. 2.18-24; *Tenakh*)

In the more sophisticated P-code (or E-code) version of creation, God makes men and women together (and perhaps androgynous) and just comes right out and gives us rule, dominion, mastery (Gen. 1.26-28). The more primitive Eden story is more subtle and yokes together consciousness, dominion, and an ambiguous marriage, soon to become fully patriarchal (Gen. 3.16).

'It is not good for man to be alone,' and in the J-code version of the creation story, there's just Adam, in the beginning, and the garden. So the Eternal makes the beasts and birds, and in the first act of human consciousness Adam names them. Which gives him dominion over the beasts: 'Because the name is the thing...and the true name is the true thing. To speak the name is to control the thing' ('The Rule of Names' [1964], *WTQ* 76).[434] The naming, however, does not give him a proper companion and 'fitting helper,' so the Eternal does the rib trick and gives the man a woman. The woman is an afterthought and created to be a helper, but is still accepted by a rather poetic and punning Adam as 'bone of my bones / And flesh of my flesh.' And, in an image of innocence, 'The two of them were naked, the man and his wife, yet they felt no shame' (Gen. 2.24).

The Hebrew for 'naked, ' though, *'arummim*, leads to *'arum*, 'shrewd' in the next verse, where we learn that '...the serpent was the shrewdest of

---

[434] Cf. Calogero and Starkey on Aeschylus's finding it appropriate (in his *Seven Against Thebes*) that Helen of Greece would prove the destruction of Troy 'because her name—naïvely derived from *helein* ('destroy') and *naus* ('ship')—marked her as a destroyer of ships. Here *nomen est omen*: the language is not merely a symbol; it corresponds to reality in its very structure.' This 'archaic sense of language' is the 'primal source' for the Eleatic philosophy of Parmenides and his school (526).

all the wild beasts that the LORD God had made' (3.1). And the rest of the story is the Fall and the establishment first of explicit patriarchal rule of Adam over Eve then expulsion from the Garden, then the birth of Cain and Abel—and then murder and, by Genesis 11, the Tower of Babel, civilization, and civilization's hubristic discontents.

The first act of complicity, then, with the monotheistic Father/Creator God was Man's unilaterally naming the beasts. Woman undoes the job, in Le Guin's version, and does it democratically, indeed, with good anarchistic participation: 'Most of them accepted namelessness with the perfect indifference with which they had so long accepted and ignored their names. Whales and dolphins, seals and sea otters consented with particular grace and alacrity, sliding into anonymity as into their element'—water, the favorite element of the Daoists, perhaps, in its yielding strength, and large bodies of water, representing Being, the Dao that can be named (if we weren't giving up naming). There is a problem with yaks for a bit: 'Unlike the ubiquitous creatures such as rats or fleas who have been called by hundreds or thousands of different names since Babel, the yaks could truly say, they said, that they had *a name.*' But it's a name 'The council of elderly females finally agreed that...might be useful to others' but was totally 'redundant' from 'the yak point of view': they didn't need a name for themselves and had never used it (*BG* 194).

Pets were a problem, especially among the 'verbally talented individuals' like 'some parrots, lovebirds, ravens, and mynahs' who 'insisted that their names were important to them.' The solution here was getting them to understand 'that the issue was precisely one of individual choice, and that anybody who wanted to be called Rover, or Froufrou...or even Birdie in the personal sense, was perfectly free to do so.' What she unnames is not the personal name any animal likes to name itself but 'the lower case (or, as regards German creatures, uppercase) generic appellations poodle, parrot, dog, or bird and all the Linnaean qualifiers that had trailed along behind them for two hundred years like tin cans tied to a tail.' The insects and fish give up their names easily, especially the fish, whose names 'dispersed from them in silence throughout the oceans...without a trace' (195). All this work of unNaming done, she feels closer to the beasts,

> far closer than when their names had stood between myself and them like a clear barrier: so close that my fear of them and their fear of me became one same fear. And the attraction that many of us felt, the desire to smell one another's smells, feel or rub or caress one another's scales or skin or feathers or fur, taste one another's blood or flesh, keep one another warm,— that attraction was all one with the fear, and the hunter could not be told from the hunted, nor the eater from the food. (195-96)

In fairness, she, the Woman, will not make an exception for herself, so she goes to Adam and says, 'You and your father lent me this—gave it to me, actually. It's been really useful, but it doesn't exactly seem to fit very well lately. But thanks very much! It's really been very useful.' She is embarrassed (it is awkward to return gifts), but, fortunately perhaps, Adam 'was not paying much attention,' and responds to what I'll call The Great Divorce with only "Put it down over there, OK?' and went on with what he was doing.' One of the reasons she, the Woman, leaves is 'talk was getting us nowhere,' but she had been prepared to talk things over. She 'fiddled around a little, but he continued to do what he was doing'—doing being what one with dominion *does*—'and take no notice of anything else. At last I said, 'Well, goodbye, dear. I hope that garden key turns up.' And Adam, oblivious, asks 'When's dinner?''

> 'I'm not sure,' I said. 'I'm going now. With the—' I hesitated, and finally said, 'With them, you know,' and went on. In fact I had only just then realized how hard it would have been to explain myself. I could not chatter away as I used to do, taking it all for granted. My words now must be as slow, as new, as single, as tentative as the steps I took going down the path away from the house, between the dark-branched, tall dancers motionless against the winter shining. (*BG* 196)

Eve has given up her name, her share of dominion, and Adam and the household of *'adam*, returning to the woods or forest or line of trees she cannot dismissively name 'forest,' or whatever. She has given up the taxons and binomial nomenclature of Carolus Linnaeus (1707-78), and, more deeply the universals and categories of Western thought going back to at least Immanuel Kant (1724-1804). Most deeply, she has redone the Western myth underlying all such naming in the Judeo-Christian-Rationalist West. Now she must face the world face to face—a truly radical Nominalist—without abstractions, and Le Guin values such immediate, unmediated contact with the world, however much to the rational (masculinist?) mind, this relationship with what is may seem like unconsciousness.[435]

Eve's act, seen this way, is also a *mâshâl* for women's giving up the ease of writing that comes with working within a tradition they have grown up with: 'The beauty of your own tradition,' Le Guin has written, 'is that it carries you. It flies, and you ride it.... It frames your thinking and put words in your mouth. If you refuse to ride,...you lose that wonderful fluency.' If women are to create their own tradition, they must drop men's

---

[435] In one old system of 'two kinds of people,' one category is Realists and the other Nominalists. Realists believe in the reality of universals, categories, abstractions; Nominalists say the categories are only words. For Nominalists, categories are more or less useful ways to group together things in the world, but have no existence except as mental constructs in human minds; reality lies in the things of the world. E.g., Rover, Lassie, and Rags exist; The Dog does not. Neither, of course, does The Nominalist, and 'Nominalists,' as a category, is problematic.

categories, which means, for at least a while, '...you have to stumble along...like a foreigner in your own country, amazed and troubled by things you see, not sure of the way, not able to speak with authority.' I think the lesson is that, like this re-visioned Eve, women must make the attempt in order to 'to speak your own wisdom' (*ER* 12).

'The Wife's Story,' 'Mazes,' 'Schrödinger's Cat,' 'Author of the Acacia Seeds,' 'Direction of the Road,' and 'Vaster than Empires' (Revisited)

In her introduction to the two stories, Le Guin states that she has *'learned to explain before I read them to an audience that 'The Wife's Story'* [1979] *is* not *about werewolves, and that 'Mazes'* [1975] *is* not *about rats'* (61). In *Buffalo Gals*, though, 'The Wife's Story' *is* about werewolves, and 'Mazes' *is* about rats, in part.

As Lillian and, more so, Leonard Heldreth have pointed out in conversation with me and in conference presentations, werewolves are a kind of allegory of human adolescence: hair starts to grow where it hasn't been before, the body changes, hormones rage, moods swing, coordination gets tricky, wild urges erupt, and, generally, one's body—not all *that* long ago brought under one's conscious control—seems to go off on its own projects. From what I've seen of female adolescents, it seems sexist and biologically silly to focus the legend on men, but, usually, it is an allegory of male adolescence: the *wer*-wolf story, from Old English *wer* for 'man,' 'male person.' The fear represented by werewolves is an ironic one. Adolescence is a transition from an arguably lower stage to a higher. At the very least, a healthy boy becomes fertile, achieving the primary male status in nature of a sperm-delivery system. Still, though, there is the fear of losing control, of being *reduced* to a beast (see 'Coming of Age in Karhide' 477-78).

In this sense, the author's explicit denial notwithstanding, 'The Wife's Story' is indeed about werewolves: about the (male) human fear of being 'reduced' to a mere animal.

The Wife in the story comes through to my ear as a lower-middle-class or working-class woman, who could be telling her story on *Oprah*. And a sensational story it is: her good, gentle husband, during the time of the dark of the moon (*BG* 67-68) becoming a monster, with the 'little one,' the 'baby' of the family, recognizing the horrible change first (69). As it had to happen, one time the change comes on at home, right outside the doorway in the 'hard sunlight.'

> I saw the changing. In his feet, it was, first. They got long, each foot got longer...fleshy and white. And no hair on them.
> The hair began to come away all over this body. It was like his hair fried away in the sunlight and was gone. He was white all over, then, like a worm's skin....

He stood up then on two legs.
I saw him, I had to see him, my own dear love, turned into the hateful one....
I was trembling and shaking with a growl that burst out into a crazy, awful howling. A grief howl and a terror howl and a calling howl....
It stared and peered, that thing my husband had turned into.... The mother anger come into me then, and I snarled and crept forward.
The man thing looked around. It had no gun, like the ones from the man places do. But it picked up a heavy fallen tree-branch.... (*BG* 70-71)

The rest of the pack come to the rescue, though, led by the Wife's sister, and the man is efficiently dispatched. The Wife goes over to look, hoping 'the spell, the curse' to be done and her husband, her true love to be there 'in his true form, beautiful.' But there's just the 'dead man' there, 'white and bloody,' and the wolves 'turned and ran, back up into the hills...back to the woods of the shadows and the twilight,' out of the sunlight and into 'the blessed dark' (71, end of story).

Dante Alighieri had called the wolf 'the beast without peace,' and 'Man is a wolf to man' has been a common expression from the Latin cliché to the last speech to the court by Bartolomeo Vanzetti before he and Nicolo Sacco were convicted and hanged in the early twentieth century (*ODQ* 551: 13). Konrad Lorenz has argued that we humans would be better off if we did treat one another more wolfishly: 'And so we find the strangely moving paradox that the most blood-thirsty predators, particularly the Wolf, called by Dante the *bestia senza pace*, are among the animals with the most reliable killing inhibitions in the world' (*On Aggression* 124; ch. 7). Similar sentiments can be found among most people who have studied real-world wolves with their pack loyalties, family loyalties, 'chivalry' and 'politeness' (e.g. Lorenz 117-18, 129-30, 232-33). And Le Guin has given some of these sentiments in her contrasting the relatively wolfish Athsheans—with their pack hunting and (culturally conditioned) aggression-inhibiting posture—vs. the civilized Terrans in *The Word for World Is Forest* (1972), where, of course, the Athsheans are the good people.

'The Wife's Tale' is about werewolves insofar as it reverses roles and the 'polarities' of our sympathies, and privileges wolves: Man acts humanly toward wolves in this story, with 'human' and 'wolf' natures closer to natural history than to human prejudices, our flattering ourselves that 'wolfish' is bad and 'human(e)' is good. If we must play favorites, Le Guin in this story (as other places in her canon) favors nonhuman animals over the human variety, dark dens and woods over the human plane of glaring light, the traditionally feminine dark of the moon to the full moon as a *man*wolf's time to howl.

In *Buffalo Gals* such a reading of 'The Wife's Tale' is almost inevitable, as is a reading of 'Mazes' in which the subject of the horrible experiments could be—except for some of the details of the story—a Terran rat. In any case, 'Mazes' begins with the word 'I,' and the 'I' takes on what I would consider the Rat-condition in a sparse, existentialist story, somewhat in the manner of Franz Kafka or Samuel Beckett's plays like *Endgame* or the *Act Without Words* (1958).

From the point of view of the protagonist-narrator, he/she/it is kept in a prison by a monstrous alien, and frequently brought out to be tortured by what should be the joy of speaking-dancing-running mazes—a positive symbol in Le Guin. The 'I' realizes that 'It'—the captor—'is intelligent, highly intelligent.... We are both intelligent creatures, we are both maze-builders; surely it would be quite easy to learn to talk together! If that were what the alien wanted. But it is not. I do now know what kind of mazes it builds for itself. The ones it made for me were instruments of torture' (*BG* 62).

A major part of the immediate problem is that the 'I' communicates through dance, and may be deaf, while the human-monster-captor communicates, we may infer and assume, orally/aurally. Another problem is a fairly typical misunderstanding about the food requirements of the 'I': s/he-it *likes* 'greenbud leaves' and would gladly eat them, but only juveniles among its species eat picked leaves, and s/he-it could get no nourishment from them (62). However, there are deeper problems, beyond mere difficulty in communication or understanding nutritional requirements. The 'I' says,

> ...it remains very hard to ascribe its behavior to ignorance.
> After all, it is not blind. It has eyes...enough like our eyes that it must see somewhat as we do. It has a mouth, four legs, can move bipedally, has grasping hands, etc.; for all its gigantism and strange looks, it seems less fundamentally different from us, physically, than a fish. And yet, fish school and dance and, in their own stupid way, communicate! The alien has never once attempted to talk with me. It has been with me, watched me, touched me...; but all its motions have been purposeful, not communicative. It is evidently a solitary creature, totally self-absorbed.
> This would go far to explain its cruelty.
> I noticed early that from time to time it would move its curious horizontal mouth in a series of fairly delicate, repetitive gestures, a little like someone eating. At first I thought it was jeering at me; then I wondered if it was trying to urge me to eat the indigestible fodder; then I wondered if it could be communicating *labially*. It seemed a limited and unhandy language for one so well provided

with hands, feet, limbs, flexible spine, and all; but that would be like the creature's perversity. (64)[436]

The speech of the protagonist-narrator here is technically and literally 'I'-'it': the captive 'I' talks about the captor 'it.' More profoundly, though, the 'I' is trying to establish communication, relationship with the captor as a 'you,' even if it is 'You—my Enemy,' while the human or humanoid captor has an (un)ethically 'I'-'it' relationship with the protagonist-narrator, studying the 'I' as if the 'I' were a thing, a *mere* animal from the point of view of an exalted human. To the 'I' of 'Mazes,' the 'it' torturing it is a kind of monster. To us, human readers, with some privileged information, the captor comes through as an ordinary-enough, indeed banal lab worker—some near-future graduate student perhaps, going for a degree in some near-future curriculum combining exobiology and xenopsychology. In the context of *Buffalo Gals*, however, civilized Man, as *'adam*, the alienated human species, is also 'solitary...totally self-absorbed'; and the cruelty to the 'I' comes from the widespread civilized lack of appreciation of anything nonhuman as capable of being an 'I.' The captor-experimenter, then, is engaged in a project deserving in its surface ordinariness—«rat running»—Hannah Arendt's damning phrase, 'The Banality of Evil': the experimenter is guilty of 'the barbarism...of treating lives as things' (*LHD* 95; ch. 7 [1969]).

After the 'I' defecates on the knobs of a device for a knob-pushing experiment, the experimenter understands the 'I' is upset by the experiment. 'The alien took me up at once and returned [me] to my prison. It had got the message, and had acted on it. But how unbelievably primitive the message had had to be! And the next day, it put me back in the knob room, and there were the knobs as good as new, and I was to choose alternate punishments for its amusement': an electric shock, nothing, or the picked greenbud plants the stubbornly ignorant experimenter thinks would be a reward for the starving subject. And, finally, we come to agree with the 'I' about the captor-experimenter: 'Until then I had told myself that the creature was alien, therefore incomprehensible and uncomprehending, perhaps not intelligent in the same *manner* as we, and so on. But since then'—since the return to the 'knob room'—'I have known that, though all that may remain true, it is also unmistakably and grossly cruel' (*BG* 65).

As a representative of us, civilized humans, the experimenter is quite familiar: I'll fill in the silences and sketch this captor-experimenter 'it' as some graduate student, desperately working on a project on alien intelligence, trusting in reports on what The Alien eats and frustrated that *this* alien won't behave and demonstrate its obvious intelligence in ways neatly quantifiable in terms of the experimental model. Or an older version of the

---

[436] If we picture the species of the 'I' descended from creatures like Terran rats, we can picture them with 'grasping hands,' used also for language. I think we should picture them that way, rendering 'unhandy language' a very elegant play on words.

'it': an assistant professor trying to get the near-future equivalent of tenure, or desperately trying to avoid getting fired because there is no job security of any kind in the near future.

Or you can fill in a stereotypical Mad Scientist.

Part of the point of the story is that it doesn't matter. If the subject beast is sentient, is an 'I,' the upshot is the same no matter what: the treatment of the 'I' is 'unmistakably and grossly cruel.'

* * * * * * *

'Schrödinger's Cat' (1974) is also a somewhat Existentialist story featuring an experiment, but it is of the comic-absurdist variety, not J-P. Sartrean grim, even if Samuel-Beckett sparse.[437]

The story is set in a world gone fast-forward: entropic but from too much energy. Stylistically, it is a very punny place, in which married couples come apart and people go to pieces—literally, in a nice mockery and use of the SF (and satiric) device of literalizing figures of speech. There is no direction to take even a story, but the Narrator has 'a severe congenital case of Ethica laboris puritanica'—the puritan Work Ethic—'or Adam's Disease,' which is curable but only 'by total decapitation' (*BG* 158). The Narrator even likes to dream and recall dreams : 'it assures me that I haven't wasted seven or eight hours just lying there' (159). So even in a world going to the dogs, there will be dreams and stories—with this Narrator, anyway.

The going to the dogs part is put off a moment by the arrival of a cat: 'All this cat can say is meow, but maybe in his silences he will suggest to me what it is that I have lost, what I am grieving for.... That's why he came here. Cats look out for Number One' (159). And then we learn of the increasing heat of everything, except in the immediate area of the cat: 'A real cool cat.' An animal with *presence* (161).

Then the story goes to the dogs, or more exactly one dog—or Coyote-style dog/person—whom the Narrator feeds and names 'Rover.'[438] Rover recognizes that the cat is Schrödinger's Cat, the cat owned by 'Erwin Schrödinger, the great physicist' (*BG* 162), the cat of the famous thought-experiment (163). Rover—simultaneously a dog and a human person—is carrying around with him paraphernalia for the experiment and concludes 'It can't be mere coincidence. It's too improbable. Me, with the box; you, with the cat; to meet—here—now.' While he sets up the experiment, the cat washes himself, and Rover explains: You put the cat in the box with a

---

[437] For a discussion of 'Schrödinger's Cat' more sophisticated in philosophy and physics than the one I shall offer, see Bittner, *Approaches* 79-83. Ben Sonnenberg reminds us that Beckett's works include 'pity and terror and (*O, horrible! most horrible!*) laughs' (16).

[438] Le Guin notes that Rover is like Coyote and '*acts* like a human person—but the Narrator seems to insist on *seeing* him as a dog' (personal communication).

gun (in this version) and a triggering device for firing the gun at the cat inside the box.

> At Zero Time, five seconds after the lid of the box is closed...[a small emitter] will emit one photon [i.e., one quantum packet of light energy]. The photon will strike a half-silvered mirror. The quantum mechanical probability of the photon passing through the mirror is exactly one-half.... If the photon passes through, the trigger will be activated and the gun will fire. If the photon is deflected, the trigger will not be activated and the gun will not fire. * * * The box is soundproof. There is no way to know whether or not the cat has been shot, until you lift the lid of the box. There is NO way!... [A]fter Zero Time the whole system can be represented only by a linear combination of two waves. We cannot predict the behavior of the photon, and thus, once it has behaved, we cannot predict the state of the system it has determined. We cannot predict it! [Contrary to Albert Einstein's insistence otherwise,] God plays dice with the world! So it is beautifully demonstrated that if you desire certainty, any certainty, you must create it yourself. (164)

Rover's main point may be the Modernist one in the last line: If we want certainties, we must create them. Or the Daoist/Handdarata point that other than death and until death there are no certainties. Anyway, we look inside the box, collapse the probability wave, and the cat at that moment is either dead or alive. Or, alternatively, two different universes come into being, one with a live cat, the other with a dead cat. But Le Guin doesn't handle that second option.

What Le Guin does do is have her Narrator make a very subversive suggestion. By looking in the box, we 'involve ourselves in the system.... [S]o when we came to look, there we would be, you and I, both looking at a live cat, and both looking at a dead cat' (164). Rover is upset by this idea and says 'You must not complicate the issue. It is complicated enough.' And the Narrator asks significantly 'Are you sure?' The whole purpose of experiments—especially thought experiments—after all, is to simplify things, to abstract a situation out of a reality far too complex for scientific investigation. And if uncertainty is the point, and certainties at best created by sentients, how can he be *sure*?

Rover is very upset now: 'Listen. It's all we have—the box. Truly it is. The box. And the cat. And they're here.... Put the cat in the box.' The Narrator pities 'the poor son of a bitch' but is about to refuse—when the cat walks over to the box, sprays an outside corner, jumps in, and brings the lid down with his tail.' Rover's response is 'Oh, wow. Oh, wow. Oh, wow' and then a deep silence. 'Nothing happened. Nothing would happen. Nothing would ever happen until we lifted the lid of the box' (165). The Narrator thinks, 'Like Pandora'—and I'll add, also like the Prince Rikard, in Le Guin's 'Darkness Box' (1963), who also is closely associated with a cat (*WTQ* 62-63).[439]

The Narrator demands of Rover 'Just exactly what are you trying to prove,' and Rover responds, 'That the cat will be dead, or not dead.' What he wants is 'Certainty. All I want is certainty.' What he sees as the one possible certainty: 'To know for *sure* that God *does* play dice with the world.' Rover isn't as bad as the Yomeshta in *The Left Hand of Darkness*, or any other enthusiasts after some transcendent certainty; he wants only the minimal security of the «stochastic universe», where at least we can depend on probabilities, even when they are Schrödinger's maddeningly 50/50 probability.[440]

In a dramatic gesture, Rover flings back the lid of the box: The cat has disappeared. Then the box disappears. Then, as with the climax of Archibald MacLeish's 'The End of the World' (1926), '...the roof of the house was lifted off just like the lid of the box, letting in the unconscionable, inordinate light of the stars' (*BG* 166).[441]

From wherever, the Narrator tells us that s/he has 'identified the note that keeps sounding.' It's an 'A, the one that drove the composer Schumann mad. It is a beautiful, clear tone, much clearer now that the stars are visible,' in part because the roof is gone, and, perhaps, the walls, too are down (though that's not in the story). 'I shall miss the cat. I wonder if he found what it was we lost' (166). In the universe of *Buffalo Gals*, and I think in Le Guin's universe(s) more generally, the cat never lost what we lost: connection with the universe that allows us *place* and *presence*, not certainty. What we have lost is embeddedness in the world that would not have as one possibility a universe gone mad with speed on one side (the beginning of the story) or isolation and cold on the other (story's end).

* * * * * * *

In *Buffalo Gals*, "The Author of the Acacia Seeds' and Other Extracts from the *Journal of the Association of Therolinguistics*' (1974) is in part corrective, in part reinforcement. The corrective part comes first from the whole idea of a *Journal of the Association of Therolinguistics*, i.e., a journal devoted to the linguistic communications of animals. It may be that all things speak, even as all things dream, as George Orr says about dreaming

---

[439] For the box in the Schrödinger experiment and Pandora's box in Greek legend, see Bittner, *Approaches* 79, 81-82. Note also the box in the tale within the tale of 'A Fisherman of the Inland Sea' (coll. under primary title of 'Another Story' in *FIS*).
[440] See *LHD*, esp. 70-71; ch. 5—and chs. 3, 12, and passim. For gambling, see *King Dog*.
[441] See below, 'The Shobies' Story' (1990), where reality disintegrates, letting in the light of the stars, and must be reconstituted (*FIS* 92, 98-104).

in *The Lathe of Heaven* (*LoH* 161; ch. 10).[442] It may be that the rocks themselves speak the words that make the Earth (*BG* 175). On the other hand, the Association of Therolinguistics sounds like a classical group of loonies of the kind Northrop Frye called *philosophus gloriosus*: the cousin of the braggart soldier (*miles gloriosus*), the 'learned crank or obsessed philosopher' (*Anatomy* 39). That nonhuman animals may have their art is an idea Le Guin wants us to take seriously, and plants and maybe even the rocks as well—but that is seriously, not so somberly in earnest one cannot joke about it.

There is also a useful corrective in the 'MS. FOUND IN AN ANT-HILL,' which may be 'an autobiography or a manifesto' (167). Human people should, indeed, get embedded back in nature, but not in the manner of ants in an ant-hill. Or at least not in the way of your usual conformist ant, but only in the way of the rebel Author of the Acacia Seeds. The ant Author declares her personhood and independence and/or urges others to do so, seeking individuality and community (*BG* 167-68; seeds 1-13). She then moves on to the philosophical statement that 'Long are the tunnels. Longer is the untunneled. No tunnel reaches the end of the untunneled. The untunneled goes on farther than we can go in ten days [i.e., forever {the article authors helpfully add}]. Praise!' (168; seeds 14-22). I'd interpret this epistemologically, in terms of the known («tunneled») and the unknown ('untunneled'). The 'Praise!' I'd take in the sense of 'Heya!' (*ACH* passim): i.e., general praise for the world. However, the 'Praise' is the first part 'of the customary salutation 'Praise the Queen!'', so the word is not only philosophical / religious but highly political (and theological). Few queens would be pleased that specific praise of their Majesties became a cry of general joy (168); 'Heya!' is different from 'Hallelujah!' because 'Praise!' without an object is different from 'Praise the LORD!'

The philosophical daring of the ant Author continues when she notes that an ant stumbling into a foreign colony is killed and even 'so the ant without ants dies'; but, in spite of this, 'being without ants'—*alone* in the gloss of the article—'is as sweet as honeydew' (168; seeds 23-29). That is, the ant Author desires solitude. Even as she cries out for personhood, independence, *and* community (seeds 1-13), she also wants solitude, at least as often as she wants honeydew. Even so with Stone Telling in *Always Coming Home*, Serenity in 'Solitude,' and Ogion and (eventually) Ged in the Earthsea trilogy; solitude, community, independence, and solidarity must be part of the rhythm of a life going with the world, which means occasionally going without other people.

The final two seeds (30-31) read, 'Eat the eggs! Up with the Queen!' The human authors resolve what seems to be a contradiction between the blasphemous 'Eat the eggs' and the patriotic 'Up with the Queen' by pointing out that 'up' has mostly negative meanings for ants; they conclude by suggesting 'that this strange author, in the solitude of her lonely

---

[442] Le Guin says she got 'all things dream' from Victor Hugo, but has forgotten where.

tunnel, sought with what means she had to express the ultimate blasphemy conceivable to an ant, and the correct reading of Seeds 30-31 in human terms is: 'Eat the eggs! Down with the Queen!'' (*BG* 169).

Le Guin agrees it is anthropocentric to assume that 'Up' is good. For ants Up is the direction food comes from, indeed, but it is also the place of 'the scorching sun; the freezing night; no shelter in the beloved tunnels; exile; death'—as opposed to Down, the place of 'security, peace, and home' (*BG* 169). Even so with humans. For us, Up has been the direction of the sky gods, transcendence, immortality—and all the *ills* those bad ideas have brought. Down is the direction into immanence, dirt, Earth (the Mother).

Further reinforcement of the general theme of *Buffalo Gals* is the acceptance in the *Journal* as scientific fact that all animals, and plants and the Earth itself, do indeed talk. And Le Guin wants us to believe that the world will indeed talk to us, if we remember how to listen, and this is true however cracked the therolinguists or phytolinguists or geolinguists (175). Perhaps it is true even given our deafness: If a tree talks in the forest, and no human hears, the tree has still talked. Within *Buffalo Gals*, nonhuman animals do talk, so the beasts may very well have their art, and the plants as well. 'Can we in fact know it? Can we ever understand it?' (174-75). Maybe—but probably not through the sort of cognition that gets into learned journals. (Perhaps *human* art can't be understood through the sort of writing that makes it into learned journals.) Le Guin's therolinguists give us some good hints as to what we might look for in animal, plant, and rock art, and the crucial concern of Time. And the President of the Association instructively editorializes that the assumption that art communicates may get in the way of our appreciating plant and rock art that just *is* (173-75).

The therolinguists are probably crazy; in the world of *Buffalo Gals*, they're also mostly right.

* * * * * * *

'Direction of the Road' tells the story of change from the point of view of a large oak tree (genus *Quercus*) at the side of a road that became a highway. It's also the story of an accident.

The first point of the story is precisely that of point of view—the literal Relativity implied in point of view. In direct address to the reader, the Oak asks if

> you have ever considered the feat accomplished, the skill involved, when a tree enlarges, simultaneously and at slightly different rates in slightly different manners, for each one of forty motorcar drivers facing two opposite directions, while at the same time diminishing for forty more who have got their backs to it, meanwhile remembering to loom over each single one at the right moment:

> and to do this minute after minute, hour after hour, from daybreak till nightfall or long after? (*BG* 88)

Well, I am sure *I* hadn't thought about that. Which brings us to the second point. Having very efficiently defamiliarized what we see when we pass trees as we drive by them, our arboreal Narrator tells us that few of us humans really see at all. Most of us, driving our cars, 'merely stared ahead. They seemed to believe that they were 'going somewhere.''' The drivers on the tree's road have these small mirrors on 'their cars, at which they glanced to see where they had been; then they stared ahead again. I had thought that only beetles had this delusion of Progress' (89), and beetles at least leave the tree alone.

Which brings us to the third point.

> For fifty or sixty years, then, I have upheld the Order of Things, and have done my share in supporting the human creatures' illusion that they are 'going somewhere.' And I am not unwilling to do so. But a truly terrible thing has occurred, which I wish to protest. (89)

There has been an accident, which the Oak very precisely describes (90), and the Tree has to hit a car and kill the driver (90-91). This is not what the Oak is protesting.

> I had to kill him. I had no choice, and therefore no regret. What I protest, what I cannot endure, is this: as I leapt at him, he saw me. He looked up at last. He saw me as I have never been seen, before, not even by a child, not even in the days when people looked at things. He saw me whole, and saw nothing else—then, or ever.
>
> He saw me under the aspect of eternity. He confused me with eternity. And because he died in that moment of false vision, because it can never change, I am caught in it, eternally.
>
> This is unendurable. I cannot uphold such an illusion. If the human creatures will not understand Relativity, very well, but they must understand Relatedness. (91)

Elsewhere in Le Guin, it is good to see the Other, and see the Other whole (e.g., *LHD* 248; ch. 18). What is not good is getting a vision that sticks, where you think you can *be* in eternity: e.g., Meshe in *The Left Hand of Darkness* (ch. 12). The Oak agrees to kill 'If it is necessary to the Order of Things,' but refuses to play death: 'For I am not death. I am life; I am mortal' (91).

The last tree I ran into that was so philosophically inclined was the tree that became the cross of Jesus of Nazareth in Old English poem, 'The

Dream of the Rood.'[443] The Rood Tree, though, was in favor of eternity; the Oak here makes some of Le Guin's favorite points: Relatedness requires being in the world and does not let you go outside it; Relatedness makes 'Progress' a difficult idea, since one needs to stand outside the world to be sure which direction is right for 'Progress.'[444] Relatedness implies mortality, and quests for immortality destroy relatedness. The Tree angrily ends, 'I will not act Eternity for them. Let them not turn to the trees for death. If that is what they want to see, let them look into one another's eyes and see it there' (*BG* 91).

****

I have discussed 'Vaster than Empires and More Slow' (1971) above, but will take a second pass at it here in the context of *Buffalo Gals*. Le Guin in her introduction to 'Direction of the Road' and 'Vaster...'—paired in *Buffalo Gals*—notes that they are different from most SF in taking a serious interest in plants and, simultaneously, '*both stories...are quite conventional science fiction,*' with 'Direction' as '*yet another point-of-view shift*' story (but with emphasis on Relativity) and 'Vaster' as '*a story about boldly going where, etc. In it I was, in part, trying to talk about the obscure fear called* panic, *which many of us feel when alone in the wilderness*' (*BG* 84). Le Guin recounts very briefly her losing the trail on a mountain in Oregon and having her '*individual relation to the trees and undergrowth and soil*' and her '*relative position in the earth-and-ocean-wide realm, as an animal and as a human...brought home*' to her, hard. She immediately goes on to note how absurd it is to be afraid of a tree and how easily we humans can (and possibly will) wipe them all out. But there was that '*obscure fear,*' the moment of panic.

Here I want to note that 'Vaster' is the most familiarly science fictional story in *Buffalo Gals*; and I want to talk about panic and about the opening four paragraphs of 'Vaster' as it appeared in its original form in *New Dimensions I* (1971). The science-fictional aspects of 'Vaster' can be reviewed very quickly: a crew of ten humans go by Nearly As Fast As Light (NAFAL) travel where, indeed, none have gone before and make First Contact with a totally vegetative sentience. One of the crew separates himself from the others and ends up attacked by—something—in the forest. The something turns out to be another crew member, and the humans themselves turn out to be in a way responsible for what hostility they really do feel from the vegetable sentience. All standard SF, out of *Star*

---

[443] A modernization of 'The Dream of the Rood' is collected as the first poem in *Norton Anthology of English Literature*, I, 4th-6th edns. The original OE poem may be found, titled 'Dream of the Cross,' in *Bright's Anglo-Saxon Reader*, Revised and Enlarged by James R. Hulbert (1935), item XXX.

[444] On the 'ideal of progress' as an idea Le Guin, speaking in her own voice, finds troublesome, see 'Is Gender Necessary? Redux' *LoN* (1989/92): 155.

Trek, many First Contact stories, and the classic 1950s science fiction movie, *Forbidden Planet* (1956).

I will assume my readers have a bit less background on minor Greek gods.

Our word 'panic' comes from the Greek god Pan, son of Hermes; Pan was a god of fertility, goatherds, and flocks and a rural god. If his father, Hermes, was a protector of travelers, Pan could be a problem for them: 'He was dreaded by travelers whom he sometimes startled; hence sudden fright without any visible cause was ascribed to him and called *panic* fear' (*Smaller Classical* 'Pan'). Edith Hamilton lists Pan as chief of the Lesser Gods who lived 'in the world,' upon Earth All-Mother. He is both god and animal, 'with a goat's horns, and a goat's hoofs.... All wild places were his home....' (40). The *Encyclopaedia Britannica* (1974) entry for him gives him the legs and ears of a goat as well as horns and hooves. More to the point for me, it adds that 'Pan' is a Doric contraction of *paon*, 'pasturer,' but the name in antiquity was 'commonly supposed...to be connected with *pan* ('all').'

The people in 'Vaster than Empires' go into a planet-wide vegetative system and feel very uneasy, eventually feeling panic; and the vegetative world, too, panics. The forest and other plants panicked because of the people. The team Biologist describes life on the planet as 'a network of processes. The branches, the epiphytic growths, the roots with those nodal junctions between individuals: they must all be capable of transmitting electrochemical impulses. There are no individual plants, then, properly speaking.... But it is not conceivable. That all the biosphere of a planet should be one network of communications, sensitive, irrational immortal, isolated....' The team's empathic Sensor picks up on 'isolated' and solves the main mystery of the fear of the plant world: "'Isolated,' said Osden. 'That's it! That's the fear. It isn't that we're motile, or destructive'— earlier it had been suggested quite plausibly that plants would fear as threats anything that moved quickly—'It's just that we are. We are other. There has never been any other.' This theory is accepted: "You're right.... It has no peers. No enemies. No relationship with anything but itself. One alone forever' (*BG* 122-23).

The forest and with it the other plants 'panicked' when faced with individuals: an Other they had never encountered. In the case of Osden, the Sensor, an Other who would be hard to miss because he sensed emotions from any entity and transmitted them back, ordinarily amplified. Osden will have to absorb the forest's (et al.'s) fear and get beyond it to bring the story to a satisfactory end; but here I want to just accept the plants' panic and ask why the people panicked.

One obvious answer, because Osden was attacked in the forest with no obvious cause, and such free-floating threats are precisely what people from Pan's time on have thought the source of panic. Another obvious answer is that they panicked because the plants panicked: a vicious cycle (*BG* 119). And both these obvious reasons are part of the answer, but the people in the story were primed to panic and felt uneasy in the forest early on.

Le Guin eliminated a hint, when she removed for publication in T*he Wind's Twelve Quarters* and later *Buffalo Gals* the first two paragraphs of the original story.

> You're looking at a clock. It has hands, and figures arranged in a circle. The hands move. You can't tell if they move at the same rate, or if one moves faster than the other. What does *than* mean? There is a relationship between the hands and the circle of figures, and the name of this relationship is on the tip of your tongue; the hands are...something-or-other, at the figures. Or is it the figures that...at the hands? What does *at* mean? They are figures—your vocabulary hasn't shrunk at all—and of course you can count..., but the trouble is you can't tell which one is one. Each one is one: itself. Where do you begin? Each one being one, there is no, what's the word, I had it just now, something-ship, between the ones. There is no between. There is only here and here, one and one. There is no there. Maya has fallen. All is here now one. But if all is now and all here and one all, there is no end. It did not begin so it cannot end. Oh God, here now One get me out of this—
>
> I'm trying to describe the sensations of the average person in NAFAL flight. It can be much worse than this for some, whose time-sense is acute. For others it is restful, like a drug-haze freeing the mind from the tyranny of hours. And for a few the experience is certainly mystical; the collapse of time and relation leading them directly to intuition of the eternal. But the mystic is a rare bird, and the nearest most people get to God in paradoxical time is by inarticulate and anguished prayer for release. (88)

What the minor god Pan represents in his person and behavior is the dissolution of boundaries: Pan is god in human form with animal parts—god/man/beast. In the folk etymology of his name, Pan is All: everything, absence of boundaries. Part of *pan*ic is the loss of the boundary between human passion and reason, with one passion—fear—overcoming reason and any passions reason might have enlisted to aid it. One source of panic fear, ironically but understandably, is the fear of loss of self, the ultimate dissolution of boundaries, when we stand in a forest or approach the ocean or any other vastness that reminds us that the price of our individuality is triviality.

If you are not a mystic, the temporary fall of Maya can be unpleasant, and the long-term fall of Maya, madness. Maya is the illusion of the world most of us call 'real': the material world divided up into human categories and organized in human relationships. Opposed to Maya is Nirvana, which is the state of the forest and other plants, the plant *world*, in 'Vaster than Empires and More Slow': 'Sentience without senses. Blind, deaf, nerveless, moveless. Some irritability, response to touch. Response to sun, to light to water.... Nothing comprehensible to an animal mind. Presence without mind. Awareness of being, without object subject. Nirvana' (*BG* 118).

Tomiko, the Coordinator of the expedition, wants to know why Sensor Osden receives fear from the plant world, and the Biologist Harfex says that the 'sentience' of such an entity 'would not be capable of conceiving of a self-moving, material entity, or responding to one. It could no more become aware of us than we can 'become aware' of Infinity.' Tomiko quotes Blaise Pascal, an early physicist (religious philosopher, mathematician) on the heavens: "The silence of those infinite expanses terrifies me'...Pascal was aware of Infinity. By way of fear' (*BG* 119).[445] The forest may be aware of the humans by way of fearing them, and the humans may come to fear the forest as we fear infinity: the dissolution of boundaries, of Self. In the context of *Buffalo Gals*, 'Vaster than Empires' undergoes, I think, a shift in focus, getting us to concentrate slightly less on the ten human actors and slightly more on what we initially thought was background, and then (in fine SF fashion) must recognize as a major actor. 'The reader can't take much for granted,' Le Guin has said about SF generally, 'where the scenery can eat the characters' (*Norton Book* 31). As synecdoche for the whole plant world, the forest becomes a character, and the humans' relationship with the forest becomes the major theme of the story.

The climax of the story, in a sense the main *action*, is Osden's getting in touch with the forest, absorbing the fear, and deciding to stay in the forest (*BG* 125-26). He has a moment of decency toward his fellow humans on the planet: 'Listen,' he says, 'I will you well.' This is an English form for the Italian 'Ti voglio bene': 'I love you,' here nonerotic love, suggesting a familial love (*BG* 126).[446] Still, his major action is one of moving away from humans to become a 'colonist' on the planet (*BG* 128). In reading the story in *The Wind's Twelve Quarters*, I saw Osden as being far more pushed away from humans than attracted to the planet and what Tomiko—a very positive character—finds as her 'intolerable experience of the immortal mindless' of the planet. In *Buffalo Gals*, however, it would be more appropriate to stress Tomiko's making sense of what Osden has done. The passage I would stress for 'Vaster' in the context of *Buffalo*

---

[445] *ODQ* 374.1 cites for the quotation Pascal's *Pensées*, § iii.206. Note Le Guin's use of the *Pensées* for 'The heart has its reasons, which reasons does not know': straight in 'The Shobies' Story' (*FIS* 79) and as a joke in *TD* (108; ch. 5).

[446] Carol D. Stevens said that when she gave Le Guin a lift from Oxford, OH, to Bloomington, IN, she asked Le Guin if she intended the Italian expression, and Le Guin said she did. My thanks to Stevens, Le Guin, and to my colleague John Romano for help with the Italian.

Gals starts with a realization that Osden would be impossible to track down and bring back.

> But he was there; for there was no fear any more. Rational, and valuing reason more highly after an intolerable experience of the immortal mindless, Tomiko tried to understand rationally what Osden had done. But the words escaped her control. He had taken the fear into himself, and, accepting, had transcended it.[447] He had given up his self to the alien, an unreserved surrender, that left no place for evil. He had learned the love of the Other, and thereby had been given his whole self.—But this is not the vocabulary of reason.
> The people of the Survey team walked under the trees, through the vast colonies of life, surrounded by a dreaming silence, a brooding calm that was half aware of them and wholly indifferent to them. There were no hours. Distance was no matter. Had we but world enough and time... The planet turned between the sunlight and the great dark; winds of winter and summer blew fine, pale pollen across the quiet seas. (*BG* 127)

Ants mindlessly toiling for ant-hill and Queen—No. Loss of ego and thereby gaining a whole Self, a Self embedded in nature and Being imaged as forest and sea—Yes. In *Buffalo Gals*, indeed *yes*. Very clearly in *Buffalo Gals*, Osden comes to a happy ending, joining in the joy of letting go Le Guin's Daoist sages in the early works, King Ashthera in the Hindu inflected *King Dog* of 1985, and the character Serenity in 'Solitude' in 1994.

In terms of the *Kulturkampf* for the hearts and minds of Americans and other Westerners who read works of the imagination, and in terms of the development of Le Guin's work, *Buffalo Gals* can be seen as a beautiful and fitting coda to *Always Coming Home*.

---

[447] For 'transcended,' see Bittner's discussion of *aufheben*: see *Approaches*, Index.

VIII.

OTHER LESSONS: PICTURE BOOKS[448]

The earliest artistic pieces I remember from my childhood are Ray Bolger's narration of *The Churkendoose* and a performance—I assume at the Goodman Theatre in Chicago—of a dramatized version of Hans Christian Andersen's 'The Emperor's New Clothes.' In addition to a comically Lamarckian view of the inheritance of acquired characteristics *in ovo* among domestic fowl—the Churkendoose is a chimera of chicken, turkey, goose caused by different birds incubating the egg—*The Churkendoose* taught tolerance of differences and that an evaluation of people 'depends on how you look at things.' 'The Emperor's New Clothes' teaches the solidly empirical and commonsensical lesson I'll paraphrase as 'I see what I see—and will speak my truth to power.' I find it disconcerting to realize how much of my approach to the world is contained in the tension between 'It depends on how you look at things' and the occasional necessity (for me anyway) to yell out that figurative emperors just *are* buck, bare-arse naked. We need not resolve this philosophical issue here nor dig into my psychology. I raise the point to give you what support I can for my assertion that I have not studied children's literature, but I take it very seriously.

Ursula K. Le Guin's picture books for children are not propaganda; they do not indoctrinate. Indeed, they are far subtler and 'open' in their teaching than, say, the propagation of Christianity in C. S. Lewis's *The Lion, the Witch and the Wardrobe* or Madeleine L'Engle's *A Wrinkle in Time*—or even the manners lessons in J. R. R. Tolkien's *The Hobbit* (see Stevens and Stevens 62-65). More significantly, perhaps, they are generally more subtle—with fewer openly didactic statements—than Le Guin's fantasy and science fiction for older children, young adults, and grownups. Part of the explanation for the subtlety may be Le Guin's maturation as an artist: most of her picture books come late in her career (1988 f.); part, though, may be just Le Guin's good manners. A picture book is a kind of guest in a child's room, and Le Guin's Shevek, as a house guest, 'kept out of the ethical mode with some scrupulousness; he was not there to propagandize his host's children' (*TD* 120; ch. 5).

---

[448] My thanks to my colleague Anita Wilson, an expert in children's literature, for discussing with me my ms. for this chapter.

A study of children's books, though, is a good way to learn what a culture, or an author, thinks most important for getting across to children: not necessarily propagandizing them or indoctrinating them with, but teaching them—with room open for interpretation, for arguing with the texts. A study of Le Guin's picture books gives a useful index to much of the continuity and change in her writing.[449] It shows her in a theater of the *Kulturkampf* where the competition for hearts and minds can be intense but gentle.

Fish Soup (1992)

Possibly the most explicit of Le Guin's teaching in her picture books is in *Fish Soup*, and the main lesson is the generally feminist, or simply sensible, one that children are 'shaped by the...expectations' held by significant others 'of what a child should be.'[450] There are also more subtle lessons about expectations, reader expectations.

In the story there is a man, the Thinking Man of Moha, and a woman, the Writing Woman of Maho, who are good friends. And that is the entire opening cast: a man and a woman. They live in any world sophisticated enough to have bridges, books, domesticated animals, dishes, dishcloths, shoes, socks, fishing rods, butterfly nets, chess, and caramel pudding—and the illustrator is undoubtedly correct in showing them in clothing and a generalized rural setting appropriate for the USA in the late twentieth century. The Writing Woman lives and makes her books—including binding them—in a 'messy house, where the mice flew through air,' literally, 'and the cats collected furballs as big as pillows in every corner,' but do not hunt the flying mice. The Thinking Man lives in a house he keeps 'neat and clean,' with no cats, no mice, and 'only an old cow in the garden, and she was a clean cow' (1-4 & passim). The woman makes a decent enough fish soup; the man is competent to make a full meal. The two friends meet frequently and engage in animated conversation (2-6).

The «inciting action» for the story is a conversation in which the Thinking Man tells the Writing Woman that he thinks 'that it would be nice if we had a child.' She wants to know 'Whatever for?', and the man replies that 'It could run back and forth between our houses and carry messages for us when we're busy.' The woman notes she's quite competent to carry on her own communication with the man; so the man suggests that 'A child...could finish the caramel pudding,' which the Woman can also

---

[449] In the following sections I cover almost all of Le Guin's picture books, but I am quite certain I miss at least one. OhioLink interlibrary loan service notes *In the Red Zone* by Le Guin, illus. Henk Pender (Northridge, CA: Lord John P, 1983), with a first edn. press run of 150 numbered copies, with one at the U of Cincinnati, 'ARB Rare Books.' Since I'm privileging readers in *Coyote*, I decided against handling a book few would get to read, unless there is a trade rpt.

[450] Quoting 'Summary' in Library of Congress Cataloging-in-Publication Data, copyright page of *Fish Soup*.

do, and does. But 'The man paid no attention. His mind was fixed on the flutter of a child's dress as she ran, and the twinkle of her feet' (7-8).

The woman leaves the man's house without offering to help him with the dishes 'knowing that he did not like the way she did it' and preferring 'to wash them himself.' On the way home she sees, or almost sees, 'the flutter of a little red dress before her on the road,' and a child's footprints; and at home the cats and the flying mice tell her 'She's here...she's here!' What 'she' is, though, is just 'a little red dress' and 'two little shoes and socks.' The woman asks where the rest of the child might be, and is answered with only a sigh (8-10).

Within the next couple of days, the woman's friend comes to Maho to see her, and the woman tells him, 'The kind of child that might be useful is a boy,' giving the man the chance to ask 'Whatever for?' and the woman the one, very utilitarian response, 'He could go fishing for us.... We never have enough fish soup.' The man «harumphs» back, 'I'll fish for myself...thank you!' and leaves without offering to help with the dishes, 'knowing that she only washed them when all the bowls and spoons were dirty.' On his way home, he sees 'a small, quiet person with an angling rod for the trout and a butterfly net for the flying fish'—but he pays no attention to the child (13-15).

When the Writing Woman next comes to visit the Thinking Man, the man tells her how he was fishing and saw 'The boy that fishes' fishing, and catching three more than the man. 'I was writing this morning,' the woman responds, 'and that girl kept sweeping up the dust, till the cats all hid and the mice sneezed.' The man doesn't want the boy catching the man's fish; the woman doesn't want the girl 'fussing about' her house. He suggests they trade (16). The woman suspects a trade won't be very easy, but doesn't argue against it; and when she comes home the cats inform her, 'He's here...he's here!' She soon spots the mice in a birdcage hanging from the rafters, 'eating barley and murmuring happily.' After some thought, the woman acquiesces to caging the mice but states the rule that pet flying mice must be fed daily, and their cage cleaned out once a week. She is answered by a giggle from the pantry (19).

Meanwhile, back at the 'neat and tidy house at Moha,' the Thinking Man is finished very carefully cleaning up his kitchen and enters his other room—to find it very untidily rearranged to be the proper mise en scène for a story of how 'brave people crossed the sea to go exploring in the wild mountains.' After some thought, the man acquiesces to the disorder, but states the rule that after play everything must be put 'back just so' (20-22).

The next morning, the Writing Woman finds a new room to her messy house, with a boy coming out of it. She wishes him good morning, and he returns the words, asking if there is any 'soup for breakfast.' There is none in the pot, so the boy goes out fishing. He returns with fish, which the woman cooks into fish soup, while the boy washes dishes, clears a spot on the table, and sets it for their meal. Allowing the possibility of such a good little boy, the only unusual thing here is that 'as he ate the soup, he began to grow, and he grew to quite enormous size.... And the house seemed to be quite full of him, so that the woman felt there was hardly room for her' (23-24). Over the next little while, his growth slows but continues, distracting the woman and making it inconvenient for the boy to move around (25).

The boy is about to 'go do something useful,' as the rather exasperated woman asks him to, but before he can leave for fishing, the Thinking Man of Moha shows up, with an animated 'little red dress and a pair of shoes and socks.' He asks concerning the girl, 'What's wrong with this child?... Why isn't there more of her,' and notes with some frustration, 'There's certainly enough of *him*!' And then the climax of the story:

> The woman looked at what there was of the girl and at all there was of the boy, and she thought (for she could think, and the man could write, too). And at last she said, 'Perhaps it depends on what we expect of them.'
> 'What did you expect of the boy?' the man asked.
> 'Too much,' said the woman.
> 'Oh, that's all right,' the boy said, but he shrank about two feet and began to smile.
> 'He doesn't have to catch *all* the fish,' the woman said, and the boy became his own size, which was just the right size to give a hug to.
> Which brings them to the girl, about whom the man said he didn't expect too much.
> 'No, indeed, said the woman. 'Did you expect anything of her at all but a twinkling and a flutter?'
> 'I did think she could carry messages.'
> 'That's true,' said the woman.
> They looked and saw two little legs dancing in the shoes and socks.
> 'I did think,' said the man, 'that she could finish the pudding.'
> 'I think so, too, said the woman.'

At which point the girl appears (28-29), and there is a brief dialog on whether or not the girl can fish. She can but doesn't like fishing; she likes to climb trees, and climbs a nearby apple tree 'right to the top'—well, almost to the top, as drawn—and tosses down an apple for each of them. The adults think the kids will do, and the kids think the same of the grownups. 'So they all lived at Maho and Moha, in and out and back and forth across the hills. The woman's house got a little neater, and the man's house got a whole lot messier.' The story closes by telling us all four of the human characters 'learned how to cook excellent fish soup' (31-32).

Necessarily left out of my account have been the illustrations, and that is unfortunate: at least two of them catch very nicely the tone of *Fish Soup*. This is important. Part of what keeps Le Guin's work almost always *teaching* works and not Sister Ursula Explaining It All is a sly sense of humor, the mature comic sense that comes from having an idea of one's place in the universe. This comedy is caught especially well in an early illustration (2-3) of the Writing Woman and the Thinking Man sitting and talking and 'waving their spoons at passing mice'—although the Writing Woman is relatively sedate at the moment pictured. Mice are in the air, except for one, either checking out a narrow space or trapped between books, and a second who sits like a miniature gargoyle at the top of a stack of books watching the Thinking Man gesticulate. The table is piled high with books, whose titles include the *Oxford Elvish Dictionary*, *Thpeaking Thornish*, *Kitty Lit: A Treasury of Cats' Favorite Bedtime Stories*, *Little Mouse [on the Pr]airie*, *Logic Made Difficult*, and *Lorenzo Bean Goes Boating*, this last one named after Le Guin's cat. The final illustration doesn't show any humans, just four mice—as much characters in the story as the humans—performing a tight-rope walk in their circus, watched intently by an audience of very innocent looking cats (32).

The MORAL of Le Guin's fable is, of course, what is identified in the Summary on the copyright page: children are 'shaped' by the expectations of their care-givers. Much less than in this story, of course, and much less than many adults flatter ourselves by thinking—but children are shaped by our expectations quite enough that we must be careful and mindful in our expectations for them. But the story also plays nicely and far more subtly with other expectations, and I wish to emphasize them.

First, note that the Thinking Man is from Moha and the Writing Woman from Maho. The place names associated with the characters should not, but may, violate our expectations: 'All female names,' as Ramchandra reminds us in 'The Pathways of Desire' (1979), 'end in 'a.' That is a cosmic constant established by H. Rider Haggard' (*CR* 183). Rationally, there is no more reason to associate a male with Maho and a female with Moha than to assume the male lead in a realistic story should come from Chicago and the female lead from Atlanta; but some of us, quite unconsciously may so irrationally assume, and this initial minor reversal is useful. Whether readers, especially young readers, associate thinking with men and writing with women is more serious, but much of the rest of the story involves fairly straightforward and highly useful «gender benders» and reversals.

The messy house-keeper is the woman; the neat one is the man. The relatively messy child who tells a story of heroic exploration is the girl; the neat, relatively quiet child is the boy. The directly useful child is the fishing boy; the less domestically useful child is the tree-climbing girl. The woman doesn't scream at the sight of a mouse, not even many flying mice. The man is a competent cook; the woman can make fish soup, but that seems about it. The woman works with her hands binding books as well as writing them; the man's work, thinking, is less manual. The man wants a child, and a girl-child at that; the woman is not very keen on the idea at first, but then prefers a boy. And the whole group learns to cook fish soup. Domesticity, readers are taught, is a major concern of human life—immanent living in the world—but domesticity is not encoded on the sex chromosomes, nor is the desire for children. Simple observation and common sense ought to teach us that parenting isn't an inherited trait in humans, but experience and common sense are not sufficient for a lot of us to learn, so presenting the idea in a story and pictures is a good idea. We don't have the extreme here of Shevek's careerist mother, Rulag, and parental father, Palat (in *The Dispossessed*), and this is appropriate; still, a child can learn from *Fish Soup* that a father might want a daughter, and that a good woman might not be enthusiastic about the idea of having any children, and, if she must choose, might want a son.[451]

Also of interest, the mother and father figures are «*just* friends» and emphatically not married or romantically or erotically involved, or living together. Within the conventions of most children's literature, the point would be muted, but still it is clear that one possible and good female/male relationship is friendship and that the 'just' in the adult expression «just friends» may underrate friendship. In *Fish Soup*, friendship is a strong enough bond for a kind of two-house but two-parent family. And from the tests, so to speak, of the caged mice and the messed up room, it looks like the two adults will make good parents: they think before they react to what the kids have done; they lay down reasonable rules that let the kids do what they want, within limits. In any event, the kids accept the parent-figures even as the parents accept the kids, and we can assume they'll all live and love happily ever after, or until they die. Properly understood, traditional family values can be achieved in nontraditional families, and parents don't need to be married. Whether or not nonmarital sex producing children is a good idea just isn't covered: the creation of the kids in this story is totally asexual.

In addition to the central moral of not expecting too much of boys and too little of girls, there is important imagery with the boy becoming a giant and the girl remaining invisible. In *The Food of the Gods...*, H. G. Wells generally privileges the huge size of the new race of young giants (Elkins 808-09), and the usual view I've encountered in American society is that parents generally and mothers in particular should be happy to be overshadowed by any children they have (especially sons) who become figurative «giants on the Earth». The Writing Woman, on the other hand, is realistically not pleased to have a house quite so 'full of *him*' (my emphasis) 'that the woman felt there was hardly room for her' (24). In *The Beginning Place*, Le Guin problematicizes kids' sacrificing themselves for their mothers, and in Big Man in *Always Coming Home*, Herman Macmilan in *Eye of the Heron*, and Bill Kopman in 'Pathways of Desire,' Le Guin presents very negative versions of male figures filling the world.[452] In *Fish*

---

[451] This is, of course, another stereotype, but one with a kernel of truth to it: fathers often want and appreciate daughters; mothers often want and appreciate sons. (My sister and I agree this was the case in our family.)

[452] See Big Man in 'Big Man and Little Man' (*ACH* 157), Luz on Macmilan in *EoH* (103; ch. 7), and Bill Kopman in Tamara's dream-vision in 'PoD' (204, 206).

Soup, Le Guin suggests mothers ought not to sacrifice themselves for their sons: such altruism is a bad idea for the mothers, and it can be very uncomfortable for a son (24-25).

The girl's invisibility relates to Alice Sheldon's 'The Women Men Don't See' (1973), which Le Guin and Brian Attebery anthologized in *The Norton Book of Science Fiction*.[453] The motif also relates to Ralph Ellison's *Invisible Man* (1952). In all these cases, part of the idea is that some people count and others don't, and that people who don't count in the world—have no clout or importance—are figuratively and sometimes literally invisible to those with power and status. In *Fish Soup*, the Thinking Man wanted a child and a girl child, but had not—either consciously or unconsciously—expected enough of her. He had to be reminded that he wanted more than 'the flutter of a child's dress...and the twinkle of her feet' (8), even as the woman wanted both more and less than a perfect fisherboy.

Little boys should not be expected to be godlike giants in training; they should be small enough to hug. Little girls should be expected to be whole human beings, and should be encouraged to follow their own bents and knacks, not conform to stereotypes. And everyone should learn basic cooking skills and learn to fit into a world where cats and fantastic flying mice have an important place in the story, and the inhabitants of civilized Cities of Men do not.

A Ride on the Red Mare's Back (1992)

Le Guin's first published science fiction story was *'written in 1963, published as 'Dowry of the Angyar' in 1964 and as the Prologue of...[her] first novel,* Rocannon's World, *in 1966'* (*WTQ* 1). It is 'Semley's Necklace': a science fiction version of a Nordic-style fairy tale, where a beautiful, young, golden-haired noble woman, of more courage than wisdom, against advice goes on a quest for the great treasure of her family. Her quest takes her on the back of a tiger-sized winged cat to see her old, alcoholic father, and from there she goes among elf-like creature (the Fiia) and among troll-like troglodytes (the Gdemiar, or clayfolk). The industrial, acquisitive, hierarchical, oligarchic—if somewhat colonial/telepathic—sexist troglodytes take the young wife on a strange overnight journey. She comes to a museum of a high-tech culture and gets back her family's necklace and returns to the cave of the clayfolk and her windsteed, she thinks, the next day. And returns home—to arrive, of course, many years later: the Gdemiar took her in a Nearly As Fast as Light space ship to another star system, and the folk motif of one night = many years is rationalized by the time dilation experienced at relativistic speeds.

In her headnote to 'Semley's Necklace' in *The Wind's Twelve Quarters*, Le Guin says she used that story to open her collection *'because I think it's the most characteristic of my early science fiction and fantasy*

---

[453] Under year and Sheldon's pseudonym, 'James Tiptree, Jr.'

works, the most romantic of them all.' She finds her stylistic progress, even as of 1972, to have '*been away from open romanticism...from this story to the last one in the volume,*' 'The Day Before the Revolution.' Le Guin notes, though: '*I'm still a romantic, no doubt about that*' (*WTQ* 1). In Roland Duerksen's term, Le Guin is among the 'Critical Romantics,' in the radical tradition of William Blake, Percy Bysshe Shelley, and John Keats: Romantics who saw poetry working in the world and politically relevant, for whom imagination could shape the world. In Le Guin's development *that* stance remains consistent, as do some story elements.

In Le Guin's 1992 picture book *A Ride on the Red Mare's Back*, a father takes his son hunting for the first time, and the son is stolen by trolls. The father despairs, and, as the flyleaf note puts it, 'because there is a baby to mind,' the mother 'must stay in the cottage.' So the third child, the oldest, the daughter, went on a quest to find her brother, walking through the winter of the North. As in many children stories (as my colleague, Anita Wilson assures me), a heroic child will venture where adults cannot or will not, even as children, in tales for children, are often smarter than the grownups.

The girl takes with her in one pocket 'the scarf she had made for her brother, and the wooden knitting needles that her father had also made for her, and the rest of the ball of yarn. In the other coat pocket she put the end of a loaf of bread that her mother had baked that morning.' And in her hand she carries 'the only toy she had, a wooden horse that her father had carved and painted for her' (13-14; § 1). The girl asks the horse directions and goes the way its head points. Fearfully walking onto a bridge, she encounters her first troll: '...over the side of the bridge, from underneath it, a great, long arm came reaching, and a great, wide hand groped toward her' (19; § 2). The girl invokes aid from the toy horse and it transforms, in a familiar motif, into 'a real horse, full size, bright red, with a bridle and saddle of flowers, and bright, fiery eyes!' (20-21; § 2). In answer to the troll's question, 'Who's that stamping on my bridge?' the horse names herself: 'Me! The red mare!' (22; § 2). The little girl asks the troll, 'Where did your brothers take my brother'—no troll sisters mentioned—and the troll demands payment for the information. The little girl gives the troll her 'mother's bread,' and the troll tells her 'The boy's in the High House' (22-23; § 2).

> "I know the way to the High House,' the red mare said. 'But it's a long way. We must come there tonight and bring your brother away before the dawn, for I have only this one night with you' (23; § 3).

They arrive at the High House, a mountain, wherein dwell the trolls. The red mare diverts most of the trolls, getting them to chase her, while the girl slips into the mountain; she must bring out her brother before dawn because the trolls 'will all go back underground at the first light... lest they be caught in sunlight and turned to stone.' And, again, the red mare has only this one magical night (27; § 3).

'The room was huge, like a cave,' where the trolls live; and it is a mess, with troll-children of various sizes running around, smashing toys and furniture and playing, significantly, King of the Mountain. 'And far across the room four or five troll-children were fighting over a toy of some kind, or perhaps something to eat.... She looked at them and saw that one of them was not a troll-child, but her brother' (31; § 4). An asexual or androgynous old troll—the singular pronoun throughout for trolls is 'it'—challenges the girl, and there follows a serio-comic brief episode where the little girl first intends to stab the troll's hand with a knitting needle if it tried to grab her but ends up giving the troll the knitting needles and yarn. The girl tries to teach the troll to knit, 'but the old troll was too stupid and impatient to listen to her,' growling 'I know how!' (34; § 4).

The adult guard diverted, the girl goes to rescue her brother, telling him that their parents grieve for him. He doesn't want to be rescued: 'I like it here. I can do anything I like here. I don't ever go to bed. I can eat rats! I can kick people! I'm going to be a troll when I grow up, and be stronger than anybody, and kill things!' (34; § 4). On her way out, the girl remembers the scarf she'd knitted for her brother and gives it to him. He takes it, says he's cold, and asks to go home; his sister may have managed to communicate with him better than their parents communicate with each other (Wilson). In any event, the girl carries her little brother out, nearly at dawn (36; § 4).

Outside, the trolls have roped and managed to get the reins of the red mare. They avoid her hooves and teeth, 'But the biggest troll came closer to her from behind, holding a long stone knife' (37; § 5). The girl cries 'Look out!' and the red mare moves to attack the big troll—when day dawns and the trolls are turned to stone. 'In the midst of the stones a little red thing lay on the snow.... Its paint was chipped and one shoulder was battered, but...[the red mare toy] was not broken' (40; § 5).

The girl knows they 'must go home,' but the boy asks 'Where is home?' All they can see is 'white snow, grey rock, black forest.' Plus 'a thin, fine, silvery thread, delicate as a spiderweb' (41; § 5)—a thread Wilson suggests we equate with parent/child love. The thread leads them home, ultimately, but most directly to the bridge, where the troll—grateful for the bread—lets them pass without incident (42-44; § 5); the girl has made a friend.[454]

Arriving home, they are welcomed with quiet joy by their sleepless parents. The father had been whittling and gives her a toy: a small, as-yet-unpainted little horse, the red mare's colt (46; § 5).

I was taught in graduate school that 'The first duty of a critic is to state the obvious,' but I'll try not to belabor it. In 'Semley's Necklace' we have a heroine on a quest, involving trolls—the Gdemiar are called 'trolls' by

---

[454] See also 'the thread of way' in the poem 'Torrey Pine Reserve' (1973) coll. *BG* (76).

the politically incorrect Ketho (*WTQ* 18)—and the heroine gets what she wants, at a price. The story is a beautiful exercise in irony and the science-fictionalization of folk motifs, but, like its folk ancestors, it teaches some lessons. Headstrong youngsters should listen to good advice; headstrong noblewomen should avoid quests; and headstrong people generally should avoid quests motivated mostly by pride; plus more recent ideas about the unintended effects of using technology (and old cautions against trusting trolls). In *A Ride on the Red Mare's Back*, the young and poor heroine does what she *must* do and, in league with the forces of nature and magic, she does it successfully.[455] She does get home; which is important, since Le Guin, in some moods, is competitive with both E.T. in the Los Angeles suburbs and Dorothy of Kansas and Oz in stressing 'There's no place like home': 'True journey is return.' Still, the girl gets home after an adventure and profits from her adventure. The costs are some bread, a pair of knitting needles, and some yarn. The profit is getting back her brother, her parents' gratitude, and a toy colt for the toy red mare.

Semley gets her necklace, has a great adventure, and demonstrates determination and courage that are admirable. She loses a big chunk of her life, her family, and possibly her mind (*WTQ* 22). Semley mostly loses; the young heroine of *A Ride on the Red Mare's Back* mostly wins. Semley, I'd say, teaches in part the good, conservative, folklore message of Caution, especially for girls and young women. *A Ride on the Red Mare's Back* teaches having the courage to do what one feels one must do, the necessity for small sacrifices for larger goals, and that even a troll can become one's friend, if one will share and give gifts and not hold fast to possessions. The story also teaches that trolls are mostly nasty and that little boys might well find the freedom of troll-life highly attractive. Especially the parts about being King of the Mountain and eating rats and hurting and killing people. But that's just a little boy's thing, and with some kindness (and maybe a gift), he can be brought around to a more loving attitude and brought home. The story teaches little girls to trust their abilities, to trust the natural order of things, their luck. And it teaches little boys that a male-bonding hunting ritual with dad might have its dangers.

Solomon Leviathan's Nine Hundred and Thirty-First Trip Around the World (1983)

> I cannot rest from travel; I will drink
> Life to the lees.
> * * *
>
> Yet all experience is an arch wherethrough
> Gleams that untraveled world whose margin fades
> Forever and forever when I move.

---

[455] She consults her toy horse as if it were an oracle and gets her way pointed out, for a combination of a faith in magic (and her luck), intuition, and following an animal's lead—a wise idea in folk tales.

> How dull it is to pause, to make an end,
> To rest unburnished, not to shine in use!
> —Alfred, Lord Tennyson, 'Ulysses' (1833/1842)

Solomon Leviathan's...Trip... tells the story of two friends and philosophers—a giraffe and a boa constrictor—who live on a forest-covered 'runcible island' far from 'the coast of Kansas.' I.e., they live in a fairly typical Le Guinian arboreal world, just more clearly fantastic than most. Kansas has no more coast than Bohemia outside of William Shakespeare's *The Winter's Tale*, and if, as I, you looked up 'runcible,' you found it's a nonsense word coined by Edward Lear, but one that sounds decorous in a world inhabited once by such intellectual talking animals as Le Guin's boa constrictor and giraffe (7).

For no particular reason I can spot, the giraffe decides that the sun's being 'halfway to noon' is the proper time to go down to the sea. So they do, and I think even grownup readers accept their going: as Joseph Campbell has shown in great detail, that's what the Hero *does*; he leaves his mundane palace or village or whatever and goes off to find a portal to the world of adventure, where he might find himself (*Hero* ch. 1, esp. §1; also pp. 245-46). There are some significant differences here between the boa constrictor and the giraffe versus the usual fairy-tale hero. First, we have two central characters starting out, not one, and «Who is the sidekick to whom?» is not a relevant question; they are equals. Second, they are both vertebrates, but otherwise the giraffe and boa constrictor don't share much biology with each other, and they—or the boa at least—differ from human readers more than we get in most fairy tales. We adults are certainly used to talking animals in folklore and more realistic stories (Le Guin's own *City of Illusions* for one example), but they are usually Helpful Animals, not our hero. Even 'The Frog King' begins from the point of view of the human princess, not that of the frog, and the frog is, of course revealed to be 'no frog but a king's son with kind and beautiful eyes' who 'had been bewitched by a wicked witch' (*Grimm's* [20]). Third, the hero is usually a hero, gendered male; only some occasional pronouns indicate the genders of the giraffe and boa constrictor, and they are male and female respectively (10, 14). And finally, the boa and giraffe are both well-bred intellectuals. When the giraffe asks the boa 'Where does your tail begin?', he asks politely and briefly justifies the question. The boa constrictor responds, intellectually, 'I am an indivisible entity to which such hypotheses are irrelevant' (8). And just a bit later the giraffe explains that, contrary to folklore, he can talk rather better than he can see (or walk) because he is 'an intellectual giraffe' (10).

Arriving at the sea, the giraffe sees the horizon and thinks of the boa constrictor's tail: even as it's difficult to tell where a boa constrictor's tail starts and stops, so it is difficult to determine 'where the sea stops and the sky starts, or the other way round' (10). They find a boat, and the giraffe wants to go to sea; the boa is less enthusiastic but goes along, apparently out of friendship (12). The boa likes the boat, called *Serendipity* in the picture on p. 13, and the two friends float off with some parody of sailors' jargon. And then stop, or, more exactly, go back and forth with the waves and backwash, 'not getting anywhere in particular' ([14]). So the boa bites the boat, lowers herself into the water, and begins 'to whirl herself rapidly,' except, of course, for her head, as the Narrator is careful to tell us. The Narrator solemnly adds that 'This is how all big ships move themselves, although instead of a boa constrictor they use a rotary screw' (15).

There is nothing ahead of them 'except that mist where the sky and sea meet,' so the two greet the horizon. 'Ahoy, horizon!' they yell. And, as adult readers will guess, 'The horizon did not answer' (15). The hawk's flight is bright 'on the *empty* sky,' the *Creation of Éa* says in the Earthsea headnotes (my emphasis); 'Heaven and Earth are not humane' as Lao Tzu gets to teach us in the headnote to *The Lathe of Heaven*, ch. 8.[456] The friends do not take well to the silence of the horizon, nor to its staying always ahead. 'We shall pursue it,' the boa constrictor replies 'grimly.' The giraffe wants to know what they'll do with the horizon when they reach it. 'Order it to strike sail,' the boa replies, 'Board it. Conquer it!' Sex and gender go deep, but speciation goes deeper: the hunter-killer female boa constrictor is more aggressive than the herbivorous male giraffe. And such hubris will bring its nemesis in stories, even in stories in worlds without gods: the delightful day at sea is interrupted by a storm (16). Not being able to bail, the friends must drink the saltwater that sloshes into the boat.

After the sea calms and all is going well—except for the discomfort of having swallowed all that bilge water—the friends and their boat are swallowed by a sperm whale.[457] They recognize that it's a whale because the giraffe knows a relevant whale Rune (with a capital 'R'), and with a little empirical investigation they figure out they've been swallowed. Having analyzed their position in the world, they reassert their identities as philosophers and determine on action: their duty as philosophers is 'to wait philosophically for whatever may happen' (22). They wait. The whale goes to the Arctic, and then south and whatever direction takes whales 'within sight of the coast of Switzerland,' where he—it's a male whale—sounds. The whale goes very deep, down to the realm of photoluminescent fish, who speak a language unknown even to whales, though the boa constrictor claims to know it (24). Readers of Le Guin might picture this place under the sea as an area quite like that from which arose Atlantis in *The New Atlantis*. In terms of plot the (relative) silence of the depths of the sea is significant because the whale hears the two friends talking and eagerly greets them (25).

The whale is, naturally, Solomon Leviathan, who has been host, moving backward in time, to 'a whole boatload of sailors,' in a story I don't

---

[456] The headnote cites 'Lao Tse: V'; the full opening sentence of this section of the *Tao te Ching* reads, in the Chen translation, 'Heaven and earth are not humane *(jen)*, / They treat the ten thousand beings [i.e., everything realized in the world] as straw dogs *(ch'u kou)*' (64).

[457] See and contrast Campbell ch. 5, 'The Belly of the Whale.'

recognize, 'a little wooden puppet fellow' (Pinocchio), a baron whose name Solomon Leviathan 'didn't catch,' but probably Baron Munchausen, and 'that fellow who started it all—the one who argued so much,' who is the one name Solomon Leviathan remembers: Jonah. This name leads to others; Solomon introduces himself, and we learn that the giraffe is Damon and the boa constrictor Ophidia.[458] And the exchange of names leads to Solomon's question of where Damon and Ophidia were going.

> 'We were sailing to the horizon,' the boa constrictor said.
> 'Sailing to the horizon!' said the whale.... My friends, I was named after King Solomon, I am the second son of the first whale, I have swum round the world nine hundred and thirty times, and I have never reached the horizon!'

The giraffe and the boa constrictor are silent for a short while. At last the giraffe said, 'Mr. Leviathan, you are older than anyone in the world, but because even you have never reached the horizon does not mean that it cannot be reached' (26). Solomon denies being the eldest: there's a much older redwood tree, and 'an elephant in India who is the first elephant that ever was. Adam named him. Lord Buddha rode him. He might know about the horizon' (27-28).

Taking an unnarrated shortcut through the Suez Canal, the friends arrive in India and Solomon makes his presence noisily known to the Eldest, who is known simply by the Adamic form: Elephant (28).

Solomon explains the situation, and Elephant explains, with what sounds to my ear as Ekumenical exactness, that the horizon 'is an effect formed by the curve of the earth, the mist on the sea, and the beholding eye. The horizon is not a place. It does not exist. I do not know how to get there. If I were you, I would simply go ahead. It seems the best way.' Solomon objects that 'The horizon must exist,' in the sense that it's their goal: 'If we want to get to it, why then, it is the thing we want to get to'—which only reinforces Elephant in his view that they should just keep going. And, in case they run into fog—which would keep them from perceiving a horizon—just *imagine* a horizon (29).

The upshot of the story is that 'The three friends have already been around the world; they have not caught up with the horizon yet, but they are having such a good time trying that they intend to go right on' ([32]).

* * * * * * *

---

[458] Some plausible the Greek possibilities for 'Damon' include the suggestion 'daemon' or 'daimon' in the sense of 'genius' or 'intellect' or Damon the Pythagorean, friend to Phintias, usually confused with Pythias (*Smaller Classical Dictionary*). 'Ophidia' is another name for the biological suborder Serpentes: snakes.

It's going to sound like a parody of presentation titles at academic conferences, but I'd like to stress in *Solomon Leviathan* a bit of ontology and intertextuality, plus a couple variations on some romantic themes generally and Le Guinian in particular.

I suggest above that *Solomon Leviathan* fits in with Le Guin's atheism in making the obvious and incontrovertible point that if you hail the horizon you will get no answer. There need to be no agency or transcendence in the universe besides the fondness of authors for irony that Damon and Ophidia's dismissal of storms as 'Childish stories' precedes, but does not cause, a storm at sea.

But there is in Solomon Leviathan's world, Jonah.

Looking from the outside into the world of *Solomon Leviathan's... Trip*, few dogmatic Christians would be happy. In the world of this story Jonah was swallowed by that 'great fish'—or aquatic mammal—Solomon Leviathan. Still, Jonah has the same ontological status in *Solomon Leviathan's...Trip* as Pinocchio. Even as a great fan of the Book of Jonah, I have no problem with Jonah as a fiction. In our world's history, it seems that there was a prophet named Jonah, son of Amittai, and he was important enough to rate mention in the Bible (2 Kings 14.25). There may also have been a historical King Arthur or a King Lear (or Lir), and I'm quite certain there was a historical King Richard III. For critics and children, though, the main or only existence of these characters is in stories, plays, movies—art. If the Book of Jonah is factual, then God worked a great *mâshâl* in history in trying to teach Jonah a lesson in mercy. For us, though, two millennia and more later, what remains is the *mâshâl* of the story, The Book of Jonah. So, as a practical matter, Jonah *does* have the same ontological status as Pinocchio: the main character in a teaching story.

Just to point it out is to overread, but it is significant that to Solomon all Jonah is is 'that fellow who started it all,' the bad precedent of people allowing themselves to get swallowed by Solomon, and Jonah is 'the one who argued so much' (25). In any event, Solomon Leviathan has no memory of being 'appointed' by God to swallow Jonah, sound, and eventually vomit him up on dry land close to Nineveh. As biblical missions go, Jonah's is, arguably, the most worthy: bringing salvation to Nineveh with no blood spilt at all. The mission from God, if it happened, though, is eminently unmemorable.

A great journey to reform a world city isn't what you have in *Solomon Leviathan's...Trip*. Salvation isn't the goal. Indeed, neither is the goal that of Ulysses in Tennyson's version: the Romantic Quest by the Romantic Hero who (a) thinks he might actually find something Out There, and (b) just can't stay still. *Solomon Leviathan* suggests that a more proper goal for people (including all philosophical animals) is a horizon: a goal given form by human perception as much as anything Out There, a goal given meaning totally by human beings giving it meaning. 'If we want to get to it, why then, it is the thing we want to get to.' More important, the journey of the three friends is a true journey because, first, it necessarily returns to its starting point—a feature of traveling full-circle around a globe—and, second, because the three friends in their quest are enjoying not only a macrocosmic immanence in their cyclical movement (and in their being embedded in Solomon) but a microcosmic one as well, in their domesticity. Long ago the three friends started their journey in and on the sea (a good symbol of immanence) and they continue with their routine:

> At noon Solomon Leviathan stops by an island, and the giraffe and the boa constrictor go out and eat lunch, while the whale goes fishing. Along in the mid-afternoon he returns; they climb back in; he spouts, and they all set off toward the horizon. When he is tired he rests on the water. The two philosophers recite Runes and Odes, and the whale tells tales from History.... (30)

Dr. Katz, Fire and Stone, and the Catwings Series (1988-94)

A Visit from Dr. Katz (1988) is described on the flyleaf as 'a fun and gently soothing book, just right for the child who knows the boredom of a day sick in bed.' It is also as close to *Ars gratia Artis* as Le Guin gets in the books I've looked at, and the one aimed at the youngest audience; or, more exactly, it is 'Art for the sake of fun' and cheering up a sick child: a worthy goal.

Marianne is a little girl, not described in the text but imaged in Ann Barrow's illustrations as young school-age, well under ten, and the book itself seems suitable for a pretty young audience: the longest and most problematic word is 'machine-gun,' and the book would work best read aloud, with the pictures resolving for a young child the riddle of Dr. Katz. Barrow draws Marianne's mother as a blond woman, briefly seen at the beginning of the book, and draws Marianne in a style that reminds me of the *Fun with Dick and Jane* books when I was a child, just drawn with more skill. Marianne as pictured is neither fat nor thin; she is cute but not what adults 'Ohh' and 'Ahh' over as 'a beautiful child.' She has a room of her own, and a nice room, and looks to me in the illustrations as a 'generic White girl,' upper-middleclass, Germanic or English in 'extraction,' as people used to say.

Marianne is sick with the flu and upset almost to crying by having to spend the day in bed. Her mother tells her to 'just lie down' (she's already in bed), and she, the mother, will 'see if Dr. Katz will come in and see you.' Marianne 'lies quietly waiting' and is rewarded with the arrival of Dr. Katz.

'Dr. Katz came in on eight white paws, and goes two different directions. Dr. Katz has long white whiskers.' If the child is being read to, the riddle here is, What sort of doctor has eight paws, long white whiskers, and can walk in two different directions? Showing the picture reveals that Dr. Katz is two tomcats: a long-hair and a short-hair. The older and more affectionate is Philip, the long-hair; the younger and more active is Lorenzo, called The Bean. Marianne gets Philip and then The Bean up on the bed with her; they warm her and wash each other; and then Marianne goes to sleep. The story ends with a picture of Marianne and Dr. Katz from the mother's point of view: 'After a while Marianne's mother looks in. Marianne and Dr. Katz have all gone to sleep. One of them is still purring.'

Again, this is a narrative without much of an agenda, but it still teaches; and it teaches parents as well as children.

First, the opening assumption is that 'The healthy animal is up and doing,' as the ethologists say—and even sick young animals will want some action. Marianne doesn't want to stay in bed: it is a given that a girl wants to act, not just be still. But as Ai and Estraven agree, 'Sick men take orders' (*LHD* 218; ch. 15)—and so do (good) sick children. They take orders, don't cry at an inevitable inconvenience, and can punctuate their activity (in good Daoist fashion) with occasional stillness and wait quietly. Good children also don't need mother with them all the time, not even when they're sick; and they learn how to deal with pets. When Marianne wants The Bean, she doesn't get out of bed and grab him but wiggles her toes under the covers. Fanatically consistent theorists might chide Marianne for colonizing cats by learning that they're «hard wired» to pounce on such wiggling motions; most adults would be thrilled that a kid has learned that you don't have to force cats to come to you.

Mothers as well as children learn a lot from what is *not* in this story: no doctors other than the cats, no medicines, no vaporizers, no special treatment except rest and sleep. Aside from wanting the mother to have left some water for Marianne, my physician would be happy with the omissions here. Even as the child can learn to work with the cats and not force them, so mother and child can learn to deal sensibly with a problem like a mild flu: basically, no high-tech attempts to force nature. We can note that such a sensible approach to dealing with—not *fighting*—the flu is something of a luxury, but the lesson to be learned from that is that it is a messed-up society that encourages people to go to work sick and sometimes forces them to send their children to school when those kids should be in bed.

* * * * * * *

Fire and Stone (1989) fits more obviously into Le Guin's canon because it features a rather realistic country 'Once upon a time' and a beautifully drawn village that could be on Sattins Island in 'The Rule of Names': your basic old-world village, but with a dragon. There are also two wise children—a chubby girl and a short boy—and a stubborn, somewhat dense (male) mayor. The two children, Min and Podo, have learned cooperation in the water avoiding the dragon's fiery breath: plump Min helps keep short Podo from sinking; short Podo helps keep plump Min mostly under water.

The dragon attacks the village crying out 'in its dreadful voice— 'RRRAAAHHHX! RRRAAAHHHX!'' And our two featured children work out between them that it might be calling for '*rocks! rocks!*' Mr.

Goose, the Mayor, wants them to keep quiet; instead the children bravely throw rocks 'straight up in the air.' The dragon catches and eats the rocks. 'DO NOT FEED THE DRAGON!' The Mayor shouts, but everyone does. The dragon lands and the villagers feed it rocks and more rocks until 'Podo fed it one last, tiny pebble.' Then 'The dragon closed its mouth and closed its eyes. It slept. All its fire and hunger had been filled up, and it was only stone.' So the dragon becomes 'Dragon Hill,' and the villagers and have learned that what looks like an enemy may not be; as with the troll in *Red Mare*, our apparent enemy may be just hungry.

The last lines of the story are the words of the sunrise song of the village:

> *Dragon brightness*
> *feeds the earth.*
> *Mother darkness*
> *gave us birth.*
> *Sun is fire,*
> *Earth is stone.*
> *Sing together*
> *at the dawn!*

The story, then, teaches not only tolerance as in *Red Mare* or but implies in the final song a universe in which the apparent and perhaps real antitheses of fire and stone, light and dark, society and nature, old and young come together to form a larger unity. This is a good Daoist lesson that fits in with the anarchistic idea (well liked by tellers of kids' tales) that two kids may know better than the mayor.

The Catwings Series

Catwings (1988), *Catwings Return* (1989), and *Wonderful Alexander and the Catwings* (1994) all feature winged cats like the windsteeds in *Rocannon's World*, only much smaller. We might say *Rocannon's World* is to the Catwings series as a windsteed is to a catwing as a tiger is to a domestic house cat. Alternatively, we could fit *Catwings* into the canon in the sense that *Wonderful Alexander* is to the first two *Catwings* books (though to a lesser degree) as *Tehanu* is to the Earthsea trilogy: same world, same premises, but with a more emphatically feminist emphasis.

Catwings is the story of an escape from an inner-city dumpster life by a litter of four winged cats out of Mrs. Jane Tabby.[459]

---

[459] Le Guin dedicates *Wonderful Alexander*... 'To the Bean'; S. D. Schindler, the illus., adds a dedication to three 'visual reference cats.' Le Guin and Schindler know cats: four is exactly the average size of the litter of a domestic 'queen' cat ('Cats' 998).

Mrs. Jane Tabby could not explain why all four of her children had wings.

'I suppose their father was a fly-by-night,' a neighbor said, and laughed unpleasantly, sneaking round the dumpster.

'Maybe they have wings because I dreamed, before they were born, that I could fly away from this neighborhood,' said Mrs. Jane Tabby. (3)

Mrs. Tabby is ready to mate again and so she sends her four flyers away. First, she wants them to take advantage of their wings and leave a bad neighborhood. As in *The Beginning Place*, *The Eye of the Heron*, 'Omelas,' and other Le Guin stories, sometimes the best thing we can do is get out: if you can't reform a place, leave it. Second, 'My work is here,' their mother tells them. 'Mr. Tom Jones proposed to me last night, and I intend to accept him. I don't want you children underfoot!' This eviction notice causes the kittens to cry, 'but they knew that that is the way it must be, in cat families. They were proud, too, that their mother trusted them to look after themselves.' So they fly away, their mother watching, with 'Her heart...full of fear and pride' (7-8).

The catwing kittens eventually find a wooded area and are very happy. 'They knew they had come to a much better place than the alley, but they also knew that every place is dangerous, whether you are a fish, or a cat, or even a cat with wings' ([17]). The local birds are not happy at all, but mostly 'had to learn to get along with the Flying Tabbies,' even as mice had learned to deal with predatory birds. 'Most of the birds, in fact, were more frightened and outraged than really endangered, since they were far better flyers than Roger, Thelma, Harriet, and James,' the four flying kittens. However, the birds 'were alarmed, and with good cause, about their fledglings.' *Catwings* isn't Disney: the kittens hunt, kill, and eat their prey. 'It took a while for the Owl to understand' the danger. 'Owl is not a quick thinker. She is a long thinker' (20), rather like George Orr in *The Lathe of Heaven*. Very much unlike George Orr, Owl is an armed predator, and in a suggestive scenelet, as scary in its spareness as the murder of Frank Poole in *2001: A Space Odyssey*—James chases bats near Owl's nest, and Owl slowly thinks "This will not do...." Then '...softly Owl spread her great, gray wings, and silently flew after James, her talons opening' ([21])—and then a quick cut to the catwings' nest and the discovery of James 'crouching under the bushes, all scratched and bleeding, and one of his wings dragged upon the ground' (22).

Now they 'know how the little birds feel' as Thelma grimly says, but that knowledge can't stop them from being cats. They must hunt to live, and that becomes a problem with Owl outside their nest: 'From then on they had to hunt in the daytime and hide in their nest all night; for the Owl thinks slowly, but the Owl thinks long' (25). Cats hunt best at night, and Owl's vigil seriously limits the catwings' hunting. At their low point, Harriet spots a human, and the kittens consult. Their mother had taught them "that if you found the right kind of Hands, you'd never have to hunt again. But it you found the wrong kind, it would be worse than dogs"; they guess these 'Hands' are 'the right kind' because the person knows not to try to grab a cat and knows to put out food. And wait. The point of view shifts slightly to the 'Hands': the human children Hank and Susan, who had put the food out for the kittens. And who wait. The kittens come to them. Susan promises Harriet she will never 'catch you, or cage you, or do anything to you you don't want me to do,' and Hank promises, too, adding that they'll never tell people about the winged cats, 'Ever! Because—you know how people are' (38). Harriet may or may not understand Susan's promise, cats and humans speaking different languages (*Wonderful Alexander* 29).[460] But whether she understands are not the promise is binding, and so they are all married—bonded—the catwings and the human children, and they'll all live happily ever after, at least to the sequel.

Note here again the commonsense lessons for children about animals, how to deal with animals, and about nature. Flying cats, are a definite maybe; they are the 'What if...' premise of the book. Vegetarian cats—no. The book also teaches the importance of patience and working with cats, not trying to force them to obey your will. And *Catwings* also teaches the hard lesson that a meal for feral kittens may mean an empty nest for an Owl, and that a new litter for a queen cat means that the last litter is shoved out on its own. 'Heaven and Earth are not humane'; nature *is*. And the book teaches that a promise is a promise, whether made to a fellow human or an Other who may not even speak your language, even a radically different Other not even of one's own species.

In the sequel, *Catwings Return*, the kittens are well into adolescence and have personalities of their own, personalities somewhat conditioned by their genders. 'Hank liked to toss kibbles in the air and watch Roger catch them, and Roger liked to catch them. Susan liked to hold kibbles in her hand while James ate them.... Thelma and Harriet took their breakfast seriously, preferring not to play games with it' (4-5; ch. 1). The human children (and their mother) still keep the winged cats a secret; 'They feared people'—adult people anyway—would try to put the catwings 'in cages, in circuses or pet shows or laboratories, to make money by owning them or selling them' (5; ch. 1). The children seem well aware of the capitalist threat; the more gothic threats of vivisection or dissection do not occur to them (they have not, apparently, seen *E.T.* or *Starman*). Nor do the children or Le Guin consider here the more benign possibility that some ethologist might want to just observe and study winged cats. In any event, the kids have no qualms or second thoughts: their mother can know about the catwings, but no other adults.[461]

---

[460] In conversation with me on 13 May 1996, Le Guin mentioned that she took care to ensure it was unclear whether or not the catwings were «bilingual» and understood English.
[461] So far in the catwings stories, Susan and Hank's father has been absent or invisible.

The children obviously love the catwings, and the catwings have become very close friends with the children. This friendship is important because the catwings have something of an ethical dilemma. James and Harriet want to return to the old alley of their kittenhoods to see their mother; Roger and Thelma think it a bad idea, in part because the children would be very sad if they found all four of the catwings gone. More important perhaps, they remember the city as a very bad place: 'Too many people in the city—it's dangerous.' And their mother had told them to use their wings 'to escape' (6; ch. 1). The catwings come to an obvious conclusion: Harriet and James will go home to visit their mother; Roger and Thelma will stay at Overhill Farm with Susan and Hank.

With trust in their Homing Instinct, and following the stench of garbage, Harriet and James fly to the city and find their old neighborhood in 'the narrowest, dirtiest alley in the oldest, poorest part of the city' (12; ch. 2). Home itself, though, their dumpster, is gone, and so is their mother. And the neighborhood is going: 'A couple of city pigeons flew by to see what the cloud of dust was. 'Knocking down another slum,' one pigeon said, and the other said, 'That's progress'' (16). 'Progress' is described in terms of men and large machines, with emphasis on the machines, knocking down buildings. Inappropriate technology here, in the service of a problematic ideal—Progress—literally moving people and things around, apparently without even a 'By your leave' to the local inhabitants.[462] In one of the buildings, Harriet and James find a black kitten, that usually says 'Me!... Me! Meeeee!', but, when angry (or frightened?), yells 'HATE! HATE! HATE!' (17-23; ch. 3). It's a scared, dirty, very hungry kitten. A kitten with wings.

Harriet and James save the kitten from death by wrecking ball and the collapse of the building it's in; and with the help of a rather rude starling they locate another cat on a roof (33; ch. 4). The cat on the flower-potted roof is Mrs. Jane Tabby, mother of Harriet and James and of the black kitten.

Mrs. Jane tells her older children how Mr. Tom Jones, her last mate, 'was called by business to another part of town' (37): Le Guin cleans up a bit feline sexuality and omits the sometimes deadly behavior of tomcats toward kittens.[463] Tomcat morality is less the point than keeping Mr. Tom offstage for a crucial scene in Mrs. Jane's narration. While Mr. Tom is out of town, 'a dreadful thing happened.' Mrs. Jane's dumpster is 'taken

---

[462] I've tried to keep my tone here light, appropriate to a work with a happy ending, but the point by Le Guin is highly serious: see esp. *ACH* for an extended meditation on appropriate technology, and consulting with *all* the 'local inhabitants,' including rivers and nonhuman animals, before making changes (33-35; Stone Telling 1 [and passim]); see 'Buffalo Gals' in *BG* for looking at «Progressed», places, inappropriately built up and paved over, as dead and deadly, outside the world.

[463] Le Guin also downplays territoriality and somewhat overstates cats' generosity, feline solidarity, and family feeling for nonlittermates (see 'Cat' 997).

away'—passive voice deleted agent, but necessarily by humans, probably men. With the dumpster gone, humans 'saw the kitten—saw her trying out her wings.... They ran to catch her,' and Mrs. Jane runs to save her. 'The poor baby, given strength by her terror, flew straight up and into a broken window high on a roof. I could not follow her,' Mrs. Jane says, and 'The people could not enter the building; it was locked.' Angry, the humans pursue Mrs. Jane, separating her even farther from her kitten. Mrs. Jane searches, is chased by dogs and finally, when she is exhausted, friendly hands pick her up, carry her indoors, and put her in the roof garden. Since Mrs. Jane is 'too old to enjoy street life any more,' she was relatively content in her elevated garden-world, living with a kind human, just very sad for the loss of her kitten. The kitten's return with Harriet and James completed Mrs. Jane's happiness (37, 39; ch. 4).

One thing remains: Mrs. Jane wants Harriet and James to take the kitten back to their home in the country. Mrs. Jane tells her grown children the kitten 'must go': 'Now that I know she is alive and well, and is with those who will look after her, all I wish is that she be safe. And there is no place in this city for a winged cat to be safe.' Mrs. Jane will 'lie in the sun in my roof-garden and dream of her flying with you, in freedom. And that will be my happiness' (40; ch. 4).

The city seems huge, and the first night of flying endless, but Harriet and James, if they do not exactly trust their Homing Instinct at least hope it 'knew what it was doing' (43; ch. 5). Finally, they find a familiar church roof and use it for a landmark—as nice a role as Le Guin has given a Christian institution—and James can tell the kitten truthfully, 'It's all right.... We're going home!' (43-45; ch. 5).

Laia Asieo Odo's tombstone says, 'To be whole is to be part; / true journey is return' (*TD* 68; ch. 3), and on a grave marker the immediate meaning is that one is part of one's planet and of the earth of one's planet, and at the end of life's journey one returns to the earth.[464] Still, in *The Dispossessed* and in Le Guin more generally, the truest journeys have approximated the full circle of the quest return: to 'There and Back Again.'[465] In *Catwings*, the kittens get out of a bad situation they cannot help to improve. In *Catwings Return*, Harriet and James as *part* of a whole litter can responsibly leave home (Overhill Farm) and return home to the old neighborhood, which is being torn down, the old dumpster, which is gone, and to their mother, who waits. In Le Guin's ongoing dialog with Le Guin, escape and freedom have been balanced by return. The demand for risk-taking and the dancing always 'above the hollow place, above the terrible abyss' (in the Earthsea formulation [*FS* 121; ch. 8]), is balanced

---

[464] I think Odo's saying also hints at a resolution to the more problematic portions of the postmodern idea of the fragmented, uncentered, nearly-abolished self. People can have the wholeness possible in our places and times by consciously participating in, being truly part of, webs of relationships.
[465] 'There and Back Again' is the subtitle to J. R. R. Tolkien's *The Hobbit* (1937 f.).

against a rational attempt to find safety, however much the world may be radically unsafe.

And we get Le Guin's pretty constant Romanticism: machines and cities usually bad (under Capitalism, statism, patriarchy, and visions of Progress, anyway); country better. And a farm with friendly, generous, and discreet kids is ideal, for cats. Harriet and James return to the farm, and introduce the kitten to her feline family and to Hank and Susan. The kitten says 'Me?', and Hank thinks her name might be 'Mimi'; Susan thinks not: 'I think...I think her name might be Jane' (48; ch. 5 unspaced dots indicate an ellipsis mark in Le Guin's text).

So at the end of *Catwings Return*, we have a moderately happy ending, with the catwings not only united and augmented with a new kitten, but that new kitten apparently brought into the world of discourse by receiving from a girl what sounds like the kitten's true name: her mother's name. The one very big exception to the happy ending, is that the kitten has said nothing else besides 'Me!' and 'HATE!' She has used language to assert her selfhood and in defense, but for no 'I-You' relationship. 'To be whole is to be part,' including being part as an active participant in a speech community.[466]

This major problem is resolved in *Wonderful Alexander and the Catwings*. Significantly, it's resolved by a point-of-view character who is a nonflying, over-privileged, male kitten who comes into relationship with young Jane.

Wonderful Alexander is Alexander Furby, a Feline American Prince with a self-esteem problem: it's much too high. Alexander is 'the oldest kitten' in his family, 'the biggest, the strongest, and the loudest,' also the only male in the litter (1; ch. 1). Hovering as he does between cat and human, he's the first-born of the litter (the inverse of the 'runt') and both the eldest and the boy in a family. Amateur students of human birth-order might predict Alexander to be intelligent, assertive, and confident. If he's overconfident—and he is—Le Guin suggests that that's because he was raised that way. Alexander bosses around his sisters and plays with them more roughly than they like. 'But Mr. and Mrs. Furby and the Caretaker and the Owner [of the country home he lives in] looked on and laughed and said, 'Alexander's all boy! Nothing frightens Alexander!... Alexander is wonderful!' And, of course, 'Alexander was sure they were right' (2; ch. 1).

In the hands of a satirist and moralist, young Alexander would have become an overindulged kitten going wrong (those familiar with the work of Anthony Burgess might picture *A Clockwork Hairball*); having been created by a very late Romantic like Le Guin, Alexander goes on a quest, going 'out the cat door all by himself' and setting off 'to explore the world.'

Alexander thinks the world ends at the fence around the garden, but he learns to his surprise 'that there was another side to the fence' (2-3; ch. 1). Very much like Shevek in *The Dispossessed* going through the opening in

---

[466] Cf. and contrast Spark's limited language abilities in *Tehanu*.

an emphatically two-sided wall to the spaceship that will take him to Urras, somewhat like Irena or Hugh going through the gate into the twilight land in *The Beginning Place*, and like any generic quester from Odysseus going down to Hades in the *Odyssey* to the SF characters played by Kurt Russell and James Spader going through a super-technological portal in *Stargate* (1994)—Alexander slips through the fence. And then he encounters his first real obstacle: 'Slipping under another fence, he found himself on a narrow, dark plain that stretched as far as he could see to the left and to the right. The trees were just on the other side of it, and he trotted bravely forward,' onto that 'narrow, dark plain' (4; ch. 1).

The illustration makes clear that the 'narrow, dark plain' is a highway. Still, I recommend that adult readers of *Wonderful Alexander* simultaneously picture both that highway and a Sartrian plain with only alienated men, plus Matthew Arnold's 'darkling plain / * * * / Where ignorant armies clash by night.' Amidst the beautiful world of *Wonderful Alexander*, adults should picture a very narrow Existentialist strip—or 'One of the holes' in the world—between Overhill Farm and the woods, and while on that strip they should momentarily picture the image in Thomas Carlyle's *Sartor Resartus* of the entire universe as 'void of Life, of Purpose, of Volition, even of Hostility,' just 'one huge dead, immeasurable Steam-engine, rolling on, in its dead indifference to grind me limb from limb' (152; 'The Everlasting No').[467] And then adult readers should see the strip again as a highway and note that the Existentialist vision may wrongly generalize to the universe and the human condition the very unusual situation of stubborn, civilized, egocentric, alienated Man Alone.[468]

Such philosophical exercise are too ponderous for *Wonderful Alexander*, but the image from *Sartor Resartus* is appropriate for this moment in Le Guin's story. Alexander hears

> a strange purring noise, far away. He wondered if it might
> be lions. His father had told him about lions. The noise
> grew from a purr to a deep roar. It must be lions, Alexander thought, but he would not be frightened—until he
> looked to the right, and saw a huge truck rushing at him,
> its headlights like terrible staring eyes. ([5]; ch. 1)

Alexander crouches down, and the truck rolls over him, bruising him, half-blinding him, and sending him scrambling for the relative safety of 'the dark shelter of the trees' ([5]; ch. 1).

In the woods, Alexander is chased up a tree by two hounds and is afraid to climb down. He both assumes and hopes that the Caretaker or his Father

---

[467] The hole in the world allusion is to 'Buffalo Gals, 'Won't You Come Out Tonight' (*BG* 40-41), q.v.; see also the places out of the world in *ACH*: what we'd call 'civilization.'
[468] I allude to Eric and Mary Josephson's anthology, *Man Alone: Alienation in Modern Society* (1962).

or Mother will find him. What he is found by is Owl, and Alexander bravely 'puffed himself up...and hissed at her.' The Owl chuckles and flies off (6-10; ch. 1). After a night in the tree, Alexander just wants to go home, but 'He did not know where his home was.' And then, at this low point, he sees 'a bird flying straight towards him.... He knew that a cat shouldn't be afraid of a bird. But last night he had seen the Owl.' It's not a bird, but young Jane. Alexander introduces himself, and Jane responds with 'Me!' (13-15; ch. 2).

Alexander asks Jane if she can talk, and in response she just 'lashed her tail a little, looking sad,' and Alexander responds with 'Well...I can't fly' (16; ch. 2), a nice introduction for kids to the idea of people's being, if not exactly 'differently abled,' at least differently disabled. Jane helps Alexander get down the tree. Alexander wants to go home because his family will be upset at his absence and his sisters will cry and be lost without him. Alexander finally just admits he's lost, and Jane says 'Me!' and pounces on his tail and then trots off. 'Alexander followed her' (17-18; ch. 2).

Alexander is adopted by the catwings and human children at the farm, and, since he has no wings, he can be most centrally adopted by Susan and Hank's mother. To perfect the situation, Alexander's Owner stops by and is pleased to locate Alexander and is even more pleased to entrust him to the children's mother. When the Owner visits he brings Alexander's parents, although Mr. Furby, Alexander's father, usually sleeps through the visits (21-31; ch. 3). Alexander finds no featherbeds or sardines laid out for him on the farm, and he's expected to be a barn cat and a working hunter of mice. Hank and Susan's mother thinks Alexander a wonderful kitten, and Alexander therefore thinks her very smart, but they cannot discuss his wonder or her intelligence or anything else: '...cats and human beings don't speak the same language' (29). More disappointing is that Alexander can't talk to Jane. During the exposition of chapter 3, Thelma tells Alexander that Jane 'has never said a word, except *Me*, and when she is frightened, she says, *Hate!*'—which is indeed the case we see with Jane and, if generalized, introduces the very common idea that fear yields hatred. The older catwings 'think something terrible happened to her when she was a young kitten, separated from our mother.' Alexander responds that Jane is 'very brave. She rescued me' (25; ch. 3).

Alexander is happy and grows fast (33; ch. 4), bothered only by the memory that he had gone off on his quest to do wonderful things.

> All he had done was get nearly run over by a truck, chased by a dog, stuck in a tree, and lost. Jane had saved him and brought him to this happy home. It was Jane who had done the wonderful thing.
> What wonderful thing could he possibly do for Jane.
> What could an ordinary cat do for a cat with wings? (33-34; ch. 4)

Alexander—in his human aspect—is caught in immanence and desires a project, and we're supposed to approve. Alexander seeks a taste of the 'rapturous consciousness of life beyond self' (Eliot 3; 'Prelude'). At least he wants to do *some*thing. What he thinks of is the obvious: He will play psychiatrist to Jane and get her to talk. The therapy is very straightforward and probably within the competence of an intelligent talking cat. Alexander knows that young Jane and Mrs. Jane got separated, 'And then machines tore down the building.' Alexander knows the experience had to have been terrible for young Jane. 'But there must have been something even worse—something so bad you can't talk about it—something so bad you can't talk *at all*. But if you don't talk, Jane, how will we ever know what it was?' (35; ch. 4). And then, in spite of some growls and a series of *HATE!*s and a bite, he stands on her tail until she talks (36-37; ch. 4).

What Jane fears and hates is rats, and Jane tells her story of being threatened by rats, rats that 'whispered' to each other, planning her destruction (38-39; ch. 4). Aside from humans' usual bad feelings about rats, the whispering is disconcerting and fits in with negative uses of whispering in the Earthsea trilogy: the gebbeth whispering to Ged thoughts of despair (*WE* 108; ch. 6), Cob's whispered promises of eternal life and 'the whispering of the souls of the dead' (*FS* 166; 'Selidor,' ch. 11)—or the whispering of the Shing in *City of Illusions* (ch. 8). Jane hides her face in Alexander's 'warm, furry side,' and then Alexander washes her and reassures her. Jane finally says 'I love you, Alexander'; and Alexander responds, 'I love you, Jane' (40; ch. 4).

So Jane is talking again and explains to the rest of the feline family that she had been afraid: 'I was afraid that if I talked, the only thing I could say would be the bad thing—the rats. And then they'd be real again.' Now, though, Jane is no long afraid she might conjure up rats with her words: 'But I know it's all right, and I can talk. Because Alexander showed me' (41; ch. 4).

The end of *Wonderful Alexander* raises the possibility of a sequel, where the catwings will return to their mother to show them young Jane can talk: 'It will make her so happy when you talk to her, Jane,' James says. Roger tells Alexander that Alexander is wonderful, and Jane agrees. "'I know,' said Alexander'—and so ends the book ([42]; ch. 4).

Wonderful Alexander and the Catwings is the most feminist of the catwings trilogy and most philosophical. The story accepts as a given that young sentients will and should want to do something 'wonderful,' something heroic. What is at issue is how we'll define 'heroic,' and what sort of heroic actions might be decorous for the different genders. *Wonderful Alexander* is quite clear on this issue: true heroism is helping others, and the gender stereotypes just do not apply. Young Jane gets Alexander down from the tree; Alexander nurtures Jane and with some «tough love» helps her break through to her fears, and helps her face and overcome her fears. Not exploring the world, not scratching a dog, not even trying to defeat an Owl: true heroic action is getting someone to where they can say, 'I love (you).'

It is well for Alexander to leave the Owner's country house and its decadence, where he could have ended up slothful like his father, or a spoiled bully. He did well to cross the dangerous highway, get back to the more natural world of the woods, and then arrive at a compromise between decadence and the wild: a farm, where he can earn his keep catching mice and still have humans feed him. But most important, he can do his one needful thing: do what he ethically *must* do and get Jane to talk. And then he can accept her love and the admiration of his new family, and fall back into the immanence and feline domesticity of a true home.

Leese Webster (1979)

> But in her web she still delights
> To weave the mirror's magic sights,
> For often through the silent nights
> A funeral, with plumes and lights
> And music went to Camelot;
> Or when the moon was overhead,
> Came two young lovers lately wed:
> 'I am half sick of shadows,' said
> The Lady of Shalott.
> — Alfred, Lord Tennyson,
> 'The Lady of Shalott' (1832/1842)

William Shakespeare's *The Tempest* (1611) is both great children's theatre and a moving meditation on art, nature, and the artist; even so with Ursula K. Le Guin's *Leese Webster* (illustrated by James Brunsman), except it is a picture book, not theatre, and so, in our time, less likely to attract the attention of critics.

One critic who did not miss *Leese Webster* was Charlotte Spivack, who notes the story's high quality and its relationship to both the Arachne myth and the Earthsea trilogy: 'the spider as an image of the master-patterner in the Earthsea trilogy' and the spider in *Leese Webster* as 'the figure of the artist' (151), even as the trilogy is a *Künstlerroman* of the life of Ged as an artist of magic.[469] In Earthsea and elsewhere, however, spiders are at least bivalent: good as images as artists, possibly bad as creators spinning traps out of their own guts. Leese Webster, though, the protagonist of this book, is definitely good. In Le Guin's first picture book, Leese's story is 'A Portrait of the Artist as a Young Spider'—to repeat the inevitable joke—and it is Le Guin's *apologia* for all artists who bring their art out into the (com-

---

[469] *Kunstlerroman*: 'artist's novel'—the story of the development of an artist. Anita Wilson notes the continuing popularity of E. B. White's *Charlotte's Web* (1952), and suggests putting 'Leese Webster' into dialog with that book.

mercial) world, and it is her Romantic affirmation of the necessity to return art to nature.[470]

Leese is born in the deserted throne room of a deserted palace (deserted by humans, that is) as one of 'a family of spiders,' with the 'family' definitely figurative: 'As soon as they had all said 'Hello' to one another, they all said 'Goodbye,' and each went off to find a place to spin a web,' as is, indeed, the nature of spiders in our world, except the part about their talking.[471] Leese wanders about the throne room and finds it too crowded—all the corners are taken—so she goes off 'exploring.' She finally locates 'a comfortable room, the bedroom of a princess long ago. She found that she had the room pretty much to herself'—'A Room of One's Own,' in arachnid terms—'which was the way she liked it; so she settled down there.'[472] And she began to spin the traditional, very elegant web of the Websters, which we're told is 'The family Leese belonged to,' and which I take to be the 'orb weavers,' or 'sheet-web' weavers.[473]

We're told that the Websters' web is 'beautiful and practical' and that all family members know 'how to weave it without giving it a thought,' i.e., in ethological terms Le Guin does not use, the Websters' weaving is literally inborn: one of the 'innate skills' of the species, an inherited 'fixed action pattern' (Eibl-Eibesfeldt 15). Leese weaves her webs unthinkingly for the first two nights in her new room. And, as the products of fixed, species-specific, fixed action patterns—again, all ethological terms I am applying, not Le Guin—each web is 'exactly the same,' which *is* Le Guin's formulation. 'The third night,' Leese says to herself, "I wonder why a web can't be a little different now and then?" So Leese Webster begins to experiment.

At first, the experiments aren't successful. But she keeps at it, 'learning and practicing, thinking out new ways to connect the threads, now patterns and new shapes.' She studies and copies patterns she sees in the carved wood and an old painting and the carpet in the room, thinking about her night's weaving during the day, when spiders rest.

Le Guin beautifully pictures the art of Leese Webster and of weaving spiders generally, and of artists as active and athletic, risk-taking, and many-faceted: an act of building and creation, a dance of Shiva over the abyss, one of the songs of god.

---

[470] The joke alludes to James Joyce's *A Portrait of the Artist as a Young Man* (1916), a much-taught *Künstlerroman* in the mid-twentieth century.
[471] *Leese Webster* is not paginated, and I will not be supplying page numbers.
[472] I allude to *A Room of One's Own* (1929), an extended essay by Virginia Woolf.
[473] 'Webster' is an old word for 'weaver.' The Micropaedia entry in the 1974 *Encyclopaedia Britannica* lists as common spiders the sheet-web weaver, taxonomic family Linyphiidae (order Araneida); the Macropaedia entry for 'Araneida' uses the style 'orb weaver' and gives the family as Araneidae (Argiopidae). See Levi and Levi 1073.

> To make the first, high thread to hold the web, she had to climb up high and then throw herself out across the dark air, hoping she would land safe on the other side. Her work was like riding the flying trapeze in the circus. It was like building bridges too.... And it was like singing, because she spun the thread out of her body, as the singer spins her voice out of the throat.... She had learned how to weave her ideas, now. Some of her webs had designs like leaves and flowers, imitated from the carpet; some had designs like huntsmen, hounds and horns, copied from the painting on the wall.

Spiders common in the United States are not social, and so it is in *Leese Webster*: 'Spiders are not sociable people. They mostly let one another be.' Still, Leese Webster gets an occasional visit from a family member or someone from other spider families, and they look over her work. 'Usually they sniffed, and traveled on.' One comments that the web Leese is working on is remarkable and asks 'Will it catch flies?' Leese must admit 'Not very well.... The old pattern works better for that.' The utilitarian spider responds with 'Waste of time.' The remark offends Leese and makes her feel 'a little ashamed,' but she improves 'her designs after that, so that her fancy webs would catch flies as well as the old kind. For that is the purpose of a spider web, after all, and spiders have to eat, like anybody else.'

Le Guin here very elegantly formulates a crucial relationship between art and economics, art and the world. Spiders and artists must eat: literally or figuratively they *must* catch flies to earn a living. On the other hand, there is the question of the esthetic dimension of the practical. It is easy enough to dismiss the utilitarian concerned totally with whether or not the web catches flies—in which case the obvious imperative is to stick with the traditional formulas for web-spinning; but the philistine spider we briefly see and hear raises an esthetic point Leese Webster recognizes and deals with: the function of a spider web is to catch flies (and other insects), and, a philosophical spider from the Bauhaus school of Weimar, Germany, or Chicago, Illinois, might insist that web-form should, on esthetic grounds, follow web-function. This is an important point. Any imaginative and talented architecture student can design a clever, unique, and perhaps even beautiful building. Genius is when you can design such a unique and beautiful building and get it built and have it stay up and function as a good place for people to live or work or play.

Leese Webster succeeds at getting beautiful webs that will still catch flies. Still, as Spivack stresses (151), Leese Webster doesn't get to eat very often—few flies go to the old room—and Leese isn't totally happy with her art. In Le Guin's words: 'Leese was used to going hungry; she liked her lonely room; she would have been quite content, but for one thing. She was never quite satisfied with the webs she wove.' Back in the throne room of her hatching, 'there had been jewels' on that empty throne, jewels that shone in colors: 'In her memory those jewels were more beautiful than anything she could weave, for there was light inside them,' whereas all of Leese Webster's weaving, even her weaving of 'jewel-shapes' and 'jewel-patterns in her web,' was still done in thread of grey. 'How do they do it?' she wondered.'

Immediately thereafter, Leese's closed world is violated by two women. For the first time in a hundred years, a human enters the room, and almost immediately utters an obscenity: "'More cobwebs,' said a disgusted voice. Bring in the brooms!'" For Leese Webster, 'The word "broom" was the worst word she knew.' The old palace was to be 'cleaned up and made into a National Monument, a museum where people could come and see how kings used to live.' The two women look at Leese Webster's work, and the first thinks the 'tapestries' beautiful—

> '...but all so dusty and spiderwebby!'
> 'The tapestries are spiderwebs,' said the second one.
> 'Spiders can't make pictures, dear,' said the first one
> laughing. But the second one, whose eyes were keener,
> said, 'Oh, don't touch them—they *are* spiderwebs!'

The two women tell the 'Authorities,' who call in the experts, and the one thing all agree on is that 'the Room of the Silver Weavings (which is what the cleaning women named it) should be kept exactly as it was, so that visitors to the Palace Museum could see the remarkable tapestries.' The experts further agree 'that the weavings,' delicate as spider webs as they are, 'must be kept under glass.' So Leese Webster's work is immortalized for the ages and all, but she is not pleased: "Stop that! If you cover my webs with glass, how can they catch flies?' Leese shouted. 'I'll starve!'" Understandably enough, since they could not hear a spider, 'The workmen paid no attention.'[474]

The cleaning women return and walk around the room admiring the beautiful web pictures. 'They were proud of what they had found and happy to have saved it, and Leese was proud and happy to have her work admired at last.' The women find Leese, and since it's bad luck to kill spiders, they put her outside. One of the women gently shakes 'her duster gently out the open window. 'There, let go, little creepy. You'll catch more flies outside!'"

Leese takes the longest fall of her life 'and landed on a broad, sunlight-speckled leaf. 'I'm dead! she cried, and lay there in a tiny ball...her eyes all shut.'

Evening comes and Leese opens one of her eight eyes and sees 'the evening star, reflected in he water of the lily pool.' Leese, rather nearsighted for all her eight eyes, infers that she sees a jewel and (therefore?) is not dead. She is impressed by the size of the room she's now in: 'It seems not to have any walls at all.' It's also 'splendidly decorated' without her

---

[474] Le Guin in conversation (13 May 1996) indicated to me that here she intended just a little joke: humans are much too big to hear the speech of spiders.

webs, and she doesn't know what to weave for it. The point is moot however; she is very hungry. What with her hunger and fatigue and having now to contend with wind and moving branches, Leese Webster's web is not even neat, let alone great art.

> As the dawn came, dew began to gather on her web.
> Leese was distressed. She tried to shake the water beads off, for she did not know what they were.... Then the sun came up. The light of sunrise struck the drops of water strung close on every thread, and they shone brighter than the jewels of the throne, brighter even than the stars.
> Breakfast came buzzing by. Leese ate it thankfully, while she watched her web glittering with diamond water beads. 'That's the most beautiful web I ever wove,' she thought.

Inside the palace, tourists visit the Room of the Silver Weavings and admire tapestries with threads 'as fine as spiderwebs.' 'But Leese, swinging joyously from leaf to branch in the endless garden, wove her wild webs every night, and every morning found them shining with the jewels of the sun.'

I find *Leese Webster* a beautiful story, and a beautifully crafted statement of important themes.

Clear to readers of Le Guin's works for older people, are the motifs of the artist and the function of art, plus such memorable motifs from romantic art as the empty throne in the deserted palace (cf. *The Tombs of Atuan*) and a fascination with jewels and the play of light in them. More central is the romantic theme of getting back to nature, with the twist of the image of 'unbuilding walls' (*The Dispossessed*) or the idea in 'An die Musik' that art generally—*Kunst*—and music more particularly 'denies and breaks down all shelters, the houses men build for themselves, that they may see the sky' (*Orsinian Tales* 145). Among human beings, in a tale set in Europe in 1938, there are problems with the destruction of shelter: a lot of houses will soon be destroyed in World War II. But for a spider thrown out (gently) into a literal garden, the exit from an old palace museum is right and proper. Leese is no delicate Lady of Shalott; she's a working artist, not a lady at all, so reality won't kill her; it nourishes her. For Leese, the proper place is outside walls; the proper shelter is the sky.[475]

Within a few years, the newest philosophies would put nature inside of art, as a rather more expansive sort of human text; but *Leese Webster* could persuasively presents a situation in which the artist can leave her transcendent artistic work to human culture and sink into a very glorious imma-

---

[475] In response to a rather angry statement of my reaction to unbuilding walls and roofs in 'An de Musik,' Le Guin raised the question, 'What if the sky is the shelter?'

nence in a world of nature that can produce beauty far beyond any creature's art. The irony is imaged very effectively: in the transcendent project of doing art within the palace of human culture, even with a room of her own, Leese is trapped. And her art is put under glass and rendered museum pieces, incapable of nourishing Leese literally; and, figuratively, her museum-enshrined art may be of only limited nutritional value to its human observers/consumers. In the immanence of nature and the garden, Leese is truly free and produces art that *she* feels, with some justification, is her best.

We have in this story a highly satisfying open-ended ending; and it is an ending we should find even more satisfying with a mild irony pointed out to me by Anita Wilson: Leese can appreciate her dew-jeweled webs fully precisely because she has seen jewels within the prison/palace/museum of culture.

At the end of *The Tempest*, the Europeans return to Europe, leaving the magic island to Ariel and Caliban and nature. The happy ending, for civilized humans (all male save Miranda), is moving out of nature back into culture. Leese Webster goes in the opposite direction, into nature, as appropriate for an artistic and cultured spider created by an author who, in some moods, is one of the last of the Critical Romantics.[476]

---

[476] For a recent variation on the theme of the picture book, see *Buffalo Gals Won't You Come Out Tonight* (1994): the 1987 story by that name printed separately as an art book with illustrations by Susan Seddon Boulet. Note, though, that 'Buffalo Gals...' is not a story for young children.

IX.

EARTHSEA REVISITED

Tehanu (1990)

Returning to the distinction between *la parole originaire* (authentic [Word, speech, idiolect]) and *la parole secondaire* (empirical), [Maurice] Merleau-Ponty says that the former, in relation to the later, is silence.... Language is of itself oblique and autonomous, it expresses as much by what is between words as by the words themselves. To understand the *parole originaire*, which gropes around an intention to make meaning, we must consider other expressions which might have taken its place and the threads of silence intertwined with the words themselves. —Philip E. Lewis (27, 26)[477]

Ursula K. Le Guin's *Tehanu* is an important short novel and one with relatively few 'incidents' (in the traditional, masculinist sense), so I'll summarize the story in some detail, in part chronologically and then mostly as events occur in the plot—and I'll supply, on occasion, some commentary.

The story of *Tehanu* starts at the beginning, the very beginning of Earthsea, when Segoy (who is the dragon Kalessin) called the land of Ea up from the sea, and, as the wind blows over the land, it produces dragons, including a dragon-person named Tehanu, who became long afterwards (to most human eyes) a little girl who would receive the use-name Therru; although, mythically considered—like Coyote—she is still Tehanu: 'She has been Tehanu since the beginning,' we learn at the end of the novel,

---

[477] Philip E. Lewis here alluding to Maurice Merleau-Ponty's 1945 work *La Phénoménologie de la perception* (*The Phenomenology of Perception* [English trans. 1962]) and directly paraphrasing Merleau-Ponty's 1960 book *Signes* (*Signs* [English trans. 1964]). Lewis notes that Merleau-Ponty here follows Ferdinand de Saussure, whose lecture notes were published in French in 1916 and in English in 1959 as *A Course in General Linguistics*.

'Always she has been Tehanu' (224; ch. 14). Then there's a very long hiatus and the story picks up in the time of the Earthsea trilogy, when Ogion of Gont visits the Woman of Kemay (who is a woman, specifically a fisherwoman, and dragon) and is sung a song telling how, '...in the beginning, dragon and human were all one. They were all one people, one race, winged, and speaking the True Language.'[478] The unity breaks down: '...the dragons, always fewer and wilder, scattered by their endless, mindless greed and anger, in the far islands of the Western Reach; and the human folk, always more numerous in their rich towns and cities, filling up the inner Isles and all the south and east.' Some humans preserved the True Language of the Making and became wizards. 'But also, the song said, there were those among us who know they were once dragons, and among the dragons there are some who know their kinship with us. And these say that when the one people were becoming two, some of them, still both human and dragon, still winged, went not east but west' and continued west until they got 'to the other side of the world,' where 'they live in peace, great winged beings both wild and wise, with human mind and dragon heart' (11-12; ch. 2 '...Falcon's Nest').

If in *Tehanu* we see *Earthsea Revisioned*, as Le Guin presents the book in a pamphlet by that title; if we are to see in *Tehanu* part of Le Guin's attempt to find 'a story for' her 'dear young hero,' then 'It will not be the old story' ('My Hero' [1994]) but something new, with a new kind of hero. If we want a formula for the new hero—one to replace the ancient *fortitudo et sapientia* (strength and wisdom for male heroes)—'wild and wise, with human mind and dragon heart' is a good place to begin.[479]

Some time after the meeting between Ogion and the dragon/woman, Ogion's former apprentice Ged brings to Gont and Ogion the Lady Tenar, as he promised her at the end of *The Tombs of Atuan*. We will later learn that Tenar had fallen in love with Ged (189-90, ch. 12; 214, ch. 13 [*ER* 15]).[480] Ogion is father and teacher to Tenar into her adulthood and offers to teach her all he knows. She learns Old Speech easily, but she declines his offer and—parallel to Ged in *A Wizard of Earthsea*—Tenar leaves Og-

---

[478] The fisherwoman reference is repeated on 196 ('Winter,' ch. 12). See Le Guin's essay 'The Fisherwoman's Daughter'; the craft of the dragon/woman of Kemay may be significant. For primal unity, cf. Androgyne as symbol in *LHD* and the initial condition of things in Red Plum's creation myth in *ACH*, 165-68 ('Time and the City').

[479] For wildness and dragons, see Le Guin, *Earthsea Revisioned* (*ER*) 21-23; see also Mike Cadden's excellent discussion of *Tehanu*, 'Buffalo Gals,' and some of Le Guin's picture-books, 'Speaking Across the Spaces...' 519 f. My translation of *fortitudo & sapientia* is correct but historically misleading: what *true* strength and *true* wisdom might be, and therefore true heroism, depends upon worldviews and is a matter of energetic contestation. See Kaske on '*Sapientia et Fortitudo*' and Tolkien on 'The Monsters and the Critics' in and on *Beowulf*

[480] Le Guin suggested that Tenar's love for Ged might have been neutralized by the chastity spell (my formulation) that comes with his being a Wizard (personal communication).

ion to seek her own way: 'Priestess of the Tombs of Atuan or foreign ward of the Mage of Gont, she was set apart, set above.[481] Men had given her power, men had shared their power with her. Women looked at her from outside, sometimes rivalrous, often with a trace of ridicule. She had felt herself the one left outside, shut out. She had fled from the Powers of the desert tombs, and then she had left the powers of learning and skill offered her by her guardian, Ogion.' Le Guin's Narrator sums up that Tenar, 'had turned her back on all that, gone to the other side, the other room, where the women lived, to be one of them' (30; 'Kalessin,' ch. 4). As Yehedarhed Havzhiva (a man) will do in 'A Woman's Liberation,' Tenar chooses to 'live on the woman's side' (*FWF* 207). Stating the matter in her own voice, Le Guin says that Tenar 'quit grad school' and, in what may or may not be a sacrifice, Tenar 'went off to be a nobody, a wife and mother' (*ER* 17).

Tenar does not seem to have been in love with him, but she marries Flint, a prosperous farmer, thereby entering the larger world and taking up women's power, 'the authority allotted her by the arrangements of mankind' (30). Tenar, or Goha, as she is called, bears a healthy, nice daughter, Apple, and later a sickly son. The son, Spark, grows up to neither love nor trust his mother enough to tell her his true name: an 'endlessly active boy,' 'driven,' with 'no patience with animals, plants, people,' silent except to *use* words 'for his needs only' (46; 'Bettering,' ch. 5). Apple marries well and happily. Spark, so radically and significantly different from Ogion, is able to make sufficient contact with Ogion to tell him (not his parents) that he wants to go to sea, and he does: eventually becoming second mate on a Gontish ship, probably running stolen goods (207; 'The Master,' ch. 13). After Lebannen starts to bring law and order to Earthsea, Spark loses his ships and heads home, arriving three years after Flint's death (204; ch. 13).

However badly Spark finally turns out, though—he is far from Daoist stillness and connectedness—Goha's marriage to Flint is fairly happy, and Goha has some status. Among the women, she is

> a foreigner to be sure, white-skinned and talking a bit strange, but a notable housekeeper, an excellent spinner, with well-behaved, well-grown children and a prospering farm: respectable. And among men she was Flint's woman, doing what a woman should do: bed, breed, bake, cook, clean, spin, sew, serve. A good woman. They approved of her.... I wonder what a white woman's like, white all over? their eyes said, looking at her, until she got older and they no longer saw her. (31; 'Kalessin,' ch 4)

---

[481] Note Arha as the 'solitary, untouched priestess, a holy thing' (56; ch. 5). In being *set apart*, Arha had been made holy or sacred, 'sacredness referred to those things in society that were forbidden or set apart...,' as suggested of the etymology of 'sacred' from Latin *sacer*, 'set off' (Streng 123, after Émile Durkheim).

I.e., she is accepted; she runs into some minor bigotry and prurient interest under female and male gaze respectively, until she approaches middle age or older, and she becomes as Alice Sheldon's title has it, one of 'The Women Men Don't See' (1973) or one of the 'Middle-Aged Women' among the Ndif in Le Guin's 'Pathways of Desire' (1979)—a potential Crone.[482]

When Flint dies, twenty years into his marriage with Tenar, Tenar becomes the holder, but not the owner of Oak Farm. Earthsea society is thoroughly patriarchal, and Tenar's tenure on Flint's property 'was contingent on there being no male heir or claimant' (191; ch. 12 'Winter'), and there is, Spark. Then an important addition to the cast arrives on Gont: Aspen, the new wizard to the Lord of Re Albi. He is a follower of Cob of *Farthest Shore* in the search for immortality, and has discovered his own, rather vampiric, way to eternal life. For some three years before the start of *Tehanu*, Aspen has kept the old lord alive, by leaching the life from the old lord's grandson and heir (118-19; 'Finding Words,' ch. 9).[483]

About the time Ged and Arren start on their quest in *The Farthest Shore* (72; ch. 6 'Worsening'), when things are going quite ill all over Earthsea, 'a very bad thing' happens among a band of tramps: Shag, Handy, the coupled pair of Hake and Senini, and Hake and Senini's daughter (?), who appears to be a girl of about six or seven.[484] The mother, Senini, has been regularly abused, but now the daughter is beaten, raped, and thrown into a fire to die. For whatever reasons, Handy gets help for the girl, and a woman named Lark gets aid from the village witch Ivy and from the widow Goha. Goha takes the little girl for her own, saying in Kargish, 'I served them and left them.... I will not let them have you' (5; see *ER* 19 f.). For readers familiar with the trilogy, 'them' here refers to the Nameless Ones, the primordial powers of darkness (ch. 1 'A Bad Thing'). Tenar gives the girl the name Therru, a Kargish word for 'burning, the flaming of fire' (21; ch. 3 'Ogion'). Later we learn that the at-

---

[482] See James Tiptree, Jr. (pseud. for Alice Sheldon), 'The Women Men Don't See' in Le Guin and Attebery, eds., *Norton Book of Science Fiction*; for Le Guin on crones, see 'The Space Crone' (1976), coll. as the first essay in *DEW*.

[483] Students of folklore will recognize in the old lord and his young wizard, the folklore character Joseph Campbell calls 'Holdfast.' On the name 'Aspen': the two witches in the story are Moss and Ivy; the two Gontish wizards have the tree names Aspen and Beech. Note Moss on how women's magic is small but 'all roots' like a blackberry thicket; wizardly power 'is like a fir tree, maybe, great and tall and grand' and ready to blow over in a major storm. 'Nothing kills a blackberry bramble' (100; 'Hawks,' ch. 8). Neither mosses nor ivies have impressive root systems, but they are ground, tree, and building huggers, water-like in their ability to get into places—and very different from majestic trees.

[484] 'Hake' is the name for varieties of food fish related to cod. 'Handy' might be an allusion to 'hende Nicholas' in Geoffrey Chaucer's 'The Miller's Tale.' It's a stretch for the analogy, but Handy Nicholas *is* associated in that story with a grab at a young woman, with over-reaching, and with a brand. See *Canterbury Tales* I (A) 3271-81, 3778-3853.

tempted murder of Therru—whatever other part he played in it—meets with the approval of the wizard Aspen (218; 'The Master,' ch. 13).

A year passes. Ged and Arren/Lebannen, ending *The Farthest Shore*, defeat the Wizard Cob. Arren 'kills' the already dead Cob. Ged closes the door between the worlds: 'It was,' this way to immortality, 'a way that led nowhere' (*FS* 183; ch. 12 'Dry Land').[485] In performing the great and good deed of closing the door between the life and death and *restoring* human mortality, Ged spills out all of his wizardly power, loses his art (*FS* 193; 'The Stone of Pain,' ch. 13), loses the light on his 'yew staff and in his face' (185; ch. 12), and leaves the staff itself 'half-buried in the sand on Selidor' 193; ch. 13).[486] As Irena helps Hugh across the worlds in *The Beginning Place* (1980), Arren takes Ged over the mountains of Pain back to life and the island of Selidor. From there, the androgynous and mysterious dragon Kalessin—the Eldest—takes Arend and Ged to Roke, where Ged kneels to Arren, the future King Lebannen, and then remounts Kalessin and flies toward Gont (*FS* 194-97; ch. 12).

Simultaneously, the dying Ogion asks Goha/Tenar to come to him at his home near Re Albi (6; '...Falcon's Nest,' ch. 2). Tenar brings Therru, and, just before they arrive at Ogion's, they are accosted by four men, whom Tenar bluffs her way past, getting so angry at them she turns red, which Therru describes as 'Like fire' (16; ch. 2). The one in the 'leather cap and jerkin' has to be Handy and the two others must include Hake and/or Shag.[487]

Even near death, Ogion is very interested in Therru. He asks her name and its meaning: 'He knew the True Language of the Making, but he had never learned any Kargish at all' (20; ch. 3), not even as tutor and foster father to Tenar, a speaker of Kargish. Ogion prophesies of Therru, 'That one—they will fear her' and tells Tenar, 'Teach her.... Teach her all!—Not Roke. They are afraid!'[488] He asks Tenar, 'Why did I let you go? Why did you go? To bring her here—too late?' and Ogion repeats his injunction, 'Teach her!' (21; ch. 3).

Ogion goes out to die 'between the roots' of a young beech tree, symbolically returning to the roots of life—and gets four more lines. When Tenar is looking after Therru while helping Ogion die, he comments, 'Never one thing, for you,' to which Tenar replies, 'No. Always at least

---

[485] See headnote to 'The Field of Vision,' *WTQ* 222.
[486] Holly Littlefield instructively reads and misreads: Somewhat, anyway, Ged 'has been symbolically feminized. He lacks his rod, his mage's staff, which was left broken on Selidor, and is left powerless, impotent' (253). The staff is whole, at the end of *FS*, but it's just a staff; Ged has no more magic—no art—to empower his staff. The key points Littlefield gets quite well: (1) Ged lost his magic potency (sexual undertones intended), and (2) in a hierarchical and patriarchal world, strong/weak = masculine/feminine.
[487] For Handy's leather cap see 109 (ch. 8), 128 (ch. 9).
[488] See Le Guin's poem 'His Daughter,' for 'They Will Fear Her' as the name of Crazy Horse's daughter (*Wild Oats* 48).

two things, and usually more' (22; 'Ogion,' ch. 3).[489] Looking west, he whispers, uncertain, 'The dragon—'. Finally, he will tell Tenar his true name, but just before that, '"Over,' he whispered with exultation. 'All changed!—Changed, Tenar! Wait—wait here for—'; he doesn't finish the sentence (23).[490]

Tenar waits. Aunty Moss, the village witch, arrives for 'the homing' of Ogion—now Aihal; and a couple of wizardly vultures (figuratively speaking) arrive to try to get the body for the honor of burying it in Gont Port or at, significantly, Re Albi. When she can get their serious attention, Tenar tells Aspen, one of the two wizards, Ogion's true name, and that he wanted to be and will be buried where he is; and she returns to the body Aunty Moss's little charm-bundle, flicked away by Aspen (24-26; 'Ogion,' ch. 3). Waiting, Tenar gets solitude and time to think, including thoughts about magic and men's power and women's; she and Therru plant a peach pit in a 'tiny grave'; Aunty Moss teaches Therru cat's cradle, and Tenar makes friends with Aunty Moss (29-34; 'Kalessin,' ch. 4). And then something both quiet and very spectacular happens: Kalessin arrives, has a brief eye-to-eye talk with Tenar (men may not look dragons in the eye, but Tenar is a woman), and drops off Ged (37-40; ch. 4).[491] Aunty Moss says that Sparrowhawk (Ged's use-name) cannot be Sparrowhawk, not if Sparrowhawk is Archmage of Earthsea: the man before her is without magic powers (42; ch. 4). For readers who remember the end of *Farthest Shore*, the answer is simple: Ged is now merely Ged, and no mage; for readers new to the series—and for Tenar—there is a nice riddle here: When is a man you know well not that man at all? (44; ch. 4).

Ged is in bad shape. Therru looks at the four white scars marking half Ged's face and asks 'Was he burned?' Tenar knows Ged was wounded by 'One of the kinship of the Nameless Ones,' but she also knows what 'burned' means to Therru and tells her Ged was 'burned' (48; 'Bettering,' ch. 5). Moss helps, without much enthusiasm, to heal Ged, and she and Tenar talk about power and men, about eunuchs and Tenar's life at the Tombs of Atuan, about the use-value of children (49). Ged, awaking, says Tenar's true name, and she kisses him, and thinks how she'd never kissed him before and how she had never kissed Ogion nor Ogion her, how Ogion (like her people at Atuan) had never touched her (56; ch. 5).

After four days, Ged is finally coherent enough to wonder about Ogion and say 'This is Ogion's house.' Tenar responds 'Aihal's house,' speaking Ogion's true name, thereby letting Ged know that Ogion is dead, having died as she later tells him, ten days past. Ged regains his strength but not

---

[489] See also 203; 'The Master,' ch. 13).
[490] For Ogion's joy, see also 28; 'Kalessin,' ch. 4.
[491] The formulation here is 'She had been told that men must not look into a dragon's eyes, but that was nothing to her' (*Tehanu* 37; ch. 4). In *WE* the quotation is 'Almost he stared into the dragon's eyes and was caught, for one cannot look into a dragon's eyes' (89; 'The Dragon of Pendor,' ch. 5). In the 'men's tongue,' *one* often means *men*.

his health (58; 'Bettering,' ch. 5) and helps around the house; unlike Flint (and like Ogion and sailors and [some] other bachelors), he was willing to do 'Women's work' (60). Tenar thinks about her past: 'the power of the dark places' that 'had run through her, used her, left her empty, untouched' and the power Ogion had offered her that she refused, choosing instead the powers of a wife and mother. But she was no longer a wife, and her children were grown; and now, like Ged, she had 'nothing in her, no power, for anybody to recognize.' But there is another 'but': 'But a dragon had spoken to her.' Tenar remembers asking Ged at Atuan 'What is a dragonlord?' and his responding, as she recalls it, 'A man dragons will talk to' (*Tehanu* 62 [exact quotation: 'One whom the dragons will speak with' (*TA* 85; 'The Great Treasure,' ch. 7)]). Tenar recognizes that whatever else she is or is not, she is most definitely 'a woman dragons would talk to' (*Tehanu* 62). Ged tells Tenar about Lebannen as King of Earthsea. Tenar has a memory/vision of Havnor as 'the beautiful city' and sees moving out 'From that bright center...order going outward like the perfect rings on water, like the straightness of a paved street or a ship sailing before the wind: a going the way it should go, a bringing to peace' (see *ER* 14).[492] "Is that it, then," she asked, kneeling, watching him—"the joy coming into the light?" that Ogion saw (64). Ged does not attempt an answer, and the perfection of those circles of order, the *straightness* of the order should give Le Guin's readers pause. Therru interrupts the visions and philosophizing and a sentimental moment to announce that Sippy, the energetic goat, has (again) gotten away. Ged looks at Therru 'as if he did not see her hideous scars, as if he scarcely saw her at all: a child who had lost a goat, who needed to find a goat. It was the goat he saw.' For good and for ill, Ged's here is a male gaze, classifying and looking for work for the gazer. Therru looks carefully at Ged—it is unusual for her to look at people, especially male people—and Tenar wonders 'Was a hero being born?', necessarily in the mind of Therru (65-66; 'Bettering,' ch. 5).

Ged heals slowly, and Tenar ponders his male 'indifference...towards the exigencies that ruled a woman: that someone must be not far from a sleeping child, that one's freedom meant another's unfreedom, unless some ever-changing moving balance were reached, like...walking' (68-69; 'Worsening,' ch. 6).[493] Immediately following, we learn just how deaf Tenar has been to what Aunty Moss has been telling her and how blind she has been to Ged's loss of power (71-72). Finally seeing, she and Ged talk seriously—if necessarily metaphorically—about Ged's former power and

---

[492] Cf. 'Rale' in *CI* (1967) as a specific analog of flowing with the Dao: 'Rale is... the right thing to do, like learning things at school, or like a river follows its course...' (136; ch. 8).

[493] Cf. comments by Ong Tot Oppong on 'The Question of Sex' on Gethen: no Gethenian 'is quite so thoroughly 'tied down' here as women, elsewhere, are likely to be'—or 'quite so free as a free male anywhere else' (93-94; ch. 7). See also Le Guin's essay on women as artists and mothers: 'Fisherwoman's Daughter' (*DEW* 212 f.), and, for walking, 'A Man of the People' (*FWF* 112, 117; § 2).

his loss: 'I went into the dry land when I was young,' Ged says, 'and I met it there'—his Shadow—'I became it, I married my death. It gave me life. Water, the water of life. I was a fountain, a spring, flowing, giving.[494] But the springs don't run, there' in the dry land of death. 'All I had in the end was one cup of water, and I had to pour it out on the sand....'[495] Tenar is hardly feeling more upbeat. Both of them have done what they have done against Cob and for Therru 'because it was all you could do' (72; 'Worsening,' ch. 6), but Tenar does feel better when she holds Therru and 'set her mind on the light of her [Therru's?] dreaming, the gulf of bright air, the name of the dragon, the name of the star, Heart of the Swan, the Arrow, Tehanu' (75; ch. 6).

A ship arrives from Havnor, with men seeking Ged to have him crown Lebannen. Ged will not deal with these men (82; 'Mice,' ch. 7), and Moss finds Ged's unwillingness totally understandable (88); but it bothers Tenar, who wonders what it might be like to have never feared anyone—or any human—as a powerful man like Ged had never needed to fear (85). Tenar tries to apply to Ged's case her own experience of power as the One Priestess of the Tombs of Atuan and then to become (in good anarchist, Daoist, feminist fashion) 'only Tenar, only herself'—therefore weak. Still, Tenar is honest enough to recognize that she was not only herself: she had become soon enough a respectable married woman with a respectable family, but she had lost all that, in the normal course of things, 'becoming old and a widow, powerless.' So Tenar does have some relevant experience to help her sympathize with Ged, except that she cannot 'understood his shame, his agony of humiliation, Perhaps only a man could feel so. A woman got used to shame.' That, 'Or maybe Aunty Moss was right, and when the meat was out' of a man—loss of power, position—'the shell was empty' (86). Tenar tells Ged her experience as Ogion's pupil. Old Speech, for her, 'was like learning the language I spoke before I was born. But the rest...that was all dead to me. Somebody else's language,' as if she tried to dress up as a warrior. The clothes wouldn't make her a hero, just uncomfortable (*ER* 18). So she gave up any dreams she might have had of power, and Ogion went along. Still, it was another matter indeed when Ogion met Therru (87; 'Mice,' ch. 7).

When Ged is away, the searchers for him visit Tenar at Ogion's house and indicate that they intend to stay in the neighborhood, with the lord of Re Albi. Therru is upset by the visitors, not looking at Tenar and making Tenar hold her 'like a block of wood' (93; ch. 7)—not the Archetypal

---

[494] For the flowing spring image, and doorways, see *Tao te Ching* ch. 6, on the undying Valley Spirit, 'named the Mysterious Female,' whose 'Doorway...Is the base from which Heaven and Earth sprang' and simultaneously 'within us.' We are told to 'Draw upon it as you will,' since this source 'never runs dry' (Waley trans., p. 149); see also *Tao te Ching* chs. 4 and 45.

[495] They go on to discuss Ged's youth, and we learn that Ged has forgotten the name of his first teacher in magic: the witch of Ten Alders (73), a name the Narrator does not give (*WE* 2-6, 13; ch. 1).

Child here or the Daoists' 'uncarved block' (a symbol of unlimited potential) but a scared little girl, tensing up in fear. Tenar knows she must act; or, anyway, she does act: reluctantly (and perhaps anachronistically), she tears a strip of paper from one of Ogion's lore books and sends a note to Ged that will send him to her home at Oak Farm.[496] Therru, who usually tries to avoid people, takes the note to Ged, going confidently out the door, 'flying like a bird, a dragon, a child, free' (94; 'Mice,' ch. 7).

Tenar spends a good deal of time with Aunty Moss, discussing philosophy and Ged, life's goal, and sex. Tenar takes the strong position for herself that 'living is having your work to do, and being able to do it....' So she knows 'in part' what's going on with Ged, but doesn't understand it. Aunty Moss has her own theory: 'It's a queer thing for an old man to be a boy of fifteen....' In *Tehanu*, we're not in a heroic fantasy and only on the edge of a fantasy world, and Aunty Moss is going to back-fill and answer a question we've probably never asked about wizards and Heroes, 'The Question of Sex' (see Christie 94-95). Moss's answer is that Ged did without sex, that wizards generally or universally do without sex (*ER* 11, 15). The sorcerer of Vemish in *A Wizard of Earthsea* has a daughter (152; ch. 9), and Ged's wizardly friend Vetch certainly enjoys a domestic, if apparently celibate, life on Iffish (*WE* 158; ch. 9), but that proves little: there could be some married wizards and still Aunty Moss's rule could hold that 'You don't get without you give as much,' and with wizards the cost of power is virginity or celibacy or continence, or, at least, never using one's power to satisfy one's own sexual lust (98; 'Hawks,' ch, 8). In her own voice, Le Guin sets the cost of wizardly power at virginity: sacrifice of 'sexual contact with women'; in the Earthsea stories as in many hero tales, masculinist 'Strength lies in abstinence—the avoidance of women and the replacement of sexuality by non-sexual male bonding. The establishment of manhood in heroic terms involves the absolute devaluation of women. The woman's touch, in any sense, threatens that heroic masculinity' (*ER* 9, 11).[497]

---

[496] *WE* started out in, the Bronze Age on culturally backward Gont. By the time of *Tehanu*, Gontish-folk have soap, drinking glasses, paper, and other amenities, and are not overly impressed by the sight of a large sailing ship from Havnor. In a work like 'The Tale of Old Venn' in S. R. Delany's *Nevèrÿon*, such changes would be remarked on, possibly at length; such changes among the 'Hilfs' in Le Guin's *PE* or among the Athsheans in *WWF* or the Kesh in *ACH*, would be noticed by someone. That significant technological changes go unnoticed indicates that *Tehanu* has an agenda different from the other works I've mentioned.

[497] Cf. superstitions about sexual abstinence before battles and football games. Note that in Sir Thomas Malory's Romance, *Le Morte Darthur* (*The Death of Arthur*, publ. William Caxton, 1485), Sir Galahad is admired for his virginity and gets to see and take communion from the Holy Grail because he is 'a clean virgin,' 'a clean maiden'; and, right after communion, Galahad kneels and prays and his soul departs 'to Jesu Christ' and goes straight to heaven. It's Galahad's father, however, Lancelot the impure Courtly Lover of Guinevere who went on to a more impressive career in popular culture. *One* formula for the ideal hero is *fortitudo &*

Perpetual virginity was not a price Aunty Moss paid, and Tenar asks her, 'Is it different, then, for men and for women?' in the magical arts. Moss answers with the rhetorical question, 'What isn't, dearie?', and Tenar answers in earnest, 'it seems to me we make up most of the differences, and then complain about 'em.' The issue of difference is not resolved, and the discussion moves on (100-01; ch. 8).

Tenar prepares to take Therru to the village to buy cloth, with her preparations including washing, drying, and brushing her own hair. Therru watches the sparks from the static electricity from the hair brushing—as Ged had seen Tenar shine in the darkness of the Labyrinth at Atuan (86; ch. 7)—and Therru says, fearfully or, more likely, exultantly, 'The fire flying out.... All over the sky!' (101). Tenar then has a vision of Ged's meeting on his way 'one of the men who had stood waiting for her and Therru on that road' to Ogion's, the 'youngish man with a leather cap,' Handy, 'the one who had stared hard at Therru'—with an unspecified version of the male gaze (103; 'Hawk,' ch. 8). Looking out from her vision, Tenar sees Handy in front of her and, quite spontaneously, follows him until he sees that he did not follow Ged's path to Oak Farm but instead went uphill 'to the domain of the Lord of Re Albi' (104).

Tenar and Therru then go to get cloth at the house of Fan, a weaver Tenar knew from her time with Ogion.[498] They all examine and admire the object that gives Fan his use-name: a large fan, with dragons on one side and humans on the other. Held up to the light, one sees 'the two sides, the two paintings, made one by the light...so that the clouds and peaks [of the dragon side] were towers of the [human] city, and the men and women were winged, and the dragons looked with human eyes' (105; 'Hawks,' ch, 8). This image of both double vision and integration is important: all people should be heroes (kings, gods), combining human and dragon, wisdom and wildness and the unowned, dispossessed freedom of both (*ER* 21-24). Human people should be at home in towering cities and towering wilderness, and human-made cities should be appropriate for such dual people to call home.

Tenar returns to her home and finds Therru missing. For whatever psychological reasons, Tenar's guilt trip on Therru's disappearance includes a stop at her knowledge 'that a wrong that cannot be repaired,' such as that done to Therru, 'must be transcended' (108; ch, 8). In terms of the structure and theme of the story, the stop at the thought of an irreparable wrong is well placed: relating Therru, malicious injury, transcendence, and dragons. In Le Guin's analysis of *Tehanu*, transcending an irreparable wrong involves dragons. If a harm cannot be healed or undone, 'there must be *a*

---

sapientia; other formulas for the hero have him good 'in battle and bed,' at 'fighting and fucking.' Whether heterosexual fucking—recreational sex—'involves the absolute devaluation of women' is a contested issue: see Moffatt 48-49, 215-25, 229-30.
[498] Cf. and contrast the Dyers of Lorbanery in *FS* as a useful exercise for pointing the difference between the heroic fantasy of *FS* and the mixed genre of *Tehanu*.

way to go on from there.... It involves a leap. It involves flying.' But not some easy, merely spiritual transcendence. The fire of the dragon's wrath—'the wildness of the spirit and of the earth, uprising, against misrule'—flashes out to meet and consume and meld with 'the fire of human rage, the cruel anger of the weak, which wreaks itself on the weaker in the endless circle of human violence.' On the cultural level, the dragon is 'subversion, revolution, change,' most specifically changes that go beyond the old order where men are allowed and encouraged 'to own and dominate women,' and, complementarily, 'women were taught to collude with them.' Most specifically, the dragon 'rejects gender.' Kalessin is neither male nor female, and Le Guin sees Therru as 'ungendered by the rape that destroys her 'virtue' and the mutilation that destroys her beauty.' In a culture of oppression, the deepest foundation 'is gendering, which names the male normal, dominant, active, and the female other, subject, passive. To begin to imagine freedom, the myths of gender, like the myths of race, have to be exploded and discarded' (*ER* 23-24)—a feminist defense of a kind of androgyny (and not one all feminists would accept).[499] To transcend the wrong done to Therru, Earthsea's human people will need to get beyond the culture that makes such wrongs possible, and likely.

Therru had been hiding from Handy, which infuriates Tenar; but she holds in her rage and promises Therru that Handy will not touch her ever again (109; ch. 8). She advises Therru not to fear Handy: 'He feeds on your fear. We will starve him' and gets angry enough to appear 'a red dragon' to Therru, with 'a shining of fire all about [her] head' in the view of Moss (110-11; ch. 8).[500] Tenar tells Moss about the man's showing up, and Moss, rigid as 'a block,' wonders why the father would show up. Tenar notes it might be to claim Therru since 'She's his property,' but she doesn't think the man she saw was Therru's father (112; ch. 8).

Tenar encounters Aspen again, the wizard of the Lord of Re Albi, who offers Tenar a job helping with the haying, quite appropriate for Flint's widow Goha, but a grievous insult to 'the woman to whom Ogion dying had spoken his true name'—and a warning (114; 'Finding Words,' ch. 9). Aspen goes beyond an oblique insult, calling Tenar a witch—which Tenar wouldn't mind—a witch followed by a 'foul imp': 'The man did well who tried to destroy that creature, but the job should be completed.' Aspen thinks Tenar 'defied' him at Ogion's burial and forbids her to even be on his lord's, and his, domain. Aspen asks if Tenar has understood him, and

---

[499] To recall part of the debate on *LHD* and to anticipate a point we will get to in later chapters: If the concept of gender precedes and reinforces oppression, then gender-based theories and politics may be suspect. Feminism itself depends upon and reinforces the concept of gender. Therefore...? See Fraser and Nicholson, esp. 31 f. Without adopting the affectation that distinguishes dogmatically between 'which' and 'that,' we should read Le Guin here to refer to the situation in a culture of repression where what is to be condemned is the gender*ing that* 'names the male normal' etc., rather than a rigorous denial of genders.
[500] For Tenar and dragons, see Littlefield 255.

she answers that she has never understood men like Aspen (115). Aspen is about to lay a curse on her when he is interrupted by courtiers, one of whom kneels to Tenar as Tenar of the Ring of Erreth-Akbe. Tenar does not know if Aspen 'had known or had just now learned that she was Tenar of the ring. It did not matter. He could not hate her more. To be a woman was her fault.... He had looked at what had been done to Therru, and approved (116). Tenar is grateful to the courtiers; still, they walk off with Aspen, talking 'comfortably' (117), which leads Tenar to think about the rumors of magic promising immortality to the Lord of Re Albi, and of the villagers' philosophy of 'Let be': 'The doings of the powerful were not to be judged by the powerless. And there was the dim, blind loyalty, the rootedness in place'—a very negative rootedness here—'the old man was *their* lord, Lord of Re Albi, nobody else's business what he did.' Even Moss felt that way, finding immortality magic 'Risky,' likely to go awry, but she does not call it wicked (119).

Tenar recalls Ogion's instructions to her to teach Therru *all* and feels momentarily uneasy that so far she has taught only cooking and spinning. She asks herself only mostly rhetorically, 'Is wisdom all words?' and tries teaching Therru 'the true names of things' starting with 'stone.'[501] That doesn't feel right, though, so Tenar starts teaching yet again with stories (120-21; 'Finding Words,' ch. 9).

That night, Tenar has trouble sleeping and finds herself in a rapidly despairing internal monolog, ending in 'Only fire can cleanse me. Only fire can eat me, eat me away like—' and she sits up and cries out a curse-turning formula in Arha's Kargish and then gets up and yells out at her attacker, 'You come too late, Aspen. I was eaten long ago.' Tenar may have the satisfaction of turning the curse and singeing Aspen, but returning to Ogion's house the next day she and Therru are followed by two little boys, boys who throw stones at them, which may foreshadow her returning home to find herself caught in a spell laid there for her, a spell that leaves her 'confused, slow, unable to decide' (123; ch. 9) and, as becomes increasingly clear as the plot unfolds, unable to speak of the source of her immediate problems. The source is of course Aspen's evil, but what is the source of that evil in Aspen? Two malicious little boys throwing stones at Therru and Tenar may give us as good a hint as we will get: some people may start out no damn good at a young age, and especially if they're male gendered people, they may be allowed by their cultures to get worse. Or 'the cruel anger of the weak' may have been turned upon those boys, and they redirect and misdirect their own rage against the still weaker. The text is silent on their motives, and a range of possibilities will legitimately fill that silence, if we want it filled. Tenar thinks 'in her own language, *I cannot think in Hardic. I must not.*' She can think, slowly, in Kargish. 'It was as if she had to ask the girl Arha, who she had been long ago, to come out

---

[501] In *Bright's Anglo-Saxon Reader* (1891...1964), the first noun to be declined is *stan*, 'stone' ('An Outline of Anglo-Saxon Grammar,' § 20): as Le Guin says in *BG*, rocks are basic and *'The stone is at the center'* (55).

of the darkness and think for her. To help her. As she had helped last night, turning the wizard's curse back on him. Arha had not known a great deal of what Tenar and Goha knew, but she had known how to curse, and how to live in the dark, and' like Falk in the Falk-Ramarren combination in *City of Illusions*, Arha knew 'how to be silent,' and, like all the wise in Le Guin's worlds, she knows *wu wei*, the wisdom of acting only when one must (123; ch. 9): going with the Dao.

Tenar/Arha leaves Ogion's house, following an 'animal sense' and taking with her only Ogion's lore books and Therru. Hardic starts to come back to her, and some words of the Old Speech, and the name 'Kalessin' helps clear her mind as she sees below her, at sea 'a beautiful ship under full sail' (125), and, although a stranger to cities or even towns, she heads toward Gont Port and ends up at that ship.[502] There Handy tries to get Therru and manages to touch Therru's arm. Tenar speaks to a sailor she initially thinks is Spark, asking to come aboard: in effect begging sanctuary for Therru. It is a ship with an all-male crew, which is somewhat disturbing to Tenar, and the sailor is not her son, but, *Tehanu* being a well-made novel, and coincidences being significant for folk of power like Tenar, the ship is the king's ship *Dolphin* with Lebannen aboard, the young man she thought to be Spark. Tenar introduces herself to King Lebannen, who is 'about to bow or even kneel to her' when she catches his hands and says 'Not to me...nor I to you!' putting her one up in protocol on Ged, who has knelt to Lebannen at the end of *The Farthest Shore*. Tenar tells Lebannen of being cursed and of encountering Handy and about what was done to Therru, and Lebannen offers to take her and Therru home, making the offer 'with delight in being able to offer it, to do it' (a male thing, perhaps: showing affection through service, but also traditional knightly service to a lady, or a king giving royal succor to one who has herself aided him). More immediately, with Tenar's permission, Lebannen takes up Therru and puts her to bed (130-32; 'The Dolphin,' ch. 10).

Tenar tries to cheer up Therru and is surprised to see her arm marked, as if branded, where Handy 'had only touched her' (133-35; 'The Dolphin,' ch. 10). Tenar seems to respond to the marked arm as a kind of symbol or omen: she'd promised Therru Handy 'would never touch her again. The promise had been broken. Her word meant nothing. What word meant anything, against deaf violence?' A while later Lebannen touches Therru very lightly (136), and the mark at least begins with that touch to go away, totally disappearing in a short time (187; 'Winter,' ch. 12).[503] Tenar is introduced to the Master Windkey of Roke and thinks of how polite they all are, 'Ladies and Lords and Masters, all bows and compli-

---

[502] For clearing one's mind, cf. and contrast Orr's telling Haber to say or think *Er' perrehnne* before effective dreaming (*LoH* 161; ch. 10). See also the Old Canon (the *Tao te Ching*) in *CI* helping Ramarren (171-72; ch. 8).
[503] Cf. and contrast *Macbeth* (ca. 1606), where Shakespeare uses thematically the idea that scrofula, 'the king's evil,' could be cured by the king's touch (4.3.144).

ments' and wonders 'at how men ordered their world into this dance of masks, and how easily a woman might learn to dance it' (138; 'The Dolphin,' ch, 10). Juxtaposed with this thought, a toothless sailor gives Therru a toy: a beautiful little carving of a dolphin. Then comes a conversation among Tenar, Lebannen, and the Master Windkey of Roke, a wizardly political weatherman who tries to 'know the way the wind blows.' The conversation starts with Lebannen's telling Tenar of his desire for Ged to crown him and Tenar's observation that Lebannen had 'learned pain' and would relearn it 'again and again, all his life, and forget none of it.' And then the thought by Tenar, 'And therefore he,' Lebannen, 'would not, like Handy, do the easy thing to do'—with no explanation of what 'the easy thing' might refer to, and the 'And therefore' sentence marked by no transition but set off in a paragraph by itself. Note, though, that Lebannen learns from his suffering and that the lessons he learns are good ones. In *Tehanu*, not everyone learns from suffering, not all of suffering's lessons push those who learn toward the good. Perhaps the easy thing for a man under patriarchy is to go along with his culture—not the Way—and try to push around those weaker than he.

The rest of the conversation is important to the meaning of *Tehanu*: it is a long response to Tenar's question to the Master Windkey of whether Ged is still Archmage. It is a delicate question, and Lebannen must press Windkey to answer. Ged isn't Archmage, of course, but neither is anyone else. The Council of the Wise meets, with Lebannen making the ninth member, but the best they can do is a vision of the Patterner that results in his crying out (in his native Kargish), '*A woman on Gont.*' An experienced teacher, but a dense, sexist, and condescending one, Windkey tells his story of the meeting of the Wise and asks Tenar if she knows 'of any woman on this isle who might be the one we seek—sister or mother to a man of power, or even his teacher; for there are witches very wise in their way' (142-43; ch. 10). Tenar is upset with Windkey, but he does not feel she can confront him: 'His deafness,' starting with deafness to his own condescension, 'silenced her. She could not even tell him he was deaf'—so she changes the subject to there being no archmage in Earthsea now, but a king.[504] And she raises the possibility that Cob could 'have such power because things were already altering,' that a 'great change has been taking place,' a change correlating with the change from an archmage to a king. Windkey responds with the non sequitur, 'Don't be afraid, my lady.... Roke, and the Art Magic, will endure.' Tenar reacts strongly, if cryptically: '"Tell Kalessin that,' she said, suddenly unable to endure the utter

---

[504] Cf. and contrast this scene with the «language lesson» scene in Le Guin's 'Pathways of Desire' (1971), where (male) Ramchandra carries on 'The great teaching tradition of the Brahman caste' to teach (female) Tamara something she is deaf to: 'People cannot hear their native language' (*Compass Rose* 181). Cf. and contrast Ged's necessary, and useful deafness to the siren call of Cob in *FS* and the frequent, negative deafness of males in *Tehanu*. Note also below, Tenar's admirable blindness to power.

unconsciousness of his disrespect,' a disrespect stemming, Tenar infers, from his having 'never listened to a woman since his mother sang him his last cradle song.' Windkey makes 'an earnest effort to amend his offense. 'I'm sorry, my lady,' he said, 'I spoke as to an ordinary woman.'' Tenar almost laughs. 'She said only, indifferently, 'My fears are ordinary fears.' It was no use; he could not hear her.' However deaf Windkey is, Lebannen listens carefully here (144-45), and Tenar soon says to him directly, in private, her thought that perhaps 'there is, or will be, or may be, a woman, and that they seek—that they need—her.' Lebannen listens 'He was not deaf. But he frowned, intent, as if trying to understand a foreign language' (146; ch. 10). And then Lebannen goes over to a language he is learning quickly: When Tenar asks him if men from Roke will come for Ged, he says, 'I will forbid' (147).

Tenar and Therru leave the *Dolphin* at Valmouth, and visit with Tenar's daughter Apple (Apple's 'young merchant husband' is absent or silent and invisible). Tenar tells Apple about Aspen, although she cannot remember his name in Hardic, or talk seriously of Re Albi at all, and Tenar makes clear to Apple and reiterates for us her interpretation of Aspen's antipathy for her—and for putting upon Tenar the spell *we* see working on her: 'For being a woman, mostly' (149-53; 'Home,' ch. 11).

Tenar arrives home at Oak Farm to find Ged sent to work herding goats in the high pastures, and she sets to her own work putting her farm aright, and finishing the dress for Therru she makes from the cloth she got from Fan. Therru tries it on, and (paralleling Ged's showing Arha herself—i.e. Tenar—in a beautiful gown [*TA* 88; ch. 7]) Tenar tells Therru 'You are beautiful.... You have scars, ugly scars, because an ugly, evil thing was done to you. People see the scars. But they see you, too, and you aren't the scars. You aren't ugly. You aren't evil. You are Therru, and beautiful' (155; 'Home,' ch. 11).

The fall equinox arrives in Earthsea, and, far away in Havnor, Lebannen is crowned. Tenar mentally rebukes Ged for not going to Havnor to crown Lebannen (although she also did not attend the coronation). Tenar doesn't dwell on such high-flown matters but, instead, resolves to make a new friend. Her getting to know the witch Moss at Re Albi piques her interest in Ivy, the local witch, and Tenar works at overcoming Ivy's dislike of her (156). Tenar's interest in Ivy is increased by the local sorcerer, Beech. Like Aspen, Beech has a tree name; unlike Aspen, Beech comes across as more mature and far better rooted on Gont. Totally unlike Aspen, Beech is a good, kind, relatively 'innocent' and 'sensitive' man (and a devout admirer of Ogion). As a man socialized in Earthsea culture, however, he too hastily and too easily interprets Ogion's injunction concerning Therru, 'Teach her all.... Not Roke' as meaning 'that the learning of Roke—the High Arts—wouldn't be suitable for a girl.... Let alone one so handicapped'—to which he adds some other male-chauvinist and condescending remarks. As a sensitive man, though, and a sorcerer of power, he can—dimly—sense in Therru 'the gift,' and he can suggest that Therru be sent to Ivy to learn healing: 'Healing befits a woman. It comes natural to her' (157-59; 'Home,' ch. 11). Indeed, Beech here gives advice that Moss might give, or might be given by any modern feminist of the feminism that sees women as essentially more rooted in nature than men, hence essentially more nurturing—or in any event just more nurturing. On a second reading of *Tehanu*, knowing Therru as girl/woman/dragon, this advice seems simultaneously wise and ludicrous, especially ludicrous in its condescension.

Tenar promises she will consider Beech's suggestion, and she does so. With good reason. Lebannen is moving with speed and efficiency to establish the King's Peace; still, though, Therru lives in fear, and that fear can both draw harm to itself and lead Therru to do harm (158-60). Also, 'most people,' either in Earthsea or most people, period, believe 'that you are what happens to you. The rich and strong must have virtue; one to whom evil has been done must be bad, and may rightly be punished' (161).[505] So it is highly important to find Therru a relatively safe place in Earthsea society, and it will be difficult to do so. So Tenar sets up a 'chance' encounter with Ivy. With an innocence stemming, I think, from her absolute blindness to power, Tenar asks Ivy if Therru has any 'gift' for magic art—'any power in her.' Ivy answers promptly and contemptuously that 'Of course!' Therru has power, but refuses to take her on as an apprentice, for the sound reason that she fears Therru. Ivy asks Tenar 'What is she?' and gets in answer 'A child. An ill-used child!' Ivy responds 'That's not all she is,' and a very angry Tenar jumps to the unfair conclusion that Ivy rejects Therru because Therru has been raped. Ivy didn't mean that:

> I mean I don't know what she is. I mean when she looks at me with that one eye seeing and one eye blind I don't know what she sees.[506] I see you go about with her like she was any child, and I think, What are they? What's the strength of that woman, for she's not a fool, to hold a fire by the hand, to spin thread with the whirlwind. They say, mistress, that you lived as a child yourself with the Old Ones...and that you were queen and servant of those powers. Maybe that's why you're not afraid of this one. What power she is, I don't know, I don't say. But it's beyond my teaching...or Beech's, or any witch or wizard I ever knew!... Beware her, the day she finds her strength! (162-63; 'Home,' ch. 11)

---

[505] Puritans notoriously suggested that worldly success is a sign of election, and the theory of Karma affirms that if you are suffering in this life it is because of evils you have done in this life or previous ones. Again, the translation of Aristotle's *hamartia* as 'tragic flaw' rather than 'tragic mistake' may indicate a strong belief that people get the misery we deserve (see *King Lear* 5.3.171-72).
[506] Cf. Myra in 'Buffalo Gals, with her one original eye and one made of pine pitch (*BG* 22, 28-19). See *ER* 21, 25.

Tenar leaves Ivy, angry at being left alone with the problem of Therru, especially angry at being left alone by Ged. In an internal dialog, Goha tells Tenar that Tenar is being unfair to Ged, that Ged had been fair to her 'Or tried to' be fair (164). Still in a mildly bad mood, she arrives home to find winter coming on and tells Therru that winter is the time to learn the great stories and songs. This leads to a brief discussion of whether or not Therru, with her burned lungs and throat, can sing—she can if 'The mind sings'—and then a brief comment by Tenar how Therru is strong and how '...strength that is ignorant is dangerous.' Therru responds with 'Like the ones who wouldn't learn.... The wild ones.... The ones that stayed in the west,' and Tenar realizes Therru is thinking of the dragons in the song of the Woman of Kemay (165; 'Home,' ch. 11). Therru starts learning the great stories with the *Creation of Éa* (not *The Deed of the Young King*, the other choice Tenar offers her), and 'By her bedtime Therru knew how Segoy had raised the first of the islands from the depths of time...the first stanza of the song of the Making' (166).

And then the farmhouse is attacked by Hake, Shag, and Handy.

The attack is narrated, and with no turning away from gory details, but it takes up only three pages of the novel (166-69). Tenar does what she can as long as she can to keep out the men and then takes up her butcher knife in a 'kitchen that was all red light in her eyes' and challenges them to enter. But it is Ged who comes in, armed with a pitchfork (169-70). Ged had come across three men and had feared them. He follows them unobserved: 'One of them kept talking. About the child,' about how he 'was going to get her back. Punish her'—and get back at Tenar. It was Hake doing the talking: if not Therru's biological father, at least a man who believes Therru is his. He had talked about 'teaching—teaching lessons'; and he is the man Ged stabbed with the pitchfork (171-72; 'Home,' ch. 11), which stops the attack. Ged assures Tenar that she did what she could. 'What you did was right. Timed right' (moving with the Great Wheel), and Tenar tells Ged, '*You* did the right thing' (175). Ged wishes he could bring himself to finish off the wounded Hake, but even after Tenar's 'Do it,' he can't, and neither can she (176). So Ged will take Hake to Ivy in the morning (apparently, without his magic, Ged is useless as a healer). Meanwhile, Tenar and Ged have tea, and the attack sequence ends somewhat cryptically, especially for readers who do not catch the allusion to Tenar and Ged's escape in *The Tombs of Atuan* (and for any who've failed to note the fire motif and fail to see here the D. H. Lawrencian fire/ darkness/color imagery):

> The fire danced in her eyes.... Flames of yellow, orange, orange-red, red tongues of flame, flame-tongues, the words she could not speak.
> 'Tenar.'
> 'We call the star Tehanu,' she said.
> 'Tenar, my dear. Come on. Come with me.'

> They were not at the fire. They were in the dark—in the dark hall. The dark passage. They had been there before, leading each other, following each other, in the darkness, underneath the earth.
> 'This is the way,' she said. (177; 'Home,' ch. 11)

Therru had slept through the attack and Ged has cleaned up his mess and taken Hake to Ivy, but Therru finds linen soaking, obviously blood-stained linen. Tenar startles herself somewhat by answering Therru's 'What happened?' with a lie about her period coming on early. Responding to the lie, Therru comes to look to Tenar 'as if her face were not human at all' but (some other) 'animal'; so Tenar becomes convinced that even as she has now lied to Therru, Therru will disobey her (178-79; 'Winter,' ch. 12). How Therru knows (apparently) that Tenar lies about the menstrual blood is hinted at but unexplained: a significant gap to be left or filled in by readers.

Ged returns, with the Oak Farm tenant Clearbrook and they fill in Tenar (and us readers) on the news. Hake is alive, but Hake, Handy, and Shag had beaten to death Therru's mother, or, anyway, the human woman who had initially raised Therru: *Tehanu* is silent on the biological aspects of producing a human/dragon child. Handy and Shag are being held prisoner in a wine cellar and will be tried in 'the King's Courts of Law' and sentenced to death by hanging or 'set to slave labor' (179-82; 'Winter,' ch. 12). We learn later that they have been sentenced to the galleys, news which Tenar and Therru greet with silence (203; 'The Master,' ch. 13).[507] Ged feels the men must be punished; Tenar feels more ambivalent: "'Punished.' That's what *he* [Hake] said. Punish the child. She's bad. She must be punished'—or so Tenar presents Hake's motive for hurting Therru. 'Punish me, for taking her for being—' Tenar doesn't finish this sentence, but it seems safe to fill the gap with 'for being a woman.' What Tenar does continue with is 'It should not have happened.—I wish you'd killed him!'[508] Ged says he tried, and Tenar agrees, and sees a little later 'in his eye the faintest, irrepressible gleam of triumph' (182).

When recounting the attack on the house to Lark, Tenar is upset that without Ged's intervention she would have trapped herself and Therru in the house. Lark responds with a rhetorical question that is both obvious and appropriate in context, and adds a philosophical remark: 'What could you do but lock the doors? But it's like we're all our lives locking the doors. It's the house we live in.' The 'we' is not specified, but the conver-

---

[507] Ged serves on a bad galley in *WE* 28 f. (ch. 2), and Arren is held on a horrific one in *FS* and finds the thought of slavery intolerable (59f.; ch. 4).

[508] For the anarchist doctrine of prison as the epitomizing institution of the State, see *TD*, esp. the boys' prison game (27-32; ch. 2). Contrast premeditated and cold-blooded imprisoning of someone with a spontaneous murder, necessary for breaking out of a kind of prison and viewed positively: Falk and Estrel escaping from the Plains tribe in *CI* (73 f.; ch. 4).

sation turns to the dead woman, who turned out to have been four-five months pregnant. 'Trapped,' Tenar says, and Lark responds with 'Fear' and the questions, 'What are we so afraid of? Why do we let 'em tell us we're afraid? What is it *they're* afraid of?...What are they afraid of us for?' Again, we have to fill in the referents for the pronouns: 'women' and 'men'—women are afraid, and men fear women (although the plot of *Tehanu* might also justify 'weak' and 'strong' or 'householders' and 'tramps'). Here the names of all the tramps are given: Handy, Shag, Hake, and Senini, with Therru supplying the correct form of the woman's name (184; ch. 12).

Lark asks Tenar if she will keep Ged on, and Tenar answers, 'If he likes.' The decision comes shortly, when Ged comes in and then Therru. Tenar almost latches the door behind them and then unlatches it. She will not imprison herself behind walls, not even the walls of her own house. Then Therru tells Ged she knows the opening of the *Creation of Éa* and says it (since she cannot sing it) for him:

> *The making from the unmaking,*
> *The ending from the beginning,*
> *Who shall know surely?*
> *What we know is the doorway between them*
> *that we enter departing.*
> *Among all beings ever returning,*
> *the eldest, the Doorkeeper, Segoy....*[509]

And (we're told) Therru recites the *Creation* on to the end with the rise from the foam of the first island. Therru looks at Ged, her face (like his) 'scarred and whole,' also (possibly unlike Ged's) 'seeing and blind' and 'fiery'—and she tells him about King Lebannen and his ship, about being sick from Handy's touch, and cured by the touch of the king. 'Some day I want to fly to where he lives,' Therru says (187; ch. 12). Tenar and Ged discuss Therru and how she is big enough now that she obeys Tenar 'only because she wants to,' which Ged thinks (in another good anarchist thought) 'the only justification for obedience.' Tenar is concerned by the 'wildness' in Therru, and concerned that Ivy fears Therru. 'But you're not afraid of her,' she says to Ged. 'Nor she of you. You and Lebannen are the only men she's let touch her' (188). Having Therru's approval of Ged, Tenar asks him to stay on, at least for the Winter, and gets to the key question: '"Well,' she said, 'which bed shall I sleep in, Ged? The child's or yours?'

Ged responds, 'Mine, if you will' and asks her to be patient with him. Tenar's response is elliptic, unanswered by Ged, and highly significant: 'I have been patient with you for twenty-five years'—i.e., for about as long

---

[509] Cf. Rilke's 'The Eighth Elegy' (of the *Duino Elegies*), *BG* 193: quoted in part for my headnote to my chapter on *ACH*. See also *Tao te Ching*: doorway (ch. 6), cycle / return (chs. 16, 22, 25, 40, 52).

as she has known him. Later she will tell him, and us, 'I have loved you since I first saw you' (214; 'The Master,' ch. 13). Ged, in the earlier scene, says nothing (stupefied?), and Tenar only looks at Ged and begins to laugh: 'Come—come on, my dear—Better late than never!... Nothing is wasted, nothing is ever wasted. You taught me that' (189; ch. 12). They embrace and end up 'that night on the hearthstone, and there she taught Ged the mystery that the wisest man could not teach him.' This is Ged's sexual initiation, a traditional rite of passage, and Tenar jokes about it: 'Now you're a man indeed.... Stuck another man full of holes, first, and lain with a woman, second. That's the proper order, I suppose.'[510] Tenar takes the joke back, asking Ged not to fear her and telling him 'You were a man when I first saw you! It's not a weapon or a woman can make a man, or magery either, or any power, anything but himself' (190; 'Winter,' ch. 12).

After Tenar tells the farm tenants about her relationship with Ged 'promptly and bluntly,' she and Ged discuss what I've suggested we might call the «negative capability» of mages: the 'emptiness' power can fill, the 'potentiality' for magery. Ged says that he was taught on Roke 'that true magery lies in doing only what you must do,' but Tenar's 'emptiness' theory 'would go farther. Not to do, but to be done to....' Tenar does not think that's quite it either. 'It's more like what true doing rises from. Didn't you come and save my life—didn't you run a fork into Hake? That was 'doing,' all right, doing what you must do....' Tenar says that as Arha she was taught 'that to be powerful she must sacrifice. Sacrifice herself and others. A bargain: give, and so get. And I cannot say that that's untrue. But my soul can't live in that narrow place—this for that, tooth for tooth, death for life' (193-94; ch. 12).[511] Tenar wants the possibility of a freedom beyond bargains, 'Beyond payment, retribution, redemption'—beyond Heroic (or Christian) sacrifice, beyond the Law of Retribution—she wants what Ged calls *'The doorway between them.'* That night Tenar dreams of the doorway in the *Creation of Éa*, which she wants to open, 'but there was a word or a key, something she had forgotten, a word, a key, a name' she needs to open it (194).[512]

Ged and Tenar discuss the true speech of dragons and Ged's theory that 'the dragon and the speech of the dragon are one,' and Tenar gives him, free gift for a free gift, her story of the Woman of Kemay, all leading to a discussion of the Patterner's line 'A woman on Gont.' Ged explicitly de-

---

[510] Cf. *WWF*: Don Davidson's (derivative) formulation is 'The fact is, the only time a man is really and entirely a man is when he's just had a woman or just killed another man' (81; ch. 4).
[511] Tenar paraphrases a standard form of the *Lex talionis*: the Law of Retaliation, or Retribution (historically *limiting* revenge) found e.g., in ancient (patriarchal) Babylonian, Judaic, and Roman cultures, and later in Islamic culture, and Germanic (as 'man-money'). See e.g., Exodus 21.22-32. Leviticus 24.17-21. Far more recently, note, e.g., 'blood money' among the Yurok of California (A. L. Kroeber, *Handbook* 28, 49; ch. 2).
[512] Cf. Shevek's dream of the wall in *TD* 26-27 (ch. 2).

nies one obvious possibility for the meaning of the Patterner's phrase: that the next archmage is currently a woman living on Gont Island.

> No woman can be archmage. She'd unmake what she became in becoming it. The Mages of Roke are men—their power is the power of men, their knowledge is the knowledge of men. Both manhood and magery are built on one rock: power belongs to men. If women had power what would men be but women who can't bear children? And what would women be but men who can?

Tenar brings up queens, but Ged calls a queen 'only a she-king,' given power by men. So Tenar asks directly, 'What is a woman's power, then? * * * When has a woman power because she's a woman? With her children, I suppose. For a while...'—or *over* her children to use a formulation Tenar does not. Tenar first learned of the distribution of power in her confrontation with Kossil. Tenar 'had the honor,' but Kossil 'had the power, from the God-king, the man,' and then Tenar asks Lark's question, 'Why are men *afraid* of women?' Ged implicitly accepts that men are afraid of women and answers, 'If your strength is only the other's weakness, you live in fear' (197-98; 'Winter,' ch. 12).

The next question is why women 'seem to fear their own strength, to be afraid of themselves?', a question Ged answers, in a therapeutic, teacherly, Talmudic, philosophical, or wizardly manner, with another question: 'Are they ever taught to trust themselves?' Tenar's attention wanders to Therru stacking wood and wishes that 'power were trust,' bringing an end to hierarchy: 'all these arrangements—one above the other—kings and masters and mages and owners— It all seems so unnecessary. Real power, real freedom,' would better lie 'in trust, not force.' Ged responds with 'As children trust their parents,' which may or may not include whatever trust Therru had for Hake and Senini; the text is silent on this point. Speaking more generally, Ged says 'As things are...even trust corrupts' and cites the trust of the mages of Roke in each other and what they do and in the goodness of their purity and power (198; 'Winter,' ch. 12).

Leading back to the riddle with the answer 'A woman on Gont' and Ogion's 'All changed.' If the change is political, perhaps it is the renewed kingship, but Tenar wonders 'if Lebannen's kingship is only a beginning. A doorway.... And he the doorkeeper. Not to pass through'—to whatever; the thought ends without specifying a destination. And then the conversation takes an intriguing and, for me, an initially surprising turn: an echo of Ogion's advice to the young Ged to 'turn and return to his beginning' (*WE* 128; ch. 7), becomes a hint of the Kargish belief in *individual* reincarnation or even the Christian idea of dying to the world and being reborn. Ged talks of how he has 'died and been reborn, both in the dry land and here under the sun, more than once'—somewhat literally in embracing his Shadow in *Wizard* and going to the Dry Land in *Shore*, perhaps figuratively in the marriage with Tenar. Ged quotes and paraphrases what he calls here 'the *Making*' to the effect 'that we have all returned and return forever to the source, and that the source is ceaseless. *Only in dying, life....*': an idea similar to Ogion's assumptions in advising Ged for the turning point of *Wizard* to 'turn and return' to Ged's beginnings.[513] Le Guin as critic comments on this dialog that 'Tenar is whole, but not single. She is not pure. The sacrificial image of dying to be reborn is not appropriate to her. Just the opposite. She has borne, she has given birth to, her children and her new selves. She is not reborn, but rebearing...actively, in the maternal mode' (*ER* 18; see *DEW* 5). I will take this to imply that Ged, too, dies and is reborn insofar as he learns 'goat wisdom' and that of sages, and «rebears» new versions of himself: finally, ego becoming Self and Brahman or dissolving into the Dao or Shiva/Shakti—the destroying/creating godhead—reforming and coming into renewed being.[514]

The conversation moves without pause from metaphysics to Ged's personal psychology, so perhaps the dying/rebirth reference means mostly that humans change, figuratively dying to childhood to become adults, etc. In any event, Ged tells how, on the mountain, the last few weeks, among the goats, he came to ask, rhetorically, why he grieves: 'What man am I mourning? Ged the archmage? Why is Hawk the goatherd sick with grief and shame for him?' Tenar tells him he has done nothing to be ashamed of, but Ged asserts he has done shamefully, that all male greatness 'is founded on shame, made out of it.' Tenar declines to argue the point, and she and Ged agree that he is starting out in life again, at about where Moss put him, a boy of fifteen (199-200). Then, with Ged thinking of his literal youth as 'An emptiness.... A freedom' (in both Daoist and Existentialist fashion). Tenar asks, 'Who is Therru, Ged?' And he responds after only a very long pause. 'So made—what freedom is there for her?' And Tenar asks in turn (in what could be a interrogation of J-P Sartre by Simone de Beauvoir), 'We are our freedom, then?' Ged thinks so. Tenar replies:

> You seemed, in your power, as free as man can be. But at what cost? What made you free? And I...I was made, molded like clay, by the will of the women serving the Old Powers, or serving the men who made all services and ways and places, I no longer know which. Then I went free, with you, for a moment, and with Ogion. But it was not *my* freedom. Only it gave me choice; and I chose. I chose to mold myself like clay to the use of a farm and a farmer and our children. I made myself a vessel. I know its shape. But not the clay. Life danced me. I know the dances. But I don't know who the dancer is.

---

[513] Cf. '...*[T]rue journey is return*' part of the inscription on Odo's tombstone (*TD* 68; ch. 3) and the Daoist river imagery in 'Another Story' in *FIS*. See *Tao te Ching* chs. 16, 25, 40, 52.
[514] For Shiva and Shakti, see *Coyote* chapter on Le Guin's poetry.

If Therru learns to dance, Ged and Tenar agree, 'They will fear her' (201; ch. 12).

Winter passes, an ending and a beginning (201), and royal officials arrive, including wizards, who, Ged thinks, are looking for 'abuses of the art.' Tenar wants to suggest that a good place to look would be 'the manor house of Re Albi!', but she cannot get the words out, and she must move on to other thoughts. In terms of the novel's magico-politics, she has been silenced by the spell (203). Among the newcomers, Spark returns to take his inheritance and show that he has grown into a young male chauvinist boar, who will not give his own mother straight or full answers, which Tenar hears as, first, Flint's half-answers to her questions during the twenty years of their marriage, and, second, lies (205, 207; 'The Master,' ch. 13). Tenar sees herself as a failure with her son since he is less than a man, jealous of Ged, dishonest, envious. Ged responds, 'Frightened, I think...not wicked' and adds, 'And it is his farm' (207).[515] We are not given enough information to judge for sure whether Spark is more frightened or wicked, but in terms of *Tehanu* we can be quite sure Spark has taken the crucial test, and flunked: he has judged and condemned Therru. Tenar quotes him as asking about Therru, 'What did she do, to look like that?' (208). The last we see of him, Spark makes one friendly gesture: he teaches Ged a useful sailor's knot (212; ch. 13).

News comes from Re Albi that old Moss is sick, and Tenar, Therru, and Ged leave Tenar's—now Spark's—farm, with Tenar taking only some personal possession and three Havnorian ivory pieces (of seven money pieces Flint saved). Spark offers her all the money, but she leaves him the four pieces as her gift to Spark's bride when he marries; the farm she freely gives him with the line 'You're the master' (211; 'The Master,' ch. 13).

And then there is another action sequence, the climax of the book: significantly, a sequence that runs only eight pages and is very straightforward, without rhetorical flourishes or elaborations.

Aspen, apparently with an audience, magically binds Tenar and Ged, forcing Tenar into humiliating postures and calling her 'Bitch' (215, 218; ch. 13). Aspen is looking for Therru but is happy to have captured Ged, 'The Lord Archmage Sparrowhawk':

> What a splendid substitute! All I can do to witches and monsters is cleanse the world of them. But to you, who used at one time to be a man, I can talk; you are capable of rational speech, at least. And capable of understanding punishment. You thought you were safe, I suppose, with your king on the throne, and my master, our master, destroyed. You thought you'd had your will, and destroyed the promise of eternal life, didn't you? (216; ch. 13)

---

[515] Cf. Spark and Irene's brother Michael in *BP* (99; ch. 4). Contrast sons' points of view in the stories of Hugh and his mother in *BP* and Shevek and Rulag in *TD*.

Ged answers 'No,' and adds, in the manner of his response to the Terrenon (*WE* 118; ch. 7), an aphorism: here, 'In dying is life.' Aspen dismisses the quotation, and dismisses Ged as 'schoolmaster!' Like Cob, he takes seriously only power, and he will show Ged and Tenar (and, if he can catch her, Therru) his power. Aspen keeps the old Lord of Re Albi alive, and continues the work of Cob.

> You did not conquer him. His power lives! I might keep you alive here awhile, to see that power—my power. To see the old man I keep from death—and I might use your life for that if I need it—and to see your meddling king make a fool of himself, with his mincing lords and stupid wizards, looking for a woman! A woman to rule us! But the rule is here, the mastery is here, here in this house. All this year I've been gathering others to me, men who know the true power. From Roke, some of them, from right under the noses of the schoolmasters. And from Havnor, from under the nose of that so-called Son of Morred, who wants a woman to rule him, your king who thinks he's so safe he can go by his true name. (215-16; ch. 13)

Tenar and Ged are imprisoned, with Tenar much humiliated: muzzled, by magic, words taken from her. And Aspen will seek out Therru, whom he sees as Tenar's 'whelp...that I planned to finish punishing, since it was left half-burned' (218).

For the conclusion of the novel and its last chapter, the point of view switches initially to Therru.[516] Therru sees Aspen 'as a forked and writhing darkness' and knows—just *knows*—that his true name is Erisen.[517] She sees Tenar and Ged as her mother and father, and sees them bound 'with a thong through her tongue and a thong through his heart.' Aspen takes Tenar and Ged behind 'a stone door. She could not enter there' but needed to fly, 'but she could not fly; she was not one of the winged ones.' So she moves to the edge of the cliff, looking carefully with her physical eye to make sure she doesn't fall. 'She looked into the west with the other eye, and called with the other voice the name she had heard in her mother's dream'—i.e. Kalessin.

Therru runs to town, passing the place where she planted the peach tree; it's not there: the peach tree will *not* be a life-symbol for Therru, ris-

---

[516] Cf. switch of point of view at end of 'Nine Lives,' and note Le Guin's justification for the switch in her commentary in R. S. Wilson's *Those Who Can* anthology (208).
[517] For 'Erisen' as a name, cf. William Blake's Urizen in *The Four Zoas* (e.g. Night the Fourth, lines 34-40) and *The Book of Urizen* (1794), e.g., ch. 2. I am not competent to discuss Blake, but I am confident a detailed examination of Le Guin's canon in the context of Blake would be highly useful.

ing from a 'tiny grave' into life (wrong author for rebirth as resurrection). Then she goes directly to the house of Aunty Moss, who has been cursed by Aspen and is dying: as a lure for Tenar. Moss asks Therru to say Moss's true name, which she does; but Therru will not fulfill Moss's more basic request, 'Set me free, dearie!' by letting her die (220-21; 'Tehanu,' ch, 14). Freedom for Le Guin does not include dying, so long as there is hope for life within the natural order.

Then the point of view goes back to Tenar as she and Ged are led to the cliff's edge, where Ged will be forced to push Tenar off the ledge and then jump himself (221, 222); but, in good villain fashion, Aspen must first mock his victims. So, before the murders we get Aspen's 'But first, maybe she wants to say something. She has so much to say. Women always do. Isn't there anything you'd like to say to us, Lady Tenar?' She cannot speak, but can and does point to the sky. Aspen says 'Albatross,' and Tenar—like the young Duny rendered speechless by his aunt's magic—laughs aloud (*WE* 4; ch. 1). 'In the gulfs of light, from the doorway of the sky, the dragon flew.... Tenar spoke then.' She yells out 'Kalessin!' and pulls Ged behind a rock 'as the roar of fire went over them, the rattle of mail and the hiss of wind in upraised wings, the clash of the talons like scytheblades on the rock.' And that long phrase is it for the resolution of the physical action of the novel: Kalessin has done the dragon thing, and we can be sure Aspen and his co-conspirators are dead (222). The 'wildness of the spirit and of the earth,' symbolized in Kalessin, rises up 'against misrule,' symbolized by Kalessin sending fire against Aspen et al. (*ER* 24).[518]

In a conversation among Ged, Tenar, Therru, and Kalessin, Ged thanks Kalessin, by the title 'Eldest.' Therru addresses the dragon as 'Segoy,' and the dragon calls her 'Tehanu.' Kalessin, it turns out, has long sought Tehanu, and she has the choice of going with Kalessin or staying with 'these.' Tehanu will stay with Tenar and Ged and humans generally, and Segoy pronounces 'It is well. Thou hast work to do here.' Kalessin promises to come back for Tehanu 'in time,' but, for now, says to Ged and Tenar, 'I give you my child, as you will give me yours'—Tehanu in both cases—to which Tenar replies, 'In time' (223). Kalessin flies off, and Tenar and Tehanu look at the meager remains of Aspen and crew. Tehanu says 'They are bone people,' and Ged responds to the line—because said in Old Speech?—with, 'Her native tongue.... Her mother tongue.' And Tenar and Ged comment on Therru's true name of Tehanu, given 'by the giver of names,' so 'She has been Tehanu since the beginning. Always, she has been Tehanu' (224)—and then Tehanu urges them on to visit the sick Aunty Moss.

For the denouement, Moss begins to recover, and it is clear that the old Lord of Re Albi will die and 'The grandson might live, if the house is made clean....' Ged asks the question Lark asked at the beginning of the novel: 'Why do we do what we do?' (3, ch. 1; 225, ch. 14). Tenar and Te-

---

[518] Cf. Arendt on spontaneous vilence to right injustice: *On Violence* 63, 64.

hanu resolve to plant more peaches. Tenar realizes she left Ogion's lore books 'On the mantel at Oak Farm—for Spark,' who 'can't read a word of them.' That is no big matter, though. Tenar likes Ogion's house and ends the novel saying: 'I think we can live there' (226; ch. 14).

'To be whole is to be part; true journey is return' as Odo's tombstone says (*TD* 68; ch. 3), and like many another Le Guinian hero—from Tenar and Ged tentatively at the end of *The Tombs of Atuan* and (in the true Gontish version) *Farthest Shore* to Luz in *Eye of the Heron* to Stone Telling in *Always Coming Home*—Tenar and Ged return with Tehanu to a place both old and new, and a true home.

Discussion

> Loss of fertility does not mean loss of desire and fulfillment. But it does entail a change, a change involving matters even more important—if I may venture a heresy—than sex.
> The woman who is willing to make that change must become pregnant with herself, at last. She must bear herself, her third self, her old age, with travail and alone. Not many will help her with that birth. —Le Guin, 'The Space Crone' (*DEW* 5)

As mentioned above, the critical consensus on *Tehanu*, including Le Guin, sees it as Le Guin's revising and re-visioning of Earthsea, filling gaps (Christie) and reinvigorating the more feminist aspects of *Tombs of Atuan*, or turning into fiction the feminist insights of 'Is Gender Necessary? Redux' (Littlefield 249-51)—or doing penance or practicing 'affirmative action' (*ER* 12). And again, I am part of this consensus. Still, I wish to stress the Janus-face of *Tehanu*, its looking backward and fitting in to Le Guin's canon as of 1990, as well as looking forward to other feminist works. This is decorous for a novel with so much stress on doorways and liminality—the space between—with so much stress on faces scarred on one side: the face of Sparrowhawk/Ged, the face of Therru/ Tehanu. Especially when we recognize Le Guin's long-standing custom of debating with herself, *Tehanu* completes some patterns left unbalanced in the Earthsea trilogy.[519] In the trilogy, the score was two to one for books narrated from a male point of view and books dealing with transcendence—as projects—more than immanence; *Tehanu* evens the score and then some: being mostly Tenar's book and ending with minimal closure with our interest in an androgynous dragon and a person both dragon and little girl.

I want to look now at two familiar themes. The first is immanence vs. transcendence. The second is the filling of gaps, but with my own twist. Mike Christie discusses how *Tehanu* backfills available gaps in the world

---

[519] On the silence of the Earthsea trilogy on 'fundamental imbalances of power and gender,' see Littlefield 252.

of the earlier trilogy, with sex being one gap and the lives of women and children and peasants and nonHeroic sorts generally being a more important other gap (Christie 94-95). I wish to look at the gaps *within Tehanu* and different ways different readers can fill those gaps. I think my discussion will make clear that *Tehanu* was intended as a feminist novel and should be read as a feminist novel but is figuratively in the doorway on the path to a fully feminist novel—part of the continuing cultural *inventing* of the feminist novel—insofar as the reader must supply some feminist filling into those gaps. To stress the point, I will, provocatively (and, I hope, usefully), occasionally fill in gaps with some *masculinist* filling, for a 'resistant' reading. I also do some resistant readings to remind my own readers that resistance is possible and far from futile. Propagandizing children is usually immoral, but a book is a pretty noncoercive thing in the hands of a grownup, for the grownup. Authors and audiences collaborate to establish meaning, and if one starts feeling uncomfortable with or hostile toward a meaning, one should identify the meaning and decline to collaborate; one can recognize and even respect the author's (apparent) intention, but resist. In *Earthsea Revisioned*, Le Guin uses one of my favorite images when she says she could not continue her hero story of Earthsea until 'as a woman and artist' she had 'wrestled with the angels of the feminist consciousness' (11). In the traditions I come out of, 'The profoundest relationship' one can have 'with the cosmos' (*TD* 12; ch. 1) is imaged as a wrestling match (Genesis 32.24-30). If Jacob can wrestle with God and Le Guin can wrestle with feminist angels, readers can wrestle, as a point of respect, with Le Guin's work generally, and more specifically with a text as rewarding as *Tehanu*.

Immanence

Immanence in *Tehanu* is very much in the sense of Simone de Beauvoir, but with values reversed.

Again, in *The Second Sex*, Simone de Beauvoir uses 'immanence' and 'transcendence' as central terms for her analysis, not of anything metaphysical but of women's situation(s) in the late 1940s and proposals for women's liberation, and finds that the 'domestic labors that fell to [woman's] lot...imprisoned her in repetition and immanence'—a bad thing. A heterosexual human couple may be 'the original *Mitsein*' (friendly society) (35), but still, women generally are most trapped in immanence in reproduction and marriage.[520] As Arha, the One Priestess at Atuan, Tenar was caught in immanence *without* marriage, and part of Le Guin's point in *Tombs* (as in 'Darkness Box' [1963]) is that some people with jobs that put them high in hierarchies may find themselves trapped worse than the most conventional Hausfrau. Penthe is a reliable, if juvenile and prejudiced, guide to Atuan; she gives a nicely vulgar, radically nonDaoist view: 'It's

---

[520] See e.g., in *Second Sex* 147, 173-5, 187; II.V.xvi: esp. 429-30, 447-48, 451-54, 456; II.V.xvii: 513, 521; 555-6, 594; II.V.xxi: esp. 598-99, 602 (see also 618-21).

always the same here. Nothing happens.' Arha replies, 'All that happens everywhere begins here,' referring I assume, to Atuan's depths and hublike stillness (*TA* 17; ch. 2). Penthe would prefer someplace else—any place else: 'I'd rather marry a pigherd and live in a ditch. I'd rather anything than stay buried alive here all my born days with a mess of women in a perishing old desert where nobody ever comes!' (40; ch. 4 [see Littlefield 248]). So readers should see Arha's becoming Tenar and escaping from Atuan as a Good Thing. If anything is bad about that escape—Tenar's rescuing Ged and being rescued by Ged—it is that that escape is justified in large part because a community of women has been presented so negatively. However, this is a community of women working for two organized religions, a community ultimately under the authority of the men who made themselves high priests and, eventually, Godkings of the Kargad Lands (*TA* 24 and passim). So the area of the Tombs at Atuan offers the same challenge for feminists as the double vision (minimally) required for a fair look at the medieval convent as an institution: women's space indeed, yet with captive women, on the one hand; on the other, like a medieval or Renaissance ghetto: both a prison *and* a fortress (see *ER* 12).

But Le Guin has had immanence both good and bad throughout the Earthsea trilogy, and usually good. Transcendent action—Heroism—as Ged emphasizes, has been a temptation for Ged, a temptation he needed to resist. And Ged learned the lesson. At the end of Ged's public life, in the second to the last speech in *Farthest Shore*, the Doorkeeper says 'He has done with doing. He goes home.' The last speech in *Farthest Shore* comes from the Gontish version of whether or not Ged crowns Lebannen. Again, on Gont they say that Lebannen forbids seeking out Ged, saying 'He rules a greater kingdom than I do'—i.e., in going alone in forest and mountains, communing with nature, (re)joining nature, and coming to know and rule himself (*FS* 196-97). In *Tehanu*, it is pretty strictly the marriage version of immanence that gets privileged. Like the young Ged, young Tenar gets offered the education—though not the life—of a mage. And, as we've seen, like Ged she leaves Ogion—but very much unlike Ged she rejects a life of masculine power and doing. As Rosemarie Arbur pointed out in 1978, Tenar reaches Ged's 'goal in life—that of *being* rather than *doing* — about two decades before he does' (*Proceedings* 151). Old Speech is a mother tongue for Tenar, but the rest of magery is a foreign language, the wrong sort of clothes: if an old word may be allowed—*inauthentic* for her.

The possible 'immanence,' or tender trap, of marriage versus a career was a major question in the 1940s when Beauvoir wrote. It was a major question for my mother in the 1950s and 1960s. It was a major question for Le Guin in her life and in the essay 'The Fisherwoman's Daughter' (1988)—and a major question for the women responding to the analysis of 'The Fisherwoman's Daughter' as it appeared in Le Guin's newspaper feature, 'The Hand that Rocks the Cradle Writes the Book.' Do 'real women' go out there and get a job and whip male butt at men's games, or do they stay home in the old 'domestic sphere'? Or do they stay home and write books and take care to do more than 'one thing' (see *Tehanu* 22, ch. 3;

203, ch. 13). Or some other choice, not yet defined for women or men? That the debate goes on is clear from a bit of commentary from late 1995 on those classics of American television, *The Mary Tyler Moore Show*, *Murphy Brown*, and *Roseanne*.

Writing in the Arts and Leisure section of *The New York Times*, Betsy Sharkey quotes and paraphrases Regina Barreca on valorized domesticity and maternity as part of the backlash against feminism:

> Regina Barreca...senses a retreat even by Roseanne, the woman generally recognized as the comic character who broke the barriers for a new generation of shows. 'In a way Roseanne's become the domestic goddess—the good mom, the good wife,' Ms. Barreca says. 'Everything that she tore apart when she was doing the most ferocious vision of it on stage has been co-opted by TV.'
>
> In the 70s, *'The Mary Tyler Moore Show'* was more cutting-edge, Ms. Barreca suggests, because the leading character was a single woman who loved her job. 'Mary's primary relationships were not romantic,'...' What an astonishing, radical thing to do! We couldn't do that with 'Murphy Brown'; they had to introduce the baby.'
>
> ...[Murphy Brown] was at first conceived as 'Mike Wallace in a dress.' Four seasons ago, a still-single Murphy got pregnant, debated abortion and decided to have the baby out of wedlock [, starting] a national debate on family values with then Vice President Dan Quayle arguing that such a portrayal of single-motherhood was irresponsible. That, Ms. Barreca suggests, was actually a conservative gesture. 'What Dan Quayle saw as a slap in the face,' Ms. Barreca says, 'I saw as absolutely rolling in with the tide. The baby maternalized this otherwise fierce figure. The 'values' that are upheld in most of these shows is that the family is the right place to be.' (29)

In *Tehanu*, as in 'Fisherwoman's Daughter' Le Guin's position is clear. Those who wish may accept what power men are willing to share (or perhaps whatever power that women in the late twentieth century can seize), but she will value also, and valorize, 'the other room, where the women live'—a domestic life (30; ch. 4). Regina Barreca may think Roseanne et al. have sold out; Le Guin seems to feel otherwise, and many feminists in the 1990s will accept such a position (see 'Fisherwoman' 233-35).

Which is far from saying that *Tehanu* celebrates domesticity or patriarchal marriage. It does not.

Most strongly attacked is rootless heterosexual promiscuity, alluded to in terms of roaring girls (as the Elizabethans said) joining the gangs on the roads and often returning home 'within the year, sullen, bruised, and pregnant' (14; '...Falcon's Nest,' ch. 2). The family relationships among the sturdy beggars (to use another high-caste Elizabethan term) is seen only in the highly dysfunctional family that abuses and almost kills Therru. Unlike the welfare mothers Le Guin celebrates as 'the superwoman of today' in 'The Fisherwoman's Daughter,' these roaring girls have made a serious mistake. In *Tehanu* Le Guin comes down against rootless gangs—men figuratively as well as literally homeless—as much as she shows negatively the wondering tribes in *Planet of Exile* (1966) or *City of Illusions* (1967), or the settled but still rootless Shing in *City of Illusions* or the Condor People in *Always Coming Home* (1985). These gang members will inflict on others 'the cruel anger of the weak, which wreaks itself on the weaker in the endless circle of human violence' (*ER* 23): the men rape and nearly kill Therru and do kill Senini, her mother; and they in turn will be enslaved (181-82; ch. 12).

Arrangements more traditionally valued than tramp groups also come off poorly. Flint dies before the start of the novel, and Tenar rarely thinks of him (and people Tenar meets do not reminisce about him); so we only get glimpses of the marriage. Still, those are not very positive views: Flint not giving Goha straight answers for twenty years, Flint keeping their few money-pieces in his money box, Flint refusing to do 'women's work' ('The Master,' ch. 13). Probably our best indication of what Flint was like—aside from the widespread indifference to his death—is Spark, who'd 'been struck off Flint' (46; 'Bettering,' ch. 5)—i.e., a chip off the old rock, with a face like Flint's 'but still narrower, harder' (204; ch. 13). Faces in Le Guin's work are important as gauges to character, as are names, and the word-play with Flint and Spark is clear. Spark is a flinty failure as a human being, and we may infer his father was not much better.

What we see with Tenar and Ged is not a good traditional marriage but a good Le Guinian marriage in old age, when Tenar and Ged 'partner.' And we see that on 'the other side,' in 'the other room, where the women lived,' there could be a strong community of women: Tenar and Moss and even (eventually) Ivy, Tenar and Lark and Apple. Among women of men-allowed power, like Arha and Kossil, there may be little love or cooperation; among women with only the power of women, *Tehanu* implies, there may be cooperation, solidarity, *Mitsein*. Contrasted with this being together—but with *no* philosophical to-do about relationship with nature or Being (or the Dao)—is the intellectual Aspen trying for personal transcendence. On one side: the women and the Tenar-Ged relationship; on the other side: Aspen with his intellectual, macho-Heroic, Dr.-Haberish quest for the ultimate transcendence for the eternal Individual, eternal life. There is no contest. *Tehanu* reinforces immanence, but almost entirely in Simone de Beauvoir's *secular* sense. Marriage and society and a family of equals obeying willingly is affirmed; striving individuals on power trips—definitely including domestic power trips—are condemned.

Silences

'Is it different, then, for men and for women?'
'What isn't, dearie?'
'I don't know,' Tenar said. 'It seems to me we make up most of the differences, and then complain about 'em.' — *Tehanu* (99-100; ch. 8)

Before The newest criticism called all in doubt / And plain-speaking critics were quite put out, there was still some speaking of 'gaps' and 'silences' in literature: based on a standard defense of the 'naughty bits' in satire, or on Erich Auerbach's essay 'Odysseus' Scar' (1946), and/or on Søren Kierkegaard's great exercise filling in the gaps in the *Akidah*—The Binding of Isaac Story (Gen. 22)—in *Fear and Trembling: A Dialectical Lyric* (1843). My own background is Auerbach and Kierkegaard but also the film and novel versions of *2001: A Space Odyssey* (1968), and my mother's complaint against people who failed to understand quickly: people who declined to make logical leaps, who needed things spelled out. Part of my mother's complaint may have been itself based on different conventions in story-telling. Following Auerbach, and throwing in a little Matthew Arnold, one might call these different sets of conventions the Hellenic and the Hebraic. As Auerbach points out, Homer in *The Odyssey* insists on filling in as much as possible. The teller of The Binding of Isaac story insists on giving only the high points. Much more recently, Arthur C. Clarke's novel, *2001* can be read as a 'Hellenic' filling in of gaps in Stanley Kubrick's much more 'Hebraic,' high-points-only film, *2001*. The idea of gap-filling, in a more contemporary form, has *Tehanu* filling in gaps in the Earthsea trilogy as a central method of revising and re-visioning this world through the nonHeroic and antiHeroic 'eyes of those that fantasy has traditionally had little time for—ordinary, middle-aged, unbeautiful, unsexy, practical women; wives or widows, with children or without' (Christie 94).

Here, I wish to turn to the silences and gaps in *Tehanu* itself, and how we readers go about filling them.

If Joanna Russ et al. have taught us to ask, 'Where are the women,' I'll ask of *Tehanu*, Where are the people of faith in forms appropriate to a very ancient world? If Odo is right, religion is 'one of the categories: the Fourth Mode. Few people learn to practice all the Modes. But the Modes are built of the natural capacities of the mind,' definitely including the 'religious capacity' (*TD* 12; ch. 1). And, of course, Le Guin's Kesh in *Always Coming Home* are a highly spiritual people, and, generally, spiritual matters are important in several of the more recent stories collected in *A Fisherman of the Inland Sea* (1994) and *Four Ways to Forgiveness*, plus 'Coming of Age in Karhide' (1995). At least outside of the Kargad Lands, Earthsea does without gods, and that is well. There are observances of the turns of the year in the trilogy—and Ogion and later Ged and other people of inner power are in touch with the Balance—but in *Tehanu* the closest we come to spirituality is Aunty Moss's presenting its possibility for women. 'A man's in his skin,' including the young wizards we see, but women have deep roots. Ogion dies at the roots of a tree and the council of the wise meet in the Immanent Grove with deep-rooted trees (22-23, 142), but it is with Moss that we get the dialog on roots: Moss is sure she is rooted, and gets her power not from sacrifice or social forms but from her roots (51-53; 'Bettering,' ch. 5).[521] Aunty Moss raises some good points, but she is 'as essentialist as Allen Bloom' (*ER* 16), and she may represent a feminism admirable in its day but now inappropriate.[522] If that is the case, what will Tenar and Ged do to expand their connectedness beyond the family—find rootedness in their world? In their daily lives, of course: living on the land and keeping goats—and in the good, Daoist philosophy Ged learned on Roke and elsewhere (e.g., 200; ch. 12). Also, probably in their relationship with Tehanu, but Tehanu's dragon-nature associates her with fire and air, not with water and earth and roots, and one must make a leap of faith to expect a human daughter to lead necessarily to deeper connections for her parents. (The stereotypical American nuclear family is not hope-inspiring for connectedness.) The dragon will include symbolic and mythical immanence only for readers who bring to Tehanu some knowledge of 'St. George's earthy worm' (*ER* 21), and of the World-Serpent surrounding Ocean. Beyond that readers must see that 'These are dragons of a new world, America, and the visionary forms of an old woman's mind,' a 'guide into a mystery,' and 'emptiness' (*ER* 22) that readers can fill as we wish. Tehanu is the girl-gendered dragon-child of Segoy, the demiurge, so she can hold a lot of symbolic meanings. And Tenar and Ged (on the hearthstones again?), move toward a feminist re-visioning of the Perennial Philosophy in their discussion of emptiness, potentiality, true magery, power, sacrifice, and a freedom 'beyond all the bargains and the balance'—moving beyond the 'balance' celebrated in the trilogy toward what Ged glimpses as '*The doorway between them*' (192-95; 'Winter,' ch. 12). But with Ogion dead, we could use some spiritual people beyond Moss to help us understand how the religious mode works in *Tehanu*, or a more explicit imbuing of everyday farm and pastoral life as life *in* the world.[523]

If we now are to learn about sex in Earthsea, we might ask about the varieties of sexual experience. There are, apparently, no gay wizards, no lesbian witches. As far as we can see, everyone in Earthsea is heterosexual or doing without among the respectable people, and at least heterosexual

---

[521] In Behavorist terms, 'skin' is the impassable barrier to the private world of human individuals (Skinner 191); for a Sartrean Existentialist, that barrier may be equally impassable. Moss suggests that skin-as-barrier, skin as a prison, is a problem with rootless males, which, for her, is a redundancy.

[522] Cleaned up and regularized, Aunty Moss's views could be restated in terms of a spiritually inflected 'EcoFeminism'; and an ecofeminist approach (as I imply *passim*) would work quite well for much of Le Guin's work.

[523] Cf. and contrast the great farm communities and religious life in 'Another Story OR A Fisherman of the Inland Sea' in *FIS* (1994).

among the homeless tramps. A witch like Moss will take her pleasure where she can, but she limits herself to men. The book certainly does not present the idea as either insult or brag that 'Feminism is the theory, lesbianism, the practice.'[524] Among the Kesh, a man might be woman-living man, like the *wergern* among the Yurok and (with other names) generally among the Indians of California and 'probably by all the tribes...north of Mexico' (Kroeber, *Handbook* 46; ch. 1)—but not among the peoples we learn about in Earthsea.

I do not think such silences should bother readers. And I for one was glad to see Le Guin showing some unheroic single people as happy: Ivy, Moss, miscellaneous bachelors who do 'women's work' without thinking about it. As critics from Sir Philip Sidney to *MAD Magazine* have pointed out, we expect art to give us better than a slice of life, so all art is selective and *highly* selected: ordered, arranged, and, in some sense, made more interesting than life. And if women got included in *Tehanu*, others will be left out: not just believers or gays or lesbians, but others we might expect to be in a book such as this. For a major example: an anarchist. As Le Guin says in *Earthsea Revisioned*, 'Old Moss is no revolutionary' (16), and Tenar, though a wonderfully complex character, is not either. In *Tehanu*, Earthsea gets itself a king, and Tenar finds him a nice boy, and a capable one: which we know he is (see *ER* 14), and Tenar approves. But another very loud silence in *Tehanu* is what we should make of kingship generally and more specifically what, if anything, King Lebannen should do about (or, Daoist fashion, set a good example on) the social problems giving rise to 'tramps.' 'Sturdy beggars' and today's homeless in reader-world history, have been produced by economic dislocation, public stinginess, and/or oppression. If we accept the openness of the ending of *Tehanu*, we also may assert our right to speculate. Ogion's final joy invites us to optimism about the future of Earthsea, but that optimism is much too extreme in Craig and Diana Barrow's statement that 'Therru-Tehanu becomes the female archmage of Roke at novel's end' (41; n. 1), which would balance the new royal power. Le Guin recognizes and honors people who are kingly, whose 'lordship is the outward sign or symbol of inward greatness' ('Elfland,' *LoN* [1979]: 87). But from *Always Coming Home*, *Tombs of Atuan*, and what I know of history, I would infer serious problems with kingship as an institution. Even a nice boy learning to forbid and command and establish law 'n' order may soon oppress his people.[525] And if not Lebannen, then one of his successors. Kingship may be a phase through which Earthsea must pass, but if we foresee Therru *eventually* becoming archmage we should also foresee her facing a patriarchy and hierarchy reinvigorated by a King. So readers foreseeing a happy new world order un-

---

[524] For movement by Ti-Grace Atkins in the 1970s from 'feminism is a theory, lsbianism is a practice' to 'feminism is the theory, lesbianism the practice,' see Echols 238 and 349 n. 164.
[525] See 1 Samuel 8.11-17 (noting that the Prophet Samuel, was far from disinterested: royal power threatened the power of the prophets).

der Good King Lebannen and Archmage Therru might do well to consider the possibility that Kings are good for punishing rapists and other scoundrels, but they are kings by right of hierarchy, and the logic of their situations means they will enforce the patriarchal groundrock of hierarchy: men over women.[526] Moreover, Tenar is right to have problems with the whole concept of punishment—she is a good Odonian anarchist in questioning guilt, punishment, deserving (*TD* 266, 288; ch. 10)—and we should be careful about wishing to Earthsea anything more than a brief phase under a king.

In my summary of *Tehanu*, I have at least implied a number of gaps in the narrative: places where readers have to supply something out of our own lives and experience. Here I will deal with some I find most important.

A big one for me relates to my feeling that 'This book,' like *City of Illusions*, 'has villain trouble.' In her introduction to *CI* (1978), Le Guin had said, 'Real villains are rare; and they never, I believe, occur in flocks....' (*LoN* [1979]: 146; 'Introd. to *CI*'). In case you are way ahead of me—men generally are *not* the villains in *Tehanu* (there are good men as well as bad in it [*ER* 14]), but I think one needs to bring to *Tehanu* a strong suspicion of the motives of men generally to make the novel work. 'Why do we do what we do?' (3, 225) is indeed an explicit and twice-repeated question in *Tehanu*, and in some ways this book is an investigation of the mystery of good and evil behavior in the manner of Shakespeare's *Othello*, *King Lear*, or *Macbeth*. Except that *Tehanu* puts the question, «Why do men do what *men* do?» and why do women—who instigate no evil in *Tehanu*—allow it?

Why does Aspen attack Tenar? In terms of the political conspiracy he is running (216-17; 'The Master,' ch. 12), it is a stupid move: Lebannen probably won't find out about the disappearance of Tenar and some goatherd she has taken on, but he might. Why take the chance? Revenge against Archmage Sparrowhawk is a motive—whenever he learns the goatherd's identity—and because Aspen has this fanatical obsession about cleansing the world of 'witches and monsters' (216), and demonstrating his power, especially over women, especially over a woman connected to the new King, and Ged. All right; in the Earthsea trilogy, Aspen would have been a perfectly well-motivated villain: the trilogy is heroic fantasy, and readers are not and should not be overly fastidious about motivation in heroic fantasy, especially the evil motives of villains. This is even more the case in fantasies with limited points of view: we may know the motives of 'Me' and 'Us' but learn little about the Others. In a high fantasy *Tehanu*, I would read Aspen's fanaticism as a straightforward *mâshâl* for racist and sexist obsessions with purity and power. But Gont in *Tehanu* only borders the world of high fantasy; in its use of conventions *Tehanu* is closer to the juxtaposition of mundane and fantasy words in *The Beginning Place* (1980), than to the rest of the Earthsea series. By that sort of hybrid

---

[526] One might also read Marian Zimmer Bradley's retelling of the rise of patriarchal Kingship in ancient Britain: *The Mists of Avalon* (1983).

standard, Aspen is only about as motivated as, say, the monsters in *Beowulf* and, more relevantly, is somewhat less realistically motivated than 'the Master' of Mountain Town in the psychological-fantasy world beyond the gate in *The Beginning Place*.[527]

We accept Aspen's villainies finally, I think, because we have been prepared for them. Most immediately because they occur in ch. 13, 'The Master,' where we have seen that under patriarchy even a son of Tenar can turn out bad: few men—or nobody—will do well in the role of 'The Master,' and we know that Aspen wants power and understands power, as Cob before him, only as dominion. More important, I think, is the question of how much sheer blind misogyny and male pigheadedness we are willing to accept as plausible in Aspen, and this will depend on how much we find, or have experienced, misogyny and male pigheadedness endemic in the patriarchal world we inhabit.

A key scene for this question is the dialog among Tenar, King Lebannen, and the Master Windkey of Roke. They have the answer to the riddle, 'A woman on Gont,' but they need to discover the riddle. We may have a variation here of the motive of the Indwellers of the Handdara for developing Foretelling 'To exhibit the perfect uselessness of knowing the answer to the wrong question' (*LHD* 70; ch. 5). The search for the right question goes nowhere in this scene primarily because Tenar cannot bring herself to talk to Windkey—or even ask him to leave—because 'His deafness silenced her. She could not even tell him he was deaf' (144).

Why, and why not?

Were we back on Karhide, with Estraven trying to give advice to Genly Ai, the problem would be clear enough: Ai's macho 'deafness' on one side, but on the other, ensuring that Estraven will have problems cracking through that deafness, is Estraven's own *Shifgrethor* and diplomatic experience and the custom of Karhide making it «not done» to give direct advice.

In Earthsea, in *Tehanu*, Tenar does suggest to Lebannen in private 'that there is, or will be, or may be, a woman, and that they seek—that they need—her.' And Lebannen listens, even if it was as if he were 'trying to understand a foreign language' (146; 'Dolphin,' ch. 10). Windkey oozes condescension for women and a generalized pomposity, but again, still, why doesn't Tenar try harder to get through to him—or politely get him to leave so she can speak then and there to Lebannen? Windkey is an intellectual, presumably with some experience handling new and strange ideas. And surely communication between women and men cannot be *that* much more difficult than between dragons and men, and Orm Embar tells Ged much—however obliquely—when he must communicate with Ged about Cob on Selidor (*FS* 153; ch. 10). The issue in the little council on the *Dolphin* at least seems a crucial one, and Tenar has a duty to offer good coun-

---

[527] Cf. and contrast the investigation of motives in John Gardner's *Grendel* (1971), a modernist, men's tongue exercise in combining fantasy, naturalism, and philosophy.

cil. Tenar is multiply situated and hardly powerless: she is indeed Goha, the Gontish widow-woman, but the universe of power is lumpy, and Goha is also Tenar of the Ring, the Lady the King himself offered not only to bow to but to kneel to, a woman who will not be bowing to the King (131). Any fear Goha might have of Windkey should be more than balanced by Tenar's confidence in her status *in this context*, if not her general, quite high, competence. Later in *Tehanu*, Tenar says that '...women seem to fear their own strength, to be afraid of themselves' (198; ch. 12), and that is a possibility some sixty-seven pages earlier, during the council scene. Alternatively, Tenar has become *mostly* Goha, and speaking to Windkey as Windkey's equal (or his superior in the immediate hierarchy) is just not, for Goha, «done».

A feminist reading of my text above, ought to see me blaming the victim: «Why can't a woman, talk more like a man?» (see 50; ch. 5). That is a legitimate complaint, but I'll stick with the reading: to pass over as seamless and *not* question Tenar's problem with Windkey means assuming the communication problem is all with Windkey. We make that assumption, I think, only if we bring to *Tehanu* the assumption or the experience that «Men are/tend to be like that», in our world, or everywhere.

As with communication problems, so with other gaps in the novel, which are frequently silences by Tenar which we either assume are justified or not. Tenar loved Ged and never spoke her love. If we take the chastity spell as a clarifying subtext—what the author knows but did not make explicit in the text—Tenar could neither know nor speak her love while Ged was around; and I for one prefer a nonromantic ending in *Tombs* rather than Ged and Tenar's sailing off together toward marriage and life happily ever after. Still, what of later? As far as we know, Ged never visits her between the time of *Tombs* and *Tehanu*.[528] Should Tenar have chided him for not visiting—or have sent a message via Ogion after Flint died to hint to him she was available? Such a message to the Archmage Sparrowhawk would be like discreetly propositioning the Pope, but 'Who allows? Who forbids?' (*FS* 137; ch. 9) in the universe of Earthsea—what is to stop her if her sense of decorum and timing indicated it was time to drop the hint? I can supply a number of answers to that question myself. The point is that if we wish to judge we are not given enough information to judge whether Tenar's unspoken love is a problem with Ged or patriarchy or the nature of magic—or at least in part with Tenar. And part of one's reading of the politics of *Tehanu* will depend upon how one fills in or skips over that gap.

Ogion never kissed Tenar nor touched her. Did she ever ask him to? Did she touch him? If she didn't ask him to, what should *we* make of that lack of touch from a man who is to Tenar father, teacher, and guardian?

---

[528] He does not visit Vetch either, his best friend from *WE*, or Vetch's young kinswoman, Yarrow (*WE* ch. 9), or Ogion; so, viewed more naturalistically than is legitimate for high fantasy, Ged may have a problem with maintaining old relationships.

Given Le Guin's use of 'touch' generally, we should think it a bad thing that Ogion never touched her (see Remington, 'A Touch'). Surely it would be terrible if Tenar and Ogion were Athsheans, where touch is 'a main channel of communication' (*WWF* 94; ch. 5), and Ogion would be radically abnormal in not touching another person who lived with him. Such lack of touch would also be a very bad sign on our Earth during the time of Falk-Ramarren: the Shing, the great Enemy never touch 'common men' or women; 'they are like gods, cold and kind and wise—they hold themselves apart' (*CI* 154; ch. 8). But 'touch' in *Tehanu* is at least bivalent: good when Lebannen or Tenar is doing the touching, evil when it is Handy, ambiguous when Therru touches Moss, and Moss feels the touch as a burn (220; 'Tehanu,' ch. 14). Indeed, touch in Le Guin has been capable of negative value since at least 'Semeley's Necklace' (1964 [*WTQ* 16]) to Dean Festl in 'The Rock That Changed Things.' Festl is 'a kind old Obl who had never raped Bu,' the female hero, although 'he had often patted her' (*FIS* 60); we are not to think much better of the Dean for merely patting Bu. If we are somewhat bothered by Dean Festl patting Bu or high-tech troglodytes touching Semley's golden hair, do we want the picture of Ogion kissing or even touching teenage Tenar? Frankly, I think this gap is best overleaped, since old Ogion is going to be damned by one group of readers or another whatever he does. As a teacher, though, of many years experience, I'd say, «Wise choice, old man; keep your hands off your students, period, even if you are a mage and must remain chaste (or virginal) to retain your power and would *only* touch.»

I'm going to say again that *Tehanu* is at least double-sided in genre, Janus-faced in terms of Le Guin's canon, and an internal debate (*dialogic*) on feminist issues. Aunty Moss can present a kind of essentialist feminism that Tenar can only partly accept, and Le Guin in 1993 rejects (*ER* 16), but which we may and I think should feel ambivalent about. Aunty Moss says she has 'roots deeper than this island. Deeper than the sea, older than the raising of the lands. I go back into the dark'—and we should know Le Guin sympathizes: at least in her early works she generally liked roots and the dark—however much Tenar got too much of the dark (*Tehanu* 52; ch. 5). When Aunty Moss says, 'Before the moon I was' (52; 'Bettering,' ch. 5), we should admire her audacity in her own context, and the greater audacity for Christian readers who know Jesus's line, as the Son, 'Before Abraham was, I am' (John 8.5). And when Aunty Moss stresses the differences between men and women, and Tenar disagrees, we should accept that both have their points (100-01; ch. 8). Moss is an essentialist on men and women, believing there are some elemental, mystic differences between us; she is also a healer who would just as soon Ged died as lived (55-56; 'Bettering,' ch. 5) and a woman with enough against men that there is 'a gleam of vengeance' when Tenar tells her about eunuchs—even though Tenar has told her, truly, that the eunuch Manan 'was the nearest to a mother I had' (53-54; 'Bettering,' ch. 5). So Aunty Moss gets her say and Tenar gets hers, and *Tehanu* ends with a re-established family—a good Le Guinian marriage—and much else left open, including Tenar's cautious question, 'What's wrong with men?' (51; ch. 5). That the question is very serious here, makes *Tehanu* a feminist novel. That it is still basically a question, is a gauge that *Tehanu* is going to be feminist in different degrees, according to the ways in which it is read and how that question is answered.

What is unquestionably feminist and highly interesting in *Tehanu* is its completion of the movement, logically more than chronologically, from *The Tombs of Atuan* (1970/71) and *The Beginning Place* (1980) to *Eye of the Heron* (1978) to 'Stone Telling's Story' in *Always Coming Home* (1985): from shared billing in terms of protagonists to definitely a woman protagonist. And a woman protagonist who declines to become a female version of the masculinist Hero. People who identify strongly with Ged might also argue that Le Guin goes out of her way to reduce him from heroic stature to domesticity. But 'We don't need another hero'—or we need a new kind of hero—is part of Le Guin's point, and she does well here to drive that point home. Masculinist, macho Heroes are part of the problem, and that becomes clear when you bring into a genre like heroic fantasy some mundane reality.[529] We lose a hero, but we gain an every-day world where a dragon might pop in now and then, and we gain the possibility for a different style than that of the Earthsea trilogy, and, to my tastes, if not a better style, a welcomed variation from the high-fantastic.[530]

Tehanu is an open-ended work that I hope is not 'The Last Book of Earthsea,' but whether Le Guin continues the series or not—what a long, great trip it's been! Le Guin has taken us to a number of intriguing places in Earthsea: geographically, psychologically, cosmologically, philosophically, esthetically, ethically, and now (more consciously) politically. In the Earthsea Trilogy, Le Guin fulfilled some of the promise of Heroic fiction to teach new myths, new morals about the Hero and his world; in *Tehanu*, Le Guin has expanded the form itself to include a much smaller world geographically, and much wider world socially and thematically. If Le Guin ends the series with *Tehanu*, leaving open the circle, Tehanu will be and remain a book worth wrestling with: a beautiful and useful gift to the English language.

Le Guin thinks '...the archetypes may change' (*ER* 13), and *Tehanu* is an important step in changing the archetype of the Heroic quest and of the Dragon, opening them up to women's experience, and changing the stereotypes of those of us the Hero meets along the Heroic way.

---

[529] Tina Turner sings 'We Don't Need Another Hero' in the 1985 film *MAD MAX BEYOND THUNDERDOME*: a study of gendered Heroism that can be profitably studied with *Tehanu*. See also, among Le Guin's other comments on the Hero, Le Guin's poem 'My Hero' (1994) in *Peacocks* 58, and *ER* 25 and passim. For Le Guin in *Tehanu* moving 'her fictional attention away from even such devoutly fair men' as her nonmilitaristic heroes 'Ged and Shevek,' see Christie 94; see also *ER* 17.

[530] For Le Guin on style see 'From Elfland to Poughkeepsie' (1973), coll. *LoN* (1979): 83-96. See also Christie 93-94 for a fine discussion of the conversation among Apple, Tenar, and Lark while cleaning up (*Tehanu* 152-53; ch. 11).

*　*　*　*　*　*　*

At least as of my writing, though, Le Guin has written 'The Last Book of Earthsea' and returned to other old universes and moved on to more mundane worlds and to different issues: among other issues, the metaphysical questions raised in 'Pathways of Desire' and in Ged's guess that 'the dragon and the speech of the dragon are one. One being' (196; 'Winter,' ch. 12). One topic coming up will be the way words make worlds. Also in the stories following *Tehanu*, the stories of the 1990s: serious handlings of the solitary life (possibly returning to the unhoused wildness of the Dragon), religion, menopause (with a reference to menstruation), sex in figurative flavors other than vanilla, men's studies, and a hero whose coming of age journey is in the androgynous form that is one meaning of the Dragon.[531]

---

[531] I used the phrase 'unhoused wildness' with Le Guin's first published story in mind: the idea of 'breaking down all the shelters, the houses men build for themselves, that they may see the sky': 'An die Musik' (1961), coll. *Orsinian Tales* (here 145).

X.

TRANSITION: THE SOCIAL CONSTRUCT OF REALITY

Readers approaching the novellas collected in Ursula K. Le Guin's *Four Ways to Forgiveness* and, much more so, the major stories in *A Fisherman of the Inland Sea* will benefit from knowing that many in the original audience for these tales could see them in terms of a debate on 'the social construction of reality.' In terms of that debate, the doctrine that 'All human knowledge is local' in *Four Ways* can be seen as a 'weak,' epistemological form of the idea that reality is locally created. And in *Fisherman*, 'Newton's Sleep,' 'The Shobies' Story,' and 'Dancing to Ganam' may be read as rather realistic fiction: not merely as literalizations of a figure of speech concerning how our psychologies, stories, and interpretations 'construct reality' but instead as representations of a pure case of the social construction of reality in action, with social construction seen as the most real of phenomena. Below I tell several stories showing why 'social constructivism' should be taken seriously and (in its 'weak' form) accepted. Readers who dislike philosophy as gyring narratives or who are offended by nontechnical sources, readers suspicious of the sciences and who dislike reformulations of subtle theories for 'first-approximation' popularization in altered frames of reference—such readers should definitely consider moving on to my discussion of Le Guin's fiction in the 1990s. Readers without a background in philosophy should note that I usually clarify technical terms within my text, but you still might want to have a dictionary handy.

So, again, CAUTION, another *Kulturkampf* zone: a discussion by someone with little training in philosophy attempting to render a fictional premise plausible. College students in courses stressing social construction should keep in mind that their instructors may find the social construction of reality the only truth there is, and my approach to that sole truth repugnant.[532]

---

[532] My thanks to Dennis McGucken for making clear to me in a long e-mail message the limits of my sources on Western Marxism (Roy Bhaskar) and Jacques Derrida (David Lehman). McGucken does a beautiful job locating Derrida in terms of a highly nuanced philosophical debate, but Lehman may be more helpful

Physics/Philosophy of Science

I was taught at the outset of Chemistry 101 (in 1961) the scientific principle, 'The observer is part of the system.' I.e., in no science can one talk of some phenomenon in itself but only the phenomenon as observed. Most famously, it is impossible to determine simultaneously both the location and (vector) velocity of an electron. I would later learn that this indeterminacy means that the universe is not a machine whose future can be (theoretically) predicted; so Enlightenment scientists like Pierre Simon Laplace (math, astronomy, 1749-1827) and other really strict determinists will be disappointed in their hopes for at least theoretical certainty and predictability (Capra 45; ch. 4). But I was not doing philosophy in Chem. 101, and The Uncertainty Principle is still beyond me; what we could understand as first-year students is that all observations either potentially change the thing observed or are necessarily limited by the range of capabilities of the observer. An ethnographer cannot effectively observe 'the village as such,' but only the village plus an ethnographer living in the village. Astronomers cannot objectively observe the Crab Nebula, not because they change a nebula by observing it but because they are limited in their observations by being human astronomers on Earth or (later) sending instruments from Earth. The most interesting things about the Crab Nebula may have to do with phenomena not detectable on Earth and/or which humans have not evolved to perceive, not even with instruments we can conceive and build. More generally, we can say along with the followers of the eighteenth-century philosopher Immanuel Kant that no one can observe and report on any 'thing in itself' because we must observe the thing and perceive it in terms of human categories ('Kantianism,' *DoP*).

If strict objectivity is impossible in the sciences, then even scientific knowledge is in some degree 'constructed.' If even scientific knowledge is constructed, in some sense (if not yet necessarily an important one), our entire vision of reality, to a significant degree may be not passively perceived but actively constructed. This much could be clear even to an orthodox materialist and empiricist in Chem. 101. Modern physics, however, goes further.

When dealing with the exceedingly small, in the quantum world of the subatomic, 'The observer is part of the system' can have a very strong meaning. This is a world in which particles are processes and arise and disappear out of a quantum field Fritjof Capra can present quite convincingly as philosophically equivalent to Dao, Brahman, Dharmakaya or Tathata: the Void of myth and mystics (*Tao of Physics* ch. 13, p. 175; ch. 14, esp. 198-201). 'The crucial feature of atomic physics,' in Capra's statement of orthodox doctrine out of Werner Heisenberg et al., 'is that the human observer is not only necessary to observe the properties of an ob-

---

for the ideas that entered the more popular discourse of the academy and America's bicoastal intelligensia.

ject, but is necessary even to define these properties. In atomic physics, we cannot talk about the properties of an object as such. They are meaningfully only in the context of the object's interactions with the observer' (126; ch. 10). In the 'S matrix' interpretation of subatomic particles, this 'impossibility of separating the scientific observer from the observed phenomenon' appears 'in its most extreme form. It implies, ultimately, that the structures and phenomena we observe in nature are nothing but creatures of our measuring and categorizing mind'—i.e. those structures and phenomena are *maya* in Hindu terms: 'illusion' (Capra 266; ch. 17).

The unity of observer and observed can go at least three steps further. Stepping in one direction, one could come to solipsistic Idealism, where we each individually dream the world between our ears, or we come to a shared, corporate Ideal: what we may call in a good sense, a «consensus reality» (Jürgen Habermas, Antonio Gramsci), or, hostilely, 'Collective solipsism' (George Orwell). Stepping in another direction, the more wildly Idealistic among speculative cosmologists have noted that the universe took many unlikely evolutionary twists to get to a state that could sustain human life—and have added to that unimpeachable assertion the idea from quantum theory that an observer is necessary to collapse probability waves and get quantum events to happen. The steps from there can lead to the idea that the universe evolved to allow for humans to observe quantum events, thereby allowing the universe to evolve. In that case, human consciousness does not just construct reality but is the literal cause of the physical universe. The Greeks had a label for such a notion, *hubris* (noble pride, leading to a fall); Ashkenazi Jews call it *chutzpah* (comic arrogance); still, it is not quite absurd, and it is, paradoxically, a wildly woolly, Idealist idea arising out of the 'hard,' material science of modern physics: the Universe may exist because people perceive it; the Universe may exist so that people can perceive it.

Biology, Physiology, Psychology

It is axiomatic in the biology I was taught that (ignoring free will),

$$\text{genotype} \xrightarrow[\text{time}]{\text{environment}} \text{phenotype}.$$

That is, the genetic complement of an organism interacting with the environment over time yields what that organism is, at least *is* in terms of what can be observed and measured. The most immediate environment for any human organism is the person's society, and (with trivial exceptions) all of the environment is mediated by the person's culture. Hence, in a formulation of Arnold Gehlen, quoted with strong approval by the ethologist Konrad Lorenz, we humans are by nature (with trivial exceptions) creatures of culture (Lorenz, *On Aggression* 256; ch. 13). Our being creatures of culture is significant for our ways of perceiving the world.[533]

In the late nineteenth and early twentieth century, the American psychologist William James postulated that the world to human infants is, initially, a 'blooming, buzzing confusion.'[534] This doesn't seem to be the case, 'Rather, even infants one or two days old are capable of refined visual discriminations' (Dember, 'Perception' 41). One reason for this is summed up in a line by the character Forest in Le Guin's 'Dancing to Ganam': '...we filter out most of what our senses report' (*FIS* 132). I.e., we individually filter out much of what we are capable of perceiving; to this add that there has been a historical filtering of data reaching us because our perceptions start out highly limited by the highly evolved organs we are born with: we see only a small part of the electromagnetic spectrum, hear only a range of sounds, and smell a millionth or far less of what an olfactorily well-equipped animal such as a dog smells. And the data received and *used* by the brain are fewer still (the lab frog starving to death in the midst of minced flies both does and does not perceive the fly meat).

As human infants grow into adulthood, our perceptions become even clearer, if not necessarily more reliable, in part because of training and expectations. Among older children and adults, there are variations in perceptions—experimentally testable variations—according to age, sex, and culture. For an example highly relevant for Le Guin, there are 'differences in the style with which people perceive' as seen in 'extremes of response to context.' Some people perceive 'the world as highly differentiated' and tend 'to resist contextual influences' and are 'said to be field independent'; people who perceive 'in an extremely diffuse style' are called 'field-dependent' and tend 'to be highly susceptible to contextual effects. Thus, field-independent people are superior in locating a simple visual figure (e.g., a triangle) embedded in a complex pattern' or adjusting a rod to vertical in the absence of visual background cues. In North American, older people tend to be more field-independent than younger people; girls, 'especially after puberty,' and women tend to be more field-dependent than boys and men. 'Perhaps these results are distinctive of cultures in which females are at least implicitly trained to be passive and perceptually diffuse, and in which males are encouraged to assume an active, perceptually articulated stance' (Dember, 'Perception' 44). *And* perhaps some Daoists, Romantics, and ecoFeminists are right in seeing children and women more embedded in nature and the world, in which case being relatively 'field-dependent' would simply correlate with women's and children's reality. What is significant here is that the world appears differently to people in even slightly different subcultures: North Americans of different age and/or gender. Little girls are more likely to perceive things as part of a whole more than boys will; little boys will see contexts—usually—more

---

[533] See Erlich, 'On the Necessary Uncertainty of Historical Criticism.'
[534] The William James line is quoted in Le Guin's 'The Field of Vision' (*WTQ* 231).

readily than old men. 'Beyond sex differences,' psychologists have found evidence that 'the type of physical environment people construct for themselves or choose to inhabit can influence their style of perceiving,' e.g., traditional Zulus and Bushmen, 'whose environments are virtually lacking in rectangular forms' see things somewhat differently—literally see things differently—from people brought up in 'the carpentered, right-angled world of people in Western cultures' (Dember, 'Perception' 44).

Sociology

> We shape each other to be human.... —Le Guin, 'Coming of Age in Karhide' (1995)

In 1966, the same year as Jacques Derrida 'subversively declared that structuralism was finished' and to be supplanted by poststructuralism (Lehman 97), Peter L. Berger and Thomas Luckmann published *The Social Construction of Reality: A Treatise in the Sociology of Knowledge*. For Berger and Luckmann, 'reality,' in quotation marks, is the *subjective world* that we human are 'biologically predestined to construct and to inhabit,' a social world of self and others. For each human, this subjective, learned world 'becomes...the dominant and definitive reality. Its limits are set by nature, but once constructed, this world acts back upon nature,' e.g., determining what of all the biologically possible foods people (ordinarily) will actually eat, what of all the possible sexual acts most people in a culture will actually perform. 'In the dialectic between nature and the socially constructed world the human organism itself is transformed. In this same dialectic man produces reality and thereby produces himself' (183 [see also 180])—i.e., produces our social selves, our roles, our identities. Burger and Luckmann present an excellent and persuasive analysis of a 'weak' form of social construction of reality, but still a powerful thesis. Human beings are socialized into human identities in specific societies, and those primary socializations give us, if not our worlds, at least our initial, and very strong worldviews: 'The child does not internalize the world of his [initial] significant others as one of many possible worlds. He internalizes it as *the* world, the only existent and only conceivable world...' ; these primary socializations give each of us, 'the world of childhood...the 'home world' (134, 136; ch. 3).

Myths of Origin

According to a very early account of Creation, that of Hesiod, 'First of all the Void,' *Chaos*, 'came into being, next broad-bosomed Earth, the solid and eternal home of all, and Eros [Desire], the most beautiful of the immortal gods....' From Earth comes Sky, parthenogenetically, and then mountains and 'the barren waters.' Then Earth lies with Sky and produces Ocean and the first generation of gods (*Theogony* II.116-53 [56]). Later creation myths had less symbolic sexual action, and more dialog. According to the Fourth Gospel of Christian Scripture, 'In the beginning was the Word,' the *Logos*, 'and the Word was with God, and the Word was God,' and 'all things were made through him' (John 1.1-3). That is, out of nothing came all, via the Word. According to the P-code, in one Hebrew version, 'When God,' *Elohim*, 'began to create heaven and earth—the earth being unformed and void, with darkness over the surface of the deep and a wind from God sweeping over the water—God said, 'Let there be light'; and there was light....' (Gen. 1.1-5, *Tanakh*). I.e., language for the P-code authors and for John, 'is not only a means of communication but also [is] an operational agent destined to produce being—it has an ontological value,' and perhaps still does (Vajda 10.184). Doing some very rough and ready creative comparative mythology, then, one could say that in the beginning was Void, Chaos—a very active and *potential* Nothingness—out of which came All. Mediating the shift from nothing to all was either Desire and a Yin-Yang-like mystic marriage of the primal deities, or there was the Word or words: the *Logos* or *logoi* or, I will suggest, a conversation among *elohim*: the gods (see Gen. 1.26).

Alternatively—and a very significant alternative it is—that which was at the beginning and is now and is all that truly *is* is Brahman, 'the one Being,' that than which there is nothing greater ('Indian Philosophy' 9.316). 'Not this...not that' but Being itself, what is left over after all things are removed, as opposed to *maya*, illusion, the 'relative' world of appearances (*Bhagavad-Gita* 74-75; VIII. 73-74; VII. 39; II). 59-60; V), the world of 'individual and separate things' (Capra 85; ch. 6). If we would free ourselves from *maya*, some mystic disciplines tell us, we must free ourselves from the chatter of the world, pre-eminently the chatter of our own stream of consciousness: 'to silence the thinking mind' (Capra 25; ch. 2), to end 'the mind's endless, idiot monologue' (Huxley 217; ch. 15). If the task at hand, though, is to recreate *maya* after immersion in Brahman, then, perhaps, the way is through «chatter» seen much more positively: the word as human conversation, social narrative, the telling of stories. As Le Guin suggests in her image of us 'huddling about the campfire' telling tales: In the beginning of the human world, and so even now, was and is the human word, telling our stories, re-forming the (human) world, if not creating ourselves, at least preventing 'our dissolution into the surroundings.'[535]

* * * * * * *

According to the J-code version of creation, '...the LORD God formed man from the dust of the earth. He blew into his nostrils the breath of life, and man became a living being' (Gen. 2.7). I.e., human beings are one, psycho/somatic being: earth plus breath. Still, in spite of the resistance of the Temple elite, and, apparently, that of some of the delegates to the Council of Nicea, both Judaism and Christianity took 'the breath of life'

---

[535] 'It Was a Dark and Stormy Night,' esp. *DEW* 28-29.

and made it into *soul*: a separable soul, dwelling in the body as a god in a temple, or a prisoner in a dungeon, with Christianity going for the soul big time.[536] Secularized, this split became, in Gilbert Ryle's phrase, 'the ghost in the machine': mind within body. To resolve the split, one could become a materialist, and say that mind is a product of matter. Alternatively one could say—and Bishop George Berkeley *did* say in the eighteenth century—that "To be,' said of the object, means to be perceived; 'to be,' said of the subject, means to perceive' ('Berkeley, George' 2.847). Among simple souls—and to the author of the *Encyclopaedia Britannica*'s Micropaedia's entry for Berkeley—Berkeley's insight got simplified to 'to be is to be perceived.' More specifically, in the *Treatise Concerning the Principles of Human Knowledge*, Part I (1710), Bishop Berkeley 'brought all objects of sense, including tangibles, within the mind,' rejecting the possibility of 'material substance' ('Berkeley' 847). So if materialism is one extreme, balancing it after Bishop Berkeley is idealism: the world as idea, and the being of matter a function of its being perceived. Hence, as our ideas of the world change, the world changes: necessarily changes, ontologically changes, *really* changes.

Linguistics/Feminism/Physics

Daphne Patai and Noretta Koertge call attention to the Sapir-Whorf, or Whorfian hypothesis (republished 1956), 'according to which the structure and lexicon of a language,' its set of grammar plus vocabulary, 'both molds and reveals a culture's basic categories of thought and perception.' In Edward Sapir's formulation, 'Human beings do not live in the objective world alone,...but are very much at the mercy of the particular language which has become the medium of expression for their society.... The fact of the matter is that the 'real world' is to a large extent unconsciously built up on the language habits of the group.... We see and hear and otherwise experience very largely as we do because the language habits of our community predispose certain choices of interpretation' (Bright 13.212). Obviously, there are limits to the theory: 'German has no single word for what we call 'efficiency,' but one can hardly claim that Germans have no such concept. The Hungarian language has no gender, yet patriarchy exists in Hungary nonetheless' (Patai and Koertge 133). Still Patai and Koertge note that the Whorfian hypothesis and other forms of social construction have been applied in very strong forms in a fair amount of recent academic work: They cite the assertion by Michel Foucault in *History of Sexuality* that there were no homosexuals before the late nineteenth century and the invention of the term/category 'homosexual.'

---

[536] The Nicene Creed insists upon affirmation that the believer looks 'forward to the resurrection of the dead, and the life of the world to come,' which allows one to be a 'mortalist' and believe that even when good Christians are dead, they are dead, and remain dead until the end of history and the universe, when, again one thing, body/breath are joined for 'the life of the world to come.'

But what are we to make of certain followers of Foucault? Bruno Latour, for example, contends that no anthrax existed before Pasteur, and Ian Hacking says there were no battered babies before 1962.... [Patai and Koertge give rational explanations: Pasteur added isolated anthrax to the 'material culture of science'; Hacking may have] merely intended to make an assertion similar to Joel Best's [in *Threatened Children*], namely, that the battering of babies was not regarded as a serious social problem until physicians defined it as a syndrome in 1962. But each author, in the argument he makes, seems to do his best to block such a charitable interpretation of his words. (137).

* * *

[Patai and Koertge note] much more startling assertions, such as the insistence of Women's Studies students in a class taught by one of us that the pain of childbirth is socially constructed by patriarchy and would not happen in a feminist society. (139)

Both Le Guin and many of her SF readers would know about the Whorfian hypothesis, including the possibility of very strong formulations, wherein language structures the world. Benjamin Whorf (1897-1941) was a famous student of Native American languages, and the daughter of Alfred and Theodora Kroeber would be unlikely to have missed exposure to his thoughts as she got informally socialized into what Carol D. Stevens has called 'the family business': anthropology, starting with the ethnography of Native Americans. Additionally, anyone sophisticated in science fiction would get an introduction to Sapir-Whorf. The restructuring of reality by language is a strong theme in Robert A. Heinlein's *Stranger in a Strange Land* (1961); and Peter Nicholls cites a number of other works using Sapir-Whorf, including Jack Vance's *The Languages of Pao* (1958) and Samuel R. Delany's *Babel-17* (1966). According to Nicholls, in the 1975 essay 'Towards an Alien Linguistics,' Ian Watson has used the linguistic theories of Noam Chomsky—with S.F. expansion—to suggest 'that there may be 'a topological grammar of the universe, which reflects itself in the grammars of actual languages.'' And, Nicholls concludes his article, Watson has 'used arguments from quantum mechanics to support the solipsistic view that the Universe exists as an external structure only through the consciousness of its participants and observers; language, in Watson's scheme, is reflexive, Nature sending a message to itself....' ('Linguistics').

Marxism

Writing in 1909, E. M. Forster could see and foresee a world in flight from the human body and the world of matter. In the beginning of the third and last section of his far-future dystopia, 'The Machine Stops,' moving toward the end of the imagined world of the Machine, Forster presents 'one of the most advanced' of future intellectuals, an antiEmpiricist historian who warns his audience to 'Beware of first-hand ideas!' and asserts that 'First-hand ideas do not really exist. They are but the physical impressions produced by love and fear, and on this gross foundation who could erect a philosophy?' Forster's crank exhorts his audience to let their ideas 'be second-hand, and if possible tenth-hand, for then they will be far removed from that disturbing element—direct observation.' Actually, the crank isn't all *that* crazy in suggesting getting a number of different points of view on a historical event, in this case, his specialty, the French Revolution. What is disturbing, though, even to those of us who want knowledge carefully located, is his idea that the farther away from events we get the better we can judge, until '...there will come a generation that has got beyond facts, beyond impressions, a generation absolutely colourless, a generation 'seraphically free / From taint of personality,' which will see the French Revolution not as it happened, nor as they would like it to have happened, but as it would have happened, had it taken place in the days of the Machine,' i.e., in their own time, as ideologically constructed. 'Tremendous applause greeted this lecture,' Forster's Narrator tells us, because it 'did but voice a feeling already latent in the minds of men—a feeling that terrestrial facts must be ignored' (Forster 191).

Not very much later in the twentieth century, advanced thinkers will bring back the idea that 'terrestrial facts' don't even exist.

According to Roy Bhaskar, there is 'abundant textual evidence' for Karl Marx's '*simple*, commonsense *realism*,' the sort of everyday, colloquial realism that asserts 'the reality, independence, [and] externality of objects': i.e., that the 'real' world we see out there is really there.[537] Most modestly stated, as a character in 'Dancing to Ganan' puts it, simple realism is 'the notion that there is, somewhere, if one could just find it, a fact' (*FIS* 118), maybe even many facts. There is also evidence, Bhaskar says, for Marx's 'scientific realism': i.e., his belief in the reality of 'the objects of scientific thought' and structures scientifically inferred—but scientific realism need not concern us. What should concern us is that 'an entire tradition' of Marxism, i.e., much of 'Western Marxism,' has 'interpreted Marx as rejecting' simple realism and has very influentially tended toward 'some variety of epistemological idealism, normally anti-naturalistic and judgmentally relativistic' ('Realism' 407, 408).

Bhaskar traces this tradition back to György Lukács's 1923 *History and Class Consciousness*, where Lukács rejects 'any distinction between

---

[537] Bhaskar carefully defines the *realism* he refers to because of the ongoing debate that got formulated in the Middle Ages as nominalism vs. Realism, where the Realists are what many would call Idealists. I.e., Realists believe in the real reality of abstract Forms, Universals. Nominalists (like me) say that those 'Universals' or forms are just names (Latin *nomen*) people give to abstractions, mere categories of the human mind. See below for highly radical nominalists becoming poststructuralists, postmodernists.

thought and being as a 'false and rigid duality.'" This anti-realist tradition 'proceeds down to the extraordinary claims made on behalf of Marx by e.g. [Leszek] Kolakowski that the very existence of things comes into being simultaneously with their appearance in the human mind' (1958...) and [Alfred] Schmidt that 'material reality is from the beginning socially mediated' [1962]' ('Realism' 408). According to Bhaskar, no less a figure than Antonio Gramsci found 'the very idea of a reality-in-itself...a religious residue.' In his *Prison Notebooks* (1929-35), Gramsci redefined 'the objectivity of things...in terms of a universal intersubjectivity of persons; i.e. as a cognitive consensus, asymptotically approached in history but only finally realized under communism.' Pushing the matter, Gramsci, in Bhaskar's reading, holds 'that human history is not explained by the atomistic theory, but that the reverse is the case: the atomistic theory, like all other scientific hypotheses and opinions, is part of the superstructure,'' i.e., part of the cultural superstructure raised up upon a deeper and more significant (human) reality. Suggesting that we take Gramsci on atomic theory quite literally—that atomic reactions happen because humans theorize atomic reactions—Bhaskar says that Gramsci's remark here 'reminds one of Marx's jibe against [Pierre-Joseph] Proudhon that like 'the true idealist' he is, he no doubt believes that the circulation of the blood must be a consequence of Harvey's theory' of the circulation of blood (*Poverty of Philosophy*, ch. 2, sect. 3). Bhaskar finds Gramsci and some other Western Marxists 'in favour of a historicized anthropomorphic monism,' maintaining that 'nature, as we know it, is part of human history.' I.e., Bhaskar says these Western Marxists teach that the world is One and that One is centered in and made by humanity and our history ('Knowledge' 258-59)—an idea Bhaskar does not seem to like. Alternatively, we can see these Western Marxists returning, ironically, to the German Idealism of Georg Wilhelm Friedrich Hegel (1770-1831), where 'The categories of human thought are...at the same time objective forms of Being, and logic is...ontology'—a path I will not follow (Fetscher 198).[538]

Whatever its sources, it is something like Gramsci's vision of reality as the 'intersubjectivity of persons' and 'cognitive consensus' that George Orwell attacks in what is sometimes called «The Grand Inquisitor» section of *Nineteen Eighty-Four* (III.3-III.5). Orwell's immediate concern was the falsification of history under Hitler and Stalin (see Crick 119); still, at least for satiric purposes, Orwell in *Nineteen Eighty-Four* comes down squarely

---

[538] We might also see them returning to a formulation by Oscar Wilde (d. 1900) complementing his idea of life imitating art: 'Nature is no great mother who has borne us. She is our creation' (qtd. David Denby, 'In Darwin's Wake,' *The New Yorker* 70.2 [21 July 1997]: 60). Denby quotes Wilde, 'Decay' (40 [my colleague J. Kerry Powell noted 'Decay' as a probable source for the quotation and recommended that essay and also Wilde's 'The Critic as Artist']. As with Orestes in Sartre's *Flies*—a murderer of his mother, acquitted by an argument privileging fathers in reproduction—note the sexual and gender implications in the lines quoted.

for old-fashioned British commonsense empiricism against the extreme idealism of Winston Smith's Inner Party torturer and instructor, O'Brien. O'Brien tells Smith,

> The first thing you must realize is that power is collective. The individual only has power in so far as he ceases to be an individual.... [I]f he can make complete, utter submission, if he can escape from his identity, if he can merge himself in the party so that he *is* the Party, then he is all-powerful and immortal.[539] The second thing for you to realize is that power is power over human beings. Over the body—but, above all, over the mind. Power over matter—external reality as you would call it—is not important. Already our control over matter is absolute. * * *
> ...We control matter because we control the mind. Reality is inside the skull.... You must get rid of those nineteenth-century ideas about the laws of nature. We make the laws of nature. * * *
> ...Before man there was nothing. After man, if he could come to an end, there would be nothing. Outside man there is nothing. * * *
> ...This is not solipsism. Collective solipsism, if you like. But that is a different thing; in fact the opposite thing.' (218-19; III.3)[540]

I doubt that Orwell's criticisms had much effect, but there was this much change in Western Marxism in the generation following Orwell: Jürgen Habermas, in *Knowledge and Human Interests* (1972), at least according to Bhaskar, allowed for the origin of 'the human species as a purely natural process' even while seeing 'reality, including nature, as constituted in and by human activity.' And Theodor Adorno, a little earlier—*Negative Dialectics* (1966)—advised giving up trying to resolve objectivity and subjectivity 'and argues against any attempt to base thought on a non-presuppositionless [sic] foundation and for the immanence of all critique' ('Knowledge' 260).

---

[539] Cf. and much more so contrast merging with the Dao or Brahman, attaining Nirvana. Cf. Le Guin's highly negative view of merging with some 'Unist'—falsely One—movement; and strongly contrast Le Guin's favorable imagery of *occasional*, fleeting touch with Reality. The temptation to lose self through merging with a Party, Church, or other mass movement is discussed in detail in Hoffer's *The True Believer*. The «Grand Inquisitor» section of *1984* can be read usefully for Le Guin's presentation of such villains as Dr. Haber in *LoH*, Cob in *FS*, and Aspen in *Tehanu*.

[540] I am not the only one to cite Orwell against contemporary Idealists. Cf. Tzvetan Todorov, 'Crimes Against Humanities,' *New Republic* 3 July 1989, cited Lehman 45-46. Lehman's Index cites Orwell eight times (314).

I'll put the matter that, by the 1970s, there was a long-standing debate on the Left that had pretty well concluded on the impossibility of finding transcendent epistemological 'Archimedean points' outside the world from which to observe the world. This meant the inevitability of 'the immanence of all critique.' We judge situations more or less from within them and cannot get a godlike overview; we are located at certain points in space-time, and that is that. So our judgments are relative. At least among people with a lot of academic philosophy—including those coming from very unMarxist positions—this lead to a kind of crisis in epistemology. Matters soon got worse. In the words of my friend and colleague John H. Crow, Modernism's 'Epistemological uncertainty yielded (to) ontological instability'—postmodernism.

Linguistics/Postmodernism-Poststructuralism/Feminism

In the fifth century BCE, in Elea, in southern Italy, the Greek philosopher Parmenides reacted against Heraclitus's theory of flux by, among other things, composing a poem 'On Nature,' privileging among the 'ways of research' the 'absolutely noncontradictory way that says only what is, Being, is really true.' If you think something, you assert its existence (an idea that will get a lot of play later, with the Cartesian variation that one must first think oneself). Reality, then, is that which can be truly thought: grasped and communicated, and that which can be thought and communicated is reality. 'The primal source of the Eleatic philosophy thus lies in the archaic sense of language, according to which one cannot pronounce 'yes' and 'no' without deciding upon the reality or unreality of the objects of the statements.' So human language is not merely symbolic but 'corresponds to reality in its structure,' and it is 'From the premise of the essential coalescence of language and reality follows Parmenides's theory of Being....' (Calogero and Starkey 6.526; see also Benjamin 8-10). Parmenides and his school, then, introduced into philosophy ideas similar to those in magic, myth, and mysticism.[541]

By the early twentieth century, the linguistic ideas of Parmenides et al. were again very fashionable in philosophy. Fritz Mauthner, one of the founders of modern linguistic analysis in philosophy, could hold that 'Every attempt to tell what is true just leads back to linguistic formulations, not to objective states of affairs'—a position that 'bears some affinities to the views expressed in Ludwig Wittgenstein's *Tractus Logico-Philosophicus* (Popkin 16.855), another road I decline to travel. By the middle of the twentieth century, there was a good deal of emphasis among the intelligentsia for placing reality in words, but there was some hope that 'The Age of Analysis' could produce, a science of 'semiology' or a

---

[541] And which would go from philosophy back into systems of western mysticism; e.g., the ongoing 'ontological value' of language in Jewish mysticism may derive from Greek philosophy as much as from the Hebraic idea of the *mâshâl* (language working in the world).

grounded philosophy of language, or (at least) an exposition of structures, that could serve well enough as a philosophy of the world.

As David Lehman tells the story—hostilely, among other things—that hope was called into question at Johns Hopkins in 1966 with Jacques Derrida's paper 'Structure, Sign and Play and the Discourse of the Human Sciences' (coll. and trans. *Writing and Difference* 1978). The key passage, according to Lehman, takes precisely the view that can easily, and I stress *can*, lead to a vision of social construction. The moment came, Derrida asserts, in the development of the concept of structure 'when language invaded the universal problematic, the moment when, in the absence of a center of origin, *everything became discourse*...that is to say, a system in which the central signified, the original or transcendental signified, is never absolutely present outside a system of differences. The absence of the transcendental signified extends the domain and the play of signification infinitely' (*Writing and Difference* 278-80). Lehman paraphrases this—usefully for us, though arguably—as 'Nothing exists ahead of language or outside it; there are no things or ideas except in words.'[542] Alternatively put, 'Il n'y a rien hors du texte,' which Andreas Huyssen renders 'there is nothing outside the text.' Possibly looking to J. Hillis Miller's statement that 'Language...thinks man and his 'world'...if he will allow it to do so' (Miller 224), Huyssen couples Derrida on the textuality of reality with the 'insight that the [perceiving] subject is constituted in language' (Huyssen 259).[543] Or in Lehman's unnuanced reading, '*Words speak us*,' whether we 'allow' them or not: '...we are merely passive conductors of language' (106). Le Guin may agree; at least she does in a 1988 poem 'For Helene Cixous' (*Wild Oats* 60).

Human beings, according to such theories, seem to be in a Westernized, secularized, language-centered version of the relationships among 'the personal self and the Self that is identical with Brahman, between the individual ego and the Buddhawomb or Universal Mind.' For the individual human mind, the mystic Huang Po taught, to go into the state of 'no-mind,' one 'must not try to think it, but rather permit ourselves to be thought by it' (paraphrased Huxley 73; ch. 4). As the comedian George Carlin could state as part of his early-1970s act, 'All we have is words,' except Carlin's *we* in this sentence may also be constructed by words, so that instead of Universal Mind thinking us, we are spoken by language.

In modernism of the J-P Sartrean Existentialist variety, there was no God to create us; our existence preceded any essence we might have,

---

[542] Some of the philosophically sophisticated may spot a figurative cloven hoof in my 'usefully' in this sentence. My one philosophy instructor was appalled to infer that I was a *pragmatist*. And I still am, in part, but nowadays I'll make that a *vulgar* pragmatist to differentiate myself from such respectable thinkers of 'a resurgent pragmatism' (in Daniel Callahan's phrase) as Richard Rorty and Linda J. Nicholson.
[543] I get the quotation from *Writing and Discourse* from Lehman 97 (my emphasis); the Miller quotation is from Lehman 106.

which was our job to create. Philosophically, the action was in the perceiving subject rather heroically making something of himself (and that's *himself*: Existentialism is masculinist). Roughly speaking, consciousness was king.

Seyla Benhabib can sum up for the (post)modern philosophers—and help illustrate why I have avoided technical sources:

> Whether in analytic philosophy, contemporary hermeneutics, or French poststructuralism, the paradigm of language has replaced the paradigm of consciousness.... [T]he focus is no longer on the epistemic subject [a potential knower] nor on the private contents of its consciousness but on the public, signifying activities of a collection of subjects.... The identify of the epistemic subject has changed as well: The bearer of the sign cannot be an isolated self—there is no private language as Wittgenstein has observed; it is a community of selves whose identity extends as far as their horizon of interpretations ([Hans-Georg] Gadamer) or it is a social community of actual language users (Wittgenstein). This enlargement of the relevant epistemic subject is one option. A second option, followed by French structuralism, is to deny that, in order to make sense of the epistemic object [something external, potentially knowable], one need appeal to an epistemic subject at all. The subject is replaced by a system of structures, oppositions, and *différances* which, to be intelligible, need not be viewed as products of a living subjectivity at all. (112)

If our (post)moderns are correct, there is no single, unified, perceiving 'I'; if the crucial structure is language, perhaps there is no world outside of the discourse among many 'subject positions'—the people who say 'I' and construct themselves and the world(s) they talk about. Again George Carlin: 'All we have is words'—literally, except the words may have us even more. If this theory is correct, all we can do (and do do) to create the «facts» of our world is tell one another fictions, stories. This is an idea Le Guin is willing to play with seriously, and possibly believe; but I think Le Guin remains with what Aldous Huxley has called 'The Perennial Philosophy'—*and* remains (as a pretty consistent Daoist) a romantic affirming the worth of anarchic individuals.[544] With her favorite old mystics, I believe Le Guin believes in the ultimate reality indeed of *only* the Dao, the Brahman, but of the validity also of individual life among the 'ten thousand things,' illusory or not, the validity of living with others in the world of *maya*.

---

[544] Huxley got the 'Perennial Philosophy' phrase from Gottfried Wilhelm von Leibnitz (vii).

XI.

THE HAINISH UNIVERSE REVISITED I

Sixteen years after the publication of *The Dispossessed*, starting with 'The Shobies' Story' (1990), Ursula K. Le Guin returned to the Hainish universe to tell stories set very late in the history of human worlds: after the rise and fall of the League of All Worlds and the victory of the Shing and the ages of chaos, after the reconstruction of the League and its transformation into the Ekumen of known (human) worlds, after the action of *The Left Hand of Darkness* and the entry of Gethen into the Ekumen (Ekumenical Year 1490-97 [*LHD* 1; ch. 1]). For the stories in *Four Ways to Forgiveness*, she went to the planets Werel and Yeowe and to Ekumenical Year 2102 and thereabouts, in the year 5467 by Werelian count (*FWF* 211; 'Notes'); by Peter Brigg's count, some time after 5000 CE ('Chronology' 18).

In *Four Ways to Forgiveness* (coll. 1995), Yeowe is the third planet out from the sun and Werel the fourth; Yeowe 'has a warm-moderate climate with little seasonal variation' and Werel a climate that is 'cool temperate,' though 'severely cold at the poles' (212, 218). There is no indication of 'double planet' with an extraordinarily elongated orbit and very long year. This is significant, since 'Werel' is the name of the world—if not the True Name of the world—in Le Guin's *Planet of Exile* (1966) and *City of Illusions* (1967), where Werel does have a notable moon and an extraordinarily elongated orbit and very long year (*PE* 26; ch. 2). To me personally and in 'An Open Letter to Peter Brigg' Le Guin asserted that she simply forgot that she had already used 'Werel' as the name for a planet: 'The two Werels are not the same planets, not the same peoples' ('Open Letter' 12). The old Werel of *Planet of Exile* (Gamma Draconis III) is only alluded to in *Four Ways*, under the name 'Alterra.'[545]

Since 'Werel' means just 'the world' (*PE* 148; ch. 7), setting the four interrelated novellas of *Four Ways to Forgiveness* on 'Werel' and its sister planet Yeowe can be seen equivalent to Le Guin's having set them on

---

[545] The lead character in 'Forgiveness Day' is Solly Agat Terwa; the 'Agat' part is our hint that the earlier 'Werel' in *PE* and *CI* is 'Alterra' here. (So I suggested, and Le Guin responded 'yes!'.)

planets that the local peoples call 'earth' (see, e.g., *PE* 26, ch. 2; *TD* passim). 'Werel' can just mean 'Anyworld,' and I wish to discuss it first as Anyworld where relatively low-technology people have been colonized by a high-tech, hierarchical, capitalistic people with imperialist leanings. I wish to take a moment then for my own thought experiment, taking the history of *Planet of Exile*'s Werel (as we learn it in *City of Illusions* or as I infer it elsewhere) and relating it to the backstory of Werel in *Four Ways to Forgiveness*, as we learn that story in 'The Notes on Werel and Yeowe' at the back of the book in *Four Ways to Forgiveness*.

The relevant Werelian history in *City*, very tentatively, would go like this. Not long after our time, the human species on Terra gets even more self-destructive than usual, and had worse luck, yielding widespread famine and ecological disaster, authoritarian government plus assorted geological catastrophes.[546] 'When civilization became a matter of standing in lines, the British had kept queue' and the cooperative were fittest to survive—but not too many other Whites cooperated, and in lands richer than the United Kingdom 'a few had thrived' but 'most had died' ('Nine Lives,' *WTQ* 123). So humanity on Terra became mostly people of color. And it was these people of color who sent a colony to a double planet very slowly circling the star Eltanin: Gamma Draconis III, taking nearly sixty-six Terran years for each revolution, each Year (*PE* 26, 29; ch. 3). The colony wasn't sent to exploit Werel for the sake of Terra. The logistics and economics of such exploitation would be unlikely to start with, and there was a far more pressing purpose for sending the colonists. The Enemy was approaching the territories of the 'League of All Worlds,' and the Terrans were sent to Werel to gain another ally for the War To Come (*CI* 132, ch. 7; *RW* 31, ch. 1; *PE* 45, ch. 5). But then the War comes, and the Terrans are stranded.

This is the premise of *Planet of Exile*, which shows the merging of the Terrans with one of the human tribes native to Werel. The Terrans are dark skinned; the local native Tevaran tribe is lighter; and the barbarian Gaal are White (*PE* 7-9, ch. 1; 101, ch. 12). Significant here, the native tribe is highly sexist and has or knows about customs including ceremonial rape of women and castration for men for sexual offenses, and the Terrans have a highly structured, somewhat aristocratic, mildly oligarchic society: ruled by an elected Council (27, 31, ch. 3; 93-94, ch. 11). The Tevarans quite openly consider the Terrans 'falsemen' (9, ch. 1 & passim); the Terrans are usually more subtle but frequently feel an equivalent bigotry (e.g. 115-16; ch. 13). Putting the two societies together—intermarrying, interbreeding, combining evolving cultures—yields 'Kelshak society...hierarchic, intensely conscious of each person's place on a scale or in an order,' ruled by 'the achinowao' (*CI* 157-58; ch. 8), a society that comes to see time and space in 'the linear, imperialistic fashion' of the Terrans on Werel—or of Terrans generally in the early Hainish universe. Kelshak culture includes

---

[546] For near-future (eco)catastrophes, see e.g., 'Nine Lives,' *The Dispossessed*, *Always Coming Home*, *The New Atlantis*, 'Newton's Sleep.'

the idea of Rale, an analog to a basic idea in Daoism: 'the right thing to do, like learning things at school, or like a river following its course' (*CI* 136; ch. 7); it also includes old Terran 'dreams of domination' (*PE* 32, ch. 3; 74, ch. 9).

> The new mixed stock and mixed culture of the Tevar-Alterran nation flourished in the years after that perilous Tenth Winter. The little cities grew; a mercantile culture was established on the single north-hemisphere continent. Within a few generations it was spreading to the primitive peoples of the southern continents, where the problem of keeping alive through the winter was more easily solved. Population went up; science and technology began their exponential climb, guided and aided always by the Books of Alterra [i.e., Terran and League knowledge].... Finally, the moon and sister-planets all explored, the sprawl of cities and the rivalries of nations controlled and balanced by the powerful Kelshak Empire in the old Northland, at the height of an age of peace and vigor the Empire had built and sent forth a lightspeed ship.

The ship goes on an expedition to Terra, establishing the premise for *City of Illusions* (*CI* 134-35; ch. 7).

A historical pattern that is backstory and background in the 1967 *City of Illusions* is brought into the foreground in *Four Ways to Forgiveness*. A 'mercantile culture' becomes a highly developed if unusual form of capitalism: sensible about technology, particularly brutal in its use of slaves. Our view of 'aggressive, progressive' imperial power is presented in narratives that recognize the lives and gives speech to the voices of those the conquerors will see as 'primitive peoples.'

* * * * * * *

The second section of the 'Notes on Werel and Yeowe' quickly moves through the physical aspects of Werel (211-12) and spends only a bit more time on the physical aspects of Yeowe, concentrating on the ecological damage done to the planet by economic exploitation (218-20). Of the eight lines devoted to the Natural History of Werel, three deal with human adaptations including 'a cyanotic skin coloration (from black to pale, with a bluish cast) and eyes without visible whites, both evidently adjustments to elements in the solar radiation spectrum' (212). The lack of whites to the eye was seen in the 1960s *Planet of Exile* and *City of Illusions*, e.g., when we first see Falk in *City* (2; ch. 1); with the skin color, there has been both continuity and a change. The dark-skinned high-civilization people in *Four Ways* are purely local: '4000-3500 years BP [Before Present], aggressive, progressive, black-skinned people from south of the equator on the single great continent [of Werel] (the region that is now the nation of

Voe Deo) invaded and dominated the lighter-skinned peoples of the north'—repeating the offstage pattern of the earlier works of dark-skinned people establishing hegemony over lighter people, but switched in the movement of expansion from north to south to south to north. 'These conquerors instituted a master-slave society based on skin color' (*FWF* 212). The Voe Dean master-slave culture has two basic categories, Owners and Assets, subdivided by sex and age, and, among Owners, to some extent by economic class. Master or slave status was entirely matrilineal: if your mother was a slave, you were a slave; if your mother was of the Owner class, you were, that far, a master. Among the Owners, there are the *veot*s, a hereditary warrior caste, and *gareot*s, Owners who may have at most one asset, or none. A gareot who cannot live directly off slave labor might have to work for a richer Owner. Slaves were field hands or other kinds of work slaves (including house-slaves), *makils* owned by the Entertainment Corporation, slave-soldiers, owned by the Army, or 'Cutfrees': eunuchs, 'castrated (more or less voluntarily, depending upon age, etc.) to gain status and privilege.' Like some of the eunuchs in the Byzantine or Chinese Empires of Terra, some 'rose to great power in various governments' and were often influential. 'The Bosses of the bondwomen's side of the compound were invariably cutfrees' (212-13).

Basically, then, we see on Werel a propertarian society (as the Odonians would say) with a vengeance, stripped to the basics of race, class, caste, gender, and based upon the most primitive kinds of property: women and slaves. And a very long-established oppressive society: 'Voe Dean economics have been based on capitalism and slavery for at least 3000 years' (*FWF* 212). The most schematic form of the Werelian system would be found on old plantations, called exactly that—plantations. On traditional plantations there is the «great house», usually called 'the House,' and the slave Compound. The House was divided into the men's side and the women's side (*beza*), with the degree of division between the sexes varying directly with the wealth of the family. 'The compound was divided in halves by a ditch running parallel to the gate wall'—the single gate in the compound walls (214). Children lived with their mothers until old enough to work (ca. nine years old), and the Owner ideal was that asset 'pups' would be produced only by careful breeding (216). Traditionally, on the plantations the grandmothers kept order most directly among the women of the slave compounds under the more final but less direct control of Compound Bosses, the eunuch 'intermediaries between the grandmothers and the Work Bosses (members of the owner family), or hired gareots, in charge of the working assets' (214).

The means of production on Werel were in the control of the Owners, but the primary means of production always remained slaves. 'Slave labor, whether simple brawnwork or highly skilled, was hand labor, aided by an elegant but ancillary machine technology.... Production, even of very high-technology items, was essentially traditional craft of very high quality. Neither speed nor great volume was particularly valued' (224).

The slavery system reinforced and was reinforced by sexism and rigorous patriarchy. Owner women were always at law male property: fathers initially, then husbands; for spinsters or widows, some other male family member. 'Most observers hold that the gender division of Werelian society was as profound and essential as the master/slave division, but less visible, as it cut across it, owner women being considered socially superior to assets of both sexes. Since women were property, they could not own property, including human property. They could, however, manage property,' including slaves (213).[547]

The Werelian slave system, therefore, was Roman in its extensiveness and tradition but chiefly like that of the American South before the US Civil War: if the US plantation system had not had to compete with the industrialized North but instead had taken it over, if there had been fewer poor Whites and almost no freed Blacks. The American analogy is completed not when Werelians discover a New World, but when they themselves are rediscovered, by the Ekumen, leading indirectly to a new Werelian age of exploration and expansion. The arrival of the 'Aliens' sends the government of Voe Deo and its allies into the 'rapid, competitive development of space technology,' leading to the incredibly rapid colonization of Yeowe. However, their 'paranoid expectation of the armed return of conquering Aliens' is not fulfilled, when the Stabiles of the Ekumen wait patiently for the Werelians to join voluntarily (217). They wait some 300 years, until just before the time of the linked stories of *Four Ways to Forgiveness*.

During those 300 years, Yeowe is colonized by corporations who own slaves corporately and becomes a world to be exploited, to a great extent as a mining colony. In this subordinate status, Yeowe / Werel ≈ Anarres / Urras—with a hint or two of Athshe / Terra (in *WWF*). But the main and obvious analogy is with the New World on Terra, the Americas from the early sixteenth century CE to more or less our present in South America and MesoAmerica—plus the 'Third' and 'Fourth World' generally in its relationships with European colonizers. Exploitation of Yeowe went from mines to timber to the oceans to agricultural, each area of exploitation run by one great monopolistic Corporation, in league with the government of Voe Deo, but by no means under its control (220-21).[548] As on Terra (and later for a short time on Athshe), the exploitation was brutal to the planet and terrible for the slaves. In a long parenthesis we learn that literacy

---

[547] For land-tenure and property, cf. *Tehanu*; for the general status of women, cf. Condor Women in *ACH*.

[548] Slave-holding on Yeowe may seem more familiar if we note that distinguishing between the Corporations and the State on the planet is to make a distinction without much difference. State ownership of slaves was fairly common in early antiquity (e.g., the helots of Sparta [Swain 1.316]) and later in Roman mining and quarrying ('Slavery...'). And the convict lease system under the 'Black Codes' of the Jim-Crow US South (1870s f.) has been called 'socialized slavery' (Adolph Reed, after Oshinsky—see Reed [46]).

among slaves was criminal. Slaves found reading were blinded with what sounds like a slow acid drip or, more quickly, by having their eyes taken out. Using a radio or similar device was punished with deafening. In a summarizing sentence all the more horrifying for its reticence, we learn that 'The 'Fit Punishment Lists' of the Corporations and plantations were long, detailed, and explicit' (223).

Initially, the slaves on Yeowe were all male. As much as they could, they established their own subculture(s): one similar in some ways to my American view of tribal structures under slavery or extreme colonialism, but also a straightforward extrapolation of aspects of the more brutal prisons, all-male labor camps, and some neighborhoods of our world. Change came when 'Prices on bondsmen kept going up, as the Mining and Agricultural Corporations in particular squandered slave life (a mine slave during the first century was expected to have a 'worklife' of five years),' and eventually the Corporations brought in female slaves for breeding and other work (221).

> On the plantations, the original all-male social structure set the pattern of slave society. Work gangs early developed into social groups (called gangs), and gangs into tribes, each with a hierarchy of power: Tribesmen under a slave Headman or Chief, under the Boss, under the owner, under the corporation. Bonding, competition, rivalry, homosexual privileges, and adoptive lineages became institutionalised and often elaborately codified. The only safety for a slave was membership in a tribe and strict adherence to its rules. Slaves sold away from their plantation had to serve as slaves' slaves, often for years, before they were accepted into membership of the local tribe.
>
> As women slaves were brought in, most of them became tribal, as well as Corporate, property. The Corporations encouraged this. It was to their advantage to have slave women controlled by the tribes, as the tribes were controlled by the Corporations. (222-23)

When assembly-line production was introduced, the already alienated labor force on Yeowe rebel, followed by a serious liberation movement in the countryside. The Uprising's initial organization is in groups of tribal women joining together to oppose the political/sexual oppression of women (225). And the initial great act of insurrection is the unlocking of the doors to the armory at the Nadami Plantation by a slave woman (226). A thirty-years' war of world-liberation follows, ending in Yeowean independence, but a troubled independence. 'No central government was able to establish itself until Abberkam's World Party, defeating the Freedom Party in many local elections, seemed to be on the point of setting up the first World Council elections,' until Abberkam and his party are accused, correctly, of corruption, and worse, and the party collapses. 'The First

Election...established the new Constitution on rather shaky ground; women were not allowed to vote, many tribal votes were cast by the chiefs alone, and some of the hierarchic tribal structures were retained and legalised' followed by tribal warfare (227).

And more or less here, in these contexts, begins *Four Ways to Forgiveness*.

The first novella, 'Betrayals,' is a variation on a Romeo and Juliet love story, but one in which the explicit Romeo and Juliet figures are minor characters who break off their relationship (25-26), and, in any event are mere background for the story of two opposed old people who find love. It is as if Shakespeare had written *Romeo and Juliet* starring the Nurse, and telling her achievement of Friar Lawrence, but a highly politicized, rather more religious—well, a lot more religious—and marriageable Nurse and Friar Lawrence.[549]

The second novella, 'Forgiveness Day,' begins from the point of view of Solly Agat, a 'space brat' and a female Mobile of the Ekumen, serving in the old kingdom of Gatay on highly patriarchal and sexist Werel. Her guard is Rega ('Major') Teyeo, a veot vet from the War on Yeowe, and his point of view is brought in later in the story.[550] These two very different people do not get along, and end up marrying: Beatrice and Benedick, for another Shakespeare analogy (*Much Ado About Nothing*), but very much more significant as a 'Forgiveness Day' story for Americans. If 'Betrayals' shows Le Guin showing her respect for Hinduism and Islam, then 'Forgiveness Day' has antiwar activist Le Guin, the author of *The Word for World Is Forest*, allowing not justice to colonial warfare, but offering compassion and forgiveness for US Vietnam vets and veterans more generally.

'A Man of the People' starts on Hain, in the Pueblo of Stse, and with the family of a youngster of the Yehedarhed family: the relatively short form of his name is Yehedarhed Havzhiva. The village of Stse could be, culturally, one of the communities in the Valley of the Na, among the Kesh in *Always Coming Home*. The people are communal, matrilineal, traditional, in touch with the sacredness of all things, and outside of history (*FWF* 93-103). To the consternation of his family, and possible betrayal of his lover, Havzhiva leaves the Pueblo, leaves the People, and becomes a 'historian,' entering history and service to the Ekumen. At the Ekumenical school he has a love affair, fails to follow his new beloved to Terra, and goes to Yeowe to serve as a Sub-Envoy under 'a clever young Terran named Solly,' the Ambassador (118)—Solly Agat Terwa, from 'Forgiveness Day' (91-92). At the beginning of his assignment on Yeowe, Havzhiva is almost killed by an attacker, but comes to love Yeowe. Havz-

---

[549] For Le Guin's earlier uses of *Romeo and Juliet* motifs, see above, the discussions of *PE* and the East Karhidish tale 'Estraven the Traitor,' ch. 9 in *LHD*.
[550] For those of us who grew up during US military involvement in Indochina, esp. in Viet Nam in the 1960s, a *veot* who is a veteran of a colonial war can easily come across as stand-in for a Viet Nam vet.

hiva loyally serves the Ekumen and «goes native» in a very positive way. Havzhiva aids the women of Yeowe in their liberation of themselves, but 'not in a rebellious spirit'; that had to be the spirit of the women themselves. His work was 'To accept. Not to change the world. Only to change the soul. So that it can be in the world. Be rightly in the world.' His *wu wei*—Daoist action through stillness—is very helpful to the cause of women's liberation. Eventually becoming a Stabile, Yehedarhed Havzhiva does not marry on Yeowe—there is no marriage nor giving in marriage there—but he forms a stable partnership and fulfills his life as a Le Guinian hero (140-43).

His partner started life as Shomekes' Radosse Rakam, 'That is, Property of the Shomeke Family, Granddaughter of Dosse, Granddaughter of Kamye [i.e. granddaughter of] the Lord God.' Her story is 'A Woman's Liberation,' and it is a slave narrative: a classic slave narrative in its overall structure, beginning in ignorance, ignominy, slavery, and alienation on Werel, and ending in consciousness, freedom, and re-integration on Yeowe. It is also a classic slave narrative in much of its more detailed structure. It begins with a brief statement of the occasion of the account, which is followed by a statement about the lateness of literacy for the Narrator, and the explicit labeling of the story as 'my narrative'—followed by a paragraph beginning 'I was born a slave...,' and specifying a place but no date (145). It involves the great moment when, in James Olney's words on American slave narratives, 'the paths of literacy, identity, freedom met' (Olney 169).[551] It is, though, a mildly science-fictional slave narrative, set finally in a post-colonial world and told from the point of view of a woman under no obligation to produce Abolitionist propaganda (see Olney 166-68), and it was a novella in a series of linked stories, and then a collected novella in a book by Ursula K. Le Guin on the theme of forgiveness. So it is a slave narrative ending in a literal and symbolic Le Guinian marriage, and stressing throughout feminist issues.[552] 'A Woman's Liberation' features Le Guin's ongoing debate with herself on epistemology and politics, on how 'all knowledge is local,' but repressive institutions are just *wrong*; on the (masculine) City as the symbol of civilization and its evils, *and* 'The city as goal and dream' and potential place of freedom.[553]

---

[551] For a 'Master Plan for Slave Narratives'—with a pun on 'master'—in US Abolitionist tracts, see Olney 152-53. For some details in 'A Woman's Liberation,' the *Narrative* of Sojourner Truth may serve as a model: see Lerner, esp. 26.

[552] As more slave narratives are studied, it may turn out that domestic relations in slavery and freedom were a common theme. Please note that I am no authority on slave narratives. My contribution here will be mostly to identify 'A Woman's Liberation' as a slave narrative—if I recognized it as one, it must be *obviously* one—and to do a close reading of the story.

[553] For 'all knowledge is local,' see the formulation of William Blake, 'What is General Knowledge? is there Such a Thing? Strictly Speaking All Knowledge is Particular' (Annotations to Reynolds 459). For context specificity as an ongoing issue with Le Guin, note that in Earthsea 'A mage can control only what is near him, what he can name exactly and wholly' (47) and that *Rules change in the*

'Betrayals'

'Betrayals' is told in Le Guin's usual third-person, limited narration, from the point of view of Yoss of the Seddewi Tribe (23). We do not get the point of view of the other main character: Chief Abberkam.

Again, the direct Romeo and Juliet figures, young Eyid and Wada are minor characters with few lines. They are from quarreling families—the Dewis and Kamanners, aspiring to village leadership and squabbling over some land: no feud yet. Whether or not there will be one is not important to the story; one of the betrayals is that the two young lovers break up and do not 'Hold fast to the noble thing,' as their religion teaches them (25-26)—and as Mahatma Gandhi taught. Le Guin suggested to me 'cf. satyagraha,' which is the name of Gandhi's doctrine of 'cheerful, nonviolent resistance to some specific evil'; more literally translated from the Hindi, it is 'the grasping for and holding on to truth.'[554] In terms of the plot and our sympathies, rather more important in the story are Tikuli and Gubu, the foxdog and spotted cat (respectively) that live with Yoss. Tikuli had been given to Yoss by her daughter, Safnan, and his main act in the story is to die, peacefully, of old age (*FWF* 15), breaking the last link between Yoss and her daughter, who is lost to Yoss in NAFAL flight to Hain (21). Gubu continues a long line of cats in Le Guin's fiction, from 'Semley's Necklace' (1964) through the picture books (1988-94) to the great hunting cats of Werel to Yoss's Gubu himself (a small but effective hunter [25]), to Rakam's cat in 'A Woman's Liberation' (1990s)

The major events in the story are minimal. Chief Abberkam had been a fighter in the War of Liberation from the beginning: from Nadami, where his brother died, finally 'leading a great movement' headed by the World Party 'for what he called Racial Freedom,' i.e., the total expulsion of everyone from Werel who had not been a slave: Bosses and Owners, however long their families had been on Yeowe, the Aliens who served the Ekumen, however much the Ekumen had helped Yeowe gain freedom (9). Just short of an electoral victory, Abberkam goes down in scandal, primarily betraying an old friend: 'A chief could indulge himself sexually, mis-

---

Reaches' (160); see chs. 3 and 9 in *WE*, 1968. For a good introduction to the question of local knowledge in 1990s feminist thinking, see Part II: *The Politics of Location* in Nicholson's *Feminism/Postmodernism*, esp. Probyn essay. See my discussion of *ACH* for Le Guin's most explicit attack on the City of Man; see Introd. to *CI* for potentially positive city, esp. *LoN* (1979): 147.

[554] I quote *Encyclopaedia Britannica* (1974): Micropaedia 'satyâgraha'; Le Guin's suggestion was a personal communication. For the theme of 'hold fast,' note the phrase as a repeated motif in *EoH* (also referred to by Le Guin): a catch-phrase, the name of a significant character, Holdfast, and the last words of Lev Shults's formal speech at the climactic confrontation in that novel: 'I speak the conscience of my people. We will hold fast' (132; ch. 9). For a negative view of Holdfast as mythic father-tyrant and 'monster of the status quo,' see Campbell 337 (2.3.3) & passim (and Susan McKee Charnas's *Walk to the End of the World*.)

use power, grow rich off his people and be admired for it, but a chief who betrayed a companion was not forgiven. It was, Yoss thought, the code of the slave' (10)—and in a story called 'Betrayals,' we are invited to consider whether or not this bit of slave ethics should be carried into freedom. Christians and some old Marxists may want (re)birth of a New Man, and the more testosterone-poisoned of the Nietzscheans may want that New Man to be a Superman beyond the good and evil set up by bourgeois Christians, following a religion made for slaves. Le Guin holds allegiance in none of these camps. The question here is a real one: what of the morality slaves practiced as slaves is intrinsic to what their culture is or what they want it to be; what is *merely* servile and to be discarded?

Yoss has gone to a small village to give up the world: to drink water and be silent and learn the holy *Arkamye*; Abberkam has come there in disgrace. Yoss is happy in Abberkam's fall, or that of any Boss or chief or man of power. Still, one night she hears howling and finally recognizes the cries 'as a human voice,' howling in pain; and, like Estraven in *The Left Hand of Darkness*, Yoss responds to that cry, and finally looks at Abberkam 'striding and tearing at his hair and crying like an animal, like a soul in pain.' And, 'After that night she did not judge him. They were equals' (11-12).

The rest of the plot consists of Abberkam's coming down with 'berlot,' a pneumonia-like disease, followed by pneumonia, Yoss's helping to pull him through, and the foxdog Tikuli's dying. Yoss doesn't exactly come to like Abberkam, but she does come to feel that he listens to her 'intently...that he was trying to understand' what she said, 'like a foreigner who did not know the language' but is trying to learn (23).[555] For the climax of the story, Yoss builds a wood fire in a fireplace made for peat, and leaves the fire burning when she goes out, leaving her cat locked in. She returns to a burned house, but Abberkam has saved Gubu, Yoss's cat. And then Yoss and Abberkam reach an agreement:

> 'I came here in shame,' he said, 'and you honored me.'
> 'Why not?' [Yoss responds] 'Who am I to judge you?'
> * * *
> 'Would there be any peace between us?' she said at last.
> 'Do we need peace?'
> After a while she smiled a little.
> 'I will do my best,' he said. 'Stay in this house a while [the house he uses].'
> She nodded. (34)

Thus ends a thirty-four page story in the HarperCollins collection. The interest here isn't significantly less in on-stage incident than in, say,

---

[555] Cf. Lebannen's listening to Tenar in *Tehanu*, 'as if trying to understand a foreign language' (146; ch. 10).

Shakespeare's *As You Like It* or Anton Chekhov's *Three Sisters* (1901), but, as with those two dramatic works, the linear plot competes for interest with character, relationships, theme, and setting (for a 'carrier-bag' sort of story). Again, though, the physical setting is not science fictional and is certainly less impressive than such literally mundane settings as medieval Orsinia or the canyon Es Toch is built over in *City of Illusions* or even Le Guin's home city of Portland, OR. What is interesting is the *social* setting. This is not the day before the revolution; 'Betrayals' covers perhaps a fortnight in the years after a major anticolonial war.

The story starts with quotations from an Ekumenical book: about the planet O, without war for 5,000 years, and about Gethen, where there still has never been a war.[556] Yoss's world is not peaceful.

> From the Uprising at Nadami on, thirty years of fighting, rebellions, retaliations, half her lifetime, and even after Liberation, after all the Werelians were gone, the fighting went on. Always, always, the young men were ready to rush out and kill whoever the old men told them to kill, each other, women, old people, children; always there was a war to be fought in the name of Peace, Freedom, Justice, the Lord.

And for less exalted causes: there were tribal fights for land in the country-side, and fights for power in the city (*FWF* 10). Warlords sent their gangs out into city streets by night, and even by day a woman in the city had to be very careful (19). So Yoss asks herself, 'What would that world be, a world without war?' And she answers herself, 'It would be the real world. Peace was the true life, the life of working and learning and bringing up children to work and learn. War, which devoured work, learning, and children, was the denial of reality' (1). So however much a feud threatens because of petty aspirations for petty families, and however stormy we foresee the future relationship between Yoss and Abberkam, in Yoss's sense 'Betrayals' is still a story set in a world moving toward reality, moving toward peace.

News reaches them, of 'a new war in the eastern province' (27), but Yoss's village is at peace—tentatively—so Yoss and Abberkam and anyone else old enough to strive for wisdom can deal with some major human issues, and therefore issues Le Guin returns to frequently, often arguing at least two sides.

Yoss wishes to let go of the world and come to the Lord Kamye with empty hands, to drink water and live simply and be silent and nurture her soul (3-4). Good things, indeed, in Le Guin, except for the god part—except, again, in these stories of forgiveness, Le Guin, I think, forgives God. At least she allows that slave peoples may need a strong faith to sur-

---

[556] I'll add that Athshe in *WWF*, before the Terrans came, had had no war and only minimal intraspecific violence of any kind.

vive, and that such a faith might be shaped into something useful in freedom. Moses may have taken a bad detour in going to Sinai on the route from Egypt to Canaan, but Martin Luther King, Jr., Nelson Mandela, and Latin American Liberation theologians may have done better.

In any event, Yoss and Abberkam are theists and followers of a religion whose central moment has two god-brothers—like characters out of Indian myth or epic—standing before *'the Five Armies.'* The younger, Enar, holds up his sword and says to Kamye, *'My hands hold your death, my Lord! Kamye answered: Brother, it is your death they hold.'* A true hero, a holy man, and God's younger brother, 'Enar dropped his sword'; read allegorically on Yeowe to mean dropping desire, and the world (4).[557]

The phrase 'empty hands' implies 'unarmed,' as when Enar had empty hands after dropping his sword, which is good; but, as we've seen with 'Pathways of Desire,' there is much to be said for filling your hands with the world, holding fast to life and love, and not letting go. The difference is what you are holding on to. When Yoss tells Abberkam about the brewing feud between the Dewis and the Kamanners, Abberkam replies (somewhat Napoleonically), 'Those shopkeepers. They have the souls of owners. They won't kill. But they won't share. It it's property, they won't let go. Never.' And here Yoss sees again in her mind 'the lifted sword' (6). This exchange comes only moments before Abberkam begins coughing the berlot cough.

The point of 'Betrayals' seems to be that one should indeed 'Hold fast to the noble thing' as the holy *Arkamye* teaches, *and* that one should hold fast to the world: that one should love the things of the world, and even hold fast to a desire to be useful (4, 8, 14, 24). What is a bad idea is holding on to things as *property*, to be hoarded and not used.

> Enar had taken up his sword to kill his Elder Brother on that battlefield, to keep him from becoming Lord of the World. And Kamye had told him that the sword he held was his own death; that there is no lordship and no freedom in life, only in letting go of life, of longing, of desire. Enar had laid down his sword and gone into the wilderness, into the silence, saying only, 'Brother, I am thou.' And Kamye had taken up that sword to fight the Armies of Desolation, knowing there is no victory. (18)

---

[557] Cf. and strongly contrast the god-brothers in the Earthsea trilogy (*WE* and *TA*), and the mythic fighting in Le Guin's filmscript, *King Dog*. Ellen Wedum (a chemist living in Oregon) notes similarities of the battle of the Five Armies in the *Arkamye* to the battle fought on the plain of Kurukshetra in the *Mahabharata*, the epic surrounding the *Bhagavad-Gita* (26); and I'll note Arunja's throwing away his bow and arrows in the midst of the battle on the plain (*Bhagavad-Gita* 34).

What is a bad idea is to attempt lordship in this life over other people, to take up the sword to kill one's sibling who may have his or her own mission and usefulness.

Giving up the world seems to be a useful ideal and appropriate for Ogion in the Earthsea series, for Handdara Indwellers on Gethen, for the Thurro-dowist 'All-Alonio' in *City of Illusions* (ch. 3). It is only partly appropriate for Yoss and Abberkam. They will do best living a simple life, but a comfortable one, outside of stirring times and history, embracing the world and each other. The story, then, ends like *Planet of Exile* (1966) in a Le Guinian marriage, but there is no integration of peoples: Yoss and Abberkam are of the same human species, from the same culture.

Where 'Betrayals' differs from the earlier works is the sufficiency of difference in this central couple that one is a woman and the other a man, and in having the emphasis on the point of view of the woman. In *Planet of Exile*'s fourteen chapters, five are told from the point of view of the young, relatively fair-skinned, native woman Rolery (1, 5, 8, 11, 13), five from the point of view of the relatively young, Black, alien Alterran Jakob Agat (3, 6, 9, 12, 14), and four from the point of view of very old, relatively fair, sexist, male native chief Wold (2, 4, 7, 10). I.e., *Planet of Exile* maintains a complex balance among points of view of native and alien, woman and man, young and old, aboriginal, low-technology light-skinned people and colonizing, high-technology people of color. 'Betrayals' privileges throughout the view of an old woman: relatively grey-skinned, a former slave and freedwoman (19), definitely native to Yeowe in birth and a 'native' figuratively in the sense of one colonized to an extreme. And her final Le Guinian marriage is to an unreconstructed and only somewhat reconciled xenophobe who had fought—by 'policy and persuasion' when he could, by force otherwise—under the sign of his World Party: 'the curved sword' (10). Instead of the marriage symbolizing the integration of human species and serving as a *mâshâl* of the integration of peoples on our Earth in our time, the marriage of true minds of Yoss and Abberkam is part of the movement toward peace and perhaps, in the far future, eventual reconciliations following an expulsion.

The curved sword on Terra is a sign for Islam. So to Gandhi (and warriors and warrior-gods from Indian Epics), Martin Luther King, Jr., and Nelson Mandela, we have to add as religious liberators relevant to this story Mohammed and his followers. The historian of the ancient Western world, Joseph Ward Swain, wrote that the initial military success of Islam in the seventh century CE 'may be best regarded as the triumph of the Orient over European invaders. Almost a thousand years had passed since Alexander [of Macedon, 'the Great'] overthrew the first Persian Empire [330 BCE]. During all that time a small aristocracy of Europeans and Europeanized Orientals had dominated a vast oriental population. Orientals now became masters in their own house once more. Except during the Crusades, they remained so until the nineteenth century' (613-14). And in the nineteenth century, the process happened again, with Christian Europeans this time and 'Europeanized Orientals' again taking over much of the lands of Islam. Rebellion followed much more quickly this time around: in the twentieth century, successful movements—nationalist and Islamic—have gotten the Europeans and Americans out of such countries as Algeria and Egypt and the Islamic states of the former Russian Empire. Partially out: This drama is still, in production; and the drama of postcolonial Islam, including the treatment of women—strongly including the frequent oppression of women—is one of the referents of Le Guin's fables of Werel and Yeowe.

Yoss's partnering 'a while' with Abberkam symbolizes a woman of Yeowe forgiving one of the local big men, a local boss. Abberkam's partnering with her is his seizing 'this beautiful chance...to hold you [Yoss], to hold you fast.' This is a good sign. The most radically xenophobic part of Abberkam's program came because he had lost faith in his cause. He tells Yoss, 'I feared the Aliens because I feared their gods. So many gods! I feared that they would diminish my Lord. Diminish him!' If God is God, God is not diminished by competition. Abberkam had not held on to the 'one noble thing'—a mostly transcendental thing—and now wishes to hold Yoss, in the immanent world of peace and domesticity (34).

In *Planet of Exile* (1966), there was integration of Werelians and Alterrans; in *The Word for World Is Forest* (1972), there was total separation and alienation of Athsheans and Terrans. In 'Betrayals,' we get something in between. There has been a successful war for liberation and an expulsion of colonists under the relatively good sign of a sword that is to be let go by most people, a sword that does not (in the old holy book) bring lordship. There's a concluding Le Guinian marriage that offers what we might call a chastened hope for further integration. Peoples may be able to come together; first, though, in a story informed by feminist and postcolonial thought, is the very difficult and problematic movement into marriage of the Le Guinian central couple: one woman and one man, both former slaves.

'Forgiveness Day'

'Forgiveness Day' is another Beatrice and Benedick story: two unlikely lovers who do not fall in love at first sight but fall instead into mild loathing. The initial point of view character is Solly (Agat Terwa), daughter of an Ekumenical Mobile; Solly goes on to become a notable Observer, Envoy, Ekumenical liaison to Terra, and finally Stabile on Hain (*FWF* 35, 92). She is half Terran; the other half may be Alterran; in any event, we're told that she is half Terran and that Terran and Alterran are the languages she usually swears in (89). She is described by one of her superiors at the Embassy in Voe Deo as 'a bit headstrong. Excellent material, but young, very young' (56). I see her as delightfully direct and vulgar for an Envoy: no lady, but a twenty-five-year old Terran/American woman who has been around the known worlds and is competent in at least one of the martial arts, a woman who can belch and say 'shit' in front of a gentleman, a woman who can take care of herself.

Solly loves Werel and the Kingdom of Gatay, and Werelians generally; she dislikes Teyeo: the veot rega assigned to guard her. She translates 'rega' as 'major' and sees Rega Teyeo as the Major: a thirty-two-year-old stuffed shirt (52): 'stonily polite, woodenly silent, stiff and cold as rigor mortis' (37). She sees him possessed by 'militaristic paranoia' (60), and he comes to represent for her 'The Man,' in his primevally pure, Werelian incarnation: slave-owner, sexist, militarist, tight-assed, puritan control freak. And so he could serve very well as «the inconvenient third» in a story in which Solly comes to love a man who is her lover for a while, Batikam: a makil slave, a transvestite bisexual entertainer—including sexual entertainer—and a liminal and very transgressive person, at least transgressive by the standards of the dominant cultures of late twentieth-century Terra. But Batikam does not transgress *Solly*'s standards, nor those of many of Le Guin's more Leftish readers; Teyeo does.

A little over ten pages into Solly's story, Le Guin switches point of view and gives us Teyeo's story, very completely: she starts with his birth and takes him up to the present, including his brief marriage, the sad death of Emdu, his wife (*FWF* 48-49), his service on Yeowe, where he tries to kill as many freedom fighters as he can (53), finally his being employed by Esdardon Aya, 'Old Music,' to help with security at the Ekumenical Embassy. Again, we have a veot veteran: a man who fought on the losing side and the wrong side of an anticolonial war of national liberation, a totally justified war of slaves to free themselves.[558] 'To understand all is to forgive all' is not always a good generalization, but there is much to be said for understanding, and understanding the life of Rega Teyeo *is* to forgive him and find him, as the slave Batikam does, 'a man of honor' (61), and a worthy mate to Solly.

The point of view then returns to Solly for the major plot of the story. A group of Gatayans Patriots trying to free Gatay from Veo Dean hegemony find out about a plot to kill the Envoy during the important ceremony of Forgiveness Day. The patriotic group kidnaps her and must take along Teyeo when he launches himself at one of the kidnappers (67). The rest of the story features Solly and Teyeo, mostly left alone, locked in a room while the story goes out that they were killed at the Forgiveness Day ceremony.

And here the story shifts from a potential Beatrice and Benedick (embedded in a complex culture) to something much more like Estraven and

---

[558] See Le Guin's *King Dog* (7) for her interest in the *Mahabharata*, and note well for Rega Teyeo that warrior is his literal *caste*. I'm not sure how far to push the point, but Aldous Huxley suggests in *The Perennial Philosophy* that it is unfortunate that the *Bhagavad Gita* (the Song of God) is part of the *Mahabharata*, which, 'like most epics,...is largely concerned with the exploits of warriors' and so 'it is primarily in relation to warfare that the Gita's advice to act with non-attachment and for God's sake only is given.' Huxley stresses that 'Non-attached slaughter is recommended only to those, who are warriors by caste, and to whom warfare is a duty and vocation'—but 'what is duty or *dharma*' for warriors 'is *adharma* and forbidden' to those of other castes (272-73; ch. 24).

Ai out on the Ice of Gethen (in *LHD* chs. 15-16,18): the simplest social unit—a prototype *Mitsein*—of two people in an extreme situation, trying at first to keep away from each other (e.g., *FWF* 76), then to make contact (77 f.). The first contact is intellectual, ethical. Even as Estraven and Ai discuss the issues central to their lives and situations, so Solly and Teyeo discuss the central issues on Werel. At dead center is Teyeo's status as an Owner. Solly and Teyeo share a small room, but they divide it up more rigorously than a Werelian House or Compound, the only difference being that the door is on her side, as opposed to Gateside being the men's side in a Compound. They share a mattress, but they never transgress the center line. They physically touch in aiji martial arts exercise, but this is only literal touch: 'impersonal, ritual' and 'a long way from creature comfort.' At all other times, from Solly's point of view,

> ...his bodily presence was clearly, invariably uninvasive and untouchable.
> He was only maintaining, under incredibly difficult circumstances, the rigid restraint he had always shown. Not just he, but Rewe, too [the serving woman given to Solly by the Gatayan king]; all of them but Batikam; and yet was Batikam's instant yielding to her whim and desire the true contact she had thought it? She thought of the fear in his eyes, that last night. Not restraint, but constraint.
> It was the mentality of a slave society: slaves and masters caught in the same trap of radical distrust and self-protection. (77)

And these thoughts lead into a dialog between Solly and Teyeo on slavery, and its near kin, sexism. Solly tells him she is 'trying to understand what it feels like to believe that two-thirds of the human beings in your world are actually, rightfully your property. Five-sixths, in fact, including women of your caste.' Teyeo objects that his family owns only some twenty-five 'assets'; Solly tells him not to quibble, and he accepts the 'reproof.' This leads to the crucial problem with slavery as Solly, and possibly Le Guin, sees it: 'It seems to me,' Solly tells Teyeo, 'that you cut off human contact. You don't touch slaves and slaves don't touch you, in the way human beings ought to touch, in mutuality,' i.e. in anarchist solidarity, parallel to Martin Buber's relationship ideal of 'I and Thou' (see *LHD* 259; ch. 18).[559] 'You have to keep yourselves separate, always working to maintain that boundary' (77).

For now, though, note the words 'separate' and 'boundary' in this quotation, contrasted with 'touch' and 'mutuality' here, and to be contrasted later with the images in the lines, 'The idea of the Ekumen was to offer a way. To open it' (79). The rigorously political and mundane nature of this

---

[559] 'I and Thou' = 'I and You, my friend' ('thou' is the *in*formal form). As always, for 'touch' see Remington, 'A Touch of Difference...'

passage in 'Forgiveness Day' is important as a gauge to the importance of separateness vs. connectedness throughout Le Guin's thought. As I have noted earlier, the great French sociologist Emile Durkheim said that 'sacredness referred to those things in society that were forbidden or set apart,' as is suggested by the etymology of 'sacred' in Latin, Greek, Hebrew, Arabic, and even Polynesian (Streng 123). In the tradition of the philosophical Daoists, native Americans, and followers of the really old-time religions, Le Guin sees the sacred in connectedness. Slavery and sexism are bad for all the obvious reasons, plus the sheer waste—*and* because of what Odo called 'The creation of pseudo-species' (*TD* 11; ch. 1): the radical separation needed to rationalize slavery and sexism. Given that pseudo-speciation, slavery, sexism, and patriarchy are social, political, and legal manifestations of a fundamental perversity, a wrong turn. If what people *do* in life is in some sense sacralize it, then slavery/patriarchy on the level of human society is a wall shutting us off from the sacred. Master/Slave is the ultimate I-It relationship, perhaps the ultimate human disconnection.

Teyeo starts unbuilding the wall between himself and Solly by telling his story, beginning 'In the war...I was on Yeowe....' (78). Teyeo tells her and us that he respected his enemies on Yeowe and gets Solly to think about her own half-Terran heritage: 'My ancestors rushed around their planet slaughtering each other. For millennia. They were masters and slaves, too, some of them, a lot of them....' And then Solly admits the possibility of more personal complicity as an agent for the Ekumen. 'Who are we to tell anybody what to do and not to do?' And we readers can realize that Abberkam and Teyeo earlier, when they've seen the Ekumen as Alien snobs and colonizers may—allowing for overgeneralization and hyperbole—have a point (see *FWF* 89). And here Solly delivers her line about how the Ekumen was to offer a way, openings, not bar peoples because they have practices the Ekumen finds evil and dangerous. Teyeo 'listened intently but said nothing until after some while,' when he responds with 'We learn to...close ranks. Always. You're right, I think, it wastes...energy, the spirit. You are open.' Teyeo is a man who can really hear what a woman is saying and admit error, and speak seriously. 'His words cost him so much, she thought.... He spoke from the marrow. It made what he said a solemn compliment' (79).

And then Solly asks about the war, and he opens up to her, letting her know what numbers can mean when they are part of one's life: He served seven years on Yeowe. 'We lost three hundred thousand men on Yeowe. They never talk about it. Two thirds of the veot men in Voe Deo were killed' (79).

More of the wall comes down when Solly is starting to lose hope, and Teyeo for the first time calls her by name and gives her two orders: 'Be still. Hold fast.' She asks him what she should hold fast to when he won't let her touch him (80). More of the figurative wall comes down when they start working out a plan with their captors, and when each gets in touch with her and his anger. Solly is used to anger and has the vocabulary to express it, most effectively perhaps when she reminds the representative of her captors, that they will need to get in touch with the Ekumen and that can be tricky: 'You kidnapped an Envoy of the Ekumen, you asshole! Now you have to do the thinking you didn't do ahead of time. And I do too, because I don't want to get blown away by your Goddamned little government for turning up alive and embarrassing them.' Rather Genly Ai's political situation in *The Left Hand of Darkness* (except I cannot picture him calling even an Inspector of the Orgota 'asshole'). In any event, in her anger at the kidnappers and Gatay, and perhaps in her anger at having to stop Teyeo from chivalrically protecting her when the guard responds to her 'asshole' epithet with an arguably nastier epithet of his own, Solly asks Teyeo 'Are you sure your country isn't playing the same game as Gatay?', i.e. going along with the story that Solly and Teyeo have been murdered to help justify destruction of all rebel forces in Gatay. 'As he understood her, slowly the anger he had stifled and denied, all these interminable days of imprisonment with her, rose in him, a fiery flood of resentment, hatred, and contempt'—for Solly (83).

Teyeo insists 'They would not betray us,' meaning the government of Veo Deo, the government he had served so loyally. When she asks him who the 'They' refers to, Teyeo comes to an insight, coming to the knowledge 'that she was right; that it was all collusion among the power of the world; that his loyalty to his country and service was wasted, as futile as the rest of his life.... He put his head into his hands, longing for tears, dry as a stone.' Literally dry—they're dehydrated—and symbolically. 'She crossed the line. He felt her hand on his shoulder.' And then Solly apologizes. She had apologized earlier when it became obvious that Teyeo's 'militaristic paranoia' about the Forgiveness Day Ceremony and Festival had proven correct. Here, though, she apologizes sincerely, adding to her being sorry, 'I honor you. You've been all my hope and help.' And for his part, Teyeo can note, 'speaking slowly and formally,' that if Solly is correct in her suspicions of Veo Deo they and their captors 'are in danger not only from Gatay but from my own people, who may...who have been furthering these anti-Government factions, in order to make an excuse to bring troops here...to *pacify* Gatay' (84) and take it over.

Teyeo doesn't believe Veo Deo could hold Gatay for long, since he thinks, apparently, that any serious violence will trigger a slave revolt. To the question of who on Werel could defeat Veo Deo, he answers 'Yeowe. The idea of Yeowe. * * * Revolution.... How long before Werel becomes New Yeowe?' His Gatayan keeper is incredulous at the idea of 'assets' organizing, but believes completely in the possibility of a Veo Dean attempt to establish complete hegemony over his country, and that the Ekumen might prevent it. Teyeo suggests his plan: contact the makil Batikam, a probable member of the Hame, 'the asset underground' opposed to Veo Deo. Batikam can tell the Ekumenical embassy staff 'that a Patriot group has rescued the Envoy and is holding her safe, in hiding, in extreme danger. The Ekumen...will act promptly and decisively' (85-86).

The plan works, and there is a rescue, quickly narrated. The rescue however, is not the climax of the story, no more than the fall of governments is the narrated climax of *The Left Hand of Darkness*—though two governments fall—or the killing of the dragon-beast is dwelt on in *The Beginning Place*. While waiting for the political maneuvering offstage, Solly wishes for some moments of darkness in her cell, contemplates long life vs. short (and the probabilities hers will be *very* short), and takes the finally step toward removing the wall and achieving touch: 'Do you think...that it would be a mistake...under the circumstances...to make love?' she asks. Teyeo responds, more or less, that, under these circumstances, it's a good idea. 'They reached out to each other. They clasped each other, cleaved together...crying out the name of God in their different languages and then like animals in the wordless voice. They huddled together, spent, sticky, sweaty...reborn in the body's tenderness, in the endless exploration, the ancient discovery, the long flight to the new world'—with 'new world' alluding to their new relationship and 'the idea of Yeowe.'[560]

Shortly after this moment Batikam arrives, and they are rescued. Tying up the story, Le Guin's Narrator tells us that Teyeo's parents die, and Teyeo frees his slaves and sells his family property. And, finally, he joins Solly as she takes her new job as 'the first Ambassador of the Ekumen to Yeowe' and later goes on to her illustrious career (91-92).

In the ending of *Left Hand of Darkness* a war is averted and a new world joins the Ekumen, with the death of Estraven to provide the 'blood bond' completing the arch of the novel and sealing Gethen into the Ekumen. The ending of 'Forgiveness Day' is more purely comic: a war is averted and Yeowe joins the Ekumen—with no cause and effect here—and we get a partnering. We do not get the standard «magic» of romantic comedy with a new and better world coalescing around a central couple, but we do get Solly and Teyeo moving out into a world that might be improved.

'A Man of the People'

¡El pueblo, unido, jamás será vencido!
(The people, united, will never be defeated!)[561]

Again, 'A Man of the People' begins among the People of Hain, in a pueblo, with a glance at the complexity of *pueblo* in the original Spanish: 'a village,' indeed, but also village people and people generally. Havz-

---

[560] Cf. and contrast the idea of Annares in *TD* (e.g., 239-41; ch. 9) and Shevek and Takver's reuniting in *TD* and, in coupling, repeating in microcosm the circling of Anarres and Urras (258; ch. 10).
[561] 'This slogan was used in Chile and then in many different resistance movements throughout Latin America'—Reed Anderson, Professor in Spanish and Portuguese, Miami University at Oxford.

hiva's town of Stse has its own local knowledge, which can be summed up as, *'typical pueblo culture of the northwestern coastal South Continent'* of Hain (*FWF* 109). It's a vaguely Amerindian culture, like that of the Kesh, and Stse is a good place for a Le Guinian Hero (especially a male Hero) to be from.

There is no controlling image strongly associated with Stse, nothing like the Circle of Life symbol in *The Dispossessed*, nor a Yin-Yang (e.g., *LHD*), nor anything like the heyiya-if in *Always Coming Home*. There is, though, an opening image of Havzhiva and 'his father,' Granite, watching the surface of an irrigation tank, where 'Trembling circles enlarged, interlocked, faded on the still surface of the water' (93): somewhat like the ring-trees in *Eye of the Heron*, but more dynamic, far more ephemeral. It fits in with the knowledge gained by Havzhiva as a young man that any one human life 'was one flicker of light for one moment on the surface' of the 'great river' of history—a thought he finds 'sometimes distressing, sometimes restful' (108), but one which we should find familiar: in Earthsea, Ogion had used the image of the stream in teaching Ged; Ged, as an adult, uses the image of a wave on the sea in teaching Arren (*WE* 128, ch. 7; *FS* 122, ch. 8).[562] Perhaps Heroes like Ged and Havzhiva can make their flickers on the surface into interlocking circles. Note that Havzhiva is told by his teacher here that 'What makes the water go that way' is the touch of arahas—small, flying mammals—coming to drink, so Havzhiva understands that '...in the center of each circle was a desire, a thirst' (94). Le Guin's Daoist and feminist Heroes perform small, crucial actions, perhaps, producing an enlarging circles of effects. And at the center of those circles is their desire, their thirsts.

Life in Stse is unexciting, traditional, domestic, immanent, and sacralized. The economy is not described in detail, but it is based on the principle that 'Wealth can't stop.... It has to keep going. Like the blood circulating' (*FWF* 94); wealth is good but it is not to be accumulated. What is to be produced and by whom is based on traditional divisions of labor (96).[563] Their technology is sufficient to their needs, but no more, and they keep their material needs simple: they do not collect gadgets among their wealth. Mothers keep their babies and children's fathers are not their biological sires but mother's brothers: maternal uncles or, if the mother lacks a brother, an adopted uncle/father. The men who sired the children might take an interest in them, but they have no parental rights, nor, apparently, is it shameful for a sire to be no more concerned about his offspring than with village children generally. People do marry, but marriage is not intimately related to child-rearing (94).

---

[562] There's also the literal stream the boy Duny enters 'Nameless and naked' to cross to Ogion to receive 'his true name: Ged' (*WE* 15; ch. 1).
[563] The injunctions are put negatively: Women don't weave; men don't make bricks, etc. The negative allows more freedom than an injunction to *do* something (and nothing else) and allows space for people gendered neither male nor female.

The people of Stse lived daily among their daily gods and were visited every eleven years by the Unusual Gods; they study their trades and lineages and dancing, and, if they have any talent for it, they study for a long time and seriously their local variant of soccer (96): possibly influenced by the increasing enthusiasm of girls and women for sport, Le Guin is opening up space for athletics. If reality is immanent and not transcendent, the body embedded in the world is as good as the mind and has no transcendent soul to compete with; and in such a world bodies may be allowed, on occasion, to show off. Plus, in a healthy society, sports would be fun.

So is sex, and sex is important in 'A Man of the People,' both as a synecdoche for desire and as simply sex.

The rules in Stse are straightforward and strict. As Le Guin has shown in *The Word for World Is Forest* (1974) and thereafter, she is well aware of taboos against «incest» within clans and moieties, but, mercifully, she spares us the details, which can get very complex. As usual in Le Guin (and very strongly believed among the Kesh in *ACH*), sex is a great «manna,» and virginity 'a sacred status, not to be carelessly abandoned' and sexuality 'sacred' and 'not to be carelessly undertaken' ('A Man of the People' 97). The people of Stse keep their pubescent children heterosexually virginal until about age fifteen, but they are not cruel about it. They allow homosexual sex, but not homosexual pairing, before fifteen, and they allow solitary male masturbation. And as among Denis Diderot's Tahitians (Diderot 64-65), there is a required coming-of-age day among the people of Stse and ritual heterosexual intercourse '...everybody must go through 'the twofold door' once,' whatever their sexual orientation or desire for celibacy. Heterosexual initiation, however, takes place only after some *real* sex education, especially necessary because Hainish men and women have the ability unique among Hainish-derived species to control their fertility, by literal *self*-control, but they must be taught how (*FWF* 97-98).

For their initiation, Havzhiva is paired with Iyan Iyan; there's really no choice given the clan requirements. Havzhiva and Iyan Iyan 'Each saw a stranger' when they approach each other for sex and think that they want to be done with the ritual. 'So they touched and that god entered them, becoming them; the god for whom they were the doorway; the meaning for which they were the word.' We're told the god was a clumsy one at first, 'but became an increasingly happy god.' So Iyan Iyan exercises her right to bring Havzhiva home with her. 'So he slept with Iyan Iyan at her house, ate breakfast there, ate dinner at his house, kept his daily clothes at her house, kept his dance clothes at his house, and went on with his education, which now had mostly to do with rug-weaving on the power broadlooms and with the nature of the cosmos. He and Iyan both played on the adult soccer team' (99).

In addition to weaving, Havzhiva has another career option. His mother, Tovo, is an important woman, the 'Heir of the Sun': a traveler and trader who dealt with strangers, an expert on rituals and protocol (94). Just before the turning point of this part of the story, Tovo offer Havzhiva inheritance of the Sun. 'Do I want to? he thought.... He knew he liked the work. Its patterns were not closed. It took him out of Stse, among strangers, and he liked that. It gave him something to do which he didn't know how to do, and he liked that' (100). Havzhiva feels himself at a crucial moment in his life, and that moment arrives with Mezha, 'the woman who had borne the children Granite sired,' and then who 'had broken the social contract, done things no woman does, ignored her lineage, become another kind of being'—a historian (100-01).

Mezha tells Havzhiva about the world of Hainish historians, how there she is not a Buried Cable woman but a woman, who 'can have sex with any person I choose. I can take up any profession I choose. Lineage matters here. It does not matter, there. It has meaning here, and a use. It has no meaning and no use, anywhere else in the universe.' Most importantly, she presents him with a highly arguable proposition important for the rest of *Four Ways to Forgiveness*: 'There are two kinds of knowledge, local and universal. There are two kinds of time, local and historical.' When he asks if there are 'two kinds of gods,' she tells him that among the historians there are no gods. There are 'souls,' though (if not necessarily the individually immortal variety).

> There are souls, there. Many, many souls, minds, minds full of knowledge and passion. Living and dead. People who lived on this earth a hundred, a thousand, a hundred thousand years ago. Minds and souls of people from worlds a hundred light-years from this one, all of them with their own knowledge, their own history. The world is sacred.... The cosmos is sacred.... You can choose the local sacredness or the great one. In the end they're the same. But not in the life one lives. 'To know there is a choice is to have to make the choice; change or stay: river or rock.' The Peoples are the rock. The historians are the river.

After a moment, Havzhiva replies, 'Rocks are the river's bed' (103-04). 'Rocks,' then, may be literally more fundamental than 'the river,' but rivers are still all right; shifting out of the metaphor, in *Four Ways to Forgiveness* lives lead in history are all right. Very differently from many of Le Guin's works, from *The Word for World Is Forest* to *Always Coming Home* to *Tehanu*, these stories allow for a life of action in the world, so long as it is action *in* the world, without illusions of transcendent vision.[564]

A short while later, Havzhiva asks Iyan Iyan to have a baby with him, and she declines. Over a year later, she asks him for a baby, and he declines. And, insightful woman that she is, Iyan Iyan jumps to the correct

---

[564] See below, the disastrous consequences of the altruistic, «theoretic», actions of elite abolitionist Lord Erod (in 'A Woman's Liberation' More generally, note here another instance of Le Guin's fascination with rivers and rocks.

conclusion that Havzhiva is going to leave. He thinks 'Nothing is right.' And that everything he does he does 'because that's how it's done'—a negative conservatism in *The Dispossessed* (*TD* 264; ch. 10)—and he is coming to feel that 'there are other ways.' Iyan Iyan is far more certain that 'There's one way to live rightly' that she knows of, which is to live in Stse, which is where she is staying (105). Havzhiva leaves, ending the first of the three parts of the story.

Part two, takes Havzhiva to Kathhad and Ve; he trains to be a historian in Kathhad, and then goes to the Ekumenical School on Ve (the next planet out from the sun). Among the historians, he is called Zhiv, and Zhiv enjoys his new being, where he thinks at first 'there are no rules,' at least not for sex. Mezha tells him a point dear to Le Guin and just about any student of culture: 'There are always rules,' especially for sex (111). Zhiv is less liberated than he thinks, intentionally seeking out Alien women to add 'exoticism' to what the Narrator gently assures us he saw as 'transgression,' however much Zhiv described his Alien adventures as 'an enrichment of knowledge.' He's again ready for love, though, and he finds it in Tiu, who is Hainish but 'a child of the Historians as he was a child of the People. He realised very soon that this bond and division was far greater than any foreignness: that their unlikeness was true difference and their likeness was true kinship.... She was what he sought' (111-12).

Lyubov in *The Word for World Is Forest* looks beyond the esthetic 'defect' of 'white skin' to see the Hainishman, Mr. Lepennon, as an expert at civilized humanity, living 'the social-intellectual life with the grace of a cat hunting in a garden,' the Hainish generally being and acting who and what they are (68; ch. 3). Similarly, Zhiv sees Tiu in possession of 'perfect equilibrium,' which he extends into a figure of walking, 'effortless, unselfconscious as an animal, and yet conscious, careful....' In his view, Tiu was 'a woman free to be fully human,' with 'perfect measure...perfect grace' (112).[565] Tiu finds Zhiv appealing and a little scary. She sees how he needs her, wants her, and 'had made her into the center of his life.' When he comes to her and says 'I cannot live without you,' she tells him, 'Then live with me a while.' They live together, and Tiu comes to accept being adored, but 'Very gradually, she began to resist the tension, the intensity, the ecstasy' of the relationship; she found it 'lovely' but somehow not right. Tiu didn't see herself so lovable to deserve Zhiv's 'passionate loyalty.... Her self-respect was an intellectual thing. 'You make a god of me,' she had told him, and did not understand when he replied with happy seriousness, 'We make the god together'' (113).

For good and bad, then, Tiu decides to go to Terra as she had planned, leaving Zhiv to follow her in a year. Zhiv does not take the news well. Tiu reaches out to Zhiv, 'scared by the darkness in him, his grief, his mute acceptance of betrayal. But it wasn't betrayal—she rejected the word,' and we are free to side with Tiu or Zhiv or remain neutral. 'Darkness' is a much-privileged word in Le Guin's writing, and we should respect it in

---

[565] For walking imagery, see *Tehanu* 68-69, ch. 6.

Zhiv, but Tiu has a point that she and Zhiv are not children and 'must not cling together like children.' Romeo and Juliet could not stand to be separated, but Shevek and Takver in *The Dispossessed* can, and if Takver can wait for Shevek, Zhiv ought to be able to wait a year or a couple of years to follow Tiu (114).[566]

He is not able to wait, however, and almost wills himself to die. People find him and sing a Staying Chant over him, and he lives, but his love for Tiu, if it doesn't die, at least becomes irrelevant for his actions. Zhiv goes to a hospital where he philosophizes at some length, arguably going beyond the modern, Enlightenment views of the Historian, Mezha—views that allow universal time, universal knowledge—to something more postmodern, poststructuralist, and/or more Daoist. These views privilege the local and immediate, the immanently experiential over the transcendentally theoretical, but simultaneously insist upon 'everything': the Dao, perhaps, the cosmos, or, for that matter, the universal quantum field.[567]

> What you select from, in order to tell your story, is nothing less than everything.... What you build up your world from, your local, intelligible, rational, coherent world, is nothing less than everything. And so all selection is arbitrary. All knowledge is partial—infinitesimally partial. Reason is a net thrown out into an ocean. What truth it brings in is a fragment, a glimpse, a scintillation of the whole truth. All human knowledge is local. Every life, each human life, is local, is arbitrary, the infinitesimal momentary glitter of a reflection of....' (116)

And here he breaks off, but having made some decisions. After leaving the hospital he returns to the Ekumenical School but changes fields of study: dropping social science, Tiu's field—and an abstract one, a temptation to formulate large-scale laws—and instead going into training for Ekumenical field service. He no longer aims for Terra and Tiu and 'All that stuff about war and slavery and class and caste and gender'—the stuff of Terran history—but wants now to go to the Werel system where war and slavery are 'current events.' He had gone to the hospital Zhiv and returns as Havzhiva again. He had seen himself as having 'betrayed and for-

---

[566] Cf. Romantic infatuation in *BP* as something definitely to be gotten over.

[567] Fritjof Capra argues strongly for the unity of 'ultimate reality.' 'The ultimate essence, however, cannot be separated from its multiple manifestations. It is central to its very being to manifest itself in myriad forms which come into being and disintegrate, transforming themselves into one another without end. In its phenomenal aspect, the cosmic One is intrinsically dynamic, and the apprehension of its dynamic nature'—by no means a transcendent, static, One 'is basic to all the schools of Eastern mysticism' (175; ch. 13). Capra's point is this ultimate reality is also the relativistic quantum field underlying manifestations of matter/energy in modern physics (e.g., 198-201; ch. 14).

saken Iyan Iyan, so Tiu had betrayed and forsaken him. There was no going back and no going forward. So he must turn aside' (116).

Havzhiva sees himself as still one of the People but incapable of living with them; he had become a historian but did not want to live among historians. 'So he must go live among Aliens.' And perhaps he can be useful. There is a beautifully maintained ironic stance here, stressed in the final image in this part of the story. The local medicine man visits Havzhiva for a kind of pre-departure checkup and after a silence asks him to walk a bit. 'You're out of balance.... Did you know it?' Havzhiva replies that he knows it, that he has 'always been off-balance.' The medicine man tells him he need not be but adds, 'On the other hand, maybe it's best, since you're going to Werel' (117).[568] Stone Telling leaves the Kesh for her father's unbalanced Condor people, who are trying to figuratively soar over the world and very bloodily make history (and corpses and cripples). Similarly, Havzhiva leaves his Pueblo to study history and then help make it. The second section of 'A Man of the People' ends though with another image, one with perhaps more positive possibilities. At very the end of *City of Illusions*, Falk-Ramarren both leaves home and heads home, in a ship moving 'across the darkness' (*CI* 217; ch. 10). Falk-Ramarren brings important knowledge back to his Werel at the end of *City*, and the second section of 'A Man of the People' ends with Havzhiva's boarding a NAFAL ship and heading out toward Werel 'across the darkness' (*FWF* 117).

Havzhiva doesn't stay on Werel long but gets promptly sent to Yeowe, 'a new member of the Ekumen of Known Worlds' (119). The thirty-years' War of Liberation is over, but the struggle for power among the former freedom fighters is still going on, including the struggle over whether to allow agents of the Ekumen to remain on Yeowe. The Ekumenical Ambassador, 'a clever young Terran'—or half Terran—'named Solly' sends Sub-Envoy Havzhiva to the Yotebber Region. Havzhiva's trip to Yotebber is only long enough to allow his observation that 'History is infamy' as he observes 'the ruined landscapes' of this world; and his acclimation time there is just enough to allow some exposition on the development of male tribal hierarchies when Yeowe was a planet-wide slave state, and on how the Liberation 'had arisen first among the women in the tribal compounds, a rebellion against male domination, before it became a war of all slaves against their owners' (118-19). And then we get the first incident in this part of the story. Against good advice, Havzhiva goes for a walk in the City Park, and he is almost killed (120-21).

The attempted murder is part of Le Guin's continuing meditation on justice, and it gets the main plot of the story going. Before the attack, we get the excellent observation that 'Havzhiva thought of justice what an ancient Terran said of another god: I believe in it because it is impossible'

---

[568] See at The Back of the Book in *ACH*, the last entry among 'Some Generative Metaphors'; under the Way as metaphor, we have '*Medicine* as keeping in balance' (485).

(120).[569] The 'justice' we get to *see* is the holoscreen picture of the punishment of the man convicted of attacking him: 'a thin human body suspended by the feet, the arms and hands twitching, the intestines hanging down over the chest and face' (122). Havzhiva's response is not a philosophical 'All knowledge is local'; hence, 'Who am I to judge you?' It's the far more psychologically realistic shout of 'Turn it off...turn it off!', vomiting, and, 'You are not people!' The last in his own language; Havzhiva is still a diplomat on duty.

The plot arrives in the person of Yeron, his nurse. She brings him a message:

> I'm a messenger to the Ekumen...from the women...all over Yeowe. We want to make an alliance with you.... Yeowe is a member of the Ekumen of the Worlds. We know that. But what does it mean? To us? It means nothing. Do you know what women are, here, in this world? They are nothing. They are not part of the government. Women made the Liberation.... But they weren't generals, they weren't chiefs. They are nobody. In the villages they are less than nobody, they are work animals, breeding stock.... I am a doctor, not a nurse. Under the Bosses, I ran this hospital. Now a man runs it. Our men are the owners now. And we're what we always were. Property.... We have to finish the job. (124)

Havzhiva asks her if the women are organized, and she responds that they are good at organizing. She doubts, though that they can free themselves on their own. 'There has to be a change,' primarily in the way men think: the men of Yeowe must stop thinking that 'they have to be bosses.' Yeron isn't quite sure how to do that, but she knows it cannot be done through violence: 'You kill the boss and you become the boss. We must change that mind. The old slave mind, boss mind.' It is 'a matter of education,' with 'education' to her 'a sacred word,' and she asks for Havzhiva's help and that of the Ekumen (125).

Yeron raises the thematic political problem for 'A Man of the People' and, later 'A Woman's Liberation': If «*To liberate* is a reflexive verb», as we used to say in the late 1960s, how can outsiders effectively and ethically serve the cause of liberation? If «Liberation requires 'outside agitators'», but if, as we will see in 'A Woman's Liberation,' top-down emancipation can be disastrous—how can privileged people usefully serve? Part of the answer may have been given by Estraven in *The Left Hand of Darkness*, who claims to have had one and only one talent: 'to know when the

---

[569] I.e., Tertullian's 'Credo quia impossible est,' which my *ODQ* gives as 'Certum est quia impossible est,' 'It is certain because it is impossible' (Tertullian was an early Father of the Catholic Church; the *ODQ* gives his dates as ca. 160-225 (CE) and cites the quote at *De Carne Christi* 5.

great wheel gives to a touch, to know and act' (189; ch. 14). The 'great wheel' is a-turning on Yeowe, and Havzhiva is able to give it a nudge now and then; equally important, as the story is plotted, he is capable of learning about this world.[570] Havzhiva is well aware of his own insignificance on Yeowe, but he also knows that 'what he did might signify' (127). So he does little things. He requests the government to invite women to a reception; when a bodyguard detail is forced upon him, he gets it made up of policewomen; he plants in the mind of the local Chief the idea that 'what is called the construction of gender' must be shown to be different on Yeowe from Werel—or the Chief will have trouble with immigrants sent from Werel 'to lessen revolutionary pressure' there (127-28).[571] And he shows up and talks and gets himself in the news at the great demonstration for women's rights. And when his boss—Solly still—calls and asks 'What the hell' he is up to, he gets her to encourage the women of Yotebber for showing 'Yeowe a model of true freedom for immigrants from the Slave World' and praise the government of Yotebber as 'a model...of restraint, enlightenment, et cetera.' Solly raises the critical questions of what will happen if the Regional Government starts shooting the demonstrators and 'Is this a revolution...?' Havzhiva perhaps answers both questions in his response to the second, 'It's education, ma'am' (130).

The suggestion seems to be that so long as the movement remains peaceful, and so long as it has a major power for a friend, that long the local powers will refrain from shooting their opponents. The powers that were in A-Io at the beginning of Ekumenical history were quite willing to shoot unarmed civilians in the political climax on Urras in *The Dispossessed*, but the point may be that there was no friendly Alien *power* on Urras—not even a real League of Worlds yet—to cause trouble over the atrocity. The Werelian Owners and Bosses and politicians had no qualms about using murder and terror to crush the rebellion on Yeowe, but they were slave-owners who made no claims to kinship with the people they exploited, tortured, and killed. In any event, the key point seems to be the point in Shevek's speech at the demonstration in *The Dispossessed*, just before the military start shooting down the strikers: 'You cannot buy the Revolution. You cannot make the Revolution. You can only be the Revolution. It is in your spirit or it is nowhere' (242; ch. 9); alternatively: '...revolution begins in the thinking mind' (267; ch. 10). What one can do for the revolution, then—always—may be 'education,' starting with

---

[570] The image used in 'A Man of the People' is not the Wheel but that 'great gods are loose' on Werel and Yeowe (*FWF* 118). Cf. and contrast Selver as god in *WWF*.

[571] Cf. the function of Anarres for Urras, Victoria for Terra in *EoH*, or the Americas in our history for Europe and China. Eric Hoffer wrote that 'Emigration offers some of the things the frustrated hope to find when they join a mass movement, namely change and a chance for a new beginning. The same types who swell the ranks of a rising mass movement are also likely to avail themselves of a chance to emigrate. Thus migration can serve as a substitute for a mass movement' (28; § 17 in Part One).

Havzhiva's educating himself within the world of the story, and Le Guin's educating us in our world of the possibility and hope of revolution.

To learn Yeowe culture Havzhiva 'must know the plantations and the tribes.'[572] He starts at Hayawa Tribal Village, the original slave compound on Yeowe 350 years back.[573] In this large and remote district, 'much of the society and culture of plantation slavery' remained. The current situation is perhaps symbolized in the first thing in the village the Narrator mentions: a large gate standing open in a 'massive frame; there were no walls' (130-31). There have been some changes after liberation—a banquet features meat, the food of the masters—but much remains unchanged: the Elder, once the slave chief, has his own path and walks his 'narrow way.'[574] Having been forbidden to waste Corporation time singing—and risking having acid poured down one's throat if heard—the slaves had developed a very quiet music. No 'shout of triumph,' of freedom, in their songs (132-33). What most remains the same is the utter subordination of women, symbolized in the coming-of-age ceremony for six boys.

The ceremony begins with the fasted thirteen-year-olds trying to jump the compound ditch, followed by a 'catechism' on 'ritual, protocol, ethics.' Havzhiva watches and lets his thoughts go 'back a long time, a long way. We teach what we know, he thought, and all our knowledge is local.' Then the boys are ritually marked, and the elders call them 'tribesmen' and 'hero.' Havzhiva thinks the ceremony is over. 'But now six more children were...brought into the plaza, led across the ditch-bridge by old women. These were girls, decked with anklets and bracelets, otherwise naked. At the sight of them a great cheer went up from the audience of men. Havzhiva was surprised. Women were to be made members of the tribe too? That at least was a good sign, he thought' (134-35). He thinks wrong.

What happens next is that these girls—two 'barely adolescent, the others...younger'—are put down by the women accompanying them and then laid by tribal elders: 'The elders' bare buttocks pumped, whether in actual coitus or an imitation Havzhiva could not tell.' And then it is the boys' turn. Recall that Stse also had a heterosexual initiation, and that Havzhiva was unlikely to be shocked by such an idea. What is shocking to him and to us is this scene and the words of the nice man who had slept with Havzhiva the night before. He assures Havzhiva that unlike the bad old days under the rule of the Corporations, nowadays the girls are drugged so they won't be hurt.

---

[572] Cf. Estraven's saying, 'The Domains are Karhide' (*LHD* 100, ch. 8; see also 6, ch. 1). Cf. knowing Rer and its environs to know Karhide: *LHD* ch. 6, esp. 47, 55 f.

[573] Even as historically minded US readers should find of interest the time-scale in *TD*, set some 200 years after the Odonian revolution in a book published two years before the US Bicentennial—even so, in the 1990s 350-400 is the approximate time of enslavement of Africans to labor in the Americas.

[574] Cf. the Nation of the Basnasska in *CI* who 'walked a very narrow, a tortuous and cramped Way' (68; ch. 4).

> These ones are lucky, privileged to assist initiation. It's important that girls cease to be virgin as soon as possible, you know. Always more than one man must have them, you know. So that they can't make claims—'this is your son,' 'this baby is the chief's son,' you know. That's all witchcraft. A son is chosen. Being a son has nothing to do with bondswomen's cunts. Bondswomen have to be taught that early.

The kind man repeats that now the girls are drugged, and when Havzhiva notes that he had called women 'bondswomen' he corrects the slip and apologizes for the old, derogatory term. Havzhiva looks directly into the face of his new friend and notes 'that his dark skin meant he must have a good deal of owner blood, perhaps indeed was the son of an owner or a Boss. Nobody's son,' Havzhiva corrects himself, 'begotten on a slave woman. A son is chosen. All knowledge is local, all knowledge is partial' (136-37).

The political and ethical moral of the initiation sequence is stated explicitly by Havzhiva, speaking into his recording device, in Hainish. 'You can't change anything from outside it' Havzhiva says. 'Standing apart, looking down, taking the overview, you see the pattern.' You see 'What's wrong, what's missing. You want to fix it. But you can't patch it. You have to be in it, weaving it. You have to be part of the weaving' (137). The Narrator tells us that 'This last phrase, was in the dialect of Stse,' reminding us that weaving was the trade Havzhiva might have followed in Stse. Readers familiar with Le Guin's earlier work will put Havzhiva in a line of weavers, most relevantly, I think, Faxe the Weaver of the Foretelling in *The Left Hand of Darkness*, who sees patterns from within them, and only for an instant, and for the purpose of denying all utility to transcendent knowledge (*LHD* 59-67, 69-70; ch. 5). Faxe: who ceases to be a ritual Weaver when he returns to the world of Gethenian politics.

The fabular moral of 'A Man of the People' is reinforced symbolically in a small section ending Havzhiva's visit to Hayawa Tribal Village, balancing the currently ironic symbol of the open gate without walls. Women are making the Yeowean equivalent of a sand painting, 'spreading dust, colored earth, making some kind of pattern or picture.' One of the women tells him that he can't see it, and he asks if she means he should not be there; she does not. The picture is only a part of some larger pattern. 'We make what we know, here,' the woman says. Havzhiva asks about the men: 'They never see it whole?' And he is answered, "Nobody does. Only us. We have it here.' The dark woman did not touch her head but her heart, covering her breasts with her long, work-hardened hands.' Havzhiva says he'd like to see the pattern: "You'll have to find a woman to teach you,' said the woman the color of ashes' (138-39).

Havzhiva's last service we see is a discussion with the Young Chief: 'the Son and Heir, the Chosen,' and (along with the open gate) a symbol of future political possibilities. The key lines are the Chosen's asserting in the words of his religion that they have held 'fast to the one noble thing' and have become 'a free people.' Havzhiva says 'You are free men.' The Chosen comes back by pigeon-holing Havzhiva as a city man who wouldn't understand tribal women, who, he says 'do not want a man's freedom.' Among tribal folk, 'A woman holds fast to her baby. That is the noble thing for her. That is how the Lord Kamye made woman, and the Merciful Tual'—the Goddess in this culture—'is her example. In other places it may be different.... Here it is as I have said.' Havzhiva nods, Yeowean style and says 'That is so,' but then goes on to tell about a picture he has seen. 'Lines and colors made with earth on earth may hold knowledge in them. All knowledge is local, all truth is partial.' And from this it follows that 'No truth can make another truth untrue.' But yet, as a political matter, some knowledge may deserve privileging. Havzhiva puts the matter either differently or more diplomatically. 'All knowledge is part of the whole knowledge. A true line, a true color. Once you have seen the larger pattern, you cannot go back to seeing the part as the whole' (139-40).

Whatever the epistemological implications of Havzhiva's lines here, the Chosen interprets it politically as a justification to change their traditional ways and, from the male tribal point of view, 'come to live as they live in the cities,' losing the tribal way of life.[575] The Narrator notes that beneath the Chosen's 'dogmatic tone was fear and grief.' Havzhiva replies to the Chosen that the Chosen speaks true: 'Much will be lost.' However, 'The lesser knowledge must be given to gain the greater. And not once only.' The Chosen says that the men of his tribe 'will not deny our truth,' and Havzhiva, sensibly, is sure that that is the case (140).

And then there is a white space for a transition of a number of years: we now have Stabile Yehedarhed Havzhiva, Ekumenical Advisor to the Yeowean Ministry of Social Justice and partnered for eighteen years (to Shomeke, as we will learn in the next story). Havzhiva returns to Yotebber to visit, and we see his visit with Yeron.

The movement has been successful—and we'll have to wait for the next story also for more hints of how—and Yerod greets Havzhiva as a saint. He demurs. She changes the appellation to hero: 'You can't deny that you're a hero,' and he doesn't 'knowing what a hero is,' he says with a laugh, 'I won't deny it' (143). And he is a hero: not so much any more for Le Guin a bringer of change like Shevek in *The Dispossessed* or even a

---

[575] On the philosophy and cultural investigation of 'Man of the People,' Le Guin says 'The intellectual underpinnings of the story come mainly from Cl[aude] Lévi-Strauss and Clifford Geertz (incompatible sources!)'—personal communication. Lévi-Strauss is the French social anthropologist who helped make Structuralism a dominant mode of analysis in a number of fields through the 1970s and beyond; Geertz is a younger American anthropologist, handling 'the sociology of religion and the theory of culture' (*Encyclopaedia Britannica: Micropaedia.* [1974]: 'Geertz, Clifford'). If someone hasn't done the essay already—in which case my apologies for missing it—the next round of analysis of 'Man of the People' might start from this comment by Le Guin.

translator of it like Selver in *The Word for World Is Forest* nor even like a midwife in the Marxists' noble image. This hero is more like the purest of Daoist sage, changing things through a kind of spiritual 'autoplasty.' Mary Douglas tells us that a 'primitive' man 'seeks to achieve his desires by self-manipulation, performing surgical rites upon his own body to produce fertility in nature, subordination in women[,] or hunting success.' This is opposed to our own 'alloplasty': 'In modern culture we seek to achieve our desires by operating directly on the external environment, with the impressive technical results that are the most obvious distinction between the two types of cultures.'[576] In what I'm calling 'spiritual autoplasty' one *is* the revolution, and that is the crucial thing for achieving true change.

Havzhiva says Yeron gave him little choice in becoming a hero, and she insists that he chose: which is, of course, the central thing traditional heroes do.[577] Havzhiva responds,

> 'Sometimes I think I was able to choose because I grew up where all choices had been made for me.
> 'So you rebelled, made your own way,' she said, nodding.
> '...I'm no rebel.'
> 'Bah!' she said again. 'No rebel? You, in the thick of it, in the heart of our movement all the way?'
> 'Oh yes...But not in a rebellious spirit. That had to be your spirit. My job was acceptance. To keep an acceptant spirit. That's what I learned growing up. To accept. Not to change the world. Only to change the soul. So that it can be in the world. Be rightly in the world.'
> She listened but looked unconvinced. 'Sounds like a woman's way of being,' she said. 'Men generally want to change things to suit.'
> 'Not the men of my people,' he said. (143)

This is an important exchange. It usefully denies some sort of essential maleness and allows for different men coming from different cultures. It also seems to imply that changing one's soul works directly on the world. In one sense, that is obviously true: if the real reality of things is immanent, changing oneself changes the world by definition, minutely, and small changes in oneself can have big effects in a world in which everything is connected to everything else: a connected cosmos in which 'trembling circles' of human desire and being and choice can enlarge, interlock, and fade 'on the still surface of the' symbolic 'water' of life (93). Still, metaphysics is pretty far from practical politics, and I would direct readers toward the very end of the story and the conclusion of the motif of walking.

---

[576] *Purity and Danger*, 1978 Routledge rpt., qtd. Wolfe [211].
[577] See Crow and Erlich, 'Words of Binding' 208, 210 and passim.

Havzhiva talks of learning at home in Stse how to 'sit still.' Being dissatisfied with that, he 'learned flying, with the historians'—i.e., trying to stand outside the world and see its patterns. Still though he could not keep his 'balance.' What he learned on Yeowe was what he needed to learn: 'How to walk.... How to walk with my people' (144). Here the suggestion is one of solidarity. Walking with one's true people, one can be in balance—a key word with the Daoist Le Guin—and one can get things done. Not utter stillness in the manner of the Pueblo: being removed from history by choosing stasis. And not being removed from history by just studying it. And not being removed from history by trying to get above what history *is* and trying to change things, godlike, from above and outside. The image here is the small 'p' people, united, walking together and making nonviolent history, bringing true change.

'A Woman's Liberation'

Rakam begins her story with how she came to write it at the request of her 'dear friend,' who turns out to be Havzhiva from 'A Man of the People.' She ends it, 'as so many stories...with the joining of two people' and raises the question, 'What is one man's and one woman's love and desire, against the history of two worlds, the great revolutions of our lifetimes, the hope, the unending cruelty of our species?' And answers her own question with, 'A little thing,' but notes that a key, too, is a little thing. Keys unlock doors (much bigger things than keys), and this is an important image to end a collection that has talked of heterosexual intercourse as going 'through "the twofold door"' ('A Man of the People' 98), has made much of Compound gates both opened and closed, and has featured as *the* liberating event the women of Nadami opening and holding open the door to the armory, beginning the Liberation of Yeowe ('A Woman's Liberation' 193 [& passim])—to say nothing of all those gates and walls and doors from Earthsea through *Always Coming Home*. Here the key is two human beings in a balanced relationship: not a 'marriage of true minds' (in Shakespeare's phrase) but bodies: 'it is in our bodies that we lose or begin our freedom, in our bodies that we accept or end our slavery' (208, penultimate sentence of the story).

Rakam's story is her movement from slavery into freedom, a journey both figurative and literal. In 'A Man of the People,' Havzhiva went from the immanence of the Pueblo of Stse into history and the Ekumen at Kathhad and Ve and ends up among the 'dust people' of Yeowe (119). So Rakam on Werel goes from the slave Compound to the House of the Shomeke Family, gets kidnapped «down the river» to the far worse Great House of Zeskra, goes to the City and a moment of freedom on Werel—a time in which she learns and helps make history, flees to Yeowe, and then must go from the village of Hagayot to Yotebber City to find a true freedom, a voice in history, and find Yehedarhed Havzhiva. The pattern is a standard one—the Journey—and stands behind the most factual of slave narratives and some of Le Guin's most extravagantly imagined works: in being one-way, it is the journey of Luz into freedom in the wilderness in *Eye of the Heron*, and, most relevantly, perhaps, the journey of Irena to the City and Hugh in *The Beginning Place*. 'O, O, Yeowe , / Nobody never come back'—which was horrible for the slaves first sent there but just as well for Rakam and others who have no place decent to go back to.

Rakam starts life as a Werelian asset whose mother serves in the House of the Shomeke family, a family that had been 'great in History'; Rakam had been sired by the Owner, making her darker than most slaves and giving Rakam's mother hopes for her. The racial analogies here should be clear to most readers and every adult US reader: it is a simple reversal of US racial hierarchies favoring the 'fair'—i.e., those with skins light in color.[578] Rakam's mother has her dreams and, perhaps, pretensions, and she gets Rakam to promise to be, with significant wording, 'tame,' not 'wild,' and gets Rakam accepted at the House (150).[579] Rakam becomes 'the pet of Lady Tazeu Wehoma Shomeke.' Her Lady 'was gentle, but she was the mistress in love,' and Rakam is 'her instrument' (152): a good reminder that patriarchy has to do with power more than XY vs. XX sex chromosomes, and that sexual exploitation, too, is primarily about power.

Young Rakam comes to feel superior to the field hands: 'We domestics of the Great House were entirely different from them,' she thought. 'Serving the higher beings, we became like them' (154). Her stay with Lady Tazeu comes to an end in Rakam's fourteenth or fifteenth year when her Lady sends her as a birthday present to her son, Erod. Erod is like a young Lord Byron, if one can picture a chaste, not-crippled, not-too-bright, non-poetic Lord Byron, with no sense of humor. In any event, he is a radical and a rich abolitionist and a golden-voiced orator. Erod knows that intercourse with a slave is rape, so he won't touch Rakam, but he does speak to her and two male slaves about abolition, liberation, and the on-going revolution on Yeowe (155-56).

When Lord Shomeke, the Owner, is dying horribly of pusworm, the Lady Tazeu shows him the kindness of slitting his throat and then cuts 'the veins in her arms across and across'—no «cry for help» but a competent euthanasia plus suicide. Lord Erod's first act is to manumit his slaves, give a rousing speech on the subject, leave them the estate and their freedom papers, and fly off to the capital with two of his male servants, but not with Rakam; he'd never touched Rakam (162). If «*To liberate* is a reflexive verb», such top-down manumission is a potential problem philosophically, and it proves to be an immediate problem practically: indeed, an utter disaster for Erod's former slaves. With Werel just having lost the war on Ye-

---

[578] That 'fair' means both good-looking and light comes from the idea that dark skin is 'foul': so says my desk dictionary and my experience of Renaissance English literature. The superiority of light skin was originally class-based, not racial—English peasants and other outdoor workers were sunburnt; the upper classes fairly pale—but the idea was readily expanded to include a racist hierarchy.

[579] See *ER* for Le Guin on dragons in the Earthsea trilogy representing 'above all, wildness. What is *not owned*' (*ER* 22).

owe, the local Bosses are not going to allow the gates to the slave compound to remain symbolically open, and the neighbors generally, those potential dangers to every utopian experiment, are going to be upset with Lord Erod's dangerous action. Under the Voe Dean law, Erod's slaves may be free, but the government's «writs don't run» so far from the City, and any laws protecting slaves 'meant nothing on the Estates' (168).

The grandmothers and the eunuchs spent all the first night of freedom 'trying to make plans, to draw our people together so they could defend themselves.' But the young men 'ran wild' and loot the House, precipitating shooting and the flying in to the estate of reinforcements for the Bosses. So the Compound gates are locked again, but from the inside this time, as the newly freed slaves try to resist their attackers. In the analogy with Terra, it is Yeowe that is Haiti, the place of a successful slave rebellion, not rural Werel. In the middle of the night of the second or third day of freedom, the attackers 'came with heavy tractors and pushed down the wall, and a hundred men or more, our Bosses and owners from all the plantations of the region, came swarming in. They were armed with guns. We fought them with farm tools and pieces of wood.' In a few days, the Compound has gone from a prison to a fortress to a killing field. 'One or two of them were hurt or killed. They killed as many of us as they wanted to kill and then began to rape us. It went on all night' (163-64). For the first time since, perhaps, *Planet of Exile* (1966), Le Guin has shown a truly negative example of 'unbuilding walls'; for the first time ever, perhaps, in her canon, she narrates a very negative example of men acting explicitly against the law.[580]

> A group of men took all the old women and men and held them and shot them between the eyes, the way they kill cattle. My grandmother was one of them. I do not know what happened to my mother. I did not see any bondsmen living when they took me away in the morning. I saw white papers lying in the blood on the ground. Freedom papers. (164)

Rakam is kidnapped and taken to Zeskra, to serve among the 'use-women' at the Great House (165). There she sees sexual exploitation extreme even in Werel's slave culture, including the murder of a little girl from Shomeke, who dies when a guest at Zestra tightens a knot too much in a sex/strangulation game. This leads to a very important brief passage, when Rakam says she'll speak no more of such horrors: 'I have told what I must tell. There are truths that are not useful. All knowledge is local, my friend [Havzhiva] has said. Is it true, where is it true, that that child had to

---

[580] In *Tehanu*, the crimes brought to trial are committed offstage; the trials are conducted offstage; and we get no details on how the new King's courts determine what is the law.

die in that way? Is it true, where is it true, that she did not have to die in that way?' (166)

As Archmage of Earthsea, Ged refused to punish, but that didn't stop him from rescuing Arren from slavers and striking their captain dumb until that captain could 'find a word worth speaking,' which we may assume was a long time (*FS* 62; ch. 4). In *The Word for World Is Forest*, among the rigorously immanent, totally unidealistic Athsheans, the Daoist-style Old Man, Coro Mena, tells Selver he has 'done what you had to do, and it was *not right*' in massacring Terrans (33-34; ch. 2, my emphasis). Knowledge may indeed be local, but it is not so local that a murderer at Zeskra can claim justification through a local value system, nor can even whole tribes claim a local truth in finding true progress in drugging girls before they are ritually raped (136-37).

With the help of the Hame (the slave resistance-movement), and The Community (the abolitionists), Rakam escapes to the City, one of her friends dying in the attempt. Holding onto her freedom paper, she arrives in the City: in this story, a good place for people.

In the City, as a free woman, Rakam gets a room for herself and shuts her door. She comes to feel a good deal of hostility toward anyone, male or female, who looked at her sexually. She was mere body to Lady Tazeu and at Zeskra and even 'to Erod who would not touch'—Rakam saw herself as 'Flesh to touch or not touch, as they pleased. To use or not to use, as they chose' (171). Having a room of one's own—and with a closeable door—is, indeed, a good thing, and Le Guin strongly believes in times of abstinence; still, there is a potential for a puritanical hatred of the flesh here—Rakam *does* hate the 'sexual parts' of herself—and Rakam's rejection of her body is not a good thing. What is altogether good is her learning to love history (171-72). She had 'grown up without any history' and is now learning its importance.

> Nobody knew anything about any time when things had been different. Nobody knew there was any place where things might be different. We were enslaved by the present time.[581]
>
> Erod had talked of change, indeed, but the owners were going to make the change. We were to be changed, we were to be freed, just as we had been owned. In history I saw that any freedom has been made, not given. (172)

'A Woman's Liberation' is, in part, a defense of history and the life of historians, both in a colloquial sense and in the sense established in 'A Man of the People' of studying history and making it, *doing* in the world, changing things. On worlds where people could talk of 'postliterate infor-

---

[581] See Le Guin's poem 'Tenses,' and its line, 'Terrible is the cage of the present tense' (*Wild Oats* 81). (See 'Tenses' also for the theme of the promise [*TD*]—and for why Le Guin is one Romantic who has refused to romanticize madness.)

mation technology' (197)—Werel and Yeowe in the far future, Terra in our time—'A Woman's Liberation' is a defense of books and book-learning and book-teaching. And it is part of Le Guin's continuing investigation of politics, including feminist politics.[582]

Rakam becomes a student and teacher of history, a friend of the Hainishman Esdardon Aya—Old Music from 'Forgiveness Day'—and a political activist, allied with, and a thorn in the side of, the Radical Party. Rakam's militant activism causes problems for Radical candidates, but she defends her action by saying 'No owner is my candidate!' When charged with egotism by Ahas, a servant of Lord Erod since their days on the estate, she claims 'I don't put myself first—politicians and capitalists do that. I put freedom first,' which sounds suspiciously like a canned phrase from Abberkam in 'Betrayals.' Rakam does not go into detail about the politics here, but she makes clear that she was a difficult ally and contributed to one problem. She admits now some truth in the accusation she was putting herself first.

> I had found that I had the gift in speaking and writing of moving people's minds and hearts. Nobody told me that such a gift is as dangerous as it is strong. Ahas said I was putting myself first, but I knew I was not doing that. I was wholly in the service of truth and of liberty. No one told me that the end cannot purify the means, since only the Lord Kamye knows what the end may be. My grandmother could have told me that. The *Arkamye* would have reminded me of it, but I did not often read in it, and in the City there were no old men singing the word, evenings. If there had been, I would not have heard them over the sound of my beautiful voice speaking the beautiful truth.
>
> I believe I did no harm, except as we all did, in bringing it to the attention of the rulers of Voe Deo that the Hame was growing bolder and the Radical Party was growing stronger, and they must move against us. (179)

The issue coming up was a divisive one for the Liberation Movement: a social issue. In the 'open' compounds in the City, there was a men's side and a women's side and, in a radical move, some apartments for couples. This was illegal given the Werelian doctrine that assets owed loyalty to Owners, not to another asset. Lord Erod and others did not want to take up this issue, feeling it was a matter of personal arrangements and got in the

---

[582] Whether or not the oppressed/newly emancipated can learn much of use from the books and culture of the oppressors is still being debated. See Chevigny for even '...Algebra as Political Curriculum': a news article with a strong text supporting effective teaching of algebra to poor Black kids and, more generally 'strengthening a culture of educational expectations' (19) among underclass African-Americans.

way of the larger issue of emancipation; Rakam and others argued that '...the right of assets to live together and the bring up children was a cause the Radical Party should support. It was not directly threatening to ownership and might appeal to the natural instincts of many owners, especially the women, who could not vote but who were valuable allies.' The debate moves to basics and an important exchange between Rakam and Erod (*FWF* 180).

Rakam says there can be 'no freedom without sexual freedom, and that until women were allowed and men were willing to take responsibility for their children, no woman, whether owner or asset, would be free.' Erod responds that 'Men must bear the responsibility for the public side of life' and goes on to make a standard «dual spheres» argument, established by 'God and Nature.' Rakam infers from this, correctly, that for women slaves emancipation will mean only the ironic freedom 'to enter the beza, be locked in on the women's side' of owners' houses (180).

All good points, and taken up by some other women at the meeting, who want the Radical Party to speak for women and to make the political more the personal in the lives of Radical leaders: letting their own wives out of the women's side, letting their own wives become active in Radical politics. Rakam looks at the argument and feels 'half-triumphant, half-dismayed.' She is seen by Erod and some others 'from the Hame...as an open trouble-maker. And indeed my words had divided us. But were we not already divided?' Of course they were already divided, and anyone who knows about the rise of the American women's liberation movement out of the New Left and «The Movement» in the late 1960s and 1970s will recognize the argument. Rakam is right in her triumph and her dismay: the radical women and far leftists in the US Movement were mostly correct in their analyses, but yet their truths *were* divisive and contributed to divisions and backlash. In Rakam's story, however, the theoretical issue must give way to an urgent, practical concern. Esdardon Aya shows up with news that the government of Voe Deo is about to force manumitted slaves to find owner sponsors. And if they cannot—and a trouble-maker like Rakam will have problems getting sponsored—they faced death, a labor camp, or auction back into slavery (181).

It is time for Rakam to get out, and very fast; Old Music can offer her a trip to Yeowe, and she accepts, with gratitude (182-83).

It looks at first that the plot-conflict in 'A Woman's Liberation' now will turn toward violence: the ship is attacked by the Voe Dean Space Defense Fleet, but this attack comes to nothing; the true conflict is elsewhere (184-85). Elsewhere appears when Rakam gets to Yeowe and gets her first taste of their version of postcolonial freedom. A teacher and historian, she is sent to a cooperative village to work the rice paddies. So is Tualtak, a chemist, and every other woman to arrive on their spacecraft.

The Hagayot Village in the Yotebber Region is a rural cooperative and not as bad as the old tribal compound Havzhiva observed in 'A Man of the People'; it is bad enough, though. The men there fear the Werelian women, 'who were not used to taking orders' from men of equal social rank; the village maintains a men's side and a women's side; the men watch the Werelian women 'with fierce suspicion and a whip as ready as any Boss's.' What the men fear, it seems, is 'Bosswomen,' their idea of the grandmothers on Werel. The men as a group wish to retain and seek to increase power over women after the Liberation because many of the men enjoy that power in itself and the privileges it brings. Their main fear is fear of losing privilege (189-90).

The men on Yeowe have continued a horrible situation for the women, horrible enough to drive to suicide a woman from the space ship from the country of Bambur, 'whipped and beaten by both women and men for speaking her language,' a language they do not understand (191). Rakam feels she has to act and her action is teaching: she decides 'to teach the village women and children to read.' Country-schools were about to be started, and it would advantage the Hagayot boys if they arrived knowing how to read; Rakam finagles permission to teach boys, girls, and women, starting with the Life of Tual for the women: unimpeachable religious training (191-92).

Tualtak wants to just walk away—the valued action in 'Omelas,' *Eye of the Heron*, and elsewhere in Le Guin's canon—but Rakam is afraid they will be raped, and she could not stand another rape. So Rakam begins organizing and a little agitating and gets, eventually, payment in cash for the women for their labor—as opposed to local script, worthless outside the village. She gets the local women to shame the men for not paying them. Not waiting to help the women of the village get the vote, Rakam and Tualtak take their earnings and catch a train for Yotebber City (193-94). Tualtak is sick, so Rakam takes her to a hospital and meets Dr. Yeron (Havzhiva's friend in 'A Man of the People'), Rakam's entrée into radical politics in the Yotebber district.

Yeron takes her to 'a meeting of an educational society...a group of democrats, mostly teachers, who sought to work against the autocratic power of the tribal and regional chiefs under the new Constitution, and to counteract what they called the slave mind, the rigid, misogynistic hierarchy' that Rakam had learned about in detail in rural Yotebber. Her experience is useful to these city people 'who had met the slave mind only when they found themselves governed by it.' Not surprisingly, the women of the society were the more militant, the men more gradualist: the women 'had lost the most at Liberation and now had less to lose.' So the women were 'ready for revolution' (197).

How you run a revolution when the government has all the weapons is most of the political topic for the rest of 'A Woman's Liberation,' except that the situation is worse than that. Even granting the power of discourse, '[W]hat good were words' when the established powers control 'the net. The news, the information programs, the puppets of the neareals.... Against that, what harm could a lot of teachers do? Parents who had no schooling had children who entered the net to hear and see and feel what the Chief wanted them to know: that freedom is obedience to leaders, that virtue is violence, that manhood is domination' (197).

And at this promising low point, an Alien shows up at the meeting: the Sub-Envoy of the Ekumen, Yehedarhed Havzhiva, bearing books from Esdardon Aya (198). These are a great gift for Rakam: 'the books gave me freedom, gave me the world—the worlds.' And this leads to the assertion that books are better than the net because the net—privileged in Stse and among the Kesh of *Always Coming Home*—gives the present; books preserve the past. They are city things, books, helping concentrate and preserve civilization, in *this* story a good thing (199).

The story quickly presses on to 'the great demonstration of women,' a kind of general strike featuring 70,000 women lying down on the tracks and stopping the trains of Yeowe (201 [also 130]). And, when the Movement loses some momentum, these activist teachers, with Havzhiva's help, take over the printing house of the University of Yeowe (202). Books 'are the body of history' Havzhiva says, and Rakam agrees, and she becomes editor of the new—subtly subversive—women's press, the one free press on Yeowe (203-04).

'A Woman's Liberation' comes to a happy ending. The incidents leading up to this happy ending are the demonstration and the founding of the press, Rakam's returning to public speaking, and her public singing of 'O, O, Ye-o-we, / Nobody never comes back' when hecklers tell her to 'go back' where she came from. Plus, the very popular Sub-Envoy's Havzhiva's working for the Liberation Movement and his determining that Rakam's cat, Owner (named for 'his' dark coat), is not a male but a female (203).

Havzhiva invites Rakam for a walk and then to come home with him, and Rakam accepts. She 'had not desired a man or a woman...since Shomeke,' touching people 'with love but never with desire.' She had thought, 'My gate was locked.' Havzhiva opened it, and we have Le Guinian touch. Then dinner, with the invitation to dinner followed by an invitation to make love, something Rakam has never done. She has *been* raped; perhaps she had had love made to her by the Lady Tazeu; but she has not *made love*. So they go to Havzhiva's bedroom, 'in the beza...in the harem.' He lives on the women's side, liking 'the view' (207).

The final paragraph of 'A Woman's Liberation' tells us 'The Amendments to the Constitution were voted, by secret ballot, in the Yeowean Year of Liberty 18'—and if you want the details of the 'events that led to this and what has followed,' we can read them in the newly published *History of Yeowe* from the University Press.' Part of this happy ending is the traditional magic: As We Like It, «They all lived happily ever after in a new and better world coalescing around a central couple.» In a political story like 'A Woman's Liberation,' that better world includes serious political reform, so if we want the happy ending we'll accept the liberating amendments on faith. Additionally, there is the living proof of Havzhiva as a man who can 'live on the woman's side.'[583] Men are not genetically predestined to *be* sexist; it is a matter of cultural conditioning—and of greed, pride, fear, and individual choice if men are male chauvinist oppressors. The men of Yeowe, we've learned, do have a sense of shame, and this can be used politically: the women of Hagayot Village did finally get paid for their labor in real money (194). The men of Yeowe owe the women a large debt for their world's liberation. And post-slavery, postcolonial Yeowe has much to gain from friendship with the Ekumen, and maybe from making Werel look reactionary, and much to lose from the Ekumen by shooting down activist women. The political logic is that Yeowean men can be accused of gaining freedom in large part for the «freedom» to oppress women. They can be accused of hypocrisy and ingratitude. Such accusations are painful, especially if true—on the occasions the accused have a sense of shame. And the women have shown they can stop the trains and thereby threaten serious economic disruption. If there is not a greater pain from losing privilege, sensible Machiavellian politicians will give people simple justice. The US Civil Rights Movement did succeed in securing rights that cost majority Whites relatively little. The more militant, and majority, liberation movement in South Africa achieved even more. The happy ending on Yeowe could happen. And 'A Woman's Liberation' may prove to be an effective *mâshâl* for postcolonial women's liberation on our world.

---

[583] Cf. Tenar in *Tehanu*, 'turning her back on all that,' the power of men, and going 'to the other side, the other room, where the women lived, to be one of them' (30; ch. 4).

XII.

THE HAINISH UNIVERSE REVISITED II

> The Last Judgment is an Overwhelming of Bad Art & Science. Mental Things are alone Real; what is call'd Corporeal, Nobody Knows of its Dwelling Place: it is in Fallacy.... I assert for My Self that I do not behold the outward Creation & that to me it is hindrance & not Action; it is as the Dirt upon my feet, No part of Me. 'What,' it will be Question'd, 'When the Sun rises, do you not see a round disk of fire somewhat like a Guinea?' O no, no, I see an Innumerable company of the Heavenly host crying 'Holy, Holy, Holy is the Lord God Almighty.' I question not my Corporeal or Vegetative Eye any more than I would Question a Window concerning a Sight. I look thro' it & not with it. —William Blake (End of A Vision of the Last Judgment, Blake 617)

A Fisherman of the Inland Sea includes two long, nicely done jokes and six short stories, all of interest for a study of Ursula K. Le Guin's teaching works. The stories show a good deal of continuity with and some change from Le Guin's earlier works. They are informed by feminism, but remind us that Le Guin 'was a feminist in 1968,' following her philosophy as well as she knew how, and with inevitable slips (*LoN* [1979]: 217). The stories continue to stress 'Marriage' as a theme (*LoN* [1979]: 143), but allow the possibility that a legal marriage might be improved if one partner were out of it—and, more important, greatly expand the possibilities for true marriage.[584] Significantly, we see single-sex marriage and marriages that include homosexual bonding and homosexual sex; and we see the possibility for living in the world in communities where one might commit to marriage or not, where one might commit to a group marriage only partially, attaching oneself 'to a brother or sister's marriage as aunt or uncle' (*FIS* 152). In these stories, Le Guin continues her critique from the 1960s

---

[584] See Le Guin's 'Solitude' (1994) for the possibility of good living with only moderate conscious commitments and relatively tenuous human connections. Cf. and contrast 'Science Fiction and Mrs. Brown,' here *LoN* (1979): 116.

of 'the Judaeo-Christian-Rationalist-West' (*LoH* [1979]: 82; ch. 6), but *Fisherman* is less interested in the monotheist Judeo-Christian part than in a critique of Rationalism. Where Le Guin differs from some recent theorists, is in knowing that the Western Rationalist part long preceded René Descartes and Sir Isaac Newton and 'The Mechanical Universe.'[585] Two of the stories in *Fisherman* deal seriously with the postmodern idea, popular in much feminist theory, of the social construction of reality. Dealing explicitly with social construction of reality may be a change for Le Guin, but *as change*, it is mostly a change of foregrounding what had been background in at least one earlier story: the Old Ones of 'Pathways of Desire' (1979) 'are gradually making a real language' out of the 'fake one' of the world they were born/dreamed-up into (*CR* 197), and with that language they are creating a culture, a new world among the Ndif. And Le Guin has enough of a background in non-monotheistic, nonrationalist, nonWestern approaches to the world, and in anthropology and recent science, to know, without much help from academic theorists, something of how human consciousness structures the world. What recent work has done quite usefully is stress the *social* construction of reality, perhaps helping to shift Le Guin's emphasis from The Dream (as in *The Lathe of Heaven*) to The Story.[586]

Prelude 1: 'The First Contact with the Gorgonids' (1991), 'The Ascent of the North Face' (1983), 'Sur' (*CR* 1982)

The two long jokes in *Fisherman* are 'The First Contact with the Gorgonids' and 'The Ascent of the North Face.'

The point of view character in 'First Contact' is Mrs. Jerry Debree when we first meet her (*FIS* 13), later, Annie Laurie Debree, the heroine of the great TV documentary shot by her husband, 'Grong Crossing, South Australia: The First Contact with the Gorgonids' (20).[587] Mrs. and Mr. Debree are Americans in Australia, and Mr. Jerry Debree is a very ugly American. He's loud, obnoxious, vulgar, arrogant, sexist. At the beginning of the story, Jerry is complaining about a local Corroboree specifically and putting down Australia more generally to two men at a bar who say their names are Bruce and Bruce (14).[588] Bruce-1 tells Jerry that for a *real* Cor-

---

[585] See Le Guin's 1982 essay 'A Non-Euclidian View of California...' (*DEW* 80-100), esp. 87.
[586] See the discussion above on Social Constructionism; see Le Guin's 'It Was a Dark and Stormy Night' (1979) esp. *DEW* 27.
[587] 'Annie Laurie' is an old folksong (in English, from Scotland), whose lyrics I checked on World Wide Web from *The Florida Star* (Jerund@aol.com), and whose provenance is given as recorded by William Douglas in 1685 (according to jfeiszli@silver.sdsmt.edu). The folksong heroine exists primarily as Bonnie Annie Laurie for the (male) singer to adore.
[588] Cf. the routine by Monty Python where the members of an Australian university philosophy department (except the new hire) are all hard-drinkers named Bruce.

roboree he ought to travel to Grong Crossing. Annie notices that Bruce-2 didn't understand what Bruce-1 meant at first, 'and that was when her woman's intuition woke up' that the Australians might be putting them on (14).

They are, of course, but Jerry buys an expensive camcorder and resolves 'to shoot me some abos' and drives, and drives and refuses to even consider turning back (15), until he gets to what he thinks is Ayer's Rock but which Annie knows from the hotel flyer she read can't be Ayer's Rock; and they arrive at what Jerry thinks is a Corroboree (16). Jerry approaches and starts to record, despite Annie's advice first to ask permission (17) and second, that 'They're not natives. They're Space Aliens. That's their saucer,' which Annie knows from the *Sun* (19)—a supermarket tabloid.

> 'Jerry,' she said...as one of the Space Aliens pointed with its little weak-looking arm and hand at the car. Jerry shoved the camera right up close to its head, and at that it put its hand over the lens. That made Jerry mad, of course, and he yelled, 'Get the fuck off that!' And he actually looked at the Space Alien, not through the camera but face to face. 'Oh, gee,' he said.
>
> And his hand went to his hip. He always carried a gun, because it was an American's right to bear arms and there were so many drug addicts these days. He had smuggled it through the airport inspection the way he knew how. Nobody was going to disarm *him*.
>
> She saw perfectly clearly what happened. The Space Alien opened its eyes.

The Alien glance turns Jerry to stone, or close enough: 'He was just like stone, paralyzed' (19). Annie is very upset and wonders, 'Oh, what should I do, what can I do?' and gets a little help from what will turn out to be 'our friends from Outer Space,' who put Jerry into the car. Annie says thanks and good-bye and drove back, eventually very fast: to get Jerry to a doctor, 'of course, but also because she loved driving on long straight roads very fast.... Jerry never let her drive except in town.' It turns out that 'The paralysis was total and permanent, which would have been terrible, except that she could afford full-time, round-the-clock, first-class care for poor Jerry...,' since it also turns out that the new Annie Laurie Debree is highly skillful on her own with cutting TV and video rights deals, and Jerry's little home video, after the aliens send ambassadors to Canberra and Reykjavik, is worth a fortune. More important to her, she is the first to make contact. 'There was only one good shot of her on the film, and Jerry had been sort of shaking, and her highlighter was kind of streaked, but that was all right. She was the heroine' (21). And so ends the story.

As Le Guin says in her Introduction to these collected stories, it is a bad idea to try to explain a joke (9); still, I will try to contextualize this one. Concentrating on Jerry, it is a dumb ___ story, where one can fill in the blank with whatever group one wishes to have a laugh at the expense of. In context, Jerry is a man, an American, and a husband, so 'Gorgonids' is, in part, a dumb American-male (husband) joke. Concentrating, as we should, on Annie, it is a wise-fool joke, and a joke in which a persecuted person, of a persecuted people (women generally or wives in particular) gets one up—big-time here—on the persecutor (e.g., see Rugoff 67-71) or any jokes of the weak overcoming the (apparently) strong.[589] More specific to the main body of Le Guin's work, we have the discomfiting of someone who wants to push things, and Others, around, and the reward of someone who will go with the flow of a situation. More specifically feminist, 'Gorgonids' presents what seems to be, and mostly is, a radically unliberated woman gaining her voice and becoming the heroine of what becomes her story.

'The Ascent of the North Face' is a beautiful send-up of the journal of the brave leader, Simon Interthwaite in this case, of, it seems, a WASPish mountain-climbing expedition from Calcutta: e.g., '2/28. Derek, Nigel, Colin, and I went up in blinding snow and wind to plot course and drive pigils [sic]. Visibility very poor. Nigel whined' (*FIS* 54).[590] Interthwaite's journal ends on 3/9, with him 'alone on the High Roof, his fellows waiting for him below, above him 'the sharp Summit, and the Chimney rising sheer against the stars.' After that, we get an editor's note (in italics) telling us that Interthwaite never returned from the High Roof Camp and his party abandoned the climb.

> *In 1980 a Japanese party of Izutsu employees with four Sherbet guides attained the summit by a North Face route, rappelling across the study windows and driving pitons clear up to the eaves. Occupant protest was ineffective.*
> *No one has yet climbed the Chimney.* (55)

The key to the joke is that the ascent is of 'the North Face of 2647 Lovejoy Street,' a fictitious address of a house that could exist on a street that does (in a residential section in Portland, OR).

'Ascent of the North Face' is a silly story, hence 'a gift...from the dark side of your soul' (*FIS* 9). Its significance, beyond self-justifying silliness, is mostly as comic reversal. Instead of very pukka-sahib British gentlemen

---

[589] See also, for contrast and comparison, 'Why Women Always Take Advantage of Men' (Rugoff 71-74), whose female (?) narrator tells how the first man got from God greater strength than the first woman, but how the woman followed the advice of the devil and got back control (Rugoff 74).
[590] For the log-entry joke, cf. opening narrative in 'The Matter of Seggri.' See Also Le Guin's more earnest discussion of heroic explorers of the Antarctic in 'Heroes' (*DEW* 171-75).

of the Raj leaving Calcutta for Nepal or the Karakorum range to ascend Everest or K2 or something else highly mountainous, they end up in urban America and try to climb a house. It makes sense: the Himalayas are the 'Roof of the World' to the people living there; if Western gentlemen have the right to barge in on the figurative house of the Nepalese and climb their mountains, why not gentlemen from Calcutta barging in on American householders by climbing an American house? 'Ascent,' from 1983, is an exercise in the mock heroic that nicely balances the true heroism, or non-heroism, in 'Sur,' from the previous year (collected in *Compass Rose* [not *FIS*]).

'Sur' is 'A Summary Report of the *Yelcho* Expedition to the Antarctic, 1909-1910.' In the story nine women—nine again in a Le Guin story!—are the first humans (probably) to reach the South Pole. Although it might not have been a good idea to make the last part of the trip: they 'were by then all a little crazy with exhaustion and the great altitude,' in a place where people have no 'business to be,' and the Narrator wishes they 'had not gone to the Pole' (*CR* 267-68). The Narrator has a point. In her own voice in 'Heroes' (1986), Le Guin says that, with reservations, what she admires in Ernest Shackleton in his expedition to the South Pole 'is that he turned back' (*DEW* 174).

The women's polar expedition in 'Sur' is different from expeditions in men's history. The women select leaders in case of grave emergency, but never have an emergency, and so act in near-perfect anarchy (*CR* 257); they practice good housekeeping, 'the art of the infinite' (260); the explorer Berta creates beautiful sculptures (262-3); and Teresa has a baby (269-70). The Narrator and her friends have their act together. They have their goal and 'success crowned our efforts.' They are world-class explorers, but also very responsible wives and mothers (256). And they claim no reward, not even fame. They do not proclaim their project, not even so much as to leave at the South Pole a single human footprint. The Narrator was and is glad they 'had left no sign there, for some man longing to be the first might come some day, and find it, and know then what a fool he had been, and break his heart' (*CR* 268).

We will return to 'Sur's' themes of heroism and the achievement of transcendent goals—and their gender inflections—with 'The Kerastion,' and the Churten Drive stories in *Fisherman*. First, though, I wish to look at another story outside *Fisherman*; as introduction to 'Newton's Sleep,' I want to look at 'The Eye Altering.'

Prelude 2: 'The Eye Altering' (1976, 1978, *CR* 1982)

A textual note to begin with: I am using 'The Eye Altering' in the revised version published in *The Compass Rose* (1982); this seems substantially identical with 'The Eye Altering (II)' at the end of *The Altered I* (168-80) but different in a couple of important ways—primarily greater stress on exile and pattern—from the initial version of 'The Eye Altering' in *The Altered I* (17-28). My references to 'Eye Altering' will always be to the revision; the initial version I will refer to as 'The Eye Altering [I].'

The setting for 'Eye Altering' is the planet New Zion, and the point of view character is Miriam, the physician for one of the Twenty Settlements of humans. She was born on Earth a generation earlier and exiled with other Jews. There are more hints in 'Eye Altering' than in 'Eye Altering [I]' about exile, but these are only hints. As with the Terrans in *Planet of Exile* (1966), the characters are exiles on a planet where they had not evolved, and that is all we need to know for the premise of the story.

Miriam finds the planet ugly, and all the exiles have difficulty living there. The local sun (NSC 641) is more orange than yellow and makes the world look strange; and the settlers from Earth are allergic to the native protein and must take pills, called 'metas,' to eat local food. One of the sickest of Miriam's patients is Gennady Borisovich, a Zionborn young man who goes by the nickname Genya. Genya is a painter.

The story opens with Miriam looking out the window of her infirmary and thinking, 'If I forget thee, O Jerusalem—' (*CR* 154), followed by a comment by the Narrator about exiles being able to forget pain, hatred, and fear, but not the beauties of one's home. The spare description by the Narrator is highly moving, especially if one knows the source of Miriam's quotation:

> By the rivers of Babylon,
> there we sat,
> sat and wept,
> as we thought of Zion.
> There on the poplars
> we hung up our lyres,
> for our captors asked us there for songs,
> our tormentors for amusement,
> 'Sing us one of the songs of Zion.'
> How can we sing a song of the LORD
> on alien soil?
> If I forget you, O Jerusalem,
> let my right hand wither;
> let my tongue stick to my palate
> if I cease to think of you,
> if I do not keep Jerusalem in memory
> even at my happiest hour. (Psalm 137.1-6, *Tanakh*)

The story then moves to Genya, one of Miriam's figurative children, who is again in the infirmary, from what Miriam initially thinks is sun stroke or heatstroke. None of Miriam's own biological children had lived, and she is very concerned about Genya at all times: now a young man of twenty-four whose practicing of 'moral genetics' has gotten between him and a desired marriage to Rachel, a healthy woman who loves him but will marry a man who can give her healthy children (158-59). Then Genya tells

Miriam he is not taking his meta pills, and she fears for a moment he is allowing himself to die (*CR* 158). Genya is not giving up, however, and Miriam goes along with an experiment where he will avoid the metas for another two weeks, but under close observation at the infirmary. What did it matter? A quiet voice inside reminds Miriam, 'Whatever you do or don't do, he will die.... The sicklies can't adjust to this world. And neither can we, neither can we' (161). The 'protein keys' on New Zion do not fit the Terran's metabolic 'locks,' so the Terrans have to change their metabolism with the metas; but that is just a least bad solution—they still do not fit into New Zion's pattern (162-63).[591]

Meanwhile, paper arrives from Little Tel Aviv, a rare and valuable item, and Genya starts painting (161-62). To Miriam's eye Genya's paintings are ugly. Only one adolescent really thinks highly of Genya's work. Young Moishe had asked 'How do you do it, Genya, how do you make it so pretty?' Genya answered 'Beauty's in the eye, Moishe' (164). Miriam had not liked Genya's painting when it has been 'vague and half created.' The painting he finishes during the time of the story, though, is 'realistic, all too realistic. Hideously recognizable': a mudscape of their world (164). Still, Miriam suggests hanging it in the Living Room, a kind of commons area loved by the older people, a place with Earthlike lighting and the community's pictures of capital 'H' Home. Genya agrees.

> 'It isn't bad, he said. 'I'll do better, though, when I've learned how to fit myself into the pattern.'
> 'What pattern?' [Miriam asks.]
> 'Well, you know, you have to look until you *see* the pattern, till it makes sense, and then you have to get that into your hand, too.'[592] He made large, vague, shaping gestures with a bottle of absolute alcohol.
> 'Anybody who asks a painter a question in words deserves what they get, I guess,' said Miriam. 'Babble, babble.'

The climax of the story comes in the following scene when Genya's painting is found by the old folks of the community in the Living Room. It is beautiful and a mystery. How could an old painting of Earth have been around without their seeing it? Who could paint a new landscape of Earth? And *paint* it must be, created from experience; the old pilot of the exiles is outraged at the first suggestion that someone copied a photograph: 'That is a painting, not a copy! That is a work of art, that was seen, seen with the

---

[591] Alternatively, one could picture the metabolic keys of Terran digestive enzymes not fitting the locks of New Zion's proteins (carbohydrates, etc.). Either way the point is excellent (and often ignored in SF): Terrans would have trouble eating native food on even Earth-like planets.
[592] See also *CR* 163 for the *pattern* of Genya's surviving a month without metas.

eyes and the heart!' (166). We know that this is Genya's painting—but it is a painting of New Zion. Miriam solves the riddle.

'Miriam looked, and she saw. She saw what the light of NSC 641 had hidden from her, what the artificial Earth daylight of the room revealed to her. She saw what Genya saw: the beauty of the world.' She explains to the other old-timers.

> 'It's here,' she said. '...It's here. Zion. It's how Genya sees it. With the eyes and the heart.'
> 'But look, the trees are green, look at the colors.... It's Earth—'
> Yes! It is Earth. Genya's Earth!'
> 'But he can't—'
> How do we know? How do we know what a child of Zion sees? We can see the picture in this light that's like Home. Take it outside, into the daylight, and you'll see what we always see, the ugly colors, the ugly planet where we're not at home. But he is at home!... It's...*we* who lack the key. We with our...meta pills!'....
> 'With our meta pills, we can survive here.... But...he *lives* here! We were all perfectly adjusted to Earth, too well, we can't fit anywhere else—he wasn't, wouldn't have been; allergic, a misfit—the pattern a little wrong, see? The pattern. But there are many patterns, infinite patterns, he fits this one...better than we do—'

Not just Genya but 'All the sicklies,' maybe: here Miriam realizes her mistake and that of the settlers. The sicklies are 'allergic to *Earth* proteins,' so metas 'just foul them up, they're a different pattern...' (167). And then a further insight that Genya and Rachel can marry. 'They've got to marry, he should have kids. What about Rachel taking metas while she's pregnant, the foetus. I can work it out'; and shortly thereafter the story ends (168).

Comments

Miriam is named, appropriately (if coincidentally?) for the sister of Moses and Aaron in the Book of Exodus, and, traditionally, the author of the oldest verse in the bible. When Pharaoh and his cavalry are drowned, Miriam 'the prophetess...took a trimbel in her hand, and all the women went out after her in dance with trimbels. And Miriam chanted for them: 'Sing to the LORD, for He has triumphed gloriously; / Horse and driver He has hurled into the sea' (Ex. 15.20-21, *Tanakh*). Le Guin's Miriam, thinking of Psalm 137, raises questions that are important for all strangers in strange lands: exiles, envoys, immigrants—but also people moving from oppression into emancipation in their own lands: familiar lands made strange by one's new status, by that kind of altered eye. What should one bring from Egypt into Canaan? From Werel to a postslavery, postcolonial Yeowe? How much of the old life should one bring into the new? The people of New Zion are appropriately Jewish as a people experienced at exile, but, from the view I am taking here, for this reason, too: Jews have been the first of the oppressed in the West to achieve emancipation, and Jewish experience can be useful for peoples of the African Diaspora, women, and colonized people generally.

Again, Le Guin's Miriam looks out of a window and laments the loss of Jerusalem. In her memory she is like the psalmist: 'Even when you try to forget it[,] you remember that Jerusalem was golden' (*CR* 154). The psalmist, though ends with a curse:

> Fair Babylon, you predator,
> a blessing on him who repays you in kind
> what you have inflicted on us;
> a blessing on him who seizes your babies
> and dashes them against the rocks! (Ps. 137.8)

The Miriam of Exodus, who did exalt at the death of Pharaoh and a cavalry unit, the Miriam of Exodus had she watched her own children being killed—such a Miriam would be quite capable of wishing payment in kind upon Babylon, and expressing so horrid a wish in excellent poetry. Le Guin's Miriam has let go of hatred and fear, we are told (*CR* 154), and anyone who knows the psalm should feel grateful.

What should we bring from Old Earth to New Zion? Our feuds we would do well to leave behind, but what should we take care to remember? The people of the Twenty Settlements, we're assured, 'remembered the words civilisation, humanity. They remembered Jerusalem' (*CR* 157). And here, I think, we have another reason for Jews in Le Guin's new world, New Zion: Jews as one of the bearer peoples of 'civilisation,' one of the peoples of Jerusalem—Jerusalem the golden, the bloody, the fought over: along with Athens and Rome one of the great, complex, contradictory embodiments in the West of 'the City as goal and dream' (Introd. *CI, LoN* [1979]: 147).

In 'The Eye Altering,' Le Guin strikes an exquisite balance between memory and necessary change, and favors a gentle transition from old to new, one not forced, one going with the Way of things, one mediated by art and the perception of beauty. What Miriam has left is the beauty of Old Earth; she must learn to see the potential for beauty in New Zion. The change-bringer is Genya, 'Auntie Doctor's' kid, and also 'A native. A feeble and unpromising native' (155), and with all the connotations of *native*, an appropriate cast-away stone to be the 'the chief corner stone' of the new world building on New Zion (Psalm 118.22, quoted Matthew 21.42).

Genya's picture gets Miriam and maybe others to *see* her world, as Genly Ai finally sees Estraven in his epiphany on the Ice in *Left Hand of Darkness* (248; ch. 18), as Shevek has his 'vision both clear and whole' in *The Dispossessed* (225; ch. 9). And this vision of the beauty of her very *mundane* world—the mudscape—correlates with Miriam's insight that Genya can live and reproduce, and that he and Rachel and the other sicklies can fit into the pattern of New Zion and produce a living human presence.

As in *Planet of Exile*, we get a classic comic-romance ending, with a new and better world coalescing around a fertile central couple, here, Genya and Rachel, bringing together two kinds of humans. But *Planet of Exile* was 1966, and 'The Eye Altering' was a decade later. Rachel is the pretty one among the Mothers of Israel, the younger sister, the desirable one (Genesis 29.16-18), and Rachel doesn't even appear in 'The Eye Altering.' In *Planet of Exile*, Rolery is a featured point-of-view character; in 'The Eye Altering,' the point of view goes to Miriam, the older woman, the mother-figure, not the wife. In *Planet of Exile*, the world is interesting and beautiful (after its fashion) to even an unaltered eye. In 'The Altered Eye,' one must come, as in *Eye of the Heron* and the later work, to see the beauty in mud.

'Newton's Sleep' (1991)

> ...psychoanalysis is unlikely to be adequate for the interpretation of identity problems in rural Haiti, while some sort of Voudun [= Voodoo] psychology might supply interpretative schemes with a high degree of empirical accuracy. The two psychologies demonstrate their empirical adequacy by the applicability in therapy, but neither thereby demonstrates the ontological status of its categories. Neither the Voudun gods nor libidinal energies may exist outside the world defined in the respective social contexts. But in these contexts they do exist by virtue of social definition and are internalized as realities in he course of socialization. Rural Haitians *are* possessed and New York intellectuals *are* neurotic. Possession and neurosis are thus constituents of both objective and subjective reality *in these contexts*....
> —Berger and Luckman,
> *The Social Construction of Reality* 177

Readers and authors are collaborators in constructing the meaning of a text (to repeat an assumption of *Coyote*), and what those readers bring to the text is important: meanings are conditioned by contexts. Obviously, I want to put 'Newton's Sleep' in the context of 'The Eye Altering,' but I'd like the reader to bring to 'Newton's Sleep' at least five other works.[593]

---

[593] I'll mention more. Please note: In most cases, Le Guin undoubtedly knows the works I mention. In some cases she may not; in some cases, the works I mention by others may be irrelevant for her writing her works. I mention them as context for *reading*, for readers' work in constructing the meaning of the texts. In old

One of the works Le Guin quotes in the title: William Blake's verses, 'With happiness stretch'd across the hills' from his letter to Thomas Butts (Blake 816-19); the other three are Joanna Russ's 'The Man Who Could Not See Devils' (1970), and Le Guin's *Eye of the Heron*, *The Lathe of Heaven*, and 'Buffalo Gals, Won't Your Come Out Tonight.'

Whether or not Le Guin knew or recalled 'The Man Who Could Not See Devils,' it is useful for a reader to put this work in dialog with 'Newton's Sleep,' or to see it as a kind of pre-existent mirror image. The protagonist-narrator of 'The Man Who...' lives in a world in which people have a Dark-Side Blakean vision: as part of their normal perceptions, they can see devils, plus 'Incubi, succubi, fiends, demons, werewolves, evil creatures of all sorts.' They see angels as well, but they are puritanical people who don't see good in the world very often. The protagonist-narrator is the hero of the story. He is a mutant, perceptionally disadvantaged in terms of his world: he cannot see devils (etc.), and, perhaps, they cannot see him (*Those Who Can* 137 [and passim]). To make Russ's short story even shorter, the hero escapes his narrow, religiously zealous, rural, parochial homelife to a city, where he ends the story about to take up a new life, thinking about the strangeness of a world in which people concern themselves with magic and all and do not 'investigate the really compelling questions,' what we'd call empirical or scientific questions. The story closes with the hero drifting off to sleep.

> I remembered my nurse, when I was little, asking me whether when the sun rose I did not see a great company of the heavenly host all crying Holy Holy Holy and I had said no, I saw only a round, red disk about the size of a penny coin.[594] And then I wondered...whether it might not be an advantage not to see demons and angels, and if it was, whether my children might not inherit the trait and pass it on to their children; and perhaps eventually...everyone would be like me, and if you asked people about the afreets, the succubi,...the angels and the fiends...they would say *Those creatures? Oh, they're just legends; they don't exist....* (*Those Who Can* 148)

I'd like to suggest here an image of a kind of Left-footed Hacky Sack: Blake to Russ to Le Guin (all good Leftists), on the subject of clerics, orthodoxy, reason, vision, and dirt. All oppose clerics and orthodoxy, so it can be a friendly game. Blake, at least in the 'Holy, Holy, Holy' passage, doesn't have much use for experiment or 'the outward Creation' or for 'the

---

technical terms, I'm not doing a source study but looking at sources, analogs, homologs, and cognates; in old-fashioned pedagogical terms, I'm looking for comparisons and contrasts.

[594] See above, this chapter, my headnote from Blake. For the triple 'Holy,' see Isaiah 6.3, quoted in Revelation 4.8.

Dirt upon my feet.' Russ's hero sees a desacralized world, but he does *see* his world and cares for it enough to want to study it. His mind isn't on the dirt but on the sun and moon and abstract knowledge—but that, in his world, is progress. It is also, in my tentatively teleological view, progress beyond Blake in the passage I quote as a headnote. Blake is in a high Idealist mode in talking about the Vision of the Last Judgment, and Le Guin seems to prefer scientists who work in and with the world, and who are willing to get their hands dirty: if not Russ's proto-astronomer, then biologists who can perceive beauty in a rat running a maze, or work *with* pear trees to produce a better pear (*ACH* 273-75). In this context, Le Guin's job can be seen as incorporating a vision that can behold—really *see*—the wonder in dirt.

* * * * * * *

For background for Isaac Rose of 'Newton's Sleep,' I would like to consider Dr. William Haber from Le Guin's *The Lathe of Heaven* (1971) and Lev Shults in *The Eye of the Heron* (1978), as prime examples, for both good and ill, of the results of the ideals of 'the Judaeo-Christian-Rationalist West' (*LoH* 82; ch. 6). Haber in *The Lathe of Heaven* (1971) is a benevolent man, but finally a villain who separates himself from the world, would control the world, and nearly destroys his world.[595] Lev in *Eye of the Heron* (1978) is, on the other hand, a traditional Leftist hero: one of the most admirable of political activists, descended, philosophically, from Russ's unnamed rationalist hero and from such martyrs as Martin Luther King, Jr., and the Mahatma Gandhi (*EoH* 51-52; ch. 4). Lev is an idealist, and, that far, a rationalist. Lev loves and is loved by, but is contrasted with, the female lead, Luz, who accepts risks but rejects abstract ideals and rejects sacrifice (115; ch. 8). Luz is right in the world of *Eye*; Lev is wrong, but if anyone «deserves» the Odonian principle, 'No man earns punishment' it would be young Lev, getting himself murdered trying hard to do right (see *TD* 288; ch. 12).

Lev's problem is one of vision; he sees too clearly, too cleanly, too rationally—too much in terms of a theory, however good and true and beautiful that theory is. Both 'Eye Altering' and 'Buffalo Gals' insist on the importance of seeing the world, really seeing it, and the transformative power of such a vision.[596] Both stories insist on the necessity of seeing with the eye(s) of a child (Myra in 'Buffalo Gals') or with the eye of an artist native to his place: one who can still see the 'splendor in the grass' and 'glory in the flower'—and not hear in those phrases merely clichés or

---

[595] See below on Dalzul and a human individual's inability to destroy *the* world.
[596] See also my discussion of 'Field of Vision' (1973): where Percy Bysshe Shelley replaces Blake as the inspiring Critical Romantic, but the same point is made about the importance of seeing not God or anything else Beyond, but the mundane world (*WTQ* 222 f.).

literary allusions.[597] In 'Eye Altering,' Genya teaches Miriam and maybe others the beauty of their world, fitting them to live on and *in* their new world. Myra ends 'Buffalo Gals' with a human eye and one of pine pitch. Looking just through her new, pine pitch eye, we may infer, she sees a yellow blur. We're told explicitly the other two options: looking with just her human eye 'everything was clear and flat; if she used them both, things were blurry and yellowish, but deep' (*BG* 26; § ii).

Le Guin's fictional Jews and Leftists, I think, are people who can produce humanist intellectuals who 'remembered the words civilisation, humanity. They remembered Jerusalem' (*CR* 157), including Jerusalem in the sense of the City as ideal, but not necessarily a home. And this is not a bad thing. The 1991 story 'Newton's Sleep,' though, is in a series of works from *The Lathe of Heaven* (1971) through 'The New Atlantis' (1975) and 'Buffalo Gals' (1987) showing the limitations and/or dangers of a single-eyed, nonspiritual view that sees little else except civilization, humanity, the City on the Hill and other ideals. Lev of *Eye of the Heron* (1978), is best of breed of Le Guin's heroes until Commander Dalzul of 'Dancing to Ganam' (1993), but even as best of breed, in an evil world such a (male) hero brings death.[598]

In 'Newton's Sleep,' we get Le Guin's standard third-person limited narration, but with cinematic precision: with the camera usually focused, so to speak, on Isaac ('Ike') Rose, Susan, or Esther Rose: father, mother, and eldest child in the Rose family, keeping them center screen or showing shots from their points of view. The most general setting is our Earth and the surrounding space in the second quarter or so of the twenty-first century, with all the immediate action taking place in the Spes Colony: i.e., a colony established by the Special Earth Satellite Society, at a gravitational balance point between Earth and the Moon (the 'L5' Lagrangian point is a likely spot).

The 'back story' is suggested on the first page and filled in with some hints here and there in the rest of 'Newton's Sleep.' Basically, the political/environmental overplot is Le Guin's usual—and uncomfortably plausible—future history for the turn of the millennium and the first part of the twenty-first century of serious environmental degradation. In 'Newton's Sleep,' the major results of (hu)mankind's rape of Gaia are famine and plagues, mainly 'the fungal plague' ([23]) 'slow-rad' death (radiation sickness? [35]) and a series of mutated retro-viruses—plus a breakdown in social order. The situation, and Isaac Rose's response to it, is illustrated, summarized, and perhaps epitomized, with the death of Ike's mother, recalled some four pages into the story. Ike's mother, Sarah Rose, will not

---

[597] Wordsworth, 'Ode: Intimations of Immortality' line 179; § 10 (*Norton Anthology* 217).
[598] For Commander Dalzul see *FIS* [107]-45, esp. 109, for Dalzul as hero; and see below in this chapter. For Le Guin on heroes and their problems—often for other people—see *DEW*, esp. the essays on literature: 'The Carrier Bag Theory of Fiction,' 'Heroes,' 'Conflict,' 'World-Making' (for Conquistadores).

go with the rest of the family to the Spes Colony and 'Live in that awful little thing, that ball bearing going around in nothing'; she stays on Earth. 'She died of RMV-3 less than three years later,' and Ike did not attend the funeral. More important, he does not go to see her while his mother is dying. He was on the way to the Colony. Ike 'had already been decontaminated; to leave Bakersfield Dome would mean going through decontamination again,' an unpleasant process, 'as well as exposing himself to infection by this newest and worst form of the rapidly mutating virus which had accounted so far for about two billion human deaths, more than the slowrad syndrome and almost as much as famine.' After not attending the funeral, Ike loses contact with his sister on Earth, either because of technological problems or because she never forgives him. 'It was an old ache now. They'—Ike and his wife Susan—'had chosen. They had sacrificed' (26): family, roots, life in the world. Sacrifice is problematic in much of Le Guin's work, but the Roses are hardly to be blamed for their choice. The villains in 'Newton's Sleep' are those who created the world in which sacrificing living on Earth for life on an artificial satellite is a relatively attractive option; i.e., among others, the villains are us, the generation(s) reading the story. Isaac and Susan Rose and their children had 'been spared,' Ike thinks, passed over to get to safety.[599]

The agent of their salvation is the SPES society and David Henry Maston, 'the 'Father of Spes,'' and a relatively admirable fan of Tom Godwin's 1954 story (and strongly 1950s story), 'The Cold Equations.'[600] 'Cold Equations' is a kind of lifeboat story: an emergency rescue ship with limited fuel is the setting; the rescue ship's pilot finds a stowaway whose added mass means that his ship has insufficient fuel to complete the mission, meaning the deaths of those he is to rescue, himself, and the stowaway. Regulations call for him to «space» the stowaway immediately; but the stowaway is a 'girl'—young woman, actually—and the plot moves toward the acceptance by all involved of 'the cold equations,' where the woman dies willingly. Maston gives the moral of 'The Cold Equations' story as 'No dead weight on board!' which is probably not what Godwin intended. That Maston so oversimplifies a somewhat complex story says much for the limits of his critical abilities as a reader of literature. That Le Guin has him find this moral says much for her abilities not only as crafter of elegant stories but also as a literary critic. Some crucial 'cold equations' that Godwin skips over in a few words are commercial equations, from human corporate culture, not The Laws of Nature; and 'No dead weight on board!' is indeed a central *implicit* moral to Godwin's story.[601] Anyway,

---

[599] Cf. and definitely contrast the Passover narrated in Exodus 7.16-12.13.

[600] Note for the name David Henry Maston that Henry David Thoreau wrote *Walden* (1854), a call for a simple life of relative self-sufficiency (except, if the rumor in academic folklore is true, Thoreau had his mother do his laundry while he stayed at Walden Pond).

[601] See in *TD* Shevek's chiding a fellow physicist for talking about 'the politics of reality'—i.e., a power struggle—and elaborating on the phrase by saying 'The

for Maston, 'no dead weight' means multiple 'excellence' for all on board, even if that meant, by the Colony's criteria for excellence, 'the lack of African-ancestry colonists.' On the other hand, in judging Maston, Le Guin allows that he is consistent enough to apply 'the cold equations to himself' and rejects the 'sentimental' gesture that would have him aboard, an old man taking up a place that could be filled by 'a working scientist' or a young genius or, in a significant phrase, 'a breeding woman.' So Maston disappears from the story, except for a reference from the point of view of Ike Rose that Maston gives advice from Indianapolis that is 'always masterful, imperative, though sometimes, these days, a bit off the mark' (35-36). Maston cannot follow, but he has pointed his people to safety.

Safety is the Colony, and it is important for readers to know that Le Guin did not need to make up men like D. H. Maston nor SPES. As a refuge in a dying world, SPES is a literalization of the lifeboat metaphor in Garrett Hardin's conceit of 'Lifeboat Ethics' (1975 f.): the idea that, in an overpopulated, overexploited world, those who have food and other resources should hoard them in their metaphorical overcrowded lifeboat—play the folklore role of Holdfast—fighting off those who might force their way on or try to get the well-off to share.[602] And imagining space habitats for humans has been a fictional exercise since at least Robert A. Heinlein's 'Universe' (1941)—and for perhaps a decade before 'Newton's Sleep,' planning real human habitats for Lagrangian points, primarily L5, had become a very earnest exercise.[603]

The space Colony and the idea of literally transcending the world to get to safety will be very important for the thematic significance of 'Newton's Sleep.'

* * * * * * *

The plot of 'Newton's Sleep' is rich in incident, and therein lies a lesson for authors of SF: If you want "'thick' description' (*FIS* 88), in a literary sense, people your stories with families; there will be a *lot* going on in

---

politician and the physicist both deal with things as they are, with real forces, the basic laws of the world.' Shevek can't see "'laws' to protect wealth' and the "forces' of guns and bombs' as having the same reality as 'the law of entropy and the force of gravity' (*TD* 164; ch. 7).

[602] For Holdfast as the mythical, not just folklore, father-tyrant and 'monster of the status quo,' who keeps the past, and, centrally, *keeps*, see Campbell 337 (2.3.3) & passim (see Campbell's Index).

[603] A World Wide Web, search for 'L5,' yielded substantial files for 'The Foundation Society' and HAL5, the very real Huntsville Alabama L5 Society. At least as of this writing, 'A Tour of the Colony' can be downloaded from
    www.nas.nasa.gov/NAS/SpaceSettlement/75SummerStudychpt5.html#HAB
—where '.gov' indicates a governmental location on the net, and NASA is the US National Aeronautics and Space Administration. See also Gary Westfahl's *Islands in the Sky*, a book originating in a desire to use SF space station to infer practical lessons for the design of Space Station Freedom (11-12).

families, especially if those families are both enmeshed in the politics of their world and conscious actors in or observers of those politics. The plot begins in the monitor center of the Colony, with Ike and two of his three children (Esther, fifteen, and Noah, eleven [the youngest is Jason]) watching the destruction of the Bakersfield Dome, the departure port for the Colony, by the 'hordes' of one Ramirez. 'A hairbreadth escape,' is Noah's response, setting up the motif of escapes and alerting us to literary allusions: Noah reads a lot, we're told, and 'discovered each literary cliché for himself and used it with solemn pleasure.' The monitors occasion a paragraph on sight: Esther has vision problems that, for now, can only be corrected by eyeglasses, 'like some slum kid,' but in the zero-pollution environment of the Colony, she might lose her allergy problems and be able to accept eye transplants and get 20/20 vision (and maybe blue eyes). We learn Ike's motive for wanting his family to watch the latest horror on Earth's surface: 'Some of the women and children on Spes were inclined to be sentimental, 'homesick'' and Ike wants them to see 'what earth was and why they left it' (*FIS* 24).[604]

During this scene in 'Newton's Sleep,' or at about that time, Esther asks why it was that 'everybody' is not off Earth and on Spes. Her mother answers 'Money,' and her father gives a speech about how few people are willing to trust reason, plan, and wait years. 'How many people can stick to a straight course in a disintegrating world?' And, of course, it is reason that, compass-like, keeps them going straight (25). Ike Rose is very much a straight-thinker: into linear thought and planning and proud of it, a 'hard-facts' man like Charles Dickens's utilitarian Gradgrind in *Hard Times* (1854), or, more charitably, like B. F. Skinner's character Frazier, the key founder of Walden Two (*Walden Two* 167; ch. 20). All in all, sensible Susan is more right than elitist, rationalist Ike; *money*, having it or lacking it, is the main reason people are or are not able to escape the decline of human culture on Earth.

The conversation in the monitor center leads to further significant information about Ike, including that he does not like the monitors and doesn't like to 'look down,' seeing the view of Earth as 'a tie, an umbilicus.'[605] He wants to 'start fresh. Absolutely clean and clear' (27). This bit of exposition leads in turn to our learning that Ike leads the Environmental Design group for 'the second Spes ship,' and that a colleague, Al Levaitis, suggested that there be no landscapes: no illusions, no dishonesty, form strictly following function in what I'll call good Modernist, Bauhaus fashion (27-28). Ike would like that, he thinks: 'It would—simplify'; Susan is less sure, fearing 'oversimplifying.' Right after the discussion of spacecraft interior design, Ike says that the worst thing about Earth was weather,

---

[604] In this ploy, Ike is like the Managers and Planners in B. F. Skinner's *Walden Two* (a safe haven rather like Spes Colony): 'Of course our children know about the outside world!', a doubter is told at Walden Two. 'We simply make sure they know the whole truth! Nothing more is needed' (*Walden Two* 206; ch. 24).
[605] See below on figurative umbilical cord in 'Another Story' (*FIS* 173).

and states his happiness at getting 'free of that stupid, impossible unpredictability' (28). Weather systems are literally chaotic, and Ike cannot stand such unmanageable disorder. Ike stops looking at the monitor to look over the illusion of New England in his family's part of the Colony, 'and saw that true shelter that lay behind it, holding them safe, safe and free, in haven. The truth shall make you free, he thought,' and he puts his arm around his wife and says that. She hugs him back and says, 'You're a dear'—which Ike sees as 'reducing the great statement to the merely personal,' which still 'rather pleases him' (29).

The next incident is a school curriculum meeting attended by Ike, Susan, and Esther. The direct issue of discussion is whether or not to continue teaching geology. Ike recognizes that the «real» issue wasn't geology in the curriculum, but the clout of three men on the Education Committee. 'The discourse concerned power, and the teachers didn't understand it; few women did.' Ike sees what is going on, but goes with the flow of the meeting, not confronting the men on their play for trivial power. In this untroubled acceptance of a power struggle as part of 'the politics of reality' (quoting *TD* 164), Ike makes a familiar mistake, and we should not be too surprised when Ike has an unpleasant surprise: Mo Orenstein went 'off into a story of how his chemistry class had learned to identify a whole series of reactions by cooking a pebble, which he had brought from Mount Sinai as a souvenir and as a lab specimen' and John Kelly interrupts abruptly with 'All right! The subject's geology, not ethnicity!' (30). Ike understands ape-descended males jostling for status in a space cave, but John Kelly's interruption he does not understand. He mentions to Esther that Orenstein 'seems to get under John Kelly's hide,' to which Esther replies 'Oh, *shit*, Daddy,' and when Ike tries to get her to explain what she means, she just repeats 'Oh, *shit*, Daddy!' Finally Susan explains to him that Timmy Kelly, the son of John and Pat Kelly, calls Ike 'Kike Rose' and calls Esther 'Kikey Rose,' to which Ike replies 'Oh—shit.' And Susan says, 'Exactly' (30-31). Mo Orenstein and his story annoy John Kelly because John Kelly is an antiJewish bigot.

Ike thinks people may have to put up with bigotry on Earth but not among the intellectual elite in the Spes Colony. Susan tells him something he has missed: 'Ike, Spes people are very conventional, conservative people,' into 'Power hierarchy, division of labor by gender, Cartesian values, totally mid-twentieth century!' She is not complaining; she chose safety, 'But you pay for safety.' Ike doesn't understand her 'attitude' toward the Spes colonists and argues that 'We risked everything for Spes—because we're future-oriented. These are the people who chose to leave the past behind, to start fresh. To form a true human community and to do it right, to do it right, for once! These people are innovators, intellectually courageous, not a bunch of gutbrains sunk in their bigotries' (32-33). Bigotry, however, had made it into a Colony that had kept out even viruses. Indeed, we learn later that antiJewish bigotry may have been around from the beginning: Ike can count only seventeen Jews among a Colony of 800 (for 2.1% [34]). Their discussion ends with Ike and Susan entering their unit, and, significantly, is followed by Noah's mentioning 'this burned woman' seen by two girls (33). This sighting by children—with the eyes of children, reported by children—is either the inciting action or turning point in the overplot of the story (33-34).

In terms of the Rose family, the major incident in the plot is also associated with the burned woman. There is a white space, and the primary point of view changes to Esther and her asking two twelve-year old girls about what they claim to have seen. In a paragraph of great technical mastery, Le Guin's Narrator introduces Linda Jones and Treese Gerlack and gives us a glimpse through their eyes of Esther. They are 'partly shy' in her presence, 'partly rude': 'because even if she was sixteen, she was really gutwrenching-looking with those glass things she wore'—Esther's glasses—'and Timmy Kelly called her Kikey, and Timmy Kelly was so incredibly gorge.' These are not *nice* little girls; still, at least Treese is happy for the attention of an older girl, and the two tell her their story.[606] They have seen what appears to be a burned woman who looks like a famine victim from what they think might have been Africa. The girls have a fairly implausible guess about the woman, and Esther rejects it, but allows that they aren't stupid—Colony IQ is high—but they've never lived outside the Colony (*FIS* 36-37). Esther had lived on Earth, and she remembers. Primarily she remembers Saviora, a Black girl who was Esther's best friend back in their apartment building in Philadelphia.[607] In a flashback, Esther remembers 'cockroaches, rain, pollution alerts,' but her strongest memory is of a lost friend. The memory of the City of (here) Sisterly Love and of Saviora allows Esther to conclude that 'maybe this burned woman was a black woman' (37).

Esther doubts there could be a stowaway and thinks 'It's just kids' playing ghost-story games, using images from old video records of the famines, a return of (repressed?) images of 'black faces, grinning with famine, when all the faces in your whole world were soft and white and fat.' And then Esther pronounces a thematically significant line: "The Sleep of Reason engenders monster,' Esther Rose said aloud,' from an engraving she had seen, with difficulty, in the Colony's Monuments of Western Art file. 'Goya, it was. The bat things coming out of the man's head while he slept at a table full of books, and down below were the words that meant 'The Sleep of Reason engenders monsters' in English, the only language she would ever know. Roaches, rain, Spanish, all washed away'—

---

[606] Cf. and contrast the two nasty little boys who throw stones at Tenar and Therru (*Tehanu* 122; 'Finding Words,' ch. 9).

[607] So long as we exclude anything supernatural, we might accept the 'a' as a feminizing ending in 'Saviora' and read Saviora as female Savior for Esther. (See though 'Pathways of Desire,' *CR* 183).

except for the memories and skills in the AI (38), except for human memory.[608]

And here Esther decides she has *got* to leave home and live in a dorm. 'The dorm couldn't be worse than home. Their incredible family...The womb within the womb!' of the Colony. Esther gets home, faces her mother 'heroically,' and makes her announcement about the dorm—and is greeted by silence until she moves close enough to see that her mother is crying. The tears are not from Esther's announcement but from news of the death of Eddie, Susan Rose's half brother. Eddie and Susan had been close and 'kept in touch.' 'He was my family,' Susan tells Esther, and Esther thinks—or the Narrator just tells us—'Maybe the word,' *family*, 'did mean something' (39). Contrary to Esther's fears, her mother thinks it will be fine if she moves into the dorm, and Ike Rose agrees, but with a condition. With only the slightest bit of emotional blackmail, he tells her, 'First get your eyes—then fly.' Esther may not want the eye transplant, but Ike sees it as the choice dictated by reason, and he's sure his daughter will 'make the reasonable choice' (40-41). In this beautiful little sketch Ike Rose is ever so reasonable and rational, but he *will* get his way on the important issue of the eye operation for Esther. Or on any other issue. If Esther wants a pleasant, nonconfrontational exit to the Colony dorms, she'll get the eye transplants. Ike tends to drive his daughter to rage: as Esther tells Susan, 'It's when he gets so, you know, like he has to control everything or everything will be out of control, I get sort of out of control' (40).

As Esther is prepared for the operation—a time-consuming and painful process—more and more people see 'the Hag,' an Asian-looking woman supplementing or supplanting the burned woman (41). The operation is not successful, and correlating with this failure is what Ike sees as the 'mass hysteria phenomena' of hag sightings, plus Susan's anger at the operation for Esther (43). Ike is heading for a low point.

Fairly soon, just about everyone in the Colony has seen strange people (43-44). 'Newton's Sleep' seems to be literalizing the Freudian slogan of 'the return of the repressed': that which has been excluded from the culture and world of the Spes Colony is returning, starting with people, and among the people starting with the burned Black woman and then an Asian-looking Hag.[609] Ike insists that what is going on is 'A group delusion,' but this is denied by Larane Gutierrez, a shop assistant, who tells him that 'nobody is hysterical. These people are here. * * * The people from earth.' Ike sees and hears her as shrill and aggressive. 'These people are here, Ike. And there's more of them all the time,' a thought Rod Bond

---

[608] See Le Guin's Introd., *FIS* 10. The injunction, 'You shall remember' is a motif in Hebrew Scriptures, which is bad insofar as memory is necessary for revenge, but good in other contexts.
[609] For apparitions on a space craft, cf. and contrast the visions from a mystic world-ocean in S. Lem's *Solaris* and the more cybernetically generated images in Gawron 's *Dream of Glass*.

agrees with. Ike responds to Larane with the challenge, 'And whatever you see is real, of course, even if I don't see it?' She responds, 'I don't know what you see.... I don't know what's real. I know that they're here.' She adds that the people she saw yesterday 'looked like they were from some really primitive culture, they had on animal skins, but they were actually kind of beautiful, the people I mean. Well fed and very alert-looking, watchful. I had the feeling for the first time they might be seeing us....' (*FIS* 45).

This is not the world of 'The Man Who Could Not See Devils' (1970), and the perception-impaired rationalist in this story turns out to be a sexist and an exponent of scientific original sin: the denial of data (46). Soon, Noah Rose is watching goldfish come out of the tap at the washstand, and Helena, the woman moving into leadership of the Emergency Committee for the Colony is suggesting 'ghosts' for as good a way as any to refer to the Colony's 'guests'—and suggests inviting them to join the regular Colonists at a Committee meeting.[610] Helena tells Ike the Colonists must learn 'how to coexist with ghosts'; it is something they *must* do. 'They are not going away. They are here, and what "here" is is changing too.' As Coyote told Myra, where the 'first people' are *is* 'here' (*BG* 32 § 2), and it looks like the 'first people' are (re)taking SPES. Ike replies with the quotation, 'Whom the gods would destroy they first drive mad' (47) and exits the meeting to find people in the corridors running after bison. 'Ike walked straight ahead, looking straight ahead' (48), providing his own «objective correlative» for his linear thinking and tunnel vision.

Soon, possibly the next morning, Susan tells Ike that there is 'a vine growing by the front door.' Ike notes, rationally, that vines 'grow in dirt. Earth. There is no earth in Spes.' Noah suggests, 'It's going backwards,' from people—'weird old women and cripples and things'—then «lower» animals, 'and now plants and stuff,' including whales in the Reservoirs and 'horses on the Common.' Ike didn't see horses, and he begins to cry (48). Susan stands silent and thinks for a while and then admits to Ike she's a little scared,

> It seems like something supernatural, and I don't think there is anything supernatural. But if I don't think about it in words like that, if I just look at it, look at the people and the—the horses and the vine by the door—it makes sense. How did we, how could we have thought we could just leave? Who do we think we are? All it is, is we brought ourselves with us.... The horses and the whales and the old women and the sick babies. They're just us, we're them, they're here.

---

[610] In addition to the Blake poetry I quote below in this chapter, see for ghosts Le Guin's *CI* (1967), *WWF* (1972), 'Solitude,' 'The Matter of Seggri' (1994).

The Spes colonists have moved into Coyote's world, or Coyote's world has moved in on them. We civilized, rationalist, Cartesian humans are embedded in reality, too, and where we are they are. Ike still doesn't believe; he refuses to 'Go with the flow' (49)—to «yield to the Dao, accept what *is*». His son plays tag football and gets dirt on his clothes; 'but Ike walked on plastic grass through dustless, germless air.' He walks through the trees—literally—straight to the hospital to see Esther. But Esther isn't there. She's gone with Saviora from Philadelphia to stay *'up in the mountains for a while,'* possibly with her physical vision restored, possibly not (50).

The conclusion of the story has Ike walking along one of the rational ways of Spes, where 'All corridors led to known places' and one could go anywhere and 'never get lost and always end up safe where you started from. And you would never stumble....' Ike stumbles on a rock. An impossible rock that could not be there. He calls out, 'Esther, I can't see. Show me how to see!' And he gets no answer from Esther. Instead he hears his mother's voice asking him, 'rather sharply'—'Isaac, dear, are you awake?' Ike does not continue straight forward but literally and symbolically turns and sees his mother 'sitting beside Esther on an outcropping of granite beside the steep, dusty trail. Behind them, across a great dropping gulf of air, snow peaks shone in the high, clear light. Esther looked at him. Her eyes were clear also, but dark'—i.e., not blue in the Rose-family fashion? unseeing, physically?—and she said, 'Now we can go down'' (51). And here the story ends.

Further Comments

The phrase 'Newton's sleep' comes at the end of the verses William Blake appended to his letter to Thomas Butts of 22 Nov. 1802.[611] The poem deals with a very general personal problem: 'Must the duties of life each other cross?' (line 43), with our obligation to one friend working against our obligations to another, our love of spouse possibly conflicting with love of sibling (lines 49-51). The problem is not resolved in the poem, but it is sandwiched between a vision and a re-vision, with prayer. The vision is of a world, 'With happiness strech'd across the hills' (line 1), and with Angels, God, and Demons about—plus family ghosts (lines 10-12). The 'I' of the poem sees his father, Brother Robert, and 'Brother John the evil one,' although 'dead, they appear upon my path' (lines 14-17). The Speaker sees the everyday world, and a good deal more,

> A frowning Thistle implores my stay.
> What to others a trifle appears
> Fills me full of smiles or tears;
> For double the vision my Eyes do see,
> And a double vision is always with me.

---

[611] For the Blake quotations, see Le Guin's Introd., *FIS* 10.

> With my inward Eye 'tis an old Man grey;
> With my outward, a Thistle across my way.
> (lines 24-30)

By the end of the poem, the Speaker has 'a fourfold vision,' but drops back to three, 'And twofold,' at least, 'always. / May God us keep / From Single vision & Newton's sleep!' (lines 87-88).

I suggested earlier—very tentatively—a series from Blake to Russ to Le Guin, but the series can be extended backwards and forwards, and in places not so tentatively.

Blake and the Romantics more generally were reacting against the Enlightenment: René Descartes (1596-1650) and Sir Isaac Newton (1642-1727) and a mechanical universe that could be analyzed with elegant simplicity through Cartesian philosophy and analytic geometry and Newtonian calculus and physics.[612] From my point of view, starting my professional life as a student of the English Renaissance generally and Shakespeare most particularly, the philosophes and the Romantics embody a far older conflict between what seem like a perennial opposition of personality types. 'Newton's Sleep' is Le Guin's contribution to this debate as a 'Critical Romantic' (to repeat Roland Duerksen's instructive phrase). It is, as she says, 'a cautionary tale' responding 'to many stories and novels' she has 'read over the years' that 'consciously or not' seem to 'depict people in spaceships and space stations as superior to those on earth' (Introd., *FIS* 10). This cautionary tale, is also a useful reminder to the 'L5' enthusiasts that in some areas they are a whole lot less cutting edge than they may think. Spes colonists are, in their rationalist way, 'very conservative, conventional people,' very 'Cartesian' in values and 'totally mid-twentieth century!' (32).

'Newton's Sleep' features another set of Le Guin's exiles (*FIS* 11) and continues Le Guin's Critical-Romantic, anarchist, Daoist critique of rationalist utopias, a central theme in *The Lathe of Heaven*, *The Left Hand of Darkness*, and among the Terrans in *The Word for World Is Forest*: Dr. Haber, the Orgota, and Captain Davidson are all, after their fashion, utopians.[613] An advantage of 'Newton's Sleep' over *Lathe of Heaven* and *Word for World* is that Ike Rose is both more normal and normative than Haber or Davidson. Indeed, Le Guin can see Ike as 'a tragic character, an admirable overreacher' (Introd., *FIS* 11), not a loner with megalomania but a family man with more everyday faults. In Le Guin's formulation, he is 'a worried, troubled man: a truly rational man who denies the existence of the irrational, which is to say, a true believer who can't see how and why the true belief isn't working' (Introd. 10-11). He wants safety (as does his wife), simplicity, neatness, and Reason. These are not bad things in themselves. The problems come in when he combines such desires and tastes

---

[612] Note also Euclid: see Le Guin's essay, 'A Non-Euclidean View of California...' (esp. *DEW* 86-88).
[613] See 'A Non-Euclidean View,' *DEW* 86-89.

with a desperate *need* for control. In this he is indeed in the tradition of Christopher Marlowe's arguably tragic overreachers, especially Doctor Faustus, but more in the tradition of Euripides's Pentheus in *The Bacchae* (after 406 BCE). In Euripides's play, the rationalist Pentheus, who rejects any data that go against his theories and prejudices and royal power, will not accept Dionysos as God of nature and is torn apart when Dionysos possesses him and drives him mad. 'Whom the gods will destroy they first drive mad' is one classic «sentence» Le Guin has Ike quote (*FIS* 47). He might have done well to keep in mind another Latin sentence and the explicit lesson of *The Bacchae*: Those who will not follow nature or fortune are dragged along; rationalists who deny the power of the unconscious and of Nature themselves risk madness, or are mad, and may find themselves destroyed by that which they have denied.

As an inheritor of the 'Judaeo-Christian-Rationalist' Western tradition (*LoH* 82; ch. 6), Ike Rose wants to transcend everyday immanence—and clutter, dirt, and complexity—and rationally look down at the world and manage a simplified world efficiently and neatly. Except he is in a space craft that literally does transcend the Earth, literalizing an important metaphor—and he doesn't like looking down. Ike will build his utopia in the clean, isolated, ecologically impoverished world of Spes. '*To be whole is to be part; true journey is return*' (*TD* 68; ch. 3), and Spes Colony is trying to be not a part: to leave and leave behind the ills of Earth. That which they would repress and leave—the people they have oppressed, the plants and soil they have tried to dominate—*those* return to Spes. If people are embedded in what really *is*, our choice is to be part humanly consciously, or to have our embeddedness forced upon us.

Ike Rose is not dragged to destruction but only bent and a little bruised. Miriam in 'The Eye Altering' knows enough on her own to let her surrogate child Genya help her learn to see. Ike needs to be knocked around a bit before he will call for aid, almost at the end of the story, from his literal child Esther: 'Esther, I can't see. Show me how to see!' Finally, at the very end of the story. we learn that even Ike Rose can return to being Isaac, son of Sarah Rose (26), and awake from Newton's sleep (51).[614]

'The Kerastion' (1990)

> He who clings to his work will create nothing that endures. If you want to accord with the Dao, just do your job, then let go. (*Tao te Ching* 24 in Mitchell trans. [1989: tape I.2])[615]

---

[614] Isaac Rose's father is not present or alluded to in the story. For Isaac as son of Sarah, see Genesis 18.9-15, 21.1-7.
[615] Mitchell's poetic rendition differs significantly from other translations I have consulted, and I do not suggest it or *Tao te Ching* ch. 24 as a source for Le Guin's 'Kerastion': 'a workshop story' (*FIS* 10) produced at about the same time as Mitchell's work. Note also Wilhelm/Ostwald trans. of *Tao te Ching* 52 on 'the

A kerastion, Le Guin tells us in her introduction to *A Fisherman of the Inland Sea*, is 'a musical instrument that cannot be heard' (10, [69]). The story of 'The Kerastion' is told in third-person, limited omniscience from the point of view of Chumo, a tanner in a culture whose technological level is low by contemporary American standards but whose level of technique and respect for craft is very high. The story begins almost at the very end of things with Chumo 'waiting for the funeral procession of her bother, who had broken the law and betrayed his caste' and had then killed himself in shame ([69], 72). The moment of the shame of her wombbrother, Kwatewa, is also the moment of Chumo's greatest pride: 'For that was her masterpiece that Dastuye the Musician held now and raised to his lips as he walked before the procession, guiding the new ghost to its body's grave' (71), Chumo's kerastion. The five pages of the story tells mostly how Chumo came to make the kerastion and how Kwatewa came so young to die.

Chumo's 'proving piece had been the traditional one for Tanner women, a drumhead,' in this case a drumhead for a dancing drum. Her 'truebrothers,' those of her caste, had joked with her, punning on 'drumhead' and 'maidenhead,' trying to make her blush. She doesn't blush: 'Tanners had no business blushing. They were outside shame.' Again, though, not outside or beyond pride, and Chumo is very proud that her drumhead lasts long, and is proud again 'when it split and gave itself to the Mother' (70-71). Her masterpiece, the kerastion, she made in the only way such an instrument can be made: a leather flute, 'and the leather is tanned human skin, and the skin is that of the wombmother or the foremother of the dead'; it is the skin of the 'wombmother of Chumo and Kwatewa.... It was a privilege which only the most powerful, the most truly shameless of the Tanners took, to make a kerastion of the mother's skin' (71-72).

Chumo had been a good wombsister to Kwatewa, mostly by taking great joy in him. When he was 'a little boy too young to have caste, too young to be polluted by the sacred,' he had looked at the river and asked 'Does it ever stop? Why can't it stop running, Chumo?' And soon after that he had decided to become a sculptor, making Chumo 'only his wombsister. He would have true sibs, now,' among the Sculptors. 'He and she were of different castes. They would not touch again' ([69]-70).

Without a pause, the story skips forward ten years to Kwatewa's proving day. Chumo comes with most of the other people of her town 'to see the sandsculpture he had made in the Great Plain Place where the Sculptors performed their art.' The wind had not yet disturbed 'the lovely curves of the classic form he had executed with such verve and sureness, the Body of Amakumo.' The Sculptors' speaker had barely dedicated Kwatewa's piece when 'a wind came out of the desert north, Amakumo's wind, the maker hungry for the made—Amakumo the Mother eating her

---

Mother of the World' and how (the?) one way to avoid danger is to be one who 'returns to the mother' (p. 50).

body, eating herself. Even while they watched, the wind destroyed Kwatewa's sculpture.... Beauty had gone back to the Mother. That the sculpture had been destroyed so soon and so utterly was a great honor to the maker' (70).

It is an honor, though, Kwatewa would as soon do without. Seeking something forbidden within his culture, Kwatewa eventually breaks a kind of ultimate taboo.

> Shepherds had found the cave where he had kept the stone, great marble pieces from the cave walls, carved into copies of his own sandsculptures, his own sacred work for the Solstice and the Hariba: sculptures of stone, abominable, durable, desecrations of the body of the Mother.
>
> People of his caste had destroyed the things with hammers, beaten them to dust and sand, swept the sand down into the river. She had thought Kwatewa would follow them, but he had gone to the cave at night and taken the sharp tool and cut his wrists and let his blood run. Why can't it stop running, Chumo? (72-73)

And here the flashback ends and present-time picks up with a return to the funeral. The Musician had come abreast of her now. 'His lips lay light on the leather mouthpiece, his fingers moved lightly as he played, and there was no sound at all.' Le Guin told us we would not get to hear it: no stops on a kerastion, and the ends are sealed with bronze disks. In the last sentence of the story we learn that 'Only Kwatewa in his woven grass shroud on the litter heard what song the Musician played for him, and knew whether it was a song of shame, or of grief, or of welcome' (73).

'The Kerastion' is a beautiful gem of a story, unique in itself and also clearly a Le Guin story. To start, it is an anthropological story: an ethnographic cameo showing a defining and epitomizing moment in a culture. The story earns its keeps in terms of 1990s debates about family values by reminding readers, or teaching them initially, that 'family' gets defined in different cultures in different ways, and one's wombmates are not necessarily one's closest relatives. In the culture of 'The Kerastion,' one's true siblings are one's caste (professional) colleagues. Equally Le Guinian, 'The Kerastion' deals with the Daoist theme of the world as a river, never stopping, with each life and each work of art a wave on the river (to combine two images from the Earthsea trilogy [and *TD* 44; ch. 2]).[616] Or the Hindu image of Shiva/Kali creating and destroying the worlds. Correlating with the river image, the story picks up the ideas from *The Dispossessed* of both 'process is all' (*TD* 268; ch. 10) and 'the deep connection between the aesthetic and the acquisitive' (*TD* 260, ch. 10; 118, ch. 5).

What I find most fascinating about this story, however, has to do with tone and point of view. In such plays as *Romeo and Juliet*, *Hamlet*, and

---

[616] For life as a wave on a pool, see Meerloo 248.

Antony and Cleopatra, Shakespeare works with an aspect intrinsic in his medium: the tension between the obviously dramatic point of view of drama versus our tendency to identify with some characters rather than others and see the plays, figuratively, from their points of view. This provides a kind of double vision, where we can see Romeo and Juliet as the gods of each other's idolatry *and* as two kids setting themselves up for disaster; or Herculean Antony with Isis-clothed Cleopatra—Egypt, the woman of 'infinite variety'—*and* see two aging lovers and losing politicians. In 'The Kerastion,' a similar balance comes from our imaginatively getting inside a culture that gracefully and consciously lives on the Daoist river, where beauty arises out of the Mother, Lao Tzu's Being as the Mother of all individual things (*Tao te Ching* 1)—and where all things beautiful and useful must return to the Mother. Inside the culture of 'The Kerastion,' it is firmly and wisely believed that if a work of craft/art 'be well done and the thing made be powerful, it belongs to the Mother.... Beauty, the most sacred of all things, is hers; the body of the Mother is the most beautiful of all things. So all that is made in the likeness of the Mother is made in sand' (*FIS* 71).

So Chumo can exclaim to her dead brother, and then ask rhetorically, 'To keep your work, to try to keep it for yourself, to take her body from her, Kwatewa! How could you, how could you, my brother?' And then Chumo even in her heart returns to silence and stands silent among the 'trees sacred to her caste' and accepts the death of her brother. Imaginatively getting inside this culture, imaginatively immanent in it, we can accept the death of Kwatewa and the pride of Chumo. In this world it is well for a Tanner to flay off the skin of the arm of her mother's corpse, and it is wrong for Kwatewa to make statue out of rock (72). But from our necessarily transcendent, god-like, vision as readers, always and necessarily *not* of the world of the story—from there we can take other views, filling in 'the silence' with some answers to Chumo's rhetorical question, 'How could you, my brother?'

Looking in on the world of 'The Kerastion,' we could say with John Keats,

> A thing of beauty is a joy for ever:
> Its loveliness increases; it will never
> Pass into nothingness; but still will keep
> A bower quiet for us, and a sleep....
> (*Endymion* i.l.I [*ODQ* 284.18]).

And we can add that, however transcendent Keats's things of beauty theoretically may be, mundane beauty is not 'a joy forever' because sooner or later it *will* 'Pass into nothingness,' whatever 'it' might be. Looking in on the world of 'Kerastion' we may fill in Chumo's silence with a good deal of sympathy for a sculptor who would like to hold onto his work at least a little while. There *is* that 'deep connection between the aesthetic and the acquisitive' because we would like to keep beauty around. Indeed, we can go further, I think, and fill in the possibility of a story in which Kwatewa is a culture changer, putting his stone sculptures out on the Great Plain Place to be shared with all who care to come out to see them as they *slowly* return to the Mother.[617]

Indeed, the Mother will take us all back very soon and all we have made, so we can, looking in on the society of 'The Kerastion' from our world, see no big deal if they allow a statue or two. Indeed, we can see the sandsculptures and their other works as *sacrifices* demanded of artists, and Kwatewa himself as a kind of sacrifice—in the canon of an author who strongly approves of taking risks, but not making sacrifices. But if the story had shown a change in culture that allowed Kwatewa to keep his stone sculptures, it would have been a change with an elitist source, coming from an Artist as Hero, and would be a change that would endanger what is a functioning, living, and admirable culture, risking moving down the slippery slope from artistic preservation to allowing acquisitiveness to (ultimately) capitalism. And so on.

We are not going to resolve this issue any more than we resolve the tensions in *Antony and Cleopatra*. To resolve the tensions would be to miss the point: the artistic power of the story lies in the balance, in the double and multiple vision. To *just* say «Good riddance!» to Kwatewa would be not only obscenely insensitive but esthetically dense. To look down on the culture of 'The Kerastion' and condemn it for killing an artist is no better. Either way is to fall into 'Single vision' and an esthetic variation on 'Newton's sleep.' In terms of Le Guin's canon, there is on the one side the communist-anarchist Anarresti in *The Dispossessed* (1974) and the Kesh in *Always Coming Home* (1985), both privileging theatre as their primary and highly appropriate art, where every theatrical performance is necessarily ephemeral—incapable of being possessed—'such stuff as dreams are made on.' There are also the four women in 'some kind of sacred space,' in 'A Man of the People' (1995); producing a sandpainting that is never seen whole and is necessarily ephemeral, except as it exists in the women's hearts (*FWF* 137-39). On the other side, there is that political radical and (arguably) cultural conservative Rakam in 'A Woman's Liberation' (1995), who fears 'postliterate information technology' far more than she has any faith in it and greatly values books in spite of the fact *and because* they preserve the past (*FWF* 197-200). On this side, too, we get Tolfink, an author whose one surviving work is preserved in Carlisle Cathedral in England: a line of runes Le Guin quotes in translation in 'It Was a Dark and Stormy Night' (1979): 'Tolfink carved these runes in this stone.' And Le Guin in this context strongly approves of Tolfink, who

---

[617] See Shakespeare's *Tempest* 4.1.148-58 for a poetic version of art and all things coming to an end; see Le Guin, 'Legends' 8, for the same idea in prose, viewed with disapproval.

'bore witness at least to the existence of Tolfink, a human being unwilling to dissolve entirely into his surroundings' (*DEW* 29).[618]

In 'The Kerastion,' we get this tension between acceptance of the transience of all human works, and of all humans, and our desire to resist—epitomized in little, and very beautifully, and in a story, 'The Kerastion,' eventually collected in a volume, *Fisherman*, in its initial edition printed on heavy paper, securely bound.

'The Rock that Changed Things' (1992)

> ...[T]he bricoleur actively pieces together different signs and produces new (and sometimes unsanctioned) meanings; the bricoleur is always in the process of fashioning new locales. —Elspeth Probyn (182)

> The most potent weapon of the oppressor is the mind of the oppressed.—Steven Biko

Le Guin classifies 'The Rock that Changed Things' as a parable and notes that she doesn't 'really much like parables' (*FIS* Introd. 10). I am going to classify 'The Rock' as one of Le Guin's *mâshâlim*: a parable, indeed, plus fable and satire, but *satire* in the old sense of a verbal attack that can work directly in the world, «magically», to make the world a little less bad. 'The Rock' is a *mâshâl*, like *The Word for World Is Forest*, and 'The Rock's' hero, 'the nurobl called Bu,' is like Selver in *Word for World*: a legitimate culture hero, a bringer of true change.[619] But Selver's word, if not a sword, inspires arrow and knife and the massacre of Terrans; Bu is more like Le Guin's Odo in being a human(oid) woman and bringing her changes through words and other symbols, without explicit bloodshed. Anyway, all we see of the revolution Bu brings is, 'dancing and singing across the terraces' and 'the first rock' flying through a window (*FIS* 67). That rock through a window is going to be one of the rocks that change things in the world of the story, but it is not *the* rock that changed things.

The rock that changed things is found by Bu 'working one day with her crew on the rock pile of Obling College' in the first sentence of the story ([57]). In the world of 'The Rock,' obls have towns and quarries and 'hunt the rock-coney' with ancient guns 'for their meat feasts' while their nurobls—significantly, '*Their* nurobls' (my emphasis)—'gather and pre-

---

[618] For more somber examples, see *DEW* 25-27: the song of Aneirin, the perhaps lone survivor of a battle remembered only in his song, for the voices of survivors of Dachau, Treblinka, Auschwitz—bearing witness.

[619] Students of Lévi-Strauss's *The Savage Mind* might also see Bu (and the other nurs) as distant relatives of Le Guin's ethnographers. If making mosaics is very far from literal 'bricolage,' it still can be related, in 'The Rock,' to 'intellectual bricolage'; see Lévi-Strauss 16-18, Heilman xvii-xix. See also Le Guin on 'The Carrier-Bag Theory of Fiction,' *DEW* 165-70.

pare stonecrop and lichen for ordinary food, and build the houses and the colleges, and keep them neat.'[620] We get the story mostly from the point of view of Bu—this is the story of Bu and her people—so the story's setting is mostly the rock piles and arranged-rock terraces of Obling College, plus a couple scenes within the college ([57] and passim).

The social setup is slavery, apparently with community ownership and quite certainly with obls controlling nurobls—but with less sexism than in the slave cultures of Werel or Yeowe in *Four Ways to Forgiveness*, or on Terra. The head of Obling College is the Lady Rectoress (65), and she carries a gun and smokes a pipe just like all the professors, which may make her a 'male-obl identified' female, or not: the Rectoress's psychology is a silence we are free to fill in as we wish. Among the slaves, female nurs work alongside males, so it is best I think to see them all as a colonized people: figuratively in the story Reason (the Professors) colonizing what they see as mostly bodies, workers merely. The nur gaze is not allowed to be cast upon obls of either gender, and rape is used to control nurs (*FIS* 58)—with just female nurs being raped or nurs of both sexes.[621]

All the obls that we see are very professorial intellectuals, not only with their Hemingwayesque long-guns and stereotypical, if soapstone, pipes but also in their delight in 'discussing history, natural history, philosophy, and metaphysics.' And then, after deep thought, '...the wisest old obls enter the colleges and write down the best of what was thought and said'—an allusion to Matthew Arnold's definition of criticism as 'a disinterested endeavour to learn and propagate the best that is known and thought in the world.'[622] Anyway, the wisest old obls select what is best and write it down in the Books of Record, which are then shelved in the college libraries. During the flood season in the spring, the obls 'stay inside the colleges,' where they 'read the Books of Record, discuss and annotate, plan new designs for the terraces, eat meat feasts and smoke.' And in an allusion to the feminist question of who served up all those feasts in *Lord of the Rings* and other heroic romances, we're told, 'Their nurs cook and serve the feasts and keep the rooms of the colleges orderly'—and then lines on how nervous (intellectual, professorial) obls beat and rape nurs (58).

---

[620] For meat as food of the slave-owners, cf. 'A Man of the People' (*FWF* 132).

[621] We can be sure only of the rape of females in 'The Rock.' In the USA of the 1990s, rape and the threat of rape functioned for social control primarily to limit the behavior of women. Note, though, the systematic use of rape of women to terrorize populations generally in the wars in the Balkans at the time of 'The Rock's' composition, and prison rape as a threat functioning to limit the behavior of American male activists in the 1960s and early 1970s. As prison populations increase in the USA, prison rape and the threat of prison rape become more obvious as a control on the behaviors of boys and young men, esp. young African Americans. The prison rape threat for males was used explicitly in the 'Scared Straight' programs in the 1970s into the 1980s.

[622] Arnold, *Essays in Criticism, Functions of Criticism at the Present Time*; I quote *ODQ* 19.12.

We learn that the rock terraces of Obling College are 'notable for the perfect order and complex beauty of their pebble-patterns' and that great obls of old spent years in 'designing the patterns and choosing the stone.' So stones must be exactly the right size and shape to fit the obls' patterns, and Bu was looking for such a one 'when she came upon the stone that changed things' (58). The stone itself wasn't some epic-impressive Terrenon stone, as in *A Wizard of Earthsea*, but a standard large oval serpentinite stone 'a palm-and-a quarter wide and a palm-and-a-half long.' What was special about this stone was that Bu was 'struck by a quality...she had never noticed before: color' (58-59, 61). In the culture of the obls, a stone's color 'is a matter of absolute indifference' (59), as is the grain and texture (63); what counts is the 'arrangement by shape and size'—allowing René Descartes's ultimate attribute of bodies: extension, by which the obls design Euclidean 'squares, oblongs, triangles, dodecahedrons, zigzags, and rectilinear designs of great and orderly beauty and significance' (62).[623] And these rectilinear designs are literally significant: signifying patterns 'about obls and what obls think'—which may include nurs and blits (children), but only in terms of patterns about obls (64).

Bu is fascinated by her serpentinite stone, perhaps even obsessed with it. "This stone is beautiful," she thinks. 'She was not looking, as she should have been, at the whole design, but at the one stone.... 'This stone is significant. It means. It is a word.'' She puts the stone into the Dean's Design, and it fits exactly. But, standing back to study the pattern, Bu thought it scarcely seemed to be the Dean's Design at all. It was not that the new stone changed the design; it simply completed a pattern that Bu had never realized was there: a pattern of color, that had little or no relation to the shape-and-size arrangement of the Dean's Design' (59). Unlike the rectilinear designs of the obls, all designed by individuals, 'The new stone completed a spiral of blue-green stones' that was mostly made (unconsciously) by Bu over the last few years but 'had been begun by some other nur' (59-60).

The Dean happens to come along just then, and the Narrator assures us that he is 'a kind old obl who had never raped Bu, though he had often patted her.' Seeing her 'crouching and hiding all her eyes,' the Lord Dean condescends to answer Bu's question on the 'verbal significance of this section of the true pattern' that she had just repaired.[624] 'This subsection of my design may be read, on the simplest level, as 'I place stones beautifully,' or 'I place stones in excellent order''; it is, apparently, a metamosaic, but 'There is an immanent high-plane postverbal significance, of

---

[623] Thought is the second ultimate Cartesian category (*DoP* 'Attributes').

[624] Nurs have three eyes (*FIS* 62), but in some stories—including that of Flicker of the Serpentine (*ACH* 283)—so do humans, with the third eye able to glimpse some of the things in heaven and earth that are missed in the philosophies of people who use only two eyes: e.g., with Shiva the third eye is 'the eye of insight beyond duality' (Buitenen 8.931). See Le Guin's poem 'Siva and Kama' (*Hard Words* 18).

course, as well as the Ineffable Arcana'—which Bu 'needn't bother' her 'little head with.' The Dean dismisses as mere «nurish nonsense» the idea of meaning in color. That night, Bu dreams of the blue-green stone and, 'In the dream the rock spoke' and the rocks around it also, but 'Waking, Bu could not remember the words the stones had said' (60). Bu raises the issue with her fellow workers, and they tell her, orthodoxly, that colors can't mean, that 'Colors aren't part of the patterns.' She tells them to suppose for a moment that they are and 'Just look.' Since they are 'used to silence and obedience' (and have not been schooled to mistrust empiricism and their senses), the nurs looked, and, across what they still see as 'the real pattern,' they see 'another pattern. A different pattern.' Bu suggests that 'Maybe it makes an immanent pattern of ineffable significance.' Ko, Bu's best friend and mate, tells her to 'come off it,' but she goes on and wonders if the blue-green rock could change the meaning of the Dean's design (*FIS* 61).

And at this point a wise, old nur, so excellent at maintaining patterns that the obls let him live even after he was maimed, enters the discussion to do some pattern criticism. For a first-order approximation reading, he suggests 'It might say, ''The nur places stones,'' and others fill in that the nur would be Bu. Ko corrects them with 'patterns aren't ever about nurs!' and Bu counters with 'Maybe patterns made of colors are.' Looking with all three of his eyes, Ko reads, '—'the nur places stones beautifully in uncontrollable loopingness...foreshadowing the seen.'' Un suggests 'The vision' but cannot figure out the last word. Bu is *very* excited, inferring that 'the patterns of the colors...aren't accidental. Not meaningless. All the time, we have been putting them here in patterns—not just ones the obls design and we execute, but other patterns—nur patterns—with new meanings.' Amid the straight lines of the obls' designs they now see, 'other designs, less complete, often merely sketched or hinted—circles, spirals, ovals, and complex curvilinear mazes and labyrinths of great and unpredictable beauty and significance. * * * Both patterns were there; did one cancel the other, or was each part of the other? It was difficult to see them both at once, but not impossible.' Had the nurs done this all totally unconsciously 'without even knowing we were doing it?' Un admits to having looked at colors, and so did Ko, plus 'grain and texture.' Un warns them to keep word of their works from the Professors: 'They don't like patterns to change.... It makes them nervous'—and nervous Professors are dangerous to nurs (62-63).

Bu, however 'was so excited and persuasive' about colors of stones 'that other nurs of Obling began studying the color patterns, learning how to read their meanings.' And the practice spreads. Soon, all sorts of nurs were finding 'wild designs in colored stones, and surprising messages concerning obls, nurs, and blits' (64) Conservative nurs—'Many nurs,' we're told—resist the trend. 'If we start inventing new meanings, changing things, disturbing the patterns, where will it end?' It is unclear just how many of the nurs believe «Mr. Charlie treats us real good»—or, as we soon see, Ms. Charlie—but certainly not Bu; she 'would hear none of that; she was full of her discovery.[625] She no longer listened in silence. She spoke.' Bu goes up to the Rectory Mosaic, wearing around her neck a turquoise that she calls her 'selfstone.' Up at the Mosaic, Bu crouches before the Rectoress and asks 'Would the Lady Rectoress in her kindness answer a question I have?' The Lady Rectoress will not. Without a word to Bu, she turns to the nearest Professor and says, 'This nur is insane; have it removed, please.' We may assume Bu is removed. The next sentence tells us Bu was punished with ten days in jail, rape 'by Students whenever they pleased, and then sent to the flagstone quarries for a hundred days.' She returns to the nest after her sentence, pregnant from one of the rapes (proving, if we needed proof, that Nurobls and Obls are the same species). Her many friends and nestmates greet her, singing songs that they 'had made out of the meanings of the colored patterns on the terraces.' Ko comforts her that night, and tells her 'that her blit would be his blit, and her nest his nest'—in an interesting variation on Ruth's promise to Naomi (Ruth 1.16-17). Bu does not give up her quest for the meaning of the stone (64-65).

Sneaking in through the kitchen, and with the help of serving-nurs, Bu gets to the private room of the Canon of Obling College, 'a very old obl, renowned for his knowledge of metaphysical linguistics,' and the sort of wise old man or animal that heroes often go to in penultimate actions in tales to get a secret meaning. Except we are in a satire here, more than a relatively innocent folktale, and the canon would have 'reached for his gun' if he hadn't been so sleepy (65-66). Returning to more folkish motifs, Bu tells the Canon that nobody else has been able to answer the question she has for him: 'Do you know if a blue-green stone in a pattern might be a word?' The Canon knows. It can *not* be a word nowadays because '...all verbal color-significance is long obsolete'; but once, long ago, 'The hue of blue-green—such as in that stone you seem to be wearing as an ornament—might, in its adjectival form within a pattern, have indicated a quality of untrammeled volition. As a noun' it might have meant, 'an absence of coercion; a lack of control; a condition of self-determination—' Rescuing the Canon from his syntax, Bu ask, 'Freedom.... Does it mean freedom?' The Canon says it doesn't. 'It did. But it does not. * * * Because the word is obsolete' (66)

Bu tells the Canon to look out the window at the terraces. 'Look at the colors of the stones! Look at the patterns the nurs make, the designs we have made, the meanings we have written! Look for the freedom!' (67) Bu goes off, and, after a bit, the Canon looks out the window:

> For a moment he thought he was dreaming again, seeing entirely different patterns than those he had seen all his long life on those terraces—wild designs of curves and colors, amazing phrases, unimagined significances, a wonderful newness of meaning and beauty—and then he opened all his eyes wide, very wide, and blinked; and it

---

[625] 'Mr. Charlie' is the folklore White-Guy-in-Charge (see Farber 100 & passim).

was gone. The familiar, true order of the terraces lay clear and regular in the morning light. And there was nothing else to see....

So he did not see the long line of nurobls coming up from the nests and work houses down below the boulder walls, carrying blits and dancing as they came, dancing and singing across the terraces. He heard the singing, but only as a noise without significance. It was not until the first rock flew through his window that he looked up and cried out in agitation, 'What is the meaning of this?' (67)

And with this question the story ends.

Comments

For the meaning of 'this' at 'The Rock's' end, I shall start with the revolutionary vision at the end of Jerry Farber's classic 1967 underground essay, 'The Student As Nigger,' which ends, 'For students, as for black people, the hardest battle isn't with Mr. Charlie. It's with what Mr. Charlie has done to your mind' (100). Or, more positively, in Le Guin's formulation, '...revolution begins in the thinking mind' (*TD* 267; ch. 10). I.e., a necessary and, perhaps, nearly sufficient cause of revolution is getting oppressed people to think. Ordinarily, the colonized oppressed will greatly outnumber the oppressors, and the «grunts» in the armed forces will almost always come from the ranks of the oppressed (the children of the privileged will find better work, at least as officers over the grunts). The problem is how to get oppressed masses conscious enough to rebel before they have rebelled (see Orwell, *Nineteen Eighty-Four* 61; I.7).

By the 1990s, one Leftist (anti)orthodoxy reformulated the problem in terms of who got to tell the stories crucial to peoples' cultures: who got to formulate what earlier in the century were called myths and ideologies, now themselves redescribed as 'metanarratives' (Lyotard, Introd.). In 'The Rock That Changed Things,' the nurs are clearly the oppressed, literally spending their working lives telling the stories of the oppressors, the Professorial obls. When Bu comes to see their work with an 'altered eye,' and gets that vision generally accepted, the nurs see that they *have been* telling their own stories and that their stories include a word now obsolete but yet always (already) with us: 'freedom.' And when the word goes forth, the first steps toward freedom are taken. The rock that changed things is primarily the rock that gives the word, 'freedom,' but also, if far less so, the rock that goes through the window to start making the word into living revolution.

Like Selver in *The Word for World Is Forest*, Bu is one of Le Guin's answers to the difficult question of how you can get true anarchistic change: you get true change by getting from among the people themselves a 'translator'; i.e., you need a person to tell the people what they already know, to bring over into consciousness and action what is already there in the Dreamtime, the collective unconscious, the prehistory of freedom, a potential within the Dao—however we formulate it.

Beyond this beginning of revolution, however, in 'The Rock,' 'The rest is silence' (*Hamlet* 5.2.347). And this is well. In *The Dispossessed*, in the high-technology civilization of Urras, the bearer of change is Shevek, and he gives a pre-Revolutionary crowd the true message, 'You cannot buy the Revolution. You cannot make the Revolution. You can only be the Revolution. It is in your spirit, or it is nowhere'—followed by the clatter of helicopters and machine guns as the Ioti State moves to crush any movement Shevek might have helped to start (242; ch. 9).

We see no automatic weapons among the obls in 'The Rock That Changed Things,' so the revolution there may have a chance. But the towns of the obls are make-believe, and it may be more important what 'The Rock' is doing for its readers' heads.

First, there is, for the synecdoche for the oppressors, Obling College, with Rectoress, Canon, Professors, Students—an armed and pipe-smoking faculty, and nurobl-raping Students. As one who did not invent the US system of higher education but partly sold out to it, I will resent the implications of Obling College, but I won't flat-out deny them. If one sees the Enlightenment and Modernism, Rationalism and rectilinear forms as major tools of the oppressors in our world, then universities and colleges are more part of the (Modern/Modernist) problem than part of the solution. If one sees the University as, ideally, a small-scale utopia, then it is important to remember Le Guin's statement in her own voice that 'The purer, the more euclidean the reason that builds a utopia, the greater is its self-destructive capacity'—and, clearly, capacity for destruction of others.[626] Second, you have the idea in 'The Rock' that what colleges and universities get inscribed and reinscribed—those rectilinear forms—have within them, if we can only see the 'colors,' other patterns, other messages. Insofar as the oppressed of the world inscribe the messages, there are also, again, if we see with more than one eye—other messages. 'Both patterns' are there, and they do not necessarily cancel each other out. 'It was difficult to see them both at once, but not impossible' (62-63). And, I believe the major message of 'The Rock' is that we should try to see all the messages: the old, rectilinear, establishment messages *and* the more colorful, nonlinear messages of the oppressed.

Indeed, that may be the most important message of 'The Rock That Changed Things.' Whether or not *this* revolution is successful, the nurs have learned that they have been telling their own stories and that they have stories of their own to tell. Whether or not this revolution is successful, Bu and her nest-mates and work-friends had brought back into the world-time of their culture the word 'freedom.' In 'The Rock,' the nurs produce their color stories collectively and, initially, with only limited consciousness. They work out their stories *immanently*, working in the rock, feeling their way through, as opposed to the obl Professors, who

---

[626] Quoting 'A Non-Euclidean View of California' (here *DEW* 87).

have a (transcendent) design that they have the nurs execute for them. Except, as we have seen, some of the nurs—like Medieval craftsfolk, not ancient slaves—have worked quite consciously with color, and even with texture and grain. In any event, we see in the story is the enlightenment of Bu and the others so that they get a relatively transcendent vision of the color patterns they have made. In this story, enlightenment in the sense of seeing patterns is not a bad thing but a good thing, to be shared among different classes and extended beyond Euclidean ideas of regular shapes to Newtonian curves and colors—and, maybe, eventually, textures and grains: felt patterns. And, just maybe, enlightenment can continue on to Einstein, and a nur/obl alliance could produce dynamic patterns, in the four dimensions of everyday reality.[627] Looking at the story this way, 'The Rock' has to do with canons: whose stories get told, what sort of stories get told, what approaches to the world are accepted as legitimate. And here Le Guin and 'The Rock' (and many feminist, postmodernist, and postcolonial critics) have an important point: *Obl* 'Patterns aren't ever about nurs!' (62), and few US college courses are about patterns valued by figurative nurs: all those who traditionally do not become Professors. And that is much of the world, far too much to be denied and excluded from college and university curricula and the major narratives of Western culture.

The Churten Effect Group: 'The Shobies' Story,' 'Dancing to Ganam,' 'Another Story OR A Fisherman of the Inland Sea'

The stories of what may be called the Churten Effect Group (or Churten Group) are quite good and important for continuity and change in Le Guin. Le Guin in these stories remains consistent in her philosophical interests, her most profound feelings about what *is*, her valuing of community, and her distrust of more or less radical individualists and masculinist heroes.[628] 'The Shobies' Story' and 'Dancing to Ganam' are also serious investigations in prose fiction of the question of the social construction of reality, of the possibility that we construct the world with language.[629]

From my point of view, a fairly Modernist, epistemological position, the practical (ethical, political) implications of a world of language is best presented by Jane Flax, who is skeptical of the extreme skepticism of

---

[627] Anything that is in the everyday world, has length, width, breadth, and duration: extension in time. That far, the four-dimensional universe is just commonsensical.

[628] See in *DEW*, 'Heroes,' 'Bryn Mawr Commencement Address,' 'Conflict,' and 'A Non-Euclidean View of California...,' esp. 88-89.

[629] Going beyond words, though, figuratively beneath them, we may also have the deeper reality of the Dao or Being or whatever Ineffable it is that mystics contact when they leave behind the chatter of social life and our incessant interior monologs. (In 'Some Generative Metaphors' in *ACH* [483-85] Le Guin has an entry for '*Language as* ' for each of her seven entries [all preceded by 'THE']: WAR/control, LORD/power, ANIMAL/relationship, MACHINE/communication, DANCE/connection, HOUSE/ self-domestication, 'THE WAY'/inadequate.)

'nothing exists outside of a text' (Flax 47) and suggests the more moderate idea that 'Perhaps reality,' however constituted 'can have 'a' structure only from the falsely universalizing perspective of the dominant group. That is, only to the extent that one person or group can dominate the whole, will reality appeared to be governed by one set of rules or be constituted by one privileged set of social relations' (49). If Jean-François Lyotard is correct, that dominance in a world of words would come from illegitimately controlling the stories we tell, determining which metanarratives will be privileged and used to legitimate all other politically significant thought. For Lyotard, though, no discourse is really privileged. 'Where, then, he asks, does legitimation reside in the postmodern era?' Nancy Fraser and Linda J. Nicholson give, out of Lyotard's *The Postmodern Condition*, the brief and intelligible answer, 'that in the postmodern era'—our times—'legitimation becomes plural, local, and immanent' (23). If all we have is words, what may constitute our truest social reality is the words of the stories we tell each other around the fire in the cave, or reconstructing the world while in a limbo after a Churten jump.

'The Shobies' Story'

Allowing Le Guin her Hainish universe in the far future—Peter Brigg puts it in 5100 CE—we have with 'The Shobies' Story' a very elegant example of a science fiction story using the principles of 'one big lie' and the wonderful gadget. In this case the one big lie is Churten theory and an instantaneous trip from Ve Port on the planet Hain to M-60-340-nolo. The crew of the *Shoby*—hence, 'the Shobies'—will turn on 'the churten process' device, and (if it works as did in extensive testing) it will 'effectuate their transilience to a solar system seventeen light-years from Ve Port without temporal interval' (*FIS* 89).[630] That's one major whopper of a lie, actually, and a pretty miraculous gadget: even as Shevek's theory allowed the ansible and instantaneous communication, so churten theory allows instantaneous travel by matter (except that 'transilience,' technically is not instantaneous travel). 'There and Back Again,' indeed, as the alternative title to J. R. R. Tolkien's *The Hobbit* (1937) has it, but not just to the rather uninteresting M-60-340-nolo. (If the *Shoby* 'arrived as a neutron bomb or a black hole event,' they would take out only bacteria and a rather ugly planet [*FIS* 91].) This trip, like that of the Hobbits or the men in the 1950 movie *DESTINATION: MOON*, is both a literal trip and a thematically significant one.

The crew of the *Shoby* differ from the crew in *DESTINATION: MOON*, or even the Bridge of any of the *Enterprise*'s in *Star Trek*.[631] The crew is a

---

[630] For 'transilience,' see *TD* 69; ch. 3.
[631] Including the original TV *Star Trek* episode, 'Is There in Truth No Beauty,' with its motif of navigating back to known space and its augmented and diversified crew. Comparing and contrasting 'Shobies' Story' with 'Is There in Truth'

group of ten from the Ekumen planets of Hain, Gethen, Anarres, and Terra. The *lingua franca* adopted by the crew is Hainish, and so the Hainish woman on board has a meaningful name: Sweet Today ([75]-76). When they are operating the *Shoby*, Sweet Today is a central figure, the coordinator.[632] The 'affective focus' of the crew, their metaphorical hearth, is the Gethenian pair Karth and Oreth, and their two children Asten (six Earth-years old) and Rig (four years). 'Oreth, who was just coming out of female kemmer' could watch for a moment 'Rig, whom she had fathered, dance with Asten, whom she had borne' (86)—an extraordinarily elegant illustration of the defamiliarization SF is supposed to get done: making strange overly familiar parental roles. Hain, the homeworld of humanity, then, supplies one center for the crew; Gethen, a very recent addition to the Ekumen, supplies another. The one member of the crew with a background to allow him some chance of understanding churten theory is, appropriately, the Cetian Gveter, from Anarres: the relevant intellectual of the crew. The remainder of the crew come from a world as marginal in its way as Gethen (distant, extremely cold) and Anarres (as desert mining colony for Urras, and a place to dump their anarchist revolutionaries); the remainder come from Terra, still recovering some 2000 years later from the ecological disasters Le Guin posits for us in her future history.[633] This last is an important point. 'The Shobies' Story' places value upon risk-taking, gambling, even taking risks with children; still, Le Guin continues her warnings, consistently and repeatedly, against *ecological* risk-taking, when any generation (necessarily abstractly and unmindfully) gambles the future of all who might follow them.

One of the Terrans is Lidi, an expert in NAFAL (Nearly as Fast as Light) flight; she is an old woman who pointedly stays away from Terra. A pair are Tai and Betton. They had been living 'in a reclamation commune on Terra,' and Tai had 'drawn the lot for Ekumenical service,' and had requested ship duty; her eleven-year-old son Betton asked to come along 'as family. She had agreed; but after training; when she volunteered for this test flight, she had tried to get Betton to withdraw.... He had refused.' The last crew member is Shan, about whom we get little background. He had trained with Tai and Betton, and he wants a relationship with both.

---

might be a useful exercise in differentiating liberal Modernism (*Star Trek*) from a more postmodern, feminist perspective.
[632] For 'coordinator,' see 'Vaster than Empires' (*WTQ* 170); for 'Weaver' in a Foretelling group among the Handdarata, see LHD_1 ch. 4.
[633] Le Guin may be mildly pessimistic on the recovery time for Terra, but probably not, given the degree of ecological disaster and the consequent social disintegration she has implied or shown from 'Nine Lives' in 1969 through *LoH* (1971), *WWF* (1972), *TD* (1974), 'New Atlantis' (1975), *ACH* (1985), to 'Dancing' (1993). The logic for such future disasters is worked out brilliantly in Frederik Pohl and C.M. Kornbluth's *The Space Merchants* (1952, 1953), and it is reiterated in Korten's 1996 'The Limits of the Earth' article, tracing the environmental implications of the assumption at the Bretton Woods meeting in 1944 that economic growth 'will not be constrained by the inherent limits of a finite planet' (15).

This Terran triad is, in a sense, where the action is on the *Shoby*. Shan tells the others about 'the tension between the mother and the son' so that it could be understood and 'used effectively in group formation.... Shan offered him fatherly-brotherly warmth, but Betton accepted it sparingly, coolly, and sought no formal crew relation with him or anyone' (78). Tai will dance with Shan 'but even then was shy, would not touch. She had been celibate since Betton's birth. She did not want Shan's patient, urgent desire, did not want to cope with it, with him' (85).

The story starts with the Shobies making their 'first consensual decision,' which is 'to spend their isyeye in the coastal village of Liden, on Hain, where the negative ions could do their thing' ([75]). The 'consensual decision' phrase indicates that this is serious social fiction, a point reinforced soon after with the definition of the Hainish term *isyeye*: '"making a beginning together,' or 'beginning to be together,' or, used technically, 'the period of time and area of space in which a group forms if it is going to form."' The reference to negative ions foreshadows 'The Shobies' Story' as hard science fiction at least so far as one needs to be sophisticated enough at physics or chemistry to know what an 'ion' is and/or sophisticated enough of a reader of SF not to care: i.e., to know that you needn't know what an ion is to follow the story's first paragraph. The reference to negative ions doing 'their thing' is a key to the tone of the story. The 'thing' of negative ions for humans is mild euphoria, as when Ike Rose is 'absolutely happy' in the Spes colony and notes that 'The negative ions in the atmosphere would have something to do with that' (*FIS* 29). And 'do their thing' is a highly anthropomorphic and fairly flippant way to talk about ions ([75]). *This* point is reinforced when we learn that Sweet Today, as a Hainish person, had 'kinsfolk of all denominations, grandchildren and cross-cousins, affines and cosines all over the Ekumen....' (76). Cosines? Indeed: 'The Shobies' Story' is going to be hard SF and social fiction—and a story, to be enjoyed and taken seriously, not earnestly, as if it were our grim duty to be instructed. 'The Shobies' Story' will have some jokes, and even a happy ending.

During their isyeye, the adult Shobies and Betton sit around a campfire and discuss churten theory: 'They talked, as human beings do, about what they didn't know.' And they talk imperfectly. These people are far more stable than the ten 'nuts' on the *Gum* in 'Vaster than Empires and More Slow'—with the craziness of the early NAFAL explorers specifically alluded to by Shan (81); indeed, they are more stable than the disgustingly competent heroes of Heinlein novels or even the officers aboard any of the *Star Trek*ian *Enterprise*'s. Still, Gveter, communist-anarchist Anarresti 'held tight to his knowledge, because he needed the advantage it gave him' (76), and, as we have seen, Tai doesn't want to be touched. It will even turn out that Tai is suspicious of men, and Karth of Terrans—and do-gooder Shan may be a control freak (95).

Sandwiched between these rounds of crew discourse, is a conversation by ansible with Cetian scientists, where, from one point of view, the Shobies get explained to them as much about the churten effect as they can understand, and, from another point of view—Shan's particularly—undergo a ritual like the ones used by Ekumen humans when they use lab animals (82).

In the first round of discourse, around the fire on the beach at Liden, the main topic is the churten effect. Sweet Today suggests their ship will travel 'by ideas?'—and Gveter says 'No, no, no, no,' but isn't sure where to go from there. 'It is not physical,' he says, 'it is not not physical, these are the categories our minds must discard' (78). Gveter, the student of temporal physics and old Lidi the navigator were convinced 'that the engineers knew perfectly well what they were doing': there had been sixty-two successful 'transiliences' (instantaneous trips). The problem was theirs: 'the difficulty human minds had in grasping a genuinely new concept.' Tai offers the analogy of blood circulation, which went on for a long time before William Harvey described it. She isn't totally satisfied with the analogy when Shan quotes 'The heart has its reasons, which reason does not know,' and Tai replies with 'Mysticism' using 'the tone of voice of one warning a companion about dog-shit on the path' (79).[634] Betton finally turns the conversation quite serious in asking what the dangers might be. Tai tells him that they do not know; Sweet Today says the obvious: worse goes to worst, and they might all die. The conversation moves on to Asten telling about the ritual animals with an earlier crew they were with. Sweet Today compliments her/him on telling good stories. Betton concludes 'So we're sort of ritual humans,' and then the others supply other possibilities. Tai: Volunteers; Lidi: Experimenters; Shan: Experiencers; Oreth: Explorers; Karth: Gamblers. Then Shan alludes to the 'nuts' who supplied personnel for NAFAL ships early in the history of the League, and Oreth asks, 'Are we stable' and says for himself: 'I like instability. I like this job. I like the risk, taking the risk together. High stakes! That's the edge of it, the sweetness of it'; and Gveter, who has been fairly silent in through here, says, 'Together' and adds 'You aren't crazy. You are good. I love you. We are ammari,' i.e., siblings (80-81).

Then comes the ansible talk with the experts about the churten. The Cetian scientists helpfully explain to them that 'The churten, in lay terms, may be seen as displacing the virtual field in order to realize relational coherence in terms of the transiliential experientiality.' Shan for one rejects at least one later bit of such jargon with the one-word typification, 'Shit!'; the Narrator, however, is more generous, noting that the scientist 'was trying to find the words, to accept the responsibility.' The Shobies and we are told that there is 'a possibility that the participation of high intelligence in the process might affect the displacement in one way or another. And that such displacement would reciprocally affect the participant.' Trying to get the words right, the scientist eventually tries, 'As the experimenter is an element of the experiment, so we assume that the transilient may be an element or agent of transilience,' which is why they wanted to send a

---

[634] Shan translates Blaise Pascal, *Pensées* § iv.277; cf. *TD* 108; ch. 5. *Pensées* also quoted in 'VEMS.' My source here is *ODQ* 374.4 (and 374.1).

group and not just one or two: 'The psychic interbalance of a bonded social group is a margin of strength against disintegration or incomprehensible experience, if any such occurs. Also the separate observations of the group members will mutually interverify.' (It is the word 'interverify' that is the immediate occasion for Shan's 'Shit!' [83].) Again, there is wisdom among the pedantry here, and foreshadowing: what happens if the 'interbalance' is weaker than it appears?[635]

The other part of the discourse sandwich comes after this conversation with the scientists and just before the churten. There is an informal ritual celebration the night before, with everyone dressing up and having a fine meal and then sitting around 'the big fireplace in the library' on the *Shoby*: it is a *big* and comfortable ship. Oreth lays a fire and later Karth lights it (artificial logs, real flames). 'Everybody gathered round' and the youngest, Rig, says 'Tell bedtime stories,' which they do. When the kids go to bed, Betton passes by his mother, 'for she did not like to be touched; but she put out her hand, drew the child to her, and kissed his cheek. He fled in joy.' The section ends with Sweet Today saying 'Stories' and adding 'Ours begins tomorrow, eh?' (88).

The next day they churten, and all seems well with the process: there is no command chain with 'hierarchic control' on the *Shoby* but rather a properly anarchistic 'network of response' and feminist basing in 'mutual empowerment, 'thick' description,' and open-ended complexity. Sweet Today, intersees or subvises, 'gestalting them, all ten at once' with the analogy Le Guin suggests of the violinist of a chamber group (88-89), plus, I will add for those who know *The Left Hand of Darkness* (1969), like Faxe 'weaving' the Foretelling. They churten, and things are not well with the result.

Among the bridge crew, Oreth on the Artificial Intelligence says 'There was no interval,' and Gveter agrees. Karth says 'Nothing happened,' and Lidi says 'We aren't anywhere.' Tai and Shan say they're at M-60-340-nolo, but 'All their words fell dead, had a false sound.' And then the ansible doesn't work, and Lidi says, 'We're going back now.' Lidi wants to return by NAFAL flight for a little over seventeen years of Hainish time. The Narrator tells us briefly but very significantly that Lidi's 'words, her tone, shook them, shook them apart' (89).

Then we get to hear what Gveter calls 'Perception variation' among the Shobies. Shan sees an ugly planet, and Gveter's instruments indicate that it is a cold planet with a lot of bacteria. Oreth sees the planet; Asten does not. Tai thinks that they somehow must determine that they got to where they are 'and then get here.' Lidi, the oldest of the group, can see stars through the walls of the ship and takes herself off duty. Rig, the youngest says s/he 'can see the stars too,' that s/he 'can see *everything!* And Asten can't' (91-93). Karth carries Rig off, and Oreth follows the rest of the fam-

---

[635] See below, this chapter, 'Dancing to Ganam' for Shan's learning the importance of interverification (however much the jargon remains ugly and suspect).

ily off the bridge and does and/or does not stay with the children (93, 94-95).

Rather than bring back only evidence Sweet Today labels, neutrally, 'Anecdotal,' Tai asks for 'a consensus about going down onplanet.' A rough agreement is reached to go—although nothing that sounds like consensus to my ear—and Betton asks to go with. Tai says no; Gveter says yes. Gveter is 'honestly puzzled' by Tai's position. 'I don't want the responsibility,' Tai says. Even more puzzled, Gveter asks why it is particularly hers: 'We all share it; Betton is crew.' Shan wants to know why they 'keep crossing...coming and going.' Gveter's answer is 'Confusion due to the churten experience,' and that is part of it (94). From a godlike, readerly position, though—*and* located ourselves within Terran history and culture—Gveter's interpretation may seem to us to miss how the 'crossing' preceded the churten experience and participates with it in a cycle. Tai, Betton, and Gveter are acting out a bit of Terran family dynamics, including what viewed positively is parental responsibility and viewed negatively is parental possessiveness.

From this point on in 'The Shobies' Story' the center doesn't hold, and we get 'a cessation of cause and effect.' In the original opening of 'Vaster than Empires and More Slow' (1971), the Narrator directly addresses the audience, starting with 'You're looking at a clock,' and tries to give us some idea what NAFAL flight is like for the occasional mystic—'intuition of the eternal'—and more statistically normal people: 'Oh God, here now One get me out of this[!].' Here, the Narrator sticks to third-person, tells us quite directly that it is difficult to narrate a switch from sequency to simultaneity and gives us a workable solution to the problem: 'As the members of the crew network no longer perceived the network steadily and were unable to communicate their perceptions, an individual perception is the only clue to follow through the labyrinth of this dislocation.' So she goes to the point of view of Gveter. Gveter talks with others about going down to the planet: 'He perceived this discussion as perfectly rational,' except it was 'interrupted by outbursts of egoizing not characteristic of the crew,' including the lines in response to Shan's 'Somebody's got to stay in control here,' Tai: 'Not the men!' and Karth: 'Not the Terrans' (95).

Gveter perceives himself going on the lander with Tai and Betton down to the planet, and then staying on board the lander as Tai and Betton go out to get samples. Betton walks easily on the planet, while Tai seems to 'be sinking into the surface,' until finally she 'sank into the formless murk' (96-97). Except then Tai's voice comes on the ship's intercom, instructing Lander One and its crew to return to the *Shoby* (97). Etc.[636] In fact, *etc.* until it seems that chaos is come again and the *Shoby*'s 'systems died away into the real silence that was always there. But there was nothing there,' or nothing except the threat of the Shobies' dying as they lose life-support (98).

---

[636] For straight-line exposition, see Shan's summary in 'Dancing to Ganam' (*FIS* 115-16).

The suns burn through my flesh, Lidi said.
I am the suns, said Sweet Today. Not I, all is.
Don't breathe! cried Oreth.
It is death, Shan said. What I feared, is: nothing.
Nothing, they said.
* * *
In her cabined solitude, Lidi felt the gravity lighten...she saw them, the nearer and the farther suns, burn through the dark gauze of the walls.... The brightest, the sun of this system, floated directly under her navel. She did not know its name.
I am the darkness between the suns, one said.
I am nothing, one said.
I am you one said.

And then one (of the Shobies?) cries out, 'Listen!' and tells them, 'We have always known this. This is where we have always been, will always be, at the hearth, at the center. There is nothing to be afraid of, after all' (99).

As in NAFAL flight, 'Maya has fallen. All is here now one' (*New Dimensions I* 88). The threat to the Shobies is that which Tolfink of Carlisle resisted in carving his runes into the stone: dissolving entirely into one's surroundings, total loss in the Dao (*DEW* 29).[637] The Shobies, must die, or they must recreate the(ir) universe. They do not die but wind up at a 'here, at the hearth,' where Oreth 'had laid the fire.' Karth lights it, and Oreth and Karth say together, in Karhidish, 'Praise also the light, and creation unfinished' (99). The one bit of ritual language Genly Ai learned from the Handdara in Karhide was 'Praise then darkness and Creation unfinished' (*LHD* 246; ch. 18). Darkness, Absolute Dao, is the source of creation: the nonBeing out of which comes Being, the Void, the Potential; but light, also, is necessary. And at a time and place where Yin seems to have conquered Yang, where nonBeing has become a threat to human life—then it is a time for light and words. So these *elohim*, human gods, will recreate the world, not by hovering over the firmament and commanding light, but in the human fashion of sitting around a fire and finding 'the thread,' of the Way (and the narrative), creating the world, establishing a human cosmos through 'Telling stories' (100-02).

In 'silence, the silence that was always there,' their voices raise some key points. First, the personal one: Betton quietly claims that 'The boy and

---

[637] One could see the metaphoric danger as falling into eternity, as Meshe did in *LHD* (ch. 12), and/or, far more innocently, the 'old mad woman' who has fallen into the mere *now* in Le Guin's 1988 poem 'Tenses': 'Terrible the cage of the present tense * * * without foresight or memory' (*Wild Oats* 81). See also Ramchandra's finishing 'PoD' bound tighter to the karmic wheel (203), more firmly enmeshed in the world by his desire for Tamara.

his mother...were the first human beings ever to set foot on that world.' Then another voice out of the silence, Lidi expressing her fears that her navigation skills would be rendered obsolete by the churten, her fear she might be too old to learn the new technique. One of the Gethenians, I think, tells briefly of their sense of loss in NAFAL time-dilation. Then I think the other Gethenian—Garth?—talks of how they bet on the new technique, 'Staking everything on it,' and then, in a favorite Le Guinian paradoxical teaching, completing the sentence, 'because nothing works except what we give our souls to, nothing's safe except what we put at risk' (103).

Frequently in Le Guin we have gotten the Romantic-Comic motif of a new and better world coalescing around a central couple (in my modification of Northrop Frye's formula). In 'The Shobies' Story,' we have that again, but with an important difference. In a voice that may be Gveter's we hear that 'actual transilience of living, conscious beings...would be a great event in the mind of his people—for all people. A new understanding. A new partnership. A new way of being in the universe.... He wanted to be one of the crew that first formed that partnership' (103-104). *Partnership* is the term for 'marriage' among Odonians and in this speech some primal couple is replaced by a crew, in the immediate context a discourse community telling their stories. But a community—a hearth—that includes pairs and families: the Gethenian family, with Sweet Today as honorary Grandmother (76), Tai and Betton, apparently without Shan. The ship's systems start up again, with the final voices speaking:

> 'They were thoughts in the mind; what else had they ever been? So they could be in Ve and at the brown planet, and desiring flesh and entire spirit, and illusion and reality, all at once, as they'd always been. When he remembered this, his confusion and fear ceased, for he knew that they couldn't be lost.'
>
> 'They got lost. But they found the way,' said another voice....

And here they notice the 'warm fresh air and light inside the solid walls and hulls' (104). Nine had spoken; the tenth is Rig, asleep with thumb in mouth.[638] They are back at Ve Port, having been gone for forty-four minutes 'into non-existence, into silence,' but they are back now to tell their stories (105), the story Le Guin has put into a complex singular: 'The Shobies' [plural possessive] Story.'

---

[638] For 9 / 10, see Le Guin's 'Nine Lives' and the Foretelling in *LHD*, esp. 65-68 (ch. 4).

'Dancing to Ganam'

'Dancing to Ganam' is a sequel to 'The Shobies' Story,' a gloss to 'The Shobies' Story,' and an extension of 'The Shobies' Story's' thematic concerns.[639] 'Dancing' is also a return by Le Guin, to such themes as music and myth, the archetypes of the Child and the Hero, the nature of reality.

The story is bracketed with a brief prolog and slightly longer epilog (neither labeled with those terms). What I am calling the epilog occurs after the action of the story, as part of the report of the point-of-view character in the story—or his responses at a debriefing or interrogation, or his testimony at some (formal?) inquiry.

The prolog is in three parts, starting with a dialog between the priest Aketa and his wife Ket, although both 'priest' and 'wife' need a good deal of explanation, especially since Ket has at least one other husband and is herself the more important priest (133). In the dialog, Aketa starts the story with the line, 'Power is the great drumming,' and adds 'The thunder. The noise of the waterfall,' which sounds nicely primitive and traditionally poetic until he identifies that waterfall as the one 'that makes the electricity.' He adds that such power-thunder-noise 'fills you until there's no room for anything else.' This is, of course, an important line for Le Guin: if her villains aren't hollow, like Haber in *The Lathe of Heaven* (e.g., 167; ch. 10), they are full of themselves like Davidson in *The Word for World Is Forest*—or full of themselves like such flawed men as the Master Windkey in *Tehanu* (ch. 10) or Jerry Debree in 'Gorgonids' or the Professors in 'The Rock that Changed Things.' Ket, however, does not develop the line immediately (that will come in a moment and in the action of the story) but instead pours water upon the ground, followed by pollen meal, saying 'Drink, traveler' and 'Eat, traveler.' If we tentatively picture these two as ancient Greeks (who know about electricity), we might think Ket welcoming or propitiating a ghost or sending water and food to one on the way to Hades. This first section of the prolog ends with Ket looking up at the volcano Iyananam, 'the mountain of power' and speculating, 'Maybe he only listened to the thunder, and couldn't hear anything else,' and asks if Aketa thinks the unidentified 'he' 'knew what he was doing.' Aketa replies that he thinks 'he' did ([107]).

After a white space, the prolog continues with some background on churten technology and theory, featuring the admonitions of Cetian temporalists and Hainish psychologists that 'You cannot say' a number of things about a churten event, including among the excluded words and concepts: *went*, *happened*, *fact*, *experienced*, and maybe *arrival*. Like old mystics or

---

[639] In his 'Hainish Chronology,' 'Dancing' is put by Peter Brigg in 5120, twenty years after 'Shobies' Story' in 5100 CE (Brigg 18). However, Betton is still living with Tai (and Shan) and is called 'boy' on the second page of the story (*FIS* 108); and Shan's relationship with Dalzul and his brief reference to his relationship with his partner Tai (126) is more consistent with a relatively young man, recently married than a man in his 40s, who has been a husband for a good while.

recent physicists, these future scientists present reality as 'Not this...not that'—what's left over, possibly, after we stop thinking. They are pretty sure that 'The reality point of 'arrival' for a churten crew' of intelligent sentients 'is obtained by mutual perception-comparison and adjustment, so that for thinking beings construction of event is essential to effective transilience.' This section ends with the experts listening to Commander Dalzul (from Terra, as we later learn) who has the idea that 'The problem' the *Shoby* crew encountered was 'interference'; therefore, 'send one man alone.' More specifically, send him (108).[640] In 1967, in *City of Illusions*, 'Go alone' was good advice to the hero; in 1993, in 'Dancing to Ganam,' the volunteering for a solo job, and for heroism, is more problematic.

The last section of the prolog is a brief dialog between Tai and her son, Betton. Betton tells Tai she should go on the mission with Shan; Tai says that if Betton isn't invited on the churten mission, Tai is not going. Shan, though, is going, and the story proper starts with Shan: Shan getting into his black-and-silver Terran Ekumen uniform to meet Commander Dalzul—and then two long paragraphs of exposition on Commander Dalzul, a genuine, big-time hero.

Shan is our point-of-view character here, but rather like Ishmael in Herman Melville's *Moby Dick*: Dalzul will be the Ahab-like scene-stealer (competing with two characters we will meet later). So we learn little more about Shan and more about Dalzul, including that Dalzul is Terran-born (from 'the barracks of Alberta') and goes back almost to the time of Terra's entrance into the Ekumen, a significant time back.[641] Dalzul has a degree in temporal physics from the University of A-Io on Urras (the school Shevek taught at), 'trained with the Stabiles on Hain,' and had returned to his homeworld as a Mobile, where 'a troublesome religious movement escalated into the horrors of the Unist Revolution'—some totalizing system, monotheistic, and for some readers surely a glance at recent Right-wing religious movements in the US and elsewhere. That last point is hardly necessary, however; theocratic takeovers are a standard SF motif, one Le Guin used in 'The Masters' (1963) and 'The Stars Below' (1973). We learn that Dalzul brought things 'under control within months' in ways that got him respect from those he helped, 'and the worship of those he had worked against—for the Unist Fathers decided he was God.' Acting with the 'all the means the Ekumen most honored'—grace, wit, patience, 'trickiness, and good humor'—Dalzul had at least 'defused the worst resurgence of theocratic violence since the Time of Pollution.'

Under the threat of renewed deification, Dalzul could no longer work on Terra and moves on to 'obscure but significant tasks on obscure but significant planets,' including Orint, the one planet from which the Ekumen had ever withdrawn, not long before whatever powers that were

---

[640] For a significant allusion to Dalzul among the Cetians and Hainish, see 'Another Story,' *FIS* 177.

[641] Brigg puts the Formation of the Ekumen in 4623, which makes Dalzul 497 Earth-years old, which, with time-dilation, is plausible.

on the planet resorted to biological warfare and exterminated humanity on their world. Dalzul had not only foreseen the destruction 'with terrible and compassionate accuracy' but had also managed to 'set up the secret, last-minute rescue of a few thousand children whose parents were willing to let them go....' Dalzul has again achieved major, unproblematic, unambiguous heroism. 'Dalzul's children, these last of the Orintians were called,' making Dalzul a combination of Janusz Korczak, 'Father of the Orphans' (see Bernheim) and Oskar Schindler—plus any other of the righteous, nonmilitaristic, life-affirming heroes one wishes to mention. 'Shan knew that heroes were phenomena of primitive cultures, but Terran culture is still primitive,' it seems, 'and Dalzul was his hero' (109). Indeed, Dalzul is strongly in contention for best of Heroes—if we need or want another hero at all.[642]

This exposition on Dalzul very neatly replaces a scene we do not see: the first meeting between Dalzul and Shan. What we do see, very briefly, is Shan's return to his partner, Tai, and relaying the offer we already know she has rejected/will reject. 'What kind of crew is that?' Tai asks—when all we know is that the proposed crew does not include (young) Betton; and she adds the intriguing rhetorical question, 'Who asks parents to leave their kid?' Good question for those of us who found problems with taking children along on the *Shoby* trip. If Shan should go, so should Tai, and she wants to take her son. But she tells Shan to go without them: 'Tai was on the hero's side,' the Narrator tells us, and Shan goes, as is necessary if we want this story (109-10).

Instead of Tai, for Dalzul plus a partnered, heterosexual couple, the crew will be Dalzul, Shan, and a partnered couple who, initially are not identified by gender or sexuality: Riel and Forest, both Terrans for an all-Terran crew (unusual in the Ekumen). Riel and Forest know Shan from training on Ollul, and, like Shan, and modal Terrans generally, they are people of color: allowing for some figurative exaggeration, Forest's face is 'an obsidian knife'—i.e., literally black, beautifully shiny, very sharp—and Riel's 'round and shining as a copper sun' (110).[643] Dalzul is the oddball in terms of color-coding: 'light hair, going grey...white-skinned'; the skin-color Shan sees as a 'deformity or atavism,' but a minor one.[644] In his first meeting with the (potential) crew, Dalzul briefly relates the story of his first two solo churtens: no problems, 'no perceptual dissonances at all.' Promisingly, in a Le Guin story, he found the trips 'magic,' 'natural. Where one is, one is.' Dalzul asks for Shan's experience on the *Shoby*, and

---

[642] In George Miller's *MAD MAX BEYOND THUNDERDOME* (1985), the literal theme song is Tina Turner's 'We Don't Need Another Hero (Thunderdome).'

[643] Among current human beings, Black people are not often black but some variation on brown or brown-black. My selection of 'Black,' 'White,' etc. is intentional: I use these terms precisely because they are *obviously* 'counterfactual' if taken literally.

[644] Cf. Lyubov's finding the Hainishman Lepennon's white skin 'a defect' to his 'Earth-formed aesthetic taste' in *WWF* (68; ch. 3).

Shan relates that they 'had some trouble deciding' just where they were. Dalzul thinks such confusion avoidable. Transilience, he thinks, 'is a non-experience,' wherein, 'normally, *nothing happens*.' He tells Shan 'Extraneous events got mixed into it in the *Shoby* experiment—your interval was queered,' in what may turn out to be a significant bit of word-choice. He thinks this time they could and should have 'a non-experience,' looks at Forest and Riel, laughs and says 'You'll not-see what I don't mean' and gets to the really good part of his story (*FIS* 110).

Dalzul says he annoyed the churten group until Gvonesh—a character we will see in 'Another Story'—allows Dalzul 'to do a solo exploratory,' coming to this decision, I assume, in consultation with her colleagues (111). Dalzul sets out to G-14-214-yomo, a k a Tadkla, called by the people Dalzul met on the planet—as Dalzul interprets what they say—Ganam. The Ekumen has a NAFAL mission on its way to Ganam, and Dalzul hopes the NAFAL mission will arrive 'thirteen years from herenow' to find Ganam already a member of the Ekumen—and everything wonderfully transformed:

> ...churten is going to change everything. When transilience replaces space travel—all travel—when there is no distance between worlds—when we control interval—I keep trying to imagine, to understand what it will mean, to the Ekumen, to us. We'll be able to make the household of humankind truly one house, one place. But then it goes still deeper! In transilience what we do is to rejoin, restore the primal moment, the beat that is the rhythm.... To rejoin unity. To escape time. To use eternity! (112)

This little speech introduces Dalzul's audio-visual show of his solo to Ganam, so it is an important speech in a stressed location.

In Le Guin's canon, the Dao *is* and is 'the beat that is the rhythm'; namable Dao is a timeless unity: in Western terms, eternal Being; in a very popular image, including with Le Guin, the eternal dance—hinted at with the printer's mark in *Buffalo Gals* (1987). Very explicitly in *City of Illusions* (1967) and *The Lathe of Heaven* (1971), Le Guin has it that one should get in contact with the Dao, touch immanent Reality, from time to time. Additionally, in the Hainish universe, we *are* children of one hearth, one household of humankind. However, and this is crucial, immanent Reality does not exhaust the human world, and where we live is less the Ultimate Dao of Nothingness or Namable Dao, but the world of Yin-Yang and the ten thousand created things. A bird in T. S. Eliot's Burnt Norton tells us that 'human kind / Cannot bear very much reality,' and Eliot liked the line enough to assign it also to Thomas à Becket in *Murder in the Cathedral* (1935).[645] In *The Lathe of Heaven*, Le Guin says, '...the bird is

---

[645] Near the end of Section 1 of Burnt Norton for the bird, in 'Four Quartets' (Burnt Norton written 1935, publ. 1939).

mistaken,' that it is 'unreality' we cannot bear (171; ch. 11); still, I think she agrees with Eliot this far: we should not try to *live* in Ultimate Reality, however pictured, and lose our identities and the world: we should not lose ourselves in the light of Being and Truth as Meshe does in *The Left Hand of Darkness* (1969) nor in the transcendent God of 'Field of Vision' (1973), nor in Brahma in 'Pathways of Desire' (1979)—nor in the 'here now One' of NAFAL flight ('VEMS' 1971 [only]), nor in the churten. So Dalzul is right to remember with a very positive passion a churten experience that was, for him, a restoration of a lost unity, a restoration of 'the primal moment.' But only as a *moment*. It is troubling that he speaks of both changing things and escaping time, and a very bad sign that he wishes 'To *use* eternity!' Le Guin makes clear in 'The *Shobies*' Story' that she is well aware that 'We all use each,' however much 'we have no right to do so' (*FIS* 82), and that is an ethical dilemma humans must feel our ways through; still, eternity is not there to be used, nor is 'interval' to be controlled, nor time to be escaped.

There are also problems with wanting to unify quite so much the household of humankind. Again, Jane Flax reminds us that 'Perhaps reality,' however constituted 'can have 'a' structure only from the falsely universalizing perspective' of some dominant group (49). White males, for example, White heterosexual and mildly heterosexist males for what will turn out to be an even more specific example.[646] False universalizing, trying to make us all one every which way, denies the reality of the Other, denies difference, denies the delight of diversity (see *LHD* 34-36; ch. 3).[647]

And here we move on to Dalzul's story of First Contact with the Gaman, the people of Ganam, which he shows on a tape (with some sound).

The adventure starts out well, even if the magic did not work perfectly. Dalzul and ship did not materialize in the stratosphere but in the atmosphere, some 100 m. up and very close to a city. In Dalzul's theatrical figure of speech, he did not have much of a 'chance to make an unobtrusive entrance on the scene' (*FIS* 113). There is soon an audience: magnificent barbarians from the City. So, Hero and competent man—and a well-trained Mobile of the Ekumen—Dalzul goes with his situation. He stresses his defenselessness by exiting his ship naked, with empty hands 'held wide and open in the gesture of offering.' He is met by a 'stunning' woman, her hair 'braided with gold into a coronet' (114), identified as Ket, the Anam, a word Dalzul will come to translate, 'princess' (133). She goes through what seems to be a ceremony of greeting, or a ritual of some sort, ending with: 'with a splendid conscious gesture,' herself undressing and standing 'naked before the naked man,' and offering her hand, which Dalzul accepts (114).

Aside from its potential erotic appeal(s), Dalzul's tape and the adventure it records is very different from the Shobies' story because of its clar-

---

[646] I believe Adrienne Rich invented and/or popularized the term 'heterosexist.'
[647] See also any US strip mall; making our Earth 'one place' has some bad implications.

ity and coherence. In Dalzul's interpretation, "What the *Shoby*'s crew discovered...is that individual experiences of transilience can be made coherent only by a concerted effort. An effort to synchronize—to entrain.' The Shobies' 'chaos experience,' Dalzul thinks, 'was an effect of the disparity of the *Shoby* crew.' They were 'ten people from four worlds—four different cultures'; Dalzul also counts 'two very old women,' which is overstating the ages, 'and three young children,' which lumps (honorary) Elder Sib Betton (*FIS* 88) with the two Gethenian children too casually: the Gethenian children are four and six E-years old, and Betton is eleven, big differences at those ages—which would help prove Dalzul's point; so this conflating of the children is a minor but potentially significant mistake; Dalzul may have blind spots about women and children (*FIS* 114-15)..

Dalzul would by-pass the problem the simplest way: 'go alone.' Forest brings up the obvious objection of the difficulty or impossibility of cross-checking on a single person, especially when, as Shan reminds them, the *Shoby*'s instrument readings were no more coherent than the Shobies' perceptions (115). From Dalzul's point of view, that is the point:

> That murk, that shit, that chaos you saw, which the cameras in your field saw—Think of the difference between that and the tapes we just watched! Sunlight, vivid faces, bright colors, everything brilliant, clear—Because there was no interference, Shan. The Cetians say that in the churten field there is nothing but the deep rhythms, the vibrations of the ultimate wave particles.[648] Transilience is a function of the rhythm that makes being. According to Cetian spiritual physics, it's access to that rhythm which allows the individual to participate in eternity and ubiquity.... [I]ndividuals in transilience have to be in nearly perfect synchrony to arrive at the same place with a harmonious—that is accurate—perception of it. (*FIS* 116)

Bright colors are good things, period and in Le Guin (e.g., 'The Rock That Changed Things'), and so is clarity, e.g. Cetian or Anarresti clarity of thought in *The Word for World Is Forest* or *The Dispossessed*, or a clear view on the Ice in *The Left Hand of Darkness*. Still, such clarity is habitually contrasted in Le Guin's work to, or balanced by, the murk of forest, the rights of the darkness, the respectability of mud (*EoH*) or even of shit, 'The color of the earth' (*LoH* 103; ch. 7). And, again, there is the point so elegantly summarized by Flax: if harmony = accuracy = Truth, it will probably be a «truth» determined by the person or caste or class with greatest power.

In Dalzul's theory, churtening by one person is safe, by ten people was an invitation to disaster; a churten by four is a 'control' (118). What he

---

[648] Cf. Capra on the quantum field; see, *Tao of Physics* ch. 13, 'The Dynamic Universe' and ch. 14, 'Emptiness and Form.'

does not add here is that he wanted to keep the emotional dynamics among the crew minimal: he wanted himself and a bonded heterosexual couple; when Tai declines, his second choice was a heterosexual male, Shan—who was more homosexual in his sexuality before his marriage than heterosexual, but Dalzul apparently doesn't know that—and the significantly named Riel ('real'?) and Forest (*forest*), bonded lesbians (126).

There is more to Dalzul's theory, a very beautiful more. The compatible group is to churten while entrained, and the entrainment is music: 'All we need to get to Ganam is music. All there is, in the end, is music,' which is an attractive theory to one who started her publishing career with 'An die Musik' (1961); so they drink, as Shan's toast, 'To music!' (*FIS* 117).

They keep isyeye—their crew-bonding time—but keep it to a minimum. During this time we overhear the first conversation among Shan, Forest, and Riel, without Dalzul. Forest notes the problem in accepting Dalzul's version of his trip 'as objective fact.' Shan notes that Dalzul's version and the 'ship's tapes agree completely,' but Forest points out that, if Dalzul's theory is correct, they would: '...he and the instruments were entrained.' Shan has to agree, but he is reluctant, finding it 'very difficult...to live without the notion that there is, somewhere, if one could just find it, a fact.' Forest is consistent, 'unrelenting,' and insistent: 'Only fiction.... Fact is one of our finest fictions.' Shan doesn't push the point, but the story will return to it. What Shan does do is assert that '[M]usic comes first.... And dancing is people being music. I think what Dalzul sees is that...we can dance to Ganam.' Riel likes the dancing idea, but picks up the implication of 'the fiction theory.' If all we have are fictions, the ship's tapes are also fictions. Dalzul is 'a seasoned observer and a superb gestalter' (118), and Forest thinks Dalzul's version 'looks and rings true.' Still, you do not have to have just come off a reading of Jean-François Lyotard, or Joseph Campbell's *The Hero with a Thousand Faces* (1949, 1968) to recognize bits of a very old metanarrative in Dalzul's story or a displacement toward the secular of 'The Meeting with the Goddess' or a fairly straight-forward version of the 'mystical marriage' (Campbell 109 f.; ch. 2.2). Forest puts it, 'There are elements of a rather familiar kind of fiction in his report.... The princess who has apparently been waiting for him, expecting him, and leads him naked to her palace, where after due ceremonies and amenities she has sex with him—and very good sex too—?' (119). Forest wonders 'how the princess perceived these events' (119). Good question. Even if Truth exists, it may look different to a dragon and a man, as Ged points out to Arren (*FS* 153; ch. 10), and in a world where all may be fiction, the princess's version may be that nothing happened at all—and then tell you she is not a princess.

After a white space, the crew sets off, with Shan confident that 'with Dalzul there would be no chaos'—not with the Dalzul taken as a god by the Unists, received reverently by the Gaman: 'Dalzul was charged, full of mana, a power to which others responded, by which they were entrained.' Dalzul has 'a brightness of being' (119) that makes him what Luz Falco calls her father in *Eye of the Heron*: 'a king, a real one' (*EH* 73; ch. 5)—or the Prince of Kansas in *City of Illusions* (99; ch. 5) or a god like Rocannon (*RW*) or Selver (*WWF*) or Bob in 'Pathways of Desire' (*CR* 189) or the god-like folk George Orr thinks we all, potentially, are (*LoH* 145; ch. 9). And Dalzul leads them in song to Ganam, where all four see sky of blue, grass of green and the approach of friendly natives (120). Shan finds this world, solidly real: 'crude, magnificent, and human. It was stranger than anything Shan had known and it was as if he had been away and come home again.' Shan briefly weeps and thinks, 'We are all one.... There is no distance, no time between us.' The section ends with native people greeting them, and the final sentence—in Gaman?—'You have come home' (122).

After another white space, there is a quick summary of Shan's experiences the first few days. The summary can be quite quick since Shan follows the generally good advice Arthur C. Clarke offers people in very strange situations in *Childhood's End* (1953) and, more directly, in *2001: A Space Odyssey* (1968): relax, experience, take it in; figure it out later. Shan enjoys himself, finding the experience a second childhood, with 'no control,' hence 'no responsibility'; he 'was part of the happening and watched it happen.' And the happening he and his colleagues see is that the Gaman will 'make Dalzul their king.' What he and the rest believe (for now) is that the king has died without a successor, and Dalzul appears 'out of the sky,' and 'vanishes and returns with three strange companions who can work various miracles; you make him king. What else can you do with him?' Forest, as well as the hilfer Riel are dubious about getting so involved in the native culture, but they have no better suggestions to make, and, if the kingship turns out to be as it appears, 'more honorary than authoritative,' then they thought going along better than resisting. Attempting to retain 'perspective on Dalzul's situation,' Riel and Forest move to a house 'where they could be with common people and enjoy a freedom of movement Dalzul did not have' (122). On Ganam as with ritual kings on Terra, the 'king-to-be...was expected to hang around the palace all day, observing taboos' (122-23), but often in the company of one Viaka. Shan sleeps at the palace, in a sort of liminal and movable position between Dalzul and the women: a Merlin, so to speak, to Arthur at Camelot and Morgan le Fay allied and in love with the Lady of the Lake. Or like Lyubov in *The Word for World Is Forest*, moving between the macho world of Davidson and the military and the more balanced world of Selver and the Athsheans. Or we can see Shan as similar to George Orr in *The Lathe of Heaven*, Child-like and moving between the world-changing (mad) scientist Dr. Haber and Orr's once and future partner, Heather Lelache.

In any event, Shan, though relatively peripheral to the action, is central in terms of point of view and as an envoy between a kind of dueling realities or, as Forest might still insist, competing fictions. Orr-like, Child-like, Shan goes with the flow, or follows the script, until we reach the turn in the story. The turn comes with some facts, or fictional elements, that do not fit in with the premise of Ganam as a world of magnificent barbarians awaiting a sky-god king. The first jarring bit of information comes when Shan gets to walk up the slope of Iyananam, the larger of the two volcanoes in the territory of the Gaman (123), and which the first section of the story identifies as 'the mountain of power' ([107]). There is in the area 'a little earth shrine,' and Shan sees from the volcano other towns or cities and learns that '...only Ganam belonged to the Gaman; those cities were other cities' (124). The really jarring part comes in a beautiful area with a sacred waterfall Shan's hosts want him to see: 'He was very much surprised to find that the sacred waterfall was employed to power a sacred dynamo.' Shan feels less happy 'to feel like a child,' and comes to feel more like a 'half-wit' trying to get his hosts to explain to him what they did with the electricity. He learns '...it comes out at the ishkanem when the basmmiak vada' (123). To clarify, they take him out onto an expertly made terrace and point downstream, where he sees something shining on the water and is told it is taboo, the first taboo he has personally run into (124).

The next jarring is far less spectacular than seeing a sacred hydroelectric generator; it involves a pruning knife Shan is using. It is not something Shan immediately thinks about, but the Narrator describes it as 'a thin, slightly curved steel blade' with a handle (124-25). Steel? Bronze for ancient barbarians, magnificent or otherwise, as in *King Dog*'s setting, which is explicitly labeled 'a society in the Bronze Age' (13) and consistently depicted as such. Shortly after these experiences, Shan and Dalzul get together for a man-to-man talk, and Dalzul tells Shan that something is wrong.

In Dalzul's story, he has developed a rival, Aketa, with whom Princess Ket has gone to live, even though she still says that Dalzul will be what he translates as 'king' (126). Dalzul is confused and seeks advice about women from Dalzul, as a partnered man. When Dalzul asks him if partnered people ever get to a place where the man knows who the woman is and (in Sigmund Freud's question) what she wants, Shan can only answer that he doesn't know and sensibly suggest that Dalzul ask Riel and Forest: 'As women, maybe they'd have some insights?' It is here that Dalzul shows his sexism and heterosexism:

> 'Women yes and no.... That's why I chose them, Shan. With two real women, the psychological dynamics might have been too complicated.'
>
> Shan said nothing, feeling again that something was missing or he was missing something, misunderstanding. He wondered if Dalzul knew that most of Shan's sexuality had been with men until he met Tai.
>
> 'Consider,' Dalzul said, 'for instance, if the princess thought she should be jealous of one or both of them, thought they were my sexual partners. That could be a snake's nest! As it is, they're no threat.'

And here Dalzul tells Shan he would have preferred the 'consonance' of an all-male crew but compromised to suit the old women of the Elders on Hain. Dalzul allows that Riel and Forest (though not 'real women') have still 'performed admirably. But I don't think they're equipped to tell me what's going on in the mind, or the hormones, of a very fully sexed woman such as the princess' (236-27). Here, Shan again feels the 'beat' skip, and he should. Perfect consonance within a group can make their figurative music boring; Dalzul's attitude, though, could break their music: if Riel and Forest are not 'real women,' what are they? To paraphrase a Gethenian saying, you do not have to be lovers to work together—but you do have to see the people you work with as fellow human beings.

Dalzul's reading of the situation is that Ket has defected, causing a schism, 'and if Aketa gains power, his supporters will wreak vengeance on Viaka and all his people. Blood sacrifice for offense to the true and sacred king's person.... Religion and politics! How could I of all men be so blind?' And Dalzul answers his own question by saying that he'd allowed his 'longings' to persuade him that they had found a 'primitive ideal' among people who have retained 'everything we lost with our literacy, our industry, our science.' Dalzul sees himself, and through him his companions, in the midst of 'a factional and sexual competition among intelligent barbarians who keep their pruning hooks and their swords extremely sharp' (127).[649]

The immediate problem for Shan is what to do faced with 'Dalzul's unexpected male-heterosexual defensiveness' that prevent Dalzul from getting help and advice from Riel and Forest. Being a sensible person, Shan goes off to see Riel and Forest, thinking about the dynamo, other cities, and a pruning hook of steel: 'How did the Gaman make their steel?' He comes upon Forest reading a native book—a book?—who greets him facetiously as 'A visitor from another planet!' getting Shan to wonder just how long it had been since he had seen them, and feeling 'a sudden tremor of unease, a missed beat so profound that he put his hands flat on the warm sandstone,' as if there had been an earthquake (128).

Shan explains the situation from Dalzul's point of view, ending with 'It's just the kind of sticky situation Dalzul was hoping to avoid,' to which Forest adds, 'And is matchless at resolving.' Shan doesn't rise to that bait but says that Dalzul doesn't understand 'what role the princess is playing.' Forest and Riel then give another version of events. If by 'princess' Dalzul means the daughter of a king, then Ket isn't one; there is no king; there has never been a king among the Gaman. Dalzul will be the divinely designated 'one who will hold the scepter,' but not a king. Forest asks for the name of the rival, and Shan tells them it is Aketa, and Forest looks at him very directly and tells him '...we are seriously out of sync,' and suspects a chaos experience (129-30). Shan says it is nothing like what he experi-

---

[649] Dalzul may see himself as Davidic king, working a slight variation on getting opponents to 'beat their swords into plowshares, / and their spears into pruning hooks' (Micah 4.3 [also Isaiah 2.4]).

enced with the *Shoby* churten, but Forest suggests that they might be 'reading the experience quite differently.' Shan notes, correctly if 'rather desperately,' that 'People always do, everywhere.'[650] Then he sees—first «surrealistically» sees, sees as metamorphosing things—then really *sees*, the book: 'In a strange writing. In a strange language. A book with covers of carved wood, hinged with gold.' Forest tells him it is probably a sacred history of the cities under the volcano Iyananam. Shan knows the Gaman are preliterate. Forest and Riel tells them that many are illiterate, but some are literate, for example, Aketa, who gave them the book to read: Aketa who is teaching them, as part of his vocation as scholar-priest (130).

To Shan, it seems that men run the city; to Riel and Forest, the Gaman are 'a non-gender-dominant society,' without much sexual division of labor, a good deal of polyandry, and homosexual group marriage for women. 'Aketa is one of Ket's husbands. His name means something like Ket's-kin-first-husband. Kin meaning they're in the same volcano lineage.' His high rank may come from his marriage to Ket. If Forest and Riel are correct about the Gaman, Shan's impressions are 'out of sync,' and Dalzul's reading is seriously wrong. Shan says that Dalzul has to see the book (131). Riel says, 'He has seen it,' and explains the apparent paradox through an old Terran anthropologists' tale of taking a smart tribesman from a remote Arctic tribe to New York City, where the tribesman spent his time studying 'the knobs on the bottom posts of staircases.' In case this newel-post-knob analogy wasn't totally clear, Forest gets quite specific. The churten problem may not just be one of impressions but also of expectations.

We make sense of the world intentionally. Faced with chaos [William James's postulated 'blooming, buzzing confusion'], we seek or make the familiar, and build up the world with it.[651] Babies do it, we all do it; we filter out most of what our senses report. We're conscious only of what we need to be or want to be conscious of. In churten, the universe dissolves. As we come out, we reconstruct it—frantically. Grabbing at things we recognize. And once one part of it is there, the rest gets built on that.

As, for example, whatever the tribesman saw in the newel-post knobs. Riel then shifts her explanation to the linguistic: Say the word 'I,' and '...an infinite number of sentences could follow. But the next word begins to build the immutable syntax.... By the last word, there may be no choice at all. And also, you can only use words you know' (132). Technically, in terms of generative grammar, you could probably extend any sentence, but the practical points are correct. As Ged in *A Wizard of Earthsea* had to learn, our choices create who we are and continually redefine the circumstances of our lives, limiting further choice.

---

[650] Note old Wold's observation in *PE* (1966), 'All men were alien to one another at times, not only aliens' (37; ch. 4).
[651] The William James line is quoted in Le Guin's 'The Field of Vision' (*WTQ* 231).

Shan has some experience in this matter: the Shobies talked and 'reconstructed the syntax of the experience. We told our story.' Forest notes that the Shobies 'tried very hard to tell it'—singular—'truly,' and Shan asks if Dalzul is lying (132). They do not think Dalzul lies but ask if he is 'telling the Ganam story or the Dalzul story' (the constant problem of the «participant-observer» generally, ethnographers most particularly). What they imply, is that Dalzul may be caught in a narrative: 'The childlike, simple people acclaiming him king, the beautiful princess offering herself...'—Shan interjects that 'she did': so they saw on the tapes. Forest responds,

> It's her job. Her vocation. She's one of these priests, an important one. Her title in Anam. Dalzul translated it princess. We think it means earth. The earth, the ground, the world. She in Ganam's earth, receiving the stranger in honor. But there's more to it—this reciprocal function, which Dalzul interprets as kingship. They simply don't have kings. It must be some kind of priesthood role as Anam's mate. Not Ket's husband, but her mate when she's Anam. But we don't know...what responsibility he's taken on.

If you know the term 'Year-King,' you can guess, though, and that guess would be reinforced by the suggestion at the end of the page that part of the job of the priests is to 'keep the city in spiritual balance,' which means, 'Sometimes, possibly, by blood sacrifice' (133).

For many readers, then, the syntax of the plot has already pretty well closed. Unless Le Guin gives us a surprise ending, or cheats, Dalzul has cast himself into the role of consort to the Earth-Mother, the consort whose major act in the story is to get killed. (And we already have strong hints on *how* Dalzul will be killed). Some of the questions remaining in the story for such readers regard character—Why does Dalzul do what he does? How do the others respond?—and theme: What should *we* make of this story? How does the plot relate to the churten experience and the structuring of reality? What does the plot tell us about Heroes?

The Narrator gets to work on these issues just before allowing Riel to throw out the crucial and only slightly misleading phrase, 'blood sacrifice.' Going into Shan's mind, the Narrator has him tell what he knows: that Forest and Riel are 'sympathetic, intelligent, trying to be honest'; that 'Dalzul is a great man, not a foolish egoist, not a liar.' But Shan also knows 'that when he was thirty, Dalzul was worshipped as God. No matter how he disavowed that worship, it must have changed him. Growing old, he would remember what it was to be a king....' And he might translate 'Todoghay, the one who holds the scepter' (133) to mean 'king.' Shan sighs and tells Riel and Forest he feels 'like a fool,' and Forest asks him, 'Because you fell in love with Dalzul?' and says that she honors him for doing so. Still, Dalzul needs Shan's help. Shan concludes that there is a *must* here: initially he thinks they must tell their story together, but he changes the thought to 'I must listen.'

> He listened as he walked in the streets of Ganam. He tried to look, to see with his eyes, to feel, to be in his own skin in this world, in this world, itself. Not his world, not Dalzul's or Forest's or Riel's, but this world as it was in its recalcitrant and irreducible earth and stone and clay, its dry bright air, its breathing bodies and thinking minds. A vendor was calling wares in a brief musical phrase, five beats.... A woman passed him and Shan saw her, saw her absolutely for a moment.... She left behind her indubitable sense of being. Of being herself. Unconstructed, unreadable, unreachable. The other. Not his to understand.
>
> All right then. Rough stone warm against the palm, and a five-beat measure, and a short old woman going about her business. It was a beginning. (134).

A beginning for building up a world, a *real* world, starting with what he sees as 'recalcitrant' and 'irreducible,' including an Other 'absolutely' a being in herself, for herself. All fiction, of course: Shan is a character in a highly improbable story. But while we are entrained into the world(s) of this story, caught up in its words and music, these are *facts* for Shan—out there, external facts—and, for a moment also, for us. This is one of the epiphanies in Le Guin, one of the moments a character achieves momentary wholeness and a momentary glimpse of the Other, wholly and clearly.[652] A moment when one can see with a kind of certainty: the 'Sureness' for which language is 'inadequate' when one has found 'THE WAY' (*ACH* 485; 'Some Generative Metaphors').

Starting from there, Shan understand that he has 'been dreaming,' a good dream, not the nightmare of the chaos experience on the *Shoby*—a good, Yinish, Le Guinian dream. But it is time for action, Tai is not there (who usually gets him moving), but Riel and Forest have figuratively shaken him awake, and Shan concludes he must do the same for Dalzul. If Dalzul will let him: 'Apparently Forest and Riel don't exist for him as women; do I exist for him as a man?' In musical terms, Shan feels his job is to add 'dissonance in the harmony, to syncopate the beat.' In a different metaphor, he thinks his job 'is to try to jolt him' (135).

To prepare for the dissonance-introduction and jolting, Shan, Riel, and Forest talk with Aketa about the scepter-bearer and the scepter and the power the scepter 'Is connected with—symbolizes?' After a brief comic episode of Shan's 'dancing a waterfall,' miming 'the little dynamo up on the volcano,' and Aketa's responses, they conclude that the scepter is associated with electricity: 'If you take the scepter[,] you're the Electricity

---

[652] Or one sees the Other and then contacts Dao; the language of cause and effects does not apply well to mystic experiences.

Priest....' Dalzul chose the scepter and, in some sense, was chosen by it. But to what end? Aketa's answer includes a word Shan tentatively interprets as 'Dead, death?' (136-37).

Shan has Dalzul over for dinner and serious conversation, and gets Dalzul's story (continued). In Dalzul's version, Ket is a virgin saving herself for the sacred marriage of the king and earth: 'So that in a sense she is the Earth. As, in a sense, I am Space, the sky. Coming alone to this world, a conjunction. A mystic union: fire and air with soil and water. The old mythologies enacted again in living flesh.' Except the Terrans 'aren't behaving in a properly sacred manner.' Dalzul thinks the Gaman primitive and therefore rigid; and from there he reasons that the Terrans are disrupting the Gaman society and that he, Dalzul, is responsible. Shan tries to get the matter in perspective, pointing out to Dalzul that the people of this world are responsible for their world, 'And they don't seem all that primitive,' pointing out the steel, electricity, literacy, and social flexibility and stability. And then goes on to give Forest and Riel's reading of their situation. Dalzul hears little of this (rejecting what doesn't fit with his story) and then exits: 'He stood up and patted the air on the back, saying, 'Good night, Forest; good night, Riel,' before he patted Shan on the back and said, 'Good night and thanks, Shan!' (138-39). Shan returns to Riel and Forest to review the problem. Shan thinks Dalzul delusional, and from the point of view of the story, which is Shan's, Dalzul *is* delusional. Still, within the story, Shan must wonder if perhaps he is the one with the delusions, 'But you and Riel and I,' he tells Forest, 'we seem to be in the same general reality—fiction—are we?' Forest says 'Increasingly so' (139).

All three go to see Dalzul, but Dalzul sees only Shan. Dalzul agrees they must leave, but only after the coronation. He sees an obligation: 'If I run out on them, Aketa's faction will have their swords out—' Riel interrupts, loudly, 'Aketa doesn't have a sword.... These people don't have swords, they don't make them!' Dalzul talks through her words (141). Shan thinks they should knock Dalzul on the head and get him offplanet: 'He could destroy Ganam instead of saving it—' and Riel interrupts him with 'Is Ganam a world? Is Dalzul a God?' And then an important speech:

> Ganam is one little city-state on a large planet, which the Gaman call Anam, and the people in the next valley call something else entirely.... Dalzul, because he's crazy or because churtening made him crazy or made us all crazy, I don't know which, I don't care just now—Dalzul barged in and got mixed up in sacred stuff and maybe is causing some trouble and confusion. But these people *live* here. This is their place. One man can't destroy them and one man can't save them! They have their own story, and *they*'re telling it! How we'll figure in it I don't know— maybe as some idiots that fell out of the sky once!'

Putting 'a peaceable arm around Riel's shoulders,' Forest reiterates the message: Aketa won't slaughter Viaka and the palace household, and Forest cannot 'see these people letting us mess up anything in a big way. They're in control.' So they should go through with the ceremony. 'It probably isn't a big deal except in Dalzul's mind.' When it is over, they can ask him to go home, and he'll take them: "He'll do it. He's—' she paused. He's fatherly,' she said, without sarcasm,' ending the section (142). The ultimate father-figure in a way, Dalzul is best-of-breed as traditional (heterosexual, unpartnered, Judeo-Christian-Rationalist Western) Hero, who comes to a decorous end.

The Ceremony of the Scepter as the Narrator describes it, and Riel interprets, is very impressive. Ket is accompanied by Aketa and Ketketa, her two husbands, with a big turnout of priests. Dalzul is dressed in his black and silver uniform, and Ket walks to him, kneels down on both knees, and says to him a sentence Riel translates, 'Dalzul, you chose.' She goes back to her husbands (143); everybody walks onto the volcano, 'all in one huge pulse. Entrained.' They get to 'an altar or low pedestal' placed in 'the shine and glitter of the water,' and on the pedestal 'a wand, not gold, unornamented, of dark wood or tarnished metal' (144). It's metal. Dalzul is told to take off his shoes, which he does, walks to the pedestal 'and around it, so that he faced the procession and the watching people. He smiled, and put out his hand, and seized the scepter.' For those who want things spelled out, there is Shan's testimony in what I've called the epilog: Dalzul was electrocuted. 'They thought he had chosen that death. He chose it when he chose to have sex with Ket, with the Earth Priestess, with the Earth. They thought he knew.... If you lie with the Earth, you die by the Lightning. Men come a long way to Ganam for that death.' Shan says that the Terrans had not understood, but he doesn't know if their lack of perception had to do with 'the churten effect, with perceptual dissonance, with chaos.' They had come 'to see differently, but which of us knew the truth? He knew he had to be a god again'; and there the story ends (145).

Discussion

At the end of 'The Shobies' Story,' the nine crew members still awake agree on a narrative and so recreate the(ir) universe and get home. It is a comic ending: not a new and better world coalescing around a central couple, but a lost universe reforming around a central group, in a kind of allegory of the establishment of human society around the fire in a cave. 'Dancing to Ganam' comes to a more abrupt and tragic ending.

I have of 'Dancing' three related question: (1) Finally, whose story is this? (2) How does this story come down on the possibility 'that there is, somewhere, if one could just find it, a fact'? (3) How does 'Dancing' fit into Le Guin's canon?

However much Captain Ahab steals the show in Herman Melville's *Moby Dick* (1851), the opening and closing belong to Ishmael, the Narrator. The close of 'Dancing' is Shan's testimony about Dalzul's death, including the assertions that the Gaman 'thought he had chosen that death' and that Shan is sure that Dalzul 'had to be a god again' (145). So Shan and Dalzul share the close between them, with some reference to the Gaman, and with Shan as Narrator, Shan having escaped to tell the story. The opening is the Gaman view, or at least that of Aketa and Ket, in a scene that occurs, I think, simultaneously with Shan's testimony. As the Ekumenical authorities close the case, as I picture these scenes, the Gaman are completing their ritual.[653] Ket wonders if Dalzul 'only listened to the thunder'—the power—'and couldn't hear anything else'; Aketa says he thinks Dalzul 'knew what he was doing' ([107]). The opening, then, is shared by the Gaman and Dalzul. I think, then, that the story is about Dalzul, from multiple points of view, Terran and Gaman, female and male.

If Dalzul knew what he was doing, then one interpretation of what he was doing was choosing to become a year-king, one of the 'Kings Killed at the End of a Fixed Term' described by James Frazer (319 f.; ch. 24.3), combined with the consort of the Earth, in the godly manner of Osiris, Tammuz, Adonis, Attis (Frazer 376 f.; chs. 29-43, esp. 378-80). This is not exactly what the Gaman think Dalzul is doing, but it is close enough. What is insane in Dalzul's behavior is his starting to conspire, wheel, and deal in the manner of a real, political king, or in the manner of a Mobile of the Ekumen to Terra, when he really was taken for God and really, in terms of Ekumenical history, achieved his greatest political success, going on to become, on Terra and on Orint, a true hero (*FIS* 109). In that case, his insanity is trying to recreate in detail his greatest role. He is also a little scary from the point of view of Shan, Riel, and Forest, in talking to people who are not there and (on another occasion) ignoring people who are—at least in Shan's version.

If Dalzul did not choose his script, then he was insanely acting like a political king going to his coronation and finding himself an electrocuted temporary lover of the Earth embodied in Ket as Anam.

Alternatively, Dalzul went to the Ceremony of the Scepter, was crowned king, and did what was necessary to get back the princess Ket and put down the rebellion of Aketa. If we have nothing else but fictions, that happy ending (for Dalzul) is a possibility—if we had heard the story from Dalzul's point of view. We did not, however, and I believe most readers take it that within the fiction of 'Dancing to Ganam' it is a fact that Dalzul is electrocuted. So Ket and Aketa imply in the opening; so Shan testifies or reports (without ever mentioning Dalzul by name) at the end of the story. So the Narrator strongly hints by standard protocols of dropping hints in SF stories and in mysteries. We can say, then, 'that there is, somewhere...a fact,' if only in a fictional world. Further, we can say that for Shan there are facts: the sensations in the market place, where Shan sees the world of the Gaman, hears the vendor's call, and most especially sees the 'short old

---

[653] From a godlike, readerly point of view—as I read—one can say that two events at serious astronomical distances are simultaneous; within the world of any fiction set in a relativistic universe, simultaneity is a problematic concept.

woman going about her business' as an Other, absolute in herself (134). Or we can say with Forest that there is 'Only fiction,' including the facts Shan makes up for himself (118); we can add to this the idea, also from Forest, that 'the churten problem centers not on impressions only, but expectations' (132)—including, perhaps, the expectations of those who know the term 'Year-King' and SF reading protocols. And we should add even to that Riel's insistence that the Gaman: 'have their own story, and *they*'re telling it!' (141). In that case, in the land of the Gaman, Gaman consensus determines reality: *they* expect Dalzul to be electrocuted; hence Dalzul *is* electrocuted (insofar as 'is' is a meaningful word).

I choose to take the modernist position (and the *very early* modernist one of Koheleth in Ecclesiastes) and believe that somewhere some facts may exist, but they are very difficult to find and will look different from different point of view. And I think I can get Le Guin on my side here as much as she is on the side of Riel and Forest.

I have compared Shan's liminality—his acting as a kind of envoy between two realties—to that of Lyubov in *The Word for World Is Forest* (1972) and George Orr in *The Lathe of Heaven* (1971), both early works but both relevant. On the one hand, both works stress the importance of the dream, always a kind of fiction. For the Athsheans in *Word for World*, dream-time is as real as world-time. And, in a sense, *all* of *The Lathe of Heaven*, except for a flashback, is set in worlds dreamed by George Orr: Orr's fictions. Still, though, within those worlds and applicable, I think, to our world—singular—we have statements that go very differently. Most succinct is Selver's assertion, 'What is, is.' If something has been brought from the dream-time into the world-time, it is in the world; to believe otherwise 'is insanity' (168; ch. 8). Selver's people have learned mass murder; in the story, that is a fact. In the story, Selver and his people have won a terrible victory, and Don Davidson has lost and is isolated on an island. To say that this is only one version and to insist on giving Davidson's equal weight is to undermine *Word for World* as an attack on US military action in Indochina and render Le Guin politically and artistically irresponsible.

Within one world that George Orr has dreamed up, within the fiction of *Lathe*, Heather Lelache thinks about her responsibility in suggesting a dream to George Orr. 'A person who believes, as she did, that things fit: that there is a whole of which one is a part, and that in being a part one is whole: such a person has no desire whatever, at any time, to play God. Only those who have denied their being yearn to play at it. But she was caught in a role and couldn't back out of it now.' Lelache suggests that Orr 'dream the Aliens aren't out there on the Moon any longer'—with bad (if darkly comic) results (106-07; ch. 7). Le Guin is well aware of the idea of getting caught up in roles—fictions, narratives—and nevertheless her Narrator rings a lot of large chimes here in having Lelache able to resist the yearning to play God because Lelache feels herself part of a larger whole, a whole that has real, extra-fictional existence. In *Lathe*, the most basic whole is the Dao. Similarly, at the turning point of *Lathe* George Orr experiences 'a sense of well-being...a certainty that things were all right, and that he was in the middle of things. Self is universe. He would not be allowed to be isolated, to be stranded.... This feeling did not come to him as blissful or mystical, but simply as normal' (139; ch. 9). Dalzul is *not* a god, able to save or destroy the Gaman (141) even if in Dalzul's mind he is, not because the Gaman outvote him but because there just aren't such gods in the world of this story.

In 'Pathways of Desire' (1979), Le Guin was willing to play again with the idea that worlds can be dreamed up and are being dreamed up; but even in 'Pathways' relatively old people are able to escape the dream—having no assigned roles except being old—and begin to create a culture. And the two central lovers can determine that even if the world we experience is all illusion, Maya, that we should stay in it and do the best we can in what reality we have. If nothing else, death in 'Pathways' seems really real, and it is also the one certainty allowed in the Handdara in *The Left Hand of Darkness* (71; ch. 5). Genly Ai makes his report as if it were a story, for the Terran view is 'that Truth is a matter of the imagination' and 'Facts are no more solid, coherent, round, and real than pearls are' (1), but pearls are quite real enough for all esthetic matters, and, in *Left Hand*, we cannot deny Estraven's death. The same is the case for Dalzul. Starting with this one apparent fact—Dalzul ends up the story dead (so says Hideo in 'Another Story' [*FIS* 177])—we can read back and privilege the perceptions of the Gaman and the growing awareness of Riel, Forest, and Shan. They are right; the Hero Dalzul is wrong and flawed and/or suicidal: a worthy *tragic* hero, in a universe where we can do without heroes. Additionally, we can privilege the Narrator's hints at facts within the story: the dynamo, the steel pruning hook, the book. What is, *is*: Brahman, Dao, Yin-Yang, the Other, a tune on the streets, a tool, a woman passing by—perhaps most if not all of the ten thousand created things of the only world most of us have.

'Dancing to Ganam' indeed uses poststructuralist ideas becoming mainstream in the 1990s, but I do not think it was a major break with Le Guin's earlier work. In some ways, the postmodern avant-garde was catching up with Le Guin and some very old ideas of Eastern thought, the Perennial Philosophy, and a very widespread tradition of down-to-earth mysticism.

'Another Story' or 'A Fisherman of the Inland Sea' (1994)

'A Fisherman of the Inland Sea' straddles the time of 'The Shobies' Story' and 'Dancing to Ganam' (Brigg 19; Le Guin, 'Open Letter'). It is a first-person narrative and a report: Tiokunan'n Hideo, a 'Farmholder of the Second Sedoretu of Udan,' on the planet O submits a report to the Ekumenical Stabiles on Hain and to the Anarresti scientist Gvonesh, working on the Churten Field at the Laboratories at Ve Port. It being a tradition of some standing, he makes his report as if he told a story (*LHD* 1), and it is a sentimental love story. Le Guin describes 'Another Story' as one of her 'very few experiments with time travel,' and notes that it 'explores the possibility of two stories about the same person in the same time being completely different and completely true' (*FIS* 9). Since the privileged version comes to a happy ending, I will call 'The Fisherman' a 'Replay' story, following Carol D. Stevens's suggestion (from the title of Ken Grimwood's novel *Replay* [1986]).[654]

In the first-play version and the replay, Hideo is born on the planet O to the First Sedoretu of Udan, and what that means is complicated. O is a world with 'a low, stable human population' of long-standing, 'an ancient climax technology,' a social basis of dispersed villages and associated farms (very rich farms) rather than cities and states—and few problems.[655] In short, human culture on O is close to Le Guin's idea of eutopia from at least her description of Karhide's hearths in 'Is Gender Necessary?' in 1976 (*LoN* [1979]: 164-165) and the 'Redux' version in 1989 (*DEW* 10-12), through 'A Non-Euclidean View...' in 1982 (*DEW* 88-96). We should not think of O's society, however, as simple; we humans tend to like complexity in life, and the ki'O add a lot of complexity to their lives with their marriage arrangements (see *FIS* Introd. 9). Unlike the Christian vision of eternal life after the resurrection 'There is no end to the making of marriages on O' (152).[656] The ki'O are born into one of two moieties, Morning and Evening, with one's mother determining which moiety one is born into. Sex between members of the same moiety is incest and punished only socially but severely. A basic marriage group, a sedoretu, is a heterosexual couple of Morning and Evening, and a heterosexual couple of Evening and Morning (each designated Morning or Evening according to the moiety of the woman in the pair): four people, who also form two homosexual pairings (male-male, called Night; female-female, called Day [reversing the usual Terran associations]). Each member of the group is expected to have sex with the two people of the opposite moiety and strictly forbidden to have sex with the person of the same moiety (*FIS* 151).

Hideo's father, Dohedri, is a ki'O Morning man, and 'rooted to his knees in the dirt of Udan Farmhold'; adding beautifully to the 'thick description,' 'thick planning'—social complexity—of the neighborhood, Hideo's father somehow got involved with a very important person of no moiety: Isako, a Mobile of the Ekumen, a Terran with an ethnic background Le Guin's readers will recognize as Japanese (150). Le Guin's

---

[654] The theme is older. It was central to a one-act playlet at the University of Illinois (Urbana-Champaign) 'Stunt Show' event, homecoming, 1960, called, if my memory is correct, 'Some Sweet, Secret Place,' i.e., a place where people might get second chances. Entering the 1980s and 1990s, correlating with an aging Baby Boom population, the theme became quite popular.
[655] Cf. 'the deep richness of the land' vs. 'the show-wealth of the city' in Le Guin's fantasy 'Olders' (1995), coll. *UA* (172).
[656] Jesus answers a trick question on a multiply-married widow's marital status after the resurrection of the dead with '...in the resurrection they neither marry nor are given in marriage but are like the angels in heaven' (Matthew 22.30)—presumably celibate. Also Mark 12.25 and Luke 20.34-35.

readers will also recognize the Terra alluded to briefly: a planet where human fertility was so decreased that 'they have to think about marrying for children' (151), where Isako sustained 'damage from her childhood, from the poison in the Terran biosphere'—a potential threat to her (173). With much ado, Isako is adopted into the Evening (155), and Dohedri and Isako marry as the Evening couple. Isako (Evening) also marries Tubdu, 'the Morning wife' (forming the female homosexual 'Day' pair); and Tubdu marries Kap, the Evening husband, who is also married to Dohedri (for the male homosexual 'Night' pair). Tubdu and Kap have two children, Isidri, who is highly relevant to the rest of the story, and Suudi, who is irrelevant. Isako and Dohedri have two children, Hideo (the protagonist-narrator) and his younger sister Koneko. Under the ki'O incest taboo, Hideo and Isidri may have sex and reproduce; Hideo and Keneko may not (151-53).

Hideo, his sister Keneko, and 'germane' Isidri have a happy childhood, much of it spent fishing. Hideo likes to 'stand heroic on a slippery boulder in midstream, the long spear poised to strike,' in a pose that probably is no longer part of the fantasy life of the kids of California and the Pacific Northwest, but once was. With the exception of the Colorado River tribes, 'every group' of Indians 'in California whose territory contained sufficient bodies of water' used the harpoon to fish (Kroeber, *Handbook* 815; ch. 54). Hideo is good at hero-style fishing; Isidri does better slipping into the water and catching fish and even eels barehanded: 'You just sort of move with the water and get transparent,' she tells him (*FIS* 153).

All together, a good childhood: sort of ideal village life, but without raids by Vikings or Cossacks, without the manorial system, without plagues, Church, lord, or synagog—and with advanced, responsible science and appropriate technology. Also with a religion very like philosophical Daoism, Hinduism, Buddhism ('godless, argumentative, and mystical,' stressing the name of the world [174-75, 177]), and with no television but a strong tradition of story-telling.[657] As a child, Hideo's favorite story is his mother's story from her homeworld, 'The Fisherman of the Inland Sea' (148 f.).

A poor but beautiful young fisherman, Urashima, Isako's story goes, is beloved and desired by the daughter of the sea king. She 'begged him to come to her palace under the sea,' but he refuses: 'My children wait for me at home,' he says, with no mention of a wife. Then Urashima gives in and spends 'a night of love in her green palace.' She tells him that if he leaves he leaves forever; he says he'll return. He leaves, and the sea king's daughter gives him a box with instructions not to open it. Urashima accepts the box and the command and returns to his village, except he knows no one there and his name is recognized only in terms of a story of 'a fisherman named Urashima [who] was lost at sea' long ago, and none of that

---

[657] 'The name of our world,' *O*, 'is the first word of its first prayer' (175). Cf. *Om*: 'a mystical Indian symbol upon which devout Hindus of all schools meditate' (*Encyclopedia of Religion* 545). See Le Guin on her stealing 'an idea from China and...a god from India,' in 'World Making' (1981 [*DEW* 48]).

family has lived in the village for a century. 'So Urashima went back down to the shore; and there he opened the box....' A bit of white smoke comes out of the box. 'In that moment Urashima's black hair turned white, and he grew old, old, old; and he lay down on the sand and died.' There is evidence for the story, too: in the Annals of the Emperors, one Urashima of the Yosa district, 'went away in the year 477, and came back to his village in the year 825, but soon departed again,' and there are rumors of a box kept in a shrine (*FIS* 149). The story, of course, is like Isako's life, as a Mobile of the Ekumen: leaving home never to return, or, if she did, to return to a world that had changed in the many years she had been away because of the time-dilation of Nearly as Fast as Light travel, as is especially clear to readers familiar with read Le Guin's 1964 story, 'Semley's Necklace.' The question of 'Another Story' is in what ways 'The Fisherman' will become Hideo's story.

Not particularly with Hideo's first goings away. He goes off to school and loves it, but comes home for the long holidays and 'dropped school like a book bag and became pure farm boy overnight,' doing good country things, including 'falling in and out of love with lovely boys and girls of the Morning' (156-57), including Sota, a Morning boy (168). As he grows older, though, Hideo takes care to avoid falling in love and even pulls away from Sota. He sits by the local river, the Oro, thinking deep thoughts and comes to a resolution: he's going to leave home. Looking back, Hideo as Narrator sees his younger self 'luxuriate in sorrow...for this ancient home that I was going to leave and lose forever, to sail away from on the dark river of time. For I knew, from my eighteenth birthday on, that I would leave Udan, leave O, and go out to the other worlds. It was my ambition. It was my destiny' (158). Coming to this decision, Hideo sees himself, at least figuratively if not also literally, 'standing again, poised on the slick boulder amidst the roaring water, spear raised, the hero!' willing to toss away the 'long, slow, deep, rich life of Udan' (160)—to sacrifice.

The major tossing involves two women in his life: his mother and Isidri. Instead of just telling Isako he was going to Hain, his immediate plan, Hideo tells her he is going to Hain 'and that from Hain I wanted to go on farther and forever.' The older Hideo, maybe retaining a bit of his youthful luxuriating in misery, exclaims, 'How cruel we are to our parents!' and goes on to condemn his own participation in 'the impenetrable self-centeredness of youth.' Hideo notes how that self-centeredness 'mistakes itself for honesty,' giving his mother instead of 'some modest hope' she might see him in ten years, 'the desolation of believing that when I left she would never see me again.' Hideo says, 'I prided myself on my truthfulness. And all the time, though I didn't know it...it was not the truth at all. The truth is rarely so simple, though not many truths are as complicated as mine turned out to be' (*FIS* 159-60).[658] He tells her he wants to be a Mobile of the Ekumen.

---

[658] On the self-centered young, note 'young Thurro' and 'his bridegroom's self-absorption' in *CI* (1967 [28; ch. 2]) and, from a parental point of view, Serenity's

Having left her people herself to become a Mobile, Isako takes Hideo's 'brutality without the least complaint' (160). Isidri, surprisingly, turns out to be another matter. She encounters Hideo in a boathouse and tells him she has been avoiding him, because she loves him: 'If you'd felt anything like that for me, you'd have known I did. But it wasn't both of us. So there was no good in it' (161). So she says good-bye and for about an hour Hideo looks 'at the world I had thrown away,' sitting, thinking in the dark in the boathouse. 'When at last I moved, I turned on a light, and began to try to defend my purpose, my planned future, from the terrible plain reality.' By dinner time, Hideo 'was in control' of himself again: 'master of my destiny,' sure of his decision (162).

He goes to Hain, a four-year trip (O time) by NAFAL, and begins his training.

> My studies and work during those years are of no interest now. I will mention only one event, which may or may not be on record in the ansible reception file.... [(]Urashima's coming and going was on record, too, in the Annals of the Emperors.).... Early in the term I was asked to come to the ansible center, where they explained that they had received a garbled screen transmission, apparently from O, and hoped I could help them reconstitute it. (163)

The message is dated 'nine days later than the date of reception' and contains words in Hideo's native language. Hideo cannot help them with this 'creased message' or 'ghost message,' and the best guess of the Receivers is that there may have been 'a double field-interference' phenomenon (164).

The next significant event occurs when Hideo is in his final year of training in temporal physics and considering going to the Cetian Worlds for advanced work, after his 'promised visit home.' Then they receive the first news 'from Anarres of a new theory of transilience,' the possibility of a 'Churten technology' that would allow instantaneous transportation of matter. Hideo says, possibly with a pun he does *not* intend, 'I was crazy to work on it.' And then, just before he 'was about to go promise...soul and body to the School if they would let' him do work on churten theory, they come and ask him. 'Judiciously and graciously,' Hideo consents and gets the chance to work with Gvonesh at Ve Port.

> The joint work of the Cetian and Hainish churten research teams in those first three years was a succession of triumphs,...defeats, breakthroughs, setbacks, all happening so fast that anybody who took a week off was out-of-date.

---

treatment of her mother in Le Guin's 'Solitude.' Cf. and contrast Rakam on her 'beautiful voice speaking the beautiful truth' in 'A Woman's Liberation' (*FWF* 179; § 3).

'Clarity hiding mystery,' Gvonesh called it. Every time it all came clear it all grew more mysterious. The experiments were exciting and inscrutable. The technology worked best when it was most preposterous. Four years went by in that laboratory like no time at all, as they say. (165)

Hideo has now spent ten of his years on Hain and Ve and is thirty-one; returning to O, he will have been away for eighteen years. So Hideo goes home (166): 'Eighteen years had made no difference at all to the hills beside the wide Saduun.... Everything was the same, itself. Timeless, Udan in its dream of work stood over the river that ran timeless in its dream of movement.' People, though, change. Hideo's parents are older, and his mother is not well: the results of her youth in the degraded environment on Terra, plus, we later learn, sorrow for the absence of her son. Hideo's sister Koneko is also older; once four years his junior, she is now four years older. 'The Second Sedoretu' of Udan 'had been married for eleven years: Koneko and Isidri, sister germanes, were the partners of the Day. Koneko's husband was my old friend Sota.... Isidri's husband, a man nearly twenty years older than herself, named Hedran had been a traveling scholar of the Discussions....He and Isidri had no children' (168). Hedran, then, was one of the 'Scholars, wandering Discussers, itinerant artists' and others on O who 'seldom want to fit themselves into the massive permanence of a farmhold sedoretu' and often do not marry (152). Hideo thinks Hedran may have a more passionate relationship with Sota than with Isidri, but he respects Isidri's respect for Hedran and her acceptance of his 'intellectual and spiritual guidance'—although Hideo finds Hedran's teaching 'a bit dry and disputatious' (174). Hedran is a strong candidate to become a comic-romance *alazon*: here, the inconvenient fifth who can be a leftover after the pairings up. He is older than the others in the Sedoretu, not in an impassioned love with Isidri, associated with 'dry' teaching, symbolically dry in his sterility. Isidri, to the contrary, is 'the hydrologist for the village and the oenologist for the farm'—working with water and wine—living a life that is 'thick-planned, very rich in necessary work and wide relationships.' Employing still more water imagery (the favorite Daoist element, Takver's element in *The Dispossessed* [1974]), Hideo says 'She swam in life as she had swum in the river, like a fish, at home' (173-74).[659]

Hideo does not feel at home at Udan. He and his mother may be attached by 'a very fine, thin cord, like the umbilical cord, that can stretch light-years without any difficulty' (173), but it is not enough to snap him back. What might be is Isidri, and in a long, dark, night of the soul he decides to ask Isidri, to help him. 'So, holding fast to that, I could at last stop

---

[659] For Takver and water, see esp. her line while pregnant, 'I am a fish...a fish in water. I am inside the baby inside me' (*TD* 191; ch. 8). See also Yarrow in *WE*—true name Kest (= 'minnow' in Old Speech): 158, 169; chs. 9 & 10.

the terrible sobbing and lie spent' until daybreak. Except he doesn't go to see Isidri. What he does do is recognize that he needs help and go 'to the shrine in the Old School' and offers worship and comes to a true recognition 'that Cetian physics and religion' really 'are aspects of one knowledge' and came to wonder 'if all physics and religion are aspects of one knowledge' (175-76), which is the case with Terran physics in our time, and Terran mysticism if Fritjof Capra is right in *The Tao of Physics*; but none of this resolves Hideo's immediate problem.

Which is the point: Hideo returns to work at Ran'n and gets by. Gvonesh churtens from one place to another around Ve Port, then farther. Then nonhuman animal tests and robot tests. Then the *Shoby* and their barely avoiding 'a death by unreality,' using 'entrainment' to rescue 'themselves from a kind of chaos of dissolution'; and 'Experiments with high-intelligence life-forms came to a halt' (176). Gvonesh feels that 'The rhythm is wrong,' getting Hideo to think about something his mother had said to him at Udan about there being something wrong to have events without intervals: 'Where is the dancing?' she had asked, 'Where is the way?' and doubted the research teams, would 'be able to control it' (170). But Hideo won't follow the 'dancing' thought because he doesn't want to think about Udan. When he does, he feels 'the knowledge of being no one, no where, and a shaking like a frightened animal' (177). He goes on to remember that his religion assured him he 'was part of the Way,' and the physics 'absorbed...[his] despair in work.' And then Dalzul arrives, and there are the two journeys from Ve to Ganam (called Tadkla here, its name on the maps of the Hainish Expansion). And then, obviously, another problem of some sort (177), though going one person at a time seems to work; and Hideo gets an idea.

He tells us that the lab groups 'had taken to calling the non-interval in time/real interval in space a 'skip.' It sounded light, trivial. Scientists like to trivialize.'[660] Hideo suggests his skipping to Ve Port and back to Ran'n. He notes that he had said he would visit Udan 'this winter' and adds, with significant repetition and, perhaps, variation, 'Scientists like to trivialize'—i.e., he suggests that a visit to Udan would be no big deal (177). Despite a 'wrinkle' in the field Gvonesh points out to him he tries the test, and it works; and he is on Ve, with 'no desire to return to O' (178).[661] Gvonesh thinks there is still a wrinkle or fold in the field they have named for Hideo: 'the Tiokunan'n Field'; she finds it 'unaesthetical.'

In physics terms, we will have to take Gvonesh's word that the wrinkle is esthetically inappropriate; in literary terms she makes it very apt. Shortly after noting the wrinkle in the field, she asks 'You got no sex, Hideo?' meaning primarily no sex life. Then she adds, before apologizing,

---

[660] E.g., 'trivializing the origin of the world by calling it the Big Bang, as if the Universe were a firecracker' (Jastrow 114). Alternatively, given the importance of being earnest in our time, one could find the flippancies of scientists endearing.

[661] 'A Wrinkle in Time' might be another appropriate alternative title for 'Another Story,' except it was used as a novel title by Madeline L'Engle in 1963.

'You got some kind of wrinkle in your life, hah' and suggests/asks, 'Maybe is time you go back to O?' (179). She can send him back, and does, via churten: 'A shimmer, a shivering of everything—a missed beat—skipped—' and Hideo is in darkness, in what turns out to be a biology lab on O, 'in some building of the Center at Ran'n' (179-80). Eighteen years earlier, 'the night after...[he] had left' for Hain by NAFAL ship (182).

'O is a good world to time-travel in. Things don't change.' In fact there is no problem at all with Hideo's return to Udan, except that he was now thirty-one, not twenty-one (182-83). So at thirty-one, Hideo goes to see Isidri, and they marry, and time passes like a river, bringing Hideo to the present and end of his report, if not quite the end of the story: 'I have lived now for eighteen years as a farmholder of Udan Farm of Derdan'nad Village...on Oket, on O. I am fifty years old. I am the Morning husband of the Second Sedoretu of Udan; my wife is Isidri; my Night marriage is to Sota of Drehe, whose Evening wife is my sister Koneko.... But none of this is of much interest to the Stabiles of the Ekumen' (185). Of interest to readers in the rest of the story is, first, what the current Hideo when newly returned to O is to do about Hideo's commitment to be on Hain; second, what will happen when the current point-of-view Hideo reaches the moment in which the initial Hideo churtened back into time—and, third, what to make of Hideo's story.

The first issue is handled very directly by Isako, who is quite healthy when Hideo returns and remains that way. However strange the situation—or perhaps especially when things get very strange—a promise is a promise, and Isako feels a 'strong sense of duty' and 'obligation to the Ekumen': she insists that Hideo 'Apologize for not coming to study, as you said you would. And explain it to the Director, the Anarresti woman. Maybe she would understand.' Gvonesh's understanding is unlikely since she will not learn of the churten for another three years; additionally, Hideo may *be* on Hain: time-travel quickly creates paradoxes. As many readers will have guessed, Hideo sends a message by ansible (for 'a staggering sum in cash' [and nine days after returning?]), and Hideo assumes 'that this was the 'creased message' or 'ghost' they asked...[him] to interpret' his first year on Hain (*FIS* 186-87).

The second issue is resolved when the time comes (again) when Hideo-1 returned to Udan to find Isidri married to Hedran, his mother sick—and so forth. About that time Hedran comes again to the village and Isidri suggests 'inviting him to stay at Udan.' Hideo successfully opposes the suggestion, 'saying that though he was a brilliant teacher there was something I disliked about him' (190). So 'the instant of transilience' passes, leaving intact Hideo-2's marriage, family, and new life at Udan (189).

What Hideo's experience means in terms of time-travel, I don't understand. Hideo's explanation involves the 'fact' that the ansible field for his message from O to Ve 'was meeting a resonance resistance caused by the ten-year anomaly in the churten field, which did fold the message back into itself, crumple it up, inverting and erasing.' It follows then, Hideo writes, that 'At that point, within the implication of the Tiokunan'n Double

Field, my existence on O as I sent the message was simultaneous with my existence on Hain when the message was received. There was an I who sent and an I who received. Yet, for so long as the encapsulated field anomaly existed, the simultaneity was literally a point, an instant, a crossing without further implication in either the ansible or the churten field' (187-88).

Hideo tries to clarify this in terms of an image of a river curving back on itself in its flood plain into an 'S' and then breaking through the 'double banks of the S and runs straight, leaving a whole reach of the water aside as a curving lake, cut off from the current, unconnected': his life on Hain and Ve as a churten researcher. He thinks, though, 'a truer image is the whirlpools of the current itself, occurring and recurring, the same? or not the same?' (188), and the two images together, I think, are central to the meaning of the story. And to the meaning of *A Fisherman of the Inland Sea* as a volume ending with 'Another Story'—and to the place of *Fisherman* in Le Guin's canon.

That 'reach of water...cut off' is Hideo's time 'outside the world' in terms of *Always Coming Home* and *Buffalo Gals*, as a 'historian,' in the term of 'A Man of the People.' His time as a research scientist is a project that was necessary for him, perhaps, but time away from his real 'life's work': 'vineyards, drainage, the care of yamas, the care and education of children, the Discussions, and trying to learn how to catch fish' not with a manly heroic spear, but with bare and empty hands (188). 'True journey is return,' indeed, but also Dorothy of Kansas's recognition, even after Oz: 'There's no place like home.' Corny, but a point Le Guin insists upon, so long as home is a true home (otherwise the moral is to Walk Away from Omelas—or just get out). '[T]he whirlpools of the current itself' refers to the quantum field where particles go in and out of existence, and to the same field seen as the Dao—or Brahman or *ch'i* (Capra 197-201; ch. 14); it makes little sense to get pedantic about nomenclature for the ineffable. As Ogion explains to Ged, to avoid becoming 'a stick whirled and whelmed in the stream,' one 'must be the steam itself, all of it....' (*WE* 128; ch. 7). As Ged explains to Arren, 'Deep are the springs of being, deeper than life, than death....' (*FS* 165; ch. 11), and each human life— 'That selfhood which is our torment, and our treasure, and our humanity'—is a momentary wave on the sea of being (*FS* 122; ch. 8).

In *Fisherman*, as in much of Le Guin's earlier and most recent work, selfhood is best achieved in immanent relationship with the world and with others, primarily a primary, central, really significant other. In 'Another Story,' Isidri is that center, but only as the center of a web of relationships with other people, 'yamas,' and a world held together with highly symbolic water. Hideo's true heroism, his holding fast, is letting go of his project of churten science and returning to his beloved. He is not caught in Urashima's story or Semley's or even his mother's but is able, as if by magic, to change the story and come to a comic-romance ending.

Further Comments: *Fisherman* and the Theme of the Hero

Hideo's rejection of traditional, macho heroism, gives a nice shape to *Fisherman*.[662] The first story of the volume, 'The First Contact with the Gorgonids' shows the development of Mrs. Jerry Debree to Annie Laurie Debree. She begins as an appendage to Jerry; at the end, 'She was the heroine.' That is 'hero*ine*,' arguably a feminine form of the hero, and a heroine with the name of a stereotypical ballad heroine: Annie Laurie. Still, that's progress for Ms. Debree, who becomes a heroine who can look out for herself and cut a sharp business deal, and not a bad place to start a volume. 'Newton's Sleep' suggests that a transcendent project like the Spes Colony has its limitations and shows the recapture of the colony by Earth and earth: the world and dirt and life. Thinking about the story, it is a strange comedy of reintegrating Spes with the planet; feeling with Isaac Rose, we experience Ike as the Hero as exile, engineer, and rationalist: 'a true believer' in reason 'who can't see how and why the true belief isn't working,' even, for his creator, 'a tragic character, an admirable overreacher' (*FIS* Introd. 11)—or not so admirable but still tragic.[663] If we learn a kind of 'double vision' from 'Newton's Sleep,' we *should* experience the story through thinking and feeling, as comedy and tragedy. 'The Ascent of the North Face' is a delightful send-up of the Hero as explorer/adventurer, Conqueror of Everest, K2, the Pole, a house at the nonexistent address (in Portland, OR) of 2647 Lovejoy Street. 'The Rock That Changed Things' shows us a Her*a*, I think, although I won't push the point. Bu did not have to be female; what she had to be was a nur: one of the oppressed of the Earth (or wherever), functioning as a midwife of the revolution—or, in Athshean terms, functioning as a god like Selver, helping her people to translate the word 'freedom' and tell their own stories. 'The Kerastion' shows the Hero as Artist, and, as we have seen, quite exactly balances the claims of the heroic artist to express himself and try to hold onto his art, and the claims of the community and the Earth-Mother as Kali: destroying and producing, taking into herself and recycling all that is, that lives, that is beautiful.

The three churten stories show a successful group project (similar to 'Sur') in 'The Shobies' Story,' and the Hero as Hero in 'Dancing to Ganam.' Dalzul is a good hero as heroes go—a savior—but also 'a hi-tech, hubristic hero' (*FIS* Introd. 9), who turns out to be a heterosexist and a bit of a sexist. He also usefully repeats the lesson of *2001: A Space Odyssey*,

---

[662] The idea of a taxonomy of Heroes that I use below goes back to (at least) Thomas Carlyle's *On Heroes, Hero-Worship, and the Heroic in History* (1841), but beyond the idea that such classifications might be useful, I tend to disagree with Carlyle.

[663] I allude to Horace Walpole's comment in a letter to Sir Horace Mann (1742), 'The world is a comedy to those that think, a tragedy to those who feel.' Alternatively: 'This world is a comedy to those that think, a tragedy to those that feel'—letter to the Duchess of Upper Ossory, 16 Aug. 1776 (*ODQ* 558.27).

the very old one that the truly transcendent project of a Hero is to become a god. *That* is overreaching! If we see him consciously choosing a role as a dying god in a universe without resurrection, then, I think, we can find him a still potentially dangerous but 'admirable overreacher' (9). What keeps him from being truly dangerous in the world of 'Dancing' is, first, that quite unlike Captain Ahab's authority in *Moby Dick*, Commander Dalzul has nothing like near total, despotic command on a ship; the Stabiles on Hain won't grant such power, nor will the members of the crew. Second, he is kept in line by a universe that *is*, massively *is*, and planets and cultures that are much smaller but still much, much too big for one man to push around. 'Another Story' gives us the scientist as Hero, returning to a theme of 'Newton's Sleep.' Here, though, the scientist does not need to have his world recaptured; *he* is recaptured by the story he says he feels 'far down deeper inside me than my bones' (177). When the churten experience puts him into contact with what *is*, Hideo's entire being goes back to Udan. He renounces his project, sacrifice, the symbolic spear of the hero, a life of never having 'an intense relationship' being 'married to a damned theory,' 'No room for love, no time'—rather like Shevek in despair, actually (*TD* ch. 6)—and he follows home that 'very fine, thin cord' that leads back to Mother in many senses: to his wife, family, and life (*FIS* 171, 175).

In this chorus of the Coyote's song the finest heroism is renunciation of heroism and returning to the world.

'Another Story' (1994) and *The Dispossessed* (1974)

Tiokunan'n Hideo and 'Another Story' generally are similar to Shevek and *The Dispossessed*: both works are structured with dual time-tracks in a significant variation on the rhetorical device of chiasmus—crossover, as symbolized by the Greek letter Chi: X (Bittner, *Approaches* 130). Both feature temporal physics and physicists; both deal with issues of transcendent projects and immanent life of domesticity; both stress the importance of pain for human development; both contain significant sexual politics; both deal with continuity and change.[664]

Implicit in my analysis of Le Guin has been a perception of a good deal of continuity in her work, and such a view, as one view, is appropriate. As Shevek says at Vea's party in the central chapter of *The Dispossessed* (178-80; ch. 7), things do endure, at least for a while: there is time's circle as well as arrow. Alternatively stated, Haber tells Orr in *The Lathe of Heaven*, 'Life—evolution—...existence itself—is essentially *change*,' and Orr doesn't disagree but says, 'That is one aspect of it.... The other is stillness' (135; ch. 9).

---

[664] For pain in *The Dispossessed*, see esp. the discussion at the party just before Shevek leaves for Abbenay, where Shevek says that 'Suffering is a misunderstanding' *and* 'Suffering is the condition on which we live' (*TD* 48-50; ch. 2). For pain in 'Another Story,' see esp. 162, 175.

In *The Dispossessed*, the emphasis is on change, uncertainty, and the unreliability of the everyday world: the dance over the abyss, 'on the brink of the world' (*DEW* 48). Shevek returning home feels something like an earthquake and feels that 'Death was in him, under him; the earth itself was uncertain, unreliable.' In such a world 'The enduring, the reliable, is a promise made by the human mind.' That bit of reliability is imaged in Shevek and his partner Takver taking hands as 'they came together and stood holding each other on the unreliable earth' (*TD* 252; ch. 10). Central to Shevek's story and his life are his relationships, primarily his love for Takver. Still, Shevek is a change-bringer; his work is important. 'Another Story' makes a similar point; the change, the difference from *The Dispossessed*, is the increased stress on relationships. In *The Dispossessed* there is a dynamic balancing of the value of Shevek's temporal physics (his theory makes possible the League and the Ekumen) and Shevek's homelife. In the world Hideo makes in his return to Udan, there is no reference in the literature to a 'Tiokunan'n Hideo doing [churten] research.... Nobody worked on a theory of a stabilized double field'—Hideo's theory. The cost of Udan is the Tiokunan'n Field (*FIS* 188-89)—the loss of Hideo's chance to be a Shevek-like, worlds-changing hero—and it is a cost Hideo cheerfully pays and hardly reckons. And we should agree: the galaxy is too big to be changed significantly by any person, or even all of Ekumenical humanity.

On the other hand, the differences with working women, especially older women, is very important for the sexual politics of 'Another Story' versus *The Dispossessed*, as is the treatment of homosexuality.

In *The Dispossessed*, Shevek's mother Rulag is cold and distant, denying Shevek touch; it is Shevek's father who nurtured him. Rulag summarizes, 'He was supportive, he was parental, as I am not. The work comes first, with me. It has always come first' (97-101; ch. 4). In 'A Fisherman,' Hideo's father is pretty much absent from Hideo's story; his mother, Isako, the Mobile who went native (*FIS* 150), has been as much of a mover and Shaker as Rulag, and she is a keen intellectual (169-70), and she is very much a nurturing parent in a story that puts strong value upon nurture. In *The Dispossessed*, there is Odo as a looming presence, but still 'an alien: an exile' on Anarres (*TD* 82; ch. 4), and Shevek was trained in his field by women: Mitis and Gvarab 60; ch. 4). The Narrator of *The Dispossessed* tells us that 'There are people of inherent authority; some emperors actually have new clothes,' and Mitis is one of them (45; ch. 2); and old Gvarab's lecture group on Frequency and Cycle introduces Shevek to 'a much larger universe than most people were capable of seeing' (87; ch. 4); Gvarab has been the unrecognized Odo of physics (130; ch. 6). But Mitis and Gvarab are minor characters in a long novel; their parallel in 'Another Story' is Gvonesh, Director of the Churten Field Laboratories at Ve Port, introduced in the salutation to Hideo's report, and a major character. Gvonesh is all *director*, her job, her function; her sex life is a mystery to her co-workers, and so was 'the rest of her existence' outside of their work (178). But Gvonesh is, if not often nurturing, very concerned with Hideo, and overall a very positive character: asking Hideo the right questions, nudging him home.

On Anarres in *The Dispossessed*, 'No law,...no punishment, no disapproval applied to any sexual practice of any kind, except the rape of a child or woman...,' and a partnership (marriage) is a partnership, 'whether homosexual or heterosexual' (*TD* 198; ch. 8). Summarizing other arguments, and overstating the case, Sarah Lefanu has said tolerance and valuing diversity may be the theory on Anarres, but what we see is different (141); and she has a valid point. We see no lesbian relations in *The Dispossessed*, and Takver and Shevek's friend Bedap is the one major male character we might describe as homosexual in primary orientation (139; ch. 6). Bedap re-enters Shevek's life at close to Shevek's low point, and they discuss 'whether or not they should pair for a while'—and Bedap helps save Shevek from despair (139; ch. 6). Still, it is Takver and a heterosexual, monogamous marriage and family that really saves Shevek, a relationship Bedap touches but is definitely outside of. Bedap ends up almost forty and asking himself, 'What have I done?... Nothing. Meddling. Meddling in other people's lives because I don't have one. I never took the time. And the time's going to run out on me, all at once, and I will never have had... that.' What Bedap meant by "that' he could not have said...; yet he felt that he understood...that all his hope was in...understanding... that if he would be saved,' as Rilke would put it, 'he must change his life' (*TD* 297-98; ch. 12).[665] This passage might mean that Bedap should find a nice young man and settle down and help raise children, but it probably does not: we see in *The Dispossessed* no homosexual domestic life: no options for gays and lesbians balancing political doing with immanent being. *The Dispossessed* suggests here that the life of social activism without family life is inadequate, and can be read that to get a real family part of what Bedap must change in his life is his sexual orientation.

Thus *The Dispossessed* in 1974, and still a light-year or two ahead of the United States in the 1990s. There is a definite change between *The Dispossessed* and 'Another Story,' where the sexual politics privilege bisexuality but are still more open, more inclusive. The central relationship is very much between Hideo and Isidri. When Isidri tells Hideo 'There was a reason...that you came back—here,' Hideo replies quite directly, 'You.' Still, she adds correctly, 'And Sota, and Koneko, and the farmhold' (*FIS* 189) Especially relevant here, Sota: Hideo's relationship with Sota is secondary to that with Isidri, but it is there, socially supported, and important. And with other, positive people in the story, the homosexual marriages are equal or primary: Dohedri and Kap (male-male), Tubdu and Isako (female-female), with Uncle Tobo, Kap's younger brother, thrown in for Tubdu as 'a bonus' (155). And 'many people never marry,' sometimes attaching 'themselves to a brother or sister's marriage as aunt or uncle,' sometimes

---

[665] 'The poet [Rainer Maria] Rilke looked at a statue of Apollo about fifty years ago, and Apollo spoke to him. 'You must change your life,' he said' (Le Guin, *LoN* [1979]: 77-78).

not (152); so, apparently, even a relatively single life is provided for, and need not be lonely, or lead to evil. So long as it is conducted, mindfully and responsibly, in the world.

XIII.

ALTERNATIVE ROUTES

'Solitude' (1994)

To see the World in a Grain of Sand,
And a Heaven in a Wild Flower,
Hold Infinity in the palm of your hand,
And Eternity in an hour.
—William Blake,
'Auguries of Innocence' (*ODQ* 73.18)

There is more than one road to the city. —*The Beginning Place* (last sentence)

If a relatively positive unmarried life is a real possibility in the world of 'Another Story'—if not for the main character—frequent solitude is privileged in 'Solitude.' If the socially-mediated complexity of human relationships is praised in all the churten stories, life in 'artificially complicated situations' (*F&SF* 87.6: 134) is just one option in 'Solitude,' and not the option chosen by the protagonist-narrator. Like any responsible character in one of Ursula K. Le Guin's stories, the heroine, Serenity (nicknamed 'Ren'), strives 'to be in the world' (141), but she wishes to be in the world relatively alone. As she said in 'Science Fiction and Mrs. Brown' (1976), Le Guin is not convinced that 'Man is the measure of all things, or even of very many things.... The great mystics have gone deeper than community and sensed identity, the identity of all,' and Serenity, if not (yet) a great mystic, at least knows part of the mystic Way and can get by with relatively little community, relatively little human *touch* (*LoN* [1979]: 116). In one way at least, 'Solitude' is like the meditation on *Mitsein* in the climactic section of *The Left Hand of Darkness* (1969), with Genly Ai and Estraven out on the Ice. Even as Ai and Estraven comprise the simplest human social unit, so 'Solitude' seems almost a thought-experiment using the simplest sort of human society, and concluding that such a society is still human. Indeed, the culture Ren adopts seems as simple as the Ndif created by Bill Kopman's fantasies in Le Guin's 'Pathways of Desire' (1979), or the post-Apocalypse cultures seen in most post-Apocalypse movies. 'Solitude' and 'The Matter of Seggri' are also thought-experiments on more or less gender-separatist societies, where men and women have little interaction. Unlike *The Tombs of Atuan* (1970/71), in these two stories the all-female societies, in themselves, are good places for women to live. However, 'Solitude' and 'Seggri' are not separatist in their politics, affirming on the contrary 'the body's obscure, inalterable dream of mutuality' ('Seggri' 29) between women and men; but they make the biological, sociological, and political point that, our function as sperm-production systems aside, men are optional: women living in solidarity can get along without.

'Solitude' is strongly anthropological science fiction, set in what Serenity's mother Leaf, a professional ethnographer of the Ekumen, considers an impoverished society. The planet Eleven-Soro in the 'Before Time' had a population of 120 billion people and 'the greatest cities every built on any world' (147); the people of Eleven-Soro risked disaster, and disaster came, and the current human population seems to have regained only 'a broken culture—not a society, but the remains of one.' From the point of view of Leaf, there remains only 'A terrible, appalling poverty' (153). It is significant for the kind of fiction Le Guin writes that it never occurs to Leaf or any of the Ekumenical researchers to rescue the Sorovians or to debate whether or not the Ekumenical 'Prime Directive,' the 'Law of Cultural Embargo' (*PE* 75; ch. 9), allows the forces of civilization to move in and make the Sorovians conquer their stasis and get with the high-tech, «high-culture» program.

The team of three Ekumenical First Observers initially sent onplanet to Eleven-Soro ran into an immediate 'communications problem.' They understood the language itself well enough for first contact; the problem was finding informants, people to talk to. Sorovian culture is strongly segregated not only sexually but also generationally, with women and children living apart from men, who in turn live apart from (post)pubescent boys. The men of Eleven-Soro live 'in solitary houses as hermits or in pairs' and would not exchange more than a few words with the male investigators. When the two male Observers entered the territory of a group of adolescent boys, the young males 'either fled or rushed desperately at them trying to kill them.' When these Observers entered one of the 'dispersed villages' of the women, the women 'drove them away with volleys of stone as soon as they came anywhere near the houses.' One woman did approach one of the male Observers, but only to mate with him, leading one of the Observers to state his belief that the sole community activity of the Sorovians 'is throwing rocks at men.' A female Observer did little better. She was allowed to move into an unused house of an 'auntring' (i.e. village) consisting of seven houses. She was never invited into another house by any of the women, 'nor expected to help or ask for help in any work. Conversation concerning normal activities was unwelcome to the other women,' leaving her only the children to talk to. This leads to the conclusion that the Sorovians learn what 'they learn when they're children'—only, which sets up the situation for the story; the Ekumenical field ethnographer Leaf is the mother of In Joy Born (a boy nicknamed Borny, eight years old) and Serenity (a girl of five), who have already accompanied their mother in fieldwork on another planet (132-33).[666]

The plot begins with Leaf, Borny, and Ren moving into a house in an auntring (134) and continues into the adulthood of Serenity. The action of the plot is Serenity's adaptation to the culture around her, while her mother does not adapt, and Borny rather falling in between. There is conflict in the plot: mostly between Serenity and her Mother, Leaf. Still, Borny is very significant. Leaf is using her children in her work but also keeping them with her (132), so there is no ethical problem with their presence on the planet (see 'The Shobies' Story' and the opening to 'Dancing to Ganam' [*FIS*]). The crisis in the story has to do with Borny's being forced to leave the auntring when he reaches puberty and head out for 'the Territory' (141) and into a 'boygroup' (140) and his later prospects for life on the planet as a man.[667] Leaf wants to go back to the ship before Borny is expelled from the village. Serenity hardly remembers and does not understand the ship; she wants to 'be here, where my soul is. I want to go on learning to be in the world.' She fears Mother and Borny, 'who were both working magic': Leaf using her authority as a mother, Borny using persuasion. Serenity says 'nothing and was still,' as she had been taught by the aunts (140-41).

Borny persuades his mother to let him go to the Territory and join the boys, without a radio, doing it 'right,' but arranging to meet her in half a year. And Borny and a friend leave the village, stopping by all the houses to say goodbye, except that there is no word in the language for either 'hello' or 'goodbye' (141). Borny's time away is torment for Leaf and an excellent opportunity for suspense—Will Borny make it back?—but it is an opportunity Serenity and Le Guin forego: 'Nobody ever came back to their mother from boygroup. But Borny did,' Serenity tells us, with the last sentence getting a paragraph to itself (142). But the return is not after six months. Instead, Serenity goes out to 'starwatch' one night to get in contact with the universe, and on her way home she is accosted by a rather Dickensian character who tells her that Borny and his friend are all right and warns Leaf through Serenity not to go to her rendezvous with Borny: 'Some boys are in a gang. They'd rape her.' The man—House on the Skyline Man—makes sure that Serenity has memorized his message, including, 'I and some others are killing the leaders' of the gang. 'It takes a while. Your brother is with the other gang' (143).

With that kind of news and reassurance, Leaf starts packing to go after her son, but Serenity tells a neighbor about House on the Skyline Man's

---

[666] If Borny and Serenity have a father, he is invisible in the plot of 'Solitude.'

[667] The end of Mark Twain's *Adventures of Huckleberry Finn* (1884/85) is Huck's decision, his book being written, 'to light out for the Territory ahead of the rest, because Aunt Sally she's going to adopt me and sivilize me and I can't stand it. I been there before.' Presenting kids literally running in packs may be only a slight and slightly satiric extension of American-adult views of youngsters (see Charnas's *Walk...and Motherlines*).

message, and the neighbor comes over to get a message across to Leaf. This is difficult. The Gethenians of *The Left Hand of Darkness* (1969) won't advise one another unless the giver of advice wants to insult the receiver; the Sorovians are even stricter. Serenity tells us the neighbor, Noyit, 'pretended to be talking to me, because women don't teach women.' Noyit repeats House on the Skyline Man's message, and gives some background on men breaking up juvenile male gangs, 'when the boygroups get wicked. Sometimes there are magicians among them, leaders, older boys, even men who want to make a gang. The settled men will kill the magicians and make sure none of the boys gets hurt,' and Noyit assures Leaf, indirectly, that Borny will be all right. Leaf isn't listening, so Noyit adds, 'A rape is a very, very bad thing for the settled men.... It means the women won't come to them' for sex (and some talking). 'If the boys raped some woman,' e.g., Leaf, 'probably the men would kill *all* the boys'—and that last gets Leaf's attention and keeps her from going after her son (143).

Borny eventually shows up, emaciated and with a damaged lip, and with no intention of going back to the Territory and having to 'hold his own among the older boys, by fear and sorcery, always proving his strength, until he was old enough to walk away' and try to find a place 'where the men would let him settle'—and then spending another three or four years 'challenging, fighting, always watching the others, on guard' to become a settled man and 'end up living alone your whole life.' Borny concludes that he 'can't do it' and says that he is 'not a [p]erson' and just wants 'to go ho[m]e.' Leaf agrees to leave; Serenity says 'No' (145).

Leaf forces the point, and they go up to the ship. Borny recovers and thrives and wants to go to Hain for education in the Ekumenical schools. Leaf just wants to go home to Hain. Serenity does not; she wants to go to her home. In a confrontation with her mother, Serenity pronounces the formula, 'You have no power over me' and says she won't go to Hain, telling her mother to go without her. Highly angry, her mother says to Serenity, 'You are one of them. You don't know what love is.' She thinks Ren has closed into her self 'like a rock,' and she concludes she should never have brought Serenity to Eleven-Soro. 'People crouching in the ruins of a society—brutal, rigid, ignorant, superstitious—Each one in a terrible solitude—And I let them make you into one of them!' If 'You have no power over me' is a crucial formula for Serenity, 'one of them' is a powerful formula for an ethnographer like Leaf: Lyubov in *The Word for World Is Forest* most fears the 'racial hatred' that would have his friend Selver 'treat him not as a 'you' but as 'one of them'' (*WWF* 94; ch. 5). Finally Serenity repeats 'You have no power over me' and shuts her eyes and covers her ears with her hands: 'She [Leaf] came to me then and held me, but I stood stiff, enduring her touch, until she let me go' ('Solitude' 148).

The impasse is resolved in part by a Gethenian archeologist, Arrem, someone Serenity can respond to: 'not a man...yet not a woman; and so not exactly an adult, yet not a child: a person, alone, like me.' Arrem finds the 'slow walking' of the Sorovian women like 'the untrance movements from the Handdara of Karhide' and other elements of their soul-formation 'like what they learn on Gethen,' which Serenity says Borny says 'kind of stopped Mother from ranting about primitive superstition.' With Arrem and Borny mediating, a compromise is reached. Borny will go to Hain while Serenity and Leaf stay on ship, for one year (149). At the end of the year, Leaf will go to Hain, with or without Serenity, who may then return to Eleven-Soro. Meanwhile, Serenity will stay, but with occasional trips onplanet, where, among other things, she helps a zoologist solve—significantly—a communications problem with a cephalopod high-intelligence life-form (150).

Whatever her other needs, most immediately Serenity needs to get off the ship. She has privacy there, 'But there was no place to be alone on the ship'; 'It was all human-made,' designed, and like Isaac Rose's mother in 'Newton's Sleep' (*FIS* 26), Serenity doesn't see a space craft as a proper home ('Solitude' 151). Serenity cannot be 'friendly and mannerly' the way everyone else is on the ship, and she feels her soul is dying, perhaps drowning in 'a mechanical sea'—or, perhaps, 'the soft hushing of the ship's systems, like a mechanical sea' is the best part of the ship.[668] In any event, Serenity needs to go home to make her soul, and Leaf needs to go home to save hers: it is just that they have two different homes, and their respective returns home will make them dead to one another (151-52). So they decide to die to each other, and both weep and embrace: Ren could hold her 'mother, cling to her and cry with her, because her spell was broken' (152). As in much of Le Guin's writing, life requires acceptance of death; to be able to touch and hold someone, we must be willing to let go.

Serenity is left onplanet and lives out her life up to the time she makes this report, as a supplement to her mother's report on Eleven-Soro. Some events in her life are significant for her and for us. The first is Dnemi's death. When Sut's baby died, Leaf had been 'angry and ashamed that she could not go and try to comfort Sut and that nobody else did.' Even the Ndif in 'Pathways' have funerals, however 'graceless' (*CR* 200-01). It was Sut's just going away with her dead baby that had elicited the complaint from Leaf, 'It is not human.... Nothing could be clearer evidence that this is a broken culture.' Serenity wonders if Dnemi's death might have changed Leaf's mind. Aid is sent to Dnemi's house while she is dying, and a watch kept over the body, with singing for her soul. The corpse is wrapped in bedding and 'given back, under a rock cairn or inside one of the ruins of the ancient city.' The theory is to take the corpse to the ruined city because 'Those are the lands of the dead.... What dies there stays there' (153)—in both a practice to keep a ghost away (cf. *CI* 69; ch. 4) and a sophisticated judgment on the cities of the Before Time. So Dnemi's death is handled with ceremony, after the manner of humans.

After death, life: the birth of a baby in the village and the beginning of Serenity's desire to have one herself, eventually, 'but not for a long time,

---

[668] On manners, cf. and contrast 'Nine Lives' (1969), where learning manners is a crucial part of Kaph's learning to be a person.

because once you have a child you are never alone.' Meanwhile, there is 'the great harmless magic, the spells cast between men and women,' which Serenity goes off to seek (154). She finds sex and a variety of love with Red Stone Man, for a while, and then leaves him, indicating to him her need 'To get away from your magic, sorceror,' and find 'a larger world to be in' (155-56). Ren wanders a while and finally returns and builds a house of her own, keeping clear of Red Stone Valley since 'The man there behaved as if he had a claim on me, a right to me.' She still likes him, but not 'that smell of magic about him, his imagination of power' over her (157). So she finds another man, and they make a daughter; later Serenity and this man, or another man, make a son (158). The story ends with Serenity's explaining why, after all these years, she called down the lander and told her story. When her daughter

> was born, that was my heart's desire and the fulfilment of my soul. When my son was born, last year, I knew there is no fulfilment. He will grow toward manhood, and go, and fight and endure, and live or die as a man must. My daughter, whose name is Yedneke, Leaf, like my mother, will grow to womanhood and go or stay as she chooses. I will live alone. This is as it should be, and my desire. But I am of two worlds; I am a person of this world, and a woman of my mother's people. I owe my knowledge to the children of her people.... To them, to the children I say: Listen! Avoid magic! Be aware! (158-59)

'Solitude' is an important story for a number of Le Guinian themes: loners, complexity, abstraction, peoplehood, marriage, projects, politics, magic, communication, self-sufficiency, and soul-formation in the world—a consideration of one extreme way of finding/making the Self that is Universe.[669]

In much of Le Guin's writing, loners come across poorly. The hermit in *Rocannon's World* (1966) gives Rocannon mindhearing, but at the cost of Rocannon's dearest friend. William Haber in *The Lathe of Heaven* (1971) sees himself as 'a lone wolf,' and 'had never wanted marriage nor close friendships' (112; ch. 8), and Haber is the villain of *Lathe* and arguably the greatest mass murderer in Terran history.[670] In *The Dispossessed* (1974), 'on the fringes of the older Anarresti communities,' there were always 'a good many solitaries and hermits...pretending that they were not members

---

[669] See also Edna in 'Ether, OR': 'All my life since I was fourteen I have been making my soul' (*UA* 107 [108]); and the Woman in 'The Woman and the Soul' (*Peacocks* 53-55). Note Ren as a liminal character, and one of Le Guin's exiles and, as we read her story, envoy (see Spencer).

[670] 'The murder of six billion nonexistent people' raises ontological questions that make it a difficult action to judge; we can be sure, though, that it is a wicked thing to do—whatever we finally decide has been done (*LoH* 75; ch. 6 [see ch. 5]).

of a social species,' and young Shevek views them negatively, a feeling readers should share, although not to the degree of the rather rigid and puritanical young Shevek (*TD* 90; ch. 4). More recently, Dalzul, though hardly a villain in 'Dancing to Ganam' (1993), is a man with serious problems, as is Tiokunan'n Hideo in 'Another Story' (1994) when he tries to be a relatively loner scientist, lost in his work. This is not surprising: the lone hero, unproblematic or angst-ridden, is a «guy-thing», usually avoided by feminist writers, with Joanna Russ's *We Who Are About To...* an important, rule-testing, and superlative exception. Still, there is the helpful, philosophical hermit in *City of Illusions* (1967), and Osden in 'Vaster than Empires and More Slow' (1971): two men who cannot shut out other people's emotions and so *must* limit their contact (*CI* 51-52; ch. 3). More admirable still, there is in Earthsea Ogion for much of his life and Ged in one version of his last days—if not the version we see in *Tehanu*. And there is the peasant boy in 'The Poacher' (1992), the protagonist-narrator of a beautifully ironic variation on 'Sleeping Beauty,' where a poor boy knows enough to leave sleeping princesses lie and learns to live and tell his own story in the solitude of an enchanted castle (*UA* 205-207). The boy's relationships with nonroyal women are highly questionable, but we are to think well of his choice of solitude.[671]

The story, 'Solitude,' is a meditation on hermetic life, the Way of one kind of sage, carefully distinguishing degrees of isolation. Serenity tells us that such a meditation is difficult, and more difficult to communicate: 'I think there is no way to write about being alone,' she writes. 'To write is to tell something to somebody, to communicate to others.... Solitude is non-communication, the absence of others, the presence of a self sufficient to itself' (154). Earlier, though, Serenity clarifies the limits to the solitude, the degree to which even Leaf had to recognize that humans on Eleven-Soro were members of a social species. Even without adults going into one another's houses or having conversations, even when '...men and women had only brief, often casual relationships, and men lived all their lives in real solitude, still there was a kind of community, a wide, thin, fine network of delicate and certain intention and restraint: a social order' (144), enough of a social order to get to Leaf word of her son and to protect him and other (nonwicked) boys.[672] Right after saying how it may be impossi-

---

[671] In the story's primary world, the Poacher did not protect his step-mother from his father when he grew big enough to do so (*UA* 197-98). In the dream-time world of the castle, he did not leave a (heterosexual) pair of sleeping peasant lovers alone but 'laid [himself]...down softly on her,' kissed her nipples, 'and came into her honey sweetness,' apparently on more than one occasion and with her smiling 'in her sleep' and sometimes making 'a little groan of pleasure' (208). When he eats food without its being consumed, the boy asks, 'Was it that as a dream, I could change nothing of this reality of sleep?' (204), and he may change nothing; so if he's in a dream, ethical issues get complicated—or very simple: dreams are amoral.

[672] Not entering other people's houses may glance at a trend in the US away from casual visits. In large US cities around the time of 'Solitude,' people may be

ble to write about being alone, Serenity expands on the ways in which the persons of her world—persons, not her *people*—are connected.

> A woman's solitude in the auntring is, of course, based firmly on the presence of others at a little distance. It is contingent, and therefore human, solitude. The settled men are connected as stringently to the women, though not to one another; the settlement is an integral though distant element of the auntring. Even a scouting woman [looking for sex, other adventure] is part of the society—a moving part, connecting the settled parts. Only the isolation of a woman or man who chooses to live outside the settlements is absolute....There are worlds where such persons are called saints, holy people. Since isolation is a sure way to prevent magic, on my world the assumption is that they are sorcerors, outcast by others or by their own will, their conscience. (154)

Serenity is not endorsing saintly isolation; Serenity, and Le Guin, endorse relative solitude as one way of being in the world, a way of a self to be, within limits, sufficient unto itself. Not Saint Simeon Stylites on his pillar, trying to transcend the world; or Star-Child at the end of *2001: A Space Odyssey*, gazing down at Earth as his new project, not even a ten-clone as in 'Nine Lives' (1969), a misguided attempt at self-sufficiency (*Those Who Can* 208), or a family man isolated in his ego and rationalism like Ike Rose in 'Newton's Sleep.'[673] Serenity rejects a transcendent position above her planet in the Hainish observation ship; she rejects a chance to go to an Ekumenical school and go off on great projects for the Ekumen. Her relationship to the stars is lying on her back looking at a star 'and the stars around it, until you feel the earth turning, until you become aware of how the stars and the world and the soul move together' (142).[674]

Daily life immanent in the auntring or out scouting or among the men may be repetitive, and repetitive daily life can certainly grow dull; but Serenity has a point in saying 'I never knew anybody, anywhere I have been,

---

physically close to their neighbors but more isolated than the women in a Sorovian auntring.

[673] Having spent time 'wearing a spiked girdle in a dark cave,' and a full summer as 'a rooted vegetable in a garden,' Simeon became a 'pillar saint' near Antioch in 423 CE I.e., after having descended into the earth, aardvark-hole fashion, St. Simeon Stylites climbed atop a pillar and stayed there, meditating, praying, and building the pillar higher, gradually raising 'himself to a height of sixty feet above the ground,' where he spent thirty years (Thompson and Johnson 56; see Pynchon, *Gravity's Rainbow* 315-22).

[674] Owen Griffiths, the protagonist-narrator of *VFA* (1978), had a similar experience 'Once out in the desert, under the stars,' when he 'turned into the earth turning on its axis'—but he has such experiences 'always alone. By myself,' and he treasures a similar experience 'on the high mountain with a friend' (*VFA* 41).

who found life simple. I think a life or a time looks simple when you leave out the details, the way a planet looks smooth, from orbit' (134). A vision from orbit is hardly to be despised, giving a whole, beautiful view of a planet; that is one truth, and it is no less true that worlds are 'dirt and rocks' up close, and in the dirt and rocks and details there is always complexity (*TD* 153-54; ch. 6). The 'heart' of Serenity's life has been her 'being alone' (154), and she can be alone and not know loneliness and boredom because she is aware of, if not necessarily Blake's 'a World in a Grain of Sand,' then certainly 'of the grain of dust beneath the sole of the foot, and the skin of the sole of the foot, and the motion of the light across the air, and the color of the grass on the high hill across the river...endlessly changing, endlessly new' (156).[675] For many mystics, the details of multiplicity in unity *is* the mystic experience.

Serenity is a *Self*, capable of a degree of self-sufficiency precisely because she is a Self in contact with the world (see *ACH* 485); she is not some mere ego trying to transcend and command the world. For Serenity and the persons of her world, wholeness is to be part of the planet, and with other humans—but *with* other humans only as that 'thin, fine network of delicate and certain intention and restraint' (144), a social order as tenuous as the cord Isako tells Isidri connects mother and child ('Another Story' *FIS* 173), or the 'silvery thread' in *A Ride on the Red Mare's Back* (1992: 42). These persons refuse to intellectualize, generalize, or universalize on the political level at all, not even thinking of themselves as a people. To get people to act together—act politically, in concert—is magic. Possibly on the basis of their horrible historical experience, to use *any* power 'to get power over other persons' is magic—'an art or power that violates natural law' (136)—and 'To live rightly a person has to keep away from magic' (144).

Le Guin allows Serenity and the philosophy of her planet to make a very strong point: 'to get power over other persons' in *any* way is magic, even if it is coming to lead a gang of boys, even if it is Borny talking to his mother on his joining the boygroup. Leaf thinks the boygroups 'Perform natural selection,' and she wants Borny to have nothing to do with the boygroups, and she has an excellent point. She wants to take them back to the ship, and Borny 'persuaded her out of it' (140). Serenity agrees with Borny, but she does not join this argument, and she will come to use methods against her mother that readers could see—and I do see—as far more harmful than arguing: shutting her eyes and covering her ears, standing stiff and '*enduring* her touch,' the touch of Leaf, her mother (148, my emphasis). Serenity is admirably guilt-free, and she is correct in setting out one exception to the naturalness of a mother's power: it is unnatural if 'used against the child's soul' (140). Still, looking back upon this scene, there is something to be said for Tiokunan'n Hideo's line in 'Another

---

[675] Among sociable people who pair for life, such attention to detail is also crucial; Shevek and a nameless truck train driver in *TD* agree it is attention to detail that makes for *variety* in partnerships (249; ch. 10).

Story,' 'How cruel we are to our parents!' (*FIS* 159), and more to be said for Rakam's somewhat rueful memories in 'A Woman's Liberation' of her (young) 'beautiful voice speaking the beautiful truth' with too little thought of immediate hurts (*FWF* 179; § 3).

In the text, there is an exquisite balance that readers may legitimately leave be or tip one way or another. *Logos* is central to 'phallologocentric'; and logic, reason, and rhetoric can be part of patriarchal oppression: 'a form of violence, a kind of tyranny' (de Beauvoir, *Second Sex* 167; ch. 20). In Le Guin's canon, Ike Rose in 'Newton's Sleep' is a rationalist, as is Dr. Haber in *The Lathe of Heaven*, and the Professors in 'The Rock That Changed Things' (*FIS*). And the anti-Logos position can be pushed quite far. In the 1980s a feminist colleague sent on to me for my information and comments a published essay she had come across arguing (sic) that 'any attempt to persuade is an act of violence,' that 'the difference between a persuasive metaphor and a violent artillery attack is obscure and certainly one of degree rather than kind.' By this sort of logic, an attempt by Amnesty International to persuade people to stop torture is equivalent to torture. In the ethicist William Schuyler's phrase, such a conclusion would 'gag a maggot.'[676] My view is that 'Avoid magic!' is bad advice if it means avoid trying to persuade people, and I have an ally in Bu in 'The Rock that Changed Things.' In that story, Bu, 'was so excited and persuasive' about colors of stones 'that other nurs of Obling began studying the color patterns, learning how to read their meanings' (*FIS* 64)—and Bu's persuasion helps bring a very necessary revolution. In 'Solitude,' though, from Serenity's view, we should take the idea seriously that persuasion is magic to be avoided.

What we see in much of the story is a moving, loving conflict between Leaf and Serenity, mother and daughter, both of whom have claims on our empathy and sympathy. Leaf is something of a cultural and intellectual snob for an anthropologist, and most of us can sympathize with Serenity for wanting more stories and songs from her 'and not so many words'—which I assume means fewer theories and abstractions. We can see the narrow-mindedness, plus flat-out error, of Leaf's dismissing as 'primitivism' the way the persons of Eleven-Soro see technology as magic. As Serenity explains, they just do *not* see the technology as magic; they see the technologists as (evil) magicians, using technological power to get political power (144). And, of course, we can see perhaps better than Leaf the wisdom of a 'cultural imperative' against 'magic.' The daughter has some

---

[676] I.e., 'cause a maggot to gag' (if maggots were capable of gagging). The quotations on persuasion = violence I recalled turned out to be from Sally Miller Gearhart's 'The Womanization of Rhetoric,' qtd. here from Jarratt 106-07. For a nuanced response to Gearhart and more generally 'The Feminist Case against Argument,' see all of Jarratt's 'Feminism and Composition: The Case for Conflict,' a thoughtful and important essay Jarratt was kind enough to give me when I requested it in the spring of 1997, in the context of my work as Student Mediator for the Miami U. English Dept.

points. On the other hand, even as we would do well to 'know how the princess perceived' Dalzul's initial visit in 'Dancing to Ganam' (*FIS* 119), so we do well to wonder what Serenity's mother would have to say about much of 'Solitude.'

Ideally, Serenity would have as native tongues both Hainish and Sorovian and could be a woman of two worlds. The universe is not set up that way, though, and Serenity must choose a world. Leaf and In Joy Born do well to figuratively walk away from a culture far less tempting than that of Omelas and leave Eleven-Soro: if they decide they want to be *in* the world, they can find a nice pueblo on Hain to do it in (see opening sections of 'A Man of the People,' *FWF*). Serenity chooses Eleven-Soro, and we have learned enough about that world to say that, for her, the choice is a happy one and a legitimate choice of a place to be.

'The Matter of Seggri' (1994)[677]

> Be careful how you pray; the gods are malicious and sometimes give us what we ask for. —Proverb and Joke

Complementing 'Solitude' is 'The Matter of Seggri.' As a phrase, 'The matter of Seggri' is what the Mobile Noem calls his report to the Stabiles of the Ekumen on the culture of Seggri (34). As a literary work in *Crank!* magazine, it is five narratives, from five different times over perhaps 1400 years of Seggrian history (see Brigg, 'Chronology' 18, n. 2). 'Seggri' is anthropological SF, including Le Guin's first long look at athletics in a culture, and the five narratives give us figurative snapshots of the planet's human culture from their first recorded contact with alien humans through their having sufficient dealings with other cultures to have some perspective on their own culture, to the beginning of change.[678]

Of the five narratives, the first and last are in the voices of men, the middle three of women. The first narrative is a log entry by an alien male; the second, notes for a report to the Ekumen by a woman who is a Mobile and a native of Hain; the third is a memoir by a woman of Seggri, telling the story of herself and her brother; the fourth is a Seggrian short story, by a woman and from the point of view of a woman, telling of the fictional woman's life and loves, including the sad romantic love a man has for her; the last is an autobiographical sketch by a Seggrian man who has worked off Seggri for the Ekumen and desires to return home as a Mobile.

The basic situation on Seggri will seem familiar to anyone who has read Sam Moskowitz's anthology *When Women Rule* (1972) or, more to the point for me, Joanna Russ's 1980 essay '*Amor Vincit Foeminam*: The

---

[677] My thanks to David Schappert for sending me on 10 July 1995 materials on 'Seggri' from the World Wide Web site for the 1995 James Tiptree, Jr. Award. I used from those materials comments from Brian Attebery, Pat Murphy, and Susanna J. Sturgis. ('Seggri' won the 1995 Tiptree.)

[678] For snapshots, see 'Winter's King' (1969/1975, coll. *WTQ* (86 f.).

Battle of the Sexes in Science Fiction.' 'Seggri' shows 'role reversals in the group relations between the sexes' (Russ 42). That seeming familiarity of role reversal, however, gets defamiliarized radically by other, different familiarities: not all the roles are reversed, 'reversal' is far too crude a term for what Le Guin is up to in this story, and, on Seggri, the sexes do not battle.

The first item in 'Seggri' is Captain Aolao-olao's Report from the log of his Wandership, apparently a generation starship, some 'six generations out' (*Crank!* #3: 3). As frequently happens on generation starships, cultural development has taken a strange turn (and/or the culture was strange to start with), and we have a report by a starship captain who looks with contempt upon the leader of their hosts for believing 'the stars to be worlds full of people and beasts, asking us from which star we descended' (4). Captain Aolao-olao's Report is a send-up of the ship's log entry of a Terran sea captain of the eighteenth- or early nineteenth-century CE: say, an Englishman or a Frenchman ca. 1767-69 or 1778 for Captain James Cook in Hawaii—or of a utopian description in the manner of Sir Thomas More's *Utopia* (1516). The Captain is a mildly fanatical monotheist and a sexist, and what he sees is a paradise of bachelors served by 'a vast superabundance' of maids and adult women (3).

The Captain opens his log entry stating that on this world he and his men have been entertained well 'and leave with as good an estimation of the natives as is consonant with their unregenerate state.' His next sentence tells us that the natives 'live in fine great buildings they call castles, with large parks all about,' and it is only in the seventh line of the entry that we learn that his comments about 'the natives' have included only men. 'Their women live in villages and towns huddled outside the walls. All the common work of farm and mill is performed by the women,' who the Captain sees as 'ordinary drudges, living in towns which belong to the lords of the castle' (3). The men spend their days in manly sporting events, and 'At night they go to certain houses which they own in the town, where they may have their pick among the women and satisfy their lust upon them as they will.' To make the dream perfect: 'The women pay them...for a night of pleasure, and pay them yet more if they get a child on them. Their nights thus are spent in carnal satisfaction as often as they desire, and their days in a diversity of sports and games' (3-4). And, after the kids are raised to be sufficiently human for men to deal with—in my formulation, not the Captain's—the 'Boys are taken from the women at the age of eleven and brought to the castle to be educated as befits a man.' The only problems from the Captain's point of view are that so few boys are conceived and live through infancy, though this is appropriate as 'the curse of GOD laid upon this race as upon all those who acknowledge HIM not'; the Captain is also disappointed by the paucity of arts and ignorance of the sciences among the (male) Seggri—occupations and projects the men dismiss as 'women's work' and 'womanish things' (4). And he is struck by the degree of competition 'in the ornamentation and magnificence of their costumes' which the Captain et al. might have thought unmanly 'were they not withal such proper men, strong and ready for any game or sport, and full of pride and a most delicate and fiery honor' (5).

The second voice we hear is from many years later, that of Merriment, a Hainish woman, in her Notes for a Report to the Ekumen. She and the Alterran man Kaza Agad are First Observers. They are separated shortly after they arrive onplanet, and Agad is sent to a Castle; in the link between Merriment's Notes and the next entry, we learn that Agad is killed, and he is absent from 'Seggri' except for Merriment's concern for him and attempt to get information about him.

Merriment stays a while in a town and then goes to a college, and her view of Seggrian culture—though based on similar data—differs greatly from that of Captain Aolao-olao. In scenes from daily life and from exposition, we learn that humans on Seggri have a world-wide monoculture with a deep division between the sexes very deeply rooted in their reproductive biology. Merriment tells us, bitterly, 'My ancestors must have really had fun playing with these people's chromosomes,' and she feels guilty—a useful occasion, she thinks, for guilt. Merriment is able to quantify Captain Aolao-olao's observation on the superabundance of women: one conception in six yields a male zygote, with many miscarriages of male fetuses and high death rates in infancy bringing the male population down to one in sixteen by puberty. 'Given their situation,' the biological gift of the Hainish founders, 'they need strong healthy men' to reproduce; so they evolved a system of 'social selection reinforcing natural selection' (8). Males have scarcity value on Seggri, but the culture is hardly the masculinist paradise Captain Aolao-olao saw. 'Their gender imbalance has produced a society in which...men have all the privilege and the women have all the power' (8-9). It has been a stable society for 'at least two millennia,' probably longer, 'But it could be quickly and disastrously destabilised' through contact with the Ekumen and 'experiencing the human norm' of more equally gendered societies (9).

The castles are supported by the towns and the men must stay in the castles except to compete in games and to go to the 'fuckeries' to service—'that's their word, the same word they use for their bulls'—the women of the towns (11). Within capitalist constraints, the women choose the men they want; the men have no more choice in the matter than bulls servicing cows.

Merriment finds much to like about Seggrian women's culture, and 'Seggri' can be read as a complex variation on the theme of the ambiguous utopia.[679] Among the Seggri, 'female homosexuality...is the central ele-

---

[679] In the Web site comments on the Tiptree Award, Brian Attebery invites comparisons of 'Seggri' with some of Le Guin's own works 'as well as the thought experiments of other gender explorers like Joanna Russ, Eleanor Arnason, Sheri S. Tepper, and James Tiptree, Jr.' (i.e., Alice Sheldon). Susanna J. Sturgis compares with 'Seggri' Arnason's 'The Lovers' and Suzy McKee Charnas's *Furies*, both nominated for the 1995 Tiptree (*Furies* is the sequel to *Walk to the End of the World* and *Motherlines)*; the worlds of the Charnas trilogy should also be put

ment of society, as heterosexuality is' in Terran societies generally.[680] The women are highly communal but respect the need to be alone; they are capitalistic and admire wealth, but they also respect teaching (6), and the flexibility of their colleges could be instructive even for the schools on Hain (10). They say 'piss' and 'fuck' and cry easily and publicly: 'There is an enviable simplicity to many acts in a society which has, in all its daily life, only one gender. And which perhaps...has no shame' (7). Indeed, Seggri is an improvement on our world for most women, and Seggri could be a dream come true for a bisexual woman sports fan from a patriarchal culture who migrated to Seggri and got rich.

On the other hand, Merriment finds some less admirable aspects to the culture. Skodr, a professorial intellectual, tells Merriment that men aren't allowed in colleges because learning is 'very bad for men: it weakens a man's sense of honor, makes his muscles flabby, and leaves him impotent. 'What goes to the brain takes from the testicles.... Men have to be sheltered from education for their own good'' (10). Some younger readers might find this passage just entertainingly silly; older readers should recognize it as one instance of simple reversal: sexist ideology about educating women reversed and applied to men. It is also a straightforward statement of classic (and sexist) American macho anti-intellectualism: the life of the mind as unmanly, male intellectuals as wimps. Merriment tries to 'be water' and accept, as she was taught, probably by the rather Daoist teachers of the Ekumen and on Hain generally; still she was 'disgusted,' and Skodr, as a *liberal* sexist intellectual, tries to placate her by telling her about 'secret colleges' often run by the homosexual men of the castles. Such colleges have produced interesting works, but Skodr can only think of two (10).

Merriment's disgust at Skodr's ideas about male intellect is based in part on what she has learned from Skodr about life for men in the castles.

> I keep thinking 'spoiled brats!' but actually these men must be more like soldiers in the training camps that militarists have. Only the training never ends. As they win trials they gain all kinds of titles and ranks you could translate as 'generals' and the other names militarists have for all their power-grades. Some of the 'generals,' the Lords and Masters and so on, are the sports idols, the darlings of the fuckeries...; but as they get older apparently they trade glory among the women for power among the men, and become tyrants within their Castle, bossing the 'lesser' men around, until they're overthrown, kicked out....

---

into dialog with Eleven-Soro in 'Solitude.' As a quiet part of that dialog, one should add Le Guin's own 'Limberlost' (1989), coll. *UA*.
[680] Quoted words from Le Guin, personal communication; I have removed Le Guin's underlining to fit her words better into my sentence.

> It sounds like a miserable life. All they're allowed to do after age eleven is compete at games and sports inside the Castle, and compete in the fuckeries, after they're fifteen or so, for money and number of fucks and so on. Nothing else. No options. No trades. No skills of making. No travel unless they play in the big games. (9-10)

So not just a military life—which Le Guin has handled negatively since at least *The Word for World Is Forest* (1972)—but militar*ist* life in the castles. And emphatically no life of the mind, because the sexist ideas outside the castles dovetail perfectly with the sexist ideas within on what manly men do when doing manly things—and it is not thinking (10). So life for the great mass of men must be, by statistical necessity, not winning in the games and trials and therefore not becoming sports champions. And 'men who don't win at things aren't allowed to go to the fuckeries.' The analogy with grand champion bulls at a state fair is quite exact, except that the Seggrian champions are joined by 'boys between fifteen and nineteen,' used for pleasure. However, Merriment's friend and colleague Kaza is not a prize stud nor a juvenile sex toy: 'He's a man, and this is a terrible place to be a man' (11).

And so ends Merriment's Notes. Again, the link (written in italics) tells us '*Kaza Agad had been killed*' and adds that Merriment's recommendation to the Stabiles to '*observe and avoid*' was not followed, with another pair of Observers sent to Seggri (both women), with their status changed after their third year to First Mobiles; and then one of them was made Ambassador. Very conscious of the guilt she felt for her ancestors' experimenting with the genome of the humans of Seggri, Merriment had been determined to upset things as little as possible (9). The First Mobiles were less cautious: '*They made Resehavanar's Choice as 'all the truth slowly*,'' with up to 200 offworld visitors a year (11).

The memoir that follows is written by a woman of Seggri for her 'dear friend,' who either is, or through whom it eventually got to, the Ekumenical Ambassador: 'You asked me, dear friend, to tell you anything I might like people on other worlds to know about my life and my world.' The Speaker here is aware of 'how strange we seem to all the others, the half-and-half races' and conscious of how her people may seem to aliens 'backward, provincial, even perverse.' She is aware that her people may change within the next few decades, that they may 'decide that we should remake ourselves' (11). The woman is happy she will be dead by the time such a decision must be made. She writes, 'I like my people. I like our fierce, proud, beautiful men, I don't want them to become like women. I like our trustful, powerful generous women, I don't want them to become like men' (12).

The story she chooses to tell is that of herself (Po) and Ittu, her beloved younger brother. Little Ittu wants to work/play with his older sister among the cattle (eventually playing hornvaulting games) even after it is time for Po to 'be doing things together with the other girls' and Ittu—approaching his eleventh birthday and going to the Castle—to be 'doing things' alone 'the way men do' (15). Ittu does not want to go to the Castle and eventually makes his feelings known. He draws the attention of Ushiggi, a mother and grandmother of boys, mayor of the town five or six times, and 'a formidable old woman' who has the title of respect 'vev': teacher. Apparently, Ittu has the inchoate idea that 'a man's body does not' or need not 'shape his fate' (14). Vev Ushiggi has another lesson for him. 'She told him that he was born to the service of his people and had one responsibility, to sire children when he got old enough; and one duty, to be a strong, brave man, stronger and braver than other men, so that women would choose him to sire their children.' He had to live at the Castle 'because men could not live among women.' Showing some of the bravery Vev Ushiggi has commanded, he asks her why not. Po quotes Ittu quoting Ushiggi's long-considered answer: 'Because we would destroy them' (15)—i.e., women would destroy the men.

Feeling 'that passion of justice that children know, the birthright we seldom honor' as adults (13-14), Po disobeys her mother and the village elders by playing with her brother and is punished by hard time in solitary confinement in the town jail. Very close to his eleventh birthday, Ittu proposes to Po running away to the agents of the Ekumen. The first thing his sister says is 'You want to get me locked up again? They said next time it would be thirty days!' Ittu replies, 'They're going to lock me up for fifty years.' He hopes the Ekumen can save him from the Castle; Po thinks running away would be 'dishonorable.' Ittu doesn't 'care about honor'; he wants 'to be free' (16). His sister won't take the risk and tries to cheer him up with clichés. 'He knew and I knew,' she says, 'that I had betrayed our love and our birthright of justice. He knew he had no hope.' So he runs away, and his sister doesn't tell, but he is caught anyway. On his eleventh birthday, he goes into the Castle, 'and the Gates closed' (17). In anarchist terms, Ittu is imprisoned, with prisons a central image of State repression and oppression (see *TD* 27-32; ch. 2).

There are three more brief paragraphs to the memoir, making explicit the image of the closing gates. Ittu becomes a Young Champion Hornvaulter and gets traded away to another castle at age twenty. When Po's daughter is born, she writes Ittu, but he doesn't answer her letters. The memoir ends with 'I don't know if it's what I want you to know. It is what I had to tell' (17).

Po's narrative is followed by a Seggrian short story, supposedly by one Sem Gridji, called 'Love Out of Place.' The introductory link distinguishes the new genre of the short story from the older Seggrian genres of drama and narrative poem (18), with the most important form the traditional Epics (33). The classical genres were initially '*written collaboratively*' and rewritten over the generations—all by anonymous authors. '*Small value was placed on preserving a 'true' text.*' The short prose narratives have identifiable authors and historical or fictional settings and characters, not larger-than-life Heroes. The epics and plays are very well known and as a set of classic works are '*one of the principal unifying influences of the*

Seggrian monoculture.' On the other hand, *'The prose narrative, read in silence, served rather as a device by which the culture might question itself, and a tool for individual moral self-examination'*; hence, conservatives among the Seggrian woman *'disapproved of the genre as antagonistic to the intensely cooperative, collaborative structure of their society'*; the intellectuals of college literature departments, as one might expect, often dismissed the genre out of hand: *'fiction is for men'* (18).

'Love Out of Place' is the story of Azak, a mill-district girl who goes to college, eventually marries well and starts her own business with her first wife; the two find a third woman for a marital triad—a strong lesbian relationship in which the three prosper and reproduce; but Azak ends up feeling, 'My life is wrong' and not knowing 'how to make it right' (25). The problem in her life, and the stuff of the story, is the Young Champion of Dance, Toddra. Azak sees him dance on holovision and is 'captivated.' His price at the local fuckery is twice that of the other men, but Azak likes sex, especially intercourse with highly potent men, and she pays it. After some very good sex indeed, Azak develops something of an obsession for Toddra (18-19); for his part, Toddra falls in love.

Toddra's love is romantic in a way that is new and subversive in Seggrian literature *'in the late sixteenth century'* (18), and was new and subversive on Terra in France and England and Western Europe fairly generally from about 1100 CE (producing, for a major example, 'The Matter of Britain') through the Elizabethan period in England in the sixteenth century CE. (Nowadays on Terra, the most common form of romance is of the Harlequin variety and definitely not subversive.) Sem Gridji, then, has helped re-invent literal heterosexual romantic love through a literal prose romance, with 'romance' suggesting 'Medieval Romance': with romance as courtly love, where the male lover wishes to belong to the woman and serve her. Toddra says, 'I wish I were your servant,' and he means it. He wants to belong to her: to serve her and only her; Toddra would die for Azak, he says (19), so great is his love (and his pathos).[681]

To confirm the point, there is a brief dialog between Azak and the manager of the fuckery, occasioned by Azak's asking if Toddra has proved as popular with the customers as the manager et al.—who owns the fuckeries is not clear in 'Seggri'—might have expected.

> 'No,' the manager said. 'Everybody else reports that he takes a lot of arousing, and is sullen and careless toward them.'
> 'How strange,' Azak said.
> 'Not at all,' said the manager. 'He's in love with you.'
> 'A man in love with a woman?' Azak said, and laughed.

---

[681] I use 'pathos' as in *pathetic*: Toddra is like the traditional chivalric/courtly lover in combining a strong dose of overly earnest masochism in his love. See below for Le Guin as a critical Romantic critiquing this variety of lover.

'It happens all too often,' the manager said.
'I thought only women fell in love,' said Azak.
'Women fall in love with a man, sometimes, and that's bad too,' said the manager. 'May I warn you, Azak? Love should be between women. It's out of place here. It can never come to any good end. I hate to lose the money, but I wish you'd...not always ask for Toddra. You're encouraging him...in something that does harm to him.' (19)

It does not come to a good end. And a Seggrian version of Captain Aolao-olao, could read the fuckery manager as the Spokeswoman for the true social norm reinforced by this story, the *real* meaning of the story: 'Love should be between women. It's out of place' in a heterosexual relationship.

Toddra has a plan. In the story-dances he usually plays women's parts; Toddra proposes to disguise himself, escape and come to Azak's house as a servant. 'I would serve you, service you, sweep your house, do anything, anything. Azak, please, my beloved, my mistress, let me be yours!' At least till she tires of him. Azak declines. She cannot take Toddra's love 'entirely seriously,' but she is touched (20-21). With other women, Toddra turns out to be a reliable stud, with a good record for healthy male offspring, which puts him in demand. Which is just as well with Azak, because she finds a woman, Zedr, and great sexual fulfillment (21). She sees less and less of Toddra and feels a little ashamed for not telling Toddra that she loves Zedr, but consoles herself thinking he would be so busy siring children he wouldn't miss her much: '...despite all his romantic talk of love, he was a man, and to a man fucking is the most important thing, instead of being merely one element of love and life as it is to a woman' (22).

So Azak marries Zedr, and they set up business and a household, and start arranging for a third partner, both for business and the marriage. Then Toddra shows up in women's dress, pleading, yet again for Azak to let him be her servant, claiming he cannot live without her. Zedr calls the police, who subdue Toddra brutally and send him back to the Castle. Two years pass, and the third woman, Chochi, is added to their business and then household. Toddra was back at the fuckery occasionally, as the year's Champion Sire for his Castle, but he was used only for reproduction, 'as he had a reputation for roughness and even cruelty.' Azak finds it difficult 'to picture Toddra behaving brutally' and concludes that severe 'punishment at the Castle...must have altered him' (23). Valuing marital fidelity, Azak has avoided the fuckery since marrying Zedr, but Chochi is pregnant and the triad would like twins—and Azak doesn't want either 'self-impregnation' with semen out of a sperm bank, nor some stranger to copulate with her; so she schedules Toddra (24). After some small talk with Azak's trying to make sure that 'all that foolishness about love is over,' Toddra undresses her, they lie naked, she fondles him, and he sneaks a knife into his hand and attacks her—the attack including his entering her and ejaculating. Toddra is subdued with violence by the men at the fuckery and returned to Castle, where 'They'll geld him' (25). Romance lovers, especially when crossed, can be dangerous to themselves and others.[682]

We do not learn whether or not Toddra impregnated Azak, or if she successfully had a child, or how her marriage or business fare; and the story ends with the lines on her life being wrong and her not knowing 'how to make it right' (25).

Why end the story there, with Toddra hauled off for castration, and Azak coming to the vaguest sort of recognition? If it is Azak's story, why not tell us more about her life than what may have been only a strange interlude with a literally hopeless romantic? Aristotle and his followers talked about a narrative having a beginning, a middle, and an end, but Le Guin question sthe idea in 'The Carrier Bag Theory of Fiction' (*DEW* 169) and is going to have a very respectable story-teller tell us, within ten pages of the end of 'Love Out of Place,' that stories don't have 'an end' (34). Why end the story here, and why can we be sure most readers will find this an appropriate place to end the story and my questions about What happened next? in Azak's life, at best impertinent?

Short answer: Because unlike the Seggri, most of Le Guin's audience are used to the prose *romance* narrative, and for us the center of 'Love Out of Place' is Toddra's unreturned, passionate love for Azak. For most of us, and for Sem Gridji, the beginning of the story is the rise of Toddra's love, the middle of the story the highly unsmooth course of that love, and the end of the story the end of that love and the violence that destroyed Toddra and got Azak to begin to recognize a problem. But what about Sem Gridji's readers, as we imagine them, or any readers of 'Seggri' (perhaps young males) unfamiliar with stories of romantic love? Or female readers very familiar with stories of romantic love who, on the basis of ideology and/or experience, are convinced that stories of romantic male lovers of women are dirty rotten lies? If the manager of the fuckery is seen as especially acute in matters of male/female love, and if Azak and Zedr are more typical of the culture, then 'Love Out of Place' is a very challenging work, challenging the idea that only lesbian love is appropriate love, true love. For those who think that 'to a man fucking is the most important thing,' or the only thing in a male relationship with a woman or women, it would be a bit of a shock to read about Toddra, a man who can have all the fucking he can handle, and who instead wants to love and serve.

It's a relevant point. Writing of his own research among his undergraduate students at Rutgers University in the 1970s and 1980s, Michael Moffatt inferred as a useful category, *Romantic Men*. About a third of the young men who wrote about their sex lives and attitudes for Moffatt's

---

[682] For a classical instance in English see climax of Shakespeare's *Twelfth Night*, where, thinking himself betrayed, the sighing and riming Duke Orsino gets murderous: 'I'll sacrifice the lamb that I do love / To spite a raven's heart within a dove' (see 5.1.111-27). Lancelot of the Lake, Romeo of Verona, and many of their brothers on the Romance circuit are also dangerous to have around.

study took 'sexual stances that could be called romantic, sometimes in opposition to what they themselves saw as the more powerful men's mainstream.... Like the neotraditionalist women, the romantic men maintained with varying degrees of conviction that the only good sex was sex with love' (Moffatt 212). By the mid-1990s, the 'Remasculinization of America' (to appropriate a phrase from Susan Jeffords) had proceeded apace, with that 'more powerful men's mainstream' rolling on, washing out much of the American branch of the male-romantic tradition. In such a context, it is well to put readers into a situation where to deny the possibility of a male romantic is to deny the existence of a character right in front of then—and to put themselves on the side of the obviously narrow-minded and sexist. For Le Guin's readers who might think that life in the Castle and fuckery could be enjoyable for at least a Champion, 'Love Out of Place' might indeed prove *'a device by which the culture might question itself, and a tool for individual moral self-examination'* (18).

The last section of 'The Matter of Seggri' is a personal narrative, an 'Autobiographical Sketch by Mobile Andar Dez,' a man who would like to return as a Mobile of the Ekumen to his native Seggri. It is a first-person, first-hand look at life in the Castle, a direct look at a man's world not possible from the point of view of Serenity in 'Solitude' and not given us up until now in 'Seggri.'

After a brief summary beginning with 'I was born'—a common opening for personal narratives on Terra, especially slave narratives, and perhaps Yeowe as well (*FWF*)—Andar Dez brings us quickly to 'the ceremony of Severance' and his entry into the small Castle at Radedr.[683] Like many of Le Guin's settings, Rakedr is 'conservative': a hinterland place where, for good and/or for ill, the old ways are clung to. Here it is mostly for ill. Dez sees the Severance as a kind of death all men on Seggri knew: 'They had turned and looked back at their whole life,' the families that raised them, their towns, 'every place and face they had loved, and turned away from it as the gate closed' (27). If the heart of tragedy is the isolation of the individual, followed by crushing that individual, then every boy of Seggri had undergone a tragedy. Not the death of the boy and the birth of the man, but in the Castles of Seggri, as Dez describes them, pure tragedy: the boys leave the world—the living world—to try to live outside the world in a militarist prison, a very small City of Man: at least figuratively a place of death.

The Castle at Rakedr, though, may have been, in its details, worse than most, although potentially promising. There is a political split between the 'collegials' and 'traditionals,' i.e., 'a liberal faction left from the regime of' the previous Lord 'and a younger, highly conservative faction.' The rule of the new Lord 'had grown increasingly harsh and irrational,' corrupt and cruel. Dez thinks he and the other boys and young men would have 'been destroyed if there had not been a strong, constant, moral resistance, centered around Ragaz and Kohadrat, who had been protégés of Lord

---

[683] See opening of 'A Woman's Liberation' (*FWF* 145).

Ishog. The two men were open partners; their followers were all the homosexuals in the Castle, and a good number of other men and older boys' (27). Resistance is needed. The Castles are indeed the everlasting boot camps inferred by the Mobile Merriment concerning Awaga Castle (9)—plus a nightmare version of a nineteenth-century English public school plus the rape and brutalization of punk-breaking rituals at your average American high-security prison.[684] Unlike an English public school, or among peoples on Werel and Yeowe (*FWF*), there is no religion in the castles nor on Seggri generally: no Kamye to give hope to the oppressed. Indeed, there seems to be no overt religious life on Seggri, with sports, perhaps, replacing religion. So the machismo and displaced militarism of the castles, where sport clearly replaces war, is not, as in Le Guin's earlier work, bracketed with monotheism.[685]

There is also no privacy in the castles, and compassion must be shown in secret. Adult consenting homosexuality and consenting sexuality between the older boys is punished with 'bizarre and appalling physical mutilations.' Yet Lord Fassaw 'encouraged the older boys to rape the eleven- and twelve-year-olds, as a manly practice.' The youngsters, and eventually everyone not of the chosen, came to dread particularly four «lords of discipline» called 'the Lordsmen'—Lord Fassaw's men, his sycophants and enforcers. Looking back, Ardar Dez says he was happy that he didn't kill himself or kill his 'mind and soul' to survive. 'Thanks to the maternal care of the collegials—the resistance, as we came to call ourselves—I grew up.' Dez calls attention to his use of the word 'maternal': there are no fathers in the world of Seggri, only sires; Dez says, 'I thought of Ragaz and Kohardrat as my mothers. I still do' (28).

Dez does not feel totally positive toward his literal mothers. The times have changed a bit, and town councils and other authorities among the women that could investigate the castles. Still, 'Any protest the resistance tried to bring to the Town Council could be dismissed as typical male whining, or laid to the demoralising influence of the Aliens,' the Ekumen here as «outside agitators» (28-29). Dez feels abandoned, but the collegial leader Ragaz tells him that they both are and are not abandoned. The women support them: food, clothing, shelter, payment for services rendered. Still, there is violence inherent in the Seggrian system—obvious violence among the males, and, among the women, what the Narrator of *The Dispossessed* (1974) called violence's 'most devoted ally, the averted eye' (206; ch. 8). Rogaz formulates the problem as collusion between the

---

[684] 'Breaking a punk' was described to me in the middle 1970s when I guest-taught at the State of Ohio's maximum security prison at Lucasville; I believe the story.

[685] We might see the lack of sky-god monotheism correlating with a woman-run culture. Note, though, that there is no visible religion among the Terran military on Athshe in *WWF* (1972)—or in most SF and other genres of popular narrative. Contrast the strong monotheism of the Basnasska Nation in CI (1967 [ch. 4]) and of the Condor people of *ACH* (1985).

sexes 'in maintaining the great foundation of ignorance and lies on which our civilisation rests'; and Ragaz foresees male independence. Dez adds, 'Independence was as far as his vision could reach. Yet I think his mind groped further, towards what he could not see, the body's obscure, inalterable dream of mutuality' (29).

Neither the vision nor the dream last long for Ragaz. However much he doubts the Town Council will hear them, Ragaz still led the attempt to have their case heard. 'Lord Fassaw saw his power threatened' and within days Ragaz is 'seized by the Lordsmen and their bully boys, accused of repeated homosexual acts and treasonable plots, arraigned, and sentenced by the Lord of the Castle' to a beating with 'Lord Long,' a tube of heavy leather, filled with lead weights. Ragaz survives the beating less than two hours. Ragaz's lover and colleague Kohadrat preaches a sports variation on the anarchist doctrine of the unity of ends and means: 'How you play is what you win.' Dez and his fellows, though, 'would not play the patience game any more. We would win, now, once for all.'[686] And they do: in The Rakedr Mutiny they kill Lord Fassaw and the Lordsmen and their supporters, and mutilate the bodies (29-30). For himself, Dez and three other mutineers grab exercise clubs and beat to death Lordsman Tatiddi. Dez comments, 'How we played is what we won' (30).

The blood and guts aside—literal blood and guts: they eviscerated at least one victim—there was a positive result of the uprising. 'It was only two months after the Mutiny that the World Council enacted the Open Gate Law. We told one another that that was our victory, we had made that happen. None of us believed it.' We should believe: the link between the stories that is the headnote to Dez's 'Autobiographical Sketch' states explicitly that the Mutiny *'directly precipitated the Open Gate Law'* (26). Dez continues, 'We told one another we were free. For the first time in history, any man who wanted to leave his Castle could walk out the gate. We were free!' As in 'A Woman's Liberation' (1995), but with gender variations, a question is, 'What happened to the free man outside the gate?' As Dez discovers when he and ten others walk out the gate, 'Nobody had given it much thought' (31). They are like ghosts returning from the dead—nearly a motif for Le Guin in the 1990s—which is a problem: societies do not make room for ghosts. Men are hounded on the streets; they cannot get jobs, not even an apprenticeship; they cannot even work at the fuckeries, absent a Castle's guarantee of their health and behavior. They are still outside the world of life: 'work, love, childbearing, childrearing, getting and spending, making and shaping, governing and adventuring—the women's world, the bright, full real world.' There was no place for them; all they knew how 'to do was play games and destroy one another' (31-32).

As he explains to his mother, Dez wants, primarily, to get married. She asks if he means marry a man, and he responds that he wants to marry a

---

[686] Contrast the rejection of violence by the Committee of the Student Action Council when in power in 'Unlocking the Air' (coll. *UA*, see esp. 138).

woman: 'a normal, ordinary marriage. I want to have a wife and be a wife' (no 'husbands' in the culture or language, only wives). His mother is shocked, but she tries to deal with the idea. Her son and a woman would 'live together just like any married pair,' establish 'our own daughterhouse' and be faithful. If they have a child, Dez would 'be its lovemother along with her.' And his mother doesn't argue, just notes that she knows no precedents and that he will have to find a way to meet women. She offers the sound motherly advice that he might want to try the fuckery: fucking is, of course, a very logical way for a man to meet women and see if they like each other—and she doesn't see why their motherhouse couldn't guarantee his health and behavior as well as a Castle could (32). For readers from a still largely puritanical culture such as that of the USA, where normative mothers do not tell their sons that fucking for money is a good way to meet nice girls, this is a moment of wry situation comedy as well as vigorous defamiliarization of a mother-son conversation. But Dez refuses this offer, explaining that as a resistance worker he had few experiences at the fuckery and those experiences were not good, 'after the tenderness of my lover-protectors in the Castle' (33).

On the other hand, women attract him 'physically as men never had,' and he is in a painful situation: surrounded by women, with no sex life. Fortunately, they have given him a room of his own, so he has physical room, and a place to masturbate. Much more fortunately, the story moves to a turning point when his sister Pado comes up to his room to tell him of an offworlder come to Rakedr to study the Mutiny. "He wants to talk to the resistance,' she said, 'Men like you. The men who opened the gates. He says they won't come forward, as if they were ashamed of being heroes.'[687] Dez blurts out 'Heroes!' and then glosses the word as a female-gendered term referring to 'the semi-divine, semi-historic protagonists of the Epics'; and Pado says that a hero is what he is: 'You took responsibility in a great act. Maybe you did it wrong,' but heroic error is hardly unprecedented, including in the Epics, and Pado sends him off to see the alien by saying 'You owe us the story' (33), and he does: it is a rule with Seggri that 'The doer of any notable acts was held literally *accountable* for it to the community' (34).

So Dez comes to talk to Mobile Noem, of Terra, and finds him 'easy to talk to.' Dez thinks, Noem 'did not seem at all masculine to me, at first; I kept thinking he was a woman, because he acted like one. He got right to business, with none of the maneuvering to assert his authority or jockeying for position that men of my society felt obligatory in any relationship with another man.... Noem, like a woman, was direct and receptive' (34). Or maybe Noem is just from a fairly egalitarian and direct society on Terra

---

[687] On the gate-opening, cf. and contrast the revolt on Yeowe, where it is the opening of the armory of Nadami Plantation by a slave woman that gives the insurrection impetus, and military weapons (*FWF* 226), and note passim in *FWF* (1995) and *ACH* the imagery of gates, especially gates closed and open in *FWF*, and the presence or absence of walls for there to be gates in, in *ACH*.

and/or was well-trained on Hain; Dez, for good reasons, tends to have a bit of tunnel-vision in terms of gender. (The Gethenians, can be highly indirect and jockey enthusiastically for *shifgrethor*, without concerns of gender [see *LHD* 14; ch. 1].)

Dez learns that his story 'has no beginning, and no story has an end. That the story is all muddle, all middle. That the story is never true, but that the lie is indeed a child of silence.' I'd prefer to put the first couple of statements that, short of the story of the universe from Big Bang to Big Crunch (or Final Whimper of Entropy), all beginnings and endings are more or less arbitrary; and that insofar as all stories are partial—as in only part, plus told from a point of view—they are never completely true. Getting as much of Dez's story for 'the matter of Seggri' as he wants, and perhaps noticing that Dez had come 'to love and trust him,' Noem asks Dez more personal, 'impossible' questions (34). Most especially, Noem asks, 'What would you be if you could be anything?' Dez's unhesitating, passionate answer: 'A wife!' He wants his own family and his own house, where he can be a grownup (not his mother's son). He wants 'A wife, wives—children—to be a mother,' concluding, 'I want life, not games!' Dez cannot bear a child, but he can 'mother one,' and Noem likes the Seggrian usage. Noem presses the point: what are the chances that Dez will find a wife? Noem doesn't think any Seggri woman has yet married a man. 'It will happen, certainly, I think'—a hedged «certainty» Dez likes. But, Noem continues, noting that the first heterosexual marriages will come at high personal costs to the couples. And Dez tries to tell him his feelings 'of having no room in my world, no air to breathe,' and Noem points out the obvious: that there is plenty of room in the galaxy, and he offers a chance for an Ekumenical School on Hain. After Dez gets at least a bit of local education (35).

So Dez goes to college, and he meets an open-minded woman. And they 'managed, tentatively and warily, to fall in love.' Both 'loathed the professionalism of the fuckery' and manage a relationship of 'communication and commonalty' that was mostly other than and far more than just genital. But Dez's story is not another prose-narrative romance. The love-match 'did not work out very well, or last very long, yet it was a great liberation' for both. Dez does *not* marry and give All for Love and the Galaxy Well Lost.[688] That is 'Another Story' (*FIS* 147 f.). His college lover married into a motherhouse and had two children, and Dez does not sacrifice himself romantically for love or altruistically for the principle of heterosexual marriage on Seggri. Instead he finishes college, leaves for Hain for Ekumenical training, and travels to Werel and Yeowe as a member of the staff of the Mobile. The autobiography we read here is submitted as part of his 'application to return to Seggri as a Mobile of the Ekumen. I want very much to live among my people, to learn who they are, now that I know with at least an uncertain certainty who I am' (36). The Gate got

---

[688] John Dryden's updating of Shakespeare's *Antony and Cleopatra* was titled *All for Love; or, The World Well Lost* (1677/78).

opened; Dez left the Castle. In earlier imagery, as at the end of *City of Illusion* (1967), the frame breaks and pattern shatters, and Dez went flying off into the great room of the galaxy. In a somewhat later image, he is one of those who walk away from Omelas. Still, Seggri has possibilities intentionally omitted in the timeless, changeless psychomythic world of 'The Ones Who Walk Away from Omelas' (1973). 'True journey is return,' and the occasion of Dez's autobiographical sketch is his trying to get back. Dez's story, so far, is of a man who affirms marriage, who affirms political action, but who would not sacrifice himself for an idea and who knew when to get out. Now that he knows 'with at least an uncertain certainty' who he is, now that he has experienced other worlds of oppression, and, maybe, now that Seggri has changed, now he can take the risk to return to what might be or become a home.

* * * * * * *

As I indicate above, 'The Matter of Seggri' is a thought-experiment in 'role reversals in the group relations between the sexes,' to use Joanna Russ's formulation (42). But it is a very complex thought-experiment: among other things it offers commentary on 'The Matter of Role-Reversals,' 'The Matter of Romance,' 'The Matter of Sexism,' and maybe even 'The Matter of the Feminist/Separatist Utopia,' or of utopias more generally.

Above I said that 'reversal' was too simple for much of what Le Guin is up to: there is at least a *dual* reversal among the Seggri. It is a reversal of patriarchy by definition, that women are in power and men are not; but the most narrow-minded of patriarchs, Captain Aolao-olao, say, can look at the Seggrian condition and find it comfortably familiar. The male conservatives of the Castles as well as the conservative women of the towns can look around them and see a culture to preserve. The men are solely masculine: the most manly of men doing the most manly of things, short of warfare, i.e., sports, competition, rule, fucking. And the women do women's work: everything else, including love, drudgery, mothering, 'getting and spending,' the life of the mind. Pushing through the reversal, following 'round the heyiya-if, so to speak, one can read the reversal to see the successful men of Seggri imprisoned in their narrowly-defined, golden cage of macho masculinity even as privileged women under patriarchy are imprisoned in a golden cage of a narrowly-defined femininity. A Seggrian pumped up Ken-doll can be seen reflecting a Terran Barbie. Less successful men among the Seggri, like all but the most privileged of Terran women, are pretty well just imprisoned. In a competitive hierarchy, as in the Castles, the great majority necessarily lose.

The basic and inevitable price for the men is that they are cut off from just about everything Le Guin defines as 'the world,' 'life.' They are also cut off from any vivifying life of the mind, but they intellectualize with a vengeance: the intellectual kick of success in sports, climbing in that abstraction, the hierarchy, finding glory among women or power over men.

Even in the best of Castles on Seggri, the men are within the gates, in prison, trapped, cut off from nature, young children, women, any possibility for real community, real work, real thought; cut off from everything except games.

The women of Seggri have a good world: if not The Good Place, at least *a* pretty good place, better than most women get in most readers' times and places. Still, 'The Ones Who Walk Away from Omelas' is a most rigorous proof that Le Guin is not going to let us approve of a Good Place bought at the Faustian price of the suffering of one child, and the good life for the women of Seggri is bought at the price of many sacrificed sons.[689]

Insofar as a Good Place for Seggri women is purchased at the price of brutalized boys, Le Guin suggests, there is a problem. Still, the Castles are *a* truth on Seggri, not the whole truth. As the military is a truth on Urras in *The Dispossessed* (1974); as the rooms of suffering people are not the only truths of Orgoreyn in *Left Hand of Darkness* (1969) or 'The Ones Who Walk Away from Omelas'—and as Lucasville maximum security prison in my own region is not the only truth about Ohio. Readers, and especially male readers, who find the Seggri women paying too much for eutopia—figuratively out of the pockets and hides of their men—should come to ask the price of male-run eutopias. The point here is not that the women should be denied their good place in the world but that the men—carefully—should be allowed to enter. How difficult that will be for the Seggri is a measure of how effective Le Guin's story is as a feminist commentary on macho excess.

'Seggri' and Feminism: The Political Le Guin

Men's Issues

'Since when was altruism an Odonian virtue?' Le Guin's Shevek asks in *The Dispossessed* (214; ch. 8), and the point is that altruism is *not* an Odonian virtue. Nor do altruism and benevolence look very good in Le Guin's *Lathe of Heaven* (1971). With very few exceptions—the most capable and confident of the elite—men on Seggri need not be altruistic nor benevolent to want to change their society; they need only be conscious. Terrans are not Seggri, but if we look at their world 'in the peculiar, devious, and thought-experimental way proper to science fiction' (*LHD* 1976: Introd.)—there are significances for us. Taking to an extreme a sexist logic (*reductio ad finem*), Seggri 'is a terrible place to be a man'; so, for most men, are the patriarchal cultures of Terra: patriarchy is the basis of a system of hierarchy and privilege in which a handful prosper, and most (men) are exploited. Industrialized patriarchal society offered few decent ways for men to live, and postindustrial society may lead to a culture like Seg-

---

[689] There are also lost options for girls with high potential for athletics, and some kinds of dance and theatre (the story dances).

gri: most of the population with no useful work, reduced to game-playing, and prison.

If sexism and patriarchy as such are problems with men that must in part—mostly?—be dealt with by men, then, 'Seggri' very usefully implies the evils of a patriarchal system *for men*.[690] In Le Guin's universe, there is no system of divine justice distributing rewards and punishments, no transcendent Goods to fulfill one's being by serving, so philosophically as well as in terms of very crass practical politics, there must be self-interests served for political action. 'Seggri' can teach that Terran feminism can help men.

Women's Issues

In Alice Echoll's words, 'The issue of lesbianism really exploded' within the Women's Movement 'on May 1, 1970, opening night of the second Congress to Unite Women' (214) and has been out of the closet and significant for the politics of feminism ever since. Into the 1970s and beyond, there was a good deal of anti-lesbian bigotry among liberals and a few radicals in the Women's Movement—and some conscious actions against lesbians in the Movement—and in the early 1970s the animosity was sometimes returned by lesbian-feminists. If one's doctrine is 'feminism is the theory, lesbianism *the* practice' (my emphasis), then one might well agree with Rita Mae Brown's assertion that 'Straight women...betray Lesbians and...their own selves. You can't build a strong movement if your sisters are out there fucking with the oppressor' (Echolls 219, 227, 238, 232; ch. 5).[691] Infighting among people who mostly agree is never a good thing; moving into the 1980s and a full-scale backlash against feminism, radicalism, and then even liberalism and 'secular humanism,' Left-wing animosities against «natural allies» became an unaffordable luxury. Heterosexist biases and actions got recognized and renounced more among heterosexual activists; biases against heterosexual «breeders» generally got dropped. The rising consciousness on gay and lesbian issues among heterosexual authors and their readers is important background for Le Guin's recent writing.

As Le Guin has gone 'forward with feminism without looking backward to fathers' (Barr 115)—no fathers in either 'Solitude' nor 'Seggri'—and 'wrestled with the angels of the feminist consciousness' (*ER* 11), she has also dealt more positively with homosexuality. In 'Seggri,' voluntary, compassionate male homosexuality comes through well, and it is clear that the lesbianism-based motherhouses we learn about, and the marriage triad we see with Azak, Zedr, and Chochi, work quite well. Further, there in-

---

[690] The oppression of women, as such, is a problem for women to be dealt with primarily by women: "To liberate' is a reflexive verb.'
[691] Echolls notes Ti-Grace-Atkinson's movement from 'feminism is theory, lesbianism is a practice' to 'feminism is the theory, lesbianism the practice' (238). I have heard the second form used as a feminist slogan.

deed *is* 'an enviable simplicity to many acts in a society which has, in all its daily life, only one gender' (7); and there is an admirable elegance and stability when that one gender is female and women can get all their needs met within that society, plus occasional professional servicing by males. But Le Guin is a critical feminist, I think, even as she is a Critical Romantic. Lesbian relations as 'the central sexual element of *society*' among the Seggri do not preclude capitalism or sexism, nor do they preclude exploitation, segregation, and—when a few men enter active society—discrimination (31-32). The Seggri are a *mono*culture, which is stable and enviably simple, but as Susan Rose warns Ike in 'Newton's Sleep,' one might well fear 'oversimplifying' (*FIS* 28). One should also fear simplifying in ways that go against 'the body's obscure,' but apparently quite real and 'inalterable dream of mutuality' (29), including the simplifying of men into mere bodies.[692]

In 'The Matter of Seggri,' Le Guin has given us feminist SF not looking backward to fathers but perhaps forward to a world in which women and men would want and find real work *and* 'A wife, wives—children—to be a mother' and to 'mother' a child (35), 'to have a wife and be a wife' (32), a challenging and radical feminist idea and ideal. In the sexual and gender politics area of one *Kulturkampf*, Le Guin will value solitude and separation, but only so long as there is the possibility of eventual social integration and on-going mutuality.

---

[692] Note that Merriment is soon 'glad to get away from the rah-rah and the swooning and the posters of fellows with swelling muscles and huge penises and bedroom eyes' (8). The jock/cheerleader aspect of Seggri culture is a satiric joke that should be taken seriously. If a women's culture segregates men and uses men for entertainment, at least part of that culture could move toward a kind of fan culture. See Moffatt for the 'recurrent motifs' in Rutgers U. dorm room decoration of 'good-looking, minimally-clad young adults of the opposite sex, which were about as common and about as near-nude in women's rooms as in men's, and favorite stars of music, television, and the movies' (80; ch. 3).

XIV.

DANCING OVER THE ABYSS WITH SHIVA AND KALI

Wild Angels **(1975),** *Hard Words and Other Poems* **(1981),**
Wild Oats and Fire Weed **(1988),**
Going Out with Peacocks and Other Poems **(1994)**

> I talk about the gods, I am an atheist.[693] But I am an artist too, and therefore a liar. Distrust everything I say. I am telling the truth. —Ursula K. Le Guin, Introd. to 1976 reissue of *The Left Hand of Darkness* (n.p.)

Poems can and regularly do tell stories,—if usually short ones, nowadays—and those stories often teach lessons. Homer wrote in verse, and he told stories so pedagogically influential that Plato would call him 'the schoolmaster of the Greeks' (Swain I.277).[694] I will handle some of Ursula K. Le Guin's poems from her four collections (as of early 1997) before moving on to *King Dog*, which started as a long narrative poem and ended up 'A Movie for the Mind's Eye' (7). Dealing with the poetry is important. As Patrick D. Murphy suggests, Le Guin may see 'her audience for poetry...composed of a much large percentage of women and gender-sensitive men' than her prose. Murphy stresses that in much of Le Guin's poetry there is 'a strong feminist perspective,' and one 'usually more explicit' than in her fiction, at least in her fiction to the time Murphy wrote, not long after 1985 (127, 129).[695] Also more explicit are anger, a sexual theme or two and, related to that, Le Guin's interest in Shiva, Shakti, and Kali in the Hindu pantheon. Le Guin talks of how, in trying to (re)make her world, she 'learned, like most of us, to use whatever I could, to filch an idea from China and steal a god from India, and so patch together a world....' ('World-Making,' *DEW* 48). To oversimplify, the idea from

---

[693] Le Guin notes the 'am' was inserted by a copy editor, changing the sentence rhythm (and making the punctuation questionable)—personal communication.
[694] Or *they* wrote stories, if you prefer 'Homer' as a group of poets.
[695] Including in that 'feminist perspective' philosophical and academic feminism: see 'For Helene Cixous' in *Wild Oats* (1988): 60.

China is the Dao, Daoism; to oversimplify greatly, the god from India is Shiva: Shiva-Linga with Parvati-Yoni, phallic god with vulva/mountain goddess; Shiva with Shakti as (male) quiescence and (female) creative energy; Shiva with Shakti, or Kali, the terrible, the destroyer; and, preeminently, Shiva as Nataraja, the Cosmic Dancer, dancing into existence the worlds (see front and back covers of *Hard Words*).[696] I wish to deal with the poems on anger, the Dao, dancing, and the gods.

Anger

As Le Guin says about Le Guin, 'I am an aging, angry woman laying mightily about me with my handbag, fighting hoodlums off,' a project she continues in some of her poems, ranging from anger over women having to travel alone with the kids to US war crimes against the plains Indians.[697]

In 'Amtrak Portland to Seattle' (1988), the Speaker would like to cry and sees 'the woman across the aisle / is crying / in silence.' The Speaker then goes on to see other women, other children, 'and no man' traveling 'with a couple of children' on the train (*Wild Oats* 41).[698] In 'The Anger' (1975), we have an ungendered Speaker demanding entrance: threatening, shouting; if not shouting herself, calling for the smashing of door latches, seeing herself as 'the exile,' standing with empty hands 'waiting in long anger / outside my home' (*Wild Angels* 28). In 'His Daughter' (1986), we hear of the death in childhood of the daughter of Crazy Horse, 'the true fragile hero / who lost what he won as he won it'; we learn that her name was 'They Will Fear Her' (*Wild Oats* 48), as Ogion says of Therru/Tehanu in *Tehanu*.

'Apples' (1986) is still angry, but much less somber. In this poem, we are told, in Coyote's vein, that 'Judeochristian men should / not be allowed / to eat apples,' since these men have been 'bellyaching / for millennia' that the Speaker's mother 'made / them eat an apple / that gave them a bellyache.'[699] Henceforth, the Speaker decrees, apple-eating will be limited to

---

[696] In more Western philosophical terms, cf. the description of 'Becoming' by Satosi Watanabe in 'Time and the Probabilistic View of the World' in *Voices of Time* (1966): 'Becoming is making of the yet-unmade. Becoming is constant death and constant rebirth. It is a simultaneous destruction and creation' (560).

[697] The quotation is from Le Guin's 'Carrier Bag Theory of Fiction' (*DEW* 168). See below for Crazy Horse: a Sioux Indian chief of the Oglala Tribe; the accusation of US war crimes comes from the US Army full colonel (Professor of Military Science and Tactics) who taught my Military Science 101 class at the U of Illinois in spring of 1961; he was expanding only slightly on the judgment of the official (if abridged) US Army history of the US Army that was our textbook.

[698] See also, 'At the Party' (*Wild Oats* 45).

[699] In the Eden myth, Adam and Eve are under one prohibition: '...of the tree of knowledge of good and evil you shall not eat, for in the day that you eat of it you shall die' (Genesis 2.17), plus additional penalties—when God finally judges— for women, men, and serpents, including patriarchy (Genesis 3.11-24). In the folklore I know, the Forbidden Fruit has been identified with the pomegranate (a

women, and 'nonjudeochristian men' who will eat apples 'without whining'—plus children if their mother says it is all right to do so, or if they can 'steal them and / get away with it.' Also, women and snakes are to renew their old, strong relationship, with women wearing snakes 'for bracelets / and her hair,' Medusa style, if they wish.[700] And women's snake-hair 'is to hiss at any man / who cannot resist her' and strike him into a Sleeping Beauty state, in which he is to be put into 'a glass coffin / like a bank'—a child's penny bank?—and stay there because 'nobody will come to kiss him' (*Wild Oats* 34-35).

Unless they are pushing a political agenda that really demands the category, few men define themselves in terms of «Judeo-Christianity», and a fair number of women and children think of themselves as Christians or Jews. 'Apples,' then helps show that such categories are more or less arbitrary and externally imposed *and* shows that such categories may be useful. Serenity, the Narrator in the short story, 'Solitude' thinks 'a life or a time looks simple when you leave out the details, the way a planet looks smooth, from orbit' (134), and she means, correctly, that such a distant view—the ground work for a *non*immanent critique—oversimplifies and thereby falsifies. Indeed, but a view from outside, and from a distance, can provide insight into similarities, including similarities missed by those embedded in the context. It is odd to lump together as 'judeochristian men' a sixth-century BCE shepherd, a first-century CE centurion, a third-century mystic, a fourth-century emperor, a fifth-century saint, a tenth-century farmer, a twelfth-century philosopher-physician, a thirteenth-century beggar, a fifteenth-century Inquisitor, a sixteenth-century dramatist, a seventeenth-century revolutionary, a nineteenth-century slave or slave-owner (or Hassid or secular Jewish socialist or Methodist capitalist), a twentieth-century Chinese engineer, African bishop or American skinhead—but it can be instructive to do so. As 'Apples' suggests, all these men may share a millennia-long belly-ache from accepting the ideology of the Fall and of patriarchy. As a political matter, 'Apples' also suggests, it might be well for women, children, and (nonwhining) nonJudeo-Christian men to define

---

popular fruit of the Eden area), the pear (from its shape [female body; male genitalia]), and the apple.

[700] In the Greek tradition, there is not only Medusa and her two sisters (the Gorgones) with snake hair but also an association with a snake for the priestess of Apollo at Delphi, called the Pythia, after Pythian Apollo, from Apollo's slaying the great serpent Python—or as a rationalization under the Olympians of an older tradition of wise snakes and wise women. In the Judeo-Christian tradition, the most famous encounter of a woman and snake is the usual picture of Genesis 3.1-6: the temptation of Eve and the Fall, with Eve tempted by a snake = the serpent, 'the shrewdest of all the wild beasts that the LORD God had made' (*Tanakh*). Note also the healing snake: on the staff of Asklepios, god of healing, and as a bronze serpent on a pole in Numbers 21.8-9. See below, 'My Hero.'

themselves in those terms and against Judeo-Christian men—who often enough lump *them* together and define them as Other.[701]

In 'My Hero' ([1994] *Peacocks* 58), the Hero of the poem might give up or turn her anger inward and become self-destructive—'drop the sword' or 'behead herself'—but probably will not: 'There are better things to do / with anger' and 'with beauty' and also with 'a headful of serpents / who can hiss wisdom.' The hero here is imaged not as Zeus and Danaë's son, Medusa-slaying Perseus but Medusa herself, a young Medusa, as a 'dear young hero' who will find a story. All we know of this future story is 'It will not be the old story.' The young Hero as woman does not have a set role to fall into but will have to tell her own, original story.[702]

A less optimistic but similar redirecting of myth appears in 'Her Silent Daughter' (1994). In this poem, Le Guin combines a current event that has angered her with the old legend of Demeter and Persephone, plus the (masculinist) image of Justice. The poem is '*For Tawana Brawley*,' and Le Guin's Speaker quite exactly states Tawana Brawley's story—the public story, the news story—as well as anyone not Tawana Brawley can know it with confidence (a grand jury rejected her story):

> She is fifteen and she is written
> foul names on and cut and rubbed
> with dog shit and stuffed
> into a plastic garbage bag.

Preceding this description, we are told that 'They'—men—'have this statue: Justice,' who is described in terms of the traditional image (as imaged by males). But 'she's not Justice. Justice / is a man,' a man who might listen to some men but who 'has never heard / one woman say one word.'[703] He also, more generally, just is not fair, just *ratio*nal in a Utilitarian fashion, measuring (*ratio*) desire and income: 'He weighs what he wants with what he gets / in these scales he made.' Following this description, we have an instance of justice, for Tawana Brawley: four statement/questions from 'the man' asking/telling Brawley 'Why did you do this / to yourself?' and demanding an explanation, ending with, 'What have you got to fear?' The final stanza has the Speaker presenting her own idea for a statue: Demeter, 'blind with tears,' looking the world over,

---

[701] If Theodor Adorno is right in arguing that all 'critique' is immanent ('Knowledge' 260), then an external view that could set up a category like 'judeochristian men'—or EuroAmericans, or European culture—is problematic. If the more radically nominalist elements in poststructuralism have got us beyond abstract categories and Structuralist dualism, then setting up 'judeochristian men' and a negation of them is wrongheaded. Insofar as I suggest that the category may be useful, I'm trying to problematicize totally immanent critique and privileging some structuralist moves in feminism. (Or, in an image I prefer, I'm sending Coyote in to nip at some ankles in a very minor skirmish on the left flank of a *Kulturkampf*.)
[702] See *ER* 12 and my discussion of the Rer story 'Coming of Age in Karhide.'
[703] Cf. the Master Windkey's not listening to Tenar in *Tehanu* (143-45; ch. 10).

> for her daughter that was taken from her,
> her silent daughter
> that the king of shit and money
> took to the garbage kingdom
> for his use forever.

The daughter taken is Persephone, the *Kore*, the Maiden abducted by Hades, brother of Zeus and king of the underworld—as Pluto, the god of wealth. The Speaker reminds us of the rest of the old story: Until Demeter finds her daughter, 'it will be winter' (*Peacocks* 30-31).

In 'The Menstrual Lodge' (1986), the Speaker, the 'I,' is a traditional woman in a traditional society, who goes to the menstrual lodge while menstruating and avoids meat and eye contact and touching herself.

> It was no use. Nothing,
> no ritual or servitude or shame,
> unmade my power, or your fear.

The 'you' are the men of her village and men generally, including the plural 'you' who beat her and raped her 'and went to boast.' The 'I' has her child at Bear Creek and 'in Bear Creek / I drowned it.' 'Menstrual Lodge' ends with both anger and the conditions for reconciliation. The woman says, 'I am the dirt beneath your feet'—which may sound degrading but is not—and asks the men, 'What are you frightened of?' She tells them to go off and engage in what I'll call transcendent projects; far more concretely and poetically, the woman tells the men to go fight wars, 'be great in club and lodge and politics'—and come back when they find out 'what power is,' what power really is. The woman knows: her blood is power; she is power.

> I am the dirt, and the raincloud, and the rain.
> The walls of my house are the steps I walk
> * * *
> The roof of my house is thunder,
> the doorway is the wind.
> I keep this house, this great house.
>
> When will you come in? (*Wild Oats* 49-50)

The menstrual-lodge woman identifies herself here with the earth and the Earth, and in that identification she is both ego-denying and very powerful. She can do without walls and roofs because she is emphatically *in* the world and hence is the world or, at least, the world's housekeeper. This is a Daoist view (see *Chuang-Tzu* ch. 6, in Giles pp. 79-80), and more generally a view of 'The Perennial Philosophy' (Huxley chs. 1 & 2, 76-78 in ch. 4). This idea is very important for Le Guin's opinion of the world—

and life in the world without walls—and for her ideas for the possibility of reconciliation between women and men, more generally reconciliation among peoples with two very different ideas of power, people who speak two, at least, very different languages.

Dao, Dancing, and the Gods

Pride of place—the last word—in Le Guin's first collection of poems goes to 'Tao Song' (1974), the last piece in *Wild Angels* (1975). This poem is four stanzas and a brief conclusion—all giving an elegant lesson in Daoism. The first and third stanza call upon a 'slow fish,' a 'green weed' and the 'bright sun' to show, grow, light the Singer the way. The second stanza makes explicit that

> The way you go
> the way you grow
> is the way
> indeed.

Nature's way—synecdochized in fish, weed, and sun—is the way that cannot be gone: 'If one can choose it / it is wrong' (stanza 4), but a song can remind one that '*No one can lose it*'—the Way—'*for long*' (last lines). I.e., as Lao Tzu taught: one cannot name and consciously choose the Dao (Wilhelm 27; I.1); but if 'Man conforms to Earth,' he—we—can be in a series in which Earth conforms to Heaven and Heaven conforms to Dao (Wilhelm 37-38; I.25).[704]

In Le Guin's latest collection (as of my writing), *Going Out with Peacocks* (1994), the last poem is also Daoist, but more subtly, and with reversals: 'The Hard Dancing' (1994).[705] In the first sentence of 'Hard Dancing's' two sentences, we learn that it is difficult, 'hard,' to dance on the sun; you burn your feet, of course, and 'have to leap / higher and higher into the dark,' finally somersaulting 'to sleep.' In the second sentence, we learn that there are steep mountains on the sun, 'rising to shadow at the

---

[704] In other chapters, dealing with only one two or a few of Le Guin's texts, I've used different translations of the *Tao te Ching* (or *Dao de Jing*), using Le Guin's eclecticism with translations to justify my own search for the most convenient rendition. I deal with too many of Le Guin's texts here for that to be courteous, so I will limit myself to 'The Richard Wilhelm Edition': i.e., the 1910 translation into German, re-issued in 1978 and translated into English by H. T. Ostwald for Routledge and Kegan Paul in 1985. 'Wilhelm' followed by a page number refers to a page in Routledge edn.; that is followed by a I or a II for Wilhelm's division of *Tao te Ching* into Part I: DAO and Part II: DE or LIFE, with the number after the period referring to the standard *through-numbering* of chapters. So Wilhelm 27; I.1: is the first chapter of the *Tao te Ching*, found on p. 27 of the Wilhelm edn.; Wilhelm 57; II.66 refers to ch. 66, found on p. 57 in Wilhelm—etc.

[705] Reminder: In my usage, 'subtle' is not superior to 'simple'; 'later' does not imply better than 'earlier.'

crown,' and valleys, even as on Earth, but very deep ones, 'and ever brighter deeper down' (*Peacocks* 82). On the sun, you must leap up to the darkness and go down into the light, keeping the traditional images, but reversing Up and Down. A transcending leap upward is necessary to reach the immanent darkness; the burrowing that on Earth takes one into the cool dark, on the sun takes one into more heat, more light. The sun is (obviously) an interesting place to visit, but an impossible place to live.[706] *Hard Words* (1981) ends with a poem called 'Uma,' about 'Beginning's daughter,' who 'sings to stone.' Like Tehanu and Crazy Horse's daughter, 'You do well to fear' Uma, although her singing is very sweet (79). Uma is the Hindu goddess Parvati, Daughter of the Mountain, and 'Beginning's daughter' if we see the mountain in the east, making Parvati child of the dawn. Or if we see Parvati as a personification of *the* Goddess, she is 'Beginning's daughter' as first child of the Mother (and the Mother herself), one mythological beginning of all—unnamable Dao and Pandora All-Giver, to conflate traditions (see Wilhelm 37; I.24). And I think Le Guin does conflate traditions in 'Uma': she describes the goddess as 'Clear water running / in a handhollow,' which is an image of Dao (or close to Dao)—and then adds the line, 'You do well to fear her' (see Wilhelm 29, 31; I.8, I.11) Dao is, and it inspires fear only for those who find themselves lost in it with insufficient practice in nullifying the ego. What scares most of us, or at least most men, is Uma as Kali. The last word in *Hard Words*, then, is about a Hindu goddess associated with Shiva. 'You can't tell a book by its cover,' usually, but the cover of *Hard Words*, with its dancing Shiva, is quite indicative.

I think Patrick D. Murphy and his source, Craig and Diana Barrow, are correct in seeing Le Guin willing to go farther in her poetry than in her early prose with ideas threatening to 'typically biased heterosexual males' (Murphy 129). In any event, Daoism is clear in most of Le Guin's prose, the 'god from India' not clear until we look at the poetry, and then *King Dog*—and then return to and reread the earlier fiction. And in Le Guin's poetry, in a gyring, reversing, widdershins sort of way, I think she moves from Daoism toward a bit more of the Dance of Shiva. Always, though—with the possible exception of the poem, 'Some of the Philosophers'—there is a return to the concrete, the untranscendent, unChristian, the natural, the world, the Self, the 'Perennial Philosophy,' the Way.[707] In 'Ars Lunga' in *Wild Angels*, there is the assertion that the Speaker does not desire the 'new heaven and new earth' promised to the saved in the Revelation to John (21.1), but 'the old ones': the old heaven and earth of 'Old sky, old dirt,' some Walt Whitmanesque 'new grass.' And she wants not 'life beyond the grave' but death and the threat of death, living

---

[706] See references to Apollo, 'god of light,' in the Introd. to 1976 reissue of *LHD*, and light imagery associated with Meshe (*LHD* ch. 12, esp. 164).

[707] 'Some of the Philosophers' denies Utilitarianism and Positivism (chiding philosophers who must 'use it' or 'count it') but allows the creative 'word' (*Wild Angels* 39).

> so that death finds me at all times
> and on all sides, exposed,
> unfortressed, undefended,
> inviolable, vulnerable, alive. (29)[708]

In 'A Lament for Rheged,' a 'bondsman / bound to the land' is chosen to return 'in the bitter weather / to the place of birth.' And he has chosen to return, 'having chosen / the heavy art': to remember and to praise everyday things—marriage, work, kindness, hearth—and to be true to 'the bond of thing, / of stone, of earth' (*Wild Angels* 35-37). In 'The Withinner,' a man named Laurus picks up supplies from a coastal trade ship and then hurries back to his canoe, and 'vanishes upstream' into the heart of a well-tree'd continent (*Wild Angels* 31), a standard image in Le Guin for moving within—'The *Within*ner'—into the subconscious, the Self, 'the vast interior spaces' (e.g., 'A Trip to the Head' [*WTQ*]).

The spirituality of 'Rheged' and 'Withinner' in *Wild Angels* (1975) is familiar in Le Guin's prose work, and such ideas can be found also in *Hard Words* (1981), in 'The Man Who Shored Up Winchester Cathedral,' in 'Invocation,' and in 'Smith Creek.' 'Invocation' invokes 'Mother,' who will not be otherwise named, and promises to honor her, praise her, with 'the great lies.' The poem speaks of yin things, traditional female things: darkness, emptiness, and of the 'silence of the valleys' and the 'north side of rivers.'[709] It ends with a plea to let the Speaker speak 'the mother tongue' and sing in it. And then moves to a vision of the Speaker becoming a Singer, of loud songs to which newlyweds and old women dance,

> and sheep will cease from cropping and machines
> will gather round to listen
> in cities fallen silent
> as a ring of standing stones...
> as the Singer sings down the walls (*Hard Words* 7).

In 'The Man Who Shored Up...,' we have the Daoist suggestions of working 'by touch' and touching 'the foundations / in the old darkness of waters / under the earth.'[710] Under mind'—the man working 'alone' shoring up rotten foundations: 'When you come up to daylight / the cathedral stands' (*Hard Words* 6). Sort of a George Orr in a hard-hat, the mole in

---

[708] See *Chuang Tzu* ch. 6, p. 79 in the Giles trans.
[709] *Yin* of the Yin-Yang of Daoist philosophy and Chinese thought generally 'is conceived of as Earth, female, dark, passive, and absorbing; it is present in even numbers, in valleys and streams' ('yin-yang,' *Encyclopaedia Britannica: Micropaedia*). One theory is that yin was originally the shaded valley, so the '*north side of rivers*' might be decorous here as the shady side.
[710] See Wilhelm 28-29; I.4, I.8.

'Totem' (*BG* 134), aiding Christians—or a fine, old building—in a very elegant brief poetic narrative.

And in 'Smith Creek' a creek flows to the sea, figuratively 'counting aloud the ten thousand things' of the everyday world, 'carrying heaven downward' (*Hard Words* 35). I'll take a stab at the meaning here, applying Lao Tzu (Wilhelm 37; I. 25) and James W. Bittner's discussion 'the Neo-Confucian *T'ai chi 't'u*,' a diagram relating the Supreme Ultimate (T'ai Chi) to everything else ('Approaches' 375-78).[711] The creek, like Dao, both is and stems from the Supreme Ultimate ('heaven') and both goes 'forward to' the sea and returns to the sea, in the process creating the multiple and mutable world by 'counting aloud'—numbering here, not naming—'the ten thousand things.'[712] And the creek remains a literal creek going to the sea, the mica in its mud reflecting the sun, and the creek providing a proper home for minnows.

In addition to Daoism, though, *Hard Words*, offers that god from India, useful in balancing philosophical Daoism, which, for all its valuing of water, is somewhat dry for a religion. Le Guin describes her 'Epiphany':

> Did you hear?
>
> Mrs. Le Guin has found God.
>
> Yes, but she found the wrong one.
> Absolutely typical.
>
> Look, there they go together.
> Mercy! It's a colored woman!
>
> Yes, it's one of those relationships.
> They call her Mama Linga. (*Hard Words* 19)

To my ear, 'Mama Linga' sounds like one of the *Loa* of Vodoun (voodoo), like Papa Legba. If so, however, she is still unlisted on the World Wide Web or made the List-of-Loa site. Until corrected, I shall read 'Mama Linga' as the incarnation of the Goddess as 'phallic' mother: Ky-

---

[711] Bittner's *Approaches*, published by UMI, prints the first four chapters of the five in 'Approaches,' Bittner's diss. I use here 'Approaches,' ch. 5: 'Le Guin's Taoism, the Romance, and Utopia.' The diss. proper concludes with an appendix, 'A Bibliographical Orientation to Taoism.' Students of Le Guin wishing to look deeper into Daoism in her works, should study her translation of the *Tao te Ching* (when it is available) and consult Bittner's 1979 diss.: University Microfilms 79-22108,

[712] Cf. the origin myth sardonically told by Atro, an old conservative Ioti aristocrat: 'The religion of my fathers informs me with equal authority [to the tales of the Hainish Expansion], that I'm a descendent of Pinra Od, whom God exiled from the Garden because he had the audacity to count his fingers and toes, add them up to twenty, and thus let Time loose upon the universe' (*TD* 115; ch. 5).

bele or Kali—in *Hard Words*, it would be Kali.[713] Or Kali/Shiva: an androgynous dancing god (see *King Dog*).

There is a lot of dancing in *Hard Words*, and a lot about God and the god/dess. The woman in 'Carmagnole of the Thirtieth of June'—i.e., a song and street dance from the French Revolution—is 'feeling mean' and dancing on the stomach of God, and on God's chest and guts and cock and eyes. This is Revolutionary Woman, going against the clergy of the old regime and all their works, including God, but rather more hopefully portrayed than the Revolution-as-Woman of French Revolutionary art; instead of leading the armed charge toward the Bastille and Liberty (and the Terror and betrayal), this woman calls upon all creation to 'Get up and dance...!' (*Hard Words* 20-21). If *this* Revolutionary Woman is not allowed to dance, she will have nothing to do with the revolution. In 'The Night,' Kali herself appears. Children fear her—with good reason; Kali is destructive—until 'Mother takes the fear away' and we have Kali as night: 'the god appears between her thighs / stands in beauty, dances, dies,' and the Speaker calls in the final line, 'O Mother, comfort me' (*Hard Words* 17). We can identify Kali and the Mother here: Parvati, Shiva's consort, is both Kali and Amba ('Mother'); except here Kali is *the* Goddess, the Lady in the Hindu pantheon, Devi; and Shiva is consort to her, and, like Western consorts of 'the Lady,' dies.[714] However we interpret Kali/Amba, it is clear that 'The Night' introduces into *Hard Words* sex, the god, and the dance, and a series of poems on Kali and Shiva together (part II. The Dancing at Tillai).

In 'Shiva and Kama,' we have a brief retelling of how Desire (Kama) came to Shiva, when Shiva was in an ascetic mood on a remote plateau in the Himalayas (*Hard Words* 18). In the legend, Shiva burns Kama to ashes with a glance of Shiva's third eye, 'the eye of insight beyond duality'—as an austere ascetic should (Buitenen 8.931). In Le Guin's version, the Speaker tells Shiva to burn Kama so 'that he may cast no shadow / being with you and before you' forever. Key roles of Shiva in Hindu myth demand renunciation of asceticism, and Le Guin, I think, has Shiva incorporate Kama—Desire—into his permanent entourage, if not his being. The highly unascetic Shiva appears in a very down-to-Earth avatar in 'School' (*Hard Words* 22), where the ever-so-elegant Dancing Master can't keep his fly shut: 'Black tie and gaping pants, / the Dancing Master laughs.' And impresses at least one of his audience ('What is that thing? A cobra?') who passes on the gossip that 'They say he uses cannabis.' She—I assume a woman Speaker—will not trust her daughter at the school of the Dancing Master, but even this apparently conventional and cautious woman thinks, 'O but how sweetly, / sweetly he can dance!'

---

[713] *Linga* (also 'lingam'): phallus symbol, for Shiva. Note also: 'ling*o*': for specialized language, with 'ling*a*' available as a feminine form; and *lingua*: tongue (esp. if we read, 'Yes, it's one of *those* relationships').

[714] Cf. Osiris, Tammuz, Adonis, Attis (Frazer 376 f.; chs. 29-43, esp. 378-80).

The call to join the earth(l)y dance is repeated in the next poem, 'Middle' (*Hard Words* 23). The title, I think, alludes to the idea expressed in 'An Orgota Creation Myth' that all who are 'born in the house of flesh' and have death following at our heels, 'are in the middle of time' and will remain so until the end of time (*LHD* 239; ch. 17). The question is what we will do with our time of mortality. One possibility is the Modernist image that begins 'Middle.' 'When the pure act turns to drygoods / and the endless yearning to an earned sum,' then the time is long past for 'the silly sniveling soul' to get itself post haste out of a Modernist wasteland and run 'stark naked to the woods / and dance to the beating drums,' a great turning dance. The dance is to be called, square-dance fashion, by the 'master,' and its effect will be to 'dance the Great Year whole.' Astronomically that would be to dance complete one cycle of the precession of the equinoxes (25,800 years). Mythically, we could follow Plato and an ancient tradition and have the Great Year, one cycle of the universe, after which, everything (possibly) recycles.[715] Alternatively—using Earthier myths Le Guin prefers—we have an annual world-renewal dance, as done in fairly recent times by the Indians of northern California (Le Guin, personal communication), which may have been done in the ancient Fertile Crescent (*High Holiday Prayer Book* 409 n.), and which may be the source of the Long Dance on midsummer eve in Earthsea: 'You stamp the earth down and make it safe' Arren is told by the chief of the Children of the Open Sea—though the sea people dance over the abyss and have no safety (*FS* 117; ch. 8). Le Guin's 'Middle' ends,

> The only act that is its end
> is the stars' burning.
> Swing your partner round and round,
> turning, turning. (*Hard Words* 23)

The 'its' in the phrase 'its end' may refer to the Great Year, or it may be the cosmic/human dance. Probably it is the dance and its sole conclusion the final combustion of the stars, and its *telos* (goal and purpose) is renewing the stars. In a world of 'turning, turning,' we should locate a partner, join the dance, and turn with it. In an Existentialist, Absurdist mood, one might join enthusiastically the dance at the end of the universe. Taking a more optimistic view, we should 'dance the Great Year whole' in the sense of healing it, renewing it, renewing the world and with it ourselves.

'A Semi-Centenary Celebration' (*Hard Words* 25-26) refers to a turning in a woman turning fifty. Addressing her 'terrible darling,' she explains at first that she is 'afraid of tigers / and in love with god,' and it is time to change that. She is angry and wants a lover, 'so little Joanie Yoni / found lovely Louie Linga': i.e., a contemporary, low-key avatar of Parvati,

---

[715] See Lasky 199; 2.4.5 and Frazer, *Voices of Time* 67-68; Eliade, *The Myth of the Eternal Return*....

seen as the personified vulva (and the rest of the human female genitalia ['Yoni']), found Shiva, concretized as the phallus (Linga). We are reassured, though, that the sexual action is 'all esoteric / and strictly in the head'—with a Chorus coming in and repeating 'Strictly in the head,' for either emphasis through repetition or undermining by protesting a bit too much (methinks) and once too often. Now, the Speaker can tango and waltz and play a sitar and is 'in love with tigers / and afraid of god.' But not very afraid. She can joke about 33,000 choices for a 'personalised brahman'; and the Speaker can image herself as Kali tiptoeing 'through the tango,' even if her 'necklace-skulls' get alliteratively 'tangled' and she scares people.[716] Ending the poem, she has a question for her 'terrible dancing partner,' her 'dear dirty Louie'—with an allusion to the early 1960s hit, 'Louie, Louie' and the phrase 'dirty dancing'? She wants to know if he knows who she really is. The answer is that she is more than Kali, although Kali is still there and a major thing to be. More exactly, though, if figuratively, mythically, mystically, she says,

> I am the dance you're dancing
> I am the loving tiger
> I am the hungry god

—and he is the drummer and the drum, but she is 'the sound of drumming.' The Speaker has lost herself in the dance so thoroughly as to become it—all: the dance, the tiger, the god at hand, and underlying all the drumming as the music, which is Brahman, which is the Dao.[717]

'Pasupati' is a love song, from Parvati, consort of Shiva, about Shiva as Pasupati, Lord of Cattle, Lord of Beasts. He is not a respectable lover. He never combs his hair, which is 'grey with ashes' (in the manner of the Pasupatas, worshippers of Shiva who smear their bodies with ashes); and he dances naked.

> He dances at the crossing
> of three rivers
> the Ganges and the one beneath the Ganges and the one
> that falls out of the stars.[718]

---

[716] Part of the joke is that 'Brahma' is the masculine form and refers to the personalized god; 'brahma*n*' is the neuter form and refers to the 'eternal, conscious, irreducible, infinite, omnipresent, the spiritual source of the universe of finiteness and change' (*Encyclopædia Britannica* Micropædia)—good luck trying to personalize *That*. A necklace of skulls is part of her iconography for Kali.
[717] See 'Dancing to Ganam,' esp. *FIS* 117.
[718] Note epigraph to *BP*: '*Qué río ésta por el cual corre el Ganges*?'—J. L. Borges: *Heráclito*, trans. Spivack (118), 'Which river is it through which the Ganges flows?'

That is, he dances where the physical Ganges intersects the River of Time and Reality immanent under all that is, which in turn meets the transcendent, heavenly Ganges of myth. For those of us who didn't know about the heavenly Ganges: The Ganges, 'personified as a goddess, originally flowed only in heaven until she was brought down by the king, Bhagiratha, in order to purify the ashes of his ancestors. She came down reluctantly, cascading first on the head of Siva, in order to break her fall, which would have shattered the earth' (Buitenen 8.932). Le Guin's Parvati praises Shiva as lord of 'all waters * * * the silences the depths,' but her last lines state her heavy-hearted tenderness for the more mundane male: 'thinking of my husband the herdsman / who never combs his hair' (*Hard Words* 27).

The last poem in the section is 'The Dancing at Tillai' (*Hard Words* 29-30), and it demands the most difficult faith or confidence—or mortification. It begins with an 'I' saying she had 'said the center / was a ring of stones' that made 'a hearthplace'; she corrects herself: 'I meant a place for bones and ashes.' The next sentence identifies the center more specifically as 'the burning ground,' the place of death. The following stanza has young Percy Bysshe Shelley 'burned by the sea,' which 'pleased Kali'—itself followed by a much large burning: Hiroshima, which also 'pleased Kali.'[719] The Speaker calls upon 'mother' for comfort—and is told to 'Find it in the ashes' and 'in the bones.' The mother (Devi, the Goddess in her more benevolent form?) tells her child, the Speaker to 'Come to the drumming at Chidambaram,' the place of the great temple of Shiva Nataraja: Shiva as the Cosmic Dancer. There, amidst the drumming and the fires, the mother explicates the text of the god, explaining the iconography of his statue.[720]

> See where my lord bears drum and flame
> his right hand says Be not afraid
> his left hand points to the dancing foot
> he dances in the heart laid waste
> the burning place
> * * *
> his lifted foot is grace
> his lowered foot is sleep
> he dances in the center
> there, and there, and there....

Shiva also has a look on his face of utter serenity, utter detachment. For those familiar with Western art—the effect is similar to the look on the

---

[719] On the orders of Pres. Harry S. Truman, the US bomber command dropped an atomic bomb on Hiroshima on 6 Aug. 1945, inflicting some 130,000 casualties (casualty count from 'Hiroshima').
[720] Again, see the cover of *Hard Words* or any correct reproduction of the Shiva Nataraja statue.

face of God in the whirlwind in the theophany in William Blake's series of watercolors (1818-21), and later plates (for graphic reproduction), for the Book of Job (1823-25). In Blake's vision of the theophany, Job sees God in the whirlwind; the sour, conventionally pious Comforters, see nothing and hear (I think) only the wind. Whatever 'true religion' may be (see *King Dog* below), it will not include easy acceptance of poets dying at thirty or infants dying at all in bombed-out cities.

'The Dancing at Tillai' ends with a three-line stanza of the mother's direct address to the thrice-invoked child, inviting her to the drumming at Chidambaram, the dancing at Tillai. The lesson seems to be the traditional one of Hinduism, Buddhism, Daoism—the mystic tradition generally: If the child will let go of her ego and get in rhythm with the drum, if she will fully join in the dance and become the dance, then she will not necessarily be happy, but well. In the ecstasy of the dance, the Self—Atman—will know itself Brahman: 'Self is universe' (*LoH* 138; ch. 9). In Aldous Huxley's words, '...the Brahman, who is one with the Atman, is not only Being and Knowledge, but also Bliss, and after Love and Peace, the final fruit of the spirit is Joy' (*Perennial Philosophy* 106; ch. 6). No comfort is offered by the mother—not as Kali-Devi, become Death, destroyer of worlds—but only the possibility of the drum, the dance, becoming again the child, and experiencing the Dancer's offer of joy.[721]

King Dog (1985)

King Dog takes an episode from the *Mahabharata* ('Great Epic of the Bharata Dynasty' [written ca. 400 BCE-200 CE]) and retells the epic tale in science-fictional and cinematic terms.

In the original story, the Pandavas are five royal brothers contesting with their uncle Dhritarashtra and his son Duryodhana for the realm of the Pandavas' dead father, King Pandu.[722] Despite the jealousy and antipathy of Duryodhana (and a murder attempt), a compromise is reached whereby Dhritarashtra and the Pandavas divide the realm (23). The Pandavas get bad land, but they clear it, build a city, and make Yudhisthira, the eldest, the king. 'Now the five brothers lived in triumph and splendour, and

---

[721] Cf. J. Robert Oppenheimer at the test of the first of the Manhattan Project A-bombs, the 'Trinity' plutonium weapon detonated 16 July 1945: 'After witnessing the awesome blast, Oppenheimer quoted a line from a sacred Hindu text, the Bhagavad-Gita: He said: ''I am become death, the shatterer of worlds.'''—From Project Guttenberg: TEXTS: ETEXT95: 1trnt10.txt' = Trinity Text, 1995. The speaker quoted from the *Bhagavad-Gita* is Krishna (e.g. *Song of God* 94; ch. 11), but I think in epiphany as godhood manifest, incorporating ALL, including Kali (chs. 10-11: 'Divine Glory' and 'The Vision of God in His Universal Form). I recall the Oppenheimer quotation as ending in 'destroyer of worlds' and therefore used that phrase.

[722] I summarize from the 'Gita and Mahabharata' introd. to *The Song of God: Bhagavad-Gita* (23-27), cross-checked with the 'Mahabharata' entry in *Encyclopædia Britannica* 1974: Micropædia.

Duryodhana hated them more than ever. His jealousy hatched a new plot for their ruin. The pious and noble Yudhisthira had a dangerous weakness for gambling [i.e., dangerous in the short-term]. Duryodhana challenged him to play dice with a clever sharper named Sakuni, knowing that the king would feel bound in honour to accept' (*Song*, summary 24). Sakuni cheats, and Yudhisthira loses, finally staking and losing 'his wealth, his kingdom...his brothers,' the wife they share (or who is spouse to each in polyandry) and himself. They were all now subject to Duryodhana's enmity until the intervention of Dhritarashtra, who restores the kingdom to them. Duryodhana arranges another dice-match, with the stakes the kingdom and the provision that the 'loser retire to the forest for twelve years,' then live in the city unrecognized for a year. Yudhisthira again loses, and he and his brothers go off to the forest, where they practice 'spiritual austerities' and heroism (*Song*, summary 25).

One adventure has the four younger brothers thirsty and tempted to drink water before they answer a series of questions from a voice. Each in turn drinks and dies. Finally Yudhisthira finds the bodies and laments. His lamentations are interrupted by a talking crane, who is actually the disguised Dharma, 'the personification of duty and virtue' (plus other things: *dharma* is a complex word).[723] The crane asks Yudhisthira, 'What is the road to heaven.' Yudhisthira replies,

'Truthfulness.'
'How does a man find happiness?'
'Through right conduct.'
'What must he subdue, in order to escape grief?'
'His mind.'
'When is a man loved?'
'When he is without vanity.'

The penultimate question is, What is the most wonderful of the world's wonders? The answer is that we see all sorts of people dying around us, and we still manage to think of ourselves as immortal. The last question is how people can find 'true religion.' The answer is, 'Not by argument. Not by scriptures and doctrine.... The path to religion is trodden by the saints.' As in Daoism, only the way that is gone spontaneously and unconsciously can be the Way. Dharma being satisfied, he reveals his identity and resurrects the four dead brothers (26).

At the end of their exile, Yudhisthira asks for the kingdom back but is refused, then reduces his request to just a village apiece for himself and his

---

[723] In Hindu belief, '...*dharma* is the religious and moral law, governing individual conduct, and one of the four ends of life, to be followed according to one's class, status, and station in life' ('dharma' in *Encyclopædia Britannica* 1974: Micropædia). For the communicating crane, cf. and contrast Lev with the heroin, *EoH* 50-51; ch. 4).

brothers. This too is refused, and the poem moves to the great battle on the plain of Kurukshetra, where armies from all of India gather to fight. This is the setting for the *Bhagavad-Gita*: the conversation between Sri Krishna and Yudhisthira's brother Arjuna before the battle. After eighteen days of fighting, Duryodhana lies dead, and Yudhisthira becomes king of all India, which he rules well for thirty-six years (26-27). The end of the story shows a pilgrimage of the Pandavas and Queen Draupadi (wife to them all) to the top of the Himalayas to abide with God.

> On the way, the queen and four of the brothers died: they were not sufficiently pure to be able to enter heaven in their human bodies. Only Yudhisthira, the royal saint, journeyed on, accompanied by his faithful dog. When they reached heaven, Indra, the king of gods, told him that the dog could not come in. Yudhisthira replied that, if this was so, he would stay outside heaven too; for he could not bring himself to desert any creature which trusted him and wished for protection. Finally, after a long argument, both dog and king were admitted. Then the dog was revealed as Dharma himself. This had been another test of Yudhisthira's spiritual greatness. One more was to follow. When the king looked around him, he found that heaven was filled with his mortal enemies. Where, he asked, were his brothers and his comrades? Indra conducted him to a gloomy and horrible region, the pit of hell itself. 'I prefer to stay here,' said Yudhisthira, 'for the place where they are is heaven to me.' At this, the blackness and horror vanished. Yudhisthira and the other Pandavas passed beyond the appearance of hell and heaven into the true Being of God.... (27)

King Dog is set, mostly, on a world that Le Guin explicitly says she wants ambiguous: it may be our Earth, or it may not. More specifically, the onplanet cinematic mise en scène is a high civilization during the Bronze Age. The government we see is monarchical, but less patriarchal than we might expect, and not at all tyrannical. The kingdom is long enough on the north-south axis to have a definite North and South, with the usual idea of the North as more rugged, less pleasant, and less civilized than the South (see Russ, 'On Setting' 149). In the North there are mountains, and there is at least one significant river. Le Guin does not mention this in the script, but even as the planet might be Terra, so the kingdom might be India (and a Bronze Age Indian setting—with some mild surprises—is a temptation few film directors would, or should, resist). The religion in the South is leaving worship of the Lady for a high god more androgynous; the North still worships the Goddess. As with the Karhiders in *The Left Hand of Darkness* in 1969, the culture here is still 'more tribal than urban,' even if 'overlaid and interwoven with a later urban pattern.'

At least in the North, to push what we see just a bit, 'the hearth tends to be communal, independent,' as Le Guin describes Karhide, 'and somewhat introverted.' There are gaps between the social classes in *King Dog* but 'no great gap between rich and poor. There was no slavery or servitude. Nobody owned anybody.' And if there are great movements of peoples 'that live by expansion and aggression against other societies' on this world, that is either in the past or future.[724] The second world in *King Dog* is the Space Ship of a very high-tech, scientifically advanced civilization. It is '*a huge ship, self-contained, a stable environment and a stable community, a very high level of technology, everything controlled: the acme of artificial environments.... Everywhere...we see bright whites and bright colors, cleanliness, comfort, order. Complex and beautiful machinery runs itself.... It is not a sterile, militaristic environment, but aesthetically rich, complex, even overloaded*' (*King Dog* 112-13).

The film is divided into six parts, with a brief prolog to begin the film and a final coda.

PART ONE: THE STRANGER COMES—set in Aremgar, the capital city of King Ashthera (the film's protagonist).
PART TWO: KING KAMMIN'S WAR—set in Aremgar and then the scenes of the war as foreign King Kammin conquers Ashthera's realm.
PART THREE: JOGEN—set in the North, in the royal fort at Jogen.
PART FOUR: KING ASHTHERA'S WAR—set various places in the Guerrilla War against the invader, ending in Aremgar, the capitol, and in Sova, a small city in the North.
PART FIVE: EIGHT YEARS LATER—set in the Palace Compound and in the countryside.
PART SIX: ON THE SPACE SHIP—on the Ship, with the final sequence back in the Kingdom.

The Persons of the Film in *King Dog* are:

In the Realm of King Ashthera

Ashthera: The King (corresponding to Yudhisthira in the *Mahabharata*)
Tassalil: Wife to King Ashthera
Shiros: Daughter and eldest child of King Ashthera and Queen Tassalil (and thereby heir to throne), later Queen
Hantammad: Son to King Ashthera and Queen Tassalil (younger child and heir to lordship of the North)
Batash: a loyal old councilor to King Ashthera

---

[724] During the second millennium BCE, India was invaded (?) by a people or peoples speaking an Indo-European language, called by the handy phrase 'the Aryans' until Hitler et al. appropriated the term and made it a problem. The quotations are on Karhide in *LHD*, from the original and 'Redux' versions of 'Is Gender Necessary?' (1979: 164-65; 1989: 161-63).

Bolhan: King Ashthera's younger brother
Fezat: King Ashthera's youngest brother
Harish Ashed: Lord of the North, brother to Queen Tassalil
Kida: a minister to King Ashthera

King Kammin: Opponent of King Ashthera, and temporary conqueror of Ashthera's realm, later taken to the Space Ship
Priestess: Servant and local representative of the god/dess honored by King Ashthera
Prince Zeham: Consort to Shiros when she is Queen

On/From the Ship:

Romond: The (space) Traveller, an anthropologist/psychologist observer, experimenter in ethics
Anduse Deji: A colleague of Romond in anthropology/psychology, who remains on board the Ship
Davdre: A woman of the Ship, specializing in ecology or similarly respectable science

King Dog starts with the arrival of Romond, the Traveller, to the realm of King Ashthera (the Yudhisthira-figure); the King will suspect that Romond is a god (corresponding to Indra and Krishna), but we know he is a visitor from another planet and will learn that he is an anthropologist.[725] If there are intimations of immortality with Romond—he doesn't age—it is a technologically mediated longevity, not the immortality of the gods. Romond travels to the court of King Ashthera. Until late in the script, Romond is an ethical anthropologist and courteous visitor: a participant-observer, but one careful not to interfere unduly with the locals, and the plot belongs almost totally to the King, not Romond.

The King and his court must deal with a demand by King Kammin for return of the Eastern Province, won by Ashthera's father in a great battle (15-16). King Ashthera wants to avoid war. He would prefer to fight Kammin in single combat, except Kammin won't accept that deal because Ashthera has a reputation as a superb swordsman (17); later we'll see him in action as a kind of Zen fencer (63-64; Part 3). What Ashthera would most like, though is to throw the dice (17), gamble for the province. Like Yudhisthira, Ashthera is a gambler, but in *King Dog*, as we might expect with Le Guin—for whom true life always involves risk—gambling is a virtue: 'The Goddess loves a gambler' (18).[726]

---

[725] Romond et al. could also be visitors from the planet's future, and, in cultural terms, they probably are. In terms of SF film protocols, however, he's an alien visitor from some*where* far.
[726] According to Robert D. Herman, 'In the *Mahabharata*...gambling with dice is frequently and prominently described; the world itself is conceived of a gambling game.' Herman also notes that Le Guin's father, A. L. Kroeber, 'tried to discover

Ashthera bets on Romond and takes him into his private space: 'The Inner Room.' Aside from what appears to be a resident cat—joined by Ashthera's dog, who follows them—about all there is in the room is a book, a cot, and a tapestry. The tapestry is significant and is described in detail.

> *Its subject is a single large figure, an androgynous dancing god/dess, holding the sun in the right hand and the moon in the left. The figure is graceful, erotic, and threatening; the face, however, is totally serene. The background and lower part of the tapestry are composed of a mass of small figures, which as the light catches them stand out...: corpses, people dying of plague, women in childbirth in prison, warriors disembowelled, a bound slave being blinded, a baby spitted on a sword, horses foundering under loads, oxen at the slaughterhouse, dogs whipped, people and animals starving thin, broken tools, houses collapsing in earthquake, altars befouled, palaces burning. All these small images form a dark, burnished mass or heap beneath the dancing feet of the god/dess; and at the bottom of the tapestry is woven the image of a wide-mouthed bowl of reddish clay, into which thin streams red, black, and gold run from the mass of tormented figures.* (21; Part 1).

The figure is Shiva Nataraja, combined with Kali, the Goddess in her destructive mode: life bound to the Wheel, an artistic imaging of the First Noble Truth of the Buddha, 'Existence is suffering.'

As Ashthera is well aware, he is not going to throw dice with King Kammin for a province. There will be a war. The climax of Part One is a ceremony at the Great Temple of Aremgar; we're told there is a goat sacrifice (26), as in the rites of Kali, and we see the military leader, Harish Ashed, and King Ashthera exit the temple, Ashed's hands and wrists covered with blood. Ashthera gives a traditionally scripted speech on 'the soldier's duty to kill or to be killed'—and gain glory in victory and a 'right to heaven' the moment he dies for King and country: 'So go forth gladly to this war, knowing that you dance the dance of God!' (27). Ashthera *holds out his arms in the same position as those of the figure on the tapestry in the inner room: his hands and arms are red with blood. The crowd shouts out its wild rhythmic chant of enthusiasm'* (27). The scene at the Temple is followed by a wordless scene of Ashthera in his Inner Room, looking dejected, still bloody from the sacrifice, his expression *'inward turned, but*

---

whether or not gambling was distributed among the cultures of the world in systematic patterns that might reveal a general association between gambling and other cultural traits' (7.867). Kroeber devoted great effort to survey gambling, an extremely broad topic.

his gaze is steadily on the tapestry, on the feet of the dancing figure' (28). And then the images break up '*into the meaningless textures of the warp and weft, and go dark,*' with a cut to the Palace's Inner Gardens and a domestic scene of Ashthera's family: his wife Tassalil primarily, but also their children and Fezat, the King's young brother. Tassalil tells Fezat that she is in her kingdom there, which Fezat characterizes as 'The inmost garden of the Inner Lands,' and they talk a bit of Ashthera, primarily of his disappearance for two days, 'In that room.' Fezat notes that as an improvement: 'At least he doesn't run off into the forest anymore.' And Tassalil adds, 'Not even to the gambling house' (30).

The final scene of Part One is a dialog between Ashthera and Tassalil in the Inner Room. A little way into the scene, Tassalil brings water, some of which Ashthera drinks, the rest of which he uses to wash from his hands and arms the dried blood. Ashthera is upset by the prospect of war, which he'll lay five to three they'll lose, but more immediately he is upset by his lying to his people. "Go kill and be rewarded, be killed and be rewarded, heaven and earth are yours by right of war!" Tassalil objects that the words are scripted, 'sacred. They're in the Book of Ashantari.' But Ashthera lied because *he* did not believe the scripted words (32). They briefly discuss other philosophical matters, and Ashthera reassures his wife he won't give up his kingship to go off to the forest; he's 'on the leash now' and will be a dutiful king. Most immediately and practically, he wants his wife and family out of the capitol and up north, at Tassalil's family fort at Jogen. The scene and Part One end quietly with Tassalil singing to her royal husband, inviting him to 'dance life over...dance death forever.'

> I sing, I sing
> The name I do not know.
> In love's name I destroy.
> I am danced by joy. (36)

PART TWO: KING KAMMIN'S WAR starts impressively, with some hints of the 'Pride, pomp and circumstance of glorious war,' to quote Othello, not Le Guin (*Oth.* 3.3.354)—until we get to medium shots of the actual fighting: e.g., '*Hand to hand combat with short swords, footsoldiers*{sic: one word} *in armor of leather, wood, and bronze; the fighting is ugly, awkward, cautious, desperate. There is no way to tell which soldier is on which side, except that some of them wear a crude hawk figure on helmet or shield*' (42). The sequence begins with Ashthera's side setting out from Aremgar in early summer. It ends in autumn, with King Kammin ascending Ashthera's vacant throne.

PART THREE: JOGEN is set in winter, in the mountains, with the King and a few surviving followers arriving in defeat. This is Tassalil's home and her space, far more than the pleasant gardens of the South can be. She is '*very much the chatelaine and chief housekeeper, alert, calm, maternal*' (48); when the warriors return, '*the women give the orders*' for their care

(53). Ashthera is reunited with his old friend Batash, and with Romond, who has followed Tassalil and Shiros. Fezat is dead, we learn, and Ashthera tells his daughter that 'We've lost more than I knew we had...'; but yet, Ashthera kneels to his daughter, tells her she is beautiful and *'tenderly yet with formality'* addresses her as 'child who will be queen!' (57). Ashthera will fight no more battles; he wants nothing more to do with armies, but he intends to lead his people to war: 'We have no army. I don't want an army. I want a rabble—thieves, cowards, robbers, cut-throats.' He plans guerrilla war and total war, allowing Kammin and his followers 'No subjects, no cattle, no grain, no rest. Dogs in the barren fields, dogs in the forest, dogs yapping at his heels. But no more victories. There are eight thousand dead besides the Ram [River].... Those were victories. The river stank. Plague in the villages.... Well, the Dancer has had her dance on the battlefields. And now the dog will have his day' (59).

That is the action of PART FOUR: KING ASHTHERA'S WAR, which he and his people win. But we knew that. In terms of suspense, the interesting conflict isn't between Kammin and his newfangled army (hawk symbols, no less) defeated by Ashthera's guerrilla tactics; when democrats, let alone a communist anarchist write movies, the people's forces win. No, the suspenseful conflict here and in the script generally is a theological argument, and a philosophical one.

In a quiet, domestic scene at the Hall of Jogen, a soldier wounded in the war asks Romond if his god-like people 'praise any gods.' Romond says 'Not with altars or sacrifice' but perhaps 'by upholding the idea of truth, the idea of justice—' and is interrupted by Tassalil. Since Romond has just stated the philosophical ideal of truth and the prophetic ideal of justice, it is an important interruption. To Tassalil, even in the Bronze Age, Romond's line is 'That old story. By righteous action God is praised.'[727] So much the worse for your people, who have so much happiness and waste it! What's cold and hunger and sickness and fear of death, what's war, even, if one could be free of soul? But to endure all that and to give praise for it—that's slavery. That's the betrayal' (65; Part 3). Romond does not answer her, which is just as well since Tassalil is speaking less to him than to the household generally and to Ashthera very much in particular. She goes on to get said what she must say, before spring comes and renewed war and what she fears is total ruin:

> No god deserves one grain of sacrifice, one word of praise. Let the Dancer dance, and make and unmake the worlds, what's that to me? What do I see of the dance but lies defeating truth, and injustice given power, and cruelty triumphing over courage? What god worth worship would

---

[727] Cf. 'The Lord of hosts is exalted through justice, and the holy God is sanctified through righteousness,' in the Amidah prayer in Judaism (from Isaiah 5.16—except in Isaiah the meaning is 'In all he does, God is just and right' [note in *Oxford Annotated RSV*]).

let a child die frightened and in pain? What god would let Kammin defeat Ashthera? I will not dance that dance. I will not ask for mercy or for justice. I will praise the one thing worth praising: our love, our fidelity, ours, not the gods. We don't live forever, not even two hundred years [like Romond's people], forty or fifty years and we die—and that's what I praise, our mortal love. We love because we die. In our death is our freedom. (66; Part 3)

And to clinch her point, she picks up on the one thing that has bothered Ashthera beyond even defeat: the lie he told his people. She says that it wasn't his but the god's. And then a final dialog:

ASHTHERA: Peace gets lost when truth does; and happiness I suppose goes with them. But there is joy, Tassalil. I know joy. I learned it first in the forest, alone; and then with you. And sometimes winning at dice, and sometimes this past year, in the war, in defeat. You can't earn it, you can't keep it, you fall into it. Joy is the abyss between myself and God. It is the river.
TASSALIL: In which you drown.
ASHTHERA: Alone, maybe. But there is...fidelity, you called it. Mortal love. Trust between us. A boat on the river.
TASSALIL: Yes. You I will trust. Not the god, but you.
ASHTHERA: Do you trust me Tassalil? You foresee me dead...and if I come again to Aremgar, will you come with me then?
TASSALIL: *(bitterly)* To the Palace gardens....
ASHTHERA: They'll be destroyed. All to do over. You are winter, you are the north, you are the dark. You only know me, you among them all. I am your truth, you said. You are my freedom, Tassalil. (66-67; Part 3)

Romond joins Ashthera and they go off to fight and win the war.

The war over, Romond goes off to visit King Kammin (much to the disgust of Batash, the old adviser), and Ashthera and Tassalil have something of a falling out or, at least—as foreshadowed—a parting of the way. Ashthera wants her to come with their daughter to the South; Tassalil wants to stay with their rather obnoxious, young, macho son Hantammad—or, more exactly, stay in his domain, and hers, of the North (86-88; Part 4). Ashthera and Tassalil part; three years or so in their future, Tassalil dies (97; Part 5).

The next scene is at the Great Temple in Aremgar. In the Courtyard, Ashthera renounces his name and all that he owns and is, and gains admittance to 'A Small Inner Room of the Temple' (89; Part 4). There Ashthera encounters a priestess of the god/dess, whom he addresses as 'Mother.' Ashthera claims to have lost his way, when he was born. The Priestess sees no problem, then, since he will 'find it soon enough. When you die.' Meanwhile she tells him, with two meanings, that he lives 'A good king's life': i.e., he leads (1) a good life, that of a king, and (2) the life of a good king. Ashthera finds it 'A dog's life, Mother,' but the Priestess tells him he has been 'a good dog.' Ashthera responds (with near-liturgical parallelism),

> Yes. I have obeyed. I have served, I have ruled. I have begotten, I have killed. I have built up and unbuilt, made and destroyed. I have danced that dance through. I have served the god. Now let me serve you! Let me dance without moving, let me speak silence. Let me lay down my kingdom and go alone. (90-91; Part 4).

'Mother' thinks he asks a great deal, wanting to go alone. There follows a catechism of renunciation. Does Ashthera desire to give up 'power, pleasure, wealth, will, and world'? He does. Speaking for the god/dess, the Priestess gives him the hard teaching that if he wishes to renounce, he must also, finally, 'renounce renunciation' (91).

Renouncing the world is easy enough to understand: those who want to find God or go with the Dao or lose themselves in that which *Is*, must renounce 'our preoccupation with 'I,' 'me,' 'mine.'' So we have the easily-enough resolved paradox that to truly possess the world we must renounce self and the world: 'Everything is ours provided that we regard nothing as our property. And not only is everything ours; it is also everybody else's' (Huxley, *Perennial Philosophy* 108; ch. 6). In this view, you must come to the world (in Le Guin's formulation) 'with empty hands.' In the case of altruism, renunciation is more difficult to do but still fairly easy to understand. Aldous Huxley quotes Fénelon, Archbishop of Bambrai, in a letter advising a questioner that, 'You have spent all your life in the belief that you are wholly devoted to others, and never self-seeking. Nothing so feeds self-conceit as this sort of internal testimony that one is quite free from self-love and always generously devoted to one's neighbours' (*Perennial Philosophy* 253-54; ch. 22). The goal, however, is total mortification: learning to have 'unstudied reactions to events—reactions in harmony with Tao, Suchness, the Will of God. Those who have made themselves docile to the divine Nature of Things...who respond to circumstances...with the love that permits them to do spontaneously what they like'—they can say they aren't acting at all, 'but God in me' (*Perennial Philosophy* 116; ch. 6). Altruism is nonspontaneous and consciously ethical behavior. The next step, though, is to give up *all* ethical ideals, including conventional, small 's' selflessness, finally even giving up the ideal of renunciation (*Perennial Philosophy* 252; ch. 21).

Ashthera does not do too badly here.

The Priestess addresses him as 'Man born a king, as all men are born': i.e., of all people, it can be said, 'Thou art That'—i.e., Atman is Brahman, Self is Universe, You are God, so definitely a king.[728] The Priestess calls upon him to give her his anger, judgment, and fidelity. 'Give me your an-

---

[728] See Le Guin's poem 'For June Jordan' (1988; *Wild Oats* 44).

ger, your indignation against untruth, your hatred of the lie.' Can this righteous king give those up? He gives up anger. 'Give up your judgment on men, your knowledge of injustice and justice, give me that, righteous judge.' He gives up judgment, making two God-like qualities he is willing to renounce.[729] Two out of three isn't bad, but Ashthera balks at fidelity, at what the Priestess renames as the very human virtue of Trust. 'Trust is an empty thing. Can't you give it up to me?' As we might have expected from his dialog with Tassalil on fidelity, 'Mortal love,' and trust (66-67)—he cannot give these up to or for the god/dess; and the Priestess tells him to 'Get up, King Dog. Get up, and take your crown, your throne, your sword, your wealth, your power, your collar and your leash. Be answerable, and be a king. There's no freedom for you on this shore of the River' (91-92; Part 4). That is, he must be King of Life and a faithful man until he dies. Or so says the local voice of organized religion.

Eight years pass, bringing us to Part Five, and Romond's return to Aremgar. Tassalil is dead. King Kammin has been deposed and is held prisoner by his nephew Morromin, who in turn is being pressed by 'another pretender.' Shiros rules as Queen, while her younger brother conspires in the North. She has married Zeham and made him prince consort; the gods apparently made him a fool: handsome but *'perfectly stupid'* (100). Zeham and Shiros have put old Batash in prison for some unwelcome scolding (98). And King Ashthera has gotten sick, crowned his daughter, and his finally gotten his wish and has gone off into the forest, giving up even his name: as in *City of Illusions*, 'A Trip to the Head,' and, with variations, 'She Unnames Them': 'A man in the forest has no name' (*King Dog* 96). Romond searches for Ashthera and finds him and offers him 'The way to the new life' (105). Ashthera is a little incoherent from his illness, isolation, 'old age and poverty' (106). Romond tries to explain to him that Romond is not the 'guide to death' nor a god, just a man who wants to take him on a journey Ashthera cannot yet understand: 'I'm taking you out of darkness to the light—to a new world, a new life. You must do as I say,' which Ashthera does, except he insists on bringing the dog (108). In *The Farthest Shore*, Ged tells Arren he would advise a king to 'do nothing because it is righteous or praiseworthy or noble [or good] to do so;...do only that which you must do....' (67; ch. 4). We see in *King Dog* that much of the knack of being a king is knowing (also) what one truly *must* do as opposed to what other people tell you you must do. In Romond's trim little powerboat, the three go out to an island in the bay—in and a very long shot *'a light rises...like a tower of silver,'* and they are headed toward space.

PART SIX: ON THE SPACE SHIP introduces us to a world where Ashthera can find life for another five to ten years, healed mostly, and with the dog fixed up very well (111). The space-farers have a translation de-

---

[729] In Judaism (hence, necessarily, «Judeo -Christianity»), 'righteous king' and 'righteous judge' are epithets applied to God, e.g., 'Blessed be the Eternal, the Righteous Judge.'

vice, so Ashthera can understand much of what the people say, but he is still confused, not being sure how to distinguish 'dream from the not-dream' (114). One source of continuing confusion: King Kammin is there, and his brother Fezat is not. That makes sense in terms of studying Ashthera's ethics: King Kammin is a control for King Ashthera, a control insisted upon by Anduse and Romond's other colleagues in anthropology/psychology. It does not make sense in terms of the Ship as Heaven. 'How can you bring Kammin here and leave Fezat out?' Indeed, from what we know of Kammin and Fezat, it makes no sense with the Ship as just a human-made refuge (115). Yudhisthira in the *Mahabharata* would not stay in heaven if his family and friends were in hell; for those of who know the earlier story, and who can feel 'The awful greed to find out what happens next' (56; Part 3), a big question now is whether or not Ashthera will, in this, be like Yudhisthira.

Ashthera finally confronts Romond in the Ship's garden, accusing him of using Ashthera and Kammin: '...you juggle us like dice.' Romond objects that 'It isn't a game....'; Ashthera says it is indeed a game, but tells Romond that Romond is not the player; Romond only rolls the dice. 'How does God play, Romond? Does God play fair, or cheat?'[730] Ashthera tells Romond what Romond thinks, which is, 'You think I'll tell you that God plays fair. And you think perhaps Kammin will tell you, in his language, that God cheats at dice. And thus you're spared decision. You needn't even bet. No stakes, no losses. Safe' (119). Romond interjects, but before he can object or ask for an explanation—Why would Romond think Ashthera or Kammin experts on God? Since when is Romond a theist to care if God plays dice or not?—Ashthera brings up a very legitimate point: Ashthera has asked for 'all sorts of impossible things, justice, peace—even freedom,' but he has 'never asked for safety!' (119).

Romond insists that he did not bring Ashthera to the Ship to play with him or control him: 'I wanted to free you. To heal your body, to free your mind—to show you what life can be—' At which point Ashthera calls Romond 'Lord Death,' although he will back down on that one. Ashthera finds Romond's kingdom too small for Death's: 'Two ex-kings and a dog.' And then he turns to more personal matters, and to the possibility of an argument that can be resolved. Ashthera misses Fezat and Tassalil and 'Even old Batash'—at which Romond tells him that Batash isn't dead but in jail (120). So Ashthera wants to return home and rejects Romond's objection that Ashthera is concerning himself with 'gossip from a little world nine million miles away—a dustmote. Quarrels no longer yours. Duties you've outgrown' (121). Ashthera responds regally, 'I will go home now,' but adds '*more gently*,' that they can keep their other king (121).

---

[730] On God's playing dice with the universe, see discussion of 'Schrödinger's Cat' and the comment by Einstein usually paraphrased, 'God does not play dice with the universe.' On Ashtera's low regard for Romond's courage here, note that Romond chose a hazardous life with Ashthera at war—Romond has a gun, but no other protection—over a safe job on the Ship.

Ashthera shakes hands with Kammin, reminding him that the people they killed are 'dust now.' He adds, 'Everything's dust, the stars and all. Stay here and be free, among these gods who do without the gods. They don't get angry, they don't judge. They live in peace, and truth, and justice. They don't keep dogs, or cats, or even lice. They're free. Enjoy your freedom, brother enemy' (122). Romond's colleagues Anduse and more so Davdre, two women of the Ship, conclude that Kammin can stay if he wants to stay, and Ashthera may go if he wishes to go: 'The whole trouble is,' Davdre says, 'Romond has been playing God,' and they vary images of God-playing with 'pulled the strings' and 'threw the dice' (123). In this script, apparently, God *does* play dice with the universe. Romond tries one last time to convince Ashthera to stay, for the last philosophical dialog in the script, and almost the last lines. Ashthera should stay with them and not throw his life away on the chance that Batash is still alive and still in prison. In voice-over, Romond is heard:

ROMOND: He's probably been free for months, telling everybody where they're going wrong. You must not waste yourself for him! Conscience must be intelligent. The guide of right action is just proportion. You know that. Measure the difference between what you have to lose and what you can win. It is an abyss!
ASHTHERA'S VOICE: In that difference is God, in that abyss is joy. My dear friend Romond, you've sailed across the ocean of the stars and never got out of sight of land. You never will, till you learn not to hedge your bets. But anyway, there's no use my staying here. There's no freedom for people like me. I'm no good for anything but life. By nothing that I do can I attain a goal beyond my reach.[731] That knowledge I owe to you. Goodbye, dear friend, Traveller. (124)

The script ends with the images of Ashthera, the freed Batash, and the dog walking down the streets of Aremgar: '*People watch, not speaking, intent, unjudging.*' The final shot is '*A large landscape, fields, forests, mountains. The three, Batash, Ashthera, and the dog, are going away from us, small figures on a long dusty road*' (125).

Discussion

Along with the relevant episode in the *Mahabharata*, *King Dog* may be read with profit with at least one Shakespearean work and several of Le Guin's works: *Rocannon's World* (1966), for an anthropologist among a Bronze-Age people; *The Lathe of Heaven* (1971) and *The Word for World Is Forest* (1972), arguably Le Guin's most Daoist books; *Always Coming Home* (1985), her unBible and fullest elaboration of the West Coast as a non-Euclidean, nature-informed, place to *be*; 'Newton's Sleep' (1991), a

---

[731] 'By nothing that I do can I attain a goal beyond my reach' is a 'Direct quote from *Mahabharata*' (Le Guin, personal communication).

story about rationalists on a space station, and 'Pathways of Desire' (1979), her earlier prose examination of a Hindu doctrine, and 'Betrayals' (1994), a later one.

When Ashthera demands to be sent to hell with his brother and wife rather than live in the 'heaven' of Ship with King Kammin, the dialog alludes to the *Mahabharata* while the stage direction has Ashthera stand 'every inch a king' (116). The stage direction alludes to *King Lear* (4.6.106), and I think it should invite readers of the script to bracket KING DOG with *King Lear*. *Lear* is an investigation in Western terms of questions of justice, divine and human, of the existence and relevance of the gods, of the meaning (if any) of human suffering; it asks, '*How shall a human being live well, then?*' in a world that can get very nasty (*ACH*; 236; *Chandi*).[732] Given the degree to which *Lear* loads the dice against assertive daughters and ambitious outsiders generally, though, it is well that Le Guin raises the same great issues in a manner that does not center on a woman but still works to include women.

Yudhisthira in the *Mahabharata* is a gambler, which causes problems; Ashthera is a gambler, but that is a strength, an unambiguous virtue. Le Guin values risk-taking in her fiction—dancing over the abyss can be fatal for humans—and that valuation remains the same in *King Dog*.[733] Whether or not the world is a gambling operation in the *Mahabharata*, life is based on gambles in any worlds in which the Nature of Things is explicable through the *I Ching* or quantum mechanics, or where people in our daily lives necessarily guess at and play the odds—and/or where 'Existence is suffering.'

Neither Yudhisthira nor Ashthera will enter heaven without the dog, but heaven in the *Mahabharata* is heaven; in *King Dog* it is a spaceship. Both heaven and spaceships are above the world, though, and people both places may feel 'superior to those on earth. Masses of dummies stay down in the dirt and breed and die in squalor, and serve 'em right, while a few people who know how to program their VCRs live up in these superclean military wordlets...and are the Future of Man' (*FIS* 10; Introd.). We should keep in mind, though, that the Space Ship is explicitly *not* military and is generally quite nice: a more rigorous proof for space-ship-as-bad-alternative (future) than some clearly dystopian ship of technologically advanced fools and militaristic technocrats. Yudhisthira for his goodness gets the highest good: he and his family pass 'beyond the appearance of hell and heaven into the true Being of God' (*Song*, summary 27). Ashthera gets what may be in *King Dog* the most central good, the freedom to head off with a dog and a friend toward forest (or gambling house?) or, at least, '*going away from us, small figures on a long, dusty road*': like figures in a traditional Chinese or Japanese landscape, or characters in a classic John

---

[732] Among the vast literature on *Lear*, see, e.g., Danson, and Erlich's chapter on *Lear*, central to 'Wise Men and Fools.'

[733] 'The dance is always danced above the hollow place, above the terrible abyss' (*FS* 121; ch. 8).

Ford Western shot: people figuratively *embedded* in the landscape, but free to move and moving away from the dead world of a camera and possibly *us*. And they do this in a world where the dog Dharma remains just a dog: the mundane, organic, and even flea-ridden preferred to the incarnation of a lofty ideal of duty and virtue. If Yudhisthira is a prefiguring of the compassionate Buddha, refusing Nirvana for himself alone, Ashthera is a more mundanely compassionate man, returning from the Ship to save from prison one friend (and, I would hope, to get the dog some decent place to play and hunt).

In *Always Coming Home*, the aggressive sorts recapitulating the invention of Terran warfare (and patriarchy, monotheism, and other bad things) are the Condor people. In *King Dog*, the most immediate enemy are King Kammin's army, with their 'distinctive style of clothing' and 'stylized hawk device' (70; Part 3). Opposing King Ashthera on another axis, and figuratively, is his friend Romond, and the high-tech world of the Space Ship. Romond is no Don Davidson in *The Word for World*, but he is a Rocannon or Lyubov crossed with a Davidson: an anthropologist and rationalist with what we think of as Western ideas of the superiority of high technology over low, highly developed cultures over the relatively—and from a distance—simple. Romond's is a way that can lead to long life, lasting health, exploration of the galaxy, comfort. His is not the way of the Kesh or Karhide or a way which Le Guin will go out of her way (or even cross the street) to endorse.

The Lathe of Heaven and *The Word for World Is Forest* affirm the Daoist principle of *wu wei*, action in stillness, and see the world of explicit, willful action as a dry land, a wrong turning, a perversion that can destroy the world. *King Dog* makes similar points, but with a Hindu inflection, and it is far less explicit—as a script—in its teaching. A produced film will necessarily remove most ambiguities as characters get concretized in actors, and settings in the mind's eye become very specific mise en scène; where battles are romantic gestures or bloody messes as a director decides—etc. More exactly, we are to see the end of *King Dog* as a happy ending: King Ashthera gets what he wants, to leave the world of action and go at least toward the forest, where, with luck, he can lose his name and himself. As a sage in the forest, he can try to join his Self with the Universe, and possess, paradoxically, through loss and mortification, Brahman, at one with the Atman, thereby achieving 'not only Being and Knowledge, but also Bliss, and after Love and Peace, the final fruit of the spirit is Joy' (Huxley, *Perennial Philosophy* 106; ch. 6).

He can be at one, joyously, with Shiva/Kali dancing the universe.

The makers of an actual film, however, should find out from Le Guin how she wants an audience to feel about dancing with the god/dess in *King Dog*.

In the poems, Le Guin, I think, mostly, would have us join the dance. I will repeat that and stress it and remove some of the hedging: my impression of the relevant poetry is that, in voices close to her own, Le Guin values Shiva/Kali and the dance of destruction and creation. Even as the Daoist symbol of water, and literal water both image and perform destruction and creation, so Kali and Shiva recycle the everyday world. But a film or even a film script invites us to *see* the dance of destruction and creation, including our seeing horrors. How many of the episodes shown on the tapestry of the god/dess should be reproduced in shots of the two wars in *King Dog*? How positively or negatively should the Priestess of the god/dess be shown? To what extent should she be imaged as a representative of *organized* religion, allowing for more positive, personal approaches to a spiritual life involving the god/dess? And how positively should we feel about Tassalil, how much *ethos* should we allow to her side of the argument?

In the short story 'Pathways of Desire' (coll. *CR*), certainly, and pretty clearly in the novella 'Betrayals' (*FWF*), Le Guin accepts Tassalil's evaluation that fidelity and 'mortal love' are to be valued more than anything else, perhaps more than even the joy Ashthera claims to have known. And Le Guin gives Tassalil a strong speech on the subject, ringing most of the Le Guinian chimes other than Joy. And Ashthera loves Tassalil—'winter...the north...the dark,' his freedom—and will not renounce her. I see her as a very strong character, worthy of love, and I would reinforce her speech on 'What god worthy of worship...' with images in the film of the horrors of the wars and their aftermath (66-67; Part 3).

I hope *King Dog* gets produced some day, with Le Guin consulting. I would also hope, though, that *King Dog* ended up a film like *Patton* (1970), or Kenneth Branagh's *Henry V* (1989): films which leave unresolved debates that should not and cannot truthfully be resolved. For what may be strongest about *King Dog* is the dialectic, its place in Le Guin's continuing argument with Le Guin over the issues she has her characters raise. Tassalil gets the great lines about 'mortal love,' but she stays in the North with her conqueror-in-training son; she doesn't go South to her daughter and to Ashthera, her husband. Ashthera gets the great lines about risk, but he never asks Romond about the possibilities for him, Ashthera, for five to ten years anyway, starting a new life exploring the galaxy. Instead, Ashthera holds fast to his fidelity: he stays loyal to his wife and family, and his wife dies, and his children have their problems. Even the favorite child, Shiros, marries foolishly and is cruel in the imprisonment of Batash. Significantly, in the rebuilt palace of Queen Shiros and her trophy consort, there is no Inner Room with a sacred text, tapestry, and resident cat. Ashthera is left holding fast to—he has traded the stars for—not a great romantic love or a fine family, but an old friend and a dog.

It could be a movie argued over for years—an excellent form of teaching.

XV.

LOVE AND DEATH AND RETURNING TO RER

> ...there must
> be a story for my dear young hero.
> It will not be the old story. ('My Hero' [1994])

Ursula K. Le Guin's Daoist spokespeople frequently advise turning and returning to one's cosmic and individual roots to get one's life in order. Returning to roots is also good advice for the study of an author's canon, or for disinterested study of a culture, for example, in a science fiction thought experiment: to know a culture, you must dig down, figuratively and carefully, into its roots, examine its bases; one must look to its origins and myths of origin, closely examine physically and politically out-of-the-way places where people still try to go with the old ways.

In 'A Man of the People' (1995), Havzhiva, the title character, is told 'that to know who the Yeowans were he must know the plantations and the tribes' (*FWF* 131): this includes facing not just past history but a living history of continuing oppression. In a more neutral context, Estraven in *The Left Hand of Darkness* implies that to know Karhide one must know the Domains (*LHD* 6; ch. 1); and more explicitly, Genly Ai's 'landlady' in Erhenrang delights in advising him to get out of the capital city into the provinces if he wants to study the basis of the culture of Karhide. Ai's landlady tells Ai that he—the landlady—is 'a Yomeshta,' a follower of the cult of Meshe, but, 'We're a lot of newcomers, see, for my Lord Meshe was born 2,202 years-ago, but the Old Way of the Handdara goes back ten thousand years before that. You have to go back to the Old Land if you're after the Old Way,' and the place to go in the Old Land is to go to 'Old Karhide, to Rer, the old King's City' (47; ch. 5).

Ai goes to Rer and from Rer to the nearby Handdarata Fastness of Otherhord (53-54), the setting for the Foretelling in 'The Domestication of Hunch' chapter in *The Left Hand of Darkness* (ch. 5). Rer itself is described briefly, but memorably, and in a way generally consistent with Le Guin's other stories using the city.

> No landboat or car can enter Rer. It was built before Karhiders used powered vehicles, and they have been using them for over twenty centuries. There are no streets in Rer. There are covered walks, tunnel-like, which in summer one can walk through or on top of as one pleases. The houses and islands and Hearths sit every which way, chaotic, in a profuse prodigious confusion that suddenly culminates (as anarchy will do in Karhide) in splendor: the great Towers of the Un-Palace, blood-red, windowless. Built seventeen centuries ago, those towers housed the kings of Karhide for a thousand years, until Argaven Harge, first of his dynasty, crossed the Kargav and settled the great valley of the West Fall. All the buildings of Rer are fantastically massive, deep-founded, weatherproof and waterproof. In winter the wind of the plains may keep the city clear of snow, but when it blizzards and piles up they do not clear the streets, having no streets to clear.... The Thaw is the bad time on that plain of many rivers. The tunnels then are storm-sewers, and the spaces between the buildings become canals or lakes, on which the people of Rer boat to their business, fending off small ice-floes with the oars. And always, over the dust of summer, the snowy roof-jumble of winter, or the floods of spring, the red Towers loom, the empty heart of the city, indestructible. (53-54)

Ordinarily in Le Guin, cities are suspect, and in *Left Hand* both the Harge dynasty's city of Erhenrang in Karhide and, far more so, Mishnory in Orgoreyn are dangerous places. But cities are not monovalent or malevolent in Le Guin or in any other complex mythos, and a Daoist view pretty much precludes the idea of cities or anything else as evil in themselves. More than Abbenay in *The Dispossessed*, certainly more than Es Toch in *City of Illusions*, and as much as any city in her canon, Rer and its civilization sybolizes not 'negative force—restraint, constraint, repression, authority—but.... The City as goal and dream,' where, perhaps, 'No word or moment or way of being is more or less "real" than any other, and all is "natural"....' (*LoN* [1979]: 147).[734]

'Winter's King' (1969/1975)

Le Guin started out on Gethen in Erhenrang and Rer: she tells us in the headnote to the 1975 reprint of 'Winter's King' in *The Wind's Twelve Quarters* that the first version of 'Winter's King' was written a year before she began work on *The Left Hand of Darkness*. In that original version of

---

[734] See also *EoH* 27; ch. 2: Luz's seeing for a moment with Lev's eyes 'the glory, the City that should be, and was,' at least as a dream, an ideal.

'Winter's King,' we have a series of pictures that give most of the high points of the story of King Argaven XVII and his son, successor, and predecessor Emran.[735] When Emran is still a small baby, Argaven is kidnapped and 'mindformed': an 'induced paranoia,' it turns out, that a healer much later tells him was likely to have caused him to 'become a remarkably vicious ruler, increasingly obsessed by fear of plots and subversions, increasingly disaffected from your people. Not overnight, of course. That's the beauty of it. It would have taken you several years to become a real tyrant....' (*WTQ* 89, 100). Argaven is released by the kidnappers and shows up on the streets of Erhenrang, drugged and brainwashed, wanting only to abdicate. Besides continuing to rule and abdication, the only other choice for him is suicide, which puts him in a dilemma foreseen by the conspirators. Suicide is held in contempt on Karhide, and the conspirators correctly counted on Argaven's 'moral veto' of the option.[736] Abdication required consent of Argaven's Council, and the conspirators correctly counted on the Council's veto of that option. 'But being possessed by ambition themselves, they forgot the possibility of abnegation'—renunciation —'and left one door open....' (*WTQ* 101), a door Argaven uses: he leaves his ring of office with the baby, Emran, and takes an Ekumen spacecraft to Ollul, twenty-four light-years away, just over twenty-four years away, Gethenian time, traveling nearly as fast as light (98).

As simply 'Mr Harge' on Ollul, Argaven is cured, attends school—widening his view of the galaxy, learning to perceive his world as part, not center, his culture as one among many (102)—and waits. What he is waiting for, it turns out, is to be of use. A Terran ethnographer tells him that 'Waste is a pity,' and Argaven's talents are being wasted: he was (and is) 'the right king' for Karhide, a ruler with 'a sense of balance,' who 'might even have unified the planet'—and 'certainly would not have terrorized and fragmented the country, as the present king seems to be doing' (103).

So Argaven Harge sets out to return to Gethen, after having been away twelve years, subjective time, thirty-six years on Gethen. He arrives back home some sixty years, Gethenian time, after he left, to be welcomed by a small group, a very small number of whom recognize him, all of whom turn out to be exiles and rebels. King Emran is now an old tyrant and an ineffective ruler; he has cut off relations with offworld humanity, ceded the Western Provinces to the Orgota, lost to them the capitol of Erhenrang, and resides now in what I'll call the île-de-Karhide, attempting to consoli-

---

[735] According to Le Guin in the *WTQ* headnote (85-86) and Elizabeth Cummins Cogell (*Biblio.* A-15), the changes to produce the 1975 version of 'Winter's King' were in pronoun references (plus, I think, other changes to render the story more androgynous). For this discussion, I have not consulted the 1969 version. For at least one significantly changed passage (*WTQ* 105-06), see Bittner, *Approaches* 142-43, n. 26: 'So 'men' became 'people' and an 'empire' becomes a 'commonality'—and a reference to the complexity of life is expanded to include 'difference'; for a discussion of the original version of the story, see *Approaches* 105-09 (ch. 4 § 6).
[736] Cf. comment on suicide in *WWF* (103; ch. 5).

date his power to the east of the mountains, in the Old Capital at Rer (*WTQ* 105-06). Argaven Harge takes up the cause of the rebellion. 'Snow and ice and guerrilla troops keep Orgoreyn at bay on the west side of the Kargav Mountains. No help came to the Old King, Emran,' when the country rises against him. Emran commits suicide in burning Rer and is succeeded by his father. The king is dead'—Argaven, dead for sixty years to his people—'long live the king,' Argaven, returned to rule again (106-07).

This original (male-gendered) version of the story has much to say about choice, renunciation, and exile, about what would become in *Left Hand* the idea of the blood-bond needed to cement the keystone in the arch: more literally the sacrifice necessary to restore a balance, to reweave a tear in the tapestry of humanity (97). It has nothing to say about androgyny because the Gethenians in the 1969 version are not androgynes; in the 1975 re-issue version, however, the Gethenians are androgynous, and in the 1975 version Le Guin uses '*the feminine pronoun for all Gethenians—while preserving certain masculine titles such as King and Lord, just to remind one of the ambiguity.*' The androgyny of the characters doesn't change the plot, '*but the pronoun change does make it clear that the central, paradoxical relationship of parent and child is not, as it may have seemed in the other* [earlier] *version, a kind of reverse Oedipus twist,*' with father killing son, '*but something less familiar and more ambiguous*' (*WTQ* 85-86; headnote). And something relevant for considerations of gender as well as generation.

Personalized and psychologized by Sophocles, Sigmund Freud, and the Freudians, Oedipus's killing the Old King, his father, and marrying the Queen, his mother, becomes a story of intrafamily rivalry and forbidden lust. Alternative to Freud among nineteenth- and early twentieth-century theorizers, we might look to Johann Jakob Bachofen and his *Mother Right* (1861), Sir James Frazer's *The Golden Bough* (1922), and other studies of early societies for the idea that one became king of an ancient city precisely by becoming the consort to the Queen, with the Queen as representative of The Mother, The Lady: the Earth. In that case, killing the old King-Father to become new King is less a psychological gesture in a family drama and more a conscious political act, and a religious act. Taking this view, one may speculate that the Oedipus legend as Sophocles handed it down is a bit of revisionist myth-making, reading patriarchal kingship into a time when gendered political arrangements were different, arguably more balanced. More immediately relevant, in *The Left Hand of Darkness* (1969), Ong Tot Oppong, Investigator, tells us explicitly in 'The Question of Sex' (ch. 7) that a Gethenian child 'has no psycho-sexual relationship to his mother and father. There is no myth of Oedipus on Winter,' although there is a strict prohibition against incest between generations (*LHD* 94, 92). The Oedipus legend in its family-drama forms does not apply in the world of 'Winter's King' in either version, and part of the usefulness of the changes in the 1975 version is eliminating Oedipus and most other ready-made categories.

Relatively young Argaven XVII, a parent, pursues to the death old King Emran, the parent's child, to retake a kingdom. If we need a legend, a more likely candidate would be that used in 'Semley's Necklace' (1963/64): the night journey that lasts years, the young parent meeting the child grown up (*WTQ* 21-22). Making the pronouns feminine should get most readers to picture Argaven's farewell to the baby Emran as a mother's farewell to her baby (96-97). Insofar as we gender the Gethenians in 'Winter's King,' then, we have Argaven as loving mother pursuing to the death her grown daughter—grown into an old and vicious tyrant. For many readers this will be much *'less familiar and more ambiguous'* than Oedipus, Laius, and Jocasta. Another part of the usefulness of the 1975 version of 'Winter's King' is its subtextual attack on the view that 'Sugar and spice and everything nice / And that's what little girls are made of': i.e., the sentimentalized view of women, occasionally endorsed—although hardly in my sardonic terms—by women, and even feminist women. But not by Le Guin. Along with Joanna Russ, Alice Sheldon, and Suzy McKee Charnas, what might be the mainstream among feminist writers of SF, Le Guin holds that XX sex chromosomes and/or the womanly condition will not guarantee a *nice* human being. This idea is implied by the violence within the human repertoire of the androgynous Gethenians in *The Left Hand of Darkness*, but there we may picture Gethenians in that novel mostly male. In the revised 'Winter's King,' we may err equally, but more likely on the side of picturing Gethenians as female. And the story's lightly-sketched frame of a series of pictures insists that we *picture* the story's ambiguous, bitter climax, of Argaven's politically conclusive, bitter victory.

> Now at last comes the dark picture, the snapshot taken by firelight—firelight because the power plants of Rer are wrecked, the trunk lines cut, half the city is on fire....
> Snow and ice and guerrilla troops keep Orgoreyn at bay on the west side of the Kargav Mountains. No help came to the Old King, Emran, when her country rose against her. Her guards fled, her city burns, and how at the end she is face to face with the usurper. But she has, at the end, something of her family's heedless pride. She pays no attention to the rebels. She stares at them and does not see them, lying in the dark hallway, lit only by mirrors that reflect distant fires, the gun with which she killed herself near her hand.
> Stooping over the body Argaven lifts up that cold hand, and starts to take from the age-knotted forefinger the massive, carved, gold ring. But she does not do it. 'Keep it,' she whispers, 'keep it.' (*WTQ* 107)

'We will bury you' is every younger generation's generous promise and implied threat to every parental generation. If all goes *well*, young survivors bury (or burn or set out for the vultures) loving and beloved parents who have died. Younger Argaven kills her old daughter and will dispose of the body after the customs of Karhide. We have no ready-made myth or legend for Argaven's deadly victory, no neat category into which to pigeon-hole and therefore make safe this act; so we must face that picture and thereby face a horror more frightening than the familiar and familiarized tale of Oedipus: a political killing in 'Winter's King,' where a parent, as a practical, uniquely historical matter—mundane not mythic, nonsexual, nonpsychological, nonpathological—has (ethically considered) killed her child.

'Coming of Age in Karhide' (1995)

> Because although half the fun is, of course, confounding expectations, the other and more serious half of the fun is the attempt to get myself and my reader NOT to gender the characters—to accept & believe genderlessness/genderbothness even amidst a seething of hormones.
> — Le Guin on 'Coming of Age,' letter, 10 Oct. 1996

When Le Guin returned to Rer, it was to tell another story of youth and age, but a very different one: not better, just different.[737] 'Coming of Age in Karhide' is not a story of royal politics, royal heroism. The only injury is a kid's broken leg; the only blood is menstrual blood. 'Coming of Age' may be Le Guin's best attempt so far to find a story for her dear young hero, a very mundane, domestic story, set in an elegantly rendered science-fictional world.

About the time Emran Harge was making her last stand in Rer, Guyr Thade Tage em Ereb, a tradesperson of Rer, was conceiving a child with Karrid Arrage, a cook (eventually head cook) of the Ereb Hearth (*Year's Best* 483). In the year Argaven XVII began his/her second reign, 'the Year One, or sixty-four-ago' (it is *always* 'the Year One' on Gethen), Sov Thade Tage em Ereb was born.[738] Fourteen years after that, 'in the Year One, or fifty-ago,' Sov came of age, entering kemmer (estrus, heat) for the first time. In this Year One, now, the sixty-four-year old Sov has 'been thinking about that'—coming of age—'a good deal' and narrates for us her/his coming of age story (471). That is the story, reasonably enough, of 'Coming of Age in Karhide'; the plot is that story sandwiched between a short introduction on the City of Rer generally and an even shorter conclu-

---

[737] Le Guin might prefer 'Coming of Age' if she sees 'Winter's King' as a 'killer story,' part of the 'wonderful, poisonous' male Heroic cycle ('Carrier Bag,' *DEW* 168 [most of the *DEW* essays marked with a square and female symbol are relevant]).

[738] It is more difficult to think the idea of Progress when one's calendar is always on the Year One. It is more difficult to value transcendent actions if your calendar is not dated from one.

sion—two paragraphs—bringing us up to date on Sov's cousin, Sether, and giving the quietly stated moral of the story. Sov has gone into radio—the main medium on Gethen—and Sether 'went into the Handdara, and became an Indweller in the old Fastness' at Rer, and is now an Adept. Sov visits the Fastness often, and Sether returns frequently to the Hearth. Sether and Sov talk, apparently of 'The old days or the new times' and the story ends with the clause, 'somer or kemmer, love is love' (486). Though they have not vowed kemmer and do not live together, Sov and Sether love one another, and, 'Coming of Age in Karhide' is a love story and a story of a marriage.

As a love story and story of a marriage, 'Coming of Age' is in the line of works from Le Guin as romantic (*WTQ* 1). Still, this is definitely not a story featuring 'dreary male heroes' (Lefanu 143) doing chivalric or even macho-manly things to win the hearts of otherwise inactive women. Nor, the androgyny of Gethenians not withstanding, is it a story of which any but the most literal-minded would ask, 'Where are the women?' Indeed, 'Coming of Age' beautifully supplies the story of family structure and the practices of child rearing Joanna Russ correctly noted were absent from *The Left Hand of Darkness* ('The Image of Women' 39). The complaint people might have starting to read 'Coming of Age' is that our world, anyway, has quite enough coming of age stories, and those of us who were regular movie-goers in the 1960s and 1970s may claim to have seen more than our quota of such stories and demand one hell of a variation on this romance theme if we are to be subjected to another. In 'Coming of Age in Karhide,' Le Guin delivers brilliantly.

First of all, time's figurative arrow in 'Coming of Age' brings in with it not one coming of age story but at least four: the main story of Sov's sexual initiation and a word or two on Sether's (483-85), the coming of age of the Gethenians in entering the Ekumen (471), and the coming to the end of sexuality by Sov's mother's sibling Dory (and a number of others), and Sov's own approaching or having reached the end to her/his sexuality (473-74). 'Coming of Age' means only puberty only for males; Gethenians are potentially male and females, and, we learn here, have menopause as well as puberty for coming of age.

Second, the arrow of time is only one of time's manifestations. Time also cycles and endures; the arrow or spear of plot is complemented by the carrier bag of—well of all the miscellaneous useful or interesting things one might put into a carrier bag.[739] In a perhaps more familiar figures of speech, science fiction tends to 'foreground the background' and characters and their stories in SF compete for our attention with their worlds. In 'Coming of Age in Karhide,' Le Guin integrates with great skill story and world, and amply justifies our attention by giving us a perfect small cameo of a story set in a very ample world.

In 'Coming of Age,' Rer, the Ereb Hearth, and the Thade family are major features: Sov is embedded in them all, rooted, woven into their fab-

---

[739] 'The Carrier Bag Theory of Fiction' (1986) coll. *DEW*.

ric—except those figures of speech are static, and a major part of the point of 'Coming of Age' is that Rer and all it contains are (like water) both static and dynamic. Rer is like the farmhold Udan in '...A Fisherman of the Inland Sea' (1994), where the protagonist returns after a number of years to find 'Everything was the same, itself, timeless. Udan in its dream of work stood over the river that ran timeless in its dream of movement' (*FIS* 167). Except, of course, the people of Udan keep changing. And Rer is no farmhold but a city, 'the oldest city in the world,' on Gethen, over 15,000 years old, with 15,000 years of changes. Rer is the place where Karhide became a nation, and the place of Karhide's first experiment in literal anarchy, where 'Sedern Geger, the Unking,' in a major change, 'cast the crown into the River Arre from the palace towers, proclaiming an end to dominion,' thereby beginning 'The time they call the Flowering of Rer, the summer Century...,' which ended when the Hearth of Harge came to power (under Argaven I) and moved the capital to Erhenrang, across the mountains (*Year's Best* 471).

Politically, the people of Rer have been blessed in what a rabbinic authority in *Fiddler on the Roof* suggests is the proper blessing for a monarch: 'May the LORD bless, and keep the Czar—far away from us!' Except for the recent warfare between Emran and Argaven XVII, the Harges have generally stayed on their side of the mountains, far from Rer; and the Harge monarchs wear only a ring of office, not a crown. They lack the political power to really push things around, to run things, Orgota fashion, with totalitarian 'efficiency,' to work their will imposing «progress» on Rer. More symbolically, but still of political consequence, Rer has not been urbanly renewed or planned but 'rebuilt forever' by her people, becoming a city 'as vast and random and ancient as the hills,' as enduring and evolving as the hills. 'Rer is all corners,' and the people of Rer joke 'that the Harges left because they were afraid of what might be around the corner' ([470]), which makes Rer not only hill-like and like an ancient farmhold, but also like a forest, like Selver's forest for one, where 'Revelation was lacking' and there is 'no seeing everything at once: no certainty' (*WWF* 26; ch. 2).

Rer is a city Le Guin can like, and it is a fitting center for the Handdara unfaith, with the Handdara's lack of Revelation, its appreciation of uncertainty (*LHD* 71; ch. 5): a good Daoist place, with tunnels and randomness and, in the Thaw, lots of running water (476, also *LHD* 54; ch. 5).

The Ereb Hearth is also a good place; to start with, it is a good place to be a kid as a member of what Charnas in *Motherlines*, with poetic economy, calls a 'childpack' and Sov calls a human 'flock, a school, a swarm.' The Thade kids run 'in and out of our warren of rooms,' doing work and getting educated and 'looking after the babies'—though their care of babies includes playing catch with them. Sov feels that such 'escapades were well within the rules and limits of the sedate, ancient Hearth,' and tells us, very significantly, that the children felt these limits 'not as constraints but as protection, the walls that kept us safe,' which statement leads into Sov's first mention of a cousin Sether, and Sether's breaking a leg trying a rope-swing from a balcony in 'Another misguided attempt at flight,' before Gethenians had learned the word *flight* from the Ekumenical 'Aliens' (472-73). Note here the elegance of intertwining of plot, background, image, and theme. Sether is to become Sov's lover, within the norms of the Thade family, and that love is central to the plot. The Hearth as a physical place is a major, if mostly neutral, setting of the story; and the Hearth with its physical and figurative walls is here a variation on a Le Guinian theme. Flying—falling upward through 'a golden light'—becomes an image for Sov's sexual initiation (484). Most important, I think, these walls, the walls to the Hearth buildings, are *not* to be unbuilt; the safety of this Hearth is an unambiguously good thing, and appreciating safety in this eutopia is legitimate.

The Thade family is special and possibly old-fashioned in three or four ways. First, it is quite large. Sov's grandmother had four children, all of whom had children, yielding Sov 'a bunch of cousins as well as a younger and an older wombsib,' about whom we learn nothing, except for cousin Sether. Second, the neighbors gossip that "The Thades always kemmer as women and always get pregnant," with someone inevitably adding, "And they never keep kemmer.'...The former was an exaggeration,' Sov tells us, 'but the latter was true. Not one of us kids had a father. I didn't know for years who my getter was, and never gave it a thought.' The reasons for the Thades' actions are not so much ideological as practical: 'Clannish, the Thades preferred not to bring outsiders, even other members of our own Hearth, into the family.' The implications, though, are quite ideological. In *Left Hand*, Ong Tot Oppong was convinced that 'The whole structure of the Karhidish Clan-Hearths and Domains is indubitably based upon the institution of monogamous marriage' (*LHD* 92; ch. 7). The Thade portion of the Ereb Tage Hearth is indubitably not, and it is the only Hearth Sov tells us about. The little eutopia of the Thade clan is, for us, matriarchal—literally, as we shall learn (*Year's Best* 478)—and presents a women's space, a nonmonogamous, nonmarried women's community, and one that is unambiguously good.[740] The implications of this local taboo against monogamy, for some of the Thade children, though, can be bad: When young people among the Thades 'fell in love and started talking about keeping kemmer or making vows, Grandmother and the mothers were ruthless. 'Vowing kemmer, what do you think you are, some kind of noble? some kind of fancy person? The kemmerhouse was good enough for me and it's good enough for you,' the mothers said to their lovelorn children, and sent them away, clear off to the old Ereb Domain in the country, to hoe braties till they got over being in love' (472).[741]

---

[740] Except, of course, 'matriarchal,' 'women's community,' and 'women's space' are our gendered terms, at most only obliquely applicable on Gethen.

[741] Note hint in *TD* on maternal tones of voice as a candidate for a cross-cultural constant (199; ch. 5): the (grand)maternals lines here read well in the accent of an Ashenazi or Appalachian grandmother (cf. below, *mahad/Mensch*).

We have, potentially, a kind of Romeo and Juliet story in 'Coming of Age': a romance of young lovers, Coming of Age in each other's love, and, in despite of their family (possibly singular in this case), vowing kemmer and killing themselves off in the love-death of a romantic-tragedy—or, for a variation, vowing kemmer and finding a way to live happily ever after, making for a romantic comedy.

Le Guin follows neither of these routes. Instead of old Capulet's patriarchal household in *Romeo and Juliet*, or older Wold's tents and Winter City in Le Guin's own *Planet of Exile* (1966), we have here the 'warmth and density and certainty'—a positive certainty—'of a family and a Hearth embedded in tradition, threads on the quick ever-repeating shuttle weaving the timeless web of custom and act and work and relationship,' and in which Sov is quite happy until she turns fourteen, and enters the Gethenian form of puberty, the first coming of age. That is why Sov remembers the year; it is not why it is memorable for most of the Thade kin, who recall it as the year of 'Dory's Somer-Forever Celebration' (473), and Sov significantly interrupts her/his coming of age story to tell that of a relative.

Dory is mother to Sether (475), and 'Mothersib' to Sov, which I would translate here as 'aunt' or 'mother's sister,' except, as we might expect from the physiology of Terran humans, 'In their last years of kemmer...many people tend to go into kemmer as men; Dory's kemmers had been male for over a year, so I'll call Dory 'he,' although of course the point was that he would never be either he or she again' (473-74). Which makes Dory roughly, and misleadingly, analogous to 'mother's brother,' a point anthropologists and students of Old English poetry can appreciate. In societies in which the mother's clan keeps the children, 'mother's brother' is an important male figure in raising those children. For whatever reasons, in old Germanic society, the mother's brother had a close relationship with at least the boys. 'Mothersib Dory' is obviously an important person in Sov's life, but 'his' role will not fit into Terran categories.

In any event, Dory is joined by age-mates 'in the middle of going out of kemmer' or who had ended sexuality but hadn't marked the passage, and they stage an impromptu ritual and throw one great party. After fifty some years, what Sov most vividly remembers is 'a circle of thirty or forty people, all middle-aged or old, singing and dancing, stamping the drum beats' in the centerhall of the Hearth, lit by fires. Like the old people in 'Pathways of Desire' (1979), they have more reality than the young. 'There was a fierce energy' in Dory et al., 'they stamped as if their feet would go through the floor, their voices were deep and strong, they were laughing. The younger people watching them seemed pallid and shadowy.' The motivation for the party was Dory's public recognition that s/he can no longer have kids or sex and has 'to get old and die'—so they dance! And Sov looks at the dancers and wonders, 'why are they happy? Aren't they old? Why do they act like they'd got free?', and this is the transition question to the story proper of Sov's puberty (473-74).

Puberty for Sov is about the same trouble that it is for large numbers of Americans on Terra, except a little worse and a little better because 'bisexual' and concentrated in time. As with us, any tissues that can erect will erect during puberty, causing embarrassment—all the more acute because one is sure *everyone* can see or smell what is going on—plus, of course, «pubescing» kids undergoing physical discomfort or real pain. On Gethen, though, there is this much advantage over the Hainish norm: everyone's 'tits are on fire' one time or another; everyone's 'clitopenis' gets 'swollen hugely' and sticks out, then shrinks till 'it hurt[s] to piss' (475, 477). Every adolescent can get the unwanted hard-on, the unexpected blood flow. Introducing for a moment Genly Ai's mistake of seeing Gethenians male, then female (*LHD* 12; ch. 1), I'm going to gender Sether male in his finding puberty 'dehumanizing. To get jerked around like that by your own body, to lose control,' and he 'can't stand the idea. Of being just a sex machine.' And here he asks Sov if she—as I'm picturing this exchange— knows about how people 'in kemmer go crazy and *die* if there isn't anybody else in kemmer? That they'll even attack people in somer? Their own mothers?' Ong Tot Oppong, in *The Left Hand of Darkness*, had said that 'there can be no unconsenting sex, no rape' among Gethenians (94; ch. 7). Sov thinks so too, but the Narrator Sov remembers that Sether said that Tharry told him of a truck driver who went into kemmer as a male and 'he did it to his cab-mate.' We can note that Sether doesn't have the word *rape*, and that in the story the driver comes 'out of kemmer and committed suicide' in shame for what he had done (477-78). And we can believe Tharry's story of the truck driver or not. I believe it: among the Athsheans in *The Word for World Is Forest*, some people do go crazy—very rarely— and murder other Athsheans, however strong their cultural and perhaps even physiological inhibitions against murder. It is possible that there have been some rapes in Gethenian history. Most of the rest of Sether's speech is the sort of tripe adolescents (and a few science fiction writers) sometimes tell one another on Terra: 'People in kemmer aren't even human anymore!... It's a primitive device for continuing the species. There's no need for civilized people to undergo it' (478).

Picturing Sether as male, we can see here one standard male hang-up, and a standard masculinist dream: rage at losing control to one's body, the desire for asexual (woman-free) reproduction. On the other hand, picturing Sether as male we get a denial of the stereotype—which lasted into the 1990s—of males in love with our bodies and thrilled with the thought of erectile tissue constantly erected.

The up-side of puberty for Sov, is that Sov gets more in touch with the mother, Guyr, and starts getting treated more like an adult. The saying Sov has heard among old people is '*We shape each other to be human,*' which s/he recalls as Guyr strokes Sov physically (perhaps with Guyr's being touched by Sov metaphorically). And Guyr tells Sov, in a metaphorical «stroke» that even 'Grand,' the grandmother, has been bragging about Sov: '...what a beauty, what a *mahad*!', with *mahad* explained as a dialect word of Rer, meaning 'a strong, handsome, generous, upright person, a reliable person': Yiddish *Mensch*, in a grandmother's mouth. The up-side is also Sether. At the end of Sether's speech on the inhumanity of sex, Sov tells Sether that s/he's human; 'even if you have to do that stuff, that fucking'—a word she hears first aloud from Sether—'You're a mahad'; and five lines into the following section, Sov is saying 'I want to go into kemmer with Sether' (478).

Sov's grandmother is pleased with this idea, although s/he must remind Sov that Sether may look older but s/he's a month or two behind Sov in pubescence. They are both 'Dark-of-the-mooners,' like Grand once was, and Grand advises Sov to 'stay on the same wavelength, you and Sether,' and grins a grin Sov hadn't seen before, 'an inclusive grin.' This 'unquestioned autocrat in the Hearth' was starting to treat Sov as an equal, a clue that s/he 'might be becoming more, rather than less human' (478). And Grand has hopes for Sov, and Sether, too, and wants Sov to spend a half-month at the Handdara Fastness: "You've got a good brain,' said Grand. 'You and Sether. I'd like to see some of you lot casting some shadows, some day. We Thades sit here in our Hearth and breed like pesthry. Is that enough?' (479). The question is rhetorical for Grand, if an open one in Le Guin's canon.

At the Fastness, Sov's ignorance is respected: in the Handdara, the Karhidish version of Daoism, they respect the Uncarved Block, the Child who has less to unlearn to contact the Dao, the Mother. Sov practices the Untrance daily—a kind of Tai Chi, it seems—and has her first menstruation, looking at 'the smear with horror and loathing.' The Indweller who sees her washing her sheet says nothing, but brings her stain-removing soap (479). After that, Sov has much better moments at the Fastness: a sense of peace 'sank into me'—and s/he feels a 'strangeness' of soul s/he associated with puberty, but now without the pain: it is part of 'an immense enlargement' (480). As in Earthsea there is the Long Dance on midsummer's eve (*FS* 117; ch. 8), so at the Fastness there is a Midsummer Chant, for four days. Sov joins in, and then truly *joins in*. Sov can no longer hear her own voice 'and heard only all the voices, and then only the music itself, and then suddenly the startling silvery rush of a single voice running across the weaving, against the current, and sinking into it and vanishing, and rising out of it again'—and then an ellipsis mark and it's time for dinner; Sov had been lost in the music and has touched something basic in Sov and in the world (480). S/he is ready for a change.

Sov's mother and 'Grand' and the elders come for Sov at the Fastness and they return home and Sov is given all new clothes. 'There was a spoken ritual that went with the clothes, not Handdara, I think, but a tradition of our Hearth; the words were all old and strange, the language of a thousand years ago'; and the ceremonial response, as among the Kesh and Native Americans, with variations, is 'Haya!' Then Sov is given one last bit of advice, and Le Guin makes explicit a point mostly implicit in *The Left Hand of Darkness* (not sufficiently recognized by Ai, just assumed by Estraven): "last advice,' they called it, since you gain shifgrethor when you go into kemmer, and once you have shifgrethor advice is insulting.'[742] Not

---

[742] Cf. 'Solitude' (1994).

very originally, but usefully, they tell Sov to be careful—not of pregnancy, since s/he won't be fertile as female or male for a year or so—but to be careful of the Doorkeeper, and more generally careful who is to be the first. They parade Sov to the Ereb kemmerhouse and leave, with the family speaking the Handdara blessings, "Praise then Darkness' or 'In the act of creation praise" (481).[743]

There is a ritual entrance to the kemmerhouse, lead by a Doorkeeper (cf. Roke in Earthsea), who is a 'halfdead,' which makes sense: he is a 'pervert,' that is, 'a person in permanent kemmer, like the Aliens,' like us. As Sov asks, what normal person would 'want to *live* in a kemmerhouse' (482). The Doorkeeper, contrary to the suspicions and prejudices of some of Sov's family, turns out to be ethical and reliable. Sov thinks, 'As I had in the Fastness, I felt the familiar reassurance of being part of something immensely older and larger than myself, even if it was strange and new to me,' and s/he feels s/he 'must entrust myself to it and be what it made me.' S/he goes with the situation, the ritual; at the same time, as is common in mystic submission, s/he is 'intensely alert' (483).[744]

The first to approach Sov is Karrid Arrage, in kemmer as a male. The family also warned Sov of Karrid, and some in the kemmerhouse mistrust him when he picks her up, erotically. Karrid responds, 'I won't hurt my own get, will I? I just want to be the one that gives her kemmer. As a woman, like a proper Thade. I want to give you that joy, little Sov.' And he undresses Sov and s/he kemmers as a woman—and Karrid moves on before they couple (483), with Sov taken away by Berre, a stranger in kemmer as a woman, and they play erotically, much to Sov's delight. And then a man comes up and engages Berre's full attention, and Arrad Tehemmy, a hearthmate in kemmer as a man and older than Sov by a few years asks to be her first, and is (484).

Sov spends the entire first night with Arrad, 'fucking a great deal'— and eating a great deal; the house's beer, though, is rationed by 'an old woman-halfdead' who won't let people get drunk. Even sober, Sov feels 'in love forever for all time all my life to eternity with Arrad'—until Arrad moves into somer, and a deep sleep, and Hama arrives: 'and it was entirely different with Hama than it had been with Arrad, so that I realized that I must be in love with Hama, until Gehardar joined us. After that I think I began to understand that I loved them all and they all loved me and that that was the secret of the kemmerhouse' (485). There are others, but Sov as Narrator remembers only one other name. By the third or fourth close encounter of the erotic kind, however, even the densest reader should realize that «the first time» can be socially sanctioned and beautiful and erotic, *and* not at all romantic in ways that validate 'love forever for all time all

---

[743] For my use of 'blessings' here, see 'Nine Lives,' where Kaph's 'Good night' or similar phrase is called, in the final word of the story, 'benediction' (*WTQ* 147).
[744] Cf. Serenity in 'Solitude' on 'To be aware,' esp. 156.

my life to eternity'—definitely *not* romantic in ways that reinforce long-term pair bonding and 'the institution of monogamous marriage.'

Coming out of kemmer, Sov meets Berre again, and when they're both in somer Berre talks a little business. S/he's 'in the radio trade,' not making radios but broadcasting, and s/he invites radio-lover Sov to visit at 'the tower.' This is how Sov finds a 'livelong trade' and makes 'a lifelong friend.' This exchange ends the narration about the kemmerhouse, and leads, without a break in paragraph, to Sov's recalling telling Sether, 'kemmer isn't exactly what we thought it was; it's much more complicated' (485). Apparently, sex doesn't have to be kept in 'a room, as it were, apart'—in Ong Tot Oppong's elegant phrase—but can be integrated into friendship, and business. And sex, reproduction, love, and friendship can be separated from marriage as an institution.

'Coming of Age in Karhide' ends with Sov's summary of Sether's first kemmer, at the beginning of autumn (for another change of the year) and 'at the dark of the moon,' a time of power. If we have been picturing Sether as a boy entering manhood and Sov as a girl becoming a woman—and I intentionally offered temptations to do that—these last two paragraphs are very important.

> One of the family brought Sether into kemmer as a woman, and then Sether brought me in. That was the first time I kemmered as a man. And we stayed on the same wavelength, as Grand put it. We never conceived together, being cousins and having some modern scruples, but we made love in every combination, every dark of the moon, for years. And Sether brought my child, Tamor, into first kemmer—as a woman, like a proper Thade. (485)

When Juliet finally makes love with Romeo, so to speak—and they do *make love*, not just copulate—Juliet *is* Romeo![745] It's a gender-bender, and Le Guin is having things at least two ways: We see women's space, women's community among the Thade family; we can see Sov as a girl becoming a young woman (including the passage of menarche), a girl in love with her cousin Sether; *and* we are refused our categories of sex and gender and sexual propriety: Sether doesn't just have nipples to get irritated in puberty, but *tits*, Sov gets unmotivated erections with a clitopenis, and when clitopenis enters vagina, it is Sov's penis in Sether's vagina—and Sether in kemmer as a man aids in the 'proper' sexual initiation of Sov's daughter. And we have a denial of romance, and an assertion of pair-bonding and love.

The very end of 'Coming of Age,' though, is the final bringing up to date, with intimations of the second coming of age, 'Somer-Forever' (or at least until death).

---

[745] The distinction between copulating and making love is developed in *TD*, e.g., ch. 10.

> Later on Sether went into the Handdara, and became an Indweller in the old Fastness, and now is an Adept. I go there often to join in one of the Chants or practice the Untrance or just to visit, and every few days Sether comes back to the Hearth. And we talk. The old days or the new times, somer or kemmer, love is love. (486)

Not sex here, not heterosexual marriage. What remains from the old times of Rer to the new Ekumenical age is the love of two humans as humans.

In 'Coming of Age in Karhide,' Le Guin may have found a story for her 'dear young hero,' and it was not 'the old story' of macho heroism. 'You have to go back to the Old Land if you're after the Old Way,' and maybe you have to return, and re-return, to the Old Way to get to the new story. In her second return to Rer, Le Guin may have again come of age as an artist; in giving Sov and Sether and their family, City, and world to us, she may have helped American SF come of age. And in unrepentantly using the androgynous characters, in getting us, at least intermittently, 'to accept & believe genderlessness/genderbothness,' Le Guin here may mark a coming of age of American feminism as a set of feminism*s,* where one of the feminisms is a strangely Daoist one that can examine in one short story: a family where children count descent from their mothers, remain with the mothers, are ruled by the mothers—*and* include in the women's space of that story that most uncompromising symbol of (sexual/gender) integration, the Androgyne.[746]

---

[746] Le Guin has written in her own voice, that through the late 1960s, 'Art was to transcend gender. This idea of genderlessness or androgyny is what Virginia Woolf said was the condition of the greatest artists' minds. To me it is a demanding, a valid, a permanent ideal'—if definitely a problem as an ideal, given 'the fact...that the men in charge of criticism, the colleges, and the society had produced male definitions of both art and gender' (*ER* [1993]: 6).

XVI.

CONCLUSION

The way up and the way down, the way back and the way forward, are one and the same. —Heraclitus

How shall a human being live well, then? (*Always Coming Home* 236; *Chandi*).

One of best literary criticism statements on the old topic of theme is Damon Knight's contribution to accompany his story 'Masks' in the anthology *Those Who Can: A Science Fiction Reader*. Knight refused to write much on the abstract subject of theme in his story because he thinks 'that 'theme' is an academic shibboleth, an imaginary entity that is read into a work by the teacher in order that the student may be required to read it out.' Knight maintains that the theme of 'Masks' or of any work is, 'Life is like this.' Knight insists that a story is not 'a kiddy-car containing a message,' but instead 'a formal structure which the author builds around you; in the process you learn to see some portion of the world in a new way and you experience certain esthetic responses....' (230). Actually, Knight does write about the theme of 'Masks,' and writes very well, but his contribution to *Those Who Can* is 'An Annotated 'Masks,'' and his major statement on theme is, precisely, the set of his annotations of 'Masks.'

Ursula K. Le Guin did contribute a formal essay 'On Theme' to accompany 'Nine Lives' in *Those Who Can*, but Le Guin at least partly agrees with Knight. In responding to the 1975 Le Guin issue of *Science-Fiction Studies*, Le Guin noted that the ideas in her Earthsea trilogy 'are more totally incarnated, less detachable from the sounds, rests, and rhythms, less often stated as problems and more often expressed in terms of feeling, sensations, and intuition' than in some of her other, arguably less artful work. 'If you dissect the ideas out of' the Earthsea trilogy, 'you get things like Don't Meddle. Keep the Balance. Man is Mortal.—Fortune-cookie ideas' (45). The implication I draw is that when Le Guin succeeds best she produces a work that is a 'formal structure' built around us, and 'in the process' of experiencing the work, we 'learn to see some portion of the world in a new way.' Hence, my method in *Coyote's Song* has been 'close reading': to a large extent sticking to the works themselves, their 'sounds, rests, and rhythms,' and supplying a system of annotations that I hope will help readers see the world in a new way by helping them do their part in constructing the meaning of the story by making connections. Most important, for me in *Coyote's Song*, the connections are with Le Guin's other works; the canon of Ursula K. Le Guin is a primary context for the works of Ursula K. Le Guin.

My general method, then, is close reading. My central conclusion and starting point is the inference that within the canon of Le Guin's works there is a large subset where theme is very strong. These are works that indeed 'mean intensely' (as Robin Scott Wilson and Robert Browning's Fra Lippo put it)—and mean intensely in terms of some of the great debates of the twentieth century, what has been called, melodramatically, a *Kulturkampf* or 'the culture wars.'[747] Le Guin's intention, I believe, is always a story (poem, film script): a work of art. The frequent upshot is a work of high art that is a *teaching* story, one that says 'Life is like this' very explicitly.

And here I had better pause and explain myself, especially explain myself to those for whom 'didactic' is a term of mild contempt, among whom even 'teaching story' and 'explicitly' are suspect. Short form (if a mildly pretentious form)—*Ars gratia artis* is not the only Latin formula around; there is also *utile et dulce*. Indeed, it has only been relatively recently (say, since the late nineteenth-century Decadents) that it has been widely fashionable to believe that capital 'A' Art exists and exists for its own sake. The more usual idea was that art (small 'a' art production and appreciation) is something human beings *do* and earns its keep by instructing and entertaining, and instructing all the more effectively by entertaining at the same time. Alternatively, one can say that the wheel of fashion has turned and—or philosophical esthetics have progressed to a point that—the idea of autonomous art is untenable. One can see all art existing in a historical/cultural matrix in which art reinscribes hegemonic values and/or resists them. In that case, if consciousness is a virtue, then consciously didactic art (when it teaches good lessons) should be valued. The works I examine in *Coyote's Song* teach in ways that are politically conscious, complex, relatively open, and useful; hence, these works should be valued. To which assertion I will add the personal point that I come out of traditions in which teaching is valued and that I define my self largely as a teacher.

In a substantial body of her work, Le Guin says 'Life is like *this*' and includes in 'this' complexity and contradictions. In a passage I find quite useful, a Le Guin character says his religion is 'godless, argumentative,

---

[747] Robin Scott Wilson's section on theme in *Those Who Can* is titled, 'Theme: To Mean Intensely.' Browning's dramatic monolog 'Fra Lippo Lippi' (1853/1855) has it that the world to the artist Fra Lippo 'means intensely, and means good' (lines 313-15 [see also lines 286-309]).

and mystical' (*FIS* 175). So is, for the most part, Le Guin's.[748] The immediate point is the word 'argumentative.' so far as the central concern of religion is ultimate things, Le Guin is often a highly religious writer who sees central to religion (in the Eastern tradition) the mystical experience of the absolute individual losing individuality, opinions, and desire in the Absolute. 'But the mystic is a rare bird' ('VEMS' 1971: 88), Le Guin asserts; the rest of us, who are not adept at mysticism, argue about the world. Le Guin argues. She argues with other authors, with her culture, and with Le Guin, and sometimes contradicts Le Guin. In much of her work Le Guin is a philosophical *auteur*, returning to a limited set of topics and examining them from a number of different angles—like William Shakespeare on political calculation vs. magnanimity, Stanley Kubrick on male violence, or Terry Gilliam on Romance. In Le Guin's argumentative religion, opposites are inseparably joined, affirming and denying inherently related. Le Guin in her works is presenting her contribution to what Aldous Huxley called 'the Perennial Philosophy,' combining different aspects in her own version of a magnanimously syncretic Eastern Mysticism.[749] In the metaphor of my title, the Coyote's song is a many-track chorus, and (occasionally) a richly, joyously dissonant chorus.

* * * * * * *

So Le Guin is a Daoist and a great respecter of the Compassionate Buddha who put off Nirvana to return to the karmic wheel to bring all of us out of multiplicity to Oneness with the Absolute—*and* Le Guin usually finds one not only the loneliest of numbers (as a bad old song has it) but a very dangerous number: the monotheist number for the One God ('Hear, O Israel, the LORD our God, the LORD is one'), the number idealized by totalitarians with one single, simple totalizing Truth, rationalists with one utilitarian motto or one mold for all to fit into.[750] Or the vision of 'the one true God, immanent in all things. Everywhere, forever' that torments the protagonist in 'The Field of Vision' (1973) and is not something of which Le Guin approves.

'*To be whole is to be part*,' as Odo's tombstone has it in *The Dispossessed* (1974), '*true journey is return*' (68; ch. 3). To be whole is to be part of a human society and culture, and Le Guin spends a good deal of time showing her readers anthropologists looking at human societies, or just showing us, without literal anthropologists, relatively good societies we

---

[748] The gods Kali (female) and the dancing Shiva (male) figure strongly in Le Guin's poems collected in *Hard Words and Other Poems* (1981). See my discussion of Le Guin's poetry.
[749] Huxley borrowed the phrase from Leibniz: the Baron Gottfried Wilhelm von Leibniz, also spelled 'Leibnitz.'
[750] I quote the usual English translation of the Sh'ma (Deuteronomy 6.4, quoted by Jesus, with approval, in Mark 12.29).

can find eutopian, or bad ones we should find dystopian.[751] But being humanly whole and part is not *just* participation in a decent society and culture; to return is to return *home,* and what home is is both complicated—a good society for being *in* the world—and the simplest thing in the universe. Literally the simplest thing. 'Return is the movement of DAO' (*Tao te Ching* ch. 40 [Wilhelm 45]); therefore true journey is return and return home: return to the One of being and beyond the One to the unnamable Dao of nonbeing.

In the response mentioned earlier to the *SFS* 1975 Le Guin issue, Le Guin said that 'The central image/idea of Taoism is an important thing to be clear about, certainly not because it's a central theme in my work. It's a central theme, period' (45). In responding to David Ketterer on *The Left Hand of Darkness* in *SFS* #6 (1975), Le Guin described herself as 'an unconsistent Taoist and a consistent unChristian' (139). Le Guin, I think, is a quite consistent syncretic Daoist if we allow a gloss from *The Lathe of Heaven* and an emphasis from the ki'O people of the planet O in 'Another Story' (1994). In *Lathe*, Le Guin sets up as an norm 'people without resentment, without hate.... People who never go cross-grained to the universe...[who] recognize evil, and resist evil, and yet are utterly unaffected by it...[who] have returned in pure compassion to the wheel,...who follow the way that cannot be followed without knowing they follow it' (99; ch. 7). In 'Another Story,' Le Guin values the ki'O: good Daoists in practice though not name, but Daoists for whom 'The name of our world is the first word of its first prayer. For human beings' on O, religion's 'vehicle is the human voice and mind' (*FIS* 175). Le Guin is very much a low-church, really-big-vessel Daoist who places people into the world, onto the Karmic wheel of everyday. That which truly *is* is the Dao, the Way, the river of (non)Being. 'But,' again, 'the mystic is a rare bird,' and most of us everyday pigeons and sparrows and noisy woodpeckers will not be transcending the world of illusion (*maya* in the Hindu formulation) or sinking into the Dao but live *in* the world, with, with luck, occasional contact with the Absolute, the Dao, the truly Real. Le Guin is philosophically a mystic but of the practical, worldly Chinese variety: a mystic who might figuratively hit you with her handbag as part of her teaching, or seem very somber while making a sly joke.[752]

From this basically Daoist ontology—idea/image of what the universe really is—follows a highly relativist epistemology, a theory of knowledge. If that which is is immanent in all things, to really touch reality is not to transcend the world and get a God's-eye view but to feel connected to all

---

[751] For Le Guin and anthropology, see Bittner, *Approaches* 88 and passim (see Barr 114). Note Carol D. Stevens's insightful joking reference to anthropology as 'the Family Business' in the title to her 1989 SFRA presentation (q.v. in the biblio. at the end of this volume).
[752] Zen masters, as Le Guin reminded me, will concentrate the attention of disciples by the Wordless Teaching of quite literally hitting them on the head (see *Tao te Ching* II.43; Wilhelm 47, Waley 197).

of the world. The early Greek physicist Archimedes is said to have said that if you gave him a place to stand and place his machine he could move the world. Archimedes knew there was no 'Archimedean point' to rest his machine on: you cannot get physically outside the world. In the Daoist view (agreed with on this point by Jacques Derrida and the postStructuralists), you cannot get outside the world even to just take a look.[753] So: one cannot physically get outside the world to push things around, and one cannot get outside the world to see where one should push things if one could. There is no avoiding 'the immanence of all critique' ('Knowledge' 260). Hence, there can be moments of insight, but no final, fixed certainty, no overarching theories of which way lies God's Kingdom or the proletarian paradise or even Progress (*LoH* 82; ch. 6 & passim).[754] More exactly, there can be and are such theories, but such theories are dangerous, as is any idea of a single transcendent God or principle or 'metanarrative' to justify such theories. Le Guin is a consistent critic of the Judeo-Christian-Rationalist West primarily because monotheists and rationalists have potentially dangerous ideas about what they—or we—can know about the world and what can be done in the world.

Politics / Ownership

From this ontology and epistemology follows a politics and a politically significant theory of ownership.

If there is no Archimedean point or mystic mountain on which to stand to get long-range, long-term visions, if the best we can hope for is an occasional flash of insight or feelings of what we must do right here, now—in that case, there is very little to be said in favor of what President George Bush once called 'the vision thing.' No place to have the visions, then no person or class can consistently and reliably claim to have such visions and obtain from them the mandate of heaven to impose such visions. Hence, no reliable, permanent aristocracy claiming privileges because they claim leadership. Hence no leaders for life, no permanent kings, no fully reliable codes of Law. Very logically (although they did not particularly approve of logic), the early Daoists became the first formal anarchists. What the Emperor can best do is *wu wei*, action through stillness, and let his people do their things, with leaders arising as needed, or not (see *Tao te Ching* ch. 43). This theory of leadership—do without hierarchical, can-do, let's get moving leaders—made the early Daoists political birds be-

---

[753] In a review that arrived while I was drafting this chapter, Andrew M. Butler says that Derrida found inadequate the Structuralist idea of everything as system, holding, on the contrary 'that system is not enough, that there is no point outside of the system from where the structure [of the system] can be seen as a structure' (113).

[754] For A. L. Kroeber on progress as a bad principle in anthropology, see *Anthropology* § 5, 'Evolutionary Processes and Evolutionist Fancies,' *Anthropology: Biology and Race* (6-7).

coming in our time almost as rare as mystics: conservatives. As Aldous Huxley wrote in 1946, with useful hyperbole, 'For the last thirty years there have been no conservatives; there have been only nationalistic radicals of the right and nationalistic radicals of the left'—and he helpfully identifies the 'last conservative statesman' he knows of as the fifth Marquess of Lansdowne, who attempted to get published a suggestion for ending World War I with a compromise (*Brave New World* Foreword xi). Le Guin speaks very positively of change, but it must be true change, radical change: bottom-up, from the *roots* change, mediated by some person or people in touch with the Dao. In traditional, Aboriginal Australian terms, such changes are changes only in the everyday world; rightly understood, they are already-present ways brought into everyday life from the timeless Dream-Time. In more Western, if ancient, terms, such changes were brought by word from a reliable oracle or a true prophet and strongly contrasted by the Prophet Samuel with the rule of a king, pushing things, and people, around regularly, systematically (1 Samuel 8.10-21).

The Daoists went further: no oracles at Delphi, no God or gods that sent the Word. The truest Oracle would be one older than Daoism: the *I Ching* to indicate what one should do to go with the Dao at this moment, throwing the yarrow sticks to see what course might prove lucky. This all means, by our standards, very infrequent change, very little action.

Le Guin usually values everyday complexity—the texture of the ten thousand things, "thick' description,' 'thick planned' richness (*FIS* 88, 173); still, her theory of ownership is very simple. In a world where Ultimate Reality is like a river, and you are ordinarily on the surface of the river, all is flux, and ideas like 'permanent address' or 'real property' or 'ownership in perpetuity' make no sense. You came into the world with empty hands; you will leave the world with empty hands; and in the meantime you can and will use all sorts of things (and plants and animals and people) but cannot legitimately or really possess them, own them. We have not been dispossessed but *are* dispossessed in the sense that we can not firmly possess anything (see *TD* 22; ch. 2). Le Guin's writing is informed with Daoist-inspired and thoroughly modern *communist* anarchism.[755]

* * * * * * *

---

[755] Those new to the study of politics and Le Guin, might do best to take the word 'anarchy' literally and only literally: 'an-archy': no government, no state. That the absence of a state would lead to violent chaos is a point to be argued, but not assumed; the historical anarchies of Native Australians and the Indians of California were quite sedate. Similarly for 'communism': take the term literally, radically, and unscientifically by Marxian standards, as just the possession and control of the means of production and administration by the community, no private property whatever, with people having rights of *use*.

Also implicit in a syncretic Daoist vision of the world are some of Le Guin's key images, two highly stressed words, a system of tolerance and solidarity, and a value judgment.

The most obvious images are the verbally described symbols in Le Guin's stories and the printer's marks in Le Guin's short story collections. The circle apparently completed is a central symbol in *Planet of Exile* (1966); the circle almost but not quite completed is the Odonian Circle of Life in *The Dispossessed* (1974) and is the shape of the story of its hero, Shevek. In the collection *The Wind's Twelve Quarters*, the printer's mark is the Yin-Yang symbol in the Yin-on-top configuration.[756] In *Always Coming Home*, the central symbol is the heyiya-if: an open-hinge, a far more open-ended variation on Yin-Yang. And in *Buffalo Gals and Other Stories* (1987), the printer's mark is a dancing woman icon: what may be an American Indian woman or a more generic Woman, dancing the world. The more subtle images are of water generally (as an 'element') and streams and rivers and oceans more particularly.[757] As an element, water can be associated, and is associated in much Chinese thought, with Yin as the yielding, the tranquil, the female principle, and water is associated with earth and the immanent as opposed to (and complementing) heaven and the transcendent Yang of the Yin-Yang dynamic (Wing-tsit 419). Water is both changing and quite constant, depending on whether you look at the surface or the depths. Water appears weak because it moves where you put it, but it is, of course, very strong: water cannot be destroyed; water wears away rock.[758] As ocean, water easily symbolizes Dao as source and place of return, like earth, the symbolic Mother. As stream or river, water also symbolizes Dao: the flowing Way, churning up the ten thousand things of the everyday world but remaining always itself. So Ogion suggests in his stream image in *A Wizard of Earthsea* in 1968; so we see with the River Oro in 'Another Story' in 1994.

The words I shall draw attention to are 'pain' and 'joy,' 'risk,' 'safety,' and 'home.' Most famously in Buddhism, pain is an unavoidable consequence of the fall from Oneness into multiplicity, i.e., into life in what most Westerners, most of the time, consider the world. Our separation from the real reality of things into empirical experience is the ultimate source of our pain. This initial Fall, though, is succeeded in history by sub-

---

[756] The Yin-Yang symbol can also be drawn with a vertical axis and arranged so that '*Light is the left hand of darkness / and darkness the right hand of light*' (Tormer's Lay, *LHD* 233; ch. 15). That is also the configuration given in *Encyclopaedia Britannica*: Micropaedia, 1974: 'yin-yang.' The flag of the Republic of (South) Korea has the horizontal configuration as in *WTQ*, with red-orange on top (yin) and azure-blue on the bottom (yang).
[757] In the West, from the time of Empedocles in the fifth c. BCE through the seventeenth c. CE, the usual elements were Fire, Air, Water, and Earth (for the dates, *Encyclopædia Britannica* Micropædia, 'elements, prescientific'). Chinese theory had it as Fire, Water, Earth, Wood, and Metal (*Encyclopædia Britannica* Macropædia 'Chinese Philosophy,' diagram of Chou Tun-i, 4.419).
[758] *Tao te Ching* ch. 43 (see Waley 197). See 'Legends' 5.

sequent falls moving us farther and farther away from life in nature into lives in cultures that alienate us from who we are, from human community, from the reality of things. So of course we are in pain, as fragments in a fragmented world: a pain underlying and augmented by all the everyday pains human flesh is heir to, plus the additional ones we—individually, in groups, as cultures—inflict upon others and ourselves. To move back into relationship moves us toward joy; achieving relationship gives us (for a moment) joy; ultimate relationship (for a moment) with All, gives us (for a moment) pure joy: in J. R. R. Tolkien's formulation, 'a fleeting glimpse of Joy, Joy beyond the walls of the world.'[759] To return to true relationship, though, almost always involves risk, leaving the apparent safety of houses, cities, and the high-tech cultures we think of as home, back to truer homes in nature. Repeatedly in Le Guin's canon, one may find most joy, most of a *heimlich*, 'home-ly' sense of joy, dancing the dance of Shiva, but without being an immortal god: 'The dance is always danced above the hollow place, above the terrible abyss' (*FS* [1972] 121; ch. 8), 'Dancing on the brink of the world' ('World Making' [1981]: *DEW* 48). As with many Romantics, Le Guin feels we may be most at home when most outdoors, in nature—exposed.

Among people who cannot find one absolute Truth, among people in pain, it is sensible to be tolerant of others and, as much as possible find solidarity with others. Still, a number of value judgments follow from these ideas and I shall stress one: a judgment on the traditional Hero. As Joseph Campbell and his predecessors and followers have documented in detail, one of the great stories of the world is the Monomyth of the Hero. Often it is a story of bringing great and apparently permanent changes, of conquests or resisting conquests—in any event, actively making things *happen*. In much of her canon, Le Guin presents an anti- or unMonomyth.[760] In 'An die Musik' (1961), *Rocannon's World*, and *Planet of Exile* (1966), we have fairly traditional (male) heroes, but from at least *The Left Hand of Darkness* (1969), *The Lathe of Heaven* (1971), and *The Word for World Is Forest* (1972), Le Guin has been interrogating and critiquing the Hero myth with insight and, especially in *Word for World* and some of her recent works, with strong feeling. In classic mysticism, warriors are important metaphors (Capra 27; ch. 2), and there are Eastern incarnation of the Hero with a Thousand Faces; but Heroes cannot push around water very successfully or for very long, and Daoism values far more the quiet Way of the Sage, the contemplative. One of the ways in which Le Guin has been a feminist from early on is her questioning of traditional male heroism and her attempt to find a different model, from anatomically and physiologically androgynous Estraven in *The Left Hand of Darkness* in 1969 to 'My Hero' in 1994 (in *Peacocks*), to the fully androgynous hero in 'Coming of Age in Karhide' in 1995.

---

[759] Tolkien's *Tree and Leaf* (1964), quoted in Jackson 154-55.
[760] See 'The Carrier Bag Theory of Fiction,' coll. *DEW*.

So, in good Daoist fashion, nothing has changed in Le Guin's work in all these years, and much has changed. Her style has gotten more colloquial, lower-flown, so to speak, if, for example, one compares the language of *Tehanu* with the language of the Earthsea trilogy, or the voice of Sov in 'Coming of Age in Karhide' to most of the voices in *The Left Hand of Darkness*. As I have indicated, her heroes have changed—they are now often women; the men are more domestic—and Le Guin's language is now more openly and sometimes angrily feminist: Le Guin as an 'aging, angry woman laying mightily about' with a 'handbag, fighting hoodlums off' ('Carrier Bag,' *DEW* 168). The *fact* of Le Guin's using the voice of an 'aging, angry woman' is significant (see Cummins, 1993: ch. 6, 'Recent Fiction'). It is important for young women to hear as an authoritative voice the voice of a woman, and the voice moreover of a woman free to get both old and angry; it is also important for boys and men to hear such voices; the embedded lessons are liberating ones.

Le Guin has also come to accept more fully the Way of tolerance pretty much required by the logic of Daoism, and to move toward a celebration of the 'ten thousand things' that includes celebration of human diversity implicit in Le Guin's Ekumen and stressed in recent feminism*s*. If there is no one transcendent, spiritual, and rather puritanical god to allow and forbid, if there is no immortal soul separate from the body and living in the body like a god in a temple—then it is odd at best to condemn simple bodily pleasures.[761] So Le Guin's stories from, say, *The Dispossessed* in 1974 to 'Another Story' and 'Seggri' in 1994, have come to deal more regularly and sympathetically with lesbians, gays, bisexuals, and women who want sex, but not particularly marriage in any sense, or love and sex, but not 'the institution of monogamous marriage' (*LHD* 92; ch. 2). In *The Dispossessed*, Bedap, the one gay character, concluded he had to change his life; in 'Dancing in Ganam' (1993) and 'Another Story,' homosexual as well as heterosexual relationships are both good (and far better than heterosex*ism*), and to be praised.

* * * * * * *

The times have changed a bit, and Le Guin has changed with them. But the times have only changed a bit. If Le Guin repeats basic themes in her stories, that repetition is justified by United States society's reproducing itself quite accurately over the generations—and repeating our mistakes.[762]

---

[761] For a rhetorical question implying that there is no god to allow and forbid, see *FS* 137, ch. 9. For 'Nothing is immortal,' most especially including 'the gift of selfhood,' see *FS* 122, ch. 8.

[762] From many points of view, the USA of the 1980s and early 1990s is not all *that* different from the USA of the Gilded Age or the 1920s; more people have been brought into the system (an important improvement for many, including me), but the system itself has been quite stable. It was and is monotheistic—Judeo-Christian now, not merely Christian (and Islam coming in)—Rationalist, Western,

If Le Guin keeps embodying a basic myth in a large part of her canon, she deals with other, more literally mundane issues in the substantial body of more mundane (or mainstream) works not covered in *Coyote*. If Le Guin frequently writes works embodying her world-view and a basic myth, so do all those works using The Hero with a Thousand Faces; so did a large hunk of the vast literature of medieval Western Christianity; so do most of the texts produced and consumed every day in the Judeo-Christian-Rationalist West, in works ranging from John Updike's Rabbit books to a film like *INDEPENDENCE DAY* (1996). For Le Guin's art that can mean one basic world-view, myth—'metanarrative'—embodied in many forms: until there *is* a change, a radical one, from the roots. And such changes are infrequent. The Monomyth of the Hero and the sky-gods—or, more exactly, their hegemony—has had a course of over 4,000 years; we need in the West other voices, with other, equally powerful myths. Le Guin has such a myth, and in a large number of works she has embodied it and given it life beautifully. Perhaps most eloquently, up to the mid 1990s, she has embodied it in 'Coming of Age in Karhide,' a quiet story of a sexual rite of passage. In this story, Le Guin combines an anthropological view and Daoist myth so completely with a new kind of hero that we may miss—consciously—the lesson taught: that we can tell stories without the old Hero, without the sky-gods, mostly without conflict. We, or Le Guin anyway, can tell a story of very ordinary people in their world, who are extraordinary to us, and so accomplish, perhaps, another artistic coming of age for Le Guin, and aid the coming of age of American SF.

As one of Frederik Pohl and C. M. Kornbluth's less reputable characters says at his moment of recognition and conversion, 'It is an axiom of my trade'—the advertising business—'that things are invisible except against a contrasting background' (*Space Merchants* 173; ch. 14). Even for those who see themselves rebelling against Western culture, the contrast Le Guin offers is useful and probably necessary. There is a Judeo-Christian-Rationalist culture, and we, even communist-atheist feminists among that 'we,' are embedded in it. To be confronted with a consistently unChristian, unJewish, unWestern, unPatriarchal, intellectual, reason-respecting but Romantic and antiRationalist position—that, for most of us, is highly educational.[763]

Kulturkampf on the Left, Revisited

> ...of quitting our animosities and factions, nor acting any longer like the Jews, who were murdering one another at the very moment their city was taken.... — Jonathan Swift, 'A Modest Proposal' (*Norton Anthology* 1.2150)

---

hierarchical and patriarchal (though more subtly so), imperial when we can do it cheaply, always capitalist.
[763] See Le Guin's 'Response' 45.

> Tell a group of Leftists to form a firing squad, and they get into a circle. — Joke, old by the 1960s[764]

Le Guin's argument with monotheists, militarists, machismo, and tunnel-visioned rationalists is straightforward. Less clear but equally interesting is what, in a review of Le Guin's *Four Ways to Forgiveness* (1995) for *New Scientist*, Ian Watson talks of as 'a subdialogue with feminist critics'; or what Le Guin refers to in *Earthsea Revisioned* (1992) as her wrestling 'with the angels of the feminist consciousness' (11). Or what Marleen Barr referred to when she spoke of Le Guin, *in malo* (in an aspect Barr does not like) as 'this female writer who seems to appeal to everyone—with the exception of feminists....' (112). Indeed, in *Four Ways to Forgiveness*, there is a 'subdialogue' with those who 'have chided Le Guin for presenting men as the doers and women as the more passive founts of being' (Watson 48)—with Le Guin answering their objections with women in the *Four Ways* novellas *doing* and being in the world, men being and doing. And, since the 1980s, Le Guin has found her own voice as a woman and has given us girls and women as primary protagonists in some works, and has gotten over her mild case of heterosexism. There may still remain, though, some residual hostility in the 'subdialogue' coming from some feminist critics, and this is the unclear part. Part of the problem stems from the use of unmodified 'feminists' as a mass-noun and Le Guin's '*the* feminist consciousness' as a simple singular. For even a first-approximation oversimplification, we still need to get more specific. Most of the complaints about Le Guin's work come not so much from feminists generally but with some academic feminists fairly specifically. (Or these complaints *did* come until some time around 1989, when Le Guin won the Pilgrim Award from the academics of the Science Fiction Research Association.)

Briefly, and as that first-approximation oversimplification, I think Le Guin has had her most basic problems with feminists who are also secular, Leftist, more or less Frankfort-School, Gramscian academics (Di Leonardo 35), unused to seeing the Enemy as the religious Right or militarists and capitalists or fascists but in a variation of the Great Satan of the Sixties: Liberals and, later, White, Euro-American liberal men and our female fellow-travelers. And still later, among academics in literary studies, seeing as basic to the struggle, 'the opposing interests of the dissident literary left and the status-quo-perpetuating literary right' (Barr 112). For these critics, I will suggest, the problem was and perhaps still is Le Guin's celebration of *marriage* and Le Guin's related celebration of increasing integration, ultimately a joyous return home: integration into the world.

---

[764] Swift alludes to a historical incident: 'During the siege of Jerusalem by the Roman Emperor Titus, who captured and destroyed the city in A.D. 70, the city was torn' by murderous fighting among Jewish factions (*Norton* I.2150 n. 5). The joke about ally-destroying Leftists is also told (with equal truth and equal falsehood) about the Right.

Obviously, there were problems early on with a celebration of literal marriage: literal heterosexual marriage is crucial for patriarchy. Moving into the 1980s, however, Le Guin's work acknowledged that the 'central glory' to a life of even a good literal marriage 'can happen and be done with by the age of twenty-two' (*BP* 102; ch. 4). Still 'marriage' for Le Guin is metaphoric as well as literal, as nicely stated in James W. Bittner's assertion (quoted in part by Marleen Barr [111-12]) that when Le Guin 'says that marriage is 'the central, consistent theme' of her work, we can understand her to be referring to any complementary, correlative, or interdependent relationship between what we may perceive as opposites or dualisms, but which are in reality aspects of a whole, or moments in a continuous process.' Since such 'complementarity, represented by the yin-yang circle, encompasses Le Guin's theme of marriage, being both more general and abstract than the idea of marriage, yet also more specific and concrete' Bittner uses it 'to define not only Le Guin's central theme, but also her fictional techniques, her modes of thought, and ultimately, her world view' (*Approaches* x-xi).

In much of her canon, Le Guin is engaged in a 'subdialogue' over marriage and over the potential for joyous being at home in the world. This idea is crucial for Le Guin and has been problematic for some—at least three major—feminist critics.[765] For two quite respectable examples: Marleen Barr in her insightful 1987 review of Bittner's *Approaches* and Rosemary Jackson, in her still influential and impressive *Fantasy: The Literature of Subversion* (1981).

Barr limits herself to Le Guin's works covered in Bittner's *Approaches*, except for *Always Coming Home*, which she adds to note an important change and improvement. Barr quotes a justly well-known passage in Joanna Russ's *The Female Man* (1975), where Jeannine Nancy Dadier claims that all she did was

> defer to The Man
> entertain The Man
> keep The Man
> live for The Man. (*Female Man* Three.I)

—plus several lines from *Female Man* Four.XI to the same effect. Barr is not referring to Phyllis Schlafly of the Eagle Forum, 'Leading the pro-family movement since 1972,' as their very professional home page slogan puts it. She is talking about Le Guin's use of male protagonists and 'the oppressor's language.' Barr's discussion is under the general rubric of Le Guin as 'The good witch of the west,' who 'waves her literary wand, unites magic and science and fiction—and, poof, she eradicates reality's oppositions and conflicts.' Alternatively put, Barr found in Bittner's analysis 'that Le Guin embraced a stance which opposes the objectives of

---

[765] The third is Sarah Lefanu, and some might add to the short list Joanna Russ. See my discussions of *LHD* and *TD*.

feminist discourse,' primarily the objectives of eschewing the language of male oppressors and developing a women's language. 'Feminist writers, particularly feminist SF writers who imagine separatist societies, advocate that women should learn the Truth about themselves and their world by moving towards the female self; Le Guin arrives at this Truth by moving away from herself. Feminism, then, is Le Guin's other hand, which remains outside her marrying of left and right hands, her universal appeal and complementarity' (Barr 112-13).

Barr goes on to agree with Bittner that Le Guin quite early moved from Isaac Asimov as literary father to A. L. Kroeber, her biological father—and finds this a radically dual act. On the one hand, Bittner, Barr asserts, 'in effect suggests' that Le Guin 'ignores half the ground from which she sprang: her mother.' On the other hand, it is major progress for Le Guin to go from Asimov to Kroeber: 'a crucial step for the development of SF in general and feminist SF in particular,' especially since Le Guin then goes from Kroeber to Odo in 'The Day Before the Revolution' to *Always Coming Home*—and a return in *ACH* to Theodora Kroeber's work in *The Inland Whale*. Barr suggests we see *Always Coming Home* as Le Guin's 'rejection of the Father and her return to the Mother,' and here Barr can use 'marriage' positively. In *Always Coming Home* (and thereafter), Le Guin 'can finally marry her own right (in the sense of 'correct') revolutionary views with the left views of feminism' (Barr 114-15).

Revolution in a correct cause married with feminism—fine; marriage in the sense Bittner identifies as 'complementarity,' however, is problematic or worse for Barr. Suspicion of complementarity is even more strongly the case with Rosemary Jackson, who in addition strongly objects to Le Guin's mystic home-comings. So Jackson may be a better example than Barr (except she is not so careful a reader as Barr).

Jackson discussed the Earthsea trilogy, *City of Illusions*, and *The Left Hand of Darkness* in the same figurative breath as the fantasies of J. R. R. Tolkien, C. S. Lewis, T. H. White, George MacDonald, and Charles Kingsley of *The Water Babies* ('a classic text of repression,' in Jackson's phrase, and an antirevolutionary, snobbish, and racist one to boot [Jackson 151]). In her brief section on Le Guin (154-55), Jackson (1) sees 'a dark 'other'' in the Earthsea trilogy 'magically defeated' in traditional romance manner, (2) objects to the combining of two into one in Falk and Ramarren in *City of Illusions*, and (3) objects even more strongly that '*The Left Hand of Darkness* synthesizes male and female, light and darkness, life and death,' and has Le Guin insisting in that book 'that left and right are synthesized, are as one.' Not exactly. In the Earthsea trilogy, the one 'other' defeated is Cob in *Farthest Shore*, and Cob is associated with grey and with the light of immortality as much as with darkness, and the way he opens between the worlds is 'void': 'Through it was neither light nor dark, neither life nor death' (183; ch. 12). The Nameless Ones in *The Tombs of Atuan* lose their tombstone symbols and get some of their real estate destroyed, but no human defeats the Old Powers of the Earth, and Ged in *Tombs* does not defeat them; he robs them. Nor could Ged defeat his

Shadow in *A Wizard of Earthsea*. In his encounter with his Shadow, Ged 'had neither lost nor won' but had become 'whole,' and Jackson can complain legitimately that the process certainly sounds like synthesis. Ged and the Shadow say 'Ged' simultaneously, and '...the two voices were one voice,' and when Ged and the Shadow reach out for each other, 'Light and darkness met, and joined, and were one' (179-80; ch. 10). But Ged and his Shadow are one as the Yin-Yang is one: light/dark, black/white, like Ged's face after Ged was wounded by his Shadow (and like Tehanu later, as girl and dragon); they are a balance, not a synthesis in the sense of mixture or even compound. As Douglas Barbour insisted and James W. Bittner developed at some length, the issue is always 'Wholeness and Balance'—a Yin-Yang balance, not synthesis (see Le Guin's 'Response').

Jackson is only mostly correct, then, in seeing Le Guin's works up to 1969 as 'romances (of integration)' as opposed to 'fantasies (of dualism)' such as Mary Shelley's *Frankenstein*, Robert Louis Stevenson's *Dr. Jekyll and Mr. Hyde*, or much of the canon of Charles Dickens. As Estraven explains to Ai, Gethenian androgynes live in biological wholeness, but they 'are dualists too. Duality is an essential.... So long as there is *myself* and *the other*' (*LHD* 234; ch. 16).[766] Jackson's emphasis upon synthesis in Le Guin's works reinforces Jackson's placement of Le Guin among the Christians and leads Jackson to place Le Guin to the right of not just mildly-liberal reformer like Dickens but also to the right of Edgar Allen Poe and Franz Kafka.

Jackson sees 'fantasies (of dualism)' allowing the interrogation of 'the cost of constructing an ego, thereby challenging the very foundation of symbolic cultural order'; whereas Le Guin's and other's 'romances (of integration)' leave 'problems of social order untouched' (155). Again, not exactly. Egos are not constructed cheaply by Ged, Tenar, Arren, or other of Le Guin's early characters, and in the Earthsea series a social order *is* being constructed; for good and for ill, Earthsea is being united under a king. In *City of Illusions*, humans live a 'good life' in the Forest, but not a life chosen; the Shing 'took choice and freedom from men.' *City of Illusions* deals with Shing imperialism and the *forcing* of people into immanence eschewing 'the great machines,' and preventing them from gathering 'in groups or towns or nations to do any great work together' (18-19; ch. 1). And *Left Hand of Darkness* contrasts rather anarchic Karhide, under a King (and the brief rule of a protofascist prime minister), with Stalinist Orgoreyn, with Karhide coming through as the more promising.

It is not fair to say the early Le Guin habitually left 'problems of social order untouched'; she dealt with political questions rather more directly than Poe or Mary Shelley in *Frankenstein* but in ways other than Sigmund Freudian or Jacques Lacanian. I don't want to put words in Jackson's mouth—I wouldn't want the psychoanalytically inclined to even begin to

---

[766] Hence, it was not *philosophically* a big deal when Le Guin came to celebrate single-sex marriage: '*myself* and *the other*' is all that is necessary for a duality; different sex is just «to boot»—additional difference.

deal with the imagery of that expression!—but I think the most useful formulation of Jackson's brief against Le Guin is that Jackson sees the psychologically, esthetically, and politically best fantasy—the fantasy worthiest of the name—as that which deals with the uncanny, *das Unheimlich*.

> As Freud points out, there are two levels of meaning to the German terms for the uncanny, *das Unheimlich*...*Das Heimlich*, the un-negated version, is ambivalent. On the first level of meaning, it signifies that which is homely, familiar, friendly, cheerful, comfortable, intimate. It gives a sense of being 'at home' in the world, and its negation therefore summons up the unfamiliar, uncomfortable, strange, alien. It [*das Unheimlich*] produces a feeling of estrangement, of being not 'at home' in the world.... *Das Heimlich* also means that which is concealed from others. Its negation, *das Unheimlich*, then functions to dis-cover, reveal, expose areas normally kept out of sight.... The uncanny...uncovers what is hidden and, by doing so, effects a disturbing transformation of the familiar into the unfamiliar.
>
> Fantastic literature transforms the 'real' through this kind of dis-covery, It does not introduce novelty, so much as uncover all that needs to remain hidden if the world is to be comfortably 'known.' Its uncanny effects reveal an obscure, occluded region which lies behind the homely (*heimlich*) and native (*heimisch*). (65)

Instead of giving us dualisms which 'dis-cover,' for example, 'bestial elements within the human,' Le Guin and other practitioners of 'Modern 'faery' literature,' Jackson asserts, give us 'miraculous unities': 'myths of psychic order which help to contain critiques of disorder. Their utopianism does not directly engage with divisions or contradictions of subjects *inside* human culture: their harmony is established on a mystical cosmic level' (154). And it is here that Jackson offers one prooftext from Le Guin, from *City of Illusions*: 'for there is in the long run no disharmony, only misunderstanding, no chance or mischance but only the ignorant eye' (189, n. 9 [quoting the London edn.]). The full quotation is significant. I quoted it in my discussion of *City* and will repeat it here, with some key lines emphasized. Ramarren, the intellectual, a high-born leader among an elite civilization,

> sought with all his trained intelligence some way in which he could turn his situation about and become the controller instead of the one controlled: for so his Kelshak mentality presented his case to him. Seen rightly, any situation, even a chaos or a trap would come clear and lead of itself to its one proper outcome: *for there is in the long run no dis-*

> harmony, only misunderstanding, no chance or mischance but only the ignorant eye. **So Ramarren thought**, and the second soul within him, Falk, took no issue with this view, but spent no time trying to think it all out either. For Falk had seen the dull and bright stones slip across the wires of the patterning frame, and had lived with men in their fallen estate, kings in exile on their own domain..., and to him it seemed that no man could make his fate or control the game, but only wait for the bright jewel luck to slip by on the wire of time. Harmony exists, but there is no understanding it; the Way cannot be gone. So while Ramarren racked his mind, Falk lay low and waited. And when the chance came he caught it.

Or rather...he was caught by it. (207-08; ch.10, my emphasis)

Ramarren thinks the lines quoted by Jackson; Falk, the Narrator, and Le Guin take a rather more nuanced view. Jackson was and is right, though—and Barr, too—that Le Guin believes in harmony, and believes that harmony has a cosmic basis and spiritual significance for which 'mystic,' in its denotations, is correct. Falk has a sense of that harmony, and he feels at home in the world. From Estraven to George Orr in the early *Left Hand* and *Lathe of Heaven* to Serenity in 'Solitude' and Sov in 'Coming of Age in Karhide' (1994-95), Le Guin's heroes typically get in contact with the universe, sometimes before important social action, or, with Serenity, *as* important social action. Quite consistently, Le Guin has suggested we should feel at home in the universe and, when that is what one *must* do, act in the universe.

But, living in a decade of tell-all tabloid journalism, I see nothing necessarily radical in any dis-coveries of a psychologically juicy nature. Living in a century where alienation and atomization cause daily anguish and frequent apathy, I see nothing good in itself in reinforcing them. And living in the late twentieth century, I will assert that really alienated people, almost totally unable to find true homes, can find substitutes in nationalistic mass movements, militant fundamentalist churches, and Aryan militias. With a nicely grotesque irony, Eric Hoffer may have become a True Believer and apologist for horrors during U.S. warfare in Indochina in the 1960s, but his 1951 analysis of fanaticism in *The True Believer* makes some sound points, relevant unto our day. What he calls 'frustration'—severe alienation—can be a precursor of mindless absolute commitment to a transcendent cause far more often than it leads to radical (and immanent) social critique. Reading E. A. Poe or H. P. Lovecraft is not likely to make alienated people into social democrats or Greenpeace activists or politically active feminists. Helping them feel more at home in the world could make it easier for alienated people to ask radical questions of our cultures and societies.

Le Guin's great contribution to this *Kulturkampf* on the Left is presenting an alternative ideology that is *heimlich*, that suggests ways of living in the world. That it is an alternative ideology very unlike Christianity, Capitalism, Marxism, and most of the fashionable academic ideologies, makes it useful just existing: the mere existence of an accessible Daoism (more generally a syncretic Perennial Philosophy) contrasts with and highlights—makes visible—some of the ideological presuppositions in even highly sophisticated political consciousness and certainly sloshing around in most of the political unconscious.

In the myth behind the Judeo-Christian-(Islamic)-Rationalist West, in the beginning was chaos and the Void, and the Word of a transcendent God brought cosmos out of that chaos. As in the beginning, even so today—for some forty percent to perhaps two-thirds of US adults, if Cornel West has his numbers correct—'A mighty fortress is our God,' holding off chaos and evil. And as in the heavens, so on earth: our Kings, rulers, and magistrates keep godly order, holding off 'chaos and even anarchy'—and, often enough, equality and democracy.[767] From the point of view of such a tradition, only God and the 'eternal consciousness in a man,' prevent a universe where, 'at the foundation of all' there is 'only a wildly seething power which writhing with obscure passions produced' and/or produces 'everything that is great and everything that is insignificant.' And from such a view, Søren Kierkegaard asks rhetorically, 'if a bottomless void never satiated lay hidden beneath all—what then would life be but despair?' (*Fear and Trembling* [30]; 'A Panegyric Upon Abraham'). Le Guin answers this myth directly, following the part of the Perennial Philosophy that gets rid of God and the Word and has the eternal Void, not 'writhing with obscure passions' but usually flowing rather serenely: NonBeing producing Being, the Dao producing Yin-Yang, producing all beings. To an alienated ego, without a personal God who loves *me*, there is only Chaos and the Abyss, and my existence is suffering while dangling over the Abyss. Le Guin says we should stop being alienated egos and try being our Selves, and join the dance over the Abyss. Live a while in the world, responsibly, consciously—suffer and enjoy—and then die and lose selfhood in Sheol or Hades or the Dry Land or whatever more or less poetic metaphor we choose for dying and being dead—or, and better, rejoin the Dao or Brahman and dissolve in the sea of (non)Being. Meanwhile, though, live in the world as *part* of the world, at home in the world.

That Le Guin offers a nearly complete, but not totalizing, *heimlich* ideology—one that includes the religious (or spiritual) mode—makes it a strong alternative to the ruling ideologies in all their alienation. For readers as unconsciously at home in the universe as many of my students, Le Guin's more gentle works are a good way to get into the habit of seeing the arbitrariness and strangeness of Western society. For those of us sufficiently alienated that we find Kafka's stories mostly just realistic, Le Guin

---

[767] Cornel West, interview in *The Progressive* 61.1 (Jan. 1997): 26. I quote from memory the first line and title of Martin Luther's 'A Mighty Fortress Is Our God,' in English, and a phrase implying that anarchy is worse than chaos, used by a student of mine, and which I have seen in the work of professional journalists.

offers a truly countercultural approach to living, the possibility for a critique of society both immanent and radical, and a Way home. This makes Le Guin a challenging and inspiring teacher in her works, and, to restate that assertion, a highly subversive author. Coyote's song, if we will listen, will act in the world.

>'Is it revolution, Havzhiva?'
>'It is education, ma'am.' ('A Man of the People,' *FIS* 130)

ABBREVIATIONS

WORKS BY URSULA K. LE GUIN

FREQUENTLY USED ABBREVIATIONS (and selected short forms):

ACH: *Always Coming Home*
BP: *The Beginning Place*
BG: *Buffalo Gals and Other Animal Presences* (Collection)
CI: *City of Illusions*
'Coming of Age': 'Coming of Age in Karhide'
CR: *The Compass Rose* (Collection)
DEW: *Dancing at the Edge of The World: Thoughts on Words, Women, Places* (Collection, mostly essays)
EoH: *Eye of the Heron*
ER: *Earthsea Revisioned*. (Lecture)
FIS: *A Fisherman of the Inland Sea* (Collection, fiction)
FS: *The Farthest Shore*
FWF: *Four Ways to Forgiveness* (Collection, four novellas)
Hard Words: *Hard Words and Other Poems* (Collection, poetry)
'Legends': 'Legends for a New Land' (Speech)
LHD: *The Left Hand of Darkness*
LoH: *The Lathe of Heaven*
LoN (1979): *The Language of the Night* (Collection, essays [original edition])
NA: 'The New Atlantis' in *The New Atlantis...*
Norton: *The Norton Book of Science Fiction*
Peacocks: *Going Out with Peacocks and Other Poems*
PE: *Planet of Exile*
'PoD': 'Pathways of Desire'
'Response': 'Response to the Le Guin Issue'
RW: *Rocannon's World*
TA: *The Tombs of Atuan*
TD: *The Dispossessed*
UA: *Unlocking the Air* (Collection, fiction)
'VEMS': 'Vaster than Empires and More Slow'
VFA: *Very Far Away from Anwhere Else*
WE: *A Wizard of Earthsea*
Wild Oats: *Wild Oats and Fireweed*. (Collection, poetry)
WTQ: *The Wind's Twelve Quarters* (Collection, fiction)
WWF: *The Word for World Is Forest*

WORKS CITED

FICTION BY URSULA K. LE GUIN

Always Coming Home. New York: Harper & Row, 1985. {*ACH*}
'An die Musik.' 1961. Coll. *Orsinian Tales.* New York: Harper, 1976.
'Another Story, OR A Fisherman of the Inland Sea.' *Tomorrow*, 1994. Coll. *FIS.*
'April in Paris.' *Fantastic* 1962. Coll. *WTQ.*
'Author of the Acacia Seeds and Other Extracts From the Journal of the Association of Therolinguistics, The.' *Fellowship of the Stars.* Ed. Terry Carr. 1974. Coll. *BG.*
Beginning Place, The. New York: Harper & Row, 1980. New York: HarperPaperbacks, 1991. {*BP*}
'Betrayals.' 1994. Coll. *FWF*, q.v.
Buffalo Gals and Other Animal Presences. Santa Barbara: Capra Press, 1987. Collection. {*BG*}
City of Illusions. New York: Ace, 1967. {*CI*}
'Coming of Age in Karhide.' *New Legends.* Ed. Greg Bear. New York: Tor Books, 1995. *The Year's Best Science Fiction.* Thirteenth Annual Collection. Ed. Gardner Dozois. New York: St. Martin's, 1996.
Compass Rose, The. 1982. New York: Bantam, 1983. Collection. {*CR*}
'Dancing to Ganam.' *Amazing* Sept. 1993. Coll. *FIS.*
'Darkness Box.' *Fantastic* 1963. Coll. *WTQ.* Toronto: Bantam, 1975.
'Day Before the Revolution, The.' *Galaxy* 1974. Coll. *WTQ.* Toronto: Bantam, 1975.
'Direction of the Road.' *Orbit 14.* Ed. Damon Knight. 1974. Coll. *BG.*
Dispossessed, The. New York: Harper & Row, 1974. New York: Avon, 1975. {*TD*}
'Ether, OR.' 1995. Coll. *Unlocking the Air and Other Stories.* New York: HarperCollins, 1996.
'Eye Altering, The.' Original version. In *Altered I*, q.v. 17-28.
''Eye Altering (II), The.' Revised version of 'The Eye Altering.' In *Altered I*, q.v. under Secondary works: 168-80.
Eye Altering, The.' Revised version of 'The Eye Altering' (= 'Eye Altering [II]' in *Altered I.*) 1976/1978. Coll. *The Compass Rose.* Toronto: Bantam, 1982.
'Eye of the Heron, The.' *Millennial Women.* Ed. Virginia Kidd. New York: Delacorte, 1978. *Eye of the Heron.* New York: Harper & Row, 1983. New York: Bantam, 1984. {*EoH*}
Farthest Shore, The. New York: Atheneum, 1972. New York: Bantam, 1975. {*FS*}
'Field of Vision, The.' *Galaxy* 1973. Coll. *WTQ.*
Fisherman of the Inland Sea, A. New York: HarperPrism, 1994. Collection. {*FIS*}
'Forgiveness Day.' 1994. Coll. *FWF*, q.v.

Four Ways to Forgiveness. New York: HarperPrism-HarperPaperbacks (Harper-Collins), 1995. Collects 'Betrayals,' *Blue Motel 1994*; 'Forgiveness Day,' *Asimov's Science Fiction* 18.12-13 (Nov. 1994): [262]-304; 'A Man of the People,' *Asimov's Science Fiction* 19.4-5 (April 1995): 22-65; 'A Woman's Liberation,' *Asimov's Science Fiction* 19.8 (July 1995): [116]-63 1995. {*FWF*}

'Hernes.' *Searoad: Chronicles of Klatsand*, by Ursula K. Le Guin. New York: HarperCollins, 1991.

'Kerastion, The.' Westercon 1990 Program Book. Coll. *Fisherman of the Inland Sea*.

Lathe of Heaven, The. New York: Scribner's, 1971. New York: Avon, 1973. {*LoH*}

Left Hand of Darkness, The. New York: Ace, 1969. Rpt. with Introd. New York: Ace, 1976. {*LHD*}

'Man of the People, A.' 1995. Coll. *FWF*, q.v.

'Matter of Seggri, The.' *Crank!: Science Fiction—Fantasy*. No. 3 (Spring 1994): 3-36.

'May's Lion.' *The Little Magazine* 14.1&2. 1981. Coll. *BG*.

'Mazes.' *Epoch*. Ed. Robert Silverberg and Roger Elwood. 1975. Coll. *BG*.

'New Atlantis, The.' In *The New Atlantis and Other Novellas of Science Fiction*. Ed. Robert Silverberg. 1975. New York: Warner, 1976. {*NA*} Also in *CR*, q.v.

'Nine Lives.' 1969. Rpt. with essay 'On Theme.' *Those Who Can....* Robin Scott Wilson, ed. New York: Mentor, 1973.

'Ones Who Walk Away from Omelas, The.' *New Dimensions 3*, 1973. Coll. *WTQ*.

Pathways of Desire, The.' 1979. Coll. *CR*, 1982. Rpt. New York: Bantam, 1983. {'**PoD**'}

Planet of Exile. New York: Ace, 1966. {*PE*}

Rocannon's World. New York: Ace, 1966. {*RW*}

'Schrödinger's Cat.' *Universe 5*. Ed. Terry Carr. 1974. Coll. *BG*.

'Semley's Necklace' (vt. 'The Dowry of the Angyar'). *Amazing* 1964. Rpt. opening of *Rocannon's World*. Coll. *WTQ*.

'She Unnames Them.' *The New Yorker*. 21 Jan. 1985. 1985. Coll. *BG*.

'Solitude.' *The Magazine of Fantasy & Science Fiction* 87.6 (Dec. 1994): [132]-59. Coll. *The Birthday of the World and Other Stories*. New York: HarperCollins, 2002.

'Stars Below, The.' *Orbit 12* (1973). Coll. *WTQ*.

'Sur' 1982. Coll. *The Compass Rose*. Toronto: Bantam, 1982.

Tehanu (The Last Book of Earthsea). New York: Atheneum, 1990.

'Things' (vt 'The End'). *Orbit 6* 1970. Coll. *WTQ*. Toronto: Bantam, 1975.

Tombs of Atuan, The. New York: Atheneum, 1971. New York: Bantam, 1975. 'A shorter version of *The Tombs of Atuan* appeared in the magazine *Worlds of Fantasy*, Winter, 1970-71, published by UPD Publishing Corporation.' {*TA*}

'Trip to the Head, A.' *Quark 1* (1970). Coll. *WTQ*. Toronto: Bantam, 1975.

Unlocking the Air and Other Stories. New York: HarperCollins, 1996. {*UA*}

'Vaster than Empires and More Slow.' *New Dimensions 1*. Ed. Robert Silverberg. Garden City, NY: Doubleday, 1971. Coll. *WTQ, BG*.

Very Far Away from Anywhere Else. New York: Atheneum, 1976. New York: Bantam, 1978. {*VFA*}

'Wife's Story, The.' *Compass Rose*. 1982. Also Coll. *BG*.

Wind's Twelve Quarters, The. 1975. Toronto: Bantam, 1976. Collection. {*WTQ*}

'Winter's King.' *Orbit 5*. Ed Damon Knight. New York: Putnam, 1969. Revised version, *WTQ*, 1975.
Wizard of Earthsea, A. Emeryville, CA: Parnassus Press, 1968. New York: Bantam, 1975. {*WE*}
'Woman's Liberation, A.' 1995. Coll. *FWF*, q.v.
'Word for World Is Forest, The.' *Again, Dangerous Visions*. Ed. Harlan Ellison. 1972. *The Word for World Is Forest*. New York: Berkley-Putnam, 1976. {*WWF*}

PICTURE BOOKS

Catwings. New York: Orchard Books, 1988. Illus. S. D. Schindler. 'A Richard Jackson Book.'
Catwings Return. New York: Orchard Books, 1989. Illus. S. D. Schindler. 'A Richard Jackson Book.'
Fire and Stone. New York: Atheneum-Macmillan, 1989. Illus. Laura Marshall.
Fish Soup. New York: Atheneum-Macmillan, 1992. Illus. Patrick Wynne.
Leese Webster. New York: Atheneum, 1975. Illus. James Brusman.
Ride on the Red Mare's Back, A. New York: Orchard Books, 1992. '[P]aintings by Julie Downing.' 'A Richard Jackson Book.'
Solomon Leviathan's Nine Hundred and Thirty-First Trip Around the World. New Castle, VA: Cheap Street, 1983. Illus. Alicia Austin.
Visit from Dr. Katz, A. New York: Atheneum-Macmillan, 1988. Illus. Ann Barrow.
Wonderful Alexander and the Catwings. New York: Orchard Books, 1994. Illus. S. D. Schindler. 'A Richard Jackson Book.'

POEMS

'Apples.' *Galley Sail Review* 7.2 (Summer 1986). Coll. *Wild Oats*.
'Ars Lunga.' First publ. *Wild Angels*.
'Carmagnole of the Thirtieth of June.' First publ. *Hard Words*.
'Crown of Laurel, The.' First published *BG*.
'Dancing at Tillai, The.' 'First publ. *Hard Words*.
'Elegy.' Trans. of the poem by Rainer Maria Rilke. First published *BG*.
'Epiphany.' First publ. *Hard Words*.
'For Ted.' *Wild Angels*. Also coll. *BG*.
Going Out with Peacocks and Other Poems. New York: HarperPerennial-HarperCollins, 1994. (Collection: **Peacocks**)
'Hard Dancing, The.' First publ. *Peacocks*.
Hard Words and Other Poems. New York: Harper & Row, 1981. (Collection: **Hard Words**)
'Her Silent Daughter.' First publ. *Peacocks*.
'Her Silent Daughter.' *Peacock*.
'Heroes.' 1986. *DEW*.
'His Daughter.' *Calyx* 10.1 (Spring 1986). Coll. *Wild Oats*.
'Invocation.' First publ. *Hard Words*.
'Lament for Rheged.' First publ. *Wild Angels*.
'Lewis and Clark and After.' *The Seattle Review*. Summer 1987. Coll. *BG*.
'Man Who Shored Up Winchester Cathedral, The.' First publ. *Hard Words*.
'Menstrual Lodge, The.' *Calyx* 10.1 (Spring 1986). Coll. *Wild Oats*.

'Middle.' First publ. *Hard Words*.
'Mount St. Helens/Omphalos.' *Wild Angels*. Also coll. *BG*.
'My Hero.' *Peacocks*.
'Night, The.' First publ. *Hard Words*.
'Pasupati.' First publ. *Hard Words*.
'School.' First publ. *Hard Words*.
'Semi-Centenary Celebration, A.' 'Shiva and Kama.' First publ. *Hard Words*.
'Shiva and Kama.' First publ. *Hard Words*.
'Smith Creek.' First publ. *Hard Words*.
'Song.' In *Wild Angels*.
'Spell.' First publ. *Wild Oats*.
'The Woman and the Soul.' *Peacocks*.
'Torrey Pines Reserve.' *Hard Words*. Also coll. *BG*.
'Totem.' *Hard Words*. Also coll. *BG*.
'Uma.' First publ. *Hard Words*.
'What I Discovered After the Earthquake / October 17, 1989.' *No Boats*. Np: Ygor and Buntho Make Books P, 1991. 12-p. chapbook.
Wild Angels. Santa Barbara: Capra Press, 1975. (Collection, poetry)
Wild Oats and Fireweed. New York: Perennial-Harper & Row, 1988. (Collection, poetry: **Wild Oats**)
'Withiner.' First publ. *Wild Angels*.
'Xmas Over.' *Clinton Street Quarterly*. 1984 Coll. *BG*.

DRAMA

The Lathe of Heaven. Dir. David Loxton and Bred Barzyk. USA: Educational Broadcasting Corporation, 1979. First shown Public Broadcasting System, 9 Jan. 1980. Ursula K. Le Guin, original novel, consulting on production.
King Dog: A Screenplay. Santa Barbara, CA: Capra P, 1985. 'Capra Back-to-Back' Vol. V, bound with Raymond Carver and Tess Gallagher's 'Dostoevsky: A Screenplay.'
Left Hand of Darkness, The. Adapted and dir. Meryl Friedman. With David Coronado (Genly Ai), Genevieve Ven Johnson (Estraven), and Karen Tarjan (Faxe). Lifeline Theatre, Chicago. Feb.-March 1995. From *LHD*.

EXPOSITORY WRITING: ESSAYS, SPEECHES, HEADNOTES

'American SF and The Other.' 1975. Coll. *LoN*.
'Carrier Bag Theory of Fiction, The.' 1986. Coll. *DEW*.
Contribution to '[David] Ketterer on *The Left Hand of Darkness* [in *New Worlds for Old*].' *SFS* #6 (2.2 [July 1975]): 137-39.
Dancing at the Edge of The World: Thoughts on Words, Women, Places. New York: Grove, 1989. {*DEW*}
'Dreams Must Explain Themselves.' *Algol* 21, 1973. Coll. *LoN*.
Earthsea Revisioned. Cambridge, MA / Cambridge, UK: Children's Literature New England / Green Bay Publications, 1993. 'A lecture delivered under the title *Children, Women, Men and Dragons* at *Worlds Apart*, an institute sponsored by Children's Literature New England and held from August 2 to 8, 1992 at Keble College, Oxford University, England.' {*ER*}
'Fisherwoman's Daughter, The ' Coll. *DEW*.
'From Elfland to Poughkeepsie.' 1973. Coll. *LoN*.

'Hand that Rocks the Cradle Writes the Book, The.' *The New York Times* 22 Jan 1989: 7.1.
Headnote to 'The Good Trip.' Coll. *WTQ*.
Introduction to *City of Illusions*. Coll. *LoN*.
Introduction to *Planet of Exile* (reissue). 1978. Coll. *LoN*.
'Is Gender Necessary?' *Aurora: Beyond Equality*. Ed. Vonda N. McIntyre and Susan Janice Anderson. New York: Fawcett, 1976. Coll. *LoN*.
'Is Gender Necessary? Redux.' 1976/1987. *DEW*. New York: Grove, 1989. Also *LoN* 1989 edn. (Original 1976 'Gender' essay plus commentary updating it according to UKL's current views.)
'It Was a Dark and Stormy Night; or, Why Are We Huddling About the Campfire?.' Conference Presentation 1979. *Critical Inquiry* 7.1 (Autumn 1980). Coll. *DEW*.
'Ketterer on *The Left Hand of Darkness*.' *SFS* #6 = 2.2 (July 1975): 137-39.
'Legends for a New Land': Guest of Honor Speech at the 19th Annual Mythopoeic Conference.' *Mythlore* 56.2 (Winter 1988): 4-10. {'**Legends**'}
Language of the Night: Essays on Fantasy and Science Fiction. Ed., Introd. Susan Wood. New York: Putnam, 1979. {*LoN* **(1979)**}
Language of the Night: Essays on Fantasy and Science Fiction. Ed., Introd. Susan Wood. 1979. Rev. edn. Ed. Ursula K. Le Guin. UK: The Women's P, 1989. New York: HarperCollins, 1992.
'Non-Euclidean View of California as a Cold Place to Be, A.' 1982. Coll. *DEW*.
'On Theme.' In *Those Who Can: A Science Fiction Reader*. Ed. Robin Scott Wilson. New York: Mentor-NAL, 1973.
'Open Letter to Peter Brigg, An.' *SFRA Review* #225 (Sept.-Oct. 1996): 11-12.
'Response to the Le Guin Issue [of *SFS*], A.' *SFS* #8 = 3.1 (March 1976): 43-46.
Rev. of *The Ascent of Wonder: The Evolution of Hard SF*, ed. David G. Hartwell and Kathryn Cramer. *Foundation* #62 (Winter 1994/95): 82-89.
'Space Crone, The.' Coll. *DEW*.
Wave in the Mind, The: Talks and Essays on the Writer, the Reader, and the Imagination. Boston: Shambhala, 2004.
'Whose *Lathe*?' *The Oregonian* 16 May 1984. Coll. *DEW*.
'World Making.' Coll. *DEW*.

ANTHOLOGY

Norton Book of Science Fiction, The: North American Science Fiction, 1960-1990. Ed. Ursua K. Le Guin and Brian Attebery, with Karen Joy Fowler. New York: Norton, 1993.

MISCELLANEOUS

Le Guin, Ursula K., story. Susan Seddon Boulet, illus. *Buffalo Gals, Won't You Come Out Tonight*. San Francisco: Pomegranate Artbooks, 1994. (Story © 1987, in *BG*.)
Barton, Todd, and Ursula K. Le Guin. *Music and Poetry of the Kesh*. Valley Productions (dist.). not numbered, 1985. Accompanies *ACH* in 1985 Harper First Edn.

SECONDARY WORKS CONSULTED OR CITED

FREQUENTLY USED ABBREVIATIONS AND SHORT FORMS:

AV: Authorized Version of the Bible: 'The King James Bible' of 1611
CIE: *Compton's Interactive Encyclopedia*
DoP: *Dictionary of Philosophy*
Ency. of S.F.: *Encyclopedia of Science Fiction, The*
NEB: The New English Bible
ODQ: *Oxford Dictionary of Quotations*
q.v.: Which see
RSV: Revised Standard Version of the Bible
SFS: The journal *Science-Fiction Studies*
Tenakh: Scholarly trans. of the Hebrew Scriptures from the Masoretic Text
UtS: The journal *Utopian Studies*
Voices: *The Voices of Time*

2001: A Space Odyssey. Dir. Stanley Kubrick. UK: MGM, 1968. Script by Kubrick and Arthur C. Clarke.
'About 'Buck Rogers'...'. Introd. note to *Armageddon 2419* (The Seminal Buck Rogers Novel), q.v. below under Nowlan; note signed D.A.W. (Donald A. Wollheim).
Abrash, Merritt. 'Le Guin's 'The Field of Vision': A Minority View on Ultimate Truth.' *Extrapolation* 26.1 (Spring 1985): 5-15.
Adams, Rebecca. 'Narrative Voice and Unimaginability of the Utopian 'Feminine' in Le Guin's *The Left Hand of Darkness* and '...Omelas.' *UtS* 2.1&2: 35-47.
Aldiss, Brian. *The Dark Light Years*. New York: Signet-NAL, 1964.
Aldridge, Alexandra. 'Origins of Dystopia: *When the Sleeper Wakes* and *We.*' *Clockwork Worlds: Mechanized Environments in SF*. Ed. Richard D. Erlich and Thomas P. Dunn. Westport, CT: Greenwood, 1983.
Alighieri, Dante. See 'Dante.'
Altered I, The : Ursula K. Le Guin's Science Fiction Writing Workshop. Ed. Lee Harding. 1976. New York: Berkley Windhover, 1978. (***Altered I***)
Arbur, Rosemarie. 'Le Guin's 'Song' of Inmost Feminism.' *Extrapolation* 21.3 (Fall 1980): 223-26.
Arbur, Rosemarie.'Beyond Feminism, the Self Intact: Woman's Place in the Work of Ursula K. Le Guin.' *Selected Proceedings of the Science Fiction Research Assocation 1978 National Conference*. Ed. Thomas J. Remington. Cedar Falls, IA: U Nothern Iowa, 1979. 146-63.
Ardrey, Robert. *African Genesis: A Personal Investigation into the Animal Origins and Nature of Man*. 1961. New York: Delta-Dell, 1963.
Arendt, Hannah. *Eichmann in Jerusalem: A Report of the Banality of Evil*. 1963. Harmondsworth: Penguin, 1977.
Arendt, Hannah. *On Violence*. New York: Harcourt, n.d. © 1969, 1970.
Arendt, Hannah. *The Origins of Totalitarianism*. 2nd Enlarged Edn. 1951. Cleveland: Meridian-World, 1958.
Arnold, Matthew. 'Dover Beach.' ca. 1851 / 1867. *The Norton Anthology of English Literature*, q.v.
Asante, Molefi Kete. 'Multiculturalism and the Academy.' *ACADEME: The Bulletin of the American Association of University Professors* 82.3 (May-June 1996): 20-23.

Attebery, Brian. *The Beginning Place*: Le Guin's Metafantasy.' *Children's Literature* 10 (1982): 113-23. Rpt. *Ursula K. Le Guin: Modern Critical Views*, ed. Harold Bloom.

Auerbach, Erich. 'Odysseus's Scar.' Ch. 1 of *Mimesis*. 1946. Trans. Willard Trask. 1953. Garden City, NY: Anchor-Doubleday, 1957.

Ayers, Alfred Jules. *Language, Truth, and Logic.* London: Gollancz, 1936. New York: Dover, 1952.

Bäby, Ian D. 'Reply to C. S. Lewis: Similarities and Differences in *The Beginning Place* and *The Lion, the Witch, and the Wardrobe.*' English 112A, Miami U (Oxford, OH), First Semester 1994-95.

Bhagavad-Gita: See *Song of God, The*.

Bain, Dena C. 'The *Tao Te Ching* as Background to the Novels of Ursula K. Le Guin.' *Extrapolation* 21.3 (Fall 1980): 209-22.

Baker, Paula. *The Moral Frameworks of Public Life: Gender, Poilitics, and the State in Rural New York, 1870-1930*. New York: Oxford UP, 1991. Rev. Michael S. Kimmel, *The Nation* 12/19 Aug. 1991: 205-8.

Bakhtin, Mikhail. 'Response to a Question from the Novy Mir Editorial Staff.' *Speech Genres and Other Late Essays*. Eds. C. Emerson and M. Holquist. Trans. V. McGee. Austin: U of Texas P, 1986.

Bakhtin, Mikhail. 'The Problem of the Text in Linguistics, Philology, and the Human Sciences: An Experiment in Philosophical Analysis.' *Speech Genres and Other Late Essays*. Eds. C. Emerson and M. Holquist. Trans. V. McGee. Austin: U of Texas P, 1986.

Bamber, Linda. *Comic Women, Tragic Men: A Study of Gender and Genre in Shakespeare*. Stanford, CA: Stanford UP, 1982.

Barbour, Douglas. 'On Ursula Le Guin's 'A Wizard of Earthsea.'' *Riverside Quarterly* 6 (April 1974): 119-23.

Barbour, Douglas. 'The Lathe of Heaven: Taoist Dream.' *Algol* no. 21 (Nov. 1973): 22-24.

Barbour, Douglas. 'Wholeness and Balance in the Novels of Ursula K. Le Guin.' *SFS* 1.3 (Spring 1974): 164-73.

Barr, Marleen. 'On the Other Hand.' Rev. *Approaches to the Fiction of Ursula K. Le Guin* by James W. Bittner. *SFS* #41 = 14/1 (March 1987): 111-115.

Barrett, William. *Irrational Man: A Study in Existential Philosophy*. Garden City, NY: Anchor-Doubleday, 1958.

Barrow, Craig, and Diana Barrow. '*The Left Hand of Darkness*: Feminism for Men.' *Mosaic* 20.1 (1987): 83-96.

Bear, Greg. 'Schrödinger's Plague.' *Analog* 1982. *The Norton Book of Science Fiction*. New York: Norton, 1993.

Beauvoir, Simone de. *The Second Sex*. 1949. Trans. and Ed. H. M. Parshley. 1953. New York: Vintage-Random House, 1989.

Beckett, Samuel. *The Lost Ones*. Trans. by SB of his *Le depeupleur*. New York: Grove, 1972.

Benford, Gregory. 'Reactionary Utopias.' 1987. *Australian Science Fiction Review*, 2nd series 3.3, whole number 14 (May 1988).

Benhabib, Seyla. 'Epistemologies of Postmodernism: A Rejoinder to Jean-François Lyotard.' 1984. Rpt. *Feminism/Postmodernism* (q.v. below).

Benjamin, Cornelius. 'Ideas of Time in the History of Philosophy.' In *Voices of Time* (q.v. below). 3-30.

Berger, Albert I. 'The Dispossessed.' *Survey of Science Fiction Literature*. Ed. Frank N. Magill. Englewood Cliffs: Salem, 1979. 548-53.

Berger, Peter L., and Thomas Luckmann. *The Social Construction of Reality: A Treatise in the Sociology of Knowledge*. 1966. New York: Anchor, 1967.

'Berkeley, George.' *Encyclopaedia Britannica: Macropaedia*. 1974.

Bernheim, Mark. *Father of the Orphans: The Story of Janusz Korczak*. New York: Dutton, 1989.
Bhagavad-Gita (The Song of God). Trans. Swami Prabhavananda and Christopher Isherwood. Introd. Aldous Huxley. 1944. New York: Mentor-NAL, 1954.
Bhaskar, Roy. 'Knowledge.' In *A Dictionary of Marxist Thought*, q.v.
Bhaskar, Roy. 'Realism.' In *A Dictionary of Marxist Thought*, q.v.
'Biblical Literature.' By several authors. *Encyclopaedia Britannica: Macropaedia*. 1974.
Biskind, Peter. *Seeing Is Believing: How Hollywood Taught Us to Stop Worrying and Love the Fifties*. New York: Pantheon, 1983. Esp. ch. 3, on SF.
Bittner, James W. *Approaches to the Fiction of Ursula K. Le Guin*. Ann Arbor: UMI Research Press, 1984.
Bittner, James W. 'Approaches to the Fiction of Ursula K. Le Guin.' Diss. U of Wisconsin, 1979..
Bittner, James W. 'The Serpent Spits Out Its Tail: 'The Pathways of Desire' as Le Guin's Last (?) SF Story.' 12th Annual Convention of the Popular Culture Association. Louisville, KY. April 1982.
Blake, William. Letter 24. 'To Thomas Butts' 22 November 1802. Coll. *The Complete Writings of William Blake....* Ed. Geoffrey Keynes. London: Oxford UP, 1966.
Blake, William. 'With happiness stretch'd across the hills,' untitled poem. In Letter 24, To Thomas Butts (22 Nov. 1802). Coll. *The Complete Writings of William Blake....* Ed. Geoffrey Keynes. London: Oxford UP, 1966.
Bloom, Harold, ed. *Ursula K. Le Guin: Modern Critical Views*. New York: Chelsea House, 1986.
Bolger, Ray, narr. *The Churkendoose*. 78 rpm recording. Decca, 1947. Narrative with sound effects and orchestra. By Ben Ross Berenberg. Cond. Mitchell Miller.
Braidish, Meghan. 'A Woman's Role.' English 113H, Miami U (Oxford, OH), Fall Semester 1996-97.
Brigg, Peter. 'A Hainish Chronology.' *SFRA Review* #223 (May/June 1996): 17-19.
Brigg, Peter. 'A 'Literary Anthropology' of the Hainish, Derived from the Tracings of the Species Guin. *Extrapolation* 38.1 (Spring 1997): [15]-24.
Bright, William O. 'North American Indian Languages.' *Encyclopaedia Britannica: Macropaedia*. 1974.
Broderick, Damien. 'Allography and Allegory: Delany's SF.' *Foundation* #52 (Summer 1991): 30-42.
Buck Rogers. Dir. Ford Beebe and Saul A. Goodkind. USA: Filmcraft, 1939. 12 chapters. Features Larry (Buster) Crabbe, Constance Moore, and Jackie Moran. Re-released on 2 VHS cassettes: United American Video, 1989, in their Cliffhanger Serials series.
Bucknall, Barbara J. *Ursula K. Le Guin*. New York: Ungar, 1981.
Buitenen, J. A. B. van. 'Hindu Mythology.' *Encyclopaedia Britannica: Macropaedia*. 1974.
Butler, Andrew M. Rev. *Reading by Starlight: Postmodern Science Fiction* by Damien Broderick. London: Routledge, 1995. *Foundation* #66 (Spring 1996): 111-114.
Cadden, Mike. 'Speaking Across the Spaces Between Us: Ursula Le Guin's Dialogic Use of Character in Children's and Adult Literature.' *Para•Doxa* 2.3-4 (1996): [516]-30.
Calogero, Guido, and Lawrence H. Starkey. 'Eleaticism.' *Encyclopaedia Britannica: Macropaedia*. 1974.
Campbell, Joseph. *The Hero with a Thousand Faces*. 1949. 2nd edn. Princeton, NJ: Princeton UP, 1968. Bollingen Series 17.
Camus, Albert. *The Myth of Sisyphus*. 1942. Trans. Justin O'Brien. New York: Knopf, 1955.
Capra, Fritjof. *The Tao of Physics*. 1976. © 1975. New York: Bantam, 1977.

Carlyle, Thomas. *Sartor Resartus*. 1833-34. 1871. New York: Harcourt, 1921.
Carrigan, Ana. Rev. *Colombia: The Genocidal Democracy* by Javier Giraldo, S.J. *The Progressive* 60.11 (Nov. 1996): 39-41.
'Cat.' *Encyclopaedia Britannica: Macropaedia*. 1974. (By the editors.)
Charnas, Suzy McKee. *Motherlines*. 1978. New York: Berkley, 1979.
Charnas, Suzy McKee. *Walk to the End of the World*. New York: Ballantine, 1974.
Chaucer, Geoffrey. *The Canterbury Tales*. 1387-1400. Ed. F. N. Robinson. 2nd Edn. Boston: Houghton Mifflin, 1957.
Chayefsky, Paddy. *Gideon*. New York: Dramatists Play Service, n.d., © 1961, 1962.
Chen, Ellen M. *The Tao Te Ching: A New Translation with Commentary*. New York: New Era-Paragon, 1989.
Chevigny, Bell Gale. 'Mississippi Learning: Algebra as Political Curriculum.' *The Nation* 262.9 (4 March 1996): 16-21.
Christie, Mike. Rev. *Tehanu: The Last Book of Earthsea*. *Foundation* #49 (Summer 1990): 93-95.
Chuang Tzu. *Chuang Tzu: Taoist Philosopher and Chinese Mystic*. Trans. Herbert A. Giles. First edn. 1889. 2nd rev. edn. 1926. London: George Allen & Unwin, 1961.
CIE: Compton's Interactive Encyclopedia (for Macintosh). 1995 edition. © 1995. Compton's NewMedia.
Clarke, Arthur C. *2001: A Space Odyssey*. New York: Signet-NAL, 1968. Based on the screenplay by Stanley Kubrick and ACC.
Clarke, Arthur C. *Childhood's End*. New York: Ballantine, 1953.
Clarke, Arthur C. *The City and the Stars*. 1953, 1956. New York: Signet-NAL, 1957.
Clute, John. 'Sturgeon, Theodore.' *The Encyclopedia of Science Fiction*. Ed. John Clute and Peter Nicholls. New York: St. Martin's, 1993.
Cogell, Elizabeth Cummins. 'Taoist Configurations: *The Dispossessed*.' *Ursula K. Le Guin: Voyager to Inner Lands and Outer Space*. Ed. Joe De Bolt. Port Washington, NY: Kennikat P, 1979. [See below, Cummins.]
Conrad, Joseph. *Heart of Darkness. Youth and Other Tales*, 1902. *Conrad's Heart of Darkness and the Critics*. Ed. Bruce Harkness. Belmont, CA: Wadsworth, 1960.
Corngold, Stanley, trans. *The Metamorphosis*. By Franz Kafka. New York: Bantam, 1972.
Crick, Bernard, ed., introd., and annotations. *George Orwell: Nineteen Eighty-Four*. Oxford, UK: Clarendon, 1984.
Crosby, D[avid]. 'Mind Gardens.' Perf. The Byrds. *Younger than Yesterday*. Columbia, CS 9442, n.d.
Crow, John H., and Richard D. Erlich. 'Words of Binding: Patterns of Integration in Earthsea.' *Ursula K. Le Guin*. Ed. Joseph D. Olander and Martin Harry Greenberg. New York: Taplinger, 1979.
Cummins, Elizabeth. 'Biographical Sketch' in 'Understanding Ursula K. Le Guin.' Ch. 1 of *Understanding Ursula K. Le Guin*. Columbia, SC: U of South Carolina P, 1990. [See above, Cogell.]
Cummins, Elizabeth. 'Praise then Creation Unfinished: Response to Kenneth M. Roemer,' *UtS* 2.1&2: 19-23.
Cummins, Elizabeth. *Understanding Ursula K. Le Guin*. Columbia, SC: U of South Carolina P, 1990.
Cummins, Elizabeth. *Understanding Ursula K. Le Guin*. Rev. edn. Columbia, SC: U of South Carolina P, 1993.
Daly, Mary. *Gyn/ecology: The Metaethics of Radical Feminism*. Boston: Beacon, 1978.
Danson, Lawrence. '*King Lear* and the Two Abysses.' *On King Lear*. Ed. Lawrence Danson. Princeton, NJ: Princeton UP, 1981.

Dante Alighieri. *Inferno.* In *The Divine Comedy.* Comp. ca. 1302. Publ. 1472. Trans. John Aiken Carlyle. New York: Random, 1932.

Davies, Anthony. *Filming Shakespeare's Plays: The Adaptations of Laurence Olivier, Orson Welles, Peter Brook and Akira Kurosawa.* 1988. Cambridge, UK: Cambridge UP, 1990.

De Bolt, Joe. 'A Le Guin Biography.' In *Ursula K. Le Guin: Voyager to Inner Lands and to Outer Space.* Ed. Joe De Bolt. Port Washington, NY: Kennikat Press, 1979.

Delany, Samuel R. *Tales of Nevèrÿon.* 1979. London, UK: Grafton-Collins, 1988.

Delany, Samuel R. *The Einstein Intersection.* New York: Ace, 1967.

Dember, William N. 'Perception.' *Encyclopaedia Britannica: Macropaedia.* 1974.

Derrida, Jacques. *Writing and Difference.* Trans. Alan Bass. Chicago: U of Chicago P, 1978.

Desan, Wilfrid. 'Sartre, Jean-Paul.' *Encyclopaedia Britannica: Macropaedia.* 1974.

Descartes, René. *The Meditations and Selections from the Principles of René Descartes* (1596-1650). Trans. John Veitch. Introd. and limited apparatus L. Lévy-Bruhl. La Salle, IL: Open Court, 1962.

Destination: Moon. Dir. Irving Pichel. USA: George Pal Production/Eagle-Lion, 1950.

Di Leonardo, Michael. 'It's the Discourse, Stupid!' Rev. *The Magic of the State* by Michael Taussig. *The Nation.* 264.10 (17 March 1997): 35-37.

Dictionary of Marxist Thought, A. Ed. Tom Bottomore. Cambridge, MA: Harvard UP, 1983.

Dictionary of Philosophy. Ed. Dagobert D. Runes. Ames, IA: Littlefield, Adams, 1960.

Diderot, Denis. *Supplément au voyage de Bougainville,* written 1772, publ. 1796. Trans. Ralph H. Bowen. *Supplement to Bougainville's 'Voyage.'* Rpt. *Peaceable Kingdoms: An Anthology of Utopian Writings.* Ed. Robert L. Chianese. New York: Harcourt, 1971.

Duerksen, Roland A. 'The Critical Mode in British Romanticism.' *Romanticism Past and Present* 7.1 (Winter 1983): 1-21.

Dunn, Thomas P., and Richard D. Erlich. 'A Vision of Dystopia: Beehives and Mechanization.' *Journal of General Education* 33 (Spring 1981): 45-58.

E.T.: The Extra-Terrestrial. Dir. Steven Spielberg. USA: Amblin (prod.) / Universal (release), 1982.

Echols, Alice. *Daring to Be Bad: Radical Feminism in America 1967-1975.* Minneapolis: U of Minnesota P, 1989.

'Egyptian Religion.' *Encyclopaedia Britannica: Macropaedia.* 1974.

Ehrenreich, Barbara. 'Once Upon a Wartime.' Rev. *Women and the War Story* by Miriam Cook, *The Soldier's Tale...*by Samuel Hynes, and *War Before Civilization: The Myth of the Peaceful Savage* by Lawrence H. Keeley. *The Nation* 264.18 (12 May 1997): 21-24.

Eibl-Eibesfeldt, Irenäus. *Ethology: The Biology of Behavior.* Trans. Erich Klinghammer. New York: Holt, 1970.

Eliade, Mircea. *The Myth of the Eternal Return... .* Original French edn. 1941. Trans. Willard R. Trask. Bolligen Series 46. Princeton: Princeton UP, 1971.

Eliot, George (pseud. of Mary Anne Evans). *Middlemarch.* 1871-72. Gordon S. Haight, ed. and introd. Boston: Riverside-Houghton, 1956.

Elkins, Charles. 'The Food of the Gods....' Entry in *Survey of Science Fiction Literature.* Ed. Frank N. Magill. Englewood Cliffs, NJ: Salem, 1979.

Elmendorf, W. W., with A. L. Kroeber. *The Structure of Twana Culture* [by WWE], *with Comparative Notes on the Structure of Yurok Culture* [by ALK]. Monographic Supplement no. 2, *Washington State University Research Studies* 28.3 (Sept. 1960).

Encyclopedia of Religion, An. Ed. Vergilius Ferm. 1945, 1959. Paterson, NJ: Littlefield, Adams, 1964.

Encyclopedia of Science Fiction, The. Ed. John Clute and Peter Nicholls, 1993, 1995. New York: St. Martin's, 1993. {*Ency. of S.F.*}

Erlich, Richard D. 'Catastrophism and Coition: Universal and Individual Development in [D. H. Lawrence's] *Women in Love,*' *Texas Studies in Literature and Language*, 9.1 (1967): 117-28.

Erlich, Richard D. '"The Elizabethans' and Other Dangerous Myths: The Uses and Abuses of Historical Criticism.' *O.C.T.E.L.A.* (Ohio Council of Teachers of English) 19 (1978): 20-28.

Erlich, Richard D. 'The Earthsea Trilogy.' In Survey of Modern Fantasy Literature. Ed. Frank N. Magill. Englewood Cliffs, NJ: Salem Press, 1983. 447-459.

Erlich, Richard D. 'The Left Hand of Darkness.' *Survey of Science Fiction Literature.* Ed. Frank N. Magill. Englewood Cliffs: Salem, 1979. 1171-77.

Erlich, Richard D. 'On Barbour on Le Guin,' *Science-Fiction Studies*, #13 = 4.3 (Nov. 1977): 317.

Erlich, Richard D. 'On the Necessary Uncertainty of Historical Criticism,' *Phi Kappa Phi Journal* (now called *National Forum*), 53 (1972): 9-13.

Erlich, Richard D. '"Praise then Darkness and Creation Unfinished': Evolutionary Ethics in *The Left Hand of Darkness.*' Ethics in Le Guin's Fiction Seminar. Convention of the Science Fiction Research Association, Waterloo, IA, 1978.

Erlich, Richard D. '"That Old White-Bearded Satan' (OR 'Sympathy for the Devil'): Outsiders Inside Some Fictive Social Worlds.' *West Virginia University Philosophical Papers* 32 (1986 [1987]): 1-14.

Erlich, Richard D. '"Trapped in the Bureaucratic Pinball Machine': A Vision of Dystopia in the Twentieth Century.' In *Selected Proceedings of the 1978 Science Fiction Research Association National Conference*. Ed. Thomas J. Remington. Cedar Falls: U of Northern Iowa P, 1979. 30-44.

Erlich, Richard D. 'Strange Odyssey: From Dart to Ardrey to Kubrick and Clarke [in *2001*].' *Extrapolation* 17 (1976): 118-24.

Erlich, Richard D. 'Ursula K. Le Guin and Arthur C. Clarke on Immanence, Transcendence, and Massacres.' *Extrapolation* 28.2 (Summer 1987): 105-29.

Erlich, Richard D. 'Wise Men and Fools: Values and Competing Theories of Wisdom in a Selection of Tragedies by Tourneur, Marlowe, Chapman, and Shakespeare.' Diss. University of Illinois (Urbana-Champaign), 1971.

Erlich, Richard D., and Thomas P. Dunn et al. *Clockworks: A Multimedia Bibliography of Works Useful for the Study of the Human Machine Interface in SF.* Westport, CT: Greenwood, 1993.

Esmonde, Margaret P. 'The Master Pattern: The Psychological Journey in the Earthsea Trilogy.' In Olander and Greenberg, q.v.: 15-35.

Evans, Mary Anne: See George Eliot.

Farber, Jerry. 'The Student as Nigger.' Coll. *The Student as Nigger: Essays and Stories.* 1969. New York: Pocket, 1970.

Feminism/Postmodernism. Ed. and Introd. Linda J. Nicholson. New York: Routledge, 1990.

Fetscher, Irving. 'Hegel.' *A Dictionary of Marxist Thought*, q.v.

Finan, Christopher M., assisted by Anne F. Castro. *Catherine M. MacKinnon: The Rise of a Feminist Censor, 1983-1993.* Pamphlet. New York: The Media Coalition, 1993.

Finch, Sheila. Letter to the Editor, *Australian Science Fiction Review* 2nd series 3.6, 4.1, whole numbers 17/18 (Nov. 1988/Jan. 1989): 40-42.

Fisher, Roland. 'Biological Time.' In *Voices of Time* 357-82.

Fitting, Peter. 'Readers and Responsibility: A Reply to Ken Roemer.' *UtS* 2.1&2: 24-29.

Flash Gordon (Rocket Ship). Dir. Frederick Stephani. USA: Universal, 1936. 13 chapters. Based on the cartoon strip by Alex Raymond. Features Larry (Buster) Crabbe, Jean Rogers, Charles Middleton, and Frank Shannon. Condensed into a 69-min. VHS feature by Video Images, 1991.

Flax, Jane. 'Postmodernism and Gender Relations in Feminist Theory.' In *Feminism/Postmodernism*.

Forbidden Planet. Dir. Fred McLeod Wilcox. USA: MGM, 1956.

Forster, E. M. 'The Machine Stops.' *Oxford and Cambridge Review* 8 (Michaelmas term 1909): 83-122. Rpt. *Science Fiction: The Future*. Dick Allen, ed. 2d edn. New York: Harcourt, 1983.

Fox-Genovese, Elizabeth. *Feminism Without Illusions: A Critique of Individualism*. Chapel Hill, U of North Carolina P, 1991.

Franko, Carol. 'Dialogic Narration and Ambivalent Utopian Hope in Lessing's *Shikasta* and Le Guin's *Always Coming Home*.' *Journal of the Fantastic in the Arts* 2.3 (1990): 23-33.

Franko, Carol. 'Acts of Attention at the Borderlands: Le Guin's *The Beginning Place* Revisited.' Rev. for *Extrapolation* 28 Feb. 1995.

Fraser, J. T. *The Voices of Time: A Cooperative Survey of Man's Views of Time as Expressed by the Science and by the Humanities*. New York: George Braziller, 1966.

Fraser, Nancy, and Linda J. Nicholson. 'Social Criticism without Philosophy: An Encounter between Feminism and Postmodernism.' *Communication* 10.3-4 (1988): 345-66. Rpt. *Feminism/Postmodernism*, q.v.

Frazer, Sir James George. *The Golden Bough: A Study in Magic and Religion*. 1922. 1 vol. abridged edn. New York: Macmillan, 1963.

Friedan, Betty. *The Feminine Mystique*. 1962, 1963 (1973, 1974, 1983). New York: Laurel-Dell, 1984.

Frye, Northrop. *Anatomy of Criticism: Four Essays*. 1954. New York: Atheneum, 1966. Third Essay: Archetypal Criticism: Theory of Myths.

Fulbright, J. William. *The Arrogance of Power*. New York: Random House, 1967. Based on the Christian A. Herter Lecture Series, 1966.

Full Metal Jacket. Dir Stanley Kubrick. UK: Puffin (prod.) / Warner (dist.), 1987.

Galbreath, Robert. 'Taoist Magic in the Earthsea Trilogy.' *Extrapolation* 21.3 (Fall 1980): 262-68.

Gardner, John. *Grendel*. 1971. New York: Ballantine, 1972.

Gawron, Jean Mark. *Dream of Glass*. New York: Harcourt, 1993.

Gilligan, Carol. *In a Different Voice: Psychological Theory and Women's Development*. Cambridge, MA: Harvard UP, 1983.

'Gödel, Kurt.' *Encyclopaedia Britannica: Micropaedia*. 1974.

Godwin, Tom. 'The Cold Equations.' *Astounding* August 1954. Frequently rpt. including *Science Fiction Hall of Fame Volume 1*. Ed. Robert Silverberg. Garden City, NY: Doubleday, 1970.

Gordon, Andrew. 'Dreams Come True: Ursula K. Le Guin's *The Lathe of Heaven* as Novel and Film. Eleventh Annual Conference of the Secience Fictin Research Association. Denver, 1981.

Grimm's Fairy Tales, The Complete. Trans. Margaret Hunt, rev. James Stern. Introd. Padraic Colum. Commentary by Joseph Campbell. 1944. New York: Pantheon, 1972.

Grixti, Joseph. 'Consumed Identities: Heroic Fantasies and the Trivialization of Selfhood.' *JPC* 28.3 (Winter 1994 [sic; appeared Winter 1995]): 207-28.

Hamilton, Edith. *Mythology*. 1940, 1942. New York: Mentor-NAL, 1953.

Hardin, Garrett. 'Carrying Capacity as an Ethical Concept.' 1975. http://www.esva.net/~leo/carrycap.html.

Hartsock, Nancy. 'Foucault on Power: A Theory for Women?' 1987. *Feminism/Postmodernism*. Ed. and introd. Linda J. Nicholson. New York: Routledge, 1990.
'Hegel, Georg Wilhelm Friedrich,' and 'Hegal and Marx.' *A Dictionary of Marxist Thought*, q.v.
'Hegel, Georg Wilhelm Friedrich,' and 'Hegalianism.' *Encyclopaedia Britannica: Macropaedia*. 1974.
'Heidegger, Martin.' *Encyclopaedia Britannica: Macropaedia*. 1974.
Heilman, Samuel. *Defenders of the Faith: Inside Orthodox Jewry*. New York: Schocken, 1992.
Heinlein, Robert A. *Starship Troopers*. 1959. New York: Berkley, 1968. New York, Ace: 1987.
Heinlein, Robert A. *Stranger in a Strange Land*. 1961. New York: Ace/Putnam, 1991 ('uncut version').
Heinlein, Robert A. *The Puppet Masters*. 1951. New York: NAL, n.d.
Heinlein, Robert A. 'They.' 1941. *Science Fiction: The Future*. Ed. Dick Allen. New York: Harcourt, 1971, 1983.
Heinlein, Robert A. 'Universe.' *Astounding* May 1941. Rpt. as book New York: Dell, 1951.
Heizer, Robert T., and Theodora Kroeber, eds. *Ishi the Last Yahi: A Documentary History*. Berkeley: U of California P, 1979.
Herman, Robert D. 'Gambling.' *Encyclopaedia Britannica: Macropaedia*. 1974.
Herring, George C. *America's Longest War: The United States and Vietnam, 1950-1975*. New York: Wiley, 1979.
Hesiod. *Hesiod's Theogony*. Trans. and introd. Norman O. Brown. New York: Liberal Arts P, 1953.
High Holiday Prayer Book. Morris Silverman, compiler and arranger. Bridgeport, CT: Prayer Book Press, 1951.
'Hinduism.' *Encyclopaedia Britannica: Macropaedia*. 1974.
'Hiroshima.' *The New Columbia Encyclopedia*. Ed. William H. Harris and Judith S. Levey. New York: Columbia UP, 1975.
Hoffer, Eric. *The True Believer: Thoughts on the Nature of Mass Movements*. 1951. New York: Perennial-Harper, 1966. Reset (with alternative pagination) 1989.
Holy Bible, The. 'Revised Standard Version.' Ed. Herbert G. May and Bruce M. Metzger. New York: Oxford UP, 1962. 'The Oxford Annotated Bible.' {**RSV**}.
Holy Bible, The. 'The Authorized King James Version.' Cleveland: World, n.d. {**AV**}.
Huxley, Aldous. 'Foreword.' *Brave New World*. 1932. New York: Harper, 1946. New York: Bantam, 1958.
Huxley, Aldous, comp., commentary. *The Perennial Philosophy*. New York: Harper, 1945.
Huyssen, Andreas. 'Mapping the Postmodern.' 1984, 1986. *Feminism/Postmodernism*.
'Indian Philosophy.' *Encyclopaedia Britannica: Macropaedia*. 1974.
Innes, Mary M.: See 'Ovid.'
'Is There in Truth No Beauty?' *Star Trek*. Episode #62, aired 18 Oct. 1968. Dir. Ralph Senensky. Jean Lisette Aroeste, script.
Jackson, Rosemary. *Fantasy: The Literature of Subversion*. London: Methuen, 1981.
Jackson, Shirley, 'The Lottery.' 1948. Coll. *The Lottery*. New York: Farrar, 1949.
James, William. *The Varieties of Religious Experience: A Study in Human Nature*. 1902. Ed. and Introd. Martin E. Marty. 1982. New York: Viking Penguin, 1985. A Penguin Classic.
Jarratt, Susan C. 'Feminism and Composition: The Case for Conflict.' In *Contending with Words: Composition and Rhetoric in a Postmodern Age*. Ed. Patricia Harkin and John Schilb. New York: MLA, 1991.

Jastrow, Robert. *God and the Astronomers*. New York: Norton, 1978.
Jenkins, Ruth. 'The Fuction of 'The Place Inside the Blizzard,' 'On Time and Darkness,' and 'An Orgota Creation Myth' in *The Left Hand of Darkness*. English 112LB, Miami U (Oxford, OH), Spring 1977-78.
Jorgens, Jack F. *Shakespeare on Film*. Bloomington: Indiana UP, 1977.
Kalish, Alan et al. "'For Our Balls Were Sheathed In Inertron': Textual Variations in 'The Seminal Novel of Buck Rogers.'" *Extrapolation* 29.4 (Winter 1988): [303]-18.
Kaske, R. E. '*Sapientia et Fortitudo* as the Controlling Theme of *Beowulf*.' *Studies in Philology* 55 (July 1958): 423-57. *An Anthology of Beowulf Criticism*. Ed. Lewis E. Nicholson. Notre Dame, IN: U of Notre Dame P, 1963. 269-310.
Kellogg, Robert, and Oliver Steele. *Books I and II of the Faerie Queene....* Indianapolis: Odyssey/Bobbs-Merrill, 1965.
Keyes, Daniel. 'Flowers for Algernon.' *The Hugo Winners*. vol. 1. Ed. Isaac Asimov. Garden City, NY: Doubleday, 1962.
Khanna, Lee Cullen. 'Beyond Utopias: Utopia and Gender.' *UtS* 2.1&2: 48-58.
Kidd, Virginia. 'Ursula K. Le Guin: Biographical Data (1996). Literary Agent media release/handout.
Kierkegaard, Søren. *Fear and Trembling* [1843] *and The Sickness Unto Death*. Walter Lowrie, trans., introd., notes. 1941, 1954. Garden City, NY: Doubleday, n.d.
Knight, Damon. 'An Annotated Masks.' *Those Who Can : A Science Fiction Reader*. Ed. Robin Scott Wilson. New York: Mentor-NAL, 1973.
Korten, David C. 'The Limits of the Earth.' *The Nation* 263.3 (15/22 July 1996): 14-18.
Kroeber, A. L. *Anthropology: Race, Language, Culture, Psychology, Prehistory*. 1923. Rev. edn. New York: Harcourt, 1948. Mostly rpt. New York: Harbinger-Harcourt, 1963. As *Anthropology: Biology and Race* (chs. 1, 2, 4, 5, and 15), and *Anthropology: Culture Pattern and Processes* (chs. 1, 6-10).
Kroeber, A. L. *Handbook of the Indians of California*. Bulletin 78 of the Bureau of American Enthnology of the Smithsonian Institution. Washington, D.C.: GPO, 1925. New York: Dover, 1976.
Kroeber, A. L. *Yurok Myths*. Ed. Grace Buzaljko. Berkeley: U of California P, 1976. Theodora Kroeber, foreword. Timothy H. H. Thoresen, 'Kroeber and the Yurok, 1900-1908.' Alan Dundes, folkorist commentary.
Kroeber, A. L., and E. W. Gifford. *Karok Myths*. Ed. Grace Buzaljko. Berkeley: U of California P, 1980. Grace Buzaljko, ed.. Theodora Kroeber, introd.. Alan Dundes, folklorist commentary. William Bright, linguistic index.
'Kroeber, Alfred L.' *Who Was Who in America (With World Notobles)*. vol. IV, 1961-68.
Kroeber, Karl. *Retelling and Rereading*. New Brunswick, NJ: Rutgers UP, 1992.
Kroeber, Theodora. *Ishi in Two Worlds: A Biography of the Last Wild Indian in North America*. 1961. Berkeley: U of California P, 1976.
Kroeber, Theodora. *Ishi, Last of His Tribe*. 1964. New York: Bantam, 1973.
Kroeber, Theodora. *The Inland Whale*. 1959. Berkeley: U of California P, 1974.
Kropotkin, Petr. *Mutual Aid: A Factor of Evolution*. 1902, 1914. Boston, MA: Extending Horizon Books 1960.
L'Engle, Madeline. *A Wrinkle in Time*. New York: Yearling-Dell, 1962.
Lamb, Patricia Frazer, and Diana L. Veith. 'Again, *The Left Hand of Darkness*: Androgyny or Homophobia?' *Erotic Universe: Secuality and Fantastic Literature*. Ed. Donald Palumbo. New York: Greenwood, 1986.
Larrain, Jorge. 'Ideology.' *A Dictionary of Marxist Thought*, q.v.
Lasky, Melvin J. *Utopia and Revolution*. Chicago: U of Chicago P, 1976.
Lawrence, D[avid]. H[erbert]. *Women in Love*. 1920, 1922. Compass-Viking, 1960.
'Le Guin, Ursula K(roeber).' *Current Biography Yearbook*, 1983.

Lefanu, Sarah. *In the Chinks of the World Machine: Feminism and Science Fiction.* London: Women's Press, 1988. *Feminism and Science Fiction.* Bloomington: Indiana UP, 1989.

Lehman, David. *Signs of the Times: Deconstruction and the Fall of Paul de Man.* New York: Poseidon-Simon & Schuster, 1991.

Lem, Stanislaw. *Solaris.* Original, in Polish, 1961. Trans. from French Joanna Kilmartin and Steve Fox, 1970. New York: Berkley, 1971.

Lerner, Gerda. Rev. *Sojourner Truth: A Life, a Symbol*, by Nell Irvin Painter. New York: Norton, 1996. *The Nation* 264.2 (13/20 Jan. 1997): 25-28.

Levi, Herbert W., and Lorna R. Levi. 'Arneida.' *Encyclopaedia Britannica: Macropaedia.* 1974.

Lévy-Bruhl, L. Introd. *The Meditations and Selections from the Principles of René Descartes.* La Salle, IL: Open Court, 1962.

Lévi-Strauss, Claude. *The Savage Mind.* Trans. *La Pensée sauvage*, 1962. English © 1966. George Weidenfeld and Nicolson Ltd. [Chicago]: U of Chicago P, n.d.

Lewis, C. S. *The Lion, the Witch and the Wardrobe.* The Chronicles of Narnia Book Two. Illus. Pauline Baynes. 1950. New York: HarperCollins, [1994].

Lewis, Philip E. '[Maurice] Merleau-Ponty' and the Phenomenology of Language.' In *Structuralism.* Jacques Ehrmann, ed., introd. 1966. Garden City, NY: Anchor-Doubleday, 1970. Re-issue of a 1966 special issue of *Yale French Studies.*

Linden, Eugene. 'Global Fever' (Climate change threatens more than megasotrms, floods[,] and droughts. The real peril may be disease.) *Time* 148.3 (8 July 1996): 56-67.

Littlefield, Holly. 'Unlearning Patriarchy: Ursula Le Guin's Feminist Consciousness in *The Tombs of Atuan* and *Tehanu.*' *Exprapolation* 36.3 (Fall 1995): 244-58.

Lorenz, Konrad. *On Aggression.* Trans, Marjorie Kerr Wilson. 1966. New York: Bantam, 1967.

Lukens, Rebecca J., and Ruth K. J. Cline. *A Critical Handbook of Literature for Young Adults.* New York: HarperCollins, 1995.

Lyotard, Jean-François. *The Postmodern Condition: A Report on Knowledge.* Trans. *La Condition postmoderne: rapport sur le savoir* (1979). Geoff Bennington and Brian Massumi. Minneapolis: U of Minnesota P, 1984.

Mann, Paul. 'Stupid Undergrounds.' *Postmodern Culture* 5.3 (May 1995), pmc@jefferson.village.virginia.edu.

Marx, Karl. *Capital: A Critique of Political Economy.* Vol. Three. [1894.] Trans. David Fernbach. Introd. Ernest Mandel. New York: Vintage-Random, 1981.

Maslen, Robert. ''Towards an Archaeology of the Present': Theodora Kroeber and Ursula K. Le Guin.' *Foundation* #67 (Summer 1996): 62-74.

McCarthy, Eugene J. *The Limits of Power: America's Role in the World.* New York: Holt, 1967.

McKibben, Bill. 'The Enigma of Kerala (one state in India is proving development experts wrong).' *Utne Reader*, no. 74 (March-April 1996): 103-12. Excerpted from *DoubleTake*, Summer 1995.

McLean, Susan. '*The Beginning Place*: An Interpretation.' *Extrapolation* 24.2 (Summer 1983): 130-42.

Meerloo, Joost A. M. 'The Time Sense in Psychiatry.' In *Voices of Time* 235-52.

Melville, Herman. *Moby Dick; or, The Whale.* 1851. Indianapolis: Bobbs-Merrill, 1964.

Merleau-Ponty, Maurice. *La Phénoménologie de la perception.* Paris: Gallimard, 1945.

Merleau-Ponty, Maurice. *Signes.* Paris Gallimard, 1960.

Metropolis. Dir. Fritz Lang. Germany: UFA, 1926.

Miller, J. Hillis. 'The Critic as Host.' In Miller et al. *Deconstruction and Criticism.* New York: Seabury, 1979.

Minkowitz, Donna. 'Wrath of God Best Sellers.' *The Nation* 262.7 (19 Feb. 1996): 25-28.
Mitchell, Stephen, trans., reader. *Lao-tzu: Tao te Ching*. Audiocassette. Caedmon (Harper Audio), 1989. CPN 2114. 2 hours.
Mitchell, W. J. T. 'Editor's Note: On Narrative.' *Critical Inquiry* 7.1 (Autumn 1980): 1-4.
Moffatt, Michael. *Coming of Age in New Jersey: College and American Culture*. New Brunswick, NJ: Rutgers UP, 1989.
More, Sir Thomas. *Utopia*. 1516. Ed. and trans. H. V. S. Ogden. New York: Appleton, 1949.
Multimedia Encyclopedia of Science Fiction, The. Grolier Electronic Publishing, 1995. Based on *The Encyclopedia of Science Fiction* by John Clute and Peter Nicholls, 1993, 1995. Book Browser Synopses by Neil Barron, 1995. Version 1.0.0. Macintosh ISBN 0-7172-3998-5.
Mumford, Lewis. 'Utopia, The City and The Machine.' 1965. In *Utopias and Utopian Thought*. Ed. Frank E. Manuel. Cambridge and Boston: Riverside & Houghton, 1966. 3-24.
Murphy, Patrick D. 'The Left Hand of Fabulation: The Poetry of Ursula K. Le Guin.' *The Poetic Fantastic: Studies in an Evolving Genre*. Ed. Patrick D. Murphy and Vernon Hyles. New York: Greenwood, 1989.
Nakamura, Hajime. 'Time in Indian and Japanese Thought.' In *Voices of Time* 77-91.
Needham, Joseph. 'Time and Knowledge in China and the West.' In *Voices of Time*. 92-135.
New English Bible, The. Donald Ebor, Chairman of the Joint Committee [overseeing translation]. 1961, 1970. New York: Cambridge UP (in collaboration with Oxford UP), 1971.
Nicholls, Peter, and Brian Stableford. 'ESP,' 'Psi Powers.' *The Encyclopedia of Science Fiction*. Ed. John Clute and Peter Nicholls. New York: St. Martin's, 1993.
Nicholls, Peter. 'Linguistics.' *The Multimedia Encyclopedia of Science Fiction*.
Nicholson, Linda J., ed., introd. *Feminism/Postmodernism*, q.v.
Norton Anthology of English Literature, The. 4th Edition. Ed. M. H. Abrams et al. New York: Norton, 1979. 2 vols.
Nowlan, Phillip Francis. 'Armageddon—2419 A.D.' *Amazing Stories*, August 1928: 422-49. And its sequel, 'The Airlords of Han.' *Amazing Stories* March 1929: 1106-1136.
Nowlan, Phillip Francis. *Armageddon 2419 A.D.* Fix-up, 1962 of 'Armageddon—2419 A.D.' and 'The Airlords of Han.' *Armageddon 2419 A.D.* (The Seminal Buck Rogers Novel). Revised Spider Robinson. New York: Ace, 1978.
Nudelman, Rafail. 'An Approach to the Structure of Le Guin's Science Fiction.' Trans. Alan G. Myers. *SFS* #7, 2.3 (Nov. 1975): 210-20.
Olander, Joseph D. and Martin Harry Greenberg. *Ursula K. Le Guin*. New York Taplinger, 1979.
Olney, James. "'I Was Born'': Slave Narratives, Their Status as Autobiography and as Literature.' In *The Slaves Narrative*. Ed. Charles T. Davis and Henry Louis Gates, Jr. Oxford, UK: Oxford UP, 1985.
Orwell, George (pseud. of Eric Blair). *Nineteen Eighty-Four*. 1949. Rpt. *1984*. New York: NAL, 1961.
Ovid. *The Metamorphoses of Ovid*. Trans. and introd. Mary M. Innes. Baltimore: Penguin, 1955.
Oxford Annotated Bible with Apocrypha, The. The Holy Bible, Revised Standard Version. Ed. Herbert G. Bay and Bruce M. Metzger. New York: Oxford UP, 1962.
Oxford Dictionary of Quotations. 2nd edn. London: Oxford UP, 1955. {*ODQ*}
Partridge, Eric. *Shakespeare's Bawdy*. 1948. New York: Dutton, 1960.

Patai, Daphne, and Noretta Koertge. *Professing Feminism: Cautionary Tales from the Strange World of Women's Studies.* New York: BasicBooks-HarperCollins, 1994. 'A New Republic Book.'

'Pharisees, the.' *An Encyclopedia of Religion.* Ed. Vergilius Ferm. 1945, 1959. Paterson, NJ: Littlefield, Adams, 1964.

Pohl, Frederik, and C. M. Kornbluth. *The Space Merchants.* 1952. New York: Ballantine, 1953.

Popkin, Richard H. 'Skepticism.' *Encyclopaedia Britannica: Macropaedia.* 1974.

Porter, David L. 'The Politics of Le Guin's Opus.' *SFS* 2 (Nov. 1975): 243-8.

Probyn, Elspeth. 'Travels in the Postmodern: Making Sense of the Local.' In *Feminism/Postmodernism,* q.v.

Putnam's Concise Mythological Dictionary. 1963. New York: Capricorn, 1964. By Joseph Kaster, based on Bessie Redfield's *Gods....*

Pynchon, Thomas. *Gravity's Rainbow.* 1973. New York: Viking-Penguin, 1987.

Rabinowitz, Isaac. 'Toward a Valid Theory of Biblical Hebrew Literature.' In *The Classical Tradition: Literary and Historical Studies in Honor of Harry Caplan.* Ed. Luitpold Wallach: Ithaca, NY: Cornell UP, 1966. 315-28.

Rabkin, Eric S. 'Determinism, Free Will, and Point of View in LeGuin's *The Left Hand of Darkness.*' *Extrapolation* 20.1 (Spring 1979) 5-19.

Rand, Ayn. *Anthem.* UK: 1938; USA: 1946. New York: Signet-NAL, 1961.

Reed, Adolph Jr. 'Socializing Neo-Slavery.' Rev. *'Worse than Slavery': Parchman Farm and the Ordeal of Jim Crow Justice* by David M. Oshinsky. *The Nation.* 262.18 (6 May 1996): 44-48.

Remington, Thomas T. 'The Other Side of Suffering: Touch as Theme and Metaphor in Le Guin's Science Fiction Novels.' In Olander and Greenberg, q.v.

Remington, Thomas J. 'A Time to Live and a Time to Die: Cyclical Renewal in the Earthsea Trilogy.' *Extrapolation* 21.3 (Fall 1980): 278-86.

Remington, Thomas J. 'A Touch of Difference, A Touch of Love: Theme in Three Stories by Ursula K. Le Guin ['Nine Lives,' *WWF,* 'VEMS'].' *Extrapolation* 18 (Dec. 1976): 28-41.

Rilke, Rainer Maria. *Duino Elegies.* The German Text, with an English Translation, Introduction, and Commentary by J. B. Leishman and Stephen Spender. New York: Norton, 1939.

Rochelle, Warren. 'The Story, Plato, and Ursula K. Le Guin.' *Extrapolation* 37.4 (Winter 1996): [316]-29.

Roemer, Kenneth M. 'The Talking Porcupine Liberates Utopia: Le Guin's 'Omelas' as Pretext to the Dance.' *UtS* 2.1&2: 6-18.

Rugoff, Milton, ed. *A Harvest of World Folk Tales.* Illus. Joseph Low. New York: Viking, 1965.

Rupp, Ernest Gordon. 'Luther, Martin.' *Encyclopaedia Britannica: Macropaedia.* 1974.

Russ, Joanna. '*Amor Vincit Foeminam*: The Battle of the Sexes in Science Fiction.' *SFS* 7 (1980). Coll. *To Write Like a Woman,* q.v.

Russ, Joanna. *How to Suppress Women's Writing.* Austin: U of Texas P, 1983.

Russ, Joanna. *The Female Man.* 1975. New York: Bantam, 1975.

Russ, Joanna. 'The Image of Women in Science Fiction.' *Red Clay Reader* 7 (1970): 35-40.

Russ, Joanna. 'The Man Who Could Not See Devils.' 1970. *Those Who Can: A Science Fiction Reader.* Ed. Robin Scott Wilson. Mentor-NAL, 1973.

Russ, Joanna. 'On Setting.' Afterword to 'The Man Who Could Not See Devils,' q.v.

Russ, Joanna. *To Write Like a Woman.* Bloomington: Indiana UP, 1995.

Russ, Joanna. *We Who Are About To....* 1975, 1976. New York: Dell, 1977.

Russ, Joanna. 'When It Changed.' *Again, Dangerous Visions*. Vol 1. Ed. Harlan Ellison. New York: Signet-NAL, 1972.
Sale, Kirkpatrick. 'Countercultural Elite.' Rev. Taylor Stoehr's *Here Now Next: Paul Goodman and the Origins of Gestalt Therapy*, and three of his editions of Goodman's work. *The Nation* 260.14 (10 April 1995): 496-99.
Sale, Kirkpatrick. 'Lessons from the Luddites: Setting Limits on Technology.' *The Nation* 260.22 (5 June 1995): 785-90.
Sartre, Jean-Paul. 'Existentialism Is a Humanism.' 1946. Trans. 1948. Frequently rpt. including Kaufmann, Walter. *Existentialism from Dostoevsky to Sartre*. Cleveland: Meridian-World, 1956.
Sartre, Jean-Paul. *No Exit*. 1944 (production); 1946. Trans. Lionel Abel. *No Exit and Three Other Plays by Jean-Paul Sartre*. New York: Vintage-Knopf/Random House, n.d.
Sartre, Jean-Paul. *The Flies*. *Les Mouches* 1943. First English trans., UK: 1946, USA: 1947. Trans. Stuart Gilbert. In *No Exit and Three Other Plays*. New York: Vintage-Random House, n.d.
Selinger, Bernard. *Le Guin and Identity in Contemporary Fiction*. Studies in Speculative Fiction, No. 16. Ann Arbor: UMI Research P, 1988.
Service of the Synagogue: Day of Atonement. Herbert M. Adler, gen. ed. Trans. Adler, et al. New York: Hebrew Publishing Company, ca. 1938. 'Reprinted from the latest and best London edn.'
Sharkey, Betsy. 'Good Girls, Bad Girls And How TV Scrambles the Signals.' *The New York Times*, Arts & Leisure, Sun. 17 Sept. 1995. Pp. 1, 29.
Sheldon, Alice (writing as James Tiptree, Jr.). 'The Women Men Don't See.' 1973. *The Norton Book of Science Fiction*. Ed. Le Guin (see above).
Siciliano, Sam Joseph. 'The Fictional Universe in Four Science Fiction Novels: Anthony's Burgess's *A Clockwork Orange*, Ursula Le Guin's *The Word for World Is Forest*, Walter Miller's *A Canticle for Leibowitz*, and Roger Zelazny's *Creatures of Light and Darkness*.' Diss. U of Iowa, 1975. Ann Arbor: UMI, 1981.
Silverberg, Robert. 'A Happy Day in 2381.' 1970. *Science Fiction: The Future*. Ed. Dick Allen. 2nd edn. New York: Harcourt, 1983.
Sixties Without Apology, The. Ed. Sohnya Sayres et al. Minneapolis: U of Minnesota P, 1984.
Skinner, B. F. *Beyond Freedom and Dignity*. New York: Knopf, 1971.
Skinner, B. F. *Walden Two*. New York: Macmillan, 1948.
'Slavery, Serfdom, and Forced Labour,' II. Slavery in Antiquity (by the Editors). *Encyclopaedia Britannica: Macropaedia*. 1974.
Slusser, George, *The Farthest Shores of Ursula K. Le Guin*. San Bernardino: Borgo, 1976.
Smaller Classical Dictionary. Sir William Smith, compiler. Revised E. H. Blakeney and John Warrington. New York: Dutton, 1958.
Smith, Philip E. 'Unbuilding Walls: Human Nature and the Nature of Evolution and Political Theory in *The Dispossessed*.' In Olander and Greenberg, q.v.
Sobchack, Vivian. *Screening Space: The American Science Fiction Film. Enlargement of The Limits of Infinity...* (1980). New York: Ungar, 1988.
Sobchack, Vivian. 'The Virginity of Astronauts: Sex and the Science Fiction Film.' *Shadows of the Magic Lamp' Fantasy and Science Fiction in Film*. Ed. George Slusser and Eric S. Rabkin. Carbondale: Southern Illinois UP, 1985.
Song of God: Bhagavad-Gita, The. Trans. Swami Prabhavananda and Christopher Isherwood. Introd. Aldous Huxley. 1944, 1951. New York: Mentor-NAL, 1954.
Sonnenberg, Ben. 'The Happiness of the Unhappy.' Rev. two collections of the works of Samuel Becket. *The Nation* 262.18 (6 May 1996): 16-18.

Spencer, Kathleen L. 'Exiles and Envoys: the SF of Ursula K. Le Guin.' *Foundation* No. 20 (Oct. 1980): 32-43.
Spinrad, Norman. *The Iron Dream*. New York: Timescape-Pocket, 1972.
Spivack, Charlotte. 'Life and Intellectual Background.' Ch. 1 of *Ursula K. Le Guin*. Boston: Twayne, 1984.
Spivack, Charlotte. *Ursula K. Le Guin*. Boston: Twayne, 1984.
Stains, Howard James. 'Carnivora.' *Encyclopaedia Britannica: Macropaedia*. 15th ed. 1974. Section on CATS (FAMILY FELIDAE): 3.936-37.
Stargate. Dir. Roland Emmerich. USA: MGM (prod.) / United Artists (dist.), 1994.
Starman. Dir. John Carpenter. USA: Columbia, 1984.
Stein, George J. 'Biological Science and the Roots and Nazism.' *American Scientist* 76 (Jan.-Feb. 1988): 50-[58].
Stevens, Carol D. 'A Response to Ken Roemer.' *UtS* 2.1&2: 30-34.
Stevens, Carol D. 'Le Guin and the Family Business: Anthropology, Nostalgia, and *Always Coming Home*, OR What She Stole, What She Changed, and Why.' 20th Annual Conference of the Science Fiction Research Association. Oxford, OH, 24 June 1989.
Stevens, David, and Carol D. Stevens. *J. R. R. Tolkien*. Starmont Reader's Guide 54. Mercer Island, WA: Starmont, 1992.
Stone-Blackburn, Susan. 'Adult Telepathy: *Babel-17* and *The Left Hand of Darkness*.' *Extrapolation*. 30.3 (Fall 1989): 243-53
Streng, Frederick J. 'Sacred or Holy.' *Encyclopaedia Britannica: Macropaedia*. 1974.
Suvin, Darko. 'Parables of De-Alienation: Le Guin's Widdershins Dance.' *SFS* #7, 2.3 (Nov. 1975): 265-74.
Swain, Joseph Ward. *The Ancient World*. 2 vols. New York: Harper, 1950 (corrected printing 1962).
Talbot, Norman. 'The Ambiguities of Utopia: A Reaction to 'Reactionary Utopias.'' *Australian Science Fiction Review*. 2nd series 3.5, whole number 16 (Sept. 1988): 11-18.
'Taoism, History of.' Michael Strickmann. *Encyclopaedia Britannica: Macropaedia*. 1974.
'Taoism.' Anna K. Seidel. *Encyclopaedia Britannica: Macropaedia*. 1974.
Tschachler, Heinz. 'Forgetting Dostoevsky: The Political Unconscious of Ursula K. Le Guin.' *UtS*: 65-66.
Tenakh: A New Translation of The Holy Scriptures According to the Traditional Hebrew Text. Philadelphia: Jewish Publication Society, 5746/1985 C.E.
Tennyson, Alfred. (Alfred, Lord Tennyson). 'Ulysses.' 1833/1842. *The Norton Anthology of English Literature*, q.v. 2.1110-1111.
Thompson, James Westfall, and Edgar Nathaniel Johnson. *An Introduction to Medieval Europe: 300-1500*. New York: Norton, 1937.
Those Who Can.... Robin Scott Wilson, ed. New York: Mentor, 1973.
Time and Space. By the Editors of Time-Life Books. Alexandria, VA: Time-Life Books, [1990]).
Tiptree, James, Jr.: See Alice Sheldon.
Tolkien, J. R. R. '*Beowulf*: The Monster and the Critics.' *Proceedings of the British Academy* 22 (1936): 245-95. *An Anthology of Beowulf Criticism*. Ed. Lewis E. Nicholson. Notre Dame, IN: U of Notre Dame P, 1963. 51-103.
Trumbo, Dalton. *Johnny Got His Gun*. Philadelphia: Lippincott, 1939.
Turner, Victor. *Dramas, Fields, and Metaphors: Symbolic Action in Human Society*. Ithaca: Cornell UP, 1974, 1975.
Turner, Victor. *The Ritual Process: Structure and Anti-Structure*. 1969. Ithaca: Cornell UP, 1977.
Twain, Mark (pseud. of Samuel Clemens). 'Corn-Pone Opinions.' ca. 1900. *Essays in English from Ascham to Baldwin*. Ed. Paul C. Wermuth. New York: Holt, 1967.

Twain, Mark (pseud. of Samuel Clemens). *Adventures of Huckleberry Finn.* 1884, 1885. New York: Norton, 1961.
Ursula K. Le Guin: Modern Critical Views. Ed. Harold Bloom. See above: Harold Bloom.
Utopian Studies 2.1&2 (1991): v-76. Forum on Le Guin's 'The Ones Who Walk Away from Omelas' plus Heinz Tschachler, q.v. {*UtS*}
Vajda, Georges. 'Jewish Mysticism.' *Encyclopaedia Britannica: Macropaedia.* 1974.
Viereck, Peter. 'Conservatism.' *Encyclopaedia Britannica: Macropaedia.* 1974.
Voices of Time: A Cooperative Suvey of Man's Views of time as Expressed by the Sciences and by the Humanities. Ed. J. T. Fraser. New York: George Braziller, 1966.
Vonnegut, Kurt Jr. *Slaughterhouse-Five, or The Children's Crusade: A Duty-Dance with Death.* 1969. New York: Dell, 1971.
Vonnegut, Kurt, Jr. *Cat's Cradle.* 1963. New York: Dell, 1970.
Waley, Arthur. *The Way and Its Power: A Study of the Tao te Ching and Its Place in Chinese Thought.* London: Allen & Unwin, 1934.
Watanabe, Satosi. 'Time and the Probabilistic View of the World.' In *Voices of Time* 527-63.
Watson, Ian. 'An anthropologist in space (Ian Watson reviews *Four Ways to Forgiveness* by Ursula K. Le Guin).' *New Scientist* 150. 2030 (18 May 1996): 48-49.
Watson, Ian. 'Le Guin's *Lathe of Heaven* and the Role of Dick: The False Reality as Mediator.' *SFS* #5 = 2.1 (March 1975): 67-75.
Welch, Holmes. *The Parting of the Way: Lao Tzu and the Taoist Movement.* Boston: Beacon, 1957.
Wells, H. G. *The Food of the Gods And How It Came to Earth.* 1904. New York: Berkley, 1967.
Wells, H. G. *The Time Machine.* 1895. Ed. Harry M. Geduld. Bloomington: Indiana UP, 1987.
Westfahl, Gary. *Islands in the Sky.* San Bernardino: Borgo P, 1996. I. O. Evans Studies in the Philosophy and Criticism of Literature, Number 15.
Whitrow. G. J. 'Time and the Universe.' In *Voices of Time*, 564-81.
Wilhelm, Hellmut. *Change: Eight Lectures on the I Ching.* Trans. Cary F. Baynes. New York: Pantheon, 1960. Bollingen Series 62.
Wilhelm, Richard, trans., ed. *Tao Te Ching.* 1910. New German edn., 1978. Trans. to English H. G. Ostwald. London: Arkana-Routledge, 1985.
Williams, Donna Glee. 'The Moons of Le Guin and Heinlein.' *SFS* #63, 21.2 (July 1994): 164-72.
Wing-tsit, Chan. 'Chinese Philosophy.' *Encyclopaedia Britannica: Macropaedia.* 1974.
Wolfe, Gary K. 'Instrumentalities of the Body: The Mechanization of Human Form in Science Fiction.' *The Mechanical God: Machines in Science Fiction.* Ed. Thomas P. Dunn and Richard D. Erlich. Westport, CT: Greenwood, 1982.
Wood, Susan. 'Discovering Worlds: The Fiction of Ursula K. Le Guin.' *Voices for the Future: Essays on Major Science Fiction Writers.* Ed. Thomas D. Clareson. Bowling Green, OH: Bowling Green State UP, 1979. Rpt. Bloom 183-209.
Wood, Susan. 'Taoism: a Study of Balance in the Hainish Novels of Ursula K. Le Guin.' M.A. Thesis. San Francisco State University, 1992.
Wordsworth, William. 'Ode: Intimations of Immortality from Recollections of Early Childhood' (1802-4 / 1807). *The Norton Anthology of English Literature*, q.v.: 2.213-18.
Wytenbroek, J. R. '*Always Coming Home*: Pacifism and Anarchy in Le Guin's Latest Utopia.' *Extrapolation* 28.4 (Winter 1987): 330-39.
Wilde, Oscar. 'The Decay of Lying: An Observation.' Coll. *Intentions.* 1891. New York: Boni and Liveright, 1920.

Zamiatin, Yevgeny (variously translated and transliterated). *We*. Written ca. 1920. Trans. Mirra Ginsburg. New York: Bantam, 1972. Zorda, Margaret Lee. 'Bahtin, Blobels[,] and Philip Dick.' *JPC* 28.3 (Winter 1994): 55-61.

ABOUT THE AUTHOR

RICHARD D. ERLICH served as a Professor in English at Miami University in Oxford, Ohio, from 1971 to 2006. In collaboration with Thomas P. Dunn, he has edited *The Mechanical God: Machines in Science Fiction* and *Clockwork Worlds: Mechanized Environments in SF*, and compiled *Clockworks: A Multimedia Bibliography of Works Useful for the Study of the Human/Machine Interface in SF*. Alone and in various collaborations he has published essays on the '*Buck Rogers* opus,' *Mad Max Beyond Thunderdome, 2001: A Space Odyssey*, Shakespeare pedagogy, Alexander Pope, D. H. Lawrence, and science fiction works by Arthur C. Clarke, Ursula K. Le Guin, Frederik Pohl and C. M. Kornbluth, Larry Niven and Jerry Pournelle, Robert Silverberg, and D. F. Jones.

www.ingramcontent.com/pod-product-compliance
Lightning Source LLC
Chambersburg PA
CBHW032026150426
43194CB00006B/173